DEAN GODSON is a journalist and biographer who lives in Washington, D.C.

For more information on Dean Godson
visit www.harperperennial.co.uk and register for AuthorTracker

'A remarkable piece of work. It is so detailed, well sourced and carefully annotated that it will inevitably become essential reading for students of Northern Ireland's interminable peace process.'
ALAN RUDDOCK, *Sunday Times*

'Ulster politics – that wilderness of distorting mirrors – at last has a guide worthy of its complexity and importance. Dean Godson's biography is ... a triumph of scholarship, readability and acute political analysis.' ANDREW ROBERTS, *Mail on Sunday*

'Godson ... has a superb instinctive grasp of political life; its calculations, compromises and passions. His story is more than one man's life, it is a portrait of power-broking at its most intense when issues of life and death hover over every politician's decision.'
MICHAEL GOVE, *The Times*

'Masterly ... Godson has an absolute command of the detail and access to sources on every side of the many political divides ... Not only is this book the definitive account of the modern history of Northern Ireland, it is also as good a guide to its embattled inhabitants as one could wish.' EDWARD AMORY, *Daily Mail*

'A feast of eavesdropped political conversations, plotting sessions in Downing Street, the White House and Dublin, and surreal glimpses of a province caught between the still-fresh battle-scars of 1689 and the 21st century.' REBECCA TINSLEY, *New Statesman*

'Dean Godson's work is magnificent in its scope and its detail and must now be placed at the centre of any historical record of the recent "peace process".'
MATTHEW PARRIS, Boo

'Essential for anyone interested in "the other side of the story".'
Irish Examiner

'A meticulous traditional political biography of a kind rarely written these days . . . If Trimble is a tough man, with a high respect for the truth, then he has found a biographer who is equally tough.'
ANDREW MARR

'This is a book about a man and a tribe: their values, their history, their struggle for survival. Dean Godson's book . . . is a formidable work of industry and scholarship. Anyone who is interested in the affairs of Ulster must read it; it is likely to be a standard text for many decades to come.' BRUCE ANDERSON, *Financial Times*

'*Himself Alone* is not only an excellent biography of Trimble, but at least as good an introduction to the curious creeds of Unionism as Ruth Dudley Edwards' *The Faithful Tribe.*' *Time Out*

'Well researched, loaded with detail and impressively sourced . . . This monumental book will be an essential source book for students of the Process for many years to come.'
MAURICE HAYES, *Irish Independent*

'As Dean Godson reminds us in this masterful biography, Trimble is a political eccentric – a loner and an enigma . . . Godson's finest achievement is bringing (his) character to life with such vividness. [Trimble] is a great man of our times, and this is a great biography.'
PATRICK WEST, *Literary Review*

'We owe a great debt to Dean Godson for writing this exhaustive and outstanding account of David Trimble's political life. . . Godson's style is fluent and he retains the reader's interest in such a way that returning to the book is a pleasure, an act of full anticipation.'
ED MOLONEY, *Sunday Independent*

HIMSELF ALONE

DAVID TRIMBLE

AND THE ORDEAL OF UNIONISM

Dean Godson

HARPER PERENNIAL

For my mother above all
but not forgetting Paul, Greta, John, Evelyn, Charlie and Gill

Harper Perennial
an imprint of HarperCollins*Publishers*
77–85 Fulham Palace Road
Hammersmith
London w6 8jb

www.harperperennial.co.uk

This edition published by Harper Perennial 2005

First published by HarperCollins*Publishers* 2004

Copyright © Dean Godson 2004

Dean Godson asserts the moral right to
be identified as the author of this work

A catalogue record for this book is available from the British Library

978-0-00-717999-2

Set in Minion by
Rowland Phototypesetting Ltd,
Bury St Edmunds, Suffolk

CONTENTS

I am Ulster, my people an abrupt people
Who like the spiky consonants in speech
And think the soft ones cissy; who dig
The *k* and *t* in orchestra, detect sin
In sinfonia, get a kick out of
Tin cans, fricatives, fornication, staccato talk,
Anything that gives or takes attack,
Like Micks, Tagues, tinkers' gets, Vatican.
An angular people, brusque and Protestant,
For whom the word is still the fighting word,
Who bristle into reticence at the sound
Of the round gift of the gab in Southern mouths.
Mine were not born with silver spoons in gob,
Nor would they thank you for the gift of tongues;
The dry riposte, the bitter repartee's
The Northman's bite and portion, his deep sup
Is silence; though, still within his shell,
He holds the old sea-roar and surge
Of rhetoric and Holy Writ.

W. R. Rodgers; from 'Epilogue' in *Poems*,
Michael Longley (Oldcastle,
Co. Meath, 1993), pp. 106–7

'Whatever an Ulsterman may be, he is certainly never
charming, and of that fact, no one is more fully aware
than the Ulsterman himself.'

F. Frankfort Moore, *The Truth about Ulster*
(London, 1914), p. 102

'I've changed, you know.'

David Trimble to his old friend, Professor Herb Wallace,
after signing the Belfast Agreement

'What do you want for your people?'
'To be left alone.'

Exchange between Sean Farren, a senior nationalist
politician, and David Trimble at Duisburg, in the late 1980s

A brief word is required about the origins of this book, not least since it says much about the character of David Trimble. I had known him since early 1994, when he was still the youngest and most junior of the UUP MPs at Westminster and was starting to carve out a discreetly distinct position from the then leader, James Molyneaux. Trimble was much more my sort of person than Molyneaux, who appeared to me to speak in whispers and incomprehensible riddles. The MP for Upper Bann, by contrast, seemed to me just what Unionism as a whole needed: a thoroughly modern man, capable of communicating with the outside world. He appeared tougher than Molyneaux, who I believed had been too deferential to the then Conservative Government but was mercifully free of those aspects of Paisleyism that made it so hard to defend Unionism beyond Northern Ireland. That said, after he became leader, I became increasingly concerned by the course which Trimble began to chart. In my view, he was willing to pay too high a price to do a deal with the forces of Irish nationalism.

Nonetheless, shortly after he signed the Belfast Agreement on 10 April 1998, I telephoned Trimble. Would he be willing to cooperate with me on a book on him and how and why he struck the treaty? Trimble declined to do so, stating he was too busy at this time. In late September 1998, he telephoned me unexpectedly. He was willing, after all, to co-operate. We discussed the matter at length, during which I made clear my profound opposition to the Belfast Agreement. In a debate with Professor Paul Bew in *The Times Literary Supplement* on 24 April 1998, I had been one of the few journalists willing publicly to oppose the accord. The newspaper for which I worked, *The Daily Telegraph*, had come close to recommending a 'no' vote in the Referendum on the deal and continued to have grave difficulties with its outworkings, especially with prisoner releases and the threat it posed to the Royal Ulster Constabulary (RUC). Did he really want me to do this? And how much time could he give me, bearing in mind that a rival biographer, Henry

McDonald – whom I knew and whose journalism I admired – was also seeking interviews and was a much stauncher 'Trimbleite' than I was?[1]

To my astonishment, Trimble still said yes. He obviously knew of our differences – which had resulted in some memorable rows – but expressed confidence in my ability to be accurate. I hope that in this respect at least, I have not disappointed him. But whatever the quality of my work, I regard it as little short of amazing that a practising politician would entrust such a work to someone whose natural sympathies lay with the main internal critics of his political handiwork. It is a sign of two qualities for which few detractors, whether nationalist or unionist, give him enough credit: his essential fair-mindedness and almost school-masterly patience. He so believed in the rightness of his course of action that he thought that any intelligent person would eventually come to see the light. And, for a practising politician working in very adverse circumstances, he has been remarkably candid.

Where has all this left me in terms of my views of Trimble and of the Agreement? When I started out, I imagined this project would take four months. In the event, it has taken well over five years. Many doubted it would ever be completed, including, at times, myself. When a senior figure in the republican movement asked me when it would be ready, I replied, 'Well, my publishers think I have learned from your strategy on decommissioning. They think I've begun the process of writing a book without delivering the actual product.' Both pro- and perhaps more especially anti-Agreement unionism have changed much in the intervening years. I remain as sceptical of the Belfast Agreement as when I started out. But I hope that I now better understand why Trimble did what he did and the myriad pressures upon him. As time went on, I became more interested in the question of whether, having treated with nationalism, he had played the new institutions as well as he might *in his own terms*. But love him or loathe him, he was the 'indispensable man'. No one else could have done what he did at that time, for better or worse. Hence the title of this book, *Himself Alone* – for the uninitiated, a play on *Sinn Fein*, Irish for 'Ourselves Alone'.

The sub-title is significant as well: it is 'David Trimble *and* the Ordeal of Unionism'. Whatever anyone thinks of David Trimble, of the UUP, and of Unionism as a whole, it seems to me desirable that the position of the Ulster-British people and its elected representatives be better understood. For many of them, the Belfast Agreement represented 'the world turned upside down', as their longtime republican tormentors achieved a degree of recognition at home and abroad which they deemed unconscionable. Their position has not, at least for much of the current Troubles, been well explained – either on the British mainland, in the Irish Republic or in the wider world. Some would even claim that it has not been well explained to Unionists in Northern Ireland by spokesmen of mainstream Unionism! On more than one occasion, I have heard this failure ascribed to the phenomenon of 'Unionist inarticulacy', or even 'Protestant inarticulacy'. But whatever the cultural and political circumstances which gave rise to the failure of Unionists to communicate their case over the last 30 years, one thing is certain: the total amount of literature on unionists of all hues, and on unionism, is thin compared to that on individual nationalists and republicans and nationalism and republicanism – as is immediately evident from a quick glance along the shelves in the excellent Political Collection at the Linen Hall Library in Belfast. And considering that the UUP was the Province's largest party in terms of numbers of seats held at Westminster, Stormont and in municipal government up to and including the 2001 General and local elections, it has suffered especially badly from an 'attention deficit'. Depending on how one categorises it, it is noteworthy that Paisley and Paisleyism have been the subjects of almost as many books as all of the six leaders of the UUP since the Troubles began!

That is not to say there has not been much excellent work on the UUP by the likes of Arthur Aughey, Feargal Cochrane, Andrew Gailey, John F. Harbinson, David Hume, Marc Mulholland, Henry Patterson and others, all of which greatly helped me in my own researches.[2] The point rather, is to observe that anyone who writes on this area has the advantage of writing on what are still relatively uncharted waters. If this book serves any one purpose, it is an attempt to assist the process of rectifying that imbalance. I have sought to chart the hopes and fears of unionists, and the often virulent divisions which obtained amongst them. In a sense, therefore, this is a 'pan-unionist' book. I have largely sought to describe those debates, rather than to adjudicate between them. None of this is to the exclusion of Irish nationalist perspectives. I have enjoyed excellent cooperation throughout from Irish nationalists, north and south of the border, and in Irish America, and their perspectives on Trimble and of Unionism were invaluable. Indeed, the conversations which I have had with senior figures in the Dublin Government, from the Taoiseach downwards, have been especially pleasurable. Obviously, I have also devoted much attention to Trimble's view of the changes in nationalism and republicanism, which made it possible in his own mind to become the first Ulster Unionist leader to share power with Sinn Fein.

There were, to my mind, sound reasons for writing this book as I did – about Trimble *and* the ordeal of Unionism. For if I had been told when I began this work that Trimble would survive entering Government thrice with Sinn Fein, with the IRA still very much in existence and massive changes to the RUC, I would not have believed it possible. But survive he did. Indeed, Trimble outlasted his counterparts in the devolved institutions set up in the other components of the United Kingdom in 1997–1999. In Scotland, where Labour enjoyed a cushion that the UUP never did, Donald Dewar died and Henry McLeish resigned. In Wales, where Labour leaders also boasted electoral margins greater than Trimble ever did, Ron Davies's career was aborted in a 'moment of madness' on Clapham Common and his successor, Alun Michael, resigned. Thus, since 1999, Scotland has been through three First Ministers, and Wales two and a half (if the abortive career of Ron Davies is included). In Northern Ireland, Trimble's nationalist 'co-premier', Seamus Mallon, retired from the post of Deputy First Minister in 2001. Trimble's life was at times endangered by both loyalist and republican paramilitaries, and after the 1998 Assembly elections, he was certainly close to becoming the 'minority shareholder' in Unionism. Yet he endured, both physically and politically, beyond anyone's and perhaps even his own expectations. For students of politics, it seems worthwhile to examine how he achieved this. Actuarially, it appeared unlikely at the beginning that he would do so. Accordingly, I sought to provide a wider portrait of the UUP and of Unionism as a whole in these times, precisely because of the precariousness of his position.

One of the reasons why Trimble survived was because of his own ability to 'duck and dive' (which he once likened to me as the UUP equivalent of the 'Ali Shuffle'). Certainly, Trimble showed a capacity to adjust to altered circumstances. The most obvious shift in the eyes of the outside world was the way in which the 'hardline hero' of Orange protest at Drumcree became a 'peacemaker'. But readers may well also notice that he has changed even during the course of the writing of this book. Thus, the Trimble of 2001–3 is noticeably different from the Trimble of 1998–9. In 1998–9, scarcely a critical word would come from his lips about Tony Blair – or, if it did, he would seek to place the best possible construction upon the Prime Minister's behaviour and motives. Not so thereafter: to a degree, it was 'never glad confident morning again'. In some ways, he is still a work in progress. It has been fascinating and a great privilege to watch, but it has made for difficulties in writing the book and even in offering an interim assessment of his career to date. Inevitably, this has entailed making subjective judgments on what is and is not of greater or lesser importance in his career and to Unionism as a whole. Thus, I devote a whole chapter to the events of Drumcree I in 1995 – which vaulted him into the national and international consciousness for the first time. He was very important to it, and it to him. I have also devoted substantial attention to Drumcree II in 1996, on similar grounds. Thereafter, I devote less attention to Drumcree, partly because the issues have been thoroughly explored in earlier chapters. Likewise, I devote much detailed attention to the repeated attempts in 1998–9 to set up an inclusive executive, and to the first suspension of the institutions in February 2000, precisely because these were novel events. But I spend less time proportionately on subsequent events, on account of what Gerry Adams rightly described as the *Groundhog Day* quality of the process.

One final word of caution is required: contrary to what some have claimed, this is not an official or even authorised biography. By this, I mean that David Trimble has at no stage seen the text of this book nor has he had veto over the contents. If he had so insisted, I would not have started work on it. I wanted the freedom to make my own judgments. Certainly, I have had cause to refer many, many things to him: when claims or accusations were made about him or, more often, for the purpose of verifying his own quotations when I had doubts about the materials, whether because of apparent contradictions in my record of his own testimony or because I was engaged in synthesisation and compression of his views. The only case in which I have as a matter of course checked materials back with him and with his wife, Daphne, has been in the case of references to his children. Everything else which I bounced off him has been done voluntarily by me, if I deemed the circumstances required it. Any subsequent excisions were ultimately my own decision. Inevitably, there has been a degree of give and take. The end product is, therefore, a biography written with his cooperation, in the sense that I have spent many hundreds of hours in his company, often tape-recorded. He also gave me access to his personal papers, of which there are remarkably few, despite spending nearly 30 years, on and off, in public life.

Many of these were stored in appallingly dusty boxes in his garage. 'Take at look at what you can find,' he told me, laughingly. They turned out to be a veritable 'mini-Linen Hall Library', bulging with pamphlets from every obscure republican and loyalist groupuscule, such as the 'Merseyside Defence Association' newsletter. I believe this approach has given me the best of both worlds – access and independence. And whilst a fuller historical verdict on the entire peace process must await the release of some of the state papers after 30 years – the full story will probably never be told – I would nonetheless like to think that my approach has certain advantages. The most notable of those is immediacy. I spoke to most of the *dramatis personae* when many of these events were fresh in their heads and sometimes even on the same day. In certain instances, I was lucky enough to be a first-hand witness to events.

One final word is required about nomenclature, so often the source of much contention in writing about Northern Ireland. My approach has been stylistic rather than ideological. To avoid repetition of names and terms, I have used synonyms irrespective of their political meaning. I have employed Northern Ireland and Ulster interchangeably, even though nationalists often dispute the use of the latter to refer to the six-county Province (as opposed to the original nine-county unit before Partition). At times, though, I have written of 'northern unionists', 'northern unionism' and 'northern Protestants' – terms with echoes of the nationalist phrases 'the North' or the 'Northern Secretary' to refer to the Secretary of State for Northern Ireland. This is employed mostly for the purposes of distinguishing them from their pre-Partition brethren in the South. I have referred at various times to Derry or Londonderry, as the case required. Thus, I have described Dr Seamus Hegarty by his official title as the Roman Catholic Bishop of Derry, though I use the term 'Londonderry' when Trimble refers to that city, not least because I think it says something about him. Again, for literary reasons, I call John Hume a 'Derryman', partly because it is how he would describe himself and partly because I think it less of a mouthful than 'Londonderryman'. Equally, I sometimes use the term 'Maiden City' as a synonym for Derry/Londonderry, notwithstanding the fact that it is a largely 'unionist' term. I have described the 1998 accord as the Belfast Agreement, largely because it is the term favoured by Trimble himself, except where a nationalist source has explicitly used 'Good Friday Agreement'.[3] But I also use the Catholic and Anglican term 'Holy Week' to describe the dramatic events of those final five days of negotiations, because it has a nice, economical ring to it – even though Presbyterians and other Protestant denominations historically never employed it. The terms 'the British' and 'the Irish' are shorthand for the Governments of the United Kingdom and the Irish Republic, respectively – even both Unionists and nationalists in Northern Ireland would obviously regard themselves as just as British and Irish, respectively, as those politicians and officials operating out of London and Dublin. Indeed, in several cases, I have used the old pejorative republican expression 'Dublin Government' – when reasons of economy, style, and tensions between Sinn Fein and the Irish State warrant such terminology. As far as names are concerned, I have used the titles by which people are best known to the public. Thus, I call John Taylor, the long-time Ulster Unionist MP for Strangford, 'John Taylor' – even though he was subsequently elevated to the Upper House as Lord Kilclooney. Likewise, Robert Armstrong, Cabinet Secretary from 1979–87, is not described as Lord Armstrong of Ilminster, and so on. For the sake of consistency, I refer to the Ulster Unionist Party (UUP), even when it was described as the 'Official Unionist Party'. The letters 'DT interview 24/03/03 etc', used in the notes obviously refer to interviews with David Trimble. The shorthand 'DT' is also used on occasion in the main text.

Such a project could not have been completed without the assistance of a great many people. My first and primary debt is to David Trimble, who so generously opened up about his life to me – even when I asked some very intimate questions. As a relationship, it has not been without its ups and downs, but I have much to be thankful about to him. His memory is not as good as it was, yet I have no reason to believe that he deliberately withheld anything from me if I asked the relevant question! Considering the strains he was under, his forbearance was remarkable. Much the same goes for Daphne Trimble, who is the model of a political wife and a generous hostess as well. Their children, Richard, Victoria, Nicholas and Sarah were also extremely tolerant of my frequent intrusions into their father's Sundays at Richmond Court, Lisburn. I am particularly grateful to Richard Trimble for extracting some of his father's old memoranda from a long-unused computer disk. I also owe debts to Squadron Leader Iain Trimble, RAF (brother) and to Rosemary Trimble (sister) for reminiscences of their Bangor childhood and for photographs. Likewise, Maureen Irwin, David Trimble's sole surviving first cousin was very helpful on family matters, as were Kyleen Clarke (second cousin) and her husband, Professor Richard Clarke. And George MacDonald MacAllister, a member of the North of Ireland Family History Society, was indefatigable in chasing up the Trimble ancestry in diocesan and land registers across the island. Alluding to Brian Faulkner's non-Ascendancy background, the poet John Hewitt observed that his family tree will 'offer little grist/to any plodding genealogist'.[4] In my position, I have every reason to be grateful to this not-so-plodding genealogist – who does it all in his unique style. He was assisted at various times by David Leahy in Limerick. Revs Janet Catterall, Stephen Lockington and Andrew Dougherty in Co Longford also helped in my inquiries concerning the southern roots of the Trimble family. Constable David Lockhart did sterling work in looking up the service record of Trimble's grandfather, who served in the RIC and RUC. William Blair QC was generous with his assistance on the Prime Minister's and his own forebears in Co. Donegal. Thanks also to Bill, who knows how much he did!

I should also like to record my gratitude to the following individuals. I have largely concentrated here on those who are not acknowledged in the text or in the notes as interviewees – or, if so, who have given further assistance beyond that of oral testimony for this book. If I have excluded anyone, save at their own request, my profoundest apologies. Any such omissions are entirely accidental and I will seek to make it up to them in any subsequent editions of this book:

Ian Wilson of the North Down Heritage Centre for his insights into local history and for a fascinating drive round Bangor; Bangor Grammar School for opening their archives; Yvonne Murphy and Alistair Gordon of the Linen Hall Library's Political Collection, and Kieran Crossey previously of that Collection for their professional help; likewise to Gerry Healey, Irish and Reference Librarian of the Linen Hall Library; to Bobby Hanvey, a true gentleman, for his kindness; the splendid Adam Smyth of Radio 5 Live, for innumerable kindnesses; Trevor Birney and Ken Reid of UTV; Ed Curran, editor of the *Belfast Telegraph* and Walter Macauley, Chief Librarian for opening their files; ditto, Geoff Martin, formerly editor of the *News Letter*; David Fletcher of the *Ulster Star*; and David Armstrong, Brian Courtney and Victor Gordon of the *Portadown Times*, who gave the warmest of welcomes.

Thanks also to Dr Clifford and Mrs Anne Smyth for much hospitality and fascinating insights; their son Martin, who was killed in a road accident in Australia during the latter stages of work on this book is much missed by all who knew him. Also to John Hunter for taking the time; Gordon Lucy for looking up countless references and many other acts of generosity – ever the gentleman and the scholar; Andrew Castles of the Ulster Society; David Jones, for sorting out that day at Drumcree; Stewart O'Fee; Robert and Maureen McCartney for their hospitality; Herb Wallace, for explaining so much; and David and Judith Brewster, for much counsel and friendship. Especial thanks are due to Anne Graham, who contributed moving reminiscences of her late brother, Edgar.

I also received much help from Government officials in London, Dublin and Washington. Some of it was routine, such as confirmation of dates of meetings; others gave help way beyond the call of duty, especially considering our profound differences of opinion! They included, from successive No. 10 staffs, Sir Rod Lyne, George Bridges, Sir John Holmes, John Sawers, Jonathan Powell, Alistair Campbell, Alison Blackshaw, Tom Kelly and Pat McFadden. Amongst past and current officials of the Northern Ireland Office and the Northern Ireland Civil Service, I am indebted to Peter Bell, Sir John Chilcot, Sir Brian Cubbon, William Fittall, Dennis Godfrey, Robert Hannigan, Bill Jeffrey, Sir Gerry Loughran, Chris Maccabe, Jonathan Phillips, Sir Joe Pilling, John Steele, Sir Quentin Thomas, Alan Whysall and many others besides. Thanks also to Arlene in the Permanent Under Secretary's office. I should record also a special mention for Sir John Wheeler, for his kindnesses, and to Andrew Hunter, MP, and the late Jan Hunter. Jan was loved by all who knew her, and will be much missed. In the Foreign Office, thanks also to Anthony Cary, George Fergusson, Paul ('P.J.') Johnston and Sir Ivor Roberts. In the Republic of Ireland, I owe a great debt to Senator Martin Mansergh, who effected countless introductions and took a great interest in this project, and his assistant, Evelyn Eager. Joe Lennon, the then Government Press Secretary was generous with his time. I also wish to record thanks to Paddy Teahon, Dermot Gallagher, Ted Barrington, Tim Dalton and others too numerous to mention. Fergus Finlay was superb. Thanks also to P.J. Mara for helping to open the door with Bono. Donne Cooney in Cyril Ramaphosa's office was ever-accommodating. In the United States, I wish to record my appreciation to Blair Hall, Sara Rosenberry, Larry Butler, Dick Norland, Jim Steinberg and Meghan O'Sullivan.

On David Trimble's own staff, past and present, I am eternally indebted to David Campbell, Graham Gudgin, David Kerr, Steven King, David McNarry, Mark Neale and Barry White. Amongst his Commons researchers, thanks are also due to Claire Kirk and Rodney McCune. And to the civil service staff in the First Minister's office – David Lavery, Maura Quinn, Dr Bill Smith and Alison Coey. Anne Rainey and Pamela Stewart were endlessly patient, not least with countless requests for telephone numbers. Jack Allen, Honorary Treasurer of the UUC, was a wonderful source of information on the rules of the party and Alan McFarland was ever courteous and helpful. Hazel Legge at UUP headquarters, Margaret McKee, assistant to the UUP MPs at Westminster, Stephanie Roderick, David Trimble's constituency office secretary, and Dianne Marshall, assistant to David Burnside, also deserve honourable mentions for their unstinting help.

Thanks also to David Montgomery, always a delight to deal with and full of suggestions; to his assistant, Sharon Hayden, for all her help; to Lord Gilbert, a very dear and old friend, for opening many doors despite his total lack of interest in this subject; to Sean O'Callaghan for his unique and often brilliant perspectives; to Ruth Dudley Edwards for much kindness and hospitality; likewise, to Maureen Carter; to Stephen Collins of the *Sunday Tribune* for teaching me so much about southern Irish politics with limitless courtesy; to Simon Walker; to Mgr Denis Faul, whose table is as good as his talk; to Sean Farren for many pleasurable hours in Portstewart; to Michael McDowell in Washington, DC, a fount of much wisdom and common sense; to Richard McAuley and Denis Donaldson of Sinn Fein; to Gary Kent, always a star; to David Hoey; to Dr Anthony McIntyre, who was always of assistance with my tedious inquiries about the geography and topography of Belfast; to Ed Moloney for helping clarify my thoughts; to John Gross for explaining Tennyson; Professor Brigid Hadfield of Essex University and Professor Andrew Le Sueur of Birmingham University for explaining points of constitutional law, and Professor Trevor Hartley of the LSE and Professor Erika Szyszczak of Leicester University on EU law; to Dr Graham Gudgin for his help on public expenditure figures; Sydney Elliott and Nicholas Whyte for all their help on electoral statistics; to Richard Moore of Millward Brown, Ulster; to Professor Des Greer for all his help; to Dr Alvin Jackson of Queen's University and Dr Tim Bowman of Durham University for their guidance on the Ulster Covenant; to John Bew for his excellent research assistance; to Chris Leibundguth for his top-notch help and to the Leibundguth family for their friendship over the years; to Kenny Markeson for the photocopying; to Jonathan and the excellent staff at Aldens, where many of the interviews took place; to Ted and Hazel McMullen for all their help and lifts; likewise, to Felicity and Michael Pearce; to Dr Anne and Ben Riley; and, of course, Ray and Joe McCluskey, the lights of my life, who managed to look after me without recourse to any paper bags.

Chris, Larry and William know who they are. Thanks for everything.

The following individuals were approached but were unavailable for interview for a variety of reasons and in some cases none: Archbishop Sean Brady; former President Bill Clinton; Rev. Bryan Follis; Sir Alistair Goodlad; Ray Hayden; Martin Howard of the Ministry of Defence; Ken Lindsay of the NIO; Heather McCombe (David Trimble's first wife); Liz O'Donnell; and Tina Rosenberg of the *New York Times*. I received no response to requests for interviews with Brian Cowen (who also half-declined an initial, oral request in person). Martin McGuinness and Dick Spring both expressed a willingness to be interviewed in principle, but for a range of reasons it proved to be impossible to arrange anything in practice.

Amongst those who gave me hospitality during my travels across Northern Ireland and the Republic, I must particularly thank Chris and Joyce McGimpsey; Chris and Isabella Hudson; James and Sasha Abercorn; Trevor and Jennifer Wilson; David and Fiona Burnside; Brighid McLaughlin; Antony and Mary Alcock; Ciara Dwyer; Gwen Halley; Eoghan and Anne Harris; Robin and Joy Guthrie; Hugh Rathcavan; William and Christine Ross; Thomas and Pauline Fleming; and Dr Mary Bew. In America, I owe much to Jonathan Foreman and to David and Danielle Frum and Richard and Leslie Perle. All, without exception, were wonderful hosts and I could not have done it without them.

At *The Daily Telegraph*, thanks to Stuart Whitelaw, now sadly departed from the company owing to illness; Ian Forsyth; Roger French; Roland Halliwell; Janis Hegarty; Jim Robinson; Roger Trippas; Eddie; Monty; Simon Scott Plummer; Toby Harnden and David Sharrock, two brilliant Ireland correspondents; Bob Bodman, the outstanding Picture Editor; Alexandra Erskine, Reference Library Manager for the Telegraph Group and its wonderful staff; Matthew d'Ancona (of *The Sunday Telegraph*), Neil Darbyshire, Sue Ryan, Sarah Sands and Alice Thomson for lending me their offices and allowing me to spread out my papers; and anyone else I may have omitted. Thanks also to two superlative secretaries, Henrietta Courtauld and Penny Cranford. The Comment Department has been very lucky indeed to enjoy their services.

Other friends and relations have also been towers of strength during this period. I would particularly like to record my thanks to Louise Aspinall; John Barnes, who introduced me to republican songs; Michael Barone; Robin Birley; Charlotte Blacker; Ahmed Chalabi, who understands all the matters discussed here instinctively; Harriet Cohen; Barbara Comeau; Anthea Craigmyle; Devon Cross; Annie Eyre; John Frieda; Leonie Frieda; Paul and the much-lamented Paula Genney; my brother Roy Godson, ever full of encouraging words; Catherine Goodman; Paul and Fiona Goodman; Sarah Gove; Miriam Gross; Robert Hardman; John Hayes; John Lehman; Kate Leigh-Pemberton; Harold; Brian, Kate, Ivo, Hubert, Christabel, Flora and Madeleine MacGreevy; Brian Markeson; Charlotte Metcalf; David Maclean, whose courage is inspirational; Simon Milton; Audrey Nickerson; Madeleine North; Kenneth Rose; Allen and Mary Roth; Kate Sells; James Sherr; Douglas Smith; and the ever-bountiful and inspirational Manny Weiss and his family. My old friend David Bar-Illan, one-time editor of the *Jerusalem Post*, who died as this project was nearing completion, was never far from my thoughts. Likewise his wife Beverly. The late Alan Clark would have approved of the completion of this project, since he always urged me not to concentrate too much on Ulster!

I owe a huge debt of gratitude to the Telegraph Group for allowing me the time to begin and to complete this book. Thanks to Charles Moore, former editor of *The Daily Telegraph* for his endless forbearance and kindness, and to his successor Martin Newland. I also owe much to Lord Black of Crossharbour for his support. His definitive biography of Duplessis, the long-time Premier of Québec, took even longer to complete than did this book and was the only precedent that excused my own tardiness in finishing. Thanks also to Lady Black, Dan Colson, former Chief Executive of the *Telegraph*, and Sarah Sands for their support. There can be few pleasanter places to work, anywhere. And Boris Johnson tolerated my prolonged absence from *The Spectator*, whilst flattering me with complaining noises.

At HarperCollins, a great thank-you to Michael Fishwick for his encouragement and for his understanding of the huge problems which writing a biography of a serving politician entails. Kate Hyde was outstanding and this project could not have been completed without her meticulousness and cheerfulness. And to Georgina Capel, my agent, for keeping my spirits up and much else besides.

The manuscript was read in full, or in part, by the following individuals: C.D.C. Armstrong, Arthur Aughey, Paul Bew, Stephen Collins, John Creaney, QC, David Frum, Brian Garrett, Michael Gove, Eoghan Harris, Jonathan Isaby, Dennis Kennedy, Patrick Maloney, QC, Patrick Maume, Andy McSmith, Frank Millar, Henry Patterson, Andrew Roberts, Justin Shaw, Siôn Simon, MP, A.T.Q. Stewart, Blair Wallace and Nicholas Whyte. In particular, C.D.C. Armstrong, Dennis Kennedy, Patrick Maume and Henry Patterson went over successive drafts and taught me much in the process. Frank Millar was particularly generous with his time: as one of the outstanding journalists of our time, he should have written this book. In addition, C.D.C. Armstrong and Jonathan Isaby were outstanding, chasing up innumerable notes and other references. I can never adequately repay my debt to all of them. They saved me from innumerable howlers but, needless to say, any remaining errors are entirely my own.

My greatest debts are to the dedicatees of this book. First, to Paul Bew, who has been like a brother to me since I first set foot in Northern Ireland, and who is an intellectual and moral colossus. In his company, I feel like a dwarf on the shoulders of a giant. And one of the best things about him has been coming to know his wife Dr Greta Jones, whose counsel has been no less valuable. Likewise, John and Evelyn Creaney opened their home to me and have nurtured me during my long stays in Belfast. They have taught me much of what I know. Nothing was ever too much for Charlie and Gill, whose friendship means more to me than I can say.

Above all, this book belongs to my mother, Ruth. She often wondered what I was doing in the north-eastern corner of the island of Ireland and what my late father, Joseph, of blessed memory, would have made of it. I hope she now understands.

ONE

Floreat Bangoria

WILLIAM David Trimble was born on 15 October 1944, at the Wellington Park Nursing Home in Belfast of respectable, lower-middle-class, Presbyterian stock. From his earliest years he was called David, apparently to distinguish himself from his father, William Sr. The gregarious elder Trimble was generally known as 'Billy', but his flinty son was to reject all such attempts to turn him into a 'Davy' or a 'Dave'. He remained resolutely 'David'. This name apparently derives from his paternal grandfather, George David Trimble, born in 1874 and a native of Co. Longford. The earliest Protestant settlement there can be traced back to the reign of James I, though there was an overspill into Co. Longford resulting from subsequent influxes of Scottish Presbyterians into Ulster at the end of the 17th and early 18th centuries. Indeed, at its pre-Famine peak, the Protestant community numbered around 14,000 and the 1831 census suggests that it comprised 9.5% of the population. As late as 1911, in the parish of Clonbroney where the Trimbles lived, Protestants comprised 18.3% of the population.[1] It is not known when the Trimbles – a variation of the Scottish Lowland name of Turnbull – arrived in Co. Longford.[2] But what is certain is that David Trimble's own line of descent can be traced back to the end of the 18th century (he is not related to the Co. Fermanagh Trimbles, whose descendants own the famed *Impartial Reporter and Farmers' Journal*. By coincidence, his wife is part of that extended family). Like most Protestants, the Co. Longford Trimbles and the families they married into – the Smalls, the Twaddles, the Gilpins and the Eggletons – were farmers, with a few ploughmen, stewards and underagents amongst them. The first available record is of one Alexander Trimble (DT's great-great-grandfather) who farmed in Sheeroe, Co. Longford. His son, also called Alexander (DT's great-grandfather), lived from 1826 to 1904 and had eight children of whom the above-mentioned George

David (DT's grandfather) was the youngest. According to Griffith's valuation of property in Ireland, conducted in the 1850s and 1860s, Alexander Trimble (II) rented a plot from one of the Edgeworths, the main landowners in the area, comprising lands of 11 acres, 3 roods and 16 perches. Its rateable valuation was £9 and 5 shillings, with buildings thereon valued at £1 and 15 shillings. But unlike most Protestants in Co. Longford, who were adherents of the Church of Ireland, the Trimbles were staunch Presbyterians: the parish registers show that George David, DT's grandfather, was baptised at Tully Presbyterian Church in 1875. They were thus a minority within a minority. History does not record how these Trimbles felt about the Ascendancy, in the shape of the Edgeworth family, nor about the Church of Ireland itself. If they keenly felt the disabilities long imposed upon Dissenters, it echoed down the years in odd ways: David Trimble himself never much cared for the traditional Unionist establishment.

The world of the Trimbles, like those of so many smallholders, would have been far removed from the elegiac evocations of 'Big House' Protestant life described by Somerville and Ross or Elizabeth Bowen. Especially during the latter half of the 19th century, they became increasingly vulnerable. There were a number of reasons for this: changing patterns in the rural economy, which led to the disappearance of farm servanthood and labouring jobs; difficulty in finding suitable local spouses, sometimes leading to intermarriage with Catholics and to conversion; and the lure of North America. Another, darker explanation for the decline in the Protestant population was the rising tide of Catholic disaffection – which took an increasingly violent form – and the attempts of some of the bigger landlords and of the British Government based in Dublin Castle to appease such anger through a variety of reforms at the Protestant smallholders' expense.[3] According to J.J. Lee, mid-19th-century Co. Longford was one of the six most disturbed counties in Ireland. David Fitzpatrick further states that in the immediate pre-Partition era, Sinn Fein membership in Co. Longford totalled between 600 and 1000 out of a 10,000 population, the highest of any county.[4] Whatever the exact causes of the collapse of the Protestant population of Co. Longford, the community undoubtedly declined by 40% between 1911 and 1926. By 1981, there were fewer than 1500 in the entire county. Census returns from Clonbroney at the time of the 2002 Easter Vestry to the Church of Ireland Diocese of Elphin and Ardagh showed that there were 43 regular worshippers – compared to 1010 in 1831.[5] In Longford as a whole, there were around 40 Presbyterians left in 2003, plus around 80 Methodists. Tully Presbyterian Church closed in the 1950s; only one, at Corboy, is left in the county. As Liam Kennedy concluded in his authoritative study of the Protestants of Longford and Westmeath, 'The Long Retreat', 'there is little comfort here for those seeking stories of ethnic accommodation along pluralist lines. True enough, by the 1930s or '40s, unlike the case of Northern Ireland, there was no minority ethnic or religious problem in the region. There was no minority.' [6] Throughout his career, David Trimble has been determined that the Protestants of Northern Ireland, and pro-Union Catholics, not suffer the same fate.

George David Trimble, DT's grandfather, was part of that exodus – though, again, his exact reasons for leaving remain unknown. Originally a farmer, he joined the Royal Irish Constabulary in 1895 (it seems an uncle, one Thomas Trimble, born in 1819, had earlier served in the Dublin Metropolitan Police from 1840–8). After tours of duty in Sligo, Armagh, Belfast and Tyrone, George David Trimble returned to Ulster's capital in 1909. He remained there for the rest of his life, attaining the rank of Head Constable. According to the official records, he received a life annuity of £195 upon the disbandment of the RIC in 1922, and then joined the newly created Royal Ulster Constabulary: his service record has neither blemishes nor commendations on it. He ended his career in 1931 at Donegal Pass RUC station and died in 1962, aged 87. Thus it was that the Trimbles came to settle in the 'greater Belfast area', as it is now sometimes called.[7]

Moustachioed Grandfather Trimble was a great 'spit and polish' man, who would daily 'bull' his boots till he could see the reflection of his face.[8] He stood at over six-foot-three and was not one to be trifled with: he had been through the severe inter-communal rioting which racked Belfast at the time of Partition and was ever on his mettle. When some relatives from the newly created Free State banged on his door in jest, shouting 'we've come to get you, Trimble', he drew his gun from his holster and repeatedly fired through the wooden panels, scattering his terrified country cousins.[9] According to Maureen Irwin, David Trimble's sole surviving first cousin, the 'Trimble temper' comes down from Grandfather George Trimble; the red hair and the florid complexion come from Grandfather Trimble's diminutive wife, Sarah Jane Sparks, daughter of James Sparks, a farmer of Cullentrough, Co. Armagh, to whom he was married in 1903. Grandfather Trimble sired three red-headed sons; the eldest, Norman, emigrated to Arizona; the middle child, Stanley, followed his father into the RUC and also attained the rank of Sergeant; Billy, the youngest, was born in 1908.[10]

Grandfather Trimble was also a staunch Presbyterian: when Stanley Trimble had his children baptised in the Church of Ireland, Grandfather Trimble was furious, believing that little separated the Anglicans from Rome. 'Were you at Mass today?' he would ask his grandchildren in later years.[11] Grandfather Trimble also signed the Ulster Covenant of 1912 – a mass pledge against Asquith's Home Rule Bill – at the Sandy Row Orange Hall. Indeed, he was a pillar of the Orange Order, rising to the post of Master of Ballynafeigh District Lodge (Ballynafeigh District's traditional 12 July parade through Belfast's Lower Ormeau Road became the most controversial Orange walk after Drumcree during the 1990s). The population of the area, once overwhelmingly Protestant, is now overwhelmingly Catholic; David Trimble wonders what kind of reception he would receive today if he returned to the string of modest terraced houses where Grandfather Trimble used to live in and around the 'Holy Land' of south Belfast (so called because of the large number of Middle Eastern street-names): at Agincourt Avenue, Carmel Street and at Jerusalem Street (where Billy Trimble was born). Latterly he lived across the Lagan at 50 Candahar Street, where the young David used to visit him on day trips.[12]

Strangely, David Trimble was quite unaware of his links to the Ballynafeigh District Lodge until he became leader of the Ulster Unionist party. This may owe something to the influence of his mother, Ivy Jack, who regarded the Loyal Orders as vulgar and who appeared unhappy when the teenaged Trimble eventually joined the Orange Order in 1962 (Billy Trimble was never a member, though he was a Mason). Ivy Jack was born in 1911, the only child of Captain William Jack and of Ida Colhoun. The lineage of Capt. Jack (DT's maternal grandfather) can be traced back at least as far as one Samuel Jack (DT's maternal great-great-grandfather), a landed proprietor of Lisnarrow in the parish of Donagheady, Co. Tyrone, who lived from 1776 to 1846. His son, also Samuel (DT's great-grandfather), became a prominent official of the Londonderry Corporation and for over 30 years served as water superintendent. His death notice in the *Londonderry Sentinel* of 16 February 1897 states that he was 'a staunch Unionist in politics . . . one of the electors who suffered "excommunication" from the Covenanting Church rather than forgo his right to vote at the Parliamentary elections'. Formally known as the Reformed Presbyterian Church of Ireland, the Covenanters were quite separate from the much larger Presbyterian Church in Ireland: they were descended from the Scots Covenanters, and did not agree with the Revolution Settlement of 1689 because it did not reaffirm the Solemn League and Covenant of 1643, which swore to recognise Christ as King of the Nation. Since the Revolution Settlement did not provide the reassurance which they sought, the Covenanters held it was inconsistent for their communicant members to vote in parliamentary elections. Most of their flock went along with this ruling, but Samuel Jack was highly unusual in his unwillingness to give up the hard-won right of Dissenters to exercise this democratic liberty.[13] A hundred or so years later, his Presbyterian great-grandson, David Trimble, would also endure a kind of ostracism – again, risking much for his rejection of what he considered to be the other-worldly purism of some of his fellow Protestants.

Samuel Jack's son, Capt. William Jack (DT's grandfather), worked for J. & J. Cooke, timber merchants and subsequently for Robert Colhoun Ltd, the building and construction firm owned by his wife's family. He was a Derryman all his life – he served on the Board of Guardians – and signed the Ulster Covenant of 1912. Grandfather Jack only left Londonderry during the First World War in his 40s: in June 1915 he was given a temporary commission as a 2nd Lieutenant in the 12th Battalion of the Royal Inniskilling Fusiliers, a support unit which furnished drafts to the 36th (Ulster) Division. In October 1916, he transferred to the southern-recruited Royal Irish Regiment and was posted to the 1st Garrison Battalion which provided guards for bases and prisoners. He then went to Egypt during Allenby's campaign in the Middle East against the Turks, but appears not to have left the place during the liberation of Palestine from the Ottomans. Instead, he spent much of his time in the British military hospital in Cairo: the service records in the PRO say nothing of wounds, as they normally would, suggesting he was felled by malaria or some other infection. After the war, he returned to his home at 5 Eden Terrace, in the city's Northland district.[14] It was some five minutes away from the house in Glenbrook Terrace where Trimble's fellow Nobel Laureate, John Hume, grew up (although, as John Hume is keen to point out, the Jack residence was in a much more up-market area).[15] It is a neighbourhood from where most Protestants have now fled. 'The biggest thing that's happened in Northern Ireland over the last 30 years is the ethnic cleansing of the west bank [of the River Foyle]', notes Trimble. 'There were 10,000 there till the early 1970s. The North Ward was Protestant. That's all gone.'[16]

Captain Jack's wife, Ida, was undoubtedly the most influential of Trimble's grandparents. Following her husband's death, she was crippled and came to live with her daughter and son-in-law until her death in 1966. Ida Jack was ever-present during Trimble's childhood and teenage years and imparted a smattering of loyalist lore to young David. She told him of how the inhabitants of Derry were reduced to eating rats during the Siege of 1689 and of how a forebear, one Robert Colhoun, had been in the Siege. She claimed that he subsequently married a daughter of George Walker, the Rector of Donoughmore and joint governor of the city during the Siege (such claims are, however, not uncommon in many old Ulster families).[17] She also signed the Ulster Covenant in 1912. Family tradition holds that the Colhouns originally came from Doagh Island off the Inishowen peninsula in Co. Donegal. They left in the early 19th century because of deteriorating land conditions and eventually came to Londonderry, via Malins, Co. Donegal, in 1860 (John Hume's family made a not dissimilar journey from Inishowen).[18] The tithe applotment books show that they settled in Elaghtmore in the parish of Templemore, Co. Londonderry. Ida Colhoun was one of seven children of Robert Colhoun and his wife Anne Walker (DT's maternal great-grandparents), the daughter of one David Walker, a leather dealer from the Diamond on the west bank of the Foyle (DT's great-great grandfather). Robert Colhoun had founded the family construction firm: their buildings included the military barracks and Roman Catholic Church at Omagh, substantial tracts of the Bogside, the Guildhall in Londonderry and the Methodist Church at Carlisle Road, also in the Maiden City. The construction firm was eventually run by his mother's first cousin, Senator Jack Colhoun, a former Mayor of Londonderry, known to Trimble as 'Uncle Jack' (prior to the prorogation of Stormont in 1972, the Lord Mayor of Belfast and the Mayor of Londonderry were ex-officio members of the Northern Ireland Senate). The company ran into financial difficulties during the construction of Altnagelvin Hospital, which was to become Londonderry's leading infirmary. Although he did not have to do so, Colhoun sold up in 1961 in order to ensure that none of his sub-contractors was out of pocket. Trimble was impressed by such probity.

Indeed, when the Northern Ireland civil rights movement denounced the 'rotten borough' practices of the old Londonderry Corporation in the late 1960s, Trimble reacted on both a personal and on a political level. Recalls Trimble: 'I thought "Well, I know Uncle Jack. And I know he's not corrupt." So I started to think about things more deeply.'[19]

Billy Trimble met Ivy Jack whilst he was working in Londonderry as a middle-ranking official in the Ministry of Labour; she was a clerk-typist in the same department. They were married in the Great James Street Presbyterian Church in the Maiden City on 7 December 1940. Billy Trimble soon returned to Belfast, where he eventually became the deputy manager of the labour exchange at Corporation Street. Known in the local vernacular as the 'Broo' (a corruption of 'Bureau'), it was the largest such centre in Northern Ireland. The Trimbles settled in Bangor, which had become something of a dormitory town for Belfast and was rapidly expanding because of the post-war baby boom. They resided at an artisan's house, 1 King Street, just off Main Street, where David Trimble lived until he was four: his first memory is of the relaxing of sweets rationing in 1947. Although Trimble could, by his own admission, often be awkward and gauche in his dealings with his parents, peers and the outside world generally, he was always the dominant sibling. His older sister, Rosemary, born in 1943, was not overly assertive; his younger brother Iain, born in 1948, naturally looked up to him.

Trimble's mother, Ivy, was, by his own testimony, 'middle class moving downwards'. Little of the Colhoun legacy came down to her, and she was obliged from the early years of her marriage to bear the burden of caring for her own mother. Moreover, her husband's career went awry in his 40s: it may have had something to do with his heavy drinking, which became even more pronounced in his later years.[20] He would return home from work, listen to the news, fidget and then put on his coat and slip away to the local pub.[21] Indeed, Trimble's earliest recollection of his drinking habit was, at the age of six or seven, of finding beer bottles under the kitchen sink – though, fortunately, there were no great public embarrassments nor huge rows in the parental home.[22] Rather, Iain Trimble recalls, he was simply not there for much of the time.[23] More obviously problematic was Billy Trimble's decision to become a guarantor of a loan on behalf of an associate, which then went wrong. In 1960, the ensuing financial difficulties forced Billy Trimble to sell the semi-detached house which he had built himself with a neighbour at 109 Victoria Road, Bangor, and move a short distance up the hill to rented accommodation in a grander Victorian villa at 39 Clifton Road.

Trimble inherited his looks and his argumentative nature from his father. But, he says, they were perhaps too alike to be really close. 'Like a lot of Ulster Protestant males, Father was emotionally illiterate,' recalls Trimble. 'He told me I was "handless" [clumsy and uncoordinated], which was true, but telling you as much doesn't help.' Efforts by his father to interest him in football by taking him to Bangor FC matches were also unsuccessful.[24] But he bequeathed his son one hobby: music. Not only was classical music always around the house, but Billy Trimble was also a prominent member of the chorus of the Ulster Operatic Company, performing in productions of such Gilbert and Sullivan operettas as *Trial by Jury* and *Patience*. David Trimble also did some acting at school – playing the part of Stanley in *Richard III* – and later for the Bangor Drama Society: he says that these performances probably did as much as anything to increase his self-confidence. During the 1980s, as chairman of the Ulster Society, he also put on several productions of the plays of St John Ervine, the Ulster writer and dramatist. Although Trimble is no singer, and does not play any instrument, music remains his greatest enthusiasm and the family drawing room bulges with several thousands of albums. His first love was Elvis Presley; later, he graduated to Puccini, Verdi and Wagner (his particular favourite). Indeed, in times of crisis, says Daphne Trimble, such as after the setting up of the first inclusive Northern Ireland Executive in late 1999, he will turn to his records for solace.[25]

Trimble's relations with his mother were not very good, either. From her, too, he encountered a measure of coldness – the origins of which may owe something to the infant David's error of throwing her engagement ring into the fire.[26] Whatever the reality of their relationship, Ivy Trimble was the dominant personality within the household. She was also determined to maintain appearances and became a pillar of suburban society, both as chairman of the Women's Institute in Bangor and of the 'B&P' (or the Business and Professional Club). David Montgomery – who later became an important Trimble ally as Chief Executive of Mirror Group Newspapers which owned the *News Letter* and who grew up 100 yards away from the Trimble family – recalls that they 'epitomised the Ballyholme-Shandon Drive society and were much more visibly upmarket than we were'.[27] If so, it was relative privilege, for when Trimble entered

Ballyholme Primary School, he was conscious of residing outside that catchment area and of coming from slightly the wrong side of the tracks. He may not have wanted for any essentials, but his home could not be said to have been 'earth's recurring paradise' – to quote Tennyson's poem 'Helen's Tower', about the folly built near Bangor by the First Marquess of Dufferin and Ava.[28]

The Trimble household could not, in the old Ulster phrase, be described as especially 'good living' – in the sense that alcohol, smoking and theatregoing were obviously indulged. Likewise, profane music and books were allowed on Sundays.[29] But certain traditional practices and forms were nonetheless observed. The family worshipped at Trinity Second Presbyterian Congregation of Bangor, whose minister John T. Carson had written several volumes, including a school story entitled *Presbyterian and Proud Of It* and *God's River In Spate*, a study of the 1859 religious awakening known as the Year of Grace; in 1966, he was called to the Moderatorial Chair of the General Assembly. Carson was in the forefront of the moderate evangelicalism of the Presbyterian Church in Ireland in the postwar era and Trimble was an enthusiastic congregant from his teenaged years through to his mid-twenties. Between the ages of eleven and fourteen, Trimble spent part of several Christmas holidays at the interdenominational Belfast Bible College and attended morning and evening services every Sunday and at midweek, as well as special services: according to Iain Trimble, he was undoubtedly the most observant member of the family.[30] He was also 'headhunted' for a variety of tasks by the kirk authorities, of whom the most influential was Michael Brunyate, an Englishman who worked as an engineer at Harland and Wolff. Trinity wanted to attract more holidaymakers to its services and to that end, the young Trimble assisted Brunyate in rigging up the sound system to blare out hymns on Main Street: because of copyright problems, they had to pre-record their own devotional music.[31] But this was not just a pastime for an awkward, bookish teenager: Trimble recalls that he was a genuine 'fundamentalist', asserting the literal truth of the Bible. Moreover, he was a 'creationist' – in the sense of believing it to be an accurate description of the order in which God created the world, though he always entertained doubts about the precise six-day timespan (he remains doubtful about Darwinian evolutionary theory to this day, but on intellectual rather than theological grounds). He would continue to be an ardent church-goer until the late sixties – though he declines to say why he stopped, on the grounds that it would be 'too complex' to explain.[32] Notwithstanding his often excellent memory, he would make a reluctant, even poor witness for the likes of Anthony Clare.

Perhaps because of the uneasy relationship with his parents, and his lack of coordination, Trimble was thrown back on his own resources at an early age. This self-sufficiency took both intellectual and emotional forms. Certainly, books were the safest refuge of all from family and contemporaries alike. His siblings recall him poring endlessly over war adventure stories: his brother Iain recalls that young David would read by candlelight after his parents switched off the lights at 9:00 p.m.[33] Later, he moved on to Winston Churchill's *The Unknown War*, about the eastern front during the First World War, and delighted in mastering the geography and history of the obscure countries described in that volume. Yet for many years, Trimble's knowledge of the outside world was largely derived from books. Despite his curiosity, he never holidayed overseas – apart from a couple of school-trips to Austria and Germany – until he married Daphne Orr in 1978. His parents could afford only cycling holidays in the Mourne Mountains or the Trossachs, where the entire family would stay in youth hostels.[34]

Such mastery of detail may have been entirely theoretical, but it served Trimble well in his own home. He established his pre-eminence in the house as much through a natural ability with words and his excellent memory, as through physical force. 'You could never argue with David because he always retained any information,' recalls Iain Trimble, who left home at fifteen to join the RAF as an apprentice photographer. 'He would always know more than you did. Which was quite frustrating. But it had the effect on me that if David said something, I'd believe it.' Whether the issue at hand was the Munich air disaster of 1958, the Floyd Patterson–Ingemar Johansson fight, or Elvis Presley, the young Trimble acquired an encyclopaedic mastery of the details.[35] Trimble is often called an intellectual snob, but this is not quite right: he could more accurately be described as a knowledge snob, whatever the subject. Even today, notes Daphne Trimble, 'he can be quite happy spending the evening at home reading, without exchanging a word with anybody in the family'.[36]

Such traits and interests set Trimble apart from his contemporaries at an early age – first at the Central Primary, then at Ballyholme Primary. In consequence, Trimble's mother entertained hopes that he might attend Campbell College (one of Northern Ireland's leading independent schools). Such aspirations were short-lived – especially after his father pointed out that they could not afford travel costs, let alone the fees. But he passed the 11-plus – the only one of the three Trimble children to do so – and in the autumn of 1956 he began at Bangor Grammar. Located within 100 yards of home, at College Avenue, it was an all-boys school of 350–400 pupils. Following his successful interview in June of that year, the headmaster, Randall Clarke – a former housemaster at Campbell College – wrote at the time that the young Trimble was possessed of good speech and manners. In appearance, he was neat and red-headed. He added that he was 'over-studious and over-conscientious. Nice child. Highly intelligent. Precocious.' He wondered: 'Has he been pushed too much?'[37]

The remark may have said something about the Trimble household, but it also said something about the prevailing ethos of Bangor Grammar: Jim Driscoll, who came to Bangor Grammar from Ballymena Academy in 1952 to teach Classics, found that 'to a certain extent, it reflected the tone of a holiday town'.[38] This, of course, is precisely what it was. Bangor, known in the 19th century as 'the Brighton of the North', was a quiet seaside resort of faded grandeur; some of the older people then had never even been to Belfast. True, Bangor Abbey, founded in 558 by St Comgall, had been one the centres of learning in medieval Europe – which explains why the spot is one of only four places in Ireland referred to in the late twelfth-century Mappa Mundi.[39] By the 1950s any such academic distinction was mostly a thing of the past and university entrants, let alone Oxbridge awards, were then comparatively rare. But such qualifications were not really needed: higher education was the exception rather than the norm and, as Jim Driscoll recalls, most school-leavers had little difficulty in finding jobs.[40] Its proudest achievements were in sports and to this day, two of the most celebrated Old Bangorians are still Dick Milliken, the former British Lion, and Terry Neill, the football player and manager. Nor does the school appear to make much of its other famous politicians: one was H.M. Pollock, the first Finance Minister of Northern Ireland, and the other was Brian Faulkner, who attended Bangor Grammar briefly before completing his education at St Columba's in Dublin. Faulkner was the last Unionist politician who attempted an 'historic compromise' with Irish nationalism in 1973–4, and destroyed himself politically in the process. [41]

Bangor and its Grammar School were also socially ambitious – as was implied by the school song, *Floreat Bangoria*, adopted in conscious imitation of the Eton motto *Floreat Etona*. Indeed, class, rather than religious sectarianism, was the sharp dividing line in this overwhelmingly Protestant town. Although the Catholic Church was on the periphery of town (the three Presbyterian and two Church of Ireland houses of worship were conspicuously in the centre) there was no such thing as a 'ghetto'. Indeed, a few Catholics were to be found amongst both staff and pupils of Bangor Grammar and the two 'communities' socialised quite freely. Nor did Ivy Trimble have any objection to her sons associating with Catholic boys, provided they came from the 'right' sort of background, such as Terry Higgins and his brother Malachy (now Mr Justice Higgins); another Catholic friend was Derek Davis, later a BBC Northern Ireland and RTE presenter. Ivy Trimble's prejudices were not untypical of the time, and David Montgomery recalls that his mother shared the same attitude to contact with Catholics.[42] If most of Trimble's friends were Protestants, it was simply because they formed the bulk of the population – but, recalls Terry Higgins, that applied equally to Catholic boys such as himself.[43]

Bangor Grammar's cocktail of physical hardiness, social snobbery and academic mediocrity did not appeal to Trimble. Moreover, he disliked Randall Clarke personally. 'He treated me like a remedial pupil,' Trimble recalls.[44] So uncongenial did Trimble find Bangor Grammar that he now regards his main achievement as avoiding sports for two years. Certainly, he was an academic late-developer, only really coming into his own when he began his legal studies at Queen's. But neither was he a disaster, as some of his own recollections imply. The programme for the 1963 Speech Day shows that he won first prize in Ancient History and second prize in Geography and Latin. Still, he received no particular encouragement from Clarke to go to university. Certainly, many of Trimble's reports are replete with references to his 'carelessness' – something to which he was prone when not interested in the matter at hand. In his final term, in 1963, Clarke commented: 'This boy has a lively mind which sometimes leads him into irrelevance which can be disastrous in examination conditions.'

Trimble's teachers now remember a nervous, highly-strung boy who was a bit of a loner. He does not disagree: his friends were so few in number that he cannot recall the names of many of those with whom he was at school.[45] It is, therefore, curious that the swottish and 'handless' Trimble was never bullied. Perhaps it was because there was something forbidding about him. Family and friends recall a terribly serious and pencil-thin Buddy Holly lookalike, who could walk straight past any number of friends and acquaintances with the most tightly rolled-up umbrella anyone had ever seen.[46] 'The only way in which David was extreme was in his music and his reading,' his closest school-friend, Martin Mawhinney now says.[47] Trimble first heard Elvis' 'All Shook Up' in the amusement arcades of Bangor in 1957 and never looked back. Once, he and his friends went to three Presley films in a day: they began with *Loving You* at the now-demolished Tonic Cinema in Bangor (with its great Hammond organ which would emerge from the floor during the interval); then to Newtownards to see *Jailhouse Rock*; the 'treble bill' would then be rounded off in a Belfast cinema. He acquired a Rover 90 for £50; and he taught himself how to drive it from the handbook. As a result, he crashed into a lamp-post on his first outing and did not drive again until he was into his 40s.

Trimble's recollections of an uneven academic performance may have owed something to his growing commitment to 825 Squadron of the Air Training Corps – the Bangor area 'feeder' for RAF ground crews (indeed, according to school records, Trimble indicated upon entry into Bangor Grammar that he wanted to go into the RAF). Leslie Cree, an older boy who was already a Warrant Officer in the ATC, recalls that 'in the early days we reckoned he was a wee bit of a boffin', with little sense of humour. But in fulfilling his tasks assiduously – which included shooting competitions with the local sub-division of the Ulster Special Constabulary, or 'B' Specials – Trimble earned respect. Cree thinks it helps explain why he was never bullied.[48] To this day, Trimble recalls with pleasure his low-flying experiences in England, hedge-hopping in a Chipmunk. It was also an institution where sectarian tensions were not high: Trimble was much impressed when one recruit personally gathered up his fellow Roman Catholic cadets and took them off to Mass in Bangor in full uniform before heading off to the parade ground.[49]

The ATC was significant to Trimble in social terms. As Cree points out 'he gradually became more acceptable and part of the human race'. Moreover, he had taken risks – such as a near crash landing at RAF Bishopscourt near Downpatrick – and actually enjoyed it. But its effects were more long-term. It was through the ATC that Trimble made the contacts which led him into the Orange Order and ultimately into politics. Although Trimble had been promoted to corporal in 1962, his poor eyesight meant he could never take up a career even in the ground crews. Those who were not going to enter the RAF had to leave the ATC by 18. Many, including Leslie Cree, went from the ATC into the 'B' Specials – then run by the district commandant, George Green, who later became an important figure in the hardline Vanguard party.[50] But Trimble's hand-eye coordination, though good enough with a .22 was less good with a .303, and potential entrants had to be proficient with both. How, then, would he stay in touch with his mates? The Orange Order provided at least a partial answer.

It was, nonetheless, a curious choice for Trimble in some ways. First of all, it obviously excluded his Catholic friends. Second, even in pre-Troubles Ulster – when the Order had a far larger middle-class member-ship – relatively few boys from Bangor Grammar joined up. As David Montgomery recalls, 'Bangor had middle-class English pretensions and therefore the Orange Order would have been seen as a bit comic.'[51] Third, neither of Trimble's parents belonged to it and his father's unionism amounted to little more than raising a Union flag on 12 July and putting up election posters for the local MP in the provincial Parliament, Dr Robert Nixon, who was also the family GP. Fourth, Orangeism in Bangor was shaped by the Church of Ireland and Trimble was, of course, a Presbyterian. Indeed, Cree, who was then a member of the Church of Ireland, recalls that it was no easy matter to persuade Trimble to join: Trimble gave a stirring defence of the 'Blackmouth', or the cause of the Dissenters. But Cree showed Trimble that the Order brought all Protestant denominations together in defence of their civil and religious liberties, and he was duly sworn into Loyal Orange Lodge 726, otherwise known as 'Bangor Abbey'.[52] Founded in 1948 by members of the Abbey Church, it was a smallish Lodge, 30 to 45 strong. Membership was in that period 60 to 70% Church of Ireland; it is still around 40% 'Anglican', as it were. It was a classless cross-section of society composed, amongst others, of civil servants, butchers and gas fitters. Unusually for a Lodge, it had no Orange Hall, meeting instead on Church premises. Trimble did not then know much about Orange culture, but he rapidly mastered its 'Consti-tution, Law and Ordinances', and for a period became Lodge Treasurer. In these early days, he attended every one of the Lodge's six or seven parades that were held each year.[53]

The mildness of Bangor Orangeism of the era may also owe something to the fact that it was quite untouched during the IRA Border campaign of 1956 to 1962. Indeed, Cree remembers that Trimble and his friends were utterly shocked when a Republican slogan was painted on an advertising hoarding in Hamilton Road, Bangor. Indeed, so solid and secure was the world of Bangor Orangeism that the word 'Loyalism' would not even have been understood, at least in its contemporary sense, back then. That was only to come to the area with the onset of the Troubles, when housing clearances brought former residents of the Shankill and east Belfast to new estates in Breezemount and Kilcooley: the paramilitary influences came with some of them. Everything was assumed, and the world-view of the area can best be summed up by the genteel, stock phrase to be found in obituaries of the time in the *County Down Spectator* – 'a staunch Unionist in politics'.[54]

It makes Trimble's subsequent flirtation with the more robust elements in Orangeism – above all, at Drumcree – all the more curious. LOL 726 did go as a whole to show solidarity with their brethren during the first 'Siege of Drumcree' in 1995, which helped to propel Trimble to the Ulster Unionist Party leadership, but not in subsequent years. Indeed, he only joined the Royal Black Preceptory, the senior organisation within the Orange family, in the early 1990s at the behest of constituents in Lurgan (his lodge is RBP 207 or 'Sons of Joseph'). This was after declining earlier offers from lodges in Bangor to join 'the Black'. In other words, he did so as an act of duty as much as out of a desire to participate regularly in its activities. Indeed, by 1972, Trimble had dropped out from regular attendance at meetings of LOL 726. Partly, it was a question of professional commitments: Trimble believes that one of the problems with the Loyal Orders over many decades has been that instead of focusing on the great political questions ahead of them, they have devoted their energies to the rituals of Orange life with its incessant round of quasi-Masonic meetings and social gatherings.[55] Certainly, it was impossible to envisage him seeking higher office either in the District or the County Grand Lodge – in contrast, say, to his parliamentary colleague, Rev. Martin Smyth or John Miller Andrews, Northern Ireland's second Prime Minister, in retirement.[56]

Such concerns were far removed from the mind of the young Trimble as he contemplated his future in his last year at school. Quite apart from the discouraging noises which emerged from Randall Clarke, his father did not believe he could afford to go to university and tried to interest him in the Provincial Bank, later amalgamated with other institutions into the Allied Irish Bank. Billy Trimble had passed the Queen's University matriculation aged sixteen, but he could not afford to attend: his son wonders whether paternal jealousy may have played a part in the counsel he gave (the contrast with the pleasure which David Trimble derived from his eldest child's success in obtaining entry to Cambridge could not have been greater).[57] There was also the fear of rising unemployment, which seemed high by the standards of the time, though it was low compared to later jobless rates. Consequently, Trimble opted for security. He saw an advert to join the Northern Ireland Civil Service (NICS) and was admitted on the basis of his surprisingly good 'A' Level results. In the following September, he was posted as a Clerk to the General Register Office at Fermanagh House in Belfast, compiling the weekly bulletin which recorded births and deaths.[58] Like his father before him, Trimble seemed destined for a life of comparative anonymity.

A don is born

TRIMBLE duly began his career in the NICS in September 1963, on a monthly salary of £35. He was rapidly transferred to the Land Registry – tucked away at the Royal Courts of Justice in Chichester Street, because it had originally been part of the Courts Service. The Northern Ireland Government, however, seemed most of the time to have forgotten the existence of this Dickensian backwater: a musty, overcrowded warren of rooms with high windows. It was primarily a place where paper was stored and when ancient title deeds would be brought out from the bowels of the registry, the member of staff would often find his clothing covered in dust. When a property transaction occurred, a change in the entry of ownership was required in the relevant folio; Trimble's job was to make a draft of the new entry. But the drudgery had a purpose. Transfer to the Land Registry afforded access to the NICS's scheme for recruiting lawyers. Under this programme, civil servants could study part-time for a law degree at Queen's University Belfast, whilst continuing their professional tasks, and then return at a higher grade.[1]

Tempting as the prospect was, Trimble asked himself whether he would be up to the task. After all, no Trimble had ever been to university. Queen's was then the only fully-fledged university in the Province and the most solid of redbrick foundations. It had been founded as Queen's College after the passage of the Irish Universities Act of 1845 as part of Sir Robert Peel's reforms. Hitherto, the Ascendancy had dominated higher education, as embodied by Trinity College Dublin. But the burgeoning middle classes, Catholic and Dissenter alike, demanded something more. Three such institutions were set up. Two of them, at Cork and Galway, were intended to serve the predominantly Catholic population of the south and the west and one, in Belfast, was to serve the overwhelmingly non-conformist population of the north-east. As such, it heavily reflected the Presbyterian ethos.[2] Although there was still a residual sense amongst Protestants, even in Trimble's time, that this was 'our University', he was initially hesitant about applying. The competition was stiff, and when the NICS scheme was pioneered in the previous year only two out of the 300 applicants had made it. But Michael Brunyate, who was still one of the greatest influences on Trimble's life, persuaded him that he would never be happy within himself if he did not obtain a degree.[3]

Trimble applied, and managed to win one of two NICS places for 1964: the other went to Herb Wallace, a friend and colleague from the Land Registry who would later hold a Professorial chair and serve as Vice Chairman of the Police Authority. Wallace initially thought the pencil-thin, ginger-haired, red-faced youth was 'a bit odd'; but they were soon to become firm friends. Again, like Trimble's family and school contemporaries, Wallace was impressed by his knowledge and authority, especially when it came to current affairs. Trimble was already a critic of Terence O'Neill, the mildly liberal Prime Minister of Northern Ireland from 1963 to 1969, as much because of his unattractive and haughty manner as because of his policies. Wallace recalls that Trimble then regarded Ian Paisley, who was starting to make waves in opposition to O'Neill's policies, as a crank.[4] Instead, he admired the two most dynamic figures in the Provincial Government: William Craig, the Development Minister, and Brian Faulkner, the Commerce Minister. He considered them both to be 'doers'. Trimble, who was irritated by the parochialism of the Northern Ireland news, was more stimulated by events further afield. During the General Election of 1964, he loathed Harold Wilson, identifying more with Sir Alec Douglas-Home; he was passionately interested in Rhodesian UDI and ardently backed the United States over Vietnam. He was also influenced in his opinion of the Cold War by the London-based monthly journal of culture and politics, *Encounter*, in which contributors often urged a tough line on the Soviets.[5]

Queen's Law Faculty was then still very much in its 'golden epoch'. Along with Medicine, it had always been the most prestigious of the University departments and enjoyed an intimate relationship with the Provincial Bar and Judiciary. Places were specially set aside for law students in the library, who then underwent a four-year course. The student numbers, though they had increased substantially since the 1950s, were still very small compared to today – around 40 in each year. It was also a place where Catholic and Protestant undergraduates mixed relatively easily. But what made Queen's outstanding in this epoch was the quality of the teaching staff. They included colleagues such as William Twining, later Professor at University College London; Claire Palley, who taught Family and Roman Law and later became Principal of St Anne's College Oxford; Lee Sheridan, later Professor of Law at University College Cardiff; and Harry Calvert, a Yorkshireman who had written what was then the definitive text on the Northern Ireland Constitution.[6] Moreover, these academic grandees set the most demanding of standards: some years could go by when no 'firsts' were awarded, and even '2:1s' would be dispensed sparingly enough; many would fail their first-year exams.

Yet although Trimble was only a part-timer, he flourished. Indeed, in some ways, he rather resembled the young Edward Heath, whose life only really 'began' after he left his small-town grammar school and went up to Oxford.[7] Oddly, perhaps, in the light of Trimble's dislike of the work of the Land Registry, he particularly enjoyed Property Law and its bizarre algebraic logic, which he took in the final two years: but, unlike other 'swots', recalls Herb Wallace, he was always very generous about sharing his copious lecture notes.[8] So absorbing did he find the work that he began to attend less to duties in the Land Registry and in his final year took leave of absence.[9] Queen's, however, spotted his academic potential and in his fourth year William Twining informed him that he ought to consider taking up a teaching post – subject to his obtaining the right result. Trimble took an outstanding first in his Finals that summer and won the McKane Medal for Jurisprudence. On the basis of that achievement, he was offered an assistant lecturership in Land Law and Equity, with a starting salary of £1,100 per annum. The front page of the *County Down Spectator* of 5 July 1968 pictured him on the front page and claimed with pride that the local boy was the only Queen's student to take a first for three years. But his graduation was marred by the death of his father the night before the ceremony. In his will, Billy Trimble left an estate worth £3078.

Why did Trimble opt to become a lecturer? He also loved Planning Law and easily had the intellectual ability to become, in due course, a well-paid silk in London (indeed, he was called to the Northern Ireland Bar in 1969 and by Gray's Inn in 1970: two of his fellow pupils in the bar finals included Claire Palley and the late Jeffrey Foote, subsequently a leading QC and County Court Judge). Curiously, despite the small nature of society in Northern Ireland, he had few contacts at the Bar who would take him on as a pupil: his mother's childhood friend from Londonderry, Lord Justice McVeigh, politely heard out Ivy Trimble's representations on behalf of her son, but opened no doors for him. When eventually Trimble was called to the Bar, he was so lacking in contacts that his memorial had to be signed by a man who did not know him well, Robert Carswell, QC, subsequently Lord Chief Justice of Northern Ireland and a Law Lord (indeed, to this day, many practitioners of the law in Northern Ireland look down upon Trimble as not a 'real' lawyer). His decision to become an academic may also have had something to do with his shyness and awkwardness, which mattered less in the more arcane realms of Property Law than it would have in the more social atmosphere of the Bar Library (the Northern Ireland Bar operates a library system, inherited from the old Irish Bar, rather than Chambers). Above all, Trimble knew that any proceeds from a practice at the Bar would be some time in coming. Legal aid had been introduced in Northern Ireland only in 1966 and prior to the Troubles, the law was still a comparatively small profession. And he now had another reason to opt for financial security: he had met the local girl he wanted to marry.[10]

Trimble had first encountered Heather McCombe from Donaghadee at the Land Registry. She was a plump and very popular girl; they were first spotted together at the office Christmas party of 1967. His friends and colleagues thought her a surprising choice. Not only was she outgoing where he was shy, but she was not obviously bookish. Nonetheless, they were married on 13 September 1968 at Donaghadee Parish Church with Martin Mawhinney as his best man; they honeymooned in Bray, Co. Wicklow – Trimble's first visit to the Irish Republic ('I had no idea how deeply unfashionable it was,' he now recalls).[11] On the proceeds of his work for the Supreme Court Rules Committee, he bought their first marital home at 11 Henderson Drive in Bangor. She soon became pregnant, and six months into her pregnancy went into premature labour. Trimble went to the hospital that evening, but did not appreciate fully what was happening and the medical staff told him to go home and to obtain some sleep. When he returned, twin sons had been born – but one had already died and the other was dying.[12] Trimble went into shock and according to Iain Trimble, withdrew into himself.[13] Subsequently, Heather Trimble became one of the first women to join the Ulster Defence Regiment, otherwise known as 'Greenfinches'.[14] It became an all-consuming passion for her and, indeed, many UDR marriages broke up in this period because of the highly demanding hours.[15] The combination of their social and work commitments soon put the marriage under intolerable strain. The hearing was held before the Lord Chief Justice, Sir Robert Lowry, and the decree absolute was granted before Lord Justice McGonigal in 1976.[16]

The unhappiness of Trimble's domestic life contrasted sharply with the growing satisfaction which he derived from his professional duties in the Department of Property Law headed by Lee Sheridan. It was perhaps all the more remarkable because he never became part of the 'in-set' around Calvert and Sheridan who played bridge and squash. He has always felt an outsider, whether at Ballyholme Primary, Bangor Grammar, Queen's, even in the Ulster Unionist Party. 'In those years I was suffering from an inferiority complex,' remembers Trimble. 'Not because the people around me are English – though that's a wee bit of it. No, it's because the people around me are confident. I'm a bit unsure of myself. Francis Newark asked me if I played bridge. I felt uneasy about saying no, but at the same time I wasn't going to learn it just to please him.' Even today, he looks at himself and says: 'It's a curious thing: deep down inside I believe I'm very good but somehow I'm not always managing to reflect that in what I do.'[17] Certainly, he was then unsophisticated. Claire Palley recalls how she and Trimble went to a French restaurant in the Strand after they completed their Bar exams: Trimble preferred the traditional British fare of steak and chips.[18] The contrast with today's Trimble – who has to order the most exotic items from the menu – could not be greater.

As throughout his life, Trimble gained self-confidence – and thus respect – by mastering his subject. His Chancery-type of mind, in contra-distinction to the kind of horsedealing required at the criminal Bar, was perfectly suited to his dry-as-dust subjects. Students would often sense self-doubt in a lecturer, but Trimble kept order by asking questions which he knew nobody could answer. And when he himself then gave the response he would be able to cite the relevant case from his phenomenal memory and without referring to the textbook. Later, in judging moots, he would search on the Lexis Nexis database to check if there were any unreported decisions so he could pull the students up short; he hates nothing more than to be wrong-footed. Some, such as Alex Attwood – who became a prominent SDLP politician – thought him colourless; but as Attwood concedes, Trimble's subjects were not necessarily those which would inspire someone imbued with great reforming or radical zeal.[19]

Others, such as Alban Maginness, who subsequently became the first SDLP Lord Mayor of Belfast, enjoyed his lectures.[20] This was because he invested his subject with such enthusiasm, and would bound about his room waving his arms around. Another plus point for many students, recalls Judith Eve – later Dean of the Law School – was that Trimble was young and local.[21] In 1971, he was promoted to Lecturer and in 1973 he was elected Assistant Dean of the Faculty, with responsibility for admissions. This appointment was a tribute to the impartiality with which he conducted his duties. Trimble later became a controversial figure in the University, but in this period his outside political activities were relatively low profile and in any case he was always assiduous in keeping his views out of the classroom (though that was easier when teaching subjects such as Property and Equity, rather than the thornier area of constitutional law). Few, if any, in this period thought twice that he conveyed the 'wrong image' – least of all to have him go round schools of all kinds and denominations to extol the virtues of law as a career.

The effects of his term as Dean for admissions were significant. Only about 10 per cent of 500–600 hopefuls were accepted in this period. But according to Claire Palley, who regularly returned to Belfast, the percentage of Roman Catholic entrants rose markedly.[22] Of course, this had little to do with Trimble, and owed far more to broader sociological circumstances. But this supposed 'bigot' did nothing to retard these developments and was renowned for meticulously sifting every application (only mature students did interviews). Indeed, so assiduous was he in discharging his responsibilities to students that when one of them was interned for alleged Republican sympathies, Trimble went down to Long Kesh to give him one-to-one tutorials; even at the height of the Troubles, he also regularly went to nationalist west Belfast to the Ballymurphy Welfare Rights Centre as part of a university scheme to help the underprivileged, taking the bus up the Falls to the Whiterock Road. And despite the subsequent growth of a highly litigious 'grievance culture', no one can remember any accusations of sectarian remarks, still less of discrimination; he was never subjected to a Fair Employment Commission case of any kind. This is why he was so vexed when Alex Attwood accused him of being distant towards nationalist students: Trimble would have been impartially cold towards all.[23] 'There was a level of reserve there, undoubtedly,' remembers Alban Maginness. 'It was fitting enough for a lecturer in the Law Faculty. He didn't engage in simulated informality in a classroom context.'[24] Nor, notes Claire Palley, a one-time colleague, was he any sort of misogynist – and he shared none of the condescending attitudes of some Ulster males towards female colleagues.[25] The truth is that he is an old-fashioned meritocrat, who deplores the excesses of discrimination and anti-discrimination alike.

Trimble may have been the only member of the Orange Order on the Law Faculty staff, but that did not preclude good relationships with those colleagues who most certainly did not share his views (others were, of course, unionists with a lower case 'u', in the sense that they believed in the maintenance of the constitutional status quo, but were not Loyalists in the way that Trimble was). Thus, he enjoyed a good, bantering relationship with Kevin Boyle, a left-wing Catholic from Newry. Indeed, when his first marriage was breaking up, Trimble would even turn to Boyle for advice.[26] Trimble's best-known academic work, *Northern Ireland Housing Law: The Public and Private Rented Sectors* (SLS:1986), was written with Tom Hadden, a liberal Protestant, who also did not share his views.[27]

Trimble and Hadden had also clashed at faculty meetings over the Fair Employment Agency's attempt to review recruitment practices at Queen's, when Trimble was one of the few with either the courage or the intellect to challenge the assumptions of that body.[28] Moreover, whereas Trimble was a 'black letter lawyer', Hadden was very much more in the jurisprudential tradition. But for the purposes of this project, their complementary skills worked very well. Trimble was teaching housing law in the context of his property courses – such as how to sue landlords – and Hadden was covering the same terrain in the context of social policy. Trimble wrote three chapters, including those dealing with planning issues relating to clearance and development and technical landlord–tenant matters in the private sector (Northern Ireland's housing then differed from that of the rest of the United Kingdom in having a substantial rented sector). It was an authoritative consolidation of this amalgam of the old Stormont legislation with the Orders in Council which came in with the introduction of direct rule from Westminster in 1972; and it vindicated the expectations of the publishers, SLS (run from the Queen's Law Faculty), that it would be of use to practitioners, and sold its entire print run.[29] So impartial was Trimble in the conduct of his duties that when eventually he did become involved in Ulster Vanguard, many of his colleagues were surprised: the first that David Moore knew of any political commitments on his part was when he saw Trimble on television during the 1973 Assembly elections.[30] Events soon ensured that it would not turn out to be an image that he would sustain for long.

THREE

In the Vanguard

'I AM a product of the destruction of Stormont', is David Trimble's summation of his political genesis. On 24 March 1972, the British Prime Minister, Edward Heath, announced the prorogation of Northern Ireland's Provincial Parliament and replaced it with direct rule from Westminster. The Troubles had already claimed 318 deaths, leading London to conclude that Ulster's devolved system of government known by the shorthand of 'Stormont' was no longer the best way of kicking the issue of Northern Ireland 'into touch'. Rather, as the Heath ministry saw it, Stormont was exacerbating the problem.[1] Many Unionists, including Trimble, believed that Heath had tyrannically altered the terms of the 1920 constitutional settlement – which they had imagined could only be done by agreement with Stormont. Since then, one of the consistent aims of Trimble's political life has been to undo the effects of this traumatic episode, by regaining local control over the affairs of the Province. His argument with Unionist critics of the 1998 Belfast Agreement centres on whether he has paid too high a price to attain that objective.

Why was this imposing edifice of Portland limestone, named after its location deep inside Protestant east Belfast, invested with such significance?[2] Before the First World War, the Ulster Unionists had bitterly resisted devolved government to all of Ireland, otherwise known as 'Home Rule'. They argued that it was little more than a halfway house to incorporation into an all-Ireland Republic, in which their liberties would endlessly be trampled upon by the island-wide Catholic majority. Led by Sir Edward Carson, they preferred to be governed like any other part of the United Kingdom from the Imperial Parliament at Westminster. But Lloyd George and the bulk of the British political class were not prepared to grant them this demand.[3] Westminster had been convulsed for at least a generation by the affairs of Ireland and the parliamentary elites now wished to hold them at arm's length. If possible, they also wished ultimately to reconcile the 26 (predominantly Catholic) southern counties with the six (heavily Protestant) northern counties. A permanently divided Ireland, many of the ruling elite calculated, could only be a recipe for further conflict and embarrassment in Britain's backyard – and a possible strategic threat in time of war. Equally, an attempt to coerce Ulster into a united Ireland would also cause fighting and embarrassment.

Lloyd George, therefore, gave the Ulster Unionists a stark choice. He conceded that the six northern counties neither would nor could be coerced into a united Ireland. Ulster could 'opt-out' and run their own unique, semi-detached institutions of government – that is, Home Rule. The Ulster Unionists, who had never wanted this anomalous arrangement, now reluctantly accepted it in the changed circumstances. Many in London had at first envisaged it as only a temporary expedient, leading to eventual reunification. But over time, the Unionists became comfortable with this settlement – maybe too comfortable for their own good. 'A Protestant Parliament and a Protestant state' was governed from 1922 by the Ulster Unionist Party: the phrase was coined in a debate on 24 April 1934 by Carson's successor, Sir James Craig, the first Prime Minister of Northern Ireland. It was made in response to de Valera's remarks about the Catholic nature of its southern counterpart (it was in the same speech that Craig also used another memorable phrase, 'I have always said I am an Orangeman first and a politician and member of this Parliament afterwards').[4] Stormont thus came to be seen by the Ulster Unionists as their bulwark against a united Ireland. Or, more precisely, it was seen as a bulwark against potential British pressure to join such a state: the experiences of 1919 to 1921 had taught the Ulster Unionists that the liberties of this small group of British subjects could easily be sacrificed where broader British interests were deemed to be at stake. Ulster Unionists may have formed a majority in the six counties, but they were in a tiny minority in the United Kingdom as a whole. Stormont thus became the institutional expression of their wish to control their own destiny and the pace of change. Indeed, the famous Unionist slogan 'Not an inch' is an abbreviation of another of Sir James Craig's pronouncements – 'not an inch *without the consent of the Parliament of Northern Ireland*'.[5]

Despite the rocky beginnings of the Northern Ireland state, successive British Governments did pay for the post-1921 settlement because Lloyd George's solution of 'semi-detachment' seemed to have worked. During

Terence O'Neill's modernisation programme in the mid-1960s, it even appeared that residual sectarian differences would be dramatically modi-fied by the 'white heat' of new technology. While allegations of discrimi-nation in housing and employment and gerrymandering of electoral boundaries were still raised from time to time by assorted British civil libertarians and Labour MPs with large Irish populations in their con-stituencies, the issue of Northern Ireland was never at the forefront of the public consciousness until the late 1960s. Even within Ulster itself, the future looked rosy: David Trimble first became interested in national and international politics precisely because he found the politics of the pre-Troubles Province to be so soporific. Unlike many of his Unionist peer group, such as Sir Reg Empey or David Burnside, he had neither joined the Young Unionists nor the Queen's University Unionist Associ-ation. Indeed, some loyalist critics of the Belfast Agreement told me privately that Trimble's apparent emergence from nowhere suggested that he was some kind of long-term plant of the British state inside the unionist community.

A simpler explanation is that times of upheaval bring improbable individuals to the fore. After 1968, the state of Northern Ireland was under relentless assault. The offensive came first from the Civil Rights movement, elements of which successfully portrayed Stormont as little more than a discriminatory instrument of Protestant hegemony, and then from the resurgent IRA. Protestants, feeling their position under threat, retaliated. The exhausted RUC could not cope and regular British troops were dispatched during 1969 to aid the civil power. Three provincial Prime Ministers – Terence O'Neill, James Chichester-Clark and Brian Faulkner – resigned or were deposed in quick succession. Worse still from a Unionist viewpoint, many of the nationalist allegations of sectarian injustices and a repressive security system now found a sympathetic hear-ing in British official and journalistic circles. As long as Stormont 'worked' (in the sense of keeping things quiet) the British were happy enough to let it be. Once it was seen as a source of discontent and international embarrassment, the British cast around for less bothersome alternatives. The allegations against Stormont shaped one of the constants of British Government policy over a quarter-century: namely, that Unionists could never again be trusted with simple majority rule on the basis of the first-past-the-post electoral system. Henceforward, they would have to share power with representatives of the nationalist minority.

To a young man like Trimble, it all had a 'disorienting effect. The established landmarks in one's life were shifting and I did not know where it would lead to.'[6] Trimble also disliked the way in which the British Army, which was accountable to central government, was introduced on to the streets of Northern Ireland in 1969. Like so many Loyalists, he felt it undermined the role of the old RUC and the locally raised militia called the Ulster Special Constabulary (or 'B' Specials), which were accountable to the Government of Northern Ireland.[7] He did not, however, initially respond by becoming politically active. Indeed, his first experience of elections owed more to informal peer pressure within the Law Faculty than to any reaction to the collapse of public order. Trimble was approached by Harry Calvert: would he help his friend Basil McIvor, then running in the 1969 Northern Ireland General Election as the Ulster Unionist candidate for one of the newly created south Belfast constituencies? Trimble knew McIvor's wife Jill, who worked in the Law Faculty. 'Even at that time I had difficulty in saying no,' recalls Trimble. 'I find it embarrassing. If people are pressing me, it's easy to say no, but if they ask nicely, it's much harder.'[8]

It was, at first glance, an unlikely pairing, for Basil McIvor was the most liberal of Unionists and a staunch ally of Terence O'Neill, Northern Ireland's aloof, patrician Prime Minister.[9] Moreover, he was one of very few UUP MPs elected to the old Stormont not to have been a member of the Orange Order.[10] Trimble, by contrast, had always disliked O'Neill's style and his increasingly flaccid response to the disturbances: he less minded O'Neill's reforms than their timing, which he felt showed weakness and which could only encourage more violence. There was, however, another attraction in aiding McIvor. McIvor's seat not only contained such unionist terrain as Larkfield, Finaghy and Dunmurry, but also included the adjacent, predominantly Catholic, area of Andersonstown: Trimble wanted to see what it was like and duly canvassed it. In February 1969, things were not yet so polarised as to preclude such an excursion and Trimble even received a good reception – so much so that he reckons that as many as 1000 to 1500 votes out of McIvor's winning total came from Andersonstown (though some of these may have been cast by Protestants then still living in the area).[11]

Subsequently, Trimble sought to join the UUP but received no reply to his letter of application. The inertia of party HQ at Glengall Street in central Belfast seemed to him to incarnate all that was wrong with the organisation of the time. Glengall Street had failed to provide a sustained or coherent intellectual response to the critique of the Northern Irish state advanced by the nationalists and their left-wing allies on the mainland.[12] In consequence, says Trimble, 'quite a few contemporaries tamely accepted this fashionable view of things – of a politically and morally corrupt establishment. There was a widespread view then of a poor, down-trodden minority. Those of the same age as me all went with the spirit of the times – Unionist Government bad, Civil Rights movement good. When things went pear-shaped, one gets the impression that the middle classes opted out of unionist politics altogether and headed for a safe port. They found it in the nice, uncontroversial New Ulster Movement and later in the Alliance party'. The reaction of one colleague from Queen's was typical of the times: driving down the Shankill Road past Malvern Street, where an organisation styling itself as the 'UVF' had perpetrated a couple of grisly murders in 1966, his companion observed 'ah, we're passing your spiritual home'. Trimble was angered by the remark, but was not deterred. Indeed, the challenge of articulating a Unionist response also appealed to the counter-cyclical, even contrarian aspects of his nature: 'My feeling that they were wrong was not entirely intellectual, it was in my bones as well. But it took me a couple of years to work things out. I usually do find myself uncomfortable with fashionable views and I have spent most of my life arguing against them.'[13]

Trimble, therefore, responded to the crisis in the only way he knew: he searched the stacks at Queen's and read, read and read. There was a dearth of material. For although there had been some 'Unionist' historical writing during the Stormont years – such as St John Ervine's biography of Sir James Craig, the first Prime Minister of Northern Ireland – there had been little Unionist political thought since the 1950s.[14] With their massive majorities at Stormont, and little opposition, Ulster Unionists had become complacent. Trimble's aim over the last 30 years, and especially since becoming leader, has been two-fold: first, to persuade Unionists to think politically and not just to wave the Union flag at election time; and, as a consequence of that, to persuade the broad unionist middle classes to re-engage in politics. Later, Trimble found one unexpected source of inspiration. These were the publications of the British and Irish Communist Organisation (first known as the Irish Communist Organisation). Many then considered B&ICO was then a self-consciously Stalinist (but non-sectarian) faction. A substantial number of its leading lights believed that the British multi-national state was invested with certain progressive possibilities (by contrast, a large number of them contended that northern nationalism, encouraged by southern irredentist elements, was a sectional diversion from the reality of class struggle). Adapting Stalin's theory of nationality to the Irish context, B&ICO had come to conclude that Irish republicans had fundamentally misanalysed the situation. Far from northern Protestants being a minority within the Irish nation, they were a distinct nation of their own, no less entitled than the Catholics to political self-determination: any attempt to coerce them would not merely be foredoomed to failure, but would also lead to a blood-bath by virtue of dividing the working class. This became known as the 'two nations' theory (at the same time, B&ICO also believed in civil rights for Catholics – and that the British state was the best vehicle for achieving these complementary ends). He was particularly influenced by three of their pamphlets: *The Economics of Partition*, *The Birth of Ulster Unionism* and *The Home Rule Crisis 1912–14*. In time, Trimble also became a fan of *Workers' Weekly*, the newsletter of an allied organisation, the Workers' Association for a Democratic Settlement of the National Conflict in Ireland – a compliment which that journal did not always reciprocate through the late 1970s and 1980s. It found him too devolutionist and Ulster nationalist for their more integrationist tastes (in its issue of 28 October 1978, following Trimble's speech at the UUP conference, *Workers' Weekly* described him as an 'advocate of getting Stormont back at all costs'). After Trimble became leader, the links with the left endured. Thus, Paul Bew, Professor of Irish Politics at Queen's and Henry Patterson, Professor of Politics at the University of Ulster – both of them formerly of the Workers' Association – became two of his strongest supporters in academe. And John Lloyd, the staunchly Trimbleista former Editor of the *New Statesman* who later worked for the *Financial Times*, had been in B&ICO itself for a time.

The retreat to the ivory tower was perhaps a predictable response for a shy academic who felt he needed to be on intellectually secure ground before entering the fray. Curiously, Trimble's unworldliness contributed in another very different way to his political education. From 1970–2 he lived for the only time in his life in Belfast – at 12 Kansas Avenue, just off the Antrim Road. He had moved into an area from which Protestants were rapidly departing. Nonetheless, he imagined that it was far enough up the Antrim Road and middle-class enough to avoid the clashes between the Catholic residents of the New Lodge and Protestants from the neighbouring Tiger's Bay. If so, it proved a forlorn hope, for Trimble regularly witnessed many sectarian confrontations at Duncairn Gardens. The experience further convinced him of the inefficacy of the Ulster Unionist establishment's approach, and that something more had to be done. But through what vehicle? Some of his contemporaries had joined the New Ulster Movement. To Trimble, however, the Alliance party did little to confront the Republican political offensive. Rev. Ian Paisley's hardline Democratic Unionists would certainly have been a possibility for a Unionist who wanted to protest against the alleged weakness of their traditional leadership. But as Trimble saw it, Paisley did too little to save Stormont for his own partisan reasons: if the provincial parliament went, so too would the UUP's patronage powers and therefore the DUP would be able to compete more equally with the UUP.[15] Trimble met Paisley for the first time during the 1973 Assembly elections on a broad loyalist platform. His reaction was mixed: 'One appreciated the broad earthy humour, and when he's in a good mood he can be charming. And, obviously, he has considerable gifts of crowd oratory. I would not have been very well disposed to him because of the inconsistencies of his background – his integrationist views and his flirtation with negotiating with Irish nationalism. Then there was the raucousness of his presentation and his purely sectarian approach. I occasionally looked at the *Protestant Telegraph* [Paisley's newspaper] and was struck by the crudity of it and that it contained too many vulgar quips from a churchman. And the more I think of it, it's an accurate reflection of his personality.'[16] For the bulk of the intervening three decades, the relationship of the two men would be antagonistic rather than cooperative. Both men are known for not mincing their words at each other.

It seemed to many, including David Trimble, that the abolition of Stormont was a precursor to a British withdrawal from Northern Ireland.[17] Even Brian Faulkner, whose energy and dynamism Trimble had hitherto admired, seemed to him to have no clue as to how to respond. Only one man appeared to Trimble to have the answers: William Craig, sacked from O'Neill's cabinet in 1968 for attacking the drift of Stormont's policy. Craig anticipated that Heath would move against the Unionists and urged that Ulstermen prepare for the coming constitutional crisis. Subsequently, he condemned Faulkner for meekly acceding to the abolition of Stormont – reckoning that Faulkner should have called a Northern

Ireland General Election to demonstrate that Heath's unilateral violation of the 1920 constitutional settlement had no popular support.[18] But Craig went further still. Although he was mild-mannered in private and was a flat platform speaker, he nonetheless had a flair for the dramatic pronouncement. 'I can tell you without boasting that I can mobilise 80,000 men who will not seek a compromise in Ulster,' he told a meeting of the Monday Club in the House of Commons. 'Let us put bluff aside. I am prepared to kill and those behind me will have my full support for we shall not surrender.'[19]

Certainly Craig – like Trimble – vaulted into the national consciousness as a hardline Unionist. But both men were far more complex than they first appeared. Indeed, when each man eventually sought to treat with the representatives of Irish nationalism, their flexibility would amaze supporters and opponents alike. Born in 1924, Craig had been a gunner in RAF Lancaster bombers during the Second World War. After building up successful solicitor's practices, he had entered the Northern Ireland Parliament for Larne in 1960. During the O'Neill era, he was portrayed (along with Faulkner) as a dynamic, modernising Wunderkind who could accomplish great things for the Province: a meritocratic, almost Wilsonian contrast with the 'big house' Unionists who largely ran the Province till 1971. Craig was also an ardent proponent of German-style federalism for the United Kingdom and Ireland. Significantly, Trimble recalls that Craig and he were the only two elected Unionists publicly to support a 'Yes' vote in the 1975 Referendum on the Common Market.[20] Moreover, most Ulster Unionists were instinctive Tories who until 1974 took the Conservative whip in the Commons – hence the latter party's official title of 'Conservative and Unionist'. By contrast, neither Craig nor Trimble were High Tories in the Enoch Powell mode.

These subtleties were, for the time being, lost in the mêlée. Unionist Ulster felt it was fighting for its life. Only a campaign of mass cross-class mobilisation – of the kind which Loyalists had launched against Home Rule in 1912 – could save the Province from absorption into an all-Ireland Republic. To a young Unionist activist at Queen's such as David Burnside, it did not then seem improbable that such a feat could be replicated. After all, it had been accomplished within living memory: veterans of the original UVF and 36th (Ulster) Division still regularly walked on Orange marches and there were large numbers of people around with military training from the Second World War.[21] Craig's chosen vehicle for conducting the struggle was the Vanguard Movement, which he launched as a pressure group within the Unionist party on 9 February 1972. Following the precedent of 1912, they produced a Vanguard Covenant. It asserted that the 1920 settlement – which partitioned Ireland into two parts, North and South – could not be undone save with the consent of the Parliament of Northern Ireland. By proroguing Stormont, and introducing an almost colonial system of direct rule from Westminster, Heath had unilaterally abrogated the terms of that bargain. The key test of political authority, the consent of the governed, was now lacking. Craig was accused of denying the doctrine of parliamentary sovereignty; but he replied that there were political and moral limits to its theoretical power to legislate as it pleased.

Such propositions would have been uncontroversial amongst most Unionists. But where Vanguard differed was that it drew some highly radical conclusions from this state of affairs. Historically, the unique Ulster-British way of life had best been preserved by Union with Great Britain. But what if Ulster was locked into a loveless marriage and her affections were not reciprocated? What if the terms of that marriage could be altered under pressure from Irish nationalists and the IRA – as exemplified by Westminster's unilateral destruction of Stormont? What, indeed, if Westminster could use its sovereign power within the Union to deliver the Ulstermen 'bound into the hands of our enemies'? The price of marriage would then have become too high. Thus, for Vanguard, the Union of Great Britain and Northern Ireland was not an end in itself, but a means to an end. If they could not regain an Ulster Parliament on satisfactory terms within the Union, then Vanguard preferred negotiated independence. The arrangements enjoyed by the Channel Islands or the Isle of Man – under the Crown but not in the Union – looked attractive. Vanguard's enthusiasm for independent dominion status would soon expose them to accusations from some supporters of Faulkner that they were no longer Unionists, but rather had become 'Ulster nationalists'.[22]

At the time, Trimble was prepared to give such Vanguardist ideas a fair wind. In an article in the *Sunday News* on 20 January 1974, he rebutted the views of Desmond Boal, QC, a leading adviser of Paisley. Boal believed that the time for greater integration of Northern Ireland with the rest of the United Kingdom had passed – but that Ulster independence had never been a runner. Instead, he favoured a federal Ireland Parliament and Provincial Parliament with 'Stormont' powers.[23] Trimble took particular issue with Boal's rejection of independence for Northern Ireland. He argued that if one accepted the notion that the British were prepared to pay large sums of money to leave Northern Ireland, then they would surely be just as happy to subsidise an independent Ulster as a united Ireland. He was implying that the coercion of Ulster into a united Ireland was costlier than independence. By contrast, independence might satisfy enough unionists and nationalists to leave behind a relatively stable entity. Intriguingly, he posited the idea that republicans mainly disliked 'British' forces, but had an ambiguous attitude towards Protestants (whom he did not describe as 'British'). Once these 'British' forces were gone, and Protestants gave a guarantee that the purpose of such an entity was not to reinforce an anti-Catholic hegemony, all but the most irreconcilable elements of the republican movement might be able to enter into some compact in a new, independent Ulster.

Such ideas must have seemed fairly fanciful as sectarian tensions sharpened. Vanguard held a series of Province-wide rallies, culminating in a great demonstration at Belfast's Ormeau Park in March 1972: the *News Letter* estimated the crowd to be 92,000, the RUC put it at 60,000.[24] Theatricality was an integral part of the Craig roadshow, who would arrive at gatherings with motorcycle outriders. It was widely reported that they were members of a uniformed group called the Vanguard Service Corps – although Trimble, for one, now doubts whether it actually ever existed in any organised sense. Trimble rebuts all allegations by the now deceased loyalist Sam McClure – that he was sworn into VSC at an initiation ceremony at Vanguard headquarters in Hawthornden Road – as 'utter balls'.[25] Some nationalists found Vanguard gatherings fascistic and even Trimble now says he was 'never terribly comfortable' at these 'embarrassing' occasions. Nonetheless, he attended many such events. He was present at Castle Park, Bangor, in February 1972, where Craig inspected 6,500 men as they stood to attention wearing Vanguard armbands (although Trimble declined to wear one).[26] He also turned up for the mass gathering at Stormont, just days after the abolition of the Northern Ireland Parliament had been announced.[27]

Given the circumstances – both civil war and British withdrawal seemed to be on the cards – Trimble did not consider Craig's rhetoric to be unjustified. 'Craig had a tendency to outbursts and to overstate things even before the Troubles,' recalls Trimble. 'But he was saying, "Look, there are a lot of people who don't like the direction of government policy and if pushed they are prepared to fight." His intention was to make Government in London sit up and think. He certainly succeeded in getting negative publicity!' Some felt that Craig was unleashing terrible forces in society, but Trimble does not agree: 'There were lots of things unleashing those forces – the abolition of Stormont, the IRA campaign. If anything, Craig's rhetoric provided an emotional safety valve.'[28] It was more than just rhetoric, though: Vanguard, after all, 'saw itself as a resistance movement against an undemocratic regime that could be shown to be unworkable when the time came'. To that end, it aimed for 'the coordination of all loyalist organisations under one banner to save Ulster'. The largest of these was the Ulster Defence Association, then still a legal organisation probably numbering about 40,000 members.[29] 'Everybody was in it then,' says Trimble. 'I was conscious there were criminal types, but they were not dominant. The organisation then was a broad popular response to a near-civil war situation. But what's happened to the loyalist paramilitaries is that the criminal types have taken over and the broad popular types have gone away' (indeed, to this day, he thinks that the conventional police wisdom is wrong and that the Ulster Freedom Fighters are not a mere flag of convenience for the UDA, but are a separate organisation). In retrospect, however, he concedes that Craig's condemnation of Protestant paramilitarism was inadequate.[30]

Trimble never saw himself as a street activist in this cause; his contribution, he thought, would be as a cerebral backroom boy. In 1972, after his flat in Belfast became too dangerous, he moved back to Bangor and resumed contact with some local Orangemen. It was they who provided him with his first public platform at the Ballygrainey Orange Hall at Six Road Ends, between Bangor and Newtownards. In 1973, the British Government had produced a White Paper, which outlined some possible political structures for the Province. The new Assembly would be elected by proportional representation rather than the traditional first-past-the-post (in fact, there had been PR elections during the early years of Stormont, but these had soon been scrapped, largely to maintain the unity of the UUP).[31] No one knew how to operate the Single Transferable Vote system – except, everyone thought, David Trimble. Trimble, in fact, had to go into the Queen's University library where he found a book on electoral systems by Enid Lakeman.[32] His description of how many candidates to run and how to maximise transfers so impressed one of those present, Albert Smith, that he called on Trimble shortly afterwards.

Trimble recalls him asking: '"Would you like to give another talk?" I said yes, but when? "Tonight!" came the reply. It turned out he wanted me to speak to a North Down Vanguard meeting at Hamilton House, Bangor. I never looked back.'[33]

There, he met up with a group opposed to the local Faulknerite Unionist establishment. They included George Green, the former County Commandant of the since disbanded 'B' Specials, who was by now an independent councillor in the area. More important still to his long-term political development, he also met a Vanguard councillor, Mary O'Fee. Her husband, Stewart, was a senior civil servant in the Ministry of Health and Social Services, who would telephone Craig and identify himself as 'the Seaside Voice'. Trimble worried that the 'tide of history' was turning against the Unionists, but Stewart O'Fee snorted dismissively and told him to read Karl Popper's *Poverty of Historicism*, which he found inspirational.[34] But O'Fee came to have an even more direct influence: he was the anonymous author of two Vanguard's best pamphlets, *Ulster – A Nation* (April 1972) and *Community of the British Isles* (1973).[35] The former, in Trimble's own words, 'hurled defiance at our enemies'. It was a trenchant rebuttal of the High Tory case for Ulster's integration into the United Kingdom along the lines of Scotland and Wales, whose best-known advocate was Enoch Powell. But O'Fee believed this approach contained profound dangers for Ulster. First, the Province would be integrated into the more urbanised, 'permissive society' of the 'Swinging Sixties' – an unattractive end in itself for a still-religious people. Second, even if it was desirable in principle, integrationists did not possess the means to achieve this: peaceful persuasion would not work since the main British parties did not want it and street protests to attain it would only alienate their fellow citizens with whom they wanted to integrate. Third, Trimble shared O'Fee's belief that pure integration, without any body which Ulster could call its own to undergird it, contained a political trap. They both believed that integration could only work if the three main parties at Westminster supported the Union. But since many in Labour and the Liberals then appeared to favour the principle of Irish unity, albeit peacefully achieved, as an ultimate outcome, integration would leave Ulster and its tiny twelve-man contingent at the mercy of the 630-strong Commons.

Ulster – A Nation concluded with a ringing appeal for Ulster to redefine her relationship with the rest of the United Kingdom. It posited the idea of a federated British Isles comprising Great Britain, Ulster and Eire, with three separate but equal regions cooperating to promote common prosperity. These ideas were fleshed out in *Community of the British Isles* which exerted an even greater impact upon Trimble's thinking. Great Britain would 'throw off the trammels of the residual sovereignty' that she exercises as a legacy of her colonial past and thus free herself of any guilt or international embarrassments which that legacy has caused her. More significant still, this would have profound implications for the Roman Catholic minority: 'The absence of British sovereignty would remove one of the causes of friction and help confront both communities [within Northern Ireland] with the realities of the situation.' Trimble was impressed both by its emphasis on taking account of the existence of the nationalist community, which would not go away, and by the possibility of creating new structures that could accommodate everyone's diverse aspirations without surrendering to Irish nationalism. Indeed, the approach outlined in *Community of the British Isles* would eventually find expression in the British-Irish Council, established under the 1998 Belfast Agreement.

Again, such speculations seemed fanciful at the time. For Unionists were then enmeshed in debating the merits of Heath's attempt to outline the principles governing new political structures for Ulster. The Government White Paper of March 1973 aimed to provide something for everyone (and was the basis of the Sunningdale agreement of December of that year). For Unionists, it contained the guarantee that Northern Ireland's overall constitutional status would not be changed save with the consent of the Province's majority. Also, the bulk of Stormont's functions would be returned to local control (with the exception of security). But Unionists could only regain their parliament at the price of accepting nationalists in the Government of Northern Ireland for the first time. Nationalists would derive further reassurance from the establishment of an 'Irish dimension' – North–South bodies which could someday prove to be vehicles for harmonising the institutions of government on both sides of the border into all-Ireland structures. Faulkner accepted the White Paper and received the endorsement of his party's supreme body, the Ulster Unionist Council, by 381 to 231.[36]

Many hardline Unionists had been toying with the idea of creating a new party to oppose the drift of policy, but they had always been deterred from so doing by the feeling that they would have more influence by staying within the existing party structures. The vote to accept the White Paper proposals convinced them that they no longer could prevent such slippage. Craig and his supporters left to form the Vanguard Unionist Progressive Party: the word 'Progressive' was included to appeal to the substantial trade union element in Vanguard, led by such men as Billy Hull (formerly of the Loyalist Association of Workers) and Glenn Barr, a shop steward and senior figure in the UDA. Although opposed to the new system, Vanguard nonetheless contested the June 1973 Assembly elections. Trimble was uncertain about whether to stand, but in the end decided to do so. There were several reasons for this. First, he thought if he remained an academic, people would not respect him; he would, therefore, have to 'get his hands dirty' in the political arena. But there was another reason, which would continue to motivate him in the coming years. 'The Loyalist parties were getting a very negative press then,' he recalls. 'But I thought "well, it will make the media and the middle classes sit up and think if they find that not all of the Loyalist candidates are ignorant working-class types".'[37] He put his name forward for the Vanguard nomination in North Down and found himself alphabetically on the bottom of the three-man slate headed by George Green. The North Down Vanguard literature had a cartoon of the master (William Whitelaw, first Northern Ireland Secretary) tossing a bone to his lap-dog (Faulkner). And it proclaimed: 'Vanguard Unionists will not accept a humiliating, powerless, consultative Assembly in place of a proper Parliament . . . they will not allow murderers and quislings to destroy Ulster and hand it over to Republicans.'

Trimble's first serious outing on the hustings was, however, disastrous: during the abortive Loyalist strike of February 1973 which Vanguard had supported, a fireman had been killed by Protestant hoodlums. Trimble received a bitter reception in many quarters – 'it was guilt by association' he recalls – and came bottom out of eighteen candidates.[38] Vanguard took 10.5% of first preference votes for seven seats. Faulkner's group, with 24 seats, was nominally the largest. In conjunction with other pro-White Paper elements (including the SDLP, Alliance and Northern Ireland Labour parties) the group held 52 seats to 26 for the broad loyalist coalition. The reality, though, was more complex. Some of those who were officially within the Faulknerite camp in fact opposed his policy. The real picture was, therefore, 21 for Faulkner to 27 against him: enough to push policies through with the help of the SDLP and others, but crucially depriving him of a majority and therefore legitimacy within the Unionist community.[39]

Despite Trimble's terrible showing, the campaign was not a waste of time. While on the hustings, he met Craig for the first time. Trimble felt an immediate sense of personal as well as ideological kinship: he always was able to anticipate what Craig was thinking. 'Craig had a penchant for surrounding himself with bright young men,' says Trimble. 'David Burnside, Reg Empey and myself have lasted the course. There was a sense with Craig of open-mindedness not associated with the "good old boy" network of Glengall Street. Unlike the others, if he discovered talent he would use it.'[40] Many of these Young Unionists had been locked out of Glengall Street – in Empey's case literally – after the split with Faulkner. Craig also cultivated another young hardline politician, John Taylor, who in the previous year had survived an assassination attempt by the Official IRA; but Taylor never made the leap. Trimble first met Taylor in Bangor in 1973 and liked him instinctively. 'He was a person who was entitled to respect. After coming within an inch of losing his life, he was still involved and not in any way intimidated.'[41]

Some felt that Trimble could be a little bit of a 'boffin' – but they also deferred to him on that basis. Isobel McCulloch, who was Craig's secretary, remembers that when Trimble referred to some legal concept by its Latin name, one of the less well-read figures in Vanguard piped up: 'Say that again, David – this time in English!'[42] The whole room, including Trimble, broke up laughing. But for the most part, observes Craig, 'he fitted in very comfortably. He became accustomed to talking with people. Events brought him out of his shell.' Craig found Trimble an ideal sounding board for fleshing out his existing ideas: this is significant since many suppose that Craig only extolled the Aland Islands – a semi-autonomous part of Sweden – as a potential model for Ulster because of Trimble's research. In fact, it was Craig who introduced Trimble to many of these concepts, as Trimble readily acknowledges.[43] Trimble was also introduced to the darker side of Loyalism in this period – including Andy Tyrie, the then Supreme Commander of the UDA. Tyrie found that Trimble was quite unlike any of the traditional Unionists of the 'fur coat brigade'. Not only was he 'great in committees, great working with people, but he had a quality I would have loved to have had – he was a good listener. Above all, he stayed with the people. Harry West [the Ulster Unionist leader] had no use for us once the crisis that had brought us together was over.

David, though, always was available – even when he did not approve of what we were doing. He would say "look, this type of violence is totally counter-productive from your point of view". Tyrie noted with appreciation that unlike most middle-class people, Trimble was prepared to fight, though he claims that he never asked him to join up. 'I would certainly have been very glad of him,' Tyrie adds.[44] Some time later, Tyrie invited Trimble to attend meetings of the UDA's Inner Council – an offer which Trimble declined, though he said he would be happy enough to draft papers. He refused because he believed that his talents lay in the realm of politics. When asked if he would have joined up to give the UDA political direction, Trimble replies, 'wasn't that what Vanguard was [already] doing?'[45] Whatever Vanguard's relationship to the UDA, there is no doubt that Tyrie trusted Trimble utterly at a political level. But did their closeness to each other make Trimble vulnerable to British state pressure years down the road? Trimble is unequivocal on the subject. 'There never was an effort by anybody – whether British or anyone else – to make capital out of my associations of the early 1970s. Which is surprising.'[46]

FOUR

Ulster will fight

IN THE autumn of 1973, Trimble became the chairman of the constituency council of North Down Vanguard and was elected Publications Officer at the entire party's annual general meeting.[1] Many in Vanguard – including Trimble – were celebrating the success of the brand-new party in the Assembly elections, but Craig counselled caution. Hardline Unionists had, in fact, suffered a political defeat. Much as Unionists disliked his compromises, Faulkner was still in business. Now that the Assembly was up and running, the stage would be set for the establishment of the second pillar of the new political order as envisaged by the 1973 White Paper for Northern Ireland – a power-sharing executive (the third being the 'Irish dimension'). The creation of this executive was announced on 22 November 1973, although the wrangling over its composition and size was reminiscent of the disagreements which bedevilled the same exercise some 25 years later. Eventually, it was agreed that Unionists would hold six of the eleven seats, with four for the largely nationalist Social Democratic and Labour Party and one for the Alliance. Faulkner became Chief Executive and Gerry Fitt, the leader of the SDLP, became Deputy Chief Executive. Although there was a bi-partisan welcome for this development in Great Britain, loyalists were enraged and vowed to destroy it.

The third and final pillar of the new institutions of government was to be the Council of Ireland. This was a reincarnation of the Council of Ireland provided for in the 1920 Act: it was originally intended that powers gradually be transferred to this body as a prelude to re-unification, albeit under the Crown. It fell into abeyance not because of Unionist intransigence, but because Dublin never nominated any representatives to it (a refusal which suited the Unionists well enough). There was, however, one key difference between the 1920 and 1973–4 settlements: the 1920

Government of Ireland Act notionally envisaged growing harmonisation, through the agency of the Council, between two devolved areas of the United Kingdom. As things turned out, only Northern Ireland accepted the 1920 settlement, whilst the southern part of the island gradually went its own way.[2] As Unionists saw it, such a formulation was more disadvantageous in the very different circumstances of the 1970s. For the 1973 Council of Ireland would have combined representatives of a devolved region of the United Kingdom (Northern Ireland) with the representatives of a fully fledged sovereign entity that had severed residual links (namely the Republic of Ireland). Only once this Council had been established would full-scale direct rule be scrapped. However, the security powers would remain a matter for Westminster for the time being.

The British Government hoped that the emerging package would be sufficiently attractive to mollify most Unionists. Under its provisions, the Unionists secured the return of a devolved local parliament, albeit with smaller majorities under the new PR system than they had enjoyed under the first-past-the-post; and they would return to office, but not on the basis of traditional majority rule. Instead, it would be in an enforced cross-community coalition with some of their harsh critics in the SDLP. For nationalists, it was the all-Ireland aspects of the deal which were most important: the gradual transfer of powers to the Council of Ireland was seen by them as possessing the potential, over time, to take Ulster peacefully out of the United Kingdom and into a united Ireland of some kind. After all, they argued, they would be acquiescing in the return of Unionists to the hated Stormont, where nationalists would still be in the minority; and they acknowledged more explicitly than before that Ireland could be re-unified only with the consent of Ulster's majority. Therefore, in order to keep their constituency happy, the SDLP and the Irish Government felt that they had to obtain a 'result' on the Council of Ireland.[3] Heath duly summoned the leaders of the power-sharing parties – Faulkner Unionists, Alliance and the SDLP as well as the Irish government – for a conference at the Civil Service College at Sunningdale in Berkshire to draw these strands together. The deal struck there contained many of the elements found in the Belfast Agreement of 1998: hence the famous *bon mot* of Seamus Mallon, now Deputy First Minister, that any subsequent settlement would be 'Sunningdale for slow learners'.[4] By this, Mallon meant that the broad outlines for any new arrangements in Northern Ireland were always going to be the same, whether in 1973–4 or in 1998–9.

According to this analysis, the hardliners on both sides were too obstinate or confident of securing an unattainable ethnic victory over the other to perceive this essential reality.

But others have invested the phrase with a meaning beyond that given to it by Mallon. Mallon may have implied that David Trimble – a trenchant critic of Sunningdale – was one of the 'slow learners'. But to pro-Agreement Unionists, it was the two Governments who were themselves slow learners. From a moderate Unionist standpoint, the Governments had asked Faulkner, the leader of the largest party representing the majority community, to bear too much of a political burden: indeed, the then Irish Foreign Minister, Garret FitzGerald, with John Hume, pushed for a more ambitious version of the Council of Ireland.[5] Faulkner called these cross-border arrangements – which, initially at least, comprised tourism and animal health – as 'necessary nonsense' that would keep nationalists happy within essentially partitionist structures. But most Unionists perceived them to be an embryonic government for the whole island. Unionists (and, above all, David Trimble) derived the lesson that it was these all-Ireland aspects of the deal – rather than power-sharing with nationalists – which were unacceptable to the mass of Unionists. That is why in the week of the Belfast Agreement of 1998 – when the very 'Green' draft settlement was rejected by Unionists – Lord Alderdice of the Alliance party brought a predecessor who served in the Sunningdale Executive, Sir Oliver Napier, to meet Tony Blair. His purpose was to explain to the Prime Minister that Trimble would end up as another Faulkner if the draft agreement was rammed down his throat.[6] The ghost of Faulkner thus hangs over much of what Trimble does: indeed, both men rose to the leadership on account of their strong Orange credentials, in Trimble's case because of Drumcree, in Faulkner's because he led a disputed Orange march down the Longstone Road in Annalong, Co. Down, in 1955.[7]

Curiously, Trimble recalls that he felt a degree of sympathy with Faulkner's dilemma even at the time. David Bleakley, who was the Northern Ireland Labour party's representative in the 1975–6 Convention, remembers being struck by the fact that Trimble was one of the very few rejectionists in that body who did not lash into the deposed Faulkner.[8] Nonetheless, like everyone in Vanguard, Trimble found the overall Sunningdale package unacceptable. The prospects of derailing it, however, seemed at first slender. Shouting abuse at the Faulknerites in the Assembly had not proved noticeably successful. When Trimble heard of the idea of an all-out strike to protest against the new dispensation, he doubted whether it would work, for he recalled the ignominious failure of the earlier protests. In a peculiar way, this was to be a key card in the hands of the loyalist resistance. There had been so many abortive acts of defiance that when the strikes became really serious in May 1974, it came as a surprise to much of the government machine. As ever Vanguard, with its extraordinary mix of town and gown, took the lead in coordinating the resistance of a variety of loyalist organisations to the emerging settlement. Craig brought Trimble to the Portrush conference in December 1973, which was the precursor to the formation of the United Ulster Unionist Council. The UUUC (or 'Treble UC' as it came to be known) was to become the umbrella group for all of those Unionists – Vanguard, DUP and anti-Faulkner Ulster Unionists – opposed to the 'historic compromise' with nationalism. The aim of the conference was to evolve a single policy statement, for which purpose Trimble was a very suitable choice. He became a leading light in the working party that adopted a federalist blueprint for the constitution of the United Kingdom. Trimble first met both Enoch Powell and James Molyneaux there.[9] 'His was a very clinical kind of approach,' recalls Molyneaux. 'He was not at that stage concerned about whose toes he trampled on. And there was the natural tendency of anyone in that age group to have a very strong idea and to take it to the limit – and to shoot down any old fogey.'[10] If Trimble was intellectually arrogant, it certainly did him little harm: he spoke in nearly every debate and he remembers Ernie Baird telling him that he was the success of the conference. Later, Craig also asked him to draft the rule book for a new organisation of which little was then known: the Ulster Workers' Council. At first, it was one of of innumerable organisations of the period, which seemed to arise and then disappear with dizzying regularity – but it would soon acquire great significance. Not that anyone, recalls Trimble, would have needed to consult such a constitution: the exercise was purely to give the organisation a veneer of procedural respectability in the event that anyone had asked. Moreover, it brought Trimble into contact with Harry Murray, a Belfast shipyard shop steward who chaired the UWC and lived in Bangor (and who often gave Trimble lifts into the city).[11]

The momentum which built up in favour of the UUUC's rejection of Sunningdale was not confined to the working classes. It was more broadly based, and as during the first two 'sieges of Drumcree' in 1995 and 1996 implied at least a level of middle-class Unionist acquiescence in street protest. The source of this discontent was quite simple: the deal did not seem to be delivering what it promised to do. The first major blow came after the Executive had taken office on 1 January 1974. The Ulster Unionist Council – where Faulkner's margins had been thinning ever since he accepted the White Paper in May 1973 – rejected Sunningdale by 427 votes to 374. The motion was proposed by John Taylor and was seconded by Martin Smyth. Faulkner promptly resigned as party leader, and although he took the Executive members and others with him, he was now completely detached from the bulk of the party machine.[12] Shortly thereafter, a former Fianna Fail Cabinet minister, Kevin Boland, launched a High Court challenge to the Irish Government's recognition of Northern Ireland's present constitutional status. He claimed that it conflicted with Articles 2 and 3 of the Republic's 1937 Constitution. When the Government mounted its defence, it emerged that they were arguing that they had not after all acknowledged that Northern Ireland was outside the jurisdiction.[13] The consent principle, so crucial to Unionists, was fatally undermined by a clever legal formulation. The effects on Faulkner were more devastating still: so much so that when the United Kingdom General Election for Westminster was held on 28 February, the UUUC defeated every sitting Unionist candidate who was loyal to Faulkner and won eleven out of the twelve Ulster constituencies. Their slogan was, 'Dublin is only a Sunningdale away'.[14]

The February 1974 election was the closest thing there would be to a referendum on Sunningdale, and for the first time rejectionists could claim to have a popular mandate. Labour were back in power, and Harold Wilson, whose personal sympathies were in favour of Irish unity, was once again Prime Minister.[15] Meanwhile, the IRA stepped up the tempo of its activities: the murder of a UDR soldier, Eva Martin, at Clogher, Co. Tyrone, evoked particular horror. The killer was Sean O'Callaghan, who later became the highest ranking ever defector from the Provisional IRA and who would come to know Trimble well – and advise him – following his release from jail in 1996.[16] In this fevered atmosphere, the UWC demanded fresh Assembly elections. The UWC had been preparing assiduously behind the scenes and were especially well organised amongst the crucial power workers. Accordingly, when the Assembly rejected a motion denouncing power-sharing on 14 May 1974, by 44 to 28, Harry Murray promptly announced that the loyalists would reduce electricity output from 700 to 400 megawatts. The next day, in response to a general strike call from the UWC, workers downed tools at the Harland and Wolff shipyard; road blocks started to appear everywhere.

The organisational skills of the loyalists were impressive then. The strike was run from Vanguard headquarters at 9 Hawthornden Road, in east Belfast, by the UDA spokesman and Vanguard Assembly member Glenn Barr, with a fifteen-strong committee that included representatives of all the main political parties. Also on that committee along with the politicians and trade unionists were Andy Tyrie of the UDA, Ken Gibson of the UVF, and Lt Col. Brush of Down Orange Welfare. As well as power cuts, the strike committee started a system of issuing 'passes', so that workers in essential services could buy petrol: anyone who wanted to move about had to apply to the strike headquarters. Initially, the politicians were told to stay away for the duration of the strike – and it suited them perfectly. For although the idea of the strike, according to Trimble, had originally come from Vanguard, they did not want it to be thought to be theirs alone or even originating primarily with them.[17] The focus of attention soon moved even further away from conventional politics and street protest: on 17 May, the UVF bombed Dublin and Monaghan, killing 33 people. It was the heaviest day of casualties during the entire Troubles. 'I was very surprised,' says Trimble. 'The whole object of the strike was that it was non-violent action. The perceived wisdom was that it was mid-Ulster UVF. I could never see the logic of sectarian attacks. This is one of the worrying things about loyalist paramilitarism, its absence of intelligence in both senses of the word.'[18] Trimble was present at Hawthornden Road on the evening that the Dublin-Monaghan bombs went off: despite Craig's instruction to key Vanguard figures to stay away so that the grassroots elements could appear to run the show, he could not stay away from the scene of the action for very long.[19]

After acting as telephone operator, Trimble graduated to printing very amateurish passes on a children's Letraset, which those who applied to the UWC could show at road blocks to go and buy fuel. Eventually, he produced the daily strike bulletin with Sammy Smyth of the UDA.[20] Smyth was a figure given to very extreme pronouncements: the *Irish Times* reported him as saying that 'I am very happy about the bombings in Dublin. There is a war with the Free State and now we are laughing at them.' For these, remarks, Smyth was 'disciplined' by the UDA – that is, beaten up – and was removed as a spokesman; he was murdered by the IRA in 1976.[21] (Curiously, until I raised the matter with him, Trimble states that he was unaware of Smyth's views, since he rarely read the newspapers in those fevered days). Indeed, at one point, Trimble was embarrassed when a professor at Queen's turned up at Hawthornden Road wondering how examinations would be run with petrol so severely rationed. 'Oh, Trimble knows all about that,' replied the trade unionist. The two university colleagues then had a strained conversation. For the most part, though, Trimble – who at the time stayed at his mother's house in Kilcooley – remembers 'an almost blitz spirit'. Local farmers, for instance, gave milk away rather than throw it out because they could not sell it. The sense of solidarity was reinforced by the knowledge that they were being listened to by the security forces. Trimble remembers watching a British soldier crawling along the ground trying to install a microphone at Hawthornden Road: he laughed loudly when George Green simply placed a radio near the device and switched it on, drowning out the loyalists' words. Trimble suspected that his mother's telephone was tapped, and his concerns were vindicated when she returned from holiday and was surprised to find that the line had been broken, which tended to occur when the primitive devices of the period were disconnected: Trimble, though, never sought to venture an explanation to her for this inconvenience![22] In fact, says one senior security source of the era, the technology even then was such that a breakdown of Ivy Trimble's telephone could not have been caused by the removal of the tap. But the source confirms that Trimble's telephone, along with many others, was monitored in this period.[23]

In these heady days for loyalists, Trimble was hugely animated. Herb Wallace, his closest colleague at Queen's, remembers that he was 'terribly excited to be associated with the leading lights on the UWC. Glenn Barr even told him that when he became Prime Minister of Northern Ireland, Trimble would be Minister of Law Reform.'[24] On the morning that the Prime Minister was to make a broadcast to the nation about the growing crisis, Trimble attended a key meeting of the strike coordinating committee. Present were Craig, Paisley, West and the workers' representatives. They had just received a draft of Wilson's address condemning the strikers in even harsher language than the Prime Minister eventually employed. Trimble, like everyone else, thought that if he went ahead with that version, there would be an explosion of uncontrollable violence. 'I reckoned: "This is madness. This will destroy the country and double the death toll overnight." [25] Word also came through back-channels that as they watched the broadcast that night, the UWC would be swooped on by the Army. Accordingly, the UWC high command went to ground and left the elected politicians behind: the Army would then find they had bagged a bunch of parliamentarians, plus the Assistant Dean of the Law Faculty at Queen's University. But before they departed, the UWC did have one serious discussion about the legal aspects of a possible declaration of martial law. Trimble had brought along a copy of R.F.V. Heuston's *Essays in Constitutional Law*, which had an excellent treatment of the subject. The strike leaders were obviously sufficiently impressed by Trimble's exposition to borrow his copy of Heuston. It was not returned – and the Army never came anyhow. [26]

Wilson, in the end, diluted his speech, but it nonetheless turned out to be his best-known pronouncement ever on Ulster, in which he attacked the loyalists for 'sponging' on Westminster. [27] The strikers promptly began to wear little sponges on their lapels, and the effect of Wilson's speech was, Trimble recalls, to send the already high levels of support for the loyalists through the roof. [28] Despite Wilson's own resentment of the strikers, neither the Northern Ireland Office nor the Army wished to confront them: why risk bloodshed, they reasoned, for the sake of a doomed executive? Faulkner, faced with a complete end to electricity supplies, more unburied dead, and untreated sewage bowed to the inevitable and resigned with the executive on 28 May 1974. The Council of Ireland died with it and Merlyn Rees, the Ulster Secretary, resumed full-scale direct rule from London. Thereupon, the *raison d'être* of the strike vanished: those who wanted to press on and secure the return of the old Stormont were left isolated. Unionists had shown that they could veto unwelcome developments, but they had neither the strength nor the cohesion to reimpose Stormont.

Trimble, though not a figure of the first rank in the strike, had impressed many of those around him by taking his stand. 'It could have ruined his career in law – but he stood up and was counted,' says Andy Tyrie. 'David Trimble, David Burnside and Bill Craig were prepared to suffer the consequences. It could have been a failure. There were no MPs there. They all ran and hid over the law-breaking. All those generals and captains in the Orange Order left and did not want to be seen as bigots and thugs. But the David Trimble of today is the product of 1974. Nineteen seventy-four was the first time that ordinary people started to question how the Unionist family operated. In 1974, no Unionist politician of any prominence took part in the strike.'[29] (Paisley had been in Canada at the funeral of a friend when the strike broke out and some paramilitaries used this to undermine him, suggesting that he had only returned when it seemed to be gaining ground.) In the euphoria which obtained after the UWC strike, it was decided that the organisation needed to have a policy. Craig, therefore, 'loaned' Trimble to the UWC – in a bid to hold back some of the wilder ideas which would emerge from some individuals at 'brain-storming' sessions.[30] Eventually, the UDA went off in their own direction and in 1975 produced a document in favour of Ulster independence; and whilst Vanguard was the largest of the Unionist movements with an affinity for such ideas, neither Craig nor Trimble plumped for that logical extreme. Indeed, both men would soon astonish the political world with their boldness, but of a very different kind.

FIVE

The changing of the Vanguard

TRIMBLE had earned his spurs during the UWC strike and its aftermath, but he was not yet a figure of any public note. All of this was soon to change as a result of the British Government's new set of proposals – one of many 'initiatives' that punctuated the Troubles. The White Paper, published in July 1974, set out a scheme for an elected Constitutional Convention. The job of this body was to consider 'what provision for the government of Northern Ireland is likely to command the most widespread acceptance throughout the community there?' The Convention was to be composed of 78 members elected by PR on the same basis as the 1973 Assembly, under the chairmanship of the then Lord Chief Justice of Northern Ireland, Sir Robert Lowry.[1] At first, though, Trimble thought he would not be a candidate. His marriage had broken up and he duly decided to withdraw himself from consideration in North Down (divorce was then much rarer in Northern Ireland than it has since become). George Green would anyhow head the Vanguard list on his home turf, making it unlikely that Trimble could win even if selected. But Craig had counted upon Trimble to be at his side in the Convention and persuaded him to put forward his name for the nomination for South Belfast, where Queen's University was located. Trimble had two rivals: Raymond Jordan (election agent for the local Westminster MP, Rev. Robert Bradford) and David Burnside. Jordan was assured of a slot, so the contest boiled down to a fight between Trimble and Burnside.[2] Trimble won out, but that did not prevent them from working together as the twin pillars of Craig's operation, with Trimble as the policy brains, Burnside as the press officer. Both men shared a common objective: to modernise Unionism. As early as 1976, Burnside favoured breaking the formal link between the Orange Order and the UUP, which is reminiscent of the trade unions' links to Labour. It was a relationship which would

endure with many ups, and more downs, over the next quarter-century
– by which time Burnside had become a prominent London PR executive
whose premises served as home to the Unionist Information Office, and
from 2001 as Ulster Unionist MP for South Antrim.[3]

Trimble's election literature showed a bookish Buddy Holly look-alike
posing in a law library, and proclaimed the traditional Vanguard message
of the necessity to restore effective devolved government. But it also
contained a teasing hint of flexibility – and one which was to prove
significant and bitterly controversial later. 'An effective local Parliament
must have an executive which conforms with democratic principles
(which includes the possiblity of coalitions freely entered into),' he
declared. 'The executive cannot be formed on a sectarian basis or with
places guaranteed to certain groups irrespective of the outcome of an
election.' In other words, whilst rejecting compulsory power-sharing with
a guaranteed place for the minority population no matter what happened,
Trimble was prepared to look at another kind of arrangement with the
SDLP. This codicil neither distressed nor enthused the electorate: to them,
it was the sixth poll in just over two years. Trimble, initially, found it
hard going on the hustings. 'I don't think that he actually liked the process
of asking little old ladies for their votes – and I'm not sure he does
today,' recalls Reg Empey, who was then chairman of Vanguard. 'I got
the impression that he saw the election as the only way into the political
process but he was uncomfortable talking about rising damp and other
problems.'[4] But more important still was the way in which Craig chose
to use Trimble in the Convention election. He fixed things so that Trimble
would be given maximum coverage, picking him as the party's representative in a Province-wide TV debate. He certainly needed the experience.
'I showed John Taylor my scripted contribution beforehand,' recalls
Trimble. 'It went "now let us dispose of some canards". Taylor, though,
just mocked me. "Nobody will understand what that means," he said.
And he was right.' On the next day, back on the doorstep in South Belfast,
the atmosphere had changed: Trimble was now a personality in his own
right and was treated as such. Trimble also stood in for Craig in a second
broadcast after the Vanguard leader was taken ill, and thus appeared in
two out of three of the party's election broadcasts. This exposure did
much to explain how Trimble was elected over Raymond Jordan, notwithstanding the fact that he came lower down the ballot paper alphabetically
and had been less well known locally than his colleague.[5] Trimble secured

2429 first preferences (Martin Smyth of the UUP topped the poll with 15,061 votes) and following the distribution of transfers was elected on the ninth count with 7240 ballots cast.[6] Trimble was the fifth of the six representatives for the seat and duly became a member of the Convention on a salary of £2500 per annum.

Trimble, like Enoch Powell, is a loner who immerses himself and finds fulfilment in the work of institutions – and the Convention was no exception. He immediately set to work on the Standing Orders, and on the last day of debate was given the task of replying to all the points made from the dispatch box. 'It was a baptism of fire for a new comer,' recalls Trimble. 'I acquitted myself well and was exhilarated having come from being an almost complete observer of things to playing a significant role.'[7] Some opponents found his style too reminiscent of the kind of point-scoring that went on in university debating societies. Nonetheless, few doubted his worth to the body's deliberations. Maurice Hayes, who served as special adviser to the Convention, swiftly regarded him as 'unquestionably the most academically capable member of the body – although there was not much competition!'[8] Sir Frank Cooper, the Permanent Under Secretary at the NIO also spotted the young law lecturer. At a time when the NIO devoted more attention to the SDLP and to loyalist paramilitaries – because they were the ones who appeared to have the clout – Trimble stood out 'as someone with whom you could have a rational and intelligent conversation. London accepted the fact that people sometimes had to make extraordinary statements to maintain their credibility. But although he was seen as very right wing and much brighter than most other people, he would not have been seen as prospective leader. He would have been 25th on a list – well after Glenn Barr, say.'[9]

A glance at the Convention proceedings gives some clues as to why Trimble excited both approbation and resentment. His speeches are larded, inter alia, with references to the writings of Arnold Toynbee and Alexander Solzhenitsyn – scarcely conventional Unionist pin-ups. Indeed, when SDLP members urged that Northern Ireland emulate the power-sharing arrangements of Belgium, Holland and Switzerland, Trimble was ready with a rebuttal. Far from proving that there should be compulsory coalitions, they illustrated the very opposite: in the Netherlands the practice had evolved over time rather than by prescription in the constitution.[10] Anthony Alcock, an English academic at the University of Ulster, who joined Vanguard after settling in the Province – and who later advised

Trimble during the 1996–8 talks – says that Trimble 'knows everything about the most obscure minority groups in the Caucasus. He is the only person I know of who can tell you about the two types of Karelians – Finnish Lutherans or Russian Orthodox.' Alcock, who had been commissioned by the Convention chairman, Sir Robert Lowry, to look at possible European models for resolving Ulster's conflict, also introduced Trimble to the intricacies of the South Tyrol question. It greatly appealed to Trimble, for it illustrates the principle in Europe of maintaining existing boundaries, while protecting minority rights within those borders. Even though there is actually a German-speaking majority within the South Tyrol, it has been accepted that this region should remain in Italy, but with special provisions through the local authority and with a proportionality rule for public service employees.[11] Such cosmopolitanism might in and of itself have been sufficient cause for suspicion, but some of Trimble's associations also aroused further doubts. After the Convention began, Trimble invited a couple of B&ICO activists – including Eamonn O'Kane, later General Secretary of the NAS-UWT – to place their pamphlets in the members' pigeon holes at Stormont. Trimble derived huge pleasure from escorting in the left-wingers, one with an obviously Catholic name. Later, he ran into a DUP Convention member, Clifford Smyth. 'David, there is such a thing as guilt by association, you know.'[12]

During the Convention, Trimble also came into prolonged contact for the first time with the British, joining Craig in seven meetings with Merlyn Rees and his officials. He also came into sustained contact for the first time with the SDLP. Trimble's maiden speech was a reply to Paddy Devlin. As the corpulent, working-class autodidact from the Belfast dockyards sat down, the pencil-thin, suburban academic stood up. As he did so, John Taylor whispered in his ear, 'congratulate Paddy on that speech'. Trimble was at a loss, since he had not actually listened to Devlin: he was searching for his notes, which he feared he had lost. Trimble duly told the chamber that Devlin was trying 'to achieve the greatest concord in this Convention. It was an approach which I welcomed and I am sure the people who sit on this side of the House with me welcomed it also.'[13] Afterwards Devlin beckoned him over. 'Can I have a word?' said Devlin. 'Any chance of getting some talks going?' Trimble said he did not know, but reported straight back to Craig.[14] Craig wondered whether Devlin wanted talks in Craig's capacity as Vanguard leader or as one of the chiefs of the loyalist coalition, or UUUC. When Trimble returned to Devlin, the latter said that either would do. For the next fortnight, Trimble spent much of his time at the Convention carrying secret messages back and forth between the two camps. Before entering the SDLP room at Stormont, Trimble looked down the corridor to make sure that no Unionists could observe him. Seeing that everything was safe, he opened the door only to find an SDLP group meeting in progress: the whole SDLP Convention party could see that Trimble was there. The consequence of such shuttle diplomacy was the inter-party talks which led to near-agreement on the voluntary coalition with the SDLP. Trimble remembers sitting alone in the members' room one morning, drinking coffee, when Craig walked in and out of the blue asked him: '"How are we going to prepare our people to bring the SDLP into government?" You could have knocked me down with a feather. And my thoughts went instinctively to Jean Coulter [the staunchly unionist UUP Convention member for West Belfast]. How are we going to get it past her? But the more I thought about it, the more I thought, "this is a bloody good deal"'.[15] Years later, after he signed the Belfast Agreement, Coulter was again an opponent of Trimble's power-sharing ideas.

Why was Craig, the great foe of Sunningdale, prepared to offer this to the SDLP? His reasoning was simple. In his view, Unionism had essentially three options in this period. First, they could either reach agreement with the other parties; second, they could by use of their majority in the Convention push a report that would be unacceptable to Westminster, and knowing that it was such then work to make direct rule more efficient; or, third, they could force a report on an unwilling Westminster, which amounted to a kind of insurrection. The latter option was not viable by this stage, for the only way that loyalists could raise the people of the Province against direct rule was in a context where Westminster had behaved unreasonably, such as in foisting Sunningdale upon an unwilling majority.[16] The second option foreclosed any real possibility of a devolved govenment and meant acceptance of whatever 'crumbs' were on the 'table' from London. By contrast, the first option, in the particular circumstances in which Unionists found themselves, looked more attractive. For after the success of the UWC strike, Unionists were in a relatively strong position: not strong enough, he noted, to re-impose the old Stormont but enough to regain some kind of local institutions on better terms than Heath had offered to them. They had shown their residual muscle. And loyalist terrorists had even taken 'the war' down south in the Dublin-

Monaghan bombings of May 1974. Moreover, a growing body of southern Irish opinion was anxious to disengage from 'the North' and effectively were telling Northern nationalists that they were now on their own and would have to cut the best deal they could with Unionists.[17] Given these circumstances, there was a real chance of cross-community agreement, without which Westminster would never accept the Convention report (a report adopted by simple majority – that is, of Unionists – would not be sufficient in political terms). But even if they failed to reach such an agreement, there were tremendous advantages to be gained by acting as reasonable men putting forward reasonable proposals. If Unionists were for once not seen to be the nay-sayers in the eyes of mainland opinion, there was every chance that they might then be able to extract other concessions from central government, such as an increase in Northern Ireland's representation at Westminster.

Trimble had no doubts about the benefits to Unionism of Roman Catholics participating in government. 'It would be of great benefit to Ulster's political debate if all Unionist parties would examine carefully some aspects of the relationship between Unionism and persons of the Roman Catholic faith,' he opined. '. . . But let us state what we mean when we say "We will accept Catholics in Government if they are loyal!" Qualifications for inclusion must mean 1. Being prepared to act consti- tutionally, and only to seek change within the law. 2. Being prepared to accept the will of the majority that Ulster remains part of the United Kingdom. 3. Being prepared to support the forces of law . . . In present circumstances it would be highly advantageous for unionism if there were Catholics, who satisfied the above conditions, and who could be included in a unionist administration. But they would have to be representative Catholics, not G.B. Newe type figures [the only Catholic brought into government under Stormont, during Faulkner's premiership].'[18]

On what terms, though, would these representative Catholics – that is, the SDLP – enter government? What was clearly unacceptable to Unionists was that they have a place in the administration of Northern Ireland as of right. Compulsory power-sharing would be outside of nor- mal British parliamentary practice. But, Craig (and Trimble) conjectured, there were other ways of ensuring that a variety of parties were represented in government: in other words, fulfilling the need for minority represen- tation without it appearing that a gun was being held at the head of the majority. If the composition of the government was voluntary – say, for the duration of a national emergency such as on the lines of the 1940–45 war-time coalition – then it might prove more acceptable. Moreover, few could argue that the circumstances then obtaining in Northern Ireland constituted anything other than an emergency. The SDLP would have a place in government, but beyond the first few years there would be no guarantee of anything. They would be bound by Westminster-style collective responsibility in the majority Unionist Northern Ireland Cabinet, whose First Minister/Chief Executive could hire and fire at will. And, above all, any such arrangements would be lacking an 'Irish dimension', such as the Council of Ireland which had contributed so powerfully to Faulkner's demise after Sunningdale.[19]

Trimble says that Craig later told him that the idea first occurred to him during his private talks with John Hume, another senior SDLP figure, at John Taylor's house in Armagh in 1973.[20] (Craig now denies this to be the case, stating that he never met Hume at Taylor's house.) But if Trimble is right, Craig only unveiled the idea when the Convention talks had stalled on the question of enforced power-sharing and the Council of Ireland. Later, when more hardline unionists had torpedoed the voluntary coalition proposal – severely damaging Vanguard in the process – Trimble would be blamed for devising the plan. He was, after all, an easy target as the cosmopolitan *éminence grise* with rum contacts, who had persuaded Craig to go down the route of compromise – even, as loyalists saw it, surrender. In fact, both men today deny this, asserting rather that it was Craig's idea.[21] That said, according to Craig's secretary, Isobel McCulloch, Craig discussed the details of the plan more intensively with Trimble than anyone else in Vanguard.[22]

But what happened next was, and has remained ever since, a subject of controversy – and the *way* in which the proposal for voluntary coalition was brought forward was as controversial as the idea itself. For its opponents, the idea was something suddenly sprung on them out of the blue, with no proper pedigree within UUUC policy-making councils. But for its proponents, there was ample scope for voluntary coalition in the UUUC's manifesto.[23] Most of the UUUC would have viewed such proposals as mere window-dressing – especially since there appeared to be no chance that they might be accepted by the SDLP. But after the initial impasse was reached, events and positions moved very rapidly. Both parties exchanged position papers on 26 August 1975 and reported the deadlock to the chairman, Sir Robert Lowry – with the specific request that he look at paragraph 8 (iii) of the UUUC document. That portion of it outlined three ways in which a coalition could be formed: first, by inter-party agreement before the election, approved by the electorate; second, by a combination of two or more minority parties obtaining a majority together; or, third, by parties coming together in the national interest during an emergency. Not only did this section – which was drafted by Craig and Trimble – appear to many in the UUUC to contradict the earlier passages on straightforward majority rule but they contended that it was not put to the UUUC Convention grouping as a whole prior to its presentation to the SDLP. That said, it was discussed by the 12-strong UUUC policy Cabinet (on which Trimble sat) and by the three appointed UUUC negotiators – Craig, Capt. Austin Ardill of the UUP and Rev. William Beattie of the DUP. Indeed, the official Vanguard account of this episode states that Beattie saw it and assented after showing it to Paisley and that it was ratified on the following day by the policy committee. The DUP leader later denied seeing it; Beattie says he only agreed to look at the early version, in which the coalition appeared to be voluntary. But when the DUP and others examined the fine print more closely, it turned out to be anything but voluntary.[24]

Whatever was or was not agreed, on 29 August 1975, the UUUC negotiators were told by Lowry that the SDLP had said that it was prepared to accept the the Unionists' position of 26 August as a basis for further discussion. As the official Vanguard record, drafted by Trimble and approved by others, then states: 'However it was recognised that further exploration was needed to see if the detail of such an agreement should be settled. Ian Paisley arrived and discussed the matter with Mr Craig. On their way out to their cars, Mr Paisley told Mr Craig that such an agreement would be satisfactory to the Unionist people if it was put in a referendum first . . . it was stated that the SDLP appreciated that there could be no constitutional guarantee within the structures of government envisaged by the UUUC and that consequently they could have no assurance beyond the life of the first Parliament and that they would be liable to dismissal if they failed to support government policy. It was also stated that the SDLP had agreed that "the first tasks of the new government would be to wage war on the terrorists" . . . they also accepted that the [Northern Ireland] Parliament should control security and have appropriate forces – indeed they said that they would prefer the war against terrorism to be waged by local forces rather than by Westminster.'[25] On

3 September 1975, according to Lowry, the UUUC negotiators came to him and requested that he prepare a paper on the voluntary coalition and the SDLP followed suit with a similar request: Hugh Logue, then an SDLP Convention member, says that although the SDLP were not at all enthusiastic about this idea, they decided that it would not be politically advantageous to shoot it down: 'Our view was "let's see if Vanguard can deliver"', he recalls. 'The problem was that had it become a real offer it would have caused tensions within the SDLP – and would certainly have triggered a vigorous debate.'[26] Indeed, Trimble remembers asking John Hume if he thought he could carry the whole of the SDLP: the Derryman calculated that they would lose three to four out of the party's seventeen-strong Convention caucus.[27]

Lowry's paper was delivered on 4 September. At the UUUC policy committee meeting that day, it became clear that Paisley would now oppose the plan. 'In the course of argument Dr Paisley conceded that there was no alternative way of regaining a Parliament but nonetheless felt that the price was too high,' noted the official Vanguard record. 'He said that all we could do was to await divine intervention. Billy Beattie privately informed a Vanguard member that the DUP would leave the coalition and said they were going out to rouse the country against this "sell-out" although he had not clearly dissented from the initiative earlier in the week.'[28] (Beattie reiterates that this was because he believed the proposals as originally presented were different from what they subsequently turned out to be.) Craig may have been under the impression that the UUUC team had agreed to his proposals; but when the matter went to the separate Vanguard and UUP Convention caucuses within the UUUC coalition, it was clear that the Unionists of all shades were split by the voluntary coalition proposal. David Trimble, addressing his fellow Vanguardists at Saintfield in the following year, laid the blame squarely at the door of the UUUC rather than the SDLP: 'At this point, the UUUC panicked. The thought of obtaining an agreement even on their own terms so scared them that they broke off talks.'[29]

Reg Empey, then a Convention member, says that Craig never consulted him about the idea – even though he was chairman of Vanguard and his running mate in East Belfast. There had been no meeting of the party's full council, nor any debate at constituency level, and once leaks started to appear in the press, local party workers started to make alarmed calls to headquarters. The Vanguard leader insisted 'that they had to strike while the iron is hot' remembers Empey. 'I observed that we had been the principal complainants under O'Neill that there had been no consultation and numerous attempts to bounce the party into decisions without debate. But Bill had made up his mind, he was absolutely rigid and inflexible. Back me or sack me was his approach. He didn't take a conciliatory approach to colleagues.'[30] Certainly, the lack of preparation of the grassroots contributed to the emerging debacle, but it was not the only cause of it. As so often in Northern Ireland, terrorist action played its part in hardening attitudes: on 1 September 1975, four Protestants were murdered by the South Armagh Republican Action Force (a cover name for the Provisional IRA) at the Tullyvallen Orange Hall in Newtownhamilton, Co. Armagh.[31]

A more important cause of the the Voluntary Coalition disaster lay in the internal dynamics of Unionist politics – or, more precisely in this instance, Protestant politics. For when word of it leaked out to Paisley's Free Presbyterian Church, the reaction of his co-religionists was unanimous: have nothing to do with this. At a Church meeting on 7 September, Paisley was told that any further dalliance with the coalition idea would divide the Free Presbyterians as well as the DUP.[32] Trimble also discerned two reactions within the UUP. The first related to their doubts about holding their own supporters in line with Paisley touring the country denouncing the proponents of the scheme as 'Vanguard Republicans'. But the second calculation was, Trimble believes to this day, more cynical: that many of them saw Craig's gamble as a way of destroying the Vanguard leader. After all, by the 1975 Convention elections, Vanguard had leapt into second place in terms of the overall number of seats within the UUUC coalition (14 compared to the DUP's 12 and the UUP's 19, even though it was still third in terms of the popular vote). Moreover, it had more capable people than the DUP and UUP. In fact, as Clifford Smyth – a not uncritical observer – notes in his biography of Paisley, such low calculation was probably not the motive of the DUP leader in this instance: whilst 'the Doc' did eventually reap political rewards from the destruction of Vanguard, there was no way of knowing this for sure on 8 September 1975. After all, no one can have anticipated that having gone up the Voluntary Coalition cul-de-sac, and been stymied, Craig would not have been nimble-footed enough to extricate himself.[33] But above all, the bulk of elected Unionists were in no mind to compromise on very much after 1974: the Convention was, in Maurice Hayes's words, 'Unionism's victory lap'.[34] So when the idea of a Voluntary Coalition was put forward at a full meeting of the UUUC Convention group, the proposal was duly rejected. Paisley then put forward a motion rejecting the presence of 'republicans' in the Government of Northern Ireland, which was passed by 37–1; although he was one of Craig's staunchest supporters, Trimble actually abstained, reasoning that there would be no point in being the sole dissenter in the room (Craig, he says, had left by this point).[35]

Craig's offer also prompted astonishment in England – and praise from unlikely quarters.[36] An *Observer* profile of 14 September 1975 likened him to O'Neill, Chichester-Clark and Faulkner, 'each a Unionist leader who tried to confront the prejudices of his supporters, and was swept aside. In each case, the British public has been mystified by the apparent transformation, at bewildering speed, from near villain to near hero. So before it happens to Craig, the British public should be warned about a significant literary genre, the Belfast Europa school of journalism. Deeply influenced by the Western "B" movie, this school's simple rule has been to identify, preferably on the journey into Belfast from Aldergrove airport, the Good Guys in the White Hat. Craig has last week been awarded his white hat.' Trimble duly noted the praise heaped on Craig by the mainland establishment, but not because it betokened to him a sell-out: rather, it illustrated to him how anxious official and semi-official circles were to latch on to any good idea. Far from having a master plan, the British state, in his eyes, was often rudderless in its aims and incompetent in its execution.[37]

Craig then proceeded to launch a media blitz to overturn the UUUC decision, spearheaded by Burnside and Trimble, and he won the support of the Vanguard Central Council on 11 October by 128 votes to 79 after a fighting speech. But the bulk of the Convention party were not with him and shortly thereafter they formed the United Ulster Unionist Movement. Then, following a five-hour meeting at Stormont Craig, Trimble, Barr and Green were expelled from the UUUC grouping. The Ernie Baird faction was admitted in their place, and Baird himself became deputy leader of the UUUC.[38] But Trimble's own expulsion was delayed. The reason had nothing to do with any innate affection for the man amongst his brother loyalists. Rather, it had everything to do with the fact that as chairman of the UUUC drafting committee he was the main author of the report which had to be delivered imminently by each of the parties. Despite some suggestions that he leave his detractors in the lurch, Trimble completed the task, asserting that it was vital for Unionism that it be done properly.[39] After the split, he also became deputy leader of the rump Vanguard party.

Trimble derived some crucial lessons from this episode. The first was that Craig should have done more to consult the average member of the Convention about the evolution of his thinking and the contacts with the SDLP. The sense of shock when these dealings emerged, says Trimble, did much to weaken Craig's position when the deal went awry and they panicked.[40] Trimble, who was part of Craig's inner circle, initially went to the opposite extreme in dealing with his Assembly party after the Belfast Agreement of 1998. According to Trimble, the collapse of Craig's initiative was one of the great political disasters to have befallen the Province during the Troubles. Had that opportunity been taken, he says, there would have been political stability in the second half of the 1970s, and an end to terrorism soon thereafter. There would have been no Anglo-Irish Agreement of 1985 – giving the Republic a say in the governance of Ulster for the first time – and none of the present political developments. And it amused him greatly when the DUP launched their *Devolution Now* document on 6 February 2004 – in which the Paisleyites extolled the concept of a voluntary coalition with the SDLP as one of three options for the future of the Province.[41]

Yet in the short term, Trimble was to suffer even more acute, personal discomfiture as a result of the Voluntary Coalition debacle. In the last debate of the Convention, on 3 March 1976 – just before its dissolution – Trimble wound up for Vanguard. His concluding remarks were directed at his UUUC colleagues, and especially at Paisley: 'In 1972, he [Paisley] was not prepared to exert himself to defend Stormont and in 1976 he does not seem to be prepared to exert himself to restore it . . .' opined Trimble. 'In the debate of the last few days I have been reminded of an old Russian proverb that I came across in the pages of *The Gulag Archipelago*, volume 2, to the effect that we should look for our brave men in prisons and for the fools amongst the politicians.'[42] It was, says Trimble, a bit of hyperbole on his part to hurt Paisley: in his view the DUP leader had always been a short-term thinker who was prepared to undermine Stormont for the sake of gaining an immediate advantage over the UUP. But the quote from Solzhenitsyn was also, he contended, a reference to his view of the way in which Paisley's rhetoric had fired up a lot of loyalist people, who had then ended up in Northern Ireland's jails. Those who did those deeds, thinks Trimble today (and then), had more bravery than those who encouraged them.[43]

Trimble was not, however, ready for Paisley's response. 'There is a story going round Queen's University that a well-known member of Vanguard and a lecturer in law at Queen's University, was toying with his personal side-arm in a young lady's home' retorted the DUP leader. 'After seemingly unloading it he pulled the trigger and surprise, surprise, it went off and a bullet embedded itself in a wall behind the girl, missing her head by a mere inch. Our man from Vanguard very quickly filled in the bullet hole with Polyfilla. One wonders how good Polyfilla is for holes in the head. Mr Chairman, that might be an apocryphal story, but tonight the hon. Gentleman was certainly toying with a situation with which he was not prepared to come clean out into the open.'[44] The attack was a clear reference to Trimble. There was uproar and shouts of 'withdraw!' from Convention members; Trimble tried to make Paisley give way, but the DUP leader declined. John Kennedy, one of the clerks to the Convention, recalls that 'it was the most chilling, lowest, moment I have ever witnessed at Stormont. The blood literally drained from David Trimble's face. Even the nimble-witted Lowry was lost for words.'[45]

Not for nothing is Ian Paisley reputed to have the best contacts of anyone in the Province – and, to this day, David Trimble does not know how the DUP leader discovered about this episode.[46] Paisley still declines to say who his source was.[47] Indeed, a large number of people – mostly, but not exclusively anti-Agreement unionists – have asked me whether I know of 'Trimble's attempt to kill his first wife' or of an attempt of kill an ex-girlfriend. One senior Ulster Unionist even suggested to me that because of this supposed attempt to murder his then consort, Trimble was exposed to blackmail by MI5 – resulting in a vulnerability to British state pressure which led him, ultimately, to sign the Belfast Agreement (there are echoes here of the allegations made by some Irish republicans against Michael Collins, to the effect that he only signed the 1921 treaty because London 'had something' on him).[48] The reality then was rather more prosaic. Far from being an illustration of Trimble's temper in the course of a domestic dispute it was, rather, an illustration of his technical incompetence. Trimble was at the Belfast home of his girlfriend and wife-to-be, Daphne Orr, in Surrey Street off the Lisburn Road. He was clearing his personal protection weapon – a nine-millimetre automatic – and had removed the magazine. He thought he had cleared the chamber and squeezed the trigger to clear the spring. To his horror, 'there was a round up the spout which fired into a wall. Even now, I find it it a bit of a shock to recall it.'[49] Daphne Trimble recalls that her reaction after the bullet hit the wall was 'quite unprintable' – and adds, reasonably enough, that if she believed that he was trying to kill her, she would have terminated the relationship. The RUC was never called, nor did David and Daphne Trimble ever tell anyone about it: Daphne, who was in the public gallery when Paisley revealed this information, was in a state of shock. The episode contributed to Trimble's decision to give up the weapon in 1978, a decision made all the easier by the fact that he thought then he was leaving public life following the break-up of Vanguard.[50]

Daphne and David Trimble had first met at Queen's in 1972, where he had taught her Land Law in her second year and then advanced Property Law in her third year for her honours classes. She had been born in 1953 at Warrenpoint, Co. Down, a small port by the border with the Republic. She was the second of four Orr sisters, the last two being twins.[51] Her older sister, Geraldine, married a Newry Catholic, Connla Magennis – whose uncle, Frank Aiken, was an IRA Chief of Staff in the 1920s who later became Fianna Fail Foreign Minister (Trimble never met Aiken, and Daphne only met him once at her sister's wedding).[52] Daphne's mother came from Scotland and her father owned Fred C. Orr, a well-known jeweller in Newry, the nearest large town. Newry was, she recalls, a tinderbox in the early years of the Troubles, and Protestant businesses were regularly burned out: she remembers that when the next shop was set alight, the arsonists were burned to a crisp. Like so many border Protestants, they came under huge pressure in this largely nationalist area, but the family remained resolutely non-sectarian. None of her family ever joined any of the Loyal Orders, though her father was a Freemason. Her parents were in the New Ulster Movement, the precursor of the Alliance party, but she freely admits that had she not married Trimble she would never have become a political animal.[53]

Initially, she had only liked him as a lecturer and felt comfortable enough to ask him for advice on an apprenticeship, for she had few contacts in the legal profession in Belfast. He directed her to his old friend from the Land Registry and personal lawyer, Sam Beattie, of F.J. Orr & Co. (no relation). It was only in the summer of 1975, after she had graduated, that they started going out with each other: the courtship was first struck up at a staff–student cricket match. Later, he took her to the bar at Stormont and taught her about classical music, especially Wagner. They were married on 31 August 1978 at Warrenpoint Methodist Church: as at his first wedding, ten years earlier, Trimble was married to the strains of the bridal march from Wagner's *Lohengrin*.[54] The reception was held in Banbridge and Trimble's new-found happiness was apparent for all to see: even today, members of his staff are struck by how his countenance lightens whenever her name is mentioned. Daphne Trimble's influence on his life has been enormous. As Herb Wallace notes, 'she is good at all the things David is not good at'. She provides the softening touch when he can be brusque or distracted – especially running the constituency office in Lurgan.[55] Sam Beattie notes that under her influence, he has become more even-tempered.[56] Above all, she provided him with four chidren: Richard, born in 1982; Victoria, born in 1984; Nicholas, born in 1986; and Sarah, born in 1992. Trimble had little contact with children prior to his marriage, but to Daphne's surprise has proved to be a good father. Since 1982, the couple have lived in a chaotic, detached house at Harmony Hill in suburban Lisburn – just off the old Belfast road heading towards Lambeg, Co. Antrim, and a mere ten minutes away from the outlying portions of republican west Belfast. More significantly, perhaps, the particular cul-de-sac in which they live is majority Roman Catholic.[57]

Despite that, Harmony Hill has provided a stable home and community in which to rear a family. It also permitted Trimble to reconnect with his spiritual roots. He had ceased to participate in the act of worship from 1968 to 1978, but resumed kirk attendance shortly after his remarriage. Daphne Trimble was born into a Methodist family, but they go every week to the nearby Harmony Hill Presbyterian Church, as much for geographical reasons as anything else. And when in London or abroad, he worships either at Crown Court Church of Scotland kirk in Covent Garden or at the National Presbyterian Church in Washington DC. Since 1992, the family has been ministered to by a liberal evangelical clergyman, David Knox, and all the children have been brought up as Presbyterians. This church is ecumenical in spirit and holds joint services with its nearby Roman Catholic neighbour, St Colman's, Lambeg: Trimble has read the lesson when the shared Christmas carol service is held at Harmony Hill, although he has never gone down the road to St Colman's itself. But there is no connection, says Trimble, between his religious evolution and his political development: he has kept a pretty rigid separation between church and state in his own life.[58]

SIX

Death at Queen's

AFTER the Convention was dissolved, Trimble stayed loyal to Craig, who was still Westminster MP for East Belfast. In 1977, Trimble helped his chief defeat the abortive DUP-led loyalist workers' strike called for the purpose of pushing the British Government to adopt a more robust security policy to crush the Provisionals: like much of the UUP and the Orange Order, Vanguard did not believe that the time was right. There were a number of reasons for this. First, unlike in 1974, there was no obvious target, in the form of a power-sharing enterprise. Second, under the new Labour Secretary of State, Roy Mason, British security policy was at its toughest anyhow. Craig and Trimble duly met with Mason on 1 and 10 May 1977 to advise him on how to deal with the disturbances. In particular, after Mason had issued a stern attack on the strikers from his home in Barnsley, Trimble urged him to tone it down: he feared that it might consolidate support for the strike, much as Wilson's 'spongers' speech had done several years previously.[1] Perhaps Mason took notice, for he did not use such language again.[2]

However valuable Craig's and Trimble's advice was to the British Government, nothing could alter the central political reality: Vanguard was finished. Craig duly wound up the party in 1978 and decided that his movement would again work for change from within, rather than from outside the UUP. Trimble duly joined the UUP for the first time in 1978 and found a berth in the Lisburn branch of Molyneaux's constituency party in South Antrim. Far from slowly working his passage, after serving on the losing side in the internal party debate, both he and Craig were soon in the thick of the action again. At their 1978 conference at Enniskillen, Co. Fermanagh, the UUP backed the idea of a Regional Council for Northern Ireland. In other words, they would rather accept the lesser level of power inherent in local authority-style devolution than share a greater measure of Stormont-style power with nationalists. There were sound political reasons for this carefully calibrated stance. The party was deeply divided between integrationists and devolutionists. The Regional Council proposal could be represented as a move towards either wing of the UUP. For integrationists, it offered the prospect of British-style local government; for devolutionists, the return of such limited powers could be the prelude to return to Stormont.[3] Trimble put forward an amendment at Enniskillen which called for a restoration of a devolved legislature working along normal parliamentary principles. He told the gathering that the party's original motion would be interpreted as abandoning devolution and adopting integration as a policy.

Such interventions did little to endear Trimble to the UUP establishment. The reasons for their distaste were personal as well as political, and ensured that he remained an outsider for many years to come. First, he was a refugee from Vanguard, which in 1973 had contributed mightily to the split in the old UUP. Indeed, there was always a whiff of sulphur about Vanguard, with its air of unconstitutionality. 'It was not just David Trimble,' recalls Molyneaux. 'There was a certain reservation in the mind of a great many members of the party. It was a little unseen question mark – particularly if they do something impulsive. That was the trademark of the Vanguard party.'[4] Then there was the matter of his character, which was light years from the backslapping bonhomie of the 'good ole' boys' at Glengall Street; nor, he admits, did he do much to make himself amenable to them.[5] Then, of course, there were the more obvious reasons for political prejudice, namely Trimble's status as a devolutionist dissident in a party that was apparently becoming ever more integrationist under Enoch Powell's influence. No doubt such sentiments help explain why Trimble came in third place when he sought to become UUP candidate in North Down in the 1979 General Election, behind Hazel Bradford and the eventual nominee, Clifford Smyth.[6]

Given these sensibilities, it was perhaps fortunate that few, if any, of Trimble's party colleagues (including Molyneaux) knew that from 1976 to 1986, he often wrote the 'Calvin Macnee' column in Fortnight magazine, which alternated between a unionist and a nationalist (subsequently, nationalist contributors wrote under a nom de plume of Columbanus Macnee). He had originally been recruited by his colleague, Tom Hadden, who found it hard to persuade Unionists of Trimble's hue to write for the journal: Hadden recalls that Trimble would leave his contributions in his pigeon hole at the faculty in a brown envelope.[7] It was characterised by an irreverent, mocking tone: two of its main targets were Molyneaux and Paisley, though Martin Smyth and Harold McCusker were recipients of the occasional sideswipe as well.[8] Trimble was contemptuous of what he saw as politicians who would wind up the public and then walk away from the consequences of their actions – in terms which would have been well understood by Andy Tyrie and others in the UDA. 'Just the other day Harold McCusker was discussing, on television, the circumstances that would lead to loyalists firing on the RUC and the British Army. It is all rather reminiscent of the days when Bill Craig went to Westminster to make his shoot-to-kill speech. Though there are differences. When Craig made his threat he had the strength of the UDA and others behind him. Also, if I remember rightly, he used the first person singular, while McCusker ingloriously refers to what others might do.'[9] In particular, he heaped scorn upon Paisley's 'Carson Trail' antics, launched in protest at the Thatcher–Haughey dialogue and which followed Sir Edward's itinerary in protest at the Home Rule Bill in 1912. At one point, the DUP leader had assembled 500 men on a Co. Antrim hillside, supposedly waving firearms certificates. 'To be impressive you must have something extra – something to show that these men mean business,' opined Calvin Macnee. 'So what do they do? They all wave a piece of paper in the air, and it is suggested that the papers represent firearms certificates . . . If the "Big Man" wants to persuade the government that he is a threat to be taken seriously, he must do better than that. I've heard it said that the demonstration might not be unconnected with the current history programmes on television, which have unearthed a lot of interesting film of bygone days. Paisley himself has made the connection by saying that he is following the Carson trail. Well, I've heard it said too that the television set at the Paisley home is faulty – that it's not the example of Sir Edward that he is following, but Frank of that ilk . . .'[10] Correctly, he warned fellow Unionists that despite Margaret Thatcher's John Bull rhetoric, she was not reliable on Northern Ireland. As he saw it, Unionists tended to respond to her positively because of the very hostile reaction of Irish nationalists to the volume and manner of her remarks, rather than because of the intrinsically pro-loyalist content of policy.[11]

Before the 1979 General Election, Molyneaux had struck up a close relationship with Thatcher, then leader of the Opposition and her

principal spokesman on Northern Ireland, Airey Neave. He had persuaded her to go for Scottish-style regional councils with no legislative
powers and had contributed greatly to the writing of the section of the
Tory manifesto on Ulster. But after Neave was murdered by the INLA in
March 1979, and the Conservatives entered office in May 1979, Thatcher
put in the much weaker Humphrey Atkins as Secretary of State. He
listened very carefully to his officials, whose institutional preferences were
profoundly sceptical of anything that might integrate Northern Ireland
more fully into the rest of the United Kingdom. Instead, in November
1979, the Government published a consultative document, *The Government of Northern Ireland: A Working Paper for a Conference*. Although it
ruled out discussion of Irish unity, confederation, independence, compulsory power-sharing or the constitutional status of Northern Ireland,
it contained none of the positive suggestions for which the UUP had
hoped. The SDLP, meanwhile, demanded the right to raise the 'Irish
dimension', which was eventually conceded in 'parallel' talks.[12] Molyneaux
reacted bitterly to what he saw as this betrayal and the UUP accordingly
refused to attend the 'Atkins talks' – whilst the DUP, to the surprise of
many, did so. Trimble, writing as Calvin Macnee in *Fortnight*, slammed
Molyneaux's 'miscalculations' and dismissed the boycott of the talks
as 'silly'.[13] Molyneaux, whose approach was always one of 'safety first',
had his own calculations: he had to fend off a challenge from the DUP.
Paisley had scored the highest number of first preferences in the 1979
European elections, the first Province-wide 'beauty contest'. And during
the 1981 Hunger Strikes, the DUP actually outpolled the UUP in the local
council elections (as Trimble correctly predicted in *Fortnight* in July/
August 1980).[14]

Trimble disagreed with Molyneaux's approach. 'Jim should not have
assumed that the Government was going to pick up his ideas and run
with them as a single option. The fact that there were talks did not mean
that they would disappear. But he was petulant. Because he was not
offered those things on a plate, it meant that his ideas could not possibly
come about. It was a terrible tactical judgement from his own point of
view. Molyneaux's negativism drove an impatient Thatcher into the hands
of succesive Irish governments. She felt she had to do something following
the Hunger Strikes of 1981, and this eventually resulted in the Anglo-Irish
Agreement of 1985' (significantly, even in this highly polarised period,
Trimble was at pains to emphasise in his *Fortnight* column that he did

not conclude from Bobby Sands' victory in the first Fermanagh-South Tyrone by-election of 1981 that the majority of Catholics backed violence).[15] Indeed, he recalls that even the South Antrim UUP manage-ment committee passed a highly unusual motion that was critical of Molyneaux's behaviour over the Atkins talks.[16] Despite these public rever-sals, Molyneaux proceeded to consolidate his internal grip on the party, prompting Trimble to form the Devolution Group in conjunction with some fellow dissidents. One of the key driving forces behind this ginger group was Trimble's colleague from Queen's, Edgar Graham, who would come to play an important role in his life. Superficially, they were birds of a feather, though in fact the two men were very different (nor were they 'best friends', as some have suggested). They had first met when Graham was a second-year law student, taking Trimble's course on Trusts. Graham, who was born in 1954, came from Randalstown, Co. Antrim and had attended Ballymena Academy. After Queen's, he had gone on to postgraduate work at Trinity College, Oxford, where he worked on a thesis on sovereign immunity. Returning from England, he was called to the Bar and taught Public Law at Queen's. He and Trimble occupied adjacent offices and became close professionally and politically, talking animatedly together in the Common Room during coffee breaks. Graham, who had been interested in politics since his teens, joined the UUP, but significantly did not join the Loyal Orders: he wanted to see how far he could progress in the party without such feathers in his Unionist cap. He was also opposed to capital punishment. He lacked the personal spikiness of Trimble, nor did he carry any of the Vanguard baggage and became one of the few intellectual indulgences which the UUP allowed itself.[17] After his election in 1982 to the Assembly, he displayed an impress-ive command of parliamentary procedure, which few could match. Many, including Molyneaux and Trimble, assumed that Graham would one day become leader of the UUP.[18]

Graham was elected Chairman of the Young Unionist Council in 1981 and in the following year was elected Honorary Secretary of the full Ulster Unionist Council. Ian Clark, a Queen's Young Unionist and Devol-ution Group activist who later became election agent to John Taylor, recalls feeling a sense of despair that Trimble, by contrast, could not have managed to be elected a party officer on the Devolution Group slate.[19] At one point, Trimble was even thrown off the Ulster Unionist Executive as representative from South Antrim and in the 1981 local elections he failed to be elected as a councillor in Area D of 'Loyalist' Lisburn.[20] Moreover, the space which he might potentially have occupied within the party was further 'crowded out' by two other capable lawyers who had recently joined up – Robert McCartney and Peter Smith. Significantly, both were critical of the drift of Molyneaux's policy. McCartney became chairman of the Union Group, which according to Trimble was founded to perform a function akin to the Bow Group or the Tribune Group. In 1982 the Union Group published *Options: Devolved Government for Northern Ireland*. McCartney wrote the foreword, while Trimble contributed the main paper. Trimble acknowledged that there could be no return to old Stormont-style majority rule and urged that a coalition be formed of all parties prepared to support common policies – that is, something along Voluntary Coalition lines. It also endorsed Sir James Craig's flexibility at the time of Partition: 'Before the 1921 Treaty, Craig had gone south to speak to de Valera while the latter was still on the run. [Trimble's added emphasis] This meant putting himself into the hands of a go-between, allowing himself to be taken, blindfolded, to an IRA hideout ... Craig negotiated the Craig-Collins pact with Michael Collins which covered the whole range of law enforcement in Ulster, including the proposal that Catholic reserve constables should be recruited specifically for the policing of Catholic districts.' The favourable reference to these discussions is significant: according to Marianne Elliott, 'the Craig-Collins pacts had held out the prospect of peaceful collaboration by the minority with the northern state. Not until the Sunningdale agreement of 1973 was another such effort made.'[21] But few invested these lines with much significance at the time; and as James Cooper, a prominent Fermanagh Ulster Unionist notes, Trimble was a master draftsman, who would be careful to emphasise that he was simply putting forward options, which were not necessarily his own views.[22] Trimble says he was even perfectly prepared to place his academic expertise at the disposal of political rivals. *Ulster: The Facts*, published in 1982 under the names of Ian Paisley, Peter Robinson and John Taylor, was, he says, largely drafted by the Unionist writer Hugh Shearman and himself. It was written in preparation for the trio's visit to America and was described by John Whyte in his bibliographical study, *Interpreting Northern Ireland* as 'the fullest recent attempt to give the Unionist case a factual basis'.[23] However, Peter Robinson and Cedric Wilson – a director of Crown Publications, the company which produced this work – state vigorously that they have no knowledge of

Trimble assisting in this endeavour. But Robinson concedes that Trimble might have worked privately with Shearman. By contrast, John Taylor states that he clearly recalls Trimble playing a leading role in drafting of the document. Whatever Trimble's precise role, it is clearly symptomatic of the divisions in Unionism that even so apparently uncontentious an issue as the authorship of a two-decades-old pamphlet should prompt such disagreement on basic facts!

Despite his skilled advocacy, much of the UUP hierarchy still regarded Trimble with suspicion as the most dangerous of the devolutionists. Those suspicions were further fuelled by the style as well as the substance of Trimble's politics. For Molyneaux's boycott of the Atkins talks and the attendant mistrust of the NIO were the antithesis of Trimble's approach: he believes in engaging political opponents head-on. In 1978, Trimble had several meetings with Allen Huckle, a young civil servant on secondment from the old Civil Service Department and later a senior member of the Foreign Office. He also met Stephen Leach, a rising civil servant in the political affairs division of the NIO, who contacted him out of the blue after reading his contributions to the Convention debates. The dialogue was a two-way process: the officials were out to influence the Unionists, and Trimble was out to influence them. Later, Leach introduced Trimble to a more senior figure in the NIO, David Blatherwick, who was on secondment from the Foreign Office and who later became ambassador to the Irish Republic and Egypt. 'Trimble came to us with a lot of suspicion not of the British state but of the Foreign Office and the NIO,' recalls Blatherwick. 'All of them, in his view, were selling out and pandering to the nationalists. You can't, of course, provide reassurance through mere words. You can only do it by consistency, by trying to explain what government is trying to do. If I had been in his position, I would have been suspicious, too. Everything normal about the Unionists' early lives had been swept away and here were these funny foreign guys from London put in charge temporarily and why should you trust them?'[24]

Trimble says he learned an important lesson from these conversations – that the Government had no master plan for the future of the Province and that Blatherwick was, in fact, grateful for ideas. Far from seeking a 'sell-out' or 'scuttle' from Ulster, Trimble contends that Blatherwick was looking for some formulation that would quieten things down.[25] The two men spoke in particular about the ideas which Trimble, Craig and David McNarry had expressed in their personal capacities as UUP members in

February 1980 in a paper entitled *Towards the Better Government of Ulster*. The document proposed a phasing of devolution which in the first stage could cover those services presently administered by the six Northern Ireland departments (Health, Education and so on), thus reserving more controversial matters for later. These reserved matters, it went on, could then be transferred within a specified period following a vote by a special or weighted majority of the members of the Northern Ireland Parliament. It added that the advantages of this procedure would be that there would be a clear incentive for all parties to work towards such a transfer. Some of these ideas were later incorporated into the 'rolling devolution' plans of Thatcher's second Ulster Secretary, Jim Prior, and the ensuing 1982–6 Assembly. Although the UUP participated in the Prior Assembly, many integrationists – and, above all, Powell – saw the body as a NIO stratagem to perpetuate the semi-detached status of the Province.

Trimble may have found discussions with officials informative, but they cost him dearly in the short term. In 1982, Enoch Powell raised a grave matter in the Commons, which came to be known in unionist circles simply as 'Sloan-Abbott'. The sequence of events was as follows: in February 1981, a young postgraduate researcher at Keele University called Geoffrey Sloan approached an upcoming NIO civil servant called Clive Abbott, for the purpose of interviewing him for his thesis. Sloan passed a record of this interview on to Harold McCusker, who in turn passed it on to James Molyneaux, who in his turn showed it to Enoch Powell. The contents of Sloan's notes were sensational. Abbott had apparently informed him that when the Tories entered office in 1979, the NIO had to tell them that the Neave (and therefore the Molyneaux) policy of greater integration was 'just not on', both because such an approach would forfeit the cooperation of the Republic in security affairs and because of past secret undertakings given to the Irish Republic on the constitutional future of Northern Ireland. The message was in line with Powell's worst fear: that civil servants were working actively to undermine the policy of the elected government of the day at the behest of a foreign power. Prior was enraged that a civil servant who could not defend himself should be named in this way. Moreover, he said, beyond the fact that these interviews took place, there was no agreeement on what Abbott had actually said. The Cabinet Secretary, Sir Robert Armstrong, had conducted an investigation. According to his findings, Abbott had not said these things: the notes contained some basic errors which, he held, no high-flying NIO civil servant could ever make (such as the misnaming of a US Congressman interested in Ulster). Above all, Prior retorted, Powell had not – as it were – 'declared an interest' in the matter of Sloan. For it emerged that although Sloan was, indeed, a researcher at Keele, he had once done research for McCusker and had also met Molyneaux on a number of occasions. When Powell raised the matter, he did not mention this and it thus appeared (erroneously) that Sloan had been acting as an entirely independent observer. Whatever the truth of the matter, the apparent errors in the interview notes and the question of Powell's omission allowed the Government off the hook.[26]

But there was a further twist to the tale. For according to David McKittrick's 'Westminster Notebook' in the *Irish Times* of 3 July 1982, the document 'has Abbott naming a prominent Official Unionist politician and saying, "he is also a personal friend, and has kept us well-informed about what is going on inside Jim Molyneaux's party for a number of years". The politician named says he has never, to the best of his recollection, met anyone by the name of Clive Abbott.' That unidentified person was David Trimble. The notes were circulated widely in loyalist circles and their contents were advertised – accurately – to the author. Key passages have also subsequently been passed on to me by a prominent UUP figure. The implications of this allegation were very serious indeed and confirmed the worst suspicions of the UUP about anyone who spoke to the NIO. For, at best, he could have been seen by his fellow unionists to have been indiscreet in front of 'the Brits'. Indeed, the most damaging claim, says Trimble, was to be described as a 'good friend' by a civil servant. Trimble states that since he had not met Abbott, the reference to him was obviously meant in a departmental sense, in the light of his conversations with Huckle, Leach and Blatherwick. He protested loudly to Blatherwick about the damage, but the UUP leader remembers that 'the NIO had gone into deep defensive mode' and would not issue a denial on his behalf.[27] Blatherwick also denies that Trimble was an informer of any kind and says that 'as a person he's honest to the point of brutality. A very proper person, very aware of his own position. That's why he took Sloan-Abbott so badly.'[28] Trimble also spoke to Molyneaux, as his local MP, to ensure that these claims were curtailed, but he remembers Molyneaux simply equivocated; Molyneaux says that he did not know what Trimble was alluding to. Even today, over two decades on, serving and retired senior civil servants are edgy about the Sloan-Abbott correspondence, refusing either to talk about it, or claiming that they cannot remember the details (or after much delay taking refuge in the Prior statement to the House in 1982). Abbott himself left the NIO a few years later for a senior position at the Home Office. Later, he held high rank in English local government and became chief executive of Cotswold District Council. He declined to talk on the record and his off-the-record comments added nothing beyond the existing public record. Sloan is now a lecturer in strategic studies and the author of an excellent tome entitled *The Geopolitics of Anglo-Irish Relations in the Twentieth Century*. Molyneaux strongly urged the author not to pursue the matter. Trimble, by contrast, is far more open about Sloan-Abbott than some of the other protagonists.

The accumulation of reversals contributed to Trimble's decision not to run for the Assembly and to contemplate leaving politics altogether. 'My first child was on the way and I was not getting anywhere personally,' recalls Trimble. 'Had it not been for Edgar [Graham] and the Anglo-Irish Agreement, my life would have gone in a totally different direction.'[29] Although Graham was by now in the Assembly – he had been elected for Trimble's old seat in South Belfast – the two men remained on friendly professional terms. Graham carried a personal protection weapon, but it was no macho indulgence on his part. The nationalist population – including many students at Queen's – had been 'radicalised' during and after the Hunger Strikes. Academia and judiciary, in particular, were becoming more vulnerable: in March 1982, whilst the Lord Chief Justice, Sir Robert Lowry, was visiting Queen's, the IRA fired four shots, wounding a professor; an RUC officer was shot in the head during an examination, though his life was saved; and Lord McDermott, Lowry's predecessor, was injured in a bomb blast whilst visiting the then Ulster Polytechnic at Jordanstown some years earlier.[30] And although the IRA did not usually target politicians, they had broken with this unwritten half-understanding in December 1981, when the Rev. Robert Bradford, Westminster MP for the constituency was murdered along with a caretaker at a community centre in Finaghy. Brian Garrett, a leading Belfast solicitor met Trimble at the opera that night and told him the news: Trimble's reaction was such that Garrett recalls that 'I felt as though I had plunged a knife into him.'[31]

By now, Edgar Graham had also come to the notice of the IRA. First, he was a relatively rare commodity – an intellectually talented Unionist politician. Second, in a debate at the Queen's University student union, he had conducted a brilliant defence of the so-called 'supergrass' trials (to which he always referred as 'turning Queen's evidence'), drawing attention to their effectiveness in Italy in combating the Red Brigades. The 'supergrass' system was then threatening to play havoc inside the terrorist organisations on both sides. Undoing it became one of the principal short-term aims of republicans and Graham was a highly articulate and plausible obstacle. Graham's colleague, Sylvia Hermon, who came to the debate to support him, never before witnessed such malignancy or hostility from some of the students. 'I felt afraid for him that day and in that environment,' she remembers. 'But I then did not realise the significance of it.'[32] There may have been other, more hidden threats as well. Trimble received a separate call after a gap of some years from Andy Tyrie to tell him that he had reason to believe a Queen's colleague, Miriam Daly, was using her post to gather information on people at or associated with the University (that is, the activity which subsequently came to be described as 'targeting'[33]). Miriam Daly was subsequently murdered by the UFF on 26 June 1980 – and was then described on the INLA headstone as a 'volunteer'.[34]

However, Graham had not only come to the attention of republicans. He had also angered the loyalist terrorists, opposing separation of prisoners in the Maze. Indeed, friends of Edgar Graham – including David Trimble – recall that at this point, he was more afraid of assassination by loyalists than by anyone else and he alluded to this threat in an Assembly debate.[35] Trimble told him that this threat was an attempt to intimidate rather than seriously to injure – on the grounds that no elected Unionist representative had been seriously attacked in the way, for example, that senior SDLP figures had been assaulted by republicans.[36] Possibly, this was because Graham knew that a leading loyalist had been warned by a prison officer that he (the prison officer) overheard a UVF prisoner suggesting that Graham might be a 'legitimate target' because of his policies (the implication being that if the IRA killed Graham, there would be no reciprocal strike against a nationalist). Certainly, Graham was regularly attacked in *Combat* – the 'journal' of the UVF – during this period and especially for his views on prisoner issues. 'Does Assemblyman Graham really speak on behalf of the UUP and its elected representatives?' it asked. 'They will be judged by their silence!'[37]

A few months later, Sylvia Hermon walked into the Law Faculty building at 19 University Square to find two men she had never seen before looking at the examination timetable. She let them depart the building, but followed behind into Botanic Avenue. She ran into an RUC officer who intercepted the pair. When pressed, one of them said that he had been looking at the timetable for his sister, who was reading geography and law – a non-existent combined course. It sounded suspicious, but the policeman could do nothing.[38] On the last day of tutorials – 7 December 1983 – Graham walked across from the main university building to the Law Faculty. There, he met a colleague, Dermott Nesbitt. Nesbitt, a lecturer in accounting and finance, had been Brian Faulkner's election agent in East Down in the 1970s; after leaving the party with Faulkner to form the short-lived Unionist Party of Northern Ireland, he had returned to the UUP fold. Graham laid down his case on the pavement and told Nesbitt that he was going over to London the next day to talk to the Conservative back-bench Northern Ireland Committee. 'John Biggs-Davison [vice chairman of the committee] is a good integrationist,' said Nesbitt, teasing his devolutionist colleague. 'Michael Mates [secretary to the committee] is a good devolutionist,' retorted Graham to his integrationist colleague.

At that point, two men ran up behind Graham and fired a number of times, at point-blank range, into his head. He fell immediately to the ground. The other plotters, who did not pull the trigger, began running in all directions to distract witnesses so as to prevent the identification of the killers. Stunned, Nesbitt looked up at the row of buildings opposite. 'Everyone was staring out of the windows,' remembers Nesbitt. 'With all the lights on during this dark December day, the hundreds of matchstalk heads looked like something out of an L.S. Lowry picture.' He ran into the faculty, where he immediately met David Trimble. 'It's Edgar,' exclaimed Nesbitt.[39] Sandra Maxwell, administrative assistant in the Law Faculty since the days of Professor Montrose, remembers that Trimble was very quick to react, thundering up the stairs to call the ambulances and the RUC.[40] But it was to no avail. Edgar Graham was dead, aged 29. Sylvia Hermon was present in the students' union when his death was announced over the tannoy: it elicited a vast roar of approval from some of the republican students. She has never been able to set foot in the place since.[41] Whilst regretting all deaths, Gerry Adams nonetheless declined to condemn the killing because Sinn Fein was not prepared to join the 'hypocritical chorus of establishment figures who were vocal only in their condemnation of IRA actions and silent on British actions.'[42]

Hitherto, Queen's had prided itself on being 'above the conflict' – a kind of safe haven where such unpleasantnesses did not intrude. Now, however, they found that the RUC investigation centred on republican students. According to *Lost Lives*, two former students were given suspended sentences for withholding information about the shooting – tariffs which the Unionists denounced as 'shameful'.[43] But Queen's was terrified at the prospect of the University being torn apart by the murder. The handling of the aftermath of the killing was therefore a matter of great sensitivity – and, to this day, Sir Colin Campbell, the Pro-Vice Chancellor, declines to say what measures he took in dealing with any member of the University.[44]

Some colleagues suspected that Queen's did not want Trimble making things worse because of what it might have considered as any injudicious pronouncements which he might have made in the heat of the moment. Trimble recalls Campbell coming up to him in University Square, with the body of Graham still on the ground, instructing him not to do any interviews on television. 'This is the University speaking,' Campbell told him.[45] Campbell says this was definitely not the case: he had no instructions at this point from the Vice-Chancellor, Peter Froggatt, and that there was no such conversation with the body still on the ground. What Campbell does say is that he was subsequently advised by Froggatt not to say anything: he says that Queen's policy in those days was not to get involved in anything which could be construed as hyping up political conflict.[46] Trimble says that, in fact, he had no intention of saying anything. But when he discovered that Queen's had no plans to make any collective institutional pronouncement, he told Campbell 'you've got to say something or I will'. He recalls that Campbell did talk to the press on the next day and that he did it 'very well'.[47] Again, Campbell's recollection is different. He says that upon seeing the massive media coverage of the event, Queen's changed its mind and gave him authority to speak on its behalf on *The World at One*. His concerns, he recalls, were twofold: first, he urged Trimble and everyone else to keep quiet to ensure that the University did not speak with a multiplicity of voices. Second, Campbell says, with one colleague already dead, he did not wish to see Trimble pushed further into the limelight.[48] But in the eyes of many of Graham's friends, Queen's had stuck its institutional head into the sand. The statement issued by the Vice-Chancellor's office, reported in the *Belfast Telegraph* on 8 December 1983, read: '[No] ... evidence been offered to suggest that these attacks originated from within the University and this University has no knowledge of any direct involvement by any member of staff or student.' Piously, it concluded: 'The University does not impose – nor could it impose – any political test for entry as a student or appointment to the teaching staff, taking academic achievement as its only criterion'.[49] To this day, Colin Campbell describes it as 'not a political event, but primarily a human tragedy'.[50] Some of Graham's friends felt this was besides the point. It was not people's views which were at stake, but their actions.[51]

Whatever controversies attended the conduct of Queen's, one thing is certain: anyone who attended Graham's funeral still describes it as one of the saddest days they can ever recall. Rev. Dr Alan McAloney, who had baptised Graham, conducted a packed service at Randalstown Old Congregation Presbyterian Church, which included the teacher who taught him his first lessons and the seven members of the Graham family who sang in the church choir.[52] The cortège then moved to Duneane Presbyterian Church, one mile from the shores of Lough Neagh, where this only son was laid to rest close to his mother's forebears. Expressions of shock and sympathy came from all over the world: Margaret Thatcher, who had met Graham earlier in the year when he spoke at the Conservative party conference, wrote to the parents to express her condolences.[53] But whatever the condemnation, the killing had a profound and beneficial effect from the IRA's viewpoint. As one close colleague has noted, Graham could have been assassinated anywhere, but the choice of Queen's was quite deliberate.[54] Trimble observes that 'the murder reinforced the "chill factor" on campus. It reinforced the tendency of Protestant children to go elsewhere for their education.'[55] Indeed, when Nesbitt returned to teach the following term, he found on one occasion a mugshot of himself on the blackboard with a drawing pin through his head.[56]

The gunmen are still at large today, and their identity is widely known. Even in the wildly unlikely event that they admitted their involvement, the semi-amnesty provisions of the Belfast Agreement would ensure that any sentence served would be minimal. It contributed to the University authorities' reappraisal of political activity by members of staff. Until then, they had viewed such forms of public service indulgently. But thereafter many contend they became more concerned lest it enmire them in further controversy. Trimble and others increasingly felt that excursions into the public arena would not help their careers.[57] Trimble has been unable to forget his fallen colleague and extolled his memory when he won the UUP leadership at the Ulster Hall in September 1995 and in a key vote of the Ulster Unionist Council of November 1999. So, too, did opponents of the Belfast Agreement: 'What would Edgar have done?' became a topic of intense debate between the two sides of the UUP. Every day, he passes the memorial stone set on the wall at the entrance of the debating chamber at Stormont. The inscription, with its quote from Euripides, was specially chosen by Anne Graham, sister of the deceased:

IN MEMORY OF
EDGAR SAMUEL DAVID GRAHAM
ASSEMBLY MEMBER FOR BELFAST SOUTH 1982–83
SHOT BY TERRORISTS ON 7 DECEMBER 1983
'KEEP ALIVE THE LIGHT OF JUSTICE'

SEVEN

He doth protest too much

WHEN the University term resumed in January 1984 many colleagues of Trimble feared that he would be next in line for assassination. But short of leaving Queen's – where any lecturer working to a set rota of lectures and tutorials would be desperately vulnerable – there was little that he could do. Ian Clark, a Queen's Ulster Unionist student who was friendly with Graham, recalls an intimidatory atmosphere at the University in those days and remembers Trimble telling him that 'if he needed any protection', he could help to provide it: Clark understood this to mean physical muscle, but Trimble says that he meant he would intercede with the Queen's authorities and the RUC.[1] Whatever Trimble actually meant, the one thing which he was determined not to do was to be cowed by the University authorities into relinquishing all political activity: if nothing else he is 'thran' (an expression common to Ulster and Scotland spelled in three different ways, meaning in this instance 'obstinate').[2] An opportunity arose in 1984, when his old friend John Taylor – who was running for his second term as a member of the European Parliament – picked Trimble as his election agent. For the first time, he found himself running a campaign from party headquarters. Although personally disorganised, Trimble proved a good organiser on behalf of the party – and Taylor won the third of Ulster's three seats in Strasburg (Paisley again secured the highest number of first preferences and Hume took the second seat).[3]

In Lagan Valley, too, Trimble sought to burnish his credentials. In 1983 he became Vice Chairman of the constituency UUP and in 1986 sought renomination for the same post. He found himself opposed for this largely honorific job and assumed that it was a renewed attempt by elements of the local Unionist establishment to be rid of him. Suddenly, the incumbent Chairman of Lagan Valley announced he was not standing again. Since Trimble had put himself forward for Vice Chairman, it could reasonably be inferred that he was prepared to run for the top job. This he duly did and Trimble squeaked by at the AGM, with votes 55 to 53. Thus it was that Trimble became chairman of one of the largest Ulster Unionist associations. More important still, Trimble – one of Molyneaux's main critics – was now the local party chairman of the party leader. Although Molyneaux could not but acknowledge his abilities, the two men were never natural soulmates – to say the least. In Molyneaux's eyes, politics and policy were the prerogative of the Member of the Imperial Parliament. Ulster Unionist associations, like their Tory cousins, were supposed to be election-winning machines which collected subscriptions and raised funds, but did not bother themselves with great affairs of state. Indeed, even in times of great crisis, such as in 1985–6, the Lagan Valley Association minute books show that surprising proportions of meetings were still spent on such routine matters as fulfilling branch quotas and the payment for the use of Association facilities for jumble sales. Trimble, by contrast, was keen to 'politicise' Unionists and accordingly set up a monthly discussion at the Lagan Valley Management Committee meeting called the 'Current Political Situation'. For example, the minute books for 11 January 1985 record that Trimble suggested that Lagan Valley affiliate to the National Union (of Conservative and Unionist Associations) to influence the ruling mainland party. This initiative was noted with interest by *Workers' Weekly* on 2 February 1985, which stated that Trimble 'has not been foremost amongst those anxious to bring Northern Ireland's wretched local politics into the British mainstream. He has been a leading spokesman for the devolutionist wing of the UUP.'

There was one other contrast between the two men. Molyneaux was Deputy Grand Master of the entire Orange Order and Sovereign Commonwealth Grand Master of the Royal Black Institution, the senior branch of the Loyal Orders; whereas Trimble was an Orangeman out of a sense of duty and was rarely concerned with the plethora of meetings which office-holders in the District or County Grand Lodge had to attend. Trimble felt that the Orange Order with its rituals and procedures was institutionally not suited to combating the *Kulturkampf* which Irish nationalists had launched against the Ulster-British way of life: in consequence of this campaign, many outsiders regarded Unionists as the 'Afrikaners' of the island of Ireland. Trimble's view of this matter had been given an extra urgency by the text of the joint communiqué which followed the 19 November 1984 summit at Chequers between Mrs Thatcher and the Irish Prime Minister, Garrett Fitzgerald. At the press conference, Mrs Thatcher had famously ruled out the three recommendations of the New Ireland Forum of the Republic's constitutional parties and the SDLP – which then became known in 'tabloid-speak' as her 'out, out, out' pronouncement. Unionists were delighted, but Trimble counselled caution. One of his reasons for caution was that in an attempt to slow down the momentum of Sinn Fein/IRA, the British and Irish Governments had agreed to give greater recognition to Irish culture in the life of Northern Ireland. Trimble could, therefore, see this emerging as the next great battle-ground.

Trimble believed that even the most balanced accounts of the island's history did not, taken as a whole, accord equality of treatment to Unionism.[4] Unless Unionists found an organisational vehicle to rectify this asymmetry, governmental support would go entirely to the Gaelic/Catholic/Nationalist side rather than the Orange tradition. Trimble reckoned that although the Orange Order was an entirely bona fide body, the 'cultural commissars' (his words) at the NIO would never dispense funds to it.[5] In some ways, he thought the Order was too exclusive a body, for the wider unionist community of Ulster was not coterminous with Orangeism. Likewise, to insert 'Protestant' into the title of any new body would also be unsatisfactory, for neither was the British community of Ulster synonymous with Protestantism: some of its most loyal citizens were Catholic. He was also anxious to avoid any hint of anti-Englishness, to which so many loyalists were prone after being let down by successive British Governments. Trimble now thought that anti-Englishness only played into the hands of Irish nationalists, and served to detach them from their natural moorings in the broader, more cosmopolitan community of the British Isles. What, then, would provide the broadest basis for fighting the dilution of Ulster's cultural identity?

'Ulster-British' – hyphenated – seemed the most satisfactory formulation. It implied a community capable of autonomous existence but which was also invested with wider associations in these isles as a whole. So following a seminar at the Park Avenue Hotel in Belfast on 25 April 1985, it was decided to set up 'the Ulster Society for the Promotion of Ulster-British Heritage and Culture'. On 28 September 1985 (the 73rd anniversary of the signing of Ulster's Solemn League and Covenant) the organisation was launched formally at Brownlow House in Lurgan.

Brownlow House – a mid-19th-century sandstone structure that served as worldwide headquarters of the Royal Black Institution and was also the largest Orange Hall in the world – became its home base. Trimble became the chairman, and a young activist from Fermanagh, Gordon Lucy, became general secretary. The first project focused on loyalist folk music and entailed the collecting of the words and tunes of traditional Orange songs and ballads which were in danger of being lost to posterity (surprisingly or not, Trimble's musical tastes do not extend to loyalist bands). The second subject concerned Orange banners, with question-naires to be sent to every lodge. Another study focused on the original UVF and 36th (Ulster) Division, which would trace and interview sur-vivors of the carnage which that unit endured on the Somme. Nor was the international dimension neglected: the Ulster Society also sought to rekindle awareness of the contribution of Ulstermen to the American Revolution.[6] Later, he was instrumental in securing a reprint of Cecil Davis Milligan's *Walls of Derry*, the authoritative work on all aspects of the defences of the Maiden City, first published in the *Londonderry Sentinel* in two parts in 1948 and 1950.[7] Trimble also reviewed books on Ulster's contribution to the development of science and technology – including Sir Hans Sloane and Lord Kelvin – and wrote a new introduction to the third volume in the *Tom Barber* trilogy of novels by Forrest Reid, an early to mid-20th-century Ulster author.[8]

Maintaining the self-confidence of the Unionist community turned out to be even more necessary than Trimble had imagined when he deter-mined to set up the Ulster Society. For on 15 November 1985, the British and Irish Governments signed the Anglo-Irish Agreement, which for the first time gave the Republic a formal say in the affairs of Ulster – on everything from security, public appointments, to the official use of flags and symbols.[9] As Trimble later noted, the 1985 Agreement did not even contain any declaration – as in the 1973 Act – stating that Northern Ireland was part of the United Kingdom, nor that it was the policy of the British Government to support the wishes of the people of Northern Ireland.[10] Worse still from a Unionist viewpoint, the Republic had achieved this role in the internal affairs of the Province without rescinding its claim over Northern Ireland contained in Articles 2 and 3 of the 1937 Constitution, which was illegal under international law. In the words of the Northern Ireland Assembly's report on the AIA – largely drafted by Trimble – 'the agreement clearly diminishes British sovereignty in

Northern Ireland by admitting a foreign government into the structure and processes of government of Northern Ireland'. The Intergovernmental conference – with its secretariat at Maryfield, on the outskirts of Belfast – was 'a joint authority in embryo, which if allowed to develop will become the effective government of Northern Ireland'.[11] Trimble now believes that the British state was disappointed with the results of the AIA and pulled back from the logical drift towards joint authority. But even though today he prefers the description of 'direct rule with the Greenest of tinges', he still shudders at the thought of the AIA effectively placing the Irish Government inside British ministers' private offices.

It was an even greater blow than the suspension of Stormont in 1972. As such, it fulfilled the Ulster-British people's worst nightmares, both in the contents of the treaty and in the manner of its negotiation. For the UUP leadership had been ruthlessly excluded from consultation about the document. But should Molyneaux have seen it coming? As is shown by his Calvin Macnee article in *Fortnight* of 2 February 1985, even a relatively peripheral figure such as Trimble spotted that something was in the works as early as November 1984, when Thatcher and Fitzgerald held their press conference at Chequers (as has been noted, the occasion of her famous 'out, out, out' pronouncement – on the findings of the New Ireland Forum of the south's constitutional parties and the SDLP). Her words had delighted Unionists, and horrified nationalists. But Trimble was not so sure. He watched the whole press conference on television with fellow delegates to the UUP's annual conference at the Slieve Donard Hotel in Newcastle, Co. Down. What she actually said was: 'A United Ireland was one solution. That is out. A second solution was confederation of the two states, that is out. A third solution was joint authority. That is out. That is a derogation from sovereignty.'[12] Trimble noted, though, that she had hesitated when the third option was mentioned and had to be prompted by a civil servant – an odd slip for someone as well-briefed as she was. He concluded from this lapse that if the two Prime Ministers really had been discussing the New Ireland Forum, she would not have needed to be prompted. It followed in Trimble's mind, therefore, that they must have been discussing something else.

But what was that something else? Thatcher, who feared that the Cabinet might leak, left the negotiations largely in the hands of her Cabinet Secretary, Sir Robert Armstrong, and one of his officials, Sir David Goodall. Increasingly desperate efforts to find out what was going on were met with ever more evasiveness as proposals emerged in the Dublin press. At one meeting at No. 10 between Molyneaux, Paisley, Thatcher and Douglas Hurd (the Northern Ireland Secretary) on 30 August 1985, the Prime Minister and Ulster Secretary simply listened and took notes but offered no guidance whatsoever on the contents of the negotiations. Many Unionists, including Trimble, could not grasp why Molyneaux – who had been aware of the seriousness of what was being negotiated for some time – waited till August 1985 to start agitating against the emerging deal; only then was a joint working group between the UUP and DUP set up. Trimble shares the conventional view of many Unionists that Molyneaux had relied excessively upon Enoch Powell, who believed that such an agreement would not be reached (and whose utility was diminished by his own highly ambivalent relationship with Thatcher). Trimble also thinks that Molyneaux might have relied too much on Ian Gow, who had left his original post as Thatcher's PPS for a ministerial slot and who inevitably no longer enjoyed the same access as in the first term.[13] Frank Millar – who was then general-secretary of the party – remembers that although Molyneaux went along with his contingency planning in anticipation of an Anglo-Irish deal, the UUP leader nonetheless believed to the last that there would be no agreement.[14]

Why had Thatcher done it? Many were astonished, especially after Anglo-Irish relations suffered during the pro-Argentinian tilt of the Haughey Government during the Falklands War of 1982.[15] First, she felt that 'something must be done' over the rising tide of violence and the growth in Sinn Fein's electoral support after the Hunger Strikes of 1981: the SDLP needed to show that constitutional politics could deliver something and the AIA would comprehensively demonstrate that capacity (though Fitzgerald admits that he continued to emphasise the degree of the republican threat during the negotiations, even after the Sinn Fein challenge had begun to wane during the May 1985 local government elections).[16] Second, she was told that it would yield all sorts of new security cooperation: a top-ranking Gardai agent in the IRA, Sean O'Callaghan, had recently supplied the information which aborted the attempted assassination of the Prince and Princess of Wales at a Duran Duran concert. She may, therefore, have believed that signing the deal would open the door to more such successes.[17] Third, her old friend, Ronald Reagan exerted some pressure: according to an authoritative biography of Tip O'Neill, the Irish-American Speaker of the US House of Representatives, the White House mollified O'Neill's anger over Administration policy in Central America by 'delivering' something to the Massachusetts Democrat on Ulster.[18] Moreover, by associating the Irish with decision-making on Ulster, the Government hoped to minimise the international costs of this engagement. And fourth, as Trimble believes, she may well have been fed up with the UUP leadership for turning down every government initiative after she did not automatically proceed with their favoured proposals in the 1979 election manifesto.[19]

Trimble actually heard about the signing of the Anglo-Irish Agreement during his sabbatical year whilst on holiday in the Costa del Sol. Daphne Trimble recalls them turning to one another and saying, 'This will mean civil war.'[20] Like so many Unionists, Trimble erroneously thought the British state was on the verge of a complete scuttle from Northern Ireland. 'After the AIA, it was perfectly obvious that normal constituency activity was useless and the MPs had completely failed,' he recalls.[21] The effects of all of this were swift and dramatic: between 100,000 and 200,000 Unionists assembled to protest at Belfast City Hall on 23 November.[22] But how would the initial surge of protest be sustained? As in the early 1970s, Unionists felt themselves to be in a bind. If they played by the rules, no one would take any notice. Yet if they resorted to large-scale violence, they feared that the rest of the United Kingdom would be disgusted and would accordingly resolve – in Peter Robinson's memorable phrase – to keep Ulster on the 'window ledge of the Union'.[23] Trimble, therefore, had three reasons for immersing himself in the gathering storm of protests. If someone such as himself did so (known to the NIO as a moderate of sorts after the voluntary coalition episode of 1975–6) then it would send a powerful signal to the system about the depth of feeling within the Unionist camp. The second reason was that if the protests were not to damage the Unionist cause, it was vital that there be some guiding form of political intelligence behind them. The third reason owed much to his responsibility as constituency chairman: he says he wanted to protect Molyneaux's back from the more extreme elements.[24]

Nonetheless, Trimble was not a figure of the first rank and was probably more peripheral than he had been in 1974–6 – as is illustrated by the fact that he registered only just in the consciousness of senior servants of the British state. Sir Robert Armstrong, for instance, recalls 'a shadowy figure, but little more than that'.[25] Trimble's chosen vehicle for protesting the accord was the Ulster Clubs: originally created before the AIA to oppose the re-routing of traditional loyalist parades, they had since then recanalised their energies to oppose the Agreement. Above all, they felt that neither the mainstream politicians nor the Orange Order were doing enough. Trimble became the founding chairman of the Lisburn branch, whose inaugural meeting was held at the town's main Orange hall. But Trimble was depressed by the combination of loose fighting talk about taking on the British Army and a lack of a coherent strategy to deal with the crisis. Indeed, he took it as a measure of how bad things were that the deputy supreme commander of the UDA, John McMichael, was the most sensible person at many of these meetings. McMichael, also from Lisburn, was the political brains behind the UDA, and the two men had a healthy mutal respect.[26] John Oliver remembered that 'McMichael thought the world of David' and over the next few years took to heart many of Trimble's strictures about the legitimate parameters of protest.[27] This contact proved important to Trimble, for without McMichael's help, he would have been unable to keep a grip on the wilder elements. But Trimble also used his own skills to chair the meetings of the Ulster Clubs. Nelson McCausland, later a Belfast city councillor, remembers Trimble's technique for dealing with the grassroots: 'What struck me was how people were talking a load of nonsense. David Trimble would then summarise their ramblings in a very articulate way, "I think what you're really saying is . . ." and the person would be gratified that he had hit upon some new insight.'[28] Trimble would also do all the talking at meetings of the Province-wide executive of the Ulster Clubs, where his colleagues again seemed to him to be equally clueless. He directed them to the strategy of the Militant Tendency. 'I said to them, "if you're aligned to mainstream organisations, but oppose their strategy as a ginger group, one thing you can do is to set up a newspaper to influence the wider debate".' So it was that *Ulster Defiant*, the Clubs' newspaper, was born.[29]

To demonstrate that the AIA had no support in the majority population, the fifteen UUP, DUP and independent Unionist MPs resigned to create a massive Province-wide by-election: the SDLP put up candidates in only four of the most marginal constituencies. On 24 January 1986, the Unionists secured an overwhelming 418,230 votes and held all of their seats bar Newry–Armagh. This took the gloss off the victory. Indeed, the rise in the SDLP vote at the expense of Sinn Fein allowed the Government to claim that its strategy of strengthening constitutional nationalism was working. The collapse in the pro-Agreement (but loosely unionist with a lower case 'u') Alliance party vote showed the virtual unanimity within the Unionist family against the diktat. Gradually, all of Ulster-British society mobilised. Eighteen councils with Unionist majorities, including Lisburn, adjourned; rates protests followed; and southern Irish goods were boycotted (Trimble thought this last form of protest to be silly, but went along with it in the spirit of the times). The culmination of this phase of struggle was the Loyalist 'Day of Action', held on 3 March, whose purpose was to bring the whole of Northern Ireland to a standstill. Lisburn, of course, was to do its bit and set up a municipal coordinating committee comprised of representatives of the UUP, DUP, Loyal Orders, Ulster Clubs and farmers' bodies. After a series of road blocks, to shut off the town, they would then adjourn for a mass rally at Smithfield Square in the town centre.

It was, though, an organisational nightmare. Trimble knew that street protests had to be managed. And the only people who could exert sufficient influence to prevent things spiralling out of control were the paramilitaries themselves. When tempers frayed, such crowd scenes could easily degenerate into full blown riots. Trimble participated in an ad-hoc action committee of 20 that included McMichael, whose purpose was to discusss the arrangements for the event. They decided on peaceful pickets of all the main arteries leading in and out of town. Trimble went around the traders in Bow Street, asking for their support: only one of them, he recalls, gave a dusty response. On the day itself, he positioned himself on the Hillsborough Road. During the course of the protest, some UDA men began to thump a bus which had been stopped. Trimble tried to stop them and they told him in no uncertain terms where to go. He rang McMichael, who duly told them to cease, and was always grateful to the UDA leader for sticking by what they had agreed.[30] Later in the day, Trimble presided at the mass rally in Smithfield Square, packed with families and farm vehicles. The *Ulster Star* – a local newspaper – reported on 7 March 1986 that he saluted the work of the coordinating committee. 'Mr Lawson Patterson and Mr Eddie Blair were thanked for arranging the tractor cavalcade and there was praise for the representatives of the Loyal Orders and Mr John McMichael, of the UDA.' But there was an uglier side to some of the subsequent protests as well. Lisburn RUC men who were put in the front line of policing the demonstrations were burned out of their homes and Seamus Close of the local Alliance party claimed it was significant that these had come on the heels of 'sinister and intimidatory' comments by UDA spokesmen.[31] Indeed, later that year, the Housing Executive reported 114 instances of intimidation against Roman Catholic families in the greater Lisburn area. 'It was a very unhappy time,' recalls Trimble. But he was determined not to allow that element to spoil the legitimate demonstrations of others.[32] In May 1986, on the occasion of the intergovernmental conference, Trimble and his fellow loyalists took over the rates office, urging householders and businessmen to withhold payments for as long as possible. He hoped that if enough people did so, the temporary shortfall would cost the Treasury £100 million in interest payments. When he eventually paid up, he did so with a giant, blown-up four foot by ten hardboard cheque for £616.16 drawn on his own and Daphne Trimble's personal account: he had derived the idea from A.P. Herbert, who once wrote a cheque on the side of a cow. When Peter Barry, the Irish Foreign Minister, visited Northern Ireland on 17 June 1986, Trimble and others chained themselves to the railings at Hillsborough Castle; he arrived at work on the next day to find a photograph of the stunt displayed on the front page of the News Letter: it certainly annoyed his supporters at Queen's such as Herb Wallace, who at the time was 'managing' his campaign to be elected Dean of the Law Faculty. In the eyes of the university authorities, it may well have confirmed their impression that Trimble was someone unsuitable for preferment.[33] Indeed, Trimble received two convictions for minor public order offences, such as parading without a permit in Lisburn with his own branch of the Apprentice Boys of Derry.

As time went on, it became clear that the Government would not budge. It correctly calculated – on the advice of Sir Robert Armstrong and other senior officials – that there would be no repeat of 1974.[34] They also came to this conclusion on the basis of assessments from the security forces.[35] For in 1974, there was a locally-based political experiment to bring down. This time, there was an unassailable international treaty signed by two governments which could not be pressurised like the Faulknerites were. The 'Irish dimension' had thus been used to outflank the Unionist majority in Ulster. Or, as John Hume was reported as saying, 'I always expected a furious Unionist reaction to the Agreement, but the Protestant boil had to be lanced.'[36] The Government also saw that hardline loyalist protests, such as the 1977 strike and Paisley's much-vaunted 'Carson Trail' of 1981 had been damp squibs: in the more straitened financial circumstances of the 1980s, loyalists were less prepared to engage in the kind of industrial militancy which had proven so successful across the United Kingdom in the 1970s. Partly, this was conditioned by the growing dependence of both the Protestant and the Catholic working classes on the subvention of the United Kingdom Exchequer. Above all, the British Government correctly reasoned that the ultra-respectable Molyneaux and the UUP would never sanction a mass uprising: indeed, Molyneaux and his party only accepted the March 1986 Day of Action when they were left with no other choice.[37]

Unionist protests became ever more desperate, partly out of frustration with the Unionist leadership. In his first major interview in the *News Letter*, on 6 November 1986, Trimble said: 'If you have a situation where there is a serious attack on your constitutional position and liberties – and I regard the AIA as being just that – and where the Government tells you constitutional action is ineffective, you are left in a very awkward situation. Do you sit back and do nothing, or move outside constitutional forms of protest? I don't think you can deal with the situation without the risk of an extra-parliamentary campaign. I would personally draw the line at terrorism and serious violence. But if we are talking about a campaign that involves demonstrations and so on, then a certain amount of violence may be inescapable.' In fact, Trimble's course in this period was seemingly contradictory. On the one hand, he wanted an escalation of protests, warning that unless the Unionist leadership improved its performance, the paramilitaries would soon take over. On the other hand, during the June 1987 General Election, he was struck by the reaction on the doorstep in Lisburn. There was hostility to the council boycott – as reflected in the Lagan Valley Unionist Association minute books – but more especially to the MPs' policy of staying out of the Commons chamber. Boycotts were to Trimble a tactic, not a principle, and if they were undermining the struggle then they would have to be wound down. But if Trimble's methods for attaining his goals were variable, so were his goals. On the one hand, he lent his support to those Unionists who responded to the AIA by urging complete integration into the United Kingdom; on the other, he flirted with constitutional forms which resembled independence. He was the most senior Unionist to campaign in a personal capacity in the 1986 Fulham by-election for his Queen's colleague Boyd Black, then a B&ICO activist, who ran as Democratic Rights for Northern Ireland candidate. And although many integrationist themes found their way into Ulster Clubs' literature (indeed, Boyd Black's election address was printed on the front page of *Ulster Defiant*), Trimble's own pamphlet for Ulster Clubs explored a much wider range of options, ranging from Powellite-style total integration to independence. The treatise was entitled *What Choice for Ulster?* and it came down on the side of Dominion status – in other words, a relationship that bore more similarity to full independence than integration. It was an unusually glossy publication by the Samizdat-like standards of Loyalist pamphlets: the front cover bore the famous propaganda poster entitled *Ulster 1914*, with the Province personified as a young woman with long, flowing hair. She defiantly carries her rifle against a Union Jack background, proclaiming the words 'Deserted! Well – I Can Stand Alone'.

Trimble declared that Ulstermen were aiming for negotiated separation rather than UDI. Not only, Trimble declared, would this new Ulster be able to rely on 'native ingenuity' but it would also enjoy food provided by provincial farmers and energy supplies from Antrim lignite and Fermanagh gas. In echoes of his first speech to the Assembly and to the Nobel Prize-winning ceremony in Oslo, Trimble acknowledged that more could have been done during the 50 years of Unionist domination to make nationalists feel at home. 'We should say to the nationalists in our midst, "a united Ireland is impossible, but a united Ulster is possible, and we invite you to be part of it",' observed Trimble. *Workers' Weekly* regarded such thoughts as 'twaddle' produced by an 'introverted Unionist', and in its edition of 22 August 1987 opined: 'What is being said here in code is more or less the equivalent of what the Provisionals are saying – get out of the house but leave the money on the table.' These musings would not be forgotten by Trimble's rivals: years later, in a televised debate on the eve of the 1998 referendum on the Belfast Agreement, Paisley dusted off the pamphlet to illustrate his belief that the UUP leader was soft on the Union.[38] Trimble, though, never took such reasoning to its logical conclusion to advocate full-scale independence – such as the 'Republic of Northern Ireland'. He held several meetings with a Presbyterian cleric from Co. Tyrone, Rev. Hugh Ross, who headed the Ulster independence movement, but remained unpersuaded. Trimble believes that the bulk of Ulster Unionists would never wish completely to relinquish the link with the Crown.[39]

How does Trimble reconcile these varying positions? After all, one of them (integrationism) is based upon the notion of the inherent inclusiveness of Unionism; the other is based upon the 'apartness' of the Ulster-British from both the rest of the United Kingdom and the Republic. Trimble argues that equal citizenship is very much the first choice of all Unionists, as was the case in 1921; but that if that is not on offer, then they will have to find some alternatives which preserve their way of life. He had concluded that the Union was in such peril that he had to set as many hares running as possible – including contradictory approaches in which he did not necessarily believe himself. If integrationism took off, all well and good. If not, then alternatives would have to be found. Another reason why Trimble could embrace both apparently contradictory approaches is that there is an element of intellectual gamesmanship in Trimble's personality, which owes much to his training as an academic lawyer: he will draft anything for the sake of an argument. What is certainly the case is that Trimble was one of very few people who straddled the two, mutually antagonistic strains within Unionism: one was the world of integrationism, of the vision of Northern Ireland as part of a broader, more cosmopolitan entity. This attracted many Unionist colleagues in the professional middle classes and amongst Queen's undergraduates after the AIA. The other world was that of 'little Ulster' which, more often than not, had its roots in evangelical Protestantism and was much remoter from the British mainstream. He was not, though, the only Ulster politician to adopt a dizzying array of positions: as Clifford Smyth notes in his study of Paisley, 'the Doc' was also perfectly capable of adopting integrationism, devolution, or independence – depending upon which of them most advanced the Protestant interest at a given moment.[40]

Such activities, which were widely reported, can have done little to endear Trimble to the authorities at his workplace. The Queen's of the 1980s was very different place from the Queen's of the 1960s and 1970s. Political activism, once regarded as a public service, was now seen as less of an asset. It was not merely that the controversy-aversive University was determined to avoid a repetition of the killing of Edgar Graham for Trimble's own sake; it was also because under the cumulative impact of fair employment legislation designed to eradicate sectarianism in the workplace, the University had become far more sensitive to such matters and its 'image'. A campaign had been launched primarily (but not exclusively by nationalists) to allege that there was religious discrimination in the composition of the teaching staff. Most of them were Protestants –

if not necessarily from Ulster – whilst the undergraduate population was ever-more Catholic. It thus echoed recent allegations contained in the MacPherson report that the Metropolitan Police is 'institutionally racist'. In the words of Alex Attwood, who was president of the Students' Union in the early 1980s and subsequently vice chairman of Convocation (a body comprised of all graduates) 'Queen's succeeded Short's as the representative employment management issue in the North'.[41] Queen's responded by settling many cases out of court.

Although Trimble was never sued for harassment or discrimination (nor, indeed, was any complaint ever lodged against him) his face did not fit in this not-so-brave new world of pious neutrality. He says that Colin Campbell bluntly told him that he would never hold a professorial chair; Campbell says that he simply gave Trimble the advice which he gave to all colleagues at that stage in their careers – that Trimble would not obtain a professorship unless he increased his output of published materials.[42] As editor of the Northern Ireland Law Reports, he would be summarising and synthesising, rather than doing original work of his own. What is beyond doubt is that Trimble did not fulfil his ambitions. The first chair which came up – to replace the departing Campbell – went to Simon Lee, a 'superstar' academic with good media credentials, and the second to his old friend Herb Wallace. Wallace, for example, also came from a unionist background, but he was not an active politician and he was thought less likely to blow his top in a crisis. Trimble also believes that his political commitments may have played a part: as Iain Macleod observed of R.A. Butler, 'Rab loves being a politician among academics and an academic among politicians; that is why neither breed of man likes him all that much.'[43]

Professorial chairs were not, though, the only avenue for advancement. In 1986, the post of Dean of the Law Faculty came vacant – an administrative post that involved much persuasion and cajoling. Normally, elections went uncontested and Trimble seemed to be certain of winning: indeed, to make absolutely sure of things, Trimble authorised Herb Wallace, as his unofficial campaign manager, to say that if elected, he would cease all active politics. Colin Campbell, the Pro-Vice Chancellor, asked Judith Eve, a colleague of Trimble's from the Law Faculty to run. According to Herb Wallace, Campbell might have viewed Trimble's political activities as detracting from the Law Faculty's reputation (a third candidate, Geoffrey Hornsey, also entered the contest though he soon withdrew).[44] In the ensuing battle royal, the 'jurisprudes' formed the core of the anti-Trimble camp, whilst the 'black letter' lawyers of his own department were the core of the pro-Trimble operation. Trimble was the more senior, and had more administrative experience, but the elegant Eve was viewed as the 'safer pair of hands'. 'She was cooler, and without moods,' recalls Sylvia Hermon, then – as now – one of Trimble's most ardent supporters. The election was so close a contest that postal votes from faculty members travelling abroad were solicited, yet the Trimble camp still thought they had the edge. One morning, Sylvia Hermon came in and picked up the *News Letter*: there, she found Trimble pictured on the front page, tied to the railings at Hillsborough Castle as part of an Ulster Clubs' protest against the intergovernmental conference.[45] 'Short of raping the vice-chancellor's wife on the front gates of the university, he could not have done much worse,' wryly recalls Brian Childs, a colleague in the department of commercial and property law.[46] It may have been decisive, for Eve scraped home by 18 votes to 16, with one abstention.

Trimble's friends began to despair of his prospects. Trimble, though, was not to be deterred for long. Some months later, the post of the director of the Institute for Professional Legal Studies became available. The Institute was part of Queen's, but was independent of the Law Faculty and was governed by the Council for Legal Education. It had been set up in 1977 for professional training of law graduates.[47] Again, he seemed to have all the experience and duly applied; and, once again, a presentable younger woman entered the field. Her name was Mary McAleese, a Belfast-born Catholic, the 36-year-old Reid Professor of Criminal Law at Trinity College Dublin.[48] Her publications portfolio may have been less voluminous than compared to that of Trimble, but she had two skills which he conspicuously lacked: she marketed herself superbly and was immensely adept with people. The 10-strong interview panel was chaired by Lord Justice O'Donnell, who led the questioning. He was assisted by Lord Justice Kelly, who as Basil Kelly had been Unionist MP for Mid-Down at Stormont and was the last Attorney General of Northern Ireland under the *ancien régime*. Trimble performed poorly, whilst McAleese dealt with the questions adeptly and she was duly appointed.[49] The upward trajectory of McAleese's career was maintained and she later became Pro-Vice Chancellor. In 1997, she received the Fianna Fail nomination for the presidency of the Republic and won the election.

Trimble's record of disappointment in university politics contrasts very sharply with his successes since his election to Parliament in 1990. 'The difference between university politics and party politics is that university politics are a closed hierarchical system, whereas party politics are open,' he explains. 'In terms of the UUP, oddly, my position wasn't very different from that at Queen's. During the Upper Bann by-election, very few unionist figures were favourable to me. I thus came in 1990, and more particularly in the 1995 leadership race as an outsider. The great thing about politics is that they are decided by wider groups. My position vis-à-vis the Unionist hierarchy was just the same as vis-à-vis the Queen's hierarchy.' So why does he have such bad relations with his academic and political peer groups? 'It's my lack of diplomatic skill,' Trimble declares. 'I know that's a rather big failing. I'm argumentative by nature and get into arguments without any consideration as to who they are with and the career implications. As I get older my arguments are couched in less aggressive terms. From the point of the view of the "Good Ole' Boys" in Glengall Street [the tightly knit clique of men who ran the party headquarters in central Belfast for years] I'm never one of them. I come from the outside and I'm a bit too ready to tell them what they should do.'[50]

EIGHT

Mr Trimble goes to London

TRIMBLE'S self-analysis was shared by many of his party colleagues. In early 1989, he was finally elected one of four honorary party secretaries at a meeting of the 860-strong Ulster Unionist Council – yet his problems with his peer group endured. What his coevals immediately saw was a man in a hurry. 'I was brought up by Jo Cunningham [later party president] that you listened for the first year,' recalls Jack Allen, the long-time party treasurer. 'David could never be accused of doing that.'[1] Likewise, Jim Wilson, the party general-secretary recalls: 'He had little time for convention and the rule book – because in the rule book you find reasons for not doing things. I suppose at that time I thought, "Hey, David you're not going to fit in here, you're rocking too many boats." And he was also suspected of leaking officers' decisions.' (Trimble says he may have gossiped, but that he never deliberately leaked.)[2] At the same time as being voluble, Trimble was not very sociable: after party officers' meetings on Friday afternoons at Glengall Street, he would not be found drinking Ken Maginnis' beloved Rioja with members of the team. Subsequently, Molyneaux was annoyed by Trimble's habit of playing with his personal computer whenever the discussion became boring.[3]

Trimble could still be wonderfully inept with larger audiences as well. When John Taylor announced his retirement from the European Parliament in 1988, Trimble was one of four candidates who sought to replace him. His main rival was Jim Nicholson – a Co. Armagh farmer who had lost the Westminster seat of Newry and Armagh in the 1986 set of by-elections (caused by the resignation of all Unionist members in protest at the AIA). Nicholson already enjoyed a substantial sympathy vote for making this sacrifice. On the night, Trimble made a brilliant speech. The only problem was that he failed to mention agriculture once – something of an omission, remembers John Taylor, since the Common Agricultural

Policy then comprised more than half of the EU budget and the room at the Europa Hotel was full of farmers! Moreover, under questioning, Trimble (who speaks passable French and German) modestly down-played his genuine foreign language skills; whilst Nicholson, an arguably less cosmopolitan figure, did just the opposite. Nicholson won with 52% on the first ballot.

But even this defeat, reckons Trimble, helped raise his profile in the party. Moreover, it was a party in which there were fewer articulate lawyers than before: Edgar Graham was dead; Robert McCartney was no longer in the party; and Peter Smith had gradually moved out of politics to concentrate fully on his legal career. As if to emphasise his new-found primacy Trimble set up the UUP legal affairs committee in the autumn of 1989. Its principal work was the party's submission to Lord Colville, a law lord then conducting a review into Ulster's anti-terrorist legislation. The document, entitled *Emergency Laws Now*, was written by Trimble himself and was partly based on the old Vanguard submission to the Gardiner Committee in 1974. Amongst its principal recommendations, it urged an end to 'exclusion orders' debarring certain Ulstermen from the British mainland – which, in Unionist eyes, treated Northern Ireland as a place apart. Trimble's profile was further raised when he participated in a demonstration with DUP members against Charles Haughey's visit to Belfast in 1990 as a guest of the Institute of Directors at the Europa Hotel. From the roof of neighbouring Glengall Street, they waved Union flags and shouted anti-republican slogans.[4] Ironically Haughey was greeted by two local dignitaries, both of whom later flourished mightily under Trimble's patronage: the head of the Institute, John Gorman, later became the senior Catholic politician in the UUP. Likewise, Reg Empey, then Lord Mayor of Belfast became one of Trimble's closest colleagues. Both men were knighted under his leadership.[5]

For all his hyper-activity, Trimble remained a figure of the second rank and all prospect of advancement at Queen's now appeared denied him. Yet, suddenly, there was an opening. Harold McCusker, the UUP MP for Upper Bann, died of cancer on 14 February 1990 at the age of 50: Trimble, like many others in the UUP knew that McCusker had been ill for many years, but the cancer had appeared to be in remission. Some in the UUP, including his widow, Jennifer McCusker, even believed that his death was hastened by the shock of the AIA.[6] Now that a vacancy had occurred, Trimble was interested. But it would not be an easy passage. After all, he did not live in the area and even if he did, he was not of the community after the fashion of McCusker – who was born and bred in Lurgan, lived in Portadown and would mix effortlessly with supporters of his beloved Glenavon FC on match days. A variety of local worthies were expected to stand, including four past mayors of Craigavon District Council and Jennifer McCusker (in so solid a Unionist seat, the victor of the selection contest would effectively be the winner of the by-election). Moreover, Trimble was scheduled to go on a long-planned Ulster Society trip to the United States which would coincide with the selection process: he feared giving that up to enter a race in which he stood no chance. Daphne Trimble, though, urged him to run: 'He was 45 and looking at boredom for the rest of his life,' she recalls. 'He was fed up with Queen's and I knew he would really love to be an MP and would always regret it if he did not do it.'[7]

Almost a fortnight after McCusker's death, whilst attending an Apprentice Boys of Derry Club research meeting at the Royal Hotel in Cookstown, Co. Tyrone, on 24 February, Trimble was approached by Robert Creane. Creane is a colourful figure of great energy who was the chairman of the Edenderry division of the Upper Bann Ulster Unionist Association (one of the Portadown branches). Creane remembers pulling Trimble aside and asking him three questions: had anyone asked him to run? Would he run? And, if he did, would he ever withdraw from the race? Trimble answered that no one had asked him to contest the nomination, that if asked to do so he would say yes, and that if he ran he would not withdraw. Creane was delighted, and on that basis began to organise support. Creane's first act on behalf of his candidate was to call Victor Gordon, an ace reporter of 20 years' standing on the *Portadown Times*, the leading newspaper in the constituency. Creane drove Gordon up to Trimble's home in Lisburn, on Saturday 3 March.[8] As Gordon recalls, 'I did not know this man, but Creane did a real PR exercise, and spoke of Trimble's love of Ulster.' In the course of the interview, Trimble announced that he would run.[9] Creane also arranged a secret meeting of twelve Upper Bann members at the Seagoe Hotel in Portadown: they concluded that Northern Ireland at this time needed something more than 'parish pump politics'. Moreover, they felt that none of the local candidates in this manufactured seat would gain support in other parts of the seat: the three main towns of Portadown, Lurgan and Banbridge all felt a keen rivalry for one another and therefore to pick a native son could prove divisive in other parts of the parliamentary division. Trimble, the articulate lawyer from Lisburn, fitted the bill.[10]

In conjunction with Gary Kennedy – a local schoolmaster who had become interested in politics after the massacre in 1976 of ten Protestant workmen near his home town of Bessbrook in south Armagh – Creane organised a series of 'get to know you' meetings to introduce Trimble to the members of the 20 branches in Upper Bann. Trimble also produced a highly professional *Letter to the Unionists of Upper Bann*. 'I know we have an irrefutable case,' he wrote, 'but I also know that in Westminster and elsewhere there is still much work to be done to persuade others of the justice of our cause and to repudiate the slanders of our enemies.' It made much of his work for the Ulster Society, based at Brownlow House in Lurgan, and referred to his activities on behalf of Vanguard during the UWC strike (there were still old Vanguardists in the seat, and one of William Craig's legal practices had been in Lurgan). It also referred to his convictions for minor public order offences whilst chairman of the Lisburn branch of the Ulster Clubs.

First, he had to overcome formidable local opposition. Jennifer McCusker had run the constituency office for her husband. But having nursed her husband through his final illness, she soon made it clear elective office was not for her. Samuel Gardiner then rapidly emerged as the favourite. His credentials were indisputable: a councillor from Lurgan, a three-time mayor of Craigavon District Council, the then chairman of the the the Upper Bann Association, Assistant Sovereign Grand Master of the Royal Black Institution (also headquartered at Brownlow House), and High Sheriff of Co. Armagh. Also running was Arnold Hatch of Portadown, another former mayor of Craigavon DC; Jim McCammick of Portadown, another former three-time mayor and past president of the local chamber of commerce; George Savage, also a former mayor and prominent beef and dairy farmer from Donacloney, whose support base was in the rural areas which used to comprise the old Iveagh seat at Stormont; Councillor Samuel Walker of Gilford, Co. Down; and Jack Allen, a senior figure from the UUP establishment.[11] Although Allen was in fact from Londonderry, he had run at the behest of Mrs McCusker and of his old friend Ken Maginnis.[12] William Ward of Lisburn also ran.

The selection meeting was held in front of 250 delegates at Brownlow House on 19 April 1990. The atmosphere, recalls Gary Kennedy, was very tense. The candidates went on in alphabetical order: several of them, including Trimble, wound up their pitch with the stock Protestant quotation from Martin Luther, 'here I stand, I can do no other'.[13] But Trimble's speech was much more than the usual 'you know what I've done, now choose me' routine of some of the local eminences. He made much of the fact that the Upper Bann by-election would be the first seat contested by the newly formed Northern Ireland Conservatives. The race would thus receive national media attention and Unionists would need a capable media spokesman to articulate why they rejected the governing party. 'We wanted somebody to elucidate our feelings in a reasoned way,' remembers Gary Kennedy. 'We couldn't any longer afford guys thinking "I wish I had said that" half-way home in the plane. We needed someone who could think on their feet – and we didn't have a Unionist MP who was a lawyer. We all believed that things were going to be all right because of the perception that Molyneaux was having cups of tea with members of the Royal family.'[14] After the first round of voting, Gardiner had 91 votes; Trimble 68; Savage 37; Hatch, 18; Allen 13; McCammick 12; Ward 11; and Walker 5. Trimble then knew he was in with an excellent chance, because he felt that Gardiner had hit a ceiling and that whilst his Lurgan-based support was 'deep', it was not very 'wide'. Ironically, for someone who excites such passions, Trimble was everyone's second choice. In the second round, Gardiner was ahead but his vote had increased to just 93, whereas Trimble's had risen to 89. Allen, Hatch and Savage went down to 6, 8 and 33 votes respectively, with McCammick still on 12. In the third and final ballot, the other candidates pulled out: George Savage was seen walking down the rows of his supporters, telling them to swing behind Trimble. He now reckons that only three of his initial 37 did not switch to Trimble. The final result was 136–114 in favour of Trimble. His lack of a local track record, far from proving to be a hindrance, turned out to be one of his greatest assets.[15]

Although Upper Bann was a solidly Ulster Unionist seat, Trimble was every bit as nervous as any other first-time candidate entering into a strange area. This hybrid seat, which straddled the northern portions of Co. Armagh and western Down, was organised around 20 fiercely independent branches: it comprised the town of Portadown, known as the 'hub of the north', which had a 70–30% Protestant–Catholic population, and which included some of the staunchest loyalists anywhere. It cherishes the memory of the first leader of organised Ulster Unionism, Col. Edward Saunderson (the MP for North Armagh at Westminster), who observed of the second Home Rule Bill in 1893, that 'Home Rule may pass this House but it will never pass the bridge at Portadown'; his presence endures to this day in the form of a statue outside St Mark's Church in Market Street.[16] Beside the local bridge, in the Pleasure Garden is a plaque to the memory of the local Protestants drowned in the River Bann by their Catholic neighbours, during the 1641 uprising.[17] Even today, the ardour of local loyalism can in part be ascribed to the fact that many of the residents are descendants of refugees from the border counties of the Republic and the more southerly parts of Co. Armagh – which are increasingly 'no-go' areas for Protestants. In this climate of increasing residential segregation, the non-sectarian, trade-union based traditions of the old Northern Ireland Labour party (which used to be quite strong amongst the light industrial workers of Portadown) had inevitably waned. Lurgan, just five miles away from Portadown, was perhaps the most evenly and bitterly divided town in Ulster, with a 50–50 sectarian split. Banbridge in Co. Down was two-thirds Protestant at the time of Trimble's selection and tended to think of itself as a cut above the Co. Armagh portions of the seat.

Like McCusker – who was known to leap over fences – Trimble set a ferocious pace on the hustings; indeed, the first remark which many people made was how much he physically resembled his predecessor (a few were upset that he did not opt to live in the constituency, because he 'did not want to live over the shop' and this still rankles with some). Then, because no one knew him, he could canvass an estate in a mere 20 minutes, but now he can scarcely do one house in 20 minutes. Partly, also, it owed much to his natural shyness which he has taken years to overcome, for he would come across on the doorstep and sway back and forth on his feet. He soon enough learned some of the politician's techniques, though: on one occasion, a voter asked him, 'Are you washed in the Blood of the Lamb?' Trimble replied, 'I'm actually here on behalf of the UUP'. More insistently, the elector said, 'No, but are you washed in the Blood of the Lamb?' Trimble thought for a second and finally assented to the proposition.[18] To further integrate into the community, Trimble joined the Royal Black Preceptory. After he signed the Belfast Agreement, many members of his lodge would be supporters of the 'No' campaign. But in those days, there was only good fellowship between brother loyalists. 'I really loved the place then,' remembers Trimble. 'There was a keen interest in politics which never existed in Lisburn or Bangor.'[19]

Nationally, the main interest in the campaign lay in the fact that it was the first time that the Conservatives were running in Northern Ireland. This was not evidence of serious integrationist intent by the Conservative Government: rather, they had been dragooned into setting up associations by a grassroots revolt by English and Scottish Tories at the 1989 party conference. Kenneth Baker, the party chairman, came to canvass on behalf of the Conservative candidate, Colette Jones (a Moira house-wife) along with the Environment Secretary Chris Patten (then a staunch advocate of the NI Conservatives' cause); and Ian Gow, who was to be murdered that summer by the IRA, boomed the Tory message on the loud-hailers. The SDP also launched one of its last, quixotic electoral forays, and Dr David Owen turned up to lend his support to the candidate, Alistair Dunn. Meanwhile, Paddy Ashdown came to Portadown to back the candidate of the Liberal Democrats' sister organisation, the Alliance party. The other candidates included Rev. Hugh Ross of the Ulster Independence Party; Gary McMichael, son of the late John McMichael (also murdered by the IRA: Trimble heard the car bomb go off in Lisburn), representing the Ulster Democratic Party, the political wing of the UDA; Brid Rodgers, a very experienced SDLP local councillor; Sheena Campbell of Sinn Fein, who was subsequently murdered by the UVF; Tom French of the Workers' Party (formerly the political wing of the Official IRA); Peter Doran of the Greens; and Erskine Holmes of the Campaign for the Right to Vote Labour.[20] Trimble loved the attention, relishing particularly his first encounter with the mainland press in the person of Donald Macintyre, who visited Lurgan for the Sunday Correspondent. Trimble's message was unremitting: he sought resounding defeat for the nationalists and an exemplary humiliation for the Tories who had signed the AIA of 1985. The voters in the 18 May 1990 by-election clearly agreed: on a 53.66% poll, Trimble romped home with 20,547, compared to the second-placed Brid Rodgers of the SDLP on 6698. The sectarian head-count in the seat made such a result inevitable, but the real story was that despite bringing in the heavy guns, the Tories lost their £500 deposit and secured only 1038 votes, or a mere 3% of the poll; they were beaten into sixth place by Sinn Fein with 2033, the Ulster Independence Party with 1534 and the Workers' Party with 1083.[21]

Curiously, the press speculation about what kind of an MP Trimble would turn out to be was rather more accurate at the time of his arrival in the Commons than when he became UUP leader in 1995 – especially in the southern press. Thus, Marie O'Halloran in the Irish Times prophesied that 'some consider him a potential future leader with a close association with the maverick Strangford MP John Taylor, while overall he is viewed as a middle class intellectual with an understanding of both sides of the integration/devolution divide'.[22] The NIO was divided within itself about the implications of Trimble's election: in this period, they were seeking to find a formula that would afford Unionists the latitude to participate in talks without scrapping the AIA. 'We were trying to break the permafrost,' recalls one former senior official. 'The election of David Trimble, who was a volatile loose cannon, was seen as changing the internal Unionist party balance, and thus could lead to what we called "creative instability".'[23] The following Tuesday, he took his seat in the Commons for the first time in the presence of Daphne Trimble, his mother and his sister-in-law and her husband. John Kennedy – who for many years was clerk at Stormont to the suspended Assembly – spoke to one of his counterparts at Westminster. 'Brains at last in the Unionist party', was their verdict.[24] Indeed, within a month or two of his election, Trimble recalls half the Tory Cabinet came and sat down next to him at the large table in the members' dining room: he was particularly pleased to come to know Malcolm Rifkind, who had been greatly admired by William Craig. 'My impression was some were coming over to have a look,' Trimble observes.[25]

It did not stop him from rebuking the Tories and Labour in his maiden speech during the Appropriations (No. 2) Northern Ireland Order debate on 23 May 1990. Initially, Trimble's speech was a fairly routine tribute to his immediate predecessor and a discussion of the history of the seat – although, characteristically, it was much more learned than the contributions of the bulk of new MPs. The former Land Law lecturer delighted in describing the critical role of the 'Ulster custom' (a special provincial form of landholding arising out of the customary rights that tenants had won for themselves) which some have claimed provided the basis of the indigenous growth of the industrial revolution in the Lagan and the mid-Bann Valleys.[26] He described the role of another predecessor, Col. Edward Saunderson, reminding the House that the father of Ulster Unionism had started out as a Liberal MP for Cavan before representing North Armagh. (Trimble would have been conscious that his Colhoun great-grandfather voted Liberal, prior to Gladstone's embrace of Home Rule.) His purpose here was to emphasise that the UUP was not a provincial party. Rather, he asserted 'we are the British national parties' in the

Province, formed as an alliance of Tories, Liberals and latterly of Labourites who had to band together in defence of their constitutional rights; indeed, Trimble reminded Labour MPs that their party did not organise in Northern Ireland. But his main target was the Conservative decision to fight the by-election. As saw it, the poll showed that there was 'no mandate' for the Government's policies. Their real aim in standing for the first time in 70 years was to 'divide and diminish' the Unionist voice.[27]

Whatever effect he had on his colleagues, there can be no doubt that Trimble took to the Commons with great gusto. He was a staunch defender of its traditions, and well after he became UUP leader denounced the new Blair government's decision to curtail the rights of backbenchers by cutting down the number of Prime Minister's Question Times from twice a week to once weekly.[28] On social and cultural matters unrelated to the Ulster crisis, he developed a moderately conservative record: he is pro-hunting; opposes the 1967 abortion legislation on the grounds that it has become abortion on demand; and on homosexuality, he takes a cautious line on lowering the age of consent.[29] Important though these issues were, they were not fundamental to the nature and scope of Trimble's parliamentary mission. Of far greater significance was Moly-neaux's decision to invite him to become home affairs spokesman. Trimble duly immersed himself in the details of criminal justice and Prevention of Terrorism legislation; it was during the committee stage of one of these debates that he came across his young Labour counterpart – Tony Blair.[30] Indeed, Frank Millar was struck by the fact that like all Unionist MPs who come to Westminster, Trimble became much more of an integrationist.[31] The consistent thread of his contributions was to illuminate how Northern Ireland was treated in a fashion very unlike the rest of the United Kingdom. Thus, Trimble spoke up when an IRA terrorist, Paul Magee, received a 30-year sentence for murdering a special constable in Yorkshire: he was outraged that the average tariff for security-force killers in Northern Ireland was a mere twelve years. Likewise, he spoke out against the fact that the only major government department without a Commons Select Committee was the NIO.[32] But these were staple Unionist themes over the years, albeit put forward with rather more eloquence and erudition by Trimble than by most UUP MPs. What was really distinctive about his contributions was his eye for the international dimensions of the Ulster crisis: he said the principles of the Organisation for Security and Cooperation in Europe, signed by 34 countries at the Paris summit of November 1990 (where the Cold War formally ended), should apply to Northern Ireland: these held that existing frontiers ought to be recognised, but that the rights of national minorities should be provided for, too. What was good enough for eastern and central Europe should, he reckoned, be good enough for Ulster.[33]

Inevitably, Trimble also took much time over his duties as a constituency MP. At first, he did not know where to collect the mail at the Commons and it piled up in a great mass for a month before he discovered what to do. He located his constituency office in Lurgan: this was closer to his home in Lisburn than any of the other possible sites, and was ably run by his wife Daphne and Stephanie Roderick (whom he met whilst she worked at the Ulster Society). He may not have been the authentic grassroots politician that McCusker was, but his academic skills could still be very useful. Thus, in 1993, the fifteen-strong Economic Development Committee of Craigavon District Council visited La Grange in Georgia, where the world-wide headquarters of Interface carpet tiles was located: it was his first visit to the United States, and Trimble played his part in persuading the Americans to create 30 jobs in Lurgan with a masterly exposition of their shared Ulster-Scots heritage (the forebears of Andrew Jackson, the seventh President of the USA, came from the Ulster area, along with those of four other Presidents. At least two further holders of the office appear to have been of southern Protestant origin).[34] But in truth, his work in Upper Bann has never defined his identity as a parliamentarian as completely as it did Harold McCusker's. Bob Cooper, former chairman of the Fair Employment Commission claims that Trimble was far less active than his predecessor in bringing anti-discrimination cases on behalf of Protestants – though, as he adds, this opinion is only possible because McCusker was so unusually hyper-active on behalf of his constituents.[35] Trimble was, deep down, far more of a creature of Westminster than McCusker and he would rarely miss a division at the Commons in order to attend a meeting of his private (Orange) lodge, after the fashion of his predecessor.

The hardest part of the job, Trimble found, was visiting the families of murdered constituents, whether Catholic or Protestant – though he usually rang the RUC beforehand to make sure that the deceased had no paramilitary links. Since his own constituency was a centre of terrorist activity, dealing with security matters occupied more of his time than had he been MP for relatively unmolested seats such as North Down or Strangford. Large IRA bombs went off in the constituency at Craigavon in 1991, Lurgan in 1992 and Portadown in 1993.[36] He also campaigned assiduously, with the DUP, on behalf of the 'UDR 4' (a quadrumvirate of soldiers convicted of the murder of a Roman Catholic in Armagh in 1983: all of them asserted their innocence, and three of them were subsequently released on appeal).[37] Trimble went to HMP Maghaberry with Ian Paisley, Jnr, and then presented materials on the miscarriage of justice to the then Secretary of State, Peter Brooke. Unusually for a Unionist MP, he was not a supporter of all forms of capital punishment: in the Commons division of 17 December 1990, he favoured it as a penalty for the murder of police and prison officers, and for killings committed with firearms and explosives, but not for any murder. Indeed, since the defeat of Enoch Powell in the 1987 General Election, probably only Ken Maginnis was a more consistent opponent of capital punishment in the voting lobbies within the Unionist family.[38] Partly, this was because of Trimble's acute sense of the possibility of miscarriages of justice. Indeed, he believed that mainland juries, in particular, had a tendency to react with excessive emotion to atrocities. 'Because of the nature of terrorism and the emotional response to it, the response of the man in the street cannot be trusted,' opined the former law lecturer during the debate on the renewal of the Prevention of Terrorism Act in 1991. He believed there was a good case for replacing juries with judge-only, Diplock-style courts throughout the United Kingdom.[39]

More disturbing still to Trimble were rumours that officials were engaged in talks with Sinn Fein. He wrote to John Major in January 1991 asking the Prime Minister to confirm that there were no such negotiations with republicans: Major replied, assuring him that the Government would not have talks with terrorists or those threatening violence to advance their agenda. Major's formulation did not, though, preclude 'contacts' between republicans and officials – a very fine distinction, but one to which ministers would have increasing recourse in the coming years. Channels of communication had been operating almost continuously in one form or another throughout the Troubles: Ed Moloney has shown that overtures were certainly being made during Tom King's period as Secretary of State.[40] But the talks to which Trimble was referring were those described by Anthony Seldon in his authorised life of Major. In late 1990, the Secretary of State, Peter Brooke, had been approached by John Deverell, a senior MI5 officer and director and coordinator of intelligence in Northern Ireland.[41] He requested that a line of communication which had existed in 1974–5 and during the Hunger Strikes of 1981 be reopened. Brooke gave his approval, subject to it being deniable in the event of exposure. His reasoning was two-fold. First, terrorist deaths had risen from 62 in 1989 to 76 in 1990 (an increasing proportion of which were by loyalists) and he was determined to do something to reduce them. Second, he was informed by John Hume – who since 1988 had been engaged in a much criticised dialogue with Gerry Adams – that republicans were engaged in their own process of revisionism. According to this conventional interpretation of events, the IRA recognised that the 'war' was unwinnable, at least as traditionally defined, and that if the conditions were right they might wish to 'come in from the cold'. They had reached a ceiling of 30 to 40 per cent of the nationalist vote and were finding it hard to break out of such electoral ghettoes in Northern Ireland – let alone the Republic, where their support remained minimal after the republican movement's decision in 1986 to end the policy of abstentionism from the Dail. The public response to this was Peter Brooke's Whitbread Lecture of 9 November 1990, in his Westminster South constituency, where he first formulated the phrase that Britain had 'no selfish strategic or economic interest' in the affairs of Northern Ireland. Significantly, an advance text was shown to Sinn Fein.[42]

At the same time as such possibilities seemed to offer themselves, the Government was also engaged in trying to coax Unionists back into the political mainstream. Partly, it was a function of British disillusionment with the AIA. First, it had not yielded the end to violence and the levels of security cooperation with the Republic for which the British had hoped. Second, as Patrick Mayhew recalls of his subsequent term in office from 1992–7, the AIA 'was like a lead necklace, not so much for its content as the secretive way in which it was foisted upon the Unionists. It precluded me from saying what I wanted to say, "trust me".'[43] It was possible, but distinctly harder, to operate 'direct rule with a Green tinge' with only minimal cooperation of the representatives of the majority community; and it was certainly impossible to obtain agreement for more broadly based, popular institutions of government, without them. But how could it be done without scrapping the AIA, or at least suspending it, the minimum requirement of Unionists? Under Tom King, Secretary of State from 1985–9, Thatcher was reluctant to make even the most tacit, public admission that the AIA had been anything other than beneficial; but where King failed to gain her approval for a gesture to win over Unionists, Brooke succeeded. The result was Brooke's other major address, of 9 January 1990, to a gathering of businessmen in Bangor: in his bid to launch inter-party talks and devolution, he urged Unionists to end their 'internal exile'. If they did so, then the AIA would be operated 'sensitively'.[44]

After the failure of the protest campaign against the AIA, Unionists were also anxious for a way out. British 'revisionism' of the AIA seemed to offer this. Aided by a 'suspension' of the AIA and the Maryfield permanent secretariat whilst talks took place, they opted to participate in the elaborately constructed, three-stranded approach, first announced by Brooke in March 1991. The concept of the three strands would provide the framework for all future negotiations and structures: Strand I, chaired by Brooke and his successors, would focus on the internal governance of Northern Ireland – with the aim of restoring some sort of devolved institutions. Although any devolved parliament or council would not be based upon majority rule, Unionists would still be the largest bloc and it would, therefore, constitute an institutional structure of sorts to protect their interests. Inevitably, nationalists always sought to hedge about and to restrict its powers. By contrast, the Strand II talks (which had an independent chairman) catered for the Irish identity. Their purpose was to create North-South bodies – of greater or lesser degrees of autonomy from the northern and southern legislatures – which, nationalists hoped, would over time acquire greater powers and thus form the basis for an all-Ireland government. Inevitably, Unionists always sought to limit their remit. Strand III dealt with the east–west dimension – that is, the wider context of British–Irish relations. For long, it was the 'poor relation' of the strands – but it was the one which most interested David Trimble.

Molyneaux seems to have calculated that there would be no agreement. On this, he was proved right and talks eventually collapsed in November 1992.[45] Nationalists had little reason to make an accommodation at this particular point. For it was the Unionists who were desperate to be rid of the AIA, not nationalists. Thus, if the talks failed, the worst that could happen would be that the Agreement would simply resume its normal workings, and another impasse combined with further IRA violence might even prompt an Anglo-Irish Agreement Mark II or Joint Authority. Nonetheless, it seemed reasonable to the UUP to suppose that if they were flexible – which included going to Dublin for the Strand II talks without the DUP – they would be rewarded in some way for taking risks. This, combined with British disillusionment with the AIA, led them to believe that the Government would then return to a more Unionist agenda. It was not altogether a fanciful conception, since during the 1992 General Election, Major had successfully taken up the theme of the Union: he particularly had Scotland in mind, but he also referred to the 'four great nations' of the United Kingdom and Brooke had attacked Labour's 'unity by consent policy' during the campaign. After the election, the NIO team headed by Patrick Mayhew was 'just about as Unionist as the current Conservative party could produce'.[46] In the meantime Molyneaux decided to play along with the three-stranded formula for those very tactical reasons. But although ministers acknowledged after the failure of the 1991–2 talks how far the UUP had moved, and that SDLP intransigence had undermined progress, the party never received a pay-off commensurate to the extent of its flexibility. This was because at the moment when Unionists hoped that the British Government might adopt such an agenda, a far bigger prize than the re-entry of the weakening Unionist community into the restructured institutions of government in Northern Ireland became a real possibility. That potential prize was, of course, an IRA ceasefire.

Retrospectively, therefore, the work of the 1991–2 UUP talks team looks rather peripheral to what was really going on. Indeed, as has been noted, Trimble devoted himself to what then seemed to be the most marginal issue of all: to develop the Strand III 'basket' of the talks, which resembled the old Vanguard concept of the Council of the British Isles. In the short term, his focus on this matter seemed largely to have had the effect of annoying his colleagues, as much on grounds of style as of substance. Ken Maginnis, who later became a staunch ally of Trimble, was less than impressed: 'I thought that he was intolerable at that time. He had a purely theoretical approach to the situation without any sense of the practicalities. And his only friend in a parliamentary party full of non-graduates was the other Queensman, John Taylor [with whom Trimble shared an office]. The two were considered to be academically a cut above the rest.'[47] Substance divided the two men as well. Whereas Trimble wanted to forge ahead on Strand III, Maginnis wanted to push ahead on the North-South bodies. Trimble was riveted by Brian Faulkner's experience: that powerful cross-border institutions could prove to be the vehicle for smuggling unionists into a united Ireland. His view was that the AIA and any such Strand II structures could be transcended by bringing them into a wider context – of regions cooperating with each other on an equal basis.[48] Maginnis thought this to be nonsense. Far better to deal with Dublin one-on-one, where Unionists had some real negotiating muscle, than in such a large community of variegated peoples. In this entity, he argued, the Ulster Unionists would end up as a small, isolated group in one vast pressure cooker. When its deliberations turned sour, as they easily could when the British had to take into account their relations with the Irish Republic and other regions, there would then be enormous pressure within the unionist family to withdraw from such a body.[49] Whoever was right, there can be no doubt that once again Trimble had done little to endear himself to his colleagues at Westminster. But the dramatic events of the coming three years made such tensions irrelevant. For Trimble would soon become the main beneficiary of the challenges posed to traditional Unionism by the British state's increasingly strenuous attempts to treat with republicanism.

NINE

Framework or straitjacket?

TRIMBLE may have been the youngest and most junior UUP MP – but he was already acquiring a reputation as the party's most intellectual elected representative. Indeed, he did remarkably well to maintain his historical and intellectual interests after his election to Parliament. Trimble's main efforts lay in two pamphlets for the Ulster Society.[1] The first, *The Foundation of Northern Ireland* (1991), sold out its complete print run of 2000: it recounted familiar events leading to Partition and immediately thereafter, but gave them a 'revisionist' twist. Far from being simply the 'gallant little Ulster' taking its stand against the Fenian hordes and a faithless British Government, Trimble painted a much more complex picture. Its real political interest lay in the fact that here – at the heart of the Ulster Society – was a Unionist MP again praising Sir James Craig for going unprotected to Dublin to negotiate with terrorists. 'At home, there were some who were ready to criticise Craig, but what was not in dispute was his enormous physical and political courage,' noted Trimble. The paper was written at the time of the Brooke-Mayhew talks of 1991–2 and its aim was to show that Unionists could once again make up for their lack of political power through manoeuvre and tactical adroitness: the Craig–Collins pact, believed Trimble, had worked in the Unionists' favour. It also provided a sharp critique of Sinn Fein's policy of abstentionism at Westminster, following their triumph in the south in the General Election of 1918. By declining to take up their seats, they were unable to affect the direction of the debates on the Government of Ireland Act 1920, and the Unionists had the field to themselves. In the following year, Trimble produced another paper for the Ulster Society, entitled *The Easter Rebellion of 1916*. Its main interest lies in its rarity value, for few Ulster Unionist MPs had ever bothered to tackle this subject seriously, and it was a competent survey of the secondary literature.

Indeed, even so formidable an adversary as Martin Mansergh, who became adviser to successive Fianna Fail leaders, acknowledges the quality of Trimble's researches in his recent collection of essays, *The Legacy of History*.

But of greatest significance to Trimble himself was the lengthy preface which he wrote in 1995 to Gordon Lucy's study *The Great Convention: The Ulster Unionist Convention of 1892*, again published by the Ulster Society. Trimble describes it as 'the closest thing to a personal political credo which I have written'. The 1892 Convention was held in Belfast as a response to Gladstone's second Home Rule Bill. Trimble believed that this body had been mis-characterised by R.F. Foster in *Modern Ireland 1600–1972* as a symbol of the Protestant Ascendancy, whereas he believed that it was an authentic popular response by the democratic majority in Ulster to the prospect of being coerced into a Catholic state. In fact, Trimble was not entirely fair to Foster on this: Foster certainly employed the term 'Ascendancy' but he also acknowledged that '[the Convention] constituted a class alliance that was underestimated by Irish nationalist and British politicians alike'.[2] Whatever the rights and wrongs of Trimble's analysis, few Ulster Unionist MPs of the Troubles era – with the exception of Enoch Powell – would have had the intellectual self-confidence to challenge Foster.[3] Even bolder in the light of Trimble's own political circumstances at the time was his foreword to the Ulster Society's re-publication of C. Davis Milligan's study, *The Walls of Derry: Their Building, Defending and Preserving*. Penned in 1996, it contains an intriguingly favourable reference to the trenchworks built before the siege by Governor Robert Lundy. To this day, Lundy is a hate figure in Ulster Protestant lore for supposedly betraying the Williamite cause by virtue of his lack of enthusiasm for resisting the Jacobite forces. Relatively recent scholarship suggests, however, that he was fainthearted or just plain 'realistic' in his assessment of the city's prospects.[4] Years later, of course, Trimble himself would be accused by his loyalist detractors of being the 'Lundy' of this era. Yet, curiously, his attempted rehabilitation of Lundy stirred little controversy at the time it was written. Whatever its actual political significance, Trimble certainly loved being 'the cleverest kid on the block' and he would have enjoyed nothing more than penning a quirky, contrarian rehabilitation of such a man.

There can be no doubt that the Ulster Society dramatically raised his profile in the Province at large: the fact that its headquarters was located at Brownlow House helped him secure the nomination for Upper Bann. And the scores of talks which he gave and attended throughout Ulster brought him into contact with hundreds of grassroots Unionists, which helped mightily when he ran for the leadership in 1995. Trimble had plenty of time for such activity, since he was scarcely part of the UUP's most inner councils under Molyneaux. Michael Ancram, who became Political Development Minister in 1993, recalls that Trimble was not some-one that ministers would come across a lot, not least because sustained dialogue had in large measure broken down after the end of the Brooke-Mayhew talks in November 1992; nor, says Michael Mates, did he accept invitations to dinner at the minister's Belfast residence at Stormont House.[5] Trimble was thus a peripheral player in the negotiations which led to the Downing Street Declaration of 15 December 1993, issued jointly by the British and Irish Prime Ministers – one the most important state-ments of intergovernmental strategy issued in 30 years.

Some such pronouncement was a cardinal aim of the republican move-ment: Major had been told as much by Charles Haughey at their summit in December 1991. Haughey said that the Irish Government's soundings led them to believe that if the language was right, a declaration of principle could help to bring about an end to IRA violence. Hume, who had been engaged in his dialogue with Adams since 1988, also said as much and had his own draft version of what such a document would look like. In essence, Hume–Adams envisaged that in exchange for a ceasefire, the British Government would become a 'persuader' for a united Ireland and would gradually 'educate' Unionists into accepting the inevitability and logic of such an outcome. Major was, as ever, very cautious. Contrary to the widespread belief in Irish nationalist circles, this was not primarily a function of his shrinking majority after his narrow re-election in the 1992 General Election, and the need for the support of the nine Ulster Unionists in the Commons. Rather, Major's caution over the emerging dialogue with republicans owed at least as much to his consensual style of management of the Cabinet and of the Conservative backbenches, whatever the numbers. Patrick Mayhew recalls that he hardly made a move without the support of the whole Cabinet Northern Ireland Com-mittee, for he wanted to be sure that any initiative he took would not be disowned if it went awry.[6] The sceptics on this inner group included not merely such well-known Unionist sympathisers as Viscount Cran-borne, leader of the Lords, and Michael Howard, the Home Secretary, but also the Chancellor, Kenneth Clarke, and, at times, Michael Heseltine. The reason for their doubts was simple: 25 years of terrorism (not least the murders of Gow, Neave, the casualties of the Brighton bomb, and the mortar attack on Downing Street) had given a new lease of life to the profound dislike and distrust of republicanism within the Conservative political elite (whatever their views of Ulster Unionism as a creed or Ulster Unionists as individuals). Furthermore, many MPs knew of servicemen or civilians from their constituency who had been slain or injured. Indeed, Andy Wood, then Director of Information at the NIO, reckoned that one of the little noticed by-products of 30 years of violence was that Northern Ireland at a human level has become much closer to the rest of the United Kingdom than it had been at the start of the Troubles. He calculates that as many as several hundred thousand troops have made their way through the Province – whereas, by comparison, hardly anyone from the mainland had been there in 1969.[7]

Major's consensual approach also governed his dealings with the Unionists. Whatever personal feelings, Major was certainly of the opinion that any new arrangements had to comprise at least the Ulster Unionists, if not the DUP. In that sense, there could be no repetition of the AIA. But how were these two objectives – bringing in the IRA whilst keeping the UUP on board – to be reconciled? After all, Hume was hated within Unionism for his dealings with Adams. It would, therefore, have been suicidal for Molyneaux to have accepted any joint declaration which emanated from them, or at least was seen to emanate from them. Major understood that Molyneaux had a hugely difficult act to perform on his own party, and was determined that he be afforded the space to do so by negotiating a formulation that was more acceptable to the UUP. *More* was the key word. For Molyneaux would never be able to throw his bowler hat into the air over a text designed to draw in the Provisionals. All that was needed, says Michael Ancram, was that he should acquiesce in it.[8] To that end, Major extensively consulted Molyneaux: Molyneaux recalls that from 18 October 1993 onwards, he and the Prime Minister met on a weekly basis. One British official who participated in these meetings recalls that Molyneaux would often say '"I don't think my folk will wear this"; sometimes, he was acting as a spokesman for the state of party opinion, sometimes he was using it as a vehicle for expressing his own discontents'. The British, in turn, would play this back in their innumerable negotiations with the Irish Government. Such confidence-building measures became all the more vital after the Shankill bomb killed nine Protestants in October 1993 and the revelations of secret contacts between British Government representatives and the Provisionals; thereafter, they would take place three times a week. After all, Major had said that such discussions would 'turn my stomach'. Was there another secret deal, asked unionists – this time between the Provisionals and the British Government? Molyneaux, who was consulted at an ever more frantic pace along with his advisers, became convinced that there was no such conspiracy. His authority was still sufficient to carry the Ulster Unionists with him – thus also forestalling a revolt from the 30 or so Tory backbenchers who might have baulked at the text of the Joint Declaration had the UUP leader given the signal.

British ministers and officials to this day remain well pleased with their work on the Downing Street Declaration. In Michael Ancram's words, 'we delivered a pretty Orange document in green language'.[9] According to this reading, the British Government was merely reiterating what it had already conceded – that it had 'no selfish strategic or economic interest' in staying in Ulster – indicating to Hume and the IRA that they were neutral rather than imperialistic in motivation, and that republicanism's real 'British question' was how to deal with close to a million pro-British subjects in the north-east corner of Ireland. The British Government was now a facilitator for an agreed Ireland – again, Hume's concept – but that was not necessarily a united Ireland. Such a polity could only come about if consent was freely and simultaneously given by the people of Ireland, north and south. Partition was secure in that Ulster folk would determine whether there would be Irish unity and not the Irish people as a whole, as the republicans wanted. Moroever, the British would simply seek to uphold those democratic wishes, be they for unity or the status quo and, crucially, would neither seek to persuade nor to coerce Ulster into any new arrangements. Unionists were told that it was significant that it was the Fianna Fail Government of Ireland – traditionally the 'Greener' of the Republic's two main parties – which acknowledged a united Ireland needed the consent of the majority in Ulster. Both Governments added that all could participate fully in the democratic process if a commitment to exclusively peaceful methods was established. In his subsequent explanation of the DSD in the Dail, the Irish Foreign Minister, Dick Spring, defined a 'permanent' abandonment of violence as including 'the handing up of arms . . .'. British ministers also made such demands – a point which annoyed Adams greatly in early 1994 when he told the *Irish News* on 8 January 1994 that 'they [the British] want the IRA to stop so that Sinn Fein can have the privilege twelve weeks later, having been properly sanitised and come out of quarantine, to have discussions with senior civil servants of how the IRA can hand over their weapons'. The terms on which Sinn Fein/IRA gained access to the negotiating table and even the new institutions of government in Northern Ireland would prove to be one of the most vexing questions of the coming years.

To someone like Trimble, the language of the Declaration ought to have made for very uncomfortable reading. First of all, there was the very fact of the statement itself: a foreign government with an illegal territorial claim was once again pronouncing upon the future of Northern Ireland. Second, it spoke of the 'people' of Ireland – whereas Trimble, who subscribed to the B&ICO's 'Two Nations' theory, believed the Ulster-British to be a breed apart. Third, though it acknowledged the right of the majority in Northern Ireland to determine its constitutional future, it repeatedly posited the idea that any changes in that status would inevitably be in the direction of Irish unity, rather than towards still closer relations with Britain. But for all his doubts (which in part centred around the fact that because Molyneaux went alone to Downing Street, he could be outmanoeuvred) Trimble was reluctant publicly to denounce the document in which his leader had such a hand. To have done so, Trimble says, would have pushed him into the Paisleyite camp and would forfeit him such limited access as he then enjoyed.[10] Any fears which the NIO may have harboured that he would be the source of right-wing opposition to the DSD were thus never realised. 'If we are suspending judgment today on this statement today, it is in the hope that it will lead to a way out of the cul-de-sac in which the people of Ulster have been condemned for the last eight years,' he observed in the Commons on the day of the signing of the DSD. Instead, he focused upon the so-called 'democratic deficit' in Northern Ireland – partly a reference to the system of legislating for the Province via Orders in Council rather than properly debated and scrutinised Bills.[11]

With hindsight, Trimble feels that Molyneaux did a fairly good job in removing the 'Greener' elements within the Hume–Adams conception.[12] It was an early indication that Trimble, unlike Robert McCartney, did not regard the peace process as a fraud designed to deliver a united

Ireland by stealth; rather, it was something which, if the terms were right, was worth studying and could yield fruit. In Trimble's eyes, that fruit was the tantalising prospect of no more impositions from above, such as the abolition of Stormont by Westminster in 1972, or the AIA of 1985. This, he hoped, would be a settlement which Unionists would be able to shape for themselves rather than being left to wait 'like a dog', in Harold McCusker's famous phrase, outside the conference chamber as the future of the Province was carved up.[13] Paisley swiftly detected Trimble's modulated position, describing him in a speech to the annual dinner of the Tandragee, Co. Armagh, branch of the DUP in early 1994 as 'plasticine man' over the DSD: Trimble was 'being made to look up, look down, look left and look right in whatever way he was punched by events'.[14]

The Provisionals, for their part, never endorsed the DSD – if only because they could never then accept that Northern Ireland was the relevant unit within which the consent principle should be exercised – but it nonetheless contained enticing amounts of 'Green' language. This was emphasised by both Reynolds and Hume, thus enabling it to become an important building block in the construction of the first IRA ceasefire of 31 August 1994 – although Adams may have gambled that the 'precondition' about decommissioning would be waived more swiftly than was actually the case. Whilst republicans debated the DSD's contents and requested 'clarification' from the British Government (in an attempt to draw them into public negotiations before a ceasefire had been called), Trimble urged that they not be allowed to dictate the pace of progress. Hume had told the British and Irish Governments that there would peace within days of the DSD, but it had not been forthcoming. 'The government have held the carrot,' Trimble observed. 'Now it is time for the stick. Militarily they should clobber the Provos.' He became the pre-eminent advocate in the Commons of the idea of the then Chief Constable of the RUC, Sir Hugh Annesley, to allow wiretap evidence to be used in court (partly, he argued, because such evidence could sometimes assist in the defence of the accused).[15] From his knowledge of European law, Trimble also urged that the Italian-style, mafia-busting investigating magistrates be brought in to deal with the IRA.[16] He named a number of alleged provisional IRA godfathers.

Trimble's interpretation of the IRA's decision to call its first ceasefire is fairly orthodox. 'The RUC were slowly winning the war of attrition,' he now recalls. 'The security forces were gradually getting on top of them and consequently for republicans in the early 1990s the picture is of a long haul where they were becoming less effective and their campaign could just peter out. So Sinn Fein's involvement in the peace process is partly about cashing in the armed struggle for a political process whilst it still has some value; but it also has something to do with the rising tide of loyalist violence after the Anglo-Irish Agreement, which was starting to hurt Sinn Fein as well.'[17] Whether or not Trimble's interpretation of the IRA's rationale for its first ceasefire was correct, there can be no doubt that unionism as a whole was thoroughly unprepared for the new phase of struggle and the challenges posed by the 'peace process'. It was especially hard for them to endure the adulation which was heaped on the heads of the Sinn Fein leadership as they sought to portray themselves as 'normal' politicians. This included visas to enter America, subsequent trips to the White House, and an end to the Republic's and Britain's broadcasting bans. Sharp-suited articulate republicans were all over the airwaves; whilst Unionists such as Paisley, remarked Trimble, would protest ineptly at the injustice of the process and be thrown out of the Commons chamber or No. 10. Trimble, though, was not himself immune to such expressions of rage: he stormed out of a Channel 4 studio in the following year, when he found himself unexpectedly appearing on a remote link-up with Martin McGuinness. 'We do not share platforms or programmes with Sinn Fein/IRA,' he thundered.[18] Years later, even when he had become a much more experienced television performer, Trimble could still explode – exemplified by his anger when he felt himself provoked by the presenter Noel Thompson on BBC Northern Ireland's *Hearts and Minds* programme on 27 June 2002.[19]

Again, Unionists asked themselves: had the British Government done a deal at their expense to secure a ceasefire? Trimble himself soon concluded that whilst there was no secret deal between the British and the IRA, there was possibly a deal between Adams, Hume and Reynolds. This would be the so-called 'pan-nationalist front' so feared by Unionists. At this period, the Unionists greatly feared this would carry all before it. As they saw it, the republican movement would trade violent methods for the adoption of at least some of its aims by the constitutional parties. Thus, he believed, Hume and Reynolds were more inclined to regard the IRA ceasefire as 'permanent' than either the UUP or the British Government, even though the IRA refused to employ the 'p' word and hoped that such an impression of reasonableness would force the British into making concessions. If such concessions were not forthcoming, the British would then be blamed by nationalists for 'foot-dragging' and for adding 'preconditions' to Sinn Fein's entry into the political process – so validating the fears of IRA 'hardliners' that they had been tricked into abandoning armed struggle. Having represented the abandonment of violence as 'permanent', the thwarted IRA could then go back to Irish nationalists, and proclaim that they had acted flexibly but that British bad faith made it imperative for them to return to armed struggle. But the 'upside' of the British Government's caution was that Unionists were gradually bound into the 'process': Trimble says that he noted in 1994 that in contrast to the ceasefire of 1972 – when the young Gerry Adams was released from internment to negotiate with William Whitelaw at Cheyne Walk within 48 hours of the guns falling silent – this time there was a much longer 'quarantine' period before talks could begin. Indeed, when Trimble was asked whether he agreed with John Taylor and the Rev. Martin Smyth, MP, that Sinn Fein would eventually be involved in talks, Trimble replied: 'Personally, I would put a very big reservation against that ... for myself, that's a matter which I don't expect to be doing.' In other words, Trimble rejected this option on contingent rather than principled grounds. Later, at the Young Unionists' conference at Fivemiletown, Co. Tyrone, Trimble urged the creation of an assembly in which Sinn Fein could take part – thus sidestepping the difficulties which would occur if they sought to gain access to all-party talks too quickly. Trimble was thus publicly raising the question of diluting preconditions for their entry into the political process, in exchange for a local elected body in which Unionists would, of course, enjoy a clear majority.[20] It appears to be the first time that he raised the topic on a public platform in Northern Ireland – though he had, in fact, already made a similar suggestion in an article in The Independent on 14 September 1994. This was a mere fortnight after the IRA had declared its first ceasefire.

But in the immediate term, the majority which exercised the minds of everyone in this period was the shrinking Tory margin in the House of Commons. Although nationalist Ireland assumed that as a consequence of this arithmetic Molyneaux exercised vast influence, the UUP did not see it that way (indeed, if anything, the reverse was the case, precisely because the Tories did not want to be seen to be bending the knee to the UUP).[21] Trimble believes that Molyneaux was wrongly accused at the time by his own tribe of not extracting enough from Major. But from his own subsequent experience as leader, Trimble concludes there was very little that could be extracted from the Tories, since although the British Government was generally weak, it was not weak in the affairs of Northern Ireland and could always call on Labour for bi-partisan support in a crisis. Trimble's private criticism of Molyneaux, rather, centred around his habit of meeting the Prime Minister alone. His objections were two-fold, on both mechanical and on political grounds. First, it was often difficult both to conduct a negotiation and to take notes – particularly when there were differences in recollection over what had been agreed. This would then expose him to accusations within the UUP of having been gulled by another Tory Prime Minister. Second, such an accusation was harder to maintain when senior colleagues were roped into these discussions.[22]

These concerns were felt particularly keenly by the younger cadres in the UUP. They would increasingly look to Trimble as their standard-bearer in the coming months, as the contours of the two Governments' detailed proposals for the future of the Province became apparent. These built upon the statement of principles in the DSD and were known as the Frameworks Documents – and, as in 1991–2, were based upon the three-stranded approach. Michael Ancram, assisted principally by the Political Director of the NIO, Quentin Thomas, had been working on them since early 1994 and Molyneaux had appointed Jeffrey Donaldson, Reg Empey and the party chairman, Jim Nicholson, as the UUP liaison. Once again, Trimble was on the periphery of his own party. Nonetheless, No. 10 thought it best to keep him sweet: Trimble was summoned to Major's suite in the Highcliff Hotel, Bournemouth, in October 1994 for a conversation with the Prime Minister. Major asked him what would he do in his position – a stock ploy which often flattered his interlocutor.[23] Trimble was taken aback – he was rather less experienced then in dealing with senior government figures – and informed Major that he would proceed in the same way but that he would test the Provisionals' sincerity against events. Major, in turn, concurred. Major then added, 'You know, I'm a Unionist.' Trimble then replied: 'I know that, I don't think you're going to sell us out in the sense of taking us into an Irish Republic. My concern is that you would see an opportunity for settling the problem and that would involve what would appear to you a minor concession but would to us be a vital interest.'[24]

The episode was curious for several reasons. Did Major already view

Trimble, the youngest and most junior of the UUP MPs, as a potential leader – or perhaps as potential spoiler of the Government's plans? Trimble himself is not sure. But Major says that he spotted Trimble as 'able and ambitious. I thought it would be useful to get to know him. He was likely to be the voice of the grassroots.'[25] This view was widely held in Whitehall by the officials, too, and they may well have drawn it to Major's attention. Thus, Dame Pauline Neville-Jones, who chaired the Joint Intelligence Committee and later became Political Director of the Foreign and Commonwealth Office, states that Trimble was already seen as a potential counterweight to Paisley – and a clever one, at that.[26] If so, it was a rare instance during the post-ceasefire period when ministers actively cultivated and sought the views of Unionist MPs. For though they handled the UUP with great skill in the run-up to the DSD, Major's whips' office touch deserted him and his colleagues during the run-up to the Frameworks. Partly, this was because after the DSD and the first IRA ceasefire, their attention was mostly focused upon the political and 'military' intentions of the republican movement. Indeed, many Unionists believe to this day that the Irish Government showed a very 'Green' draft of the Frameworks Documents to Sinn Fein/IRA before its publication in order to secure an IRA ceasefire and to bind them into the process – though Irish officials still deny that this was the case. Whatever the truth of the matter, Trimble himself believes that in the attempt to draw republicans into conventional politics, they tacked so far in a nationalist direction that they forfeited the UUP's acquiescence, for a short while at least. Thus, at the time of the IRA ceasefire Molyneaux – seeing that his three appointed representatives were no better informed of the two Governments' plans – again offered to run an 'Ulster eye' over the Frameworks, as he had with the DSD. Mayhew wrote to Molyneaux to say that this would be very helpful but that the document was still very much at the drafting stage and that it would not quite be the done thing for the UUP leader to talk to civil servants.

In the eyes of the civil servants, there were sound, time-honoured reasons of Whitehall practice about this: the Frameworks were, they insist, a quite different kind of document from the DSD. First, Frameworks was a negotiating document, not a definitive statement of principle. It was a starting point, and therefore to prenegotiate it with any one party, especially one which almost held a balance of power in the Commons, would expose the British to accusations of adopting an uneven approach. Such pious formalism contrasted with rumours emanating from Dublin. Most worrying from a Unionist perspective were the claims made by the former Taoiseach Albert Reynolds (whose Fianna Fail-led Government had fallen in November 1994 following a scandal and had been replaced by a coalition led by the more instinctively anti-republican Fine Gael leader, John Bruton) that all-Ireland bodies with executive powers had been agreed between the British and Irish Governments. This, of course, would have been a reprise of the Council of Ireland which had proven so offensive to Unionists during the abortive Sunningdale experiment of 1973–4 – or worse. Trimble was also receiving his own warnings from his old Vanguard colleague on the UUP liaison committee with the NIO, Reg Empey. These indicated, he believed, that NIO civil servants had 'run amok'.[27] Molyneaux tried to engage Major in a 'control' exercise, but by the time Major was prepared to show him a draft it was too late. Indeed, Molyneaux remembers that when Major invited him into the Cabinet room to look at the draft version, the Prime Minister said he would leave him sitting at the Cabinet table whilst he went upstairs – and the UUP leader should ring the bell when he was finished. Major pushed the explosive paper across to the septuagenarian Ulsterman; the Ulsterman promptly shoved it back in the direction from whence it came. Molyneaux pointed out that he could not influence its basic direction and that by looking at it on Privy Council terms he would thus become acquiescent in its provisions.[28]

Such concerns soon ceased to be the preserve of the Unionist political classes and became dramatically clear to the Unionist population and to the world at large. In January 1995, David Burnside was shown a draft copy of the Frameworks Documents. Before he placed it in the press, Burnside went to see Molyneaux. 'I have seen them and it is terrible and disastrous.' 'What do I do?' asked Molyneaux, taken aback. 'Go and see Robert Cranborne,' said Burnside, referring to the most ardent Unionist in the Cabinet. 'I don't want to compromise his position in the Cabinet.' Burnside flared up: 'For Christ's sake, this is the Unionist cause we're talking about here.' Burnside also told Trimble of its contents, though the latter never saw the document and thus was unable to evaluate any later changes that were made when the final paper was actually published.[29] The extracts were then shown to a *Times* leader writer, Matthew d'Ancona, a prominent Trimble fan in the London print media. It turned out to be one of the greatest journalistic coups of recent years. No. 10

and the NIO were enraged: the 'spin' was that d'Ancona had endangered the 'peace process', although ultimately it had the opposite effect. *The Times* front page pronounced that the Frameworks brought 'the prospect of a united Ireland closer than it had been at any time since partition in 1920 . . . today's disclosures will alarm many Unionists who were promised by Mr Major last week that the draft would contain "no proposals" for joint authority'.[30] It posited extensive all-Ireland bodies with executive powers. Although it was pointed out that some of the proposals in this draft had already been excised in the intergovernmental negotiations, the damage was nonetheless done. Major's pep talk to the Conservative backbenches and to the nation rallied the party and mainland opinion; but in Unionist circles, Trimble recalls, Molyneaux was once again seen to have been overly trusting of a British Prime Minister.[31] No. 10 felt that the leaks were less about the substance of the proposals than about the internal power struggle within the UUP. Realising that his flank had been exposed and that he had been unable to pull off the same success as over the Downing Street Declaration, Molyneaux asked Major to see three members of his own party in the Prime Minister's room in the Commons behind the Speaker's chair. The three included Trimble – potentially his most dangerous internal party critic – and two close allies, William Ross and Rev. Martin Smyth. Trimble took the lead, employing his lawyerly skills to assault the leaked paper. Nothing that Major said in any way reassured the Ulstermen.[32] Trimble had already appeared to distance himself from the Tories: the Government noted that along with John Taylor, he abstained in the tight Commons vote on fisheries policy on 18 January 1995. With the exception of Ken Maginnis, the other UUP MPs voted for the then Government.[33]

Major had to persist, even though he knew that the Frameworks Documents were still-born: to have abandoned them, he felt, would definitively have proven to nationalist Ireland that the British Government was in hock to the Unionists. Instead, he opted to shave down the most controversial parts – much to the irritation of the Irish – in the hope that elements of the Frameworks would prove to be a basis for negotiation at a later date. When the Documents were published in Belfast on 22 February 1995, Unionists were not mollified. Mitchel McLaughlin of Sinn Fein seemed happy enough, telling a conference at the University of North London that 'John Major, by the very act of publishing the Frameworks Documents in the teeth of opposition from right-wing

Conservatives and the Unionist leaderships has demonstrated that his government is not totally hostage to the mathematics of Westminster'.[34] The Strand I proposals posited a 90-member assembly, elected by PR, serving four- or five-year terms, with all-party committees overseeing the work of the Northern Ireland departments; their activity would be scrutinised by a three-man elected panel (Hume had envisaged a six-man panel, with EU and British and Irish Government representatives: this was his way of circumventing Northern Ireland's in-built Unionist majority, but it was negotiated away by the British, not least because they feared that it would inflame neuralgic Eurosceptic sensibilities on the backbenches and in the Cabinet: ministers were mindful of the problems that might arise if the causes of Euroscepticism and Unionism became bound up with each other). Strand II, on the North-South dimension, reiterated many of the principles of the December 1993 Joint Declaration and stated that such bodies were to exercise 'on a democratically accountable basis delegated executive, harmonising and consultative functions'. The designated topics for harmonisation would include agriculture and fisheries; industrial development; consumer affairs; transport, energy, trade, health, social welfare, education and economic policy. The remit of the body should be dynamic, enabling progressive extension by agreement of its functions to new areas. Its role should be developed to keep pace with the growth of harmonisation and with greater integration between the two economics. Furthermore, the Irish Government pledged to make changes to its Constitution which would fully reflect the principle of consent and which would show that no territorial claim of right contrary to the will of Northern Ireland's majority be asserted.[35]

Major claimed that this renunciation was 'crucial' and that any such North-South bodies would not be free-standing but would rather be democratically accountable to the assembly. Nor, he said, was there a predetermined list of such functions as they would exercise: indeed, the definition of harmonisation in education, as revealed under paragraph 33, included such prosaic notions as mutual recognition of teacher qualifications. The NIO held this to be evidence that they had, once again, delivered an 'Orange document in Green-speak'. Despite these glosses, and despite Major's reiteration of the 'triple lock' – the formulation whereby any deal had to have the endorsement of the Westminster Parliament, and the people and the parties of Northern Ireland – the Unionists were not reassured. Nor were many on the Tory backbenches. If devolution, proportional representation and a Bill of Rights were so unsuitable for Great Britain, why were they suddenly so beneficial for Northern Ireland? In and of themselves, these were not great issues for David Trimble, though. Certainly, Ulster's anomalous treatment vexed as much as it always had done, but Trimble was no purist defender of English constitutional norms as he saw them and he believed in a continent of empowered regions. Rather, Trimble's worries focused on paragraphs 46 and 47: as Unionists interpreted them, these held that if the assembly ever collapsed, the default mechanism would allow the two Governments to continue to operate North-South bodies without any local input. Those bodies would be free-standing and not be set up by the assembly. They could, therefore, easily become the vehicle for creeping, even rolling unification. That this would be the case was proven by the fact that their functions were invested with a character that was described as 'dynamic', 'executive' and 'harmonising'. The 'd', 'e' and 'h' words assumed a great importance to Trimble, as did the authority under which they operated: during the negotiations leading up to the Belfast Agreement of 1998, Trimble devoted great amounts of his energy and political capital to excising these atrributes and to making sure that the Strand II institutions were explicitly accountable to the assembly. Even as they stood, the listed of areas of cooperation – such as health – were amongst the most sensitive for many unionists. After all, Catholic values still held sway on the medical ethics committees of hospitals in the Republic. How would greater integration with such a system affect the freedoms of Ulsterwomen within the NHS? Moreover, any hint that priests might have a hand in the upbringing of Protestant children was potentially explosive. Trimble further warned that British-Irish ideas for harmonising key welfare policies would threaten the right of the Province's taxpayers to equality of treatment with the rest of the United Kingdom, for which Sir James Craig had fought so hard. Would Northern Ireland be harmonised down to the Irish level or would the Republic be harmonised up to the British level? Nor was Trimble satisfied with the apparent withdrawal of the Irish constitutional claim over Northern Ireland. Whilst the Irish undertook in Frameworks to withdraw the claim to jurisdiction, they did not satisfactorily expunge the claim to territory and thus denied Northern Ireland explicit legitimacy in southern eyes.

But the failure to keep the Ulster Unionists on board was much wider than just Major's inability to tie the Irish down more precisely. Some senior figures in the Government felt that the failure to repeat the delicate balancing exercise of the DSD could be ascribed to the fact that whereas the DSD was mainly formulated out of No. 10, the Frameworks was mainly drafted in the NIO; and that officials such as Quentin Thomas had become too close to their Irish opposite numbers such as Sean O hUiginn and that they failed to see the political wood for the bureaucratic trees. Certainly, Molyneaux believed this and told Major that 'they've double crossed us again' – a variant of his old line that 'the rats have been at work'.[36] Was this really the case, though? It was always easy to blame civil servants, especially under the circumstances of direct rule in Northern Ireland. There, they wielded exceptional powers under ministers who were not MPs in Ulster and thus were not democratically accountable in the normal way. Moreover, much of their information on the correlation of political and military forces inevitably derived from secret organs of state. Certainly, Michael Ancram believes that Thomas had an instinct to undo Lloyd George's historic error in agreeing to partition Ireland and that he frequently restrained Thomas from going too far.[37] Not so, says Thomas. He claims that he was, in fact, trying to stabilise the status quo but that he also believed that British rule in Ulster was inevitably subject to a higher set of legitimacy tests than was the case for the Irish (as exemplified by the vastly greater protests whenever the RUC would shoot terrorists than when the same act was perpetrated by the Gardai). He says, rather, that he always believed that Northern Ireland's general position should be determined by the consent principle.[38] Other colleagues, such as Peter Bell, say that Thomas' key conception was that Sinn Fein were lobsters and that the task of British statecraft was to tempt them into lobsterpots.[39] At the time, Trimble also believed that attitudes such as those attributed to Thomas did much to explain why the Irish had won 'hands down' over the Frameworks. But there was also a bit of useful play-acting in all of this: officials such as Thomas were convenient bogeymen for Unionists, since it was much easier to lay the blame on treacherous advisers rather than the ruler himself. Appealing over the NIO's head to No. 10 thus became a stock Unionist ploy, and one which would be played even by Trimble – who himself had little faith in the leaders of the modern Conservative party. Sometimes, it even worked, for successive occupants of No. 10 liked to flatter themselves that they could work their magic in ways that mere departmental ministers could not. At other times, the dance might even have been pre-choreographed between No. 10 and the NIO as part of a 'hard cop, soft cop' routine: it was sometimes useful to give Unionists the illusion that they were making progress, thus binding them ever more thoroughly into the process.

The effects on Molyneaux of the Frameworks debacle were immediate. Ken Maginnis, for one, told John Bruton that he thought that William Ross, a robust opponent of power-sharing, would be the beneficiary and succeed Molyneaux.[40] On 18 March 1995, at the AGM of the UUC, a 21-year-old student named Lee Reynolds ran as a 'stalking horse' candidate against him. Reynolds declared that 'the leadership record since 1984 is one of successive defeats and an ongoing weakening of the Union'. His seconder was one of Trimble's closest associates and a Unionist intellectual, Gordon Lucy. Many supposed that Trimble was behind the challenge. Not so, says Trimble – a point confirmed both by Lucy and John Hunter, another close associate at the time. If anything, Trimble was worried that people would think just that and accuse him of disloyalty. Normally, the post went uncontested, but Reynolds received 88 votes to Molyneaux's 521 or 14 per cent of the total.

Worse was to come for Molyneaux. Two days later, the independent Unionist MP for North Down, Sir James Kilfedder, suddenly died of a heart attack. The UUP chose Alan McFarland, a former regular Army officer, as its candidate in the by-election in this most middle-class of seats (many NIO civil servants also lived there, helping to make it in some ways the most recognisably 'English' division in Ulster). It was not, though, promising DUP territory. Who, then, would carry the torch for Carsonian Unionism and the concepts of equal citizenship? A more than suitable candidate emerged in the shape of Robert McCartney, a QC originally from the Shankill Road who had become one of the Province's top-paid silks and lived in a spacious house at Cultra near Belfast Lough. Not only had he carved out a reputation as the most trenchant critic of the 'peace process'; he was also a non-Conservative who refused to join the Loyal Orders. He thus appealed both to the prosperous middle classes and to ordinary voters (although that summer, substantial portions of the bourgeoisie were also in a militant mood, as exemplified by their hostility to the attempt by Queen's University to stop playing *God Save the Queen* at graduation ceremonies and to replace it with the EU hymn, Beethoven's *Ode to Joy*).[41] McCartney – running under the 'United Kingdom Unionist' label but without a formal party organisation – beat the

UUP candidate by 10,124 votes (37.0%) to 7232 votes (26.4%) on a 38.6% per cent turnout.[42] Even though his native Bangor was in the seat, Trimble did not canvass for the UUP candidate: he says that he was not asked to do so.[43] After 17 years in the UUP, he was still not a conventional party man.

TEN

The Siege of Drumcree (I)

THE high politics of the Frameworks were of little interest to the mass of the Ulster-British population, but many of them felt that their national destiny was anything but secure. Every night on their television screens, clever and articulate Sinn Fein/IRA spokesmen seemed to win the battle of the airwaves hands down. It was part of the unremitting diet of defeat which the unionist community had suffered since 1985. But few Unionists, including Trimble, can have foreseen where their countrymen would choose to draw their line in the sand. That spot would be at Drumcree church two miles from Portadown town centre, in the heart of Trimble's constituency. There, ever since 1807, local Orangemen had attended divine service on the Sunday before 12 July (it was the oldest recorded Orange service in the history of the Orange institution, and was almost as old as the Order itself). Thence they would march back to Portadown itself. There they would arrive to the 'crack of the cane' on a lambeg drum, their colourful banners – often depicting Biblical scenes – fluttering high. This scene has changed little from 1928, when the Belfast-born Catholic artist, Sir John Lavery, painted a Portadown 12th: he claimed in his diary never to have seen anything to equal its 'austere passion'.[1]

Why was this? Because Portadown is, in the words of Sir John Hermon, a former Chief Constable of the RUC, 'the Vatican of Orangeism'.[2] Trimble also notes that local lodges boast a total of 1100 to 1200 members – in a town with a Protestant population of 20,000. Of these, over half are women and a quarter are juveniles, which means that perhaps as many as one in six of the eligible population are in the Order. Portadown District Lodge is numbered LOL No. 1, and as Trimble says, it regards that as being more than just an accident.[3] A challenge to its prerogatives and traditions would not be suffered lightly. Disaster had narrowly been averted in the mid-1980s, when the town's growing nationalist population demanded that parades through or close to Catholic areas be curtailed. Following negotiations with the RUC, the Orangemen surrendered the custom of passage down Obins Street. In exchange, they believed that they had won permanent right of passage down the Garvaghy Road – their traditional route to the town centre after completing the Drumcree church service on the Sunday before 12 July. They were reinforced in this belief by an RUC statement in 1986 claiming that 'unlike the Tunnel area [where the Orangemen ceased to march], Garvaghy Road is a major thoroughfare in which Catholics and Protestants reside'. The RUC denied that any specific guarantees had been given about the Garvaghy Road – though they acknowledged that such restrictions rarely applied to major thoroughfares. Whatever the precise understanding, the parades had nonetheless gone off relatively quietly in the intervening years in the presence of the new local MP, David Trimble, who was invited as matter of courtesy to march with the District Lodge.[4] Although scarcely an active Orangeman, Trimble was happy enough to take his place out of a sense of duty. Indeed, John Hunter remembers that Trimble loved turning round and watching the ranks of bowler-hatted brethren streaming down the hill to Portadown.[5]

But this time-honoured pageant was about to undergo its greatest challenge ever – which vaulted it into the forefront not merely of provincial concerns, but of national and international consciousness as well. For the Garvaghy Road Residents' group, which claimed to represent the inhabitants of the nationalist housing estate which comprised part of the route of the Drumcree march, indicated that they were unhappy about the parade. They had become far more active in recent years and claimed that demographic changes in the area justified a re-routing of this offensive and intimidatory march. The Orangemen retorted that the march only skirted the nationalist estate and that in any case, the protest was orchestrated by Republicans in the person of Brendan Mac Cionnaith, convicted for offences related to the bombing of the Royal British Legion Hall in Portadown in 1981 (a point of particular significance since it was the ex-servicemen's lodge which led the march down the Garvaghy Road). Many Orangemen saw the threatened street protests as an expression of aspects of TUAS – the IRA's post-ceasefire strategy of Tactical Use of Armed Struggle. Republicans would thereby seek to heighten street tensions in order to provoke Orange reprisals. These would then enable them to portray themselves as defenders of the embattled Catholic community.

Supporters of this contention rely on reports that Adams admitted in private to a Sinn Fein gathering at Athboy, Co. Meath, that the protests against a number of parades had not been spontaneous but that 'three years of work went into creating that situation, and fair play to those who put the work in'.[6] On the other side of the coin, Mac Cionnaith and other residents denied this and claimed it was simply a legitimate expression of nationalist rights.

On the morning of 9 July 1995, Portadown District prepared for their annual ritual in glorious sunshine, which would take them from Carleton Street Orange Hall in the town centre to the Drumcree church. The march out to Drumcree – not via Garvaghy Road – passed off quietly enough, and the service began at 11:15 a.m. During the course of it, Gareth Watson, then Deputy Master of LOL 273 spoke on several occasions to Superintendent Jim Blair, the RUC sub-divisional commander for the area. Watson had been formally appointed as Blair's contact shortly beforehand and stayed outside the church throughout the service. As the Rev. John Pickering, the Church of Ireland Rector of the parish of Drumcree concluded his sermon and the singing of the National Anthem began, Watson saw a large number of RUC Land-Rovers heading for the church, apparently blocking the return route to Carleton Street. Subsequently, Blair called with some disturbing news for the Orangemen. He told them that there had been a disturbance on the Garvaghy Road, with sit-down protests by the residents. Blair said that the RUC blockage was there for the Orangemen's protection, since a hostile nationalist mob might attack them, and that he would like to talk to the District officers. Portadown District duly brought David Trimble with them, relying upon him for political guidance. That said, Trimble had no master plan of action, nor any overall project in mind. Rather, he simply felt that he could not walk away and had to stay there out of a sense of personal honour and obligation to the men there.[7]

The Orangemen claim that the RUC did not immediately clarify the purpose of the blockage of the route in these talks: but they gave the impression that they were playing for time so that the police could clear the road. David Trimble told Gordon Lucy that neither he nor the District officers were told that the march would be 're-routed'.[8] To increase pressure upon the RUC, some Orangemen went to Portadown to keep their brother loyalists informed. Two hundred Protestants soon blocked Corcrain Avenue, where they were serenaded by the Portadown Flute Band.

Their number was joined by Billy Wright and boys, the commander of the UVF's mid-Ulster brigade known widely as 'King Rat', who was suspected of the murders of numerous Catholics and republicans. Wright called the Nationalist residents a 'rent-a-mob' and threatened to match their numbers by bringing in loyalists from elsewhere in the Province. Wright was utterly convinced that the march was halted by the Government at the request of Cardinal Cahal Daly (the Roman Catholic Primate of Ireland), John Hume and Gerry Adams. As Lucy notes, even if Wright's contention was wrong, after the AIA and the start of the 'peace process' loyalists were in a mood to believe such charges.[9] Wright et al. therefore determined to make a ban on the parade even costlier than letting the march down the road.

The RUC were thus in an extremely difficult position. They were obliged legally to do whatever was necessary under the Public Order (Northern Ireland) Order 1987 – to minimise the threat to life and property. But in this context, it was hard to define what 'minimisation' meant. Did it mean locally, or Province-wide? Blair Wallace, then Deputy Chief Constable for Operations, recalls that the potential nightmare for the RUC was to allow 1000 loyalists to march in the teeth of the opposition from the residents as well as the possibility that 'heavies' might infiltrate the recesses of the nationalist estate in ones and twos without the knowledge of the residents. If this resulted in bitter hand-to-hand combat, the RUC would be condemned both for imposing Orangemen on the community and for allowing the two sides to fight it out. At a minimum, says Wallace, the RUC feared that there might be distasteful scenes comparable to those outside Sean Graham's bookmakers at Belfast's lower Ormeau Road on 8 July 1992, when Orangemen in Belfast had taunted nationalists at the scene of an earlier massacre by the UFF – which had helped to turn the Ormeau Road into another flashpoint during the marching season. If reproduced on television, such scenes would not only make a settlement of that dispute harder to achieve, but would also have a 'knock-on effect' upon other contentious parades such as at Bellaghy, Co. Londonderry. Moreover, recalls Wallace, it was the first year of the first IRA ceasefire, which was looking shaky. This was especially the case following nationalist riots on 3 July, triggered by the release of Private Lee Clegg of the Parachute Regiment, who had been convicted of the murder of a Catholic girl (a conviction that was subsequently quashed).[10]

Such were the circumstances in which Assistant Chief Constable

Freddie Hall, who commanded the southern region, would decide whether the march could proceed under the terms of the Public Order Order.[11] At 12:15, he decided to halt the march in consultation with his senior colleagues in southern region. At 12:50, Trimble took the first symbolic steps down the road, followed by 803 other Orangemen. There, they were faced by a phalanx of the RUC's grey, Hotspur armoured Land-Rovers. The RUC contingent comprised six to seven Mobile Support Units, each with four to five Land-Rovers, consisting of one Inspector, four sergeants, and 24 constables. At this stage, they were all in soft gear as opposed to full riot mode. Rev. John Pickering called to his wife at the Drumcree Rectory, 'Quick, you might never see the likes of this again.'[12] Trimble walked at the head of the brethren and when he arrived at the road block he decided not to stop but rather continued walking on the route until he could not go any further – 'as was my right'.[13] From his perspective, Jim Blair recalls that Trimble charged straight into the nearest officer, who staggered back. There, the two men stood eyeball to eyeball. 'That was the first demonstration of physical contact between an Orangeman and the police, and was seen by all of the officers of Portadown District,' says Blair. 'It was an indication of how he was prepared to wind the situation up.'[14] Later that afternoon, Trimble and Harold Gracey, then Master of Portadown District No. 1, went into Portadown to talk to the assembled loyalists, where Trimble urged them again to keep the protests going; they were almost prevented from returning to Drumcree by an RUC road block. According to Gordon Lucy, the two men then had their first serious conversation. 'If this goes badly, you and I have to be the last two people to leave,' Trimble told Gracey.[15] He remembers thinking that failure was more likely than not – hence, he believes, the possible reluctance of Rev. Martin Smyth, Grand Master of the Grand Lodge of Ireland to turn up (Smyth states that he had commitments in London and wanted to stay in touch with the Government – and therefore sent Molyneaux, who held high rank in the Loyal Orders, to Portadown. He claims that he thought all along that the Orangemen would win).[16] Trimble's doubts were assuaged by the massive numbers who spontaneously turned up in support of Portadown District. Those present would be entertained by the bands, some with mighty 17th-century lambeg drums, weighing 40 pounds and three foot in diameter and depth, which rejoiced in names such as the 'Earl Kitchener the Avenger'.[17] These unalloyed expressions of solidarity buoyed up Trimble in the subsequent negotiations with the RUC. Trimble claimed on the basis of information from Orange sources that, at times, there were a mere 30 nationalist protesters who could easily be swept away. Hall, though, denied this was the case and said that the opposition to the march would be much more substantial. Jim Blair states that the actual numbers were closer to several hundred, with who knows how many 'hard men' hidden away.[18]

Trimble and Gracey then briefed the crowd on events, and the local MP introduced the District Master to the assembled journalists. The next day, the *Belfast Telegraph* quoted an RUC officer's observation that Trimble was 'grossly irresponsible'.[19] But it was Gracey's remarks which were of greater significance on this occasion. He told them 'be it days, hours, or weeks, we will stay until we walk our traditional route'.[20] It was now to be a fight to the finish to preserve Ulster-British culture. Everything, they felt, had been taken away from them: their Provincial Parliament; their locally controlled security forces; the right to display pictures of the Sovereign; the right to fly Union flags and to wear Glasgow Rangers T-shirts in the workplace; and much else besides. All of these, in their eyes, had fallen foul of the Dublin/SDLP/Sinn Fein/IRA-inspired reforms, to which weak and duplicitous British Governments had acceded in order to buy themselves a quieter life. Now even their marches, already greatly reduced in number, were to be re-routed or even banned, and that in the year of the 200th anniversary of the Battle of the Diamond in Co. Armagh, which led to the formation of the Orange Order.

The numbers began to build up further, and by 10:15 p.m. Ian Paisley had arrived. The relationship between Trimble and Paisley was never going to be an easy one, not least bearing in mind Paisley's past attacks on Trimble. Some, such as Jim Blair, thought that Trimble was in awe of the 'Big Man'; but others, such as Rev. Pickering, thought that Trimble was very much in the lead role in his own constituency and that Paisley deferred to him more often than not. Indeed, Pickering remembers that at a subsequent gathering, Paisley kept looking at his nails until Trimble was fetched – he would not brief those present until the local MP arrived.[21] Whatever the truth of the matter, it was at this meeting that Trimble suggested a compromise, whereby a smaller but still substantial contingent would go down the Garvaghy Road. Hall discussed it with Chief Superintendent Terry Houston, the RUC divisional commander. All they undertook to do was to examine the possibility of allowing the half-dozen

Portadown District officers to march. This was unacceptable to the Orangemen but Trimble acknowledged that, from their perspective, this was at least a move in the right direction. Paisley then went and addressed the crowd and denounced the reduced numbers suggested by the RUC, and thereafter went to see Blair Wallace to try to persuade him to change the ruling. Other observers described 'a surreal atmosphere – a mixture between a military camp and a scout jamboree', with accordion and flute music playing to keep up the morale of the protesters. That night, Trimble tried to obtain some rest in his Renault Espace: he never went home during Drumcree 1995, nor was he able to shower and change clothes. But he was constantly interrupted by 'alarums and excursions', such as Paisley returning from his meeting with Blair Wallace. Scrambling to put his shoes on, Trimble emerged dishevelled and with his tie askew. Paisley then told him that Wallace could not help in the way they would have wished. Later, Trimble was again pulled out of his car, bleary-eyed, this time in order to becalm the Orangemen who were becoming aggressive towards the RUC. His techniques could be unorthodox and showed a sure grasp of street confrontation: when the loyalists became convinced that they would be the recipients of a rush attack by the RUC, Trimble took the lead and stood with his back to the police, making it psychologically harder to baton charge the Orangemen. 'They're not going to charge with my back to them,' advised Trimble. The idea was picked up by some of the Orange stewards, who employed later it on. In the process, recalls Houston, 'he could become very red in the face, so much so that we were concerned about his blood pressure'.[22]

The next day, Trimble attended a meeting at Carleton Street Orange Hall between senior Orangemen and the RUC. Relations between Trimble and Hall, the key figure on the RUC side, were anything but easy. The Upper Bann MP disliked what he saw as Hall's penchant for such fashionable concepts as 'conflict resolution' techniques, which he had learned at training courses at Police Staff College at Bramshill and with the FBI. In fact, Hall was an officer with much front-line experience, during the course of which he had incurred serious wounds; in 1977, he was awarded a Queen's Gallantry Medal. Whatever the rights and wrongs of the situation, the two men proved to be ill-matched for each other during these tensest of circumstances and Trimble began to criticise Hall's conduct of the crisis. 'Mr Hall, one of your problems is that you do not listen,' snapped the local MP.[23] Hall did not, however, respond to Trimble's accusations and held his peace. But little came out of these tense exchanges. At 5:30 p.m., they met again, this time in an RUC vehicle. Trimble reiterated his compromise of allowing a 'substantial' number of Orangemen down the road. Yet Trimble felt more optimistic than before. Far from melting away, ever greater numbers of Orangemen were assembling; with loyalist womenfolk bringing copious quantities of food, they were better provisioned than the RUC. By now, Larne was blocked and protests were erupting everywhere, and in the Fountain estate in Londonderry, the last Protestant enclave on the west bank of the River Foyle, residents had erected barricades. Then came the news that the Garvaghy Road Residents would begin direct talks at 7 p.m., rather than demand unilateral re-routing of the parade. The Orangemen felt that this was not possible because of Mac Cionnaith's conviction for terrorism and, in any case, Trimble and others would be attending or speaking at the mass rally scheduled for 7:30 p.m. Nonetheless, some kind of progress was being made. At the suggestion of the RUC – and with the agreement of the residents and of Jeffrey Donaldson – the Mediation Network had already begun to explore the possibilities for an agreement. The Mediation Network, now Mediation Northern Ireland, had originally been established in 1987 and stated that its mission was to be an 'impartial "outsider" in situations of conflict assisting people to resolve or manage difference in ways which promote human dignity and mutual respect'. As Terry Houston recalls, the RUC knew that they had no 'in' with the Garvaghy residents. It was agreed that Mediation Network would shuttle back and forth between the parties.[24]

The rally by Drumcree church attracted 25,000 to 30,000 loyalists from all of the Province's counties, as well as Orangemen from Cavan and Monaghan in the Republic and representatives of Scottish lodges. Trimble was forced to leave the platform during Paisley's speech after he was told that there was trouble brewing down by the police lines. Trimble mounted one of the RUC Hotspurs and sought to quieten the crowd, but instead he was booed. Gracey and Trimble then sought to obtain a passage through RUC lines to speak to senior officers. Trimble indicated his desire for a parting of the solid police line so that he could make his way through; this was obtained and just after Trimble secured entry a T-shirted young loyalist sought to rush after him further to breach the cordon, as it were. The RUC ranks closed promptly and a mêlée ensued. Stones began to fly from the Orange side and police reinforcements charged forward, leaving Trimble exposed behind RUC lines with stones flying from behind and riot squads charging straight at him: with his face down, one of the policemen almost did not recognise him and he narrowly escaped injury. He was then invited to take shelter in an RUC Land-Rover. Harold Gracey, who frequently had strong disagreements with Trimble thereafter, still had no doubts as to his physical courage. 'There was no fear in him, nor did I ever hear him swear once,' recalled Gracey. 'Although his hands did move and wave about like a Frenchman!'[25]

Trimble returned to Drumcree church hall for fresh negotiations with the Mediation Network. The Mediation Network reported that they had discussed a range of issues with Mac Cionnaith. These discusssions were then interrupted by news of further disturbances, as Orangemen sought to envelop the police lines and more plastic baton rounds were fired. Trimble and Donaldson arrived and agreed with the RUC to conduct further talks at Edward Street station in Portadown centre. The RUC now seemed to the Orangemen to be closer to accepting Trimble's compromise about 'substantial' numbers going down the road, if not the traditional full complement – in other words, Portadown District and nobody else from outside the area. The Orangemen then offered to go down six rather than two abreast to allow the parade to pass off more swiftly and without a band. Hall, though, did not give a 100 per cent guarantee. Both sides present were worried, each for their own reasons, about raising expectations – a point which Trimble emphasised by raising and lowering his hand off the table. But from the Orange perspective, this represented further progress: the focus of the conversations now became 'how', rather than 'whether'.[26] The RUC were also more optimistic after this: Trimble now appeared to accept their contention that 200 loyalists could not commence a surprise march down the road at 4 a.m., which would trigger major disorder, and that there would have to be some kind of prior tacit arrangement with the residents. (The point about the Garvaghy residents' likely reaction had been forcibly made by Brendan McAllister of the Mediation Network at the meeting.)[27] Trimble went back to the Orangemen, partly to segregate the Portadown from the non-Portadown Districts in the hope that some such compromise might come off. But privately he was becoming ever more anxious. The closer that they came to 11th night, with great Province-wide bonfires on the eve of the 12th July, the greater the likelihood of massive disturbances in support of the thwarted Portadown brethren. Portadown District Lodge proclaimed that unless the affair was resolved by 7 a.m. on the morning of 11 July, they would march at a time of their choosing.

Portadown rose the next morning to what Brendan McAllister of the Mediation Network, surveying the scene from the hill at Drumcree, describes as 'the orange glow of the dawn, with the sun rising to sounds of lambeg drums'.[28] Slowly, the police Land-Rovers began to move down the hill, away from the Orangemen, and to point towards the nationalist residents. By this time, they feared that the march might go ahead; growing numbers were already sitting down on the Garvaghy Road. The Land-Rovers reversed course back towards the Orangemen. Trimble was worried that some Orangemen had gone home believing that there was an agreement to march; things could go nasty if it turned out that the decision was then reversed.[29] The local MP duly went to the Drumcree Rectory and telephoned RUC headquarters at Knock, where he spoke to the other Deputy Chief Constable, Ronnie Flanagan, the senior duty officer. He warned Flanagan of the gravity of the situation, and then rang Molyneaux to ask that he use his influence with the Chief Constable, Sir Hugh Annesley, to secure a speedy resolution to the affair and to overturn the ban: Molyneaux had greater standing with the RUC as the long-time leader of the Province's largest party. At around 8 a.m. Houston shifted position and stated that he would seek to take the Orangemen down the road as quickly as possible. The final ruling was delayed until Blair Wallace and Flanagan arrived from Belfast to oversee the new decision. A compromise of sorts seemed to be emerging. It appears to have been understood that Portadown District only would go down, with no bands, and minimal police presence. This meant that Trimble could not walk since he was only there in an ex officio capacity, nor could Paisley. Trimble was not very happy with this, but accepted for the sake of the march in the years to come. Instead, he would meet the marchers by Shillington's Bridge, once they were safely past the controversial part of the route and were well on their way to returning to Carleton Street Orange Hall. But the events which surrounded the closing of the deal remain controversial. The nationalists believed that there was no question of parades going down that route next year without the consent of the local community – a point which the Mediation Network organiser relayed to Brendan Mac Cionnaith and which persuaded many nationalist residents to voluntarily remove themselves from the road. The Orangemen claim that they would not have been party to any oral agreement that denied their right to march.[30] According to Flanagan, the agreement was that there would be no march on the next day – 12 July itself – and subsequently the Orangemen made no serious attempt to walk the route on that occasion. Whatever was actually agreed, the episode had the effect of enhancing the nationalist sense of grievance when the main march went down the road in 1996.[31]

Meanwhile, the Orangemen would have to fall back to facilitate disengagement of the two sides. Jim Blair then walked the length of the RUC line. As he went along, he tapped each Hotspur with his 30-inch blackthorn swagger stick (a prerogative of senior policemen since the days of the old Royal Irish Constabulary, but banned after the RUC's replacement by the new Police Service of Northern Ireland) thus signalling that the vehicle should move back.[32] At 10:30, Gracey led the 800 or so Orangemen down the hill, past the silent residents of the Garvaghy Road, who had removed themselves from the thoroughfare at a given signal. According to Gordon Lucy, those who participated remembered above all else the sound of tramping feet. By the time they arrived at Shillington's Bridge, an atmosphere prevailed that was reminiscent of the 1974 Ulster Workers' Council strike: Jim Blair in all his years as a policeman never saw a scene like it, with ex-servicemen weeping tears of joy.[33] Trimble, who rejoined them now, was exhausted rather than emotional. As the march swept up to Carleton Street, the Orangemen came to a halt. A shout went up for Gracey and then for Trimble and Paisley. Paisley, though, seemed to be forging ahead. Trimble knew that he had to do something to maintain his status as Paisley's equal. 'My thought was, "I don't want this fellow walking in front of me, upstaging me."' Thus it was that the two men clasped hands at chest level, as they took the salute of the admiring throng. 'By this gesture I made sure that we would both be walking side by side,' Trimble says.[34] 'No words were spoken,' recalls Paisley. 'It was a spontaneous gesture.'[35] But he had no realisation of how this episode would be seen, nor even that cameras would be present. Thus was born the idea that Trimble had danced a jig with Paisley down the Garvaghy Road in full view of the Catholic residents – though, in fact the episode took place approximately a mile away on Carleton Street, in front of loyalists. If Trimble's account is right, the walk with Paisley down Carleton Street was born of opportunism and relief, rather than innate triumphalism. But the oddest part of this episode is that no one viewing the video of the event could ever suppose that any kind of dance was going on. The idea that the two men performed a jig may originate with the editorial in the *Irish News* of 12 July 1995 (the day after) which accused Trimble of 'dancing' over the feelings of his nationalist constituents, but this was obviously meant in a metaphorical sense only. Certainly, neither the *Irish News* nor the *Belfast Telegraph* of 11 or 12 July mentions either Trimble or Paisley 'holding hands' or 'dancing'; and, as was shown years later in his comments on the iniquities of 'line dancing', Ian Paisley took a dim view of jigging with women, let alone male political rivals. One theory advanced by the writer C.D.C. Armstrong is that the comedian Patrick Kielty in his BBC Northern Ireland comedy show in the autumn of 1995, showed the film of Trimble and Paisley holding hands and put it into reverse at high speed, thus making it appear as if they were dancing. Whatever the strange origins of this myth, it became ever more embedded in the consciousness of nationalist Ireland. Shortly thereafter, Trimble would compound the anguish of local nationalists by denying that there had been any compromise struck with their representatives, and this would make it harder to resolve the crisis in the following year. Trimble acknowledges that the image of him 'dancing a jig' down the Garvaghy Road was 'unhelpful' and that it was exploited in ways that were detrimental to the Orange interest. He was determined to ensure that it did not happen again and he pointedly refused to be 'chaired' by the crowd during Drumcree 1996.[36] The bitterness which attended the close of proceedings obscured the real achievement of the RUC and the Mediation Network – to have secured some sort of agreement between the Orangemen and the nationalist residents. It was certainly the last occasion on which there was any kind of consensus and henceforth the march would either effectively go down by *force majeure* or not at all.[37]

In the eyes of the British Government, the first 'siege of Drumcree' confirmed their suspicion that none of the Unionists could be trusted; one civil servant who observed Patrick Mayhew at close quarters remembers that it confirmed him in his conviction that the Northern Protestants were *sui generis*. Even now, Mayhew says that Trimble's performance was 'undoubtedly triumphalist, and there's no point in saying it wasn't'.[38] He remembers that the Irish Government – not understanding how the relationship between police and politicians differs between Northern Ireland and the Republic – assumed that the Ulster Secretary could just snap his fingers and obtain the result he wanted. Fergus Finlay, the special adviser to Dick Spring, the Irish Foreign Minister, recalls coming back from holiday to find a new hate figure in the Department of Foreign Affairs in Dublin – David Trimble.[39] The television critic of the *Irish Times* was scathing: 'Ruddy, gloating and pompous, David Trimble's face filled the screen.'[40] Nuala O'Faolain, writing in the *Irish Times*, thought that the irresponsibility of men such as Trimble and Paisley would turn places such as the Garvaghy Road into 'little Mostars' (a reference to the scenes of devastation in the Bosnian War). 'They don't have to live, of course, where their neighbours hate them and they hate and fear their neighbours. They just do what harm is to hand, and go home to their comfortable houses,' she observed.[41] To many of his critics, Trimble's behaviour was reminiscent of nothing so much as John Hewitt's description, in his poem 'Minister', of the young Brian Faulkner – who initially made a name for himself as a hardliner for his role in ensuring that an Orange parade went down the Longstone Road in Annalong, Co. Down:

> Not one of your tall captains bred to rule
> that right confirmed by school and army list
> he went to school, but not the proper school.
> His family tree will offer little grist
> to any plodding genealogist;
> his father's money grew from making shirts.
> But with ambition clenched in his tight fist,
> and careful to discount the glancing hurts,
> he climbed to office, studiously intent,
> and reached the door he planned to enter, twice
> to have it slammed by the establishment.
> A plight that well might sympathy command,
> had we not watched that staff of prejudice
> he'd used with skill turn serpent in his hand

> Frank Ormsby (ed.), *The Collected Poems of*
> *John Hewitt* (Belfast, 1992), p. 141

Why did Trimble arouse such hostility in nationalist Ireland and amongst mainland progressive opinion? Trimble shrugs his shoulders and says that such anger is of 'no interest to him', but it is worth examining the reasons for it. To his detractors, both nationalist and now loyalist, there has always been 'something of the night about him' (to quote Ann Widdecombe's description of Michael Howard in his time as Home

Secretary).[42] Like Howard, Trimble may also have aroused liberal revulsion, precisely because many right-thinking people feel that someone of his intelligence and professional standing ought to have known better. Trimble was, therefore, potentially much more dangerous than someone such as Ian Paisley precisely because he was both hardline *and* a thoroughly modern man, who could not be dismissed as a throwback to the 17th-century Covenanters. He had secured the support of much of the London quality print media without compromising his principles, or playing the liberal Unionist. Thus *The Times* took 'the presence on the march of the moderate Unionist MP, David Trimble' as evidence of 'the broad appeal which the Orange Order still exercises in the Province'.[43] Then there was also the undercurrent that Trimble was engaged in sheer opportunism, of playing to the mob. Some, such as Jim Blair who observed Trimble closely in those days, believe that Trimble saw the entire issue as a magnificent opportunity to burnish his Orange credentials in preparation for a leadership bid.[44] Certainly, as he readily admits, there was opportunism in his behaviour at Carleton Street once it was all over, but that does not mean that it was governed by such considerations all along.[45] It was a huge risk, as is attested to by Trimble's nervousness during the crisis (Gordon Lucy remembers that at moments, his arm went into a spasm) and he knew he would suffer the brunt of any recriminations if either they did not go down the road or else did so with large-scale casualties. Indeed, Gordon Lucy recalls that he shouted to Trimble on the Monday night, 'this will be the making of you', but that Trimble demurred. Trimble also said to Lucy afterwards that he feared that 1996 would be an unmitigated disaster and that the Orangemen would not 'get away with it' two years running.[46] Drumcree was, therefore, subject to too many variables for it to be a truly satisfactory launching pad for Trimble's leadership bid, at least when the crisis began. Rather, Trimble appears genuinely to have been swept along by his sense of duty as the local MP. It was a predicament which even internal rivals such as John Taylor understood. 'If I'd have been the MP for the seat, what on earth would I have done?' asks the veteran politician.[47] But Trimble was also swept along by the emotion of the occasion, which was bound up with such hallowed loyalist concepts as the right to 'walk the Queen's highway' – to which he heartily subscribed. During the crisis itself, he told several people that if the march went through, it would be as significant a development in the history and folklore of Orangeism as the events at Dolly's Brae in 1849 (when, according to Protestant lore, the Catholic Ribbonmen sought to prevent Co. Down Orangemen from completing their march via their preferred route through the Mourne Mountains). As Trimble's friend Ruth Dudley Edwards observes the historical romance of the events at Drumcree would have appealed to the theatrical streak in his personality – and it explains his request to Lucy to write his book, which was begun in August 1995.[48] In so far as he was thinking in a calculated way about political effects, Trimble felt that street protest was the only way to obtain results under direct rule – a system which he once described to me in deliberately hyperbolic terms as 'dictatorship moderated by riot'.[49] 'Old thinking', perhaps, to use Gorbachevian terminology, but scarcely evidence of a preordained stratagem on Trimble's part to advance his career. Indeed, for much of his career, he has drifted into situations and improvised rather than pursued a detailed, preordained game plan.[50]

Joel Patton, who went on to found the 'Spirit of Drumcree' group within the Orange Order as a vehicle for protest against what he saw as the insipidity of the leadership, says that one of the weaknesses of loyalism is that they need men on white horses: they cannot accept that Drumcree was their victory, so they alighted upon Paisley and Trimble as explanations for that success. But Patton also expresses the view which many loyalists have held since the Belfast Agreement – that the British state, and particularly elements of the British intelligence services, wanted to give Trimble such a victory in order to build up an apparently 'hardline' Unionist who would then have the credibility to effect an historic compromise with Irish nationalism.[51] In Trimble's eyes Patton's views are just another example of loyalist conspiracy theories. 'Many of these anti-Agreement Unionists decided after the Belfast Agreement of 1998 that I was a bad 'un and therefore had to have been a bad 'un all of the time,' responds Trimble. 'These anti-Agreement Unionists have a problem. They have to avoid the lurking doubt that I might still have good reasons as a Unionist for what I am doing post-1998. If I was a good 'un in 1995, how can I have been a bad 'un? People like simplicity and they have difficulty in coping with the complexity of political life.'[52]

What is certain, both during Drumcree 1995 and 1996, is that the British politicians, including the Prime Minister, were taken by surprise.[53] The point is confirmed by Sir Robin Butler, the then Cabinet Secretary, who recalls that 'there were problems with marches the whole time and to us, it seemed as though all the protagonists were like a child crying wolf'. According to Butler, Major's attitude was to ask whether 'it was reasonable that the loyalists be so insistent about marching down this piece of road'.[54] Indeed, after the second 'Siege' of Drumcree, Mayhew told Paul Bew that 'no one told me what would happen'. By this, Mayhew did not mean that he was totally ignorant of the fact that some sort of trouble was brewing, simply that it was possible that many of those Unionists who were telling him that such crises would occur may have had a vested interest in hyping them up to secure the result they wanted (such as Trimble himself). Some of those within the NIO who were meant to provide advice on what would actually happen may not have done so with sufficient vigour: when he subsquently raised Mayhew's concerns with a senior civil servant, Bew was told by the official that it was not his role to provide this sort of 'tribal advice'. As the official saw it, the best traditions of the British mandarinate were those of impartiality. Bew also derived the impression that after the AIA it became perceived career death amongst some officials to state the 'Unionist line'; and in any case, everyone had seen the Protestants faced down before, as in 1985–6, and may simply have assumed it would happen again.[55] Peter Bell, then British joint secretary of the Anglo-Irish Secretariat, recalls that at this point, Drumcree was seen as a public order issue. It was therefore primarily a problem for the RUC and the Army (from which the Government could and arguably should stand back) rather than as an issue of the first political magnitude. This perhaps reflected an enduring lack of empathy for Unionist concerns on the part of many NIO officials from outside the Province and a reluctance on the part of some local civil servants to speak out lest they be thought of as 'sectarian'.[56] Speaking to loyalists on 12 July 1996, Trimble offered his own interpretation why the state was blind-sided during successive years' disturbances. He said this was because the leading intelligence operatives had all perished in the RAF Chinook crash on the Mull of Kintyre in August 1994. Had they lived, Trimble opined, it is unlikely that they would have failed to see the loyalist protests coming.[57] Again, this is pure speculation – and in any case, grievous as the losses were, men such as John Deverell (the senior MI5 officer in Northern Ireland) would have been retired by the time of Drumcree 1995. As with the disaster over the Frameworks Documents, the likeliest explanation is that the state as a whole was so focused on republican intentions during the first IRA ceasefire that they became tone deaf to sensibilities on the loyalist side. If so, Trimble was again the unexpected beneficiary of a Government cock-up – although he denies that Drumcree had much to do with his subsequent election as leader. Justly or unjustly, though, it was the benchmark by which much of the world, and his own community, judged his subsequent performance.

ELEVEN

Now I am the Ruler of the UUP!

AFTER a year of set-backs, James Molyneaux finally resigned as UUP leader on 28 August 1995 – the day after his 75th birthday. Trimble says he was surprised by the timing of the departure, of which he had received no advanced warning (in contrast to Major, who was notified by Molyneaux some two weeks before).[1] Indeed, John Hunter remembers Trimble dismissing the notion of a Molyneaux resignation when he raised the subject shortly beforehand at a barbecue given at the home of Drew Nelson, a leading Co. Down Orangeman. But when the news came, Trimble rang Hunter and said, 'well, you'll be happy this morning, the sun is shining'. Trimble knew that Hunter was a staunch opponent of Molyneaux, but insisted he had made no definite decisions himself.[2] However, Daphne Trimble recalls her husband saying that if he did run, he would win.[3] By contrast, the man who definitely thought that the sun was shining that morning was John Taylor. Trimble knew that the Strangford MP would seek the leadership, nor was he entirely averse to the prospect of a Taylor victory, since he was sure he would become his right-hand man.[4] Much of the political class agreed with this analysis. Thus, Jack Allen recalls that much as John Taylor was disliked by some, the majority of the party officers thought he would win – with or without Trimble in the race.[5] The NIO agreed: according to Sir John Wheeler, the security minister, Ancram's senior officials wanted Taylor precisely because he was seen as a good 'deal-maker'.[6]

Trimble soon weighed the pros and cons of running. His plus points, as he saw them, were that he was articulate, could hold his own on television, and because over the previous year he had distanced himself 'slightly' from the Frameworks proposals. He reckoned these points would weigh heavily with the UUP's unique electoral college, despite the fact that he was the youngest and most junior of the UUP MPs and was without formal standing within the Loyal Orders (beyond the reputation which he had acquired at Drumcree). If the choice had been up to the populace at large, Maginnis would be the victor. He enjoyed a good reputation amongst Unionists on security issues – the ex-UDR Major had been the intended victim of at least a dozen assassination attempts – but without compromising his non-sectarian credentials (as was evidenced by his success in holding the constituency of Fermanagh-South Tyrone, with its narrow Roman Catholic majority, in successive Westminster elections). And thanks to his personable manner, he was able to communicate on southern Irish television in a way that few other Unionists could match. Indeed many Unionists believed that he was far too willing to treat with the South, as exemplified by what they saw as his excessive generosity in the Strand II 'basket' of the 1991–2 talks in Dublin. If it were up to the MPs, Ross was reckoned to be the likely winner; and if it were up to the councillors and the business community, Taylor seemed to be favourite. But none of these groups formed the electoral college. Because the decision would be made by the Ulster Unionist Council, an 860-strong body with representatives from all of the then seventeen constituencies and other affiliated bodies such as the Orange Order and the Young Unionists, Trimble might stand a chance. The UUC was, he then reasoned, full of people with a greater knowledge than the man in the street, but was at the same time possessed in his eyes of a detachment which the full-time MPs and councillors did not have. In so far as there was an Orange constituency – and it was wider than just the Order's own delegates, since ordinary branch representatives might also be individual members – Trimble calculated that he had it sewn up. This, he maintains passionately, was not because of Drumcree but because of his work for the Ulster Society. His doubts were, therefore, not about his viability as a candidate, but whether he actually wanted the position itself at this juncture. He knew that it would be an uphill struggle to accomplish anything and, in any case, 1995 was scarcely the best year to become UUP leader after the debacle of the Frameworks Documents.[7]

Such apparent ambivalence accounts for the initial reports that Trimble had ruled himself out of the race. Thus, *The Times* editorial on the day after Molyneaux's resignation stated that 'it is regrettable that Mr Trimble, MP for Upper Bann, seems disinclined to stand' and on the back of that decision decided to endorse Taylor.[8] What Trimble had actually said to the journalists was that he did not consider himself to be a runner, but added that 'if other people are keen for me to run, then I will give it serious consideration'. In retrospect, it looks like a classic piece of political ham-acting ('if the people want me, who am I to refuse?'). According to Gordon Lucy's private diary of the campaign, Trimble was annoyed that the journalists, with the exception of Dick Grogan and Frank Millar in the *Irish Times* on 30 August and Victor Gordon of the *Portadown Times*, had failed to pick up on the nuances. Gordon, writing without a by-line in the local free-sheet called the *Craigavon Echo* on 30 August 1995 also correctly divined that Trimble had not ruled himself out of the contest. In the *Portadown Times* of 1 September, Gordon also reported that Trimble was '95%' certain to announce his candidature. Trimble stated that since he had said he 'might' run, 'my 'phone has been red hot with messages of support'. Trimble asked Lucy whether he should run, and Lucy said that of course he would support him and work for him – but that it was his decision and that he would have to live with the consequences of it. Lucy subsequently learned from Daphne Trimble that this was the wrong answer, since she wanted him to say 'yes'.[9]

Trimble was left with the impression that his natural supporters felt let down by his apparent reluctance, and that he would damage himself if he did not run. He was also discovering that in the eyes of many delegates, John Taylor was not universally popular. According to Lucy, Trimble finally made up his mind to enter the race on 30 August. The Upper Bann MP then telephoned John Taylor and told him that he would be going forward as a candidate. Taylor replied that he would be sorry to see this happen. Taylor's then aide, Steven King, states that Taylor did not in fact think that he could win after Trimble entered the race, and that henceforth his heart was never quite in it.[10] Trimble discussed his platform with Lucy: it was not so much an appeal for more right-wing Unionism as for more proactive Unionism, for a new style at least as much as new substance. Trimble planned to announce his candidature at Belfast's Europa Hotel on 1 September. He knew that he would have no heavyweight endorsements, neither from fellow MPs, nor party officers, nor from any constituency chairmen save his own, George Savage. As an outsider, as it it were, he was certain of one thing: he did not wish to repeat the errors of John Redwood's failed bid for the Conservative leadership earlier in the summer. Indeed, he told Gordon Lucy and John Hunter that their presence at the launch would have the same effect upon his bid as the support of Teresa Gorman and Tony Marlow had on the challenge of the former Welsh Secretary. Instead, inspired by Nicholas Jones' book *Soundbites and Spin Doctors: How Politicians Manipulate the Media – and Vice Versa* he opted for a bit of DIY choreography. He decided that he would be accompanied by four relatively unknown figures, all of whom would represent portions of the new Unionist coalition which he was assembling. They included Elaine McClure (a young woman); Lt Commander Bill Martin (whose service background symbolised the traditional backbone of the party); George Savage, his constituency chairman and a farmer (thus seeking to corral the substantial agricultural vote); and Nigel Connor of the Queen's University Unionists (to emphasise his appeal to youth). From there, Trimble and Lucy repaired to Hunter's house off the Upper Malone Road to plot out strategy. Two crucial steps were taken. First, an alphabetical list of all UUC delegates was obtained from Glengall Street, so that he could send out *A Personal Message From David Trimble*. The package made much of the complimentary remarks which Trimble received from both *The Daily Telegraph* and *The Times*: a key Trimble theme was the notion that it was crucial for Unionists to influence key decision-makers and opinion-formers in London, rather than sit there and let change envelop them. Second, Hunter and Lucy, who had assisted in Drew Nelson's 1992 campaign in South Down, were convinced of the merits of telephone canvassing – still a new concept in Northern Ireland, at least in Unionist circles, where many traditionalists thought it not quite the done thing. But Lucy and Hunter, correctly, believed that attitudes towards use of the telephone were changing, even amongst the older generation where resentment of such intrusions tended to be greatest. Accordingly, extra telephone lines were installed in Trimble's Lurgan office. Two young women were recruited to do the telephone canvassing as volunteers.[11]

The professionalism of the Trimble campaign, though scarcely sophisticated by standards elsewhere, contrasted with the relative amateurism of its rivals' efforts. Whereas Trimble's team would 'cold call' anybody, Taylor would only ring those he already knew. Taylor's campaign suffered a further blow when he appeared on BBC Northern Ireland's *Spotlight* programme at 10:45 p.m. on the eve of the poll on Thursday 7 September. There, he attacked Trimble for 'prancing in the streets with Ian Paisley'. By this, Taylor was seeking to appeal to that segment of the UUP electorate which rejected Paisley's populist style. Often, this would have been a correct appraisal of the party's mood, but Drumcree I was a spontaneous popular eruption which, like the UWC strike of 1974, enjoyed an exceptional degree of middle-class Unionist acquiescence, if not active support. Taylor's remarks were thus taken by many ordinary Unionists as an implicit attack on their relief over the outcome. Meanwhile, Ross's campaign never really took off. One of his main supporters, David Brewster – a solicitor from Limavady, Co. Londonderry and the constituency party secretary – had his practice to run. He found that many who would have backed his local MP were now opting for Trimble.[12] Martin Smyth's campaign was dogged by a lack of organisation, which made few inroads beyond his South Belfast constituency association and some Belfast Orangemen. Smyth concedes that many of his brethren in the Loyal Orders felt that he had stood aside from the events at Drumcree, though in fact he was attending to his duties at Westminster. Maginnis made a game effort, but his perceived liberalism counted against him in the circumstances.

Lucy meanwhile was busy putting the finishing touches to the Trimble campaign. He drafted Trimble's *News Letter* article which appeared on the day of the poll, Friday 8 September 1995. Significantly, Trimble approvingly quoted the definition of the consent principle offered by the leader of the Opposition, Tony Blair, 'as meaning that the people of Northern Ireland could choose between an all-Irish state and the Union' rather than any of the Conservative Government's glosses. Moreover, he counselled that 'a purely negative, unimaginative unionism that simply turned a "hard face" on the outside world is vulnerable to an appeal over its head to the wider society'. But despite such efforts, Trimble remembers that when he arrived at the Ulster Hall on the night of 8 September, he was in a very nervous state – whereas Daphne was quite calm (with customary candour, she says that she merely concealed her own worries).[13] The packed Ulster Hall had been the scene of many of the great events in Unionist history: there, in 1886, Lord Randolph Churchill launched his campaign to save Ulster from Home Rule.[14] But Trimble's nerves were misplaced. The candidates spoke in alphabetical order, with Ken Maginnis first: the ex-UDR Major did his 'soldier and statesman' routine. Smyth's address was full of Biblical allusions but the rest of it was every bit as disorganised as his campaign. Ross's was the best delivered of the five, but in Lucy's words was 'a brilliant speech for leadership circa 1930'. Taylor, though, was the greatest disappointment to his supporters. His address was delivered off-the-cuff, and in the words of Denis Rogan, the then party vice chairman, was 'the most arrogant speech of his life – and that's saying something';[15] Steven King claims that he in fact had 'a fit of nerves' on the night.[16] Taylor retrospectively concedes that he was not that keen to assume the leadership.[17] Trimble, who was the last speaker, read his speech like a lecture, but Lucy remembers that the audience nonetheless listened.[18] As Trimble recalls, 'mine was the only political speech whereas the others were saying what great chaps they were. But I also said I would go anywhere and speak to anyone. I was signalling that I would go to Dublin and talk to Sinn Fein, though that was not stated. It was in nobody's mind at the time, except John Dobson, who was smiling.'[19]

After the first round of balloting, Trimble's appointed scrutineer, Mark Neale of Portadown, told him of the result:

Smyth – 60 (7%)
Ross – 116 (14%)
Maginnis – 117 (15%)
Taylor – 226 (28%)
Trimble – 287 (36%)

'Oh, that's not what I f . . . ng wanted to happen,' declared Trimble. 'Well, what do I do now?' asked the Upper Bann MP. 'Tell your wife and start writing an acceptance speech,' replied Neale. Trimble duly proceeded to do so – but not before he had pulled his new 'Seige [sic] of Drumcree' medal out of his pocket. As Neale recalls, even at this moment of maximum drama, Trimble did this less out of loyalist pride than out of a desire to point out the spelling error.[20] When this result was read out in the hall, Jim Wilson, the party chief executive, immediately saw the mounting astonishment on the faces of the MPs. 'This was the UUC saying "let's jump a generation".'[21] In the heat of battle, Trimble also thought back to the Upper Bann selection of 1990, when the first-round winner, Samuel Gardiner, had been overhauled by himself in the final ballot after hitting a ceiling. He feared that Taylor could still do the same to himself. But Trimble's support was wide as well as deep, and in any case there was no way in which Ken Maginnis would ever throw his support to Taylor as George Savage had done for Trimble in 1990. After Smyth dropped out, the chairman, Jim Nicholson, read out the results of the second round:

Ross – 91 (11%)
Maginnis – 110 (13.5%)
Taylor – 255 (31.5%)
Trimble – 353 (44%)

Trimble now knew for sure that he would become the 12th Unionist leader since the formation of the UUC in 1905, and felt utterly flat inside. There was thus an inevitability about the final result as far as the cognoscenti were concerned – as Trimble's rivals sat with arms folded and legs crossed. Ross could not break out from his core of supporters from the farming community west of the Bann, dropped out. So, too, did Maginnis: he could see that not only did Trimble do well outside of the greater Belfast area generally, but that he had made substantial inroads amongst some of his own constituents in Fermanagh, notably in the Newtownbutler, Rosslea and Lisnaskea areas close to the border. After the third ballot, Nicholson announced the result of the run-off:

Taylor – 333 (42%)
Trimble – 466 (58%)

Trimble remembers one big blur; whilst Daphne Trimble says that 'on one level I went into shock. Nothing would ever be the same again. Part of David didn't want it at all; a part of him wants a quiet life – to sit at home and listen to music and to go to the opera. But at least as far as the house was concerned, his election didn't make much difference since he doesn't do the normal things that husbands do like the gardening. When we married he at least made an effort and we definitely had shelves put up.'[22]

How had he done it? After all, here was a man who just a few years earlier could not even win a council by-election in ultra-safe Lisburn. Moreover, this bookish academic had now been elected as the leader of one of the least intellectual political forces in the United Kingdom; indeed, he was the first university graduate since the foundation of Northern Ireland to lead the UUP, for many of his patrician predecessors had served in the forces but never attended a university (Carson was a graduate, but effectively handed over the leadership to Craig upon the foundation of the state; and Faulkner matriculated at Queen's in the autumn of 1939, but never graduated).[23] Nor did he seek to make himself congenial to his colleagues – indeed, in some ways the very opposite. 'Drumcree' was an obvious answer, and is certainly the explanation for his victory most favoured by senior colleagues. Likewise, Caroline Nimmons, who did much of the telephone canvassing of the delegates, says that Drumcree was referred to positively more often than any other issue.[24] Others, such as Jim Wilson, are not so sure: they think that it may have cost him as much as it gained him, and Trimble certainly said as much in his first interview with the *Portadown Times* after his victory.[25] Gordon Lucy, one of Trimble's closest aides in the contest, attributes his victory to a wider range of causes, though he does not doubt Drumcree's importance. He notes that Trimble had built up a profile well before that. Such sentiments were expressed to Ruth Dudley Edwards during her visit that summer to Aughnacloy, Co. Tyrone for 'Black Saturday' (the last Saturday in August, when the Royal Black Preceptory hold their most important procession). Clogher Valley Blackmen told her that Molyneaux's successor should be higher profile and more combative. 'We've been too stiff-necked and proud to explain ourselves,' said one. 'We've got to change.'[26] They also wanted someone who would resist the pan-nationalist juggernaut and not be taken in by the British Government (hence Trimble's pledge never to go into No. 10 alone). Finally, the hated media had made John Taylor the favourite. 'There may have been an element of pig-headedness in voting for Trimble,' noted one UUC member. 'Delegates wanted to buck the trend.' In a group as 'thran' as the Ulster Unionist grassroots, that cannot be discounted. Indeed, it was an utterly paradoxical victory: here was Trimble, an untelegenic figure with crooked teeth (who stormed out of studios and distrusted the local media hugely), running as the improbable herald of almost Mandelsonian modernisation. Yes, he was articulate, but his TV performances were often larded with obscure references to the arcana of the talks process – and were scarcely populistic either in content or delivery. Thus, a vote for Trimble was, paradoxically, a vote both for change and for cussed defiance of Ulster's many enemies.

The reaction in portions of the Irish media would doubtless have vindicated the UUC grassroots in their choice – if, that is, any of them read southern newspapers. Dick Grogan, then Northern Editor of the *Irish Times*, stated that 'he clearly regards compromise as a surrender, and that bodes ill for all-party talks ... His quick temper and truculent manner will indeed bring a drastic change of image to the party leadership and align it more closely to the manner of political conduct favoured by the DUP.'[27] But Trimble's allies in the media were delighted. Ruth Dudley Edwards, writing an open letter to Trimble in the Dublin *Sunday Independent* on 17 September 1995, advised him to 'learn from your enemies: Sinn Fein has much to teach you. First, its leaders have had the humility and good sense to learn painstakingly how to present themselves. We may laugh at their Armani suits, we may sneer about their use of image consultants but the fact remains that they leaped straight from enforced media silence to a mastery of the media. So please do what every other political party does and have your spokesmen take basic courses in television technique. And persuade them that it is not un-Protestant to smile or demonstrate that sense of humour they exhibit in private . . . one last tip: if the UUP is intent on modernising itself, isn't it time it invested in an answering machine for your Glengall Street headquarters?': one such device was soon acquired, and Trimble himself bought a mobile telephone. Significantly, she counselled Trimble against forming a pan-unionist front with the DUP, and urged him to surround himself not with 'hardline friends' but with liberals such as Ken Maginnis and Reg Empey; this, of course, is exactly what happened and may well be what Trimble wanted to happen all along anyhow (though it remains open to question how much influence she exerted towards that end). *The Daily Telegraph* also stated that despite his uncompromising line on decommissioning, 'it would be wrong to conclude that his election necessarily represents a setback for the peace process . . . a strong Unionist voice is badly needed to redress the imbalance that has been allowed to develop within the peace process'.[28] But it was not only instinctive Unionists who were pleased: Andrew Marr in his *Independent* column correctly predicted that despite the images of Drumcree, 'the great Crustacean is shedding its shell. David Trimble's election as leader of the UUP is only the first stage in what is likely to be a dramatic reshaping of Unionist politics . . . he is something rather new, a modernising but utterly committed Ulster Unionist. To bien pensant opinion that probably sounds about as likely as finding a vegetarian head hunter or a druid with a PhD. But it is real and fascinating and of great importance . . . I think he will be difficult, and sharp, and unfamiliar, and it is clear that these are exceptionally dangerous and sensitive times. But it seems a little odd to go on for years about stupid Unionists and then panic when you get a clever one. That's part of the lesson of the past twelve months. This man has a conscience and a fast mind. And for the time being he is the future of Northern

Ireland.' Unsurprisingly, Marr was in regular contact in this period with No. 10, the NIO – and with Trimble's friend, Ruth Dudley Edwards.[29]

Handling the press was, appropriately enough, Trimble's first task after his victory. He held a one-and-a-half-hour press conference at Glengall Street the following morning. Trimble immediately acceded to this idea. But, as ever, Trimble's approach was more complex than his pronouncements suggested. For although the new UUP leader understood the importance of the media better than anyone, his personal engagement with the press was much less 'proactive' than his election manifesto suggested: often, it had to be laid out on a plate for him. If rung by any journalist, he would certainly give very generously and courteously of his time. But as Matthew d'Ancona observes, Trimble never went out of his way to cultivate or even to contact somone as sympathetic as himself – an approach which d'Ancona characterises as 'light years removed from the attitude of a New Labour Cabinet minister'.[30] Charles Moore, erstwhile editor of *The Daily Telegraph*, and Michael Gove, assistant editor of *The Times*, likewise confirm that unless they contact Trimble, they would never hear from him from one year to the next; and although he is a long-time subscriber to *The Spectator*, Trimble never made much effort to contact successive editors. Nor did any of these mainland outlets receive many press releases from the UUP: their support for Unionism predated his arrival on the scene and subsequently owed little to Trimble's own actions. Indeed, Trimble came to know key figures in the London print media in the early to mid-1990s largely through the agency of David Burnside, who wanted to build up Trimble as a putative deputy to John Taylor, in preparation for the post-Molyneaux era. Having come to know the London quality press, Trimble enjoys their company and values their good opinion. But to woo them would, in his world-view, have smacked too much of 'brown-nosing'. In that sense, he started out as the most unconventional of British political leaders – and remains such to this day.

TWELVE

The Establishment takes stock

AS Trimble and his supporters celebrated their victory, members of the British-Irish Association were enjoying their post-prandials in the very different surroundings of St John's College Cambridge. Most of those who attended this annual conference of the great and the good fully expected that the winner would be the pragmatic John Taylor or perhaps even the liberal Ken Maginnis. But when Frank Millar, now the London editor of the *Irish Times*, conveyed the news in the bar, there was a general sense of horror.[1] Many of the guests would have shared Marigold Johnson's distaste for 'that ghastly man Trimble'; now, they feared that the far right had taken over the UUP and that the victor of Drumcree would end the 'peace process'.[2] (She would later come to change her opinion of him for the better and believed he was the best choice of leader for that time.) The British and Irish states, though, could not afford such self-indulgence. Now, they had to work with him. Yes, there was apprehension – as always occurred with any 'changing of the guard' in the remarkably stable Northern Ireland party system. Indeed, one minister was reported as saying that 'I choked on my Frosties' when he read in a *Times* editorial that the newly elected UUP leader was a 'moderate'.[3] The minister in question was Michael Ancram, who now claims that he did so out of surprise rather than disgust.[4]

But when all was said and done, the British state's private audit of Trimble's election was more finely balanced than is commonly supposed. According to John Bruton's contemporaneous note of a conversation with the British Prime Minister on 23 September 1995, 'Major said David Trimble was a prickly man, into detail, not grand conceptions. Don't reject his ideas too quickly . . .' Woodrow Wyatt's diary for 17 September 1995 records the British Prime Minister as observing that 'there was nothing to worry about because he's a clear thinker but it shows the IRA and Sinn Fein that he's a tough customer. He said "He's a lawyer and a very good one and, being on the right wing of the Ulster Unionists, he'll be able to make them agree to things which his predecessor couldn't."[5] Likewise, Major's Assistant Political Secretary, George Bridges, who was with his chief when news of Trimble's victory came through, says that Major was not at all displeased.[6] In so far as they were worried, the British Government's main worry, says Patrick Mayhew, was Trimble's weakness.[7] They believed that he had won the election without the public support of a single MP, and amongst constituency chairmen only enjoyed the backing of his own in Upper Bann. For the last thing that the NIO mandarins wanted on their hands was 'another Faulkner'. They wanted someone who could deliver the party, and it did not matter that much to them who that person was. A secondary worry was Trimble's volatility, for he was seen as driven more by his temperament than his intellect (considerable as they conceded it was). But on the positive side of the ledger, as they saw it, was Trimble's ambition. No. 10 was not sure where this ambition would lead. Some thought that Trimble wanted to be a Law Officer in a Conservative Government, but Mayhew was convinced that Trimble wanted to be Prime Minister of a devolved Northern Ireland (all of which Trimble says was then untrue).[8] In this respect, Trimble was an improvement on the gentlemanly Molyneaux, who was too old for the position and who would not in any case have wanted it on grounds of integrationist principle. But there were also officials such as Peter Bell – the joint head of the Anglo-Irish Secretariat at Maryfield – who argued it was vital that the UUP be led by someone with intellectual self-confidence, rather than someone who would assume that any negotiation was bound to be disadvantageous to the Unionist cause. Elements of the system thus saw Trimble as much the most 'modern' of the Unionist MPs, along with Peter Robinson (on such occasions as the DUP deputy leader could escape from Dr Paisley's shadow).[9]

These calculations, though, did not necessitate any fundamental reappraisal of the grand strategy of the British state. The officials had a long-held view of where a 'balanced' settlement between the two traditions lay. Trimble's election did, though, affect the state's tactics, most obviously towards the new Unionist leader himself. The NIO immediately contacted Rod Lyne, the Prime Minister's Private Secretary for foreign affairs: they then began a pincer movement. It was reckoned that Trimble was open to flattery by No. 10 – few would be exempt from it, especially from a minor party at Westminster – and made sure to advertise that there was an open door to him whenever he needed it. Indeed, on one morning shortly after his election, Trimble spent three hours at No. 10 talking to Lyne, who provided him with further reassurance about the British Government's intentions towards Northern Ireland: after the Molyneaux years, when the then leader kept the key details of discussions with Government very much to himself, Trimble found that the conversation made him more comfortable about state policy.[10] This process of cultivation took place on many levels: Daphne Trimble remembers that at Major's behest, Lyne gave the whole family a tour of No. 10, including the Cabinet Room, during the Christmas break.[11] Meanwhile, Sir John Kerr, who had just taken up his position as British ambassador to the United States, wrote to Trimble suggesting that he come to America as soon as possible to meet with senior administration officials.[12] Andrew Hunter, MP, the chairman of the Conservative backbench Northern Ireland Committee was asked twice by Mayhew for an assessment of Trimble's personality and was then told to maximise his contact with the UUP leader. Later, his instructions became more explicit still: on 22 May 1996, Hunter noted following a meeting with Major that 'we have a chance of winning the election if we can hang on until May next year. You can help us. Do everything you can to keep the Unionists happy.' (Discussing the AIA, Major also told Hunter that 'I'd like to tear it up . . . Margaret got it wrong . . . the government assured the UUP that there was nothing going on. All along Margaret was planning it.') Trimble immediately grasped what was going on here and became defensive, thus making it very hard for Hunter to report back to Government ministers. 'He didn't know if I was a spy or a friend,' says Hunter. 'He knew that I was playing two roles and that I was partly a spy for the Government.' Because of his status, Hunter was also regarded as being partly on 'the team' and frequently cleared his pronouncements with No. 10. Hunter now says that he is 'ashamed' to have been a conduit for so much Government 'spin' to the Unionists: this sense of guilt partly explains why he campaigned for a 'No' vote during the 1998 referendum on the Belfast Agreement.[13] It was the start of a journey which would ultimately take Hunter into the DUP.

The reason for the British state's curiosity was that Trimble had immediately begun an almost Gorbachevian whirligig of activity. This was not so much antithetical to their interests as it was unpredictable.

For if he had a detailed game plan, he certainly shared it with very few people, though the broad outlines – scrapping the AIA, regaining a measure of local control through devolved institutions, and ending the marginalisation of Unionism – were well enough understood. The frenetic round of meetings had been implicit in his Ulster Hall election speech, where he pledged to go anywhere, anytime to promote the Unionist cause (the only exception turned out to be the Forum on Peace and Reconciliation in Dublin, which he declined to attend on the grounds that it was a 'nationalist body').[14] His priority, as he saw it, was to free Unionism from ideological taboos which restricted its freedom of manoeuvre – such as the terms on which Unionist leaders could go to Dublin to talk to the Irish Government. The first opportunity to do this presented itself on the Monday following his election. Notwithstanding his unhappiness over Trimble's election, one of the UUP's best-known left-wingers, Chris McGimpsey, contacted Glengall Street with some important information. His fellow progressive, Proinsias de Rossa, the Irish Social Welfare Minister, was in town for one of his regular meetings with his colleagues in Democratic Left. Would a meeting be possible?[15]

This suggestion was, in the Northern Irish context, less improbable than it might at first glance appear. Democratic Left had emerged from the split in the old Workers' Party, once the political wing of the Official IRA. These previously pro-Moscow Marxists were arguably the most anti-nationalist political force on both sides of the border and had been deadly rivals of the Provisionals (who had split from them in 1970–1). Many of them regarded the Provisionals as fascists, and the Provisionals reciprocated their loathing, accusing the 'Stickies' (as the Officials were nicknamed) of betrayal of national ideals. Prior to embracing constitutional politics, de Rossa himself had been a republican activist: in May 1957, he was arrested at Glencree in the Wicklow mountains, was remanded and then sentenced to two months' imprisonment for declining to account to the Gardai for his movements – a crime under the Offences Against the State Act. Whilst in Mountjoy jail, the southern Government introduced internment against the IRA, which had begun an unsuccessful border campaign that lasted until 1962. De Rossa was thus kept inside – only this time at the camp run by the Irish Army at the Curragh, Co. Kildare, where he remained until February 1959. But now, he was one of three party leaders in the 'Rainbow Coalition' and a member of the Irish Cabinet's Northern Ireland Committee. John Bruton, the Fine Gael

Taioseach – who was more instinctively hostile to the most atavistic forms of nationalism than almost any other holder of that post – felt closer to de Rossa on northern questions than any other member of his Government. Indeed, a poll of UUP delegates conducted at the party's annual conference by Liam Clarke of *The Sunday Times* showed that de Rossa was the Irish politician most trusted by Ulster Unionists – and, as such, way ahead of John Bruton, Dick Spring and John Hume. No doubt this was because of his anti-Provisional credentials.[16]

When Trimble learned that de Rossa was visiting Belfast, he immediately invited him to visit UUP headquarters: had any other Irish Cabinet minister been visiting he would not have moved as he did. Above all, this particular encounter had the virtue of sending out the signal that Unionists would talk to those who had genuinely embraced constitutionalism – whilst simultaneously annoying the Provisionals.[17] Its significance was largely symbolic and little of substance was discussed: for his part, de Rossa recalls that 'I wanted to knock for six the notion that David Trimble was an obstacle to peace. Ruth Dudley Edwards, who knew him socially had said as much and she was influential in this regard. I got some hassle over it, though Democratic Left loved it.' De Rossa remembers that throughout the 30-minute meeting, Trimble displayed a nervous exuberance. But he was left with the distinct impression that the UUP leader was willing to talk to all political leaders in the Republic, including the Taoiseach.[18] Whether or not the meeting seriously annoyed the Provisionals, it certainly set alarm bells ringing at the Department of Foreign Affairs in Dublin. Fergus Finlay recalls that it was interpreted as an attempt to create a 'back-channel' to the Taoiseach at the expense of the Foreign Minister and Tanaiste, Dick Spring: Unionists saw Spring and his department as far more hostile to their interests than John Bruton.[19] Shortly thereafter, Trimble also stated that 'some unionists at the moment would have difficulty envisaging Gerry Adams coming to Glengall Street, but that's because they see Adams as he is today. But if we have a situation where people have proved a commitment to exclusively peaceful methods and have shown that they abide by the democratic process, that will put them in the same position as Proinsias de Rossa is today.'[20]

The unhappiness of elements of the Irish Government over the meeting with de Rossa was one thing; a discontented UUP parliamentary caucus was quite another. It was not so much the substance of such exercises in free-thinking which vexed them: after all, as Trimble never tired of pointing out, Martin Smyth had been the first MP to declare that Unionists might have to talk to Sinn Fein, subject to a surrender of weapons.[21] What really annoyed them was the manner in which the meeting took place. Trimble had met with de Rossa before he had met with his colleagues. Indeed, he did not meet the Westminster MPs for weeks afterwards – either collectively or one-on-one. Partly, it was his own personality. It was not his style to dabble in the little touches in man-management at which Molyneaux excelled, such as solicitous inquiries after wives and children. Indeed, Trimble says that he knew he had serious problems with his fellow MPs, but that it did not occur to him to meet with them until Parliament resumed in the following month. Ken Maginnis – who became one of Trimble's strongest supporters – still thinks it was a cardinal error of judgment which has damaged him to this day.[22] Trimble, though, believes that levels of resentment were such that he doubts it would have made very much difference.[23] Certainly, in the case of William Ross, the gulf between the two men was probably so enormous as to be unbridgeable. Ross, a magnificently 'thran' sheep farmer from the Roe Valley near Dungiven, finished his elementary education at the age of fourteen and is very much out of the 'School of Life' Brigade; he would soon emerge as Trimble's most forthright critic in the Westminster team. Ross regarded Trimble as a clever butterfly who moved from one group to the next – from Vanguard to the UUP to the Union Group to the Ulster Clubs and finally on to the Ulster Society. Although no fool, Ross's conservatism was of the heart, not of the mind. This proved to be the essence of his differences with Trimble. He felt that Trimble had no gut understanding of the malignancy of republicans because he came from the most English part of Co. Down, where there was a tiny and largely quiescent nationalist population. By contrast, Ross's native Dungiven, which was one-third Protestant when he grew up, was now almost completely Catholic and the local IRA units were much in evidence. Talk of a balanced accommodation, Ross believed, was all very well – unless you were on the receiving end of ethnic cleansing.[24]

The member of the parliamentary party with whom Trimble then felt more comfortable was his closest rival for the leadership – John Taylor. The two men had an older brother–younger brother relationship since Vanguard days: Taylor, first elected to Stormont in 1965, was then the longest-serving elected representative in Northern Ireland.[25] But for all their compatibility, Taylor was also the only Unionist who could conceivably threaten his leadership. A role had, therefore, to be found for him. But of what kind? Trimble rang Taylor from his Lurgan office and asked to come to the latter's home near Armagh. He knew that if Taylor had won, the older man would have appointed him as chief whip. But to have done the same for Taylor would have been beneath Taylor's dignity. On the drive down, a solution occurred to him. He remembered that the parliamentary party was not governed by UUC rules. Harold McCusker had been elevated to the deputy leadership of the Unionist caucus in the 1982–6 Prior Assembly. Armed with this precedent, Trimble made his offer to Taylor. The Strangford MP duly accepted, though Trimble acknowledges that this action, too, inflamed some in the parliamentary party.[26] But it was worth it: they could not decide Trimble's fate, whereas Taylor, with his 333 third-round votes, easily could. Indeed, as Reg Empey recalls, 'Trimble needed Taylor more than Taylor needed Trimble'.[27]

The move had been foreshadowed earlier in the month when Trimble took Taylor with him for his first meeting with John Major at No. 10: he was determined to tie him into his policy. The reluctance to go alone to see the Prime Minister was, says Trimble, a reflection of his own weakness. As a token of his esteem, Major greeted Trimble on the doorstep of No. 10 (the meeting, which began at 10:30 a.m., ran well over time, and ensured that Trimble had to run frantically across Whitehall for his 12:00 noon appointment with Tony Blair, the leader of the Opposition, at the Commons).[28] The encounter at No. 10 was dominated by one subject, which in the words of Sir John Chilcot 'lay there at the heart of the process like a coiled snake: decommissioning'.[29] Trimble remembers that Major rounded on him for letting down the Government by holding too soft a position on decommissioning. If so, it was an acute reading of Trimble's remarks at his first press conference at Glengall Street. He demanded that both the Irish and British Governments stick to their original interpretation of paragraph 10 of the Downing Street Declaration, which demanded the establishment of a commitment to exclusively peaceful methods. In subsequent interviews, Trimble appeared to harden the UUP postion by requiring the disbandment of paramilitary groupings, as well as decommissioning. But amidst this smokescreen, Trimble was sending other signals, which would have eluded most ordinary Unionist supporters. For Trimble also hinted that this commitment could be shown in a variety of different ways. The point was underlined by the interview he gave to the *Belfast Telegraph* the day after his election, where it was revealed that senior Ulster Unionists (that is, himself) were considering proposals for a new assembly that could help end the deadlock over decommissioning and all-party talks.[30]

It was an early illustration of how carefully Trimble used language. As Dick Grogan correctly observed, 'Mr Trimble [though] is not averse to the use of nuance when it suits, and his avowed precision is a tactical weapon carefully employed only within certain closely cordoned areas where he chooses to engage and damage his enemy ... but he would not, or could not, specify or even speculate on – the nature or quantity of evidence he will require in order to be satisfied that these sweeping conditions have been met.'[31] Major's annoyance was, however, understandable. The Government had sought, through decommissioning, to supply reassurance to the nine Ulster Unionists and Conservative back-benchers that Sinn Fein/IRA would not be brought into constitutional politics without proper 'sanitisation'. The Government had, therefore, paid a price for supplying such reassurance in the shape of 'Washington III' – Mayhew's demand of 7 March 1995 that the IRA start decommissioning prior to entry into all-party talks as a confidence-building measure. That led to tensions with nationalist Ireland and to some degree with the United States. And now, here was a 'hardline' UUP leader quietly pulling the rug from under their feet.

In the longer run, the British Government had reason to be grateful to Trimble. For he thus afforded them the space to resile from Washington III. Not that anyone thought the Government's stance to be immutable, if they could find a way off the hook (which may partly explain why Trimble chose to pre-empt them by implictly waiving the Washington III criterion, and in exchange cashing in other gains that he thought were of greater long-term value). Indeed, Trimble recalls that whilst he and his fellow party leaders assembled in the first-floor waiting room at the Foreign Office for his first Remembrance Day ceremony at the Cenotaph, he was approached by Blair and Paddy Ashdown: was Major really committed, they asked, to decommissioning? If so, they would support him as part of the new tri-partisan consensus. Trimble confirmed that Major was committed. Blair again stated that he was prepared to support Major on the weapons issue, but said that he thought it was the wrong issue: he preferred to fight on the consent principle. If Trimble staked everything on that, he would have the support of every democrat in the land. What again impressed Trimble was the solidity of Blair's commitment to the consent principle. He did not have the same degree of confidence in the Tories' adherence to it: no Unionist could do so, he long thought, after the AIA of 1985. Indeed, the attitudes which led to that debacle were, in Trimble's view, still there. He appeared to believe that 'imperialistic' attitudes lurk deep in the heart of English Conservatism (*vide* the Frameworks Documents). By contrast, at least Labour – for all its faults such as its powerful Irish nationalist fringe – was a genuine believer in the democratic imperative.[32] But Trimble's distrust of the Conservatives in this period was not just a matter of Tory culture; it was personal as well. Unlike all of the other Unionist MPs, Major had not known Trimble when he served as Northern Ireland Office whip from 1983–5. Trimble certainly enjoyed the ritual of going to Downing Street, yet he felt that Major was such a constructed personality that he was never sure whether he was meeting the real man – nor did he ever quite understand where Major's much-vaunted 'Unionism' came from.[33] Trimble was also disconcerted by Major's habit of starting off meetings by giving an apparently off-the-cuff summary of the current situation at any given moment, but which in fact he contended was a carefully calibrated way of guiding the discussion in a direction that he wanted. Andrew Hunter also recalls that much as he (Hunter) enjoyed going to No. 10, briefings from Major could often become worthless because the PM would repeat back what Hunter said at the last meeting in order to illustrate that he (Major) was basically on the same side.[34]

The failure to establish a truly trusting relationship with Major was all the more surprising because Trimble – like all UUP leaders – would seek to cultivate a 'special relationship' with the Prime Minister of the day. The purpose of this gambit was to circumvent the NIO officials and ministers, whom Unionists alleged were in hock to Dublin's agenda. To some extent this was a delusion (or convenient fig-leaf). Coordination between No. 10 and the NIO was very close and Mayhew and Major enjoyed an excellent personal rapport. Driving a wedge between No. 10 and the NIO became all the more of an imperative for Unionists because the personal relations between Trimble on the one side and Mayhew and Ancram on the other were so bad. Again, in the first instance, this may seem peculiar. Mayhew had been widely criticised by nationalists for the decision not to prosecute on the basis of the findings of the Stalker–Sampson inquiry on the RUC's alleged 'shoot to kill' policy when he served as Attorney General and was also a known sceptic of the way in which the AIA of 1985 had been secretly negotiated.[35] Ancram was a Catholic Scotsman who now sat for an English seat and who frequently touted his Unionist credentials. But whatever credentials either man had enjoyed beforehand, they counted for little with Unionists once in office. For despite his track record, Mayhew says he had made little time as a Law Officer to come to know the Unionist MPs; rather, he made it his particular business to look after the Northern Ireland judiciary.[36] Even his admirers thought, in some ways, this quintessentially viceregal figure was oddly un-political (in contrast, Trimble notes, to the highly political Ancram). 'Paddy was a patrician who saw politics primarily as declarations from above,' says Andrew Hunter, who observed the relationship from close up for some years. 'He never understood the subtleties and innuendoes of pavement politics.'[37]

But Mayhew's difficulties were more personal still. His height (six-foot-five), bearing, voice and family background all counted against him in the eyes of hardline Unionists. Daphne Trimble recalls that 'David was famously public in criticising Mayhew's "grand" accent – which really is something the poor man couldn't help. Maybe it was inexperience in dealing with secretaries of state – not that he liked Mowlam, either.'[38] Andrew Hunter ascribes the deteriorating relationship in part to the petit bourgeois academic lawyer's sense of social and professional inferiority to an eminent silk and scion of the southern Ascendancy (though Trimble says that what he really objected to was Mayhew's exaggerated patrician manner).[39] Mayhew's forebears had come to Co. Cork in the 13th century but as he himself observes, 'families like mine had very few connections with Protestants in the north. Living in the south, Anglo-Irish families tended to think of northern Protestants as denizens of the wild woods; and one of the things I was so grateful for as Secretary of State was coming to know them.'[40] Andrew Hunter, though, feels that Mayhew had little sympathy for Unionists.[41] Sir John Wheeler, who served as Security Minister from 1993–97, also says that 'Mayhew never understood Unionists or the Loyal Orders. Even though he was the first Secretary of State to visit an Orange Lodge [at Comber, Co. Down, in 1995], I don't think that he had that instinctive understanding of how they feared their position within the United Kingdom was being eroded. It took me a little while to understand it but when I did, it enabled me to deal with them.'[42] There was, notes Michael Ancram, a further reason for the mutual antipathy: 'David Trimble was very good at being very, very rude – to both of us. Paddy would sit there afterwards and ask me why did I take it whenever David accused us of being liars or whatever. It was mutual hatred. David's nostrils would flare, his eyes would go very wide and his cheeks very red. Partly, it was histrionics, but partly it was genuine. David was a new type of Unionist who was far more mistrustful of the Conservatives.'[43] Trimble preferred Ancram on a personal basis: 'He was good company and one could even trade insults with him in jocular fashion,' says Trimble. Moreover, he felt that Ancram (the heir to the Marquess of Lothian) had fewer airs and graces than his boss. That said, Trimble never took Ancram's 'Unionism' terribly seriously either and he was intensely suspicious of his key officials in the Political Development Directorate of the NIO – principally Quentin Thomas and Jonathan Stephens.[44]

One minister who kept a close eye on Thomas's activities was Viscount Cranborne, leader of the House of Lords. To Cranborne, Thomas embodied 'the habits of decades of imperial decline. This habit brought about the cast of mind of British officialdom of assuming that the most expedient way of tackling any difficulty is finding the most elegant path of retreat – and most emphatically so in Northern Ireland. Considerations of improving or advancing the interests of your own loyal people are now totally alien to the British official mind, and I suspect have been since the 1920s. As a result, I think they saw David Trimble as yet another little colonial problem to be managed.'[45] Probably no senior Tory has enjoyed so dark a reputation in nationalist Ireland since F.E. Smith, who was loathed for his part in the Home Rule crisis of 1912.[46] Cranborne's Unionist credentials derived partly from the record of his forebears, but also from his own career: when he retired from the Commons, aged 40, in 1987 he cited his disgust with the Anglo-Irish Agreement as one of the reasons. And now, it was alleged, he was placing obstacles in the way of the 'peace process'. He was credited with so much influence that one senior Irish official describes him as having been 'effectively Prime Minister in respect of the affairs of Northern Ireland'.[47]

Yet was Cranborne's reputation justified? And what was his relationship to Trimble? Certainly, Major came to depend on him not merely to manage the peers but also to run his re-election bid after he resigned the Conservative leadership in June 1995. More significantly, Cranborne had asked for, and was rewarded with membership of the Cabinet's Northern Ireland Committee. This body met monthly (or more often, when necessary) in the Cabinet Room. It also included Major, Mayhew, Kenneth Clarke, Michael Heseltine, Ancram, Wheeler, Alistair Goodlad (the Chief Whip). Following Redwood's leadership challenge that June, the balance on that body had marginally tilted away from the Major–Mayhew line because of the resignation of Douglas Hurd. Hurd was a key figure in formulating the Anglo-Irish Agreement and his replacement, Malcolm Rifkind, did not share his enthusiasm for the subject. Mayhew would start the meetings, with Ancram presenting the political picture and Wheeler the intelligence briefing. Cranborne scarcely dominated these gatherings: he would sit at the end of the table in the Cabinet Room so that he could see everybody and would not look pushy. In any case, he notes, these were not occasions for great passionate arguments – confrontation was distinctly 'non-U' – and much was left unsaid.[48] 'Robert's importance was that he knew and was trusted by all Unionists,' says Mayhew. 'After we had a row with the Unionists over the Scott Report [in February 1996, the Ulster Unionists voted against the Government over the inquiry into the arms for Iraq scandal] things were very bad between us. I'm not good at the Realpolitik of reconciliation. But Robert is different. He was very understanding of Trimble.'[49] Yet curiously, Trimble and Cranborne were not personally close. Indeed, Cranborne observes that Trimble would rarely come to see him in this period. Rather, it was Cranborne who sought out Trimble. Cranborne feels that Trimble always saw him out of politeness and says that he has never met a politician who plays his cards closer to his chest than Trimble (the UUP leader retorts, 'What cards do I have?'). Trimble trusted Cranborne as a genuine Unionist, though he feared at times that Cranborne might not always be in the loop or else might be used as a channel for spin.[50] It said much about the British state's successful alienation of Unionist affections that even this relationship was characterised at times by a degree of wariness.

THIRTEEN

Something funny happened on the way to the Forum election

TRIMBLE'S first major speech after assuming the Unionist leadership was to address a reception on the 90th anniversary of the foundation of the UUC. Gordon Lucy was summoned to help and assumed that it would be an historical *tour d'horizon* concerning Unionism past, present and future. He was not merely to be disappointed, but shocked when Trimble informed him that he was thinking of 'bringing in the Provisionals from the cold' ; shortly thereafter, John Hunter was told much the same. Hunter listened and says that he took this to be simply a throw-away remark. Trimble says that he did not quite say this: he was just trying to urge his party 'not to display the usual stock hostility to [republicans] and all their works'. Whatever the actual content or significance of the remark, Trimble's line of thinking ultimately led to a series of breaches between both men and the UUP leader.[1] Trimble's chosen first step for accomplishing the task of weaning the republicans off violence was an elected forum. On the night of the address, at the Balmoral conference centre in south Belfast, Trimble reiterated his public position on decommissioning. Then, he added: 'It could be that both these matters could be resolved in the one way. Sinn Fein could obtain a democratic mandate and show a commitment to the democratic process if there were elections, say, to a new Assembly. By standing, taking their seats and contributing to the debate they could show whether they are committed to the democratic process and the principle of consent. In such elections it would be very interesting to see what support Sinn Fein actually has. If they took their seats we would recognise their position and could debate with them across the floor and thus talk to them at a time when they have not fulfilled all the requirements of the Declaration and thus be unable to move into formal inter-party talks. An Assembly could bridge that gap until they do meet the requirements of the [Downing Street] Declaration.'[2] The address was classic Trimble and it pointed up the complexity of Trimble's actions. For although he disclaimed any intention to recreate Stormont, Trimble saw merit in facilitating dialogue with Sinn Fein in an inherently partitionist body. If they did so, all well and good; but, if not, then their refusal to accept Northern Ireland as the relevant political unit (and thus the consent principle) would be apparent to all. It would stop the obsessive concentration on decommissioning. But Trimble also thought that such a forum could provide a training ground for the younger Unionist cadres whose aspirations were stymied by the current political arrangements. Local government was so powerless as to offer little to any rising stars; and members of the ageing parliamentary party at Westminster showed scant inclination to retire.[3]

Trimble recalls that the speech caused excitement in No. 10: Downing Street was looking for flexibility and his speech afforded them the necessary space to 'get off the prior decommissioning hook'. But the reaction elsewhere was less favourable. William Ross, who was listening with his wife Christine, was shocked. 'Did he say what I think he said?' she inquired. 'And where does this leave us?' 'In one bloody awful hole,' replied the East Londonderry MP with customary candour.[4] From the other side of the divide, the SDLP – which would be critical to the success of any such venture – was scathing. Thus, Mark Durkan mocked the illogicality of Trimble's willingness to engage with Sinn Fein in an assembly but refusal to hold all-party talks without decommissioning.[5] Many felt that the reason for SDLP hostility to the Trimble plan was that the party feared it would do badly in any contest with Sinn Fein, which had been legitimated by the 'peace process' and which was a much younger and more dynamic party. Significantly, though, the plan was not dismissed out of hand by the Taoiseach, John Bruton.[6] The emerging relationship between Trimble and the Irish state would be critical to the UUP leader's willingness to engage in the talks and ultimately to sign the Belfast Agreement. It was to be a tortuous and sometimes tempestuous process – on both sides – and its beginnings were inauspicious. Fergus Finlay, Dick Spring's adviser, recalls that when Trimble was elected leader, the Department of Foreign Affairs in Dublin (known as 'DFA') feared that the relationships forged with liberal Unionists in the early 1990s – with figures such as Ken Maginnis and the McGimpsey brothers – counted for nothing. It was assumed that those whom the Irish knew best would now be marginalised. Moreover, states Finlay, 'he was a total stranger to us. All we knew was stuff we didn't like, which everyone knew, like Drumcree. But no one had ever had lunch with him, or really encountered him on a prolonged basis.'[7] Finlay was not entirely correct: Sean O hUiginn, the head of the Anglo-Irish Affairs division at the DFA had first met Trimble almost 20 years before in the post-Vanguard period. O hUiginn had huge reservations about the conduct of Trimble at Drumcree, but also found in his election intriguing parallels with the rise of Daniel O'Connell, the leading campaigner for Catholic emancipation of the early 19th century. O hUiginn noticed that as with O'Connell, Unionists laid huge stress on how 'articulate' Trimble was: the classic response of a grouping which feels itself to be voiceless (the analogy held up in another way, too, since both men could be very splenetic!).[8]

Trimble still saw the Republic as a political, if not a cultural enemy.[9] In the early 1970s, he thought that 'the Republic was very close to waging proxy war against us. The role of the Irish Government in creating the Provisional IRA was the turning of blind eyes. Things changed under [the government of Liam] Cosgrave in 1974–5 and as far as the Irish public was concerned. Northern Ireland had gone off the boil and they were anxious to have things settled. The Irish state was then wholly sectarian. Changes had started with Vatican II but they were taking a long time to work their way through Irish society. Only in the last decade – partly under the influence of the divorce referendum, and the exposure of the paedophile priests – has social life ceased to be controlled by the [Catholic] Church. And then, of course, there was the embattled, declining southern Protestant community. I remember attending one Apprentice Boys of Derry function in the late 1980s at Raphoe, Co. Donegal, and them telling me "don't end up in the same hole as us".'[10] Subsequently, though, in his UUP annual conference speech at Portrush, Co. Antrim, on 21 October 1995, Trimble approvingly quoted John Whyte as stating that the Republic was not merely a poorer society, but also a more unequal one on account of its retrograde housing and education policies.[11] In fact, much of Trimble's analysis of the southern economy and society was already out of date. He tended to underrate the rise of the 'Celtic Tiger' as a source of self-confidence to nationalists on both sides of the border, making the price which they would ask for any deal all the higher.

Such was the baggage which Trimble carried on his first visit to Dublin as leader of the UUP. There was still a degree of reticence on the Unionist

Sgt George David Trimble,
Royal Irish Constabulary and
Royal Ulster Constabulary,
Trimble's paternal grandfather.

Ivy and Billy Trimble, on
the seafront at Ballyholme,
Co. Down, in the mid-1950s.

The young Trimbles. Left to
right: Rosemary (sister),
Billy Trimble (father) with
Iain (brother) on his
knee, and David.

825 Squadron, Air Training Corps, based in Bangor, Co. Down. David Trimble is in the back row, second from the right. Leslie Cree, who introduced Trimble into the Orange Order, is sitting in the front row, second from the right.

David Trimble, second from the right, at play with some of his peers in the Air Training Corps.

William Craig, Trimble's friend and mentor, at a rally at Stormont in 1972.

The Vanguard Convention candidates, 1975: William Craig is in the front, in the middle; Reg Empey to his left. Ernest Baird, later a staunch foe of the 1998 Belfast Agreement, is standing at Empey's left shoulder. Trimble is directly behind Craig.

The Queen's University Law Lecturer in the mid-1970s.

IN MEMORY OF
EDGAR SAMUEL DAVID GRAHAM
ASSEMBLY MEMBER FOR BELFAST SOUTH 1982-83
SHOT BY TERRORISTS ON 7 DECEMBER 1983

"KEEP ALIVE THE LIGHT OF JUSTICE"

A lost leader of Ulster Unionism: Edgar Graham,
Trimble's colleague in the Queen's Law Faculty.

Civil disobedience in action, A.P. Herbert-style: Trimble protests the Anglo-Irish Agreement in Lisburn, 1986, by handing in a giant cheque for his rates bill.

Two academics in politics: David Trimble and Mo Mowlam meet for the first time at the British-Irish Association, 1989.

Trimble vaults into the international consciousness: the walk with Ian Paisley down Carleton Street, Portadown, after the Orangemen's victory at the first 'Siege of Drumcree' in July 1995. Nationalists accused Trimble of 'dancing a jig down the Garvaghy Road', thus humiliating local Catholic residents.

The moment of victory: Trimble is elected UUP leader in the Ulster Hall on 8 September 1995.

The Cold War thaws on the island of Ireland: Trimble greets the former republican internee, Proinsias de Rossa – now Irish Social Welfare Minister – at UUP headquarters in September 1995. Reg Empey of the UUP is in the middle.

Early days: Trimble leaves No 10 with John Hunter (left) and Jeffrey Donaldson (right) after meeting with John Major in 1996. Both men would later break with him.

side about accepting this kind of invitation. Molyneaux had gone to Dublin Castle in 1992 as part of the Strand II segment of multilateral talks, but had not gone to bilaterals with the Irish at Government Buildings, where the Taoiseach's office is located. Indeed, not since Terence O'Neill's meetings with the then Taoiseach, Sean Lemass, at the Mansion House in 1965, and with his successor, Jack Lynch, at Iveagh House in January 1968, had a UUP chief gone south for this sort of exchange. Again, Trimble's purpose in so doing was to kill such taboos once and for all.[12] He wanted to do so at this particular point when he was under relatively little pressure, rather than be forced to abandon this stance under duress during a crisis in the talks. But Trimble also wanted to make another point. He wanted to be seen to be meeting first with the Taoiseach rather than Dick Spring, whose department had day-to-day responsibility for Northern Ireland. Such a meeting also contained the implicit message that Trimble was the potential Prime Minister-in-waiting of Northern Ireland, the two men dealing as equals.

After breakfasting at John Taylor's house near Armagh, the Unionist team crossed the border. Their first task was to launch a book at the Mansion House written by two Unionist policy analysts, Esmond Birnie and Paddy Roche, entitled *An Economics Lesson for Irish Nationalists and Republicans*, which charged that a united Ireland made no economic sense and that the Republic in any case could not afford reintegration of the national territory. Under the gaze of Daniel O'Connell – whose portrait hangs in the Mansion House – Trimble signed the visitors' book and wrote his address as 'Lisburn, Co. Antrim, UK'. At the reception, afterwards, which was attended by de Rossa and the new leader of Fianna Fail, Bertie Ahern, Trimble signed copies of the book. The reception had another significance in the longer run. For it was at this event that Trimble first met Eoghan Harris, the *Sunday Times* columnist, former Workers' Party political strategist, and scriptwriter for the television series *Sharpe*. Harris describes himself as 'a sort of Andrew Neil without the charm, a sort of Peter Mandelson without a party', and had guided both de Rossa and Mary Robinson to their respective triumphs in the European election of 1989 and the presidential election of 1990.[13] Harris was spotted in close conversation with the UUP leader, causing one journalist to remark, 'he's probably looking for an advice contract. They must be the only political party who he hasn't advised.' 'Who said he hasn't?' responded another. The reporter's hunch was prophetic.[14]

The encounter with Bruton was in and of itself relatively unmemorable. Trimble stated his belief that all-party talks could not possibly begin by the end of 1995 because of Sinn Fein/IRA's intransigent stance on the weapons issue. Bruton found Trimble to be not particularly *au fait* with the nuances of southern politics, but he noted that the UUP leader was prepared to take the chance of finding out more.[15] A new channel of communication was established and regular meetings would be held in future. The media reaction was mostly positive: *The Times* of London speculated that Gerry Adams had met his match.[16] Mary Holland of the *Irish Times* was impressed by Trimble's boldness and reckoned that because of Drumcree he now had a stock of political capital to persuade his own community that the structures of government in Northern Ireland would never again be based upon majoritarian principles.[17]

Holland also restated nationalist fears that John Bruton would be seduced by Trimble. But were these justified? Bruton, who was elected as the youngest TD in the Dail for his native Meath in 1969 was not merely the guardian of Fine Gael tradition – the party which founded the state and set up the institutions of law and order. Bruton's own origins lay in the Centre Party, one of the successors to John Redmond's Irish Party which until its final eclipse in the 1918 General Election at the hands of the old Sinn Fein had demanded Home Rule for Ireland within the United Kingdom (a picture of Redmond even hung above Bruton's desk, and he enthusiastically devoured Paul Bew's rehabilitation of Redmondism, *Ideology and the Irish Question*, of which he had been given a leather-bound edition by his officials for his 48th birthday in 1995). One of the sources of Bruton's visceral anti-nationalism was the death of one of his closest friends, Senator Billy Fox. Fox was a Protestant legislator from Co. Monaghan who had been murdered by the Provisionals in 1974 whilst visiting his girlfriend (Bruton recalled the episode to effect in his debate on RTE with Ahern during the 1997 general election: Bruton also was advised by the ubiquitous Eoghan Harris).[18] This episode inevitably informed his dealings with republicans. Bruton declined to give 'sectarian coalitions' public recognition of the kind which Albert Reynolds accorded them, notably the dramatic three-way handshake between that Fianna Fail Taioseach and Hume and Adams on the steps of Government Buildings in Dublin in September 1994.[19]

Whatever Bruton's own views, he was leader of an unlikely agglomeration known as the Rainbow Coalition – comprising Spring's Labour party and de Rossa's Democratic Left. Dick Spring as Minister of Foreign Affairs was much the most important since he ran Northern Ireland policy on a day-to-day basis. Spring came from a staunchly republican family in Tralee, Co. Kerry, and had inherited his seat in the Dail from his father, Dan: Spring *père* had been a staunch supporter of Charlie Kerins, a senior IRA figure executed in Mountjoy jail by the de Valera government in 1944 for murdering a Garda Sergeant.[20] Spring, a former rugby inter-national, saw his own role in the government as a balancing act – not unlike the former West German Foreign Minister, Hans-Dietrich Genscher of the FDP, who switched from supporting the SPD of Helmut Schmidt to the CDU/CSU bloc of Helmut Kohl in 1982. He acted as a restraint on the instincts of the Fianna Fail-led Government of Albert Reynolds (backing the idea of a 'suspension' of the AIA in 1992 to make it easier for Unionists to enter into three-stranded talks); after moving over to a Bruton-led coalition in late 1994, many saw him as rectifying the new Taoiseach's instinctive sympathy for Unionism and keeping republicans on board. The policy of the Irish state was largely settled, so any 'innovations' by Spring were as much about presentation as about substance. Trimble certainly genuinely disliked what he saw as Spring's excessive solicitude for the republicans; but it was also because he felt the excessively 'green' spin which the Tanaiste and DFA officials placed on events made it that much harder for him to nudge the unionist community into accepting the full logic of the three-stranded process.

Trimble was thus enraged when Spring told the UN General Assembly on 27 September 1995 that it was time for the British Government to abandon its insistence on a handover of IRA weapons ahead of all-party talks.[21] And writing in the *Irish Times* on the morning of his first meeting in Dublin, Trimble stated that the British Government was now taking a principled stance on the issue of decommissioning. 'Wobbling out on a limb, however, is the Tanaiste, Mr Dick Spring, who appears to have "gone native" with the zealots in the DFA and is now demanding that the IRA be allowed into all-party talks without the removal of any weapons or a commitment to permanent peace . . .' Trimble's dislike of the DFA was shared by almost all Unionists. An elite corps of over 300 diplomats, the DFA was quite unlike any other foreign ministry in the world. In most countries, foreign ministries are the least nationalistic of government departments. In Ireland, it is the most nationalistic (its foil is the Depart-ment of Finance, whose culture on northern questions is partly informed by a dread of paying for the absorption of Ulster into the Republic).[22] Certainly, Trimble felt that until the Ahern era, 'the DFA's policy was that Ulster is the fourth green field [the term given to the four Provinces of Ireland, only three of which, in the view of nationalists, have been liberated]'. In Trimble's view, they always ran rings around British officials – not because of superior ability, but simply because they were convinced of the rightness of their cause and were comparatively guilt-free. In particular, Trimble disliked the DFA's leading light, Sean O hUiginn, head of the Anglo-Irish division since 1991: he believes that O hUiginn's departure for the United States as Irish ambassador in September 1997 enormously improved the atmosphere in the talks.[23] Whatever the accuracy of Trimble's assessment of O hUiginn's position, the DFA often were able to 'punch above their weight'. They may not have enjoyed the resources of the Foreign and Commonwealth Office, nor of the British intelligence services, but they secured results because, in the words of one Irish minister, 'they are driven by the zeal of the second division side seeking to knock a premier division club out of the cup in a local derby'. Moreover, because the Irish state is small and has relatively few crucial policy objectives compared to the United Kingdom – Northern Ireland, EU budgets and the maintenance of neutrality – its very best servants can specialise in these areas.

It was Trimble's belief that no meaningful dialogue was possible with Spring which made him so reluctant to meet him on a regular basis. This view was widely held in the UUP, and was most memorably expressed by John Taylor who pronounced Spring to be 'the most detested politician in Northern Ireland': Trimble says that once his deputy started the name-calling, he could not very well repudiate him (Nora Owen claims that Trimble always behaved differently when Taylor was present and was much more hardline).[24] In the end, says Fergus Finlay, Spring decided to put up with the abuse for the sake of the peace process. The first bilateral between the two was duly held at Glengall Street in late October 1995. Finlay remembers that it was a surreal occasion, and that Trimble made only one reference to past attacks. 'You and I are men of affairs,' Trimble intoned, 'and you recognise that these are things that have to be said to satisfy one's public.'[25] Indeed so: Trimble needed the bogeyman of Spring to afford cover for his overtures to the south, although his dislike of the Tanaiste was genuine enough. Finlay remembers that Trimble was constantly interrupted by Ken Maginnis and hardly spoke for the rest of the meeting.[26] Finlay reckoned that Trimble was devoting far more time and attention to his position as the leader of Ulster Unionism than to his relations with both the British and Irish Governments. Finlay's problem with Trimble was not so much that the UUP leader had to engage in such posturing, but rather that he was much ruder than he needed to be in order to achieve the desired effect in his own community. In that sense, he was utterly different from the courteous Molyneaux. From Finlay's viewpoint, this was not necessarily bad for the 'peace process'. Molyneaux was exquisitely polite, but impossible to pin down; whereas Trimble could be very discourteous, but was at least 'engaged'.[27]

Given such antipathy, it was scarcely surprising that Trimble should persist in his efforts to cultivate Bruton and to sideline Spring. Trimble sought to work on a back-channel via Paddy Teahon, Secretary-General of the Taoiseach's Department. But the DFA soon got wind of the UUP's attempted approaches and immediately contacted the Taoiseach's Department and any such proposed back-channel of communication was soon terminated.[28] Thereafter, it was all done on a more formal basis. Partly, it was a turf war within the Irish Government, but there was also a genuine fear in the DFA that to give such recognition so soon to the Bruton–Trimble relationship would elevate the UUP leader to such a level as to make him less willing to make concessions to northern nationalists. As they saw it, the full fruits of such summitry should be bestowed after a deal, not beforehand. In any case, they feared an unstructured dialogue when no one was clear as to Trimble's ultimate intentions. Did he, for example, really want to be Prime Minister of a new Northern Ireland (in the sense of being willing to pay a price on Strand II to achieve his Strand I objectives)? For, if not, there was a real danger that Trimble would simply 'pocket' the meeting, return to Northern Ireland and proclaim 'I've confronted the lion in his den' – thus humiliating the Taoiseach in exchange for nothing. Far better, some DFA officials reasoned, slowly to 'sus' him out. In this respect, the state of knowledge amongst the British about Trimble's goals was rather more accurate than their Irish counterparts; many of them were worried by the failure of the southerners and Trimble to forge a satisfactory relationship, which made a settlement that much more remote. Indeed, much as John Bruton tried to reassure Trimble that the Republic was not on for a tribal adventure and sought only stability, the UUP leader never felt that he could risk doing the deal in these circumstances. This was because in his view

Bruton did not fully control his own coalition government's policy towards Northern Ireland and could only intervene from time to time – an impression that was reinforced by Trimble's trips south of the border.[29] If Fine Gael came to an accommodation with the Unionists (which would inevitably include a referendum on the revision of Articles 2 and 3) they would always be vulnerable to accusations from Fianna Fail that they had betrayed the nation. Even though Bruton instinctively wanted no part of the pan-nationalist front, the fact remained that no Taoiseach could shun Sinn Fein/IRA once the 'peace process' had started. 'As Sinn Fein saw it, the pan-nationalist front meant that the Irish Government would act as buffer and conduit for their views rather than behaving with a mind of its own,' says Finlay. 'In their analysis there were only two protagonists of significance in this conflict, themselves and the British.' Finlay recalls that in discussions with the Irish Government, they displayed little interest in the evolution of Unionist politics, such as Trimble's election as leader (a point confirmed by British ministers and officials of the period). Certainly, the traditional republican view of Unionists and Unionism was dismissive. According to this line of reasoning, Loyalism was a mere creation of British imperialism. These local surrogates would disappear once their colonial paymasters in metropolitan Britain faced them down, forcing them into an agonising reappraisal of where their true interests lay. But republicans were coming to a more nuanced, if no less hostile view of their neighbours. Thus, the pseudonymous Hilda Mac Thomas, commenting on Trimble's election as leader in the Sinn Fein newspaper, *An Phoblacht/Republican News* on 14 September 1995, was noticeably free of the sanctimonious and disapproving tone which characterised the reactions of some constitutional nationalists and much of Ulster's chattering classes. Whether or not Trimble forged a pan-unionist front with other loyalist parties, it concluded, 'this does not change the context in which [he] has got to work ... The question is, will Trimble push his party in the same cul-de-sac, or will he be the one to lead them to a new agreement with the people in Ireland. An even more presssing question for him will be that of preventing the fragmentation of the Official Unionist Party [sic], as those unionists who would have adopted a more pragmatic line leave or are edged out.' In retrospect, Hilda Mac Thomas was only really incorrect on the last point, for if anything it has been anti-Agreement Unionists who have been 'purged' (and then without much efficiency).

Hilda Mac Thomas was not the only republican with a nuanced view of Trimble's election. Andrew Hunter met with Mitchel McLaughlin of Sinn Fein at the Clonard Monastery in west Belfast in December 1995. According to Hunter's extensive notes of the discussion – and he told McLaughlin he would be reporting back to the British Government – the Sinn Fein chairman described Trimble as 'a formidable politician, not to be underestimated ... McCartney will eventually succeed Paisley as leader of Unionist hardliners. Trimble is on his guard against this: hence the populist stand which Trimble sometimes adopts.' McLaughlin expressed grave reservations about Trimble's idea of an elective route to negotiations, but he did not rule it out: he opined that one reason why Trimble wanted elections was to demonstrate how derisory was the support for the UDP and PUP, the parties representing the UDA and the UVF. This, McLaughlin said, would destroy the credibility of Gary McMichael, David Ervine and other loyalist politicians whose participation exasperated mainstream Unionists.

Over the longer term, McLaughlin was confident that republicans would obtain what they wanted, which was nothing less than the Frameworks Documents. This was because in his view, 'ordinary Unionist people and the Unionist business community are far more realistic' (this was also the NIO line of the post-ceasefire period). Whilst preferring not to have a Northern assembly under its Strand I proposals – on the ground that it would confer some legitimacy upon the six counties – McLaughlin said that Sinn Fein would accept it in the context of a 'transitional process' if there were sufficient checks and balances to prevent a return to majoritarian Unionist domination. If satisfied on this point, Sinn Fein might tolerate an assembly for a short while as a tactical concession. When Hunter asked him why unionists should cooperate in creating a united Ireland, McLaughlin replied: 'We accept there must be a transitional process but it will be an interim phase on the way to a united Ireland. It will enable unionists to adjust to change. They will grow to accept a united Ireland.' Later, the tone became harsher still. McLaughlin told Hunter that 'the British are spoiling for a fight. If they want one, they can have it.' (McLaughlin's office states this was said in a purely political sense.) But the IRA was already preparing its devastating response to the 'log-jam' in the 'peace process'. Hunter suspected that all was not well. Likewise, Trimble was alarmed by the increasing numbers of punishment beatings and terrorist training and targeting. Thus, at their first meeting after he became UUP leader, on 14 September 1995, when John Hume told him that he felt that the IRA would not go back to violence, Trimble viewed the claim with much scepticism.[30] His fears would soon be terribly vindicated.

FOURTEEN

Go West, young man!

IF David Trimble stands for anything as leader of his party, it is for the modernisation of Ulster Unionism. This is not simply a question, as he often likes to say, of making Unionists 'think politically rather than simply presenting a hard face to the world'. It is also a question of overhauling party organisation and of bringing on energetic young cadres who would become the Unionist First XI of the future. Many thought that this was largely a matter of breaking or reforming the party's traditional links with the Orange Order, but it was more ambitious in scope than that. It took up much of his time in his early months as leader; Conor Cruise O'Brien paid his first visit ever to Glengall Street shortly after Trimble's election and was struck by how absorbed the new leader was in internal party management and with establishing his credentials within the broader Unionist family.[1] Fergus Finlay derived the same impression and concluded that such imperatives would preclude rapid progress in the 'peace process'.[2]

The party which David Trimble took over from Jim Molyneaux was antiquated in its culture and structure. Thus, until the mid-1990s, claims Jim Wilson (the chief executive of the UUP from 1987 to 1998) the party would send out press releases in black taxis to just five obvious outlets, such as the *News Letter*. Then there was the matter of the party's federated structure. Its organisation resembled that of the Tories prior to William Hague's reforms of 1997–8. There was, however, one crucial difference with the Conservatives: whereas the power of Tory associations via the old National Union and Central Council was more apparent than real, the analogous UUP structures were invested with genuine democratic significance. The party was a collection of highly independent local associations and affiliated bodies which came together in something called the Ulster Unionist Council. This met annually, usually in March, to elect the officers and the leader. Crucially, a mere 60 signatures was required to trigger a meeting of the UUC, a rule which was to bedevil Trimble's life in the coming years. The 860-member UUC delegated to the leader and the officers collectively the task of employing the staff of the headquarters organisation. The officers, in turn, were also subject to the scrutiny of the 120-strong party executive, whose job was to make policy in consultation with the leader. Because of local autonomy, there was no common membership list throughout the Province and Glengall Street thus had little idea of the party's total strength. Indeed, in many places the lists were held in exercise books and people would be deemed to be members of the UUP if they donated an apple pie to a Halloween fundraiser.[3] And then there was the vexed issue of the UUP's links with the Orange Order: as well as the obvious individual party members who happened to be Orangemen, the Orange Institution as a whole sent around 120 delegates to the UUC. Those delegates could be appointed by people who were not necessarily members of the UUP; indeed, as Jack Allen observes, as much as two-thirds of the members of some County Lodges could be supporters of the DUP.[4]

Concern about the UUP's organisational obsolescence predated Trimble's election as leader, but little came of it. There was always something else on the agenda in terms of the peace process, and the important invariably yielded pride of place to the urgent. The group of dynamic young hardliners who had pushed Trimble for the leadership were, however, determined to change things. But it is hard to know, even in this area, what Trimble really wanted to do, as opposed to any casual talk of radical reform in which he may have indulged others before 1995. Prior to his victory, says John Hunter, Trimble always wanted a 'clean-out' of Glengall Street and that he spoke derisively of its 'good ole' boy' culture.[5] The 'Young Turks' appear to have been operating on the asssumption that they were ridding the sovereign of his 'turbulent priests'. Denis Rogan, then UUP vice chairman recalls that 'either they were promised or in the campaign thought there would be a gutting of Glengall Street – a whole series of young advisers brought in to drive a new policy'.[6]

A counter-offensive was soon launched by the old guard. James Cooper spoke for many senior party stalwarts – few of whom declared for Trimble in the leadership race – when he opined that Trimble had been elected with too narrow a base from the right wing of the Orange Order (at this point, says Cooper, there were also doubts about Trimble's stability and his willingness to stay the course).[7] But Trimble was for now the leader and they would have to work with him. The question was on whose terms? The Young Turks' or the party establishment's? Jim Nicholson's recollection of the first officers' meeting was that 'it was fairly difficult and edgy. A lot of officers didn't trust what David Trimble would do – an attempt to do a clean sweep of party people who did great service.'[8] Jeffrey Donaldson, an honorary secretary of the party, says that at this first meeting, Trimble was told in no uncertain terms that he was not to conduct any widespread purges.[9] Jack Allen recalls that 'Jim Nicholson would muse that times were changing and that there was now a new regime but it soon became clear that things would go on as before. I told Jim Wilson "David Trimble can't sack you." The leader doesn't really have that power, though he can influence things.'[10] Allen's last remark accords with Trimble's own analysis. Trimble says that he was gravely embarrassed by Hunter's claims of imminent purges, 'none of which I could have done if I'd wanted to'. He notes that Ulster Unionist leaders are in a very weak position vis-à-vis the party organisation compared to Paisley's DUP (which, Trimble believes, operates on a top-down basis, rather than a bottom-up basis). The leader has no capacity to hire and fire the chief executive, which is in the hands of the officers and UUP Executive collectively, of whom the leader is just one. But obviously a leader could, if he was so minded, recommend it.[11]

But why did Trimble not seek to move his colleagues in a more radical direction through persuasion and influence? Partly, because he can be disorganised and often cannot see things through to their conclusion: in that sense, his *déformation professionelle* is as much that of the chaotic, overburdened university lecturer as it is the hyper-legalism of the academic lawyer. There is also a sense in which he is like a butterfly: he often cannot stick to an objective and rapidly moves on to the next, more interesting topic. (Jack Allen recalls that in his frenetic early days as leader, he would not delegate to anyone, to the point of insisting on doing the photo-copying himself. In this sense, he was rather like Molyneaux.)[12] But it is also the case that party reform was less than radical because the UUP establishment grew accustomed to his face – and he grew comfortable with them. Moreover, as he lost his original base of 'Young Turks' because of his compromises with the British Government and with Irish nationalism, he increasingly needed the old guard to push through his policy on the peace process. A complete overhaul of the UUP party risked stirring up a hornets' nest of vested interests, which could imperil his immediate policy objectives. Indeed, Trimble was to discover that he could construct a kind of 'New Unionism' with 'Old *Unionists*'.

But one seemingly minor change in the way that party business was conducted turned out to Trimble's great long-term advantage: shortly after he became chairman in early 1996, Denis Rogan increased the numbers of party executive meetings from four to six per annum, including two on Saturdays. The purpose was to ensure that the party was more thoroughly involved in the decision-making process, a concept which Trimble heartily endorsed.[13] As a result, crucial moments in the 'peace process' were punctuated by these meetings, which ratified their leader's decisions. Would he surmount the extra hurdles at each stage of the emerging deal? It could have turned into a disaster for Trimble, but in fact he turned them to his advantage. First of all, by giving at least the appearance of openness, he sought to scotch the notion that secret deals were being cooked up at No. 10 or elsewhere between the UUP leader and the two Governments. Second, by giving Trimble a chance to speak more often, it played to his strength – mastery of complexities of the talks process, allowing him to 'blind them with science'. Third, by having to account to this increased number of meetings, which could have rejected his policies, Trimble was able to create a sense of crisis. He thus used his weakness to give himself extra bargaining leverage with the Governments, because he had to give the UUP Executive something when they met.

But such innovation was a rare exception. In practice, Trimble has proven reluctant to pay much of a price to achieve party reform. This tendency was illustrated by his reaction to the debate on the link with the Orange Order, at his first party conference as leader. Trimble had never wanted to break the connection entirely, but he did want it substantially modified.[14] Partly, he was motivated by a wish to see the UUP as a voice of new, civic unionism which would attract Catholic members put off by its sectarian tinge. But he also knew that even if such change was accomplished, there would be comparatively few gains amongst the Catholic population. Rather, his real motive was to make the UUP attractive once again to middle-class Protestants who found the connection to the Loyal Orders an embarrassment. Trimble felt that Unionism could ill afford the Protestant middle classes' continuing opt-out from politics – to which he was such a marked exception. At the party conference at

Portrush, Co. Antrim in October 1995, he pitched not only for a common membership but also for reform of the delegate structure. Henceforth, the UUC and the Executive would be composed only of association and branch representatives. In other words, no one would sit on them as representatives of the Orange Order *per se*. Of course, individual Orangemen would still sit on the ruling councils of the party as constituency representatives, and he hoped that this innovation would actually stimulate more of them to participate: many supposed that if the Loyal Orders were formally represented then they need do nothing themselves.[15] But despite the standing ovation which he received for his address, and notwithstanding what the *Orange Standard* called his almost Harold McCusker-like 'cult figure' status amongst the brethren in north Armagh, reforming the link with the Orange Order proved harder to effect in practice.[16] Partly, he did not succeed because of the unexpected. During the debate at Portrush, Drew Nelson pronounced that 'in a sense this party was a child of the Orange Order, but the child has now grown up': much heckling and booing ensued.[17] Trimble believes that Nelson's undiplomatic sally polarised debate and caused it to go off the rails. The officers then had to calm things down and they opted for a compromise resolution calling for a top-level review.[18] It was passed by a two to one margin, but little change has been effected since.[19] Many compared this task to Tony Blair's recasting of his party's relations with the trade unions. In truth, Trimble failed not because of Drew Nelson's candour but because he had not done the necessary preparatory work; for all his admiration of New Labour, he lacked the Blairite zeal and organisational ruthlessness to push such changes through. Later, this would greatly irritate Irish nationalists, who believed that a failure to purge such elements made for perpetual crises in Unionism and condemned Trimble to endless narrow margins within the UUC.

Similar ineptitude characterised Trimble's dealings with the parliamentary party. Shortly after the election, a very senior UUP source told Frank Millar that 'we have five MPs who I wish would just go, announce that they intend to stand down at the next election'. The five named were Ross, Smyth, Cecil Walker (North Belfast), Roy Beggs (East Antrim) and Clifford Forsythe (South Antrim).[20] Trimble says that he knew he had a generational problem: indeed, in early 1996, the *Belfast Telegraph* noted that the combined age of the nine UUP MPs was 560 years, or an average of 62.2 (with Trimble as the youngest at 51). Whilst most Ulster parties tend to be older on average than their mainland counterparts, the UUP's record was then the most gerontophile. Some of the Young Turks were pushing for deselections, notably the Oxford-educated North Belfast councillor, Nelson McCausland, who had targeted Walker. Trimble says that he did nothing to dissuade McCausland, but nor did he help him either (Trimble would later change his view of Walker dramatically for the better).[21] David Brewster, then Treasurer of the East Londonderry Association, says that Trimble's backing helped him to win one of the party's four honorary secretaryships at the 1996 AGM of the UUC. Brewster thinks that Trimble had a reason for this: he told the younger man that if he wanted his support to take over from Ross, he would have it. Brewster had no interest in making such a challenge against Ross, and would subsequently become a leading critic of Trimble in the Union First Group after the signing of the Belfast Agreement and in December 2003 joined the DUP.[22] McCausland's challenge in North Belfast fizzled out, partly because of the endemic factionalism in that association, which as Brewster observes, 'makes Kosovo look simple by comparison'.[23]

Trimble also appeared to flirt with the idea of recreating a pan-unionist front – an idea which resurfaces every time that loyalists feel under threat. The idea was that Unionists would opt out of the process *ad interim*, build up their strength, modernise their structures, and then return to the table stronger and better equipped to repel the advances of their enemies. After Drumcree I, the conditions for such a recoalescence of pro-British forces appeared more auspicious than they had for some time. Certainly, Paisley welcomed Trimble's election as leader and ascribed his success to his identification with a stance closer to that of the DUP. Within ten days of his election, Trimble had met with Paisley at the latter's home in Cyprus Avenue (a street made famous in the Van Morrison song on the album *Astral Weeks*). The two men expressed their unity of purpose on the Union and the Frameworks Documents, but made little further progress.[24] But this *démarche* failed – largely because the UUP feared it would end up co-opted into a Paisleyite front in which it would become the junior partner. The other significant Unionist party leader, Robert McCartney of the UKUP, was soon to develop doubts about Trimble as well. Initially, McCartney had also welcomed Trimble's election as leader, judging him to be the candidate most willing to work with the leaders of the other Unionist parties.[25] A week after the election, Trimble contacted McCartney, who duly invited Trimble to his home, where the two men discussed the future of Unionism. As Trimble was leaving, McCartney said to him: 'David, you are now leader of the largest Unionist party and as such you will not want for advice. There are people in London, Dublin and Washington who will take you to the top of the temple and they will say, "all of this can be yours if you do what you are told". According to McCartney, Trimble simply nodded, smiled and left.[26]

Washington was not so sure whether Trimble was quite so biddable as McCartney feared. Nancy Soderberg says that the US administration knew little about Trimble, apart from what had been observed on the television screens at Drumcree earlier in the year.[27] But for all their doubts, the Clinton administration had to make the effort to see whether the new UUP leader would become 'engaged'.[28] Trimble did so with gusto. For unlike so many of the older generation of Unionist politicians, Trimble carried no anti-American baggage, either culturally or politically – although he disliked the activities of many Irish-Americans and of Nancy Soderberg in particular. Prior to serving as senior staff director for European affairs on the President's National Security Council with specific responsibility for Ireland, Soderberg worked for Senator Edward Kennedy. For this, and above all for her role in helping Gerry Adams obtain a visa over British Government objections in 1994, she became a hate figure amongst Unionists, earning the soubriquet of 'Nancy Sodabread'. Moreover, she forged a close working relationship with Jean Kennedy Smith, the American ambassador in Dublin and a sister of Senator Kennedy, who had out-gunned her counterpart in London, Raymond Seitz, over the Adams visa. But Soderberg and her colleagues also understood that it took 'two sides to tango'. Having 'engaged' with Adams, they would now have to work much harder with Unionists to convince them that they, too, had a stake of sorts in the 'process' and that the United States was not utterly hostile to the interests of the Ulster-British population. They were keen to emphasise their desire to promote a peaceful settlement and did not care that much about the precise terms of the deal. As Nancy Soderberg observes, 'the truth is we were knocking on the unionist door for some time and Trimble was the first one to answer'.[29]

Trimble was indeed the first Ulster Unionist leader of recent times to answer the call on a sustained basis, but the links went further back than Soderberg's remarks suggested. Terence O'Neill as Prime Minister of Northern Ireland sought to make much of Ulster-Scots heritage in his dealings with both the Kennedy and Johnson administrations, and his

Christmas card of December 1964 showed him meeting with LBJ at the White House: on St Patrick's Day of that year, O'Neill had presented the Commander-in-Chief with a book on the Scotch-Irish and banqueting cloths (which delighted the Linen Guild back at home).[30] Charles Reynolds, an Ulsterman living in America, also organised information campaigns on behalf of the pro-Union population following the outbreak of the Troubles, the highlight of which was a highly effective tour by Brian Faulkner in June and July of 1972.[31] And efforts were made at various points in the 1980s by David Burnside, Frank Millar and Harold McCusker. Likewise, Peter Robinson, Gregory Campbell and others undertook activities on behalf of the DUP.[32] However, during the long tenure of James Molyneaux, such activities were not given a notably high priority by the UUP. Towards the very end of Molyneaux's long tenure in office, arrangements were put in place for a UUP North American bureau with offices donated by Tony Culley-Foster, a Washington businessman who grew up in Londonderry. One of his employees, the Scottish-born Anne Smith of McLean, Virginia, was seconded to work for it, officially for one day a week.[33]

Nancy Soderberg acknowledges that the UUP North American bureau did provide some kind of reference point which had not previously existed, and other Administration officials have been courteous enough about Smith's contribution.[34] Nonetheless, Smith was neither from Northern Ireland nor could she be described as a 'heavy-hitting' Washington lobbyist type who 'packed a punch inside the Beltway'. Trimble stuck doggedly by her and refused to entertain any suggestions to have Smith removed. Moreover, this outfit had nothing like the resources of Sinn Fein's North American organisation. It has remained determinedly low-key in the years since then: David Burnside says that he had secured a pledge of $250,000–$300,000 for a full-time professional lobbyist, but the offer was rejected.[35] According to Trimble, Burnside offered a lobbying firm to raise money. But the idea was partly rejected by the UUP officer team on the grounds that it would be embarrassing if the North American office spent more money per annum than Glengall Street. More important, says Trimble, was the point that the money could have come from conservative American sources who wanted it to be used for partisan, anti-Clinton purposes. This was something he was not prepared to countenance, despite the fact that the US Administration was close to a low ebb at this point following the Republicans' takeover of Congress in the 1994 mid-term elections.[36]

Trimble's election also coincided with a change in key personnel amongst British and American officialdom in 1995, notably the appointment of Sir John Kerr as British ambassador to Washington, and that of Blair Hall as Political Counsellor at the US Embassy in London. Both men earned Trimble's admiration and trust, in a way that Soderberg never did: she realised that Unionists had to be brought in, but carried so much baggage by this point that she was unable to do it herself. Kerr and Hall were thus crucial to the task of facilitating the Unionists' admission into the international mainstream. Kerr was a Glaswegian Protestant married to a Catholic of Irish descent: Trimble certainly felt that as a native of the west of Scotland, he had a greater instinctive feel for the problems of Ulster than a more conventional 'Oxbridge type'. Kerr arrived in Washington on the heels of Sir Robin Renwick's devastating rebuff over the Adams visa. The British Embassy was enormously defensive towards Capitol Hill and the media. Kerr determined to reverse this through a variety of measures. In March 1996, Kerr broke with tradition by hosting his own St Patrick's Day party in the Lutyens embassy residence; Dermot Gallagher, the then Irish ambassador retorted that he would throw a St George's Day drinks party to even the score. But there was a serious message behind Kerr's move. Its essence was that Irishness was not the sole preserve of Irish nationalists or of the Irish state.[37]

America need not necessarily have been stony ground for Unionism. As a *News Letter* editorial of 9 November 1995, 'Selling Ulster', put it: 'the Unionist message has never been fully explained on the other side of the Atlantic and this has undoubtedly been to the detriment of a majority population who enjoy a kin relationship with up to 25 million of US citizens, descended from the quarter of a million Ulster-Scots Presbyterians who emigrated to the American frontier 200/250 years ago. Of the 40 million Americans who would claim to have Irish blood in their veins, an estimated 56 per cent come of Ulster Protestant stock. Whilst the knowledge of the political nuances in Northern Ireland may be extremely limited, this section would be broadly susceptible to the unionist argument and the importance of effectively dealing with terrorism conducted by a tiny unrepresentative group of people.' Trimble wholeheartedly agreed with these sentiments. Indeed, according to the American website *Political Graveyard*, no fewer than seven Trimbles have been elected to the US Senate and Congress since the inception of the Republic – mostly from Kentucky and from neighbouring Ohio (the most recently elected

Trimble had, ironically, served in the US House of Representatives as a Democrat from Arkansas from 1945 to 1967). There was even a Trimble County in Kentucky, named for Robert Trimble, who became an Associate Justice of the US Supreme Court and an intimate of the great John Marshall, Chief Justice. His forebears had orginally come from Co. Armagh in the 1740s. And General Isaac Trimble of Virginia – a descendant of a Trimble who emigrated from Co. Antrim in the early 18th century – had led two brigades of Pender's division during Pickett's charge at the Battle of Gettysburg. He was captured by Union forces after the lower third of his leg was amputated near the battlefield.[38]

This was the heritage which, in British eyes, lent Trimble such significance in America. For a long time, the US Administration had been influenced by the notion that the Unionists were mere puppets of the British and of the Tories in particular. This idea had been assiduously fostered by Sinn Fein via Irish Americans. Patrick Mayhew, with his patrician manner, was not the best man to correct this impression with American audiences and his visits became more infrequent. Trimble's manner was obviously not patrician. His accent alone was proof that there were intelligent and reasonable residents of the geographic entity of the island of Ireland who wished for no part in an all-Ireland state. Moreover, the British Government understood that the Unionist population were fed up with the ceaseless reminders of Adams' film-star status in America. If it continued unchecked, they could easily conclude that the 'peace process' was irremediably stacked against them. They would then become even less willing to cut some deal with Irish nationalism. The British also understood very well that many Unionists have always had a craving for respectability, perhaps more than some of their critics and admirers have supposed. This included the UUP leader. 'Trimble went to America a huge amount,' recalls Sir John Wheeler. 'It played to his ego. He loved his Washington jaunts and was made much of. Suddenly, here was the man from Vanguard who walked with kings and princes.'[39]

William Crowe, the American ambassador in London, and Blair Hall, the Political Counsellor at the embassy, also recognised that a one-sided process would be inherently unstable. But initially, it looked as if these overtures might go disastrously wrong. Anthony Lake, the National Security Adviser, came to London in October 1995 and met Trimble in the sunlit corner room of the US ambassador's residence in Winfield

House, overlooking Regent's Park. There was an exchange of pleasantries which well matched the Gainsborough pictures and the flowered arm-chairs. It all passed smoothly until Lake urged Trimble to 'exert leader-ship' over prior decommissioning and ventured that his community would understand. 'Don't tell me what my community thinks!' ex-ploded Trimble. Lake appeared shocked, and it confirmed the Americans' fears of Trimble's volatility (Lake and Soderberg also expressed scepticism about Trimble's elective assembly).[40] It is possible that Trimble wanted to show that he was no pushover, and that he chose deliberately to foster what Richard Nixon called the 'madman theory': that he needed to be handled with great care lest he go off the rails. Trimble denies this to be the case, though he is calculating enough in other ways.[41] It may be that he behaved thus out of genuine annoyance at a foolish suggestion which showed no comprehension of the balance of forces within Unionism.

The British were determined to persist with the UUP's 'outreach': Trimble recalls that John Major had told him that if he pressed for a meeting with the President, the request would be favourably received. It was accordingly arranged that the President would make a 'drop-by', 'spontaneous' meeting whilst Trimble was in Vice President Al Gore's suite. This was the form employed when the President did not yet want to bestow a full Oval Office tête-à-tête, but from a Unionist perspective it was a significant step to parity of treatment with John Hume.[42] Sir John Kerr says that there was huge interest in Trimble when he came to town. Attention particularly focused upon internal relations within the UUP, notably between Trimble and Taylor. Nobody, says Kerr, had studied Trimble in advance and they did not know what to make of him (such uncertainty did not affect the hardline republican Irish American Unity Conference, which took out an advert in the New York Times on 30 October 1995 entitled 'A WELCOME TO DAVID TRIMBLE, THE "DAVID DUKE" OF IRELAND' and likening the Orange Order to the KKK. The next day, David Duke expressed anger that his name had been blackened by such unfavourable comparisons!). Following a breakfast meeting with Edward Kennedy, the senior senator from Massachusetts singled Trimble out as the most important political leader in the Province and said that 'all of us here in Congress know that Mr Trimble is going to play a vital role in settling the future of Northern Ireland. Whatever is worked out will be worked out for the future of Northern Ireland by the people of Northern Ireland.'[43] This belied the rancorous nature of

Trimble's meeting with the Ad Hoc Committee on Irish Affairs, including Congressman Peter King, a Long Island Republican and an energetic supporter of Sinn Fein. All relentlessly peppered him with hostile questions, and Trimble responded in kind. At the White House, Trimble met with Gore for half an hour and they were joined by Clinton for ten minutes.[44] Trimble again pressed his idea of an elected assembly, but little of substance was achieved. One thing would impress him above all others: he presented Clinton with copies of two Ulster Society publications: Ronnie Hanna's book on American servicemen in Northern Ireland during the Second World War, *Pardon Me Boy* and Gordon Lucy's lively study of the Ulster Covenant – which he brought into the White House in a grotty plastic bag. When the President made his first visit to Belfast some weeks later, he had read both from cover to cover, and was able to put the British Prime Minister right on points of fact. The White House noticed one other thing about Trimble during these early visits: according to Anthony Lake, the UUP leader would glance across to John Taylor to see his deputy's reactions.[45]

In truth, Trimble made a mixed impression on those he met. He seemed to many of his interlocutors to be very prickly, and very much on the look-out for insults and slights. Partly, it was inexperience: he handled the US media in a confrontational manner more appropriate to a rowdy Unionist gathering back at home. But, says Anne Smith, it was also because many of his interlocutors were either hostile – as was the case with the Ad Hoc Committee – or else uninformed. As she observes, the most common question which Trimble had for years to endure on his visits to America was 'why won't you shake hands with Gerry Adams?' They always, says Smith, wanted Trimble to make the first move, because that is the way that reasonable men settle their disputes in the United States. It would take some years for Americans to understand the reasons for Trimble's reluctance – namely, the reaction of ordinary Unionists to the idea of such a meeting.[46] That was because such understanding of the Unionist case as was achieved was entirely functional: no Unionists, no process. But there was no year-round constituency created with a positive understanding of the merits of Unionism. There was, eight years later, no pro-Unionist bloc to counteract the influence of the Irish-American lobby.

In some ways this was understandable. After all, when it came to the affairs of Ireland, the Scotch-Irish Protestant immigrants of the 17th and

18th centuries were more thoroughly assimilated than the Gaelic Catholic Irish of the 19th and 20th centuries. That said, many small peripheral peoples without limitless resources such as the Chechens had set up Washington offices on a shoestring basis and had successfully mobilised far more support for their cause. Indeed, in the 1980s, even a figure such as the military dictator of Guatemala, General Efrain Rios Montt (who was pushing a rather worse case than the Unionists of Ulster) had managed to garner some support amongst his fellow evangelicals in the United States for his regime. Why then did the UUP not succeed in making in-roads? Anne Smith states there was simply no time to cultivate the 'Bible Belt', partly because of what she claims to be the size and fragmentation of the community.[47] But Unionists did little better with secular conservatives 'inside the Beltway'. Despite widespread conservative disgust with the Clinton administration, Unionists were unable to cash in much on his granting of a visa to Gerry Adams at the behest of that great right-wing *bête noire*, Edward Kennedy. Indeed, Sinn Fein/IRA was allied to many bitterly anti-American 'national liberation movements' such as the PLO: the historic hostility of Irish republicans to US foreign policy objectives throughout much of the world remained one of their best-kept secrets until 2001. Nor was the UUP leader aware of the existence of the extended Trimble clan in Kentucky and Ohio, despite his own historical enthusiasms. Trimble himself recognised that the UUP ought to do more, but was too busy and too disorganised to do anything about them. There was, however, another aspect to his failure to deliver. Did Trimble really want to build up a network of support amongst Congressmen from the Deep South, who might act as a counterweight to the Kennedys et al.? When the idea of such an 'outreach' operation in America was broached to him at the October 2000 Conservative party conference in Bournemouth, he said, 'No, I can't be associated with yahoos.'[48] Certainly, he never reached out on a regular basis to such natural allies as Senator Jesse Helms, who held the chairmanship of the Senate Foreign Relations Committee throughout that period, and who loathed the Provisionals. Partly, this was because Trimble had gradually became acutely self-aware of his status as a pillar of the international 'civilised' order. And because he is naturally shy, he liked to engage only with a few people in the United States, or anywhere else: what mattered to him above all else were his dealings with Clinton. It was a pattern which would eventually be replicated in his dealings with Clinton's admirer – Tony Blair.

FIFTEEN

'Binning Mitchell'

TRIMBLE'S tetchy approach in America and at home may have won him few friends; but intentionally or not, it served him well enough in his dealings with the unionist community. For every time the two Governments resiled from their positions on decommissioning, Trimble would eventually follow suit. But because he often did this with ill grace, it masked the extent of his acquiescence in the intergovernmental strategy. This was particularly true of his acceptance of the 'Twin Track' procedure in 1995–6. In essence, what happened was that the British accepted that Mayhew's 'Washington III' demand for IRA decommissioning prior to a republican entry into talks was no longer viable: the IRA simply would not decommission. Since the purpose of British state strategy was to secure an all-inclusive settlement which stopped nationalists and unionists fighting each other and thus harming British interests, the price of upholding Washington III became too high to pay. The only question was how to wriggle off the hook of prior decommissioning without obvious humiliation and without inflaming Tory backbench sensibilities. The two Governments hit upon 'Twin Track' as the vehicle for accomplishing this.[1] It entailed setting up an international commission to arrange for the terms of decommissioning simultaneous with the start of preliminary all-party talks: in other words, parallel decommissioning as opposed to prior decommissioning. It enabled them to say they had not abandoned the principle, but simply altered the timing and the mechanism.

Trimble publicly signalled his willingness to go for a Twin Track procedure in an *Irish Times* interview on 11 November 1995. Trimble stated that despite his serious misgivings, he had never ruled out Twin Track – so long as it was linked to his assembly proposal. As Patrick Mayhew notes, if the UUP had rejected this formulation, and stuck to Washington

III, the two Governments would have been in trouble, not least with the Tory backbenches; but it was Trimble's willingness to go along with it, subject to certain conditions, which convinced Mayhew that the UUP leader was ultimately serious about doing the deal.[2] Indeed, Trimble sometimes behaved as if immediate decommissioning was a tactical device which could be downplayed and then resurrected and traded for some other, more sought-after, objective. Thus he told Andrew Hunter to keep up the pressure on decommissioning, even as he sought to dilute the concept for the sake of more valuable gains.[3] His decision not to put too many eggs into the decommissioning basket at this point was also conditioned by his inner belief that ultimately the two Governments were not that serious about it anyway. It would always be subject to broader political imperatives. And in November 1995, the most urgent of those was the forthcoming visit of President Clinton to these islands.

Drafts of a formula on the Twin Track mechanism had been shuttling back and forth across the Irish Sea throughout the autumn. Now, both Governments wanted something in place before Clinton's arrival. They hit upon a three-man international commission, which would report on how disarmament should be achieved by the end of January 1996. It was to be chaired by George Mitchell, the half-Lebanese, half-Irish-American former US Senate Majority leader, who was mistrusted by many Unionists because of his ancestry. He would be 'counterbalanced' by the former Canadian Chief of the Defence Staff, John de Chastelain, a great favourite of the UUP Security spokesman, Ken Maginnis; and Harri Holkeri, a former Finnish Prime Minister. The deal was sealed at a dramatic, late-night summit on 28 November between the two heads of government in Downing Street.[4] The British were well pleased with themselves. True, the Commission further 'internationalised' the conflict – a concession that almost precipitated a Tory backbench revolt. But on the positive side, from the British Government's viewpoint, the formula was remarkably similar to that of September 1995. This, of course, had initially been accepted by the Irish and was about to be announced at a summit when the Dublin Government was bluntly informed by the republicans that to set up a disarmament body on those terms would prompt a crisis in the peace process and so the Irish duly pulled out of the summit. This time, things were different, and the 'Rainbow coalition' agreed to the international body.[5]

Trimble knew of the possibility of a backbench Tory revolt, and that if he had chosen to stick to Washington III he could have forced the Government to reject Mitchell. But he feared that if he did so, he would lose the battle for public opinion in England and would only have the support of *The Daily Telegraph* (in fact, decommissioning, unlike Orange parades, was one of the areas where English opinion was sympathetic to the Unionists' position, as polls subsequently showed). But he also knew that he could not sound too positive a note about Mitchell in the first instance. This was typical of his *modus operandi*: tactical, rhetorical escalations to mask a line of strategic retreat. He described the communiqué as 'shameful' and a 'fudge', and observed that 'we have had all this rushing about and a press conference at 11 p.m. last night, all that so that John Major could meet Bill Clinton and say "what a good boy I am, I've done what you told me"'. As Jeffrey Donaldson observes, this was classic Trimble: he was bargaining that many Unionists would listen to the volume, rather than the content of what he said.[6] But as the day progressed, Trimble moderated his tones and did not rule out an alternative to decommissioning, if the international body came up with something acceptable.

Trimble's changing tone might have had something to do with his imminent encounter with the US President. Trimble was a particular target of Clinton's attention on this visit – again, on the principle, that if you treat him 'like a statesman', he will become one. 'And he did grow in confidence and stature, within his own community and beyond,' recalls Anthony Lake.[7] Like all presidential visits, it was organised on the principle of 'taking care' of the mythological Chicago alderman. This required photographic acknowledgement of the stature of the individual local worthy, who poses in time-honoured fashion with the Commander-in-Chief. Blair Hall and the White House advance men ensured that Trimble had a substantial measure of private time alone with the US head of state. They also took care to ensure that the form of presidential favour would be especially impressive to Trimble's community. They therefore arranged for the ultimate accolade: Trimble would take the short ride from the Whitla Hall at Queen's University to the Europa Hotel with Clinton in the presidential limousine. This was no easy thing to organise, since the limousine is the inner part of the presidential cocoon. But the Americans were determined that Trimble be seen entering and leaving the car. In time, the strategy became more elaborate still. Administration officials concluded that even Trimble's rudeness could be turned to good effect. He had to be seen to beat his breast and to win over the US Government to his position (exemplified by his extollation of Unionist work in North America in his address to the 1996 UUP party conference).[8]

Trimble was well satisfied with Clinton's visit to Belfast, which on this occasion he found very even-handed; he particularly liked Clinton's address at the neutral venue of Mackie's plant on Springfield Road, where the President told the paramilitaries that 'you are the past, your day is over' (it was not, of course, to be: whilst Clinton was there, the IRA was making preparations to end the ceasefire).[9] That night, the two men took their short drive together back to Clinton's hotel. 'He was tired, I was tired,' Trimble recalls. 'But he referred to the books I had given him in Washington. He had read them, and especially liked Ronnie Hanna's' (on American servicemen in Ulster during the Second World War). Clinton asked Trimble what he saw as the final outcome: the Unionist leader dwelled very much on Strand III of the Talks, outlining his vision for a Community of the British Isles. Trimble was thrilled with the meeting, and spoke about it to colleagues for some days afterwards. But contrary to what some believe, Clinton applied no direct pressure whatsoever on Trimble, either then or in the subsequent negotiations.[10] Clinton would never say, for example, 'don't make decommissioning a precondition to all-party talks'. It was a more subtle process than that. Rather, Clinton would call Trimble and say something along the lines of 'now what can I do for you at this stage in the process?' or 'how can we help?' Often, the mere fact of a call from the President was pressure enough to maintain the momentum of the process. Clinton's involvement was thus not a case of rape, but of seduction. Trimble undoubtedly gave the Americans a greater understanding of his position, but this 'influence' over American policy was bought at a price: the Americans now had a purchase upon the party leader's calculations which they had never enjoyed before. Indeed, Jeffrey Donaldson recalls that Trimble's fear of forfeiting unionist 'gains' made in America was an important factor in his decision to remain in the talks after Sinn Fein's admission on easier terms in 1997.[11]

Mitchell met with Major three times during his deliberations, with Ancram more often. Mitchell recalls that 'the British repeatedly told me that David Trimble was in a difficult position politically, that there's a political division in Unionism and we've got to help him work his way through that'. Ancram, he says, 'told me that the elective route is very important to David Trimble and we want to see it in there'.[12] Trimble, obviously, made similar points.[13] Trimble's position was strengthened by a poll in the *Belfast Telegraph* on 17 January 1996, which revealed that seven out of ten respondents in Ulster wanted a new elected body as the next step towards negotiations, including two-thirds of SDLP supporters and half of Sinn Fein's constituency. But when Mitchell showed his report to the British Government, prior to publication, the results were not what they had hoped for. Mayhew's secret paper, sent to his colleagues on the Cabinet's Northern Ireland Committee on 23 January 1996, noted 'Senator Mitchell and his team were given a hard task . . . not surprisingly [they] have produced something of a curate's egg. It is disappointing that they have accepted, without question, that the paramilitaries will not start decommissioning in advance of negotiations.' Instead, it suggested decommissioning in parallel with negotiations. Mayhew had no problem whatsoever with the six Mitchell Principles of democracy and non-violence, which he recognised would prove difficult for Sinn Fein (such as an end to punishment beatings) and the International Body's rejection of the notion of equivalence between security force weapons and illegally held stocks. It noted that the Body 'also recognises that an elective process, if broadly acceptable, could contribute to building confidence despite Sinn Fein and the SDLP's public opposition to unionist proposals'. And it went on 'we know that Sinn Fein expect the Body to pose some particularly hard (if not impossible) challenges for them. They also antici-pate that the Body will not endorse Washington 3. Reporting indicates that Adams hopes that the British Government, by giving a premature negative reaction to the Body's failure to endorse Washington 3, will relieve Sinn Fein of all responsibility for giving a positive response to the challenges posed to them by the Body's report.'

But how would the British Government respond? Mayhew indicated there were three broad options:

'(a) Reject the Report. This would be highly damaging. HMG would be exposed. There would be stalemate. Sinn Fein – as we know they hope – would be let off the hook. The nationalists and all their sympathisers, including the Americans, would stand together in holding HMG responsible for the continued impasse.'

'(b) Accept the approach the Report canvasses. I do not believe that would be the right approach, without further consideration and develop-ment in consultation with all the parties. As it stands it provides too uncertain a basis for the necessary confidence. We need to test the response of the paramilitaries, and to take view of the parties including of course the UUP.

'(c) Take a positive line in response to the Report, in no way abandoning Washington 3, but promote a modified way ahead involving an elective process, as identified by the Report albeit rather faintly, requiring broad support within the political track as the next stage.'

Mayhew continued: 'I consider the third option offers the best way ahead. It enables us to take the initiative both in responding positively to the report and in putting forward a route to negotiations which builds on unionist ideas but will be difficult and damaging for nationalists to reject out of hand.' As for the proposals for an assembly, Mayhew noted that 'the attraction of some elective process is that it builds on unionists' own idea. The DUP, UUP, and Alliance Party have all proposed some form of time-limited elected body. They have all said they would be prepared, without prior decommissioning, to sit down with Sinn Fein after an election for discussions . . . nationalists are opposed to such a body, but I believe their concerns could be met if:

– elections clearly gave direct access to substantive negotiations (ie without further insistence on prior decommissioning);

– those negotiations remained on the three-stranded basis agreed in 1991;

– there was a proper role, as in 1991, for the Irish Government in appropriate strands and the British Government in all strands;

– the negotiators themselves were drawn from the pool of elected representatives, avoiding unwieldy 90-member negotiations although the full body of elected representatives could be consulted at key points;

– HMG maintained its position that there could be no purely internal settlement.'

The document demonstrates several points. The first is the central importance of the UUP to the then Government's thinking: no UUP, no process. This was a genuine article of political faith (though it was functional rather than ideological in character) which pre-dated the parliamentary arithmetic. Rather, the Government saw it as the Realpolitik of the Northern Irish political scene. The second is how even at this stage, the Government were seeking formulae which would dilute and even divest the elective route of its content as envisaged by the UUP, to make it bearable to nationalists. That, of course, was to be a hallmark of the peace process: for every advance by one side, there would be a counter-balancing measure in the next round.

Above all, does Mayhew's paper show that the Tories 'binned Mitchell', as nationalists contended – thus showing their bad faith and tilting the balance in the IRA back to the 'militarists' as opposed to the exponents of the 'political route'? For one thing, as was demonstrated during the trial of the Docklands bombers, plans for the resumption of full-scale IRA violence began prior to Mitchell's appointment to the International Body, let alone before Major responded to his report.[14] But on the point of 'binning', the record is less clear. It was not binned in the sense of the first option canvassed by Mayhew. But nor was it accepted in toto, either. Rather, the response can be interpreted as classically Majorite fudge: make positive sounds without giving the report wholesale endorsement, and seek to play up those elements of it that most suited the Government's needs.

When Trimble was briefed by Ancram on the Mitchell Report, he shared the Government's disappointment: in particular, he found the principles and the reference to the elective route too weak. Trimble made it absolutely clear that if Washington III was abandoned without compensating gains, he would be 'blown out of the water'. To this day, he believes that his warnings were responsible for the strength and tone of Major's response to Mitchell in the Commons on 24 January 1996.[15] The strength of Major's response may also have been partly conditioned by a rough ride meted out to Mayhew at the meeting of the backbench Northern Ireland Committee when they were briefed on the report. The Irish claim they also received a faxed copy of Major's remarks an hour and a half before he was due to deliver his official response in the Commons. Fergus Finlay recalls that the DFA felt that it was written by 'John Major, the Chief Whip', looking at it from the point of view of his parliamentary majority, rather than 'John Major, the Prime Minister'. As they saw it, the assembly idea was another 'precondition', meaning 'elections first, and then we'll see'. Indeed, there was no date set for the commencement of all-party talks. Finlay says there was a huge sense of shock that this risk had been taken with nationalist Ireland in order to keep David Trimble on board (whom the DFA believed to be far stronger than he made out).[16] Major responded much along the lines which Mayhew had outlined, but his tone was more insistent; significantly, Tony Blair, the Opposition leader, maintained the bi-partisan approach and offered unqualified support (thus upsetting Labour's 'Green' wing, which often took its cue from John Hume). Trimble, who spoke third, praised Blair for his willingness to facilitate legislation on the assembly. He also tweaked Hume's tail with an aside about the degree of sympathy for the elective route amongst SDLP supporters: this may have contributed to the Derryman's mood and, in a rare misjudgment of the mood of the Commons, he lashed out at Major and the Conservatives.[17] For the first time in years, an Ulster Unionist leader was making the political weather, and nationalist Ireland did not like it.

SIXTEEN

'Putting manners on the Brits'

AT 7:02 p.m. on Friday, 9 February, the British and Irish official elites were assembling for pre-prandial drinks at the Foreign Office conference facility at Wilton Park. At that precise moment, a massive bomb detonated at South Quay in London's Docklands, ending the IRA ceasefire. Within minutes, the news had been relayed to Ted Barrington, the Irish ambassador to the United Kingdom. Barrington told his fellow guest, Quentin Thomas, what had occurred. The Political Director of the NIO was stunned. So, too, was Martin Mansergh, special adviser to successive leaders of Fianna Fail. The next day, he paced around the gardens, alone, seemingly in a state of shock. The attempt to draw this generation of republicans into constitutional politics – one of his life's main goals – appeared for the time being to be in ruins. According to Thomas, the two men had spoken a few minutes earlier, when Mansergh had expressed optimism about the future.[1] Meanwhile, John Major was in his Huntingdon constituency when the news came to the No. 10 switchboard at 6 p.m. that RTE had received a call from the IRA stating that the ceasefire was over: the codeword was genuine.[2] The White House rang shortly thereafter to say that Adams had called with the same information. According to Anthony Lake, Clinton's National Security Adviser, the Sinn Fein President was 'elliptical and sounded concerned. But we didn't know what he meant. And I still don't know whether he knew what was going to happen.'[3] At Stormont House in Belfast, Sir John Wheeler, the Security Minister at the NIO, was making his way through paperwork: it was his turn to be the duty minister. His Private Secretary immediately came on the line with the news. Wheeler stayed up till 1 a.m., reintroducing many of the security measures withdrawn after the ceasefire began.[4]

But despite the shock of the South Quay bomb, the British state did not alter course: there was no fundamental reappraisal of the nature of republicanism. Wheeler says that at no stage did the Government even contemplate the notion that there should be anything other than an inclusive settlement so long as the IRA was on some kind of ceasefire; or, as Cranborne puts it, 'it was treated almost as though it was a *cri de coeur* from a delinquent teenager rather than a full-scale assault on British democracy'.[5] Andrew Hunter recorded in his diary of 21 February 1996 that even as Mayhew expected another IRA 'spectacular' on the mainland, the Government still were looking for signals that some kind of process was possible. Indeed, one senior NIO official was shocked within weeks of the blast to find the Government negotiating again with Sinn Fein: he concluded from this episode that if even a Conservative ministry with a narrow majority could do such a thing, then a serious question mark had been placed against the viability of the Union. The official was therefore prepared to toy with the idea that negotiating a federal Ireland was a possible means of 'getting the Provisionals off the Prods' backs' and to minimise their leverage over the system.[6]

John Steele, the then Director of Security in the NIO, states that as he saw it, 'the IRA were cracking the whip. They were demonstrating that bad things could happen. But the break in the ceasefire was a carefully calculated signal, not a wild lashing-out.' Steele recalls that even Wheeler – the minister most sceptical of the IRA – only wanted to respond with enhanced intelligence gathering. The Security Minister suggested neither the reintroduction of internment, nor did he advocate letting the SAS use lethal force.[7] Nor were the prisoners released during the first ceasefire recalled, and the border was not sealed. Mary Holland correctly observed the 'surprisingly mild' response to that atrocity. 'We heard almost nothing from the British side about the spirit of the bulldog breed,' she noted in her *Irish Times* column of 29 February.

The British were convinced that such measures would prove counter-productive at home and abroad. At home, they concluded, it could be a recruiting sergeant for the IRA. Abroad, principally in America, old-style counter-insurgency was deemed diplomatically too costly – even if set in the context of an overall 'carrot and stick' approach to the republican movement. Thus, Cranborne also had no purist scruples about offering the republicans the 'carrot' of political development – provided they were prepared to abandon armed struggle entirely. But he also believed that the political forms of the 'stick' were not being employed properly either. He therefore sent Major 'an intemperate memo' suggesting that the

Government was totally inactive in trying to defeat the IRA. Cranborne wanted 'to put our money where our mouth is and appoint a counter-terrorist supremo in the Cabinet in charge of winning it on all levels'. This supremo would be responsible to the Prime Minister, special Cabinet committee and the Intelligence and Security Committee of the Commons. Cranborne knew that the 'mandarinate' would oppose his plans, on the grounds that they would cut across existing lines of departmental responsibility and chains of command in the security forces and the police (although the creation of the National Criminal Intelligence Service had shown that there was scope for innovation). Major was deeply uncomfortable with the idea and the Cabinet Secretary, Sir Robin Butler, shot it down completely. Butler and Major met with Cranborne and instead offered improved intelligence coordination but no radical overhaul.[8]

Curiously, for all his rhetoric, David Trimble did not really push a return to an old-style security crackdown; nor, even then, did he think that the republican movement would necessarily be beyond the pale in the future. Mayhew notes that Trimble did not ask the Government to scrap the 'peace process' as a concept now clearly based upon false premises. 'I think he always had it in his mind to do something more than spend the whole of his political career leading a minority party in the Commons,' says the former Secretary of State.[9] Fergus Finlay also states that Trimble never asked the Irish Government to endorse the concept of a deal without Sinn Fein: without them, Finlay believes, the UUP leader could never realise his ambition to be Prime Minister of a stable Northern Ireland.[10] Again, this was partly because Trimble felt that the British state from the outset was not going to place republicans beyond the pale, and would work tirelessly to restore the broken ceasefire. Indeed, Major told Trimble that the decision to return to armed struggle was taken by a curiously informal grouping of 20 senior republicans and not through the more 'formal' mechanisms of the IRA Army Council; the actual operation was run by a very tight group based in the Republic, not involving Northern Irish 'assets', though some of the participants were northerners. Trimble drew the inference that the South Quay bomb may not have been the settled view of the whole organisation. Indeed, he says that there are many unanswered questions about the role of Adams and McGuinness in that bombing.[11] On 1 March 1996, Trimble told the *Irish News* that if there were to be an IRA ceasefire which means 'a change of heart' he would not want to create 'unnecessary obstacles about Sinn Fein's involvement in all-party talks'. All he asked for was adherence to the terms of the Mitchell Report. 'Mitchell does talk about parallel decommissioning, not prior decommissioning. If we had reasonable commitments we would be able to move in that direction.'[12]

In his first lengthy disquisition on the end of the ceasefire, published in *The Daily Telegraph* on Monday February 12, Trimble stated that the purpose of the bombing was to stop elections to his proposed body from taking place. This later turned out to be unlikely, for the simple reason that the IRA's decision to return to 'war' was taken well before the Forum idea was accepted by the British Government. But whatever the real reasons for their actions, it was certainly inept of Trimble to identify this as a cause of the bomb: it implicitly validated the nationalist notion that Major's actions in 'binning' Mitchell and alighting upon the glancing reference in the International Body's Report to the elective route had in some way precipitated South Quay. But did the IRA resumption of violence work from their perspective? Many in nationalist Ireland, and not a few Unionists, certainly believed as much, pointing to the announcement of all-party talks made on 28 February 1996 at Downing Street by Major and Bruton.[13] Bruton disagrees with this notion, observing that the decision to set a date for such negotiations had been taken in principle when the British Government accepted Mitchell as Commission chairman in November 1994. Bruton also notes that the log-jam on prior decommissioning had already been broken by the elective route of the Forum: he feels that Trimble received insufficient credit for this idea.[14] But the manner and timing of the announcement of a date for all-party talks made it appear as though the Provisionals had 'put manners' on the two Governments.

Trimble decided straight after the South Quay bomb to head to the United States to brief Clinton on what had happened, taking the advice of John Holmes, the Prime Minister's new Private Secretary before he did so. When Ken Maginnis and Donaldson arrived at the White House on Monday 12 February at 2 p.m. they found a President who seemed ill at ease. Trimble said he was surprised at the timing of the bomb. 'Yeah, it was stupid, damned stupid,' lamented the Commander-in-Chief, referring to the fact that the blast took place at the very moment that there was a chance of all-party talks. But Trimble says he never asked Clinton to place the Provisionals beyond the pale at this moment: 'They [the US Administration] know best what leverage they have,' Trimble explains.

'There is no point in telling them what to do.'[15] He shares the conventional British wisdom that this blast came as a tremendous shock to Clinton, thus prompting a reappraisal of White House attitudes towards Northern Ireland. In fact, Trimble's recollection is not quite correct: he asked that Adams' visa to the USA be rescinded and that there be a ban on fund-raising by Sinn Fein, but both these options were rejected by the US Administration. Mike McCurry, the White House spokesman, rejected this reasoning, stating that 'Mr Adams is an important leader in this process because he speaks for Sinn Fein. It is hard to imagine a process making progress towards peace without the active involvement of Sinn Fein.' Partly, the White House's unwillingness to place Adams beyond the pale can be ascribed to the fact that the British Government did not want to do so, either: they favoured Adams' admission to the USA and for the doors then partially to close on him as a sign of displeasure as exemplified by the Sinn Fein president's exclusion from the annual St Patrick's Day party at the White House. Trimble did, however, attend a dinner of the American-Ireland Fund on St Patrick's Day at which Gerry Adams was present – another small breach in the wall of taboos surrounding the republicans (Trimble had initially not wanted to attend, but feared the consequences of 'exclusion' if he did not turn up).[16]

Once the immediate shock of the South Quay bomb had passed, the attention of the political classes on both sides of the Irish Sea moved to the form of election to the new assembly and to the format of the talks. Trimble and the UUP did relatively badly in this. Indeed, Andrew Hunter noted in his diary of 21 February 1996 that 'Secretary of State [Mayhew] worried about the case for elections to a Peace Convention. Believes it is difficult to find solid, objective justification. Michael Ancram and I argued that elections justified on pragmatic grounds; no other way to get Unionists into all-party negotiations ... Not much optimism in our discussion. Implicit agreement that PM overegged elections in his Mitchell response.' Yet Trimble was himself partly responsible for affording the British Government the space which it needed to make the elective process 'work' vis-à-vis nationalist Ireland. As early as 24 December 1995, he had suggested in a *Sunday Tribune* interview that the assembly 'could take evidence from the Republic, from the Irish Government and other interested bodies' about possible North-South cooperation. The new body would not be a recreation of Stormont, he noted, but rather would be time-limited to two years (though it was a point which he never had much success in conveying). Trimble's proposal was very considerably short of joint management of the talks but Irish offficials approvingly noted the UUP leader's flexibility. Later, Trimble indicated that if the questions were framed in the right way and if it was clear that it was not an island-wide referendum, he might under certain circumstances back John Hume's idea of a plebiscite in both jurisdictions simultaneous with an assembly election (concerning the right of the Irish people, north and south, to self-determination and their right also to determine the method whereby that might be achieved). There was, of course, another imperative behind his need to obtain an elective process: Trimble says that if he won an election, he would greatly increase his authority within the UUP.[17]

Trimble's position within the UUP helps to explain his concerns about nationalist successes in diluting the Assembly idea: he was worried at least as much by the appearance as the substance. In a memorandum to Major, dated 22 February, entitled 'UU outline talks scheme', Trimble stated that there was some limited flexibility on when the Provisionals could begin decommissioning – effectively a green light to the British Government considering the other pressures on them. But on the presentation, there was no such hint of flexibility: 'The announcement of the elections for the Peace Convention and the associated talks should avoid the usual Anglo/Irish style, i.e. it should avoid the language typical of Stormont Castle/Iveagh House joint productions,' stated Trimble. 'There should be no references to the two Governments jointly sponsoring or jointly managing the Peace Convention or the talks.' In the end, the Ground Rules for Substantive All-Party Negotiations paper produced by the British Government in March 1996 gave precisely that impression: to the intense annoyance of Trimble, it was sent out while the Unionist leader was in America and suggested that the Irish Government be the joint coordinator of the negotiations.[18]

The crucial next step of setting a date for all-party talks was complicated – and dramatically so – by the Government's parlous position in the Commons. Lord Justice Scott's report on the Arms for Iraq affair was scheduled for debate on 26 February 1996. If the Government was defeated in the House, it would trigger a vote of no confidence. Not all Conservative MPs were solidly behind the Government and attention again focused on the Unionists' intentions. From the Conservative Government's viewpoint, the initial signs were not hopeful. In an interview with Roy Hattersley, Trimble had told the former Labour deputy leader that he was appalled by the use of Public Interest Immunity certificates (the gagging orders produced by the Attorney General, Sir Nicholas Lyell, which were said to have prevented ministers from revealing information on national security grounds that would have shown that the defendants in the Matrix Churchill case had acted with the state's approval).[19] He was thus less worried by the Government's Iraq policy than by the fact that innocent men might have gone to jail for *raison d'état*. No less important, the former law lecturer believed that Lyell gave poor legal advice – and had stated as much as early as the original debate on the Arms for Iraq affair in November 1992.[20]

But Trimble could not now afford the indulgence of thinking like some independent-minded backbencher. The UUP's stance would have also to be based upon the Realpolitik of Unionist interests. It was a close call. On the one hand, Trimble was dubious about how much he could extract from a weak Government. 'Major can't deliver much on his own,' he told Hattersley. '[I would prefer] a strong Government with the confidence to take difficult decisions.' Hattersley stated that Trimble did not believe that such a Government existed then. 'Ireland [sic] cannot go right for Major in any big way before the election,' predicted the UUP leader. 'It can only go wrong. That means that we are likely to have another year of stalemate.'[21] On the other hand, although Trimble may then have felt that the prospect of New Labour was more congenial, there was still much short-term business to be transacted with the Conservatives (whom Labour would broadly back as part of the bi-partisan approach towards Northern Ireland). The most immediate item on the agenda was the method of election to the new body proposed by Trimble: he feared that the Government was at this stage leaning to a variant of the DUP's preferred system (which, for a variety of complex reasons, also benefited the SDLP and thus mitigated nationalist hostility). The Paisleyites wanted a Province-wide poll based on a party list system, as in the European Parliamentary elections, which was well suited to maximising the large personal vote of their chief who would then barn-storm the Province. The Ulster Unionists, by contrast, wanted a single transferable vote in the constituencies, which would maximise their greater strength in depth further down the ticket. If a Paisley-friendly system emerged, it could conceivably destroy Trimble and inflict a serious blow to his conception of New Unionism. His fears of a deal were confirmed when one colleague heard from Paisley himself that the three DUP MPs would not enter either lobby for the Scott vote; indeed, Paisley's deputy, Peter Robinson, recalls that the Government communicated via NIO civil servants that an electoral system more in line with DUP needs would be introduced – though, as he points out, the linkage was hinted at rather than being 'crudely made'.[22] Trimble believes that the NIO has quietly favoured the DUP over the years as a means of weakening the solidarity of the Unionist bloc and specifically of its largest component, the UUP. But perhaps of greatest significance to the Government was the fact that the DUP might potentially participate in such a representative institution with Sinn Fein at some point in the future – assuming there was a ceasefire and that republicans would then take up their seats in such a body. Quentin Thomas had been impressed from the early to mid-1990s by the point made to him by senior DUP politicians that they could not voluntarily agree to share power with nationalists; but, they added, if such an outcome was forced upon them and sanctioned by a particular kind of electoral process (as on District Councils, where committee chairmanships were shared out proportionately according to party strengths) then the DUP would not decline to fulfil their democratic mandate and take up their allocated slots.[23]

But Trimble still had to treat with the Tories, and examine what, if anything, they had to offer. If they offered something very tempting (approximating to the UUP's preferred system of election) Trimble could not possibly say no. But if the Government made no such offer, Trimble might as well stick to his principles and obtain a bit of credit with an increasingly powerful Opposition. What happened next remains a matter of dispute between the Tories and the Ulster Unionists. To this day, Conservatives assert that Trimble appproached the Government to make a deal; Trimble says that on each occasion, he was approached by the Government. Trimble met twice with Major on the night of the vote, in the Prime Minister's room behind the Speaker's chair. On the first occasion, between 6 and 7 p.m., Major urged Trimble to support the Government. Trimble explained to Major that he was in some difficulty because he had reason to believe that the Prime Minister had done a deal with the DUP: irrespective of the merits of the Scott case, he would look 'bloody stupid' if he supported the Government that week and then a week or so later an election system emerged that ruined his party's chances. 'I'm not in the business of damaging the UUP,' replied Major.[24] But Trimble noted that the Prime Minister did not contradict his assertion that there was some understanding with the DUP. Major added that he could not say what kind of electoral system he would deliver since he had not told anyone else and could not have it said that he had preferred one party over all others. On the second occasion that night, Trimble says he was approached in the tea room by the Conservative Party chairman, Brian Mawhinney. 'The boss wants to see you,' Trimble recalls Mawhinney saying.[25] Mawhinney, by contrast, says that he asked Trimble in the course of a more general conversation if he wanted to see the Prime Minister. In other words, states Mawhinney, he gave Trimble the option of speaking to Major and the UUP leader chose to make the effort to avail himself of it.[26] When Trimble arrived, Major was in the room with Michael Heseltine; the chief whip, Alistair Goodlad; and Mawhinney. Trimble expected Major to say something, but he did nothing of the kind. Instead, the two just sat there and looked at each other. One witness to the scene recalls Major stating that 'I will not do a deal with you' and Trimble replying that 'I will not ask you to do a deal': it was as if both men were waiting for the other to make the first move.[27]

Trimble says he did not believe the Government's assertion that there could be no deal. He thinks they were, indeed, in the market for trading policy concessions in exchange for UUP support. Rather, it was simply not their first choice to rely on the UUP, especially after the furore in nationalist Ireland over the British response to the Mitchell report. They needed to show that they could not be bought specifically by the UUP. A DUP abstention was, by contrast, somehow a less explicit assertion of the Unionist family's 'hold' over the Government than a UUP vote for the Government. The support of the DUP was arithmetically less valuable and ideologically less predictable than a link-up with the UUP (and they were less close to the Tory backbenches than the UUP). Thus, in a peculiar way, the DUP was in these circumstances less threatening to nationalists. Specifically, a deal with the DUP afforded certain advantages to the SDLP: if enough votes haemorrhaged from the UUP to the DUP, the SDLP might receive the huge boost of becoming the largest party in Northern Ireland. The DUP and SDLP also had strong personalities at the top of the ticket, namely Paisley and Hume. But ministers still entertained doubts over the reliability and deliverability of the DUP. Because the Government was not sure until the last minute what the DUP might leak, it kept its options open. The likeliest explanation of what happened is that once it thought it had the DUP in the bag, Major et al. sought to make a virtue out of not doing a deal with the UUP.

Trimble next remembers coming out into the division lobby after the vote – in which the Government scraped by with 320 votes to 319 – to be met by a torrent of abuse from the Tories.[28] This, he suspected, emanated from Mayhew who had alleged that the UUP leader sought to blackmail the Government. Mayhew never felt comfortable with political horse-trading (he himself admits that Michael Ancram was much more comfortable doing such deals) and his distaste for the political arts emerged that night. According to Mayhew, he was crossing the lobby when he was met by the BBC's Jon Sopel. 'What do you think of the result?' asked Sopel. Mayhew replied: 'Delighted, and the more so because the Unionists tried to do a deal and the Prime Minister sent them away and we've still won.' Mayhew says he thought the conversation was on lobby terms but claims that within minutes his remarks were broadcast to the nation; Sopel denies that Mayhew's name was used, since as an experienced lobby journalist, he would have known better. Whatever the precise sequence of events, Trimble was enraged and shortly thereafter went up to Mayhew, scarlet with anger. 'It was a hostile act,' fumed the UUP leader. 'It was a hostile act to try and bring us down,' retorted Mayhew.[29] Major was even angrier over the events of that evening. Andrew Hunter recorded in his diary that he twice met the Prime Minister in the division lobby: according to the backbencher, he felt 'betrayed; furious; he had done so much for them; UUP had tried to make a deal; he would never play party games over peace. What deal [was offered]? About elections.' Later, Hunter met Ancram in the smoking room, where he was nursing a large whisky. According to Ancram, Trimble had offered a constituency-based electoral system, elections before proximity talks and no guarantee that such elections would lead into proximity talks. On the next day, Mayhew contacted Hunter whilst the latter was at Heathrow's Terminal 1, on one of innumerable semi-official missions both to Ulster and the Republic which he undertook during these years. According to Hunter's account, Mayhew told him that the UUP had offered one year's support in exchange for their tariff of demands, and had given the British Government one and a half hours in which to think about it. Indeed, when Hunter met Trimble in the lobby, he remembers telling Trimble that he had blown it. Trimble did not need to make the offer which he did, asserted Hunter, not least because Hunter believed that in conjunction with other backbench supporters he could guarantee Unionist interests. In so doing, the Tory said, Trimble had demeaned himself. Moroever, he had soured relationships with backbenchers who might lose their seats in any elections precipitated by the UUP voting with the Opposition. It was a further illustration of the point that for all of the complaints of nationalist Ireland, Trimble's hold over the Government was in practice severely circumscribed (or at least was much more complex than that simplistic analysis suggested).

But the mess illustrates another point: what was Trimble playing at all through the 1995–7 period? What was his strategy vis-à-vis the mainland parties, and from whom did he really think he could obtain the best deal for Unionism? The evidence is contradictory. According to Paddy Ashdown's diary for 27 February 1996, Trimble said that he would have abstained in a no-confidence vote that might have followed any Government defeat on Scott and added '"we hate this crew and the sooner they go, the better"'. Ashdown then commented: 'The old line. I wonder if he means it?'[30] But Woodrow Wyatt's diary for 27 November 1996 records a *Spectator* party at the Savoy, at which Trimble told him that 'it was very much to Major's credit that he'd managed to get some kind of peace going for so long. "I make a face every now and again for the hell of it, but yes, we'll back him [Major]. He'll be quite safe until he wants to call an election."'[31] Trimble says that the situation altered sharply in the months between these two conversations: Labour knew by November 1996 that it was on for a big victory and therefore had no need of Trimble to bring down the Conservative Government quickly, lest the situation change to the Tories' advantage.[32] The implication is that he might as well have continued to enjoy a few months more of limited leverage. These contrasting remarks to Ashdown and Wyatt illustrate two other points: the obvious desire that both men report back to Blair and Major, respectively, things that each party leader would want to hear. Indeed, as Paddy Ashdown noted in a conversation with Blair on Remembrance Sunday 1995: 'I told [Blair] that I had had a brief chat with Trimble at the Cenotaph earlier in the day, when Trimble had made it clear that he couldn't support the Government. Blair said "but can we trust him?" I said I thought we could, though it was the nature of Irish [sic] politicians to face both ways at once, as it was necessary for their survival.'[33] These contrasting bits of evidence do, however, also show that Trimble had no detailed, preordained game plan and may well have been making it up as he went along.

Indeed, all sides played at horse-trading of this kind during the latter part of the Conservative Government's life. John Bruton sought to reduce Major's dependence on the UUP by volunteering to ask John Hume to vote for the Government in the debate (Bruton felt that there were echoes here of the possibilities opened up by Parnell's flirtation with the Tories in 1885 – a strategy predicated upon the notion of not putting all of the Irish party's eggs into the Liberal basket. Parnell in the end returned to the Liberal fold when the Grand Old Man outbid the Tories by converting to Home Rule in the following year).[34] The leader of Fianna Fail, Bertie Ahern, attacked Bruton and asserted that it was not the role of the Taoiseach 'to be helping the British Government as an assistant whip hours before the vote'; but Bruton's effort was unsuccessful in its own terms, for Hume would not break with his Labour colleagues in the Socialist International. As an exercise in intergovernmental diplomacy, though, Bruton's intervention was more successful. It contributed to the attainment of a key Irish objective in the summit communiqué of 28 February, which the British withheld until almost the last moment: the start of all-party talks on 10 June 1996 (which would only become inclusive upon the restoration of an IRA ceasefire). The summit communiqué also stated, inter alia, that political parties would be asked to attend proximity talks to consider the structure, format and agenda for the all-party talks, and discussions would be held finally to determine the form of elections that would lead to the all-party talks. Moreover, there was no mention in the communiqué of prior decommissioning.

Trimble now acknowledges that the elections lost a lot of their value to the UUP. In part, he says, this was because of 'collateral damage' which he suffered as a result of the bruised relations with the British Government after the Scott vote (though he feels that nationalist pressure would have eroded much of the UUP's advantage, anyhow). He now concedes that his own inexperience at the time played a part in these reverses and that his own proposal should have made clearer the link between the elected body and the talks. Trimble had in mind something like the Convention of 1975–6, which included serious debates but also had the potential for informal negotiations arising in the corridors. He was alerted to this problem when he met Mo Mowlam, the Labour spokesman on Northern Ireland, in the corridors at Westminster and she informed him that the linkage between the elective body and the talks was not sufficiently explicit. 'I don't need to make it explicit – it'll happen organically,' Trimble told her. However, he says he underrated nationalist 'paranoia' about the Unionists 'pocketing' the concession of what the Irish saw as a 'new Stormont' – and, having obtained what they wanted, then stalling on the negotiations. The UUP would thus have regained something akin to their Parliament, whilst nationalists would not have obtained their cross-border bodies and other reforms.[35] Whatever the alleged diplomatic short-comings in the presentation of Trimble's election proposal, the fact remains that both he and the DUP pointedly stayed away from multilateral consultations about the format of the forthcoming talks, which began in the following week at Stormont. In the following weeks, recalls one senior official of the period, much complex mathematical work was done in the NIO to come up with the 'correct' electoral system. He believed they needed a system that satisfied the UUP entitlement to a majority of the majority community (though they did not in the end, manage it) but which would at the same time give due weight to the DUP and the smaller loyalist paramilitary parties. At the same time, the NIO obviously also had to consider the effects of any electoral system on the internal balance of forces within the nationalist community. Could they avoid handing a victory to Sinn Fein against the ageing SDLP – and in any case was that so wrong, they asked themselves? After all, senior NIO officials reasoned, the more that Sinn Fein expanded and stretched in support, the more diluted their ideology would necessarily become and they would be unwilling to lose new-found supporters by returning to full-scale violence. Over the long term, the NIO reasoned, this would help Adams and those who wished to go down a more political route. It would enable them to show to the apolitical militarists that the electoral route could yield greater gains than the armed struggle of the old variety. In consequence, the British came up with a hybrid of the constituency and list systems: electors voted for parties rather than people in the new, expanded number of eighteen constituencies, each of which returned five representatives. Two extra seats would be allocated to each of the ten most successful parties in the Province as a whole, thus guaranteeing representation to the small loyalist parties with minuscule levels of public support. The outcome of these deliberations was, in the view of one senior official, 'the least democratic election of all time. It shows that Governments can tweak voting systems and how careful you have to be with reforming the mainland system.' In the background all of the time were the Americans: Anthony Lake recalls that he would have long discussions with Sir John Kerr in his office in the West Wing of the White House to determine what kind of electoral method would be used for the elective route (that is, Single Transferable Vote, etc).[36] It was a remarkable illustration of the degree of American interference in internal United Kingdom matters.

Indeed, Brian Feeney, a former SDLP councillor in Belfast with a regular column in the *Irish News*, spotted the irony in the system which was set up for the elective route into negotiations. It was, he asserted, the most un-British, un-unionist formula ever devised. 'Professor Umberto Eco, who knows about these things, says all structures in the west display a Protestant or a Catholic mentality. If Protestantism is all about individualism the list system is fundamentally the opposite of a political system where people vote for individuals rather than parties. This political Protestantism reaches its peak in the USA where Democrats and Republicans do their own thing on the floor of the Senate ... but thanks to David Trimble, we've got a Catholic continental system where the individual is subsumed within the party discipline and dogma. Only Sinn Fein has adopted an innovative approach. They have fielded candidates from the Republic who will be elected. Also in a number of areas they have placed at the top of the list prominent figures who have been convicted of high profile IRA activities. No doubt these men unambiguously support the armed struggle. They will certainly be elected. So thanks to David Trimble and his political acumen, the pro-Union vote will be divided a dozen ways and more overtly republican candidates than ever before will be elected under a system as mysterious as a papal conclave. Take a bow, David.'[37] Feeney was being customarily bilious about the Unionist leader (whom he nicknamed the 'Portadown Prancer' after Drumcree I) and it was undoubtedly unfair of him to blame Trimble for the kind of system adopted. But Feeney's observations were invested with one underlying truth. Like so many of Trimble's victories, the elective route into negotiations blew up in his face. Thus, Trimble reproved Robert McCartney for splitting the Unionist vote in the 1996 Forum elections. McCartney replied that but for Trimble's elective route into negotiations – which required that anyone who wanted to be at the talks table had to stand for the contest – he would never have set up the United Kingdom Unionist Party (prior to that, McCartney sat as an independent Westminster MP for North Down but had no Province-wide party organisation).[38]

Trimble duly sought to make the best he could of his unexpectedly bad hand in the run-up to the elections, which were to be held on 30 May 1996. As ever, he set a cracking pace. Elaine McClure of the Ulster Society recalls that Trimble was perhaps 'the only Unionist leader with the guts to canvass the main street of Newry [an overwhelmingly nationalist town]. There was always an excuse for not doing the town, such as the top part of Hill Street. But he took his red, white and blue bus there, and it was a huge psychological boost to those remaining Unionists.'[39] But Trimble's aim was also to reach out to those members of the Catholic community who were not so staunchly nationalistic. The encouragement which Trimble gave to the candidature of John Gorman typified this approach. Gorman was a third-generation Catholic Unionist: his maternal grandfather, Dr Patrick O'Brien, had been a close friend of the moderate southern Irish Unionist, the Earl of Midleton, at the start of the century. Gorman's father, a native of Co. Tipperary, had served as a major in the Royal Horse Artillery Irish Guards in the First World War and was thereafter the last Adjutant of the the Royal Irish Constabulary. He moved north – as loyal Catholics and Protestants from the south did after Partition – and served as County Inspector of the new Royal Ulster Constabulary for Londonderry and Fermanagh. Later, he became deputy head of the RUC mission in Greece during the Civil War in the Hellenes in the mid to late 1940s. Gorman himself fought in the Second Battalion, the Irish Guards, in the Second World War, winning a Military Cross in Normandy; the Intelligence Officer of the Battalion was Captain Terence O'Neill, later the Prime Minister of Northern Ireland from 1963–9. After the war, Gorman joined the RUC, becoming District Inspector for Ballymoney, Co. Antrim. Gorman and Trimble came to know each other when Gorman subsequently headed the Housing Executive, and Trimble was the foremost authority in the Province on housing law. Gorman, who would have become actively involved in Unionist politics much sooner than he did but for the Orange link, was precisely the kind of man whom Trimble admired. For he embodied the diversity of traditions and allegiances that had been obscured by 30 years of Troubles. Trimble further addressed this topic in his speech at the 1996 UUP conference in Ballymena, Co. Antrim, when he extolled the Catholic Unionist tradition as personified by Sir Denis Henry, who was present at the creation of the Ulster Unionist Council in 1905, represented South Londonderry at Westminster, and was subsequently appointed as the first

Lord Chief Justice of the newly created Province of Northern Ireland.[40] Forge an enduring settlement, believed Trimble, and such allegiances could reassert themselves. Trimble later recommended that Gorman become the chairman of the elected Forum, and he received a knighthood in 1998.[41]

Gorman was not the only Catholic whom Trimble sought to recruit to be a flag-bearer for the Unionist cause. He endorsed the appointment of Patricia Campbell, the daughter of an RUC constable, as organiser of the Unionist Information Office in London. This was set up in 1996 under the aegis of David Burnside, which held twice-yearly receptions and occasional briefings for journalists. Under Burnside's tutelage, she edited a magazine, *The Unionist*, brimming with anodyne articles. These were accompanied by pictures of kittens and puppies frolicking with each other, bearing such italicised captions as *Reconciliation is possible* and a cover photograph of a cherubic sleeping new-born in swaddling clothes headlined *Let's keep The Peace For Their Tomorrow.*[42] It prompted some mirth in journalistic circles that so ruthless an operator as Burnside (affectionately known in the PR trade as 'the kneecapper') should produce such sentimental copy; a more serious point was that none of these treacly images did anything to increase any real understanding of the Unionist cause. Even when Unionists finally grasped the importance of PR, they could only rise to the challenge by coming up with images that erased their distinctive message almost completely. Nonetheless, Campbell's appointment – like that of Gorman – incarnated a mood of change that seemed to abound in certain Unionist circles during this period. Indeed, keen as Trimble was for more women candidates, only seven were actually selected for the Forum elections (out of a total of 78) – of whom only one was successful.[43] Selecting standard bearers remained a local affair, where Trimble's personal preferences counted for little. 'New Unionism' was for much of the time a glimmer in his eye, rather than a reality.

Trimble was especially exercised during the campaign by the remarks of the Tanaiste's special adviser, Fergus Finlay, on Channel 4's *Dispatches* programme. Finlay stated that talks without Sinn Fein were 'not worth a penny candle'.[44] Bruton was also furious, because he believed the remark took the heat off the Provisionals.[45] Why, he wondered, should the IRA call a new and this time more credible ceasefire if they knew that the process could not go on without them? The only way in which republicans would do so was if they feared that there was a possibility that a settlement could be achieved by the constitutional parties alone. Finlay concedes that the remark enabled Unionists to say that his boss was surrounded by fellow travellers of the Provisionals. From an Irish prespective, Finlay's remarks had 'reactionary consequences', as the Soviets used to call them. Finlay remembers Sean O hUiginn's regretful remark: 'True diplomats learn early in their careers that the truth is sometimes best served by silence,' opined the head of Anglo-Irish affairs. As far as O hUiginn was concerned, the problem with Finlay's remark lay with its overly stark presentation, and not its substance.[46] The Provisionals could now sit pretty and wait for the two Governments to come to them. The British were doing this anyhow, as exemplified by Major's *Irish Times* article of 16 May 1996, in which he further diluted the Tories' demands on when decommissioning would have to be carried out. But keen as Major was to obtain a renewed IRA ceasefire, he could never move quickly enough for the Provisionals.

Trimble, though, was also in trouble. The novel electoral system, just as he had predicted, would 'shred' the Unionist vote: a poster appeared in the closing days of the campaign depicting a splintered Union flag, with the words 'Division and Weakness, Or Unity and Strength'. Such fracturing also occurred in his own party: at the UUP manifesto launch at Belfast's Laganside, the late John Oliver recalled Martin Smyth looking round at the large numbers of outsiders whom Trimble had brought in and remarking: 'You'd have thought this was the Ulster Society campaign, not the UUP campaign.'[47] Smyth's observation pointed up the deep unease about Trimble within the UUP, which long predated the Belfast Agreement: namely, that as a latecomer to the party, he was not really one of the UUP tribe. For his part, Trimble also found the party organisation at the grassroots to be in worse condition than he imagined. His fears were vindicated. In the 30 May elections, on a 64.5% turnout, the UUP remained the largest single party, with 24.2% of the vote, winning 30 seats; the DUP won 18.8% and 24 seats; the SDLP won 21.4% and 21 seats; Sinn Fein won 15.5% and 17 seats. Two points were significant: first, despite the IRA's return to violence, Sinn Fein turned in their best performance ever, garnering 116,377 votes. Trimble was in no doubt as to the reason for the republicans' success. In a lengthy interview with the editor of the Dublin *Sunday Independent*, Aengus Fanning, Trimble observed that many SDLP voters had crossed over to Sinn Fein under the illusion that it would be a vote for Adams' peace strategy and against republican militarists. These nationalists had succumbed to this logic because 'the boundary lines between Sinn Fein and the SDLP', he believed, 'had been blurred by the Hume-Adams pact'.[48]

The other significant aspect of the Forum elections of 1996 was the shredding of the Unionist vote, which fell 5.2% on the 1993 council elections result. Consequently, the UUP won under 50% of the vote of the majority community; the DUP took 18.8% of the total; McCartney's UKUP took 3.6% for three seats; whilst the PUP and UDP took 3.5% and 2.2% respectively. Neither of the latter two would have won seats in the main constituency system, but they squeezed in under the Province-wide top-up system which guaranteed two extra places to the ten largest parties.[49] Moreover, the UUP's failure to win half the vote meant that when the rules for the talks were finally settled, the UUP was dependent upon at least one other unionist grouping to push through its policies (under the rule of 'sufficient consensus', any important proposal had to win the support of the representatives of over half of each communal bloc). This proved crucial especially after September 1997, when the DUP and UKUP walked out. For it left the UUP dependent upon the smaller loyalist paramilitary parties, who had their own objectives on such issues as prisoner releases that were not necessarily congenial to constitutional unionists. This played a part in forcing Trimble to acquiesce in those demands on Good Friday 1998. Trimble believes that Ancram was very pleased with these results, because they increased the divisions within Unionism. It had long been the policy of the British state, Trimble contends, to wear down the Unionist family, so as to make them more pliant to the broader needs of central government. Ancram disagrees with this analysis: it would have been far easier, he says, if Trimble had won a majority, thus diminishing his worries about Paisley and McCartney (who were then still in the talks).[50] But whoever is right, what is beyond dispute is that the Forum election was the first of a series of poor UUP electoral results under Trimble's leadership – though the decline long predated his ascent to the top job.

SEVENTEEN

The Yanks are coming

THE days following the Forum elections presented Trimble with the severest test yet of his leadership. For it was in the fortnight leading up to 10 June 1996 – the date set by the two Governments for the commencement of all-party negotiations – that the pattern of the talks was settled. Ever since the South Quay bomb, despite sometimes fierce disagreements between the two sets of negotiators, intergovernmental policy had been drifting in a pro-nationalist direction. This included the terms of entry into negotiations; when and how decommissioning would be dealt with; and, most dramatically, the issue of who would chair the talks and his remit. Unionists understood the reasons for this slippage only too well. Under ceaseless prodding from the Irish, the British were always tempted by the idea that they could win the prize of a second ceasefire. The nature of the game, as ever, was to give republicans enough whilst not losing the Unionists. But how would Trimble respond? If presented with a *fait accompli* by the two Governments, would he bring the current process to its knees – by withholding the consent of the largest Unionist party? Or would he break with his brethren in the DUP and UKUP, who adamantly opposed any resiling from earlier commitments, to keep the current talks process alive? No one knew for sure on what terms the UUP leader would settle. And as Viscount Cranborne observes, no one he has ever dealt with in public life plays his cards closer to his chest.[1]

The UUP's public position, as outlined by Trimble in the *Irish Times* on 29 May 1996, was simple enough. He referred back to the Major–Bruton communiqué of 28 February 1996, in which they stated that the opening session of talks would deal with first a 'total and absolute commitment' to the Mitchell principles of non-violence. In accepting this report, Trimble noted, the UUP had acknowledged the validity of the Mitchell compromise – that there had to be a decommissioning in parallel to negotiations. The commitments would have to be given immediately and honoured shortly thereafter – and not 'parked' as a fourth Strand which ran independently of the rest of the talks and whose success or otherwise could not affect the rest of the process. Secondly, there was the question of the agenda. Unionists were especially upset that the rules on the emerging Strand III were too intergovernmental in character and excluded them from any serious role in renegotiating the AIA. The whole thing, he believed, smacked of a classic Anglo-Irish imposition from above, instigated at the behest of those he called 'the little Hitlers' in the DFA and their 'collaborators' at Stormont. Strong words – but what did he really mean by them?

As ever, Trimble's supporters in the Conservative party were fired up by his language. They worried that the Government would dilute the conditions on decommissioning in order to secure a second IRA ceasefire (such as 'parking' the issue). On 19 May 1996, Andrew Hunter faxed the following concerned message to Trimble regarding his intentions: 'Robert Cranborne and I both feel there are too many grey areas, but see little point in demanding more than you are reported to find acceptable'. Trimble replied on the same day: 'I have not agreed anything with Major. There are too many grey areas. I find difficulty in seeing any differences between Major and Spring in terms of his procedures: tho' John claims they are different. I do not want to sound too hardline during the election. But I will insist on clarity before 10 June.' It may well have been that Trimble had not agreed anything in a formal sense, though the Prime Minister had picked up on the 'vibes' which the UUP leader was exuding. Major recalls thinking – correctly – that Trimble's hostility to Mitchell was 'more sound and fury than genuine opposition'.[2] So what was the purpose of Trimble's denial of such an agreement? He frequently preferred that unionist sympathisers on the mainland make the running for him – 'doing my dirty work' was the expression he often employed – rather than for himself to make a fuss. Thus, he appears perfectly capable of encouraging English Unionists to maintain the pressure *ad interim*, whilst planning an accommodation all along. 'Calling off the dogs' too soon would have resulted in a worse deal.

The final words of Trimble's response to Andrew Hunter were significant. 'I am also going cool on [Senator George] Mitchell since an unsatisfactory response yesterday from Anthony Lake [Clinton's then National Security Adviser] to my request for assurances that Mitchell was still committed to his report.' Nationalist Ireland was keen on a key role for Mitchell in the talks, in particular as chairman of Strands II and III, regarding this as a symbol of the further internationalisation of the conflict (and thus the dilution of British sovereignty). Trimble was concerned for several reasons. He liked Mitchell personally and could endorse his report – which he believed presented the Provisionals with some difficulties – but he feared that in a presidential election year the former US Senate Majority leader would be susceptible to pressures from Irish-Americans, who would force him to resile from his own report.[3] He wrote to Major on 20 May 1996 to state that he had spoken to Lake who 'told me that Senator Mitchell was acting in a private capacity, independently of the US administration and Mr Lake said he would be annoyed if the Senator was approached by anyone involved in the US elections. On decommissioning, Mr Lake said he had not spoken recently to the Senator but that he had no reason to believe that the Senator had changed his mind.

'In view of the somewhat ephemeral and indirect nature of the assurance on the second issue, I would not be able to agree to any involvement by Senator Mitchell *as matters stand* [author's emphasis]. Last Monday, however, you mentioned the possibility of arranging a private discussion for me with the Senator. If you are minded to pursue the possibility of the Senator's involvement in the process, I would now need to have such a discussion before I could agree to such involvement.' In this letter, Trimble attached his note to UUP candidates in the forthcoming Forum elections. In this message, however, he appeared more inclined to exclude Mitchell: 'I have made it clear to Major that we want a non-political chair for those stages of the talks [chairing Strands II and III] i.e. not Mitchell. Mitchell did a fairly good job in the Report on decommissioning. It is possible that he could help to persuade the paramilitaries to accept his report and commence actual decommissioning alongside talks. We have not agreed any such role, but we have not closed the door either.'

At Trimble's next formal meeting with the Prime Minister on 3 June 1996, Major said that he wanted Mitchell to be the overall chairman of the talks process. Trimble says he was surprised by this step, and that he told the Prime Minister that the choice of Mitchell would be unpopular with the Unionists. Major, though, was quite determined to do so. The Government believed that the appointment was important for relations with the United States and in any case there was no one else available.[4] John Hunter, who accompanied Trimble to this meeting, states that when Major told Trimble that Mitchell would be the chairman, the UUP leader swallowed hard – but made no real attempt at that meeting to fight the appointment.[5] Andrew Hunter recorded in his diary entry of 4 June that when he met Major in the division lobby, the Prime Minister denied that he would concede on Mitchell. This was because: 'a. He could not deliver because Unionists would not live with it; the negotiations would break down; there would be too many empty chairs. b. Even if he could deliver he would not. c. To entice further comment I nebulously agreed. d. PM said "we simply aren't in this business to let the Irish have it all their own way. They may do little other than cause immense trouble and be exceedingly tedious but we are on the Unionists' side."' But Major's notion of being 'on the Unionists' side' depended on a reading of where the Unionists were. Increasingly, it would not be alongside Andrew Hunter and other like-minded friends of Ulster in Great Britain.[6]

The next day, most of the headlines were devoted to the question of when decommissioning would be addressed. Trimble agreed that the opening stages of talks could begin while a deal on arms was worked out over the summer break, though the UUP would not let the negotiations proceed to a substantive phase until they saw actual 'product'. 'The Prime Minister said he will not agree to this issue being sidelined,' stated Trimble.[7] But that, of course, was precisely what was happening – and Trimble acquiesced. Partly, it was because he feared that if he joined the DUP and UKUP in opposing Mitchell in principle, and brought about a stalemate, he would create enemies in America where he was trying to 'win friends and influence people'.[8] But he may also have calculated that the Provisionals would not call another ceasefire – in which case the issue of when decommissioning was addressed was entirely academic, since their political wing could not gain admission to the talks without first ending the violence. Indeed, the events of those June days in 1996 would have appeared to support such an analysis. On 5 June, the IRA issued a statement that it would never decommission short of a final settlement; and on the 7 June, an IRA unit killed a Garda officer, Jerry McCabe, during a mail van robbery at Adare, Co. Limerick. Bruton was enraged by Sinn Fein's refusal to condemn the act, for which the IRA admitted responsibility a week later, and there was a wave of revulsion in the Republic.[9]

But the killing did not take the pressure off Trimble by illustrating the irreformable nature of the republican movement. Indeed, if anything, the pressure was increasing upon him daily. On 6 June, the British and Irish Governments produced a joint paper which gave Mitchell the role of chairing the plenary sessions as well as the subcommittee on decommissioning; whilst Mitchell's colleagues General John de Chastelain and the former Finnish premier Harri Holkeri would be independent chairman and alternate respectively of the Strand II segment of the talks.[10] The Unionist community was deeply uneasy. Paisley and McCartney were irrevocably opposed; Trimble appeared to be opposed to this paper as well, though with reservations.

What happened next remains, again, a matter of controversy. Trimble knew that when the Unionist community was under pressure, there was a widespread desire for a common approach. Accordingly, he decided to meet with Paisley and McCartney at Castle Buildings on 8 June to hammer out an agreed line. All were as one, says Trimble, on not wanting the Frameworks Documents, nor the Ground Rules paper. According to Trimble, McCartney noted that he had reserved his position on the appointment of Mitchell, but was keen to know what was the UUP leader's real position. Trimble states that he replied 'we'll have to see when we get there – but it could be difficult for you'. Trimble says he thought he had clearly signalled that he was not opposed to Mitchell per se, but rather to his powers as envisaged by the two Governments.[11] Paisley and McCartney, however, were convinced that they had agreement with the UUP to fight the appointment of Mitchell; McCartney says that the agreement was based upon a document which he faxed to Trimble on the day before. He adds that he was never, at any stage, made aware of reservations by Trimble.[12] Trimble felt that the DUP and UKUP might work with him to dispose of the Frameworks Documents, but that any such achievement would always be secondary to gaining party advantage over the UUP: he feared that if he rejected Mitchell, he would vindicate their contention that the process was rotten all along, and they would then be able to hijack Unionism for their form of protest politics.[13] His preferred solution was for the Northern Ireland parties themselves to write the rules of procedure (including the chairman's role) rather than have the two Governments impose them. Thus, he could claim a victory, even if the Ulster-British had suffered a symbolic defeat through the internationalisation of the conflict in the person of Mitchell.

McCartney noticed that Trimble, who had held his ground on Monday 10 June, was 'weakening' in his opposition to Mitchell by Tuesday 11 June: he sensed that some dealings were occurring between the UUP and UDP/ UDA and the PUP/UVF.[14] Between them, these three parties would have over 50 per cent of Unionist community support on the basis of the Forum elections and thus would satisfy the rules of 'sufficient consensus' for proceeding with the talks if they chose to accept Mitchell. The pressure from the two Governments was ferocious. Partly, it reflected the invest- ment of time and prestige by both Major and Bruton, who had come to launch the talks. Any failure would reflect badly on them, with attendant effects on the UUP's relationship with the two Governments. The talks had already started badly enough. Sinn Fein leaders, who claimed entry into the talks on the basis of their mandate in the Forum election, were denied admission because the IRA still had not declared a ceasefire. But they arranged for a piece of street theatre: to the intense annoyance of Mayhew, senior republicans turned up at the gates of Castle Buildings so their exclusion would be on view for the whole of mankind, and especially the Irish portion of it.[15] Moreover, George Mitchell and his two colleagues had been waiting for nearly two days whilst the parties wrangled over his appointment and the procedures. As far as the Governments were concerned, the friend of the US President was being 'humiliated'. Mayhew and Spring repeatedly apologised to Mitchell for the delay in seating him: they feared he might pick up his bags and go home (though Mitchell reassured them that he would sit it out till some kind of conclusion).[16]

But the pressure on Trimble was redoubled because key Irish and British players reckoned that such techniques might work. Nora Owen, the Republic's Justice Minister recalls thinking if Trimble really wanted to reject Mitchell, he would never have come to Castle Buildings with the American already designated as chairman.[17] British officials calculated similarly. 'I think that Trimble came to the negotiations knowing he would have to accept Mitchell as chairman,' observes one senior civil servant. 'But in the process he wanted to establish himself as the key figure who had to be dealt with – in other words, he was saying "don't think that you can go off and deal mainly with Adams and the DFA". He therefore played along with Paisley and McCartney to extract the most he could on the rules and procedures. He was saying "I'm a serious character, I don't care about being bolshie."' But it was a tactical escalation amidst a strategic retreat: John Taylor declared that to put Mitchell in charge of the talks 'was the equivalent of appointing an American Serb to preside over talks on the future of Croatia . . .'.[18]

Late on Tuesday 11 June, in his office on the fifth floor of Castle Buildings, Mayhew told Trimble of his decision. There were, he said, no alternatives to Mitchell. Trimble went silent; according to one official, the pause 'seemed like an eternity'.[19] The UUP then withdrew to their own offices. Trimble finally decided to go along with Mitchell, but extracted a price for it. He had determined that the *quid pro quo* would be a blank sheet on the rules governing the talks – that is, not the Ground Rules paper nor the document of 6 June. At 5:30 p.m., Trimble visited the Irish Government's rooms for direct talks to see if they would back this compromise. Shortly thereafter, Nora Owen and Proinsias de Rossa visited the UUP rooms and were happy to supply Trimble with the sort of reassurance he wanted. 'The agenda is not written in stone,' said Nora Owen. 'That's very interesting,' replied the UUP leader.[20] Nigel Dodds, the then DUP party secretary, remembers Trimble moving back and forth with drafts of how the talks would be structured. 'I've always made it clear I may part company with you [on the issue of the chairmanship],' Trimble told the DUP.[21] Trimble recalls that when he kept reporting to Paisley and McCartney the nature of his conversations with the Government, the DUP leader warned him 'to consider the personal implications of what I was doing. Up till then there had been no question of attacks.'[22] McCartney, though, asserts that Trimble never told the other Unionist parties of his intention to accept Mitchell.[23]

Even the physical imposition of Mitchell in the early hours of Wednesday 12 June had to be organised 'like a military operation'. Mayhew feared that a hardline Unionist such as Cedric Wilson (then of the UKUP) might try to prevent Mitchell from being seated in the chair; Wilson was certainly hovering in the general vicinity. Accordingly, a politician and an official – Ancram and Stephen Leach – were deliberately sat in the co-chair before Mitchell approached the spot. Mayhew remembers propelling Mitchell by the arm into the conference room; the politician and civil servant moved only seconds before he arrived. The DUP reaction was, to say the least, forthright: Sean Farren, a senior SDLP negotiator observed in his notebook that 'Trimble [was] taunted with remarks like "remember Brian Faulkner"'. As hardline Unionists raged, the twelve- to fourteen-strong Irish team led by Owen and de Rossa repaired to the Anglo-Irish Secretariat to celebrate. The Irish ministers formally toasted the officials; the officials responded in kind. The seal had formally been set on a long-time Irish goal – the internationalisation of the conflict. 'There was a huge sense of achievement,' states Nora Owen. 'We already had the New Ireland Forum Report [of 1984, composed of nationalist parties north and south of the border, but from which Unionists absented themselves]. But we did not have the majority community there. Now we did. Mitchell was in as chairman, with Ulster Unionist agreement and they had not walked. Without this, there would have been no process.'[24]

British ministers, such as Patrick Mayhew, were also impressed that Trimble had braved huge pressure in his own party and within the wider Unionist community.[25] But to senior officials, the events of June 1996 began to have a familiar pattern or – in the opinion of one civil servant – 'an almost algebraic rhythm'. This ran as follows. A proposition would be put forward by the British and Irish Governments. The Alliance party and SDLP would offer broad support, though possibly not Sinn Fein. The small Loyalist parties would then often back the Government. The DUP and UKUP would express outright opposition, whilst the UUP would express grave doubts but not close the door completely. The accept- ance of the proposal would then depend upon Trimble, for whom all sort of dances would have to take place till he had established his creden- tials within the wider Unionist community; only then could he proceed.[26] But how much did this approach profit him? Trimble was under no doubt that it had brought about substantive gains. He had obtained his blank sheets on the rules for the talks. The all-powerful chairman, as envisaged in the two Governments' paper of 6 June, would now be more of a facilitator than an enforcer – or, in John Taylor's revised description of Mitchell, 'a Serb with no powers is acceptable'.[27] Trimble noted with pleasure to how he had shaved the Governments down. In the first Irish draft, the Government of the Republic proposed that 'the two Govern- ments with the assistance of the chairmen will consult the parties'; the UUP objected. In the second, the Irish suggested 'the chairmen, with the assistance of the two Governments will confer with the parties'. Again, it was rejected by the UUP. The third draft read: 'The chairmen, the two Governments and the parties will confer.' Trimble accepted this version.

But Trimble's Unionist critics (and the SDLP) regarded his victories as the window-dressing – the illusion of control rather than the reality. According to this analysis, the two Governments were perfectly prepared to let the parties mess around with the small change of the talks once the big accounts had been settled, notably with nationalist Ireland and the United States. Decommissioning had again been postponed. Mitchell came with the blessing of the President of the United States: his mere presence was enough to constrict the UUP leader's room for manoeuvre. For once the prestige of the American Commander-in-Chief was bound up with the process, it would be ever harder for Ulster Unionists to walk away. For all of the reassurance offered to Trimble about his role, Mitchell was not insulated from the presidential election and he even played the role of Clinton's Republican opponent, Senator Robert Dole, in the mock debates that preceded the live television exchanges between the two nominees in October 1996.[28] And although Mitchell had not disavowed his own report of January 1996, he moved on with the intergovernmental consensus – which entailed constant dilution of the timing of its provisions.

Above all, Mitchell personified the internationalisation of the conflict. As Peter Bell observes, all players in the Ulster crisis increasingly looked towards the United States. 'We are now rather like those minor cast Asian potentates described in Polybius' history of Republican Rome,' he states. 'There we are, in that neo-classical setting in Rome on the Potomac, imploring Senators for favours.'[29] Irish nationalists might not have obtained all that they wanted, but the appointment of Mitchell and the willingness of Trimble to fracture the Unionist bloc could be represented as gains nonetheless. To northern nationalists such as Sean Farren, it was a far cry from the Unionist stance of 1996 and that of 1991–2, when they still regarded political discussions over the future of Northern Ireland as essentially an internal United Kingdom matter.[30] And to obtain revision of the rules, they had even turned to the Irish Government, further legitimising the southern role. Above all, it was done with the agreement of one man, David Trimble, who a mere six years earlier had been standing on the roof of Glengall Street protesting against the visit of the then Taoiseach, Charles Haughey. Paisley was in no doubts as to what the events of that night meant. 'That's it,' he told his party colleagues in the DUP room at Stormont. 'There's going to be an agreement now. Our task is to ensure that the people outside know what is going on and we keep Trimble to what he said. But he won't work with us any more.'[31]

EIGHTEEN

The Siege of Drumcree (II)

THE praise bestowed upon Trimble by 'world opinion' for his statesman-ship in helping to seat Mitchell proved shortlived. The reason could be summarised in two words: Drumcree II. Trimble's Unionist critics saw the new, unprecedented levels of opprobrium that were heaped upon him for his role in the Drumcree stand-off as all too predictable. They felt that it illustrated the pointlessness of basing key political decisions on the need to propitiate the 'international community'. Unionists only ever won plaudits for the concessions they made; by contrast, any attempt to stand up for their vital interests in a vicious inter-communal conflict was regarded by many 'right-thinking' people as the moral equivalent of such IRA atrocities as the South Quay bombing. According to this analysis, Unionists should just concentrate on defending their way of life – since good PR came at a price and of its nature could never endure. Indeed, men like William Ross believed good PR was like a monster which had endlessly to be fed and which would end up devouring the traditional Ulster-British way of life.[1] From a very different perspective, Frank Millar of the *Irish Times* also wondered whether the UUP leader had not blown a golden opportunity in taking the stance that he did during Drumcree II. As he saw it, there was a brief window of opportunity in the Republic, where opinion had turned against Sinn Fein after a series of terrorist attacks. These included the killing of Garda McCabe on 7 June and the bombing of Manchester on 15 June.[2]

But such calculations seemed at the time to be far removed from the real world of life in Portadown. There, tensions had once again reached fever pitch over the planned Orange march down the Garvaghy Road. For although Trimble liked to take the long view, especially now that he was leader of the UUP, he could not overlook the obvious: he was still the MP for the area, and no politician likes to say goodbye to a substantial portion of his electorate unless he absolutely has to do so. But it was very much a role thrust upon him – and it was a duty which the new, emerging Trimble scarcely relished. Indeed, Harold Gracey recalled that between July 1995 and July 1996, he hardly heard from Trimble, even though everyone knew the crisis was bound to come.[3] There is other evidence that Trimble simply did not want to deal with the issue at all until he was forced to address it. The Garvaghy Road Residents Group claims that they wrote three times to Trimble in 1995–6 requesting talks to avoid a repetition of the stand-off, but received no reply. Trimble now states that his failure to respond owes something to laziness: he would have to have replied himself and would not have relished a correspondence which would have taken on the air of a debate. This last point was a source of frustration to him. He felt constrained by the rut into which loyalists had inserted themselves by adopting the tactic of not talking to the Residents Group – which in his opinion was then exploited by their wider republican enemies as evidence of intransigence.[4] Since the option of talking to the residents was not open to him at this stage – indeed, he did not dare do so till 1999, well after he entered face-to-face negoti-ation with Sinn Fein/IRA's leadership – he may well have wanted to avoid thinking about a tricky subject which he could not even handle on his own preferred terms.[5] Indeed, many of the local Orangemen treated him as if he was one of their own in the security forces, such as the RUC Reserve and Royal Irish Regiment, and would not tell him the game plan. Gordon Lucy confirms that Trimble had remarkably little to do with the extensive Orange planning and preparations for the 1996 stand-off (by comparison, 1995 was a spontaneous protest).[6]

Trimble was in Stirling on Saturday 6 July for the Boyne anniversary Orange walk, as a guest of the County Lodge of Central Scotland, when his mobile telephone rang with dramatic news: the Chief Constable of the RUC, Sir Hugh Annesley, had decided to re-route the march. Until the last minute the UUP leader had been hopeful that the march could be taken down the road quickly and quietly.[7] Annesley stated that purely operational considerations governed his decision, but few Orangemen believed him – and in this crisis it was again perceptions which counted for most on both sides. Trimble spoke for the Loyalist mainstream when he asserted incorrectly that the decision was taken by 'those members of the RUC who regularly visited the Anglo-Irish Secretariat in the run-up to the decision ... I think the strategists of the Department of Foreign

Affairs believed, if Orangeism could be faced down during this summer, this would create a situation in which Sinn Fein could be enticed into talks.'[8] Speaking on Radio 4's *Today* programme on the following Monday, he warned that Annesley's decision was 'placing at risk the tranquillity we have enjoyed over recent months', a comment which Lucy says was principally construed as a reference to the fragility of the loyalist cease-fire.[9] For this act of 'scaremongering', Trimble was criticised by Gary McMichael of the Ulster Democratic Party, the political wing of the UDA: 'I don't think they [the UUP leadership] should be talking about the loyalist ceasefire being broken ... [loyalist paramilitaries] shouldn't be prompted by people like David Trimble.'[10] Annesley later said that Mayhew offered him no advice on Drumcree. Annesley told him that either of the two options could potentially lead to disorder.[11] Yet Annesley's ban did not find particular favour in the NIO, illustrating that the decision to re-route was not taken because of instructions emanating directly from the intergovernmental conference. 'The Chief Constable took a principled decision,' opines one senior civil servant but 'It was not pragmatic and the result was near civil war.'[12] Sir John Wheeler remembers that even if Mayhew had been motivated by a political agenda relating to obtaining a new IRA ceasefire (the prospect of which appeared to have receded in recent weeks, anyhow) the Secretary of State would always have been hamstrung by his lawyerly belief in the constitutional proprieties concerning operational independence of the Chief Constable. Wheeler does, though, confirm the accuracy of one of Trimble's conten-tions, that the Irish DFA wanted the Orangemen to be taught a lesson. 'It was implicit in their arguments that we would have to do whatever was necessary to keep them from going down the road,' says the former Security Minister. 'Though it was never explicitly stated, it was implicit in the course of action that they were urging upon us that we would have to shoot down our countrymen if necessary!'[13]

It was into this seething cauldron that Trimble returned on Sunday 7 July. He left his RUC personal protection unit at Carleton Street – they could not accompany him to an Orange event – and joined the brethren in the field; that night, he slept on the floor in the church hall at Drumcree. An amazing cross-section of Ulster society was to be found resting there that night, including the Star of David Girls' Accordion Band![14] But one innovation enabled him to stay in touch with the wider world in a way that had not been possible in the previous year. In the intervening months, he bought a mobile telephone, which became a kind of omnipresent trademark. By Sunday night, it was estimated that 10,000 Orangemen had turned up out of solidarity. The RUC was starting to feel stretched. Road blocks disappeared as swiftly as they emerged; on Monday evening alone, they would have to police 230 small to medium-sized parades. The atmosphere swiftly darkened, rioting occurred over-night in Belfast, Ballymena, Carrickfergus, Londonderry and Portadown. The next morning, the body of Lurgan taxi driver, Michael McGoldrick – a 36-year-old Catholic, newly graduated from Queen's, with one child and a pregnant wife – was found in his cab near Aghalee, Co. Antrim: he had been shot twice in the head.[15] No one claimed responsibility. Trimble said that 'if it should turn out to be a sectarian murder, it will be condemned unreservedly'. He went further: 'This is the sort of thing we don't want to see. It is just the sort of thing that we have repeatedly appealed to persons in paramilitaries not to do.'[16] Not everyone was as robust. David Ervine of the PUP-UVF initially said that his party did not engage in the 'politics of condemnation' – reminiscent of the formula sometimes employed by republican spokesmen when commenting upon IRA actions.[17] Suspicion immediately focused upon the highly indepen-dent mid-Ulster Brigade of the UVF, headed by the dissident Portadown loyalist, Billy Wright. Later, McGoldrick's family claimed that 'fire and brimstone speeches' and 'loose talk' by politicians had partly been respon-sible for the taxi driver's death.[18]

As the protests mounted, Trimble wrote to George Mitchell to inform him of the UUP's withdrawal from the talks until the authorities 'come to their senses'.[19] The M1 and A1 were blocked, and Aldergrove airport was sealed off. Eventually, Larne harbour closed as well. David Kerr recalls driving with Trimble to a meeting with Mayhew in Belfast: shortly after they turned off the Birches roundabout on to the M1, the UUP leader saw three plumes of smoke rising eerily in the distance. 'That's Lurgan, that's Portadown, that's Craigavon,' he noted.[20] At one point, David Campbell, a young Orangeman who was organising the protests in Lagan Valley met with Trimble and John Hunter by the Drumcree church hall. Campbell noted the support that the demonstrations enjoyed. 'Give the word, the people are there and willing to do it,' Campbell told the UUP leader. 'Let's take the country.'[21] According to Hunter, Trimble gulped at that moment.[22] And he added: 'No, we don't need to do that.'[23]

By comparison, there were few serious disturbances at Drumcree itself, though the tension rose further. Such was the strain that the Orange leadership suggested that crush barriers be used to separate the two sides, as might be erected on the occasion of a Royal visit. The RUC agreed to the creation of barriers, but the Orangemen misunderstood their short-hand and it soon emerged that what was being put up was concrete and barbed wire akin to those on dangerous border crossings. When the Orangemen asked to see the intended barrier (Trimble was worried what would happen if the Loyalists were pushed up against the wire) they were told that they could inspect it at St Paul's Roman Catholic School. A group of marshals, accompanied by Trimble, went down to the school – only to find nothing there and that the wire was already being set up. Just then they heard the noise of a fracas coming from Drumcree. They were told on their mobile telephones that the police had begun to charge the Orangemen and to push them back. Trimble drove swiftly in an unmarked vehicle to the scene through the police lines at the end of the Ballyoran estate with truckloads of regular troops looking on. As they ran through the last of the police lines to reach their brethren, they found that the RUC had entered the cemetery, assuming their new position atop several graves: according to Harold Gracey, the RUC had promised him that they would never enter the cemetery.[24] Although they offered no resistance, one Orangeman complained bitterly that it was the resting place of his father. Trimble gestured to the crowd to calm down in the face of what he, too, saw as an 'escalation by the RUC' and urged them to sit down on the road: it would then be harder for the RUC to charge them again. He then went back to the cemetery where he was filmed gesticulating a lot at the riot squad and urging them to pull back. He suddenly noticed one officer pointing a baton gun towards him. Trimble could not see the number on his tunic – thus precluding the possibility of making a complaint since it would be impossible to establish the constable's identity. 'As the officer was eyeballing me I thought to myself, "this bloody man is quite capable of shooting me".'[25] It remains the most memorable image of Trimble in that year: quite apart from the nationalist community, it horrified many Unionists as well. 'Unionists of my genera-tion found it unacceptable to poke a finger at the RUC,' says James Molyneaux.[26] Curiously, for all of their differences, Mayhew did under-stand Trimble's predicament. Andrew Hunter noted in his diary of 9 July 1996 that Mayhew said to him in a telephone conversation that 'Trimble can't afford not to be there'. Summarising the attitude of the Orangemen towards the UUP leader, Mayhew observed, '"We put you there, now do the stuff." [Trimble is being] reasonably responsible.'

Trimble spent the night of Monday 8 July 1996 at home: unlike the first Drumcree, he was better organised and managed to return to his house for some sleep and a shower. The next morning, he and Daphne Trimble went to London. His reasons were two-fold. First, he had sought an appointment with Major to discuss the crisis – along with Paisley, McCartney and Rev. Martin Smyth in his capacity as Grand Master of Ireland. Second, he had been invited on the night of Tuesday 9 July 1996 to the state banquet at Buckingham Palace in honour of Nelson Mandela.[27] Trimble knew he had to put on a display of Unionist unity because the community wanted it and there was in any case no point in holding separate meetings.[28] McCartney, though, recalls that Trimble objected to his presence and that it was Paisley who insisted that all of the Unionist leaders be there. 'You're being allowed into this meeting – but you're not allowed to dominate it,' Trimble told McCartney. To McCartney, this was a clear indication he was there on sufferance and he exploded. 'You pompous posturing ass, how dare you speak to me in those tones!': personal relations between the leaders of the various strands of Unionism were by then much worse than those which obtained between the leaders of constitutional and physical force nationalism.[29] But once they were in the Prime Minister's room in the Commons, the three party leaders emphasised that if the march did not proceed, the authorities might have eight or nine different Drumcrees on their hands.[30] But it was the dealings which took place outside of the formal context of that meeting which were most significant. Before he went into the meeting, Trimble communicated to Major that he planned to ask the four main church leaders in Ireland to intervene in the Drumcree crisis: the Church of Ireland Primate of All Ireland, the President of the Methodist Church in Ireland, the Moderator of the General Assembly of the Presbyterian Church in Ireland and the Roman Catholic Primate of All Ireland. Trimble also entertained the idea of a *quid pro quo* whereby the nationalist residents would remove their objection to the Orange march if they were allowed the equivalent of a St Patrick's Day parade. Trimble offered this because he says they knew that the Government wanted the dispute resolved by negotiation rather than by *force majeure* and that the Major ministry would view their case sympathetically if the Orangemen took the initiative and negotiations then broke down. Major duly endorsed the plan. After the three Unionist leaders emerged from the session with the Prime Minister, Trimble separated himself from the others and announced this initiative which he did not reveal over the table.[31] The church leaders' meeting, which was inconclusive, took place in Armagh the next day: its significance lay in the novelty value of a Unionist chief meeting all of the church leaders together.[32]

That night, Trimble and the Prime Minister again found themselves under the same roof – this time at the Mandela state banquet in Buckingham Palace. The Queen was 'most solicitous' he recalls, but the Duke of Edinburgh pointed at Trimble and teased the UUP leader with the words 'oh, ho, ho – so they managed to drag you away from the barricades?'; afterwards, Trimble told fellow Loyalists privately that the Sovereign's consort had a good grasp of the situation at Drumcree.[33] Jeffrey Donaldson claims that when Trimble returned the next day, the UUP leader told him, 'Major will give me a victory', so long as they went through the motions of conciliation. Trimble says that the state banquet was very conveniently timed, but he denies that Major promised him that the march would go down the road; and Major agrees with Trimble's recollection that no such pledge was given.[34] Whatever really occurred between the Prime Minister and the UUP leader that night, the visit to London did Trimble little good amongst the brethren in the fields outside Portadown. Many of them felt that he had gone to sup with a terrorist, in the person of Mandela; others saw the pictures of Trimble in white tie and tails and felt that he had let down his own people by abandoning his post to enjoy the high life.

The scene when Trimble returned on Wednesday 10 July was about as far removed from the niceties of Buckingham Palace as it was possible to imagine. The Reverend John Pickering, the Rector of Drumcree parish, had been unable to sleep all night and at around 1:45 p.m. was packed off to bed by his wife. According to his private diary, he was still lying down in the late afternoon when he received a telephone call. A huge mechanical digger was moving round at the top of the hill – and metal was being welded on. Pickering informed Trimble, who said there was no such device. 'You'd better take another look,' said Pickering. When he saw the digger, Trimble became very concerned.[35] Trimble recalls that senior RUC officers were also very worried about the digger – it had been nicknamed 'police buster' – and contacted Trimble to see if the UUP leader could do anything about it (there were also rumours that slurry tankers filled with petrol were being readied to spray the RUC). Key players such as Harold Gracey did not know where the digger came from, though Denis Watson believes it must have originated in a local construction firm. Trimble went up to the digger and clambered on to the vehicle, which according to Denis Watson was manned by loyalists in boiler suits. Billy Wright sat there, calmly sunning himself on a deck-chair, whilst the men welded on more armour plating. 'What on earth do you think you are doing?' Trimble asked them. They gave him short shrift and one of them denounced him as an MI5 agent. He was rescued by some Orangemen: Denis Watson says that 'David Trimble is a very lucky man he wasn't murdered at that stage.'[36] Harold Gracey recalled telling Trimble '"David, go you out of the way" – and he did.' Gracey then spoke to the men, whom he said that he had never seen before or since, and they switched off the engine. 'Okay, we'll do it for you, but not for him' (that is, Trimble).[37]

But the danger of them driving the digger at police lines during the night remained. Trimble then knew that there was only one option open to him. He had to find the one man reputed to enjoy influence upon these militants: Billy Wright, who had acquired an almost folkloric status amongst hardline loyalists in the region as 'King Rat'. Trimble had never met Wright before – the UUP leader states that Wright was not visible to him at Drumcree I – though the Portadown loyalist was certainly known to him as an aggrieved constituent. Wright had once turned up in his Lurgan office to complain about alleged harassment by soldiers of the Ulster Defence Regiment/Royal Irish Regiment: Trimble's secretary, Stephanie Roderick, recalls that Wright was very polite but that he had the coldest, most piercing blue eyes she had ever seen.[38] According to Trimble – who had the matter verified by his security spokesman, ex-UDR Major Ken Maginnis – some UDR/RIR soldiers had put a bounty on Wright's head: those soldiers on patrol who observed Wright obtained a £50 bonus, whilst there was a £25 bonus for sightings of Wright's side-kick, Mark 'Swinger' Fulton. Indeed, in a Commons debate on media coverage of terrorism that he himself had introduced in 1992, Trimble had con-demned a Channel 4 *Dispatches* programme, entitled *The Committee*, which alleged that there was a secret body consisting of senior RUC officers, businessmen and politicians to plan the assassination of republi-cans. Wright appeared on the programme, leaving Trimble with the impression he engaged in paramilitary activities with the approval of the police.[39] 'I hold no brief for Mr Wright,' declared the MP for Upper Bann. 'I am told that he is a gangster who tries to cloak his crimes with political motivation, occasionally gets involved in sectarian crimes about which he then boasts to journalists, giving interviews to them regularly. Whether he has committed all the offences of which he boasts I do not know, but I can hazard a fair guess as to why he collaborated with *Dispatches* and gave credence to the accusation that some RUC officers collude with paramilitaries ... He had a clear interest in harming the police force.'[40]

The full truth about Wright will probably never be known. What can be ascertained is that Wright was 35 years old in 1996. He apparently joined the Young Citizen Volunteers – the YCV, or the youth wing of the UVF – aged fifteen after the massacre of ten Protestant workmen at Kingsmills in his home patch of south Armagh in 1976.[41] Like so many who had felt the sharp end of republican terrorism, he moved to the northern part of the county where he determined to make a last stand. At that stage, he had never been sentenced for any offence, though in the early 1980s he had been remanded for one year on charges of murder and attempted murder; these were dropped.[42] He originally supported the loyalist ceasefires of September 1994, but soon became disillusioned. Wright reserved particular disdain for the 'doveish' Belfast leadership of the PUP-UVF. Much of the PUP-UVF ideology was based upon the notion that they had hypocritically been pushed into 'fighting the war'. The PUP-UVF asserted that the Protestant working class had suffered as much from Stormont's neglectful policies as their Catholic counterparts. Since their men had been dying and going to jail to maintain the privileges of the Unionist elite, they were now entitled to an independent political perspective. At times, the PUP spoke of how much they had in common with the Provisionals in terms of shared experiences of deprivation. Such talk was anathema to Wright. Leave politics to the politicians, he asserted, and let us provide the muscle. Wright believed that the PUP-UVF were putting their socialism ahead of their Unionism and that the UVF should be a broad church in terms of its ideology. He regarded men like David Ervine as traitors and saw the PUP as the pawns of British intelligence, seeking to create further splits in the Unionist bloc. They, in turn, believed that Wright was a drugs dealer who used the cause of Ulster to further his criminal ends.

Trimble met with Wright twice, once in a room in the church hall, once in the vicinity of the digger. On one level, Trimble found it disgusting.

Wright told Trimble 'quite mendaciously' that he had not been involved in the killing of McGoldrick. On the other hand, recalls Trimble, 'he was rational. He wasn't stupid by any means. It was easier to talk to him than the men on the digger.' Trimble suggested the option of a St Patrick's Day parade by nationalists as a *quid pro quo*. Initially, Wright opposed it, Trimble says, but Wright soon came to understand its necessity in the context of the talks then going on to achieve a resolution of the crisis (Paisley, believes Trimble, did not agree with this proposed compromise and therefore sought to scupper it).[43] Wright later said that 'Mr Trimble spoke to me on the basis of anti-violence. He asked me to use any influence I had to ensure there was no violence during the protest. It was not a pre-arranged meeting. He believed I had influence on the wilder elements at Drumcree and on the streets of Portadown.'[44]

Wright might have done so, but his main aim was not conciliation. Rather, his objective was victory for his people at Drumcree. Trimble also says that Wright informed him that if the RUC and Army were about to move forward on the loyalist crowd – and he had reason to believe that they would do so at 2 a.m. on Thursday 11 July – then the paramilitaries might retaliate. Trimble states that he rang Mayhew and asked him to pull back the security forces in the light of the warning; the Ulster Secretary, for whatever reason, agreed to the request and Army manoeuvres and the police profile were lowered by 7 or 8 p.m. on Wednesday 10 July. Wright denied that this part of the conversation took place, but whatever the truth of the matter one senior RUC officer is under no illusion as to the impact of 'King Rat's' presence: 'Wright's threats were a part of the reversal of the ban on the march,' he states.[45] Jim Blair also believes that 'the Wright factor' played its part in this decision, though he is not sure that it was necessarily the main element in the ultimate ruling.[46] Trimble now says of the 'digger episode': 'At the end of the day, looking back at it, I now think it was all a bluff.' Gracey subsequently even said to Trimble that he had an understanding with Wright dating back to 1995 that nothing serious would happen.[47] At the time, though, the threat appeared real enough. Daphne Trimble recalls that Trimble was desperately worried that bloodshed could both end his career and the chance of peace. If things went wrong, and the whole country erupted in violence, he would be blamed as MP for the area and any prospect of a deal with nationalist Ireland would be lost – perhaps for ever. This explains why he took the huge risk which he did in meeting Wright, even though he knew that if it emerged it would cost him dearly in terms of opinion on the British mainland as well as amongst Catholics.[48]

Trimble's entreaties to the Government were becoming ever more desperate. With 11th night almost upon them – and bonfires being lit all over the Province and especially in Belfast on the eve of the Boyne anniversary – he feared an explosion if the march was not put down the Garvaghy Road swiftly. Whatever the cause of the intelligence failure, the effects were becoming dreadfully apparent. Mayhew expected, on the basis of RUC and military advice, that around 60,000 loyalists would converging on the vicinity and he was conscious of the digger and the slurry tanker. 'Respectable people were turning out in masks who were more normally seen at the golf club,' recalls the former Northern Ireland Secretary.[49] At a crisis meeting at RUC headquarters at Knock in east Belfast, Mayhew surveyed the situation in the Chief Constable's office along with Annesley and Lt Gen. Sir Rupert Smith (the new GOC). Barbed wire was rapidly proving to be no longer enough. 'Can you hold the line if we fail?' inquired Annesley of Smith. 'Yes,' replied the GOC. 'Provided I can use ball' (Army jargon for live ammunition). As far as Smith was concerned, he was being asked to be the last resort and to stand between a large Protestant mob who had already overcome the police and who were intent on penetrating a frightened and probably armed Catholic housing estate. In these circumstances, he wished to be able to act as a soldier rather than as a surrogate policemen.[50] As Mayhew observes, 'He [Gen. Smith] knew perfectly well it was out of the question.' Annesley replied, 'In the light of that, the position is untenable.' Mayhew was surprised by what he saw as the inability of the RUC and Army to hold the line, but concedes that he underestimated the degree to which the Orangemen had worn down the security forces Province-wide.[51]

But the public order crisis was not the only element affecting the Government's thinking. Cranborne believes that the effect on Trimble's credibility after he took the risk of accepting Mitchell's chairmanship counted heavily: if the march did not go down the road, the UUP leader would have been destroyed, and with it any prospect of an inclusive settlement.[52] Nora Owen also recalls from the Irish side a general feeling emanating from Major that the march had to be expedited for Trimble's sake.[53] As Fergus Finlay noted, 'We had our ogre of IRA violence, and they [the British] had theirs of David Trimble's position being undermined.'[54] The final decision was taken at 11:45 a.m. on Thursday 11 July, when it became apparent to Annesley that the efforts of the four church leaders had failed. At 12:05 p.m. the Press Association reported the news that the march would go down its traditional route, which brought a nationalist demonstration on to the Garvaghy Road. At 12:25 a Tannoy announcement requested that the 1300 Orangemen of Portadown District and their musical accompaniment, the Star of David Girls' Accordion Band assemble for the parade. They were asked to march in files of four 'without any show of triumphalism' behind a single Union Flag, their bannerette and two sword bearers. To the beat of a single drum, the lodge and band went down the road. Once past the Garvaghy Road at Shillington's Bridge, the lodge was rejoined by Trimble: according to Gordon Lucy, he believed the crowds were even greater than in the year before.[55]

Nationalist Ireland exploded in anger. The first to feel the heat was the British team at the Anglo-Irish Secretariat at Maryfield. Initially, of course, the Irish had praised the Chief Constable for his decision; but when they learned what would happen, the RUC and the Secretary of State were subjected to a torrent of strong language.[56] The simple, one-word Irish News headline 'BETRAYED' summed up the views of many northern nationalists. John Bruton told the Nine O'Clock News that 'a state can never yield to the threat of the use of force'. A major row ensued. An enraged Mayhew retorted: 'The Chief Constable said it [sticking to his original decision] was not worth a single life. How many lives does Mr Bruton think it was worth?'[57] Trimble remembers receiving a frosty reception when he returned to the Commons on the following Monday. There, Mayhew told the House that 'all this represents, without doubt, the worst setback for many years'. He again defended the decisions taken by the Chief Constable, which he said had been undertaken without political interference. Mo Mowlam, the shadow secretary of state, agreed that the RUC had been placed in a very difficult position but added: 'Does he [Mayhew] accept that his failure to act, as we and many others have urged for many months, in a proactive way to help to resolve disputes and contentious parades makes him partly responsible for failure to reach a local agreement.'[58] She demanded details of the proposed review of marches and urged the Ulster secretary to consider suggestions for an independent commission. It was the most serious disagreement between Government and Opposition over Northern Ireland since Blair became Labour leader and the breach in bi-partisanship forced Mayhew's hand into setting up the North Committee which inquired into the matter. This proved to be the genesis of the Parades Commission, which was to give Trimble so much trouble in later years.[59]

Sir David Steel, the former leader of the Liberal Democrats, had few doubts as to who was to blame for the debacle: 'We are entitled to expect parliamentarians who describe themselves as loyalists to show a higher standard of leadership than we saw last week.'[60] Hugo Young, writing in *The Guardian* on 16 July 1996, also spoke for much of left-liberal English opinion when he asked: 'Does the leader seek to bring out the best in the people, or gratify the worst? . . . David Trimble has quickly proved a disastrous leader of the Ulster Unionists. The disaster is the greater because he gives the impression of being a modern man, capable of speaking the kind of language that reaches beyond the steeples of Fermanagh and Tyrone. Last week the proportion of time Mr Trimble was prepared to allocate to cultivating the good as opposed to the bad instincts of the people who look up to him reflected badly on his judgement. He seemed scarcely to be trying to defuse the tribalism of the Orange marchers . . .' Young concluded: 'If the mass of the people could have their way, some concessions for peace would be worth making on every side. They've tasted what it might be like. But Gerry Adams cannot bear the thought. And nor can David Trimble.' *The Economist* placed Trimble on its front cover on 13 July 1996, in his sash and surrounded by policemen in riot gear, with the headline 'Wedded to the past'.

Worse was to come for Trimble on the day of the Mayhew statement. That night, *Panorama* revealed that he had met secretly with Billy Wright at Drumcree (BBC Northern Ireland's *Spotlight* programme revealed in October 1996 that they met twice: Trimble still claimed that 'I don't know then or now, exactly who he was).'[61] Shortly thereafter, the SDLP withdrew from the Forum, never to return and henceforth it became a Unionist 'talking shop'. The SDLP added that by speaking to Wright, Trimble had deprived himself of any excuse for not talking to the Garvaghy Road Residents' Group, nor indeed to Sinn Fein.[62] Trimble defended himself against the accusation of double standards in talking to Wright but not to Brendan Mac Cionnaith of the Garvaghy Road Residents (who had a conviction): 'The two don't weigh in the same balance because you're using the word "talk" quite inappropriately,' the UUP leader told Frank Millar. 'I was not involved in any formal talks with Mr Wright and those who use that term are misrepresenting the situation. My relationship with Mr Wright is not similar to Mr Hume's relationship with Mr Adams. We were not engaged in joint political action, we were not engaged in joint action from the point of view of a demonstration, we were not coordinating activity in any way whatsoever.'[63] Trimble also said that the organisation with which Wright was alleged to be associated was 'on a ceasefire' and its political representatives (that is, the PUP) were taking part in the Stormont talks, where all of those present were content to talk to them. 'Whereas, with regard to representatives of Sinn Fein/IRA, they're not on a ceasefire,' added Trimble. The UUP leader certainly did not defend himself as well as he might have done: under the pressure of events, he seemed not to recall that he had been the first MP specifically to denounce Wright in the Commons.

As far as Trimble was concerned, the reason for the controversy over Drumcree (and his role in particular) was simple enough. Large swathes of the nationalist middle classes of Ulster settled back in the first ten days of July to watch the spectacle of the Orangemen being taught a lesson. Trimble never saw the events of July 1996 as a 'victory', but there were some undoubted losers.[64] Maurice Hayes, who was later appointed to the Patten Commission, has no doubts whatsoever that Drumcree II fatally soured the northern nationalist bourgeoisie on the RUC and drew the whole of the SDLP closer to Sinn Fein.[65] Trimble disagrees with this – perhaps inevitably, since it would imply some responsibility for this state of affairs – and asserts that the middle-class Catholic change of perceptions of the police began well before and continued long after that (not least because of the ongoing Sinn Fein/IRA propaganda campaign). As for himself, Trimble acknowledges that in meeting with Wright, he handed his foes a very obvious stick with which to beat him. But he does believe that Drumcree II did erase the anger which existed in some areas of unionism over his role in the seating of Mitchell as the talks chairman.[66]

Before the multi-party talks resumed in September 1996, Trimble met with John Hume in a hotel at Aldergrove International Airport for a 'clearing the air session'. Trimble raised the question of the SDLP returning to the Forum, but they never did so. The two also discussed the question of what to do about the small loyalist parties.[67] On 28 August 1996, the Combined Loyalist Military Command ordered Billy Wright and the former UDA commander for South Belfast, Alex Kerr, to leave Northern Ireland within 72 hours or face 'summary justice'; subsequently, a bomb exploded at the home of Kerr's parents. On the following day, Peter

Robinson of the DUP demanded that the UDP/UFF and PUP/UVF be expelled from the talks for a breach of the Mitchell principles on non-violence. Trimble stated that mediation should be attempted and insisted that the threats be rescinded for the sake of the democratic process.[68] He helped to draft a 'rescue package' to enable the parties to stay in the process if they committed themselves to the Mitchell principles and distanced themselves from the threat.[69] His worries were two-fold: first, that if the fringe loyalist parties were thrown out, the UFF and UVF would have no stake in the political process and formally abandon their cease-fires. Second, after the row over the imposition of Mitchell, Trimble knew that the DUP and UKUP might not stay in the negotiations. Without the presence of the small paramilitary parties, he would lack the support of over half of the majority community (the UUP won just under 50% of unionist votes in the May 1996 Forum elections). The two Governments opposed the loyalists' expulsion and according to George Mitchell's account, even the DUP did not want it pushed to the point of no return: they simply sought the lifting of the 'fatwa' on Wright. Shortly thereafter Wright formally founded a breakaway group, the Loyalist Volunteer Force.[70] In 1997, Wright was removed from the scene when he was sentenced to ten years' imprisonment for intimidation, though he continued to communicate with the outside world through his mobile phone.[71]

The episode was illustrative of Trimble's strained yet ambiguous relationship with the loyalist paramilitary parties. As far as both the UDP and PUP were concerned, Trimble was less 'hypocritical' in his dealings with themselves than most Unionist politicians. Gary McMichael – whose murdered father John had been a friend of Trimble – recalls visiting the UUP leader at his house soon after his election in 1995, along with John White and Joe English. McMichael was one of the UDP leaders who found Trimble a bit 'right wing' for his tastes. But they nonetheless took the initiative because they felt that the loyalist side lacked cohesion compared to the nationalists and sought to make good that deficiency by developing a closer relationship with the UUP.[72] Both loyalist parties felt that they had a key role to play in 'affording Trimble the space' in which to assume a more flexible posture. They saw themselves as slaughtering certain 'sacred cows' of Unionism, from which UUP would eventually benefit. 'We took chances they couldn't,' states McMichael. These included going to Dublin to meet in bilaterals with the Irish Government and debating with republicans (such as McMichael's encounter with Mitchel

McLaughlin at the 1995 Liberal Democrat conference in Glasgow).[73] The PUP took a similar view. But tensions also arose because from time to time, the UUP urged loyalist decommissioning to put the IRA under pressure. These entreaties were invariably dismissed by the UVF. Trimble's explanation for the loyalists' reluctance to decommission is ingenious: because the economic base of loyalist paramilitarism is not as strong as that of their republican counterparts, guns are proportionately more important to them as a means of maintaining their rackets. 'If the UVF, say, gives up its guns it also gives up territory and rackets to the UDA.' Indeed, for the most part, UUP pressure on the loyalists was not exerted by Trimble personally in an 'in your face' way: he preferred to leave the task to others. As throughout much of the 'peace process', Trimble never pushed the question of decommissioning with singlemindedness. At other times, he pushed it with apparently passionate intensity. It was all part of his unique political style – which despite his flinty candour, made him as slippery a customer as any of his contemporaries. And without such skills, he could never have survived.

NINETEEN

Fag end Toryism

THE 1996–7 period proved frustrating for Trimble. The initial bloom of excitement following his election to the leadership had passed. Having delivered the Forum elections – which had proved so explosive in nationalist Ireland – the British Government was not going to take any more big risks to help him. Especially following Drumcree II, he found himself coming up against the limitations of the power of any UUP leader, and of the image of Unionism generally. His problems also owed much to Major's desperation in this phase of his premiership to obtain a second IRA ceasefire; John Hume constantly told the Prime Minister that this prize was attainable if he waived the preconditions that had been set for Sinn Fein's entry into talks.[1] But would the terms of such a ceasefire be so abject as to make them impossible for the Government to accept? And would the Unionists' friends in the Tory party allow Major to do so, even if he was so minded? On 18 November 1996, Andrew Hunter recalls Hume telling him that the republicans' terms were:

- guaranteed immediate entry into substantive negotiations
- a guideline time frame for the talks
- an end to demands for decommissioning before or during talks
- and confidence building measures (including action on prisoners)

Hume also told Hunter of the form of words which the republicans had proposed that the British Government should use to secure an immediate ceasefire. Hunter reported this to Major and concluded that the effects would be three-fold. First, 'there would be very grave disquiet on the backbenches; [second,] the UUP and DUP would withdraw from the talks – and withdraw their fragile support of the Government; [third,]

the concessions would encourage the Provisionals to increase their demands, believing that (once again) violence had yielded dividends. In short, I believe that to follow "Hume's route" would be disastrous for the process.' John Holmes, the Prime Minister's Private Secretary, replied to Hunter on 20 November stating that Hume's view of what was happening was not shared by the Government. 'There is certainly no question of making concessions *of the kind which concern you*' (author's emphasis added: with hindsight Hume's summary of the IRA position was not misleading). Conservative backbench and UUP suspicions had been increased by the growing vagueness of the Government's responses to their inquiries concerning the definition of a 'credible' ceasefire, which would be a prerequisite for all-party talks.

Trimble was also concerned by the latest Anglo-Irish proposals on decommissioning. Mayhew had written to Trimble on 25 September 1996, informing him that 'we have worked very hard with the Irish to achieve agreement on this and there does not seem to be any further room for manoeuvre. It goes as far as we believe is possible to meet your stated concerns while remaining consistent with the two Governments' policy positions. I want to ask you to weigh the paper very carefully before reaching any conclusion on it ... I recognise that this paper will raise difficult issues for you, requiring the most careful consideration. I am ready to do my best to present the case for moving forward on this basis to plenary in the most positive and sympathetic manner.' But Mayhew went on to make clear that the commitment by the two Governments to bring forward legislation to set up decommissioning bodies by Christmas 'of course assumes a supportive Parliamentary climate which in turn would be influenced by the perception of continuing constructive engagement in the negotiations as a whole' – which could be interpreted as a clear threat that the promised decommissioning body would be contingent upon Trimble making concessions in the talks process and not holding the Government to ransom in the Commons. Pending the creation of the arms body, Mayhew proposed a committee of the plenary would do the necessary preparatory work. As Trimble noted, this committee would operate as a kind of unacceptable fourth strand, thus 'parking' the issue.

It appears that the UUP was briefly determined – at least rhetorically – to 'up the ante' on decommissioning after the IRA bombed Army Headquarters Northern Ireland in Lisburn on 7 October 1996. Hitherto, the IRA had confined its major attacks to the mainland; but this was the first serious IRA attack within Ulster since the ceasefire ended. Only reports that there were no immediate fatalities caused the loyalists to hold their ceasefire, though one of those injured, Warrant Officer James Bradwell, subsequently died.[2] Trimble accused the IRA of a policy of 'carrot and stick', of alternating bombs with hints of an imminent ceasefire which they hoped would induce Major to make further concessions. But in practice, Trimble continued to acquiesce in the dilution of the criteria for Sinn Fein's admission to the talks. This was not immediately obvious, since the immediate beneficiary was the SDLP. On 14 October Trimble emerged from Castle Buildings to say that the UUP had switched its principal focus from decommissioning to how to determine the credibility of a ceasefire. A five-point document was agreed between the UUP and the SDLP, which was accepted by all of the parties present, save the DUP and UKUP. It represented a small, but symbolically important shift in the UUP position: decommissioning was to be only the second item on the agenda for the opening plenary.

Trimble, though, received only scant reward for his flexibility. He became more anxious about the substance of his conversations with John Holmes at No. 10. His private notes of conversations (few were taken on the UUP side) point to an intensified round of diplomatic efforts in the last months of the Major ministry. The UUP leader was worried because the British paper on IRA entry into the talks given to the Irish was different from the impression given to him about that document in conversation with Major: in consequence of a more optimistic briefing that shaded key questions, he may have been bluffed into giving his assent to proposals to which he never would have agreed in cold print. He wrote to Major, although it is unclear whether he sent this letter on 26 November 1996:

At the briefing you said that there would be an express statement that the requirements of the legislation would have to be met. You then set those requirements as an unequivocal restoration of the ceasefire and establishing a commitment to exclusively peaceful means and showing a willingness to abide by the democratic process. However, there is no express restatement of these requirements in the paper. When I mentioned this to Ancram he referred to passing reference to paragraphs 8 and 9 of the White Paper and claimed that this read into the paper all three requirements. This attempted rescue is clearly unsustainable as further up the same page there is an express statement that the only precondition to entry to talks is an unequivocal restoration of the ceasefire. The result is that HMG's position is now virtually the same as that of the Irish, namely that a ceasefire and subscription to the Mitchell principles suffices [after the South Quay bomb, both Governments had said that any new ceasefire had to be 'permanent'] . . . Conclusion: I find the whole process to [be] intensely disappointing. These exchanges began with a request by us for definition of a genuine ceasefire. This we believed would make it easier to deal with decommissioning. At first you agreed that after the Lisburn and other bombs, the hurdles would have to be raised. We have ended up with a weak statement of a ceasefire, to which has been added many matters designed to act as inducements to Sinn Fein/IRA. After Hume made his approach, I was assured that I would be shown all the relevant papers. Indeed, I was told that it was only on that basis that Government decided to proceed. At one early stage your language assumed that I had seen certain papers. It has now been denied to me that there was any decision to show me the papers other than just before publication. On the other hand we were rarely offered meetings. Most, if not all of the meetings that actually occurred resulted from my requests. At those meetings we were generally given only vague language and no papers . . . the result was that on Monday morning the enemies of the Union had all the information available to them while Ancram was refusing my request for information – a clearly intolerable situation. As I said to you last night, I do not think that there has been any genuine consultation and I have been put in a position of being contaminated by a process over which I had no discernible influence . . . As I said to you last night, you have ended up accepting the Sinn Fein/IRA agenda: you are already offering them most if not all their demands.

Thus, many of the problems which Trimble encountered when Labour took office owe their origins to the decisions taken in the last days of the Tory Government. The curiosity is why he found them so much harder to tolerate under Major than under Blair. Partly, it was a matter of personality and the superior 'chemistry' between Blair and the UUP leader: one of Trimble's aides recalls that when Anthony Seldon's author-ised biography of Major was published shortly after he had left office, the UUP leader bought a copy and rushed to the index to check the personal references. Trimble was not surprised to discover that for all of Major's much vaunted 'unionism', mentions of himself and the UUP were not especially warm (though the two men were reconciled after Trimble signed the Belfast Agreement, which may explain the warmer tone of Major's own memoirs, published in 1999).[3] Likewise, Trimble's relationship with Mayhew and Ancram remained fraught so long as they were in office. At a fringe meeting at the Conservative conference in Bournemouth in 1996, Trimble even urged Major to remove them in a reshuffle – though in retrospect, the UUP leader concedes that Mayhew was 'one of the better secretaries of state'.[4] But it was also the case that as Trimble saw it, the Labour Government did its 'dirty work' comparatively openly, whereas the Tories did theirs sneakily. 'I never had occasion to address Tony Blair in the same way,' recalled Trimble in 1999. 'You can see why I wasn't inspired to help John Major.'[5] Indeed, in March 1997, Sir John Wheeler – who was more trusted by Unionists than any other direct rule minister, with the possible exception of Roy Mason – was asked by the Government chief whip, Alistair Goodlad, to undertake a 'private tour' of Unionist MPs to see what they would do in the event of a hung Parliament. Six out of the nine said they would back the Tories. But Wheeler did not even have to ask Trimble about his intentions: he believed that the answer would have been 'no'.[6] Later, Trimble would come to revise his view of Blair and seek out a much closer relationship with the Tories: as in the 1970s and 1980s, he could hold a dizzying array of positions on the political spectrum.

Why, though, was Major so desperate to dilute his own criteria for a ceasefire? After all, as Sir John Wheeler observes, on the basis of the intelligence then available, the Provisionals were certainly not going to call a ceasefire *before* the election because they regarded the Conservatives as so paralysed by their alleged dependence upon the Unionists. If anything, they would deliver for Blair.[7] Major may still have hoped against hope that he could pull something off and win an election on the basis of 'peace in Ireland' (although any deal might well not have proven cashable in any party political sense). Likelier explanations are that he saw it as his legacy to history. Indeed, Cranborne states that 'having realised that the election was lost, Major wanted a peace agreement more than anything else'.[8] And if he could not obtain it himself, he wanted to bequeath as much of a clean sheet to his successor as possible (notwithstanding his alleged personal dislike of Blair) to create the conditions for an 'inclusive settlement' within the Union that comprised a substantial portion of the republican movement. Whatever his true motivation, Major was unable to move as far as Hume wanted; Kenneth Clarke, Cranborne, Michael Howard and Peter Lilley persuaded the Prime Minister that to compromise his previous position would not be acceptable to the backbenches. On 28 November 1996, Major replied to the IRA proposals in the Commons in response to a question from Andrew Hunter, but by then it appeared as though he was going through the motions on a still-born initiative.[9]

The other cause of Trimble's vexed relationship with the Tories lay in the very set of circumstances which supposedly gave him his iron grip over the Government – the parliamentary arithmetic. It was thought by nationalist Ireland that almost any policy decision (such as Government pressure to secure the exemption of Ulster's BSE-free herds from the beef ban and the creation of a full Northern Ireland Grand Committee to examine legislation, thus bringing Ulster into line with Scotland and Wales) was bound to be the result of a 'corrupt bargain'.[10] But as time went by, the threat of Trimble bringing down the Government diminished. With a year to go, Trimble mattered. With six months or less, he did not matter nearly as much. Mayhew's letter to Trimble on decommissioning thus illustrates that the UUP leader was as much a hostage to the Government as the Government was to him. He calculated that he could not bring Major down anyhow. 'Major was only at risk on the European issue,' recalls Trimble. 'On every other issue "the bastards" [Major's term for Eurosceptic Cabinet colleagues] were with him. The [Nick] Budgens [Enoch Powell's pro-Unionist successor in Wolverhampton South West] wouldn't vote for us to do so.'[11] But there was another aspect, too. In a hitherto unpublished note to a colleague on 12 February 1997, Paddy Ashdown recorded Trimble as telling him that in those last months of the Conservative Government, Labour were not aiming to bring Major down. 'He [Trimble] didn't believe Labour were "trying". He had said to them that he couldn't understand why they had not approached him for "help" (to get rid of the Government). He had made it clear that he would be happy to support them on specifics and to help them defeat the Government. I replied that the likelihood was that Labour were quite sensibly deciding that they couldn't get themselves into a position where they "owed debts" to either side of Northern Ireland, because this would make it impossible for them to deal with the situation after the election.' Trimble then told Ashdown that '"the Government has only one further thing to do for me. They promised me something back last July on the Northern Ireland Grand Committee." It is clear that the Tories have given the Irishmen [sic] undertakings on a Northern Ireland Grand Committee but have not yet delivered. Trimble said "we all know why they haven't delivered it yet. They are keeping us on the hook as long as possible."' Ashdown concluded: 'I did not get the impression that he would pull the plug on the Government early. He might, if Labour offered him some kind of a deal. But since they are not going to, he obviously believes that it is best to stick with the Government, to give them time to build up in the polls against Labour in the hopes of getting a narrow General Election result in which they will continue to have overwhelming influence.'

Trimble's dealings with the British Government may have proven to be a disappointment, but he made some progress in a narrowly partisan sense. In late December 1996, the leader of the Referendum Party, Sir James Goldsmith, approached Trimble with a proposition: Goldsmith's group in the European Parliament (where he sat as a French MEP) known as *L'Autre Europe* had lost one of its members. This meant that it was below the quota required to be a fully recognised bloc with attendant privileges. Goldsmith suggested that the Ulster Unionist MEP, James Nicholson, move to his grouping from the centre right European People's Party in exchange for a donation of £250,000 – to be spent on a referendum campaign on the single currency. It made good sense to Trimble, since he was sceptical of a single currency, and the EPP was an increasingly federalist party.[12] The deal was sealed at the London offices of David Burnside, despite the scepticism of some party grandees. Trimble greatly enjoyed this kind of cosmopolitan wheeling and dealing: it represented the kind of unconventional move which distinguished him from his predecessor and which still alarmed some of his more staid party colleagues.

Trimble's other success came in the allocation of seats between the Unionist parties before the General Election of 1997. The Boundary Commission for Northern Ireland had increased Ulster's representation in the Commons from 17 to 18, creating several new seats in the process. Normally, in constituencies where there was some kind of serious nationalist challenge, the incumbent Unionist – whether UUP or DUP – would be given a clear run for fear of handing the seat to the SDLP or Sinn Fein. Two seats, though, were bones of contention: the newly created division of West Tyrone and the substantially redistributed seat of North Belfast. In West Tyrone, both the UUP and DUP had candidates whom they felt had legitimate claims. In North Belfast, the Ulster Unionist Association was riven by splits and the 72-year-old incumbent, Cecil Walker, could scarcely be said to be the most effective MP at Westminster; the DUP were pushing their Party Secretary, Nigel Dodds, an immensely capable Cambridge graduate with a double-first in law who had secured the highest number of first preferences in that seat in the May 1996 Forum elections.[13] Moreover, Hume baulked at the prospect of a sectarian voting pact with Sinn Fein and the SDLP and the republicans fought each other in numerous constituencies. But in the negotiations between the UUP and DUP, Trimble ensured that the Paisleyites stood down in some seats. 'At the end of the day, the DUP knew we were ahead in West Tyrone,' claims Trimble. 'Theirs was a feeble threat and they weren't going to split the vote' (and thus let in Sinn Fein's Pat Doherty).[14] Likewise, in North Belfast, the DUP accepted arguments that a Dodds challenge risked letting in Sinn Fein or the SDLP. But it also did so on the basis of a promise by Walker that this would be his last campaign.[15]

The 1997 General Election campaign in Northern Ireland was largely uneventful. Even Trimble's refusal to state that he would 'never' sit at the same table as Gerry Adams ('of course, one cannot rule out that Mr Adams will see the error of his ways') caused little controversy.[16] In the end, he secured the best result under his leadership. The UUP polled 32.7% of the poll and picked up one seat – West Tyrone, where the majority nationalist vote was split between Sinn Fein and the SDLP.[17] Trimble was delighted by the outcome in this seat and compared it favourably with neighbouring Mid-Ulster, where the DUP incumbent, Rev. William McCrea, was ousted by Sinn Fein's Martin McGuinness (indeed, Province-wide, the DUP was pushed into fourth place by Sinn Fein in terms of the popular vote). McCrea had appeared on a platform with Billy Wright in September 1996 and in so doing had further polarised the two communities in his constituency. Although the DUP vote was little changed on the 1992 result, McCrea's image shifted the balance within the nationalist population. Many of them concluded that supporting a terrorist was no longer beyond the pale and that they, too, could now opt to be represented by the most hardline advocate of their communal interests. By contrast, the public image of Willie Thompson, the UUP candidate in West Tyrone, was rather less contentious then: only later did he become known as a high-profile political opponent of accommodating republicanism. Because of that, a significant section of the SDLP vote had felt able to spurn the tribal drum of Sinn Fein knowing that it might let in a Unionist, but a Unionist who was tolerable to the less aggressively nationalistic portion of the Roman Catholic electorate.[18] Yet for all the risks which Trimble would take to bring nationalists into the fold, substantial cross-community voting remained largely a glimmer in the UUP leader's eye. This saddened him – but did not deter him as he proceeded to the next phase of the Trimble project.

TWENTY

The unlikeliest Blair babe

TRIMBLE rapidly adjusted to Labour's landslide victory in 1997, even though it entailed the loss of the Unionists' leverage in the division lobbies of the Commons. His surprising level of confidence in the new Government owed much to the personality of the new Prime Minister. So total was Tony Blair's grip, in Trimble's eyes, that he never much worried whether the new, massively enlarged parliamentary Labour party contained a few sympathisers who would try and pressure the Government to impose an AIA Mark II (or some other diktat).[1] The two men had met when Blair was the shadow Home Affairs spokesman under John Smith and Trimble was his UUP counterpart under Molyneaux. 'It was the first time that I'd come across a Unionist politician at all,' recalls Blair. 'People saw he was very clear, a real intellect with a genuine interest in ideas.'[2] Blair asked for Trimble's assistance in shifting Labour away from its hostility to key provisions of the Prevention of Terrorism Act. When Trimble asked Blair in a private session whether he was hemmed in by the very 'Green' shadow Northern Ireland Secretary, Kevin McNamara, Blair just rolled his eyes. 'It's a good job nobody is recording this conversation,' quipped the future Prime Minister.[3] It was the kind of signal which Unionists greatly appreciated. McNamara had been a hate figure to loyalists since the 1960s. Shortly after his arrival at Westminster in 1966, McNamara became associated with the more nationalistic elements in the emerging civil rights movement and in 1988, he expressed the aspiration that he might become the last Ulster Secretary before re-unification. He was thus the personification of Labour's 'unity by consent' policy.

There was no doubting that Blair was very different to McNamara, but the nature of those differences was rarely examined by Unionists (nor, indeed, the origins of Blair's own position on the Ulster Question). Blair was not the 'civic unionist' imagined by some of Trimble's supporters and also some Irish nationalists – who divined from some early Prime Ministerial pronouncements that he saw the creation of new political institutions in Northern Ireland as part of a programme of constitutional reform set firmly within a United Kingdom context. But nor was he the neo-McNamara-ite pursuing the Old Labour agenda by cleverer means, as latterly envisaged by Robert McCartney. As ever, Blair pursued his much-vaunted 'third way', and without much sentimentality. Blair appears to have been little affected by his Ulster Protestant ancestry. His mother, a Corscadden, came from Donegal Protestant stock who lived for many generations in Ballyshannon. (The *Belfast News Letter* of 31 December 1799 contains a petition in favour of the Act of Union signed by the citizens of Donegal, including many Corscaddens and Lipsetts, who come from the same areas.)[4] Nor does he appear to have been much influenced by spending school holidays in one of Ulster's three 'lost counties' or by having cousins who still live in unionist areas of Counties Londonderry and Tyrone.[5] This is in marked contrast to the warm ties of kinship which inform the attitudes of figures from nationalist backgrounds, such as Clare Short (whose family came from Crossmaglen in the republican heartland of south Armagh).[6] Some loyalists thought it significant that Blair's wife came from a Liverpool Irish Catholic background – though the degree of her influence on Northern Ireland remains unknown. Nor, despite his famous declaration in the Good Friday week of 1998 that the 'hand of history' was upon him, did Blair display any great knowledge of Northern Ireland's past.

What, then, was Blair's track record on the subject? He certainly visited Northern Ireland to lecture as a barrister during the early 1980s – and was sufficiently struck by the way in which his hosts would look under their cars for bombs to refer to it in a critical address in Belfast in October 2002. John Lloyd – who was one of Trimble's strongest supporters in left-liberal journalistic circles in the 1990s – knew Blair and his wife Cherie when they all served on the General Management Committee of the old Hackney South and Shoreditch Constituency Labour Party. 'Ireland', as it was invariably described, often came up as an issue. Lloyd had been a former B&ICO activist who believed in the pro-partition 'Two Nations' theory, and he would often challenge the Trotskyite contingent in the CLP intellectually; but Blair always kept his counsel on the subject. Indeed, Lloyd recalls that Blair was always reluctant to discuss anything from first principles. Rather, his attitude was 'whatever works'. Years later, when

Lloyd was on home leave from Moscow, where he worked as *Financial Times* bureau chief, he again met Blair who had by then become leader of the Labour party. Lloyd congratulated Blair upon moving McNamara shortly after he became leader and expected Blair to pick up the theme with enthusiasm. Instead, all Blair said was: 'McNamara's a bit long in the tooth'. As Lloyd observes, it was a contingent rationale based upon generational and personal considerations, rather than anything more substantive.[7]

Blair appeared to move carefully on the subject of Northern Ireland. Several MPs were struck by the formulation which Blair adopted during the 1994 leadership contest. During the campaign, the contestants were asked their view on a series of topics: when it came to Northern Ireland, Blair never said 'I think'. Instead, he said in the devolution portion of his manifesto that 'the conflict in Northern Ireland is the gravest and most protracted problem facing the British and Irish peoples. The pursuit of peace and reconciliation in Ireland [sic] should be one of the highest priorities of a Labour Government. The Labour Party is committed to the aim of Irish unity by consent and the principles contained within the Downing Street Declaration.'[8] In other words, he contented himself with a factual statement of the status quo rather than giving any indication of his own views. Blair's public caution was all the more noteworthy since Labour had taken the first slow steps away from its 1980s position under John Smith's brief stewardship. The 'unity by consent' policy of the Foot–Kinnock years, forged as a compromise during the party's dramatic lurch to the left, had become a liability. Because the policy had a pre-determined anti-Unionist bent, it precluded any kind of inclusive dialogue with the majority community and thus cut Labour out of any serious role in an emerging settlement. During the 1992 election campaign, the then Ulster Secretary, Peter Brooke, had been able to make capital out of this one-sided policy, which was portrayed by the Tories as part of Labour's broader penchant for constitutional adventurism, leading to the break-up of the United Kingdom.[9] Moreover, Labour's hostility to the Prevention of Terrorism Act could be portrayed as a residue of its 'Loony Left' phase on law and order issues generally – a point which particularly exercised Blair after Michael Howard adopted a far more robust line at the Home Office from 1993 onwards. Blair, as his shadow, had felt uncomfortable about voting 'no' to the renewal of the Prevention of Terrorism Act on 9 March 1994 – on the very day that Heathrow had been mortared by the Provisionals.[10]

When the 1992 election yielded a narrow Conservative majority – and the Ulster Unionists assumed a statistical importance at Westminster which they had not enjoyed since 1976–9 – it became even more necessary to revise elements of the party's explicitly anti-Unionist policy. Smith's first important move was to offer bipartisan support to the Conservatives on the Downing Street Declaration of December 1993: its 'Green' language kept Labour's pro-nationalist contingent happy, but its emphasis upon the consent principle was also, as has been seen, just about acceptable to the UUP.[11] It was thus the first signal of a shift from a policy which explictly stipulated that Irish unity was a desirable outcome, to one of neutrality on the subject. Labour's move to a new cross-party consensus on the overall constitutional status of Northern Ireland came about partly because of its own interests, but also because of the Tory Government's shift towards an apparent enunciation of explicit neutrality on the Union.

The gradual abandonment of wholesale hostility to the PTA turned out to be the extent of Labour 'revisionism' in the area of security policy. Far more dramatic, at least at first glance, was the personnel shift embodied by the appointment in October 1994 of Mo Mowlam as shadow secretary of state for Northern Ireland, replacing McNamara, who moved to the civil service portfolio.[12] Notwithstanding her stint as McNamara's deputy in 1988–9 – she had, in fact, been appointed at his behest – Mowlam carried less baggage than he. Because she was not McNamara, she was able to cultivate contacts in the Unionist community in a way that no senior Labour figure had done for years.[13] In the early days, this 'charm offensive', as Trimble describes it, attracted relatively favourable notices in some Unionist circles: she called in at Trimble's Lurgan office and wandered up the High Street. And she even stayed with so staunch a sceptic of the peace process as William Ross after addressing local Ulster Unionists at their AGM on 4 February 1995 at the Royal British Legion Hall in Garvagh, Co. Londonderry (where she astonished some of those present by apparently declaring she did not feel British).[14] But the novelty of her approach was such that these doubts did not reach crisis proportions. Indeed, even Trimble was not worried by her declaration that 'the status quo is not an option' – which some Unionists interpreted as inevitably entailing a dilution of Ulster's constitutional position within the United Kingdom.[15] Trimble, rather, interpreted this as a reference to the undesirability of retaining full-scale direct rule.[16] Perhaps he ought to have been more concerned: it was indicative of her mindset that in her memoirs published in 2002, Mowlam declined to refer to the Province as Northern Ireland, but rather as 'N.Ireland'.[17] The revised edition of Liam Clarke's and Kathryn Johnston's biography of Martin McGuinness also illustrated her high 'comfort level' with senior republicans: the transcripts record the then Secretary of State openly discussing her career prospects with McGuinness and vouchsafing her desire to deliver on long-time demands of Sinn Fein, such as an inquiry into the murder of the slain Belfast solicitor, Pat Finucane.[18]

On a personal level, Trimble was not impressed by Mowlam. Daphne Trimble states that even prior to Mowlam's appointment as Secretary of State in 1997, the UUP leader never really liked her.[19] In some ways, there were odd similarities between the two: both were provincial academics of lower-middle-class/upper-working-class origins who had 'made it' on their own merits.[20] Both could be astoundingly rude to those around them and were, in their respective capacities, completely different from those who had preceded them. Both were often more comfortable with, and interested in, foreign political cultures – Trimble in Europe, Mowlam in the United States (she obtained her doctorate from Iowa State University and had a deep interest in American politics). But the similarities ended there. 'She is hail fellow well met and over the top,' comments Daphne Trimble. 'He is inherently shy. She is so dismissive of formalities. There are times when a little bit of formality is appropriate for a situation and she doesn't do it at all. It's quite deliberate on her part.'[21] Such traits were perhaps always there, but they became much more pronounced after her illness and operation for a brain tumour in early 1997. Neither senior NIO civil servants, nor pillars of Ulster's civil society, were exempt from such lapses. Indeed, Peter Bell recalls during the Dublin Castle talks of February 1998 that she arrived and declared to her officials, 'Look, I've got this submission from Tony Beeton [a civil servant who later died in the Paddington rail disaster] and he needs more stuff. Which of you is in charge here?' 'I am, Secretary of State,' replied Quentin Thomas, the NIO Political Director. 'No, Quentin, love, you're not. That's why I've promoted someone else.' She then hurled a bundle of papers at her Permanent Under Secretary, Joe Pilling. According to Bell, Pilling 'sat there like a Buddha about to be blown up by the Taliban'.[22] The Trimbles felt that at least Mayhew had some sense of the Viceregal aspects of a Secretary of State's job inherited from the Governor in 1973: the dignified as distinct from the efficient part of his functions (the Ulster Secretary's official residence is the Governor's old mansion at Hillsborough Castle, Co. Down). To Trimble, all this betokened her lack of traditional boundaries and, by extension, her lack of political boundaries in dealing with Sinn Fein/IRA. 'How can you have any sense of your country's dignity when you have no sense of personal dignity?' Trimble once exclaimed to his wife.[23]

Some colleagues of Mowlam's, such as Tony Worthington, thought that some of Trimble's difficulties with her stemmed from the inability of macho Ulster males to cope with a woman in a position of authority.[24] Certainly, Mowlam did talk to associates about the need to 'civilise' the Ulster male. As far as Trimble is concerned, the allegation of misogyny is unconvincing – and is rejected by Mowlam as well as the UUP leader himself (if anything, Trimble prefers female to male company). Instead, as Mowlam observes, 'I don't think there is really a problem with the personal chemistry between us. I think the difficulties are really of a political nature.'[25] On one level, she is right to assert that the issues mattered more than the personalities: Trimble believed that when she took over in 1997, her anti-Unionist tilt so alienated pro-British opinion in the Province as to make it much harder for him to effect the necessary compromises. But the matters of personality and policy could not be separated. Trimble is a voracious reader who devours briefs and then expostulates on them with great precision. He believed that Mowlam was far less inclined to do so. Others disagreed, contending that she entered the job as one of the best-prepared Secretaries of State (Frank Millar, for one, believed that she knew the positions of all the participants in the process inside out and sometimes better than those participants themselves).[26] But her performance on such issues in office was by some viewed as less impressive, perhaps owing to her illness: for example, she did not shepherd key items of legislation through the Commons in 1997–8, including the Emergency Provisions, the Police and Parades Bills. Some observers detected a tinge of intellectual superiority on Trimble's part. He would come to view what he saw as her imprecision as almost disastrous for the peace process, which was predicated upon a set of carefully constructed, almost theological formulations. But he underrated Mowlam's usefulness to Blair. This lay partly in her role within the Labour party – and with nationalist Ireland – both before and after 1997. As Tony Worthington, her deputy in Opposition observes, Mowlam kept the McNamara and Livingstone wings of the party on board (the two were distinct – McNamara's approach was of the more traditional nationalist, 'Emerald Isle' variety, Livingstone was more 'republican chic').[27] Indeed, as Frank Millar observes, perhaps her most significant contribution was in Opposition. She successfully reassured Dublin and Sinn Fein that notwithstanding Blair's tactical support for the Conservative Government, Northern Ireland would indeed be a high priority for Labour once they entered office.[28] The question is whether nationalist Ireland became more obdurate during the latter Major years, suspecting a better deal was on offer.

So much for Labour's new men. But what of their measures? Here, the picture was yet more complex. The initial phase, of reshuffling personnel, was relatively simple. It was a recognition of political reality designed to 'close down negatives', as American political consultants might put it, in the run-up to the General Election. Indeed, the limited nature of Blair's aims in this period was pointed up by the writer Ronan Bennett, a former republican internee whose subsequent, initial, conviction for the murder of an RUC officer was overturned by the Northern Ireland Court of Appeal. Blair told Bennett, apparently much to the latter's chagrin, that he regarded the Ulster problem as 'insoluble'.[29] But Labour's own liabilities were another matter – and the most obvious of these was the 'unity by consent' policy. As Trimble notes, the mantra of 'unity by consent' was nonsensical anyway: since the consent of Ulster's majority was never going to be forthcoming, there would be no unity. At a series of seminars from 1994 onwards the shadow team took apart the 'unity by consent' policy bit by bit.[30] 'If we were going to have a Labour Government, you couldn't have a Government seen as hostile to the majority of the population,' recalls Worthington. 'We were working off a 1981 policy.'[31] Blair signalled a further shift in policy in a full-page interview with Frank Millar of the *Irish Times* on 4 September 1995, declaring that Labour would live with whatever the people of Northern Ireland wanted.[32] On 14 September 1995, McNamara resigned from the front bench. One of a number of reasons which he gave for this decision was the uncritical support given by Labour to the Conservative Government's Northern Ireland policy.[33] Blair's *Irish Times* interview impressed Trimble hugely – though he may have read too much into the attendant discomfiture of Labour's Greener elements.

Such misreadings concerning the nature of Labour *policy* would have been reinforced by Blair's tactical support for Major's stance on decommissioning, including Mayhew's 'Washington III' criteria. Trimble's confidence was further bolstered by Blair's backing for Major's decision to go for an elective route to negotiations as part of his response to the Mitchell Report of January 1996 – which angered John Hume, who was widely admired in Labour circles. Blair told his hosts at one Irish embassy luncheon that he had to do such things prior to the election: the peace process was Major's one great achievement and he could not be seen to cut across his bows.[34] As leader of the Opposition, he did not see it as his role to be an advocate on behalf of any one side and would frequently declare in this period, 'I'm not a player in this.' But all would change once he entered office. New Labour identified two senses of 'exclusion' in Northern Ireland and determined to address them both energetically. The Unionist sense of exclusion derived from what they saw as the arrogant Tory style of decision-making in the development of new political institutions (*vide* the AIA and the Frameworks Documents); the nationalist-republican sense of exclusion derived from what they saw as basic inequities in the state and society of Northern Ireland and from the Tory 'preconditions' on decommissioning before Sinn Fein could enter talks. Labour hoped that Unionists would be grateful enough to them for addressing such feelings of disempowerment (often simply by consulting them and granting enhanced levels of access) and therefore might be more willing to acquiesce in Blair's policy for addressing the 'disempowerment' of republicans and nationalists. Of course, much of this approach was implied in the Tory policy since Peter Brooke's time, as embodied in both his Bangor speech and Whitbread lecture of 1990. But although Labour felt that the peace process was one of the few achievements of the Major ministry, the Tories had become tired by this point and were too dependent upon the Unionists to do anything dramatic to maintain momentum.

Trimble rarely seemed to appreciate how different Blair's basic view of the Ulster question was from his own. The new Prime Minister declared in his first address in Northern Ireland on 16 May 1997, that he 'valued' the Union. But there were few concrete aspects of the existing Ulster-British way of life that he appeared to 'value'. Thus, portions of his Stranmillis College address of June 1999 – and, indeed, his Labour party conference address of 2001 and his speech at the Belfast Harbour Commissioner's office in October 2002 – would not have vexed a civil rights activist such as Michael Farrell, who dissected the *ancien régime* in his polemical tome *Northern Ireland: The Orange State* (Farrell's book was spotted on Blair's desk by John Taylor, who asked the Prime Minister, 'What on earth are you reading this awful book for?').[35] Thus, Blair declared that 'there can no longer be a Northern Ireland based on other than the principles of justice, fairness and equality and recognition that sectarianism is a thing of the past. Many republicans do not believe that Unionism will share power with them. Unionists must prove them wrong.'[36] Considering the gains which nationalists had made under direct rule, few Unionists would have recognised this as a fair characterisation of the events of the last quarter-century plus: it was almost as if Blair thought that Unionists still ran Stormont under a system of undiluted majority rule and the state-sponsored reforms of the past three decades (often urged by the SDLP) had not occurred. What, many wondered, had been unjust, unfair and unequal about housing allocation or criminal justice under successive Tory and Labour Governments? Indeed, 'sectarianism' was mentioned only in the passage addressed to Unionists (with David Trimble patronisingly exempted from such strictures) but was not mentioned in those passages addressed to republicans. Moreover, Unionists could not but notice that the Stranmillis speech implied that alleged 'inequality' and 'unfairnesses' were on a moral par with the IRA's retention of a terrorist arsenal.[37]

Some veteran Blair-watchers thought that there was little ideology in all of this: having done one 'nice' thing for the unionists (that is, acknowledging the consent principle) he then had to do something 'nice' for nationalists to even up the score. But there was a substantive component as well. There was a radical edge, a certainty about Blair's 'pro-nationalist' speeches; by contrast, his 'pro-Union' pronouncements were far more carefully qualified (in the Stranmillis address, he stated 'we have resolved the key constitutional issues' – but perhaps out of deference to nationalist sensibilities, did not say how). Moreover, there was a disjuncture between Blair's willingness, on the one hand, to remember and to make an apology on the 150th anniversary of the Irish Famine and the absence, on the other hand, of any planning for official celebrations of the 200th anniversary of the 1800 Act of Union.[38] Other New Labour figures continued to propagate this worldview, even as they revised their opinions shifted on most other issues. Thus, Peter Hain, a Foreign Office minister, couched the Ulster question in unmistakably nationalist terms to an audience in Delhi on 20 November 2000: 'In 1921 the Irish

Free State was established. That left the six counties of Northern Ireland, with their majority Protestant population, in the United Kingdom. But it was an unsustainable settlement, the Protestant majority in the North ruling oppressively in a devolved administration and denying the Catholic minority basic human rights which it felt could therefore only be achieved by re-unification with the independent Irish state in the South, an objective which some nationalists pursued by terrorism.'[39] After the events of 11 September 2001, the British Government also increasingly promulgated an 'international ideology of Northern Ireland' – derived from their experiences of dealing with Ulster – which was effectively a more elaborate version of Blair's famous mantra on law and order: 'tough on crime, tough on the causes of crime'. Implicitly, it was the old Unionist state and society which was a key 'cause' of the Troubles.

Blair's solution to Ulster's ills would be a McNamara-ish, almost Livingstonian approach to 'reserved' issues – security, 'demilitarisation', the RUC, reform of the criminal justice system, the 'equality' and 'human rights' agendas (significantly, Northern Ireland policy was one of the areas where the former GLC leader felt able to offer Blair almost wholehearted support when he became Prime Minister: indeed, Mowlam tried too have him appointed as a junior minister in the NIO in 1997).[40] These 'reforms' would be implemented even if there was no agreement at the talks. Trimble was perfectly well aware of this aspect of Labour policy from an early stage.[41] When Labour voted against the second reading of the Emergency Provisions Act shortly after the South Quay bomb, Trimble declared that they did so because Mowlam was looking over her shoulder at 'certain elements among Labour backbenchers'.[42] Later, Trimble and Mowlam would also disagree over Drumcree II, and Mowlam's proposed solution for the parades issue in the shape of an independent commission.[43] But despite such disagreements, Trimble largely concerned himself with those aspects of the Blairite stance which most suited him – the institutions of government and constitutional questions. Indeed, it can justly be said that he did little to educate his followers on the true nature of the New Labour synthesis, and by focusing largely on the Blairite 'prizes' gave an incomplete impression of what the incoming ministry's programme would be. Certainly, Blair did not mislead the unionists about the broad outlines of his programme, at least in this period – nor, it must be said, did Mowlam. Indeed, when problems arose – *vide* Mowlam's remarks about the 'status quo' not being 'an option' –

Trimble's method of dealing with them was to employ the formula 'the sovereign can do no wrong', and that difficulties should be laid at the door of 'wicked advisers' (a concept described by some medievalists as 'naive monarchism').[44]

Certainly, there were differences between Blair and Mowlam. But, for the most part, they did not relate to overall *policy* either in Government or in Opposition. Rather, they seemed to relate to personality, style and perennial tensions between No. 10 and departmental ministers about turf. Indeed, even prior to the General Election, some senior NIO officials urged that Blair and Mowlam set up a division of labour, with Blair largely handling Trimble (as was already the case under the Tories) and Mowlam largely directing her efforts to republicans and nationalists. Mowlam denies that there was any conscious attempt to choreograph a 'hard cop, soft cop' routine of this kind, but it certainly appeared to evolve that way under the impact of events once Labour were in office.[45] (Intentionally or unintentionally, she may also have served the purpose of 'spooking out' unionists into signing up to the new institutions – and thus into supporting Trimble.) But personality differences had profound political implications. Once Blair was convinced of Trimble's bona fides as a modernising Unionist leader who was prepared to share power with Catholics, he was sometimes prepared to pay a high price with nationalist Ireland to sustain Trimble within the unionist community. Blair's support for Trimble was strongest on procedural matters – elections to Assemblies, suspensions of Assemblies, and postponements of elections – rather than on matters of policy *per se* (such as the RUC, the criminal justice system or fair employment legislation).

It is possible that Trimble thought that in practice Labour would not have the time to 'engage' on a sustained basis once in Government and would simply seek to 'shut things down': no 'high wire acts' and an updated version of Roy Mason's 'safety first' approach (a reference to the Labour Secretary of State from 1976–9, who became something of a pin-up to Unionists for his no-nonsense, anti-republican attitudes). Trimble was not alone in believing that Blair would not devote that much effort to the subject. Even the US Embassy – which had considerable dealings with New Labour in Opposition – also underrated the amount of time which Blair would devote to the subject of Northern Ireland once in Government. In the early days of Blair's leadership, the Irish noted an unwillingness to commit, too. Fergus Finlay recalls that when Blair came to Dublin as Opposition leader and called in on the DFA, his eyes glazed over when his hosts raised Northern Ireland; he only really became animated over dinner when he pumped the Irish Finance Minister Ruairi Quinn – just back from an Ecofin meeting – for information on the extent of Kenneth Clarke's divergence from official Conservative Government policy on EMU.[46]

As the election neared, Blair took more of an interest in these matters. He and his Northern Ireland team attended a 'preparing for Government dinner' in late 1996 at the Travellers' Club, at which senior civil servants such as the NIO Permanent Under Secretary, Sir John Chilcot, played a prominent role. But other, less formal, influences were also working away to stimulate Blair's interest. David Montgomery, Trimble's contemporary from Bangor Grammar, had by now become a Blair ally as chief executive of Mirror Group Newspapers. In particular, Montgomery worked assiduously to bring New Labour and Trimble closer together, fearing that if Unionists said 'no', the 'Brits' might pull out. The Mirror Group chief had a ready-made opportunity to effect such introductions at the 1996 Labour conference in Blackpool – the last such event before Blair became Prime Minister.[47] Chris McGimpsey, the Ulster Unionist councillor for the Shankill – himself an ardent socialist and a pillar of the Unionist Labour Group – offered to organise a fringe meeting at the Labour conference and Trimble eagerly accepted. A perfect platform was found in the shape of New Dialogue. New Dialogue was a non-partisan grouping set up on the night that Major became Prime Minister, one of whose main aims was to create an integrated education system in Northern Ireland. It was run by Harry Barnes, in conjunction with his assistant, Gary Kent (a former Troops Out movement supporter who changed under the influence of Democratic Left stalwart, Seamus Lynch), and Bert Ward, a Communist trade unionist from Middlesbrough who had once run the CPGB's National Advisory Committee on Ireland.[48]

David Montgomery recalls that Trimble initially felt uncomfortable in Blackpool – and that he was right to be so. He was, after all, the first Unionist leader to visit a Labour conference, let alone address the Labour fringe.[49] Initially, even relatively sympathetic Labour MPs such as Calum Macdonald wondered whether Trimble himself really believed in 'civic unionism', within the overarching context of the EU – rather than in the more traditional right-wing forms of Loyalism (which were anti-EU).[50] Moreover, Trimble came with a lot of baggage: Drumcree and his personal flintiness both counted against him. Gary Kent says that when he walked behind Trimble in the Winter Gardens, heads turned in astonishment. The meeting was also addressed by Denis Haughey, International Secretary of the SDLP, and Eamon Gilmore of Democratic Left; even Geoffrey Robinson, the proprietor of the *New Statesman* and the co-host, also came along.[51] But the significance of the occasion lay less in what Trimble said than in the very fact of his presence.

But for all Trimble's belief that Unionists should 'think politically', his personal conduct appeared to others to be anything but. That night, Montgomery suggested to Trimble that he join his party for dinner: Mowlam and other important Labour figures would be there. Trimble declined, saying that he was otherwise engaged. But when Montgomery arrived at the dining room at the Imperial Hotel, he found Trimble sitting there alone with his bottle of red wine. Montgomery walked over and asked him to join his table, which by then included the shadow Chancellor Gordon Brown and the film mogul and Labour supporter David Puttnam. 'I'm pretty happy here,' said Trimble. 'That left an indelible mark on my mind,' says Montgomery. 'He was strong enough to want to be alone.' Trimble says that he cannot remember Montgomery coming over, but recalls Margaret Beckett and her husband inviting him to join them. Trimble did not know them well and conversation in a group of three would have required a far greater level of effort than joining a large party; he duly declined the offer. Shortly thereafter, Brown himself came over and asked Trimble to join them. But having declined Beckett's offer, he felt he could not then accept the invitation from Brown, whom he knew better, without causing grave offence to the Becketts.[52]

Whichever version is correct, the effect of the episode was to make Montgomery conclude that only Blair could woo Trimble effectively. He took the UUP leader to the Mirror Group reception, where Trimble was finally able to 'mix it' with the top brass. According to Montgomery, the MGN event was normally an occasion for the Labour leader to 'glad-hand' the newspapers' senior staff. But on this occasion, Trimble was set up as the focus of the attention, and the journalists present knew it. 'Blair was charm personified,' recalls Montgomery. 'For the first time in what had been pretty hostile terrain, Trimble was made to feel like an important national figure. I was banging on to Blair about how important it was to get Unionists to change. I told him that Trimble had never really left Ulster, in the sense of working outside of the Province, until he got to

Westminster. Yes, he has got a chip on his shoulder, but unless you get close to him and get him onside there will be no deal. He may not be the greatest, but he's the best you've got.'[53] Trimble acknowledges Montgomery's role in this period: 'Monty [his nickname] was hugely important to us. He was used as the conduit for dialogue with the Labour leadership. Along with Burnside, he helped convince both sides [Labour and the UUP] that an agreement could be made.' (Montgomery's significance to Trimble lay in these contacts, rather than in his proprietorship of the *News Letter*, which he regards as far less important than the *Belfast Telegraph*.)[54] Although Montgomery was not a regular 'back-channel' to Trimble, he was nonetheless useful to the Labour leadership when Blair entered No. 10: from their perspective, Montgomery could at times talk to Trimble frankly and report back accordingly. Indeed, such was the perceived disorganisation of the UUP's talks team that Blair's No. 10 found it sometimes could not discern the UUP's true bottom line through conventional means and needed therefore to have recourse to such back-channels as Montgomery. No. 10 felt it knew what Trimble did not want but had no clear grasp of his wider 'game plan'. 'I'm meeting Trimble tomorrow,' Blair would ask Montgomery. 'What's the mood?'[55] It was a reasonable question to ask: Trimble's moods were so shiftable that even relatively up-to-date assessments of where he was could swiftly be overtaken. But at another level, he need not have worried, since Trimble's basic strategic course was set for a long time.

Blair certainly handled Trimble with consummate skill on a personal level. He visited Northern Ireland in December 1996, and made a point of calling upon Trimble in his constituency. It came at a time when vigorous attempts were being made to lift the beef ban in Northern Ireland and Blair wanted to highlight the Tories' incompetence by visiting a farm. Daphne Trimble was given the task of finding a suitable farm and alighted upon Hewitt's Farm off the Dungannon Road in Portadown. After Blair completed his tour, he commented, 'I've never seen a farmyard as clean as this!'[56] But there was an awkward moment. It was reported that the new Grand Master of the Orange Order, Robert Saulters, had observed that Blair was disloyal because he was married to a Catholic.[57] The journalists gathered at the farm repeatedly pressed Trimble how he felt about this. At that moment, Blair stepped in and said: 'Can I say that since the remarks obviously concern me that I think it's important that we move on.' 'Absolutely,' chimed in a relieved Trimble.[58] As the press and politicians bantered, Trimble said to Blair, 'That's Ken Reid [then Political Correspondent, and subsequently Political Editor of UTV]. He's two thirds of the news market.' Blair shot back, 'That's the one we want.' It was the second time that Trimble helped Reid in this way: the two first became friendly at the Conservative conference in Bournemouth in 1994 when Trimble had introduced Reid to Major at the ITN party (partly, Trimble rewarded Reid thus because he felt him to be more acute than many of his counterparts in BBC Northern Ireland). It was certainly a rare instance when Trimble cultivated a journalist with any skill. Indeed, in the coming years, according to Alastair Campbell, Reid would be given greater levels of access to the Prime Minister than any other regional television journalist. It was yet another indicator of the importance which the British state increasingly accorded to the task of 'bringing peace to Northern Ireland'.[59]

Trimble was left with one other overwhelming impression from this visit: the solidity of Blair's commitment to the consent principle, which he found to be much stronger than that of the Tories. But Trimble's attraction to Blair ran deeper than that. As has been noted, Trimble was no High Tory in the Powellite mould and was keen to take his place in the proposed Blairite constitutional dispensation. This meant devolution all round, thus settling the old 'integration versus devolution' argument, since devolution would now be in line with the rest of the United Kingdom; and the incorporation of the European Convention on Human Rights into British law. These reforms would afford certain protections against the unilateral exercise of Westminster's sovereign powers that might run contrary to the interests of Ulster. Indeed, on major national issues, the only great disagreement between them was Trimble's opposition to the single currency, though Blair's caution on this subject made this a moot point. Trimble was fascinated by New Labour, a fascination which increased as a result of the May 1997 election, and craves a Blairite remoulding of the institutions and culture of the UUP (his lack of ruthlessness and efficiency in accomplishing this end is most un-Blairite, and would frustrate No. 10 in the coming years). But it may be something personal as well. One aide who has overheard conversations between Trimble and Blair believes that the UUP leader's tone when on the telephone with the Prime Minister is qualitatively quite different from his manner with anyone else in these islands, including Bertie Ahern. The listener believes that there is a measure of awe there: not grovelling, but just the respect of a senior pupil talking to the schoolmaster, even though he is Blair's elder by nine years.[60]

From Trimble's viewpoint, the dialogue with New Labour had one overwhelming purpose. 'One thing I did achieve speaking to them [Labour] was so that they could form a view before officials got at them,' says Trimble. 'It could have been crucial to Blair's decision to come to Belfast on 16 May 1997 [Blair's first visit to Northern Ireland as Prime Minister and his first official trip outside London]. I was hugely pleased he did that.'[61] The conduits for conveying his wishes were David Montgomery and David Burnside. The two men drafted a memorandum for the Prime Minister in waiting, whose inheritance of the keys of the Kingdom they confidently expected (Trimble says he did not wish for his own fingers to be on the document out of caution in all such matters).[62] But although Montgomery had access to Blair, the MGN boss had never worked in Government. Neither he nor Burnside was experienced in the arcana of Whitehall. For that, they turned to an old friend of Montgomery: Lord Donoughue, formerly Bernard Donoughue, and a one-time head of the No. 10 Policy Unit from 1974–9. Donoughue had always been interested in Ulster and during the last Labour Government attended the meetings of the Northern Ireland committee of the Cabinet. He was then more on the 'Green' side of the divide – some of his forebears came from Counties Kerry, Mayo and Wicklow – and had been rapporteur for the Cabinet Office committee established in 1974 to examine every option for Northern Ireland, including withdrawal.[63] Donoughue now firmly believed that Ulster could not be coerced and that the consent principle would have to be observed. He served on Mowlam's shadow arts team as the Labour's Lords spokesman in the mid-1990s and they had stayed in touch. 'When things started moving in 1996 I began to regain an active interest [in Ulster] and began to communicate with the leadership,' recalls Donoughue. His particular contacts were Blair's chief of staff, Jonathan Powell, and Pat McFadden, who handled Northern Ireland affairs for Blair in Opposition. Donoughue was convinced on the basis of his experiences in 1974 – when an incoming Labour Government was faced with the severe challenge of the Ulster Workers' Council strike – that things could again go very wrong and he told the Blair entourage as much.[64]

Donoughue's role was to scrutinise the text of Montgomery's and Burnside's memorandum. He immediately concluded that it would look 'unattractive to Tony Blair'. He knew how Prime Ministers reacted to paperwork, having sent in so much to their red boxes over the years. He therefore set to work on the Montgomery–Burnside rough draft so that it could be immediately absorbed into the governmental system. Dated 24 April 1997, Donoughue cut out much of the detail about the size of the Assembly – it was too detailed, he reckoned, for the purposes at hand – and the affectionate reference to Roy Mason. Donoughue also removed the attacks on John Hume, whose prestige was high in New Labour circles. The memorandum urged Blair to take the initiative by launching an elected administrative assembly in the Province (that is, something closer to the Welsh level of devolution that resembled a glorified county council than the more fully fledged government envisaged for Scotland). It thus placed UUP policy squarely within the planned Blairite constitutional settlement. It envisaged scrutiny of government through a committee system largely based on the six existing Northern Ireland departments – and saw the SDLP as participating, but not Sinn Fein. It urged that the Government seek the good will of Dublin and Washington to obtain the assembly, to which end the role of Senator George Mitchell should be made permanent. It also urged new anti-terrorism measures such as the use of wiretapping evidence in court and the power to imprison members of proscribed organisations on the word of a superintendent or above (as in the Republic of Ireland under the Offences Against the State Act).[65] This aspiration proved wildly unrealistic in the light of the incoming ministry's long-advertised wish to prune, rather than to expand the scope of emergency legislation in Northern Ireland.

Trimble believes the document had a crucial impact upon Blair's approach: it was one of the very few moments, either before or since, when Unionists were in some way 'ahead of the curve'. It all certainly dovetailed with Blair's agenda at that time. For Blair was then determined to present himself to the Unionists as their friend and to make the most of his bona fides. Blair took the measure of Trimble and concluded that he was a very emotional man who loved escaping from the hot-house atmosphere of Belfast and who revelled in the state banquets, the garden parties and the international summitry: that was partly why they always saw what they regarded as 'the best side of him', rather than the flashes of ill-temper which characterised his dealings with Mowlam.[66] It was a measure of Blair's skill in handling Trimble that Blair chose to meet the UUP leader before he met John Bruton, on 7 May 1997, in the Prime

Minister's room in the Commons (just days after taking office). Curiously, Trimble had initially been reluctant directly to contact the new Prime Minister on a regular basis. 'He was rather timid,' recalls David Montgomery. 'He had to be told – you can get access any time you want. I encouraged him to go directly to Tony, and Tony honoured that. Trimble would say, "I don't want to bother the PM about this", but I said, "You must."'[67]

Once Trimble broke the shyness barrier, he could not have enough of such contacts: indeed, his wife Daphne states only half-jokingly that the Trimble telephone line is probably the only one which lists the Downing Street exchange amongst its designated BT's 'Friends and Family' numbers – thus entitling them to reduced rates on account of the volume of calls made.[68] Certainly, Blair struck a note of informality straight away and 'call me Tony' was his watchword. Unlike Major who met them over the great table in the Cabinet room, Blair in shirtsleeves would talk to the UUP in a small room on the ground floor. Moreover, with the exception of a few occasions in the early months of the Labour Government, the bulk of these meetings were held with Blair and the No. 10 staff alone, rather than with the Northern Ireland Secretary present, as was the case under the Tories. Eventually, these meetings became embarrassingly routine as Blair became ever more immersed in Northern Ireland. 'They took on a Clochemerle quality,' observed Reg Empey after the Kosovo War of 1999 (a reference to Gabriel Chevallier's 1934 novel set in a small French town, about a municipal row over the siting of a lavatory). 'Here was Blair, first on the world stage, with thousands of soldiers under his command and now he had to focus on "Ballygobackwards". It went too far.'[69] But such levels of immersion had been demanded by the Unionists themselves, who did not trust Mowlam. Bernard Donoughue was shocked to be told by a senior Cabinet Office civil servant that the Prime Minister spent around 40% of his time on Northern Ireland (levels unthinkable under Callaghan and Thatcher).[70]

The changed atmosphere also affected the No. 10 staff. As Unionists saw it, one of Blair's first steps towards building trust with Trimble was to instruct John Holmes, the Private Secretary for foreign affairs, to become far more accessible to the Unionists than he had been under Major (Blair looks in astonishment at the suggestion that he might have given Holmes instructions to this effect).[71] In some ways, Holmes was in a more powerful position than before as the No. 10 'institutional memory' and soon earned Blair's respect and trust. The son of a schoolmaster from Preston, Holmes attended the local grammar school before taking a first in Greats at Balliol College Oxford and entering the Foreign Office in 1973. Those who knew him well say that he carried little personal baggage on the Irish question, but his attitudes on conflict resolution had been informed by his experiences in various departments dealing with the Middle East. He saw the matter of handling the Unionists as resembling the debate in the Foreign Office on how to deal with Israel. One way was to 'play hardball' and to push the Jewish state to the wall; the other was to understand their fears and to bring them along. Holmes was very much in the second camp.

Holmes worked closely with his former Foreign Office colleague, Jonathan Powell, Blair's chief of staff (and younger brother of Holmes' predecessor but three, Charles Powell). Until his appointment as Counsellor at the British Embassy in the spring of 1991, Powell had been ignorant of Northern Ireland, after the fashion of most Foreign Office diplomats. This was despite the fact that his first marriage was to an Irish-American and that he had done his post-graduate thesis at the University of Pennsylvania on Scots-Irish Presbyterian loyalists during the American Revolution. But as part of the briefing process for a job which would require substantial dealings with the Irish-American lobby, he spent several weeks in Ulster in 1991 – and loved it. He also read such standard texts as Robert Kee's history of Ireland.[72] His tour of duty coincided with the tense period of the Adams visa and Powell found himself at the sharp end of dealings with the Kennedys and their allies.[73] In consequence, he was none too impressed with elements of the Irish-American lobby. This counted for much with Trimble, who therefore thought him 'basically pro-Union' (later, there were times when Trimble would not think Powell was quite so onside).[74] It was during this period when he had first met Tony Blair (and David Trimble). Powell also enjoyed the closest of ties and an especial generational affinity with the political echelons of the Clinton administration. These linkages were a further plus point as far as Trimble was concerned, since he believed No. 10 could continue the process of 'educating Bill' without any of the baggage carried by the Conservative administration whom the Americans thought had been 'dragging their feet'. Over the years, as Private Secretaries came and went, Powell became the most important point of contact for the UUP at No. 10. And after a while the UUP noticed one other aspect of Powell's role: that when security matters were discussed, Blair would often turn to his chief of staff.

But Blair's relationship with Trimble was not just about style, or scheduling or personnel matters at No. 10 or the NIO. Above all, it was based upon profound political empathy. For Blair sought to understand Trimble's relationship with his own party and the rest of the Unionist community: he believed that the wider the Unionist constituency became, the likelier they were to support Trimble. Thus, as No. 10 saw it, the 110-member UUP executive was likelier to support him than the ten MPs, the 860-strong Ulster Unionist Council likelier to support him than the executive, and the public likelier still. Blair reckoned that he could always appeal to them over the politicians' heads (though No. 10 often felt frustrated that Trimble did not lead opinion as much as he should). Trimble saw this sympathy as a political necessity on the part of the Prime Minister. 'The most crucial thing is if London wants to achieve anything in Northern Ireland, then they need the help of the leader of the UUP,' states Trimble. 'That's so, whether the Prime Minister has got a majority of two or of 180. He needs the support of a majority of Unionists. That is the factor. Everything else is minor. But you [that is, the UUP leader and his party] only have that kind of leverage if you try to do something and don't just sit there with a stony face. To get something done, both must move. And what Blair was trying to achieve in Northern Ireland was not incompatible with what I was trying to achieve.'[75] Trimble, though, only sought to accomplish that with Blair. As very senior Irish officials observed, Trimble had virtually no positive relationship with any figure in the British system other than Blair (just as he would tend to focus upon the Taoiseach in his dealings with the Republic). It was, of course, a two-edged sword: when things went well, he could use this special relationship to override the NIO, and Mo Mowlam in particular. But if it ever went wrong, this exclusive dependency could leave him desperately exposed. Indeed, such was Trimble's level of confidence in Blair that he never took notes at meetings with the Prime Minister during the whole period of the negotiations. 'It was not wise not to keep notes, though my memory is very good on a short-term basis. But in any case those meetings were partly a matter of educating UUP colleagues, who assumed Downing Street was against them. That was not an accurate perception. They would do most of the talking and I would try and steer it in the right direction. If you're stuck in Belfast listening to *Good Morning Ulster* [the main current affairs programme on BBC Radio Ulster] how can you have a grasp of reality?' quips Trimble. Indeed, one reason why Trimble further welcomed Blair's massive majority was that it put paid to any illusions which some Unionists may have entertained about focusing solely upon opinion within Northern Ireland. Now, Trimble reckoned, Unionists would no longer be able to stick two fingers up at mainland opinion and the sooner they understood this reality the better.[76]

Once Trimble became convinced that Blair's aims were not incompatible with his own, he was remarkably incurious about both the Prime Minister and the rest of the party. David Montgomery states that whereas Blair would pepper him with questions about Trimble (invariably along the themes of 'is he serious?' and 'can he deliver?'), the UUP leader would rarely ask any questions about the Prime Minister.[77] Nor is he much good at tapping natural sources of political intelligence amongst Labour MPs known to sympathise with him: for instance, Kate Hoey also confirms that the UUP leader very rarely asked her about the state of play in the Labour party.[78] Only in early 2001 did he start having regular conversations about Labour policy with another embattled figure, Peter Mandelson – but as one wag observed, 'it was more mutual therapy – a "Politicians Anonymous"'. Indeed, Norman Godman – who till his retirement in 2001 was chairman of the backbench Northern Ireland committee – states that even Willie Thompson and Martin Smyth (scarcely cosmopolitan figures) inquired more about what was going on in the PLP in the 1997 Parliament than did Trimble.[79] This omission was all the odder since much of the PLP was actually a blank sheet when it came to Northern Ireland and could in some ways have been 'educated'. Whilst many of those who cared most passionately about Northern Ireland were on the 'Green' side of the debate, they were a minority of the total Labour caucus. Even so experienced a figure as George Robertson, who was born within sight of Northern Ireland in Argyll, had never been there till he became Defence Secretary (Robertson comes from a police family and his brother had, by coincidence, been one of Roy Mason's bodyguards). Robertson observes of the Ulster Unionists that 'they have a tendency to be very clubbable amongst themselves – and not just the Unionists. The Irish at Westminster are very much a tribe, though a few, like Ken Maginnis, will stop and talk.'[80] Significantly, Trimble never sought to make much contact with Robertson either, even though he feels a particular affinity with Scotland and has been an assiduous attender of Scottish questions. Others, such as Alan Johnson – a former General Secretary of the CWU, at least sixteen of whose members had been assassinated during the Troubles – were even staunch supporters of Labour organising in Northern Ireland. Yet despite Trimble's own long-time support for Labour organising in Northern Ireland, Johnson confirms that they have had no significant conversations with each other. Again, for all of his desire that Unionists must 'think politically', the fact remains that Trimble's personal behaviour often remains profoundly apolitical.

Trimble's conviction that Blair was basically on his side rested upon Blair's 16 May 1997 speech in Belfast. It was the new Prime Minister's first big engagement outside of London – a point which was noted with pleasure in the Province. The speech was intended as both a form of reassurance to Unionists and an ultimatum to republicans – that the settlement train would be leaving without them unless they restored the ceasefire. But it was the first aspect of Blair's agenda which elicited most comment at the time. 'I am committed to Northern Ireland. I am committed to the principle of consent. My agenda is not a united Ireland,' declared the Prime Minister. 'Northern Ireland is a part of the United Kingdom, alongside England, Scotland and Wales. The Union binds the four parts of the United Kingdom. I believe in the United Kingdom. I value the Union. I want to see a union which reflects and accommodates diversity.' Then came the crucial passage: 'Northern Ireland is part of the United Kingdom because that is the wish of the majority who live here. It will remain part of the United Kingdom for as long as that remains the case. This principle of consent is and will be at the heart of my Government's policies on Northern Ireland. It is the key principle. It means there can be absolutely no possibility of a change in the status of Northern Ireland as a part of the United Kingdom without the clear and formal consent of a majority of the people of Northern Ireland. Any settlement must be negotiated [by the Northern Ireland parties] not imposed; it must be endorsed by the people of Northern Ireland in a referendum; and it must be endorsed by the British Parliament.

'Of course, those who wish to see a united Ireland without coercion can argue for it, not least in the talks. If they succeeded, we would certainly respect that. But none of us in the hall today, even the youngest, is likely to see Northern Ireland as anything but a part of the United

Kingdom. That is the reality, because the consent principle is now almost universally accepted ... so fears of betrayal are simply misplaced. Unionists have nothing to fear from a new Labour Government. A political settlement is not a slippery slope to a united Ireland. The Government will not be persuaders for unity.'[81] Andy Wood, soon to be removed as the director of information in the NIO, was startled. 'I don't believe what I've just heard,' he thought to himself. 'That's the most Unionist speech ever given by a Prime Minister. And I looked at the 17- and 18-year-old waitresses in the Balmoral Centre and I said: "If even the youngest in this room won't see a united Ireland in their lifetime, that's at least 50 years away. That's a hell of a long time to see no constitutional movement."'[82] Trimble believes that Blair ad-libbed the words about there being no Irish unity in his lifetime.[83] The credit which Blair amassed in Trimble's own mind for this speech was considerable – but, again, he may have read too much into it. John Lloyd questioned Trimble shortly thereafter and found him almost ecstatic. But when he subsequently interviewed Blair in No. 10 (who peppered him with questions about Trimble: Lloyd was determined to convey his conviction that Trimble was neither anti-Catholic by instinct nor by intellect) the Prime Minister dismissed the notion that it was an expression of 'civic unionist' principle. Nor did he rule out the idea that the Union was up for discussion.[84] Rather, it was simply a functional statement of a current reality which could not be ignored.

TWENTY-ONE

The pains of peace

TRIMBLE accepted Bernard Donoughue's next suggestion – relayed by David Montgomery and David Burnside – that he should respond positively to Blair's 16 May speech. The earlier document was reworked and forwarded to Blair by Donoughue on 4 June 1997. 'Enclosed is a serious proposal from David Trimble and the Ulster Unionists for a new Settlement in Northern Ireland based on an all-party Administrative (not legislative) Assembly,' the new junior Agriculture Minister told the Prime Minister. 'Their approach assumes that the present peace process will run into the sand. I hope not. But if it does, you may need some such fresh initiative, or else the men of violence will move into the political vacuum. This proposal could be seen as having several attractions: (1) the Ulster Unionists are here uncharacteristically positive, inclusive and flexible. They have readily accepted suggestions to exclude traditional loyalist rhetoric, to work with the nationalist dimension, and to agree that the proposed sector committees develop relations with the republic. (2) Their involvement and endorsement ensures major – possibly majority – support in the Province (providing they can deliver their own troops). Certainly no "solutions" can work without their support. Past failed initiatives usually had an element of imposition on them. (3) The proposal embraces the constitutional nationalists, offering them chairmanships of key sector committees. (4) It – bravely for them – offers involvement to Sinn Fein. This might attract the Adams wing, who may (as with Michael Collins earlier) be looking for a more constructive political role and may not be content with forever murdering people . . .

'The downside of the proposal is that it is clearly a Unionist settlement and if presented by them triumphantly as such will alienate the nationalists whose involvement is essential for success. Certainly Dublin and Washington would need to be kept on board, at least not opposing it.

However, it is more moderate, constructive and inclusive than anything I have seen from them before ... naturally welcoming the end of any real prospect of a United Ireland in our lifetimes, but also accepting that the past Protestant hegemony is over and they must work with nationalist fellow citizens and build relations with their Irish Republic neighbours ... you may also want to encourage this new flexibility in mainstream Unionist thinking, led by Trimble and respond accordingly. If attracted, you might also want to consider how to "de-unionise it". And perhaps even adopt aspects as your own initiative and extract them as concessions from the Unionists. But you will know best how to handle that.

'My apologies for my unlikely (Catholic!) involvement in all this. My anonymous role, established by an intermediary long before being in Government, has been as a postman and remote assistant draftsman. Virtually all my drafting was done before becoming a minister and I don't expect to be further involved. I have deliberately never met the Unionists in this context and don't think they know of me. But I gather they fear that its contents, being radical and progressive, might leak from "normal channels", so they sought a direct approach. (Not leaks from Mo, but from officials in the Northern Ireland Office or Stormont, who apparently they do not trust). It would be a pity if reactionary Unionists were alerted and they moved to try to block the proposal's conciliatory elements before it could be considered.

'Mo does not know of this particular initiative. But we have worked together trustingly before and she knows I am periodically used as an Irish channel and has not discouraged that.'

The actual document this time included reference to Trimble's much-vaunted east–west dimension – though the name had been amended from 'Council of the British Isles' to the 'Council of the Isles' by Montgomery, Burnside and Trimble 'so as not to offend nationalist sensibilities'. It reiterated the UUP's wish for a Welsh-style administrative assembly, on an enhanced local council model, rather than a fuller Scottish-style legislative body with tax-raising powers: it urged that it be established by the end of the year as evidence to the wider unionist community of the viability of Trimble's approach rather than Paisley's form of protest politics. Although Donoughue was correct to state that the document did not specifically exclude Sinn Fein/IRA participation in the political process, in principle, the general tone was very much in line with the traditional Unionist hankering for a deal with the SDLP alone. Indeed, it was very optimistic about the willingness of constitutional nationalists to go along with any new structures without the presence of republicans – even in the absence of a ceasefire. 'It would be necesssary to attract the support of constitutional nationalists for the assembly' noted the authors. 'That should be possible since it offers them rapid partici- pation in a democratic political and administrative system dealing with bread and butter issues which concern all sides in Northern Ireland, and they may, in the light of recent election results, be re-thinking their relationship with Sinn Fein.' Possibly some in the SDLP did so, but not John Hume himself. Indeed, the rise of Sinn Fein offered the SDLP certain opportunities which they had not hitherto enjoyed on their own: as a result of the District Council elections of 21 May 1997, unionists for the first time lost overall control of Belfast City Council, resulting in the election of Trimble's old pupil, Alban Maginness, as the first SDLP Lord Mayor.[1]

Trimble in the short term appears to have thought that the Government would not dilute their conditions for entry into talks so thoroughly as to make that a viable option within a very rapid time frame. He therefore felt able once again to compromise on decommissioning. He told re- porters at a briefing on the fringe of the Forum on 6 June 1997 that he would allow the talks to move from the preliminary to the substantive stage without a clear commitment to prior decommissioning, thus creating movement in the talks with the SDLP.[2] Initially, the gamble appeared to have worked. For despite Blair's declaration of 16 May that republicans could have a place at the talks if they restored an 'unequivocal ceasefire' and committed themselves to exclusively democratic means, there was little public sign of a de-escalation of violence. In the late morning of 16 June 1997, two RUC officers, Constables John Graham and David Johnston, walked past David Trimble's office on Queen Street, Lurgan, where they waved at his constituency secretary, Stephanie Roderick.[3] They then continued their foot patrol to Church Walk, where shoppers and schoolchildren were gathering in the midday sun. Suddenly, two men in women's wigs came up behind them and fired into their heads at close range. Both men died almost instantly: Graham was 34, married with three daughters, and Johnston, a full-time reservist was also married with two sons.[4]

Condemnation was swift and predictable: after consulting the Prime Minister who was in Amsterdam for the EU summit, Mo Mowlam suspended official contact with Sinn Fein/IRA and said that the planned meeting between civil servants and the republicans would not be re-scheduled (Mitchel McLaughlin, Sinn Fein's chairman, did not condemn the murders).[5] Trimble saw it as further evidence that Sinn Fein/IRA would not be giving up their campaign any time soon. Nor was the choice of Lurgan an accident: 'It is six miles from the location of the disputed Orange church service due in two weeks' time,' he told the US National Committee on Foreign Policy in New York. 'It is a cynical attempt to raise tension by provoking loyalist violence.'[6] But the NIO interpreted the killings differently. John Steele recalls that it was seen as the action of a particular individual who was out of control rather than a strategic strike authorised from the very top of the republican movement (such as the attack on Thiepval barracks in Lisburn in October 1996).[7] Other senior figures in the NIO believed that such tactical escalations did not preclude another halt to 'military' operations and that Sinn Fein's refusal to condemn the killings had something in common with Adams' decision to carry the coffin of one of the Shankill bombers, Thomas Begley, in October 1993 – as a necessary act to maintain his credibility so as to be able to obtain another ceasefire.[8] It was this knowledge – that a ceasefire was 'there to be had' – which lent the Lurgan killings a quality of particular cynicism.

Trimble continued to press the two Governments and the SDLP to make a deal without Sinn Fein – though, significantly, he again refused to say 'never' to the idea of talking to republicans.[9] For the ground was slipping under his feet all of the time. On 4 June, the British and Irish Governments presented a proposal to the plenary session of the talks suggesting parallel talks and decommissioning. There would be two new subcommittees to deal with decommissioning and confidence-building measures, as well as an international commission to supervise the arms handovers. The DUP and UKUP rejected the proposals of the Govern-ments. But Trimble, as so often, reserved the UUP's position: he expressed doubts (sometimes even shrilly so) but nonetheless acquiesced sufficiently to afford the British state enough coverage to proceed with its core strategy.[10] Indeed, after emerging from 90 minutes at No. 10, Trimble told reporters that 'we could go along with decommissioning going along-side talks provided that's what actually happened. Our concern in dis-cussions with Government is to ensure that the procedures and mechanisms are clearly there to ensure that decommissioning takes place.'

The most important 'procedural factor', he added, was the establishment of an international committee to verify that weapons really were being removed from circulation. Trimble eventually obtained these mechanisms to achieve decommissioning, but no actual handover of arms. Ian Paisley denounced the UUP compromise, declaring, 'There will be no leader who will be able to survive if he sits down with Sinn Fein, especially on these terms.'[11] Paisley was right to point to the fact that Trimble had further diluted his position, but was wrong to think that it would cost him the leadership.

The arcana of decommissioning soon, however, took a back seat. For in the latter part of June and early July of 1997, the Province was once again gripped by the familiar ritual of the Drumcree stand-off.[12] The view of the NIO – as expressed in a memorandum written by Trimble's old contact, Stephen Leach, was in favour of a controlled march down the Garvaghy Road as the 'least worst outcome'.[13] This was taken by many in nationalist Ireland as evidence of the bad faith of the British Government and of the alleged influence of the 'securocrats' – for whom the Drumcree negotiations were a charade to conceal a preordained outcome which came about because the loyalists had once again played the 'Orange card'. Certainly, the public order dimension was the crucial factor in the Government's thinking. But, once again, the effect upon Trimble's position was an important secondary factor. Blair's own instinct was also to let the march go ahead. If it went through, he calculated, there would be a lot of trouble but it would essentially be a 'one-off' – as eventually turned out to be the case.

Trimble did not doubt the importance of ensuring that the march went down its traditional route, but how he comported himself during the stand-off was equally significant. He decided that whatever happened, he would not walk with his brethren (though he would await their return from church).[14] What enraged him subsequently was the justification for this decision that was forwarded by the Chief Constable, Ronnie Flanagan, who announced that the authorities had opted for the lesser of two evils: if the march had been stopped or re-routed there would have been greater loyalist retaliation against Roman Catholics.[15] Sean Farren of the SDLP observed in his notebook of 7 July 1997 that '[the] meeting with Mo Mowlam one of the most fraught I have ever attended. She looked haggard and quite depressed. Not in a position to fight her corner.' She appeared to regret the decision – which she upheld in the interests of preserving life – and promised new legislation to deal with next year's parade. For all of her emotional literacy, which so contrasted with Mayhew's proconsular hauteur, even Mowlam could not wish away the then balance of forces on the ground in Northern Ireland.

Rioting broke out all over Northern Ireland. But despite this success, many in the Orange Order were concerned that the image of their institution was being tarnished by repeated confrontations. They had been persuaded by Sean O'Callaghan and Cranborne (who despite his departure from office in May 1997 still enjoyed the confidence of many senior unionists) that confrontation with the residents' associations could provoke stand-offs that could discredit loyalism and play into the hands of Sinn Fein. After much soul-searching, it was announced that four contentious parades scheduled for 12 July would be cancelled. Trimble deliberately did not involve himself in these discussions and states that they would not have been stopped if Drumcree III had not gone ahead.[16] At the time, he said that he had 'mixed feelings' about the decision and said that he was sure the Orange Order 'do not wish their decision to be taken as being a permanent decision. It is a purely temporary gesture that is being made.' It remained to be seen if the loyalists' actions would be reciprocated.[17]

In fact, they were reciprocated – though not necessarily in the way that the Orangemen expected. For Martin McGuinness told senior NIO officials that the cancellation was an important element in the Provisionals' decision to call a second IRA ceasefire – and republicans credited the British Government with that move.[18] If so, this was a compromise on the republicans' position of several months earlier: according to a memorandum written on 17 April by the LSE academic Brendan O'Leary following a conversation with Sinn Fein's Mitchel McLaughlin, there could be no repetition of Drumcree II. Pushing a march down the road by *force majeure* would, it was asserted, cause problems with IRA hardliners. This was one of a set of proposals which O'Leary – then acting as a channel of communication between republicans and the Labour party – brought back to London as part of the package which included a second ceasefire. In fact, what appears to have happened is that the position of both sides was shaved down. Trimble needed another victory at Drumcree as a *sine qua non* for 'political development'. Likewise, republicans in the end had to put up with another Drumcree, but they did obtain their goal of restrictions on future parades, thus helping them to call a second ceasefire.[19]

So despite the Drumcree crisis, dialogue proceeded apace. This was notwithstanding clear assurances from both Blair and Mowlam that contacts between officials and Sinn Fein/IRA had been suspended ever since the murders of two RUC officers in Lurgan. 'The Prime Minister made it absolutely clear that after the killings in Lurgan, we would not have relationships between our officials and Sinn Fein in relation to the peace process. That has not changed. We have not made any approach,' Mowlam told the Commons. 'On the second point, so that I am clear about this – I believe in being honest and open – Sinn Fein has telephoned twice the officials that it has talked with, asking for further meetings and the answer was "no".' When Trimble then asked her point blank whether 'having no relationships meant having no contact and no communication – nothing?', Mowlam appeared to raise her thumb. Trimble certainly read it that way though it is possible that she simply misunderstood him.[20] Indeed, when the contacts leaked on 14 July, Trimble ran into Helen Jackson, Mowlam's PPS (who had shared 'Troops Out' platforms with Sinn Fein/IRA representatives before the ceasefire in the 1990s). 'I can't understand why she did that,' said the UUP leader. In Trimble's view she had been unambiguous.[21] Mowlam stated that these dealings fell into the category of 'clarification' rather than negotiation.[22]

It was another severe blow to the relationship between Trimble and Mowlam – though, as ever, he did not blame Blair for any of this. But it made his task much harder in the coming days, not only because he felt that he had been misled again, but also because it would make the UUP and the unionist community as a whole far more mistrustful of what was being hammered out behind closed doors between the British Government and republicans (and thus cut down Trimble's freedom for manoeuvre if he needed to make any compromises). For events were moving ever more rapidly. The text of the decommissioning document of 24 June – suggesting talks and weapons handovers to take place in tandem but finally dispensing with the 'Washington III' criterion of a prior weapons handover – was pushed through by the British and Irish Governments on 16 July with only one question permitted. The DUP and UKUP temporarily withdrew from the talks, but the UUP again opted to stay inside. The document was meant to supply a further incentive to republicans, proving to Sinn Fein/IRA that the 'preconditions' to their participation which had been erected under the Tories no longer obtained. On 18 July, the British Government also published the text of a letter to

McGuinness of 9 July, in which it was stated that following a ceasefire, Sinn Fein could participate in negotiations without any arms handover – so long as they adhered to the Mitchell principles (this, of course, left open the question of what the IRA would do). No timetable or require- ment for decommissioning was specified, even of the very diluted variety outlined in the 24 June statement which said that weapons should be handed over during talks. The letter to McGuinness made clear that once admitted, Sinn Fein could not be expelled from the negotiations because of failure to advance the decommissioning issue. Moreover, if the talks failed notwithstanding their efforts, the two Governments 'will continue to make rapid progress to an overall agreed settlement acceptable to both unionists and nationalists'.[23] Trimble made it clear that he could not endorse the document as it stood: Frank Millar reported on 18 July 1997 that 'it is understood Mr Trimble bluntly told Mr Blair that his leadership of the Ulster Unionists would be destroyed if he agreed to Sinn Fein participation without a clear commitment that decommissioning would take place in parallel to the negotiation process'.

On the following day, the IRA announced a restoration of the 1994 ceasefire and on 23 July it was announced that republicans would be able to join full-scale negotiations, scheduled to begin on 15 September. This would be following a six-week quarantine period – far shorter than was the case under the previous Conservative Government. At the end of this period, Mowlam would certify whether the cessation was genuine in both word and deed. As after the first ceasefire of 1994, Unionists again feared that another deal had been done behind the scenes between the British and the republicans. Who knows, many wondered, what guarantees they had been given beyond those publicly acknowledged? These suspicions were heightened when McGuinness declared that 'the IRA have said that they will not decommission a single bullet and I have not heard any statement from them saying they have changed their position'.[24] The DUP and UKUP left the talks – permanently. But what would the UUP now do and would their constituents tolerate it? Every guarantee they had sought now seemed worthless and they faced the prospect of sitting for the first time opposite those who had murdered them and their constituents over the past three decades.

Trimble was not much surprised by the fact of another IRA ceasefire. Indeed, according to Sean O'Callaghan, he thought the Provisionals were beaten and would have called another cessation sooner or later – but was amazed and angered that the British Government should be prepared to pay such a price in order to bring it about so quickly. O'Callaghan says that Trimble always believed that the same result could have been had in the fullness of time on far more advantageous terms. But the fact that he was surprised by its terms points up another feature of Trimble's behaviour as a political animal. Trimble derived an impression about the likelihood of another Provisional ceasefire but either misunderstood or was misled as to the fine print. Since the minutiae are crucial to Trimble – whatever else may be said about him – the latter interpretation of being misled is likelier. Indeed, something similar may well have occurred in the spring of 1999 during the deliberations of the Patten Commission on the RUC, when Trimble told Les Rodgers, then chairman of the Police Federation of Northern Ireland, in all sincerity, that the force's name and badge would be preserved.[25] 'He often thought he had something in the bag when, in fact, he did not and got shafted on the details,' notes Sean O'Callaghan.[26] Frank Millar also swiftly noted that the UUP paid far more attention to the unionist-friendly portions of Blair's 16 May speech and his general attitude than to Mowlam's behaviour. This was seriously to underestimate her role. In particular, Millar cited Mowlam's remarks of 21 May 1997 on BBC *Newsnight* that the 'settlement train' would leave without unionists if they walked out of the talks, thus proving to republicans that the 'unionist veto' over their participation had been removed.[27] To this day, Trimble believes that Mowlam was trapped by the interviewer rather than said it deliberately and states that he was not worried by her comments.[28]

Whether Trimble was surprised or not by the quick ceasefire, the fact remained that the UUP seemed to be impaled upon the hook of prior decommissioning and there appeared to be no way to wriggle off it. In such a febrile atmosphere, Trimble accused the British Government of 'duplicity' in giving secret assurances, but as so often before he was using tough rhetoric to obfuscate the fact that he would ultimately seek to go along with the inter-governmental approach – if he possibly could do so. After emerging from Downing Street on 21 July, Trimble insisted that the British and Irish had to stick to their pledge to seek decommissioning during the talks but added that 'there are some possibilities for progress' – a reference to the fact that an independent commission on disarmament would be set up under de Chastelain. Trimble now says that he did not want to come out of No. 10 and simply say 'no' to the Prime Minister.

So he came up with the idea of a consultation period within the community as a whole. It was the first time a UUP leader had done such a thing, beyond the confines of the UUC. The Government knew that he was not prevaricating unnecessarily. Blair was keen to afford Trimble the necessary space to stay in the process and, says the UUP leader, accordingly instructed Alastair Campbell not to brief against him. No. 10 also provided the language for the press conference – levels of collaboration unthinkable under the Tories.[29] As Jeffrey Donaldson believes, 'here was the start of Trimble's major entrée into the world of spin-doctoring. He believed he had to create a context in which he could stay in the talks. He had to show that he had a broad mandate within the party. Going through the consultation was as much about presentation as about consultation.'[30] John Taylor is even starker about the purpose of the consultation: 'It was window-dressing for what happened anyway – though it was nice to say it was a "consultation".'[31]

The issue, as Trimble saw it, was not so much whether he would receive the backing to stay in – he was confident enough of that as time went on – but upon what conditions. He would place the options on the table and let people discuss it amongst themselves so that they could draw their own conclusions. 'People who say that I should "educate" the unionist community and UUP have a fundamental misunderstanding about the party,' notes this former law don. 'If I go barnstorming it makes for a negative effect. I would never make an emotional, DUP-like appeal. Nor would I try an indirect approach like Jim Molyneaux. When I started the consultation exercise it was obvious what I wanted. But isn't it better to let them work it out for themselves with a little bit of guidance? Anyway, I've always preferred tutorials to lectures.'[32] His day-to-day behaviour resembled a whirling dervish, but his strategic posture could be very passive, allowing time and circumstance to grind down established positions. Many Unionists privately felt that such retreats were now necessary: they just did not want to be told it explicitly. This method of political leadership proved astonishingly successful in its own terms – of coaxing the UUP along paths which a few years earlier would have been unimaginable. He was able to abandon his own long-held positions with such apparent ease for a number of reasons. Partly, because immediate decommissioning was not always his foremost priority, at least in this period: Frank Millar recalls routinely asking Ken Maginnis if the UUP was serious about it in the light of what he believed were contrary signals from

Trimble.[33] But it was also because in the eyes of his partisans he was a supreme pragmatist – or opportunist, in the eyes of his unionist critics – who was prepared to work within the confines of state policy.[34] He bewailed the Government's position loudly but did nothing about it: he was always far more reluctant to employ the UUP's 'nuclear option' of withdrawal from the talks – thus depriving them of cross-community legitimacy – than Sinn Fein/IRA were to employ theirs (the threat, genuine or otherwise, of a return to violence). He firmly believed that protest politics had run their course. Unionists had entered the process in order to rid themselves of the burden of the AIA of 1985, and nothing would deflect them from that task.

Foremost amongst Trimble's concerns was the fear that the UUP would be blamed for any breakdown in the talks if they did not participate. 'Unfortunately, the world seems to think SF/IRA are freedom fighters and the unionists are the bad boys,' noted one senior UUP source at the time. 'If the unionists are not there, they would be branded as running away.'[35] Was this fear justified, though? Trimble's unionist critics contended that BBC television and radio might often toe the Government line – but, they asked, would *The Times*, *The Daily Telegraph* and the *Daily Mail* have turned on him? Then there was the question of the Conservative party. Trimble later told Sean O'Callaghan that he would not have stayed in the talks in September 1997 if he had felt sure of the Tories' support – but he did not, in this period, think that the Tories were up for much of a fight.[36] But he did little to find out if this was a real possibility. In fact, such was the ideological hegemony of Unionism within the modern Tory party in Opposition that William Hague and the then Northern Ireland spokesman, Andrew Mackay, probably would have backed him up if Trimble had made a serious pitch for Conservative support: certainly, neither Hague nor Mackay has any recollection of Trimble seeking to contact him in this period to ascertain whether he would support him.[37] Moreover, notwithstanding the massive Labour majority, the Government was sufficiently insecure about elements of its Ulster policy to seek desperately to maintain bi-partisan support: Mackay was surprisingly able to rattle them in the coming years with some fairly pedestrian criticisms.[38] But such was Trimble's residual disdain for the Tories even once they had left office that in the very short term, at least, meaningful cooperation was ruled out.

Whilst Trimble might well have been blamed by elements of British mainland and Irish opinion in the short term for walking out, would this necessarily have had disastrous policy consequences for Unionism? He certainly appears to have believed so. Thus, he stated that 'with Ulster Unionists at the table, there will be no united Ireland; there will be no joint sovereignty; no joint authority (actual or disguised)'.[39] It was all true, but his loyalist critics believed that none of those were real options, even if Unionists had left the table: in that sense, they thought he was knocking down a straw man. Thus, one very senior NIO official of the period states that if the UUP had opted out in September 1997, it would have returned matters to the limbo which obtained in the 1994–6 period, but it would not have resulted in the imposition of Joint Authority with the Irish Republic or some other such Unionist nightmare. 'That bogeyman was a paper tiger,' notes the mandarin. 'For without the Unionists there would have been no credible settlement. The "Frame-works Plus" formula would have been suicidal.' The official says, however, that work on the 'equality agenda' and other reforms would have pro-ceeded apace if the Unionists had stayed out – though, again, they did so even with Trimble as First Minister.

Trimble's strategy was to leave his colleague, Dermott Nesbitt, in charge of the consultation – whilst he went on holiday in Switzerland and then in Tuscany (where he stayed a few miles from the Blairs and, as he observes characteristically, 'paid through the nose'). He appeared relaxed enough, partly because he knew he had the support of the local print media for staying in the talks. The *Church of Ireland Gazette* argued in an editorial of 8 August that Trimble should confront his backwoodsmen and take the risk of sitting down at the talks with Sinn Fein in order to expose the republicans' ambiguous attitude to democracy: it claimed he was fudging his position at present because Paisley was breathing down his neck. Trimble's own constituency association in Upper Bann also recommended unanimously that the UUP stay in the talks, though it argued that 'concrete' moves had to be made on decommissioning before full negotiations began.[40] But the most dramatic event in the consultation exercise was not any internal debate within the unionist community as a whole or the UUP, but the visit of Trimble and his colleagues to the Roman Catholic Primate of All Ireland, Archbishop Sean Brady in his house, Ara Coeli (literally 'altar of heaven') beside St Patrick's Cathedral, Armagh, on 1 September 1997. A dialogue of sorts had begun some time earlier when the UUP chairman, Denis Rogan, had invited Archbishop

Brady to a Unionist businessmen's lunch at the Reform Club in Belfast and had found the archbishop to be approachable.[41] Nor was it the first time Trimble and Archbishop Brady had met, but never in so formal a context nor in the symbolically significant location of Armagh City itself. They sat on either side of a long table in the Archbishop's library, surrounded by huge bookcases, and spoke for 90 minutes. The UUP was represented by Trimble, Reg Empey, Dermott Nesbitt, and Denis Rogan; the Roman Catholic side was represented by two laymen, Archbishop Brady, Dr Gerard Brooks (the Bishop of Dromore), Dr Michael Dallat (the Auxiliary Bishop of Down and Connor) and Dr Seamus Hegarty (Bishop of Derry). Trimble regarded the last-named as the most interesting and politically acute of the clergymen, who asked questions, he says, about the British-Irish Council. There was, says Hegarty, no tension – though Trimble felt that some of the hierarchy appeared very nervous.[42] After the meeting, Trimble declined to comment in detail, feeling that there ought to be no political *obiter dicta* in the wake of the death of Diana, Princess of Wales. It was surely the right decision from his viewpoint: almost any gloss on the discussions might have contained hostages to fortune.[43] Indeed, by late August and early September, Trimble's critics were starting to become more vociferous after the summer break. William Ross called on Trimble to stay away from the talks. 'The view of many is that we should have nothing to do with these thugs,' opined the MP for Londonderry East. It was also reported that his sentiments were shared by three other colleagues in public and two in private.[44] It was during this period that relations between Trimble and the UUP parliamentary party at Westminster became cosmically bad – never to wholly recover for the remainder of the 1997–2001 Parliament. The meetings of this caucus took place in Trimble's office in the Upper Committee corridor of the Commons every Wednesday when the House is in session.[45] Trimble, though, was philosophical about them: 'Stormont and the Westminster party had abominable relations from 1921–72' says the UUP chief. 'Without intending to do so, this situation was instantaneously reproduced in the relationship now. The Forum and talks teams, as well as the Assembly party subsequently, were not disposed to take direction. This is one reason why the Westminster party feel hurt.'[46] There may have been an element of turf-consciousness about the MPs' attitudes, but that would be to underrate the profound objections of principle which men like Ross felt towards the process. Indeed, perhaps they sensed Trimble's ultimate objectives. A little later that year, Trimble met with Sean O'Callaghan, Ruth Dudley Edwards and Jeffrey Donaldson. 'I know why I can sign up to this deal when I couldn't sign up to Sunningdale.' O'Callaghan was not quite sure what those reasons were, but asked: 'When are you going to tell your supporters?' Trimble grinned and said: 'They're going to have to wait for the night itself.'[47] When reminded of this episode, Trimble said: 'Obviously, I wanted an agreement, but I couldn't say it. Molyneaux, Ross and Smyth would have destroyed me. But I wasn't sure where the precise lines of a settlement would come.'[48]

Equally vexing to Trimble was the opposition of the DUP and UKUP; yet vexing is all it was. Indeed, Peter Weir (then a UUP talks team member) states that for all the rallies, such as a thousand-strong gathering in the Ulster Hall addressed by both Paisley and McCartney, the abuse heaped on the UUP for staying in the talks in September 1997 was much reduced from June 1996, when Trimble accepted Mitchell as talks chairman.[49] But would the final deal of April 1998 have been any better had the UKUP and DUP remained in the talks? Certainly, some very senior British officials are absolutely convinced that although the departure of Ian Paisley served the DUP's electoral interests – in that it enabled them to carry on their campaign against the UUP – it also meant that Unionism as a whole was deprived of the negotiating skills of Peter Robinson. Quentin Thomas, for one, was an unlikely admirer of Robinson and at times would wax lyrical about the MP for East Belfast.[50] Thomas believes that Robinson's presence would have ironed out the rougher edges of the accord from the majority community's perspective. Having the DUP inside the tent would therefore have enhanced the Belfast Agreement's 'deliverability' (Thomas draws a contrast between what he sees as the DUP's more pragmatic stance and McCartney's more purist approach).[51] Not everyone in the NIO shared Thomas's enthusiasm for Robinson: Peter Bell recalls approvingly telling a locally-based colleague about Thomas's conviction that Robinson was the man 'to deliver' on any deal. 'That man couldn't deliver the milk' was his jesting view.[52] Jeffrey Donaldson also believes that if the UKUP and DUP had remained at the table, the agreement would have been very different – or perhaps would not have been struck at all. Donaldson says his position was hugely affected by the departure of the UKUP and DUP. By forcing Trimble to depend upon the small loyalist paramilitary parties, it made the UUP far more vulnerable to their demands on prisoners (where they had common interests with Sinn Fein/IRA).[53] By contrast, neither Trimble nor McCartney believes that had the DUP or UKUP remained, the outcome of the talks would have been very different: McCartney states that Trimble (with the backing of the small paramilitary parties) had 52% of the unionist community and could still do whatever he wanted; if the UKUP had stayed, it would simply have been soiled by the process (because the talks were governed by rules regarding confidentiality, says McCartney, participation would have constricted his ability to speak out). Moreover, asks McCartney, if Trimble was not dissuaded by the opposition of one-third of his own UUP talks team to doing the deal, why should an outsider such as himself have succeeded?[54] Trimble, for his part, thinks that with the DUP and UKUP there he could possibly have obtained a slightly better deal on the political institutions and the constitutional issues. And he adds that those aspects of the deal which caused such pain in the unionist community were prisoners and decommissioning – both of which were negotiated bilaterally between the Governments and the paramilitaries.[55]

But the purist unionists who opted to stay out of the talks were not nearly as irritating to Trimble as the Secretary of State, Mo Mowlam: she was in his view the greatest recruiting sergeant for the rejectionists in this period.[56] As the UUP consultation period neared its close in late August, Mowlam gave an interview in the *Belfast Telegraph* on 28 August 1997, in which she stated that she did not necessarily define consent in terms of numbers or 'in a functional geographical sense'. This pronouncement meant that Mowlam at least appeared to throw into doubt the principle upon which rested the intergovernmental strategy for securing unionist participation in the 'peace process' (not to mention the loyalist ceasefires). Trimble heard about it on his now ever-present mobile telephone from Mark Simpson – then of the *Belfast Telegraph* – as he was walking with John Taylor and Jeffrey Donaldson from the Commons to No. 10. The newspaper was about to publish the interview with Mowlam, and Simpson read out the sentence about consent. Trimble declined to give a reaction but immediately raised the matter with Blair and Mowlam upon starting the meeting in the ground-floor room. 'Mowlam started flannelling,' Trimble claims. 'She said, "I didn't say that." I said, "We took very careful notes of what Simpson said." She replied, "What they've done is to conflate two answers." By this point Blair was irritated and virtually told Mo to go and get the text of the interview. At the end of the meeting we came back to this. She said she didn't have the text. Jeffrey said, "Yes, you have" and reached over. And sure enough, Simpson was quite right. Mo was being economic with the truth. It was quite a picture to see Blair. He was embarrassed but wouldn't disown her.'[57] Jeffrey Donaldson remembers that 'Trimble saved his explosion till he got inside Blair's room. He took her to pieces. Blair tried to calm DT down.'[58] She had been humiliated in front of her Prime Minister and as far as Trimble was concerned she never recovered and thereafter Trimble's important dealings with Government were exclusively with No. 10.[59] Blair also sought to reassure Trimble on the consent principle. Mowlam said she was misquoted and that she too believed in the consent principle; latterly, she says she could not remember the episode.[60] Privately, Blair's reaction, according to one No. 10 official, was 'quite unprintable'.

Trimble's poor relations with Mowlam further bedevilled his attempts to obtain 'confidence-building measures' (CBMs) on behalf of the UUP. On 31 July 1997, Trimble presented Mowlam with a list of possible CBMs – small but significant concessions which would ease the pain of the majority community in the run-up to the great leap of faith made by the UUP in sitting down with Sinn Fein/IRA. These included greater openness and transparency with regard to the operation of the Inter-governmental Conference and the Maryfield secretariat; more cooperation with the Forum (regarded by Unionists as the Assembly in embryo form); enhancement of the power of local authorities; rectification of the bias in favour of nationalist culture, as exemplified by the superior provision for the Gaelic language over Ulster-Scots and the absence of adequate funding for the 36th (Ulster) Division's war memorial at Thiepval on the Somme; appointment of more elected public representatives to quangos and the future of legally held firearms (often by ex-members of the security forces); the implementation of assurances that parades and policing legislation would be subject to the parliamentary scrutiny of a full Bill rather than the Orders in Council (the latter were effectively rule by decree); measures to recognise and to support victims of terrorist violence; and vigorous implementation of the decommissioning timetable outlined by the Government on 16 July.

But when Trimble received a reply to these requests from the NIO, he was profoundly depressed. On 4 September 1997 he wrote to the Prime Minister (he used the formal title rather than the first names that were now in vogue) in the following terms: 'Overall we found the letter very disappointing. Reg Empey summed it up as "ten-nil" ie ten for officials and nothing for us ... the reason for Reg's comment is that there was nothing immediate or concrete that we could refer to next week as a reason justifying the change of position in which the Government is asking us to acquiesce ... [it] merely restates the constitutional guarantee that Northern Ireland will not cease to be a part of the United Kingdom without the consent of the majority of its people. This statement, however, is not inconsistent with the Secretary of State's assertion that consent has no functional significance. Together the constitutional guarantee and the Secretary of State's assertion coincide with what we call the McNamara definition of consent, namely that consent only applies to the final transfer of sovereignty over Northern Ireland to the Irish Republic and does not apply to any arrangement relating to Northern Ireland, including arrangements intended to bring about that transfer – the creation of the "dynamic" north-south bodies mentioned in the framework document. The "McNamara" definition of consent is intended to facilitate republican ambitions and it is noteworthy that this Monday the *Irish News* carried an article by Gerry Adams in which he described consent in the same terms as the Secretary of State. It is therefore essential that consent is properly defined numerically, geographically, and that the government makes clear that the talks are to be governed by the consent principle. The latter has, I think, two aspects. First, that any outcome to the talks must be agreed, at least within the "sufficient consensus" criterion. It is essential that we receive an assurance that the first element of the triple lock – the agreement of the parties – will hold in all circumstances, and that and that there is no question of government imposition.'

The immediate cause of Trimble's need for these assurances were the meetings of the 110-strong Ulster Unionist Executive and the 860-strong Ulster Unionist Council which would have to ratify the decision to stay in the talks. Latterly, Trimble did win some concessions from the Prime Minister. These included a satisfactory reiteration of the consent principle, the indispensability of decommissioning in parallel with talks, recognition for victims, district council powers, firearms legislation and appointing an Ulster Unionist representative to the Assembly of the Council of Europe for the first time in 20 years (it turned out to be John Taylor) – but it was a tremendous battle for him.[61] But why did the NIO fight so hard against giving him any 'collateral'? It may be the case that the NIO was not minded to move quickly because it knew that the UUP leader, for all his rhetoric, was confident enough about the outcome of the consultation and therefore had no need of making further concessions to Trimble. Trimble, though, has another explanation. He states 'you have no idea how hard it is for the NIO to get things out of the Northern Ireland Civil Service' (the NIO was the direct rule superstructure over the six Northern Ireland departments). He cites the 1974 Northern Ireland (Temporary Provisions) Act as introducing a novel concept whereby the Permanent Secretary is the head of each department, who acts on the direction of the Secretary of State. Trimble argues that because of direct rule, political control had attenuated and there was therefore a far greater possibility of inertia in the Ulster bureaucracy than in Whitehall.

Whether or not this was so – and as Trimble is fond of pointing out 'government is not a monolith' – it may underrate the degree of choreography in respect of Northern Ireland policy. It was imperative that Blair appear to come to the rescue of the Ulster Unionists over and over again, thus creating a degree of psychological dependence upon the Prime Minister (who could then demand much in return for favours granted). Whilst no doubt elements of the Northern Ireland Civil Service may have been unresponsive, there were enough ambitious civil servants there who would have been only too pleased to facilitate their new political masters. In the first instance, that meant Mowlam and her team but it also meant Blair, who by now was spending at least a third of his time on Northern Ireland. Indeed, Mowlam's gaffe in her *Belfast Telegraph* interview also forced Trimble to expend valuable chips on reiterating the consent principle ever more conclusively – something which appeared to have been nailed down long before that. Throughout the process, Unionists kept having to buy the same horse over and over again at an ever greater price.

TWENTY-TWO

When Irish eyes are smiling

BY September 1997, Trimble had no doubts at all that he enjoyed the necessary margins to stay in the talks, though he knew it would never be easy. 'Reg [Empey] said there would be good days and bad days, and certainly going in there resembled a fifteen-round heavyweight contest,' recalls Trimble.[1] But his worries were not solely party parochial. He was concerned lest Wales vote against devolution in the 18 September 1997 referendum: he wanted all of the non-English parts of the United Kingdom to enjoy the diffusion of power. Local self-government all-round was Trimble's solution to the old 'devolution-versus-integration' argument and would end Ulster's anomalous status, creating in constitutional terms 'equal citizenship'. But, Trimble adds, even in the unlikely event that Scotland as well as Wales had turned down the Blairite reforms, he would still have sought to have stuck with the political process.[2] The eventual 'yes' results in both plebiscites pleased him, giving him real hope that his idea of a Council of the Isles could now become a reality.

But Trimble had more pressing worries closer to home. On 9 September 1997, Sinn Fein signed up to the Mitchell principles on democracy and non-violence and two days later, the IRA issued a statement in its own name in *An Phoblacht*, in the form of an interview with a member of the Army Council. 'As to the IRA's attitude to the Mitchell principles per se, well the IRA would have problems with sections of the Mitchell principles. But then the IRA is not a participant in these talks.'[3] This came on the eve of the UUP Executive meeting. It forced Trimble to describe republican leaders as 'scoundrels' on an RTE interview: as so often, people looked at the volume with which he said things, rather than their precise content. He decided to stay in the talks but to boycott the opening session. Blair sought to reassure the Unionists by pointing out that the IRA and Sinn Fein were 'inextricably linked' and by also reiterating the 'triple lock'.[4]

Blair's statement was sufficient for the UUP Executive; further reassurance came on 15 September, when the British and Irish states again emphasised that the talks would be governed by the principle of consent. As the Ulster Unionists were pondering how to handle their entry into the talks plenary on 16 September, a 350lb van bomb exploded outside the RUC station at Markethill, Co. Armagh. The police were shielded by the bomb-proofed building, but the cattle market was wrecked and several cows perished.[5] Trimble immediately scrapped the plan to go up to Castle Buildings (the talks venue) and sped to Markethill at 100 mph.[6] The security forces regarded it as the work of republican dissidents; Trimble now thinks it was the work of Continuity IRA, though he acknowledges the possibility of nudges and winks from south Armagh Provisionals. At the time, though, Trimble had no doubt as to who was reponsible. There was, he said, prima facie evidence of IRA involvement and consequently made a formal request to the talks chairman, George Mitchell, for Sinn Fein's expulsion from the negotiations.[7] But when the two Governments eventually responded to the UUP indictment of Sinn Fein later that month – based both upon the IRA interview and Markethill – they made it clear that the form of words in *An Phoblacht* was too vague to constitute a disavowal of the Mitchell principles and that though some Provisionals were involved in Markethill there was nothing to suggest that the main body of the organisation was behind it.

After a day's delay, the UUP decided to enter the talks for the first time with Sinn Fein. The public presentation of this act turned out to be of crucial importance. Forty delegates from the pro-Union parties – that is, the UUP and the two paramilitary-linked groupings, the PUP/UVF and the UDP/UDA – walked in together as a show of strength. 'Our vulnerability was going in ourselves alone, with the other Unionists denouncing us,' says Trimble.[8] It was not just a matter of numbers: implicit in the decision to go in together was the notion that it was hard (at least at this stage) for the DUP to depict the political representatives of the paramilitaries as 'soft' on Sinn Fein – though that was the view which many Unionists later took of the PUP. Not all the Ulster Unionists were happy about being associated with the loyalist parties in this way. 'Here we were protesting about the Provisionals and now we were displaying double standards,' says Peter Weir, a talks team member.[9] But whatever the internal debates within Unionism, it was undoubtedly an historic moment. As one senior British official observed to Mowlam, 'I've worked ten years to achieve this.' The mandarin was 'really chuffed' not so much by having Sinn Fein in the talks, but by securing UUP participation – with a leader who had the political coverage in his community to do it.[10]

The pragmatism which animated Trimble's decision to walk in with the loyalists applied also to his decision to sit down with Sinn Fein/IRA. 'If there's a job to be done, you have to do it,' says Daphne Trimble. 'I don't think he found it a pleasant experience. These are people murdering Ulstermen and women. Somebody has to do it and nobody else volunteered. You have to put your personal feelings to one side.'[11] Likewise, when Trimble first saw Adams at Castle Buildings he found it a 'negative' experience. He was never sure whether he would strike the correct emotional note in these encounters – he would let his feelings get the better of him – so he kept his contacts with Sinn Fein to a minimum (when Adams tried to engage him in conversation in the lavatory, Trimble told him to 'grow up').[12] Then there was the question of how these encounters looked in the eyes of the unionist electorate. As Antony Alcock, a member of the Ulster Unionist talks team, noted in his private diary for 15 October 1997: '1:30 p.m. we had a [UUP] negotiating team talk. One of the issues was how to deal with SF questioning of the UUP. DT said we didn't want minutes released revealing any sort of dialogue between us and them, yet not to give hostages to fortune by declaring we would refuse to dialogue with them. The strategy is to hold our fire, vaguely saying we would deal generally with matters raised, and then put the boot in when the time came for decision-making.'

This was 'New Unionism' in embryo form: its proponents argued that it was pragmatic and 'boxing clever' to avoid blame in the media-conscious CNN era; the critics of New Unionism argued, by contrast, that it would weakly abandon long-held views about the integrity of the democratic process for the sake of short-term publicity gains. Certainly, the New Unionism was about as minimalistic as the drawing room of Peter Mandelson's erstwhile Notting Hill home: it was no longer the ornate, Pugin-esque structure of the by-gone days of yore, with the Gothic touches so beloved of such traditionalists as William Ross. Essentially, New Unionism was centred upon the defensible intellectual laager of the consent principle – a worthy but unambitious position in a post-Soviet Europe where all sorts of peoples were obtaining autonomy. The consent principle was arguably a humble aspiration for a grouping – the Ulster-British – who formed a provincial majority in one of the world's oldest and most stable democracies. Indeed, as Paul Bew noted in the Britishness edition of *The Times Literary Supplement* on 16 March 2001, the consent principle is scarcely new: it had even been accepted by Gladstone who advocated an essentially nationalist view of Irish affairs (though it has waxed and waned in government circles since). Moreover, New Unionism very rarely offered a specifically unionist/loyalist analysis of the Troubles. Instead, it made democratic arguments that could just as easily have come from such Irish constitutional politicians as John Bruton. According to loyalist critics of the Trimble strategy, it initially seemed quite clever to rationalise the abandonment of long-held positions in nationalist language. Thus, the UUP press release on the day they went into the talks sharply declared, 'whatever happens here, the result will be a partitionist settlement'. This may have irked republicans at the moment itself, but in the view of traditionalists such as Clifford Smyth, such terminology became ideologically ever more corrosive.[13] Nor, for that matter, did it answer the question of what *kind* of partitionist settlement would replace the existing dispensation.

From the other side of the divide, Sean Farren, a senior SDLP negotiator, noticed after a while how the UUP analysis of the conflict had changed between the 1991–2 talks and 1997–8. Back in the early 1990s, Farren found that he could empathise more with the DUP policy statements which though very forthright at least acknowledged another tradition; whereas, as he saw it, although UUP language was more genteel, it never properly recognised nationalists as an authentic national minority: instead, as Farren saw it, Ulster Unionists seemed to regard northern nationalism as a political force which would inevitably wane when faced with proper integration into the United Kingdom. By the time Trimble entered the talks in 1997, the UUP analysis was – in Farren's view – much closer to that of the SDLP.[14] Indeed, the record of the Strand II meeting of 24 February 1998, summarised by a UUP aide, Dr Thomas Hennessey, illustrates the point: 'Unionism was no longer arguing for majority rule, nor for total integration within the United Kingdom. Unionists were not opposing a recognition of the validity of the Irish identity of nationalists, or of their sense of belonging to the Irish nation, or asking them simply to accept that they were British. It should also be recognised that Unionism was no longer a monolith. In fact, there were no longer two homogeneous blocs in the community, but a collection of different minorities. It was important that nationalism recognised where Unionism had come from and how far it had moved – perhaps not as far as nationalism would like, but there had to be compromise.'

Farren now attributes the intellectual shift to Trimble, though he is also keen to acknowledge the supporting role of his own former colleague at the University of Ulster, Professor Antony Alcock, a highly respected authority on minority rights who had written the definitive work on the South Tyrol question. Alcock is an Englishman with a Hungarian mother, educated at Harrow, who did his national service in the Seaforth Highlanders. He then entered academe and came to Ulster from Brussels in 1974 – whereupon Trimble's European-minded mentor, Bill Craig, invited him to join Vanguard. Some years after the dissolution of Vanguard, he followed Trimble into the UUP and the Ulster Society, for whom he wrote a volume published in 1994 entitled *Understanding Ulster*. Whatever Alcock's actual importance, he exemplified the point that the UUP talks team of 1997–8 was certainly a very different crew, culturally as well as ideologically from its predecessor. Whereas the 1991–2 talks team represented what Alcock calls 'Orange and rural values' – men very much like Molyneaux, with no tertiary education – Trimble's team included a high percentage of lawyers and academics (indeed, of the key players in Trimble's crowd, only Molyneaux's protégé, Jeffrey Donaldson, had not attended university).[15] This flowed from a conscious desire by Trimble to have a better and more broadly based team than had been at Molyneaux's side in 1991–2.[16]

Alcock was by no means the only outsider on the UUP team. Much of the leg-work on the constitutional issues was done by Austen Morgan, an historian who had recently been called to the English Bar – who was not even a member of the UUP. Morgan, a lapsed Derry Catholic, was born in 1949, and was educated at St Columb's, the Roman Catholic grammar school whose alumni include John Hume and Seamus Heaney. He had joined the People's Democracy march from Belfast to Derry in 1969 whilst in his first year at Bristol University, where he spent much of his time mediating between such sects as the International Marxist Group and the International Socialists. But he always felt uncomfortable when the standard left-wing 'anti-imperialist' orthodoxies were applied to his native island. 'I have usually declined to answer whether I am a catholic or protestant atheist, being distressed by the sectarian enthusiasm of too many British radicals and socialists, bent upon a Manichean search for oppressors and victims,' wrote Morgan. 'More than one educated

English person has welcomed, in my presence, the reported death of a member of the security forces in Northern Ireland.' After entering academe – Morgan taught at Warwick and at Queen's – he wrote biographies of Ramsay MacDonald (1987), James Connolly (1988) and Harold Wilson, and a study called *Labour and Partition* (1991).[17] Morgan believed that Unionists only behaved in 'irrational' ways because they were backed into a corner and if they were allowed to cast aside their siege mentality they could be encourged to create a more pluralistic society which was perfectly willing to cooperate with the Republic.[18]

Some of the UUP team were completely new to these negotiations, or indeed any sort of political activity at all. One such newcomer was Dr Thomas Hennessey, a young English historian of southern Irish Catholic parentage who was a believer in the old 'Two Nations' analysis of the B&ICO. His thesis – which later was published as *Dividing Ireland: World War One and Partition* (1998) – had already attracted the attention of Trimble. He was working in the Belfast offices of the think tank, Democratic Dialogue, when he received a call from Trimble. At first, Hennessey – who was hung over – thought it was a 'wind-up', but the UUP leader soon explained his purpose. Hennessey had been recommended to Trimble by his one-time assistant, Gordon Lucy.[19] Trimble said that he was looking to strengthen the talks delegation and Hennessey soon found himself in the middle of the Strand II team, dealing with cross-border bodies (John Taylor was the chairman and other members included Alcock, Donaldson and David Campbell). They were joined by Peter Weir, one of the 'baby barristers' brought on by Trimble who attracted so much notice; the others were Peter King and David Brewster, a solicitor from Limavady and a prominent Co. Londonderry Orangeman, both of whom formed the 'Second XI' on the Strand I team headed by Reg Empey (others, such as John Hunter and Arlene Foster, a solicitor from Enniskillen, would also come up to Stormont on a more occasional basis). Because of their career commitments, none of the 'baby barristers' were able to be up at Castle Buildings all of the time. Trimble – who was very proud of the fact that the six elected members of the Forum under the age of 35 were on the talks team – hoped in his own mind that the experience of participating would 'educate' these up-and-coming party cadres.

Although it was the colourful characters and the younger elements who attracted much attention as evidence of the changing nature of the UUP, Trimble nonetheless relied mainly upon the advice of senior colleagues. Shortly after he had become leader, Trimble had turned to his then adviser, John Hunter, and wondered aloud, 'Can I trust Reg?'[20] Trimble was referring to his old Vanguard colleague Reg Empey – who, to this day, declines to say for whom he voted in the 1995 leadership contest. But Trimble soon answered his own question by bringing him ever more closely into the innermost counsels of the party; Empey, for his part, came to believe that only someone such as Trimble, who enjoyed the support of hardline loyalists, could come to an accommodation with nationalism (though he also said that the support of that hardline loyalist element tended to be forfeited very quickly once compromises were made). Empey was an exemplar of what the aggressively working-class PUP-UVF would disdainfully refer to as the 'fur coat brigade' – a middle-class businessman who made his money in ladies' retailing and who lived in the leafy Knock district of east Belfast some 200 yards from where he was born. His mother's family came from generations of Belfast businessmen; his father was a Co. Louth Protestant who was 'invited' to leave following the foundation of the Free State. After attending the Royal School Armagh, Empey had graduated from Queen's University and became vice chairman of the Young Unionist Council. He had joined Vanguard and was elected to the 1975–6 Convention and upon returning to the UUP fold was elected to Belfast City Council in 1985. Though he stuck to it out of party loyalty, he privately opposed the post-AIA boycott of government ministers.

The twin experiences of the anti-AIA protests and his years on Belfast City Council were crucial to Empey's approach to the talks. His friends said he was a realist, and the best negotiator that Unionism had; his critics charged that he was a rank defeatist. During the anti-AIA protests, Empey was struck by the 'sheer impotence' of the unionist community. 'We couldn't stick to a cause the way republicans could stick to it,' notes Empey. 'Our folk aren't up to the long war like the republicans are. Look at all of this aping of republicans, such as the "Long March" rallies [a reference to the Province-wide loyalist demonstrations of 1999]. How can we win a battle in which we effectively destroy our own country? Riots work for republicans but they don't work for us.' Some of his critics thought that such attitudes were a set of clever rationalisations for Empey's own lack of fight. Above all, it was the changing balance of forces in his native Belfast which impelled Empey towards a settlement before it was too late. He had seen the substantial unionist majority in Belfast slide to narrow minority status in the years of direct rule: he attributed this less to the IRA than to what he contended were the unaccountable administrative actions of the Housing Executive (which many unionists, rightly or wrongly, believed built more and better homes in nationalist areas whilst demolishing substantial tracts of many unionist neighbourhoods such as the Shankill). Empey believed that a return of local self-government to Stormont – even in a power-sharing context with nationalists – would ensure that the unionists had a greater direct say in the running of such public bodies.[21]

One reason for Empey's growing importance to the talks team was that he was in Belfast full-time (except when he was in Brussels for meetings of the EU Committee of the Regions). For unlike Trimble – and Jeffrey Donaldson and John Taylor, for that matter – Empey had no responsibilities at Westminster. He thus provided a key element of continuity in the talks team. Some on the team, however, feared that this shifting cast of characters also opened opportunities for the UUP's opponents to 'try it on' since different Unionist negotiators were not necessarily aware of the nuances of what had or had not been agreed by their colleagues.[22] Such was the confusion in the talks team that, at times, No. 10 even found the semi-clandestine republican movement to be easier to read than the ill-disciplined and disorganised UUP. Indeed, the UUP leader recalls that as he was waiting outside Castle Buildings on the day that the Unionist parties entered the talks with Sinn Fein in September 1997, his mobile telephone rang. It was Blair on the line. The Prime Minister's voice was a little uncertain, and he asked, 'Where exactly are we now?' 'In the outer car park,' replied Trimble, dead-pan. 'They kept telling me you wouldn't do it,' said Blair – that is, enter the talks.[23] It was obvious, says Trimble, that Blair was unsure what the UUP was going to do, and indeed the Prime Minister said that he had been told 'by some people' that Trimble was just stringing him along. Sean Farren's notes for this period confirm the point: 'Brits tell us that pressure being mounted by Blair and that DT is reneging over promises to enter. So we were now left waiting and Markethill happens on the 16th [September] and gives the UUP an excuse to stay out. Then they announce that an indictment will be made against Sinn Fein's participation, sounds more like cover.'

The UUP entry into the talks helped build British confidence in his intentions, but Trimble nonetheless found Blair's inquiry very surprising:

apart from all the signals that he had sent out (and the positive vastly outnumbered the negative, although he may have sought to increase doubts as the talks deadline approached), he asks himself, 'How could [British] intelligence not know?' The UUP leader speculates that there is possibly a time lag between the collection of the information and its dissemination in Whitehall. If so, Trimble says, he has been wasting his time these past few years: he often deliberately says certain things over the open telephone line which he believes are being monitored. Indeed, in July 1999, when the UUP was negotiating 'The Way Forward' document with the British and Irish Governments, Trimble told his assembly group gathered in Castle Buildings, 'It's all being monitored – but don't worry about it. What is crucial is what the intelligence community picks up about our morale and cohesivenesss.'[24] But it is also possible that the Prime Minister genuinely did not know the answer because of the highly fissiparous nature of Unionist political organisation. In other words, Blair was confronted on a political level with the same problems which John Steele had identified in respect of loyalist violence: indiscipline, randomness and lack of central control which at times baffled even the mightiest in the land.

Trimble's 'ducking and diving' owed everything to keeping his interlocutors and internal adversaries off balance. This entailed a combination of cussedness and demonstrating to his own 'folk' (the term which he often used) the new-found respect in which their tradition was held. As ever, there was no better token of this esteem than a visit to the White House. For his part, Trimble had become ever more comfortable with the Americans. This was noted by such Irish-Americans as Congressman Peter King: 'David Trimble changed after the second IRA ceasefire,' the Long Island legislator recalls. 'He was more accepting of the role we had to play.'[25] Partly, this was because the Lake-Soderberg team on the National Security Council had been replaced in the early part of the second term with Sandy Berger (Lake's former deputy), Jim Steinberg (who replaced Berger as the No. 2, and who played a far more regular part on Northern Ireland affairs than his new boss) and Larry Butler (a career diplomat with 23 years' service whose last posting from 1996–7 was as deputy chief of mission in Dublin). The Americans, says Butler, were deeply conscious of the risk which Trimble had taken with his own constituency and that, at a minimum, he had to be given parity with Adams.[26]

Trimble and Taylor met with Berger at 11:30 a.m. on 7 October 1997, in the National Security Adviser's West Wing office; Clinton and Gore both 'dropped by' halfway through the discussion. Berger told his visitors that there 'would be no third bite at the apple' for Sinn Fein if the IRA again broke its ceasefire (which was duly reported in the provincial press).[27] Trimble appeared to agree with his hosts that it was better for the IRA to be removed from the State Department's list of proscribed terrorist organisations so as to increase the leverage over republicans not to resume violence. Trimble made two particular points: first, he hoped that Sinn Fein was locked into the process now (though both he and Taylor seemed to think that they would only obtain Welsh-style committee chairmanships in a new assembly, rather than the full ministerial slots along the Scottish model). Second, he was worried that there was no serious discussion between the UUP and the new Fianna Fail-led Irish Government.

There were clearly identifiable reasons for what turned out to be a five-month-long hiatus until proper dialogue began between Fianna Fail and the UUP. The first aim of the Irish Government after the June 1997 election – at which point there were still no 'inclusive' negotiations – was to steer through the shoals of another Drumcree march and to secure another IRA ceasefire. Their focus was, therefore, largely on Republicans. The early atmospherics were not good: first, there was talk that the increasingly pro-republican former Taoiseach, Albert Reynolds, might become the 'special envoy' to Northern Ireland. Moreover, Trimble especially disliked Ray Burke, the new Minister of Foreign Affairs, who had day-to-day responsibility for Northern Ireland policy. But the problems gradually resolved themselves. The idea of Reynolds as special envoy to 'the North' died a quiet death and Ray Burke resigned both as Foreign Minister and as a TD after allegations of yet another scandal afflicting Fianna Fail.[28] He was replaced by David Andrews, who had previously served in the position in the early 1990s and who Trimble disliked less than Burke. Therefore, Andrews did not act as a 'drag' on the emerging North-South relationship. One other change within the Department of Foreign Affairs was almost as significant: in August 1997, another Unionist *bête noire*, Sean O hUiginn, left his post as head of the Anglo-Irish division of the ministry to become ambassador to the United States. His replacement was the outgoing head of mission in America, Dermot Gallagher, who had previously run the Anglo-Irish section from 1987–91. Gallagher was widely regarded by Unionists as a more emollient figure than O hUiginn.[29]

'Sean was demonised by the British, but there was no difference in policy between the two men,' recalls David Andrews. 'Sean is more abrasive. It was, however, only a difference of style, not substance.'[30]

The key figure was Ahern himself. He was a brilliant campaigner and tactician who regularly topped the poll in his home base of Dublin Central. This non-ideological technician had risen to the top of his party negotiating 'national pay agreements' and had hitherto shown little public track record in 'the North'. Nor, despite his father's participation as a teenaged runner for the 3rd Cork Brigade of the IRA in the War of Independence, which ensured that he remained on Gardai Special Branch files till the 1970s, was Ahern much haunted by the ghosts of the past.[31] He came from that segment of the Dublin lower-middle and working classes for whom Association Football rather than Gaelic Football, was the second religion. And one of his mentors was Billy Attley of SIPTU, the amalgamation of the Irish Transport and General Workers Union and the Federated Workers Union of Ireland, who was no friend of the Provisionals. From Trimble's point of view, therefore, Ahern's background was not at all unpromising – and he was told as much by his southern interlocutors, such as Eoghan Harris. Trimble had his first prolonged discussion with Ahern when the latter was leader of the Opposition at the annual conference of the British-Irish Association in September 1996, held at St John's College, Oxford.[32] They spoke for half an hour: the UUP leader was still hugely exercised by the events at Drumcree II during the previous July. Subsequently, they had met in early 1997 at Armagh in the drawing room of the Church of Ireland Primate, Lord Eames, where Ray Burke (as the shadow foreign minister) and Martin Mansergh, the Anglo-Irish *éminence grise* to successive Fianna Fail Taoisigh from the days of Charles Haughey, were also present. Though in opposition, Ahern had already begun to keep a close eye on Trimble's pronouncements. 'I started reading a lot of his speeches and he started reading mine and so we probably built up a common ground,' recalls Ahern. 'I thought irredentism was dead. I was saying things that differed from what was expected from a nationalist leader.'[33]

Trimble knew he wanted a deal. But the 'choreography' of the event – rapidly becoming one of the buzz-words of the peace process – was all-important to him. Where would it be held? Would journalists be told of the location? Would the two delegations arrive and leave separately so there would be no photographs together? The Irish did not much care where the event was held, but Trimble did. As he had observed at the White House during his meeting with Sandy Berger, Paisley and McCartney enjoyed the support of 40% of the Unionist population. London was duly hit upon as the venue and although the Irish offered their embassy overlooking the gardens of Buckingham Palace, a neutral location was thought to be better. Ted Barrington, the ambassador, opted for the nearby Sheraton Belgravia and the meeting was duly fixed for 20 November.

On the UUP side of the long table, Trimble was accompanied by John Taylor, Ken Maginnis, Jeffrey Donaldson, Reg Empey and Patricia Campbell of the Unionist Information Office; Ahern was accompanied by David Andrews, Dermot Gallagher, Ted Barrington, Paddy Teahon (Secretary-General of the Taoiseach's Department), Martin Mansergh and Joe Lennon (the Government press secretary). 'It was the first time a Fianna Fail leader had picked a delegation who would work with me and with the leader of the Ulster Unionists all the way through [the talks process],' says Ahern.[34] Ken Maginnis was especially impressed that Andrews was placed at the end of the table, thus symbolising to him the centrality of Ahern's role: Unionists wanted to sidestep the DFA and deal directly with what they saw as the less ideological Taoiseach's Department. Ahern, unlike Bruton, had the political latitude, arithmetically as well as ideologically, to indulge Trimble in this relationship. The Ahern–Trimble relationship caused some irritation to northern nationalists, and Seamus Mallon subsequently warned against any attempt to reach a settlement outside of the formal negotiations at Stormont; Liz O'Donnell, Andrews' deputy, struck a jarring note when she warned Trimble not to use Ahern as 'court of appeal' against the Stormont talks process.[35] But both the southern Government and northern nationalists eventually took the view that bestowing attention on Trimble and the Ulster Unionists was worth the irritation if it helped to bring about a settlement.[36]

Over a lunch of quail and monkfish, Ahern sought to put his Unionist interlocutors at ease. 'I don't like the IRA' Ken Maginnis recalls him saying. 'He also said that we don't have much time. We have all got our constituencies, but that if he did a deal on the 1937 Constitution he would stick by his word.' (Ahern was referring, inter alia, to republican opposition to any renegotiation of Articles 2 and 3 and their hostility to any Northern Ireland Assembly, which was reflected amongst the 'Greener' elements of Fianna Fail.)[37] Ahern adds: 'Again, I was emphasising all of the time the non-threatening nature' (of the cross-border bodies).[38] At one moment, Teahon leaned over to his chief and whispered 'you really need to move this on a bit', but Ahern replied 'Paddy, be patient': he would soothe the Ulster Unionists in his own way. For as the Irish saw it, Trimble was determined to see whether – as the necessary quid pro quo for cross-border bodies – they were prepared to go beyond the formula on Articles 2 and 3 asked by Major of Albert Reynolds at the EU summit in Greece in June 1994. Known as the 'Corfu test', Major sought both the removal of the territorial claim (Article 2) as well as recognition of the legitimacy of Northern Ireland's position within the United Kingdom. But this test had been fudged by the British in the negotiations leading up to the Frameworks Documents of February 1995. The Irish 'holding' position – set out in paragraph 21 of the Frameworks – was that the Republic would support changes to the Constitution to implement the relevant portions of the Downing Street Declaration of December 1993; that these would 'fully reflect the principle of consent' in Northern Ireland; and be 'demonstrably' such that no territorial claim of right to jurisdiction over Northern Ireland is asserted contrary to the will of the majority there, while maintaining the right of everyone born in either jurisdiction to be part, as of right, of the Irish nation. Trimble, though, claimed that the offer was negated by the Supreme Court ruling in the McGimpsey case and wanted constitutional change to be 'judge-proof' (indeed, the Irish offer of 1995 kept the language in the 1937 Constitution upon which the judges had ruled in the McGimpsey case). Trimble required not merely the abandonment of the de jure claim of jurisdiction, but also a redefinition of the national territory.[39] Although Ahern publicly stated that the Republic had already made the necessary compromises in the 1995 Frameworks Documents, some say by the autumn of 1997, the Irish had quietly come to the view they would have to go beyond that formulation.

Such changes were emblematic of something that was very important to Trimble: '. . . the rhetoric [of Dublin] screws up northern nationalists,' he observed in the January 1998 issue of *Parliamentary Brief*. 'How can northern nationalists accept a position that is lower than Dublin's rhetoric? Northern nationalists feel they must operate in line with the rhetoric of Dublin – that they are not letting down the nation. So, lowering Dublin's rhetoric and bringing it into line with reality is actually very necessary to make life easier for northern nationalists. Ever since 1922, Dublin governments have acted in a partitionist manner but because they use anti-partitionist language, they have prevented northern nationalists from coming to terms with partition.' Unionists of all hues were agreed upon the unacceptablity of such rhetoric and their apotheosis in Articles 2 and 3 and that they played a part in inflaming the Ulster crisis. But Trimble's critics wondered whether he had not got things the wrong way round. They felt that he had underrated the degree to which it was northern nationalists who dragged their southern brethren into the Ulster morass and constantly forced them to adopt a more irredentist position (citing, for example, the way in which they believed John Hume urged the cautious Cosgrave Government into a more maximalist position on the Council of Ireland at the time of Sunningdale).[40] Trimble's critics thus felt that his analysis underrated the autonomous dynamic in northern nationalism and the dialectic of conflict on the ground with loyalism.

Trimble was reassured enough by what he heard in the two-and-a-half-hour meeting at the Sheraton Hotel. Indeed when the UUP leader looked out of a window to see the cameras present at this supposedly secret meeting, Paddy Teahon was struck by the fact that he seemed utterly composed.[41] Likewise, Ahern was impressed by the fact that John Taylor – who was seen as more hardline than Trimble – walked to the door with him.[42] But longer-term effects on his view of the Irish Republic's intentions were more important still. 'Bertie's given me this opportunity to negotiate the Irish Constitution and to separate nation from state,' Trimble told Austen Morgan at Castle Buildings. And, lowering his voice, he added, 'I want an agreement.'[43] There were other reasons for his enthusiasm: the Irish Government placed renewed emphasis on the Strand III track in recognition of Trimble's needs.[44] One of the reasons for his enthusiasm was his conviction that 'if a deal is going to be done, Fianna Fail is going to be the party to do it, since they could deliver'. And he further contended: 'The problem [under the previous Government] was not Bruton or Fine Gael, but Spring. He appeared to be in charge of Northern Ireland policy. So my meetings with Bruton, while very cordial, had no follow through. When Bertie was in Opposition [during Bruton's term of office] it seemed like Ray Burke ran the policy and Bertie was the front man. But I underestimated him.'[45]

TWENTY-THREE

Murder in the Maze (or the way out of it)

DESPITE Trimble's emerging dialogue with Ahern, the end of 1997 appeared to be fraught with difficulties for him. For much of the period, the British Government appeared to operate on the assumption that the IRA ceasefire might not endure for very long (an assumption which he shared, as illustrated by his pessimistic remarks in the report stage of the Emergency Provisions Bill).[1] 'There was a two-and-a-half-hour talks team meeting,' noted Antony Alcock in his diary entry of 5 December 1997. 'We heard that intelligence sources believed that the IRA ceasefire would end in January and for that reason HMG was "filling Adams' stocking" with goodies – visit to No. 10 Downing Street, transfer of prisoners to Ireland, N & S, longer Christmas leave, to buy ceasefire for as long as possible . . . But the upshot was that the UUP was being seen as a soft touch, ineffective.' Certainly, Sinn Fein were turning up the heat on the two Governments. Thus, Francie Molloy, a leading Sinn Fein member, told a republican gathering in Cullyhanna, Co. Armagh, on 16 November 1997 that if the Stormont talks fail that they will 'simply go back to what we know best'.[2] Molloy later said he meant Sinn Fein's peace process. Trimble now says that he looked at the whole text, but concluded that it did not necessarily mean that republicans would return to armed struggle: the phrase, he believes, was meant to reassure the faithful and to 'spook out' the British without committing the leadership to anything specific.[3] Of perhaps greater importance was the creation, in December 1997, of the '32 County Sovereignty Committee', a group of republicans opposed to the policy of the Sinn Fein leadership. At a minimum, the very existence of the group – which some in the security forces thought to be a 'managed' split rather than a pre-choreographed deceit – set limits upon how far and fast the Sinn Fein high command could move towards democratic politics for fear of losing members.

Indeed, even at this point, the dark hints of what might happen were not solely rhetorical. Daphne Trimble alerted the RUC after a suspicious-looking letter arrived at her husband's office in Lurgan: upon inspection, it turned out to contain a crude but viable explosive device.[4] This was later claimed by a previously unheard-of republican grouping.

Certainly, the 'optics' were not good for Trimble. On 13 October 1997, Blair held his first meeting with Adams at Castle Buildings – the first such encounter by a serving British Prime Minister and a republican leader since the outbreak of the current Troubles. 'Blair made damn sure that there were no photos,' says Trimble. 'He felt it was something he had to do, even though it was not especially welcome.'[5] Indeed, Blair first shook hands in public with a leading member of Sinn Fein in December 1999, at the inaugural meeting of the British-Irish Council in London. Even then, it was with the new Health Minister of the Northern Ireland Executive, Bairbre de Brun, who had no 'military' record: for someone apparently so confident of republican bona fides, he left remarkably few such hostages to fortune.[6] When Adams subsequently went to No. 10, Trimble made the appropriate noises – 'I don't think it's a dignified position for the Government to be in. It's going to be an embarrassment to the Government, particularly if there is a return to violence and it's going to damage confidence here in Northern Ireland' – but did little about it.[7]

Trimble's main source of vexation with Mowlam in this period was the Parades Bill – another long-heralded item of Labour legislation for which he never dreamed of blaming Blair himself.[8] It had its origin in the widespread feeling in nationalist Ireland, which was rapidly conveyed to the Labour benches in the Commons, that there must be no repetition of the three sieges of Drumcree. The solution was an unelected Parades Commission with executive powers to ban marches, though the Chief Constable could still overturn their decision on public order grounds (however, some felt that the threshold for doing so was now politically that much higher). Unionists felt that the way in which the legislation had been drafted discriminated against their forms of culture, such as marching, but left 'offensive' forms of nationalist self-expression untouched. In particular, Trimble cited the car cavalcades of Gaelic Athletic Association supporters who would travel at high speed through predominantly Protestant rural villages on Sundays: he stated that Protestants felt 'threatened' by these intrusions, and were sometimes unable to make their way to church.[9]

The Parades Bill was one of many matters – but perhaps the most urgent item on the agenda, since it was about to reach the Upper House – that were discussed at a two-day 'Unionist unity' conference held at Hatfield House, Hertfordshire, the ancestral home of Viscount Cranborne's family. The event was attended by the UUP, DUP and UKUP leaders, as well as Andrew Mackay, and left-wing friends of Trimble such as Kate Hoey, Gary Kent and John Lloyd. Trimble was initially sceptical about the event: he was worried that the DUP and McCartney would railroad him into a more hardline stance than he wished to adopt.[10] But Trimble's anxieties were assuaged by Sean O'Callaghan, the former head of IRA Southern Command, who had conceived and helped to organise the event: the ex-Provisional was determined to show the Government that unionists could still coordinate together and retained an option on pan-unionist unity (as things turned out, this would be the last such event. It became all but impossible after the breach caused by the signing of the Belfast Agreement). Perhaps only O'Callaghan could have persuaded Trimble to participate. Since his release from prison in December 1996 under the royal prerogative, he had gained the confidence of many Unionists, not least Trimble himself. They met just days after O'Callaghan was freed – in what Trimble describes as a 'surreal experience'. The Unionist Information Office was holding its Christmas drinks at Buckingham Street by Charing Cross railway station, attended by Trimble and Ruth Dudley Edwards (who had become friendly with O'Callaghan when he was in jail). Dudley Edwards told Trimble that she was meeting O'Callaghan at a nearby wine bar after the UIO function and would like to introduce them. Trimble thought it would not be possible: fraternising with men who had blood on their hands, even in the person of so high-ranking a defector as O'Callaghan, would appal large portions of the unionist community. Could he trust him, Trimble wondered? 'David, trust me,' she said. Dudley Edwards fetched both the drinks and placed O'Callaghan and others on a bench in the nearby Embankment Gardens. Finding the gardens shut, the party was forced instead to perch on the wall of the footpath. Gradually, more and more guests from the party filtered out, and a second party began.[11] Trimble attests to O'Callaghan's subsequent role in moulding his perceptions of the key republican personalities and strategies – notably the growing importance to them of making electoral inroads in the south and the attendant implications for them of their behaviour in Northern Ireland.[12] Certainly, O'Callaghan's insights are unique and his organising skills are formidable, but the Hatfield episode also pointed up broader deficiencies in Unionism. 'Try and imagine the same event taking place on the republican side,' says O'Callaghan (probably the only man to have worked intimately with both Trimble and Gerry Adams). 'Imagine Adams having such a lack of control over his own party that he could be bounced into participating in a conference organised by a former high-ranking UVF man at which both Ruairi O'Bradaigh [president of the rejectionist Republican Sinn Fein] and Michael McKevitt [another rejectionist] were present. It's simply not possible.'[13]

Ruth Dudley Edwards, who also played a key part in organising the Hatfield gathering, had first come to know Trimble in 1986 at a conference at Keele University. He seemed to know no one, so she invited him to a party, where he stayed to the very end. To her surprise, she found him good company, and that he relaxed after a few drinks. 'Clearly, your problem is that you're permanently three pints under par' (this was not literally true, since Trimble is not teetotal, but it expresses a widespread Irish feeling about Ulster Protestants in general and the UUP leader in particular). Dudley Edwards was born and raised as a Dublin Catholic. Her father, Robin, was a distinguished historian and through him she was related to the Fianna Fail dynasty, the Lenihans. Dudley Edwards worked as a marketing executive in the Post Office and as a civil servant in the Department of Industry in London before taking up full-time writing. Her seventeen books include biographies of Padraic Pearse, Victor Gollancz and the official history of *The Economist*. When Trimble was elected as an MP, she invited him for lunch to Auberon Waugh's Academy Club in Soho. Dudley Edwards, though, wasted little time in coming to the heart of the matter for anyone from a Catholic nationalist background – even one who was a divorced atheist and had relentlessly debunked the pieties of the *Volk*: 'How much of a bigot are you?' she asked him. She would also tease him, likening Trimble's walk down Carleton Street with Ian Paisley at the time of Drumcree I to a pair of the principals at a gay wedding (Trimble laughed heartily at the idea). Dudley Edwards learned from such reactions that Trimble was anything but the caricature Unionist: indeed, it was the first of many friendships which she struck up with members of the Loyal Orders, culminating in her best-selling study of

Orangeism, *The Faithful Tribe.* Indeed, when Trimble saw an article in *Fortnight* which teased Dudley Edwards for her 'near-erotic fascination with the Ulster Protestant male', the UUP leader quipped, '*Near-erotic???*'[14] Certainly, few outsiders can ever have sought to explain the fears and aspirations of loyalists in general, and of Trimble in particular, with the assiduity of Dudley Edwards. For this, she was roundly abused by many of her countrymen for what they saw as an act of apostasy. Although Dudley Edwards modestly down-played her role, Trimble nonetheless gladly acknowledges his considerable debt to her.[15] She was neither an Irish Mata Hari who had seduced Trimble into a bad deal – as some loyalists imagined – but nor was she a mere Gaelic wallflower in a garden of Orange lilies, either. Such was Trimble's debt to her that at moments of high drama in 1999, he took the time to say a few words at the launch of *The Faithful Tribe* at Politico's bookshop in Westminster.[16]

Two of Trimble's associates were conspicuous by their absence from the Hatfield conference: Eoghan Harris and Paul Bew. Harris felt it had too much of the air of 1912-style resistance to Home Rule, with Unionists coalescing with what he saw as reactionary elements on the mainland. Harris also prevailed upon Bew – his old comrade from Workers' Party days – to opt out of the event as well. Bew, the Professor of Irish Politics at Queen's, was by now becoming a ubiquitous figure in the media. Born in 1950 of a northern Protestant father and a southern Catholic mother, Bew had joined the Northern Ireland Labour party Young Socialists whilst in his teens at Campbell College. There, he followed Michael Farrell and Eamonn McCann, helping them, inter alia, to organise a projected hairdressers' strike in Belfast. But within a few months, these student radicals had become world news and Bew had joined his coevals in People's Democracy – the far-left grouping which triggered some of the first large-scale disturbances of the Troubles when they marched through loyalist areas after the fashion of the 'freedom walks' of the American civil rights movement. Bew was present (along with his Campbell and Cambridge contemporary, Bruce Anderson, then in his Marxist phase) at the most dramatic moment in the story of People's Democracy, when their march from Belfast to Derry was violently ambushed by enraged loyalists at Burntollet in Co. Londonderry in January 1969. Later, he cut the leaflets produced by PD in defence of the Ballymurphy riots of 1970 and was to be found on numerous security force files of the period. But Bew soon ceased to subscribe to the conventional left-wing view of the 'progressive' nature of '1969 and all that'. After all that he had seen at first hand, he did not think that the Protestants were the carbon image of white American southerners, nor indeed that they were unprovoked by the nationalists. As time went on, he concluded that the 'progressive' uprising was far more sectarian and reactionary than he had originally understood it to be. Bew, like Trimble, was also profoundly influenced by the writings of the B&ICO and by the early 1980s had found his way into the Workers' Party, the political wing of the Official IRA which gradually weaned the 'Stickies' off armed struggle. Later, Trimble – who had something of a penchant for ex-'Stickies' – also supplied Bew with research materials for his study of relations between the Redmondites and the Unionists during the period of the Home Rule crisis, *Ideology and the Irish Question*.[17] In late 1997, Trimble gave *Between War and Peace: The Political Future of Northern Ireland* (co-authored by Bew, Henry Patterson and Paul Teague) to John Holmes, the Private Secretary to the Prime Minister, who read it and in turn passed on portions of it to Blair.[18]

Much attention was lavished upon Trimble's variegated ideological *galère* – probably the most cosmopolitan and unusual crew that was ever placed at the disposal of a UUP leader. Ruth Dudley Edwards jokingly observed as much to Daphne Trimble during the UUP conference in Enniskillen in October 1999. 'David's surrounded by Catholics, a Communist, an ex-Provo, a homosexual and a Jew.' 'I know,' laughed Daphne Trimble. 'Isn't it marvellous?'[19] As Trimble observes, all of these individuals had sought him out in one way or another rather than him seeking them out: partly, this derives from his own shyness, but partly also because he is very self-contained and does not really seek out company when he has his reading and his music to catch up with (though he is happy enough when such associates make contact, especially if they are outsiders). Some took the presence of these exotics to be a symptom of the enfeebled nature of the UUP: they needed this sort of 'unhired' and spectacularly unconventional help, as it were, to make good their deficiencies. Trimble, though, does not see things that way and on major policy decisions tends instead to rely on senior colleagues such as Taylor, Empey, Nicholson, Maginnis and Rogan. The function of the 'colourful characters', as Trimble calls them, is that he can let his hair down with them, safe in the knowledge that his *obiter dicta* will not reverberate around the party. 'I have to bite my tongue in party groups,' he laments.[20]

At times, Trimble also had to bite his tongue in a broader sense and could not reveal the full extent of his plans: in such a context, the outsiders served the useful purpose of floating trial balloons before turning to a sceptical UUP.

But the pro-Agreement forces on the penumbra of the UUP were, at this point, by no means confident that their mission would meet with success (perhaps less so than Trimble himself). Quite apart from terrorist violence, they still feared the Irish DFA 'maximalism' would play into the hands of rejectionist unionism.[21] Their worries were vindicated on 29 November 1997, when the Irish Foreign Minister, David Andrews, stated that the secretariat which would implement the decisions of the North-South bodies would have 'strong executive functions not unlike a Government'. As Antony Alcock recorded the atmosphere in the UUP talks team in his private diary entry of 1 December 1997: 'Apparently Andrews' statement has really rattled the UUP rank and file. The problem is that after DT's meeting with Ahern . . . when he said things had gone well and there was an opportunity for movement, it looks as if the UUP is part of the Andrews scenario, or has agreed to it, so we don't come out well and are ripe for attacks by DUP, UKUP'. Trimble swiftly contacted Ahern on his mobile telephone, but privately he was not especially worried about Andrews' remarks: according to Jeffrey Donaldson, he did not see Andrews as a significant player (much as he saw Mo Mowlam) and preferred instead to cultivate his relationship with Ahern and Teahon.[22] There may have been an array of explanations for the statement, but Sean Farren of the SDLP observed in his private notebook: 'D. Andrews faux pas dominates exchange and becomes the basis for huge Unionist reaction. DA backs down (goes against advice in apologising).' Later, Ahern distanced himself from Andrews' remarks both in a Dail speech and in an interview in the *Financial Times*: in the latter, he said that he 'assumed' Trimble would be head of a new Northern Ireland administration. The effect of a Taoiseach giving a UUP leader such 'parity of esteem' was considerable.[23]

The point was further underlined shortly before the talks broke up for Christmas when the SDLP talks team pulled away from an agreement which they appeared to have reached with their UUP counterparts – again, partly under pressure from Dublin.[24] As Antony Alcock described it in his diary entry for 9 December 1997: 'At Castle Buildings. Apparently on Monday UUP and SDLP agree at the Plenary sub cte a list of areas on which agreement was necessary. Martin McGuinness stormed out saying it would be "bodies on the streets". The issue was, in fact, rather whether an Assembly should be on the list for agreement, not whether there should be an Assembly. SF asked for an adjournment of today's meeting starting at 10:30. The meeting reconvened and lasted two hours. After, DT said the Irish Government was sheltering the Provos. There'll be another meeting tomorrow.' Alcock's colleague from the University of Ulster, Sean Farren, remarked in his notebook on 15 December 1997: 'SM [Seamus Mallon] and DT find common ground on our paper with the addition of a reference to an Assembly in Strand I; SF very opposed unless reference is also made to their proposals for regional councils and to "demilitarisation". UUP not able to agree to any such language. In a bilateral with SF I point to the irony of their position; making it appear that progress depends [on] them talking directly to UUP is admitting a veto to the latter.' At this stage, Trimble was not especially optimistic that there could be an agreement with Sinn Fein and in any case was rather more worried about the increasing nervousness of the Unionist community. On 23 December 1997 four Ulster Unionist MPs – Roy Beggs, Clifford Forsythe, Willie Ross and Willie Thompson – released a letter suggesting that the party should withdraw from the talks.

It was a gloomy end to the year: Ahern, for one, feared that without political progress, the Christmas break would turn out to be a 'dire period'.[25] His fears were dramatically vindicated when on 27 December 1997, Billy Wright, the LVF leader, was assassinated by two INLA inmates whilst waiting to take a prison visit from his girlfriend in the Maze: they had been able to smuggle in a gun with impunity. It seemed an almost unbelievable episode, even by the astonishingly lax standards which successive Governments allowed to obtain in the Province's penal regime. Thus, the INLA prisoners were housed in the same block along with loyalist rejectionists.[26] As Antony Alcock noted in his diary for 31 December 1997: 'To Glengall St p.m. UUP leaders had met "Mo" a.m. and it was disastrous, although it appears she has agreed to an independent inquiry into the Maze events. DT made no secret of the fact that he wants (and hopes) such an inquiry would blow her out of her job, that is his objective. Ken Maginnis said the events at the Maze (a tunnel, arms, a murder) should mean resignations of the Maze governor, the NIO staff i/c security [John Steele] but told "Mo" it would be unfair for them to go before her . . . Yesterday's meeting with the PUP-UVF equally disastrous. Expectation they will not be at the Talks on 12th [January]. Gloom that violence unavoidable in next 10 days. If PUP don't show and [UVF] go to war difficult for the UDP to restrain the UDA and if peace collapses the UDP would find it difficult to be at the Table and if they go the UUP wouldn't have the majority of the Unionist community [because the DUP and UKUP boycotted the negotiations] so UUP wouldn't have the majority of the U community, so talks can't produce a cross community consensus, and we will be forced to say that we need an adjournment of the Talks until at least one loyalist group has climbed back on board.'

Trimble saw the loyalist ceasefires as 'crumbling' after the LVF had committed two murders in retaliation before the year ended.[27] That weekend, the UDA/UFF prisoners – who even before Christmas were unhappy with the flow of concessions to republicans – voted to withdraw their support for the Stormont talks.[28] Gary McMichael of the UDP/UDA recalls the atmosphere: 'Some of the prisoners went daft because Wright was so close to them. It looked as if we couldn't convince them to return to the negotiations. David Trimble suddenly offered to go to the Maze to talk to them.' Trimble had previously taken the view that it was possible to talk to the UDP because their position was different from that of the IRA: the Combined Loyalist Military Command ceasefire statement of October 1994 had expressed 'abject and true remorse' in a way the Provisionals never had and they were still on ceasefire (if by now only just).[29] The UDP admired Trimble's courage in being willing to undertake so public a move. They also remembered that Trimble had also visited them in October 1996, when the loyalist ceasefire had looked no less shaky after the bombing of Thiepval barracks, and had met with such notorious UDA figures as Johnny 'Mad Dog' Adair and Michael Stone, the pony-tailed Milltown cemetery killer.[30]

Jeffrey Donaldson, who accompanied Trimble on his visit to the Maze on 6 January 1998, says that at a human level, Trimble was anything but comfortable about rubbing shoulders with the hard men – whether of the UDA/UFF or the UVF (whom the UUP also met with separately).[31] Adair, who was especially worried about Articles 2 and 3 and the role of the Dublin Government, was reassured by Trimble's analysis. 'If Johnny Adair found it credible politically and it was presented by someone he had confidence in, that would carry a lot of weight inside the prison and outside,' says John White. 'That helped us [the political representatives] a lot.'[32] Trimble recalls urging the prisoners to 'hang in there. It would be a long and difficult talks process. Michael Stone was the most sensible. The others were OTT in their manner of discourse and excitable.'[33] This discussion was subsequently all but forgotten in the excitement over Mowlam's much better known visit to the loyalist prisoners, which contributed mightily to the cult of the 'emotionally literate' 'St Mo' soothing the men of violence. Curiously, one of her greatest PR triumphs owed much to Trimble: she, too, harboured doubts about the idea, but found it much easier to justify once the UUP leader had taken the first bold step – a point subsequently confirmed by Mowlam in her memoirs.[34] Even then, she might not have done it but for the encouragement to take the plunge by her new Permanent Under Secretary, Joe Pilling, who had been director general of the Prison Service in England and Wales: several of Pilling's colleagues observed that this would have been a step too far for his predecessor, Sir John Chilcot (Chilcot later acknowledged in an interview in the Spring 1999 issue of the *Pembroke Martlet*, the newsletter of his old Cambridge college, that although it may well have been the right decision as things turned out, he would definitely not have given such advice).[35] Indeed, whilst no voices were raised against the visit within the NIO, No. 10 was not that happy. But they could do nothing about it. As Trimble was fond of pointing out, 'government is not a monolith' and Secretaries of State are 'big beasts' in their own way – who, if they set their minds on something, can steamroller it through (especially if Downing Street does not know about it in time). On this occasion, they did know about it, but despite their reservations did not feel so strongly as to stop the visit. Certainly, the UDA/UFF extracted a political price from both visits – which showed that they were taken seriously and helped them to take a decision that they wanted to take anyway (that is, not to return to 'war').[36]

Sweet words, though, were not enough for the hard men of loyalism. Trimble needed to show them and the law-abiding unionist community that he could now quickly deliver an outline of a settlement – preferably on a single sheet of paper – with which they could live. Such a deal would, implicitly, also ensure the release of many of those prisoners from jail. Trimble, therefore, sought to revive the discussions which had been aborted before Christmas thanks to Sinn Fein pressure on the Irish Government. Such a combination could normally frustrate unionist designs, but the situation after the killing of Billy Wright was distinctly abnormal. Trimble anticipated that the Irish Government would put up a considerable struggle even then, but No. 10 believed that the killing of Wright had 'a catalytic effect'. No. 10, conscious of the approaching Easter talks deadline, had been pushing for movement before Christmas but the events of 27 December and thereafter enabled them to push the Irish much further than was thought possible a fortnight previously. In this frenetic period, Trimble spoke on six occasions to the Prime Minister and he realised for the first time quite how much time Blair was prepared to invest in the process.[37] Indeed, no sooner did Blair return from his winter holiday in the Seychelles than he departed on an official visit to Japan, where from his Tokyo hotel suite, catching two to three hours' sleep per night, he commenced negotiations with Trimble and his Irish counterpart (who was on holiday in Spain); Paddy Teahon recalls that on the weekend of 10/11 January 1998 alone, some 300 telephone calls were made between the offices of the two heads of government (the two sides almost came to grief over whether to use the more minimalistic term 'equity', which was favoured by the British, or the more broad-brush word 'equality'. It was the British version which appeared in the final text).[38]

The essence of the gruelling negotiations, as described by Trimble, was recorded by Antony Alcock in his diary entry for 8 January 1998: 'Then at 2 p.m. a Team Talk with DT briefing us on his talks with Blair and RI officials in the last days. Blair had come up with a "Heads of Agreement" doc, which, DT said, we could live with 90% (consent, changes to the Articles, Assembly with devolved exec & leg powers, Council of "these" islands, N-S council with each side accountable to their assemblies & decision by mutual agreement). Clear that UUP will now shelter behind this doc, and see how Blair stands up to RI objections.' On the following day, Alcock noted: 'DT had leaked the Blair paper to the PUP and UDP and [their] decision not to boycott the Talks might have been made also in the light of that paper. In the meantime the second RI paper arrived and DT considered it disastrous (Blair – there will be a NI Assembly; RI – there could be an NI Assembly).'

But although the UUP were still unhappy with aspects of Heads of Agreement on the morning that the final paper was to be released (12 January 1998) there was enough there for them to sell to the majority community. Blair had remained firm enough and, in the eyes of nationalist Ireland, Trimble appeared to have successfully played the 'Orange card' once again. Sean Farren noted in his notebook on 12 January 1998 that 'a joint Dublin-London paper in the offing ... we see the Irish and told it was the best that could be achieved, "executive" dropped from North-South body, replaced with reference to ministers with executive responsibility and implementation bodies but all-island becomes the description of the remit, Council of the Isles also to be established. Best that can be achieved at this stage, obviously SF not going to be happy.' To George Mitchell, it was another instance of Trimble turning his weakness to his advantage: Mitchell accepted the British assessment of Trimble's predicament and shared their approach of accommodating him where possible.[39] One Belfast republican told Ed Moloney that the ecstatic reaction of the UUP leader reminded him of the day that the Orangemen marched down the Garvaghy Road in Portadown in 1995.[40] Worse still from the point of view of republicans, the negotiation of Heads illustrated two related points: first, that the Irish Government would submit to the superior muscle of the British state if the latter ever chose to exert itself. Second, that the SDLP would break with Sinn Fein in certain circumstances.

'Heads of Agreement was hugely important to me,' recalls Trimble. 'It gave me a general picture [of where any settlement would lie].'[41] Trimble's delight was to prove costly, though. The UUP leader decided to 'spin up' the document on the morning of publication. In the view of the Irish, he overplayed his hand and in the logic of the peace process this inevitably meant that the other side would have to be given a 'win' in the next round of the talks to be held in late January at Lancaster House in London (some very senior Irish officials even believed that he was trying to drive Sinn Fein out of the talks). Trimble now agrees that he hyped his success too much: 'We went in after saying this is a victory for Unionism. We shouldn't have done that, since it put backs up. But I had to convince the Unionist population that it could enter into the process and come out with something. Post-1985, the belief arose that the process meant defeat. I needed to show this was not so.'[42] In any case, the Irish Government believed that this Unionist victory was largely presentational: in their view, Heads was a summary of the long-term outlines of the settlement in language that was acceptable to Unionists. But although it was not the whole Frameworks Documents, it bore at least a family resemblance to it.

The broad outlines of the settlements may have been increasingly apparent to all, the rising tide of sectarian bitterness on the ground nonetheless threatened to undo it all. By the time that the Lancaster House conference opened in London on 26 January, loyalists had killed eight people (the INLA had killed one). Some of the loyalist killings were ascribed to Wright's own LVF, others to elements of the UDA/UFF (represented at the talks by the UDP). Under the rules of the talks, if it was proven that one of the participants represented a group that violated the Mitchell principles on non-violence, the guilty party would have to leave. The two Governments were very anxious to avoid such an outcome if at all possible lest the whole edifice come crashing down, but if the Chief Constable of the RUC certified that the UFF were involved they would have little choice as co-sponsors but to act. On 22 January, Flanagan confirmed that the UFF were responsible for three of the recent murders.[43] On 23 January, the UFF announced it was restoring its ceasefire after what it called a 'limited military response'.[44] This admission of involvement effectively sealed their fate and forced the hand of the two Governments.

The Lancaster House talks were, therefore, initially dominated by the fate of the UDP. Alcock again recorded the event in detail in his diary for 26 January 1998: 'DT said [to Mowlam] UDP should be expelled. We feel the end result is that they'll be expelled for a short period and then readmitted if no more killings for a few weeks – but KM[aginnis] and RE[mpey] emphatic that UUP, if it does not take a hard line on UDP, risks appearing indifferent to the killing of Catholics – this has been said by Alliance, Labour, Women's Coalition – and this is doing us damage . . . after lunch the UDP left the talks voluntarily, having received warning they would be expelled, but John White felt they'd be readmitted in the not too distant future.' White was correct: the UDP returned after a few weeks' absence. But from the UUP perspective, worse was to follow. When Empey caught a glimpse of the intergovernmental draft, it contained long quotes from the Frameworks Documents of 1995, which were anathema to Unionists and which they saw as a blueprint for a united Ireland. The next morning, Trimble contacted Blair, and told him very forcefully that the UUP had still not had the chance to study anything properly. A few hours elapsed and still nothing arrived whilst the Irish and British Governments argued over its contents. Trimble then rang John Holmes, Blair's Private Secretary, and said he was still waiting. Holmes expressed surprise but, again, nothing came. Eventually, Paul Murphy (Mowlam's deputy) came with a copy. According to Alcock's diary for 27 January 1998, 'enraged DT had an immediate bilateral with the Irish government.

We told them we felt humiliated and betrayed. Reg outraged because the leaks on the December UUP-RI talks identified his home address. P.m. Reg answers SF in the plenary about "engagement" [directly] with a moving speech about acceptance of the unionist community, focusing on such themes as consent ... Francie Molloy [of Sinn Fein] ended up by saying an NI Assembly & Partition couldn't be sold to his constituency.' During the lunch hour, the UUP held a press conference at which they reasserted the unacceptability of the Frameworks: Jeffrey Donaldson symbolically ripped up Alcock's copy of that 1995 document (according to Peter Weir, he had to make some preliminary tears to soften the paper up so that it would rip properly on camera). Trimble says that he knew nothing about it before it happened – and says that had he known, he would have opposed such a gesture, since it treated the Frameworks as a serious ongoing threat and thus played into the hands of Paisley and McCartney.[45] Later that day, on the evening of 27 January, the UUP held a bilateral with Blair and Mowlam: according to Alcock's diary 'DT bluntly accused Mo of treachery and said PM an accomplice. Blair said he was always being accused of having an open track for the UUP. PM shaken.' Although Unionists frequently accused British Governments of 'treachery' over the years, it was a very rare occurrence under this ministry for Trimble's anger to attach itself to Blair himself. Blair's remarks are also of particular interest: he obviously believed that the provision of access by himself to the UUP was in and of itself a significant act that was not politically cost-free.

Alcock was struck by Sinn Fein's relentless attempts to 'engage' and to secure a bilateral with the UUP: in one of the plenaries, McGuinness described Empey as a 'decent man' and praised his contribution to the debate. On the next day, Adams wrote to Trimble asking for such a meeting, addressing him in Irish as *A Chara* (dear friend) and concluding *Is mise* (I remain).[46] Eventually, he responded to Adams – not directly, but through a statement issued to the *Irish Times* published on 4 February. Trimble declared that the UUP would not talk directly to Sinn Fein because it alone of the parties represented at the negotiations did not accept the principle of consent. Moreover, Sinn Fein/IRA had never apologised for the thousands of casualties, Catholic as well as Protestant, which it had inflicted over the years. But, again, he refused to say 'never' to such a meeting. Trimble's caution was understandable: large parts of the UUP caucus in the Forum were unhappy. Antony Alcock noted in his diary for 31 January 1998 that 'at a meeting of party members we discussed the issue of "engagement" with SF. One of the delegates said that if the UUP did negotiate with SF there may be resignations in his branch. He added that he thought DT would have to resign too. DT replied that perhaps that was one of the aims of SF.'

The issue of Trimble's reluctance to meet face-to-face with Adams arose again on the Prime Minister's visit to the United States, when he met key Congressional figures at a breakfast on 5 February 1998 hosted by the new British ambassador to Washington DC, Sir Christopher Meyer. A record of the meeting was sent in letter form to Ken Lindsay, then Mowlam's Principal Private Secretary, by John Holmes. The memorandum was leaked somewhere in the system – Trimble believed by a DUP sympathiser. Certainly, in terms of traditional unionism, the document offered cold comfort. In answer to a question from Senator Edward Kennedy (D-MA) as to how a settlement could be sold which fell short of the aspiration for a united Ireland, Blair said that such a deal would have to include meaningful North-South bodies and action on 'equality issues'. He added that the nature of the issues was changing with the emergence of a modern society in the Republic and that 'in these circumstances, national boundaries obviously became less relevant over time'. The legislators were full of praise for Blair's decision to set up the Bloody Sunday inquiry and Senator Christopher Dodd (D-CT) welcomed the Government's 'work on bringing prisoners closer to their families'. But Blair was determined to make one point which went against the grain of his interlocutors' thinking – about Trimble himself. When Congressman Richard Neal (D-MA) asked what the British Government would do if the Unionist 'veto' were applied at a critical juncture, Blair replied: '. . . the Unionist community felt isolated in many ways. The Irish Government supported the nationalist side, whereas the British Government obviously had to take account of both communities. This led Unionists to resist all change. The important thing about the Propositions [on the Heads of Agreement] paper was that the Unionists had signed up to North-South structures. There was an obvious presentational dilemma in all this, since the two sides needed to present any outcome in different ways. But the differences of substance were not as great as often thought.' Later, when Congressman Peter King (R-NY) criticised Trimble for not talking directly to the Sinn Fein leadership, Blair was equally firm: '. . . Engagement all-round was desirable. Sinn Fein could help by accepting the consent principle, in line with all the other parties, North and South. He believed that Adams and McGuinness wanted to stay on the political path but we should not be starry-eyed about their organisation. There was a long history of terrorism which would be hard to put behind them . . . as far as Trimble was concerned, he had come a good deal further than many Unionists wanted him to, for example accepting North-South structures. People on the US side could help enormously by making clear that they understood the position of the Unionists. It was important to remember that Trimble was under constant attack from Paisley and McCartney, so that giving comfort to the Ulster Unionists was vital . . . the roots of Unionist resistance to change went deep and were hard to deal with. But he thought it important to keep open his own lines of communication with Paisley. Again this illustrated the difficulties of the position of Trimble, who had to be an advocate of change without making himself vulnerable to charges of betrayal.' At this point, at least, Blair understood that Trimble was the 'Fabergé egg' of the process, a politically delicate object that needed to be carefully conserved.

Any remote prospect that Trimble might meet with Sinn Fein – and some senior Irish officials thought that, at a pinch, he would do so – was eliminated by a sudden outbreak of republican violence. On 9 February 1998, Brendan 'Bap' Campbell, a drugs dealer, was murdered in Belfast by the IRA operating under the *nom de guerre* of 'Direct Action Against Drugs'; on 10 February, a south Belfast UDA activist, Robert Dougan, was murdered in Dunmurry by the Provisionals; and on 18 February, a Lurgan man, Kevin Conway, was murdered by what the Government called 'local IRA elements'. These were the first killings by the IRA since the July 1997 ceasefire.[47] Once again, the Government was reluctant to act: the talks were all about inclusivity. Explusion of Sinn Fein along the lines of the punishment meted out to the UDP risked losing the republicans for ever. The wrangle over the expulsion of Sinn Fein thus dominated the next leg of talks in Dublin. Again, Mowlam stated that Flanagan had given her his assessment that the IRA was, indeed, involved in the murders of Dougan and Campbell.[48] The IRA were therefore in breach of the ceasefire and Sinn Fein were duly suspended for a fortnight, until 9 March, or six negotiating days – half the tariff imposed upon the UDP for the UFF's violations of the ceasefire.[49] Sean Farren, a senior SDLP negotiator, also found it very depressing and observed in his notebook for 15–22 February: 'Talk about the worst week in politics – from Sunday through for the rest of week SF dominate the headlines and marginalise virtually everyone else. No movement from Brits early '98 on prisoners. SM[allon] points out v. slow movement on this issue. SF complain no in depth meetings with SDLP despite close neighbours at Castle Buildings. Mowlam says Gardai agree with RUC . . .' On the Wednesday, Farren also noted that 'in the course of SF's response, Martin McG makes one of the most bitter anti-unionist speeches I have ever heard and am ashamed of him as a nationalist representative, Gerry Adams much more measured in his remarks – obviously a hard/soft approach is the tactic. Meeting with the Taoiseach on Wed turns out to be v. useful one – Ahern displeased SF gives nothing. Despite vicious SF attacks, they said they wanted to be part of settlement, transitional and all.'[50] These were not the only provocations endured by Unionists as the talks deadline approached. On 20 February, a 500-lb car bomb planted by Continuity IRA exploded outside the RUC station in Moira, Co. Down – near to the residence of the local MP, Jeffrey Donaldson. Although there were no deaths, considerable damage was inflicted. On 23 February, another 300-lb republican bomb was planted in Trimble's constituency in Portadown town centre, with similar effects.

But the most dramatic moment of the run-up to the talks was occasioned not by republican violence, but by a loyalist atrocity. On 3 March, LVF gunmen strode into a bar in Poyntzpass, Co. Armagh and murdered two men – Damien Trainor and Philip Allen. Trainor was Catholic, Allen Protestant. They were best friends and the former was to have been best man at the latter's wedding.[51] The atrocity took place in the parish in which Seamus Mallon lived, and the owner of the bar was a good friend. Whilst Mallon was doing an interview on the next day, a car pulled up, from which David Trimble emerged and the SDLP deputy leader asked him to join him. 'I felt sorry for David Trimble finding himself in that position, having so often found myself in similar circumstances in another constituency and hoping that someone would be nice to me,' recalls Mallon. 'So we went to Allen's house. And then he said, "I'll walk to the next house" [the Trainors]. And I said, "Let's walk together. People here will be glad to see us together." So here, for the first time, were two people poles apart politically, doing this together. It had a bonding effect – and in that sense, it was helpful.'[52] Trimble did not hold back. 'I am ashamed to think the perpetrators of this deed were Protestant,' he declared. 'They were serving no cause and on behalf of the Unionist community I repudiate them and I repudiate their associates.'[53]

Not that such strong words helped Trimble much in America, when he visited Washington shortly thereafter for St Patrick's Day: sixteen US Congressmen subsequently wrote to Blair denouncing Trimble for 'obstructing the quest for peace' and that other parties in Northern Ireland had 'demonstrated courage and a willingness to compromise'.[54] Nor was the UUP delegation's own meeting with Clinton, Berger and Steinberg on 17 March plain sailing. Clinton told Trimble that he had spoken with Hume and Ahern and that Sinn Fein would go along with the Assembly and constitutional change just so long as there were North-South bodies: they believed that if Trimble did not meet with Sinn Fein, the republican movement would not sign up for a deal. Trimble responded that he could not do so since all of Sinn Fein's papers spoke of moving towards a united Ireland, and they did not accept the existence of Northern Ireland. Clinton retorted that he thought it was 'pretty clear' that Sinn Fein accepted the consent principle. Again, Trimble disagreed.[55] Frank Millar observed that it was 'incredible' that the Americans expected Trimble to agree to talk to Sinn Fein whilst in Washington – in a country still distrusted by many Unionists – when he felt unable to do so at Stormont.[56] But Trimble's stance helped him in his own community. One leading UUP activist observed that 'people were relieved when Trimble refused Clinton's request that he negotiate directly with Sinn Fein. He certainly proved his mettle. The pressure on a Unionist leader doesn't come much greater than that.'[57]

Upon returning to London, Trimble immediately went with Jeffrey Donaldson to Chequers. Blair had a clear purpose in mind: to determine the UUP's bottom line (some No. 10 officials thought that even Trimble did not know exactly where it lay on such issues as the committee system for the Assembly and that these would only emerge in the very late stages of the talks with the SDLP. Even as late as the Asia–Europe summit in London in the last week of March, Blair still lamented to the Irish that he did not know the Unionists' real position).[58] Jeffrey Donaldson remembers arriving at the door of Chequers to be greeted by Cherie Blair. The couple were celebrating their wedding anniversary. 'I hope this is going to be worth it,' she told the UUP visitors. 'I hope you realise you're taking my husband away from me.' Trimble and Donaldson sat alone in the Prime Minister's study – lined with biographies of Prime Ministers – with Blair and Holmes. Trimble handed Blair a submission on the constitutional issues written by Austen Morgan. The quadrumvirate talked about the various strands of the talks and then moved on to decommissioning. 'The Prime Minister gave us an understanding he would support the UUP position linking the holding of office with prior disarmament,' says Donaldson. Moreover, he says, Blair also appeared to be closer to the traditional UUP position that any devolved institutions would have to resemble the Welsh-style committee system rather than a Scottish-style ministerial system (it would be easier to cope with Sinn Fein as glorified council committee chairmen than as ministers in a full Government).[59] So successful was the meeting that Trimble recalls that both he and Donaldson left feeling 'comfortable – reassured regarding the position of the Government on their general orientation'. But he also believed that the price of protecting the core interests of Unionists would be many painful compromises. 'Nerves of steel will be required,' he told the anxious AGM of the UUC in Belfast on 21 March. He was speaking as much of himself as of the party.[60]

TWENTY-FOUR

Long Good Friday

THE fortnight running up to the talks deadline proved to be, in Trimble's subsequent phrase, 'a white-knuckle ride'. As the 9 April deadline approached, vast amounts of the detail had still not been settled – and, over the coming days, many doubted if ever they would be. Trimble assumed that the talks would continue at Stormont between the parties and what he never expected was that the two Prime Ministers would have to come to Belfast to take charge of the final phase of the negotiations. He reasoned that since Heads of Agreement had been negotiated in January without physical apparitions of Blair and Ahern, there was no need for such direct intervention.[1] But whilst the UUP was immersed in the details of the Stormont talks, another, parallel, show was going on over the water in No. 10: Blair and his staff were discussing with Ahern and his staff their input into the draft agreement. The independent chairman, George Mitchell, aimed to have the contributions of all the parties stitched together in draft form by Friday 3 April but he was asked by both Blair and Ahern in a conference call to delay the release of it until the two heads of Government had completed their talks and fed in their amendments.

This was what the Unionists always feared: that in the heat of a four-hour negotiation held in their absence, No. 10 might agree to something which looked unimportant to them when viewed from London, but which looked very important to the representatives of the British majority in Northern Ireland. The essence of the UUP's concern was that the Irish were returning to the agenda of the Frameworks – even to the Council of Ireland that was part of the Sunningdale agreement. In their eyes, this entailed free-standing, all-Ireland institutions, with powers devolved directly to them from on high by London and Dublin, thus by-passing the Unionist majority in the Assembly. The UUP talks team also believed rumours that the delay was caused by Ahern telling his British counterparts that if they agreed to cross-borderism on the lines of the Frame-works, the IRA would call a permanent ceasefire and recognise the Assembly.[2] Meanwhile, Ahern toughened his stance, declaring that 'the Irish Government will not be moving any further. What we need now is for the other parties to make those moves. I hope Prime Minister Blair can use his influence on those other parties. David Trimble would need to understand that my compromises have been completed.'[3] On Sunday 5 April, Trimble telephoned Blair twice and again explained the dangers from a Unionist perspective. Blair said that whilst the Irish understood Trimble's views regarding the accountability of North-South bodies, the problem was that the Unionist model would give Belfast a veto and thus they could never be certain that the cross-border entities would ever do anything. Blair thereupon undertook to tone it down.

But when Mitchell received the (unchanged) Anglo-Irish document that night, he was not so sure about its acceptability. 'As I read the document I knew instantly that it would not be acceptable to the union-ists. I didn't know what communications there had been between Blair and Trimble, but I knew that Trimble would never, could never accept this.' He also noticed that some key officials on both sides were unhappy with the departure from the normal channels of the process.[4] John de Chastelain confirms Mitchell's account: 'We felt the paper was far too "Green". Tony Blair was reported to do so as well. Well, it was his paper!'[5] Moreover, Mitchell was told the two Prime Ministers' work was unamend-able and should be presented as Mitchell's own work; the former US Senate Majority leader acceded, reluctantly, though he knew that it was part of his role to take the blame off the two Governments' shoulders. Recalling this episode, John de Chastelain says, 'I now understand why Britain had an empire and kept it for so long. They were playing hardball. They took the view that "we may lose a few pawns" – but the imperative was to reach an agreement.'[6] When Trimble received the 'Mitchell' draft document late on the night of Monday 6 April, he was profoundly dis-turbed by what he found during the course of an initial, cursory reading – especially on North-South bodies. Peter Bell, the British Joint Secretary of Maryfield, who had a better feel for Unionist sensibilities than most NIO officials, handed it over to the UUP with the observation that he would not like to have to sell such a document to the UUC. The flamboy-ant Steven King was almost tearful at what he saw as this betrayal: many in the UUP were also terrified lest the document be leaked to the DUP, which would have vindicated the Paisleyite analysis and made any deal impossible.[7]

Trimble would not come to a final view, though, and split the document up into segments for his closest aides. By the time that Trimble arrived at Castle Buildings on the morning of Tuesday 7 April, 'it looked worse'.[8] Seven of the eleven pages detailed a wide range of all-Ireland functions. Indeed paragraph 7 of the Mitchell paper made it clear that the eight implementation bodies for North-South programmes would be established directly by Westminster and the Dail from the inception of the agreement – that is, before the election of an Assembly, thus diminishing accountability to it. Moreover, Annex A listed 25 areas for immediate cross-border cooperation, Annex B listed 16 and Annex C listed eight. 'Some were modest,' noted Trimble, 'but others included the harmonis-ation of further and higher education and general hospital services, as well as the creation of all-Ireland bodies to run trade and the arts.'[9] Trimble also declared that the proposal for an independent international commission on the future of the RUC was 'quite horrifying'.[10] Even then, states Daphne Trimble, her husband's attitude to the Mitchell document was not '"this is over", but this document must be changed'.[11]

Trimble went down to see George Mitchell and told him that he had a problem about the way in which the draft document had appeared. 'I told him I was in contact with the Prime Minister all weekend and I know Blair asked you to put in the stuff reflecting Unionist concerns,' recalls Trimble. 'But Mitchell said that when he asked for the Prime Minister's changes [to be included] the Irish officials said that it can't be renegotiated and the British officials appeared to back them up.' This explains why Trimble did not blame No. 10, pointing the finger instead to a reversion to collusive 'intergovernmentalism' between the NIO and the DFA (again, he rarely criticised Blair).[12] According to Reg Empey's account, Trimble stormed into Mitchell's 5th-floor room at Castle Build-ings, thumped the document on the table, and declared, 'It's awful!' Mitchell was placid, even unsurprised by the UUP leader's verdict: as his memoir implies, he was the unwilling postman for a draft document produced by two Governments that he knew would not work.[13] Downing Street had already informed the Prime Minister that things were adrift, as had the Irish Government: Blair then tried to reach Ahern, but in his absence could only reach Paddy Teahon at 11:45 p.m. on the night of Monday 6 April. Teahon was told by Blair that Trimble was very upset and the Prime Minister asked the Irishman to talk to the UUP leader and to tell him that Ahern was very anxious to speak to him. Teahon reached Trimble after midnight and conveyed that message, urging him not to do anything sudden.[14] But Trimble was not assuaged. On the morning of Tuesday 7 April, Trimble rang Blair to say that he could not accept the document; Blair told Trimble that he knew as much when he saw the long list of cross-border bodies in the Schedules. Trimble also rang Holmes to say he would soon be in receipt of the UUP statement and that he thought the Prime Minister should come over as soon as possible. Holmes replied that Blair had decided to do so anyway.

Trimble was especially keen to discover the reaction of his deputy, John Taylor – a bell-wether for many UUP stalwarts. 'What do you think, John?' asked the Ulster Unionist leader. 'David, I'm not on board, we're going to have to go different ways,' replied Taylor. He was surprised by the Mitchell document since he knew that his leader had been in such close contact with Mitchell and Blair. 'I agree,' said Trimble. Trimble then took Taylor into his confidence and asked him not to tell their colleagues that the Prime Minister was soon coming over. Taylor said that he had an invitation to attend a gala concert at the Royal Albert Hall, as a guest of Sainsbury's, in honour of Andrew Lloyd Webber's 50th birthday (Taylor had been playing a part in negotiating with Sainsbury's to open a supermarket in his constituency). Taylor told Trimble that he would still attend this event but would stay in touch: he would be able to return in time for the serious business the next day.[15] But before he left Northern Ireland, Taylor came out with one of the most memorable lines of the peace process, concerning the Mitchell document: 'I wouldn't touch this paper with a 40-foot barge pole.'[16]

By then, also, everyone knew that the Prime Minister who felt 'the hand of history upon our shoulders' had arrived in Northern Ireland.[17] But he was not at Castle Buildings: instead, he was at Hillsborough Castle, Co. Down. The reason was simple. After the night of Sunday 5 April, Bertie Ahern's mother had died at the Mater Hospital in Dublin. Under the informal understandings which governed the peace process, the British Prime Minister would only attend the formal negotiations whilst his Irish counterpart was there. And since Ahern would not be available until after the funeral of his mother on Wednesday 8 April, an alternative venue had to be found for the urgently needed bilaterals. 'How are we going to do this?' Paddy Teahon asked Blair. They duly came up with the idea of Hillsborough, which presented no such dilemmas of protocol.[18] Significantly, in the late afternoon Blair asked to see Trimble alone at Hillsborough over supper – something which the UUP leader had said he would not do when he took over from Molyneaux.[19] Trimble did not expect it would be a detailed discussion: that, he says, is why he went alone. He told the Prime Minister beforehand that all he wanted was support and a general preliminary steer. Instead, he arrived at around 6 p.m. to find that the Prime Minister – accompanied by Holmes and Powell – had already worked out detailed proposals. In the course of a meeting which went on for nearly two hours, Blair made some specific suggestions regarding Strand II – notably the accountability of the North-South bodies and the numbers of them (Trimble thought the former was still not sufficiently explicit). But Trimble concedes that he was not ready for Blair in terms of the detail on the RUC. It was agreed on the following day that Ken Maginnis would address the matter with John Steele, the director of security in the NIO, and Jonathan Powell.[20] He also told Blair that evening that once he had the Assembly bedded down, he would like to see the integration of Northern Ireland into the mainland party system – that is, for the Labour party to organise in Ulster. In this latter aspiration, he eventually achieved a partial success: Powell, in particular, was worried about the nationalist reaction. One other request yielded more fruit. Trimble asked Blair that if the negotiation came off, two people who had done much to bring it about should be recognised. They were Reg Empey and John Gorman (honouring the latter would also acknowledge those who had been in the Forum but not in the talks team.)[21]

Trimble was still not altogether happy about these discussions. Antony Alcock noted in his diary entry for Wednesday 8 April that 'DT enraged in the morning. At Hillsborough last night he was engaged in detailed discussions with Blair and found much concentration on rights issues [by this Alcock means 'policing, prisoners, Irish language, etc.'] about which, he said, he was not briefed and was therefore ill prepared ... Clear from what DT had to say that SF would be ready to join the Assembly even if our version of N/S was accepted so long as they had their Rights issues and therefore our only hope of excluding them – thereby reducing the risk of the Assembly being collapsed – would be under a clause not allowing them into the Assembly unless there was decommissioning, about which there is nothing in Mitchell's document.

We have prepared an appropriate draft clause.' The policy behind that draft was outlined in an internal memorandum by Trimble of 8 April: 'As agreed last night more is needed on this point. The Prime Minister suggested that there should be a starting date, immediately on signature of the Agreement. This could only bind parties to the Agreement. Sinn Fein could decline to sign, stand for election and seek to take up the place in government that their statutory right to proportionality would give them. In that case John Holmes' exclusionary provision in Strand I would be ineffective, for that requires a sufficient consensus, which would *never* [Trimble's emphasis] be available against Sinn Fein over a failure to prove their commitment to peaceful means [Trimble was referring to the support of the SDLP which he feared would not be forthcoming]. So we need a more effective provision to prevent paramilitaries walking into government with their organisations intact and armed. Moreover a starting date on signature could result in the loyalist parties not signing also. The result is that the best provision is that agreed on at Chequers, namely a statutory provision that paramilitary related parties cannot have the benefit of the proportionality rule unless they have commenced and undertaken substantial decommissioning.'

Later on the evening of Tuesday 7 April, at Hillsborough, Blair suggested to George Mitchell that he call Ahern to give his independent view – that the document had to be renegotiated. By this point, Mitchell was very pessimistic about the outcome: sitting in his office at Castle Buildings at around 2 a.m. on Wednesday morning with General John de Chastelain and Harri Holkeri, the Strand II co-chairmen, the former US Senate Majority leader asked his Canadian colleague what were the chances of success. 'Twenty per cent,' replied the Canadian – and Mitchell put it at even less.[22] But Mitchell was unable to reach Ahern.[23] From the moment that his mother had suffered a heart attack on Sunday 5 April, Ahern had stood vigil by her bed in the Mater Hospital through Sunday night and Monday morning when Julia Ahern died.[24] As Ahern prepared to go to the first of the services for his mother on the evening of Tuesday 7 April, upon the removal of her remains to the church, his aides told him of the UUP's opposition to the draft treaty and the demand to renegotiate the document agreed by the two heads of Government. Ahern's aides counselled against renegotiation and he went into the service. 'Tell them to stand firm' were his last words before departing. But after he emerged, he went back to Drumcondra and wandered the streets for some time 'my security guys half with me and half not'. He contacted Teahon and told him he would go to Belfast and renegotiate.[25] 'I realised that if I didn't go up nothing was going to happen,' recalls Ahern. 'I could have stuck to my guns – that I had signed off on a deal with the British Prime Minister and his senior officials in No. 10. I was totally within my rights to say that's it. But I'd built up a good relationship with Tony Blair right from Opposition. I believed that he was stuck and I believed Mitchell that he couldn't move.' Ahern says that while traumatic, the events also gave him an opportunity to think – something which he would not have had the opportunity to do with all of the distractions of normal affairs of state. 'Everyone says you're going through the mourning process but in actual fact what you're really doing is hanging round,' notes the Taoiseach.[26] Teahon had called Trimble shortly after Ahern's mother died to explain what had happened and that the Taoiseach would be coming up as soon as was practicable. 'Please convey to him my deepest sympathy,' replied Trimble. 'But I have to tell you, you've pushed things over the edge in this document.'[27]

Ahern's schedule the following day was frenetic. He flew by helicopter to the Province to breakfast with Blair at Hillsborough early in the morning of Wednesday 8 April; went on to Castle Buildings in Belfast for a bilateral with the UUP later on in the morning; returned by helicopter to attend Requiem Mass for his mother; followed by the funeral in the Republican plot at Glasnevin cemetery; only to return to Northern Ireland late on the Wednesday afternoon.[28] Blair bluntly told his guest that the long list of cross-border bodies had occasioned much of the very emotional Unionist reaction. If the Irish did not withdraw the annexes, the whole thing would collapse. Ahern feared that the North-South dimension would be salami-sliced into oblivion. But Blair told the Irish that Trimble was serious in trying to find a way forward. Like everyone else, he had doubted it at times, but now he was sure of the UUP leader's bona fides.[29] Blair recalls telling the Taoiseach: 'David Trimble can't be expected to go further. He's under a lot of pressure. Ahern was totally understanding.'[30] At the subsequent meeting with the UUP at Castle Buildings, Jeffrey Donaldson noticed hints of flexibility in the Irish position, a point confirmed when the UUP again saw Blair. In the afternoon, the UUP met with Blair once more. In the evening, there was a trilateral between the British, Irish and the UUP: it was fairly brief and dealt with the general principles concerning the accountability of North-South bodies. Subsequently, a further bilateral took place between the UUP and the Irish Government which went on until 1:30 a.m.[31] It was during the course of these discussions, which were finally resolved by another intervention from Blair on the Thursday, that the Strand II portion of the deal took shape. There was an absolute commitment by the British and Irish to set up a North-South Ministerial Council, with elected Ulster representatives, and implementation bodies to carry out its decisions. But the three annexes of the Mitchell draft had been reduced to one, with twelve areas earmarked for possible cross-border cooperation. The language was no longer so prescriptive, and the phrase 'may include' was inserted, thus leaving the selection of those areas to the Assembly. Nor would they be described as 'dynamic', 'executive' and 'harmonising', as they were in the Frameworks Documents. As Peter Bell told Paul Bew, 'the cross-border aardvark-pruning schemes are well under control'.[32] Late on Wednesday, Trimble also extracted a 'mutual assured destruction' clause from Blair. Since Unionists wanted an Assembly, and nationalists wanted North-South bodies, each side feared that the other would sabotage their cherished aim. Unionists saw this as a gain: they loathed the Frameworks Documents because they appeared to suggest that if the Assembly collapsed, North-South bodies would nonetheless continue.[33]

It was Trimble's greatest triumph during the talks. Thomas Hennessey, a junior member of the UUP talks team, remembers Trimble drifting in and out of the party room on Wednesday evening and opining, 'I've just witnessed the ritual humiliation of the Irish Prime Minister.' Hennessey asked what he meant and the flushed and excited Trimble replied, 'They've agreed to our Strand II model.' Indeed, when Hennessey asked Trimble how this deal had been achieved, the UUP leader reported to his aide that he had asked Blair the same question. Trimble reported Blair's account as follows: the Prime Minister claimed to have told Ahern that if the Irish did not agree to the UUP's Strand II model, then he (Blair) would blame the Irish for the collapse of the talks process; Blair, unsurprisingly, denies this to be so.[34] Not quite the 'ritual humiliation' of the Taoiseach that Trimble had alleged, but possibly a clear demonstration of the muscle of the British state in a negotiation with its Irish counterpart. Trimble believed that he had obtained a better deal on Strand II than had Faulkner at Sunningdale, notwithstanding the erosion of Unionist demographic and political power over the intervening 25 years. Whilst the British state's conception of Unionists enjoying a veto over further expansion of

North-South institutions remains broadly the same as then, the areas for cooperation were more precisely delineated in the 1998 Agreement than in the 1973 accords. At Sunningdale, their remit was potentially very wide, at least on paper, whereas in 1998 they were rather more limited – at least on paper. Moreover, the North-South bodies posited under the 1998 agreement were more clearly under the control of the Assembly than was the 1973 Council of Ireland. But to achieve a reduction in the Strand II proposals, Unionists paid a massive price in other areas such as Strand I, the RUC and prisoners. Paul Bew, for one, argued that once the principle of their accountability to the Assembly had been satisfactorily settled, there could have been 150 cross-border institutions, all doing very little – checked by the Unionist majority in the devolved legislature. But the ghosts of 1973–4 haunted the Unionists: they fired endless rounds of valuable ammunition into the corpse of Sunningdale long after all life had drained out of it.

Why did Blair fail to spot that the first 'Mitchell' draft was going to be so unacceptable to Trimble, especially after he had held so many meetings with the UUP leader? John Taylor asked as much of Blair when they met at Castle Buildings on Wednesday 8 April: 'Very good of you to come, Prime Minister, but why was it necessary for you to come over?' Blair was embarrassed and gave no answer.[35] George Mitchell, also, assumed that any agreement was 'pre-sold' to both sides and was astonished to find this was not the case: he cannot offer an explanation as to why this was so.[36] So was Blair less good at ascertaining the state of the Unionist political marketplace than many supposed? Or was it the case, as Jeffrey Donaldson suspected, that the whole episode was pre-choreographed, with unacceptable portions deliberately inserted – which would then be removed at the behest of the British so as to foster the illusion of a UUP 'victory'?[37] In other words, was the Mitchell document a cock-up or a conspiracy – and, if so, whose cock-up and whose conspiracy?

Certainly, the episode of the Mitchell document proves the old dictum that 'success has a thousand parents whereas failure is an orphan'. Trimble ascribes the near-disaster to the post-1985 collusive habits of the NIO and the Irish DFA. 'Never forget the limited power of Downing Street,' he says. 'I don't want to sound like a little Sir Echo of No. 10, but Blair can't focus on everything.'[38] Trimble is correct in so far as the annexes, listing areas for cross-border cooperation, were negotiated between the DFA and the NIO in Belfast. What appears to have happened is that those Irish panjandrums who were in No. 10 in the week of 30 March to 3 April, negotiating the no less important issue of the legal status of the North-South institutions, made it clear that unless they covered themselves politically for making concessions on Articles 2 and 3 of the Irish Constitution, they would be crucified by the 'Greener' elements in Fianna Fail. (Trimble never believed this and regarded it as part of the standard negotiating stock-in-trade.)[39] David Andrews, though, acknowledges that the republicans dangled the promise of a 'permanent' ceasefire before the Irish Government, thus leading to the 'greening up' of the Strand II proposals.[40] One republican privately said that Sinn Fein's strategy was to cause the UUP to bolt by 'greening up' the Mitchell document, and that they were delighted by Taylor's '40-foot barge pole' comment. They were ultimately willing, though, to accept as a fall-back a minimalistic version of Mitchell in exchange for lots of 'collateral' in 'reserved' matters, such as prisoners. They were shocked to discover that the changes to Mitchell were far more extensive than they had imagined, causing them, in turn, to threaten to bolt.

No. 10 appears not to have regarded the lists of cross-border bodies which were being negotiated as central to the basic principles involved and only saw them late in the day – a mistake which they concede terrified the Unionists. 'We were not as closely engaged as we should have been,' recalls one Blair aide. Blair offers a similar explanation of those events. 'Frankly, as soon as I saw it, I realised that it wouldn't work,' recalls the Prime Minister. 'But I was busy with a lot of other stuff and people had been working on set tramlines under the previous Government. It was always going to be subject to a fair degree of amendment, and the deal which emerged is a significant improvement on what was on offer before. But the refreshing thing about David Trimble is that he is always completely blunt.'[41] When No. 10 did receive them on Monday 6 April, they were horrified by the 'Anglo-Irishese' and verbiage, but Quentin Thomas assured them that the UUP wanted a long list, which would give a more concrete feel to what was being proposed, as opposed to a more ill-defined and diffused list. Thomas does not recognise this account. He says he was not party to the Prime Ministerial negotiations that went on in London – he was in Belfast at the time – and that the entire episode illustrates the dangers of detailed talks taking place outside of a process designed to carry them forward.[42] (Peter Bell adds that in that last week of the talks, there were so many face-to-face encounters between the two heads of Government, apparently with no else present, that it was sometimes hard for officials on both sides to know exactly what had been agreed between them – not least since their respective accounts of those encounters could diverge.)[43] The Irish say they knew that Blair's priority in relation to any subject was to 'get on with it' and not to worry too much about the details. Since they could not agree on the precise list, they appear to have rushed the negotiation towards the end – knowing that much of the Irish shopping list would have to be taken out anyway. Teahon recalls that afterwards Holmes used to tease him, saying, 'Weren't you clever to put all those bodies in the annex so we could take them out when the Unionists got angry.'[44] (Holmes, when asked about this, is adamant that he saw it as no joking matter at the time, and that it was never part of any pre-choreographed plot.)[45] Another senior figure on the Irish side also believes that the list of areas for cross-border cooperation was put in by a 'pro-SDLP zealot on our side. Most of us realised it was excessive. But I suspect the British knew what they were doing. In their eyes they were signing up to something they could cut out. But they weren't going to die in the ditch and cause a fight off their own bat as the Ulster Unionists themselves could take care of it.'

Whichever interpretation is correct, Blair did come over to Northern Ireland and was prepared to facilitate some kind of victory for Trimble. To close observers of the scene such as Paul Bew, the significance of this was that he wanted some kind of majority community participation in a settlement badly enough to risk losing Sinn Fein (who sought a maximalist variant of North-South bodies). In that sense, to use a phrase coined by the republican ex-prisoner, Anthony McIntyre, Blair may not have been an ideological unionist, but he was 'structurally' pro-Union.[46] According to this view, Unionist participation – and therefore Trimble's preservation – was a *sine qua non* of any deal. But is this view of Blair's intervention completely correct? As Antony Alcock's private diary for Wednesday 8 April indicates – the morning after Trimble's tête-à-tête with Blair at Hillsborough – the UUP leader appears to have been told at least as early as the night of Tuesday 7 April that Sinn Fein would participate in an Assembly (of which they were publicly still sworn foes) and that they would participate in these new institutions even if the UUP's model on Strand II prevailed. If Blair did know this as early as Tuesday or even before (either directly from the republicans or from intelligence sources, or both) it suggests that he took rather less of a risk in coming over and facing down Ahern than some of the standard Unionist narratives have hitherto suggested. Alcock's diary, however, suggests that Trimble knew rather more about the likely outcome of the talks than he let on – though the UUP leader now says that his remarks to the talks team were an optimistic spin designed to maintain the UUP group's morale before he was fully assured of the kind of outcome he wanted on Strand II.[47] But whatever the real truth about the Mitchell document – whether pre-choreographed in some way or not – the effect of the episode was to increase Trimble's sense of indebtedness to Blair. So strong was this sentiment that even some senior pro-Agreement colleagues such as John Taylor thought him overly grateful to the Prime Minister, causing him to pull his punches at certain moments in the years that followed.[48]

Vital as it was, Strand II was only a part of the picture. Much else remained to be settled, and it was settled in distinctly unorthodox circumstances. The No. 10 and Cabinet Office entourages swept into the 5th floor of Castle Buildings, with Blair himself occupying the offices of Tony Worthington, the then Under Secretary of State. Blair and Ahern were a study in contrasts during the three days at Castle Buildings: Blair would remain in his temporary offices, whereas Ahern – who as he observes, had been in negotiations throughout his public career whether in the trade unions or with the EU – wandered around 'talking to everyone – including loyalists I had never even met before'.[49] Perhaps on account of this febrile atmosphere, the UUP made some odd choices – most notably on the Strand I negotiations on the Assembly and internal institutions of government, which was meant to be the jewel in their crown. If Strand II was settled mainly between the UUP and the Irish, then the key players in Strand I were the two largest parties in Northern Ireland, the UUP and the SDLP. Sinn Fein played no part in any of the 38 drafts: later on Thursday night, when Pat Doherty approached Seamus Mallon and said that Adams and McGuinness wanted to talk urgently, the SDLP deputy leader recalls using language that was 'quite unprintable'.[50] When the Mitchell draft arrived, the Strand I proposals were very vague and much of it was 'square bracketed'. The original Ulster Unionist proposals on Strand I were for an administration operating after the fashion of a souped-up local authority – the so-called Welsh model. This would have executive committees but would not have ministers per se, reflecting the party's historic opposition to institutionalised power-sharing. How, the

UUP asked, could they share collective responsibility with the Provisionals? At least if it was like a local authority, it was not so offensive to the sensibilities of the majority community and in many districts Unionist councillors rotated chairmanships with republicans (though this was usually after an initial refusal to do so, and occurred in municipalities where there was either a hung or a majority-nationalist council). Unionists urged that these local government-style committees be formed on a proportional basis under the d'Hondt system: the largest party would have first pick of committee chairmanship, followed by the other major groupings, until the process began again. But the SDLP were always unhappy about operating in a local government model. First, local government within the United Kingdom smacked too much of the integrationist agenda, and they sought a traditional executive with proper ministers (this, of course, held the danger for Unionists that Sinn Fein would serve as full ministers, something which they would not do under the UUP's own model).[51] Second, even if chairmanships were allocated under the d'Hondt system, a proportionally based committee system would look too much to them like a return to majority rule.[52]

Such arguments certainly impressed Reg Empey, who led the Strand I negotiations. 'You don't understand how important full executive powers are to the SDLP,' Empey told the talks team in the final days of the talks.[53] But Empey had other reasons as well. He came to accept that it was not practical to have 90 'councillors' (108 was, in fact, the final number) running an administration along Welsh lines. 'The problem with committee systems is that they run reasonably well in local government which has limited functions,' says Trimble now. 'But even there, there are considerable technical problems. How can you get any coherence of decision-making? You have got to have some way of centralising decision-making and [making] trade-offs, rather than the proposals for local government which are rather like a hollow polo mint.' In fact, as things eventually worked out once the Executive was set up, under the provisions of the Northern Ireland Act 1998, the individual ministries enjoyed much more autonomy than was originally supposed and the power of the centre was more limited.[54] The UUP thus traded off their traditional political stance for largely illusory administrative gains. Empey claims that the Unionists would have been happy enough with a lower-profile Assembly – without legislative input – but it became clear that as time went on all of the other parties were keen on grabbing as much power as they could (the

UUP, he claims, successfully resisted the return of tax-raising powers). The comparison with Scotland, especially, would have looked embarrassing; indeed, he observes that 'if you're on an investment drive in the States and your hosts are faced with a choice of meeting a chairman of the Northern Ireland Economic Development Committee or the Economic Development Minister, it's no contest'. Empey says that Trimble, in fact, resisted a full cabinet government to the last and had to be ground down.[55] Trimble appears also to have been swayed in favour of a more maximalist form of government by political as well as administrative considerations. 'If we've scored on constitutional and North-South then we've got to give the SDLP something to work with,' says Trimble. 'We can't push the SDLP to the limit. We'd then be doing to them what the SDLP and the Irish and Whitelaw did to Faulkner [at Sunningdale in 1973]. We had to give them enough to defend themselves.' The UUP leader believed that he had more flexibility on Strand I than on Strand II: what mattered was the 'big picture', as Blair would put it, namely that the Unionists would regain their Assembly.[56] Indeed, the terms on which they regained it were a secondary issue. Trimble recalls that the issue was settled late on Thursday night with the SDLP. When he told them that he was accepting a full government, 'I thought Hume was going to burst into tears. Hume then hugged Taylor and Taylor responded with gusto.'[57]

There were distinct, if perverse advantages to the UUP in the d'Hondt system: if any party won about 15% of the votes, that grouping would automatically win Cabinet places.[58] This provided a fig-leaf: any decision to accept an all-inclusive consociational form of government could now be explained away as the compulsory outworkings of an imposed electoral method, rather than as a decision taken voluntarily by themselves which would violate their traditional scepticism about power-sharing.[59] Such reasoning might appear eccentric, but then Unionism has always been more about maintaining appearances than many of its critics and admirers have understood. The maintenance of appearances was not about a better image to the outside world: it was about their self-image. Far from lacking a political aesthetic, Unionism had it in spadefuls, but of its own bizarre, narcissistic kind, in which substance was often a secondary issue. Unionists paid a huge price for such fig-leaves.

But the greatest problem with the d'Hondt system of proportionality for Unionists was that a system which was acceptable in local authorities was now much less so in a full government. For if Sinn Fein accepted the new institutions and were not excluded by some provision about decommissioning, they could immediately take up seats in government. Trimble, though, claims that at this point in the proceedings, he gave little thought to Sinn Fein: he says that he presumed it very unlikely that Sinn Fein would agree to these new institutions such as the Northern Ireland Assembly, nor that their democratic bona fides would be sufficient to obtain admission to the halls of power.[60] The evidence does not wholly support this assertion. As has been noted, Trimble told the talks team the day before that Sinn Fein would be participating in the Assembly. Trimble's extraordinarily generous last-minute offer to the SDLP on Strand I may even have had the effect of further contributing to republicans' willingness to participate in new institutions. Perhaps this is what he meant by his off-hand remark to Sean O'Callaghan towards the end of the previous year – to the effect that his supporters would have to wait for the night itself to see what was in store for them; Trimble, though, denies that this was his intention.[61]

Trimble did better in two other areas – Strand III issues and the Constitution. When the UUP read the Strand III portions of the Mitchell draft, they were struck by the emaciated structures which it envisaged. The disparity between these and the detail of the Strand II proposals was obvious. Trimble duly instructed Weir and David Campbell to see that the reduced Strand II structures maintained compatibility with an enhanced Strand III. The British-Irish Council (BIC), created to match the North-South Ministerial Council, consisted of the the British and Irish national Governments, the devolved executives of Northern Ireland, Scotland and Wales, as well as the authorities of the Channel Islands and the Isle of Man. But despite Trimble's belief that the BIC would help draw the Republic back into the United Kingdom orbit, it never bothered nationalists greatly.[62] Instead, some of them privately saw it as 'necessary nonsense' (to use the dismissive phrase often attributed to Faulkner in respect of the 1973–4 Council of Ireland) which Trimble required to sell the deal to his own constituency.[63] Indeed, bearing in mind the speed with which the Republic set up consulates in Edinburgh and Cardiff – enabling them to 'schmooze' the new devolutionary political elites in Scotland and Wales – there was every chance that even the Strand III structures could be turned to the Unionists' disadvantage. Frank Millar, for one, speculated whether these missions reflected Dublin's suspicion that devolution would lead to the wider break-up of the United Kingdom (which itself would greatly increase the prospects for Irish unity).[64] By 2003, there were still no countervailing UUP offices or Northern Ireland Executive Bureaux in either Edinburgh or Cardiff (though one was established in Brussels). Nor, for that matter, did the Irish set up a consulate in Belfast – a clear indication that Northern Ireland was part of a foreign state – as Trimble desired. But one fig-leaf that was keenly sought by Trimble and the whole UUP was eventually granted: the elimination of the Anglo-Irish Agreement and the supporting Maryfield Secretariat. Trimble secured Blair's accept-ance of this at Chequers on 29 March. But after he had gone to bed on the night of Thursday/Friday (9/10 April) Peter Weir took a call from Jonathan Powell, Blair's chief of staff. Powell suggested to Weir that there had been an oversight and that Maryfield would not now formally be scrapped. With Trimble's approval, Weir contacted Powell and obtained a verbal assurance.[65] Trimble then went back and obtained a letter from Blair pledging closure, of which he made much when he emerged on Good Friday itself to announce that he had signed the deal. The AIA of 1985 was gone and he had played his part in negotiating the new treaty known as the British-Irish Agreement. This contrasted favourably to the 'diktat' of 1985 imposed with no consultation whatsoever, and with the old Articles 2 and 3 still in place. Indeed, Article 1 of the new British-Irish Agreement, unlike its 1985 predecessor, referred to 'Northern Ireland's status as part of the United Kingdom . . .'. The two Governments would now have to consult on their deliberations with the First and Deputy First Minister, who would have the right to attend meetings of the Intergovernmental Confer-ence. And whereas under the AIA, the Republic could make proposals affecting the entirety of government, they now forfeited this right via this particular route in those areas which had been devolved by Westminster (namely, the six old Northern Ireland departments – Finance, Education, Environment, Agriculture, Health and Economic Development). But that did not mean that the Irish right to make proposals in respect of Northern Ireland was eliminated, which was the impression given in UUP election literature. Certainly, the bricks and mortar of Maryfield were effectively 'decommissioned', but the secretariat itself and the very same staff relocated to Windsor House in the centre of Belfast. Indeed, the work of the new British-Irish Secretariat was canalised more efficiently than ever into the most sensitive areas, where powers were 'reserved' by Westminster – policing, prisoners, demilitarisation and the courts.

Trimble certainly felt himself to be very much better off on the constitutional questions by the end of Holy Week. Although Trimble had known for quite some time that extensive revision of Articles 2 and 3 would be undertaken, the Irish held off for a very long time before they revealed their final draft: they did not want a debate on the amended text to rage outside of the context of the whole Agreement and the attendant benefits which nationalists would derive from it (otherwise, they feared that Sinn Fein would make electoral gains in the Republic at their expense). As part of the necessary preparatory work, Ahern and Mansergh spoke to the entire Fianna Fail parliamentary caucus (the 100-or-so strong bloc of TDs, Senators and MEPs) in groups of 20 based on geographic location. On the weekend of 4/5 April, Austen Morgan and Peter Weir continued negotiations in Dundalk and with the Fianna Fail representative, Brian Lenihan Jr. On the night of Thursday 9 April, Donaldson, Weir and Morgan tried to move the Irish further, but did not succeed. But Trimble was happy enough with what the intergovernmental communiqués called 'balanced constitutional change' on the grounds that the Union was safer than before. The old Articles 2 and 3 would go, as would Westminster legislation, namely Section 75 of the Government of Ireland Act. The UUP could, however, credibly claim that he had struck a good deal in this area – as was evidenced by the fact that the constitutional issue was not a prominent feature of the 'No' campaign in the subsequent referendum on the Belfast Agreement. Article 2 had been based upon territory: 'The national territory consists of the whole island of Ireland, its islands and the territorial seas.' It would now, instead, be based upon people. 'It is the entitlement of every person born in the island of Ireland to be part of the Irish nation.' Article 3 (which had declared that 'Pending the reintegration of the national territory, and without prejudice to the right of the Parliament and Government established by this Constitution to exercise jurisdiction over the whole of that territory, the laws enacted by that Parliament shall have the like area and extent of application as the laws of Saorstat Eireann and the like extra-territorial effect') would still articulate the will of the Irish to unite the entire territory but it recognised for the first time since 1937 that this could only be done with the consent of the people 'democratically expressed in both jurisdictions in the island'. Trimble argued that the revised Irish Constitution recognised that Northern Ireland is not part of the national territory. And despite Ahern's claim that the nation remained a 32-county entity, the State was limited to 26 counties and would no longer have a new territorial claim.[66]

Trimble rebutted the belief of nationalist Ireland – underwritten by anti-Agreement Unionists – that the elimination of the last vestiges of the Westminster Parliament's 1920 Government of Ireland Act had, in turn, undermined British sovereignty over Northern Ireland. Moreover, nationalists argued, the Act of Union of 1800 (which was the key item of legislation) was subject to the doctrine of implied repeal in the Northern Ireland Act 1998 which created the new institutions in British law. There was, therefore, no raft of Parliamentary Acts to back up an absolute territorial claim and according to Gerry Adams, at the Sinn Fein *Ard Fheis* of 10 May 1998, Northern Ireland's status within the United Kingdom had now been reduced to 'one hinge' – namely the will of the people of Northern Ireland. Bertie Ahern likewise claimed at an Easter Rising commemoration that 'the British Government are effectively out of the equation'. Trimble ascribed what he saw as a mischievous interpretation to the need to help the Sinn Fein leadership ram the 1998 deal through the *Ard Fheis*, but he also immediately grasped the damage which the Taoiseach's claims might inflict upon pro-Agreement unionism during a difficult referendum campaign. He rebutted Ahern at length in an *Irish Times* article on 18 May 1998. Trimble was quick to point out that the Belfast Agreement (and the subsequent Northern Ireland Act 1998) neither expressly nor impliedly repealed the 1800 Act – citing Lord Wilberforce's judgment on the Irish peerages legislation of the 1960s, which the distinguished jurist held did not imply repeal of basic constitutional legislation. As for the elimination of Section 75 ('Notwithstanding anything contained in this Act, the supreme authority of the Parliament of the United Kingdom shall remain unaffected over all persons, matter and things in Northern Ireland and every part thereof') it had nothing to do with the British territorial claim. This, Trimble observed, rested upon the United Kingdom's title in international law to Northern Ireland. Section 75 was, rather, a saving provision concerning the undiminished power of the Westminster Parliament to make laws for Northern Ireland. Indeed in her authoritative study of the constitutional aspects of the 1998 Agreement, Trimble's former colleague at Queen's, Professor Brigid Hadfield, noted that this was a standard feature of all devolutionary settlements and was even retained in the new Northern Ireland Act 1998. Section 75 was of significance only in the context of the 1920 devolutionary settlement which had been obsolete since 1972, and its elimination represented the final symbolic break with that dispensation but nothing more than that. In any case, Unionists had no particular historical affection for Section 75: the civil rights advocates of the 1960s looked to it as the means by which Stormont would have reforms imposed on it from London. It supplied the legal basis for direct rule and the radical improvements in the social and economic position of the Catholic middle class.[67] Unionists thought that if nationalists wanted to claim that Section 75 was an offensive claim of British sovereignty on a par with Articles 2 and 3, so be it: they believed that they had got the best of this particular trade.[68]

These considerations did not greatly impinge upon the Unionist grassroots. Throughout the week, calls had been coming in from unionists urging Trimble not to sign the deal. Anthony Alcock noted in his diary for 2 April 1998: 'Also in the morning [someone from Tyrone] rang through to complain about DT having broken all his promises, especially on decommissioning, i.e. we wouldn't enter the talks until there was decom.; we wouldn't sit down with SF; Willie Thompson and Willie Ross were right; and he wasn't going to vote for UUP at the next election, etc., etc. . . . DT said these types of calls should not be put through to the Talks venue.' Similar misgivings were expressed at a meeting of the Westminster party which took place every Wednesday night. The parliamentary party gathered round a speaker phone in the Commons for a conference call with their leader, who was in Belfast (along with Taylor, Donaldson, Maginnis and Cecil Walker). Those present included Ross, Smyth, Forsythe, Beggs, Thompson and Molyneaux (peers are members of the parliamentary party, too). Ross observed that the parliamentary party had not yet seen the Mitchell document. 'You're preparing to sell us out,' cried Ross. 'No, I'm not,' replied Trimble's voice out of the telephone. 'I'm trying to do my best for the people of Northern Ireland.' 'And we will do the same,' thundered Ross. Ross was much the most forthright of Trimble's colleagues. I once asked him if he had also said to Trimble in this period, 'You've betrayed Ulster, you wee bastard.' 'Wrong, laddie,' responded Ross, 'I never said "wee".'[69]

Such was the atmosphere in which Trimble addressed a specially called meeting of the 110-strong Ulster Unionist Executive at 6:30 p.m. on the evening of Thursday 9 April at Glengall Street. Trimble's decision to hold this was heavily influenced by his experience of watching Molyneaux during the 1991–2 talks, when he felt that his predecessor 'rationed' knowledge about what was taking place. Trimble, by contrast, decided to err on the side of greater 'openness'. 'The culmination of that was on 9 April 1998,' says the UUP leader. 'We had previously foreseen that the last week in April was going to be crucial so we arranged a party executive for 6:00 p.m. I requested a meeting of the talks team to review things – which operated on an open-door basis. There were a fair number of spectators, maybe 22 in that room. I would go round all of them before we went to the Executive. Then I said to the 22, "By the way, how many are going to the Executive?" Nineteen were going in one capacity or another. Then I looked round at Austen Morgan. And I said, "Austen, are you not going to the Executive?" "Ah, sure, I'm not a Unionist," he replied. I am not sure how many knew about Austen's background as a Roman Catholic or indeed Tom Hennessey's.'[70] As Trimble arrived at Glengall Street, he was met by two noisy demonstrations: one composed of loyalists shouting 'traitor, traitor, traitor' and singing 'The Sash', the other composed of Boyzone fans at the rear entrance of the nearby Europa Hotel shouting 'we love you Ronan we do' (the star, Ronan Keating, was in Belfast to receive the Hot Press Rock and Pop awards).[71] Daphne Trimble – who would not normally attend an Executive, but who felt she had to give him support on this occasion – was worried. But any nerves which Trimble felt evaporated when he walked in and received a standing ovation. Trimble told the Executive that the UUP was still holding out for a committee system of government in line with traditional party policy; it did not dawn on much of the Executive that the UUP successes on Strand II might mean significant losses for the party on Strand I. Prisoners never arose as an issue, but when Ken Maginnis and Cecil Walker (the MP for North Belfast who had been given the task of assisting the UUP security spokesman) entered the room Trimble declared 'Ken and Cecil have saved the RUC.' Jeffrey Donaldson turned to his colleague Peter King and said 'I rather suspect it's a stay of execution.' Privately, he felt that Trimble had done a brilliant job of smuggling a bad deal past the Executive on his usual 'blind them with science' principle.[72] The meeting was then adjourned until 10 a.m. on Saturday.[73]

Trimble's claim that Maginnis and Walker had 'saved' the RUC is worth examining. Trimble had certainly played little active day-to-day part in this subject, either before or during the Good Friday week. So totally did he apparently depend upon Maginnis in these areas that he took his eye off the ball and found himself unready to discuss them during his first meeting with Blair on the evening of Tuesday 7 April 1998 at Hillsborough. Maginnis says that they did know that there was always going to be a commission of some sort on the future of policing: the issue was apparently so contentious that it could not be settled in the talks context.[74] The question then was what kind of commission, and its format, remit and composition. Maginnis did secure some minor revisions to the policing sections of the Mitchell document – including a reference to the RUC and its sacrifices – prompting Peter Bell to observe with dark humour on Good Friday itself that 'the RUC are no longer to be referred to as a bunch of Serb paramilitaries!!'[75] But the final text was largely unchanged. Critically, the policing commission would have to address composition, recruitment, training, ethos, culture and symbols. Most of Maginnis's efforts were directed towards ensuring that it was handled by a Royal Commission rather than an international commission. But the Irish and Sinn Fein were unhappy and the tired British ministers did not feel strongly enough about it at this late stage in the talks to fight hard. So the Governments stuck to the suggestion of an independent commission with international and expert participation, which was outlined in the Mitchell draft (though there was an understanding about the need for a British chairman, which was achieved partly at the behest of the UUP. That Briton turned out to be Chris Patten – another Unionist 'victory' which they subsequently had great cause to regret). Loyalists believed it was typical of the UUP's priorities to concentrate on the aesthetics of the policing issue rather than its substance. Thus, Trimble wrote during the referendum that 'the Prime Minister has been very reasuring on the position of the RUC. It is a professional force with nothing to fear from a Royal Commission. We will not have a two-tier police force, nor will we see IRA men in police uniform.'[76] This was a curious formulation from one who used words so carefully: there was no Royal Commission. Trimbleistas claimed that it was royal in all but name. But, sceptics asked, what was the use of having a Royal Commission without that title?

Much of this was lost in the mêlée of the final hours of the talks – and few UUP Executive members were going to subject Trimble's claims to much scrutiny in such a time of crisis. Nor did the 'baby barristers' appear too unhappy with the deal which was taking shape. For by this point, it was mainly the 'Orange' portions of the deal which were in evidence. Articles 2 and 3 would go, an Assembly would return to Stormont, Strand II had been minimised.[77] Indeed, up till the Good Friday itself, Trimble still claims that he did not expect Sinn Fein to be part of any agreement: they could not accept the consent principle, especially since the institutional and constitutional arrangements had been settled in ways that he deemed were acceptable to the Unionists.[78] This may partly explain why the UUP expended so few chips on ensuring that those who did not decommission their weapons would be excluded from the Executive, and why those provisions of the accord proved so inadequate from their perspective: they simply did not believe that Sinn Fein would be on board. In such an atmosphere, Trimble felt able to catch a few hours' sleep at the nearby Stormont Hotel, where Denis Rogan had booked him a room. (Unionists always had this fear of being deliberately kept up all night by the two Governments and then agreeing to some foolish concession in their exhaustion.)[79] But the match was by no means over: David Kerr also recalls meeting Eamonn Mallie at 4:30 a.m. that morning and telling the Downtown Radio journalist that there was no way both sides could be on board for the deal. 'You're wrong,' Mallie retorted.[80] Oddly, the UUP (mis)perception was shared by very senior figures on the Irish side, who thought that Sinn Fein was 'lost' late on Thursday night: even very eminent participants in the process were all being conditioned by the relentlessly pessimistic republican 'spin' on the television, which was matched by Adams' grim mood in private. But all of them underestimated in one way or another the self-discipline and determination of the republican movement. 'Sinn Fein are superb at taking the last slice off the salami,' says one very senior Irish official. 'Sinn Fein were reasonably dormant in the previous 24 hours as they observed the to-and-fro-ing of the two leaders with the UUP. But they thought: "Now that they think that they've seen it all, now let's give them a run at it. Just give it one more twist and that will do it."' The republicans duly sat down with Ahern for one last fling, and they came up with over 70 demands, ranging from cross-border bodies to prisoners. The Irish knew this technique, and in their own minds would almost automatically subtract 50% – but that still gave Sinn Fein plenty of room for manoeuvre. Ahern then went to Blair and produced the republican demands. 'Ah, for Jesus' sake,' responded the British Prime Minister. 'This is impossible.' But the Taoiseach was determined and resolved to go through it with republicans line by line: the worst thing from a Fianna Fail point of view would have been to enter a southern referendum campaign with Sinn Fein portraying themselves as defenders of the 1937 Constitution. At around 10 p.m. on Thursday 9 April Ahern and Mowlam left to see Adams. 'Do you think the Taoiseach can do this?' Blair asked Paddy Teahon. 'Well, I've seen him do it before,' replied the Irish mandarin.[81]

At the top of Ahern's agenda were prisoner releases. As one very senior Irish official observes, the question of prisoners was one of those highly sensitive issues which 'stayed slightly under the bed [throughout the talks] – as though all of the politicians knew it had to be dealt with but could not be talked about "in front of the children". It was an area – one of those awful necessities of conflict resolution – where they would prefer to be presented with a fait accompli. Whilst there had been a fair amount of discussion between ourselves and Sinn Fein, there was no specific detail till the end. The Irish Government wasn't going to expose itself too early on this one. And nobody wants to be overzealous.' No. 10 also regarded it as one of the successes of the Agreement that they were able to negotiate these emotional issues very late in the day – issues which they regarded as not being at the core of the new constitutional settlement (one senior NIO official of the period described these issues as the 'necessary *pourboires*' to bind nationalist Ireland into a partitionist structure). The Irish knew that the shots were ultimately called by the Prime Minister on the subject of prisoner releases. But the southerners also felt able to proceed because the UUP did not send out very negative signals – at least not to the point whereby they would declare that they would not sign because of prisoner releases. Had they said no to the very concept of early releases, declares this official, there would have been no way that Sinn Fein/IRA and the loyalists would have signed up to any agreement. Trimble and his key supporters confirm that they did not dig in their heels against the principle. Trimble says he firmly believed that he could not influence the matter, which would mainly be negotiated between the paramilitary parties and the two Governments. Although he was very unhappy about it, he had to decide at the end of the day whether the prisoners issue was so bad that he had to throw up the whole agreement because of it.[82] Denis Rogan, the UUP chairman, confirms the point and adds that there was a commonality of interests between the loyalists and Sinn Fein/IRA in extracting their prisoners from the jails, though not necessarily total agreement on the precise terms; Rogan says the UUP feared that the loyalists might refuse to sign up at all if their 'boys' did not 'come home'.[83]

The issue then became the details of such releases. Maginnis wanted a five-year release scheme, but Sinn Fein's minimum was for all prisoners to be released within a year. When John Steele learned about it, he expressed his concerns to Mowlam, and urged her to go and see the Prime Minister. The Prime Minister was concerned about both the referendum and the passage of the Bill which would be required to effect the early releases. 'Could we get it through [on the shorter time frames of up to one year]?' he asked.[84] John Steele told Blair that the referendum would be lost if the prisoners were out within twelve months. 'So this is how long it's taken me to find out what the NIO professionals really think!' exclaimed Blair; his private secretary, John Holmes, uttered an expletive.[85] Blair and Ahern duly went to Sinn Fein to claw back the lost ground and to return to the idea of two years. As he was leaving the talks, Blair turned to John Steele and said, 'John, thanks – you stopped me making a mistake.'[86] Trimble, though, was not so happy and told one very senior Irish official who had supported the prisoner release scheme, 'You bastards have ruined almost all of this. We intensely dislike what you do and you almost scuttled all of this.'[87]

Curiously, neither of the key UUP players in this area fully realised what a huge issue prisoners would become. Partly, this was because of Trimble's own legalistic, overly-logical mindset. He reasoned that there was no great issue of principle here. Prisoners had always been released after the end of previous IRA campaigns (such as the 1956–62 border insurgency). Moreover scores had already been released in the last few years in a willy-nilly fashion. He was thus implying that what was done in the 1998 Agreement was simply a matter of degree, rather than a radical departure. Trimble recalled that UUP members had told him over the years how as they went about their daily business, they had to endure the indignity of meeting terrorists who had killed their loved ones.[88] Moreover, Maginnis believed that such schemes as were envisaged under the Agreement had to be placed in the context of 'conflict resolution situations' all over the world. 'Neither of us got very excited about it,' says Maginnis. 'To some extent we both misjudged the mood of society.'[89] Trimble is less inclined than Maginnis to engage in 'constructive self-criticism' and tends to blame others. He believes that the prisoners became a huge issue only because the Balcombe Street gang were released for the triumphalist Sinn Fein *Ard Fheis* in May, at which they were greeted by hundreds of cheering republicans, and which was shown again and again on the television. He says that he will never forgive the NIO for the timing of the prisoner releases and the lack of conditions attached to them. The attendance of the prisoners at these rallies gave fuel to what he regards as a hyperbolic and overly emotional reaction in the referendum.[90]

After the receipt of this document, noted Alcock, 'everyone split up to study the various sections, and then the Talks Team met. It was soon clear that there were massive reservations about accepting the document, and for the next five hours the debate raged. Gradually, the rooms began to fill up with Forum members, MPs, party officers, and the atmosphere inside became gloomy while outside the other parties who were all in favour waited with increasing impatience and, indeed, anger. Outside media hype was frenzied. About 2 p.m. the Talks Team had a meeting. 10 were present plus Jack Allen, David Kerr and Tom Hennessey. I saw it as 6–3 for a deal – but with great misgivings that not to accept would be even worse [DT, John D. Taylor, K. Maginnis, Antony Alcock, Reg Empey, Dermott Nesbitt versus Jeffrey Donaldson, Peter Weir, David Campbell].' No vote was actually taken and Donaldson says that Trimble did not express himself very strongly: rather, as so often, he let the debate run its course before expressing a definitive opinion.[91] Like the ex-lecturer that he was, he preferred his pupils to come to their own conclusions, to guide by inference rather than prescription. Taylor also behaved characteristically: according to Thomas Hennessey, Taylor initially expressed great scepticism in the talks team meeting, running through eighteen things which he disliked about the accord, but did not pronounce definitively against the deal.[92] As he did this, Steven King kept running in and informing Taylor that Downing Street was demanding this or that. 'We'll not be panicked,' said Taylor. 'This is just what they did to Faulkner at Sunningdale, putting us under pressure.' Trimble then interjected and said that if the UUP walked out, it would still have to put up with all of this (prisoner releases, RUC reform, etc.) and would in addition have to endure an Anglo-Irish Agreement Mark II.

Alcock next recorded in his diary: 'DT then announced that we could make a last effort about one issue – which should it be? The answer was SF in government without decommissioning. DT went off again. He also said he would call in the party officers on the decision.' Alcock recalls Trimble announcing to the talks team: 'We'll have to ditch the prisoners.'[93] The UUP leader then went up to see Blair to address the inadequacy of this section of the agreement. The No. 10 team were exhausted. 'We were in this ghastly building with very little sleep,' recalls Jonathan Powell. 'Tony Blair had slept on two seats, put together, and John Holmes had lain on the floor. At one point I even slept upright against a door.'[94] Such was the atmosphere in which Trimble went up to see the Prime Minister. The UUP leader told Blair that he believed that the issue of safeguards before the republicans could enter an Executive was a Strand I matter which related to the internal government of Northern Ireland and that any improvements could be agreed to by him without talking to Ahern. Blair agreed – though John Holmes later told Trimble that the Irish had, in fact, been consulted about this proposed 'safeguard' and had stopped something stronger. What Trimble in fact obtained was a side-letter to the Agreement (he cannot remember whose idea the side-letter was).[95] According to Jonathan Powell, it was drafted very quickly by the Prime Minister himself; Powell typed it.[96] When Trimble eventually came back with the original letter in his breast pocket – Powell says there was no time to make a copy – Trimble tapped it confidentially. 'We've got something,' he told those gathered round him. 'But it's not watertight.'[97] It read: 'Dear David, I understand that your problem with paragraph 25 of Strand 1 is that it requires decisions on those who should be excluded or removed from office in the Northern Ireland Executive to be taken on a cross community basis [a reference to the unwillingness of the SDLP to exclude Sinn Fein/IRA if they defaulted]. This letter is to let you know that if, during the course of the first six months of the shadow Assembly or the Assembly itself, these provisions have been shown to be ineffective, we will support changes to these provisions to enable them to be made properly effective in preventing such people from holding office. Furthermore, I confirm that in our view the effect of the decommissioning section of the agreement, with decommissioning schemes coming into effect in June, is that the process of decommissioning should begin straight away.' John Holmes claims that 'it seemed to have helped to give David Trimble renewed heart to persuade his colleagues' – an analysis which is by no means incompatible with the contention of republicans and Trimble's loyalist critics that this was nothing more than a comfort blanket designed to sell the deal to a doubtful unionist population.[98] Moreover, they said that it enjoyed no legal status, because the parties to the Agreement merely had to use their best efforts to bring about decommissioning rather than to deliver actual 'product'. But Trimble viewed it differently. He says that he knew that he could not obtain cut and dried assurances on this matter at that moment but contended that the British Government's view was that decommissioning should begin by June 1998. This, he argued, would put him a stronger position politically when the next round of wrangling began.[99]

Trimble then went into a UUP officers' meeting and locked the door so they could have some peace and quiet: present were Denis Rogan, Taylor, Maginnis, Donaldson, Empey, Jack Allen, May Steele, Jeffrey Donaldson, Arlene Foster and Jim Wilson. While they were talking, Jonathan Powell, the Prime Minister's chief of staff shoved a note under the closed door. Austen Morgan met Powell outside the UUP room. 'You've really got to trust Tony on this,' he told Morgan.[100] Alastair Campbell was soon outside briefing the press and distributing the Blair letter before the Agreement had been formally endorsed by the plenary, thus building up expectations and making it harder for UUP doubts to reassert themselves. If the Unionists said no to the package now, they would be blamed.[101] Much the same message was conveyed by other sources. Whilst the talks team meeting was underway, David Montgomery of MGN took a call from Blair. 'This isn't going to work,' the Prime Minister told the newspaper executive. 'It's all going badly. They're just not moving.' At this moment, says Montgomery, Jonathan Powell grabbed the telephone. 'Can you try to talk to Trimble?' the Prime Minister's chief of staff inquired with much urgency in his voice. As soon as Montgomery rang for Trimble, Taylor reached for the telephone. 'We will never accept this,' Taylor stated. 'Look, if you don't accept this, whatever the rights and wrongs, the rest of the world is just going to judge the Unionists as obstinate and you will be blamed. You'll never win another PR battle.' Taylor promptly hung up.[102] According to the diary of Denis Rogan for 10 April 1998, 'we then got a call from President Clinton to offer him help. David said if he would ring Bertie Ahern and John Hume to get them not to criticise our letter from PM and it would greatly help. This Clinton promised and we subsequently know he did.' Clinton's call to Trimble was his penultimate intervention of the day and was made from the Oval Office at 11 a.m. Eastern Standard Time (4 p.m. Belfast time). 'I have my colleagues here,' Trimble said. 'We're in a mess.' He had Taylor and Donaldson on either side and opined that if he signed up, he would lose one of them. But he gave no firm indication of which way he himself would go. The Americans noticed that he seemed angry – possibly out of tiredness. Trimble made his request of Clinton to talk to Adams and Hume, and the President concluded with the words 'hang tough'.[103]

Trimble's presentation of his internal party position was by no means inaccurate – though Taylor was, to use American political vocabulary, 'hardballing' and by then believed the side-letter to be good enough.[104] For whilst he realised that both Donaldson and Arlene Foster had displayed unease, it had not registered that they might defect. This is curious, since Arlene Foster distinctly recalls that Trimble showed Donaldson the Blair letter and asked, 'Is this enough?' Donaldson said it was not enough because it was not in the Agreement. According to Denis Rogan's diary of the final afternoon of the talks, 'Geoffrey [sic] then declared he would not agree to deal and was supported by Arlene who said that two other Hon Secs – Brewster and Rodgers – would also say no.' Rogan pulled Donaldson aside. 'You've picked a hell of a bad time,' the UUP chairman remarked.[105] Donaldson says he cannot remember this portion of the exchange taking place, but both are agreed that he told Rogan that 'my conscience won't let me go along'. Donaldson was referring to his constituents and especially to policemen and their families (two of his relatives in the RUC had been murdered during the Troubles). By contrast, Donaldson's detractors believed that he knew all along that these would be the terms of the deal but that his courage failed him at the last. Donaldson says that he remained inside the process because he thought he would enjoy more influence that way, observing that 'you can't pull the safety cord by the track-side'.[106] What can be said is that Donaldson was, in fact, not making a bid for the leadership of the UUP as some have alleged. For one thing, he knew that after less than a year in the Commons, he was not yet ready for it. Moreover, as Sean O'Callaghan testifies, Donaldson had been urging him since before Christmas 1997 to use his influence with Trimble to restrain the UUP leader from making even more concessions than he was already doing. O'Callaghan argues that a more cynical individual would have allowed Trimble to make his concessions and then to strike, rather than striving behind the scenes to put the brakes on an emerging deal.[107]

Above all, defying the leadership was temperamentally not an easy decision for Donaldson who had grown in the UUP. A native of Kilkeel, Co. Down, Donaldson was steeped in the culture of loyalism and unionism. He played the flute in the Pride of Ballinran Flute Band and had served in the UDR. His cousin, Sam Donaldson, was the first RUC officer to be murdered by the IRA during the Troubles; another cousin, Alexander, subsequently died in the IRA mortar attack on Newry RUC station in 1985.[108] He had been active in the Mourne branch of the South Down Ulster Unionist Association (where he served as full-time constituency agent for Enoch Powell in the 1983 General Election and the 1986 by-election). With much trepidation, he picked up the telephone to his constituency chairman, Donn McConnell, and his vice chairman, Barry Fitzsimons. Both men, he says, advised him to do what he thought was right.[109] Arlene Foster – who at 3 a.m. that morning had been typing bullet points in favour of the Agreement – was even more distraught. She was tearful, she says, because of lack of sleep, and talked to Reg Empey. Empey, who was part of the 'lost generation' who had been deprived of the prospect of office by the destruction of Stormont in 1972, understood the emotions of the Young Unionists. Then he told Foster: 'Another chance like this won't come along for me. And whatever you might say about the man [Trimble] he's shown great leadership.' Foster, originally from Lisnaskea, Co. Fermanagh – whose father was an RUC constable who had survived murder attempts by the Provisionals and whose husband was also a serving officer – was unpersuaded.[110] As far as anti-Agreement Unionists such as David Brewster were concerned, Empey's remarks were evidence of the price which Trimble's lieutenant was prepared to pay to fulfil his long frustrated ambitions.[111]

To Trimble, though, the logic of the deal seemed so self-evident to him that he did not really consider whether other people might not see the light with the same clarity as himself: indeed, according to Daphne Trimble, at the time he could never understand why John Hunter and other former associates had abandoned him.[112] She is undoubtedly correct, but it beggars belief that anyone who knew John Hunter could actually think that he would have been party to a deal which brought Sinn Fein into government and released terrorist prisoners. It partly reflects the fact that Trimble is often not intensely interested in the motivations and thought processes of those around him. Daphne Trimble notes that he is so focused on the tasks before him that he will work with whoever is there to advance those things in which he believes. He does not ask too many detailed questions about where they have come from and where they are going to in political terms. So consumed was he in the job at hand that he only learned that Donaldson had left the talks after he had given his press conference after the final plenary session at which he signed the deal – and then from the journalist Eamonn Mallie. Trimble, though, says that he was unaware of what Donaldson was doing because he had derived a different impression from the MP for Lagan Valley. 'Are you coming up?' asked Trimble. 'No, leave me out this time.' Trimble took this a sign that Donaldson was hanging back – but not bolting.[113]

Trimble's internal critics misread him, too, in this period. He was more determined to do the deal than they realised. According to Denis Rogan's diary, 'Trimble voiced opinion we had gone too far to leave. Taylor, Maginnis and Empey spoke in favour. Trimble paused for what seemed like an eternity – he was staring impassively into the distance – and then simply declared "right, I'm going for the agreeement". We wandered across the corridor to inform the talks team and others.' Trimble then called George Mitchell. The former US Senate Majority leader recalls in his memoir that 'it had all come down to this last call from Trimble ... I took a deep breath and picked up the phone. "Hello, David". "Hello, George". "How's it going?" "We're ready." "Are you all right?" "We're ready to do the business". "That's great". "Congratulations".' Mitchell then decided to call a plenary vote as swiftly as possible: he knew from his days as US Senate Majority leader that unless a roll call was called quickly when he had the necessary support in the bag, that backing could swiftly melt away under other countervailing pressures.[114] He need not have worried that much for by this late stage the only serious pressure was on the pro-Agreement side. The previously sceptical Taylor told those assembled that 'this is a wonderful deal, look at what we've got' – and extolled its merits in as categorical a form as he listed its demerits just hours earlier.[115] Trimble has always said that he could not have sold it without Taylor: he decided simply to sit back and to let Taylor draw the teeth of the opposition.[116] Trimble reiterated his intentions and Councillor David Browne of the Castle electoral area of north Belfast inquired, 'What if it all goes wrong?' Trimble retorted: 'Well, as they say, everyone's expendable' (i.e. himself).[117] According to Reg Empey, when Trimble stepped into that airless room, with no windows and 50 or so Ulster Unionists present, there was nothing irreversible about the officers' decision. 'Trimble's performance in that fetid atmosphere was *the* seminal moment of the talks,' recalls Empey. 'People were standing on tables. If the room had turned against him, that would have been it.'[118]

At 5 p.m. the UUP went up to the plenary to sign up formally. When Trimble's turn came to affirm, he simply said 'yes' and then – on John Taylor's advice – went out to be the first of the local party leaders to face the world's media. 'Right, you take over,' he told his deputy.[119] When he emerged outside, a storm was raging and hail was bouncing off his head: everything, he says, was a blur and he had no time for deep philosophical speculation. Instead, his main worry at this time was that the rain would smudge the original copy of the Blair letter which he was reading out.[120] Daphne Trimble was in the car park at the Marks & Spencer store in the Sprucefield Centre near Lisburn when she heard the news over the car radio: she was convinced there would be a deal and bought extra food for a celebration dinner. 'I felt quite emotional,' she says. 'Thank G-d we're there. It's been worthwhile. And I thought of David.' When Trimble arrived back at Richmond Court that night, there were no tall tales to tell. Instead, says Daphne Trimble, 'He was quite matter of fact, as if it was another day's work. But remember, this is David we're talking about. He's not going to show that sort of emotion.'[121] Meanwhile, on the Prime Ministerial jet back to RAF Northolt, the atmosphere was ecstatic: Jonathan Powell recalls the team bursting into fits of giggles.[122]

Why had Trimble done it? At the most obvious level for any politician, there was personal ambition. During a canvass in 1997, he was asked by children if he was the Prime Minister. 'Not yet,' came the reply.[123] The temptations of international acclaim were also present, and he was certainly not unaware of them.[124] That said, he took a more considerable risk, both personally and politically, than either Blair or Ahern would ever have done had they been in his shoes. Though the rewards subsequently turned out to be great, it did not always look that promising at the time he had to make the key decisions. Back in 1998, it looked as though he could lose everything. First, as one senior nationalist politician privately observes, not even Faulkner faced the threat of assassination by fringe loyalists after Sunningdale.[125] Shortly after Heads of Agreement emerged in January 1998, Trimble surveyed his future with his wife Daphne at their home in Lisburn. 'I can go for an agreement, but some of the party will be unhappy with it and I can't be sure they will endorse it – or even the people,' he told her. 'The risk is that I could lose the leadership and lose my [Westminster] seat. I could find excuses for not reaching agreement. We'll get a bit of the blame if we do that. It can be done, but it carries the risk of being out of a job altogether.' But his wife sensed that he wanted to do the deal and encouraged him to push forward. Indeed, it was on this occasion that she enunciated what became known in the Trimble household as the 'Daphne principle': that he would obtain just enough support at every stage of the process to carry on to the next round, but never quite enough for comfort.[126] As Daphne Trimble remarks, there is a gambler's streak to his personality, and he has never played for safety. Had he done so, she says, he would have opted for a Molyneaux-like stance. She adds, though, that his risks are calculated risks.[127]

Certainly, Trimble's calculations were not always those ascribed to him by his critics, nor were they even necessarily those of his ardent supporters. He did not sign up to the Agreement because of defeatism. He says he did not believe that if he did not sign up, an Anglo-Irish Agreement Mark II or Joint Authority was inevitable (though he invoked its spectre at a key moment in the talks to point the party in the direction he wanted). Not only were there no such plans but very senior figures in government such as Jonathan Powell were not even aware by mid-1999 of what the concept of Joint Authority was all about.[128] Even if they had wanted to, it is not certain that they would have succeeded in effecting such impositions: the British state of the late 1990s was rather less self-confident than it had been in 1985.[129] Nor, as some Irish journalists have speculated, did Trimble sign up to the Belfast Agreement because he was secretly threatened by Blair with a United Kingdom-wide referendum on the future of Northern Ireland that would inevitably result in the ditching of the unionists: both Trimble and, significantly, Jonathan Powell are clear that such suggestions are rubbish.[130] Rather, he was motivated by a belief that an excellent opportunity would be lost to bring back provincial self-government. This might not arise again for another decade. He was driven by his sense of dissatisfaction both with the 'democratic deficit' inherent in the direct rule system – of mainland politicians who were not accountable to the local electorate making decisions with viceregal impunity – and the futility of AIA-style protest politics. Both led to a sense of helplessness which, he believed, had profoundly demoralising effects.

Trimble's decision to sign up to the Belfast Agreement was not much motivated by worries about the sectarian head-count. According to this clichéd analysis, which sometimes surfaced in the nationalist press, Unionists had to cut the best deal now (with appropriate guarantees for the Province's minority-in-waiting) before a new political dispensation was imposed upon them by the *force majeure* of demographic change.

Certainly, Trimble – like everyone else – was conscious that the demographic balance was far from being around two-thirds-to-one-third in the Protestants' favour. Indeed, he told the Israeli daily *Ha'aretz* on 15 November 2002 that 'if you are going to have a stable political structure, then you are going to have some way in which that 30–40% [of the population which is nationalist] becomes involved and participant. You can tolerate a situation where a small percentage completely withdraws from participation in society, but when you get to that sort of percentage, if they wish to disrupt and cause problems, they can do so. It is much better to have a decent structure within society, to find some way of ameliorating and encouraging people to participate. So it was in our interest – and we keep saying that in meetings – to make Northern Ireland work. It is not in our interest for Northern Ireland to appear to be a failed political entity, or something that does not work.'[131] He genuinely believed that if Sinn Fein were sucked into Stormont, they would be operating British institutions and would thus become 'structural' as opposed, obviously, to 'ideological' unionists (the expression 'structural unionism' had been coined by Anthony McIntyre, a former IRA prisoner who became the most articulate opponent of the Adams approach, to describe British state strategy, but was then taken up by some Trimbleistas to describe republican behaviour).[132] Trimble believed that republicans could be integrated into existing, albeit reformed, state structures because the traditional ideology that drove them was dead or dying; in so far as it still existed, he believed that it was an embarrassment for the likes of Gerry Adams.

But although Sinn Fein had grown in electoral strength, Trimble firmly believed that there was no chance of a majority in favour of Irish unity any time soon. His confidence was illustrated by his proposal for a border poll on the Province's constitutional status at the UUC meeting on 9 March 2002. It was further vindicated by the subsequent results of the 2001 census – which gave Protestants a 53%–44% edge over Catholics, in defiance of some of the wilder predictions of near-parity.[133] Indeed, he had believed this for a considerable time. As far back as October 1994, Trimble had appeared on a UTV discussion and stated that the Catholic birthrate was falling dramatically (Trimble also noted the same trend in Holland, which was an implicit reference to the diminishing hold of the Catholic Church on its faithful). More to the point, Trimble observed that confessional allegiance did not necessarily result in a nationalist voting pattern.[134] Indeed, his remarks to *Ha'aretz* suggest that he believed that the opportunities opened up to Catholics in a reformed Northern Ireland would reconcile them to the Union. He claimed that between 20–25% of those who regarded themselves as nationalists were not keen to leave the United Kingdom, not least because their society had evolved differently from that of the rest of the island of Ireland. In this, he proved rather optimistic: much of the research data on the Catholic community suggested that Catholic unionism had diminished substantially during the 'peace process', partly because of the boom in nationalist self-confidence which derived from the success of the 'Celtic Tiger' economy and partly because of the growth of Sinn Fein. But there were still enough Catholic supporters of the Union – in 2001, the Northern Ireland Life and Times Survey put it at 15% of the Catholic community – to make the constitutional status quo a viable option.[135]

Trimble's real demographic calculations were rather different and, it might be argued, more subtle. They related, instead, to the internal social and political balance within the pro-Union bloc. Here, Trimble's concerns related not so much to quantity as to quality. In the first instance, as leader of the largest party in the Province (just) he was worried by the increasing difficulty in persuading pro-Union electors to vote – especially in the majority Protestant east of the Province, as was evidenced by the results of the 1998 Assembly elections. Second, it was becoming ever harder to persuade the Protestant middle classes to participate in Unionist politics, which led to a poor quality of candidates and general stagnation of the party. Third, it was becoming even harder to persuade bright, middle-class children to attend universities in the Province and more difficult still once they had gone to mainland institutions of higher education to persuade them to return (according to Trimble, as many as 40% of undergraduates at Dundee University, for example, may be from Ulster Protestant backgrounds).[136] The life-blood of the Ulster-British intelligentsia was flowing away and had been for some time. One symptom of this trend was the increasingly Catholic nature of the Bar Library in Belfast, as exemplified by the high proportion of new Catholic silks.

There was a multiplicity of reasons for all three predicaments, but there was also a common theme connecting them – the powerlessness of the Unionist community. In one way or another, the UUP had engaged since 1972 in a form of protest politics which Trimble believed had run its course. It was now pointless to vote for a party which could change nothing – which could not hold office, nor offer patronage (whereas the SDLP did so via the Irish Government, in the shape of the Anglo-Irish Agreement), nor pass laws, nor direct spending priorities. Direct rule ministers did nothing about what many from Unionist backgrounds regarded as the increasingly uncongenial, anti-British environment at Queen's University – known as the 'chill factor'.[137] But if the UUP regained a measure of local power (even at a very high price and under very restrictive circumstances in terms of the requirements for cross-community support) then they believed there was a fighting chance that some of these losses could be reversed. In their view it would be harder for certain key institutions to 'diss' unionist sensibilities – as much of respectable society had done since the humiliation of the AIA in 1985 – with even a few Unionists in the new Executive. And because a new, inclusive system of government would, Trimble hoped, make for stability, this would make it all the likelier that young people would opt to stay or even to return to Ulster.[138] Once back in office at Stormont, the UUP would again become respectable in the eyes of a swathe of middle-class Protestant society that had opted out of politics since the Troubles (for example, in the old Ards division of the pre-1972 Stormont, most head-masters of state secondary schools were members of their local UUP; within a short period after the prorogation of Stormont in 1972, hardly any remained. No doubt this pattern was replicated in other places, as the bourgeoisie declined to be associated with the party which was seen either as ineffectual or else, at times, yoked to Paisleyism and Orangeism).[139] Partly, this would be contingent upon reforms of the UUP – notably ridding the party of the link with the Loyal Orders. And if he managed it, there was a possibility that some less nationalistic Catholics might vote for or even join the party.

In so far as Trimble was motivated by defeatism, it was in a media-conscious way. He believed that Unionists could not be seen to be blamed for bringing the process to a halt (he was, says Jeffrey Donaldson, very conscious of the Downing Street 'spin doctors' hyping up the expectation of a deal on the Good Friday itself).[140] The desire to avoid such an outcome led him into making more concessions than he intended at the outset. Indeed, often he had no long-term game plan and lived, politically speaking, for the week or even the day (his decision in the final week of the talks to opt for Scottish-style legislative devolution, rather than a Welsh-style administrative model, is a case in point). And, says Empey, he was convinced that Blair would be in office for the next ten years and remoulding the United Kingdom: here would be the chance for Northern Ireland to be part of that rather than out on a limb.[141] Crucially, he trusted Blair in a way that he never did the Tories. Blair might have difficulty making good his principles and pledges, but Trimble felt that at least he believed in them and was less committed to the Frameworks formula of 1995 than the Tories.[142] Trimble the historian also felt that good relations with London were at a premium. He often recalled how Craig had benefited in Whitehall and Westminster from his own emolli- ence after he went the 'extra mile for peace' during the Craig–Collins pact of 1921–2. Only time would tell if these assumptions proved correct – but, meanwhile, he had to win a referendum. And he cannot have expected how hard that would turn out to be.

TWENTY-FIVE

'Let the people sing'

THE meeting of the Ulster Unionist Executive – which had been adjourned on the night of Thursday 9 April – resumed at 10 a.m. on the morning of Saturday 11 April at Glengall Street.[1] Denis Rogan, the chairman of the party, was keen that John Taylor (who had helped administer the *coup de grâce* to Faulkner in January 1974 at the UUC) should propose the motion, which he agreed to do. After three hours of debate, the UUP Executive passed the motion by 55 to 23 – a 71%–27% margin in favour of the deal.[2] As Trimble approached the next stage – a meeting of the Ulster Unionist Council on Saturday 18 April – he was further buoyed by a *Guardian/Irish Times* poll indicating 73% support for the Belfast Agreement. The UUP leader jauntily told republicans at a press conference that they had failed to attain their objective of a united Ireland and that 'this agreement is as good and fair as it gets'. Reg Empey was also dismissive of the prospect of Sinn Fein participating in an Executive, asserting that Gerry Adams in government would be like 'Hitler in a synagogue'.[3]

Doubts about the deal began gradually to surface within the unionist community once the fine print began to be examined: only later did the steady flow become a raging torrent. These doubts focused mainly on prisoners, policing and the prospect of Sinn Fein in government. The Grand Lodge of Ireland, though resisting pressure from the hardline Spirit of Drumcree faction to declare open hostility to the Belfast Agreement, nonetheless expressed grave misgivings.[4] The County Grand Lodge of Armagh, representing 6000 Orangemen – many of them in Trimble's constituency – stated that it was unable to recommend to brother loyalists to accept the deal.[5] Trimble believed he could win about 70% of UUC members – and ended up securing 72% on the main motion (William Ross's amendment was rejected by 68%). Upon hearing the news at the

Two men who made it the hard way: Major and Trimble reconciled at the 1998 Conservative conference in Bournemouth.

Farewell to the Union or 'sensible Cross-border bodies'? Dick Spring, Irish Foreign Minister with Sir Patrick Mayhew, Northern Ireland Secretary, at the opening of the Shannon-Erne Waterway in 1994.

Two modern European politicians: John Bruton, Fine Gael Taoiseach 1994–97, with Trimble in Dublin.

The spoils of office: Trimble presents bath-robes to the Clintons at the White House in 1996, made by a company in his constituency. His deputy, John D. Taylor, is second from the left. It is not known what happened to the bath-robes.

For God and Ulster: Billy Wright, Commander of the Loyalist Volunteer Force. A constituent of Trimble's, he played an important role in the Drumcree stand-off of 1996. Trimble met him twice during the crisis.

David and Daphne at home in Lisburn: Sarah (aged seven) is on the far left.

The old school tie: David Montgomery, a childhood acquaintance of Trimble from Bangor Grammar School, later proved an important backchannel between Trimble and Blair as chief of Mirror Group Newspapers and the *News Letter*.

Two trusted aides: Blair with John Holmes (right) and John Sawers (left), successively Private Secretaries at No 10 with responsibility for Northern Ireland.

The professional: Jonathan Powell, Blair's chief of staff, who over time became a key figure in the British state in the affairs of Northern Ireland.

Bertie Ahern, Fianna Fail Taoiseach since 1997, with his *éminence grise*, Dr Martin Mansergh, later a Senator.

The critical relationship: Trimble talks to Tony Blair at Hillsborough, on the evening of Tuesday 7 April 1998 at the start of the final week of the talks.

The unionist opposition to Trimble.

The Establishment comes riding to Trimble's rescue: Viscount Cranborne campaigns on Derry's Walls for a 'yes' vote in the 1998 referendum along with the Ulster-born and bred Labour MP Kate Hoey.

'New Unionism' personified: David Trimble receives a makeover during the 1998 referendum campaign.

Three men in the same boat: Trimble, Blair and Hume during the 1998 referendum.

Sinn Fein *Ard Fheis*, Gerry Adams told the assembled republicans 'well done, David'.[6] Optimists took it as a sign of the emerging new politics; others saw it as a crude sectarian wind-up to increase the discomfiture of the unionist community, of which there was to be much more in the coming days. Trimble thought Adams' remark to be 'childish' since it was bound to be repeated by Paisley. 'It confirmed my opinion of him as not genuine, petty and limited intellectually' notes the UUP leader. 'McGuinness doesn't have the same obnoxious features.'[7]

At this critical juncture, Trimble chose to fulfil a long-standing engagement in the United States – he was speaking at the University of Chicago – rather than to maintain momentum in the referendum. Some saw it as further evidence of his chronic 'visititis', whereby he could not turn down the prospect of just about any foreign trip, but there was more to it than that. Trimble subscribed to the view expressed by Reg Empey that because the party was divided over the Agreement it was foolish to try and force each branch to campaign for it. Instead, Trimble decided that the way to avoid a split was to do as little as possible and to let the Government go out and win the referendum. 'The calculation was wrong, but it was rational,' says Trimble.[8] He obviously, therefore, did not regard his presence in Northern Ireland as essential at all times. No. 10 noticed Trimble's lacklustre campaigning, but wrongly put it down to Trimble's own ambiguities about the deal – that he was, as it were, 'conflicted' within himself. But they did accept his advice, contrary to Blair's own initial instincts, that it would be better if President Clinton did not come and campaign for a 'yes' vote (which some in the White House regarded as his 'victory lap').[9]

The same lack of urgency afflicted prominent colleagues: Ken Maginnis, who had gone on holiday in northern Cyprus immediately after the talks ended, returned for the UUC vote and then headed straight back to the Mediterranean.[10] And although substantial amounts of money came in from sources who had not contributed to the UUP in years – Jack Allen, the party treasurer, calculates that around £200,000 came in over a two-to three-month period in late spring and summer – senior officers were not in the first instance sure whether they wanted to spend much money on the referendum: according to Thomas Hennessey, who worked on the campaign in Glengall Street, they ultimately decided to hold back and, rather, to concentrate upon the Assembly elections.[11] By contrast, Trimble's anti-Agreement opponents were the antithesis of passivity –

even though they were comparatively underfunded and enjoyed far less access to the mass media. There were a number of reasons for the disparity between the quality of the two campaigns. Trimble believed that whereas the pro-Agreement unionists came to the campaign 'physically exhausted and strung out emotionally', the rejectionists had not been a party to the negotiations and thus came fresh to the referendum.[12] But it was also the case that many on the pro-Agreement side were uncomfortable with the moral compromises inherent in the deal, whatever their calculations of Realpolitik in its favour. Significantly, cross-border bodies and the constitutional questions, on which Trimble had negotiated relatively satisfactory settlements, hardly arose as major themes of the 'nos'. Their appeal was summarised by the logo and badge produced by the campaign – A Heart for Ulster, with a Union Jack-coloured heart – and rallies were held the length and breadth of the Province. By 19 April, a joint Belfast Telegraph/UTV poll showed the unionists to be profoundly fearful with 45% undecided.[13]

But anti-Agreement unionism was by no means a monolithic force. There was, obviously, the DUP; Robert McCartney's UKUP; and six out of ten Westminster MPs from Trimble's own party of whom four (Ross, Thompson, Martin Smyth and Roy Beggs) appeared on anti-Agreement platforms with other parties.[14] By far the most carefully calibrated position was that taken by Jeffrey Donaldson and associates; moreover, Trimble recognised it as such and it was the faction upon which he lavished most attention in order to bring them round to his way of thinking. Donaldson decided to pursue his own brand of 'constructive oppositionism' but away from the 'United Unionist' rallies.[15] He was not opposed to the principle of power-sharing and could live with some of the Strand II aspects of the deal. Rather, Donaldson feared that the Blair 'comfort letter' to Trimble of Friday 10 April on decommissioning was insufficient and that the process would therefore founder upon its ambiguity. The electorate was not, he observed, voting for the Blair letter, but for the Belfast Agreement itself.

By Easter Monday, Donaldson was already under huge pressure. Whilst at his London flat, he received a call from Blair, who had joined his family on holiday in Spain. 'Prime Minister, I'm surprised to hear from you,' teased Donaldson. 'MPs only normally hear from Prime Ministers on holiday if they're offering them a job.' 'Anything's possible,' retorted Blair. The Prime Minister wasted little time on pleasantries and came to the point: he wanted to meet with Donaldson and his colleagues upon his return to discover their objections. Donaldson told him that he wanted legislative safeguards to deal with the ambiguities over decommissioning. When Blair came over for his first visit during the referendum, he duly met with Donaldson, Brewster, Arlene Foster, Drew Nelson and John Hunter in Mowlam's offices at Parliament Buildings.[16] 'What would it take you to say "yes"?' asked Blair. Foster expressed her concerns about the inadequacy of funding for victims' groups: the next morning, an extra £5 million was injected. 'I thought, "this is a bit of a buy-off"', recalls Foster. Blair told her, 'It's very easy to say "no"'. Foster replied that on the contrary, it was very hard to go against party policy: indeed, this stance would cost her dearly in the forthcoming Assembly elections, when she was not selected as a candidate in Fermanagh/South Tyrone by her local association.[17]

There were further pressures from within his own party. Donaldson's constituency chairman, Donn McConnell, urged the local MP to tone down his opposition: McConnell believed that since the UUC had decided the matter, Donaldson had to accept their verdict. But Donaldson, who canvassed much of his local association, believed that he had majority support amongst Unionists in Lagan Valley as a whole. Donaldson's sentiments were also shared by his predecessor as MP for the seat, James Molyneaux. Molyneaux was struck by the way in which Trimble was given just fifteen minutes on the Good Friday afternoon to decide whether to accept the deal: he remembers how as a magistrate, he had always ruled that confessions made under duress were inadmissible (Trimble retorts that Molyneaux had fifteen years in which to make up his mind). Trimble privately sought to persuade Molyneaux not to speak out publicly and thus to break a lifetime of loyalty to the party line, and for much of the time it appeared that his former chief would confine himself to characteristically cryptic hints.[18] But towards the end of the campaign, Molyneaux finally decided to come off the fence.[19] Like Donaldson, Molyneaux did not appear himself on anti-Agreement platforms during the campaign. It relieved Trimble hugely: 'If Molyneaux had led an open campaign against me, I'd have been finished,' says Trimble. 'And especially in those early days of the referendum.'[20]

The 'antis' were soon to receive an enormous boost – but from the actions of Irish republicans rather than their own efforts. On the Good Friday, Adams had reserved his position until he could obtain approval from the Sinn Fein *Ard Fheis*. Trimble saw it as a holding operation by a man who knew that if he rejected the deal, his strategy would have been destroyed.[21] But despite the doubts of senior colleagues, Adams was able with great tactical adroitness to persuade the movement that they had 'ownership' of the process. Indeed, the manner in which Adams sought to obtain republican endorsement would cause Trimble great difficulties. Senior figures in the Irish state believed it to be 'touch and go' and they feared that the republicans would go with the deal in Northern Ireland but vote against it in the Republic – to the point that senior Irish officials fretted that they might be printing literature in the south against the abolition of Articles 2 and 3. In order to create a 'positive dynamic' as they saw it, the Irish calculated that they would have to release terrorist prisoners. These men would have the authority to push a reluctant movement into acceptance of the new institutions.[22] Accordingly, at the second Sinn Fein *Ard Fheis*, held in Dublin on 10 May 1998, 27 republicans held in jails on both sides of the border were given temporary parole to attend. They included members of the Balcombe Street gang (who had been transferred to Portlaoise jail, Co. Laois, from English prisons for a campaign of terrorism in London in the 1970s).[23] They were hailed by Adams as the 'Nelson Mandelas' of the republican struggle and received a foot-stomping, ten-minute ovation.[24] Adams and McGuinness duly received the support of 331 out of 350 delegates for constitutional change to allow them to participate in elected institutions on the island of Ireland – including, implicitly, a reformed Stormont.

But the effects of this triumphalism on Unionists were traumatic. 'We were knocked absolutely flat on our backs by the Balcombe Street episode. It reinforced my belief that they wanted the Agreement to fail, but wanted the Unionists to [walk out and] do it themselves.' Curiously, though, Trimble only really became aware of its effects on the day after when he went to speak to unionists in Armagh city and discovered from his own activists that some UUP members there were now scared even to ask people for support. Trimble was furious at being surprised in this way and says he was never consulted by the NIO with a view to preparing his members.[25] He was likewise angered by what he saw as the NIO response to the release of the loyalist killer Michael Stone to attend a similar UDP/UDA rally, which also horrified respectable unionist opinion: Trimble understood that one of the conditions of Stone's release was that he would go nowhere near the Ulster Hall gathering. He complained bitterly about the rally to John Holmes at No. 10, who told him that Blair had no knowledge about what would happen. The Prime Minister, too, was horrified by the 'insensitivity' of it and to Trimble it was – once again – evidence of how little power a Prime Minister can sometimes have, even in a very centralised government.[26] As so often, he placed the best possible construction upon Blair's motives. Trimble now reckons that but for the 'Balcombe Street fiasco' he would have obtained 70% of the unionist vote in the referendum rather than 55%. Trimble's estimate of 55% is probably on the high side, but he was undoubtedly right about the disastrous effect of the Sinn Fein and loyalist rallies. 'It is of much greater significance that those voting against the Agreement were much more likely than yes voters to have been affected by the temporary release of IRA and loyalist prisoners to attend the respective party conferences' noted the UMS exit survey. 'This clearly indicates that these events were of great significance in persuading many to oppose the Agreement.'[27]

By the time that Blair arrived in Northern Ireland for his second visit of the referendum on 14 May, the unionist 'yes' campaign was seriously traumatised. Trimble had launched a *Say Yes For the Union* campaign on the previous day, with a glossy leaflet showing both himself and John Taylor standing in front of Stormont, but he derived little momentum from it (Trimble was always convinced that Taylor's support was crucially important: the latter subsequently made a personal appeal in a UUP advertisement in the *Belfast Telegraph* which showed him in his hospital bed after he had been shot in the face by the Official IRA in 1972).[28] Blair's response to the eroding unionist support for the Agreement was the Balmoral address of 14 May. In this speech, he declared that before republicans could hold office, or even benefit from prisoner releases, they would have to fulfil four conditions: first, a clear commitment to an end to violence for good and that the 'so-called "war" is finished, done with, gone'; second, that the ceasefires had to be complete and unequivocal, including punishment beatings and a dismantling of para-military structures; the third requirement was full cooperation with the Decommissioning Body; and the fourth was that no other groups were to be used deliberately as 'proxies for violence'.[29] The speech was greeted with polite applause, but as Trimble points out it had little immediate impact upon public opinion. A joint UTV-*Belfast Telegraph* poll published on 19 May found the unionist community split almost down the middle, with 34% intending to vote in favour, 32% against, and 31% still undecided.[30]

The Trimble camp, though, still had a few cards to play. What they needed was not so much the great and the good as figures of unimpeachably pro-Union credentials with a bit of *élan*. It occurred to Sean O'Callaghan and Ruth Dudley Edwards that the figures whose public profile most closely matched those requirements came from both sides of the political divide: Viscount Cranborne, then leader of the Conservative Opposition in the Lords, and Kate Hoey. Both Dudley Edwards and O'Callaghan mentioned it to Trimble who duly gave the go-ahead. Cranborne assented, but was keen to make two things clear: first, his profoundly sceptical view of the 'peace process', which he always regarded as doomed; second, the conditions which he would stipulate in exchange for participation in the referendum. The game as he saw it was to make sure that those who were responsible for any failure would 'carry the can'. Thus, if Unionists said 'no' they would not win the referendum *and* they would be scapegoated. 'The nature of the beast is to play the shot late,' says Cranborne. 'What David Trimble had to do from the beginning was to ensure that the spirit and the letter of the Agreement were observed by the Government and that they were held to it endlessly. And Blair was so desperate for a "yes" vote by this stage that he would give undertakings in writing which would help to build up the case that the Unionists had gone even further than was wise for the sake of peace. David Trimble said that he would agree with that in principle but he was only persuaded to say so very reluctantly. He was very reluctant to do so because he wanted to hold their feet to the fire and wanted to preserve his own "wriggle room".'[31] Cranborne was referring here to the Prime Minister's subsequent handwritten pledges. Cranborne and Hoey duly did a photoshoot with Trimble atop Derry's Walls; Cranborne emphasised that he was one of '27 heroes' who had voted in the Commons against the Anglo-Irish Agreement of 1985;[32] Trimble was certainly satisfied with the day's work: 'The Cranborne–Hoey visit was absolutely critical in getting the Ulster Unionist "yes" campaign off the deck. They may not have been universally known amongst the masses, but they were very important from the viewpoint of the Unionist political classes. This filtered down to the grassroots. And having Cranborne and Hoey was much better than having John Major campaign.'[33]

Trimble then returned to Belfast on the evening of 19 May for the unlikeliest event of the campaign. Tim Attwood, brother of the west Belfast SDLP politician Alex Attwood, knew Bono of U2 and suggested that he appear alongside Hume to drum up support for the deal.[34] But Bono – whose father was an Irish Labour-supporting Catholic trade unionist from Dublin's north side and whose mother was Church of Ireland – had an instinctive feeling for how difficult the political situation was. He believed that the Unionists were feeling estranged from the fanfare of the peace process and that people in the south had more sympathy for them than they realised – and he wanted them to know it. 'John, I don't feel that our value here is to reinforce you with the national-ist community,' Bono recalls telling Hume. 'It's to reinforce Trimble with the Unionist community. If you can put something together, we'll be happy to inter-face.' After much to-ing and fro-ing, Attwood came back with the news that the Trimble camp would participate in some such event, which was to take place on 19 May. Bono asked to see both men in Belfast's Waterfront Hall beforehand. 'You've go to listen to me now,' Bono told the leaders of constitutional unionism and nationalism. 'You're going on stage at a rock and roll concert and neither of you have ever done anything like this before.' Trimble, says Bono, looked as though he was about to say 'what on earth is he about to ask us to do?' 'You're not going to have to say one word,' Bono told them. The two politicians looked at each other. 'Look, this is a picture,' said the singer. 'People don't trust your words . . . This is a rock and roll audience and I'm going to do something never done before at a rock and roll concert – I'm going to ask for a minute's silence. I don't know if we're going to get anywhere with this.' Bono cannot remember who it was who suggested that Trimble and Hume take off their jackets, but he does recall choreographing the entry of the two, one from the left, the other from the right. By the end of this discussion on stage management, neither of the leaders had said a word, nor looked at each other. 'I've got to go and tune a few guitars and you two have a lot to talk about,' said the founder of U2. In fact, he did not have to do anything of the kind, but had been struck by the lack of communication between them.[35] Kate Hoey, who had accompanied Trimble from Coleraine, noted in her diary for that day: 'We waited at the side of the stage for David to walk on with John Hume. DT was looking ill at ease and quite nervous as we listened to the screams of the hundreds of teenagers and the ear-piercing music. This was more nerve-wracking for him than anything else he had done so far on the campaign. The handshake was very stage-managed, but at the same time quite moving as the two stood on either side of Bono.' In fact, once it became clear that nobody would have to say anything – especially Hume, Trimble recalls, teasingly – he relaxed.[36] Above all, he knew that because 'a picture says a thousand words', the 'nos' would be kept off the front pages for several days, and so it proved.[37]

Still, the polls did not look good for Trimble. On Monday 18 May 1998, private government surveys had showed a 56% yes vote – a near disaster. Again, Blair sought to address unionist concerns in a speech at the University of Ulster at Coleraine on 20 May, with Kate Hoey joining his entourage for the occasion: for some time she had made suggestions via the Prime Minister's chief of staff, Jonathan Powell, about how Blair might appeal to the pro-Union community (on the Prime Ministerial aircraft on the way back to London, Alastair Campbell had asked her, 'Why do the Unionists hate us?' She explained that it was because Labour until comparatively recently had a very nationalist policy on Northern Ireland and refused to let people from the Province join the party).[38] Once again, Trimble played his reluctant part: Anji Hunter, Blair's aide, spotted Trimble's shyness and urged Hoey 'make sure David keeps up with the Prime Minister', and Hoey duly thrust the UUP leader into the picture with Blair.[39] The audience at Coleraine included church leaders and members of the Orange Order. He offered five simple pledges: no change in the status of Northern Ireland without the expressed consent of the people of the Province; power to take decisions returned to the Northern Ireland Assembly, with accountable North-South cooperation; fairness and equality guaranteed for all; those who use or threaten violence to be excluded from the government of Northern Ireland; prisoners kept in unless violence is given up for good.[40] The presentation of these pledges was the subject of much debate between No. 10 and some in the NIO. But according to Alastair Campbell, the last paragraph of the pledges – the hardest of all to phrase – was penned by John Holmes.[41] Some of the NIO feared that the handwritten pledges of the Prime Minister would come back to haunt Blair, but they undoubtedly had an effect – to the point that Mitchel McLaughlin, the Sinn Fein chairman, complained about the 'lovebombing of Unionists'. 'It is almost as if Unionists' votes are more important than republican or nationalist votes,' he added. But he conceded that Blair had stopped short of rewriting the terms of the Agreement.[42]

Blair was not yet done with his messages to the people of Northern Ireland. On the morning of 22 May 1998, he wrote in both the *Irish News* and the *News Letter* that 'representatives of parties intimately linked to paramilitary groups can only be in a future Northern Ireland government if it is clear that there will be no more violence and the threat of violence has gone. That doesn't just mean decommissioning but all bombings, killings, beatings and an end to targeting, recruiting, and all the structures of terrorism': this was a more watertight commitment than the better-known handwritten pledges of earlier in the week. The 81% turnout was the highest in Northern Ireland since the foundation of the state in 1921: 676,966 (71.1%) voted in favour, with 274,879 (28.9%) against. In the Republic, 1,442,553 voted in favour of the deal and constitutional change – 94.4% on a 56% turnout. A Coopers and Lybrand survey for *The Sunday Times* calculated that 96% of Northern Ireland's Catholics backed the deal, but only 55% of Protestants (the result was so narrow on the unionist side that many opponents of the Agreement believe that they actually won a majority of the Ulster-British population). Significantly, 95% of eligible nationalists voted, whereas only 70% of eligible unionists voted: the most abstentions were in Protestant areas, such as North Down and East Antrim (and, unlike in mainland Britain, abstentionism tended to afflict affluent as much as impoverished areas).[43] This belief that politics was pointless went very deep in elements of the majority community, and altering this perception would prove to be a key test of the success or failure of the 'Trimble project'. Polling suggested that Ian Paisley's North Antrim was the only seat to oppose the deal, with Jeffrey Donaldson's Lagan Valley backing it by a mere 52%.[44]

No sooner was the referendum won than Trimble had to turn his attention to the Assembly elections on 25 June 1998. Curiously, there was some speculation about whether he would stand for the devolved body.[45] Trimble, in fact, never had a serious choice about whether to run, but what the ambiguity did point up was the fact that if a gun was held to his head and he was forced to choose between remaining a member of Stormont or the Commons he would undoubtedly plump for Westminster.[46] It was one of many apparent contradictions of his political personality: the long-time devolutionist who was most at home in what Unionists of an older generation would refer to as 'the Imperial Parliament'. Some regarded this sub-Cincinnatan display of indifference to the baubles of office as somewhat bogus – an 'if the people want me, who am I to refuse?' routine. But as his old friend Herb Wallace observes, such was Trimble's boredom with the day-to-day administration that it would not be surprising if he genuinely thought twice before plunging in.[47] For he already was enjoying the 'fun' side of the job with visits to No. 10 and the White House and could continue to do so as UUP leader. Indeed, of the four main party chieftains – himself, Adams, Hume and Paisley – Trimble would be the only one to opt to hold office in the new institutions. In order to stand for the Assembly, Trimble required a special dispensation from the party officers from rule 21 of the 1989 constitution of the UUC which denied elected Unionist representatives a 'dual man-date' – that is, sitting in more than one legislature.[48] Both Trimble and John Taylor duly received it: Trimble wanted somone with government experience at his side, but emphasised that it would be a one-off.[49] Far thornier, though, was the question of whether Jeffrey Donaldson and the 'soft no' dissenters would be allowed to stand ('hard noes' like Ross wanted nothing at all to do with the new institutions). At a private meeting at Rogan's house in south Belfast on the Sunday after the refer-endum – attended by Trimble, Empey, Rogan, Nicholson and Maginnis – it was decided that only Trimble and Taylor would be granted the dispensation to allow them to stand for the Assembly elections. The effect of this ruling was to prevent the MP for Lagan Valley running for the Assembly.[50] Ruth Dudley Edwards, a long-time admirer of Donaldson, sought to intercede on his behalf with Trimble, who was more inclined to seek to bring the 'soft noes' back into the fold than the others. If they had no stake in the Assembly, she argued, the Donaldsonistas would be far more troublesome than if included. But Maginnis, in particular, was militantly opposed to rewarding Donaldson for what he considered to be 'treachery'. Had Dudley Edwards won out, the history of the coming years might have been very different.

But candidate selection was not the only problem which beset Trimble in this period. Comparatively few people were present on a regular basis at headquarters during the Assembly campaign – exemplified by Jim Wilson, the party's chief executive, who was fighting in his home seat of South Antrim. The UUP organisation as a whole was in a parlous state – partly because of long-term decline, partly because of short-term prob-lems relating to the internal splits over the Agreement. These kinds of problems were also very apparent to Mark Fullbrook, a high-flying Con-servative agent who left the Tories after 1992 to form his own consultancy called Parliamentary Liaison Services, and was employed by the UUP from early 1998 to revamp the party's organisation and especially to train a new generation of election agents. He soon discovered that autonomy of local associations was such that not all accepted the centrally produced literature for the Assembly campaign, further ensuring that there was no uniform message throughout the Province.[51] But the UUP problems were not just organisational, massive though they were: as Bertie Ahern was once heard to observe, he had never been asked to stretch his constituency in the way that Trimble was asked to do to his own folk.[52]

Trimble was also asked to stretch himself in unexpected ways. He had long been gloriously indifferent to his own appearance, especially by the telegenic standards of the Blair era.[53] Accordingly, at the behest of Ken Maginnis, Trimble acquired a personal assistant for the duration of the campaign – Jane Wells, then chairman of the Institute of Public Relations for Northern Ireland and managing director of John Laird Public Relations. 'Could we not smarten him up a bit?' asked Maginnis. Wells responded in the affirmative. The first thing which Maginnis was determined to persuade her to do was to prise his omnipresent mobile telephone out of his hands, which he observed was not very voter-friendly and gave an image that he was more interested in the important caller down the line rather than engaging directly with voters. She had some success – though the minute they were back in his car, he would snatch the device back. Harder still were clothes. 'They were not on top of his agenda and we had only four weeks,' recalls Wells. 'I could, therefore, only iron out the most obvious wrinkles.' She knew that she could not persuade him to go shopping, so she rang Daphne Trimble and asked for his sizes: she specifically requested 'easy-to-iron' shirts. Armed with this knowledge, she went to Parsons and Parsons, a respectable outfitter close to Glengall Street. She would run back and forth persuading Trimble to try on different suits – always plain, since exotic colours could make suits look psychedelic on television – but he never complained. Nor, indeed, did he ever inquire where they came from: John Laird put them on his account, but Trimble assumed that they appeared as if by magic. Wells, fearing the classic shot of candidates on the stump panning from the feet upwards, also worried about his shoes: his favourite pair were in terrible condition, with the laces frequently undone. She duly took him to Reid's on Sandy Row, and also persuaded him to go to the barber's in Clarendon Street, where he had a short back and sides for the campaign:

as he emerged, Trimble's RUC protection unit quietly gave her the thumbs-up. But even after this whole exercise, Trimble did not automatically insert such considerations into his thinking: shortly after the Omagh bombing that August, Trimble was about to do a couple of major UTV and ITV interviews, but found he had no suitable clothes and no make-up. Wells duly bought some Max-Factor translucent cream puff which would smooth down his reddish complexion.[54]

In such circumstances, it is perhaps amazing that the UUP did as well as it did. No. 10 certainly thought Trimble was on the defensive throughout much of the campaign and that he did not really go out and make the case for the future of Northern Ireland. Trimble's problem on this occasion, though, was not passivity but rather his focus. He seemed to feel as though the constitutional matters had been settled and therefore he could quite happily concentrate upon 'real' issues such as hospitals and schools. He recalls attending a fraught meeting at Cookstown during the referendum campaign, when a little old woman piped up at the front: 'Will the decision on South Tyrone hospital be made by someone that we vote for?' 'Yes,' replied Trimble. 'That's okay,' she said.[55] Trimble believed that with normal politics returning, the UUP would not – could not – win less than 30 seats, at bottom, in the new 108-member Assembly (some forecast around 33, perhaps even more).[56] But he underestimated the sharp DUP and UKUP campaigns, which tapped into the residual unionist fears about prisoners, policing and decommissioning. The DUP knew that it enjoyed the support of militant oppositionists: what it needed was to expand its constituency, which it accomplished by repositioning itself as the guarantor of Blair's referendum pledges ('Vote DUP – It's Your Only Guarantee'). Nor was Paisley the centrepiece of the election broadcasts.[57]

Such was the success of this campaign in keeping the issue of prisoner releases on the boil that the UUP was forced to respond in its voting in the House of Commons. For in the middle of the campaign, the Sentences Bill – giving legal effect to the early release scheme under the Agreement – was making its way through Parliament. Trimble had appointed Donaldson as his point-man on the Bill as a sort of compensation for not receiving dispensation to run for the Assembly elections.[58] But this arrangement did not work tremendously well. First, the two men differed in their respective degrees of willingness to link up with the Tories in opposing certain provisions. Second, although Trimble wanted to obtain a greater degree of linkage between decommissioning and prisoner releases in the legislation, as outlined in the Prime Minister's referendum pledges, he was only prepared to pay a distinctly limited price with Blair in prosecuting his case. Donaldson, by contrast, felt no such inhibitions, as was illustrated by his speech of 17 June at Committee stage.[59] Even in the midst of a very tough election campaign, Trimble remained very understanding of Blair's predicament, whereby the Prime Minister found himself caught between trying to sustain the pro-Agreement Unionists in a tough Assembly campaign on the one side and the Irish, prodded by Sinn Fein and the SDLP, on the other side.

When the Sentences Bill was published on 7 June 1998, Trimble declared that it contained the substance of the Prime Minister's four Balmoral pledges of 14 May 1998 – that those parties which wished to be in government and to benefit from release schemes would have to show their commitment to democratic, non-violent means. Certainly, he believed that there could be some tightening of the legislation to ensure that all those paramilitary parties which were cooperating with the international body on disarmament could enjoy the fruits of the statutory scheme, but had no fundamental objections to the release, *per se*, as part of an overall package.[60] In fact, as Whitehall sources told Frank Millar years later, prisoners could only have their licences revoked on an *individual* basis in the light of evidence from the police about activities in breach of their release terms. However, short of an end to the IRA ceasefire after the fashion of 9 February 1996, there was no *collective* sanction.[61] But as Trimble went into the division lobbies after the debate on the second reading on 10 June 1998, he found himself alone amongst his colleagues. John Taylor was acting as teller for the 'noes' after failing to obtain assurances from the security minister, Adam Ingram, that actual decommissioning would be required before releases, whilst Ken Maginnis (the other pro-Agreement UUP MP present) abstained. Trimble duly trooped into the 'no' lobby alongside his anti-Agreement colleagues – which at second reading stage meant a clear vote against the principle of the legislation (Trimble says that he intended to vote 'no' all along, and simply did not wish to make a great fuss about it in his speech, since voting counted for little in this Parliament).[62] The confusion did not end there: both the UUP leader and the Tories sought to bring in separate amendments to tighten the legislation. Moreover, as Frank Millar observed, it reinforced the fears of nationalists that he could not deliver his own troops.[63] It was no surprise that under such circumstances, an *Irish Times* poll showed that support for the UUP had fallen from 33% to 27%: typically, on the day it was published, Trimble was keen to put forward UUP proposals about a radical restructuring of administration and quangos for Northern Ireland.[64]

The election campaign was the toughest in living memory – especially in Upper Bann, where Denis Watson, County Grand Master of Armagh, was running as an independent Unionist. John Dobson, Trimble's first election agent, says that the reproaches on the doorsteps came mainly from RUC wives who were enraged about prisoner releases.[65] But the hostility was not solely verbal: anti-Agreement elements smashed the bullet-proof windows of Trimble's Lurgan office and Councillor Arnold Hatch's van was sprayed with paint.[66] Considering such pressures, it could be argued that the results were encouraging for the new dispensation as a whole: the vote for pro-Agreement parties was 75% (up from 71% in the referendum) and the anti-Agreement parties gained only 28 of the 108 seats (as opposed to 30 for the UUP and the PUP-UVF combined). This meant that the 'noes' were two votes short of the crucial 30-seat mark which could deprive pro-Agreement unionists of the necessary level of consensus to push through measures under the rules of the Assembly. But on another level, things were much gloomier – not least because with such thin margins, the smallest number of defectors could hold Trimble and the process to ransom. The SDLP overhauled the UUP as the party with the largest number of first preferences – 177,963 (22%) as compared to Trimble's 172,963 (21.3%). This represented a fall of 2.9% from the 1996 Forum elections; the DUP vote declined slightly, but it obtained 18.1% of the vote, along with 4.5% for McCartney and 2.9% for independent Unionists. Sinn Fein recorded its 5th increase since 1993, and its best result ever, with 17.6% (this was 2.1% higher than in 1996, and further narrowed the gap with the SDLP. As Sydney Elliott notes, whereas the nationalist vote split 70%–30% in favour of the SDLP in 1992, it was now 55%–45%). The allocation of seats under the quota system yielded 28 seats for the UUP, 24 for the SDLP, 20 for the DUP, 18 for Sinn Fein, 6 for the Alliance Party, 5 for the UKUP, 3 for the independent anti-Agreement unionists, 2 for the PUP, and 2 for the Women's Coalition (the UDP obtained no seats – a failure which would have destabilising consequences for the Agreement.)[67] The detailed results made for very mixed reading – prompting loyalists to shout at him

'Clinton and Bono can't save you now.'[68] On the one hand, Trimble topped the poll in Upper Bann with 12,338 first preferences – the highest number of any unionist in the Province, including Paisley. But whilst Trimble could claim a sort of personal vindication, his coat tails were not very long: only one of his running mates, George Savage, was elected on the 14th count with a mere 669 first preferences. Indeed, as a bloc, the pro-Agreement Unionists barely outpolled an assortment of antis in the seat. Thus, the Trimbleistas secured 14,559 to the noes' 14,279. Victor Gordon of the *Portadown Times* believes that whilst gains were made, notably amongst elements of the Alliance-voting Protestant middle classes who were previously disillusioned by Trimble's stance over Drumcree, these were outweighed by losses amongst the loyalist family, especially in Portadown.[69] This reaction in large part accounts for the 4855 first preferences given to Denis Watson. Trimble's constituency office secretary, Stephanie Roderick, reports that although Alliance and a few SDLP voters did give her chief second preferences, there was no large-scale cross-community voting, even in the heady days after the Belfast Agreement was signed.[70] The contrast with Paisley's performance was obvious: the DUP leader handily carried two running mates to victory in North Antrim, including Ian, Jr (this may also owe something to the DUP's superior management of its core vote, ensuring that first preferences were better spread around). The psychological balance, which had been narrowly in the pro-Agreement direction up till then, was now narrowly in the anti-Agreement direction.[71] Indeed, Gerry Adams – who was at Belfast City Hall for the count on the day after the poll – was under no illusion as to what the emerging results meant for Trimble and told Frank Millar that it would thereafter be 'trench warfare all the way' for the new institutions.[72]

Why was this? Sam Lutton, a long-time UUP activist in Lurgan, believes that there was a number of factors at play here: 'First, you had Tony Blair causing a lot of problems [the unkept referendum pledges] and David Trimble got the blame for it. If you go round and ask people do they trust Blair, 80% would say no. Also, David Trimble had spent most of his time at Westminster and had not put time into the constituency. A lot of people still resented him living in Lisburn and not in the constituency.'[73] There were other reasons, too. According to Sydney Elliott, the UUP was also harmed by its 'no dual mandate' rule: this meant that the DUP, Sinn Fein and the SDLP all ran a far higher number of their best-known personalities, which pushed up their vote. But under PR systems, with multiple candidates from a single party, the name is especially important, more so than under the first-past-the-post Westminster model. Elliott says that in consequence, the UUP performed most disappointingly in areas such as Lagan Valley, where Jeffrey Donaldson was prevented from running because of the 'no dual mandate' rule.[74] Curiously, these disappointing election results vindicated Trimble's long-time analysis about the increasingly 'depoliticised' nature of segments of the majority community, especially in the east of the Province: the turn-outs were higher in nationalist-republican terrain than in unionist areas. Thus, North Down recorded a 60.17% poll, East Antrim 60.87% and Strangford 61.59% – compared to 77.27% in Newry-Armagh, 73.72% in South Down and 70.47 in West Belfast (the highest of the Belfast seats).[75] But if Trimble had diagnosed the illness correctly, he had not yet found the cure for such demoralisation. Notwithstanding the return of local self-government, his problem was that the Unionist 'victories' under the Agreement were in complex areas which few properly understood, such as the details of cross-border institutions and constitutional law; by contrast, their 'defeats' on such issues as prisoners were all too comprehensible.

The most obvious effects of the election results were felt in terms of the establishment of new institutions. Prior to June 1998, the SDLP and the two Governments interpreted the Agreement as requiring the rapid creation of a 'shadow executive' in July 1998, including Sinn Fein shadow ministers, prior to the full devolution of powers. Only once the full shadow executive was in place could the cross-border dimension be negotiated. The consensus was, therefore, that once Unionists had shown themselves to be 'serious' about the creation of an 'inclusive' polity and society, any excuse for republicans to retain an option on armed struggle would vanish. But the UUP leader's desperately narrow margins meant that he was better able to insist that any transition period would now have to take place in a manner and at a pace much closer to his own needs; deadline after deadline was missed. This meant that he would not allow the d'Hondt formula to be run, thus identifying Sinn Fein ministers even in 'shadow' form, until republicans proved their democratic bona fides over a much longer period (the longer time frame also allowed the unionist population to adjust to the new dispensation, or so many Trimbleistas believed). Trimble's timetable thus ran as follows: the week after the Assembly election, the new body would meet to appoint the First and Deputy First Ministers-designate (that is, Trimble, who as leader of the largest party in the Assembly was entitled to the post, and an SDLP colleague). Ministerial portfolios would not be allocated until the number of government departments was reviewed. Only after that, in November/December, would the shadow executive be set up (if then). In the meantime, the First and the Deputy First Minister would represent the new system in the initial phase of that transition. This meant that the UUP and SDLP would negotiate the number of cross-border implementation bodies alone – a set-up which suited the former more than the latter.[76]

But who would be the Deputy First Minister? After taking soundings at a caucus meeting at the Wellington Park Hotel in south Belfast on the first day of the Assembly, Hume decided to stand aside for his deputy, Seamus Mallon, who for much of the time had led the SDLP on a day-to-day basis at the talks. Unionists, including Trimble, were divided on the subject. On the one hand, he told Frank Millar at the time that he feared that the elevation of a deputy who might have to refer back constantly to Hume would detract from the stature of the Executive (in that Hume was the better known of the two).[77] On the other hand, he believed that Mallon took a more sceptical view of the republicans than his chief, and that he had a better feeling for Protestant sensibilities (he lived in majority-unionist Markethill, Co. Armagh). Indeed, on the basis of his experiences in the last days of the talks, Trimble felt that 'when the chips were down, the SDLP preferred to deal with us than with Sinn Fein'. But it was by no means the last turn of the wheel in this relationship, in which there would be many more ups and downs and by early 1999 relations had begun seriously to decline. 'When we got into the period of the shadow Executive in 1998–9, Mallon's approach was not in line with what we expected. He positioned himself close to Sinn Fein and no gaps opened up [between them] so that he couldn't be accused of selling out the nationalist interests and on the RUC wanted to show that he was a tougher nut than Sinn Fein.'[78] Trimble, for his part, found Mallon frequently moody – describing him when exasperated as a 'nasty man'.[79] So poor were relations that even when Mallon made a move in Trimble's direction – notably his offer at the SDLP conference on 13 November 1998 to vote for the exclusion of Sinn Fein from government if republicans had not decommissioned by the time of the 22 May 2000 two-year deadline for implementing the Belfast Agreement – the UUP leader remained unimpressed.[80] He thought it too vague and unrealistic, much to the relief of some nationalists, who feared that Trimble might take it up and run with it. But Mallon did not mince his words either. 'Seamus finds David Trimble hard to understand,' observes Sean Farren. 'There is no warmth on a personal basis. Seamus sees him as an amateur playing cards, not as a serious poker player, as indecisive – witness the whole transition period from June 1998, which took till December of that year to resolve.'[81] But one who observed them together said that whilst on one level they were 'chalk and cheese', on another level they were very similar: both men like to be right and both can become very angry indeed. Only intermittently – most obviously at the time of Drumcree IV – did this partnership become the driving force of the new dispensation.[82]

The first meeting of the new Assembly took place at Castle Buildings on 1 July 1998: it only returned to the refurbished Parliament Buildings that September, much as the first meeting of the old Northern Ireland Parliament in 1921 took place in the Council Chamber at Belfast City Hall. On this occasion, though, there was no Sovereign to open the legislature; nor were they even graced by the presence of the Prince of Wales, as occurred in 1932 when the future Edward VIII inaugurated the buildings (indeed, it was noticeable that the Queen opened both the new Scottish Parliament and the new Welsh Assembly upon the devolution of powers to those bodies in 1999, though she did eventually visit Stormont in 2002).[83] Moreover, the insignia of the new Assembly were carefully shorn of any signs of Britishness. Subsequently, it adopted a neutral pattern depicting the flax flower, as a reminder of the history and importance of the linen industry (though the Speaker of the Assembly did write to Garter King of Arms confirming the flax flower as the body's official emblem, and also to the Secretary of State to request that the motif be submitted to the Queen for her approval).[84] It was not, perhaps, the most auspicious of motifs: the dramatic decline of flax-growing and the linen industry exemplified the economic travails of the Province for much of the 20th century.[85] Nor does the First Minister of Northern Ireland write to the Queen when he or she resigns, as Trimble's Scottish counterpart is obliged to do. Rather, as in Wales, he would have to write to the presiding officer of the Assembly. Trimble had little time for those who complained about this symbolic no-man's-land. Partly, he believed that those who alighted upon the removal of such emblems 'were looking for excuses to oppose change'. But it was also because he believed that he had won a great victory in securing nationalist and republican participation in what for practical purposes were British institutions. By comparison, the symbolic issues were small beer. 'I'm an equity lawyer,' he observes. 'I prefer substance to form.'[86]

Trimble was feeling far from elated as he arrived at Stormont. 'How do you feel on this historic day?' asked the Channel 4 crew making a documentary about his life. 'Fed up with hearing it's a historic day,' replied Trimble. 'There are lots of important days.' Trimble and Mallon were duly elected to their respective positions on 1 July 1998 by 61 votes to 27 – a majority of each community, though Sinn Fein abstained. He also directed some of his most pointed remarks at the republicans. Recalling Edgar Graham, he observed: 'A number of Members who are here today have done terrible things. I do not need to elaborate, though I should say the people concerned are not all in one corner of the Chamber ... We are not saying, and we have never said that the fact that someone has a certain past means that he cannot have a future. We have always acknowledged that it is possible for people to change. That is fundamental to one's view of society.'[87] Trimble also sought consciously to echo the words (wrongly) attributed to his hero, Sir James Craig, the first Prime Minister of Northern Ireland from 1921–40, who was widely supposed to have spoken of a 'Protestant Parliament for a Protestant People'.[88] Trimble, though, spoke of a 'pluralist Parliament for a pluralist people'. But his aide, David Campbell, did make sure to obtain what was thought to be Craig's old desk from the bowels of Parliament Buildings.

Despite his new position and his grand rhetoric, Trimble enjoyed few of the trappings of office. When both he and Denis Rogan arrived in his temporary quarters at Castle Buildings, the two men found that nothing was ready for them, and even the telephones were not working.[89] Only in September was the First Minister-designate able to assemble the full-time staff which he wanted. The model which Trimble used was that of 10 Downing Street: if Blair had his Chief of Staff and Press Secretary, so would he. Accordingly, he appointed David Campbell to the 'Jonathan Powell' slot. Campbell was a farmer with excellent Orange credentials, who was director of the Somme Heritage Centre. He had served on the talks team (where he opposed the Agreement) but stayed loyal to Trimble. Because of his often doleful countenance, he was nicknamed 'the under-taker'. His face could appear impassive, but Trimble believed it concealed an excellent sense of humour.[90] For the 'Alastair Campbell' slot, Trimble retained David Kerr, who had gradually carved out that role for himself during the latter part of the talks. But Trimble took no less care over his non-political appointees. As Principal Private Secretary, he specifically chose David Lavery, a highly capable official, whose parent department was the Courts Service. Lavery was a qualified barrister and a graduate of Harvard Law School, who had written the definitive textbook on *Road Traffic Law in Northern Ireland* before serving as Private Secretary to the then Lord Chief Justice of Northern Ireland, Sir Brian Hutton; he had come to Trimble's attention during a period of secondment to the talks, when he dared to disagree with Quentin Thomas. So heavily did this instance of insubordination count in his favour that Trimble fought bureaucratic resistance to Lavery's appointment by going directly to No. 10 Downing Street. As Private Secretary, Trimble chose Maura Quinn from the nationalist stronghold of Coalisland, Co. Tyrone, who had previously worked for Sir David Fell, the then head of the NICS. Above all, Trimble now had one priceless asset: his Assembly group. For here was the makings of a new Unionist political class. They were dependent upon the institutions which he had created and were then paid £29,500 plus a secretarial allowance of £15,000. Moreover, they were dependent upon him for patronage in a more day-to-day sense as well – in a way that the Westminster party or even the UUP Executive and Ulster Unionist Council were not. These patronage levers included his right as nominating officer to appoint ministers and to elevate Assemblymen to the chairmanships and deputy chairmanships of their preferred committees.

Such considerations seemed like quaint high politics as the Province geared up for Drumcree IV.[91] On 29 June, the Parades Commission banned the march from the Garvaghy Road, scheduled for Sunday 5 July. Trimble was shocked: he had assumed after the 1997 march had gone ahead and the reaction on the ground was relatively muted compared to 1996, that the 1998 parade would be less problematic.[92] The Orange Order stated that it would stay at Drumcree for so long as it took to ensure that the march went down the road.[93] But much as he hoped for a satisfactory resolution of the dispute, Trimble decided on the advice of his RUC detail not to go down to Drumcree in this year: a group of around 20 loyalists were planning to attack him.[94] Indeed, the only respite which he enjoyed during the Drumcree crisis came during the deliberations on what would become the Northern Ireland Act 1998: senior British officials were astonished at his 'extraordinary good humour' and ability, even at the height of this emerging disaster on 11 July, to focus upon both major and minor points of law. At one stage, the First Minister-designate did not hesitate to point out that as a former clerk in the Land Registry, he was particularly well-qualified to pronounce on the redundant features of the land purchase annuities scheme in the soon-to-be-scrapped 1920 Government of Ireland Act.[95]

Trimble thought that the Parades Commission's decision had the capacity to doom his leadership. According to No. 10, he made 'pretty apocalyptic noises about how hundreds of thousands of Orangemen would descend on Drumcree and how he couldn't answer for the consequences' – which, in the light of what had happened in the three previous years, was not altogether fanciful. Yet on this occasion his needs were not necessarily uppermost in the minds of the British. Blair was not prepared to exert pressure to reverse the ban on the march 'in the national interest', as had occurred with the preliminary determination at the start of the referendum campaign.[96] No. 10 feared the prospect of a pan-nationalist withdrawal from the Assembly even more – as the SDLP had done with the Forum after Drumcree II in 1996.[97] There were other reasons, too, for this. First, there was a 1997 Labour manifesto commitment to 'reduce tensions over parades'. Therefore, at some level, the commission was 'their baby'. Second, Trimble says that John Holmes told him that Alistair Graham's reaction to No. 10's request to delay announcement of the preliminary decision of the commission at the start of the referendum campaign, for tactical reasons, had been so 'nuclear' that they were almost afraid to speak to him.[98] Blair was more concerned about the impact upon Anglo-Irish relations, not to mention relations with the United States.[99]

Nationalists need not have worried. Flanagan and Lt Gen. Sir Rupert Smith, the GOC, were operating in a new dispensation and had three previous 'sieges' to hone their methods. On the day that the march should have taken place, burning barricades closed roads across the Province and up to 7000 Orangemen were present at Drumcree. By 8 July, police reports indicated that there had been 400 attacks on the security forces.[100] Last-minute appeals by both Trimble and Mallon to the Portadown District and to the Garvaghy Road Residents, respectively, failed; the Deputy First Minister-designate was barracked.[101] 'There was no prospect of the Orange Order walking away and the Parades Commission wouldn't change,' recalls Trimble. 'The Republicans were happy to see the Orange

Order facing the Army. If we woke up on the morning of 12 July and in the middle of the night a soldier had killed some respectable solid citizens – elderly Orangemen – I don't know what would have happened. We were in the lap of the Gods' (in fact, at least two people were seriously injured by plastic baton rounds at Drumcree).[102] As he sat in his bleak temporary offices at Castle Buildings on Saturday 11 July, matters looked desperate. The First Minister-designate was a powerless figure waiting upon events. He had no power over the loyal orders, over policing and scant influence over the British Government: the 'democratic deficit', which he sought so keenly to close, looked wider than ever.

As so often during the peace process, Trimble was then rescued by an unexpected tragedy. At 4:30 a.m. on Sunday 12 July, three young brothers – Richard, Mark and Jason Quinn – died in an arson attack in Ballymoney, Co. Antrim. Trimble was very upset when he took the call informing him of the news. Mallon and Trimble then issued a joint appeal to the Orangemen to end their protest. Addressing them 'not as First Minister but as their member of Parliament. I know that they have tried to conduct their protest peacefully. But those responsible have used those protests as an excuse and an occasion for an appalling act of barbarity . . . We can come back to the issue again, come back to the question of their desire to complete their traditional route at another time. But today, in the light of what has happened, the thing to do is to go home.' When Trimble was asked at the joint press conference why he had not asked for the Orangemen to disperse sooner, Mallon conspicuously intervened to defend his new colleague.[103] Many loyalists drifted away, but a hard core remained until they were allowed to exercise their traditional freedoms: the effort to enable them to do so would consume much of Trimble's time in the coming year.[104]

In subsequent disturbances, a Catholic RUC constable, Frank O'Reilly, was murdered by loyalists. It was reflective of the increasingly bitter sub-culture had grown up within north-Armagh/mid-Ulster loyalism which at times was as liable to turn its ire upon traditionally 'unionist' targets as upon nationalists. Fringe loyalist literature of 1998–9 focused mostly upon Trimble and his UUP colleagues. *Leading the Way*, the journal of the LVF, pictured Trimble, Taylor and Maginnis on its back cover with the caption, 'The UUP: The Only Party You Can Trust To Protect Your Interests In The New All-Ireland Socialist Republic'; likewise, *The Volunteer*, the magazine of the Loyalist Volunteer Corps, pictured

Trimble on its front cover in late 1998 with the headline 'Trimble Surrenders Ulster's Future For Self-Gain And Profit' observing that he would be handsomely rewarded for his 'treachery' with a First Minister's salary of close to £90,000 plus other perks; *The Wright View* (dedicated to the memory of Billy Wright) pronounced him 'Traitor Trimble: The Most Dangerous Man In Ulster' and pictured him with a demon-eyes mask captioned with the slogan '"New Unionism: New Danger"' (modelled upon the Tory attacks upon Blair during the 1997 General Election). Trimble was always unfazed by these attacks. 'The paranoia comes from the Unionist sense that every other man's hand is against them,' says the UUP leader. 'Obviously, you don't trust the nationalists and the British Government is plotting against you and large numbers of your own side have been bought. So there's a reason for it and it's not irrational and it reflects that experience in the early years of the Troubles, when there was a huge avalanche of negative press coverage. It means you're up against this tendency, an ingrained assumption that things will go wrong. And what we've had here [under the Belfast Agreement] isn't a clear victory for us, it's a points victory and many people don't believe it. It's easier to accept a simpler explanation of yet another betrayal and sell-out.'[105] Trimble's conception of what constituted a Unionist victory – based upon the consent principle – was closer to the definition favoured by many senior British officials than that of wide swathes of his own community.

TWENTY-SIX

A Nobel calling

AFTER these instalments of the 'white-knuckle ride', David Trimble departed for a much-needed month-long holiday in the Moselle valley. So total was his isolation from the affairs of the Province that he did not even know about a 500lb republican car bomb which caused extensive damage in Banbridge on 1 August 1998 – the town in his constituency which remained most supportive. The subsequent silence from the First Minister-designate's office was widely commented upon, even by supporters. 'It is the lot of any great statesman to be there for the people, all the time,' noted the *News Letter* tartly. 'In these days of instant communication, Mr Trimble needed to do no more than lift the telephone to ensure that the media would carry his message back to Ulster.'[1] Indeed, he was still unaware of the Banbridge attack on the last night of his vaction on Saturday 15 August 1998: David Campbell, his new chief of staff, reckoned that if there had been loss of life, he could not have survived as First Minister-designate, and he later told Daphne Trimble that for so long as her husband was in office he could no longer be incommunicado whilst on holiday.[2] At 10 p.m. on 15 August, he had done his packing and was in bed, ready for the drive across Europe to one of the Channel ports in his Hiace van packed with children and luggage. Suddenly, there was a knock on the door by the owner of the guest house: there was an urgent call from Canada. On the line was David Campbell, his chief of staff, who was staying with relatives in Toronto. Had he heard the news? That afternoon, at 3:10 p.m., 28 people were killed and 200 were injured by a 200–300 lb republican car bomb detonated in the heart of Omagh, Co. Tyrone. One of them was a woman pregnant with twins; a 29th victim died three weeks later. It was the greatest single atrocity of the Troubles in Northern Ireland, for which responsibility was claimed on Tuesday 18 August by the Real IRA. Though no one knew it at the time, the make-up of the casualty lists would, however, turn out to have a profound political significance: the dead came from both communities. Seventeen Catholics perished (including some from republican areas) and eleven Protestants; eleven of the victims were under the age of 18. But this, obviously, was only by chance. So massive was the reaction from the public on both sides of the border that the Real IRA suspended 'military' operations on 18 August, followed by the INLA on 22 August. Certainly, Blair hoped that 'people power' would finish off the dissidents once and for all – which turned out to be a highly optimistic assumption once the initial horror over the bombing had passed.[3]

'David just went very quiet,' recalls Daphne Trimble of the moment he heard of the atrocity.[4] Indeed, had it not been for this call, Trimble reckons he would again have driven off early the next day with his mobile telephone switched off and might not have heard about the Omagh bomb until he arrived in London on the morning of Monday 17 August 1998. He returned to the Province on the Sunday night and was taken straight to Hillsborough Castle, where he met the Prime Minister. Blair was, he recalls, 'badly shaken up by what he had seen in the intensive care unit at the Royal Victoria Hospital'.[5] Trimble was only able to grasp the full human and political significance of what had happened after he toured Omagh on Monday 17 August. 'There is a huge difference between the pictures and seeing it three dimensionally,' he says. 'And smelling it.' Trimble first went to the home of the local MP, Willie Thompson: although internal party foes, this was obviously no occasion for factional disagreement and they visited the widow of Fred White, the treasurer of the Omagh branch of the UUP, who had been killed along with his son. But after consulting the UUP officer team at Glengall Street, Trimble also made very sure to go to Roman Catholic funerals as well, including those which happened to be held in staunchly republican areas of Northern Ireland. 'I had no hesitation about that,' he recalls. 'I always knew I had to go and I knew that there would never be a better chance than this to break the ice.'[6] When Trimble and Rogan attended mass at St Mary's, Buncrana, Co. Donegal – for three boys from the Republic who had been amongst the victims – it even prompted a few calls within the Orange Order for both men to be disciplined. But nothing ever came of these rumblings. This was scarcely surprising. Certainly, Phelim O'Neill (later the second Lord Rathcavan and first leader of the Alliance parliamentary party) had been expelled from the Orange Order in 1968 for attending a Roman Catholic service.[7] But as C.D.C. Armstrong has observed, there was also a venerable tradition of UUP leaders attending the funeral services of their Catholic counterparts: Sir Edward Carson and Sir James Craig attended John Redmond's funeral mass at Westminster Cathedral in 1918; Richard Dawson Bates and John Miller Andrews, both Orangemen, attended the funeral in 1934 of Joe Devlin, the northern nationalist leader of the early years of the century; Andrews and colleagues were present at the funeral in 1946 of T.J. Campbell, a County Court judge and a one-time nationalist MP at Stormont; and, in 1970, Harry West had attended the requiem for the former politician Cahir Healy at St Michael's Church, Enniskillen, Co. Fermanagh. Healy had been a very controversial anti-treaty republican in his younger days, who had been interned as a security risk in Brixton prison during the Second World War.[8] Some viewed the controversy over Trimble's attendance at the Catholic funerals as evidence that this was a less gracious era; others described it to me as evidence of the coarsening effects of Paisleyism, which itself was partly a reaction to the growing ecumenism of older Protestant churches. But there is another possible explanation: that the likes of Carson and Craig were afforded a certain latitude because they were trusted. Trimble, by virtue of signing the Belfast Agreement, had forfeited the trust of many of his compatriots.

The effect of Trimble's decision to attend the mass was startling in nationalist Ireland. Before the Final Commendation, at the end of the liturgy, the Bishop of Derry, Dr Seamus Hegarty, addressed the congregation. 'I spoke at the end of the service,' recalls Hegarty. 'I had acknowledged President McAleese. But in Trimble's case I thought simply to acknowledge him in the same way was an inadequate recognition of what he had done, the courage he had shown.' Hegarty stated: 'This is a new and welcome development ... we know it is not easy. We want to assure you that you are here among friends, among people who are looking to you and your colleagues to give us the type of climate in Northern Ireland which will be conducive to the building of a genuine and lasting just peace ... We wish you well and a fair wind in all your endeavours as you resume in the autumn.' As he did so, there was a spontaneous outbreak of applause in the church: Hegarty believes that this was one of the high points of Trimble's popularity amongst Roman Catholics in Northern Ireland.[9] As Trimble rose to leave early for the White funeral in the Omagh area, he tugged the sleeve of Mary McAleese, who was sitting in the pew in front and he apologised that he could not stay for the inter-ment; his old rival from Queen's responded by reaching for his hand. After the White funeral, he proceeded to another Catholic funeral. His chief of staff, David Campbell, asked him: 'Did you know that Martin McGuin-ness is here?' Trimble did not, since the Sinn Fein/IRA chief negotiator had not been mentioned during the service. He was worried that if McGuinness made eye contact he would walk over and embarrass him. He moved to pay his respects to the family and slowly walked to his car.[10]

Senior figures in the Irish state knew that the centre of gravity of Real IRA activity was south of the border and that it was imperative for the confidence of Unionists – and, indeed, the loyalist paramilitaries who might have been contemplating retaliation – to be restored quickly. So when Trimble went to discuss the matter with Bertie Ahern in Dublin, the southern administration was ready. Ahern gave Trimble details of the Republic's proposals to toughen anti-terrorist legislation, including restricting the right to silence, widening provision to allow suspected members of illegal organisations to be indicted on the word of a senior Garda officer and for property to be confiscated. The Irish system moved swiftly to recall the Dail to introduce the necessary legislation – more so than the British (a point not lost on Trimble). Partly, this was because the Irish system is smaller and has certain in-built efficiencies because of its size, but also because the New Labour Government was sceptical about the efficacy of draconian measures. Indeed, Ahern told his bio-graphers, Ken Whelan and Eugene Masterson, that Blair was not itching 'to do any of this for two weeks and then they had this thing in the British papers about the civil liberties stuff and all that'.[11] Trimble also wondered whether the British Government was now embarrassed by its premature decision the previous year to scrap internment, which resulted in a situation where the Irish could not implement administrative deten-tion because dissident republican terrorists could now skip over the border to a new safe-haven – Northern Ireland![12]

No. 10 officials conceded privately that the new Criminal Justice Bill was an exercise in gesture politics – but they believed that a gesture was what was needed. The measures would be, as Blair told the Commons, 'a proportionate targeted response to deal with small, evil groups of violent men'. By this, Blair basically meant groups which were outside the tent of the Belfast Agreement (Real IRA, Continuity IRA and the LVF) who lacked large organised political wings. By implication, he was saying that such measures would be ineffective, even counterproductive against groups which did have substantial amounts of public support – such as the Provisionals. The word of a senior police officer would now be admissible, though not necessarily decisive, as evidence concerning membership of a specified proscribed organisation. And the arrangements for confiscating property were brought more into line with those in the Republic. Trimble, though, did not use the occasion of his speech at second-reading stage to turn the heat on Sinn Fein/IRA, instead reverting to the impressive, wide-ranging legalese with which he was so comfortable. Trimble reserved his strongest words for the Prime Minister's remarks about the reintroduction of internment. Since internment could only work as a surprise measure, it would be utterly ineffective to bring back the provision and then to arrest. Instead, Blair asserted that in certain circumstances he would not rule out first interning the suspects and then bringing in the legislation to give it legal effect. 'That is a very dubious way of proceeding, but that is what the Prime Minister implied,' he noted: even in such trying circumstances, this ex-academic lawyer was no knee-jerk 'hanger and flogger'.[13] The House appreciated his remarks and Clive Soley, a Labour MP – and no friend of the Union – offered compliments at the outset of his speech. 'When he became leader of the largest Unionist party in Northern Ireland, I expressed severe doubts whether he could offer the quality of leadership that the Unionist people were crying out for. In recent months – indeed, for longer – he has proved me wrong by his actions and words, and I am delighted to say so publicly. The Unionists are getting the leadership that they need and I am delighted by that.' Soley's sentiments were echoed when Trimble and Mallon made a joint appearance before the Labour conference in Blackpool on 30 September 1998 and won a standing ovation (although when Mowlam leaned forward following her own address to embrace the two Northern Irish leaders, Trimble offered only a handshake as opposed to Mallon's kiss).[14] To Trimble's admirers, such praise vindicated his stance. Yes, painful compromises had been made, but the Union had been renewed on new terms with men like Soley willing to listen to Unionist concerns as never before. But to Trimble's Unionist detractors, such praise was evidence of the massive, even suicidal, compromises he had made: any UUP leader could win left-wing plaudits for a relentless stream of concessions.

On the day following the Commons debate on the new legislation,

Clinton visited Northern Ireland for the second time during his presidency. But Trimble had a problem: there was no way, logistically, that he could attend the entire proceedings at Westminster and be in Belfast in time for his meeting with Clinton on the next morning. He solved the problem by hitching a lift on Blair's aircraft from RAF Northolt. Blair sat facing the cockpit, with Cherie opposite him in a two-seater configuration; in the four-seater configuration on the other side of the aisle sat Alastair Campbell and John Holmes, with Trimble and Jonathan Powell opposite them. As Trimble sat talking to Campbell, the No. 10 Press Secretary began a loud conversation with the First Minister-designate on the iniquities of proportional representation – which the Ulsterman took to be for Blair's benefit. Cherie Blair then stood up and Blair gestured to Trimble to join him in the empty seat. Campbell was by now working on the text of Blair's speech at the Waterfront Hall in Belfast and threw his scribbled amendments over to the Prime Minister. 'There's something you might like to include in your speech today,' said Blair. Trimble looked at it. 'I say that's pretty good,' replied Trimble. 'I've got a similar passage in my speech.' Blair examined the Trimble text. 'But Alastair's got quite a way with words.' Campbell's amendment to the UUP leader's remarks read as follows: 'And I say this to those who are crossing the bridge from terror to democracy. Every move you make towards peace, I welcome. Every pledge you make to peace, I will hold you to it.' Blair's amendment read as follows: 'And as First Minister, I will work with anyone who has the interests of peace at heart. I will be frank. I will be fair. Each part of the Agreement, including decommissioning, must be implemented. But if you take the road of peace and do so in genuine good faith, you will find me a willing leader in the journey.' As Trimble delivered those words, he looked straight in the eye at Adams and McGuinness; curiously, these were the remarks for which he was much criticised on both BBC Northern Ireland and in the *News Letter*: '. . . this confrontational demeanour was more suited to a UUP rally in the Ulster Hall,' opined the *News Letter* on 4 September.[15]

Like all such events, the organisation of the Clinton visit had been fraught with difficulties. First, the President had to demonstrate support for the new political institutions. Second, he had to provide due recognition for victims of violence and for the process of reconciliation. The first element would be symbolised by a visit to Stormont. But even with the support of both Trimble and Mallon, a visit to Parliament Buildings was by no means a done deal. 'You can't do this,' many senior republicans told Blair Hall, the acting American Consul General.[16] Obviously, in republican eyes, it would confer a legitimacy upon a hated symbol of Protestant hegemony. Indeed, the White House was conscious that to meet Trimble in this setting would rankle with many Irish-Americans: they expected as of right that the first person with whom the President should normally meet would be John Hume and then Gerry Adams. The White House advance men – some of them good Irish-American Catholics – were conscious of the point as they scouted Parliament Buildings. 'Hold me up, the RUC used to torture my ancestors in the basement here,' said one of them, only half-jokingly. In reality, the Americans had no choice but to acknowledge the institutions set up under the Belfast Agreement in which Clinton – for better or worse – had played his part. 'The only thing which I cared about was getting Clinton into Stormont,' says Trimble.[17] But the manner in which they did so was important. For Stormont, with its statues of Craig and Carson, was a symbolic nightmare for the President: any photographic juxtaposition of Clinton with those Ulster Unionist icons was not necessarily the message which the embattled White House wished to convey to Irish-American Congressmen as he faced impeachment in the US House of Representatives. So the idea of a reception in the grand hallway, with the life-size statue of Craig at the top of the stairs, was ruled out as a venue for a presidential meeting with the Assembly members; instead it took place informally in the Long Gallery, with the speeches at Belfast's Waterfront Hall.

Clinton's decision to visit Stormont was intended to convey two other messages. First, it was meant to send a signal to republicans that if the most 'engaged' President ever in Irish terms was happy to give Stormont his seal of approval, then the new institutions were sufficiently reformed to make it worthwhile for them to play their full part. The intention was, therefore, to afford them the space with their constituency. Second, Clinton also sought to send a signal to Trimble that given the new, inclusive nature of the institutions, it was time he sat down and spoke to the republicans. Trimble was prepared to do this – but on very particular conditions. During the summer, Trimble had insisted upon a statement that the 'war is over', the appointment of a republican representative to the decommissioning body, actual decommissioning and an end to punishment beatings.[18] Immediately after the Omagh bombing, Trimble again urged Adams to end what he called 'word games' and to declare that 'the war is over'.[19] The British and Irish Governments vigorously sought to find some form of words and concrete actions which would give Trimble the space in which to sit down with Sinn Fein and begin the process of setting up an inclusive executive. From the Governments' perspective, there was some movement: in an *An Phoblacht* 'interview' of 3 September, an IRA spokesman said that the Omagh bombing had 'damaged the republican struggle for independence and that [Real IRA] should disband . . .' On the next day, Gerry Adams stated that 'Sinn Fein believe the violence we have seen must be for all of us now a thing of the past – over, done with and gone.' On the day after that, Sinn Fein appointed Martin McGuinness as its representative to the international decommissioning body. Although sceptics charged that close textual analysis of Adams' form of words simply meant that the violence of the past was in the past, the appointment of the Derryman was deemed by Trimble to be significant. 'They have put themselves on an escalator and that escalator will inevitably lead to actual decommissioning,' claimed the First Minister-designate – though he later added that he would not prescribe the particular method of verifiable destruction, which could be done by the IRA itself.[20] Certainly, the form of words employed by Adams was less than the UUP leader had sought. According to Trimble, Blair claimed that he wrote these words himself – and that they effectively meant that 'the war is over'.[21] Trimble says that he accepted this more limited formulation because the statement represented some sort of advance in itself and that a large number of people would read it that way. 'If it's the spirit of what you are looking for, anything else looks like excuses,' he observes.[22] Some Ulster Unionists were unhappy that No. 10 talked up the expectations of a direct meeting between Sinn Fein and the UUP as a direct consequence of such moves, but they acquiesced in the final analysis. 'Downing Street brokered the arrangements and David couldn't say no,' recalls Reg Empey, his closest lieutenant.[23] In other words, he had scored one and a half out of his four goals – a senior republican on the decommissioning body and a form of words about the 'war', but no actual decommissioning and no end to punishment beatings. Overall, therefore, the Omagh bombing had ground both sides down: the republicans were put on the defensive, and forced to appoint McGuinness to the decommissioning body, but Trimble had also been pushed into meeting Sinn Fein sooner than he might have wanted.

By the time that Clinton arrived, a Trimble-Adams meeting was a virtual certainty. But Trimble still had to overcome the profound scepticism about a meeting which took place considerably short of what had at least appeared to be the party's terms for bestowing such legitimacy upon Sinn Fein. Rogan says that when the proposal to meet with Adams was put to the UUP Executive on 5 September, there was little opposition. 'Omagh increased the likelihood of meeting Sinn Fein,' states Rogan. 'It pulled everyone up short. It made people realise that the decisions we make have serious implications for people's lives and that we would do all we could to make sure it wouldn't happen again. It reinforced in people's minds the progressive things some of us were trying to do and the consequences of not getting those things right.'[24] Rogan's explanation thus goes some way towards validating Adams' claim in a *Playboy* interview of March 1999 that 'I think the reason [Trimble] finally agreed to talk with me had to do with the number of civilians killed.' But more sceptical Unionists were appalled by this line of reasoning. According to them, Real IRA were sometimes in a competitive relationship with the Provisionals, but no less frequently were in a symbiotic relationship. Real IRA was thus a wonderful bogeyman to hold up to Unionists and the British to lever more concessions out of them. As anti-Agreement unionists saw it, the mainstream republicans' message was 'help us – or else'.

Trimble's decision to meet for the first time with Adams did not prompt a great explosion of anger in the Unionist community. Even so, Trimble made sure to handle the event in as inoffensive a fashion as possible. The chosen venue was a round-table discussion at Castle Buildings, without an independent chairman such as George Mitchell present, at which the First and Deputy First Ministers-designate would consult with all of the parties about their report on new structures for the Assembly. This enabled Trimble to present it simply as an extension of the multilaterals during the 1997–8 talks, but the key difference was that he would be in the chair.[25] However, on *Breakfast with Frost*, Trimble stated that he would not be shaking hands with the Sinn Fein president. 'There is a point about hands being held out open to show they are not containing any weapons but Mr Adams cannot do that,' observed the UUP leader. '[His] hand was not a friendly hand.'[26] Indeed, as late as 2002, Martin McGuinness complained that Trimble still had not shaken hands nor taken a drink with him and the UUP leader would only make such a gesture in mid-2003.[27] The first official bilateral between a UUP leader and Sinn Fein in 75 years took place on 10 September, following a larger meeting with Mallon and other Sinn Fein representatives. Again, it occurred behind closed doors. After the first gathering ended at 10:15, Trimble and Adams rose and went into the annexe of the next room alone, without notetakers. Trimble also recalls that the encounter between the two of them was 'stilted' but that he was determined to convey two matters: first, that he believed the historic compromise between the two communities would endure, but that he did not know if this particular arrangement would work (or, indeed, with himself at the helm). Trimble said that he had doubts about the republican commitment to peace and emphasised his feeling that Sinn Fein would not take the process seriously until it was almost over the edge. Trimble remembers that during a key session of the Mitchell Review in October 1999 at the American ambassador's residence at Winfield House, Adams recalled this conversation. The UUP leader subsequently learned from other sources that the Sinn Fein president was worried about his insouciant attitude – 'I don't have to do this, I could get myself a life' attitude.[28]

Many wondered what these meetings were like. In fact, they were frequently rather banal: there were no great arguments, after the fashion of the Lincoln–Douglas debates; nor could it be said that Trimble and Adams 'glowered magnificently' at one another, silently, after the fashion of Sir James Craig and Michael Collins at their first encounter with each other in Winston Churchill's room at the Colonial Office in 1922.[29] A flavour of these discussions is provided by the record of a later meeting which was written up in the private diary of Trimble's then press secretary, David Kerr, on 17 February 1999. Trimble began the substantive part of the encounter with the words: 'This meeting is appropriate at this point in the process. With regard to the UUP, the party is in good shape. There are fragmentations like [Peter] Weir [the Agreement-sceptic UUP Assemblyman for North Down] who is now floating away. Those people will always be there, but the position and line of the UUP is clear ... the formation of the Stormont Executive must happen before 10 March 1999, but the circumstances need to be right for this to happen. What is absolutely essential before we form the Executive and transfer powers is that there is a credible and verifiable start of the process of decommissioning. With the opportunity to transform society here, we would prefer to have you on board, but there must be a credible and verifiable start to the decommissioning process before 10 March ...'

Adams replied: 'We need to move ourselves together on an inclusive basis. There are parts of the Agreement that we don't like and there are parts that you don't like. If we look at this in a way that allows you to be unionists and us to be republicans, I don't see any way around these problems unless we accommodate each other. Our value to our communities is in our ability to deliver. We have to take the long term view.' But when Trimble reiterated the crucial importance of decommissioning before the 10 March 1999 deadline for devolution, Adams became irate and stated 'it cannot happen'. Trimble retorted, 'We have to deal with the central problem. There is no point in getting into debates on the Agreement. We believe if we have a credible and verifiable start to the process of decommissioning, we can carry the majority of unionists and Ulster Unionists with us . . . you say "it can't happen". I am saying to you "it has to happen"! We need to look at arrangements to facilitate this. At the moment, I am designing choreography with Washington, London and Dublin.' 'You need to explain what is meant by choreography,' said Adams. 'This means there must be a credible and verifiable decommissioning and the setting up of the Executive. We need reassurance from de Chastelain and yourselves that when the process starts, it will follow right through.' Adams then pointed out that 'the UVF is rearming', prompting John Taylor to cut in with the words 'well, I'm not a commander of the UVF'. Shortly thereafter, Taylor asked Adams, 'Do you think we are genuine about sharing power with you? I need an answer.' 'I don't know,' replied Adams. Empey eventually picked up on McGuinness' remark that Unionists 'didn't want a Fenian about the place'. 'We want that phrase done way with,' said Empey. 'Some elements hold that view, but we don't.' Mitchel McLaughlin then spoke up for the first time. 'The war is over and we have to now deal with this problem together – but we need more time.' 'Who are Orange Volunteers [a Loyalist splinter group]?' asked Bairbre de Brun. 'They are low-life,' replied Trimble. The discussion then focused on dissident loyalism, with Sinn Fein accusing the UUP of not doing enough to stop it. McGuinness then intriguingly remarked: 'It was Sinn Fein and republicans who stopped the Real IRA, not British or Irish legislation. It is only a matter of time before someone is killed by these loyalist groupings.' These sessions often meandered around, jumping from issue to issue and back again. But like Dr Johnson's remark about women preachers, the remarkable thing was that they were taking place at all.

Trimble found these encounters to be deeply unpleasant occasions. 'I hate that man, I hate that man ... despicable,' said Trimble to Steven King as the latter went into his office at Parliament Buildings whilst Adams left it. Indeed, according to King, the UUP leader loathes his 'sleekedness' (an Ulster expression for 'creepy' or 'devious' – an assessment which purist republicans would share).[30] Trimble tended to prefer McGuinness, whom he regarded as a more straightforward individual; but even in this case, there was little mutual admiration of the kind which evolved, say, between F.E. Smith and Michael Collins during the 1921 Treaty negotiations.[31] According to Ken Reid of UTV, who knows both men well, Trimble was far less curious about Adams than Adams was about Trimble – notwithstanding Trimble's unusual interest, for a Unionist, in the history of republicanism.[32] But that was always an academic interest rather than a personal inquisitiveness. Indeed, when Trimble does inquire about the key personalities in Sinn Fein, he relies principally upon the word of Sean O'Callaghan rather than through personal engagement. But this trait is characteristic of so many of his dealings with people in general. The pattern was also noticed by other observers of the interaction between the two groups. Thus, one civil servant was struck by the degree of republican curiosity about the shifting coalitions within the UUP – such as the role of John Taylor and whether he and Trimble were consciously playing a 'hard cop-soft cop' routine and the significance of the return of Jeffrey Donaldson to the inner counsels of the UUP in June 1999. Sometimes, republican frustration with Trimble's internal party difficulties would stem from a secretive, militaristic elite's lack of understanding of a fissiparous, even chaotic entity. Senior republicans would often ask, 'Why doesn't he just manage them?'[33] At times, republicans appeared to recognise Trimble's difficulties, but their tolerance was tactical and thus their patience was short. Trimble, for his part, was prepared to give Adams et al. leeway with their movement. When one associate asked why the Sinn Fein leadership was not undertaking a programme of education of the grassroots about the inefficacy of armed struggle – much as Cathal Goulding and Eoghan Harris had done in the 1960s and 1970s as part of redirecting the Official republican movement towards constitutional politics – the UUP leader answered that more time was needed. After a quarter-century of conflict, Adams and McGuinness were riding a far more dangerous beast than 'the Stickies'. 'The Stickies', as he saw it, were a largely southern-based movement impelled far more by a particular interpretation of republican ideology than were the northern-based

Provisionals. By contrast, the latter's roots, he believed, lay in ethnic rage and 'Defenderist' traditions: hence, Adams' increasing use of the term 'Catholic' as part of the effort to displace the SDLP. But Trimble also discerned what he regarded as another difference between Goulding-Harris and Adams-McGuinness: 'Adams' total moral cowardice. He never does anything in the open. He never tells the grassroots anything other than what they want to hear. Yes, some now are talking about decommissioning but he wants others at the grassroots to do the spadework. He wants to hold the option for as long as possible. If Adams had been in my position at Drumcree last year, he would have been at the top of the hill.'[34] Some republicans retorted that of course Adams had to move carefully: William Ross would not shoot Trimble dead, no matter how bitter their arguments became.

The question of which one of the two was 'failing to provide leadership' and to 'face down rejectionists' bedevilled republican-unionist discourse. But the two men did have very different styles. Certainly, Trimble was the far less experienced of the duo. Adams had, after all, held very senior positions in the republican movement since the early 1970s when he was in his early 20s, and was something of an ideological 'blue-blood' via his connections with his mother's family, the Hannaways.[35] Trimble, as he was fond of pointing out, came from anything but the 'Ascendancy' and was very much a latecomer to political influence. He was thus on a much steeper learning curve than his Sinn Fein opposite number. Sean O'Callaghan, who worked closely with both men during the course of his remarkable career, believes that the differences between their political styles owe as much to personality as to the varying structure and culture of republicanism and unionism. 'Whereas Adams is hugely cautious, Trimble has far more of an erratic gambling streak,' observes the Kerryman. 'Even during the hugely emotional time of the Hunger Strikes, I remember Bernadette McAliskey saying that people were losing their tempers but that Adams never lost his. Trimble has far more obvious mood swings: with Trimble, you get the sense that the policy might be based upon how he happens to feel that day. On the basis of traditional stereotypes of the two communities, you would think that Adams was the Protestant and Trimble the Catholic. And then compare what Adams did in the run-up to 1986 [the year that Sinn Fein voted to end their policy of abstentionism from the Dail] and what Trimble has done since 1995. When Adams moved in 1986, he had Ruairi O'Bradaigh [his purist predecessor, who subsequently left to found Republican Sinn Fein] totally isolated and he had done that over the seven previous years. Can you ever imagine Trimble taking seven years to seize the leadership and change its policy, effectively isolating opposition? There was loads of opposition to Adams but he managed to keep his internal opponents off-balance – shaving off people here and there. In the build-up to 1986, he introduced a motion declaring that abstentionism is a tactic, not a principle. He won, but not convincingly and knew that he wouldn't do so. But it enabled him to smoke out his enemies and he appointed twelve respected organisers to go round the country to the cumainn [branches] to persuade the doubters and he got the necessary majority in the next year. Again, you couldn't see Trimble doing that. Think also of the people whom Trimble was promoting – the John Hunters and the David Brewsters. He lost them all. Did he seriously think they would go with him? Again, you couldn't see Adams making that kind of mistake. On the other hand, Trimble has a far more formidable pure intellect than Adams, who has no real grasp of detail.'[36]

The emerging Trimble–Adams relationship thus had distinct limits. As the countdown for the Nobel Prize announcement began, speculation began about who would win it from Northern Ireland – and, specifically, whether Trimble could accept the award if both he and the Sinn Fein president had received it (a fear shared by No. 10, which saw its destabilising potential, although they deny knowing anything about who would win the prize beforehand). If, for example, Hume, Adams and Trimble won it, there was always the danger that it would appear as though two nationalists were dragging one Unionist along the 'path to peace'. Whenever his aides sought to talk about possible scenarios which might arise, the First Minister-designate declined to discuss the matter (he never much likes taking decisions far in advance, anyhow). 'You needn't worry about that – there's no chance of me getting it,' he would tell them with customary self-deprecation. The news, though, would come through whilst Trimble and Mallon were on an investment tour of North America. Maura Quinn, Trimble's private secretary, who accompanied him on the tour told him that he would hear one way or another at 3 a.m. Denver time. 'Should I wake you if you win?' she asked. 'No, under no circumstances wake me till 7 a.m.' Quinn duly diverted all calls to her own room. At 3:10 a.m., the call came through: Trimble and John Hume had won. The minute it was announced – and it was already 10 a.m. in London and

Belfast – Quinn came under enormous pressure to grant interviewers access to her boss. 'The press was going mad, so I took an executive decision,' she recalls. 'So at 5:45 a.m. I woke him. After a delay DT came to the door, blinking. "Congratulations, you've won the Nobel Prize." "So the nightmare hasn't happened?"' he replied.[37] By this, Trimble was referring to the now averted prospect of Adams as a third co-recipient, which he feared would have obliged him to refuse.[38] Hume and Trimble thus became the second duo from Northern Ireland to receive the award – the first going to Betty Williams and Mairead Corrigan, co-founders of the 'Peace People' in 1976 – with prize money totalling £576,678. On the basis of the Kroner–Sterling exchange rate in 1998, Trimble's share came to £288,339. What he did with the bulk of his Nobel money proved to be a matter of some controversy in a community in which many opponents believed he had 'sold out'. At one point, he appeared to suggest that he would use the funds to set up a political foundation, but Daphne Trimble revealed some years later that the couple were thinking of keeping the money. 'That might have to be a pension fund,' she told *The Daily Telegraph* on 23 June 2001.[39]

Trimble felt quiet pride in his award: after all the years of failure and marginalisation at both Queen's and the UUP, he would not have been human had he been completely indifferent to this achievement. 'Whatever happens, nobody can take this away,' he told Daphne Trimble. 'If it goes wrong, I've done my best.' But, she adds, he would have been very disappointed if the new dispensation did not work. Immediately before the award ceremony in Oslo, both men visited Washington to receive Averell Harriman Awards at a dinner of the National Democratic Institute honouring the main protagonists in the political process.[40] Earlier, the UUP leader had called upon the US National Security Adviser, Sandy Berger, in his West Wing office, when Clinton burst in. 'Gee, I'm so happy for you,' said the President, repeatedly. Tony O'Reilly, chairman of H.J. Heinz and also of Independent Newspapers in the Republic, loaned both Nobel laureates his private jet to fly them from Washington so they could be in Oslo in time for the start of the Nobel festivities the next day.[41] There was little conversation between the two men on the trans-atlantic flight, but there was some thawing of the relationship by the time the week was out and increased warmth between the two delegations. Trimble's included his own immediate family; his sister Rosemary, who today lives on a housing estate outside Belfast that was festooned with

'Traitor Trimble' graffiti; his brother, Iain, then a Flight Lieutenant in the RAF; his fellow Old Bangorian and then East Belfast Assemblyman, Ian Adamson; John Gorman and some of the party officers.[42]

Trimble was nervous enough about receiving the award, and before he stood up to speak before the King and Queen of Norway in the Great Hall thought about his parents. His anxiety showed in his demeanour, as he awkwardly clutched the medal and certificate in either hand on stage: beforehand, he had joked that his main worry was about tripping on stage. Certainly, Hume seemed far more at ease and coordinated.[43] But when Trimble stood up to speak, he soon found his voice. The address was drafted by Eoghan Harris. 'Harris is always such a stimulus to thought,' says Trimble. 'I don't always agree with his suggestions. But they are always worth thinking about. I like that sort of thing – people who will punt you ideas. He's clearly in a league of his own.'[44] Replete with a wide range of quotes from Edmund Burke, Rousseau, Amos Oz and the American diplomat and historian George Kennan, Trimble's address attracted far more comment – both positive and negative – than did Hume's. 'We [in Northern Ireland] have a few fanatics who dream of forcing the Ulster British people into a utopian Irish state, more ideologically Irish than its own inhabitants,' he noted. 'We also have fanatics who dream of permanently suppressing northern nationalists in a state more supposedly British than its inhabitants actually want. But a few fanatics are not a fundamental problem. No, the problem arises if political fanatics bury themselves within a morally legitimate political movement. Then there is a double danger that we might dismiss legitimate claims for reform because of the barbarism of terrorist groups bent on revolution. In that situation experience would suggest that the best way forward is for democrats to carry out what the Irish writer Eoghan Harris calls 'acts of good authority'. That is, acts addressed to their own side. Thus each reformist group has a moral obligation to deal with its own fanatics. The Serbian democrats must take on the Serbian fascists. The PLO must take on Hamas. In Northern Ireland, constitutional nationalists must take on republican dissident terrorists and constitutional unionists must confront Protestant terrorists.' But Trimble also noted another danger: 'Sometimes in our search for a solution, we go into denial about the darker side of the fanatic, the darker side of human nature. Not all may agree, but we cannot ignore the existence of evil. Particularly that form of political evil that wants to perfect a person, a border at any cost . . . What we need is George Keenan's [sic – he should have said Kennan] hard-headed advice to the State Department in the 1960s for dealing with the state terrorists of his time, based on his years in Moscow. "Don't act chummy with them, don't assume a community of aims with them which does not really exist, don't make fatuous gestures of goodwill."' If policy-makers succeeded in fulfilling these aspirations, they might be able to leave behind 'the dark sludge of historical sectarianism. We can leave it behind if we wish. But both communities must leave it behind because both created it. Each thought it had good reason to fear the other. As [Lewis] Namier says, the irrational is not necessarily the unreasonable. Ulster Unionists, fearful of being isolated on the island, built a solid house, but it was a cold house for Catholics. And Northern nationalists, although they had a roof over their heads, seemed to us as if they meant to burn the house down.'

To loyalists, it was the most prominent indication to date of Trimble's 'revisionism' concerning the record of the Northern state from 1921–72, of which there would be further evidence in the coming year – which prompted him, in the view of some, to make pronouncements more commonly associated with 'guilty Prods' who had left their Unionism behind. But if Trimble's speech left them uneasy, it stimulated a more hostile public reaction in nationalist Ireland. Martin McGuinness described it as 'abusive' of republicans and dismissive of their efforts; Vincent Browne, a veteran foe of Eoghan Harris, believed that Trimble was guilty of not engaging in acts of 'good authority' towards his own hardliners in slowing the pace of establishing a new, inclusive dispensation. 'He joined last July in the chorus which insisted that the very essence of Protestant civil and religious liberties was at stake in Drumcree, a chorus that must have echoed in the ears of those who burnt the Quinn boys in their home,' noted Browne. 'Not much good authority there.'[45] Tim Pat Coogan wrote in *Ireland on Sunday* on 13 December 1998 that 'if one appoints a horse a consul, I suppose one can't be surprised if the animal craps all over the hall . . . to paraphrase Yeats, "a most Uncouth Beast has slunk back from Oslo to Belfast".'[46] Trimble's friend Ruth Dudley Edwards was appalled by such comments. 'Reactions to Trimble are a fascinating test of nationalist bigotry,' she opined. 'You might think that someone who has put his life and career on the line to do a deal, not just with nationalism but with republicanism, might be given some benefit of the doubt . . . But in fact Trimble seems to annoy our bigots far more than does Ian Paisley, who has for them the merit of justifying nationalist/ Catholic prejudices. That Trimble is the best read and most cultivated leader in these two islands, whose passion for European art and music is surpassed only by his profound interest in history, politics and philosophy, seems to be an additional affront. And that he wants to make his party more welcoming to Catholics drives them mad.'[47] But on this day, nothing could dampen Trimble's spirits – not even John Hume crooning 'The Town I Loved So Well' (about his hometown of Derry), with the composer Phil Coulter on piano, at a reception; Hume then proceeded to do an impersonation of an elderly Orangeman marching along to the strains of 'The Sash'. The Orangemen who were present, such as Jim Nicholson and Jack Allen did not mind: indeed, Allen – also a native of the Maiden City – crowed with municipal pride over the Coulter song. 'It's so evocative,' he observed in an aside to the author. 'Now you'll have to sing,' said Hume to his European Parliamentary colleague, Jim Nicholson. Nicholson duly gave a rendition of his party piece, 'The Boys from the County Armagh'.[48] But the atmosphere of 'all Irishmen together' did not impress Trimble: both he and Josias Cunningham remained at a safe distance from the rest of the group at the other end of the room.[49]

The atmosphere at home was less convivial. The negotiations between the UUP, the SDLP, the British and Irish Governments over the number and scope of cross border implementation bodies – as well as the number of Northern Ireland departments – were deadlocked.[50] Mallon was under relentless attack from Sinn Fein for entering into the UUP-SDLP First and Deputy First Minister-designate arrangement without them, and for staying in post as the Ulster Unionists sought to insert the decommissioning 'precondition' which had eluded them on the Good Friday.[51] But Trimble's room for manoeuvre was very limited as well. The Belfast Telegraph conducted a poll of UUP Assemblymen on 1 October 1998. They asked two questions, of which the second was the more significant: 'Will you maintain support for David Trimble if Sinn Fein is allocated seats on the Executive without decommissioning?' Four answered yes; twelve were equivocal; and nine answered no. One of those nine was Trimble himself, at least according to his own address to the Young Unionist conference later that month.[52] And on 9 October, the Union First pressure group, a grouping of Agreement sceptics and outright antis – whose leading light was Jeffrey Donaldson – was launched formally in Belfast.

Trimble was reinforced in his attitude by Martin McGuinness's article in the *Irish Times* of 29 October 1998, in which the senior republican declared that 'the Agreement is not a peace settlement': it was clear that he at least purported to see it as transitional and thus would not bring about the stability within the Union that the Ulster-British community craved. McGuinness made his remarks in the run-up to an IRA convention held in the Republic which was designed, officially at least, to review the ceasefire. But according to Ed Moloney, the real agenda was to change the IRA's constitution. The purpose of such a manoeuvre, it was believed, was to restore to the ruling army council – on which the Sinn Fein leadership had a decisive say – control over weapons; as things currently stood, only a convention, which was dominated by much less political grassroots elements, could do so. It was hinted that this would make a deal on decommissioning at least possible. But that would require a *quid pro quo* from Trimble.[53] Indeed, the two Governments and the Americans were convinced that such a deal would entail Trimble agreeing to an ample measure of North-South cooperation and also to compromise on the number of government departments. This would make the move towards politics worthwhile for the republican movement. At a minimum, the two Governments told the UUP, if new inclusive institutions were up and running, it would remove every excuse that the IRA had not to decommission; Clinton said as much to Trimble when they met in the White House on 8 December 1998.[54] The implication in all this was that if the IRA were still recalcitrant, republicans would be blamed. Trimble responded accordingly. If the IRA was sucked in and lived up to its obligations, all well and good. If not, he reckoned he would be vindicated and could hope to begin the next round of the process at a considerable advantage. His calculations were partly predicated upon winning the blame game, but he also genuinely wanted to end the 'cold war' on the island of Ireland. On 2 November 1998, both he and Mallon welcomed Ahern to Parliament Buildings. On 20 November, he met with Ahern at Government Buildings in Dublin: according to an Irish Government spokesman, they agreed to 'at least six' implementation bodies, the minimum posited under the Agreement.[55] Trimble recalls that he listed other possible areas of cooperation and that the Irish pocketed it and added more. But he deliberately held back on giving his assent in one area – EU programmes. Subsequently, Trimble addressed the Irish Association at Glenview Hotel, Glen O' The Downs, Co. Wicklow, and cautioned against 'unrealisable expectations' for the North-South implementation bodies. As Trimble left the hotel, someone left a scapular for him – a small Roman Catholic token of esteem intended to wish him 'Godspeed'.[56] Certainly, the Irish Association address came at the height of his reputation in the Republic – as was evidenced by RTE's decision to broadcast the occasion live on radio.

Blair visited Belfast on 25 November 1998 for further consultations with Ulster's party leaders. The broad trade-off which appeared to be emerging ran as follows: the Ulster Unionists would abandon their opposition to ten departments in Northern Ireland. From a Unionist perspective, this was the worst number since it brought about a 5–5 parity in the Executive on the basis of the June 1998 Assembly elections, notwithstanding a roughly 50%–40% edge enjoyed by unionist parties of all stripes over their nationalist rivals. Above all, it meant two republicans in government as opposed to one. In exchange, the British would agree to back the UUP in their opposition to far-reaching SDLP-Irish proposals for cross-border implementation bodies handling EU programmes, Trade Promotion, Inward Investment and Business Development. From a UUP perspective, these appeared to threaten harmonisation of tax and grant structures, and the amalgamation of industrial development bodies in both jurisdictions – all of which meant that a set of circumstances had been created whereby Northern Ireland effectively ceased to exist as an independent economic entity in the eyes of the outside world.[57] Trimble had signalled to the SDLP in November, via David Campbell and David Lavery, that the UUP would settle for ten departments. Trimble says that once the Agreement postulated the idea of up to ten ministries, it was obvious that the new institutions of government would end up this way. 'Politics is about jobs,' he explains.[58] Unionists were, however, quite prepared for confrontations over investment, where Trimble knew that the British would be more inclined to back him: the Irish Government's lower levels of corporation tax would have threatened a compromise rate that would have reduced revenues accruing to HM Treasury.[59] To that end, he would do nothing to alienate Blair. Thus, when David Kerr, Trimble's press aide, 'spun' a story to the News Letter and The Daily Telegraph on 25 November 1998 – to the effect that Trimble would confront Blair over his side-letter on decommissioning – the UUP leader was desperately concerned about the article's tone. 'He was very upset and visibly worried about how Blair would react,' noted Kerr in his diary for that day. 'I was thinking to myself, "I couldn't care less how Blair feels, that's the way it is." DT wanted me formally to complain to the *News Letter* but I didn't. I left it to later in the day and told Mervyn Pauley [the newspaper's veteran political correspondent] that it was over the top. Put in the context of Sinn Fein and SDLP pressures and Paisley's warnings about a Trimble cave-in, I think the *News Letter* and *Daily Telegraph* front pages were fine.'

The events of the coming weeks were to undermine Trimble's hope that the two largest constitutional parties could be the fulcrum of the new dispensation and left a residue of bitterness on the SDLP side. By early December, the two Governments were very anxious that no agreement had yet been struck – indeed they had missed the opportunity they craved to announce the deal in time for Blair's visit to Dublin, where on 26 November he became the first British Prime Minister to address the Oireachtas. They had two, related fears. First, if the schedule slipped much further, it would be impossible to secure passage through the Commons in time for the devolution deadline of the end of February. Second, and partly as a consequence of that, they feared that political vacuums over the Christmas break tended to be filled by the men of violence (*vide* the December 1997 murder of Billy Wright). So worried were they by the deadlock that they decided that the time was ripe for a further injection of Prime Ministerial magic. Blair arrived at Stormont late on 2 December to great general excitement. The Prime Minister was, however, tired and very fed up. He always wanted to concentrate on the 'big picture', as he liked to call it, of keeping momentum going and said as much on occasion to Trimble.[60] Instead, Blair was forced to deal with matters of cross-borderism that were so abstruse as to make the Schleswig-Holstein question seem broad brush by comparison. Accordingly, Blair held – in EU parlance – a number of 'confessions' with the party leaders at Stormont. Again, Blair was mainly talking to the UUP and SDLP, with Sinn Fein fuming on the sidelines about their perceived marginalisation. The questions centred on such matters as whether trade and business development should be an implementation body and should it include inward investment. Trimble, moreover, was a staunch opponent of a tourism body: he feared that Ulster would be marketed as a sub-section of the South in an all-Ireland body and that it would syphon off all of the Northern visitors. The officials eventually realised that the only way to circumvent Trimble's hostility was to bring in 'experts' who would seek to reassure him with the telling detail: his initially strong theological objections to cross-borderism would then often be ground down when he entered what one official calls 'the comfort zone' with a particular concept. In the end, a formula was found which both sides could live with: tourism became a publicly owned limited company established by the southern Bord Failte and the Northern Ireland Tourism Board providing international marketing programmes, to be monitored by the existing tourism boards and by the relevant ministers in the two jurisdictions meeting under the the the auspices of the North-South ministerial Council. By late 2001, the first campaign to market the island of Ireland as a single destination was unveiled jointly by Empey and the Republic's tourism minister, Jim McDaid.[61]

The SDLP, though, interpreted the very discussion of such items as tantamount to agreement; whereas in Trimble's mind they remained no more than options. Blair left after midnight, disappointed that he had not brought the two sides closer. Once the Prime Ministerial helicopters had gone, Mallon emerged at Stormont to tell the press that agreement had been reached in the early hours of Thursday 3 December. He had reason to be pleased: Blair had promised transport to Mallon, but when presented with the option, the UUP demurred and in the end it became a matter for 'cooperation' rather than an implementation body. Trimble believes that Mallon went 'OTT'; this, in turn, frightened elements of the UUP Assembly group into believing that he had made concessions.[62] In their view, eight implementation bodies were too many. Indeed, Trimble told Clinton when he met him at the White House on 8 December 1998 that three members of the Assembly party were against the proposed deal (the sceptics included John Taylor: Trimble was often as worried about the quality of opposition as the quantity). Mallon, likewise, recalls a one-on-one meeting with Trimble where the UUP leader told him '"oh, I have to do this for party reasons" – something that I came to hear a lot of'.[63]

In this case, the political really was the personal. According to Mallon, he told the UUP that he would have to be going into hospital at 3 p.m. on 17 December 1998 to have his gallstones removed. Instead of negotiating with him before he left, Trimble arranged an appointment to visit Banbridge and Portadown.[64] By the time Trimble returned to Stormont, Mallon had departed for his operation. Mallon's friends believe to this day that Trimble deliberately delayed his return so that he could negotiate a more favourable deal without him there – exemplified by the fact that only on that day did the UUP present their final plan for the ten departments of the Northern Ireland Executive. Whichever interpretation is correct, negotiations started to make more progress in the absence of Mallon, though he kept in touch by telephone through the night.[65] Eddie McGrady, SDLP MP and MLA for South Down, took over and by 7 p.m., news emerged that the two sides had agreed a company rather than a state administrative structure for tourism. The UUP Assembly group then endorsed the leadership's approach: six implementation bodies (in line with the UUP's insistence upon the minimum number stipulated in the Belfast Agreement) of Inland Waterways, Food Safety, Trade and Business Development, Special EU programmes, Language and Aquaculture and Marine matters. Areas for cooperation – dealt with through the mechanism of existing bodies as opposed to the new implementation bodies – were transport, agriculture, education, health, environment and tourism. Health, for instance, included such apparently innocuous areas as accident and emergency planning and education included teacher qualifications and teacher exchanges.[66] By 4:30 a.m., Trimble went into the SDLP room and told them that it was time to settle as the Ulster Unionists were threatening to leave. 'I was absolutely knackered and I was saying I was ready to go,' recalls Trimble.[67] It was duly settled and later that day, the UUP Executive endorsed the 18 December accord by a 70–30 margin.

Trimble had won some significant victories on the cross-border arrangements, albeit at a high price in terms of the provisions on the internal government of Northern Ireland. But that would be a battle for another day.[68] In any case, as Paul Bew observed, Trimble's game was not so much to score a knock-out blow on his opponents, which he could not achieve anyhow, but rather to stay in office for so long as to force them to accept the revised rules of the game. In that sense, the figure whom he perhaps most resembled was W.T. Cosgrave of Cumann na nGaedheal (the precursor of Fine Gael) and President of the Executive Council of the Irish Free State from 1922–32, who rather more brutally forced the anti-treaty forces to adjust to the new Free State.[69] In any case, there were few obvious organisational vehicles for overthrowing Trimble, as there were with Faulkner: the Union First cadres within the UUP were not ready for cooperation with the DUP, fearing absorption. McCartney's UKUP was suffering from serious internal tensions: four out of five UKUP Assemblymen left McCartney to form the Northern Ireland Unionist

Party.[70] Some in the DUP had feared the UKUP's purism, which threatened to outflank them amongst those opposed to the Agreement. But once the UKUP grouping fell apart, they were comparatively free of the need to look over their shoulder. This meant that they could take their quota of two ministerial departments out of ten, with relative ease, if they wanted. This more modulated position would make things easier for Trimble in the coming months and years (indeed, as late as 2004, British officials looked back upon this episode as a strategic turning point).

Much of this speculation was with the advantage of hindsight. At the time, Trimble seemed to be in remarkably good shape considering the 'white knuckle ride' which both he and the UUP had undergone that year: Paul Bew described him in a year-end article for *The Times* on 28 December 1998 as the 'Flinty Moses of the Unionist Tribe' and for the first time references to the First Minister-designate in the press began to outstrip mentions of Adams.[71] Indeed, on 18 December, Trimble received yet more good news: as the first voluntary act of decommissioning, the LVF handed over nine guns, 350 bullets, two pipe bombs and six detonators to the International Commission. He certainly hoped that it would place further pressure upon the IRA (and other loyalist paramilitaries) to do the same.[72] The act of destruction was memorable enough. John de Chastelain deliberately chose saws which had diamond-cutters' round blades which would do the job most effectively – but which, by happy coincidence, would also generate plenty of spectacular sparks.[73] Indeed, only days before, whilst addressing a peace seminar in Stockholm on the second leg of his Nobel Prize visit, Trimble had said that the one 'absolute and irreducible requirement' of decommissioning was that a television camera had to be there.[74] Much of the coming year would be dominated by attempts by the two Governments and the UUP to ensure that this performance was repeated – but, in this expectation, they were to be gravely disappointed.

TWENTY-SEVEN

The blame game speeds up

NINETEEN NINETY-NINE was dominated by one issue: decommissioning and the setting up of an Executive. Republicans and much of nationalist Ireland believed that an inclusive Executive ought to be set up first, as part of the full implementation of the Belfast Agreement. Only then, when politics was seen to be working, would Sinn Fein be prepared to make a full effort in the context of that deal to address the issue as stipulated in the treaty text. In their view, this did not necessarily mean actual decommissioning, and certainly not at the behest of the Unionists and the British (or even the Irish Government). The republicans repeatedly told their British interlocutors that Trimble was only demanding decommissioning at the behest of his own hardliners and was exaggerating his own weakness for bargaining purposes.[1] British officials sought to explain to them that these problems were not hyped. But after a while they concluded that republicans – at least in the first half of the year – were relatively uninterested in Trimble and therefore would do little or nothing to bolster his position. If he fell, another Unionist leader could always come along, who would still have to do business with them. This mystified the officials, the ablest of whom understood Trimble's crucial role. 'David Trimble's future is as important to them as it is to him, and in some ways more so,' noted one senior civil servant. Some Trimbleista critics of British policy wondered why these officials necessarily assumed that Sinn Fein/IRA would want to preserve the UUP leader. Certainly, the British needed Trimble to make the vision of a new, agreed Northern Ireland work, but republicans did not necessarily share that preferred vision: many of them believed that given a choice between the continuation of the peace process on the one hand and the cross-community political institutions with Trimble at their head on the other, the two Governments would ultimately opt for the former. If Trimble fell as a result of their refusal to decommission by the 10 March deadline for devolution, they believed that they would continue to benefit from those aspects of the Government's reform programme – changes to the RUC, prisoner releases and the equality and human rights agendas – whilst those aspects which were of less interest to them such as the Assembly (with its Unionist majority) would disappear. Only a Government threat to suspend prisoner releases and/or RUC reforms could have supplied the necessary leverage, but these were never regarded as serious options by either the British or Irish states.

There were, however, concrete manifestations of Trimble's difficulties – exemplifed by his unwillingness to move against the rebel Assemblyman for North Down, Peter Weir, after the latter had lost the party whip for voting with the DUP against the 18 December accords on 18 January 1999. Eoghan Harris, as a good one-time Leninist, counselled in favour of ruthless purges of those bent on creating, as he saw it, oppositional factions within the party; but this was not possible in the UUP, which was the antithesis of the democratic centralism of the old Workers' Party (when Weir was eventually expelled from the UUP in 2001 and then joined the DUP in 2002, Trimble was hugely relieved). As Trimble told journalists in America during his St Patrick's Day visit in 1999, the entire Unionist family in the Assembly was now evenly split between pro- and anti-Agreement forces. 'Technically I could continue if I dropped one or two more members, but morally I would be defeated and could not carry on for much longer,' he noted.[2] Trimble and his supporters felt physically vulnerable, too: he was roundly abused by anti-Agreement unionists when he arrived to speak in Fivemiletown, Co. Tyrone.[3] Certainly, such anti-Agreement demonstrations were comparatively rare and poorly attended, but the broader communal mood made any bold initiatives suicidal. For many of the headlines in January–February were dominated by continuing provocations from republican (and loyalist) paramilitaries. Above all, the punishment beatings confirmed the suspicion of Unionist sceptics that Sinn Fein were still not a normal political party ready for government. Of greater concern still to Trimble was the killing on 27 January 1999 of former IRA terrorist, Eamon Collins, who had become a prominent critic of the organisation. He had been horribly murdered, and Trimble feared for the safety of his own friend, Sean O'Callaghan (who was moving from safe-house to safe-house).[4] Consequently, in the first months of 1999, it was the republican movement which appeared to be under the greater pressure.

But the most significant political intervention came from an unexpected source. In an interview in *The Sunday Times* on 14 February 1999, Ahern stated that Sinn Fein's participation in an Executive would not be possible 'without at least commencement of decommissioning, and that would apply in the North and in the South'. According to an MRBI poll in the *Irish Times*, 45% of respondents agreed, whilst 39% thought that it was not possible to have decommissioning before the formation of an Executive.[5] Some senior Irish officials were horrified by the Taoiseach's bluntness, not to mention Sinn Fein: a republican briefing paper leaked to the *Sunday Independent* and reported on 7 March described Ahern as 'the biggest danger to the peace process – bigger even than Blair'. It added ominously: 'We have been pushed too far. If [Ahern] believes he can push us to where he thinks he wants us to be, he will get his answer before mid-March.' The UUP leader, though, was delighted by Ahern's pronouncement. As Denis Rogan recalls, 'at that stage David Trimble was quite confident decommissioning was a done deal'.[6] He believed that the process was now irreversible and that republican militarists had nowhere else to go. But contrary to what some believed, Trimble was not hellbent on causing a split in republican ranks.[7] Rather, he saw decommissioning as an either way bet. If they disarmed and an inclusive Executive was formed, all well and good. He would then have won the prize of a stable Northern Ireland. And if not, Sinn Fein/IRA would stand 'exposed' before the world as the recalcitrant party. Privately, though, some sources close to Trimble were already saying that he would accept a relatively minimalist gesture 'up front', coupled with a guarantee underwritten by de Chastelain that the IRA would complete the task by May 2000. In fact, the issue of decommissioning did not quite turn out to be the either way bet he had hoped for: the republican movement successfully held out for long enough to receive other concessions from the two Governments that made Trimble's position very uncomfortable indeed. His anger with the Governments stemmed from his belief that they did not have to make those concessions. 'They [Sinn Fein/IRA] know what they've got to do, so there's no point in Government paying them to do what they're going to have to do anyhow,' he would frequently declare in this period.

Meanwhile, Trimble proceeded with the strategy of setting up all of the institutions and then – he hoped – of turning the heat on Sinn Fein. On 16 February, the Assembly voted by 77–29 to endorse the structures of government proposed in a report by Trimble and Mallon. On the

Unionist side, the vote was much narrower – 29 apiece. Even this result was only secured at the last minute by a letter from Trimble to the Assemblyman for East Antrim, Roy Beggs Jr (son of the anti-Agreement Westminster MP for the same division) promising that the party would not allow the appointment of Sinn Fein ministers to the Executive until the IRA had begun decommissioning. Meanwhile, the process of setting up the institutions of government continued: the British and Irish Governments signed four treaties on 8 March 1999 providing the legal framework for the North-South implementation bodies and other such manifestations of the Belfast Agreement.[8] But Trimble's carefully constructed plan to put the republican movement on the spot, by completing his side of the bargain by 10 March, foundered upon Mowlam's decision to shift the deadline: he saw it as a deliberate attempt by her to let the paramilitaries off the hook.[9]

Once again, Blair was able to becalm Trimble. Before the UUP leader left for America for the annual St Patrick's Day celebrations, the Prime Minister also advised him – in the words of one official – to 'play the reasonable, sensible guy, bringing the community along'.[10] He tried to take this advice, rhapsodising to John Sweeney, President of the AFL-CIO, about the 'vision thing'; communing with Senator Edward Kennedy; and even making sure to be seen to go over and talk to Gerry Adams at the Speaker's lunch.[11] But what should have been something of a lap of honour as the first St Patrick's Day since the signing of the Belfast Agreement and his Nobel award was marred by news from his constituency: on 15 March 1999, Rosemary Nelson, a prominent Lurgan solicitor widely loathed amongst elements of the loyalist community for her defence work on behalf of republicans, was murdered by a bomb placed under her car. The attack was claimed by a group called Red Hand Defenders.[12] The killing, though, did not stop him from pursuing the arms issue vigorously with Clinton and with Adams. The UUP leader mentioned to the President that he needed to meet with Sinn Fein, and Clinton promptly offered to let the two provincial party leaders meet at the White House. They met alone in the private residence and they hit upon the notion of 'jumping together' – that is, forming an Executive simultaneously to decommissioning.[13]

Such talks no doubt brought Trimble the kudos of being seen as a reasonable man in Washington, London and Dublin, but came at the price of losing support within the unionist community. In his leader's address to the annual meeting of the UUC the following weekend, Trimble informed the party's ruling body that IRA decommissioning would take place. It was not a question of whether, he said, but when. Trimble obtained a standing ovation, but as the session was closing, some delegates began to heckle. They wanted to know what Trimble meant by 'credible'. When he replied 'significant', there were shouts of 'fudge' and 'shame' and the president of the UUP, Josias Cunningham, swiftly curtailed the session by calling for the singing of the National Anthem.[14] Of greater significance were the results for the annual election of the UUP officer team. The vociferously anti-Agreement William Ross nearly overtook Jim Nicholson in the contest for one of four vice presidencies and the more politely sceptical Martin Smyth topped the poll in that contest with 501 votes. In the contest for the four honorary secretaryships, all of the anti-Agreement incumbents – David Brewster, Jeffrey Donaldson, Arlene Foster and Jim Rodgers – beat off challenges from Trimble loyalists.[15] There was thus no change in any of the officerial positions, but considering Trimble's new-found authority as First Minister-designate and a largely loyal Assembly group, it was a relatively poor performance by the leadership (Ken Maginnis further observes that Trimble displayed his greatest organisational ability within the party at the time of the leadership election in 1995 and has never been able quite to match it since!)[16]. Certainly, the 'antis' were more motivated. But it was also the case that opinion had genuinely shifted in the direction of the 'noes' at the grassroots, so that the constituency associations were returning far more sceptical delegates to the party's ruling body. In the Executive Council elections on 16 April for the party chairmanship, vice chairmanship and assistant treasurership, pro-Agreement stalwarts won out – but the results overall indicated a rough 60%–40% split in favour of the deal. This meant that support had declined from the 70%–30% ratio registered on both the Executive and the UUC in April 1998.[17] This balance of forces pertained during much of the coming year: the 'antis' could not remove him, but Trimble's room for manoeuvre was further constrained. And it continued not because of the personal popularity of prominent individuals within the 'no' camp – in fact, the very reverse was often the case – but because of what ordinary Unionists saw as the relentless pace of concessions to republicans.

Trimble's room for manoeuvre was narrowing, but there was little sign of any movement from republicans either – or at least so the two

Governments believed. There was now only one way to break the impasse, as had occurred at previous moments of crisis: another injection of Prime Ministerial magic. Blair and Ahern duly held court in the Lady Grey drawing room at Hillsborough Castle from 29 March, chosen in part because it represented a welcome change from the bleakness of Castle Buildings at Stormont: they were attracted by the notion of wrapping it all up on the anniversary of the Belfast Agreement. Yet it appears to have occurred to no one in the British Government until it was too late that the Easter period, with all its associations with the 1916 uprising, was not the best time to push the Provisionals. Trimble was concerned about the atmospherics of holding such a summit at Hillsborough, away from the Assembly group, which could lead to all kinds of rumours about the concessions which the UUP leader might make in such a 'pressure cooker'. Accordingly, after a 'warm-up' on the first day, Trimble, Empey and Rogan took a collective decision to bring the 28-strong UUP caucus down to Hillsborough and to keep them informed as they had done in the immediate run-up to the 18 December accords, when Reg Empey and others briefed them on an almost hourly basis.[18] Initially, the caucus was quartered in the White Gables Hotel at Hillsborough, but Trimble saw that they were insufficiently active – and, in any case, there were rumours that the group might be besieged by anti-Agreement loyalists, which would make some of the more nervous Assemblymen likelier to reject any settlement. The calculation proved correct, even though the barracking continued whenever a pro-Agreement Unionist was spotted at the window: thus, some of them shouted 'backs to the wall' at appearances of the flamboyantly homosexual Steven King, John Taylor's aide-de-camp.[19] With the UUP Assembly group there, Trimble insisted that they engage with other parties such as the Alliance and SDLP to find out what was going on: better that, he thought, than just talking amongst themselves and becoming ever more depressed ('an Ulster Unionist characteristic,' notes Trimble). 'Educating' his party was not his aim at Hillsborough, he adds, though it was a consequence of it. This, he says, helped further to bond the Assembly group, giving them more confidence and thus enabling them to take more risks over time.[20] It also proved to be an education for the Prime Minister – who in a fast-moving summit was anxious for everyone to be on hand and to close on any deal quickly. Above all, Blair wanted to make sure any deal stuck, rather than having to refer back the next day to the UUP Assembly group (when all kinds of doubts could emerge in the intervening period). Eventually, John Taylor asked Blair, 'Prime Minister, why don't you take a break from the talks and talk to our people?' Taylor – who on the eve of the summit had again offered Trimble's resignation if Mowlam triggered d'Hondt without decommissioning – says that he wanted the Prime Minister to realise the strength of feeling in the UUP.[21] David Campbell anticipated Taylor's concerns about ditching even residual forms of prior decommissioning. He told his leader that he feared that if the First Minister-designate did not have Taylor with him, he could not carry the UUP: he accompanied the UUP deputy leader as the latter did his rounds to observe Taylor's influence on the Assembly group.[22]

A group of Assemblymen gathered around Blair at the foot of the stairs. They included Roy Beggs, Jr and Ken Robinson (both from East Antrim), Billy Armstrong (Mid-Ulster) and Jim Wilson (South Antrim and the chief whip). It was Armstrong who took up the bulk of the Prime Minister's time. 'They're lovely people,' Blair told Trimble and Taylor. 'But they're politically naive.'[23] Was Blair right, though? He believed that relatively small matters such as the order in which decommissioning and the formation of an Executive took place needed to be set against Unionism's success in securing its big demand – the consent principle. But to men like Armstrong, who had lived through the past 30 years, matters did not run along such clear lines. He was no intellectual but rather was a dairy farmer who had joined the RUC part-time reserve after two British soldiers were blown to smithereens in his home town of Stewartstown, Co. Tyrone. Also injured in the attack was Charlie McConaghy, the community policeman whom Armstrong had known since childhood when he did his rounds on his bike: McConaghy lost his sight and much of his hearing in the attack, and later became chairman of the Disabled Police Officers' Association. Armstrong himself had been wounded in the arm when the car in which he was travelling was raked by Provisional gunfire, but he could live with that. What he felt worst about was helping a friend, Jack Scott, to sign up to the RUC Reserve: a while later, Scott was shot dead whilst driving his milk tanker.[24] As he contemplated letting an unrepentant Sinn Fein/IRA into government, Armstrong remembered those who had fallen and wondered how much had really changed.[25] Indeed, the coming years tended to show that it was Blair, the world leader and his staff of urban sophisticates, who had the more naive view of Northern Ireland – and not the farmer from the heart of rural Ulster.

Most of the serious business was done in bilaterals between Blair and Ahern and one of the local party leaders (Trimble often went alone, but Adams came with McGuinness). On the last night, Adams also insisted on no notes and no officials in his sessions. This could make subsequent debriefing of the heads of Governments by officials quite difficult, thus increasing the danger of misunderstanding. The Irish read-out did not always conform with the British read-out and Sinn Fein's recollections could easily be different from those of the Governments.[26] Interestingly, as on Good Friday 1998, Mowlam appeared to both senior UUP and SDLP figures to have been largely cut out from some of the main discussions, and often sat in the Prime Minister's outer office.[27] According to Sean Farren, 'she wandered round like an uninvited guest at the party and looked after everyone'.[28] Given that there were around a hundred people from all delegations present, that was no mean task: Seamus Mallon was forced on the last night to sleep on the floor of the Throne Room in his suit, whilst the Prime Minister vacated the Queen's Bedroom for Ken Maginnis. Maginnis recalls the humorous circumstances. Before he got off to sleep Mowlam passed by to make sure everyone was all right. 'Good night, Mo!' barked Maginnis, and she promptly disappeared. So soundly did Maginnis sleep that night – he was used to kipping in slit trenches and Observation Posts as an ex-major in the UDR – that Blair was later able to enter the room, shower and change without the UUP security spokesman noticing.[29]

During the course of the discussions, several key themes emerged. On a date to be set, nominations would be made under d'Hondt to identify those who would take up office as ministers, for which changes would be required to standing orders of the Assembly; at a date to be proposed by the Independent International Commission on Decommissioning, but not less than a month after the nomination date, a collective act of reconciliation would take place which would see some arms put 'beyond use', on a voluntary basis; there would simultaneously be ceremonies of remembrance of victims of violence to which all Churches would be invited. At about this point, powers would be devolved and the institutions would come into force. A month after the nomination of ministers, the decommissioning body would report progress; if not, then those appointments would have to be confirmed by the Assembly. The latter point was especially important. The old standing orders had said no further vote was required after the initial identification of ministers. But now, another vote would be needed to put Sinn Fein ministers into office – as opposed to a motion to keep them out. From the UUP viewpoint, this was a great improvement, since a vote to exclude would never win the necessary cross-community support from the SDLP. By contrast, another vote to put them in required UUP support and thus gave the pro-British majority a veto. Republicans were seething over this last point, especially with the Irish Government. 'Serves them right for murdering 2000 people,' observed Steven King.[30] Greater public attention, though, was lavished upon the proposal for a Day of Reconciliation, which many Unionists felt placed victims of terrorist violence on a moral par with terrorists shot *in flagrante delicto* by the security forces: would the families of shot policemen be standing alongside the families of shot gunmen? The idea appears first to have been mooted by the Church of Ireland Rector of Glenageary, Dublin, and also the Archdeacon of Dublin, the Venerable Gordon Linney. He was inspired by the monumental statue of Christ of the Andes located on the Chilean–Argentinian border and which was made out of materials of war between the two countries. The Archdeacon duly approached Dr Martin Mansergh, a communicant member of the Church of Ireland, who was interested and passed on the idea to Irish Government colleagues.[31] 'It was not my cup of tea, but if it made things easier for other people, well and good,' recalls Trimble.[32]

Adams later came to believe that the Day of Reconciliation was a good idea and there was even some evidence that he made a stab at selling it to fellow republicans during the summit itself. Indeed, as Sinn Fein came under intense pressure from the Irish Government, it appeared at one point on the final night of 31 March/1 April that agreement was tantalisingly close. Paul Murphy, then the Political Development Minister, believed as much, as did Seamus Mallon. 'My understanding when I lay down in the Throne Room [his berth for the night] at 3–4 a.m. [on 1 April] was that they had signed up,' stated the then SDLP deputy leader. 'I got that from very senior British and Irish officials. At 10 a.m. that morning that was still my understanding. They [Sinn Fein] were invisible and were walking around in the gardens with people I had never seen before from other organisations.'[33] By this, Mallon was referring to some of the IRA's ruling Army Council who turned up at Hillsborough after Adams and McGuinness had driven into the night to meet them for several hours at a secret location.

Some NIO officials detected a change in the body language of Sinn

Fein when other comrades turned up; it all became much frostier after the trip into the night. Trimble wanted Blair to seal the deal there and then, but the Prime Minister was prevailed upon by Ahern that the Sinn Fein leadership needed more time. 'Ahern said there had been progress but the judgment was that if they were pushed too hard now we will lose it,' recalls Trimble. 'It implies that significant elements in the republican movement would like to sell it.' Trimble had evidence of his own to back it up. When the IRA's niggardly Easter statement was published during the summit, Trimble told Adams that a number of people were very disappointed by it.[34] Adams, he says, was obviously taken aback. 'Who told you it would go further?' asked the Sinn Fein president. 'Journalists,' said Trimble, as Adams visibly calmed down. In fact, Trimble had been told this by both the British and the Irish. It was further evidence to the UUP leader of the direction in which the process would take republicans, no matter how hesitant or slow they were.[35] According to senior British sources, the two republicans personally thought the declaration was reasonable. So as the two Prime Ministers read the text of the Hillsborough declaration on a gloriously sunny Good Friday afternoon – with the UUP, SDLP and Sinn Fein hierarchies clustered at their feet – there was no obvious sign that anything was dramatically amiss.

But as Adams and McGuinness consulted their followers further, a very different picture emerged. According to Ed Moloney, the declaration went down very badly with the grassroots – as evidenced by the poor turn-outs for the political speeches after the colourful Easter republican parades.[36] Indeed, so intense was the criticism of the Taoiseach in nationalist quarters that key Irish officials gradually came to believe that the two Governments had drifted too far to the Unionist side and the tack needed to be changed.[37] 'The republicans got at the Fianna Fail grassroots,' recalls Trimble. 'Every time Bertie says something helpful to me, they go and beat him up. So I don't expect him to say things very often. If he says them every now and again, that's enough for me.'[38] Trimble was very understanding of the difficulties of others: time and again, he displayed a lack of ruthlessness with other 'principals' in the process.

This confusion was brought to an end after twelve days when Sinn Fein formally rejected the Hillsborough declaration. It pronounced the declaration an attempt to rewrite the Belfast Agreement, which made devolution dependent upon IRA decommissioning.[39] After a meeting between Trimble and McGuinness, Reg Empey declared that the pre-Hillsborough stand-off had resumed.[40] But Trimble was most vexed by Mowlam, who, as he saw it, in the face of the paramilitaries' refusal to disarm, simply appeared to throw up her hands and accept their decision. 'Oh well, if everybody's against it, that's it,' he recalls her saying.[41] In the coming days, the republicans were able to persuade the Irish Government that because the institutions of government were not in place, their position vis-à-vis the dissidents had weakened and that their trust in Trimble was at a low ebb. The republicans conveyed a similar message to the British.[42] Thus, as so often during the course of the peace process, the pendulum was now swinging back in the other direction. As the height of the marching season loomed, Blair was more determined than ever to have the institutions fully functioning. The stage was thus set for what Trimble calls the 'son of Hillsborough': an attempt to re-run that abortive summit, but with a shifting mix of proposals.[43] However, in the run-up to this gathering, Blair had less time, both because of family commitments and because of the Kosovo campaign. He was, therefore, less patient as he shuttled between the factions which were assembled in Downing Street on Friday 14 May. But this underlying irritation was not immediately obvious as Trimble and the UUP team arrived at around 11:30 a.m. They included John Taylor, David Campbell (chief of staff) David Kerr (press secretary) and David Lavery (principal private secretary). However, the Assembly team as a whole was very much not there, unlike at Hillsborough. Even Reg Empey, who might normally have attended such occasions, chose to remain in Belfast for the mayor-making at City Hall: the margins were so narrow now on the Council that he felt that every vote mattered vitally. In any case, says Empey, the Downing Street discussions appeared beforehand not to be particularly important.[44] Trimble was struck by the sight of republican delegates walking proprietorially around the garden, where the damage of an IRA mortar attack of 1991 was still visible. On the stairwell by the garden, Trimble also noticed a photograph of the War Cabinet during Lloyd George's premiership. He pointed out to Blair that it contained two Unionist leaders, Edward Carson and Walter Long. Blair, Trimble says, interpreted it as a hint that he should be in the Cabinet too.[45] At one point, recalls David Kerr, a tremendous racket was heard in the garden. It was the Blair boys playing football with some friends. 'Oy, stop mucking about,' shouted Blair. The boys immediately ceased. But with the Prime Minister safely back inside again and out of earshot, the game resumed as before.[46]

Blair first met with Trimble alone (and, significantly, without John Taylor). He then met Blair with Taylor and later with others. 'I believe that I can get them to say they believe decommissioning will happen if an administration is formed,' said Blair with his salesman's pitch. The bones of a deal soon began to emerge. As Frank Millar later observed, the final draft – which presumably bore at least a family resemblance to the earlier versions – carried no reference to decommissioning as an 'obligation', much less anything resembling a commitment by the IRA to start the process or to have it completed by May 2000. Nor was there any mention of sanctions to be applied against Sinn Fein if the IRA failed to deliver – a reversal of what appeared to have been agreed at Hillsborough.[47] Instead, it simply stated that 'all parties agree to the full implementation of all aspects of the Good Friday agreement including the objective of achieving total disarmament and complete withdrawal of all weapons from politics in Ireland [sic]. They accept that the issue of arms must be finally and satisfactorily settled and will do what they can to achieve decommissioning of all paramilitary arms within the time frame set down in the agreement. The International Commission on Decommissioning will now begin a period of intensive discussions with all parties and report back on progress before 30th June. All parties anticipate, without prejudice to their clear positions on this issue, a devolution of powers by 30th June.' Thus, the Ulster Unionists would have to form an Executive on the basis of a report from de Chastelain but without any actual 'product'.

Oddly, Trimble did not see these Downing Street proposals as demonstrably inferior to those put forward at Hillsborough some six weeks earlier. Indeed, according to one observer of the day's proceedings, he was disappointed that Hillsborough had failed and was anxious to find a way through the impasse (when he ought ideally, says this witness, to have displayed indifference).[48] He was confronted by a shirtsleeved Prime Minister who was affecting his best bedside 'trust me, I'm Tony' mode. Anyone else who presented Trimble with such a lack of detail would have been cruelly exposed by the UUP leader, but not Blair: as the Prime Minister outlined his proposals, Trimble would lean forward and move to the edge of the sofa. One of the Irish delegation states that at the first meeting between Trimble and his full team on the one side and Blair's and Ahern's teams on the other, it was David Lavery who declared that the emerging 14 May proposals would compare very unfavourably with the previous month's document. Lavery just managed to make it into the meeting with Trimble and Taylor. John Sawers, the Prime Minister's Private Secretary for foreign affairs, who had succeeded John Holmes in February 1999, blocked the entrance to the room and thus prevented David Campbell and David Kerr from joining them. As Lavery completed his interjection, recalls one of the Unionists, Sawers administered a put-down – as if to say, 'don't intervene again'.[49] Blair was also vexed, and his icy manner resembled that of the car salesman who sees the husband is keen to buy but is stymied when the wife objects to the colour and size of the vehicle. Trimble looked concerned, but he did not abort nor even raise major worries. Both Campbell and Kerr had already expressed their reservations after Trimble and Taylor had met alone with Blair, but the UUP leader was equally intolerant of these objections. He created the impression that he believed that this formula was the last chance that the Unionists would have. Curiously, John Taylor, whose antennae for the mood of the unionist population were usually very sensitive, encouraged the emerging 14 May formula. 'I do feel there is something here,' he opined: he was especially pleased that the idea of a Day of Reconciliation, positing a degree of moral equilateralism between terrorists and the security forces, had not survived the rejection of Hillsborough.[50] Things appeared promising enough to the leadership at mid-afternoon on Friday, so that David Campbell contacted the UUP chief whip, Jim Wilson, to say that a proposal would be ready for consideration by the Assembly group on the next day in the party room at Stormont.[51]

Taylor left Downing Street at 4:30 p.m.: his wife was ill back at home in Co. Armagh and he had to catch the next flight home. Trimble was not concerned about being left alone with two junior aides and a civil servant, facing heavyweight delegations from the British and Irish Governments, plus Sinn Fein and the SDLP (indeed, so relaxed was he throughout much of the day that at one point an astonished Blair came upon him in the Cabinet Room reading a volume of Cromwell's letters and speeches, which included missives from Ireland). Trimble also teased Seamus Mallon about Cromwell's description of the taking of Newry, one of the two main urban centres in the SDLP deputy leader's constituency: the UUP leader informed his nationalist counterpart that it 'fell without a fight'. Mallon, he recalls, smiled wanly.[52] Such reading was something of a habit of Trimble's: at another moment of crisis, an aide found the First Minister-designate engrossed in a copy of Toby Harnden's *Bandit*

Country, about south Armagh. The former Queen's land law lecturer was especially intrigued to find out if the book contained anything about Thomas 'Slab' Murphy's farm, which straddled the border – and conjectured as to its rateable value. The description of the farm outbuildings and the mill indicated to him that the Murphys were a comparatively well-off family.[53]

The increasingly impatient Blair and Trimble duly met alone again after Taylor's departure; another document emerged in time for the final meeting between 7 and 8 p.m. Some of the Irish officials were astonished that Trimble appeared willing to agree to a final version of the draft agreement which gave him so little; at one point, Ahern even came in and said to his team 'we've got to give something to Trimble'. One Irish official also remembers Blair in his shirtsleeves telling them 'David Trimble is prepared to do this', to which the Irish replied 'on what basis?' The Irish further claim that in a multilateral session Trimble confirmed that he would be prepared to go ahead and that they asked Lavery and Campbell whether the UUP leader could deliver his own party.[54] No Ulster Unionist can remember any such expressions of tender Irish concern at the time itself, though amongst themselves, the southerners may well have been astonished by Trimble's flexibility. They had expected radical language from the Provisionals at the start of that week – along the lines of, if not exactly, 'the war is over' – and when it was not forthcoming they expected Trimble to come back at them and bargain. But instead of bargaining, Trimble simply signed up. Frank Millar was struck by Ahern's body language as he emerged that night from No. 10: he looked miserable, and Millar later learned from his Irish sources that the Taoiseach believed that Trimble had concluded an unsellable deal. Likewise, David Andrews recalls that Ahern was very surprised, not least by the deadline. 'Deadlines are preconditions,' declared the Taoiseach.[55] The British side also believed that Trimble would try and sell the deal; as far as they were concerned, it was not for the Prime Minister to say what Trimble could and could not persuade his own folk to do. 'He could see the potential of such an arrangement and thought he would go and do his best to explain it to [his people]', Blair recalls.[56] Accordingly, No. 10 told the editors of the Sunday newspapers to clear the way for a major announcement at 5 p.m. on Saturday 15 May.

By this point, Blair was even more tired and anxious to peel away to join his waiting family. Trimble recalls during the latter part of the proceedings, Blair appeared to be disengaged, but is also adamant that during a walk in the garden, he backpedalled and told the Prime Minister that he could not sign up there and then. Rather, he would have to refer it to his Assembly group. He says that as the evening wore on, he had become increasingly unhappy with the proposal and perhaps it would have been better if he had left sooner.[57] It is not clear why he should have become sceptical so quickly after having been prepared to give it such a fair wind; indeed, Alastair Campbell now says that it was unclear what exactly Trimble had agreed to do, though he adds that the UUP leader seemed happy enough on 14 May itself.[58] The UUP leader thus left No. 10 in what he calls a 'foul mood' thinking about how he would let Blair down. The delegation then went to a Pizza Express, where he telephoned the UUP chairman, Denis Rogan, to tell him what had happened.[59] Rogan recalls Trimble as reporting to him that Taylor had to leave early. 'That's rather unfortunate – you would have been better to leave as well and not to be left there,' said Rogan. Trimble replied: 'You're probably right but I wanted to finish it.' Although Trimble sounded not 100% happy with the negotiations as he put the telephone down, Rogan was nonetheless convinced that the UUP leader was going to come home to sell it.[60]

As Trimble and his team made their way to the airport on Saturday 15 May, he was contacted by No. 10: could he come back for the press conference that was scheduled for 5 p.m. that afternoon? Trimble declined. He had a job to do in Belfast and having slept on the matter, felt no more inclined to support the proposal than he had the night before.[61] Whilst at the airport, Trimble ran into John Taylor, who had missed his flight the night before.[62] The NIO wondered whether Trimble had a 'handling problem' with Taylor and feared that he was going to be 'offside'.[63] But the NIO official concerned was wrong on this occasion. Trimble had briefed Taylor at Heathrow before the meeting of the Assembly group in Belfast; but when Taylor arrived later at the caucus after Trimble briefed his colleagues, the UUP deputy leader endorsed the Downing Street plan. Normally, he enjoyed playing the role of sceptic who restrained his colleagues, but on this occasion, says Trimble, 'his position was more advanced than mine'.[64]

As Trimble presented his introductory comments to the Assembly group, at Stormont, he looked up and noticed that most of his colleagues were sitting with their hands down: it was a rare instance, he says, when he observed the body language of the Assemblymen. Indeed, David Kerr recalls that even Empey – who normally was to be found beside Trimble at such meetings – sat at the opposite end of the table.[65] (Empey says that any such positioning was entirely coincidental.) But Trimble ploughed on in his usual matter-of-fact way, running through the sequence of events of the previous day. He told them that although he did not particularly like aspects of the deal, he did not want to say 'no' outright and wished to have authorisation to renegotiate. This proved unsustainable: crucially for Trimble, Empey was against the deal as it stood. Some reports at the time suggested eight out of the 28 UUP delegation were opposed, but the actual total appears to have been higher still.[66] Moreover, there was little inclination to take such a big risk with the European elections taking place in the following month.[67] Trimble duly telephoned the Prime Minister in person to convey the Assembly group's verdict. 'I'm sorry, my people aren't going to run with this,' Trimble told Blair. If even that body was so strongly opposed to the intergovernmental proposal then what chance was there that the more sceptical UUP officers, executive and council would accept it? Blair was courteous enough there and then, but at 5 p.m. on 15 May, he delivered his rebuff: an absolute deadline of 30 June for full devolution of power, in line with Scotland and Wales. The last point had appealed to Trimble, and the 30 June deadline was at least partly his own idea. But that was only in the context of putting it up to the Provisionals on a 'take it or leave it' basis. He did not anticipate that the concept of the 'pressure cooker' would rebound on himself and that it would be proffered on anything but his own terms. The Prime Minister had obviously expected him to make a serious effort at selling the document and was furious when it appeared to him that Trimble did not do so – this at a time when all the media had been notified to expect a big announcement.[68] The signal appeared unambiguous: that it was time for the UUP to put up or shut up and to ensure that the matter was resolved once and for all, even if there was no actual decommissioning. There was even the hint, asserted volubly by the SDLP and Sinn Fein, that the Assembly would be closed down. Worst of all, Trimble – who had staked so much on Blair's goodwill – had now apparently lost the favour of the metropolitan suzerain.

Many regarded this as the lowest ebb of Trimble's leadership to date, and Daphne Trimble states that he was annoyed with himself for losing control of the situation.[69] How did it come about? Certainly, he appeared not to have seen it coming and to have violated some of his own rules about managing such situations. He was left virtually alone with other delegations and the Prime Minister (the latter was something which he swore not to do when he replaced Molyneaux, and though it was scarcely honoured in the letter, it had symbolised in Trimble's mind the idea that a UUP leader would not be suborned by the occupant of No. 10). Second – and flowing from the first point – he had run ahead of opinion in the Assembly group and not kept them properly informed. Third, if one side had the advantage during a summit – as the Unionists enjoyed at Hillsborough – the pendulum swung back towards the other side in the next round (just as, in early 1998, the Unionist-sounding Heads of Agreement was followed by the nationalist-sounding Lancaster House communiqué). Both Governments, moreover, accepted that Adams had made what they considered to be a genuine effort. Thus Adams stated on 11 May – the day that he was to meet Blair at No. 10 – that the Belfast Agreement was 'in tatters' and his warnings were taken seriously. But a more sinister message lay behind this *cri de coeur*. Trimble had certainly been told several times by John Sawers, Blair's Private Secretary, about the threat of dissident republican attacks on London between the time of Hillsborough and 14 May 1999, though the UUP leader did not take them that seriously.[70] Indeed, Reg Empey states that when he and Trimble met with Blair after Hillsborough, he challenged the Prime Minister on whether there had been a renewed terrorist threat. Empey says he did not receive a direct reply to his direct question.[71] Thus if the two Governments could not press one side to yield, they would turn the heat on the other. In that sense, they followed the path of least resistance. No. 10 also believed that the UUP Assemblymen were so in thrall to their salaries plus expenses – a very substantial income in Northern Ireland – that they would not ultimately do anything that seriously jeopardised their financial security. But the theory did not stand up. As Frank Millar observed, it was a miscalculation, and the apparent threat had the opposite effect at Saturday's meeting of the Assembly group.[72]

Personality factors also played their part in the outcome of 14 May. At some level, Trimble hero-worshipped Blair and was loath to say no to a politician still at the height of his powers. One observer of many of their meetings – who, significantly, was not from the UUP delegation – offers the following observation. 'David Trimble negotiates very hard until he gets to No. 10. But having gone there, he frequently, but not always, concedes. His preoccupation with detail works against him. The Prime Minister says "look, you've got to look at the big picture and I'm Tony and you've got to trust me". Ken Reid of UTV, who observed the events of 14 May, states that at that point, Trimble was still 'like the little boy from Clifton Road, Bangor, who has become friends with the Prime Minister. He loves the trappings of No. 10 – but not the social side'.[73] There is some evidence that he was 'turned': Graham Gudgin, then his special adviser, was present with other counsellors when Trimble spoke to Blair on the telephone prior to the meeting. The Prime Minister tried to press Trimble to dilute his positions but, Gudgin recalls, the UUP leader rebutted Blair with concision and firmness.[74] But everything changed when he was faced in the flesh by an occupant of No. 10 who was unaccustomed to failure. Blair had relished riding to the rescue with the Taoiseach and applying Prime Ministerial magic where lesser politicians and officials had fallen short. Increasingly, however, this formula proved to be not enough – rather like an antibiotic which had been employed once too often. Nor did the UUP believe that they had much sympathy from John Sawers, the Prime Minister's Principal Private Secretary for foreign affairs, who had replaced John Holmes in February 1999 upon the announcement of the latter's appointment as ambassador to Portugal, and whom Trimble found to be a 'cold fish'. Holmes had been the Unionists' principal interlocutor and had provided the element of continuity between the Major and Blair ministries. But it was another illustration of how Unionists were far more driven by their emotions about personalities than is commonly supposed. Again, the Irish picked up on this apparent *froideur* and came to believe that the UUP had 'no friend at court'.

No. 10's conviction that the matter had to be settled quickly was reinforced by polling evidence suggesting surprisingly strong Protestant support for the Belfast agreement – such as the Ulster Marketing Surveys study for the *Irish Times* and RTE on 27 April which put it at 73% (though 71% of Protestants opposed the creation of an Executive without decommissioning). No. 10's impatience and setting of the 30 June deadline owed as much to ignorance as to pique: Paul Bew spoke to Jonathan Powell a few days after the Downing Street summit and was astonished to find that the Prime Minister's chief of staff appeared to be unaware that European elections in Ulster were upcoming and that there was a serious danger that if pushed into a bad deal, the UUP might lose one of Ulster's three seats.[75] So precarious was Trimble's position within the party that when a trilateral working breakfast was reconvened between the parties at Downing Street on 20 May, the First Minister-designate was not present: he could not afford to be seen to be suborned again, nor further to jeopardise his relationship with Blair by saying 'no'. Yet despite this debacle, Trimble's opponents – either inside or outside the UUP – could not land the killer blow on him. This astonished Reg Empey, who regarded it as one of the most dangerous moments of his leadership: for the first time, the Assembly party, Trimble's bastion of support, was against him.[76] A step was open to the antis: to convene a special general meeting of the UUC, which could have been triggered by collecting just 60 signatures. On 17 May some UUP Westminster MPs burst into John Taylor's office and angrily demanded to know what had happened over the weekend; and there were further reports that plans were afoot to depose Trimble as leader of the parliamentary party.[77] Certainly, no other party leader was then under as much pressure as Trimble – and few others displayed his powers of recuperation in adversity. Although No. 10 still refuses to admit that it miscalculated in its attempt to 'bounce' Trimble on 14/15 May 1999 and in June/July 1999, there is some evidence that they began to understand that having acted in haste and risked the loss of the UUP leader, they should pull back. On 17 May, Jonathan Powell wrote to Trimble and reassured him that devolution would not occur without Unionists.[78] In part, the Government's retreat from the hard-edged pique of the weekend was reinforced by the message it was receiving from such occasional 'back-channels' as Paul Bew. He spoke to Jonathan Powell straight after the 14 May summit and told him that the emperor had appeared casually to shift his buttocks and in the process to squash the beetle.[79] Shortly thereafter, Bew met Powell at a private residence in Pimlico. Bew sought to explain to Powell the Prime Minister's growing credibility problem within the majority community, stemming from the perception of broken referendum pledges. He noted that Northern Ireland's best-known poetry magazine was called The Honest Ulsterman and that the Prime Minister had somehow to live up to those provincial ideals.[80] In early June, a dinner was held in the small dining room on the first floor of No. 10 which put an end to the period of froideur, with Trimble, Taylor, and Empey from the UUP and Blair, Powell and Sawers from the British Government. It was at this meeting that Taylor again raised his idea of a Welsh-style committee structure, rather than a fully fledged Government. Taylor had long believed that there would be no IRA decommissioning at an acceptable price. He therefore concluded that the principle of inclusivity could only be preserved in a way that was tolerable to the majority community by downgrading the form of devolution, so it would be possible to say that it was not really a Government and more like the power-sharing arrangements that had already existed on local councils. Blair was interested, though he recognised it would be hard to sell to nationalists. One of those present says that Trimble remained silent during this – as if to connote lack of enthusiasm.[81]

The worsening mood – which so often played into the hands of rejectionists – was reinforced by the matter of the 'disappeared'. The 'disappeared' were victims of the Provisionals who had been abducted and whose bodies had been disposed of in hidden locations. After months of campaigning, three sets of remains were found.[82] It entrenched attitudes in the run-up to the European elections – which were going to be difficult enough anyway. For some months, Jim Nicholson, the incumbent Ulster Unionist MEP, had been accused of marital infidelity: at one point, a foe of the former UUP chairman had even played tapes down the telephone to Daphne Trimble, which he claimed were tearful discussions between Nicholson and his mistress (Daphne Trimble held the telephone away from her ear).[83] Trimble himself stood by his embattled colleague. The Trimbleistas believed that Nicholson had been a good MEP and recalled that he had been very supportive in selling the Belfast Agreement. Trimble, who had been divorced, genuinely believed that a private affair which did not affect one's ability to conduct public duties was of comparatively little concern (Trimble also told Steven King that Nicholson's personal problems would mainly be an issue amongst those segments of society where the UUP had relatively little support – such as rural evangelicals).[84] According to Reg Empey, when Trimble informally consulted senior party officers at Parliament Buildings, they were faced with the lack of any viable pro-Agreement alternative to the incumbent MEP.[85] The problem for anyone who wanted to be rid of Nicholson was that he had already been reselected by the party executive and any coup would have required him to go quickly. Trimble states that Nicholson would have fought tooth and nail – though Empey thinks that if Trimble had pulled the plug, Nicholson would have had to go. 'David didn't have the killer instinct,' notes his lieutenant. 'Loyalty played a greater part than the cold cynical view. Some argued for such ruthlessness, in that a loss [of the euro-seat] would have been catastrophic.'[86] Trimble was, however, reinforced in his desire to keep Nicholson because many of those who were urging this course of action were opponents of the Belfast Agreement.

One exception was John Taylor, whom Trimble retrospectively saw as playing the role of 'candid friend'. Taylor pointedly refused to endorse Nicholson's candidature.[87] But at the time, Trimble was sufficiently intrigued about his deputy's stance to seek the opinion of Steven King, then Taylor's aide-de-camp. King remembers that Trimble was annoyed by Taylor's non-endorsement of Nicholson and was keen to keep him quiet on this subject. There was generally, said the UUP leader, a lot of feeling in the Assembly party that Taylor ought to be brought into line – which he supported, but which he feared could lead to Taylor's resignation as deputy leader of the parliamentary party. King also reckoned that his then employer was annoyed that he had been pushed into only serving two terms in the European Parliament (1979–89), on the basis that this was quite sufficient – whereas Nicholson, having given a commitment, was now about to enjoy his third stint in Strasburg.[88] (Taylor regards this as total nonsense, stating that he could not keep both jobs. Rather, he says he feared that the Nicholson affair would damage the UUP in the following election.)[89] But Ken Maginnis, a close friend of Nicholson and a long-time foe of Taylor, believed Trimble took some time to come out strongly in favour of the incumbent MEP because of the UUP deputy leader. Eventually, these private tensions boiled over into the public domain on this issue. 'David was torn between John Taylor and his own desire to stick by Nicholson,' says the former UUP security spokesman.[90] Later, Taylor hit back at Maginnis: 'I think someone who sun-bathes in northern Cyprus during part of the European election campaign has no room to speak'[91] – a charge which Maginnis rejected.

So parlous did Nicholson's position appear that at one point there were fears that he might be pipped at the post by Robert McCartney of the UKUP; others believed that McCartney might obtain enough votes inadvertently to allow Mitchel McLaughlin of Sinn Fein either to win or at a minimum to come third on first preferences after Paisley and Hume. Trimble says he was never really that worried: he thought that nationalists would be so keen to see Hume beat Paisley for the first time since direct elections to the European Parliament were introduced in 1979 that a portion of Sinn Fein supporters would opt for the SDLP leader (which would be a huge psychological victory for the minority community). This, in turn, would mean that Unionists would react by plumping for

Paisley – notwithstanding the DUP leader's supposedly waning appeal. In such a context, believed Trimble, Nicholson's personal problems would turn out to be marginal.[92] Others agreed with him: to Sean Farren of the SDLP, the surprising absence of a mass public outcry about Nicholson's private life was evidence of how much the cultural mores of the unionist community had changed in the last 20 years.[93]

When the votes were counted, Paisley topped the poll for the fifth successive occasion with 192,762 first preferences, with Hume just behind on 190,731. Nicholson scraped in third at 119,507, just ahead of Sinn Fein's 117,643 first preferences. McCartney came sixth with just 20,283: the unionist electorate had decided to punish Blair (and, by implication, Trimble) by going over to Paisley and had then transferred to Nicholson to keep Sinn Fein out.[94] But at a mere 17.6% of first preferences, it was the worst-ever result in Ulster Unionist history – and brutally confirmed the downward trend in the party's vote under Trimble's leadership. Despite this narrow escape, in which four out of five unionists opted for parties which campaigned on a 'no guns, no government' stance, the Government ploughed ahead anyhow. The British regarded Nicholson's victory as a vindication of their stance, and when Trimble cited the thinness of his margins, the British team would cite the focus groups that showed the enduring popularity of the Belfast Agreement (Trimble was sceptical of these, claiming that Ulsterfolk are reluctant to express their preferences, especially when they do not know the political identity of the survey caller).[95]

'The fact that Nicholson survived almost worked against us,' recalls Empey.[96] But what also may have worked against them in terms of British willingness to cut the Unionists further slack was Trimble's emollience even in the midst of the European election campaign. In a *Belfast Telegraph* article on 3 June, Trimble offered to name potential ministers, so long as this was followed by actions which would show that violence was over. First, ministers would be identified under d'Hondt, but there would be no shadow Executive; second, the paramilitaries would make their move; third, the Executive would be formed and power devolved. He returned to the theme which Adams had put forward in March 1999 – of 'jumping together'. Whatever may have been said about Trimble by nationalists during the first few years of his leadership, by mid-1999 there was no doubt that he wanted republicans to play their part in an inclusive Northern Ireland Executive – if not at any price, then at a very high price.

TWENTY-EIGHT

No way forward

IF Unionists imagined that the dinner at Downing Street heralded a shift in policy back in their direction, they were soon disappointed. Kate Hoey, still a Home Office minister, wrote to Jonathan Powell about the widespread perception in the Unionist community that Trimble had been abandoned and emphasised how important it was for the Prime Minister to make another speech which shored up the UUP leader's position. 'If Trimble goes down, all goes down,' was her message.[1] The British and Irish understood this in varying degrees, and keenly hoped for his survival, but they were unwilling to pay that much of a price to achieve it. In fact, although Trimble shared Hoey's expectation that Blair might produce another address which appealed to their sensibilities – something, say, along the lines of his speech of 16 May 1997 – the very reverse turned out to be the case.[2] Blair's chosen forum was Stranmillis University College, a teacher-training centre in south Belfast. Trimble had got wind of its contents on 14 June 1999, the day before it was delivered. 'I don't know if it's going to help me,' he told Ken Reid of UTV.[3] He was right. Although there was a reference to the more anoydne portions of the 16 May 1997 speech, Blair's comments were suffused with the kind of 'moral equilateralism' which so upset Unionists – treating the concerns of democrats on a par with those of the paramilitary parties. 'Unionism must share power with the nationalist and republican community,' said the Prime Minister. 'There can no longer be a Northern Ireland based on other than the principles of justice, fairness and equality and recognition that sectarianism is a thing of the past. Many Republicans do not believe that Unionism will share power with them. Unionists must prove them wrong.'[4] Then came the damning line for many: 'I believe David Trimble is sincere in his desire to make this all work. And I say to those who attack him within Unionism: he has taken the hard road. And he has more integrity doing so than those who undermine him without the faintest clue as to a strategy to put in place of his.' Trimble was thus ever more explicitly associated with the Blairite project of reforming what, by implication, was a rotten, discriminatory society. It was an analysis with which few unionists agreed, however much they saw the necessity of an accommodation with the minority community.

As Frank Millar later observed, '[Trimble is] plainly torn between the expectations of his powerful Prime Minister and the demands of his party. [He] sits alone at Westminster contemplating the nuclear options presented – fearing himself damned if (and politically dead) he does, and guaranteed much the same fate if he does not.'[5] According to a BBC *On the Record* poll later in the month, seventeen out of nineteen Unionist Assemblymen stated that decommissioning was an obligation and precondition. Indeed, at least one MLA told Frank Millar that if this was not achieved, he would sign the DUP-sponsored motion which ensured an immediate priority Assembly debate on a motion to exclude Sinn Fein from the Executive – forcing other UUP dissidents into the very awkward position of deciding whether to vote in favour of placing the Provisionals' representatives into the Government of Northern Ireland. If five defected, Trimble would only be able to count upon 24 pro-Agreement Unionists, against 34 anti-Agreement Unionists, thus giving the rejectionists a critical 60% blocking share of the total Unionist complement in the Assembly.[6]

This intra-communal balance of forces was especially pronounced in the run-up to the 12 July Boyne anniversary celebrations. Chris McGimpsey, the most liberal of Unionists, made this very point in remarks at the Byrne Perry summer school held in Gorey, Co. Wexford. 'I can think of 51 other weeks in the year which would have been more suitable for it,' he observed.[7] London and Dublin, though, were convinced that Trimble himself still wanted to oblige them – and, as Ken Maginnis observed, the British Government was ever more determined to secure a deal in Ulster after Labour's debacle in the European elections.[8] Trimble's informal cadre of advisers was also divided: after Sean O'Callaghan wrote him an open letter in *The Daily Telegraph* on 6 July urging the UUP leader to hold firm, Trimble rang him. 'You're giving me the opposite advice to Eoghan Harris' (who was privately urging that Trimble take the risk and seize the 'moral high ground'). Later, Trimble asked O'Callaghan, 'Do you think I should walk away from it all?' 'No,' replied the former O/C of Southern Command of the IRA, 'but you've got to stand up to Tony Blair.' 'If I say that, I'll be destroyed by the British media,' said Trimble.[9] In fact, under pressure from his own folk, Trimble did ultimately say no – and was *not* destroyed by the British media.

Unionist fears were further increased by events on the ground. On the day after Blair's Stranmillis address, a well-known Provisional defector, Martin McGartland, was shot six times by two gunmen who scaled the garden wall of the terraced house where he lived in exile at Whitley Bay, Northumberland.[10] Trimble immediately stated that the shooting was a breach of the Provisional IRA ceasefire – a conclusion apparently supported by the local police. But although the shooting was the first time that the Provisionals had struck on the British mainland since Blair became Prime Minister, it was not deemed a breach of the ceasefire and no prisoners were recalled under the Sentences Act 1998, nor were any conclusions drawn about Sinn Fein's eligibility for government. Indeed, the very reverse appeared to be the case: on 22 June, Patrick Magee, the Brighton bomber, was released from jail to angry protests from the Conservatives.[11] Soon thereafter, 300 lb of fertiliser and explosive devices were intercepted by the Garda Siochana in a van at Manorcunningham, Co. Donegal, as it was being driven towards the border. The two men subsequently charged by the police were later accepted on the Provisional IRA wing at Portlaoise high security prison; they were later acquitted, but at a political level, the reports cannot have improved the Unionist mood at the time.[12]

On the morning of 22 June, Trimble held a press conference in London at David Burnside's Unionist Information Office. It was a largely uneventful occasion, until Trimble opined that 'one of the great difficulties we have had in implementing the Agreement, particularly in the run-up to the formation of the Executive, has been the widespread lack of confidence in the commmunity, particularly among Ulster Unionists, with regard to what the Secretary of State will do'.[13] By lunch that day, Trimble's remarks, which were interpreted as a plea for the removal of Mowlam, formed the splash in the *Evening Standard* ('MO MUST BE SACKED') and were carried prominently on many of the evening television and radio broadcasts as well as the next day's newspapers. Before lunching with Trimble that day at the Howard Hotel in London, David Montgomery rang Mowlam, as he so often did, to find out what was on her mind. He found her 'in a state' about something, but she did not specify what was bothering her. Montgomery duly ploughed ahead and 'probed' Trimble. Trimble said nothing over lunch about what had happened at the UIO press conference: it was not so much that he was withholding information, but rather that he saw his observations as unremarkable and therefore scarcely worth reporting to his luncheon companion. In so far as Trimble conveyed anything, it was that he appeared to be under the impression that the UIO gathering was a private rather than public event. Thus, when Montgomery rang the Secretary of State afterwards he was still 'blind-sided' as to what had happened. 'Fuck off, I'm not talking to you, I'm not talking to him, I'm too fucking angry to talk,' she exploded. 'I'm not angry with you, but I can't stand him [Trimble].' 'Mo, what's happened?' asked Montgomery, but the then Ulster Secretary rang off before he could extract any more information.[14] When put to her, she could not recall the exact detail of the conversation.

In the immediate term, at least, Trimble's intervention was counterproductive. As Paul Murphy, Mowlam's one-time deputy, observes: 'If a Unionist leader says someone must go, the Prime Minister cannot react to just one side in a two-sided story. The same goes if Gerry Adams or Martin McGuinness demanded it. It couldn't be seen that one side in the equation was choosing who would be the Secretary of State.'[15] Indeed, Kate Hoey recalls that at the PLP meeting on the next day, Blair began by referring to the Ulster Secretary: 'Where's Mo?' he asked. 'Oh she's not here at the moment.' He then stated that Mowlam had his total confidence, and there was a huge cheer.[16] Trimble now acknowledges that his comments at the UIO press conference helped Mowlam to survive for a bit longer in the job, though he is correct to observe that his remarks, in and of themselves, were scarcely novel. Curiously, he did not particularly set out to call for Mowlam's resignation: his remarks, rather, emerged by accident, possibly as a result of the long-term exhaustion from which some close associates believed he suffered.[17] Whatever the reason, 'Mo must go' was not necessarily the message he should have been conveying that day – namely, putting the British Government on the spot for allegedly letting down the democrats. It personalised things and pitted him against the most popular politician in the country. Whatever her administrative shortcomings in the eyes of the cognoscenti (including some at No. 10), she was still regarded by millions as 'St Mo'. Indeed, in mainland PR terms, he would probably have done better to have attacked Blair himself. Once again, despite his avowed wish to improve the Unionist image in Great Britain, he had missed a trick –

partly, perhaps, because of his emotional aversion to Mowlam, which hindered rational calculation on his part.

At other times, though, Trimble behaved very unemotionally indeed. On the morning of Saturday 19 June 1999, Trimble had paid a visit to the Lisburn office of one of his most dangerous opponents – Jeffrey Donaldson.[18] Its purpose was to secure the return of the MP for Lagan Valley to the UUP's negotiating team, which Donaldson had left on the afternoon of 10 April 1998, as the Belfast Agreement was about to be signed. According to Denis Rogan, the idea of a Donaldson return to the fold had been broached after the European elections at a meeting held in his home, which included Reg Empey, James Cooper, Jack Allen and Ken Maginnis. 'There was not a good reaction amongst some of those present,' says Rogan. 'Trimble loyalists were shown that you could criticise him all you like and still be brought back in. "David, are you sure that's a good decision?" I asked. "It's what I'm doing," he replied. He wanted to heal the wounds of the party and thought it was better to have Donaldson inside of the negotiating team.'[19] Some Trimbleistas believed he would then be tied in and less able to oppose the leader's policy. Trimble briefed Donaldson on his plans for well over half an hour: the latter recalls that Trimble told him that Blair was determined to make progress and wanted the matter of guns and government resolved. He believed that the Prime Minister would not be unsympathetic to the Ulster Unionists and that pressure could be applied to the Provisionals for a form of commitment to decommissioning. Trimble spoke of a 'sequencing' of events whereby action by republicans would be matched by moves by the UUP to set up an Executive – effectively 'jumping together', hopefully on the same day. Although it would depend what exactly was on offer, Trimble said that he would not quibble if decommissioning took place a few days after the creation of an Executive. Donaldson asked whether days would in practice mean weeks and Trimble said that it meant what it said – days. Donaldson also thought it important to have clear lines of accountability, since he was not in the Assembly but rather was there as a party officer. He therefore wanted anything of importance to be decided upon by the UUC. 'Our bottom lines were the same and on this basis I rejoined the negotiating team,' recalls Donaldson. 'Party policy was clearly stated in the Assembly and European election manifestos and in the May executive council meeting, in that the UUP will not sit in an Executive until they began a credible and verifiable process of decommissioning.' After consulting his constituency association officers in Lagan Valley and some senior figures in the UUC, Donaldson wrote to his leader on this basis on 21 June and Trimble responded on 25 June.[20] The ripples were immediately felt throughout the political process: No. 10 saw it as bad news, since they feared that Donaldson would act as a brake upon Trimble, though it made little ultimate difference to their conduct of negotiations. Likewise, Donaldson's recall certainly made an impression upon Sinn Fein, who during the subsequent Mitchell review told Trimble that they regarded it as evidence of a lack of genuine UUP commitment to the Belfast Agreement.[21]

The inclusion of Donaldson partly closed down Trimble's exposed flank within the UUP, but obviously could not solve his problems with the two Governments. On 22 June in the Dail, Ahern said that an Executive would have to be formed before paramilitary weapons were disposed of and that only in that context could the issue be solved.[22] When Hague asked Blair in the Commons on the next day about whether he would give an undertaking not to ask Trimble to form an Executive until there was a 'credible and verifiable start to decommissioning', the Prime Minister sidestepped the question.[23] With prior decommissioning and even the simultaneous creation of an Executive alongside decommissioning slipping off the agenda, the Prime Minister understood that he had to give Trimble something without losing nationalists. That 'something' was along the lines of the 'Mallon plan', as first enunciated by the Deputy First Minister-designate at his party's annual conference on 13 November 1998 – when the SDLP deputy leader appeared to indicate that he would agree to Sinn Fein's removal from the Executive if decommissioning was not completed by the May 2000 deadline. Mallon publicly revived his plan on 17 June 1999 after lengthy private discussions with both Blair and Ahern, extolling the 'inescapable obligation' to decommission and the need for 'collective responsibility' should the May 2000 deadline be breached. It was then that Blair embraced the concepts of 'certainty of achievement' and 'certainty of sanction'. In outline, this meant that the first steps would entail nomination of the Executive; then the devolution of powers combined with a new de Chastelain report and a timetable; then a start to decommissioning; and completion by May 2000.[24] From a Unionist perspective, this element of the plan (sanctions) was certainly an improvement of sorts on both the 1 April 1999 Hillsborough declaration and the 14 May 1999 summit at No. 10, but the question was whether 'better' was 'good enough', especially for the Assembly group and UUP Executive. Sources close to Trimble – at times a euphemism for the UUP leader himself – stated that 'certainty of achievement' was not enough and that only an acceptance of an 'obligation' to decommission would be enough, which would have to be accompanied by a starting and finishing date.[25]

After Blair and Ahern had met in London on the occasion of Cardinal Basil Hume's funeral at Westminster Cathedral on Thursday 24 June 1999, the two heads of Government left for Belfast. The basic principles were agreed on Friday 25 June – namely the creation of an inclusive Executive exercising devolved powers; decommissioning of all paramilitary weapons by the 22 May 2000 deadline; and that process to be carried out, in a way to be determined by the International Commission headed by Gen. de Chastelain. But there were major differences on the timing and implementation of any plan and the two Prime Ministers agreed to return to Belfast on Monday 28 June to sort out such critical details as the terms of suspension; whether only the Northern Ireland Assembly would fall, or whether other aspects of the Belfast Agreement such as cross-border implementation bodies would be 'frozen' along with it.[26] Blair further elaborated his thinking in an article in *The Times* on Friday 25 June 1999, when he stated that Sinn Fein could be in government if it gave a clear guarantee of decommissioning under a ten-month timetable combined with failsafe measures to close down the institutions if they defaulted on their commitments on arms. It was clear from this that all the parties – whether democrats or paramilitaries – would be out of the Executive under these circumstances (rather than one party excluded). This was a sign that although Blair had once supported the exclusion option, he had been unable to secure the support of the Irish Government and the SDLP. After four and a half hours of talks, Sinn Fein committed themselves to decommission in a way that was to be determined by de Chastelain – which the Governments saw as a major advance on their previous position of simply using such influence as they possessed to achieve decommissioning. But the republicans still could not guarantee such an outcome.

The pressure on Trimble was further increased by the announcement on Monday 28 June 1999 by the Parades Commission that it had decided to ban the annual Drumcree march for the second year running. Trimble had again called for the decision to be postponed, but the British still felt disinclined to intervene so directly.[27] Jonathan Powell had spent much of the weekend in Northern Ireland trying to reconcile the positions of the nationalist residents, led by Brendan Mac Cionnaith and approved representatives of the Portadown District, including Trimble, his chief of staff David Campbell, and several other prominent Orangemen. Huge amounts of time had been spent over the previous year on the running sore of Drumcree – not to mention the expenditure of much political capital on Trimble's part (perhaps only the issue of decommissioning consumed more energy). At one level, there was something peculiar about his allocation of slender political resources: here was Trimble, the 'New Unionist', who had effected so many painful compromises for the sake of modernising the image of his party in the eyes of the outside world, expending great numbers of chips on what – even to relatively sympathetic outsiders – was the most incomprehensible aspect of the Ulster-British cause. Meanwhile, in this period, he spent relatively little time on such issues as prisoner releases and the RUC – both of which had a resonance even with relatively unsympathetic mainlanders. Such a concentration would also turn off that segment of middle-class Protestants who disliked Orangeism and whom Trimble was determined to woo back into the UUP. Critics of Trimble's disproportionate emphasis on this subject argue that even if he managed via negotiation to ensure a march down the Garvaghy Road, the anti-Agreement loyalists would still not be satisfied: there were now so many obscenities in their eyes about the new dispensation in Northern Ireland that they had, as it were, moved beyond Drumcree to other issues.

Trimble fundamentally disagreed with this critique. At its heart lay the obvious point that he was not merely First Minister-designate for Northern Ireland as a whole, but was also MLA for Upper Bann – and, at least as important to him, Westminster MP for the constituency. Whilst Trimble could undoubtedly scrape back into the Assembly on a minimal number of first preferences under the STV system – however humiliating that might be – it would be harder to do so against a united anti-Agreement candidate under the first-past-the-post rules for Westminster. As has been noted earlier, he was acutely aware that a very high percentage of the Protestant male population of Portadown are in the Loyal Orders. Even if his efforts came to naught, he had at least to be seen to be making an effort. But he also felt a genuine, sentimental loyalty to the Portadown District whom he believed to be decent people. As for the hard core of irreconcilables, Trimble believed that if the Drumcree issue was resolved, then dissident loyalist paramilitarism would be deprived of its principal focus of discontent and it would be far easier for the police to deal with (nightly protests had continued since the 1998 march was blocked by the RUC and the Army).[28] At a minimum, if a portion of the Orange constituency engaged in potentially fruitful dialogue, it would prevent the protests from gaining critical mass – both physically and politically.

Finally, Trimble was very aware of the threat and the potential of Drumcree vis-à-vis his broader agenda. It was vital to him that he not be seen to be trading off some kind of march at Drumcree in exchange for a dilution of his position on decommissioning – the District Lodge, for one, would not have wanted it – and was very sensitive to Ian Paisley's accusation that he done just that.[29] But for all the denials of linkage, the two issues could not be separated. David Montgomery, who worked as an informal intermediary between No. 10, Trimble and the Orange Order – as well as some republicans – wrote a memorandum to Jonathan Powell on 20 April 1999 to say that 'Trimble has an ace to play: if he can persuade Sinn Fein to help him get a settlement in Drumcree, then the confidence it will promote among the Orange and Unionists generally may enable him to stretch his party far enough to clinch a deal on the Executive.' Indeed, according to David Campbell, even at the height of the June/July negotiations on setting up an Executive, scarcely two hours went by when he did not ask for an update on the Portadown situation – not to mention asking Blair and Jonathan Powell to meet with Portadown District at that critical juncture.[30] The First Minister-designate hoped to create a situation in which the parade could go ahead – but that could only happen (a) if the Parades Commission changed its mind or (b) if the Orange Order could achieve an agreement with the nationalist residents (which, in turn, would prompt the Parades Commission to reappraise its attitude). If the Portadown District could be persuaded to negotiate with the residents, at least via proxies, that would help them to regain the moral high ground. To persuade them to do that, Trimble was also determined to create a relationship (again, partly via proxies, such as David Montgomery) between Harold Gracey and the Prime Minister. He hoped that a prolonged engagement would show the Government and the wider world that the Portadown District were reasonable men whose efforts at compromise were undermined not merely by the intransigence of local nationalists but also what he saw as the bias of the Parades Commission.

Trimble repeatedly called for its abolition during 1999, arguing that it was the product of the era of full-scale direct rule and that in the context of devolution it would be better if the issue was handed to a body based upon the Assembly.[31]

But the Drumcree issue also opened possibilities for Trimble, at least as Montgomery saw it. On 20 April, Montgomery wrote to Jonathan Powell and informed him that 'Trimble intends to pull Gerry [Adams] into the process in that hope that he can influence Mac Cionnaith. In follow-up contacts between Trimble and Mac Cionnaith, the challenge is to release the prize of funding for Portadown [an economic initiative was one of the main planks of any settlement plan] by resolving Drumcree for all time ... if Trimble and Sinn Fein can collaborate to bring this about it would augur well for the future. It is also consistent with the proposition that the political leaders work together on the challenges as if they were in Government. If you extend that to the parties collectively tackling the decommissioning issue, behaving like a coalition government, neither the UUs nor Sinn Fein needs to give ground, thus providing a way out of the present impasse. It entails the parties jointly accepting responsibility for decommissioning and working together on resolving it. Drumcree could be the test-bed for this approach.' Over the weekend of 26–7 June 1999, Trimble, Campbell and others appeared to have achieved some success in devising an acceptable package. Acting with the approval of Portadown District, who were in the next room, he negotiated with the nationalist residents at Stormont House (which also served as 'spooks' quarters' on the government estate in east Belfast) under the chairmanship of Powell.

They came up with a deal which won the lodge's backing by a 70 to 5 margin and which had also stimulated positive noises from the other side. Trimble's plan went as follows: first, the two sides would finally meet; second, Portadown District would call off all protests; third, a local civic forum would be established to discuss these issues; fourth, the annual Drumcree march would walk back down the Garvaghy Road; fifth, the Portadown District would attend the local civic forum at a high level; sixth, a socio-economic initiative would be announced; seventh, from September onwards, the parties and local civic forum would commit themselves to working together, with the format facilitated by the First and Deputy First Ministers; eighth, the deal would be signed by the Prime Minister and the parties.[32] So optimistic were many of those involved that there were rumours that the Prime Minister had been told that he might have to fly over on Sunday 27 June to set the seal on the package at Hillsborough. But time was running out rapidly on the Drumcree negotiations – more so, even, than on the main talks themselves. For the Parades Commission was scheduled to rule the next day on the following Sunday's march. If, as many loyalists believed, Mac Cionnaith reckoned that the march would be banned anyhow, then he could simply spin things out until the new body ruled against the Orange Order: why should he make any compromise if the Parades Commission delivered everything he wanted, and with the full force of the law behind it? Trimble persuaded Powell to try to obtain a 24-hour delay in the announcement of the determination, which the latter secured, he claimed, with great difficulty.[33] But it was only a stay of execution from the point of view of Trimble and the Orange Order. Mac Cionnaith refused to sign off on any deal until there were direct talks between Portadown District and the residents and on the next day the march was officially banned; and despite the Prime Minister's role in talks between the two sides later in the week, compromise was never achieved.[34]

Disappointing as this outcome was for Trimble's team, they consoled themselves with the belief that Powell and the Government had seen how obdurate the residents were and that the Parades Body – which Labour had created – was not the fount of all wisdom.[35] As they saw it, it represented a turning point in Government thinking which contributed to the reconstitution of that body early in the following year.[36] Perhaps the Orangemen had shown themselves to be reasonable and had proven their bona fides to the satisfaction of the Government: in fact, by mid-2003, neither the 1998 nor the 1999 marches had gone down the Garvaghy Road. The Parades Commission had worked in the Government's own strategic terms, tactically bothersome as the timing of some of its decisions might sometimes be. For in the new dispensation, Orangemen could no longer set the pace on the ground as they had in 1995, 1996 and 1997. With Trimble at their side on the barricades, outside of the framework of the institutions of state, the Orangemen could win. With Trimble absent, negotiating on their behalf in the salons of the high and mighty, the Orangemen were easily containable. The case of Drumcree thus invalidated a key canon of Trimbleism – that it was better for Unionists to be inside the tent, with all of the compromises it involved, than outside of the tent. In fact, they were more marginalised on this issue in the new dispensation than they were before; not even the surprise decision of 4000 Orangemen to disperse at Drumcree at 2:30 p.m. on Sunday 4 July, so avoiding the violence of past years, helped them to attain their objectives.[37] Nor did the Government, at the end of the day, really need to deliver a settlement on this issue for the Unionists themselves. David Montgomery wrote to Jonathan Powell on 26 July 1999, after Senator George Mitchell had been recalled to conduct a review of the faltering process, that 'the prize of getting them down the road peacefully is potentially greater than ever. It will set the scene for the Review, give Trimble a boost and ultimately help deliver the Unionist people into power-sharing.' Ultimately, however, Trimble and his colleagues were prepared to make that leap without a march on the Garvaghy Road – and the Government knew it.

The Parades Commission's decision made an already difficult task even harder on the Unionist side – though, conversely, it helped to undergird the Provisionals' ceasefire. Indeed, when the full negotiations resumed on Tuesday 29 June at Castle Buildings, the bulk of the two Governments' attention was focused upon the republican movement, in an attempt to tease a statement out of them that would enable Trimble to make a positive recommendation to the UUP. So serious were these discussions that the Sinn Fein room was visited by a succession of up to 50 senior republicans, including members of the seven-man IRA Army Council. Although Martin McGuinness had asserted on BBC's *On the Record* programme that weekend that he could not speak on behalf of the IRA and thus could not deliver their weapons, his line changed as Blair pushed him to give something.[38] The two Governments were deeply impressed by these and other intimations of movement, so much so that they believed it would have profound implications for the de Chastelain report. The issue was obviously going to top the agenda when Blair and Ahern held a working lunch with de Chastelain and his colleagues at Stormont House on Tuesday 29 June. De Chastelain was on Blair's right and noticed how quickly the Prime Minister ate his food. 'I thought I learned to eat fast when I was at Fettes but you eat faster,' he quipped, referring to his own and the Prime Minister's *alma mater*. 'We've finished our report,' said de Chastelain. 'You asked us to produce by the end of June. We are ready to present you with one. We have to say at this stage, we don't think there is any sign of imminent movement.' 'Yes, we are having discussions which would affect what you have to say and delay by two days,' replied Blair. 'Well, it's your report,' said de Chastelain. 'If we're to delay, you tell us' – which was then done. De Chastelain simply assumed that the Governments' greater optimism about Sinn Fein could be ascribed to new intelligence available to them at the time – but not to the Decommissioning Body. As far as de Chastelain was concerned, once an IRA point of contact with his body was named, then it should be only a matter of weeks before actual decommissioning took place. This was, notes de Chastelain, one of the premises upon which the subsequent Mitchell review of September to November 1999 was based.[39]

So what was the nature of the offer which Sinn Fein/IRA had made? Late on the night of 30 June–1 July, Alastair Campbell told the assembled press pack at Castle Buildings that there had been a 'seismic shift' in republican thinking, a line repeated by Blair on the next day when he stated that there had been 'historic, seismic shifts in the political landscape of Northern Ireland'.[40] How, therefore, could the UUP say 'no' to this major new advance? Some of the Unionists particularly feared incurring the ire of Blair, who had been forced on account of these negotiations to miss the inauguration of the Scottish and Welsh devolved institutions on 1 July (such fears may have been genuine, but they were also played upon by British officials). At 1 a.m. on that morning, the Unionists were told by John Sawers, the Prime Minister's Private Secretary, that Blair was sufficiently irritated that he would pack up and go. In this period, things did not usually go wrong for Blair, but the republicans noted that when they did, he had a tendency to throw up his hands and ask 'what do I do?': the Provisionals were unimpressed by his stamina in real crises.[41] Three junior NIO ministers – Paul Murphy, Adam Ingram and John McFall – lobbied the UUP Assemblymen intensively. The tension in the UUP room at Castle Buildings was enormous, not least because they were constantly monitoring the effects of briefing on television and radio. The British started briefing that the UUP had to accept because of the 'future of the children' – prompting one UUP Assemblyman to snort 'I don't fucking like children.'[42] So great was the pressure that when one Trimbleista walked into the room in the early hours of Thursday 1 July 1999, he found a scene of chaos and demoralisation. Some were asleep on the floor; another was walking around the room insisting 'it's so unfair, it's so unfair'; others said 'I want to go home'; others simply wanted a drink. Many were ready to walk out there and then, but Trimble – whose face was purple with tension – urged continued engagement.

One veteran of the civil rights marches who observed the scene was struck by the Unionist political class's lack of stamina, which contrasted so unfavourably with the energy and discipline of Sinn Fein.[43] As Peter Bell observed, 'For the most part, they [the UUP] simply don't have the experience of certain Sinn Fein veterans of armed struggle.'[44]

But at another level, the UUP's confusion was understandable. For it was very unclear on what basis they were being asked to make this leap, not least because Sinn Fein did not want to put anything on paper because of its own internal problems.[45] 'It was never clear what was being said and by whom and on whose behalf,' recalls Peter Bell of the British-Irish Joint Secretariat.[46] Blair, though had no such doubts. 'It was a commitment by the republicans, as I understood it, and indeed do understand it,' recalls the Prime Minister. 'The problem is that it's a huge totem for them in their movement.'[47] Blair appears to have indicated to Trimble that there was an intimation, if not a proposition from the republicans, that if an Executive was set up now, commitments to decommissioning and then actual decommissioning would follow later.[48] Some reports indicated that this could take place as much as six months later, though Trimble said in a *News Letter* article on 16 July 1999 that a process of decommissioning would begin within days of devolution, leading to actual weapons handovers within weeks. But whereas previously, Sinn Fein had said that it would use its influence to attain decommissioning, this time it had come close to suggesting that it was confident that it would succeed in influencing the IRA to decommission by May 2000. Earlier statements had offered no prospect of success.[49] In short, if the peace process unfolded to the IRA's satisfaction, they would draw up an inventory and present it to de Chastelain.[50] The British also believed that there was evidence that the republicans were prepared to issue a statement saying that 'the war is over'; one Irish source claims that Ahern had even drafted words for Sinn Fein which employed language reminiscent of de Valera's address of 24 May 1923 which called a halt to the campaign of the anti-treaty forces in the Irish Civil War.[51]

Trimble's problems stemmed from the fact that whilst Blair was making these claims on behalf of the Provisionals, he could detect no such movement himself. Trimble recalls that when Adams and McGuinness came to his room late in the evening of Thursday 1 July to meet with himself and six colleagues, including Jeffrey Donaldson, the two republicans tried to convince them that there would be a significant movement

– though the commitment was insufficiently solid to warrant a positive recommendation from the UUP.[52] Ken Maginnis recalls that at one point, Adams said, 'I'm going to make an important statement.' 'Let's hear it,' said Maginnis. 'I can't tell you, it's very sensitive for republicans,' replied Adams. 'Well, if you can't tell us, what use is it to anyone?' wondered Maginnis.[53] Reg Empey recalls McGuinness as 'letting the cat out of the bag' when he said 'we'll try our best – but we may fail'.[54] Though No. 10 was convinced of republican sincerity, it also believed that 'Sinn Fein find it very hard to be straight with Unionists. They have this insulting superiority complex and only want to deal with the British Prime Minister and to ignore their Unionist neighbours.'[55]

So unconvincing did the UUP find the republicans' pronouncements that it began to cast doubt upon the quality of the intelligence which was being fed to the Government by the security forces. Blair had indicated to Trimble and others that he had secret intelligence suggesting a genuine shift, but Ken Maginnis had his own sources of information which suggested a very different picture.[56] So when Trimble brought Maginnis to see Blair, the UUP security spokesman bluntly told him, 'Prime Minister, this is a load of shit. There is nothing, but nothing to indicate a commitment by the IRA.' Blair looked at him and said: 'But Ken, if you're right, then I'm going to look very foolish.' He then added: 'I would like you to talk to my people.'[57] Blair was referring to officials who handled the classified information, but Trimble did not go himself and left it to Maginnis: he would sometimes be inexplicably reluctant to attend formal security briefings. 'Let like speak unto like' is Trimble's rejoinder to those who wonder why Maginnis went alone.[58] Maginnis duly went down to Stormont House, where he met with Paul Priestley, a senior NIO civil servant who served as head of liaison between the Secretary of State and the Director and Coordinator of Intelligence (invariably a high-ranking MI5 officer). 'We're getting indications of a change in [republican] thinking,' said Priestley. 'Is this strategic or tactical?' asked Maginnis. 'If it's tactical, I can understand it, but if it's strategic, I'll be very surprised.' Priestley responded: 'It's strategically tactical.' Maginnis looked at him astonished. 'Do you think I came up the Blackwater in a bubble?' retorted the UUP security spokesman (an Ulster expression basically meaning 'do you think I was born yesterday?'). But, says Maginnis, Priestley never offered him any evidence of what the shift constituted.[59]

In fact, by this point, the republicans were starting to row back from such intimations as they had made to the two Governments. Partly, this was because talk of 'seismic shifts' had frightened key players in the movement, and partly because what they had offered was so intangible anyhow. Pat Doherty, the vice president of Sinn Fein, emerged to tell the press pack that 'it's a cod' (an Irish term for a hoax, jibe or sham).[60] Further evidence that any Sinn Fein offer was not deliverable or clear enough emerged in the following week, when Toby Harnden of *The Daily Telegraph* obtained a copy of a secret report of a briefing given to republican activists in Newry, Co. Down, on Wednesday 30 June. Two prominent local republicans, Brian Tumilty and Brian Campbell, had just spoken in Belfast to both Gerry Kelly and Mitchel McLaughlin and told their comrades: 'Sinn Fein negotiators are acting for Sinn Fein and Sinn Fein only [i.e. not the IRA] . . . no matter what the media report, Sinn Fein will not be giving any commitments on decommissioning, timetables, etc. If there is going to be decommissioning, it will be up to the IRA – and at present they have made their position extremely clear, i.e. no decommissioning.' The report also disclosed that Sinn Fein's 'strategic objectives' in the talks were 'to maintain the cohesion of the republican movement, to increase the strength of the movement and to create confusion and disunity among their political enemies . . . Sinn Fein intend to pressurise unionism by insisting on the formation of an Executive without any decommissioning . . . the media and the British Government are expected to put a completely different interpretation on the form of words issued, particularly should David Trimble need help with selling the issue to the Unionist party.' They added that Kelly and McLaughlin had said that Sinn Fein had little to lose if the Agreement collapsed. 'The Ulster Unionists insisted on an Assembly in the Good Friday Agreement and at the time Sinn Fein had to accept that. Therefore, should the formation of the Assembly fail and the peace process collapse, Sinn Fein realise they can escape relatively unscathed.'[61] Trimble states that the Tumilty-Campbell memo was a factor of sorts in increasing the UUP's scepticism about what was on offer, though he regarded it as the sort of thing which Sinn Fein were bound to say to reassure their grassroots activists during the course of a tense negotiation. As far as Trimble was concerned, it was far more significant that Richard McAuley, Sinn Fein's press chief, was dismissing Alastair Campbell's optimistic briefing.[62] The confidence of the UUP in the judgment of the two Governments was not increased when Taylor and Donaldson met with senior Irish officials at Castle Buildings. The MPs asked their interlocutors whether the republican statement would come from Sinn Fein or the IRA. 'I'm not aware there is anybody in this building from the IRA,' said one of the Irish present.

The 'seismic shift' remains a subject of contention to this day – and, as with the draft Mitchell document of April 1998, no one really wants to claim responsibility for it. The phrase is generally attributed to Alastair Campbell, whom Ken Reid recalls using it first in the press tent on the night of 30 June/1 July.[63] But the former No. 10 Press Secretary says that he is '95% sure' it was not he who coined the phrase, but rather the Prime Minister in a meeting.[64] Whoever thought it up, what is certain is that the Irish were not at all pleased (or at least so they claimed in retrospect). 'Phrases like that cause huge problems,' says one senior figure on the Irish side. 'The Unionists ask, "Where is it – we haven't seen it" and republicans, who may not yet have had a chance to brief their grassroots, are then forced to pull back because of the heightened expectations.' It was not that the Irish did not believe in this shift; on the contrary, after some vigorous exchanges with the republicans, the Irish were the first party to become convinced of the bona fides of the Sinn Fein leadership and according to one participant were 'rushing around like religious proselytes at Castle Buildings, sure that the Provisionals had undergone a religious conversion'. Rather, the Irish were unhappy because once the British had come to accept their interpretation, the No. 10 spin machine had *publicly* jumped the gun, prematurely turning understandings made with a nudge and a wink into something much closer to a formalised commitment. Trimble agrees with much of this assessment. 'Ali Campbell [sic] doesn't know what he is dealing with. It's okay for London politics. [When you are] overspinning here, especially with the paramilitaries, you have got to be careful. Hyperbole doesn't mean much on the mainland – for example when one party says "this is the end of the NHS as we know it". But stating "this is the end of the IRA as we know it", well, that has a quite different effect!'[65]

If republicans had to backpedal, so did Trimble. Because for all his *ex post facto* robustness and dissection of the inadequacies of the republican 'offer' as described by Blair, he nonetheless sought to give the Prime Minister's proposals a very fair wind; fairer, perhaps, than most of his Assembly group, whose reactions he was constantly probing for signs of flexibility. Nonetheless he told the Prime Minister of the widespread scepticism in the UUP. 'I'll talk to them,' said Blair late on Thursday 1 July. Trimble, who increasingly negotiated one-on-one with Blair, was not sure whether this would work. According to Steven King, Trimble was convinced that the Assembly group would savage the Prime Minister, not least because of the widespread belief that the Prime Minister had broken his handwritten referendum pledges.[66] Trimble opted not to attend the meeting: he states he thought that the Assemblymen might speak more candidly about genuine concerns if he was not there.[67] He did not coordinate with Blair beforehand about what the Prime Minister should say, though the distinguished visitor did speak to Trimble's Principal Private Secretary, David Lavery, alone in the conference room on Level 5 of Castle Buildings. 'You have to remember that they're not professional politicians,' said Lavery. 'They're representatives of their community and they feel that they have given their word and that means a lot in our culture. You can't finesse it. Not one of these men have not been touched by the Troubles. I don't like to be overly emotional, but my best friend at university was shot dead by the Provisionals [John Donaldson, an apprentice solicitor murdered in 1979 whilst leaving Andersonstown RUC station on a motor-bike]. I remember them at times like this and I'm not even a Unionist – so think how much harder it is for these people, all of whom have a story like that about a friend or a brother or a son. It might seem odd to a sophisticated English politician like you.'[68]

But Blair did not fully internalise the message. He walked into the small, stuffy UUP room at Castle Buildings with Alastair Campbell at around 8 p.m., in his shirtsleeves with his tie pulled down from his neck. There was mild applause as he came in, and he sat down in the centre of the room surrounded by the Assemblymen. 'Hi, guys,' he began. 'I'm working for you.' Although he tried to be chummy and to create an atmosphere that they were all on the same side, his discomfort soon became evident from the shrugging of the shoulders and the gesticulations with his hands.[69] In fact, Blair was treated very politely, though some of Trimble's advisers felt that they were not acute enough to ask the pertinent questions. The Prime Minister was told by Sir John Gorman, the only Catholic in the Assembly group, that 'not all Catholics think like the IRA'. But the essence of Blair's message was that he was working on a plan whereby if the Provisionals failed to deliver, Sinn Fein would be excluded. This went down well and immediately afterwards, the meeting was adjudged to have been a success. But UUP satisfaction turned to anger on Friday 2 July, after the proposal had been explored in greater detail. For whilst Sinn Fein would indeed be thrown out in the event of a default, what Blair's presentation had not made explicit was that it would be in the context of all of the institutions being closed down – that is, with Unionists and everyone else being suspended alongside the republicans. Blair had thus elided a crucial difference, prompting much of the Assembly group to believe that they had been misled again.[70]

Had Blair done so deliberately? Certainly, the Prime Minister's address was an example of what Peter Mandelson has described as Blair's 'charming ambiguity'. Blair felt very upset at being misunderstood and was possibly angry with himself for having made this error with a group which culturally so valued plain speaking.[71] But Paul Bew believed that the Prime Minister had, at a minimum, sought to exploit the politeness and deference of a provincial audience and one which Blair himself had thought was politically naive when he met them at Hillsborough at Easter. For had the UUP Assembly Group read Blair's article in The Times of London of 25 June, they would have known that Blair now recognised that he could not obtain the support of the Irish Government or the SDLP for an exclusion model and had been forced to settle for a 'suspend them all' approach.[72] Of course, hardly any of them had read The Times – and, as Trimble observed during the run-up to the subsequent May 2000 meeting of the UUC, only the News Letter, Belfast Telegraph and The Daily Telegraph really registered with Unionist opinion.[73] Trimble now regards this fiasco as being as much down to the failure of his colleagues to listen carefully to the gaps in what Blair said, though he acknowledges that the Prime Minister 'got carried away and didn't watch himself carefully enough. The qualifications were in his mind.'[74] As ever, Trimble put the most benign construction upon Blair's actions. But he also drew some conclusions for the longer term. Till this moment, the UUP Assembly group had a fairly good opinion of Blair. Now, however, he was 'damaged goods'.[75]

Clinton, likewise, sought to reassure the Ulster Unionists. Whilst expressing his understanding of the 'legitimate problems of Sinn Fein with the decommissioning issue' he added that 'there has to be a resolution of it which enables the leadership of Unionism, Mr Trimble and others who fought for the peace, to survive, to sustain their position and to go forward and get everybody on their side to honour the Good Friday accords. One thing I would say to the Unionists is that they can walk away from this if the commitments aren't made at a later date ... they can bring this down at any time if the commitments aren't kept.'[76] In fact, once the Ulster Unionists had done the deal and republicans defaulted – as occurred in February 2000 – Clinton did not robustly back them up. But whatever the sincerity of Clinton's remarks, his intervention, like that of the British, was back to front. Instead of concentrating upon giving Unionists a failsafe in the event of an IRA default and tightening that up to their satisfaction – which was in the Government's gift – it first made claims about 'seismic shifts' in IRA thinking which were certainly not in its gift and which were not discernible to the UUP.[77] So much damage had been done by this point that when the UUP met with Blair the next day, they were in no mood to succumb to Prime Ministerial entreaties. When the core UUP negotiating team entered Blair's room at the second such meeting that day, the Prime Minister was sitting alone in the Secretary of State's office on level 5 of Block B of Castle Buildings, in shirtsleeves, staring out of the window. 'I've been praying that you'll be able to accept this, because I really believe it's the best we're going to get,' said Blair.[78]

There was thus no stopping Blair from issuing his statement with Ahern, known as 'The Way Forward', on the steps of Castle Buildings on Friday 2 July. The choreography was overwhelmingly nationalist: the two Prime Ministers were flanked by the Sinn Fein and SDLP delegations. So, too, was the substance. The immovable deadline of 30 June had been moved back to 15 July, when the d'Hondt procedure to nominate ministers would be run, with devolution to take effect on 18 July. Trimble thus had nearly two weeks to obtain something better from the Government and the republicans. All the parties would reaffirm the principles (1) of an inclusive Executive (by virtue of the fact it came first, this was obviously the most important objective. It was a further nail in the coffin of the notion of prior or even simultaneous decommissioning). (2) Decommissioning of all paramilitary arms by May 2000. (3) Decommissioning was to be carried out in a manner determined by the de Chastelain body. The de Chastelain body, which was due finally to produce its delayed report on Friday 2 July, would confirm a start to the process of decommissioning, then begin discussions with the paramilitary interlocutors, and would specify that actual decommissioning was to commence within an allotted time. There would be three progress reports – in September and November 1999 and finally in May 2000. A 'failsafe' clause would be introduced, in accordance with the review provisions of the Belfast Agreement. If commitments under the Agreement were not met, either in relation to decommissioning or to devolution, then the two Governments would automatically and with immediate effect suspend the operation of the institutions. Ahern told reporters that if the issue was not resolved within a fortnight, the Assembly would be suspended – a clear threat to Unionist legislators, who valued the body so highly. More significantly, though Sinn Fein had issued their statement on the evening of Thursday 1 July, there was still nothing from the IRA. Commenting upon the Sinn Fein document produced the previous night, Trimble noted that it used words such as 'can' and 'could' when instead they should be using words such as 'must' and 'will' disarm.[79] There was no 'certainty of achievement' and no certainty of sanction. Indeed, when Frank Millar asked a senior Irish source whether actual decommissioning was guaranteed, the southerner replied, 'What's a guarantee?'[80]

Trimble says that he made up his mind that he could not run with the proposal as it stood on Friday 2 July, though he did not definitively reject it. The failsafe was just not safe enough for him, certainly in internal UUP terms, but also in terms of what he now wanted in his own mind.[81] 'Sinn Fein/IRA still appears to retain hopes of bringing its armed movement into the heart of government,' wrote Trimble later. 'This would carry the danger of creating a mafia state in Northern Ireland while the IRA retains a future option on finishing the job. I can quite simply illustrate the problems that could arise. It is possible that we could have, for instance, a Sinn Fein health minister in charge of anti-drugs policy while associates in the IRA used armed force perhaps even on ministerial advice to exploit the supply of illegal drugs.'[82] At the UUP officers' meeting on Saturday 3 July, Trimble took his colleagues through the document. He told them that his strategy would be to go back to Blair and tighten up the legislation. But so unpopular was the plan that by then, Trimble had decided on the advice of colleagues not to call a widely expected meeting of the full 860-strong UUC to ratify it, lest such an event split the party down the middle.[83] Indeed, such was the unanimity of opinion within unionism as a whole concerning the unacceptability of the Government proposals that even so staunch a foe of Trimble as Robert McCartney came over to the UUP leader late in the week and shook his hand. 'If Paris was worth a Mass, then even a temporary "no" is surely worth a handshake,' comments the UKUP leader.[84] Journalists say that even Gerry

Adams privately acknowledged that it was a quality performance by Trimble in the face of overwhelming odds – two sovereign Governments standing shoulder to shoulder with the US Administration and the entire spectrum of northern nationalism.[85]

Blair sought to respond to some of Trimble's themes in his Commons statement on 'The Way Forward' negotiations on Monday 5 July, when he gave his strongest indication to date that he would support moves to exclude Sinn Fein from the Executive in the event of a default.[86] He explained why he thought it a better deal than that struck at Hillsborough in March/April 1999, which offered a token act of decommissioning, dependent upon reciprocal steps by the British and Irish Governments, with no clear framework for completing the decommissioning process by May 2000. By contrast, he asserted, this proposal entailed the UUP jumping first, but it did guarantee a complete process with a failsafe combined. There would be certainty built in for republicans – that an Executive would be set up – but there would also be certainty for Unionists in that they would not be expected to continue sitting in an Executive with fully armed republicans. Trimble's intervention focused upon the unfairness of the suspensory arrangements, effectively reiterating the argument about throwing off all of the passengers because of one fare-dodger. But he also asked what had happened to the Prime Minister's efforts at the start of the previous week to secure a Sinn Fein declaration that 'the war is over' and an IRA statement. On the first point, Blair hinted at the possibility of amendments in the forthcoming legislation codifying the failsafe. He also spoke more vaguely of what might come out of any review of the Belfast Agreement which would follow a republican default as evidence that not all of the pain would be suffered by the innocent parties.

Trimble insisted upon no 'knee-jerk' dismissal of the Blair proposals, but the Assembly group rejected an invitation to talk to the Prime Minister at No. 10. That said, the Prime Minister's vagueness in the Commons on key issues also left Trimble uneasy. Blair had sidestepped William Hague's question about whether the suspension would not just apply to those aspects of the Belfast Agreement which Unionists valued, such as the political institutions, but also those aspects especially valued by national-ists, such as prisoner releases, changes to the RUC and the development of the Human Rights Commission. But there were other issues, too. Would Dublin give the reassurance that if the institutions were suspended, the changes to Articles 2 and 3 of the Republic's 1937 Constitution would remain in effect?[87] Would the cross-border implementation bodies fall with the institutions and, if so, when? The Irish Government was only prepared to go a short distance towards helping Trimble – principally on the matter of securing an IRA statement which would affirm that they were bound by Sinn Fein's commitments. It was also reported that the Irish were prepared to offer an Orange centre on the site of the battlefield of the Boyne in Co. Meath – worthy enough, but scarcely sufficient to meet Unionist concerns.[88] The Irish did not reject the principle of the failsafe legislation, but were determined that it should remain within their conception of the Belfast Agreement. The broad view of the Irish state was that because of the enshrinement of the Belfast Agreement in international law, it would not be possible unilaterally to alter its provisions in the UK Commons.[89] This was not a view held by Trimble, nor by his one-time colleague, Professor Brigid Hadfield, both of whom believed that the Belfast Agreement preserved the sovereignty of Westminster in the final analysis – as Peter Mandelson was to prove early in the following year. But in the immediate term, Irish pressure did much to limit the concessions which Blair could offer to Trimble. So grim was the situation that, according to David Kerr's private diary, Trimble told a meeting of senior colleagues at the Dunadry Hotel in Co. Antrim on 8 July that 'he feared that by next Friday, the whole process would be in melt-down. "If by next Friday we don't have an Executive, we will be pitchforked into a review with the Assembly suspended." The indications are that Mo will go and Mandelson will take over.'

In such an atmosphere, it came as no surprise that the Ulster Unionist Executive on Friday 9 July baulked at endorsing 'The Way Forward' document. The UUP Executive described it as 'fundamentally unfair and unbalanced'. But Trimble himself did not say that he could not support the intergovernmental plan. Instead, as so often before at UUP gatherings, he gave a factual blow-by-blow account of the pros and cons of the deal: it was as if he was just testing opinion.[90] The UUP Executive was then adjourned until Wednesday 14 July, the day before the new deadline expired.[91] Trimble maintained his efforts to persuade the British to accommodate his demands. He emerged from an hour-long meeting at No. 10 to say that there were still 'continuing problems' with the emergency legislation giving effect to the failsafe referred to in 'The Way Forward'. Published on the night of Monday 12 July, its provisions included a failsafe to be activated if de Chastelain certified that the paramilitaries had defaulted on their obligations; a trigger mechanism which could be activated by the Secretary of State if it was decided that any of the parties had failed to meet their commitments; the Executive, Assembly, North-South Ministerial Council and Council of the Isles would be suspended; the Assembly would be summoned within seven days to debate the situation which led to the suspension of the institutions; London and Dublin would then review the process; once it was completed, there would be another Assembly debate to vote upon any recommendations; then the parties could vote to exclude the defaulting party.[92] To republicans like Danny Morrison, such legislation was evidence of how much emphasis had been placed upon David Trimble's internal difficulties – an updated version, as it were, of British Governments succumbing to the 'Orange card'.[93]

The principal concession which Trimble appears to have won concerned the right afforded to the Secretary of State to call two meetings of the suspended Assembly, (a) to debate but not to vote upon the situation leading to suspensions and those matters which would be reviewed in accordance with the provisions of the Belfast Agreement and (b) on any proposed reaction arising from a review (Seamus Mallon complained bitterly during the Committee stage of the failsafe legislation that the proposals in the Bill would favour the Assembly over all other institutions).[94] This concession did not go as far as the Ulster Unionists wanted in terms of calling the Assembly more often during any suspension.[95] Trimble's disappointment in what he saw as the niggardly quality of the Government's concessions was shared by the Conservatives. In fact, the UUP–Tory cooperation on the Bill represented a new high-water mark in relations between the parties, and Trimble deputed his Principal Private Secretary, David Lavery, to work on amendments throughout Tuesday 13 July with Malcolm Moss, a junior Tory spokesman and a former NIO minister. Trimble had hitherto not wished to become too close to the Conservatives, but this was one of the few occasions on which he was willing to tap into a growing concern on the mainland about the pace of Blairite concessions to the paramilitaries (as exemplified by the concerns of the relatively unpartisan John Major). No 10 had briefed Hague and Mackay extensively on their plans and were alarmed by what they saw as the increasing strains upon the bipartisan approach, as exemplified by Blair's aside in the Commons on Monday 5 July.[96] It became an increasing feature of Labour backbench discourse that the Tories were not treating their Government as well as they had treated the Major ministry when Labour formed the Opposition. In fact, even at the height of New Labour's 'revisionism' on Northern Ireland, they never offered the then Tory Government a 'blank cheque', as exemplified by Mowlam's attacks on Mayhew's handling of Drumcree II in July 1996 and amendments offered to emergency powers legislation.[97]

At 3:55 p.m., the Commons began an eight-hour debate on the Northern Ireland Bill. Trimble was under as great, if not greater, strain during this period as at any moment during his career and certainly more so than any of the other party leaders caught up in the crisis. Kate Hoey, who spoke to him several times during this period, told one friend that he seemed utterly alone in the Commons during the passage of the Bill – 'one chaotic man on his own with a word processor, drafting amendments'.[98] But with characteristic qualities of endurance, Trimble arose nearly an hour later, apparently fresh, after opening speeches from Mowlam and Mackay. He began by observing that his reluctance to allow Sinn Fein into a devolved Northern Ireland Executive before decommissioning would be seen by some as an unwillingness to share power with Catholics. Not so, he said. He had no problem about dealing with people who had genuinely given up violence and alluded to his relationship with Sean O'Callaghan. But he did have difficulties with those whose path from violence to democracy was not yet completed.[99]

Trimble's intervention was, however, eclipsed by that of John Major. If democrats were being pressured to take risks, argued the former Prime Minister, then there had to be superior safeguards for democracy. Specifically, he urged that the Prime Minister and Secretary of State announce their support for the publication of detailed schedules for disarming by de Chastelain, and that if there were a breach in that schedule at any point that this would trigger the expulsion mechanism. Moreover, the continuation of the prisoner release scheme when a paramilitary-linked party was expelled from government was quite unacceptable. According to Trimble, he never discussed this intervention with Major beforehand. Nonetheless, he says, 'It had a seismic effect on the Government. In view of the Major speech, they would have to put more into it.'[100] Trimble's amendments – and with all of the professional pride of the academic lawyer, he made a point of telling the House that he had drafted the replacement clause on prisoner releases himself – were all rejected. Indeed, it was reported that he became so frustrated that he did not vote in the Third Reading stage of the Bill and left the House at 10:45 p.m. that night (at other points, he was so bored that he played solitaire on his laptop computer).[101] The most which Paul Murphy was prepared to commit the Government to was that if the process was suspended because the decommissioning requirements were not met, that would weigh very heavily upon the Secretary of State's judgment as to whether a paramilitary organisation was still eligible for prisoner releases, as it would if in any review a party was expelled from the Executive on a cross-community basis. But Murphy was 'behind the curve'. For in his winding-up speech at Third Reading, Andrew Mackay informed the House that Michael Brunson had just stated on *ITN News* at 11 p.m. that the Government would move to incorporate some of the Ulster Unionist and Conservative amendments. Blair had summoned Mowlam and officials to No. 10 late that night to discuss the options for changes at the Lords stage of the Bill's passage. At 9:45 a.m. on Wednesday 14 July, Blair spoke to Ahern: rumours swirled of an Anglo-Irish rift. 'We have given our views on the amendments,' said the Taoiseach. 'Some of them we would not have difficulty with.' At 1 p.m., the Prime Minister called Trimble, who at 2:15 p.m. gave them a cautious welcome. It soon became clear from Blair's answers at Prime Minister's Question Time on Wednesday 14 July that the amendments would focus on making sure that disarmament occurred in accordance with a specific timetable laid down by de Chastelain and that any breach of it would lead to automatic suspension, as suggested by Major in his speech of the previous day.[102] At 3:10 p.m., the Lords began their debate on the Bill and at 5:50 p.m. Blair appeared on television to urge Unionists not to 'close the door' on the 'best chance for peace in a generation' – though he alluded to the possibility of putting it on hold.[103] But by this point he knew that the Unionists did not have enough to allow them to proceed and thus all prospect of an IRA statement had receded. At 7 p.m. the Ulster Unionist Executive resumed the adjourned session of Friday 9 July: in less than half an hour, Trimble had emerged to say that his party was not prepared to support the failsafe measures.[104] Indeed, one other significant, but little-noted development emerged from these meetings of the Ulster Unionist Executive. In his diary entry of 14 July, David Kerr recorded Trimble telling a meeting of senior Ulster Unionists that 'if we say tomorrow that we have faced them [the Governments] down, perhaps if we've banked some things we may be able to go for this in September. I would like to say this to Blair that I can put hand on heart that we can go for it in September.'

Trimble's worries for the next day were three-fold. First, the Irish and the SDLP were constantly pressuring Blair to run d'Hondt. Thus, even if no Unionists were nominated (ensuring that any Executive was not sustainable owing to lack of cross-community support), the sight of the creation of an inclusive devolved Government being scuppered by Unionist reluctance to share power with Catholics would, as they saw it, hand nationalist Ireland a substantial public relations victory. Second, rumours were swirling that Mallon was going to resign as Deputy First Minister, taking Trimble with him: it was widely assumed that the two posts were inextricably interwoven with each other and that in a consociational Government the one could not survive without the other. The SDLP were thus determined to deny Trimble the 'soft landing' which he had sought – the status quo of an Assembly, himself as shadow First Minister and a review whose terms were yet to be determined. Third, the DUP had announced its intention of sponsoring a motion seeking Sinn Fein's exclusion, which required 30 signatures to be eligible for debate (half the total Unionist bloc). By Wednesday 14 July, they had garnered 29 votes, including the smaller anti-Agreement Unionist parties. Only one more Ulster Unionist was needed to break to trigger the motion, and five to six were reckoned to be wobbly. If such a motion was debated, Trimble would have to abstain on it, but it was much better that there be no such event at all: for he neither wanted to appear to be 'soft' on Sinn Fein, nor did he want to be seen to vote for an exclusionary agenda set by the rejectionists. Moreover, whilst such a vote would have no practical effect without SDLP support, if the DUP succeeded in detaching at least some of the more nervous Ulster Unionists in order to have it debated it would expose the fact that Trimble had become what Frank Millar called the 'minority shareholder' in Unionism.[105] Furthermore, the UUP feared that the DUP might opportunistically be tempted to take their seats in the Executive, thus giving the devolved Government cross-community legitimacy. The DUP's stance was at least Janus-faced, if not politically schizophrenic: on the one hand seeking exclusion of Sinn Fein – but, on the other hand, if it failed, still seeking to fill their quota of ministerial seats to represent the interests of their electors in what they saw as a rotten dispensation. In that sense, it was a continuation of their 1998 Assembly election strategy, whereby they repositioned themselves by campaigning to hold Blair and Trimble to their pledges rather than frontally campaigning against the Belfast Agreement. The UUP's fear of DUP intentions was fuelled by the DUP deputy leader Peter Robinson's declaration on Wednesday 14 July – at a moment when some Unionists felt he did not need to do so – that his party would be acting as 'ministers in opposition'.[106]

Initially, Trimble says, No. 10 appeared to agree with his desire to scrub the whole day.[107] But this is not what happened, for reasons that he says he does not entirely understand to this day. He speculated whether No. 10 failed to pass the message on to Mowlam and the NIO – or else assumed that Mowlam and the NIO pursued their own agenda of making the UUP pay the maximum price without the support of No. 10. Indeed, according to David Montgomery, Trimble believed that she was in cahoots with Seamus Mallon to do just that.[108] The other possibility, which Trimble does not countenance, is that No. 10 also believed that Trimble should pay some political price.[109] As Jonathan Powell recalls, Downing Street *did* back up Mowlam to 'even up the score'. They knew that running d'Hondt would be a meaningless symbolic victory, but felt that national-ists needed such a boost after the UUP had said no to the intergovern-mental document (Powell's recollection is confirmed by the leaked transcripts of a conversation between himself and McGuinness on 16 July, reprinted in the revised edition of Liam Clarke's and Kathryn Johnston's biography of the republican leader).[110] Trimble responded by adopting what one senior British official calls 'a bizarre boycott tactic'. Fearing that the less committed Assemblymen might peel off and give the DUP the necessary 30 signatures for their exclusion motion, he summoned the UUP group to Glengall Street at 9 a.m. on Thursday 15 July and kept them there – a safe distance from east Belfast – until such time as the danger had elapsed. Significantly, following a discussion with Jeffrey Donaldson that morning, Peter Weir was persuaded to withdraw his name from the list of 29 signatories of the DUP motion.[111] At 10:50 a.m., Lord Alderdice began to run d'Hondt. To great hilarity amongst national-ists, he called upon the absent Trimble to nominate ministers first, as was his right as leader of the largest party. When no reply came, the Speaker gave the absent Trimble five minutes to do so. At 10:55, John Hume nominated his fellow Derryman, Mark Durkan, to the SDLP's first ministerial slot, and at 11:15 Gerry Adams named Bairbre De Brun as the first-ever Sinn Fein minister in Northern Ireland. But with the DUP,

Alliance and UKUP refusing to join them, all ten slots went to nationalists. At 11:48, Alderdice announced that these nominations were voided on grounds of insufficient cross-community support and two minutes later Seamus Mallon commenced his resignation speech. Trimble recalls that Mallon had virtually said he would quit in his Second Reading speech on the failsafe legislation in the Commons on Tuesday 13 July.[112] But Mallon never said so to Trimble directly, nor was it communicated by any of the Deputy First Minister's staff to their counterparts in the First Minister's office: Mallon says that he would have done Trimble 'the courtesy' of informing him in person, but the First Minister-designate had not been in his office at Stormont that day. Nor did Trimble seek to pre-empt it by a personal, face-to-face intervention. 'That would have been counterproductive,' says the UUP leader. 'Seamus certainly doesn't like to be told by me what he should do. He is very prickly and likes to consider himself more experienced than me.'[113] Once they found out, the two Governments desperately sought to dissuade him from doing so. They feared that if Mallon went, Trimble would be obliged to go as well. And because of the shift in the balance of forces within unionism as a whole since Trimble was elected as First Minister-designate in June 1998, he could never again secure a return to the job if a fresh vote had to be taken, thus destroying the prospects for cross-community government. Mallon's reasoning, according to one senior colleague, was as follows: if the two Governments believed that there had been a 'seismic shift', that should have been good enough for Trimble and that he was not entitled to extract greater concessions off the back of such footdragging and prevarication. By resigning, he wanted to force Trimble to resign as well so that he would pay a political price for months of such delay in setting up the new institutions. The threat of a Mallon resignation or an actual resignation would therefore compel the two Governments to put pressure upon Trimble to form a Government. The SDLP, which was genuinely committed to the principle of inclusivity, was now being lambasted by Sinn Fein for collaborating in a 'Unionist-friendly' shadow arrangement which comprised only themselves and Trimble's party. They were thus affording the UUP leader the cross-community coverage which they could ill afford themselves. In other words, if Trimble imagined it could be 'business as usual', with the UUP and SDLP set above the rest of the pack, he was sorely mistaken. If the SDLP was to regain its self-respect, it could only enter a review on a level playing field, with all parties as equals, and that was where the resignation came in.[114] As Alderdice was about to commence proceedings in the Assembly chamber, Blair telephoned Mallon. 'There are things you can do,' the then SDLP deputy leader recalls telling the Prime Minister. 'You can suspend the Assembly, as would have been required under the legislation. You can suspend the offices of First and Deputy First Minister. These are steps in the default legislation. Call my office if you meet those requirements.'[115] He then switched his telephone off and told the Assembly that the UUP 'used this crisis to bleed more concessions out of two sovereign Governments. To bleed this process dry.'[116]

Trimble's first reaction was that he would have to resign, too. According to Barry White, his Westminster assistant, he gave farewell presents to his private office, including a Commons headscarf for Maura Quinn.[117] But when he asked David Lavery to look into the matter, he discovered that the Northern Ireland Act 1998 only inextricably linked the offices of First and Deputy First Minister once devolution had already taken place – but not in the shadow phase which then obtained. Moreover, the two shadow posts were operating under the Elections Act 1998 and the Assembly's Standing Orders which did not link the two posts. He instructed Lavery to communicate this to the SDLP on the morning of Thursday 15 July, but it obviously made little difference to the outcome.[118] Even if his position was sustainable legally, for 24 to 48 hours Trimble was not sure that this was the case politically: he feared that he would be accused of 'clinging to office' by a legal contrivance. Lavery spoke to No. 10 to persuade them to make public their feelings on the undesirability of such a step. But there was greater reluctance on the part of the NIO to do so. NIO civil servants were already preparing new Standing Orders which would effectively remove Trimble from his position. Again, Lavery had to ask No. 10 to intervene to stop them (Mowlam's public stance when asked about whether Trimble would have to go was 'we're looking at the legal implications of that').[119] Taylor, Empey, Maginnis and David Campbell all urged him to stay on, pointing out that it would be much more difficult, if not impossible, to resume his position. Steven King rang Trimble's informal group of non-party associates such as Paul Bew, Ruth Dudley Edwards, and Eoghan Harris urging them to plead with Trimble to stay. The next morning, when Trimble came into the office, he said – only half-ironically – that to his surprise, all of the calls had suggested that he remain in place![120] For all his talk of being able 'to get a life' elsewhere, and his indifference to the profession of politics, Trimble appeared remarkably easy to persuade to stay on, even in times of great stress. Indeed, as the dust cleared, it became clear that Mallon's dramatic gambit had failed, at least in the immediate term. Far from the opprobrium of the world turning on Trimble and the UUP for not nominating, the proceedings in Parliament Buildings had turned into a farce, and an incomprehensible one at that to most laymen. Nor did it yield any of the other outcomes which Unionists feared. The two Governments did not, in consequence, immediately redouble their efforts to pressure Trimble into forming an Executive; indeed, the very reverse was the case, since they understood that if they lost him in such circumstances he might never be reinstated as First Minister-designate. Moreover, Mallon's move could be said to have further undermined one of the crucial functions of the SDLP – as the only party which could form a viable working relationship with the Ulster Unionists.

What were the effects of this debacle? The main consequence of 'The Way Forward' was that Trimble regained control of the UUP after a very shaky few months starting with the 14 May episode at No. 10.[121] There is some evidence to suggest that he knew that no deal could be cut in these circumstances and was simply playing for time. There were a number of reasons for his limited room for manoeuvre: the results of the European elections, the marching season, and the feeling of injured communal pride. For once the Provisionals had been allowed to reject the Hillsborough declaration of April 1999, no self-respecting Unionist could then be seen to buckle when the pressure then turned on him. Indeed, when Paul Bew asked Trimble on 13 June 1999 – just days after the European elections – whether there were things which the latter could not do in July but which he might be able to do in September, the UUP leader replied 'that's a nice point' and beamed a toothy, knowing grin at him.[122] He spent much of his time pushing for amendments which he knew that the Government would not support – namely non-inclusion in an Executive (which the Government saw as an important remaining IRA *casus belli*). The subject came up again that week when Trimble went to No. 10 to discuss some amendments accompanied by Maginnis, David Campbell and David Lavery. Portions of the conversation were drowned out by the noise of aircraft overhead, not least Trimble's own softly spoken remarks. But a British participant remembers that one exchange was perfectly heard by all participants. 'Even if you got these changes – and

I am not sure that we can do them,' asked Blair, 'are you sure you could accept this package?' Trimble could not answer in the affirmative. It was scarcely surprising that senior British politicians and officials frequently found him to be an infuriating interlocutor – but if the alternative was political oblivion, such irritation was a price he would have to pay. Far from becoming the prisoner of rejectionists, as some appeared to suggest, such stances bought him the credibility to escape their embrace.[123] Indeed, the leaked transcript of Jonathan Powell's conversation with Martin McGuinness of 16 July suggests that the Prime Minister's chief of staff understood this.[124]

What else was Trimble playing for throughout that week, when he must have known that there was little prospect of success? At one level, he was following Eoghan Harris's advice about simply being seen to be reasonable in negotiating, rather than walking away. But it is also possible that he was seeking to take his party through a necessary learning process – to 'educate' them on the limits of what was doable vis-à-vis the two governments, so that the next time they would negotiate around a more 'realistic' proposition. Effectively, he was letting them marinate so that they would think carefully about the consequences for the Union of a second rejection of an intergovernmental plan.[125] But there is a further, more intriguing possibility – that he subtly undermined 'The Way Forward' not because it was insufficiently prescriptive but because it was too prescriptive. The remark to Blair in the garden of No. 10 suggests someone who was not altogether enthusiastic about failsafes. At one level, this was a technical point. 'There were huge difficulties in framing the amendments,' he notes. 'The problem is that you have got to define precisely the circumstances in which suspension would take place. Defining precisely is very hard because you're dealing with future hypothetical situations.' Above all, 'it [failsafe] appears as if the primary objective is to legislate for failure. It undermines the capability to wrong-foot Sinn Fein as it anticipates that they will not live up to it and you then can't complain when they don't. If you want to blame them afterwards, you have to create the impression that you think they will [disarm].'[126] Nor did he show much enthusiasm for an eminently Blairite 'Third Way' between the demands of the British Government and the Unionist grassroots. During the course of the fortnight, Paul Bew suggested to Trimble the idea of a 'post-dated cheque' (many are credited with paternity for this idea, including the human rights campaigner, Henry Robinson, but Bew pushed it hardest with Trimble at this stage). Bew believed that Trimble should agree to trigger d'Hondt 'under protest' while placing a post-dated resignation letter in the hands of the presiding officer, Lord Alderdice. In such a scenario, Trimble would take control, rather than be cast either as Blair's loyal provincial satrap or the captive of the UUP hardliners. Blair would be tied to the decommissioning timetable he outlined in the Commons on Monday 5 July and Trimble would have his own 'failsafe' rather than anyone else's. An early leadership challenge would be fore-stalled by the guarantee that the Northern Ireland Executive would be collapsed by his own hand if decommissioning had not begun by a particular date – perhaps 22 May 2000. This would afford Blair the space to test the 'seismic shift', whilst retaining the option put forward by Clinton of being able to walk away.[127] But Trimble then found this option 'tacky' and too limiting of his freedom of manoeuvre; again, he thought it smacked too much of anticipating failure.[128] Nor, for reasons that he never thoroughly explained, did he show much interest in the 'Taylor option' that was put forward by his deputy earlier that year: that legislative devolution with Cabinet government be scrapped in favour of Welsh-style administrative devolution and no Executive.[129] So uninterested was he in the available alternatives that it suggests that he was a more committed believer in the principle of full governmental inclusivity than many nationalists gave him credit for.

Trimble's other *sine qua non* was the 'blame game' and one of the articles of conventional wisdom was that the Unionists would not be forgiven if they declined to accept an intergovernmental proposal. Cer-tainly, Gerry Adams urged Blair to challenge the 'Afrikaner ethos' of the Ulster Unionists and maintained that Trimble did not want republicans 'to get their hands on the wheel of power'.[130] Others believed that Union-ism had committed political suicide by not accepting 'The Way For-ward'.[131] In fact, nothing of the sort happened in terms of the mainstream of British opinion. The British media did not turn on Trimble: *The Daily Telegraph, The Sunday Telegraph, The Times, The Sunday Times* and the *Daily Mail* all weighed in heavily on his behalf. On the day after Mallon resigned, the strap on the masthead of the *Daily Mail* – which had as sharp a commercial nose for the sentiments of Middle England as any news organisation in the country – pictured Trimble with the words 'A shy man, he has taken great risks walking the tightrope of peace. It would now be a travesty to brand him the villain.' The relevant article was accompanied by a leader along much the same lines.[132] Even non-unionist commentators and publications – such as Mary Holland and *The Economist* – also understood his position.[133] In the political classes, too, there was no generalised sense of condemnation and much understanding. 'Political suicide' would only have taken place if Unionists had been faced with tripartisan attack. Moreover, the Conservatives were in absolute lockstep with them, to the point that backbench Labour attacks in the Commons on the afternoon of Thursday 15 July 1999 were at least as much directed at Andrew Mackay as at the UUP for his alleged breach of bipartisanship.[134] But it was a sign of Labour's shakiness over its Northern Ireland policy that even a weak Opposition party could rattle them with pedestrian criticisms. Trimble thus had the Tories where he wanted them: occupying his right flank, 'doing my dirty work for me' as he liked to put it.[135] Significantly, Trimble had built this informal coalition to resist the imposition of 'The Way Forward' by making a largely moral appeal to the mainstream of British opinion – on the basis of the unfairness of punishing democrats for the sins of paramilitaries. He rarely did so, largely for fear of offending Blair. But at this juncture he had no choice, and it had worked – so much so that even elements of the Labour party warmed to it. Tony Benn suggested in the Commons on the day after the UUP rejected the document that 'old Unionism' was not interested in sharing office with Catholics, but the very fact that it was Benn who said this pointed up the marginality of that viewpoint.[136] In fact, during the Committee stage of the failsafe legislation, at least two backbench Labour MPs, Frank Field (Birkenhead) and Dr George Turner (Norfolk North West) spoke up for the Unionist position on decommissioning and were critical of the Government.[137]

Ultimately, the Government, for all its frustration with Trimble, had to grasp the Realpolitik of his position. 'The Way Forward' debacle had, after all, turned out to be what Steve Richards called 'the lowest moment in Tony Blair's premiership' to date.[138] At one point, John Sawers of No. 10 had suggested with acerbity that 'maybe David Trimble doesn't want to be First Minister of Northern Ireland and wants to spend his time in the wilderness'.[139] But their frustration partly stemmed from the fact that they felt that they could not do without him. Alternatives to Trimble within Unionism, let alone a process without unionism, were even less palatable than indulging the UUP leader and his quirks. His methodology may have been bizarre and inelegant, as exemplified by his decision to keep the Assembly group at Glengall Street during the sitting at Stormont on Thursday 15 July – but it worked. If Frank Cousins of the TGWU was 'the awkward warrior', then Trimble could surely be said to be an 'awkward peacemaker'.[140]

TWENTY-NINE

RUC RIP

ON 15 July 1999, George Mitchell was unwinding in his London hotel suite at the end of one of the most momentous days of his life. He had earlier received his honorary knighthood at Buckingham Palace for his role in chairing the 1996–8 talks. Suddenly, the telephone rang: it was Mo Mowlam on the line. Would he be willing to head up a review which would 'break the log-jam' and try to set up the inclusive Executive for the first time? Soon afterwards, Ahern rang with a similar request. Mitchell discussed the matter with his wife, but by the time that Blair telephoned him shortly thereafter, he had decided that he simply could not decline. Following briefings with Bill Jeffrey of the NIO – who had replaced Quentin Thomas in 1998 – and Dermot Gallagher of the DFA, Mitchell met with Blair and then with Trimble at the NIO's London headquarters at Millbank.[1] Trimble reacted positively to the idea of his return and Mitchell agreed with him that the review of the talks should focus on the Northern Ireland parties to the exclusion of the two Governments. This suited No. 10, who now recognised the limitations of the two Governments doing a deal on behalf of the local communities and of high-profile set-piece negotiations. Mitchell well understood the severe difficulty which Trimble would face in selling his party 'jam tomorrow' in respect of decommissioning. Mitchell told Trimble that mistakes had been made in July, notably the overselling of the 'seismic shift'. The Governments had wanted a swift review, but the American did not agree and he prevailed. He furthermore insisted that two parallel processes not go on and that it would helpful if the two Prime Ministers did not engage directly in this phase of discussions. This would ensure that neither Trimble, nor any other party, could go over Mitchell's head to the Prime Minister or Taoiseach. Trimble was not disturbed by any of this. The UUP leader, in turn, suggested that the former US Senate Majority leader should chair the bilaterals between the UUP and Sinn Fein. Significantly, he also agreed that during the review, the parties would never occupy rooms in Castle Buildings so that there would be no 'media circus': in July, these facilities had been made available to anti-Agreement parties and Trimble felt that they had used them to upset some of his 'own folk'.[2] Above all, he felt that the presence of a neutral chairman in the bilaterals would show him (and the world) who were the 'good guys' – and who weren't.[3]

If Trimble imagined that such public exposure of the rights and wrongs of any given situation would result in the stigmatisation of the defaulting party, he was sorely mistaken. For on 26 July, the FBI arrested three Irish citizens in Fort Lauderdale, Florida. The trio were accused in court of being part of a sophisticated ring organising the importation of weapons from the United States for use in Northern Ireland.[4] Any republican terrorism was bad enough, but it swiftly emerged from their initial statements to the American authorities that far from being 'dissidents', they were affiliated to the Provisional IRA.[5] Worse was to come. On 30 July, Charles Bennett, reputed to be a low-level informer for the security forces, was found shot dead on waste ground at the rear of St Galls GAA club, Milltown Road, in west Belfast.[6] Gerry Adams expressed his shock and sympathy for the family – the killing had taken place in his 'backyard' – and senior republicans attended the funeral. Nonetheless, suspicion again swiftly alighted upon the Provisionals. Whatever the internal politics of the republican movement, the implications for Trimble were immediately obvious. Could he remain in the upcoming review with republicans not merely declining to forswear coercion but continuing to use it in the most blatant way – especially if it was subsequently proven that it was the Provisionals who perpetrated it? Indeed, so big a blow was it that Reg Empey believed that had the rejectionists moved then, it could have been the issue which landed the 'killer' punch upon Trimble in the Ulster Unionist Executive, obviating the need to go on to the larger UUC: only the 'antis' fear of losing stopped them, he says.[7] It is also possible that the 'antis' felt they did not have to push that hard since things were moving their way anyhow. Thus, Trimble believes that John Taylor's subsequent decision not to participate in the Mitchell review had the effect of becalming the 'antis'.[8]

Trimble's response was as mild as it could have been given these conditions. It appeared to him as though Bennett had been killed to prove to the hardliners that there had been no 'seismic shift' in the Provisionals' position on decommissioning at the start of the month.[9] He was far more worried about the importation of arms, which he (correctly) claimed the authorities knew to be merely one of many such operations. He (incorrectly, it appears) suspected that it was significant that handguns, rather than AK-47s, were being brought in by the IRA: to him, this implied that they wanted weapons that were suitable for policing 'their own' areas rather than for killing British servicemen and loyalists.[10] Whatever the accuracy of Trimble's analysis, the weeks rolled by. Speculation mounted about the Provisionals' role in the killing of Bennett and what Mowlam would do if informed by her security advisers that the Provisionals indeed had a role. On 25 August, the RUC Chief Constable, Ronnie Flanagan, told BBC Northern Ireland's *Straight Up* programme that he had 'no doubt' that the Provisionals were responsible for the killing and that Mowlam was in no doubt, either, of his opinion. But, he added, the question of whether the ceasefire had broken down and what the consequences might be were for the politicians to decide. Mowlam pronounced on the next day: 'I have left Sinn Fein in no doubt that all violence, for whatever reason it is perpetrated, is unacceptable, and have called on them to use their influence to ensure that there is no repetition.' The Secretary of State had taken account of her duties under the Sentences Act 1998 as to whether an organisation could continue to benefit from the prisoner release scheme if their ceasefire was in doubt. 'On that basis, although the situation in relation to the IRA is deeply worrying, I do not believe that there is a sufficient basis to conclude that the IRA ceasefire has broken down. Nor do I believe that it is disintegrating, or that recent events represent a decision by the organisation to return to violence. I have therefore decided not to use my powers under the Sentences Act at this time. But I want to make it entirely clear that I have come very close to judging that the IRA's ceasefire is no longer for real . . .' The British had plenty of hints from republicans that any tough response could jeopardise the process: Sinn Fein refused to give a promise to participate in the Mitchell review if Unionists used these events to bring about their exclusion, a threat subsequently reiterated by McGuinness.[11]

Trimble found the decision to be 'deeply disappointing and flawed' and observed that Mowlam's definition of a ceasefire appeared to be closer to that of the IRA – as being a cessation of operations against military forces of the Crown, rather than against civilians in Catholic areas.[12] He had been telephoned by Mowlam some 30 to 40 minutes before she announced her decision. He was not surprised by her approach, but tried instead to influence the presentation of her statement. He advised her to build in the line of John Bruton, the then leader of Fine Gael, about imposing the highest possible standard as the test of the ceasefire. According to Trimble, she said afterwards that she had rewritten the announcement at his behest – which made him wonder quite how much worse her statement could have been.[13] Trimble's interest in cooperating with Mowlam in this instance was obvious: a weak statement by Mowlam would have had the effect of further outraging Unionist opinion, destabilising Trimble's own position and making it impossible to participate in any review. He had little success in this endeavour – Mowlam's statement still angered many Unionists – but it offered further evidence of how calibrated his position had become. The point was widely noted in intergovernmental circles.[14] Indeed, in his Omagh address of 23 August 1999, Trimble openly stated that the Belfast Agreement would 'not work as well as it could without Sinn Fein'.[15] Once again, far from trying to drum Sinn Fein/IRA out of the Mitchell review, Trimble was in fact affording the republican leadership the space they needed to stay in the process.

Trimble could afford no such careful calibration in his 'headline' responses to the Patten report on the future of policing.[16] For at least a month prior to publication of the document on 9 September, the rumours concerning its findings had been very bleak from a UUP viewpoint. On 25 August their worst fears were confirmed when the *Belfast Telegraph* published a leaked version of substantial tracts of the report. The RUC would be renamed the Northern Ireland Police Service; it would have a new badge; officers would no longer take an oath of loyalty to the Crown; the Union Flag would no longer be flown from stations; district policing boards, congruent with the 26 district council areas, would be able to levy extra on the rates so as to buy extra policing services, raising the spectre that Sinn Fein-controlled municipal authorities could purchase 'security' from paramilitary-dominated firms.[17] Trimble treated the leaks with suspicion and assumed they could be part of an attempt to frighten Unionists into bolting from the process: he thought they were only a starting point, 'not holy writ' and was reassured when he visited No. 10. Indeed, he was told by John Sawers that 'the security services can do an awful lot but at the end of the day it is RUC Special Branch we depend on'.[18]

But the *Belfast Telegraph* turned out to be largely accurate. In Unionist eyes, many of the 175 recommendations in the final 128-page report added insult to injury.[19] True, Sinn Fein/IRA's stated agenda of wholesale disbandment had been averted and a unitary structure was maintained, thus avoiding 'regionalisation' and the most obvious perils associated with differential levels of law enforcement. There would be no explicit 'two-tier' policing. Many of the recommendations, such as the 'downsizing' of the force from 13,000 to 7500, were either 'security sensitive' – that is, dependent upon the advice of the Chief Constable and the GOC as to the level of terrorist threat – or else uncontentious, such as the new police training college.[20] Much of it was riddled with the 'management speak' which characterised much discussion of contemporary policing elsewhere, with all of the pseudo-market jargon about service delivery. Indeed, British sources made much of the point that many of the recommendations were derived from Flanagan's own Fundamental Review of the force, conducted when he was Deputy Chief Constable from 1994 to 1996. All of this went some way towards explaining Sinn Fein's cool response towards the report, although they later insisted that it was a matter of holy writ which had to be implemented 'in full'. But in terms of the *existing* culture and ethos of the force, the Patten report was very radical indeed and resulted in the erasure of the symbols of Britishness. Moreover, it offered very little in the way of visible recognition of past sacrifices beyond the proposal that existing memorials to slain officers be retained in police buildings: some Commissioners feared that a peroration on the sacrifices of the RUC might be used by republicans as an excuse not to sign up, and that they would accuse Patten of 'buying into RUC propaganda' (one loyalist, recalling the force's underwhelming PR, rejoins 'what RUC propaganda was there?'). Indeed, Patten believed that both sides had 'equally passionately felt' stories to tell: to Unionists, and many on the mainland, this was outrageous 'moral equilateralism'.[21]

Nor could Unionists fail to notice what they saw as the unbalanced presentation of such issues as the failure to recruit young Catholics (in November 1999, only 7.73% of the total of 12,514 officers were Catholic).[22] Patten appeared to them to ascribe this disparity as much to the symbols of Britishness in the force as to concerted republican murders of Catholic officers (one obvious example of this in their eyes was the Patten report's euphemistic reference to 'peer group pressure'). In addition, the part-time reserve would be expanded, especially in those republican and loyalist areas which had been alienated from the RUC: Sean O'Callaghan high-lighted this proposal to Trimble as being the most dangerous of all, since it was an inadvertent but in his view surefire way of infiltrating subversives into police stations.[23] The distinctive identity of Special Branch would be eroded by yoking it more closely together with CID under one assistant chief constable. Generous redundancy packages were offered, further transforming the old force.

When the UUP leader emerged to deliver his verdict on the report, his face was red with rage – very much in the style of the old Trimble. He described Patten as the 'most shoddy' report he had seen in his years in public life.[24] The essence of Trimble's position was as follows: Patten had misunderstood the nature of the Belfast Agreement. The accord was not about the obliteration of symbols of both communities, as the report had proposed, but their more sensitive use. What, Unionists wondered, could more thoroughly express the concept of 'parity of esteem' than the cap badge – with crown, harp and shamrock? Moreover, as Trimble saw it, Patten had not understood that the Belfast Agreement was about nationalist Ireland affirming for the first time the legitimacy of Northern Ireland's position within the United Kingdom, to be determined by the consent principle. This confirmation of Ulster as part of British sovereign territory, Trimble reasoned, would inevitably have consequences for symbols, in the police and elsewhere.[25]

Patten was swift to rebut Trimble's critique and at the press conference for the report remarked, 'What on earth did they think they were signing up to?'[26] In other words, Trimble had signed up to the Belfast Agreement, with its 'unionist' bits, and could scarcely complain when the 'nationalist' bits of the accord yielded outcomes which he did not like. The manner in which Patten sold his report showed little consideration for the damage it could do to Trimble's position: in so doing he had validated at a stroke Paisley's and McCartney's analysis that in signing up to the Belfast Agreement, the UUP leader had undermined the Ulster-British way of life, of which the RUC was a crucial component. So aggressive and conde-scending was Patten's mode of discourse, both at the press conference and at the subsequent meeting of the British-Irish Association in Cam-bridge, that even senior NIO civil servants believed that he was being profoundly 'unhelpful' to Trimble, who was already in a difficult enough position as it was. 'A better politician would have done all that he could have done to help David Trimble at this point,' says one senior official.[27]

Indeed, there can have been few such 'blue ribbon' commissions which have been so coolly received on the mainland, especially considering that it was examining as unfashionable an organisation as the RUC. Even *The Economist*, no particular friend of Unionism, was scarcely ecstatic about Patten's findings in its edition of 11 September 1999 – precisely because of their effect upon David Trimble.

How did this Unionist debacle come about? After all, Patten had told Henry Patterson over supper earlier that year that he had four constituencies to please – those headed by Gerry Adams, Ronnie Flanagan, John Hume and David Trimble. Patterson was not sure this infernally hard trick was possible, but was reassured at the time that Patten seemed at some level to have a notion of protecting David Trimble's essential political position.[28] Indeed, Patten appears to have known what the minimum Ulster Unionist requirements were: defending himself in *The Times* on 10 September 1999 from the surprisingly hostile editorial comment which greeted his report, he said that 'in the consultations I conducted before drafting the report, a leading Unionist politician said to me that it didn't matter if we got the substance more or less right. What mattered was the symbols: if we touched those, we would have blown it.' The leading Unionist referred to in that *Times* article was David Trimble himself. But this raises the question of *when* Patten realised this – and with what vigour Trimble expressed himself.

Certainly, Trimble's public pronouncements around the time that Patten was published suggest that this issue was of fundamental importance to him. Indeed, he raised the issue of the RUC at virtually every meeting with the British Government since September 1999.[29] However, Trimble's zeal on this subject had not been so apparent throughout the course of the Commission's deliberations – and many insiders knew it. No. 10 believed that in September 1999, Trimble was acting mainly because of pressure from within the UUP, not least because it reckoned that so many members of the party had relatives in the force.[30] Even as late as 8 September 1999, when Trimble met with George Mitchell at Castle Buildings, he told the former US Senate Majority leader that much of what was going to be in Patten had already been contained in the Flanagan Fundamental Review and the HMIC report. He was not sure about the implications for Special Branch, and had serious concerns about accountability and the District Partnerships. The symbolic issues would cause difficulties, but he left the impression that he could pretty well weather the coming storm and that the issue of the RUC was not so crucial as to prompt a UUP walk-out from the talks.[31]

Likewise, Andrew Mackay adds that from his conversations with Trimble in the Commons tea room he knew the UUP leader was concerned about Patten but that his worries were of a 'totally different gear to what he actually said'. The then Conservative spokesman adds: 'I was surprised by the vehemence of Trimble's language – he was much stronger and more emotional than I had seen him in the past on this subject.'[32] Viscount Cranborne, who later played an important role in the 'Defend the RUC Campaign, is more explicit still and describes Trimble's performance over much of the period as 'little short of disgraceful'.[33] Cranborne had good reasons for making this remark. For contrary to the Paisleyite analysis – which held this sort of outcome to be inherent in the Belfast Agreement – there was much crucial detail to play for once the Patten Commission had been set up. Indeed, the roots of the UUP's defeat in the policing battle lie in the period immediately after the Agreement was signed. Trimble had paid little attention to the issue in the talks and delegated almost everything to Ken Maginnis. At one point in the final week, Cecil Walker, then MP for North Belfast and till 28 March 2001 one of the few parliamentarians not to have spoken on the floor of the Commons in the 1997–2001 Parliament, was assigned to co-handle the negotiations on the RUC. Trimble believed that if policing came into the main body of the talks, then the chances of reaching agreement at Castle Buildings would have been slim. Therefore he, like the other parties, deemed it best that the issue of policing be 'long-fingered' on to a Commission. Indeed, Trimble was told by the NIO on a 'nudge, nudge, wink, wink' basis that a Commission would handle the matter sensitively in a way that his community could live with (it is not, however, clear as to why Trimble, with his long-time history of dislike of the NIO, should have accepted such assurances, especially under Mowlam's stewardship).[34] Hence Trimble's claim at the Ulster Unionist Executive of 9 April 1998 that 'Ken and Cecil have saved the RUC'. Jeffrey Donaldson correctly observed at that point that it was merely a stay of execution, but Trimble and Maginnis did not use the intervening year and a half until publication of the report greatly to strengthen their position. Indeed, whenever I asked Maginnis how the panel's work was proceeding, the UUP security spokesman would invariably declare 'we've educated Patten to the realities of policing' (Maginnis disagrees with this interpretation: he says that what he meant by this was that Patten fully understood the UUP case, but was less than sure that the former Hong Kong governor would act upon it in his final report. He adds that both Trimble and himself relied upon what they believed were Patten's assurances that he would contact them if the Commission's findings were at variance with the UUP's core needs.)[35] Les Rodgers, then Chairman of the Police Federation of Northern Ireland, recalls Maginnis telling him a mere fortnight before publication that rumours about a change of title were unfounded. 'It's nonsense – we've got the name!' said Maginnis.[36] But even if Trimble had known in advance that such an outcome was going to emerge from the Patten Commission, the UUP leader says that he would never have believed that the British Government would subsequently treat the report as 'holy writ'. He believed that since even British Government White Papers are not necessarily implemented in full, why should the work of an external body be regarded as so special? 'It was wholly alien to the British way of doing things,' observes the UUP leader.[37] If so, Trimble was being highly over-optimistic, if not naive. After all, the bitter reaction in nationalist Ireland in January 1996 to what they regarded as the 'binning' of the Mitchell report on disarmament suggested that they would insist upon strict adherence to such documents.

This pattern of wild over-optimism began with the selection of members of the Commission. According to several sources – including one close colleague – the choice of Patten had originally been the idea of Joe Pilling, the Permanent Under Secretary of the NIO, a Home Office civil servant with experience of the Province stretching back to the 1970s. And he was not thought of as a great friend of the RUC. 'Pilling rarely had had nice word to say about the police,' recalls Colin Cramphorn, an Englishman who served as the Deputy Chief Constable from 1998–2002 and who is now the Chief Constable of West Yorkshire. 'Pilling was often patronising towards the cops and viewed them as the problem and not the solution. He believed that senior officers had ridden rough-shod over senior civil servants and went instead direct to Secretaries of State. Pilling seemed to me to believe that the RUC had acted beyond its rightful position and needed now to be put in its place.'[38] Certainly, Pilling did the RUC few favours in recommending the chairman. The British believed themselves to be under great pressure to name a chairman who was not from the United Kingdom. But Pilling had concluded that it would be much easier to carry any proposals which emerged if the chairman was a

Tory. The officials soon alighted upon Patten, who they believed amongst Conservatives was especially open to change.[39] Pilling's suggestion of Patten found a very ready audience with the Government, and especially with Mo Mowlam. The former Hong Kong governor remembers being telephoned by her whilst in New York City on a lecture tour of the United States. During the course of a 'most friendly' conversation she offered him the job, whereupon he consulted with his wife. It was 13 years since he had served as an NIO junior minister, but it did not take him long to decide, since he had long viewed Northern Ireland 'not as the equivalent of exile to a Siberian power station, but rather as the most important topic in British politics'. It was at such moments that Mowlam's tenure at the NIO was crucial to the outcome of the process: Patten, for one, believes that if Peter Mandelson had been Secretary of State in 1998, he might never have been appointed. Mandelson does not agree, but says that he would have spoken with Patten and tried to influence at the margins some of the judgment calls which the former Hong Kong governor made.[40]

The Government's calculations about Patten's appointment certainly proved correct. The Tories were silenced for much of the Commission's deliberations, thus preventing a possible breach in the bipartisan approach. For if Labour started feeling the heat for dismantling the police and thus appearing 'soft on terrorism', they might be forced to make difficult choices between political damage on the mainland and changes which were vital to secure nationalist and perhaps republican acquiescence in an agreed Northern Ireland. Certainly, Andrew Mackay, the Conservative spokesman told me he was extremely reluctant to speak out too loudly and too often against Patten before September 1999 lest there be headlines of 'Tory splits'. It is difficult to know what signals Mackay sent to Patten during the course of several long private conversations: they do not appear to have been very strong signals, since Patten recalls that 'I hardly spoke to Mackay or anybody else in the Tory party and only saw him a couple of times. And I didn't consult with him before the report was published.'[41] But Patten certainly appears to have sent some sort of general signals, since Mackay was not surprised by the final outcome of the Commission's deliberations; nonetheless, Mackay did not sound the alarm bells earlier. Indeed, considering the very strong pro-RUC feeling on the Tory backbenches, Mackay's position was curious. He now regards it as 'unfortunate' that both Patten and Trimble 'personalised' the debate in the immediate aftermath of the report's publication and as a 'low point in both men's reputations' (Mackay thus casts both Trimble and Patten as equal villains of the piece).[42] Eventually, 30 Conservative backbenchers from all wings of the party, led by John Hayes, sent a letter to *The Daily Telegraph* during the October 1999 Tory conference in Blackpool: it pushed a more vigorous line than did the front bench.[43] Trimble did not object to any of these Tory campaigns on behalf of the RUC, regarding them as part of the necessary task of mainland unionists to do his 'dirty work' for him. But his comparative silence throughout much of the Commission's work communicated itself to senior Tories and therefore placed a ceiling on the willingness of others to do battle during the critical phase of 1998–9. As Patrick Mayhew – who was especially worried about the prospect of Patten affecting the operational independence of the chief constable – put it in this period, 'I felt I could not credibly "out-Trimble" Trimble himself.'[44] Like so many on the mainland, Mayhew could not be *plus royaliste que le roi*.

If the Government's calculations about the importance of appointing a Tory proved to be correct vis-à-vis the Conservatives, they proved to be even more so vis-à-vis the UUP. Far from being disturbed by Patten's record in the NIO during the 1980s, both Trimble and Maginnis welcomed the former Hong Kong governor's original appointment. Thus, the UUP security spokesman noted the choice of a 'UK establishment figure', adding: 'Chris Patten, from my experience of him as a minister here, is a man of outstanding ability and someone who will understand the implications of having had to police a community like ours.'[45] Maginnis now admits that he 'misjudged Patten. I expected more of him. I thought he would be far more realistic and pragmatic.'[46] But their reaction to the choice of Patten was not the only misjudgment in respect of the appointments to the Commission on policing – nor was it necessarily the most important. For the Commission consisted of far more than just the chairman. For the creation of a balanced Commission meant that at least one of its members would have a 'particular insight into the thinking' of the Unionist community (just as there would be those who enjoyed insights into the nationalist perspective). Trimble's and Maginnis's first choice was Paul Bew. But Bew declined partly for personal reasons. After discussions with the NIO, Maginnis and Trimble accepted John Steele's suggestion of an eminent silk.[47] Their choice seemed sound enough from a UUP perspective: Peter Smith, QC. Smith had known Trimble since the 1960s, when he had been an assistant lecturer at Queen's. He had first joined the Unionists in 1968, had left in 1971, only to rejoin in the 1980s. Then, he appeared to be a 'coming man' in the party. He was even elected one of four Honorary Secretaries of the UUC, but later left the party to concentrate on his legal career. Maginnis sounded out Smith and *assumed* that he would ensure that core unionist communal and political interests were not ignored. What Maginnis did not do was to define those core interests, such as the name and the cap badge. Instead, he took it for granted that he did not need to spell it all out. Indeed, he says that any attempt to do so – to dictate, as it were, the terms of Smith's mission – would have been counterproductive and would have been resented by Smith.[48] He was correct in this assumption, at least: Smith says that he would have declined the appointment if there had been any attempt to set the conditions of his service. An attempt to ascertain Smith's views might have been thought to be a necessary prerequisite of his appointment, since Smith says that he was never a 'flags and emblems man'.[49] In a literal sense, Smith is correct: his pamphlets of the 1980s make no direct reference to the issue. Nonetheless, his very hard-hitting writings against the AIA make specific reference to Article V of the treaty, which empowers the Irish Government to make representations regarding symbolic issues. Considering the generally robust tone of the pamphlet, the UUP might have inferred that Smith implicitly found those aspects of the increasing Irish remit over everyday life in the Province unaccept-able as well.[50] That said, it was extraordinary, given that their fortunes were so dependent upon the outcome of the Commission's work, that neither Trimble nor Maginnis asked Smith what his views were. It is, of course, perfectly possible that a man's views might have changed in the intervening period (although Smith says this was not the case). Nor did John Steele of the NIO inquire about Smith's views at the time: he says that he went on personalities rather than on views.[51] Indeed, according to Maginnis, Steele told him that the Commission needed a barrister to provide balance and expertise from the legal profession. At one point, the idea of appointing Sir John Wheeler was raised with Maginnis, but the UUP security spokesman ruled it out on the grounds that the Govern-ment may not have found him acceptable.[52] Again, this assessment was based upon dubious reasoning: if the Government had rejected Wheeler, the UUP would have had perfect grounds for publicly denouncing an attempt to 'stack' the Commission. But it would have been extremely unlikely that the Government would have gone against Trimble and Maginnis in such a matter, unless their appointee was blatantly unsuitable. This would clearly not have been the case in this instance: in 1997, the then Home Secretary, Jack Straw, confirmed the appointment of Wheeler as Chairman of the Service Authorities overseeing the National Criminal Intelligence Service and the National Crime Squad.[53]

Smith claims that it rapidly became apparent within the first month of its deliberations that the Commission would be inclined to disassociate policing from the state and thus to 'depoliticise' it, as it were. He remembers this approach as first coming together during a dinner of the Commissioners – and, unusually, the secretariat – at the Strand Restaurant on the Stranmillis Road in south Belfast. This would inevitably entail a purge of symbols of Britishness such as Union flags. Smith regarded this as being squarely within the terms of reference of the policing Commission as described in the Belfast Agreement, which he observes were far more tightly drawn than the rest of that treaty. To Trimbleistas this seemed to be an excessively pious, not to say priggish conception of the Commission's work: the purpose of the Patten report was not to be above politics, but rather was a key building-block in helping to make consociational politics work and thus to ensure Unionist adherence to the new dispensation. Anything which made that task harder was objectively unhelpful, as Peter Mandelson appeared to recognise in a series of gestures apparently designed to palliate the effects of Patten. In the 'zero-sum' communal politics of Northern Ireland, such cultural and symbolic 'neutralism' was bound to be seen by vast numbers of nationalists as a great gain, whereas for Unionists 'even-handedness' represented a great loss. An outcome along the lines of Patten could have been averted if Smith had been prepared to issue a minority report. But Smith does not appear at any stage to have been inclined to do so, at least on the issues of symbolism: he says that he would only have signed a dissenting minority report if the majority of the panel had opted for regionalisation or 'two-tier' policing.[54]

Yet to this day, Smith asserts that he was profoundly concerned with the effect of any report on Trimble's position, and thinks that the body produced a report of exquisite balance between the two 'extremes' of the status quo and disbandment (in fact, this was no longer Sinn Fein's real position and had not been so for some time: according to Brendan O'Leary's summary of Mitchel McLaughlin's views in early 1997, republicans sought wide-ranging reform of the RUC rather than its formal disbandment).[55] As Smith saw it, the report *did* address and look after core Unionist anxieties and interests. But he supposed that the UUP leader would play things totally differently at a political level. Again, although Trimble and Maginnis approved Smith's appointment, Smith did not conceive of himself as the Ulster Unionist representative. He imagined that Trimble would do as Sinn Fein does – to ignore those parts of a report that he did not like and to alight upon those parts which chimed in with long-time Unionist aspirations (such as the prospect of a return of local security powers, which Faulkner lost in 1972, leading to the collapse of the old Stormont). Then, he imagined, Trimble might say to the republicans, 'Look, we have signed up to terms of reference under the Agreement, will you now recommend that young republicans join up to the police force?', thus putting Adams et al. on the spot.[56] Maybe so: but few Unionists would have been much turned on by the prospect of young republicans in the force of the future, even as a tactical device to throw Sinn Fein on to the defensive. In that sense, Smith had a very odd view as to the likely reaction of most Unionists at the time. Again, this raises the question of whether Trimble and Maginnis could reasonably have been expected to be aware of how Smith would actually perform on the Commission. Paul Bew, for one, says that few can have anticipated that Smith would be completely swept up with the *esprit de corps* of the Commission – so much so that Smith told Bew that Chris Patten 'is the greatest unelected statesman of our times'. That said, the one obvious way to have ascertained Smith's real views would have been to quiz him rigorously. But even after Smith's appointment, Trimble never spoke to him during the year and a bit of the Commission's work (Maginnis only spoke to him twice, during the course of a Commission visit to Dungannon in early 1999 and in the week before publication). Such an omission was typical of Trimble's special form of political autism and was to cost him dear in the coming months. Indeed, when Trimble met Peter Smith on the aircraft heading to the British-Irish Association in September 1999, he initially ignored Smith. When they came face to face, Smith asked, 'Are we going to the same place?' Trimble exploded, declaring, 'You're a fool!' When one aide asked about this episode afterwards, Trimble replied, 'At least I didn't hit him.'[57] It was typical of Trimble that instead of seeking to talk to Smith when it might have had effect, he huffed and puffed when the deed was already done. Indeed, at an election post-mortem held at Denis Rogan's office – when it was apparent that the issue of the RUC had cost the UUP heavily in the 2001 Westminster poll – Trimble acknowledged that it was remiss of the party not to have 'sat' on Smith during the deliberations on Patten.[58]

But what of the other Commissioners? They included Maurice Hayes, who had been a senior Northern Ireland civil servant and who had written the report on the reform of the police complaints procedures; he was also a Senator in the Irish Parliament.[59] Patten had much admired him when he served in Northern Ireland as a junior minister, an admiration which was wholly reciprocated (both men also served on the board of Tony O'Reilly's *Independent* Newspapers chain).[60] Many believed that he would be a key influence on the Commission. Indeed, when Trimble met Peter Mandelson for the first time as Secretary of State on 12 October 1999, the Unionists told him of their worries about the proposed powers in the report for DPPBs to raise up to three pence in the pound on local rates to buy in extra policing services. Mandelson asked, 'Who thought these ideas up?' 'Maurice Hayes, principally,' replied Bill Jeffrey, the NIO's Political Director (Hayes states that it was quite true that it was his idea, but that the intent was different from what Unionists believed: it was not to hire 'goons', but rather to pay for extra police overtime or lighting in areas where police commanders were hard pressed for resources).[61] Other members not from either of the two main traditions included Lucy Woods, a British Telecom executive; Kathy O'Toole, an Irish-American with a record in law enforcement but who in consequence was perhaps viewed with a degree of suspicion by some nationalists and republicans; Sir John Smith, the former Deputy Commissioner of the Metropolitan Police (again, Maginnis believed that Sir John Smith would be 'solid', but when he invited the former senior policeman to the Commons, he found himself to be in total disagreement with the ex-peeler); and Clifford Shearing, a Canadian academic. In a volume which he co-authored with Mike Brogden called *Policing for a New South Africa*, Shearing wrote sympathetically of efforts to create an alternative system of ordering in the townships. They described the main form of punishment meted out by these courts, namely whipping, as enjoying 'the particular benefits of immediacy, of calculated, measured punishment' and as affording 'a public shaming experience of immediate duration'. The authors argued that South Africa should adopt a two-level system of policing in which such informal community methods co-existed alongside the regular, reformed state police.[62] Paul Bew drew Maginnis's attention to Shearing's writings early on in the proceedings. The UUP security spokesman shared Bew's concerns, but generally Maginnis did little to sound the alarm in public and to try to condition the climate in which the Commission operated. One reason in this instance for not sounding the alarm may have been because he had been told that Shearing was not part of the 'inner circle' within the Commission, who some said comprised Patten, Hayes, O'Toole and both Smiths. He was certainly correct in this belief, but Patten subsequently told Maginnis that the Unionists had underrated Shearing politically. He could have been the catalyst for a potentially damaging minority report which would have been issued if Patten had not been radical enough. (Patten, though, claims there was never any danger of a minority report from a 'Green' perspective, as it were, since this would have vitiated the purpose of the Commission, namely to create a police service which could command cross-community assent.)[63] The last Commissioner to be appointed was Gerard Lynch, president of John Jay College in New York and a prominent Irish-American: he received his assignment after the Irish complained bitterly that the panel was weighted against them.[64] Yet although the Commission contained few, if any, known partisans of the old RUC, neither Maginnis nor Trimble ever sought to portray it as inimicable to their interests.

So much for the composition of the Commission. But did Trimble and Maginnis do enough to influence its deliberations once the body was up and running? Or would even a vigorous campaign have made any difference? On one level, probably not. The Commission, according to one member, was neither influenced by the well-orchestrated republican campaign to pack public meetings of the Commission in nationalist areas, nor was it much influenced by the pro-RUC tenor of meetings in Unionist areas. Of greater significance was the behind-the-scenes lobbying of the Irish Government, which was even more inclined to take a 'pan-nationalist' viewpoint in security and policing matters relating to Northern Ireland than on institutional and constitutional questions.[65] By contrast, the British under Mowlam tended to play it far more conservatively and to treat the Patten Commission as a genuinely independent body. And when the British did respond to Commission requests, not all elements of the system were necessarily helpful to the RUC. One of the reasons for the niggardly praise of the force may have been the briefing given to Commissioners by the Cabinet Office on allegations of collusion between the security forces and loyalist paramilitaries. This was based on the findings of the Sampson, Stalker and Stevens reports, which one Commissioner was delegated to read in their entirety.[66] Although this related more to the Army, there was enough in it about the RUC to tar the force in the eyes of some Commissioners.[67] But nor did the RUC help their own case, often appearing divided: according to Patten, one of the most recurrent criticisms which the Commissioners heard came from uniformed officers alleging that parts of Special Branch were operating as a 'force within a force' and that station commanders would often not know what they were up to.[68] But such internal divisions did not apply solely to splits between uniformed officers on the beat and their counterparts in Special Branch, with the inevitable clashes over who had first call on resources. There were also conflicts between the priorities of police regulars and reservists – differences which eventually contributed, *inter alia*, to Ken Maginnis's resignation in 2000 as parliamentary adviser to the Police Federation.[69]

Unionists were thus bound to lose something, perhaps much, under this process. But the *extent* of the Unionist 'defeat' on Patten does owe much to the party's lamentable performance in its own terms. One senior civil servant who observed the Patten process closely opined that Unionist contributions to consultative processes have been historically weak and that Patten was no exception. Thus, some saw Maginnis's submission of 15 September 1998 as an example of this. Part of it also included a personal proposal – not formally endorsed by the UUP – for a 50–50 recruitment ratio between the two communities, notionally over a ten-year period.[70] The intention, says Maginnis, was to achieve a force that was 22.5% Roman Catholic within a decade and so to avoid the massive imbalance that would have been caused by a one-off surge. The idea was incorporated into the Patten report, although it is not clear how much Maginnis's backing for the proposal was taken by the Commissioners as a 'green light' or whether they would have done so anyhow: according to Peter Smith, the UUP security spokesman's espousal of 50–50 may have given the Patten Commissioners some comfort, though it was probably not fundamental to their final decision.[71] Whatever the actual impact of Maginnis's suggestion, the fact remained that nationalists extended no such reciprocal courtesies to Unionists, nor to the RUC. It also emerged later that the 50–50 proposal was potentially in violation of one EU directive establishing a framework for equal treatment in employment and occupational status. Indeed, to ensure that they were not acting outside of European Law, the British Government sought an exemption for the national legislation governing police recruitment in Northern Ireland. It was highly unusual for this Government to try to derogate from the anti-discrimination provisions of EU law, which have enjoyed a high constitutional status, thus further underlining how Ulster remained a place apart.[72]

Trimble and Maginnis did dine twice with Patten himself, the first time at Paradiso e Inferno restaurant in London on 6 January 1999. It was at this meeting that Maginnis says that he first began to twig that all might not be well on the name of the force and says that he objected vehemently.[73] Patten says that 'at that stage, we were still beating through the shrubbery, though we had an increasingly clear idea where we would finish up'.[74] The UUP leader and security spokesman again met with Patten in London as the report reached its final stages and once more emphasised that the badge and the royal title were very important. According to Trimble, Patten was clearly taken aback and stated how he was struck by how the new Assembly had arrived at its own symbol with Unionist agreement – which was free of any British associations. He said it would be much better if the issue of names and emblems could be left to the same body to decide. Such a course of action would certainly have suited Trimble.[75] Patten's recollection is different. He states that he believed that it was always the job of the Commission (rather than the Assembly or a Policing Board whose membership was heavily derived from that body) to make the tough decisions about the name and symbols. According to Trimble, Patten also promised that he would be speaking to the two men regularly in the immediate run-up to the report to 'market test' its findings: Trimble says that he never did this.[76] Again, the recollections of what was said differ. Patten says that he emphasised in no uncertain terms that whilst he undertook to let Trimble know in advance what the Commission was going to say, he never gave any assurance that he would engage 'in a sort of running seminar to test the political acceptance of our recommendations on the part of Unionists, the British Government, or anyone else'.[77] The purpose of such discussions would have been informative rather than consultative – to give Trimble time to prepare his position with his own community rather than to alter the report's contents. If so, it suggests that Patten knew that a name change and other reforms could cause great unhappiness amongst all shades of Unionists – though he believes that these issues mattered to the Unionists because such symbols were so disliked by non-unionists. In other words, Patten believed that Unionists were less motivated by positive allegiance to a living British culture than by a negative desire to use them for their own sectarian ends. Quite apart from the fact that few Unionists would agree with this basically nationalist interpretation of their motivation, there is little polling evidence to suggest that Catholics were ever quite so wound up about the symbols as Patten implies. Whatever the merits of the case, Patten was undoubtedly right on one thing: whilst there were parts of the report which Trimble might not like, he says he knew that Trimble would not leave the Mitchell process on this subject.[78] Indeed, even at a moment of considerable crisis for his leadership, Trimble was very careful about what he said. He simply stated this 'shoddy' document would have disastrous effects on Unionist support for the new dispensation.[79] This was an analytical point, albeit one made with great anger on that particular occasion. What he did not, though, do was to make any threats. Thus, he did not say 'If I do not get what I want on this crucial subject, I am getting out of the process', as republicans often did when their core interests were at stake.

Indeed, Trimble's references to the RUC in 1998–9 do not suggest someone who was preparing to engage in a campaign of militant opposition to substantial symbolic changes. That much was clear from his speech to the Forum on 17 April 1998; his 20 November 1998 speech to the Irish Association in Co. Wicklow; and his New Year's message to the UUC of 8 January 1999.[80] Indeed, when an unauthorised preliminary draft of the Patten report was published in the Irish Times on 18 November 1998 – and its expected radical proposals turned out to be largely correct in respect of symbolic changes, if not in other matters – Trimble did not 'go ballistic'. Instead, he was reassured after a 30-minute meeting with Patten. And, as was clear from his discussions with Clinton in Washington in late 1998, he was keen to downplay the issue of the RUC, presumably lest it 'frighten the horses' as he was trying to set up the Northern Ireland Executive. One cannot be certain what reassurance Patten offered to Trimble: most of the public rebuttals from the Commission related to the status of the document, rather than to the unacceptability or acceptability of these proposals per se. Throughout much of this period, Trimble was reluctant to speak out publicly on the subject of the RUC: from October 1998 onwards, he turned down no fewer than nine invitations from *The Daily Telegraph* to draw a 'line in the sand'. He finally took up the invitation in March 2000.[81] This, of course, was well after 'the horse had bolted from the stable'. Even this he only did under considerable pressure from Viscount Cranborne and Ruth Dudley Edwards and then sought at the last minute to dilute the message. But as Sean O'Callaghan observes, Trimble does not really believe in sustained public campaigns and prefers instead to concentrate on behind-the-scenes lobbying of the Government; the one-time head of IRA Southern Command speculates that he had his fill of campaigning during the abortive loyalist protests of the 1980s and may have believed that such efforts were now foredoomed to failure.[82]

Why did Trimble and the UUP punch so dramatically beneath their weight on the issue of policing? After all, the RUC was an issue of great importance to the Unionist community. Indeed, it was in some ways far more central to the Ulster-British identity than it had been at the outset of the Troubles, if only because the force in 1968 was 3031 strong (plus the 'B' Specials mobilised for full-time duty) whereas in September 1999 it was 12,514 strong.[83] Therefore, a very high percentage of the unionist population had passed through it in a period of a quarter-century plus, all of whom had friends and relations in a tight-knit community. In consequence, it was scarcely surprising that a poll by Ulster Marketing Surveys for McCann-Erickson in February 2000 showed that the name and culture of the RUC ranked ahead of the Crown and the Union Flag as an aspect of identity which was important for all adults; amongst Protestants, it ranked ahead of the 12th of July.[84] Yet as with the prisoners issue, Trimble seemed to have what Sean O'Callaghan and others called a 'blind spot' on the issue of the RUC. Indeed, his scale of priorities was quite *sui generis*: very few others, if anyone else at all, from the Ulster-British tribe believed that Strand III mattered more than the RUC. He seemed to care far more about the creation of long-term political institutions than what, at times, could be seen as a one-off issue which was a response to the winding down of the terrorist campaign.

Some NIO officials thought that Trimble, like so many lawyers, had a deeply sceptical view of the police; others believed that like so many other loyalists, he had been soured by RUC behaviour during the anti-Anglo-Irish Agreement protests of 1985–6 and during successive stand-offs at Drumcree. This seems unlikely: Trimble's record on policing and security issues generally ('reserved matters'), as has been noted, was fairly conventional by Unionist standards during his Vanguard years and right up till he became leader: shortly before the UUP leadership election, for example, Trimble had raised the issue of disabled police officers in a Commons debate on 6 June 1995.[85] Trimble was as much a lawyer then as he was after he became leader, so it seems unlikely that 'legalism' accounts for his later behaviour. As for the question of RUC handling of loyalist protests, it is clear that the anti-AIA demonstrations did not alter his stance on speaking up for the security forces. This raises the question of whether subsequent events at Drumcree soured him irreparably on the force. Certainly, Trimble's relations with senior RUC officers were tense: his friend Herb Wallace, vice chairman of the old Police Authority, recalls that whenever the names of certain individual RUC officers came up, Trimble did not have a good word to say about them, though Trimble denies that the events in Portadown influenced him in his attitude.[86] Trimble also seems to have felt that many police officers did not feel that strongly about the name change and other reforms and that many were only interested in it for the money and redundancy packages: as Sir Ronnie Flanagan observes, few policemen resigned in protest against the symbolic aspects of the Patten reforms.[87] Indeed, Trimble believed that the Police Federation were 'just a bunch of trade unionists'.[88] Moreover, he may have been disinclined to make too much of a fuss when Sir Ronnie Flanagan appeared prepared to embrace most of these changes. When Peter Mandelson asked Bill Jeffrey on 12 October 1999 at a meeting with the Ulster Unionists as to what was Flanagan's view of the name change and DPPBs issues, the NIO Political Director told him that 'it was a bitter pill to be swallowed, but that if it was in the general good, so be it'. If Flanagan had come out against it, or resigned, the Government would have been in serious trouble. Instead, he endorsed the main thrust of the report.[89] The Federation also turned out to be more 'moderate' than some in Government had feared – not least, contends Flanagan, because he strove mightily to try to ensure that they had 'ownership' of the structural (as opposed to symbolic) aspects of his own Fundamental Review of 1994–6.[90]

Subsequently, Flanagan was also invited by the Conservative peers to address them at a crucial stage in the Lords' deliberations on the Patten Bill: the RUC Chief Constable told them that 'the name means as much to me as anyone else'. But he successfully conveyed to them his belief that the battle to save the title should only be fully engaged by the Lords if they had certainty of ultimate victory.[91] As such, his approach was certainly an extension of his argument to the component parts of the police family – including the Police Federation, the Superintendents' Association, the widows and the Disabled Police Officers' Association – after the *Belfast Telegraph* leaks. 'If we mount a vigorous public campaign and then lose, we will be humiliated,' was Flanagan's essential message to them. Indeed, he was sceptical of the chances of success of *The Daily Telegraph* 'Defend the RUC' campaign precisely because he thought it gave false hope to these organisations.[92] Later, he also urged the RUC widows and the disabled officers to embrace the new PSNI rather than to see it as a step towards forgetting their own and their loved ones' sacrifices.[93] But as his critics saw it, Flanagan was like the man who meekly accepts unfair arrest – 'Come along quietly now, sir, there's a good lad' – and thus makes things easy for the authorities.[94]

Certainly, Trimble's views on the RUC would not have been apparent to many ordinary UUP members. Indeed, such views were even not apparent to many of Trimble's closest associates before 1995, including John Hunter and Gordon Lucy. Perhaps they should have spotted the signs: Trimble had written extensively in several pamphlets about the Craig–Collins pact, in which he described those provisions of the accord which sanctioned the policing of Catholic areas by Catholic special constables and of Protestant areas by Protestant officers in distinctly uncensorious terms. Such quirky views on policing – which were reiterated in Trimble's *Daily Telegraph* interview of 18 November 1999 – showed up his view of the profoundly sectarian nature of Ulster society. Indeed, such views at least implied the long-term possibility of cantonisation of Northern Ireland. As has been seen, Trimble was remarkably unsectarian at a personal level – but in public affairs tended not to seek to transcend those divisions, exemplified by his lack of enthusiasm for taking up the issue of integrated education. That said, Trimble believed intellectually – if not emotionally – that the RUC was an issue of importance to 'our folk' as he liked to call them. But even when he sensed that all might not be going as well as it might on this issue, he did not take personal charge of the matter, as he had on other important issues such as Strands II and III. Instead, he chose to defer to Maginnis's judgment in these matters for much of the time and would brush off calls for action with the words 'that's Ken's job'. Others thought that the issue was not one which he really understood and therefore was not disposed to be much interested. Trimble's oldest professional friend, Herb Wallace, recalls trying to raise policing issues with him. The UUP leader listened to him, but there was going to be little in the way of 'action outcomes'. Wallace derived the impression from the UUP leader that he was too preoccupied with other more pressing concerns.[95] Although Trimble's closest political associate, Reg Empey, and Leslie Cree, one of his oldest personal friends, also served on the old Police Authority, the UUP leader only intermittently consulted them on the RUC. So ill-prepared was he on the subject that he complained after his critical meeting with Blair at Hillsborough in the Good Friday week of 1998 that, in his opinion, he had been poorly briefed on policing issues. Indeed, David Lavery was very struck by Trimble's response upon receiving an early copy of the Patten report, some 48 hours before publication. Lavery briefed him that many of its recommendations had been contained in Flanagan's Fundamental Review: Trimble seemed to recognise that the greater part of the reforms on non-strategic issues was necessary. And he added: '[But] you'll understand if I'll have to shake the spear [on symbolic issues].' As Lavery recalls, the UUP leader greatly disliked the name change, but also thought that many of his own tribe were making a meal of it – and that when the issue of policing came up, it had very little resonance for him compared to the parades issue.[96]

If defending the RUC was not a political priority for him, what, then, did Trimble want as the outcome of Patten? Sean O'Callaghan thought for a long time that Trimble was prepared to entertain a measure of cultural and symbolic reform in exchange for a return of local security powers – a conception which he thought would appeal to Trimble's historicist mindset as representing a kind of 'closing of the circle' over a quarter-century after Faulkner lost them in 1972.[97] He does appear to have been willing to entertain some kind of symbolic reform, as is evidenced by his remarks on the former Hong Kong governor's report: 'The curse of Patten is that we could have lived with a compromise on the name but Patten went overboard and nationalists now see it as something which they have already got,' he laments.[98] In other words, no one in the game of Northern Irish politics ever gives something back once they have a concession in the bag – even if what they ended up with was not originally a *sine qua non* of their participation in the process. Trimble would certainly have found a compromise such as Mgr Denis Faul's suggestion of a dual name such as RUC/PSNI police service of Northern Ireland to be perfectly acceptable.[99] He may have imagined that he could humour, as it were, a modest reform programme – which then spun out of control because of what he saw as Patten's own misunderstanding of the Belfast Agreement. Perhaps he trusted Blair to take the sting out of the worst of it, as with his late intervention over the Strand II portions of the Mitchell draft document in April 1998. Yet in contrast to April 1998, Trimble never threatened to bolt over Patten, either before or immediately after publication of the former Hong Kong governor's report: again, Trimble says there was no comparison between the two situations, since he thought that the British Government would no more treat the Patten text as sacrosanct any more than it did Mitchell's April 1998 draft. To have 'gone ballistic' over the *Belfast Telegraph* or earlier *Irish Times* leaks would simply have alarmed his supporters and the unionist community, to no good effect.[100] But Mitchell's draft of April 1998 was never published at the time and it would have been much harder for Blair or Trimble to re-negotiate it if it had been released either officially or unofficially. As has been noted, the UUP leader was well aware that nationalists were unlikely to compromise on something they had won from a body such as the Patten Commission. Again, Trimble appears to have been wildly over-optimisic in his belief that Patten could have been seriously re-negotiated after publication – as was subsequently shown to be the case, even with a more sympathetic successor to Mowlam at the NIO. Certainly, Trimble tried his best to claw back lost ground in late 1999–2001, but by then the big issues had been settled.

Did Trimble seriously seek a return of local security powers? And did he imagine that his own community would appreciate this in the midst of a massive cultural and symbolic defeat? O'Callaghan's explanation for Trimble's behaviour has logic to it, but the evidence for his assertion is not overwhelming. For in this period Trimble made the scantest of *public* bids to secure a return of local policing powers. He only raised it in a Commons debate on policing – chosen by the UUP as one of its precious supply days per session – in April 2000 and then almost casually as a kind of throwaway remark towards the end of his speech.[101] He was distinctly testy about the subject when Frank Millar subsequently raised it in an interview in the *Irish Times* on 17 April 2000, protesting almost too much that he was 'extremely serious' about the Patten Commission's proposal for a resumption of Stormont's role in policing. Indeed, in an earlier interview in the *Irish Times* on 21 January 2000, Mandelson had specifically told Frank Millar that Trimble had *not* raised the issue of a return of security powers. Trimble denies this and says that he did raise the issue; but as Mandelson observes, if Trimble did raise the topic, he certainly did not do so in a strong enough way to make it register in this period.[102] One source indicates that he also raised the matter in No. 10, but they say that he often did so in a 'jocular' fashion. Unlike Sinn Fein, Trimble often seemed embarrassed about asking for things from government.

Others, though, were not so generous and detected rather different reasons for Trimble's non-performance on the issue of the RUC. One civil servant who observed him closely during this period says that Trimble often appeared to be embarrassed by the preoccupation of much of his community. 'He reminded me of the clever only child from Northern Ireland who goes away to an English university and cringes when he meets up with his former school friends during the holidays,' states the source. Increasingly, he thought he should be above all this.[103] The last point found a resonance amongst some of his fellow officers in the UUP. According to Denis Rogan, a group of senior figures in the UUP took a decision not to run a campaign defending 'our RUC' lest it give credibility to the notion that it was a sectarian force and the preserve of one political party. 'It was good politics,' says Rogan.[104] Some in the 'Defend the RUC' campaign thought this to be an utterly flawed strategy: the RUC was in any case being attacked as a sectarian force, and these assaults did not in any way stop on account of this pious neutralism by the UUP. Perhaps Trimble simply thought that it was a losing cause over which he ought not to expend too many chips. Indeed, when the subject of the RUC arose in a meeting with some academic supporters in his room at Parliament Buildings on 27 November 2001, Trimble's basic message was that 'you've got to make compromises in this world'. It seemed as though he was reconciled to, even relaxed about this outcome now the deed was done.[105] Maybe it was an inevitable outcome: but many Unionists also felt that they had the right to expect their elected representatives to make the maximum effort, after the fashion of Sinn Fein. It was hard to argue that Trimble and the UUP had done that to the best of their abilities.

Trimble believed that he did go full tilt – but thought that such influence could best be exercised in private. As many in the 'Defend the RUC' campaign feared, this turned out to be a delusion. Trimble had no cards to play in *private* with a New Labour administration whose residual radicalism found powerful expression in its attitude to the security powers of the British state in Northern Ireland. Rather, his only hope was a highly *public* campaign which sought to tap into the sense of anger in Middle England over the perceived sacrifice of a fine force to appease unrepentant terrorists (as embodied by the *Daily Mail*'s focus on the subject).[106] An elected British Government would certainly have been less impervious to such sentiments than the Patten Commissioners or the Irish state – especially if linked to broader questions of Labour's failings on law and order. For as the issues of Europe and the countryside illustrated, the Government acted as though their arithmetical majorities in the Commons did not necessarily give them sufficient cushion for their policies in the nation at large. Even if this approach did not work, advocates of such a campaign believed that as with Sinn Fein's losing 'No Return to Stormont' slogan of late 1997/early 1998, the logic of the peace process meant that the Government would have had to supply some 'collateral' to counterbalance the pain felt by one side (thus, Sinn Fein were compensated for their sacrifice in agreeing to an Assembly by such 'sweeteners' as a quicker pace of prisoner releases). But Trimble did not want to make the Government pay such a price, and his reluctance to do this inevitably set a ceiling on what any of the mainland campaigns for the RUC could accomplish. He did attack Blair once in the Commons on 19 January 2000, as Mandelson was about to announce the Government's response to Patten, but did not believe that he could exist in any kind of state of what he calls 'permanent war' with Downing Street.[107]

Indeed, Trimble maintains that he actually obtained a better deal from Blair than he would have done under the Conservatives, who he says would have been even more ruthless towards the RUC (though, curiously, Trimble's mistrust of that generation of Tories did not initially appear to apply to Patten himself). But as John Major points out, Trimble's analysis in this instance beggars belief. Irrespective of his own views, Major says that it is worth looking at the balance of forces in the last Government: it consisted of an NIO in which policy was made by such defenders of the RUC as Mayhew and Wheeler; a Northern Ireland Cabinet committee filled with such unionist sympathisers as Viscount Cranborne; plus with 30–40 unionist-minded backbenchers led by Andrew Hunter under a Government with a wafer-thin Commons majority.[108] Trimble thought he knew more than most of his compatriots about mainland politics, but in reality his comprehension of the British system could at times be deeply flawed. Perhaps there was an element of *ex post facto* rationalisation in all this. Some thought that he felt guilty about what had happened. But others disagreed. They attributed his passivity on the RUC to a quite conscious calculation. An attempt to sound the alarm on a sustained basis early on in Patten's proceedings might have so frightened the unionist community that they could have bolted the process altogether. Conversely, one Commission member says that the outcome of Patten made it much easier for Sinn Fein to live through and stay in the Mitchell review. 'Trimble knows that in unionist terms what was done by the Patten Commission to the RUC was a sin, a wrong thing to have done,' says one who worked closely with Trimble. 'But the problem was that if he had walked out over it, it would have been an intrusion into his broader strategic objective.'[109] That objective was the return of accountable Government to the Province. His critics in the Parliamentary party and elsewhere might have seen him as a callow intellectual who was incapable of commanding their respect, but they underrated his determination to do the deal. So, too, did much of nationalist Ireland – and he would prove all of them wrong in the coming months.

THIRTY

By George

TRIMBLE moved with great determination towards the goal of an inclusive Executive – a most unMolyneaux-like aim – but he did so with an
almost Molyneauxesque indirectness of style. Many conflicting signals
were sent out during the early days of the Mitchell review, which may
have confused both his internal party detractors and elements within
nationalist Ireland. Thus, on the one hand, he backed the High Court
case brought by Michelle Williamson, whose parents had died in the
Shankill bombing of 1993. She claimed that Mowlam's decision-making
methods in continuing with prisoner releases after the Bennett killing
and the arms importation by the Provisionals violated her statutory duty
under the Sentences Act 1998 (the Secretary of State claimed the ceasefire
was intact). If the suit was successful, then the republicans might well
have pulled out of the Mitchell review. On the other hand, a mere 48
hours after Williamson was granted leave for judicial review, it emerged
that Trimble was still talking to Sinn Fein. Williamson was enraged by
what she regarded as Trimble's double standards. Trimble, though, had
no doubts: 'I see no inconsistency in supporting Michelle Williamson's
legal action to stop prisoner releases, and our attempts in the review to
secure decommissioning and a permanent end to violence by the IRA,'
he observed.[1] Indeed, he saw the two as mutually reinforcing and wished
that the Government would do more to 'rattle Sinn Fein/IRA's cage'
so that they would have an incentive to fulfil their decommissioning
obligations.

Trimble had good reason to 'duck and dive' – and, indeed, he was a
better politician than some gave him credit for, at least in terms of keeping
the UUP quiescent. John Taylor withdrew from the Mitchell review, citing
continuing IRA activity as his main reason.[2] Jeffrey Donaldson piled on
the pressure in the run-up to the UUP Executive on 13 September, warning

that Trimble's position would become untenable if he sought to move away from the 'no guns, no government' commitment of the 1998 and 1999 UUP manifestos. But despite these warnings, the 'antis' could never succeed in pushing Trimble into withdrawal from the review. For one of the advantages of the Mitchell process from Trimble's viewpoint was that it was structured in such a way as to make it hard for the 'antis' to know when a surprise might be sprung – both because of the conditions of confidentiality which governed the review's largely in camera proceedings and because of the relatively small numbers involved in those talks. On one level, this ran against Trimble's desire to have as much of the party present as was reasonably possible so that they felt consulted and thus agreed to his course of action. But the events of the summer convinced him that in these circumstances, a truly watertight review might just do the trick.[3]

The absence during the Mitchell review of a media circus, and the attendant anti-Agreement demonstrations, certainly enabled Trimble to steady the nerves of his party. But the demonstrators melted away for another reason. For despite their rhetoric, the DUP's position appeared in its own way almost as contradictory as Trimble's. Irrespective of whether they did or did not launch street protests any longer, the key point about DUP behaviour was that despite all that the Provisionals had done over the summer, they never declared that they would go into full-blown oppositionist mode in the Assembly. In other words, by their silence, they were indicating that they would take up their two ministerial slots to which they were entitled under the 1998 Assembly elections. According to Nigel Dodds, after the referendum, there had been a tense debate over what the DUP's role ought to be. They concluded outright oppositionism to be futile: from their visits to South Africa, senior DUP figures derived the 'lesson' that the right could not be left out.[4] (It was curious that even anti-Agreement unionists began to think of themselves in categories to which they had first been assigned by Irish nationalists.) Instead of street opposition to the Agreement, they behaved as though their role was to act as an insurance policy against its excesses. But John Taylor has no doubt that the DUP's relatively passive stance in this period and in the coming months made Trimble's position that much easier. Taylor says that had they refused to take up their positions, leaving the UUP as the sole unionists to do so, then it would have been impossible to go on – and that Donaldson would then have been in a much stronger position.[5] Certainly, Trimble was most troubled by opposition from within, rather than from without his own party. As he saw it, the DUP's real position was that they wanted the new dispensation to work more than they ever let on; but, at the same time, they wanted the UUP to take the risks in setting it up, to destroy itself in the process, thus leaving the DUP to clean up electorally afterwards.[6]

In such circumstances, to move forward remained a risk for Trimble – but a calculated risk. Trimble's chosen methodology for proceeding was to fly trial balloons and that those trial balloons should be flown by outside sympathisers rather than by party insiders. At a meeting of the Assembly party on 21 September, Trimble secured agreement for his idea of an 'away day' for the UUP Assembly group on 25 September at the Post House Forte Hotel in Glasgow where the process of 'educating' the party might continue.[7] The trio of speakers whom he chose were Paul Bew, Eoghan Harris and Malachi O'Doherty.[8] Bew was the best known to those present, but Trimble also wanted Harris for his knowledge of southern society and O'Doherty for his knowledge of northern republicanism.[9] It was Harris who made the most memorable contribution, which he repeated in the following month before a larger audience at the UUP annual conference at Enniskillen. If the British Army, the RUC and the Garda had failed to accomplish decommissioning over 30 years, what hope had the UUP of doing it? If they took the leap and formed an Executive, the UUP would have the moral high ground and the responsibility would then be on the two Governments to protect Unionism and to make good on their pledges to ensure that the republicans delivered their side of the bargain. 'You are in the business of making peace, of making an historic accommodation (with republicanism) and thus securing the union,' said Harris. 'Look, Sinn Fein fought for 30 years. It's like a kid wanting a bike for Christmas. The bike they wanted was a united Ireland. They didn't get the bike. Please give them a few stickers.'[10] Jim Wilson, the UUP chief whip in the Assembly, recalls the stunned faces of Assemblymen who had never heard anyone quite like Harris before. 'It wasn't shocking language but it was the language of shock,' says Wilson. 'But there was no point in going to a workshop with people praising us. Let's have an electric current through us – we wanted to open minds to some realities.'[11] When Harris subsequently addressed the annual conference, Trimble was concerned that the Corkman might go 'OTT', producing a massive reaction the other way. Again, Harris deployed the same 'Blitzkrieg' rhetorical style which he employed to such effect as chief ideologist of the Workers' Party. At one point during his address at Enniskillen Harris adverted to the journey which he had travelled – from republican to defender of Unionist rights. Trimble was listening to him in the press room with Ruth Dudley Edwards and Daphne Trimble. Trimble started saying at the monitor, 'Sh, sh, sh.' Dudley Edwards said to him, 'Come on, David – they all know that.' Trimble shot back, 'Only some of them know that!' At the end, he commented, 'We'd have almost got away with that if he hadn't said he was from the Official IRA.'[12]

The invitation to Harris and others to speak on a media panel at the UUP conference was certainly novel – and as some observers pointed out, it would be hard to imagine any other party in these islands asking outside observers such as the journalist, Eamonn Mallie, to address them. Trimble's own address also contained hints of further flexibility on the arms issue: '. . . if I had taken the advice of some of my parliamentary colleagues, I would not be here now, for, had I taken their advice I would have resigned,' quipped Trimble. 'But let me tell you one thing about David Trimble and resignation. I have resigned myself to the long political struggle to secure the best interests of unionism and to make sure that our position within the United Kingdom is copper-fastened and to pro- mote the benefits of the Union to all. I will not lead this party into a never-never land of false hopes or imitation Carsons without the gritty realism of Craig, nor will I court popularity by hyping solutions that I know are not attainable. I remember when Daphne and I discussed the possible outcomes of the talks over two years ago. She predicted that I would probably obtain just enough support at each stage to go on, but that it would prove to be a constant uphill struggle.' (The 'Daphne principle', as it came to be known in the Trimble family, would prove even truer in the coming months.) Trimble then delivered the punch line: 'Do not be misled by those spreading alarm and despondency. Our position has not changed. We want devolution. We want decommissioning. To me the words "jump together" "choreography" and "sequencing" all refer to the same thing, namely the procedures by which we make sure that devolution is accompanied by decommissioning.' But it was significant that he placed devolution as first in the order of priorities.[13]

Republicans believed that Trimble would do little before the UUP con- ference and therefore made no moves towards any kind of accommodation in the early phases of the Mitchell review. The first meeting of the UUP with Sinn Fein took place at Castle Buildings on Monday 20 September and it was a testy affair. According to the *Sunday Business Post* of 26 September, Ulster Unionists left Adams and McGuinness in no doubt of their feelings about the Bennett killing, the arms importation, and the expulsions and punishment beatings by the IRA; and Sinn Fein utterly refused to offer a *mea maxima culpa*. Reg Empey recalls the 'awful' atmosphere in the early autumn exchanges, so much so that he thought republicans were trying to pave the way for an 'exit strategy': 'It was a whingeing session, with republicans deliberately trying to provoke David Trimble,' he says. 'They acccused him of leaking stuff to newspapers, to get a rise out of him. But David did not fall for it. And, of course, he loves historical footnotes. Adams also fancied himself on such footnotes and Trimble would elaborate on themes – such as the fact that there had been paramilitary disarmament on the island of Ireland, when the original UVF handed over its weapons upon the outbreak of World War One.'[14] Trimble says that he recalled a couple of sentences in A.T.Q. Stewart's history of the 1912 Home Rule crisis; in which the authorities were concerned after the Easter Rising of 1916 that UVF firearms might fall into the hands of nationalists and approached the Ulster Unionist leadership: in consequence, the largest part of the UVF armoury was lodged in RIC stations and their commanders were given receipts.[15] Many observers, learning of these meanderings, came to the conclusion that Mitchell would have to set a deadline for the end of October to complete his review.[16]

In this atmosphere Trimble was not much inclined to move. It was a sentiment which would have been reinforced for so long as Mowlam was Secretary of State. He also wanted reform of the Parades Commission. Trimble raised these matters at his meeting with the Prime Minister at the Labour conference in Bournemouth. 'What the Unionist community really needs to know is, if direct rule is renewed, that it will be treated fairly and with the same respect as nationalists,' Trimble told Blair in a room at the conference centre with just Jonathan Powell present. He also suggested that if there was no agreement with Sinn Fein, the Prime Minister ought to consider keeping the 'spirit of devolution' alive by letting both himself and Seamus Mallon continue as junior ministers under a direct rule-like structure. The UUP leader added that the current dispensation had no credibility. Blair looked at Powell as if to ask what was Trimble's meaning. 'Your Secretary of State, Prime Minister,' came the Chief of Staff's reply.[17] Trimble had never made any secret that he wanted to be rid of Mowlam, and he dropped repeated hints about her replacement. The question of whether Mowlam had outlived her usefulness also was vexing such intermediaries as David Montgomery. After 'The Way Forward' debacle, Montgomery went to see Jonathan Powell. 'This situation isn't fair on anybody – neither on the Secretary of State nor the Prime Minister,' the then MGN chief told Blair's Chief of Staff. 'Trimble's being encouraged to go behind her back to the Prime Minister and the Prime Minister is effectively being Secretary of State with no court of appeal. Consequently he's identified with every decision taken.' The two men then discussed Mowlam's position and concluded that it was unlikely that Trimble would soften his attitude. Again, Powell raised the issue of 40% of Prime Ministerial time being taken up with Ulster in this period. Also on Powell's mind, after Mowlam had dug in her heels and refused to leave the NIO, was the issue of the wider political management of the Cabinet: Blair needed to be seen calling the shots, rather than one of his underlings.[18] He was right. Such was her defiance of the Prime Minister that back in July, she even discussed her own chances of surviving a reshuffle over the telephone with Martin McGuinness: 'I'm fighting like fuck to stay, but I don't know what will happen,' she told the Derryman. 'But as soon as I know I'll let you know ... my intuition says it just depends how awkward [Blair's] being because I'm gonna stay unless he takes me, he leaves me here, ahm, I'll go on the backbenches. Which he can't do because I'm too popular. So I'm gonna dig in and I just hope I can win.' McGuinness expressed his fond hope that she would remain as Secretary of State.[19]

The UUP leader's preferred candidate to replace her was Peter Mandelson – then still in exile following his resignation as Secretary of State for Trade and Industry in December 1998. It was rare for Trimble to be so 'up-front' and blatant in making such demands: he did not believe it was the right way to do business and normally considered it to be 'crude' and 'tacky'. He had been given an insight into how government operates when he demanded a series of confidence-building measures around the time that he took the risk to remain in the talks in September 1997, and had not done well out of that exercise. Since then, he had pounded the table a few times – such as his insistence in obtaining David Lavery as his principal private secretary – but it was not really his preferred *modus operandi*.[20] When he did so, it was often in a half-joking way, or he would ask others to do it for him. In the end, Trimble secured two of his core aims – the removal of a Secretary of State and a partial reform of the Parades Commission. Whether securing these particular aims was the wisest way in which to spend slender political capital was another matter entirely. For example, he might have given a higher priority to delaying either Patten or prisoner releases until decommissioning took place; or even his long-held objective of persuading Labour to organise in Northern Ireland. Indeed, at his first meeting with Mowlam's successor on 12 October 1999, Trimble only asked for consultation on the security 'normalisation' strategy – a procedural and choreographic demand, rather than a substantive one. Likewise, despite changes to the Parades Commission, Trimble was little further along the way towards resolving the Drumcree issue to his satisfaction. As for Mowlam, it could have been argued that she was on the way out anyhow, as much for internal Labour party reasons as for having offended the Ulster Unionists.

Trimble not only had his wish fulfilled in terms of ridding the NIO of Mowlam, but on 11 October he had the additional pleasure of seeing her replaced by his own choice, Peter Mandelson. Had it been another one of the other widely-bruited candidates, such as Dr John Reid, Trimble felt it would have been a sign that Blair had more or less given up on progress and had entrusted things to a 'safe pair of hands' rather than a 'Wizard'.[21] Curiously, the two men both confirm that neither really had a proper conversation with the other prior to Mandelson's appointment, beyond fleeting contacts in the division lobby (Mandelson says he was told that Trimble was lobbying in favour of his appointment in July 1999).[22] Trimble appears to have entertained some hope that Mandelson might take a view similar to Herbert Morrison, Mandelson's grandfather, and had looked up some of Morrison's speeches (Morrison believed that Northern Ireland should be rewarded for its wartime contribution, which was in such stark contrast to the neutrality of the South, and played a key part in pushing through the pro-Union 1949 Ireland Act).[23] In fact, Mandelson's track record on the subject was mixed. As a young researcher on Brian Walden's *Weekend World* in the early 1980s, Mandelson would visit both Northern Ireland and the Republic, where he would meet with all shades of opinion. Recalling these visits, Ronan Fanning found that 'he did not show the remotest intellectual or emotional sympathy for unionists, nationalists, or republicans'.[24] This un-ideological, coldly pragmatic approach also impressed Trimble, who tended to put the best possible construction upon the *Weekend World* experience: he recalled that Mandelson had been to see the then General Secretary of the UUP, Frank Millar. 'From our point of view, knowledge is as good as sympathy,' he notes. 'The problem is gullible Englishmen led up the garden path.' In fact, Mandelson's views appeared to be rather contradictory. He was alleged to have come out in favour of a united Ireland in the early 1990s, though Trimble was sceptical of the accuracy of these reported remarks.[25] At the same time, Mandelson had laboured behind the scenes to dilute the 'unity by consent' formula of the 1980s.[26] But the real attraction of Mandelson's appointment as far as Trimble was concerned was his closeness to the Prime Minister. The UUP leader now 'needed someone you couldn't put a cigarette paper between – and someone strong enough at Stormont to impose a London view on the officials'.[27] But Mandelson also grasped Eoghan Harris's advice in an open letter in *The Daily Telegraph* on 13 October 1999. The ex-'Stickie' told the new Ulster Secretary that he was coming to the job in the middle of a match in which Trimble and the Unionists were three–nil down, partly because of what he believed to be Mowlam's bias. He had therefore to tack towards the Unionists to counteract the appalling presentation of the Patten report and to allow every police family to hold their heads high. Mandelson certainly sought to reassure the police families when in office and appeared to have some instinctive sympathy for what they had been through. On one occasion, just before meeting with Gerry Adams, Mandelson received the relatives of the last two RUC officers slain by the Provisionals – Constables Johnston and Graham, murdered in Lurgan immediately prior to the second ceasefire in 1997. 'I've just spent the last hour talking to the families of police officers murdered by the IRA,' a visibly shaken Mandelson told the Sinn Fein president. Adams did not respond and pulled out his notebook to commence the business at hand.[28] But despite Mandelson's relationship with the Prime Minister and the importance of being tough on law and order to the New Labour project generally, policing was one area where the then Ulster Secretary could never count upon full support from Blair and the No. 10 staff.[29]

The appointment of Mandelson gave Trimble the confidence to proceed full steam ahead with the Mitchell review. Much of what happened during that process remains shrouded in mystery, partly because many of the participants took its vows of confidentiality seriously. But what is known is that the talks did not make much headway until the parties went to London in early October. A staple theme of contemporary negotiating technique is to take the adversaries out of their own environment, as it were, and into more neutral terrain. There, new dynamics could develop away from the pressures of one's own communal bloc. But the general theory was of little use in picking a suitable venue. Lancaster House has particular resonances of earlier imperial scuttles, such as the negotiations which paved the way for the transition from Rhodesia to Zimbabwe.[30] Eventually, according to Empey, Trimble suggested Winfield House, the residence of the US ambassador and Clinton appointee, Philip Lader, as fitting the bill. Set in 12 acres within Regent's Park, it was secure and largely inaccessible. Mitchell duly approached Lader with his customary diplomatic finesse, since he was not sure if the large-scale renovations had been completed. But his message was unmistakable. 'There is an impasse and a change of scenery, if not of mood, is required,' Mitchell told Lader. Lader accepted Mitchell's proposition with alacrity: the refurbishment had indeed been completed. So under the 200-year-old wallpaper which had been removed 25 years ago from an Irish country house and reinstalled at Winfield, and the pictures of the Hudson River School, the UUP and Sinn Fein began their most intensive sessions yet on 13 October.[31] Each side at this still secret location started off with teams of five to six apiece, under the chairmanship of Mitchell, with no representatives of either Government present. Mitchell would rarely intervene, and then only to point out the consequences of failure. Mitchell sat in the armchair in the Green Room, with the fireplace behind him and facing the window, occupying the apex of the triangle. The UUP and Sinn Fein were on either side, sitting on sofas.[32] The UUP delegation comprised Trimble, Empey, Maginnis, Danny Kennedy, Fred Cobain and Alan McFarland, with back-up from David Kerr, David Campbell and David Lavery. Sinn Fein were principally represented by Adams, McGuinness and Aidan McAteer.

One feature of these sessions which was much commented upon after the location was discovered was Mitchell's insistence that all sides take food together and talk about anything but politics – opera in Trimble's case, fly-fishing in that of Martin McGuinness. At one point, Ken Maginnis showed pictures of his grandchildren to Martin McGuinness.[33] In fact, says Trimble, there was much nonsense talked about the importance of these meals: people often continued to sit in their own groups and tended not to mix with other delegations.[34] One other participant recalls a 'huge nervous self-consciousness at dinner, with Trimble talking through the chairman rather than directly to Sinn Fein'. Indeed, both Fred Cobain and Danny Kennedy of the UUP were so discomfited by the prospect of being seen that they closed the shutters so that they would not be caught by any telephoto lenses.[35] There was something surreal about the atmosphere, as old enemies dined side by side: so much so that at one of the dinners, when the first course was porcini mushrooms, one Ulster Unionist observed that 'for a moment, I thought they were magic mushrooms. I actually believed that I was dining with Martin McGuinness and Gerry Adams.'

At the start, the sessions alternated between the repetitive and the testy: there were only so many original thoughts that anyone could come up with on the theme of guns and government. The meetings, says Trimble, would last anything between 90 minutes to well over two hours at a stretch. At an early stage, Adams introduced the idea of a Sinn Fein statement that would provide a building-block of confidence for the Unionists: eventually, a set of interlocking statements, from Sinn Fein, the IRA and the UUP, would provide the basis for the 'sequencing' which led to the setting up of the Executive in December 1999. At one point, Adams offered a 'masterly' analysis of Trimble's position which, says the UUP leader, was even better than he could have done himself and was fully cognisant of the strength of rejectionist unionism (until then, McGuinness had been reiterating the standard republican line about Trimble's habitual exaggeration of his internal difficulties).[36] Indeed, Trimble told Sean O'Callaghan that this was the moment at which he knew Adams was serious about engagement.[37] Later in the review, Adams recalled their first one-to-one conversation at Stormont in the autumn of 1998. Trimble says that the Sinn Fein president's recollection of his own remarks was accurate. The UUP leader had said that the underlying trend was towards the process working, but that he was worried that republicans would not take the issue of decommissioning seriously until it was virtually over the edge. Trimble had added that though the process would work in the long term, maybe this particular Agreement would not do so and perhaps without himself as head of the UUP. Trimble concluded that his line about 'getting a life' away from politics had some effect on Adams – and says the fact that the Sinn Fein leader mentioned it in this context shows that it worried him.[38]

Despite hints in the last week of October that matters had become 'more civil', there was still no deal.[39] On Wednesday 27 October, Mitchell resumed discussions in Belfast which were billed as the 'last chance'; later that day, it was reported on Downtown Radio that he had told the British that he intended to leave by the weekend. Everyone knew that something was happening, but no one was quite sure what – which deprived the rejectionist Unionists of an ability to move since they had no precise idea what they were meant to move against.[40] Thus, at the UUP Executive on Friday 29 October, Rev. Martin Smyth, the UUP chief whip in the Commons, pointed out that the Government had provisionally cleared business on Monday for possible emergency legislation to give legal effect to any deal to bring about devolution. Talks continued over the weekend of 30–31 October at Castle Buildings and broke up on Saturday after eleven hours. By this point, the teams had been reduced to just Trimble and Empey on one side and Adams and McGuinness on the other. On the last day at Winfield House, David Lavery had been asked to provide an 'illustrative sequencing', which was later submitted formally to Mitchell in Belfast. The aim was to create a sequence of events which would lock both sides into the process. On the republican side, it would involve the IRA appointing an interlocutor to talk to the decommissioning body, then determining how that might occur, then agreeing with de Chastelain a timetable leading to completion of decommissioning. This would enable Trimble to argue to his supporters that a 'process' of decommissioning had begun. On the UUP side, the reciprocal steps would include the nomination of ministers leading to the creation of a shadow Executive and setting up of the panoply of institutions outlined in the Belfast Agreement. The question was the order in which these steps might be taken, or over what timeframe.[41] The critical day turned out to be Sunday 31 October. Trimble and Empey were reluctant to go for fear of further inflaming a tense situation by offending their sabbatarian colleagues, but they also knew that Mitchell was very anxious to pull things together and would be greatly vexed if he was left sitting there. Some participants wanted another full day at Castle Buildings, so as a compromise Mitchell hosted a fish lunch for the five (Trimble, Empey, Adams and McGuinness and himself) in his hotel suite at the Belfast Hilton by the Lagan.[42]

The arrangements to choreograph the statements of the parties – which had largely been agreed by then – were finalised over this working lunch. Particularly significant to Trimble was the initial report which de

Chastelain would make in early December stating that he had made contact with an IRA interlocutor and that the General would report on progress by 31 January 2000. Trimble also attached great importance to the fact that it was the IRA, and not a Sinn Fein interlocutor (in which latter position McGuinness had served since September 1998). Trimble believed that once such a representative had been appointed, the republicans were on a conveyor belt towards decommissioning, from which they could only depart at the cost of massive international opprobrium and thus lose the 'blame game'. Sinn Fein came to the meeting to see whether they could have more time than the three months stipulated under this understanding. But according to Trimble, Mitchell said to Adams, 'Gerry, I want it to be clearly understood that 31 January is the final cut-off date.' Trimble states that the republicans did not say 'yes', but that they clearly understood.[43] Neither Mitchell nor the republicans have publicly provided their own account of this episode, and Trimble's version of events was broadly confirmed on 13 April 2000 by Seamus Mallon in an *Irish Times* interview with Frank Millar: the then SDLP deputy leader stated that he believed decommissioning would begin by the end of January following the devolution of powers. Mitchell briefed Blair on this understanding on Wednesday 3 November and then flew to Washington to do the same for Clinton. But according to one White House official present, George Mitchell only said that he believed that Trimble believed that there would be serious decommissioning.[44] Trimble promptly flew off to the United States on 3 November, ostensibly for a long-standing engagement in Indiana. He was criticised for leaving at this crucial juncture, but such 'away days' were vital to his mental well being, and he always came back refreshed. But his real political agenda was to inform the White House of what had happened: however, he felt that Jim Steinberg, the President's deputy National Security Adviser, had not fully grasped the nature of the understanding reached and he was forced to return some weeks later to drive the point home.[45]

But none of this – even the details of the sequencing – emerged for several weeks. For although there had been effectively an agreement within the review, the two republicans present needed time to square their supporters. In particular, Unionists needed to see if the IRA would vouchsafe a sufficiently good statement of intent and an engagement with de Chastelain that represented an improvement upon the General's claim in July 1999 that if an Executive was formed, actual decommissioning would have to begin within weeks. Before Trimble went to America, he also gave Adams the draft of a statement from the IRA stating that 'the war is over', which had been put together by himself, Empey and Ken Maginnis.[46] According to the *Sunday Tribune* of 7 November, IRA leaders then briefed their members to expect a deal in the coming weeks, combined with a republican commitment to engage in 'tactical' decommissioning. This was meant to suggest to a sceptical republican grassroots that beginning a process – that is, appointing an IRA representative to the decommissioning body – was not irreversible. Moreover, it was dependent upon Trimble giving satisfactory reciprocal guarantees that he would take any change in policy to the UUP and prevail. Trimble also states that Adams toured all Provisional O/Cs north and south of the border in early November, but claims that he assured them that it would not lead to actual decommissioning.[47]

Trimble received a boost on 4 November whilst he was in the United States. On that date, it emerged that the RUC had conducted a raid on Saturday 30 October on Stoneyford Orange Hall, in southern Co. Antrim, not so far from Trimble's home. There, they had found stolen security force files with 400 republican names, addresses, telephone numbers and photographs – including some of leading Provisionals in south Armagh – and six arrests were made. Two men were subsequently jailed for arms offences. In so doing, they had smashed a potentially dangerous operation by the dissident loyalist grouping known as Orange Volunteers.[48] Significantly, Peter Mandelson wrote to Ronnie Flanagan afterwards to congratulate his officers upon their efforts. But the raid on Stoneyford had what John Major might have termed 'not inconsiderable' political implications, at least as Trimble and Reg Empey saw it. For as Empey observes, the arrests sent a warning shot across the bows of rejectionist loyalist paramilitaries across the province. Not only did some of these other groups have the ability to attack nationalists but a number of them were also a general source of agitation and were in a position to place pressure upon members of the UUC. Likewise, Rev. Robert Coulter, Assemblyman for North Antrim, also reported apparently separate instances of intimidation by extreme loyalists, urging him not to cave in.[49] Trimble, for his part, also found that such loyalist activities might influence some Assembly members.[50] Coulter says such threats stopped after the raid – and it certainly made things easier for Trimble and Empey.[51] Trimble agrees that in the run-up to the UUC meeting in late November, there were no paramilitary attempts to pressure the Assembly group as in 1998–9.[52] But the raids certainly impressed the Americans. Indeed, according to Jim Steinberg, Stoneyford was significant in that it showed to the White House and nationalists that the British were prepared to act unilaterally against dissident loyalism.[53]

But helpful as this was to Trimble, he was not out of the woods yet. When he returned from America, the IRA statement turned out to be 'minimalist' and was no basis for recommending to the UUP that they should change their policy and set up an Executive: the document had been delivered over the weekend of 6/7 November in the southern part of Co. Londonderry to Reg Empey and Martin McGuinness. The two men sat in Empey's silver-grey Rover 800 and the ex-Vanguardist read it.[54] At a meeting of the UUP Assembly group on 9 November, Trimble reported that the Mitchell review would be over soon. Over the weekend, he had seen the IRA statement: it was not good enough. He would, however, receive the revisions soon and would then have something serious to put forward. Later that night, Trimble told a meeting of colleagues that the Provisionals had not come back with the full changes requested by the UUP and that they had refused to include the purpose of interlocuting with de Chastelain. He then said that he detected from both Mandelson and Mitchell that they would not support a further push and that the Provisionals had reached their bottom line. The question now was 'have we [the UUP] got enough to run with?' Danny Kennedy and Fred Cobain, who attended the meeting, both expressed their unhappiness and said that in the absence of certainty of achievement, it would be very hard to sell the deal to the UUC. But Michael McGimpsey and Alan McFarland both believed there was enough in the deal as then constituted to proceed. Trimble was then asked what the timetable was and he said that Mandelson was pressing for a decision by tomorrow (10 November).

As things turned out, the republicans came back with an altered version which took on board 'two and a half' of the UUP's suggestions. Thus, by the night of Wednesday 10 November, Trimble had secured the appointment of an IRA interlocutor – which he had previously dismissed as insufficient evidence of republican commitment – and a Sinn Fein statement condemning punishment beatings and violence. He also had an expectation, which had gradually crystallised during many discussions at Winfield House and at the Belfast Hilton, that the IRA would decommission if he formed an Executive.[55] But when Paul Bew told him on

Friday 12 November that Mandelson had praised his negotiating skills, Trimble wearily dismissed it with the words 'he knows I've not got half of what I wanted' (Mandelson and Blair tended to make suspiciously much of Trimble's abilities in this department, though he certainly could annoy them both).[56] Gone was the notion of 'jumping together', let alone prior decommissioning. Nor was there any kind of timetable for decommissioning, either in the shape of a start date or a completion date. Nor was there any declaration that 'the war is over', merely a reiteration of Adams' formula after the Omagh bombing that the 'conflict is a thing of the past' and the commitment of the IRA leadership to the achievement of a 'permanent peace'. Trimble, though, consoled himself with the knowledge that republicans did things in their own language 'rather than our language'.[57]

Yet despite this disappointment, Trimble decided to proceed. Why? The key difference between the June/July proposals which he and the party ultimately rejected and now was that most elusive of concepts – trust. Trimble and Reg Empey had looked into the 'whites of their eyes' and believed the senior republicans to be sincere. Indeed, Daphne Trimble recalls meeting Empey at an evening at the ballet at the Opera House in Belfast that was hosted by the American Consul General, Kai Fort, and that he declared 'either they want this to work or else they're the best actors I've seen'.[58] Likewise, Trimble told Bew, 'I can say that I trust Adams and McGuinness.' Bew expressed concern about this and Trimble told him, 'We will walk if this does not work out.' Moreover, when faced with what he calls this 'key' decision on the night of Wednesday 10 November, he said to himself 'this is it – it isn't going to get any better'.[59] Indeed, at moments, there was almost a pathetic quality to his acceptance of the new terms. Writing in *The Times* on Wednesday 24 November, he said that 'for our part, we have reluctantly accepted that it was not possible to persuade the IRA to lay down its arms prior to setting up the Executive, nor even to do so on the same day ... such simultaneity would have been more than fair, but considerations such as this cut little ice with the paramilitaries'.

Trimble duly decided to take this package to the Assembly group and convened a meeting for the afternoon of Thursday 11 November. There was one item of good news for the First Minister-designate: British officials appeared to have found a way for Seamus Mallon to withdraw his resignation of last July, thus obviating the need for a risky cross-community vote to reinstate both men.[60] The consultations took up much of the whole day, as Trimble brought the Assembly members in groups of between five and six to read the documents in his office. He did not want all the doubters together in one group. Those who were unsure, in greater or lesser measure, included Fred Cobain, Danny Kennedy, Billy Armstrong, Roy Beggs Jr, Ken Robinson, Pauline Armitage, Sam Foster and Derek Hussey.[61] 'It didn't look as though we could do it,' recalls Trimble. 'They had two questions: will it work? And what if it doesn't?' John Taylor, who had returned to Stormont at 12:35 p.m. that day, after having absented himself from the review process, told Trimble, 'I'm disappointed with this. I don't believe you can sell to the party.' The UUP deputy leader was still haunted by the Faulkner era splits in the party. 'Northern Ireland can only survive with a strong UUP. My strong advice is not to sell it but to reject it.' Empey retorted that Sinn Fein would walk out of the Assembly if the UUP rejected the document. But, as so often before, Taylor's assessment had a considerable impact on Trimble's thinking. At 1:35 p.m. Trimble met with senior figures in the Assembly group and told them, 'I'm going to give you my assessment why we're not going with these proposals at present. I think the gamble would work, but we must keep the party intact and it comes down to a lack of certainty but we must settle this thing [i.e. the new dispensation] down without losing everything [that is, Sinn Fein walking out and the two Governments concluding that the process was over]. Otherwise, we are in deep shit [that is, the UUP would be blamed for the breakdown].' The Government, he said, was aware of these doubts and Mandelson had asked to meet the Assembly group. Jim Wilson stated that he felt there was no point in having Mandelson to such a session and that he was personally disappointed that Trimble had no chance to put the IRA to the test. 'Trimble is delivering the IRA,' declared Michael McGimpsey, triumphantly.[62] McGimpsey said that if the IRA defaulted, then they would take the blame; if they decommissioned, all well and good. And he added: 'History will judge us very harshly if you do not run with this.'[63] The UUP leader, though, was privately not so sure, at least at the level of political 'saleability'. He said that if there was certainty on guns, then an Executive could be set up first.[64] At 2:00 p.m. Trimble met with the full Assembly group, with only two MLAs absent. He said that without a greater degree of certainty, he could not carry the UUC.

Trimble duly returned to Castle Buildings at 2:30 p.m. with Empey and

Michael McGimpsey. Present were Mandelson, Bill Jeffrey, George Mitchell, Adams and McGuinness. 'There had not been a vote, he explained, but the opposition was too strong,' wrote Mandelson's biographer, Donald Macintyre. Mandelson, apparently, was 'gobsmacked', expressed disappointment, and declared that Trimble's decision would have calamitous consequences for the UUP and Trimble personally. 'Can I ask you a question, David?' Adams intervened. 'Did you actually try and persuade your people and make a case for the Agreement?' Macintyre records that Trimble was very irritated and that how he dealt with the UUP was his own business. But Adams persevered. 'I think that we are entitled to know whether you tried to persuade them.' Macintyre further claims that it had not occurred to Mandelson till then that Trimble had merely 'reported' rather than actively sold the deal to his Assemblymen. Mandelson then intervened himself. 'Well, I think we are entitled to know whether you tried to persuade the Assembly members to accept the settlement. I think that at least I am entitled to speak to the Assembly members as I believed you agreed earlier I could.' 'Well, we can discuss that separately,' responded Trimble.[65] Trimble confirms that Macintyre's account is largely accurate and that he was irritated because Mandelson and Adams were telling him how to handle his Assembly group. But this annoyance was about much more than mere *amour propre*: rather, it was because they did not understand his unique *modus operandi* with that unique body, with its own unique set of sensibilities. As has been noted, he prefers 'seminars to lectures' and deliberately wanted them to 'stew in it' – that is, to think over the consequences of rejection and to ask who exactly it was that was opposing the deed. Indeed, whilst he was away at Castle Buildings, some of the less vocal Assemblymen found their voice and were critical of the doubters. But Trimble was damned if he was going to reveal his party-handling methodology to the British Secretary of State and Sinn Fein president.[66]

Trimble went back to Parliament Buildings and again addressed the Assembly group. He had met with Sinn Fein and Mitchell and told them what the position was. 'Everyone ganged up on me,' explained the UUP leader. Mandelson had requested to speak to them, as had Gerry Adams. The intervention of the latter would, obviously, have been unhelpful – but Trimble and the Assembly group agreed to listen to Mandelson.[67] Between 4:30 and 5 the message came through that the Secretary of State should make the short trip to Parliament Buildings. It was a card which

Trimble could not have played, nor would wished to have played for so long as Mowlam was in charge. 'DT being DT doesn't come up with a game plan,' recalls Mandelson. 'But he wanted me to help put the case across and to give those reasons and those safeguards which only HMG could do. What the Unionists were concerned about is being abandoned by Britain.'[68] Yet although Mandelson was not the Unionist hate figure which Mowlam had been, he did start with a significant disadvantage – he was following in Blair's footsteps after the Prime Minister had appeared to mislead the same audience during 'The Way Forward' negotiations of the summer.[69] Mandelson, however, proved himself to be a better performer than either Blair or Mowlam in the context of this audience and in private sessions, though there was little difference in the substance of his policy (Unionists, as has been noted, are far more susceptible to style than is generally realised). He was determined not to make any errors of overpromising or making excessive claims.[70] As Reg Empey recalls, 'Mandelson was not condescending. Blair was in his shirtsleeves on a chair in the middle of the room and reminded us of the atmosphere of beer and sandwiches. Mandelson, though, sat at the top of the table in Room 277 at Parliament Buildings with his jacket on.'[71] The manner of presentation, which so contrasted with Mowlam's informality, was just as had been outlined by Eoghan Harris in a string of private memos to Mandelson, and jelled perfectly with the innate conservatism of the Assembly group. Mandelson recalls it as 'certainly the most difficult group of people I'd had to address – not because of who they were but because of the issues which we were dealing with and their acute suspicion of the British Government's aims and motives'.[72] 'I understand and share your misgivings,' said the Ulster Secretary. 'I won't pretend what is on offer is perfect, or offers complete certainty. Since I arrived [in Northern Ireland] I have sympathised with and understood the Unionist position. You have a friend in Government and I'm not going to change. Where I differ from you, however, is in my view there is a reasonable expectation that decommissioning will follow.' He went on to to say that he was fed up with Sinn Fein using excuses, but that the Assembly party was on the verge of giving them another 'let-out' if they turned down the deal. If de Chastelain was not persuaded by the republicans, then he (Mandelson) would take action to stop the game, even if it meant throwing the institutions into crisis. He told the Unionists that the current deal was much better than 'The Way Forward' document of that summer (in fact, this was not quite right in terms of formal British and Irish support for legal sanctions in the event of republican default, as outlined in the abortive failsafe legislation of July 1999). Mandelson went on: 'If you don't take this opportunity, I don't know what I can produce. I feel with all my soul that this is the best shot.' Indeed, according to the private diary of James Leslie, MLA for North Antrim, for 11 November 1999, '[Mandelson] had plenty of war-like stuff about how he would treat Sinn Fein if the IRA didn't deliver ... he also said he would not touch the RUC till all this was sorted out ... It would be for him [the Secretary of State] to judge what to do and it would be his duty to bear the burden. I then said we'd just had experience of a Secretary of State using her judgment and reaching a conclusion that to us was incomprehensible [the Bennett and the Florida arms importation cases] and that therefore we couldn't tolerate anything being left to the judgment of the Secretary of State. The consequences of non-delivery had to be certain. [Mandelson's] come-back was that he first had to give the SDLP a chance to exclude Sinn Fein. I said that I could just about bear that as the only rider, and a short-lived one too ... suspension of the Executive would be immediate, at which Trimble and I exchanged glances.' Danny Kennedy complained about the lack of certainty, and that whilst the proposed Sinn Fein statement had gone a long way towards this, that of the IRA did not. Mandelson replied that there was no certainty, but only relative certainty. 'But what do we stand to lose?' he asked. In response to a question from Sir John Gorman, he said that the Unionists were at risk (a) of being judged harshly by the world and (b) he would not lock the Unionists into an Executive with Sinn Fein if the republicans defaulted. George Savage and James Leslie backed the deal as it was presented to them: later in the discussion, Leslie opined that the UUP would have to run with this, since if it did not, the party would lose all leverage over Patten. Trimble then brought matters to a close and reminded Mandelson that Gerry Adams did not have to take a comparable risk with his own constituency. Mandelson left at 5:53 p.m. Trimble says that he later 'generously' told Mandelson that he succeeded in swaying two Assemblymen.[73] Certainly, it was an achievement in this climate not to have alienated anyone.

The internal debate resumed after Mandelson's departure. The late Tom Benson – an Assemblyman for Strangford – immediately spoke up: 'I'm more convinced than ever that we should take this to the UUC.'

Alan McFarland agreed and he was firmly of the opinion that Sinn Fein were 'up for this'. Trimble responded that he did not ever think he would trust the IRA, but that this was not a matter of trust. Rather, he said, 'it was a matter of doing business'. The Assembly group had to bear in mind that if they rejected this package, nobody would negotiate with either himself or Empey. It had not been his intention to ask the Assembly group to vote on this matter, since it was really a matter for the UUC. However, in these circumstances, he needed to consider whether he had sufficient weight in the Assembly group to carry the UUC. Trimble then proceeded to undertake a secret straw poll of the Assemblymen at 6:55 p.m. and collected the slips. He never showed the actual results of this poll to anyone save to Denis Rogan, the party chairman. The results were the subject of much ill-informed speculation on UTV and the BBC – including the notion that he had lost by 14–13.[74] This was not in fact the case. As so often, Frank Millar's understanding of the UUP proved the most accurate: he reckoned that Trimble had won a majority of the Assembly group, with only seven or eight naysayers.[75] In fact, the actual result – never hitherto revealed in public – was eighteen for, with seven against.[76] A mere five defections under the rules of the Assembly would give the 'antis' the critical 60% of the Unionist representation in that body.[77] But Trimble's assessment depended more on the quality than the quantity of the opposition: it included not just John Taylor but several other senior colleagues whose names surprised Denis Rogan.[78] Even Empey, who says he backed Trimble, believed that it was too risky to proceed with such levels of opposition. Trimble believed that some others were hostile to the emerging accord because they had no ministerial job in the offing. But whatever the reasons, if it was that hard to push it through the Assembly group – the segment of the party believed most likely to back any deal – what hope was there in the Ulster Unionist Executive or in the UUC? Empey says that he and Trimble therefore concluded that they could not carry on.[79] At one point, according to several who observed him at close hand, Trimble was talking about resignation.[80]

So it was with the heaviest of hearts that Trimble returned to Castle Buildings to tell Mandelson that he could not sell the proposals. The two men met in the 5th floor office of Bill Jeffrey, the political director of the department, with Jeffrey and Tom Kelly, the chief spokesman, in attendance. Mandelson was by now becoming used to Trimble's mood swings and was ready for him (initially, he had been shocked when at their first meeting after his appointment as Secretary of State the UUP leader had blasted Tony Blair with the words, 'we'll never trust him again, he deceived us', prompting Mandelson to ask his officials 'what was all that about?')[81] 'I don't have the votes,' Mandelson recalls a depressed Trimble telling him. 'I haven't got my people. If I force the issue, I'll split the party and I just can't do that to my party.' But Mandelson talked Trimble round quickly enough. What would the world think if having won a substantial majority in the Assembly group, the Unionists would not now proceed? 'He'd negotiated a deal which he believed was the best that could be got and therefore he owed it to history to proceed,' Mandelson recalls telling him. 'Not to go ahead would mean a rejection of his leadership and he would still be hated. He would be accused of leading them up a cul-de-sac for nothing. Why was it any worse than putting his case to the party, arguing his corner and seeing it rejected?'[82] Bucked up by what he describes as these 'first-class arguments', Trimble decided to proceed: it was perhaps Mandelson's single most important, and effective, intervention as Secretary of State, and all the more so since it was obtained at so cheap a price. Indeed, Trimble appears to have demanded little to nothing in return at the very moment at which he had maximum purchase over the British state. One associate who saw Trimble afterwards said that the impact of Mandelson's words was 'like a slap in the face when somebody is panicking'.[83]

The meeting had not even formally concluded before Trimble started ringing colleagues to put together a meeting that would decide how to sell the deal. He first called Ken Maginnis in Dungannon, Co. Tyrone: if Maginnis was against him, then he had no chance whatsover of selling it and prevailed upon him to come to Belfast that night. He then rang Denis Rogan, with the notion of using his secluded house in the Malone area of south Belfast as a convenient meeting point.[84] Present were Trimble, Rogan, Maginnis, Empey, Michael McGimpsey, Jim Wilson and David Campbell. Trimble told them, 'I'm going with this' – without telling them the figures in the straw poll. The discussion, he says, centred on the tactics of 'how do we go for it?' He also told Jim Wilson to say to the Assembly group, as a holding measure, that he was sleeping on the proposals.[85] But he had another objective: to firm up Reg Empey. Indeed, he eventually came to believe that Empey often got cold feet whenever there was a tough decision to be made. Trimble thought that

Mandelson's argument about the world not understanding the UUP's failure to embrace a deal supported by the majority of Assemblymen would be a 'clincher' with his close colleague.[86] Back at Parliament Buildings, Trimble began to work on the Assembly group once again. Three of the opponents were not quite as irreconcilable as he had first feared: they would accept a majority verdict in the UUC in favour of the deal and would not campaign against it. Indeed a vote of the UUC, the supreme decision-making body, would let them off the hook in terms of any pledges they had made to their constituency associations.[87]

But Trimble appeared, at one point in these proceedings, to be almost alone: according to the view of one witness, although Empey had almost as much 'ownership' of this deal as Trimble, he had retreated into his shell.[88] Trimble, whose mood swings could be considerable, entirely recovered his poise by the time he returned to Stormont on Friday 12 November. He went straight to Mandelson at 9 a.m. and told him 'we are going to go for this' and said that the sequencing should begin on Monday 15 November. But what he needed was a news blackout of acceptance of the final deal, which would prevent the possibility of news organisations and the 'antis' pressuring some of the more nervous Assemblymen over the weekend, forcing them into public positions from which they could not resile. Together, Trimble and Mandelson then went to see Mitchell at 9:30 a.m. Mandelson helped the UUP leader to persuade Mitchell not to tell the other parties that the UUP were on board until Monday morning.[89] Trimble then went to the weekly UUP officers' meeting at Glengall Street to report on the recent events. Although no decisions were taken, he told them that they might have to reconvene soon to call a special general meeting of the UUC should there be a successful completion of the Mitchell review. There was also the question of whether he would take the matter to the 110-strong Ulster Unionist Executive, as he had promised to do at its last meeting on 29 October, and where the 'antis' were probably in a stronger position than in the 860-strong UUC.[90] Significantly, he added that if the experiment in forming an inclusive Northern Ireland Executive went awry, 'we will walk' – though he did not specify what precise form that 'exit strategy' would take. The prospect of a great battle with his foes had so reinvigorated him that by the next day he was in sufficiently good humour to be convinced that he was irreplaceable and that the 'crazies', as he termed the hard core of rejectionists, would never take over; he also felt that Jeffrey Donaldson was 'damaged goods' following numerous failures to defeat Trimble's policy; that Ken Maginnis was too liberal; and that John Taylor did not want the job and preferred a 'ringside seat'.[91] *Himself alone*, once again.

Trimble returned to Stormont on the morning of Monday 15 November ready for the sequencing which would take place on that day and on Tuesday 16 and Wednesday 17 November. Mitchell's and de Chastelain's pronouncements would come on the Monday, followed by the Ulster Unionists on the next day, then Sinn Fein and only thereafter the IRA. Then, the officers of the UUP would summon a meeting of the UUC for the purposes of deciding what action might be taken in response to the new circumstances (it was widely anticipated that the meeting would take place on Saturday 27 November). Mitchell's report, his first public statement in ten weeks, reaffirmed his belief that all sides now understood each other better. He based his report upon the three principles enunciated by Blair and Ahern in Belfast on 25 June 1999 – an inclusive Executive; decommissioning of all arms by May 2000; and a programme of disarmament which was to be carried out in a manner prescribed by the de Chastelain body. Mitchell further called upon the parties to respond to a new de Chastelain report.

The UUP responded accordingly: 'The UUP recognises and accepts that it is legitimate for nationalists to pursue their political objective of a united Ireland by consent through exclusively peaceful and democratic means.' Its statement went on: 'The UUP is committed to securing equality and mutual respect for all elements of our diverse culture.' It also pledged to strive to eliminate the causes of disadvantage and to promote greater prosperity for all. The most remarkable aspect of these statements was the part which both sides played in drafting the pronunciamentos of the others; thus, according to Trimble, Sinn Fein played a 'slight' part in the UUP draft. 'They wanted us to confess to all sorts of sins,' he recalls. 'It was done through other channels, but not in formal meetings. I amended slightly the word "discrimination" and turned it into "disadvantage".'[92] To anti-Agreement traditionalists such as Clifford Smyth, the declaration was profoundly depressing: Unionists were again acknowledging that the destruction of their country was a worthwhile aspiration, so long as it was pursued by peaceful means. As he, and others, saw it the statement represented the further ideological degeneration of the UUP to the point whereby Unionists no longer spoke in a distinctively Unionist political language.[93] Instead, they used the language of democrats

– anti-violence, to be sure, but as much concerned with the methods whereby goals were achieved as those goals themselves. In this sense, too, the UUP position had been shaved down by years of negotiation into something closer to the British state's position, which concerned itself more with republican means than ends.

The Sinn Fein statement contained no such acknowledgment of the legitimacy of the UUP position, though it did aver that the organisation 'wishes to work with, not against, the unionists and recognises this as yet another imperative. For Sinn Fein cooperation and accommodation is the objective of this process' (loyalists pointed out that this was simply a variant of the republican strategy which envisaged enlisting a more 'realistic' portion of the Unionist elite into helping bring about their objectives in a peaceful way). Adams reiterated that 'we are entering into the final stages of the resolution of the conflict. IRA guns are silent and the Sinn Fein leadership is confident that the IRA remains committed to the objective of a permanent peace. By providing an effective political alternative we can remove the potential for conflict. This thing must for all of us now be a thing of the past, over done with and gone.' On arms, Adams added that 'Sinn Fein accepts that decommissioning is an essential part of the peace process. We believe that the issue of arms will be finally and satisfactorily settled under the aegis of the de Chastelain Commission as set out in the Agreement.' It would remain a voluntary act and collective responsibility. 'Sinn Fein has a total and absolute commitment to pursue our objectives by exclusively peaceful and democratic means in accordance with the Good Friday Agreement. For this reason we are totally opposed to any use of force or threat of force by others for any political purposes. We are totally opposed to punishment attacks.' This last portion of the statement was a particular aim of Trimble's.

Trimble thought this, combined with the forthcoming IRA statement, was a considerable achievement. Consequently he was as conscious of the perceived threats to his republican interlocutors' position as to his own. When I visited him to conduct a prearranged on-the-record interview on behalf of *The Daily Telegraph* on the afternoon of Tuesday 16 November, I found a tetchy Trimble who was profoundly anxious lest one word out of place unravelled the whole deal. When I asked Trimble about whether he feared that Adams and McGuinness might end up like Michael Collins because of the 'risks' which they had taken, Trimble exploded: 'You shouldn't ask questions like that!' – even though the comparison was commonplace and he himself had publicly speculated along these lines in the past.[94] At one point, David Kerr, Trimble's press secretary, came in and claimed that Brian Rowan, BBC Northern Ireland's security correspondent, was running with the story from some of his republican sources that there would never be any decommissioning. Trimble again exploded: 'He's going to look an absolute fool when it happens, quite apart from the huge damage which it could do to this whole operation [that is, in terms of Unionist acceptance of the deal]. He's talking to fellows on the ground and they don't know yet of the arrangements.' He thus obviously believed that actual product would be delivered. The next day, on Wednesday 17 November, he was rewarded with a statement from the IRA which backed Sinn Fein and termed the Belfast Agreement as a significant development which could bring lasting peace. They pledged to nominate a representative to the de Chastelain body once the Executive and the cross-border bodies were up and running. But there was no statement from the IRA that the 'war is over'; no commitment to 'product'; no credible and verifiable beginning to decommissioning; no public acceptance of the obligation to achieve goals according to the timetable set out by de Chastelain; and no reference to decommissioning save the appointment of an IRA interlocutor, to be effected following the creation of the inclusive Executive.[95] Moreover, there was even less chance of expulsion of Sinn Fein from the Executive than in June/July at the time of 'The Way Forward' proposals. In short, no 'jumping together'. It was all procedural and bureaucratic formulae – an IRA statement which cross-referenced to a Sinn Fein statement and vice versa – from which commitments might be inferred. All that Trimble really had was the understanding with Adams at the end of the Mitchell review as to what would happen if he jumped first – and the circumstances of that were not made public. The point was taken up by Mandelson when commending the emerging deal to the Commons on Monday 22 November. Mitchell believed that the basis now existed for both devolution and decommissioning. 'However, if there is default, either in implementing decommissioning, or indeed for that matter devolution,' stated Mandelson, 'it is understood that the two Governments, British and Irish, will take the steps necessary to cease immediately the operation of [all] the institutions ... a heavy price will be paid by those who default.'[96]

Many Unionists saw all this as a terrible compromise. Five of the Westminster MPs issued a statement on Wednesday 17 November rejecting the deal and the IRA statement as totally inadequate: Trimble promptly disowned them. He was more worried about elements of the support network for Unionism on the mainland, notably Viscount Cranborne. Cranborne had been critical in Trimble's eyes in steadying the Unionist political class during the referendum campaign of 1998, though his engagement had principally been tactical and related to the 'blame game' rather than because he was a particular believer in its intrinsic virtues. 'Robert was obviously unhappy,' recalls Trimble of their meeting in the UUP leader's office in the Upper Committee Corridor of the Commons in the late afternoon of Wednesday 17 November. 'He said: "You'll be sucked in, sucked along."' Cranborne again put to Trimble the idea of a 'post-dated cheque', an idea first put forward by Paul Bew in the previous summer and endorsed in an *Irish Times* editorial on Saturday 13 November. As Cranborne saw it, Trimble should sign and date a letter of resignation. After meeting with Cranborne, Trimble resolved that this should be deposited with Josias Cunningham, the party president, and that it would be triggered in the event of no IRA decommissioning. However, Trimble urged that there be no public indication of any such plan and as late as the eve of the UUC meeting told Frank Millar that the claim that he would quit if there was no decommissioning was inaccurate and that he would 'regard publicly setting a date as wholly counterproductive'.[97] He was, in the narrowest of terms, accurate: he did not set a *public* date, but a private one. Indeed, when Steven King had pushed the idea of a four-week-long 'suck it and see' experiment in his *Belfast Telegraph* column on 8 July 1999, Trimble exploded. 'I'd be very grateful if you'd stop promoting your madcap ideas.'[98] Trimble, as has been seen, was perfectly capable of being blunt to the point of rudeness *and* of sending out misleading signals. In a curious way, the former quality afforded him credibility that enabled him to pull off the latter. Trimble thought it a 'tacky' device and feared that it might give Sinn Fein an excuse to claim that he had injected another 'precondition'. Mandelson also knew that this was the view of the UUP leader, and Paul Bew told him when they met at Hillsborough Castle in the early evening of Sunday 14 November that Trimble feared having his hands tied.[99] However, Trimble provisionally decided to settle upon this as perhaps the only way of making it through a meeting of the highly sceptical UUC. Initially, he did not tell anybody about it, fearing attempts to dissuade him, and then only told Cunningham and Taylor and maybe a handful of others.[100] On the afternoon of Wednesday 17 November, Trimble had another significant meeting with Molyneaux – his predecessor and perhaps his greatest foe (Molyneaux was leaning strongly against the deal and would eventually come out against it in a letter to UUC delegates).[101] He told Molyneaux, as a tease as much as anything else, that he would first take the matter to the Ulster Unionist Executive before going on to the UUC. At this point, he detected what he believed was a change in Molyneaux's body language, as though his predecessor was licking his chops in anticipation of Trimble taking the proposal to a body in which the current leader would probably lose. His assessment of Molyneaux's reaction decided Trimble once and for all against taking the matter to the Executive.[102] Trimble could sometimes be more cunning than his impetuous and emotional demeanour suggested.

As ever, Trimble did it his way. Thus, Sinn Fein wanted him to launch a 'referendum-style campaign' to sell the deal to his grassroots.[103] However, Trimble thought that was the last thing which was needed. His style was the antithesis of Sinn Fein's and, for that matter, the Millbank style manual. Partly, it was a matter of disorganisation. But it was also a matter of deliberate choice in how to handle the UUC – a unique body, with its own bizarre political aesthetic which endlessly baffled outsiders. A frontal assault on his opponents could have been counterproductive in the circumstances: hence his decision to 'pull' attacks on Union First. Perhaps he was sure enough that he could obtain a sufficient majority in the UUC because he had the post-dated cheque up his sleeve, though he would have preferred to avoid that device if at all possible. Or perhaps it was sheer over-confidence on the part of some of his key supporters. Indeed, Steven King believes that 'the "yes" campaign was like John Taylor's losing leadership campaign of 1995 all over again. We had the constituency chairmen and the councillors on our side, but then the backwoodsmen came in. Trimble's staff was busy writing articles for him, but what they should really have been doing was to get on the phone to delegates and to "schmooze" them. The whole thing had too "establishment" a feel about it.'[104] In fact, as will be seen, more of this kind of 'delegate massaging' did go on, but not on anything like the scale envisaged by King.

Trimble's reluctance to launch a referendum-style campaign was perfectly understandable in one sense at least. He knew that after the perceived breach of Blair's handwritten pledges of May 1998, Prime Ministerial visitations would not work (Blair did make sure to extol Trimble's 'incredible courage' on the *Today* programme on Monday 15 November, but praise from the Government for the UUP leader's 'courage' or 'negotiating skills' tended to be a bad sign and was capable of being construed by critics as a consolation prize to conceal that he had done poorly in the talks).[105] Trimble says that Mandelson offered the Prime Minister to come and speak but that he declined.[106] Instead, Mandelson largely concentrated on trying to ensure that the atmospherics were right, often from behind the scenes. The highlight of this effort was the announcement on Tuesday 23 November that the RUC would be given a collective George Cross for bravery, as had been awarded to the entire population of Malta for their courage during the Second World War.[107] Some viewed it as a cynical exercise in the days approaching the critical UUC meeting – effectively 'thank you and goodbye' – and it is impossible to know if this gesture repelled more Unionists than it reconciled. But whatever Mandelson's motivation, he certainly carried less baggage vis-à-vis the unionists than either his predecessor or the Prime Minister. He offered to go out and sell the deal to the associations, arriving on the night of Tuesday 23 November at the Edenderry Orange Hall in Trimble's constituency to be greeted by some anti-Agreement loyalists shouting abuse.[108] 'I'd never seen such hostility before,' recalls Mandelson. 'There were two rather menacing-looking men towards the front and I remember saying afterwards to my RUC detail, "I'm surprised you chose to stand at the back of the hall in these circumstances." And they replied "Who do you think the two men beside them were?!"'[109] Mandelson said that it gave him a far better grasp of the kind of difficulties which Trimble faced – and that there were certainly no meetings like it in Hartlepool.[110] Yet despite this greater appreciation of Trimble's problems, Mandelson did not deliver the one speech which might have really helped Trimble – a kind of 'Balmoral II' akin to Blair's first speech in the Province as Prime Minister on 16 May 1997 which had given the UUP leader sufficient confidence to stay in the process. In the view of the Trimble camp, Mandelson muffed both of the opportunities to make such a contribution. First, he addressed the Women's Coalition conference at Newcastle, Co. Down, on Saturday 20 November and then on Thursday 25 November the pupils at Victoria College in south Belfast. But although he added some language towards the end of the latter address which implicitly stated that if the institutions collapsed there would be no move towards

Joint Authority with the Republic, the language was insufficiently dramatic to have any impact upon the UUC delegates.[111] The 'forces of conservatism' in the NIO, which always made sure that ministerial pronouncements showed an exquisitely calibrated balance between the two communities, militated against anything more stark. Indeed, one senior NIO official opined to Paul Bew that just as he had sought to counterbalance Mowlam's more 'green' inclinations, so he now sought to do the same in the other direction now that Mandelson was there. It may, of course, also be that the NIO's private polling was overly optimistic about Trimble's prospects and that they calculated that they did not need to make such a gesture to the UUP.[112]

In fact, it was the republicans who did Trimble most damage rather than the British. On Friday 19 November Toby Harnden, of *The Daily Telegraph*, reported that Martin Ferris, a senior republican, had told an audience in St Louis, Missouri, on Tuesday 16 November that it would be 'political suicide for Trimble [to withdraw from the Executive – that is, if the Unionist interpretation of the decommissioning issue was not satisfied] as the rejectionists already don't trust him and those few unionists who support the peace process would then be against him as well. He predicted a UUP split almost down the middle if that happened. He felt Blair was even less likely to bring down the Agreement because of a lack of decom[missioning], phrasing it thus: if the IRA guns are silent, the Executive is up and doing business, the Assembly is up doing business, the cross-border bodies are working, and the British-Irish Council is working, why on earth would Blair collapse all of that over the non-decom[missioning] of guns that are silent anyway?' Ferris disagreed with the account. But worse was to come. On Friday 19 November, Pat Doherty visited the editorial board of the *Boston Herald*. He was asked if the IRA would disarm in the weeks and months ahead. 'No, no, no,' replied the Sinn Fein vice president. When the journalists said that this would surely lead to a collapse of the institutions, Doherty rejoined: 'Do you think it's conceivable that if the institutions are working and the ceasefire holding, and that the arms are not being used, that the whole thing would be collapsed? That would be lunacy.' The comments appeared in the *Boston Sunday Herald* on 21 November. Trimble was swift to respond and called upon Sinn Fein to disown the reported comments: 'Were Sinn Fein to continue to give the impression that they are going to double-cross me, I would cancel next Saturday's UUC meeting.' Doherty stated that he was quoted out of context and remained '110 per cent' loyal to the Adams line.[113] According to Congressman Peter King, Rita O'Hare, Sinn Fein's representative in America, said, 'Pat Doherty fucked up.'[114] Adams himself pointed out that 'David Trimble has asked me to clarify Sinn Fein's position on decommissioning. I am happy to do this again.' Trimble duly responded on UTV's *Insight* programme on Monday 22 November, describing Adams' comments as 'significant'.[115]

Despite the disavowals, there can be no doubt that the remarks did much harm to Trimble as he entered the final week of the campaign. So what did Trimble have going for him? Certainly, the great and the good were on his side – the Province's three main newspapers, the business leaders, and the heads of the mainstream churches. Owen Lamont, president of the Northern Ireland Chamber of Commerce and Industry said that if momentum was not maintained, new investment would be lost. A group of 300 church leaders took out a full-page advert in the three main provincial newspapers.[116] Men with Northern Ireland connections now living in England, such as Sir Fred Catherwood, a prominent businessman and Tory MEP, appeared on BBC Radio Ulster to warn of the consequences of rejection.[117] Extravagant claims were also made in the heat of the moment. Ruth Dudley Edwards, ever drumming up support for Trimble, stated in the *Belfast Telegraph* of 24 November 1999 that 'Trimble will be in the driving seat in an unprecedentedly strong position to fight, for instance, the battle for the independence and integrity of the RUC.' She turned out to be wildly optimistic, but some delegates no doubt believed her analysis to be correct at the crucial time. In the view of some anti-Agreement Unionists, Trimble was also helped by the announcement by Ian Paisley that the second largest Unionist grouping would be taking up its ministerial seats in accordance with their electoral mandate, though they would not formally sit in meetings of the Executive.[118] Trimble believes he would have been in real trouble from 1998 onwards had the DUP sought to boycott the Assembly, leaving himself alone there with nationalists, and barnstormed the country in a reprise of Paisley's 'Carson Trail' of the 1980s; but, for whatever reason, the DUP had decided that they could not bring down the dispensation by such methods (nor, indeed, did they systematically disrupt proceedings in the chamber after the Executive was set up, after the fashion of some of the anti-Faulknerites in 1973–4).[119] Above all, Trimble had the Assembly group – though some wondered whether men such as Dermott Nesbitt were really best suited to selling the deal to a sceptical UUC.[120] (As Frank Millar opined on Thursday 18 November, 'David Trimble has not been helped by the TV appearances of colleagues whose enthusiasm for the new process will lead to an unintentional loss of urgency regarding decommissioning.') Finally, there was the desire to 'get on with it' – to put the conflict in the past (which critics termed defeatism). Not all of the arguments put forward by this strand of opinion within the UUP were especially rigorous. Thus, one delegate was quoted as saying that 'we are only 30-odd days away from the New Millennium, and I suppose that changes have to take place'.

But as the countdown to the vote began, few who knew the UUP well supposed that this kind of support would prove to be enough. In so tight a contest, the position of John Taylor, who had opted out of the Mitchell review in September, would prove pivotal. Mandelson's reassurances in the Commons on Monday 22 November regarding what would happen in the event of a republican default were insufficient for the UUP deputy leader.[121] It was the latest instalment of the cat and mouse game which Taylor played with both the British Government and his own party and left the cognoscenti guessing for days. Did he still want the top job – to round off the ministerial career which had been cut off so precipitately by prorogation of Stormont in 1972? Or was he now happy enough just to be courted at times of crisis whilst he criss-crossed the continent for the Council of Europe? Were the two engaged in a 'hard cop, soft cop' routine? Or was Taylor genuinely 'freelancing' but on behalf of the UUP leader, believing that a bit of brinkmanship was necessary to secure a bit extra to make the UUP feel like it counted? Or, as he once observed of himself, did he simply 'enjoy winding people up' and revel in the attention? Or a bit of all of these? Even so senior a figure as Denis Rogan – no particular fan of the deputy leader – has stated that 'as always with Taylor, we don't know what the hell he's playing at'.[122] Trimble says that 'I never thought that Taylor would be on the platform denouncing me, as he had done to Brian Faulkner [in January 1974]. I may just have a sentimental view of him, but it was certainly not on the basis of anything he said, just my belief. And he knew about the post-dated cheque.'[123] But at the time, Trimble was less sure and at one point asked one of his intimates, 'What's the bugger playing at?'[124] For he knew as well as anyone that Taylor would keep everyone guessing: the UUP leader commented at one point to Ruth Dudley Edwards that Taylor tended to be far more emollient in private than in public.[125] This appparent inconsistency explains why Trimble peppered Taylor's aide-de-camp, Steven King, with inquiries into the deputy leader's thinking. Indeed, according to King, 'DT would get very frustrated with John – the Nicholson business, the Mitchell review. At the British-Irish Association meeting in September 1999, DT thought that Taylor intended to wound him but not to topple him.' At one point, says King, Trimble expected a 'full denunciation' of the deal from Taylor, but if that was indeed his intention the deputy leader certainly pulled his punches.[126] Others, though, thought Trimble most indulgent towards Taylor, rather as he had been towards Donaldson.[127]

Whatever Taylor's motives, the practical task of ascertaining his precise intentions was made all the harder by his peripatetic movements. Indeed, Trimble says that it was the 'biggest problem' in the last week.[128] On Tuesday 16 November Taylor left for Teheran, as part of the first British parliamentary delegation to Iran since the fall of the Shah in early 1979.[129] The British Government was also deeply curious: No. 10 sought to ascertain Taylor's intentions from the then ambassador, Nicholas Browne. Taylor says that he was then leaning against the deal – and that he hinted at that inclination to the head of mission.[130] According to Browne, the UUP deputy leader appeared so unconcerned by the news from home (he kept in constant touch via his mobile telephone) that Browne calculated from Taylor's general demeanour that he would most probably be supporting the deal.[131] This was the least of the attention lavished upon Taylor by British officials and ministers in the coming days. One night, the telephone rang at his home in Armagh. Mary Taylor answered. 'Geoff who?' she repeated several times. 'Does he know who you are?' Taylor immediately grasped who it was. 'Give me that phone,' he insisted. It turned out to be Geoff Hoon, the new Defence Secretary, who had served with Taylor during the latter's final term in the European Parliament from 1984–9. Hoon was on his first visit to Northern Ireland as Secretary of State, to see the armed forces in south Armagh. Could he come to see Taylor? Taylor acceded and Hoon landed at the joint regular Army-Royal Irish Regiment barracks at Drumadd on the outskirts of Armagh city, a walk across the fields from the Taylor home. Later, Peter Hain, Minister of State at the Foreign Office, telephoned Taylor. He hardly knew the UUP deputy leader but he had an offer to make. Would Taylor like to head the delegation of British parliamentary observers to the elections in Mozambique from 20 November to 6 December 1999? This weighty overseas assignment would have coincided with the UUC meeting on Saturday 27 November and Taylor duly declined.[132] According to Trimble, David Campbell also came up with the idea of appointing Taylor as British ambassador to Turkey. No. 10 looked at it, but the idea was hard to implement, not least because a perfectly good envoy was in place. Likewise, No. 10 kicked around the possibility of Taylor becoming ambassador to the Council of Europe, but Taylor said no. Finally, the idea of a peerage was floated. But Taylor denies any suggestion that he received a letter from either the Prime Minister, No. 10, or through any intermediaries making such an offer at this time; he says he first heard about the peerage when canvassing in the 2001 Westminster elections.[133] Inevitably, Mandelson contacted him directly. He wrote Taylor a letter marked 'personal' on 18 November in which he admitted that 'few can know better than you the suffering that guns have brought to Northern Ireland . . . no one can offer absolute certainty – except the certainty that unless we move forward we will get neither guns nor government. What has started now is a process which leads to *both* [Mandelson's emphasis] guns and government. Adams and McGuinness will have no credibility left if the IRA does not deliver. This is a process they have helped to put in place, not one they can claim was imposed over their heads. They know what's expected of them. I don't believe they would have started unless they were confident they would deliver . . . If the UUP takes this step now, you can be assured the Government will stand with you. If Sinn Fein don't deliver, you will not be alone. I believe most of the world will condemn them. Certainly we shall – we won't pull our punches if they default now.' Mandelson then invited Taylor to Stormont on Friday 19 November. 'Your decision is terribly important,' said the Secretary of State. 'Everybody's asking what does JT think?' During the course of a one-and-a-half-hour discussion, Mandelson tried again to convince him to form an Executive and to put the IRA on the spot. 'There's no way we hold the UUP together till May on that basis,' Taylor told him. 'There's no point in agreeing to something if you can't carry people.' Taylor then went to see Trimble. 'I'm not with you on this,' Taylor recalls telling the leader. He then went to Sofia, Bulgaria, for a meeting of the Inter-Parliamentary Union on Wednesday 24 November and Thursday 25 November. Whilst he was in the legislature, his mobile rang. It was David Trimble on the line. Taylor rose and went outside into the freezing cold. Trimble stated that he would run with the idea of the post-dated cheque, signed for 5 February. 'Fair enough,' said Taylor. 'For the sake of six weeks we can hold the UUP together for just that length of time.'[134] According to Steven King, the two men spoke daily in the last few days, and in so far as there was any 'choreography' between them it was in that final period; from a conversation with Taylor on the weekend of 20–21 November, King derived the impression that Taylor was in support of the leadership (an impression shared by No. 10).[135] Taylor missed the flight he had intended to catch from Heathrow to Belfast on the evening of Friday 26 November and thus did not attend the meeting of his Strangford Ulster Unionist Association management committee in New-townards that night: instead, he simply sent them a message by telephone stating that he would support the leader's position, though he said nothing about the post-dated cheque. This leaked into the *News Letter*, resulting in a banner headline about Taylor's embrace of the Trimble line.[136]

Trimble certainly needed whatever help he could find from whatever quarter. On the day before the meeting of the UUC, *The Daily Telegraph* published an extensive survey of the delegates. Peter Foster, the journalist who compiled the tallies, found that 430 were for Trimble and 432 against; some thought that the closeness of the poll helped to decide Trimble upon the post-dated cheque, but he denies this was the case. Jeffrey Donaldson, for one, was convinced that the 'antis' would win, whereas Trimble was equally convinced that the 'yeses' would win by 60–40 – especially after a last-minute coup in the Lagan Valley Unionist Association. According to Trimble, Donaldson had been hoping to obtain a public commitment from the officers of his constituency party for a 'no' vote (Donaldson denies doing so and states that he had always enjoyed massive support in his association).[137] But Donn McConnell the chairman held back from making a decision until he and other senior figures had spoken to Trimble and Mandelson. When the MP met with his officers, Donaldson again tried to push them to say 'no'. During that meeting, McConnell floated the idea of a qualified decision now and a reconvened UUC in January or February to take stock of the situation. 'The great attraction was that this stymied Jeffrey,' says Trimble. 'The chairman of the association was identified with this [option] when I got to the Waterfront. And the person who seconded the motion was Barry Fitzsimons, the Lagan Valley vice chairman.'[138] Donaldson confirms that both McConnell and Fitzsimons came up with the idea of delaying a final decision.[139]

It was undoubtedly gratifying to Trimble to be able to make such incursions on to Donaldson's patch. But according to *The Daily Telegraph* poll, Donaldson was well in line with the general mood in his constituency association, which along with East Londonderry and Mid Ulster was the strongest area for the 'nos' by a 70–30 margin.[140]

The tension was enormous as the delegates began to arrive at the Waterfront Hall in Belfast in time for the 10 a.m. meeting on Saturday 27 November. Trimble observed that the event formed quite a contrast with 15 November 1985, with Unionists such as Harold McCusker waiting outside the gates of Hillsborough Castle to discover how two Governments had carved up their fate between them – with only an RUC officer willing to give them a text of what had been settled.[141] Now, said Trimble, the world's press and Governments were themselves waiting outside the gates to see what the UUP had decided: in that sense, he believed, Unionists had regained a substantial measure of control over their own destiny.[142] Anti-Agreement Unionists, though, believed that any such 'control' was entirely illusory. As they saw it, the UUP was effectively being given no choice at all: sign up or the world will fall on your heads, was the implied message. According to this analysis, Unionists were no more in control than the man who commits suicide by jumping out of the window before his enemies and supposed friends push him.

Trimble was scheduled to speak twice, the first time for about fifteen minutes to propose the motion and then to have the last word in response to the speakers. Six would come from each side, and it was widely expected that John Taylor would be amongst them.[143] On the platform with Josias Cunningham were only Trimble and the party's then general secretary, David Boyd.[144] Trimble recalls that he began 'a bit flat'.[145] But the UUP leader knew he would have to provide some extra reassurance if things did not work out as planned. Trimble's first and second speeches, which have never hitherto been published verbatim, were secretly recorded by a member of the UUC and supplied to the author. About halfway through the speech, he informed the UUC as follows: 'Some people have talked in terms of post-dated cheques, post-dated resignations and all the rest of it, and at first I thought I did not like the idea. It seemed a bit tacky, and there was a serious disadvantage in that it would be seriously counterproductive to put the date in the public domain. And I wondered how you could do it without a date. But then on Monday of this week, speaking to a couple of people whose judgment and support I greatly value, it became clear to me that there was a way of resolving the date problem and that it would be highly significant from a point of view of confidence to do this. Now, of course, we got promises by Governments to act. Promises had been made this week by the British Government and the Irish Government, but with the experience the Unionists have had over the last 30 years, I don't blame anybody who says "I don't trust the British Government to act and I don't trust the Irish Government to act." I am even told that some people don't trust me to act but that is by the way! So I decided to do things in such a way that would make it absolutely clear. I saw the president [Josias Cunningham] on Tuesday. I had beforehand written out a letter of resignation as First Minister. And I tell you this in case anybody is worried about it. As a lawyer, I can tell you my letter of resignation that I wrote out is legally effective. And I saw the president and I said, "this letter is to go in if there is no actual decommissioning by the day that is mentioned and if the Secretary of State has not acted to suspend the operation of the institutions then you put that in". And I will require any person who is nominated as Minister from this party to sign exactly the same letter so that the absolute certainty is there, and when those letters go in, then the Executive collapses and consequently the North-South council and British-Irish Council come down with it. So I am saying to you, you don't have to trust nationalists, you don't have to trust me. Only trust yourselves. I dated the letter, I signed the letter, I put it in an envelope and sealed it and it is out of my hands. Jo has it. And subsequent letters will be written to Jo. And so you can rest assured that there is going to be no temptation and no ability on my part to be sucked in and to be strung up . . . I should have added that the letter in – my resignation letter – the date in my resignation letter is not May. It is a darn sight closer than May. It is not really all that very far away. Beyond that I am not saying what it is. We are saying that the president reconvene this council in February and it will be for him to choose the date in February and at that point the ball will be at your feet and it will be for you to decide in the circumstances what happens. So I am saying to you, trust yourselves.'

Trimble then ceded the floor to other speakers. Inevitably, more people wanted to address the UUC than there was time for them in which to do it: they had to be out by 2 p.m. (which meant budgeting time for the count) so that the hall could be cleared for a pop concert later that day. Trimble's summing-up speech was a more effective performance than his first address, although the text (again, secretly recorded by a UUC member and supplied to the author) is less fluent. 'Now the other thing that has come out in this debate has been people's feelings about violence in the past, and the pain and killings and murders that have occurred. And names coming back. I am fortunate I suppose in this, that I have not had any close member of my family murdered. But I have had friends murdered, and the names of two of them were mentioned – Edgar Graham and Robert Bradford.' At this moment, a heckler interrupted Trimble's remarks: 'AND YOU HAVE LET THEM DOWN, SHAME ON YOU.' Trimble deliberately let him have his say. 'At that point, you could have heard a pin drop,' recalls the UUP leader.[146] Trimble slowed down and went on: 'I know that if Edgar had not been murdered he would probably be standing here speaking to you today, not me, and I am fairly certain he would be saying what I am saying!' There was further heckling. Then came the *coup de grâce*. 'As you recall, Robert was a good friend of mine and by coincidence, when my wife came home, when Daphne came home from shopping yesterday, she found a little note which had been handed in. I will read it out, it's very short. It just says "Dear David, hang in there. Be strong and courageous. God Bless. Nora Bradford."' It was rare for Trimble to employ such 'emotional literacy': he would normally have regarded it as 'tacky', but such were the circumstances that he presumably felt that he had no other option. Such were the paranoia levels amongst some anti-Agreement loyalists that at least one suggested afterwards that the exchange between the heckler and Trimble had been choreographed deliberately by MI5. This is hilariously implausible. For the heckler was none other than John Hunter, Trimble's erstwhile friend and ally, who now believed that he had betrayed everything he had once stood for; and it was hard to imagine John Hunter being controlled by anyone, especially MI5. The Bradford letter was certainly handled brilliantly by Trimble, but many of those who were close to Edgar Graham were by no means reconciled to the UUP leader's course of action and resented his memory being played in aid in this way. As one very close friend of Graham observes: 'For goodness sake, the world has changed massively since 1983 – not just here but the end of Communism, the collapse of the Berlin Wall and so on. And nobody can say with any kind of certainty where Edgar would be today in the light of those changes. I couldn't claim him for my view – but then nor, really, if he was being honest, could David Trimble.'[147] Whatever the merits of Trimble's or

Hunter's claims, it was undoubtedly the most dramatic moment of the meeting. Trimble believed it might have been 'worth a couple of percentage points', though both he and Cunningham were convinced that the vast bulk came to the Waterfront with their minds made up.[148]

The tension grew throughout the count. Then, suddenly, David Boyd emerged with a piece of paper with the figures and passed it to Trimble. He had won by 480–349.[149] Barry White, his Westminster aide, saw Trimble do the percentages on his Psion organiser. It was 58%–42%. 'What do you think?' asked Trimble. 'It's enough,' replied White. Empey then asked: 'What do you think?' 'Anything less than 55% and we were dead,' replied Trimble.[150] Jeffrey Donaldson shook Trimble's hand. 'Till the next time,' said the Lagan Valley MP; Trimble just smiled. Donaldson is absolutely convinced that his side would have won without the device of the post-dated cheque.[151] Trimble, however, draws attention to one other factor: 'Real IRA and Continuity IRA were the dogs that didn't bark. Imagine the effect on the UUC if there had been a big bomb in Enniskillen or Lisburn. Ronnie Flanagan thinks that because the review was so tight there was an element of surprise and that therefore there was no time for Real IRA to get their act together. On the other hand, Mickey McKevitt [a key figure in dissident republicanism] may not have wanted to save Adams and McGuinness and gave them enough rope to hang themselves.'[152] Certainly, the security forces were working overtime during this period, especially in the west of the Province, stymying attacks. But did the security forces also enjoy the tactical acquiescence of the Provisionals in so doing? Or did the Provisionals have a few quiet and not so quiet words with the dissidents – as occurred in 1998 after Omagh? And is this what leading republicans meant about helping Trimble do the deal in their own way?

As the leading Unionists were filing off the stage, Trimble asked Empey: 'What should I say now?' 'Over to you, Gerry [Adams],' said Empey.[153] In fact, Trimble's brief remarks at the press conference – 'We have done our bit. Mr Adams, it's over to you. We've jumped, you follow' – owed as much to the language of his friend Ruth Dudley Edwards in her *Belfast Telegraph* article of 24 November.[154] It was, he says, all 'quite unplanned' and as so often in his career, he was flying by the seat of his pants.[155] But whatever the circumstances of his victory, there was much satisfaction in No. 10, the NIO and the American Administration that Trimble had won. One No. 10 source says – improbably, in the light of the intelligence-gathering resources of the British state – that the Prime Minister's office knew nothing about the post-dated cheque until after it was announced. The National Security Council in Washington understood Trimble's difficulties, but felt that deadlines were counterproductive and could see that 'in the particular logic of republicanism' that there had to be more time for Sinn Fein/IRA given that there had already been a delay of nearly a year in setting up the institutions.[156] Indeed, Jim Steinberg advised Anne Smith, the UUP representative in Washington, on following the lines: 'Tell David that kind of language is not that helpful. He ought to be a little more diplomatic.'[157] Steinberg believed that setting a *formal* deadline made it less likely that the IRA would make a move on decommissioning under the *informal* timetable which had formed the understanding between the parties at the end of the Mitchell review.[158] Such rebukes derived ultimately from the unhappiness of the republican movement, and in particular of Gerry Adams. Although the Sinn Fein president was suffering from bad 'flu, he nonetheless arose from his sick bed on the afternoon of Saturday 27 November to call in to Downtown Radio in Belfast. Adams' motive was to tell the station and its listeners that they had been misled by Paul Bew, who had been debating with Brian Feeney, the *Irish News* columnist. Bew had said that he believed in the Sinn Fein president's sincerity and that there was a deal on weapons along the lines which Trimble had suggested at his press conference. Adams denied there was any such deal with Trimble – and the differences over what was actually agreed between the two men would dominate the politics of much of the coming year.

THIRTY-ONE

'And the lion shall lie down with the lamb'

FULL-SCALE direct rule from Westminster came to an end at midnight on the evening of 1/2 December 1999, and junior ministers Lord Dubs and John McFall duly vacated their posts. Powers over the six old Northern Ireland departments were then devolved to the new, inclusive Executive – whose first meeting was held at 3 p.m. on Thursday 2 December at Stormont. It had all the feeling of boys and girls on their first day at a new school, with the Unionist ministers sitting alongside Sinn Fein. Trimble, though, sat detached from the rest of his party team and was sandwiched at the head of the table between Mallon and John Semple, the then head of the Northern Ireland Civil Service.[1] The actual executive meeting, which went on for 75 minutes, was unremarkable enough, but the optics were significant. 'The Executive is a curious body,' observed Sean Farren, a new SDLP minister, in his notebook. 'In the absence of the two DUP ministers [who boycotted meetings whilst taking up their slots] the Unionists are outnumbered by the SDLP and Sinn Fein [4–6]. DT is competent in the chair along with SM. They are joint chairs and SM insisted on making the point quite forcibly when John Semple only passed a note to DT and Seamus insisted that he have sight of it as well.'

The events which preceded this meeting – the process of Cabinet-making – turned out to be of far greater significance to the viability of the Executive. As Trimble observes, the d'Hondt system for picking ministers is effectively an opinion poll amongst the eligible political parties for deciding which were the most desirable ministries: thus the UUP, as the largest party, would have first choice, followed by the SDLP as the second-largest, then the DUP, then Sinn Fein. The process would then start again, with the same parties able to make their second choices. Only the UUP and the SDLP had enough support to secure a third seat each. 'I therefore only had one totally free choice before Sinn Fein got there,' recalls Trimble. 'There were ten departments to look at and I had to decide which is the most important to society, and the most politically significant, and with the most discretion.'[2] Reg Empey was the first in line as Trimble's closest lieutenant in the UUP, and he chose Enterprise and Investment, one of the smaller ministries with a budget of £288 million in 2000/1 and a staff of around 1000. Mark Durkan of the SDLP came next and opted for the Department of Finance with direct influence over the entire £6.0 billion of departmental expenditure over which the Assembly had discretion: one of his main tasks was to put in Northern Ireland's bid to the United Kingdom Treasury, which provided funds amounting to £9.6 billion, including social security. Two-thirds of this was offset by taxes raised in Northern Ireland, but this money by-passed the Assembly going straight to the Treasury (just under £1 billion of this £9.6 billion went direct to the NIO, again by-passing the Assembly, to be spent on items like the RUC and prison officers).[3] Trimble saw this bidding game as precisely the kind of 'structural unionism' which would lead to nationalists being sucked into operating British institutions – which he had predicted they would in 1975 if the SDLP ever accepted William Craig's proposals for a voluntary coalition.[4] In a way, ministers of all parties came to resemble Sir James Craig: they played the politics of the begging bowl vis-à-vis Whitehall, just as Northern Ireland's first Prime Minister had done, and there was intense competition to obtain the credit for successful raids on the Treasury.[5] Next came Peter Robinson of the DUP, who opted for Regional Development, with a budget of £403 million and a staff of 4800 – which handled all forms of transport, energy and 'strategic planning'. But he would not sit in the Executive itself, nor meet with Sinn Fein ministers, nor sit on the North-South Ministerial Council. These were largely symbolic distinctions which the DUP invested with much significance.

Then came the big shock: Martin McGuinness wholly unexpectedly opted to be Education Minister, with a budget of £1.243 billion, and responsibility for such controversial issues as the future of the 11-plus exam. It would have been enough of a problem for most unionists to put up with any kind of Sinn Fein minister, but to have this particular republican in charge of children's schooling was little short of sensational. One Trimbleista who observed him says that the new First Minister seemed 'slightly shocked', as was Empey, and that they then moved into 'damage limitation mode' by placing Newry-Armagh Assemblyman

Danny Kennedy into the chairmanship of the education committee, to which McGuinness would report. Trimble apparently reasoned that Kennedy, who came from an area where Protestants had been in a shrinking minority, was well used to dealing with republicans. The UUP took the fifth slot: Sam Foster, aged 67, one of two Ulster Unionists from Fermanagh–South Tyrone became Environment Minister with a budget of £84 million. Foster had taken the slot after John Taylor decided not to be a minister and his appointment was, as Trimble pointed out, a reward for personal and constituency loyalty: if the poll in *The Daily Telegraph* on the eve of the UUC was accurate, then Fermanagh-South Tyrone had been the most ardently pro-Agreement constituency association. And there was one other consideration in his appointment. Without him, there would have been no Ulster Unionist ministerial representation from west of the Bann in the new Northern Ireland Executive. Sean Farren of the SDLP became the sixth minister, with responsibility for Higher Education, and a budget of £527 million. Nigel Dodds of the DUP took Social Development, with responsibility *inter alia* for housing, urban regeneration and social security, totalling £3.842 billion. Sinn Fein's Bairbre De Brun took Health with its £2.029 billion budget and 45,000 doctors, nurses and other employees and Michael McGimpsey of the UUP took Culture, Arts and Leisure, with its tiny allocation of £64 million and staff of 350. Brid Rodgers of the SDLP took the last remaining post – Agriculture, with a budget of £167 million.[6] At the apex of it all sat Trimble and Mallon. Trimble's total salary was £102,344 – plus various allowances as an Assemblyman and a Westminster MP.[7] It was a dramatic contrast from what he earned as a Land Law lecturer in 1990. Indeed, he was comfortable enough by mid-2000 to be able to move away from his London flat in Elephant and Castle to a larger property in a far more salubrious area north of the river.

All this left Sinn Fein in charge of over 60% of the discretionary budget. According to Irish Government sources, Gerry Adams was astonished at the choices made by the Unionist parties.[8] And for many Unionists it was profoundly demoralising, if not downright wrong, to have one republican running schools and another running the largest employer in the Province. Meanwhile, their own representatives had opted for three minor departments, which comprised 8.21% of the total budget for 2001/2. The more sophisticated critics of the UUP's choices, such as Paul Bew, asked themselves the following question: was it really worthwhile for Reg Empey to become regional economy minister when even the United Kingdom Chancellor of the Exchequer had little power in a globalised economy? Initially, Trimble was unrepentant about the tactics of Cabinet-making, and was proud of having ensured that the process was technically flawless from a UUP point of view: he was the only nominator who did not need an adjournment to think about who to place in what slot, right down to Assembly committee chairmanships and deputy chairmanships. Later, Trimble had still not understood the basic political point, and asked Steven King in December 1999, 'Have they got over McGuinness?' (as Education Minister). 'No,' came the firm reply.[9] Bill Clinton certainly grasped the political significance of McGuinness's choice and opined to Trimble when they met at the White House on 20 December 1999 that 'Martin McGuinness took the Education portfolio to help boost his own profile and soften up elements within his movement who were nervous about decommissioning.' Only much later, in December 2001, did Trimble publicly concede in *Parliamentary Brief* that the UUP's choice of ministries might have been a mistake.

Why had Trimble and Empey done it? Both men believed that the presence of Sinn Fein ministers in any slots would have severely enervated a portion of the Unionist population and that some kind of offence was therefore unavoidable. No less important was Trimble's belief that he 'owed' Empey – who had stood by him throughout the talks process.[10] But there were other reasons as well. Empey observes that Trade and Investment linked up with the most significant cross-border implementation bodies – tourism and trade. That way, he says, he could keep a rein on creeping unification. Similar considerations governed Michael McGimpsey's decision to take Culture: imagine, says Empey, if Sinn Fein had taken Culture, as was widely expected, and a Sinn Fein minister was responsible for 'defending' Northern Ireland's interests in the face of demands from the cross-border language body. As it was, McGimpsey could keep an eye on that institution. By contrast, McGuinness and De Brun had no access to cross-border implementation bodies. The UUP also thought it would look bad if Sinn Fein took the Economy slot after 30 years of republican efforts to wreck the Province – which Sinn Fein had done during the abortive running of d'Hondt in July 1999 at the time of Mallon's resignation. And they miscalculated that the DUP, as the third-ranking party, would still want Education, thus keeping it out of the hands of Sinn Fein. Trimble also reasoned that Education and

Health are effectively the departments responsible for closing schools and hospitals – something for which few politicians, anywhere, would wish to take responsibility.[11] Curiously, Empey says he would have taken Education if Trimble had asked him to do so.[12] Indeed, in so far as he blamed anyone for the debacle, Trimble fingered the DUP for taking the Regional Development portfolio rather than Education (Paisley rationalised the choice, claiming there were 5000 cases of housing discrimination against Protestants).[13] Trimble, though, never coordinated with the DUP over portfolios. But then he rarely had a long-term plan of action, even when big issues were at stake. When King asked him, 'What is our strategy for February?' (a reference to the widely expected UUC meeting to review UUP participation in government if there was no decommissioning) Trimble replied jocularly, with a big grin, 'We've never had one till now.' In fact, he did have a strategy of sorts, but he let very, very few people in on what exactly it was.[14] But the poor decisions over the allocation of portfolios also owed something to the UUP leadership's misunderstanding of the new institutions. As they saw it, Enterprise and Investment might have a small budget, but it also has huge discretion. By contrast, Health and Education may have huge budgets, but enjoy relatively little discretion once the statutory requirements and reforms of the 1980s such as Local Management of Schools are taken into account. According to this view, McGuinness was little more than a figurehead. Trimble soon discovered that the ministers had rather greater autonomy than he had originally envisaged. He states that the Northern Ireland Act 1998 was drafted in such a way as to diverge from the Belfast Agreement and the legislation vested executive authority in individual ministers rather than the Executive as a whole. Whether he is right or not about such alleged discrepancies between the Agreement and the Act, the fact remains that each department enjoyed considerable latitude on policy pronouncements, if not necessarily in its financial ability to deliver on those policies. This became apparent when McGuinness sought to scrap League Tables for schools and to question the 11-plus exam, thus frightening middle-class Catholics and Protestants alike.[15]

Yet Trimble – who was immersed in the detailed drafting of the Bill – did not make good these shortcomings at the time. This was despite being informed of many of these systemic shortcomings in a confidential draft memorandum dated 4 September 1998 written by Graham Gudgin and others. Perhaps this was because the bulk of the UUP leader's concerns, at the relevant meetings with the British officials on 11 July and 3 October 1998, were still focused on tightening the clauses pertaining to the North-South bodies. Even when the Northern Ireland Act 1998 replicated the standard British model, the effect turned out to be negative from a Unionist viewpoint. Thus, as in Whitehall, individual ministers are legally responsible for their departments – but without the counter-balancing informal aspects of control from the Prime Ministerial centre (namely, the power to hire and fire). The only patronage powers which Trimble (and, indeed, all the nominating officers of the eligible parties) enjoyed was the capacity to appoint and get rid of his own party's choices for jobs under the d'Hondt procedure. Thus, unlike Blair, or even the heads of the other devolved administrations in Scotland and Wales, Trimble could not himself dismiss wayward republican or Paisleyite ministers.

Whatever the rights and wrongs of Trimble's choice of portfolios, the new First Minister certainly did not push a Unionist agenda very hard in the early days of the Executive – partly because he feared that excessive 'proactivity' might give republicans an excuse not to decommission.[16] Trimble's passivity was illustrated by his conduct at the first meeting of the North-South Ministerial Council on Monday 13 December. Once again, the 'optics' of the occasion presented an obvious danger for Unionists. Thus, when the Irish Government, Sinn Fein and SDLP representatives were added up, the Unionists would be in a small minority. 'The First Minister is keen to limit the overall size of the first meeting, both in terms of number attending and expenditure,' wrote David Kerr in a memo to his colleagues on 3 December 1999. 'He is mindful of the sensitivities in relation to the issue within the Unionist community.' But after lengthy negotiations with the Irish about how the photo calls were to be handled – and an appeal from Ahern, who said that all of the southern Cabinet wanted to come – he settled for vague promises regarding the seating and for the numbers of people who would speak on either side. Such restrictions proved difficult to enforce. The event was duly covered in much of its glory, with Ahern describing it as the 'biggest thing that has happened in my political life'.[17] The most memorable aspect of the day was the arrival of the fleet of 12 Irish ministerial 98D and 99D Mercedes cars (plus Ahern, Mary Harney the Tainiste and Progressive Democrats' leader, and David Andrews by Air Corps helicopter).[18] This put the total number of representatives of nationalist Ireland at the meeting to 21, compared to just four Unionists. To Mary Holland, it appeared that the Irish were rubbing the Unionists' noses in it. 'My own impression was of an invading army arriving to dictate surrender terms to the defeated army,' she wrote in her *Irish Times* column of 16 December. To others, it was comic in effect: more like a mafia funeral as the black saloons came over the hill.

But in so far as substance was concerned, the meeting was very light – so much so that Trimble, in classic fashion, spent much of the time reading his papers whilst Ahern addressed the group. As soon as the meeting commenced, Irish ministers began to circulate an expensive booklet produced by Armagh Council about the North-South Ministerial Council, for signature by all of those present on this historic occasion. Trimble noticeably omitted to pass his copy around.[19] Perhaps of greatest significance to the Trimble project was one of the least-noticed items: the appointments to the management boards of the North-South implementation bodies. For the list of beneficiaries contained few new names. Certainly, there were party worthies, such as Jack Allen on the Foyle, Carlingford and Irish Lights Commission, and Bertie Kerr on the advisory panel of the Food Safety Promotion Board. Of greatest symbolic significance was the appointment of the Duke of Abercorn to the Trade and Business Development Board. As Marquess of Hamilton, he had sat for Fermanagh and South Tyrone at Westminster in the Commons between 1964 and 1970: like much of the Ulster aristocracy he had declined to participate in the UUP during the Troubles (indeed, after 1970, he did not vote at all) and his sympathies lay with the Alliance party. This was because of what he saw as the UUP's harsh treatment of Terence O'Neill and of Brian Faulkner. Certainly, he had been prepared to engage in public service – since 1987, he had served as Lord Lieutenant of Co. Tyrone and as chairman of the Laganside Corporation – but these obviously were apolitical appointments in the gift of the Sovereign and of direct rule ministers rather than of the UUP. But despite Abercorn's willingness to accept this offer from the new First Minister, there was little evidence as yet that another key element of Trimble's project – of reconnecting the UUP with great swathes of the Protestant middle classes – had yet borne fruit. Indeed, Trimble concedes that when he and his lieutenants were making the appointments, they had to scratch their heads to find enough suitable candidates to fill all of the posts.[20]

The inauguration of the North-South bodies, however circumscribed their activities, was always going to be awkward for Trimble in presentational terms. By contrast, the inauguration of the British-Irish Council (or East-West-Strand III dimension) was supposed to be 'his' day. After all, he had pushed for this institution to counterbalance the North-South pull of cross-borderism ever since his days in Vanguard in the 1970s.[21] So on 17 December, in the mirrored room at Lancaster House, the new body held its first meeting. It brought together representatives from the two sovereign Governments, the heads of the three devolved executives of Northern Ireland, Scotland and Wales – Trimble, Mallon, Donald Dewar and Alun Michael – plus the Channel Islands and the Isle of Man.[22] The long-term Unionist agenda was later described by Dr Esmond Birnie, party spokesman on the BIC. It envisaged joint studies of problem estates in Manchester, Dublin and Ballymena. 'There are [also] several potential areas for BIC involvement in cultural activities, such as the common Viking heritage and the commemoration of the First World War,' Birnie added. 'If Britain were to host a football World Cup, some matches could be played in the Republic and (subject to the building of a national stadium) in Northern Ireland. We would also wish to build on some of the excellent work carried out by the Ulster Orchestra in promoting music composed in Ireland, which was part of (or on the edges of) the standard classical repertoire of the 19th and 20th century music (e.g. Stanford, Wood, Ferguson).'[23] The two-hour conference agreed to work together on five issues of mutual concern – such as e-commerce and social exclusion: it was all very worthy, but was scarcely enough to compensate for the shock to the unionist political psyche of republicans in government. Indeed, Bairbre De Brun, the new Health Minister, made history by becoming the first member of Sinn Fein to enjoy a public handshake from the British Prime Minister: hitherto, all such encounters had been in private.[24] Again, few Unionists will have seen this as evidence that republicans were becoming 'structural unionists' by virtue of operating within United Kingdom institutions. Rather, many saw it as representing further legitimation of their tormentors.

Indeed, there was every chance that the BIC might rebound on Unionists: as Frank Millar observed, it was the Irish who were ahead of the game by opening consulates in Edinburgh and Cardiff once those two countries had voted for devolution in the 1997 referendums, and whose representatives there were already 'romancing' the new local political elites.[25] By contrast, by 2004, Trimble and the Northern Ireland Executive had still not set up Northern Ireland bureaux in any of these cities, let alone UUP offices (though bureaux were established in Washington and Brussels). Given this disparity in influence-peddling, there was every chance that the BIC could end up being a forum which the Irish could use further to bend the Unionists – and that it could thus become the 'pressure cooker' which Ken Maginnis feared during the 1991–2 talks. Trimble, though, was unconcerned by the impact of these Irish missions: rather, he saw it as evidence that they were 'engaging' with other British peoples.[26] Much later, Trimble told Paul Bew in an interview in the December 2001 issue of *Parliamentary Brief* that '"Strand Three" has not worked. Initially this was because of a lack of a dedicated secretariat. There was a degree of apathy on the part of the British and Irish governments.' Indeed, the only east-west structures which really worked from a UUP perspective were the Joint Ministerial Committees to coordinate, say, health policies between the centre and the devolved institutions (and which were not, strictly speaking, part of the Belfast Agreement).[27]

Once the BIC was over, attention shifted to the British-Irish Intergovernmental Conference – the reformed successor to the Anglo-Irish conference set up under the AIA. As one official notes, 'far from retreating, the Irish felt that their *droit de regard* in respect of Northern Ireland had actually increased under the Agreement'. Attention soon focused upon the British Government's paper on demilitarisation. The Irish sought far more extensive commitments from the British, including a timetable, than the latter were willing to give (on account of the enduring threat, especially from 'dissident' republicans). Partly, the Irish did this because they wanted to show the Provisionals' grassroots that 'politics was working'. The intention was to shore up Adams' position so that the republicans might, at a pinch, be able to provide some kind of gesture to satisfy de Chastelain that sufficient progress was being made. On Wednesday 22 December, the Government's paper *Return to Normality* was published: it pledged closure of the last RUC holding centres at Gough Barracks in Armagh and Strand Road in Londonderry as soon as was practicable; committed the Government to a lower proportion of Diplock or 'juryless' trials; the closure of HMP the Maze; and the withdrawal of three emergency battalions to reduce the total troop presence. It also noted, *inter alia*, the removal of security barriers, the removal of the Oath of Loyalty to the Queen, and looked forward to the implementation of the Patten report. To republicans such as Gerry Kelly, it was short on specifics. But what was really significant was the very muted Unionist response: the role of the Irish Republic and of Irish republicans in shaping security policy was now almost an accepted part of the Province's political life.[28] Indeed, Trimble's concerns were as much about adequate consultation as about substance.

Certainly, Trimble was going to do nothing to make IRA decommissioning less likely – and, indeed, was willing to go a very long way to help it happen. Thus, in January 2000, he and Ken Maginnis visited Sir Ronnie Flanagan at RUC headquarters. At one point in the discussion, Trimble said: 'Ken's going to do his nut when I say this.' The 'this' turned out to be an inquiry as to whether Flanagan could ask the Army GOC whether some security installations in south Armagh could be removed (including the Borucki sangar in Crossmaglen). As he understood it – presumably from the British or directly from the republicans – the stumbling block to movement on decommissioning was coming from Provisionals in that area. Flanagan responded that any such removals would have to be based on a security assessment.[29] Trimble says he wanted to see whether there was any flexibility on what south Armagh republicans see as a 'totem pole' and withdrew the suggestion when the system was explained to him, but it was nonetheless an amazing proposal to make.[30] For it was a sign of how far Unionism had moved and what a huge price it was prepared to pay even for a fig-leaf gesture on decommissioning. Here was the leader of the UUP and First Minister of Northern Ireland – who was meant to look after the interests of all law-abiding people – quietly 'inquiring' of the Chief Constable of the RUC whether he, in turn, could 'inquire' of the Army commander to lower his guard in one of the most lawless parts of the country.

Trimble was prepared to go the 'extra mile for peace', but it was not the only part of his strategy in this period. He was also determined, having moved himself, to ensure that the basis on which he did so was fully grasped by all concerned. If things did then go wrong, the blame would fall upon those who had failed to deliver on their obligations – namely, the republican movement. At the lunch at No. 10 following the BIC on Friday 17 December, he gently reminded Ahern and Blair of the understanding reached between himself and Adams in George Mitchell's hotel suite in the Belfast Hilton at the end of October, and quoted the words then used by the former US Senate Majority leader.

But he was especially worried lest the American Administration, including Clinton and his point man on Ulster, Jim Steinberg, had not entirely grasped the nature of the deal. Having initially been very keen on Steinberg, Trimble increasingly realised how 'green' the American was (some British officials also had problems with him). But the meeting proved hard to arrange – so much so that Trimble, who was well aware that there was very little time available if the IRA were to make a move, stated that he would never again meet with Clinton if something was not arranged before Christmas. When Trimble finally met Clinton, his fears were realised. At the meeting, on 20 December 1999, Clinton told Trimble that 'some of them [Sinn Fein] want to do this' (i.e. decommissioning) but that the republicans had several concerns, notably defections to Real IRA. Trimble told him in no uncertain terms about the resignation letter lodged with Josias Cunningham, and emphasised that the important event was not the planned UUC meeting but the de Chastelain report at the end of January. According to David Kerr's note of the meeting, Clinton 'understood he [Trimble] could not have got the deal through UUC without making provision for another meeting in February 2000 . . . [Clinton] did not think at the time the First Minister would get the plan through the UUC.' Despite his problems with Clinton, Trimble still loved his 'away-days'. Indeed, as Trimble told Graham Gudgin only semi-jocularly, 'If I don't spend a lot of time away, I'll behave oddly.'[31] In his penchant for absences from the Province, he was certainly less self-indulgent than Sir James Craig – 'whose health provided both a reason and an excuse to escape from Northern Ireland for increasingly long holidays', first to the south of France and then on trips to Commonwealth countries of anything up to six months; but then that was a more leisurely era.[32] There were certainly enough 'away-days' as the 'dignified' aspects of the new dispensation were formally inaugurated. Apart from the first meetings of the new institutions, Trimble was also appointed an officer of the French Legion of Honour.[33] The investiture took place at the Quai d'Orsay: he thereafter has often worn the pin of the Legion of Honour in his left lapel.[34] For all of the anxiety and stress he had undergone, the process was sometimes rewarding. The point was further underlined when Trimble and his family were invited by the Blairs to the Millennium celebrations at the Dome in north Greenwich on 31 December 1999. After attending the reception hosted by the Lord Chancellor, Lord Irvine, in the House of Lords, the Trimbles travelled with other VIPs on the specially commandeered Jubilee Line tube train; the UUP leader told Blair that Mandelson was doing well and Blair again said that he remembered what the UUP leader had said some time ago – that the Prime Minister 'needed to get a Secretary of State'. Trimble also reminded Blair of the importance of the date of 31 January, when the critical de Chastelain report was due.[35] But for many of the families of victims of terror, the winter holidays were less uplifting. That Christmas, only one prisoner remained in the Maze. The rest had all been let out on parole, including the Milltown cemetery killer, Michael Stone; the Shankill bomber, Sean Kelly; and James McCardle, part of the IRA team that blew up Docklands in February 1996.[36] Although Government had long discounted such developments as part of the necessary pain of a settle- ment – a viewpoint which Trimble largely shared – many in the Province did not. There was a relentless 'drip-drip' effect eroding the position of pro-Agreement Unionism.

'Optics' of this sort explain why the new Executive turned out to be such an unpleasant experience for Unionists. Certainly, Trimble could never declare, as did Brian Faulkner after the fall of the 1974 power-sharing executive, that those months were some of the 'best of my life'.[37] At one point in February 2000, he told Steven King that 'everyone will think it's been the best ten weeks ever in history – in fact, it's been ghastly and we've been lurching from crisis to crisis',[38] Indeed, Daphne Trimble recalls that during this period he was more tense and would often come home exhausted: a classic sign of tiredness and stress was that he would talk less and listen more to music.[39] Nor, despite his reputation as a 'policy wonk', did he display great interest in the detail of policy per se: one who observed him closely in this period says that he would happily go to Waterstone's and buy three or four books, but would sometimes appear not to have read a three-page brief on A4 paper on the work of the Economic Policy Unit.[40] But his lack of immersion in the details of administration may also have owed something to an awareness that he had one big task to perform before he could settle down to 'real politics', namely the resolution of the decommissioning issue. And since that was very obviously still up in the air, anything he did had a contingent feel. Indeed, Daphne Trimble recalls that after he became First Minister in December 1999, they were given the option of choosing pictures for his room at Parliament Buildings from the Ulster Museum. They therefore came early to a reception at the gallery and chose a North African scene painted by the Catholic Ulster artist, Sir John Lavery, and a landscape looking down on Belfast from Cavehill. 'Look, don't do anything about this at the moment' were Trimble's words as they made their pick (later, for his departmental office in Stormont Castle, he also picked Lavery's portrait of Sir James Craig).[41]

Certainly, the very temporary feel to the new institutions played a part in Trimble's unwillingness to combat the nationalist agenda: why get into fights over something which may collapse anyway? Moreover, if Sinn Fein defaulted, he hoped for SDLP support and therefore, in Unionist terms, let them have their 'pound of flesh' in some areas of policy.[42] Trimble's ideological passivity in the face of a nationalist 'march through the institutions' communicated itself to the Assembly group – who in any case were not themselves the most politically aggressive body of men and women. Certainly, few were ready for the new forms of political struggle which Sean O'Callaghan, for one, envisaged when urging Unionists to back Trimble.[43] There were a number of reasons for this. Even so experienced a politician as Reg Empey, claims Steven King, was terrified of being accused of 'sectarianism' – hence his reluctance to attack McGuinness (many Unionists had now been so conditioned by republican propaganda that they appeared implicitly to accept the Sinn Fein view that to attack any nationalist was perforce 'anti-Catholic'. Empey disagrees with this interpretation. Rather, he says, he could not see how UUP ministers could attack Sinn Fein ministers when he and his colleagues were trying to form an inclusive Executive with republicans).[44] This 'conditioning' affected others, too. Trimble's English special adviser, Graham Gudgin, was astonished at how few Assemblymen overtly disagreed with the nationalist critique of what they saw as the discriminatory nature of the old Stormont regime from 1921–72. This was scarcely a novel point of view amongst Irish nationalists, or liberal Protestants, but it would have been profoundly controversial within Unionist caucuses in past elective bodies such as the Prior Assembly.[45] In fact, there was some truth to the old nationalist line that Trimble had not 'educated' his party, but in a very different sense from which they meant it. By 'educating' his party, nationalists meant Trimble forcing his people to accept a set of new realities and institutions which at least implicitly acknowledged that all movement was in the direction, ultimately, of Irish unity. But what is surprising is that Trimble, who founded the Ulster Society, never sought to 'educate' the Assembly group in the sense of giving them much ideological self-confidence – even in terms of taking on their adversaries within the context of the Belfast Agreement.

Nor did the UUP Assembly group generate a great deal of policy analysis from within its own ranks (hence the dependence upon an English social democrat such as Gudgin). Although UUP Assemblymen often averred during the year and a half of the shadow Assembly from June 1998 to December 1999 that they could not wait to deal with 'real politics' – that is, schools and hospitals as opposed to the sterile positioning on constitutional questions – the reality was that too many of them were not very expert in these areas either. As Gudgin observes, the UUP lacked much of the culture of policy-making – a tendency reinforced by Trimble's habit of wanting to keep policy in his own hands.[46] Indeed, Michael Farrell, the former People's Democracy activist who had written *The Orange State* – the radical text which continued to exert a considerable influence on perceptions of the Troubles – visited the new Assembly in mid-2000 and was struck by the contrast between the UUP and DUP Assembly groups. The DUP was rushing around energetically, making a go of the new institutions however much they may have deplored the principles behind them and the manner of their negotiation. By contrast, the UUP seemed lost. 'It was as though the DUP had negotiated the settlement and was now reaping the rewards, whereas the UUP had stayed out and was in inert opposition,' recalls Farrell. The UUP did not seem to resent the new institutions; rather, they seemed, often, to make little use of them.[47]

Trimble was initially very defensive about the Assembly group, but over time he came to take a more realistic view of them. 'Can you think of anything they make a song and dance over?' asked the UUP leader rhetorically of the author in early 2002. 'They're not accustomed to political action. They're not very good at issuing statements. I'm not very good at that. The business of going on radio, acting aggressively, doesn't come naturally to them. They're polite middle-class folk. The DUP aren't polite and part of the reason why they're Ulster Unionists is that they don't like the way Paisley behaves. But while they may not be as aggressive and as demonstrative as some might want, there is no doubting their commitment and they've been asked to cope with political issues of an intensity and complexity that very few British politicians have had to deal with in the last half-century. As a group they have become more cohesive and confident as time has gone on.'[48] The UUP Assembly group was certainly an odd bunch. It contained many people who had little political experience, save at the local council level. Such is the parochialism of wide swathes of the UUP Assembly group that eighteen of the Assemblymen surveyed by Henry Patterson for his researches had also come up through the local government route. Only nine of the 24 interviewed by Patterson regularly read a mainland British broadsheet (this figure excludes Trimble and John Taylor). Likewise, the 'higher professions' are thin on the ground, with only two junior barristers in their number. The absence of any influx of new talent was also underlined by the nature of the Assembly group: only four out of 28 MLAs had joined the party in the 1990s. All this left Trimble – who had no experience of government – to bear much of the burden. Indeed, until late 2001, Trimble was the only party leader who served as a minister: Adams, Hume and Paisley all left those jobs to subordinates, leaving them to concentrate on political strategy and party management rather than administration.

The passivity of the UUP Assembly group stood in stark contrast to the 'in-your-face' energy and dynamism of Sinn Fein – transforming the entire landscape of Northern Ireland, if not administratively then at least in terms of the Zeitgeist and the public mood. Over Christmas, it emerged that Bairbre De Brun had refused to grant permission for the flying of the Union Flag from departmental buildings during the holiday season. Trimble's reaction in public – perhaps because he wanted to do nothing that might jeopardise decommissioning, perhaps also because he really believed he had 'won' – was relatively mild. 'My reaction is more one of pity than anger,' stated the First Minister in a New Year's Day article in the *Belfast Telegraph* entitled 'My Vision for Ulster'. 'To pretend that Northern Ireland is not part of the UK and that Ministers in the Executive are not Ministers of the Crown is a self-deception. The agreement contains clear recognition of the Northern Ireland state.' Many Unionists, though, did not take so apparently relaxed a view of the transformation of the public space.[49] De Brun also displayed an unwillingness to say she would work with the RUC on drugs policy (again, both these elicited little in the way of counterblasts from the UUP).[50]

But a substantive issue then arose which went to the very heart of the workings of the new dispensation. De Brun decided to centralise regional maternity services in Belfast at the Royal Victoria Hospital – which happened to be located in her constituency of overwhelmingly Roman Catholic west Belfast – and to close the Jubilee ward of the City Hospital (in the mixed, but still majority Protestant seat of south Belfast). Protestants from the south and especially the overwhelmingly Protestant east of the city would thus have to make a longer journey into terrain where many of them, notwithstanding the ceasefires, rarely wandered. Indeed, as Trimble himself states, she had simply followed the advice of her officials in rationalising the provision of these services in accordance with long-time profession advice.[51] In normal circumstances on the British mainland, this might not have caused a furore. But these were not normal circumstances. In the climate of distrust that obtained after 30 years of the Troubles, De Brun's decision appeared to conform to many unionists' worst nightmare of what Sinn Fein rule might be like: republicans using the organs of government to advance their communal interests at Protestants' expense. Worse still, in the eyes of many unionists, the decision had been made despite a 7–4 vote in the Health, Social Services and Public Safety Committee against closing the unit – a majority which included such local Assembly members for south Belfast as Carmel Hanna of the SDLP and Monica McWilliams of the Women's Coalition.[52] Thus, at a stroke, De Brun had appeared to bring into question the notion that ministers were accountable to the Assembly, even though many unionists had been led to believe that Executive members were unable to do anything without the approval of the majority; just as they knew that they, in turn, needed a substantial tract of nationalists to push through anything controversial. As Rick Wilford has observed in respect of De Brun's subsequent record – notably her unsuccessful attempt to terminate GP fund-holding – there was no real mechanism for the Assembly to remove her even in the event of a cross-community no confidence vote (in fact, the GP fund-holding episode was one of the few cases when, to Trimble's delight, the Assembly did supervene over the will of a minister).[53] The only way she could actually have been removed would have been at the behest of her own party leader and nominating officer, Gerry Adams. Thus, the exigencies of inclusivity came ahead of those of accountability.[54] Indeed, Sir John Chilcot had made the general point to Paul Bew at Stormont House in early 1995, 'we had a choice between good government and peace – and we chose peace'.[55] Bew was discussing the over-elaborateness of the Frameworks proposals, but it could be said to apply to the Belfast Agreement as well.

Empey explains that 'any minister can make decisions in defiance of their departmental committee. The committee can't get into all the minutiae. It was never supposed to be departmental decisions taken jointly with Assembly committees, though the Assembly as a whole must agree to the financial arrangements.'[56] Empey further notes that whilst De Brun could close facilities, she would never have been able to build additional new ones on other sites, since any such decision had financial implications which would have required the approval of the then Finance Minister, Mark Durkan, and the rest of the Executive.[57] Indeed, de Brun's decision was eventually quashed by judicial review in 2000, on the grounds of a breach of procedural fairness.[58] A poll published in the *Belfast Telegraph* on 23 February 2000 showed that although 87% of Protestants wanted to remain part of the United Kingdom, 36% either thought it very likely or quite likely that there would be a united Ireland within 20 years. It was this conditioning of the public mind, and the relentless republican attempts to dominate the public space, which made it so hard for Trimble to make headway.

THIRTY-TWO

Mandelson keeps his word

TRIMBLE's relative passivity in this period owed something to exhaustion, but more to his desire to do nothing that might hand republicans an excuse not to decommission. And in any case, he believed that the terms of the Mitchell deal were such as to make it impossible for them to resile from their commitment without a massive political fall-out. There is much evidence to support the contention that Trimble genuinely thought he had a private understanding that they would fulfil their obligations (a confidence not shared by his deputy, John Taylor, who all along believed that there would be a return to full-scale direct rule).[1] Thus, Daphne Trimble states that he believed at least up till Christmas 1999 that there would be decommissioning.[2] Denis Rogan says that he first heard Trimble express some doubts about the prospects of decommissioning taking place at a lunch for local newspaper editors held at Antica Roma restaurant in Belfast shortly before Christmas – though even as late as 23 January, at a meeting of senior figures held at his offices in south Belfast, Trimble felt able to tell the UUP chairman that they would obtain decommissioning. 'Why do you say that?' Rogan asked. 'Denis, it just is,' came the reply.[3] It was, he reasoned, very much in Sinn Fein's political interests to decommission, not least because of their electoral aspirations in the Republic.[4] But the Ulster Unionists, and the British, also believed that there was another dynamic at work within republicanism: that in consequence of the Mitchell review process, Adams and McGuinness had come to understand that Trimble was the 'best' Unionist leader with whom to deal.[5] If he fell, to be replaced by someone mandated to pursue a less accommodating policy, they would be desperately exposed amongst their own purists as having 'gone the extra mile' in diluting traditional republicanism and still not satisfying the Unionists. Therefore, since they knew that Trimble was on such thin ice with the

UUC after 'jumping first' in November 1999, it stood to reason that the republicans would make at least a token gesture. After all, Trimble's margins in the UUC had shrunk from 72% at the time of the Belfast Agreement in April 1998 to 58% in November 1999.

Sinn Fein may or may not have developed a greater appreciation of Trimble's internal difficulties during the course of the Mitchell review, but they were only prepared to pay a very limited price to extricate him from his difficulties. Such sentiments had been powerfully reinforced, as they saw it, by Trimble's post-dated cheque, which as the IRA statement noted at the time of the devolution of powers 'was not part of this context [entering discussions with the de Chastelain body] and in our view represents a clear departure from the terms of the Mitchell Review'. Mandelson now says he first heard that Trimble had actually decided upon a post-dated cheque on the morning of the UUC meeting, Saturday 27 November – though he claims he had earlier told Trimble supporters who were pushing such a course of action 'please, no hostages to fortune, don't start making elephant traps for yourself'. The official view was that the 22 May deadline under the Belfast Agreement would have been far more suitable and would have had far more moral sanction. According to Frank Millar, whilst Mandelson shared Trimble's general understanding about what ought to follow if Unionists jumped first, there was a world of difference between that and Trimble's specific interpretation which held that it must happen by 31 January.[6] Even Trimble's phrase 'we've jumped, you follow', was felt by the Secretary of State to be 'too stark. It was an ultimatum, to which they [republicans] couldn't be seen to respond.'[7]

Mandelson recalls that Adams told him throughout January that there was 'no way' that the republican movement were going to do anything by 31 January and probably not by the 22 May 2000 deadline stipulated under the Belfast Agreement. 'Adams looked me in the eye and said "Peter, it's not going to happen."' When Mandelson asked what de Chastelain would then be able to say in his report, Adams replied, 'Don't worry, there will be a positive de Chastelain report by the end of January.'[8] Authoritative sources also state that no indication was ever given to the de Chastelain body at any one of three meetings held, supposedly in Dundalk, with the IRA's representative that decommissioning would take place. There were plenty of positive noises that the ceasefire was intact, but he made much more about the anger of republicans over the post-dated cheque and the discovery of a bugging device found in Gerry Adams' car than about 'delivering product'.[9] The public stances of the republican movement indicated mostly truculent defiance as well: on 23 January Adams, McGuinness and de Brun attended the reinterment of Tom Williams, an IRA terrorist hanged in 1942 for murdering a Catholic RUC officer during the Second World War (Williams had till then been buried at the prison where he was executed).[10] Adams referred to the 'martyrdom' of IRA casualties during the Troubles, but made no reference to decommissioning. The *Daily Mail* picked up on the episode and pictured the Sinn Fein president on the front page with the massive headline 'AND NOW HE DANCES ON THE RUC'S GRAVE'. It was significant that a newspaper with as strong a commercial nose for 'Middle England' should highlight the issue in this way, though Trimble was never especially energetic about tapping into this agenda to extract the maximum political price from the Government on the policing issue.[11]

Despite all this, the Irish Government implied to their British counterparts, including Mandelson, that it would somehow be 'all right on the night' and that something would turn up.[12] Privately, the shrewdest Irish officials were less convinced. I was told in early January 2000 by one authoritative source that Adams and McGuinness did not have the votes in the 'Army Convention' (a gathering of representatives of IRA active service units) for even a gesture on decommissioning – assuming, of course, that they really wanted to deliver such a gesture. One Dublin insider also claims that the Taoiseach told him before Christmas 1999 that there was trouble down the pike with the British and that, in consequence, he needed a fresh foreign minister who would stand up to Mandelson. The Taoiseach's interlocutor interpreted this as meaning that there could be major disagreements on decommissioning – notably what constituted a republican default on the terms of the Mitchell review.[13] Perhaps, also, they thought that Ferris and Doherty were correct and that the British would not collapse the institutions once up and running. Certainly, No. 10 believed that despite the new dispensation, one canon of Irish nationalist theology had not been abandoned by their counterparts: that when it came to a crunch, the British would be able to snap their fingers and order the Unionists to abandon their post-dated cheque. This presupposed that the British would be willing to do this, and that even if they had been willing, the UUP would have jumped. It also raises the question of why the British were unable successfully to convey to nationalist Ireland that they would back up Trimble – despite clear warn-ings from Peter Mandelson to Niall O'Dowd of *The Irish Voice* at a lunch at the British Consul General's Residence in New York on 9 December 1999 that the British Government would do just that and that Pat Doherty's analysis was wrong.[14] Likewise, Jonathan Powell also states that it was always made clear to the Irish that if there was a default, then the British Government would suspend.[15]

If Trimble was not prepared to do anything which would give republi-cans an excuse not to decommission, nor were the British. So determined were they not to give offence that they further weakened Trimble's pos-ition and that of pro-Agreement unionism. The British also wanted to give Adams et al. enough concessions to enable them to tell their grass-roots that politics was working – such as wide-ranging reform of the RUC. The British Government's differences with nationalist Ireland were largely over timing, manner and pace, especially as they concerned Union-ist sensibilities in this difficult period for them, but the fundamentals were never in question. Indeed, at a meeting with Blair at No. 10 on 13 January 2000 – the first big formal meeting between the Prime Minis-terial and the UUP teams since the end of the Mitchell review – Blair had already reiterated that Patten and demilitarisation would proceed. Trimble stated that how Patten was handled was critical, and that the symbolic issue would determine if the reforms were acceptable or not. Mandelson said that they had looked at the 'Faul option' – a dual NIPS-RUC name suggested by Mgr Denis Faul, parish priest of Carrickmore, Co. Tyrone – but stressed it would create further problems and that the RUC itself did not want it. There would, he emphasised, be safeguards in the legislation on the District Policing Partnership Boards and their ability to 'buy in' extra policing services, which many unionists feared would result in republican-controlled private security firms being given security powers (though some of these safeguards were subsequently diluted when the legislation itself was introduced in June 2000). Trimble complained about the lack of consultation and said that he did not think the English public would put up with this relentless stream of concessions to republicans. 'We do have a Labour majority, you know,' replied Mandelson.

Mandelson was not always so confident, though. When Eoghan Harris blasted Mandelson in his column for the Irish edition of *The Sunday Times* for planning to forge ahead with the Patten reforms, which he charged 'has dealt a mortal blow to moderate unionism', the Secretary of State suddenly came on the line.[16] He was apparently deeply upset by the strong words written by one of his greatest admirers in the Republic. 'What better time is there on Patten?' Mandelson asked Harris. 'It would be better after the de Chastelain report and the meeting of the UUC,' replied the former chief ideologist of the Workers' Party. 'But that would be rewarding Sinn Fein for being bad boys.' 'Well, I'm assuming, Peter, that everything would be changed by context,' retorted Harris. 'I mean, if they don't deliver, I wouldn't give them anything. Fuck them.' 'Oh well, if we're going down that road,' sighed Mandelson. 'So no matter what Sinn Fein do, you won't alter Patten?' inquired the Corkman. 'My worry is not only the USA,' said the Secretary of State. 'It's bombs in London.'[17] Mandelson confirms the accuracy of this account, but says that he had an additional concern: that if he did not make his intentions clear about the implementation of Patten, it could then be used by republicans as an excuse for not moving on decommissioning. Trimble was delighted by Harris's description of the exchange, but it could not detract from the central problem in this area. For the Government believed that the essence of police reform stood on its own merits, almost irrespective of the need to keep the Irish and the Americans on board (though these two elements powerfully reinforced such tendencies).

It was a startling reminder of the limits of the consent principle – not quite the McNamara definition whereby it applied only to the last stage of the transfer of sovereignty from the United Kingdom to the Republic, but certainly not the Trimble definition either. Indeed, the doctrine of the need for parallel consent, enshrined in the Belfast Agreement and the workings of the Assembly, did not really obtain in respect of policing and other reserved matters. The reforms thus proceeded despite a 350,000-strong petition, organised by the Police Federation of Northern Ireland and handed into Downing Street in January; a 50–42 vote in the Assembly on 24 January rejecting the Patten report; and a Police Authority Survey of 1200 people showing that only 45% of Catholics would be likelier to support a renamed police force, whereas 51% thought there would be no change following such a reform.[18] It was this approach which prompted Trimble's outburst at No. 10 that day: 'When are you going to do something for us?' inquired Trimble. 'What can we do?' asked Blair. 'What would be helpful?' 'Save the RUC.' Mandelson – who unlike Mowlam now attended meetings with the Unionists at No. 10 and was always anxious to prove to his boss his knowledge and toughness – replied, 'Oh, come on, get real.' As Jonathan Powell subsequently observed to one of his interlocutors, one of the distinctive features of Trimble's negotiating style was that he either asked for the impossible or else for concessions that were so insignificant as to make little real impact upon his own supporters.[19] One witness thought that Trimble was just going through the motions as much as hoping for a result and that these gatherings were as much exercises in party management as anything else. Trimble then said that as things stood, he could not retain his seat at Westminster and that Blair had no idea what harm was being done by all this to pro-Agreement Unionism. 'Is the Executive itself not popular?' asked Blair. Perhaps he was being a *faux naïf*, or else he was so in the grip of conventional wisdom about the therapeutic effects of an inclusive Executive on the wounds of Ulster society that he simply could not imagine that it would be anything other than a success. Trimble also asked whether there was any intelligence on what would happen at the end of January: Blair did not answer the question and then said, 'I'll come back to you.' Trimble told the Government representatives that his letter of resignation had been submitted to Josias Cunningham and would be activated at the beginning of February.

Mandelson duly announced the Government's response to Patten in the Commons on 10 January 2000.[20] Important as the RUC issue was in its own terms, it raised another even more important matter. Why inflict this humiliation on Unionists now, at this moment, weeks ahead of Trimble's tryst with destiny at the UUC where he might well have to make good his post-dated cheque? In a seminal article in the *Irish Times* on 25 January, Frank Millar quoted a trusted source who thought that Mandelson's handling of the policing matter meant one of two things: either that he knew from his intelligence chiefs that the Provisionals were going to deliver something and that the defeat of the Unionists on the RUC represented some sort of 'down-payment' of good faith towards that end; or else, that Mandelson knew that nothing was coming down the pike from the Provisionals, that the situation within republicanism was far more serious than anyone had hitherto realised, and that he had accordingly decided that Trimble's survival could only be bought at too high a price by suspending the institutions and thus enraging nationalist Ireland. Having put the squeeze on the Provisionals to deliver, and failed, might not the pressure as so often before turn back on to the UUP? The suggestion that he might be about to ditch Trimble enraged Mandelson, to the point that some thought his sensitivity on the matter meant that it must have had some truth (of which more later). But whatever the Secretary of State's actual motives, the announcement on Patten bought neither Mandelson, nor Trimble, much immediate credibility with either Sinn Fein, the SDLP or the Irish Government that might have prompted them to respond on the decommissioning issue.

The British were especially disappointed by the Irish Government's approach. Mandelson recalls that the Taoiseach's approach was quite contradictory. On the one hand, he repeatedly said that suspension would be a 'disaster', destroy the institutions that they had worked so hard to set up, and could sweep away the Sinn Fein leadership which had gambled so much on them. On the other hand, he would frequently say, 'Tony, we can't lose Trimble, that would be the end.'[21] Ahern knew that the clock was ticking away in the run-up to the publication on 31 January of the next de Chastelain report and that if Trimble resigned he would never be re-elected in the Assembly and the inclusive process required for stability on the island of Ireland would be done for. This appeared to imply that suspension – putting the institutions in deep freeze but obviating the need to re-run the election of First Minister – might be necessary. This approach, of course, was squarely in line with the sympathetic noises made by the Taoiseach in the Dail in November 1999, suggesting that he would stand behind Trimble if he jumped first and the IRA did not follow suit, and to the South African Institute of International Affairs in Johannesburg on 12 January 2000.[22] Thus, the Irish did begin to push the republicans in January, and Adams went on a tour of IRA units around the country; but they concluded that the Sinn Fein president gave up after a quick try. Indeed, when Trimble and his colleagues met with Ahern and his team on 20 January 2000 at Government Buildings, the Taoiseach made a particular point of telling the UUP that he had informed the republicans that Trimble had no room for manoeuvre. Republicans, he said, were mainly concerned about the possibility of an internal split, but a consequent negative de Chastelain report on 31 January (indicating no movement) would also be a catastrophe and the two Governments would then have to take stock. Significantly, one senior Irish official observed that McGuinness apparently stopped going to IRA meetings when he was appointed to the Executive, so as to keep a clear division between ministers and 'the movement'. Trimble's broad response was that in the event of a negative de Chastelain report, the two Governments would immediately have to go into a review.

Why were the Irish so 'conflicted'? The loss of Trimble would obviously have been a disaster to them, so much so that Dermot Gallagher, the then head of the Anglo-Irish affairs division of the DFA in Dublin, subsequently told Paul Bew that without him, Northern Ireland politics would enter a ten- to fifteen-year wilderness.[23] They wanted him to survive, but like the republicans were prepared to pay only a limited price towards that end – especially after the UUP leader injected what Sinn Fein saw as the extra precondition of the post-dated cheque. Sinn Fein's displeasure over that move placed serious constraints upon Fianna Fail's willingness to make good any pledges to Trimble. In any case, ever since the southern local and European elections of June 1999, Trimble says that both John Taylor and Reg Empey had discerned a qualitative shift in the policy of the Republic, which they alleged had become 'greener'.[24] Sinn Fein recorded 6% of the vote in the south in the European elections, and though they did not win as much in terms of aggregate percentages in the council elections, they nonetheless dug into traditional Fianna Fail terrain in the border areas, winning the chairmanship of Monaghan County Council and the mayoralty of Sligo. Whilst elements of the Fianna Fail establishment saw Sinn Fein as a threat – principally to their patronage powers and networks – Fianna Fail voters were happier to see them in the Dail on sentimental grounds. There were, therefore, both positive and negative reasons for embracing a more nationalist approach. One was to take the wind out of Sinn Fein's sails by tacking to a more anti-British line – although this would be by no means the last turn of the wheel in respect of Fianna Fail's attitude towards Sinn Fein, as increasingly became apparent in 2001–2. An opportunity to strike an apparently 'greener' posture was provided by the long-expected retirement from the Cabinet of the 65-year-old Minister for Foreign Affairs, David Andrews, on 26 January 2000.[25] His replacement was the far more aggressive Brian Cowen, a 40-year-old TD for Laois-Offaly. He owed his first ministerial appointments to Albert Reynolds, and appeared in tears on RTE on the night that the latter resigned as Taoiseach. But when Ahern, Reynolds' rival, became Taoiseach in 1997, he made Cowen Health Minister.[26] Some of Ahern's aides thought Cowen's appointment to the DFA showed how the Taoiseach did not hold grudges. But he may also have had two further calculations. First, that a disgruntled Cowen – who appeared to affect a certain doziness to conceal his own sharpness and ability, not least of which was a superb skill at mimicry – could be a danger to him. Second, he may have wanted to build up a counterweight to another potential heir, Micheal Martin. These considerations, as well as the need to have a heavyweight to combat Mandelson, account for his elevation to the position of Foreign Minister. The British initially viewed his appointment favourably, but they rapidly found that his apparent lack of sympathy for certain unionists made things worse (as a leaked memorandum from the British ambassador to Dublin, Ivor Roberts, made clear).[27] He took a maximalist position on erasing the symbols of Britishness from Northern Ireland. Trimble immediately understood the significance of the reshuffle: 'The fact that the Irish state acquired such a Foreign Minister complicated things,' he notes.[28] Privately, he told aides, 'We may now have to start to pay more attention to the DFA.'

The internal politics of the Republic thus set the stage for the Anglo-Irish ructions of the next few weeks – which would have profound implications for Trimble's position. The Trimbleistas knew that the worst thing that could happen to them would be a cloudy de Chastelain report on 31 January. As they saw it, if the report announced the decommissioning of actual 'product', or its imminent arrival, all well and good: the Provisionals would have 'blinked' and Trimble would have been vindicated in the eyes of the UUC for making the leap and for attaining decommissioning, albeit with some dilution on the timing. Or, if the report said that the Provisionals had not seriously engaged – that is, that there was no real evidence of a commitment to decommission – then the republicans would have defaulted. They would then lose the blame game in the eyes of the world because of this default and thus create a context in which Mandelson could suspend the institutions with (Unionists hoped) the support of the Irish and the Americans. The institutions could then be put in the deep freeze pending a review which might just yield better terms for Ulster Unionists on the renewed admission of Sinn Fein into the Executive. But what if under pressure from the Irish, and perhaps the British, the Provisionals appeared to give de Chastelain just enough on procedural matters relating to 'modalities' to secure a more positive report? In other words, something which might be enough for the two Governments to enable them to fudge collapsing the new institutions and then effectively to say to Trimble and the Unionist leadership, 'just give them a bit more time'. This, though, would never be enough for the UUP: indeed, as the DUP never tired of pointing out, the UVF had agreed modalities in 1998 but still militantly refused to decommission.[29]

But there was another possibility, which is where the state of Anglo-Irish relations came in. For there might be no agreement between the British and Irish Governments over what, precisely, constituted a default. This was not a matter of a breakdown in communications – contacts were so routinised that Blair and Ahern, for instance, spoke to each other at least six times between January and early February.[30] Rather, it reflected different priorities and cultures, even in this era of Anglo-Irish inter-governmental convergence. The British, who were more sensitive to the nuances of Trimble's position, were insistent upon a more extensive set of IRA commitments that would enable de Chastelain to report positively, and sought more keenly to achieve it within some kind of timeframe that would be of use to Trimble – though that did not mean that their position was identical to his, since he was not the sole consideration of policy (and, as will also be seen, different players in the British Government had different priorities). The Irish also wanted an advance on previous republican positions, but were ready to be satisfied with a vaguer language and commitments. They therefore did not give Trimble's survival as high a priority as did the British. So what if the Provisionals gave enough to satisfy the Irish but not enough to satisfy the British? Would the British still suspend without the backing of the Irish?

Mandelson, therefore, sought to probe and to test Trimble repeatedly to see whether there was any flexibility in his position. On 28 January 2000, the Secretary of State again met with Trimble at Castle Buildings. Mandelson asked how Trimble was. 'I will be worse,' retorted the First Minister. Mandelson stated that he thought that Sinn Fein/IRA were in turmoil, and that they only really appeared to be focusing on the issue of weapons now – and were becoming desperate. They would not be able to deliver by Monday 31 January, but the NIO was seeking an IRA statement of intent and details of modalities of disarmament. Mandelson said he was asking three questions: (a) would he succeed in obtaining the bare minimum requirements from the IRA – again noting the absence of McGuinness from meetings with the Provisionals; (b) is the bare minimum enough for you (Trimble) and (c) if it is not enough, what do I (Mandelson) do? He said that Adams was hotly contesting the provisions for default (that is, suspension, for which there was no legal provision). But it was also the case that his soundings inside the Unionist community were indicating that people who were previously solidly for the Agreement were now fraying. Trimble responded that the questions which Mandelson posed would not cut much ice with him and the party and that he was shocked to find out that the Sinn Fein leadership had only begun seriously to engage in that week. The UUP leader said that a requisition had been received for an extraordinary general meeting of the UUP Executive, and advised Mandelson for the first time that the 'post-dated cheque' delivered into the hands of Josias Cunningham was dated for Friday, 4 February 2000.[31] (As Trimble subsequently recalled to the author, he had deliberately left almost a week's gap between the de Chastelain report and the Cunningham letter, so as to give time to the Government for the suspension legislation to be introduced. The letter was conditional on *two* events: failure to decommission *and* failure to suspend.)[32] 'I know you feel let down, so does the Prime Minister, but we have to operate on the basis of the Agreement for which the deadline is May 2000,' replied Mandelson. Trimble then became angry and accused Mandelson of encouraging him to take the leap in November and now preparing to rat on him. 'No one is ratting on you,' said Mandelson. 'And what if you get a positive report from de Chastelain?' 'What is a positive report?' asked one of Trimble's colleagues. 'De Chastelain reports progress and expects decommissioning by May 2000,' said the Secretary of State, who then appealed to Trimble not to raise the temperature. Trimble then became very red-faced and replied that Adams had left things too late. He accused Mandelson of setting him up: republicans would continue with the peace process and the blame would fall on his own (Trimble's) head. Mandelson responded with the offended air which he could easily adopt: 'There is no benefit in casting aspersions on my motives. If you want to cast aspersions you're better off not to share them as they only cause ill will.' It was one of a string of very testy exchanges between the two men, which culminated in Mandelson observing to one colleague after a meeting, 'How can you work with anyone as rude as that? I've never encountered anyone as rude in my life.' On another occasion, an exasperated Mandelson even told Trimble, 'I wouldn't talk to my dog in that way.' But, as Mandelson recalls, if Trimble did become very rude it was because he was under enormous pressure – perhaps greater than that endured by any other figure in the process. And Mandelson would rather have Trimble vent his fury on himself as Secretary of State than on the nationalist community. Like so many of his predecessors, Mandelson would act as a sort of punchbag for the various parties.[33]

But beyond the personality clashes, the UUP drew two conclusions from this meeting: first, that Mandelson had raised the issue of how could he go about suspending the institutions when there was no mechanism to do so. Second, that he was still looking to 22 May rather than 31 January – although within days, the Secretary of State would imply in the Commons that even the 22 May deadline was not sacrosanct, either. But Trimble knew one thing throughout these exchanges: that any sign of wavering on his part would be seized upon by the British as a way of weaselling out of any obligation they might feel to pressure the Provisionals.[34] Indeed, Mandelson probed at all levels of the UUP to see whether there was more room for manoeuvre: at a dinner held by the shores of Strangford Lough at the home of Sir Dennis Faulkner (brother of the late Brian Faulkner) Mandelson raised the matter of delaying the post-dated resignation letter with another guest – Josias Cunningham. Cunningham recalled he did so in 'an off-handed way'. 'If we had an extra week, that would be useful.' Cunningham was prepared to be flexible – but if Mandelson thought the UUP president could be squared away after receiving a knighthood in the New Year's Honours List, he was sorely mistaken.[35] Cunningham's first loyalty was to the UUP, and he was quite secure enough in his social and political position to have no need of ten minutes' approbation from metropolitan elites for 'statesmanship' (his grandfather had covered the costs of the German guns sent in via Larne to arm the original UVF at the old family home at Fernhill in west Belfast).[36] In fact Cunningham was not the last representative of 'big house' Unionism, as he was so often portrayed. Rather, he was the last representative of that other breed – the independent Presbyterian capitalist class who attended private schools on the mainland.[37]

So concerned were senior Ulster Unionists, including Trimble, by Mandelson's apparent 'wobbliness' that he had recourse to the oldest of Unionist stratagems in dealing with successive Secretaries of State: to find reassurance at No. 10. This, of course, was the very thing which Mandelson's appointment was supposed to end. Indeed, on 28 January – the same day as Trimble met with the Secretary of State – John Sawers rang David Campbell, and told him that in the next week they would choreograph events to ensure that the UUP leader's position was protected (that is, that the blame would not fall on Trimble). Jonathan Powell also telephoned Campbell on Monday 31 January to ask what was best for Trimble. Campbell told him that they would need to have suspension by the end of that week: he was determined, like his boss, to prove that the Ulster Unionists were most certainly not bluffing on this occasion about pulling the plug in the event of what they saw as inadequate progress.[38] No. 10 took the prospect of Trimble's resignation more seriously than anyone else and both Sawers and Powell were adamant off the back of such information that Trimble must not be allowed to resign. As senior Ulster Unionists saw it, it was these officials who stiffened Mandelson's spine. Indeed, there were numerous reports in this period of tensions between No. 10 and the Secretary of State – especially between Powell and Mandelson, who at times was viewed by elements of the No. 10 high command as something of a potential liability. Both Eoghan Harris and Paul Bew spoke to Mandelson in this period and were struck by his jumpiness and insecurity, as though he felt himself to be very much on trial vis-à-vis the Prime Minister. Indeed, when Bew told Mandelson, 'You're going to have to move', the Secretary of State responded very edgily. 'What do you mean?' Mandelson asked nervously. Bew had to explain he meant 'move to suspend' – not to leave the Northern Ireland job and move to a mainland Cabinet portfolio![39] Mandelson's apparent brittleness was certainly picked up by the Irish Government and by Sinn Fein. This perception of Mandelson partly accounted for the determination which some displayed in late January/early February, and would have profound implications for their treatment of Mandelson later on.

The extent of Adams' desperation as the de Chastelain deadline approached was illustrated by his remarks on BBC's *Breakfast with Frost* programme on Sunday 30 January, urging Unionists 'not to hardball or go down to the wire'. He said he wanted Trimble to remain in place.[40] More ominously, he also warned that suspension would likely result in the withdrawal of the IRA interlocutor with de Chastelain. The report of the International Commission had orginally been expected on Friday 28 January, but had been delayed to allow for a further weekend of intense diplomatic activity.[41] Adams' desperation may also have owed something to the apparent reaction of constitutional nationalism, north and south of the border. On Thursday 27 January, the *Irish News* printed a front-page editorial calling for decommissioning and on Friday 28 January, after a 90-minute meeting with the Taoiseach in Dublin, John Hume intervened to call for just a gesture from the IRA to keep the institutions alive.[42] But it was to no avail. When the de Chastelain report was delivered to the two Governments at 1:30 a.m. on the morning of Tuesday 1 February –

one and a half hours after the intended deadline – it made for bleak reading.[43] '. . . our sole task is decommissioning,' the report noted, 'and to date we have received no information from the IRA as to when decommissioning will start'. There was no decommissioning, no schedule for it, nor any commitment to it in principle, now or at any time in the future. This was patently not enough for the UUC, for David Trimble himself, for the British Government – and, the British Government supposed, for the Irish Government as well. As they saw it, the republicans had clearly falsified the basis on which Trimble took the leap in November 1999. To avert the delivery by Josias Cunningham of the post-dated letter of resignation on Friday 4 February, the British would now have to introduce suspension legislation in the Commons with, they hoped, the support of the Irish and the Americans. But the Irish had other ideas. Now that the threat of suspension seemed to be more serious than ever, they wanted to give another push to the republicans so that de Chastelain could make a more positive report, thus averting the shut-down of the institutions: if they came up with enough for the Irish and hopefully the British, the ball would then be back in Trimble's court and he would have to chose between refusing to accept (so losing the blame game) and facing down a substantial portion of his UUC, so risking a split. But then if someone had to suffer a split, the Irish seemed to prefer it be the Unionists rather than the republicans. Irish officials duly applied more pressure to the republicans. According to John de Chastelain, he understood they showed Sinn Fein a copy of the decommissioning body's report.[44] The Irish officials candidly told the republicans that their failure seriously to engage really would mean suspension.

Sinn Fein then 'consulted' with the IRA. The message which came back by the afternoon was that they would seriously engage with de Chastelain and seek to resolve the crisis (in fact, notes de Chastelain, he felt the IRA was not unhappy with his report: at least, he says, 'their supporters could see that their leaders had not sold the farm').[45] The Provisionals later produced a statement which reiterated the Provisionals' 'total' commitment 'to the peace process, that the IRA wants a permanent peace, that their declaration and maintenance of the cessation, which is now entering its fifth year, is evidence of that, that the IRA's guns are silent and that there is no threat to the peace process from the IRA'. Sources close to the republican movement yet again claimed that it represented an implicit acknowledgment that 'the war is over'.[46] Even the

Irish Government recognised that it contained nothing new, but they invested huge importance in the mere fact that it was extracted at all and hoped to come up with greater specifics on intentions and timing in the coming days. Ahern called Blair and told him that this was significant and that more time was needed. He therefore pushed postponement both of the publication of the de Chastelain report, which would have made Trimble's case unanswerable, and of any suspension legislation; he also told the Dail that if the institutions were not functioning, there would be no chance of obtaining decommissioning.[47] The message was reiterated by Brian Cowen when he met with Mandelson at 4 p.m. in Iveagh House, arguing that the de Chastelain report was the property of both Governments. Some Irish officials portrayed this encounter as the Irish Foreign Minister successfully facing down a British Secretary of State for Northern Ireland hell-bent on suspension. After the meeting with Mandelson, Cowen publicly identified the positive elements, as he saw them, in the Provisionals' statement – in Irish.[48]

In fact, the key decisions may already have been taken elsewhere between Blair and Ahern. Wherever they were taken, and whatever their scepticism about the feasibility of success, the British acceded and decided to try to give it another 48 hours. The announcement about the plans to suspend would be postponed till Thursday 3 February – though some of the Irish felt that two days' grace was not quite enough and indicated that, even then, the Taoiseach would still oppose bringing such legislation before the Commons. On one level, Trimble expressed fury that the Irish helped let the IRA off the hook by the suppression of the de Chastelain report, which undermined its independence.[49] For this, Trimble blamed Mandelson rather than Blair.[50] Moreover, it meant that the British (and himself, perhaps) would have to ask Cunningham to postpone the delivery of his letter. On the other hand, though, Trimble must also have known that immediate publication of de Chastelain's report would give him no coverage at all vis-à-vis the UUC, whose worst fears about republican intentions had been vindicated. For if de Chastelain's negative report was published, Cunningham might then be forced into releasing the letter on Friday 4 February for the sake of party unity. So, in light of the fact that the British had decided to give the Provisionals a period of grace, maybe it was best from Trimble's point of view that it was suppressed: the process tied protagonists to one another in all kinds of bizarre ways. Trimble was also said to be furious that he had not been allowed to see the report, in contrast to Sinn Fein. To this day, he denies that he was shown it by Mandelson. Indeed, if he could not see a report upon which his political life depended, many Unionists asked, what was the point of having a First Minister, with all the compromises which had been made to regain office after a quarter-century?

On Wednesday 2 February, Mandelson and Trimble met at Castle Buildings at 4:30 p.m. Trimble again complained about the non-publication of the international body's report. Mandelson replied that they were still working out the details of the proposed suspension legislation, and that the time was being used for the Irish to pressure Sinn Fein, with meetings going on in Dublin all night. He thought that a genuine struggle was taking place within republicanism and that Adams was trying his best but was not prepared to put his leadership on the line. Again, Mandelson tried to probe Trimble for signs of weakness. But of one thing the UUP leader made absolutely sure: he had to have an announcement that a Bill would be introduced, if only to satisfy Josias Cunningham. He specifically needed the announcement of forthcoming suspension legislation by Thursday 3 February. The meeting of the UUC was pencilled in for Saturday 12 February. If that legislation was to make it through the Commons by then – Trimble's only hope of surviving as leader without a Provisional IRA volte face of unimaginable proportions – the House had to be notified in the previous week and since Friday was effectively only a half-day, that meant Thursday 3 February. The Irish would have known that, too. So not only did the Dublin Government maintain its strategy of pressing the republican movement to come up with something: they also appeared to employ a particularly lethal tactic to back Trimble and the British into a corner. After five leading republicans saw the Taoiseach at Government Buildings – including, significantly, McGuinness – the Irish Government again contacted their British counterpart. They hoped to have new proposals on the table which could materially alter the planned British course of action. Blair was in the west country on the next day for a political tour and the Irish proposed to call upon him whilst 'on the road'. The British support for such a meeting was conditional upon there being something new from the republican movement, whereas the Irish seemed to want it whatever happened (though if they did have something significant, so much the better). The probable reasons for their enthusiasm soon became clear – and lay in the timing. The meeting which was originally planned for the morning of Thursday

3 February was gradually put back to lunchtime, then to the early afternoon, and then to the evening – by which time the Prime Minister was in Cornwall. The British believed the Irish agenda could have been to postpone until the last possible moment. If they did that, then they could have hoped it would be too late for Mandelson to make the announcement in the Commons on Thursday – the last feasible time for clearing the legislative timetable for the suspension Bill that had to be put through Parliament in the following week. Stop the announcement, and it would make it impossible, or at a minimum much harder to bring in the legislation.[51] Finally, in the early evening of Thursday 3 February, the Irish Government Gulfstream IV jet took off with Ahern, his top aides in tow. They were driven to the Prime Minister, who was accompanied by Campbell, Sawers and Bill Jeffrey, at a hotel in St Austell in Cornwall, and talked for two hours till around 11 p.m. There, Teahon forcefully put the legal case against suspension (increasingly, Teahon would say bluntly the things which Ahern did not wish to say himself to Blair). Both men called for 'clarity' on decommissioning – code for republican pledges to do something concrete within a particular timeframe – but there was precious little that would add to earlier republican offers.

Some Ulster Unionists feared that this latest bout of Anglo-Irish summitry would blow the British off course. Trimble had certainly spent several nerve-racking days, wondering whether the British would actually announce the legislation (as so often in such situations, he relieved the tension by taking himself off in a red bus and buying stacks of CDs at Tower Records). His doubts had again been fuelled on the morning of Thursday 3 February, when he met with Mandelson at the NIO's London offices at 11 Millbank. Barry White, his Westminster assistant, recalls that he came back to the Commons afterwards and said that the Secretary of State was very wavery and that he would not commit himself to guarantee the legislation; moreover, Mandelson told Trimble that the First Minister should not castigate the Provisionals too much in any remarks he made, since that would merely stir them up.[52] Again, he found himself turning to No. 10 – and again, Jonathan Powell reassured him. Indeed, when Trimble's friend Ruth Dudley Edwards rang to find out whether the UUP leader would be 'shafted', the Prime Minister's chief of staff replied, 'Balls!' And he added, for good measure: 'We do not desert our friends.' As far as some Trimbleistas were concerned, this parting sally was only mildly reassuring![53] But Powell did not mislead Trimble. For at 7:13 p.m., as the

Taoiseach was setting off for Cornwall, Mandelson stood up and went much further than the Irish wished. He stated that the Bill would be published the next day, which would allow him to suspend and to bring back direct rule by the end of the following week when the measure would receive royal assent – while continuing efforts with the Irish Government to achieve a resolution that would make such a step unnecessary. Mandelson told the Commons that his understanding relating to the Mitchell review was that whilst there was no guarantee of decommissioning by the end of January, nor was there any ambiguity about the notion that something would happen if the Unionists jumped first. He declined to play the blame game, though he implicitly laid responsibility at the IRA's door. But the most significant interventions of the night did not come from Trimble or the UUP, even though it was their political lives which particularly depended upon the legislation. Seamus Mallon, Deputy First Minister in the Northern Ireland Executive, stated his opposition to suspension. Then, however, he formulated two of the most oft-quoted questions of the period, which he urged General de Chastelain to direct at the paramilitaries: 'will you decommission?' and 'if yes, when will you decommission?' Mandelson should then inform the Commons of the answers, consult with the Irish and only thereafter decide how to proceed. Again, Mandelson emphasised that he had no answers to those questions, and if that remained so he would have to choose the least bad of the options. More disturbing to Unionists was his answer to a question from Dominic Grieve, a first-term Conservative member. When Grieve inquired as to whether Sinn Fein would continue to benefit from the Belfast Agreement even if they had not decommissioned by the 22 May 2000 deadline, the Secretary of State replied: 'The hon. gentleman – perhaps inadvertently – puts his finger on a thorny issue. The problem for members of Sinn Fein as they would presently see it, if they had taken up their seats here and were to respond to him directly, is that, whereas the Good Friday Agreement was signed 18 months and more ago, the Executive and its institutions came into effect only last December. Therefore, they think that the timeframe has become somewhat concertina-ed. It is a matter for them to make the case on their own behalf – I am certainly not going to do so for them – but it is not unreasonable to take that into account even though it does not provide an excuse for the inaction that we have seen.' Notwithstanding Mandelson's formal disavowal of making the republican case for them, he was as good as endorsing their position on the matter of timing. The 22 May deadline was effectively bust, and they would indeed have more time to assess the quality of British concessions across a range of issues, including policing. Nor did he respond directly to John Major's question – whether Sinn Fein had presented a decommissioning plan to the IRA, and sidestepped John Maples' inquiry as to whether he had the full backing of the Irish.[54] Given such evasions, it was little wonder that Ulster Unionists were so nervous. But the statement proved sufficient to delay the delivery by Josias Cunningham of Trimble's post-dated letter of resignation.[55]

The Irish had not wanted the British to play things this way by announcing the legislation, but at another level it gave them extra muscle in their dealings with the republican movement over the weekend of 5–6 February. It was now quite clear that the British were serious about protecting Trimble's position – in some measure, if not as comprehensively as the UUP leader would wish. Three very senior Irish officials headed for Northern Ireland for the second weekend in a row.[56] Another IRA statement emerged on Saturday 5 February, as ever in the name of 'P. O'Neill': 'The British Secretary of State has accused the IRA of betrayal over the issue of decommissioning . . . we have never entered into any agreement or undertaking or understanding at any time whatsoever on any aspect of decommissioning . . . The IRA believes this crisis can be averted and the issue of the arms can be resolved. This will not be on British or unionist terms, nor will it be advanced by British legislative threats . . .' Trimble expressed disappointment over the statement, which gave no answers to Mallon's two questions – though once again Irish officials felt that the mere fact that the Provisionals were saying something was an acknowledgment that the issue had to be dealt with. For the UUP leader, it was a further agony, for he had to sit it out waiting for the Irish officials to succeed – especially when his own fifteen-minute meeting with Adams on Saturday 5 February was totally unproductive. It emerged by the following week that the first building-block in the proposed deal would entail a concrete IRA commitment to decommission in exchange for a firm schedule for British 'demilitarisation'.[57] There certainly was no doubt that the tempo was quickening: significantly, McGuinness reappeared on the scene and, according to Trimble, Adams went on a tour of every IRA 'unit'. There were days, claims the UUP leader, when he did nothing other than move from farmhouse to farmhouse in the border areas.[58] At the same time, Adams tried to ease the pressure on the republican movement by hinting that he might not stick around for ever if, as he saw it, he and his community were let down.[59] Trimble believed that Adams was trying to play his own game on a 'copycat' basis.[60]

Despite Adams' meeting with Blair at No. 10 on Tuesday 8 February, debate on the suspension legislation finally began at 3:42 p.m. Mandelson angered the Conservatives by refusing to publish the de Chastelain report, claiming it was the property of both the British and Irish Governments, and by declaring that 'anything that smacks of surrender is unjustified; nobody is seeking to humiliate anyone in these circumstances. I cannot think of anything that would be more destructive.' But he went on: 'Any cause that unites the Irish Government, the American Government, editorial writers in Dublin, Cork, Boston, Washington, and New York, the leadership and rank and file of the SDLP and public opinion in the north and south of Ireland surely cannot be wrong [Mandelson was in the habit of using nationalist territorial vocabulary accidentally/on purpose through much of his period as Ulster Secretary]. All that coalition – that breadth and wealth of opinion – has stated unambiguously that the time for decommissioning is now, and that a start must be made by the Provisional IRA.'[61] Mandelson was right enough to assert that the editorials in the leading American newspapers had all, effectively, come down against republicans for falsifying the basis upon which Trimble took the leap in November 1999 – and that gave him and the Government much confidence in pressing ahead with the suspension legislation.[62] Trimble had more to cheer about in this opening speech than from the previous week's announcement of the legislation. 'If we do not put the operation of the institutions on hold, subsequent events would so severely compromise and shatter their operation, that they would rapidly and irreversibly unravel,' said Mandelson at Second Reading. 'No hon. Member should doubt – I do not believe that any hon. Member will doubt – that the First Minister and his colleagues would resign their positions in view of the loss of confidence in the Executive and the institutions. We must be clear about what would ensue if we lost the First Minister from his position. First, the Deputy First Minister [Mallon] would automatically cease to hold office at the same time. I cannot choose, or wave a magic wand, to change that. As sure as night follows day, consequences would follow. No other credible candidates would secure a majority of Unionists and a majority of nationalists in the Assembly. An alternative First Minister and Deputy First Minister would have to do that if they were to stand any chance of election. The cross-community majority would not exist for another ticket. In such circumstances, I would be obliged within six weeks to call fresh Assembly elections. At best, those elections would cement the existing stalemate. At worst, they would further polarise the divisions that have emerged, and make conducting a successful review almost impossible – let alone reverting to the existing Executive and institutions. The last thing to have emerged from those circumstances would be another consensual, cross-party Government in Northern Ireland. The Government of Northern Ireland would simply cease to operate. I will not let that Government simply collapse into a black hole.' At Third Reading, Mandelson was more explicit still: 'We are not considering any individual. We are not trying to save the skin of the right hon. Member for Upper Bann [Mr Trimble], although his skin is pretty valuable and worth saving if we can. I believe that because he has shown admirable leadership of his party; because we would never have formed the Executive and set up the institutions without him; because he has a great deal of leadership left in him; and because, if he relinquished the leadership of the UUP, I would fear for the consequences for Northern Ireland, given his likely replacement.'[63]

These were the clearest admissions to date by a senior British minister that Trimble had, indeed, become the minority shareholder in Unionism. Trimble's own contribution at Second Reading stage was a summary of events leading to the Mitchell deal in November 1999 and an explanation of why he took the jump – though in response to an intervention from the former Conservative Cabinet minister, Douglas Hogg, he declined to give details of where and when he received the undertakings from republicans about what would happen if he moved first. He was also certain that even if the IRA answered the two Mallon questions of Thursday 3 February, it would not be enough. And even certain kinds of gestures would not be enough, either: 'Some people in the press are saying that, in the past, the method used by the IRA in similar situations was to dump their arms. It has been suggested that they might be sufficient in the present circumstances. However, may I say to the Secretary of State – in case he is not fully aware of it – that some very misleading impressions have been given about the dumping of arms? The instruction issued by the leadership of the IRA in, I think 1925 [in fact, in 1923], to its members to dump arms was not an instruction to disarm and no disarmament occurred. Arms were put in dumps, but they were put in them for future use.' He counselled members to read Sean O'Callaghan's book, *The Informer*, in which the exiled Kerryman dug old 'dumped' weapons out of the ground when the Troubles began: if weapons are stored properly, they do not rust.[64] It was a remarkable performance, as much for the occasion as for what he actually said: for here was a man who ten years earlier, on 8 February 1990, had been an obscure, middle-ranking academic at a provincial university, on the periphery of his party. Ten years on, here he was at Westminster – with the Commons, Whitehall, the Irish Government, the White House, and much of the world's media focused on how to avert his resignation. And in the debate, only three well-known sympathisers for a united Ireland – Tony Benn, Jeremy Corbyn and John McDonnell – had sided against him. Against that, there was an overwhelming consensus of Tories, Liberal Democrats and even many other independent-minded Labour MPs (as well as the payroll vote and the usual loyalists) who understood his dilemma. The Bill passed by 352 votes to 11 on Second Reading. Most significantly, these 11 noes included the Deputy First Minister, Seamus Mallon: he said he would hold Unionists and republicans equally responsible and that there would 'be no such thing as a soft landing' if the institutions were suspended.[65] But at a personal level, Trimble was exhausted for much of this debate and the preceding announcement of the Bill's introduction on Thursday 3 February: on both days, there were moments when he nearly fell asleep in the chamber.

The vigour with which Trimble pursued the point about the unacceptability of the dumping of weapons suggested that even at this late stage, he feared that the British Government might still prove susceptible to such a last-minute offer. There was no shortage of ideas floating around: on Wednesday 9 February, the Roman Catholic Bishop of Derry, Dr Seamus Hegarty, suggested in the *Irish News* that he was willing to play the role of guarantor and supervisor of IRA weapons for a year under the auspices of de Chastelain. This step had the full support of Archbishop Brady, the Catholic Primate, and was welcomed by the SDLP and UUP alike. 'Effectively, it was another way for the Roman Catholic Church to offer to facilitate decommissioning,' recalls Trimble.[66] Privately, he opined to his intimates that, hitherto, the hierarchy had not appeared committed strongly either way on decommissioning: it added to Trimble's feeling that the UUP now occupied the much-vaunted 'moral high ground'. It was a welcome boost as Trimble went to No. 10 for a midday meeting with Blair. Alun Michael had been forced to resign as First Secretary of the Welsh Assembly that day and Trimble darkly joked that the Prime Minister might be about to lose a second leader of a devolved administration. The Prime Minister told the UUP leader that the ball was in Sinn Fein/IRA's court. He believed that Sinn Fein were trying to do something, but that he did not hold out any great hope at the moment of a breakthrough and that if the institutions went into suspension it was important to sustain some form of dialogue with the republicans (an early hint that he did not wish Trimble to go too hard on Sinn Fein/IRA in playing the 'blame game'). Blair was particularly anxious not to lose the support of the US Administration, but Trimble said that the editorials in the American newspapers had been excellent. The First Minister of Northern Ireland expressed one particular fear: that there might be an 'accident' with Josias Cunningham. The UUP president had control of the post-dated resignation letter and might bump into Lord Alderdice and hand it to him there and then.[67] Trimble left with no doubt of Blair's resolve, but he still felt that if the Provisionals came up with something – either in the shape of a promise to do something in future or a procedural engagement with de Chastelain – then Blair would say to the UUP 'Oh, you'll have to move.'[68] There was also much speculation that Ahern might rush to London for a last-minute summit with Blair prior to the expiry of the week's grace on Friday 11 February, prior to the UUC meeting scheduled for the following day. Yet when Trimble arrived in Dublin on the next day for meetings at Government Buildings – to secure the support from Ahern which he imagined he had obtained in November 1999 – the Taoiseach had no dramatic progress to report. Yes, Adams and McGuinness were working on something and Ahern said that he had told the Sinn Fein president that he had to visit Trimble and explain personally to the UUP leader what he was trying to do.[69] Again, Trimble obtained the impression that Ahern was still very much against suspension – a point which the Taioseach had made explicitly in the Dail earlier, asserting that it would run contrary to the Belfast Agreement.[70]

But the main significance of the meeting lay in the renewed Irish emphasis upon the legal and constitutional difficulties with suspension. When the British had first heard this in late January, they had wondered how serious their counterparts in Dublin were – and so for a period of days did not apprise Trimble lest he think that this represented a hint that their resolve was weakening. Broadly, the southern Government felt that having taken the Belfast Agreement by implication into their new Constitution (which changed the old Articles 2 and 3), any suspension of those institutions would be unconstitutional. If the Irish Government joined with the British, they could expose themselves to a republican challenge in the southern Supreme Court. Whilst they would not definitely lose, defeat would be a catastrophe for the Dublin Government. Trimble, who was perfectly competent to deal with such arguments from the experts, believed that the Irish were bluffing on this issue: he argues that law is a creative art in this area, not a science. Yet he took it seriously enough to direct his principal private secretary, David Lavery – himself no mean lawyer – to go through the matter with the then Irish Attorney General, Michael McDowell.[71] Any British suspension Bill would also require matching primary legislation in the Republic: provisions automatically to return the powers devolved by the two Governments to the North-South Ministerial Council and the BIC (the BIIGC would continue to operate as before so that the British and Irish could still discuss the most sensitive of Northern Irish matters). But would the six cross-border implementation bodies go, too? Or would they continue their 'harmonising' functions during suspension, without any supervision from Ulster's elected ministers and Assembly? The British were solid about putting these in the deep freeze, but the Irish were less so, asserting that they would have to remain in being because of contractual obligations to staff and reassignment of responsibilities. This lacuna would have exposed Trimble politically within Northern Ireland, and caused further friction between the Ulster Unionists and the Irish in the weeks to come.[72]

With the Assembly hurtling towards suspension, Trimble began to focus on the 'how' rather than the 'whether'. He was persuaded of one thing by Barry White, his Westminster assistant: that if members of the Ulster Unionist Council had gone to bed on the night of Friday 11 February without hearing about the suspension on the 6 p.m. news they might be in a state of panic by the time they arrived at the meeting in Belfast on Saturday 12 February (especially those from the west of the Province who left their homes in Fermanagh and Tyrone at around 7:30 a.m. the next morning).[73] Trimble accepted the suggestion: Reg Empey also recalls him saying that it had to be on the nightly news as many of his 'folk' would not read the newspapers in the morning and that if the announcement missed the tea-time bulletins on the night before, that was it.[74] The UUP leader duly made the point to Mandelson. But the drama shifted back to the efforts of the top Irish officials to persuade the republicans to move at the 11th hour, partly in the hope of securing an offer that was good enough to allow for another Anglo-Irish summit, perhaps in London. The three civil servants were collected by a republican Toyota at around 11 p.m. on Thursday/Friday 11/12 February from Jury's Hotel in Belfast under what one senior British official calls 'a huge cloak of mystery'. They were then driven to a house somewhere in nationalist west Belfast (they knew not where precisely) owned by an elderly couple. They waited for two hours, talking about everything under the sun except the issue at hand. When the owners asked what they were doing there, the officials simply said that they were 'up and down for a few days'. They were then collected and driven to another part of west Belfast. There, waiting for them in a terraced house, were Adams, McGuinness, Aidan McAteer (McGuinness' special adviser) and Gerry Kelly. 'It was one of the hardest meetings ever,' recalls one of the veteran participants. The republicans asked if the Irish believed that Trimble would be prepared to withdraw his threat of resig- nation. They suggested that if Trimble were put up against the wall, then the Unionists would cave in – and the UUP leader would have set up the Executive in July 1999 had he really been pressed by the British. As they saw it, Trimble had 'more in his tank' than he had let on, not least because he was so keen on office. If he fell, he would fall a great distance and so was not in any kind of position to dictate terms. If the republican movement now 'jumped to it' on the basis of the post-dated cheque, they would be bedevilled, as they saw it, by one Unionist precon- dition after another. The Irish officials assured the republicans that Trimble would not withdraw his resignation, at least on the basis of what was currently on offer. They soon proceeded to the substance of the negotiation. The Irish officials were not allowed to take away the draft IRA statement, but they could copy it down in their own long-hand – and they made frequent amendments to the republican document, with words crossed out and reinserted. It was not as good as the Irish had wanted it to be, yet it was better than they feared. The Irish sought three things in particular: first, a statement that a solution to the conflict could be reached by exclusively peaceful means; second, that arms would be put 'beyond use'; third, given that arms would not immediately be put beyond use in a way that would satisfy others, what gesture/confidence- building measure could be offered 'up front'? They obtained the second of their aims: effectively, the formulation had originally been crafted at

Hillsborough in March/April 1999 by the Irish as a polite way of describing the destruction of weapons. There was also a possibility of attaining the third goal. There was a lot of to-ing and fro-ing in and out of the room, and the Irish team were regularly asked to go into the kitchen whilst the northern republicans deliberated amongst themselves over the acceptability of the reformulation. The officials feared it was too distant an offer in time terms and too imprecise for what Trimble required; but they also believed that it was probably 'in advance of what the Army would tolerate' ('the Army' referred to in this instance is the IRA). The Irish mandarins then repaired to Jury's Hotel at around 3 a.m., where they typed up the statement on a laptop borrowed from the British-Irish Secretariat at Windsor House: significantly, they did not plug it in but operated the machine on battery power for security reasons. The officials then flew back in the early hours to Dublin on a Beechcraft aeroplane and headed for the Grand Hotel in Malahide, Co. Dublin, where the Taoiseach and the Foreign Minister had gathered with other colleagues for a routine Fianna Fail party meeting on election strategy.

The officials took Ahern and Cowen through the paper. The IRA document, though, came with procedural conditions attached: it was only communicated to the Taoiseach and Prime Minister as a republican leadership paper that was private to those two heads of Government. But the key negative aspect was that it was not to be given to David Trimble. Partly, this was because the statement, as they saw it, was so far in advance of anything they had put forward to their own grassroots that they feared the internal movement reaction to any leaks by Ulster Unionists. And there was another condition attached: if it was to be given to Trimble, it would have to be on the basis that the British would have to accept it first. Ahern and Cowen decided it was not as good as they wanted – but nonetheless felt that it could be built upon further. The Taoiseach duly telephoned Blair soon after 10 a.m. He sought to persuade Blair that he, in turn, should try and convince Trimble that it was good enough – although how he was supposed to do that when the UUP leader could not have sight of its contents was unclear (it may be that Ahern calculated that the British would effectively inform him of its contents, anyhow). 'Let me look at it,' said Blair and it was duly faxed over to No. 10 (which, in turn, informed Mandelson, who was in Belfast).[75] According to Mitchel McLaughlin, the chairman of Sinn Fein, both Ahern and Blair accepted the document that morning in conversations with Gerry Adams.[76]

Certainly, the British were happy enough to look at anything. 'Both the Prime Minister and Taoiseach agreed it was serious, and potentially significant,' recalls Mandelson. 'But something more had to happen.'[77] That 'something more', Blair concluded, was that both Trimble and de Chastelain would have to see it. Adams duly agreed that the text should be shown to de Chastelain. He would thus be able to incorporate any new developments into his next report about republican intentions to disarm. The effect of this new development was that suspension, which had been originally scheduled for midday on Friday 11 February, was put back until 2:30–3:00 p.m. De Chastelain was told at midday that there was a draft IRA leadership statement available, but his problem was that he had no idea of what could be said on the record. Without that public assurance, Trimble definitely could not move, and Blair said as much to Ahern when they spoke again at around 12:30 p.m. Meanwhile, he urged Adams to go and see Trimble and give him a confidential briefing as to what was in the IRA statement so that the Ulster Unionist leader might be able to judge for himself whether there had been any movement within republican ranks and thus to forestall suspension. Initially, Adams appeared happy to do this, but there was to be a further twist to the tale.

By midday, Trimble was at UUP headquarters at Glengall Street with members of the Assembly group. There, he took a call from Mandelson, who briefed him – but not in great detail. The Secretary of State reported that the IRA would make a statement in the context of the 'full implementation' of the Belfast Agreement (i.e. swifter 'demilitarisation' etc.). Trimble again told Mandelson that there was no certainty of intent and no timetable in this. The IRA proposal was thus insufficient and he would resign if there was no suspension. As the Trimbleistas saw it, Mandelson was clearly 'flirting' with the IRA statement as a basis for postponing suspension. Jonathan Powell rang at about this time and again reassured the Unionists that the British Government would not blink – but that a couple more weeks would be helpful in order to test the seriousness of the IRA offer. Again, the Ulster Unionists declined to budge. Shortly thereafter, No. 10 rang once more and gave further details – designed, again, to buy a bit more time. It was, they argued, essential that Sir Josias Cunningham not release his resignation letter in the light of the significant IRA statement. They said that the IRA was claiming (1) that the peace process contained the potential to resolve the conflict and (2) that in the context of full implementation of the Belfast Agreement and in the context of ending the causes of conflict (that is, a process leading towards the end of Partition) they would engage in a process finally to place weapons beyond use. It also emerged that there was no clarity and no timescale for the latter offer. As No. 10 saw it, the proposal represented a commitment in principle – indicating that the IRA had blinked – but it lacked specificity. There were four possible options: (a) to suspend; (b) not to suspend (which would destroy Trimble and was thus an impossibility); (c) Trimble postponing the UUC meeting and (d) a post-dated suspension. This meant Mandelson would sign the suspension order, but that it would only make it effective four weeks hence, seven days after another de Chastelain report. Trimble did not dismiss (c) and (d) out of hand when it was presented to him, but he did not think that the UUC could wait for a few more weeks. Indeed, when Trimble showed himself to be determined, No. 10 rapidly moved off this effort to present alternatives.

Trimble was becoming increasingly detached by this point – indeed, according to one participant in the day's events, it was almost as if he was reconciling himself to a life after politics. Cunningham was on his way to Parliament Buildings to see Alderdice at 4 p.m., and time was rapidly running out. There was now only one person who could persuade Trimble that the offer was serious and that he should pull back from the brink: Martin McGuinness, who had gradually re-emerged from his ministerial purdah in recent days, supposedly to 're-engage' with the IRA. Trimble had always preferred him to Adams, regarding him as more straightforward and more crucial to delivering the apolitical militarists in the republican movement. According to Stephen Collins of the *Sunday Tribune*, the meeting was arranged by Mandelson.[78] So when McGuinness arrived shortly after 2 p.m. at Trimble's office at Parliament Buildings, some in his circle thought that it was a hopeful sign: the Derryman would surely only come if there was something substantive to discuss. But McGuinness gave no hint of what it might contain. Instead, he gave Trimble three ultimata in a totally calm and clinical way. First, that the UUC meeting of Saturday 12 February had to be cancelled and that there were to be no further meetings of that body of this nature; second, he had to countermand and withdraw the letter of resignation; third, the suspension legislation had to be revoked. There was no effort whatsoever to explain to Trimble what was contained in the IRA offer. Trimble, for his part, did not push McGuinness to tell him what was in the document. 'I was in listening mode,' he recalls.[79] It is obvious that Trimble did not want to push McGuinness into making an offer which might be enough for nationalist Ireland, but would place him in an impossible position between the UUC and the British Government. Afterwards, Trimble observed: 'I think I'm being conned.' Paddy Teahon, who spoke to McGuinness later, expressed frustration that he had made no effort to sell the deal to the UUP leader. 'He didn't ask me,' replied the Derryman. But since Sinn Fein had moved, Teahon was also frustrated with what he saw as Trimble's lack of flexibility.[80] Meanwhile, Trimble's office began to fill up. Sir Josias Cunningham arrived, and the entourage included Taylor, Empey, Michael McGimpsey and David Campbell. The tension was rising: Empey recalls that Trimble was pacing the room, fiddling with the newspapers and making lots of telephone calls.[81] Cunningham had the letter with him and said that a cut-off was needed and Taylor opined that matters had to be brought to a head. Trimble called Mandelson shortly after 3 p.m. and told him that Cunningham and the entire group were determined to hold firm. 'On the basis of what I have heard, I can't budge and I would be voted down tomorrow if I did,' said Trimble. 'I have the president here' – and handed the telephone to Cunningham. At 12:45, Cunningham had already turned down an earlier offer from Mandelson's then principal private secretary, Nick Perry, to meet with the Secretary of State, on the grounds that there was nothing constructive to talk about. ('I don't want to be brainwashed,' Cunningham recalled saying at the time.) He was equally firm on this occasion. When Mandelson told the UUP president 'we should be courteous to de Chastelain and await upon his report before suspending', Cunningham retorted, 'I am all for courtesy but there is a limit.' He went on: 'Unless we have an awful lot more, I will put the letters in. Why don't we just get on with it, I'm not going beyond 4:30.'[82] The Ulster Unionists soon learned from Nick Perry and Bill Jeffrey that suspension orders had been prepared and were en route to the Secretary of State at about 4:30 p.m. At this point, the British had some indication of what de Chastelain might say in his anticipated, second report – but it was much weaker than they needed to persuade Trimble that it was worth looking at. Had the IRA produced a concrete public statement committing itself to decommissioning and a timetable (the answers to the two Mallon questions) the British would not have suspended – even at this late stage.

At around 4:20 p.m., Blair told Adams that suspension was now inevitable.[83] Although Adams remonstrated that this was in breach of the

Belfast Agreement, he was nonetheless keen to leave the telephone quickly. The reason for this soon became apparent: if suspension was bound to happen, the republican movement had to avoid taking the blame by taking the bad gloss off the first de Chastelain report. Much better, from their point of view, to turn it back on the British for their alleged perfidy – which would provide a compelling narrative for nationalist Ireland and split the British Government from its Irish counterpart. If it could at least be seen that the republicans had made a dramatic last-minute offer, which had then been thrown back in their face by the British who had again succumbed to an updated version of the 'Orange card', then something might yet be salvaged. So Adams hurriedly left the telephone to draft a 'flexible' new statement – in which he claimed there had been an unspecified 'significant proposition to resolve the arms issue'. He announced it at 5:15 p.m., some twelve minutes after Mandelson signed the suspension order but forty minutes before the suspension was made public at 5:55 p.m.[84] Adams' announcement made it sound as though he had heard nothing about an impending suspension.[85] Thus, when news of suspension did emerge, it appeared to many Irish nationalists that the British, and the Ulster Secretary in particular, had been so hellbent on suspension that they had ignored a courageous last-minute initiative from the Sinn Fein leadership.

In fact, for all of the Irish anger subsequently directed at the Secretary of State, the Ulster Unionists believed that it was No. 10 which was more solidly in favour of suspension than Mandelson. For reasons which will become apparent, it suited nationalist Ireland and especially the Irish Government to blame not the Prime Minister but, rather, one of his principal lieutenants (Blair was certainly very regretful over the telephone to Ahern when suspension actually took place). Mandelson had sought every way out of suspension, perhaps even more vigorously than No. 10. But, as he observes, 'even if we had got a workable [de Chastelain] report, what could we do for Trimble and the Unionists – we had literally run out of time'.[86] When Trimble heard the news of suspension, he did not smile: instead, those present took a stiff glass of whisky, rather than uncorked champagne. Despite the most dramatic political victory won by a Unionist leader in years – a reassertion of British sovereign power at his behest by a Labour Government in the face of the collective opposition of the Irish Government, SDLP and Sinn Fein/IRA and the neutrality of the US Administration – he was utterly flat. When he saw

Daphne Trimble that night for a Mahler concert at the Waterfront Hall, she recalls that he was utterly phelgmatic. 'Well, that's that,' he said, much as he did when he came home on the night on which the Belfast Agreement was signed on 10 April 1998 ('you know how un-dramatic David can be,' she adds).[87] Indeed, some minutes before Mandelson signed the suspension order, Adams had also called Trimble. Despite the enormous tension, it was not an acrimonious conversation: Trimble told Adams that they must make sure that they did not lose the whole process. 'I had no alternative,' Trimble told the Sinn Fein president regretfully. 'I would have had to have resigned. There is not enough in this.' One observer noted the UUP leader's calmness in dealing with the enemy, which formed such a contrast to his dealings with some of his own folk. Although he was not triumphalist about it, Trimble nonetheless saw the last-minute IRA statement as a vindication of his belief that the Provisionals only moved if they were given a serious jolt. He was also amazed that in offering too little, too late, 'they made things so easy for me'.[88] In retrospect, even some senior Irish figures conceded that Trimble was right to have done what he did in holding the Provisionals' feet to the fire.[89]

Salvaging something from the process, and the exigencies of the 'blame game', now became the main consideration in the aftermath of suspension. Elements in the highest reaches of the British Government felt that they could have identified Sinn Fein as the defaulting party – much as President Clinton in the same year would point the finger at the late Hafez al-Assad of Syria for the failure of the Geneva summit with Israel and Yasser Arafat for the failure of the Camp David talks. But they concluded that to have done so would have 'knocked republicans out of the process for good'.[90] So at around 6:20 p.m. Jonathan Powell rang the Unionists to say that when the second de Chastelain report came out, they should be as positive as possible: having dragged republicans so far, No. 10 did not wish the efforts of the Sinn Fein leadership to be utterly damned.[91] Trimble largely acceded to this request. Partly, it was because the UUP were genuinely grateful to Blair. As Powell recalls, the Unionists really believed that the Government would let them down over the crisis, and were pleasantly surprised when the British did not do so![92] But Trimble did not pull his punches solely out of deference to Blair, who had saved his political skin. The UUP leader also did not rub salt into the historic enemy's wounds because he genuinely lamented the collapse of the inclusive Executive which he still saw (on the right terms) as the best guarantee of the Province's stability.

Trimble was thus the least of the British problems. The further difficulty with which they had to contend was that 'the waters were now so muddied' (to use the words of one senior official). Not only was it quite unclear what was on offer from the IRA, but also on what basis and especially what could be said to whom. In the half-hour to hour following the signing of the suspension order, intense discussions took place between de Chastelain and the republicans revolving round what the General could say in public on the back of the new IRA statement that would form the basis of his second report; even the Irish Government was not fully aware of what was going on between them. At 6:45 p.m. the first (and suppressed) de Chastelain report of 31 January was published, which soon prompted much speculation about the imminent publication of the next instalment (republicans claimed this negative first report had been leaked to afford Mandelson cover for his decision to suspend). At 9 p.m., the second de Chastelain report, dated 11 February, was released. Paragraph 5 revealed that the IRA had told de Chastelain that 'the IRA will consider how to put arms and explosives beyond use, in the context of the full implementation of the Good Friday Agreement, and in the context of the removal of the causes of conflict'. Paragraphs 7 and 8 of the second de Chastelain report further added that the Provisionals had made clear to the Commission 'the context in which the IRA will initiate a comprehensive process to put arms beyond use, in a manner as to ensure maximum public confidence. The Commission believes that this commitment, on the basis described above, holds out the real prospect of an agreement which would enable it to fulfil its mandate.' The Irish regarded this as a hugely significant development in the history of republicanism: Deaglan de Breadun, then Northern Editor of the *Irish Times*, claimed to have been told by unnamed 'senior political sources' that republicans held out the possibility of a permanent end to the IRA's 30-year campaign and a standing-down of the Provisionals. But this required restoration of the institutions and full-blooded participation by the Ulster Unionists in the institutions. Moreover, the Provisionals were not prepared to take any steps before 22 May 2000, arguing that the clock started ticking with the creation of the Executive in December rather than with the 1998 referendum.[93] The Irish Government was surprised by the timing of the new IRA announcement, but thought it would be enough to reverse suspension. Neither Trimble nor the British believed this to be the case, though the UUP leader recalls Mandelson nonetheless telling him at the time that he thought that the new IRA statement could definitely be built upon.[94] Trimble, too, did not close the window on such reasoning. He told the *Breakfast with Frost* pro- gramme on BBC1 on Sunday 13 February that 'the question is, of course, whether the republicans are genuine, whether they do have a plan or whether what we saw at the last minute was just a PR exercise' – scarcely the sign of someone who wanted to place Sinn Fein beyond the pale.[95] Much of this, however, was lost in the mêlée. Republicans rounded on the Irish Government for not doing enough to avert suspension; and whether because of that, or in anticipation of such attacks, the key figures in the southern state appeared ever more aggressive in their dealings with the British. At one point, during the course of a conversation between Ahern and Blair, Paddy Teahon became so irate that he was handed the telephone by the Taoiseach – and proceeded to give the Prime Minister an earful about Mandelson: he did not believe that the British had been straight about their intentions or the *ex post facto* rationalisations for what they had done. Unbeknownst to Teahon, Mandelson was of course listening in on the other end of the line, having been plugged in by the Downing Street switchboard.

Of greater concern was the Provisional IRA response to these develop- ments: 'P. O'Neill' informed de Chastelain that the IRA statement of Friday 11 February was off the table and that he, the representative, was breaking off contact with the Commission. Indeed, according to Trimble there was a 'serious wobble' in the republican leadership on the afternoon/early evening of Friday 11 February and the IRA representative had to be replaced by another.[96] (De Chastelain, though, says that there was never any change of representative, whoever that may have been.)[97] The two Governments knew about this development over the weekend of 12/13 February and it was publicly confirmed in an IRA statement on the night of Tuesday 15 February. But even then, de Chastelain recalls him saying, 'John, I hope we will be working together again.' The implica- tion was that it was goodbye, but not farewell. There was nothing personal, and what he had to say, believed de Chastelain, was more in sorrow than in anger. It seemed that he was much more annoyed with the British, and especially with Mandelson and his advisers than with Trimble and the Unionists. The representative said that more time was needed to prepare the grassroots for progress towards decommissioning.[98] Sinn Fein's public line was full of dark hints. Indeed, Mitchel McLaughlin says that the situation has similarities, as far as republicans were concerned, to that which obtained in 1996–7, when British demands on decommissioning, as much as the Unionists, caused the difficulties which led to the breakdown of the first IRA ceasefire.[99]

Did, then, Trimble's 'post-dated cheque' play a large part in Adams' failure to deliver? Republicans claimed that they would have moved had Trimble not stepped outside of the terms of the Mitchell review. Significantly, however, republicans never made good their threat of early February – that they could, in the event of suspension, produce documents showing that there was no basis in the proceedings of the Mitchell review for such an act.[100] There is also evidence to show that some of the darker concerns of certain British officials were not without substance – and that the republicans never intended to move on arms, whatever Trimble had done at the UUC meeting. First of all, the reported Ferris–Doherty remarks were made before the UUP leader issued his post-dated cheque in late November. Nor, subsequently, was there much in the way of concrete intelligence suggesting that the republicans would move (whereas there was stacks of secret information to suggest they would not do so). And as Mandelson notes, there was insufficient evidence of preparation of the republican grassroots, either in the run-up to November's deal or thereafter: the republicans never seemed to expect there to be any successful conclusion to the Mitchell review. When the republican leadership did take the new proposals to the 'volunteers', the response was a dusty one at best – and, as Mandelson recalls, it was at times threatening.[101]

Meanwhile, Mandelson was swiftly repositioning himself. For he was being hit by a tidal wave of abuse from nationalist Ireland – far more so than Trimble. And it was an apparent anger which bound together those who came from northern physical force traditions with those cautious bureaucrats who had spent their lives within the confines of the greater Dublin area. In the words of one senior figure in the Irish state, 'the king of spin met his match'.[102] That Mandelson received the blame said much about his and Blair's respective operating modes. Indeed, both Ulster Unionist and Irish Government narratives of the suspension crisis have one thing in common: both believe that Blair was basically on their side. Thus, Trimble believed that Mandelson wobbled in the run-up to suspension, whereas the Irish (and republicans such as Mitchel McLaughlin) believed that Mandelson was far more hellbent on doing it.[103] Possibly there was some pre-choreography whereby Mandelson allowed Blair to play the 'good guy' to everyone. The alternative explanation is that Blair used Mandelson ruthlessly and was quite happy to allow a very close subordinate to 'take the flak'. Partly, also, Mandelson was blamed because the Irish chose to play it that way. For Ahern was reported to have quickly sent out the word to his key subordinates that whilst the British were to be blamed for the crisis, Blair had to be exempted from any criticism: the old ploy of blaming wicked advisers rather than the king.[104] It is not clear how grateful Blair was for being thus exempted, and what he was disposed to give in return. But what is also intriguing is how rapidly republicans grasped the necessity of not attacking Blair: the responses of pan-nationalism were remarkably similar, and remarkably disciplined.

There were also personality-related factors militating against Mandelson. 'He is gay, Jewish and English,' says Trimble. 'His tone, his coolness and his hauteur further irritated nationalist Ireland. They can't dump on Blair. He stood there in the Dail [on his visit in 1998 after the Belfast Agreement], is married to an English Roman Catholic and has an Irish mother [of Donegal Protestant stock].'[105] Stephen Collins, of the *Sunday Tribune*, one of Dublin's leading journalists, is not so sure if Mandelson's homosexuality and Jewish origins were relevant, since many Irish nationalists would certainly be unaware of the latter (Mandelson, in any case, is not Halachically Jewish, since his mother was a gentile, and he was not brought up in the faith, and certainly does not practise it). Rather, Mandelson's unpopularity owed much more to his style. Many nationalists felt he behaved more like a Tory minister than a Labour one. His lofty manner provoked a negative response, particularly from people with strong republican views. In that sense, he was more like Mayhew than Mowlam.[106] Nor did he much warm to the camaraderie and bonhomie of Irish socialising, whether in Northern Ireland or amongst the diaspora: he did not find it easy to engage in back-slapping in bars.

Moreover, the Irish felt that he had not levelled with them over suspension – though, in fact, he was inconsistent rather than consciously mendacious. It was certainly a shock to Mandelson, who had never previously been caught in the cross-fire of ethnic politics. For he believed beforehand that he really did have the Irish on board and that both Governments would stand shoulder to shoulder. But he drew few long-term conclusions about the nature of Irish state culture from this episode: instead, he subsequently sought to blur the differences between himself and the Irish, and not always successfully. The most obvious example of his desire to insinuate himself into the good books of nationalist Ireland occurred during his interview with Marian Finucane on RTE in the following month. There, he recalled watching Trooping the Colour in childhood, and described the Foot Guards as 'chinless wonders', thus prompting an outcry from relatives of soldiers slain in the course of the Troubles; General Sir Charles Guthrie, then Chief of the Defence Staff, was also inundated with apoplectic calls from retired Guards officers.[107] Mandelson offered a demi-apology to the Commanding Officer of the Household Division, but some in No. 10 wondered whether the Ulster Secretary was not always one bright remark away from trouble.[108]

Above all else, nationalist Ireland was upset by the substance of the suspension fiasco. 'Mandelson succumbed to the unionist veto' stated an IRA spokesman in *An Phoblacht/Republican News* of 17 February. 'So responsibility for the crisis rests squarely on his shoulders.' It was evidence to them that 'the Orange card' could still successfully be played, even under a Labour Government with a massive majority, and under a dispensation that was meant to have banished this sort of thing for ever.[109] They saw it as an illegal act, whereby the British chose to place their domestic law over international obligations in the shape of the Belfast Agreement (in fact, no Sinn Fein legal challenge materialised).[110] But for all of that anger, British officials still could not understand why all of the key components of nationalist Ireland – the southern Government, the SDLP and Sinn Fein/IRA – miscalculated so badly on suspension. As Peter Bell observed, reflecting on his days in the NIO: 'Why is it that Anglo-Irish relations should still be bedevilled by mutual misunderstanding and recrimination some fifteen years after the Hillsborough accord of 15 November 1985, despite the unparalleled intensification of routine meetings? And why should this have obtained between two Governments which prided themselves on their "civilised" and very "modern" natures – which were headed by two men who sought so self-consciously to banish the ghosts of the past and to create an "era of good feelings"?'[111] Trimble recalls a certain complacency: 'Bertie would tell me he was still working on things and that there was movement. But my sense of the whole period was reluctance to face hard facts, a degree of wishful thinking. It's like somebody brushing away what he doesn't want to hear.'[112] Again, personality factors may have been crucial here. 'You can't ignore Bertie's political character,' believes one Dublin insider. 'He's nice to Trimble, and to anyone else, so long as there is no real price attached to it. If he can, he puts off crucial decisions. But in a crunch, he can revert to a more traditional Fianna Fail sort of response. I think it was easier for him to blame the British than to take on republicans.'[113] Indeed, one of the reasons why nationalist Ireland gave the British this roasting was precisely because they never wished to endure such an experience again, and were determined to drive home to their counterparts in London just how costly they could make such ventures in future.

Hitherto, British officials had been struck by how warm the Trimble–Ahern relationship had been: whatever the DFA or other Irish officials advised the Taoiseach, the First Minister was sure that as a fellow politician his southern counterpart would understand his predicament and would come through at the end of the day. In fact, there was profound disappointment on the UUP side when Ahern did not do so. In private, he expressed anger with the Irish and had some fierce exchanges with both Cowen and his deputy, Liz O'Donnell. On 8 March at Castle Buildings, Trimble told them that he had a 'major problem' with how the Irish Government had acted following suspension and that a major breach of faith had to be repaired. Cowen ignored this remark, preferring instead to ask what kind of review the UUP leader wanted (to which Trimble had earlier made reference). After some discussion of this matter, Cowen asked Trimble what was the 'breach of faith' to which he referred. The First Minister (suspended) replied that there would never have been devolution but for the assurances which he had been given, both privately and publicly – therefore it turned out that in his view the word of the Irish Government was 'worthless'.[114] Yet although Trimble felt let down, he thought the Irish had failed him mainly out of weakness rather than malignancy. He never appears to have taken the darker view: that the Irish knew that a crisis was coming and regarded Trimble (as one Irish figure told Reg Empey) as 'a necessary road kill'.[115] Indeed, the Irish appear to have anticipated that there was trouble ahead but did little: as has been noted, this author knew from senior Irish officials in early January that Adams et al. did not have the votes in any 'Army Convention' to do anything on arms – knowledge to which Ahern must have been privy. At a minimum, what can be said is that if Ahern had wanted to prepare the Fianna Fail caucus for the task of making good any guarantee to Trimble, he would have done so: after all, in early 1998, well ahead of the Belfast Agreement, he had patiently explained to his party in the Oireachtas that the scrapping of Articles 2 and 3 was indispensable to any settlement in 'the North'. In consequence, the constitutional changes did not become a serious issue in the May 1998 referendum in the Republic. That Ahern did not do this between November and February suggests that backing Trimble (and the British) was a price he could not or would not pay in changed circumstances two years on. Indeed, senior Irish figures were very relieved that their stance forestalled any serious degree of internal party criticism of the Taoiseach – and it never approached the levels reached during the extradition battles of 1987.

Trimble's relatively mild public reproof to the Irish Government for not standing by him in his hour of need was not the only instance of his reluctance to push home his moral advantage. Some months later, Frank Millar interviewed Seamus Mallon in the *Irish Times*. Mallon pointed out that the SDLP had not been party to the understandings reached between Mitchell, the UUP and Sinn Fein, but that the former US Senate Majority leader had told him about what was agreed. Millar inquired as to what that was, and Mallon 'for the first time, and without hesitation' offered corroboration of Trimble's understanding of what was decided. 'What we were told by George Mitchell very clearly was that his understanding was that devolution would be set up on 29 November and that decommissioning would begin end of January.'[116] It was significant that so crucial an item of corroboration was secured by an independent journalist such as Millar, rather than Trimble himself. Indeed, Trimble never followed up on Mallon's remarks, either personally or in the media – even though, as David Campbell saw it, it was one of the most helpful gestures which the SDLP deputy leader had made towards the UUP.[117] Trimble feared it could have been construed as putting Mallon on the spot. 'Seamus can be a bit touchy on these things,' observed Trimble. 'It could have been counterproductive.'[118]

If he could not ask Mallon to confirm the understanding of the previous November, why not Mitchell himself? Again, Trimble and his entourage thought it was unfair 'to put George on the spot', and were worried about breaches of confidentiality concerning the Mitchell process.[119] Trimble himself stated that 'the important thing was that Mitchell has not publicly controverted me' – and claims that one of the reasons why the former US Senate Majority leader did not return after suspension to carry out another review was that he would have to confirm the UUP version of events. Trimble accepted this state of affairs as though it was entirely reasonable; he was also reluctant to ask people to do things which they should be doing anyhow out of their own innate sense of honour.[120] His approach was the opposite of Adams – for if the positions had been reversed, and Mitchell would have been able to confirm that Sinn Fein's version had been accurate, there can be no doubt that republicans would have insisted upon public vindication of their stance from the former US Senator. But then Trimble, a comparative newcomer to high-level politics, never played 'ethnic hardball'. Indeed, he was noticeably solicitous and understanding of the political needs of 'top people' and was very anxious not to antagonise them. Partly, this stemmed from a personal sense of awe at being on high table, as it were. But it also stemmed from his belief, shared by so much of the Unionist political class, that Unionism's margins were very thin and that it could not afford to push things too far with the international 'grown-ups' lest they turn on him. The Unionist community had been so traumatised by the events of 1985 that so long as they were not explicitly blamed for what happened, they were grateful enough. To press home their advantage was pushing their luck.

This, in turn, explains the absence of recriminations with the American Administration. Clinton repeatedly said that 'I don't understand why they [the Provisionals] don't do it' (on arms) and never explicitly told Blair not to suspend; indeed, Trimble says that Blair never gave the impression that the United States was 'unhelpful' (this was not surprising: they would not have wanted news of an Anglo-American rift to leak, and any such impression would only have made Trimble more nervous and likely to trigger the post-dated cheque).[121] But when the crunch came, the White House was not there – either for Trimble or Blair. Certainly, as Jim Steinberg recalls, the White House agreed with the British that the loss of Trimble would be disastrous.[122] But as one British diplomat observes, 'the [Clinton] NSC says they understand Trimble's problems on decommissioning, but effectively blame the Unionists when it all falls down'. According to Donald Macintyre's biography of Mandelson, when Blair started to sketch in the background of the day's events to Clinton, the President cut him off. Surely, Clinton said, Trimble understood that this was a breakthrough? Blair was solid in his response. Adams had held off making his best offer until the suspension order was signed. Clinton asked if suspension could be reversed. 'No,' came the firm reply from the Prime Minister.[123]

The White House neither criticised nor endorsed Blair's actions. It thus appeared to many in Britain as though the Americans were indicating their deep unhappiness over London's decision through deafening silence. Not so, says Jim Steinberg. He says that he did indeed regard the last-minute movement by the Irish republicans as significant, but that notwithstanding that *declined* to criticise the British. The implication is that considering the White House's private reservations about the British move to suspend, the act of 'keeping mum' was in itself a sign of the solidity of the Anglo-American relationship and that Clinton had done the right thing by their British friend and ally.[124] Maybe so: but it was still astonishing that a US Administration should effectively chose to be neutral between, on the one side, an ideologically compatible British Prime Minister who had stood by the President during his personal travails and during the Kosovo War and, on the other side, one of the world's most consistently anti-American terrorist organisations and its political wing. As Peter Mandelson recalls, 'there was a tendency – not a uniform one but a tendency nonetheless – to view tactics for dealing with republicans more through a Dublin than a London lens'.[125] But although Blair stood by Trimble, it was not the kind of choice – between the UUP leader and the President of the United States – which he relished having to make.

Curiously, Trimble never asked Clinton to stand up and point the finger at Sinn Fein the defaulting party.[126] 'I didn't do so because of the political situation he is in,' says the UUP leader. 'He's got to think of the vote he courted and the vote his wife is courting' (as US Senate candidate in New York).[127] Once again, he showed solicitude for Clinton, a man who would never face re-election, rather than look after himself: it showed that there was something in Ruth Dudley Edwards' assertion that he was rather too nice for this game. Certainly, Trimble was delighted when the *Washington Post* editorial on 3 February criticised Clinton and Edward Kennedy for not demanding decommissioning, but would rarely himself take up those themes in public: he was frequently contented to let 'others do my dirty work for me' (one of his favourite phrases). So little did Trimble hold grudges that later in the year, he gladly acceded to Clinton's request for a 'lap of honour' in Belfast – the Arkansan's third visit as President. Again, it was quite enough for him that Clinton 'never criticised me for walking'. Trimble may also have felt a sense of residual gratitude to Clinton for intervening on his behalf on Good Friday 1998, when the President afforded him coverage by urging Irish nationalists publicly not to rubbish the Blair side-letter on decommissioning.

Trimble and his entourage certainly felt gratitude to No. 10 for what they had done. 'I want to thank you for standing by us,' David Campbell told Jonathan Powell after the deed was done. 'There was no question of us not,' replied Blair's chief of staff, coolly.[128] Trimble did indeed have cause to be grateful to Blair: after all, here was a New Labour Prime Minister standing by a Unionist leader in the face of bitter opposition from Sinn Fein/IRA, the SDLP, the Irish Government and the US Administration.[129] Yet although Trimble had won the greatest victory of any Unionist leader in 30 years, he made little of it in terms of reconciling Unionist opinion to the Belfast Agreement. The UUC on Saturday 12 February was not a footstomping celebration of democracy: instead it was fearfully anti-climactic. The task of conveying a pro-Agreement Unionist message was also impeded because his attention was focused upon relatively trivial bureaucratic matters. So whilst Trimble was genuinely anxious not to appear to be clinging to office after the resumption of direct rule at midnight on 11/12 February, and moved swiftly out of the First Minister's office to party rooms on the second floor of Parliament Buildings, he was also keen that his staff and some of his special advisers continue to be paid so they be kept in the deep freeze until such time as the institutions were de-suspended. However, says Trimble, elements of the NIO-Whitehall nexus were anxious to make things as difficult as possible so as to create the incentives for the Unionists to be more accommodating and to return to office as swiftly as possible. 'It required a huge struggle,' recalls the UUP leader.[130] The struggle may have been titanic, but it was not exactly 'big picture' stuff, as Blair might have put it. In his own way, Trimble kept his 'eyes on the prize', yet was unable to communicate the fact to more than half a dozen people around him, if that.

Part of the explanation for that failure lies in British policy, and specifically the Blair–Trimble relationship. The crisis had proven to be something of a shock to the British, who were convinced that they had the support of the Irish for suspension following Ahern's undertakings in the Dail in the previous November. However, they swiftly resumed business as usual and had no wish for a prolonged spat. As one loyalist privately saw it, British behaviour was like an act of courage which is swiftly regretted by the man who performed it. Thus, when Mandelson spoke to Paul Bew on 6 March 2000 at a dinner at the Queen's Vice Chancellor's lodge at Lennoxvale in south Belfast, Mandelson reproved him with the words, 'I understand it [the post-dated resignation letter] was your idea. I wish you hadn't done it.'[131] Publicly, Mandelson was soon speaking of a 'Mexican stand-off' between the UUP and Sinn Fein: not once did Trimble publicly reprove him for this characterisation of the impasse. Nor, indeed, did Trimble ever reprove the British for what many Unionists saw as the unfairness of the suspension procedures, which penalised democrats and defaulting paramilitaries alike – a key theme of the debate on the 'failsafe' legislation 1999.[132] The British wanted to muddy the waters and to pull back from confrontation after having made good their pledge to Trimble, and urged him not to push home his advantage – and he acceded. This was largely a result of his respect for Blair. But it was also a matter of his own inclusive vision and his personal temperament. He had sacrificed much in terms of traditional Unionist values for the sake of winning the 'blame game', yet his definition of 'victory' did not extend to driving the republicans out of the process and trying to form an Executive without Sinn Fein (or even a renegotiation of the Belfast Agreement).[133] Indeed, he even told a *Newsweek* interview after suspension that he did not 'necessarily' blame the Sinn Fein leadership for the IRA's failure to decommission, citing difficulties with local units.[134] He had expected some sort of decommissioning would happen right up till 31 January (as was evidenced by his opening remark at his first meeting with Adams and McGuinness after suspension – 'what went wrong?') As ever, the ex-law don believed in seminars, not lectures. In consequence, most ordinary unionists had no grasp of the scale of the victory which had been secured. Trimble now had a seemingly compelling refutation of the anti-Agreement Unionist narrative, which held that the British Government would betray a Unionist leader because of fears of bombs in London – but made next to nothing of it. The old Irish nationalist allegation, that he had not sold the Agreement with sufficient vigour, was absolutely right – though, once again, not quite in the sense which they used it. Reminding everyone of the supremacy of Westminster was not the name of the game as the two Governments desperately scrambled to restore the institutions. Blair, who had done so much to make Trimble First Minister, prevented him from 'telling his story' – with potentially fatal consequences in the months to come.

THIRTY-THREE

The Stormont soufflé rises again

THERE was, retrospectively, a highly calibrated, even ritualistic quality to the rage of Sinn Fein/IRA concerning the suspension of the institutions. The purpose of this display of anger was less to convey the message that 'we are leaving town for ever' than 'don't you dare think of doing that again'. Adams even told Mandelson that the republican movement would 'go to town on you over this'. Certainly, the Irish Government did little to palliate this campaign of abuse, and when Adams attacked Mandelson in the presence of Brian Cowen, the Republic's Foreign Minister would not support him. This contrasted starkly with Mandelson's solidarity with Cowen when Trimble would criticise the latter in post-suspension trilateral meetings with the UUP.[1] Indeed, Cyril Ramaphosa of the ANC, who subsequently came to play a part in the resolution of the impasse, states that the republicans were much more angry with the British than they were with Trimble. Ramaphosa notes that the republicans still saw the British, rather than the Unionists, as their main interlocutors; and to the extent that they had to deal with the Unionists, it was mainly in the context of how it affected their over-arching relationship with London.[2] Of course, the Sinn Fein message depended on the target audience in question: Sean Farren's notes of the suspension period reveal that at a meeting with senior SDLP figures 'Sinn Fein were quite aggressive toward us naming myself, Mark [Durkan] and Seamus [Mallon] as the culprits for having advocated "product" [that is, of weapons to decommission] . . . Gerry Adams did most of the talking and indicated the present leadership of Sinn Fein no longer has much influence over the IRA; members were leaving the party, unable to indicate in what circumstances things could be got together again. John Hume exasperated when they indicated that [the IRA leadership offer] might not be possible.'

For all the sound and fury of the suspension drama, it soon became apparent that none of the major protagonists wanted that hiatus to last indefinitely: all of them had too much invested in the process to want to see a return to full-scale direct rule. The question, therefore, was not whether the institutions would be restored, but on what terms – given both Trimble's and Adams' needs to manage their internal constituencies. Trimble gave a clear hint as to his real aims in an interview with Frank Millar in the *Irish Times* on 26 May 2000, as the UUC was again contemplating re-entering government with republicans. 'If this didn't work and we decided to withdraw, it would be for the same purpose as in February, namely giving people [Sinn Fein] a jolt to force them to move further down the path of implementation and their part of the Agreement.' In other words, he did not want republicans put out irrevocably: suspension was, rather, a tactical political escalation, along a broad line of strategic inclusivity. Conversely Sinn Fein/IRA, as Trimble told the National Press Club of Washington DC on 17 March 2000, had adopted a 'tactical posture . . . of disengagement'.[3] And he even acknowledged publicly that the only argument for not proceeding immediately with decommissioning 'is the need to manage the situation and to ensure you don't provoke too big a reaction from dissidents'.[4] Trimble was perhaps the only Unionist leader of the Troubles who saw it as part of his role to calculate the effect of his actions upon the internal balance of forces in the republican movement.

After the ferocious abuse he received, Mandelson was more prepared than ever to play his part in restarting serious dialogue. He reassured nationalist Ireland that he would proceed apace with implementing the rest of the Belfast Agreement, notably Patten and demilitarisation.[5] Mandelson also began to look at redefining the concept of decommissioning. As part of that process, he began also to revise his account of the events surrounding the suspension. Thus, in a speech at the Irish Management Institute on 8 March 2000, he opined: 'Unionists say there must be certainty about decommissioning, before they will participate in the institutions. Republicans say that certainty about decommissioning can only be achieved when the political institutions have been functioning for some time.' These postures were, Mandelson declared, 'mutually exclusive. The end result . . . is not guns and government but no guns and no government. It is reasonable to ask . . . whether we risk the one becoming an obstacle, rather than a stepping stone, to the other. The integrity of positions on both sides is easy to preserve. They can just maintain some sort of Mexican stand-off. But the inevitable consequence of the decommissioning stalemate is political instability, thus threatening the very peace which everyone wants to preserve.'[6] In other words, Mandelson wanted to build on the IRA leadership position of 11 February, and to secure public answers to the two Mallon questions to the republican movement – will you decommission and, if so, when? Private IRA asides to de Chastelain counted for nothing with Unionist opinion: few, if any, believed them (this was in contrast to the White House view, which was that Trimble would now have to put up with less than publishable guarantees). But Mandelson, and the rest of the Government, were increasingly of the belief that these worthy goals could only be delivered after the institutions had been restored and not before.[7]

From a Unionist perspective, Mandelson's talk of 'Mexican stand-offs' represented a rewriting of history. It implied what many of them saw as 'moral equilateralism': that the intransigence of all sides, themselves included, was equally responsible for the current impasse. As Unionists saw it, of course, they had done everything asked of them in the previous November by 'jumping first', especially after the debacle which had befallen the RUC thanks to the Patten Commission. Moreover, the recent suspension had put all parties out of the Executive, defaulters and innocent alike. Why, therefore, was everyone now an equal villain of the piece – implying that all would have to move from their previous positions which already represented massive compromises on core democratic and unionist principles? Certainly, Trimble became very frustrated with Mandelson during the suspension. He believed that the Secretary of State had 'collapsed' to the Irish on the terms of re-establishing the institutions.[8] According to David Campbell, after meetings the UUP leader would often telephone No. 10 and give the 'read-out' to Jonathan Powell to express his unhappiness.[9] But this irritation remained largely private, and only really burst out in an interview with Frank Millar in the *Irish Times* on 17 April 2000. In practice, Trimble acquiesced in Mandelson's rewriting of the history of the previous months and now states that he was 'not excited' about the 'Mexican stand-off' remarks.[10] So low were Ulster Unionist expectations about what they could extract from the British state that Reg Empey believes that 'when you have a Secretary of State who blames both sides as opposed to just blaming Unionists – well, that's progress!'[11]

Trimble may have been disappointed with Mandelson, but having been disappointed, he also proceeded to think about the new realities which the Secretary of State's repositioning had created. If the Government was moving, he would eventually have to move, so he might as well obtain the credit for doing so on what he supposed to be his own terms. Indeed, according to David Lavery, he also concluded around the time of suspension that decommissioning in the sense of a televised LVF-style public cutting-up of weapons would not take place in the immediate term (although he never ceased to work for a more ambitious form of disarmament). Instead, he began to think in almost American legal terms about such concepts as 'escrow' – meaning, in this context, a phase in which weapons would be impounded rather than destroyed. He also met at Stormont with Father Alec Reid, the Redemptorist priest based at Clonard monastery in west Belfast, who assured him of the Provisionals' sincerity.[12] The question for Trimble was to find the context in which he could move without damaging himself beyond repair. By the time the UUP met with the SDLP on 13 March, there were already hints of a rethink. 'Meeting with UUP good and it was obvious that "product" not what they [are] after as a first step but [rather] a commitment to process assuring that the war is really over,' observed Sean Farren in his notebook.

Trimble would astonish all of them in the days to come – in the unlikeliest of venues for a Unionist leader. On 17 March 2000, he was in Washington for the St Patrick's Day celebrations, which were Clinton's last in the White House. At a briefing to reporters at the National Press Club, Trimble told the audience that 'I am prepared to recommend to my party that we try again. I am prepared to go back to the party and say "let us have fresh sequence" but I can't just do that simply in the abstract, I can only do that in circumstances where there is good reason to believe that this time it will work, and at the moment I am not in a position to do that.' When asked whether an IRA declaration that 'the war is over' would be sufficient, Trimble responded that 'obviously it would be significant if they were, even if just to say that in their view, the conflict is over'. When asked if he was saying that the IRA should declare that violence was over and that decommissioning should be dealt with further along the road, Trimble declared that 'I am not going to be specific on this.'[13] It represented a political bombshell of the first order: despite what many Unionists believed to be the republicans' ill-faith in not delivering on their side of the Mitchell review, here was Trimble again abandoning prior or maybe even simultaneous decommissioning in order to 'kick start' the process. 'Great speech, David, great speech,' Jim Steinberg told the UUP leader at the British Embassy later. 'I didn't say anything new in it,' replied Trimble. 'Oh I know, it isn't, but it's a great speech.'[14] The reason for Steinberg's pleasure was obvious. As the former deputy US National Security Adviser recalls, 'it was a crucial moment. It helped Clinton hugely in his meeting with Gerry Adams. It was a sign that Trimble was moving.'[15] Indeed, senior American officials confirm Trimble's contention that the effect of his 'statesmanlike' intervention was to redouble the pressure on Adams (though the Americans may have been less impressed when Trimble and the UUP team subsequently visited the Oval Office and one of their number opened the adjoining passage-way to have what Trimble calls a 'good gawp' at the spot where Clinton enjoyed a tryst with Monica Lewinsky).[16]

But the British were not so happy: they instinctively feared the reaction in the unionist heartland, and they were right.[17] Likewise, Trimble's friend and informal adviser in Washington, DC, Michael McDowell – who had been urging the UUP leader to make some kind of move – was concerned about the timing and location of these particular remarks. A journalist by profession, McDowell had known Trimble since his days as a reporter on the *Belfast Telegraph* in the 1970s. McDowell stayed in America after a year as Nieman Fellow at Harvard in 1978 and subsequently specialised in Northern Ireland issues at the Carnegie Endowment. Latterly, he came to know an energetic young diplomat called Jonathan Powell. Although McDowell – an ex-Northern Ireland Labour party member and now Alliance sympathiser – had originally been highly sceptical of Trimble, he was now a firm if not uncritical admirer of the UUP leader. His most important role was as an informal back-channel on behalf of Trimble to both the US Administration and Jonathan Powell. But, as McDowell told the US deputy national security adviser, 'He's gone rather further than I would have expected.'[18] Frank Millar was rather blunter in his column of 20 March 2000, 'has David Trimble lost the plot? Is he deliberately goading the Willies (Ross and Thompson) to challenge his leadership directly? Or is he close to doing a Faulkner – finally cutting his losses and formally splitting his party in a last bid to save the Good Friday accord? . . . Yet with a very few words, Mr Trimble had seemingly given legs to the Irish-led search for an "alternative context" in which the decommissioning issue might be addressed. He had done so, moreover, while 4,000 miles from home: in the context of a distinctly green event; without prior notice to many of those presumed close to him, and while his aides and allies fretted about the prospects for an already problematic meeting of the UUC on Saturday.' As Trimble put it more pithily still, 'Many thought I had committed political suicide.'[19]

Certainly, as with Trimble's remarks at the Unionist Information Office in June 1999, when he called for Mowlam's resignation, the 'sequencing' offer just seemed to drop out of the UUP leader's mouth spontaneously. Daphne Trimble, for one, was taken by surprise by her husband's comments.[20] In fact, they were rather more deliberate than that implies – a point observed by Frank Millar, who noted that the remarks had been repeated no fewer than three times to make sure that the journalists present fully understood them.[21] So why did Trimble take the risk? He feared the possibility of an 'ambush' from the Administration, prodded by the forces of pan-nationalism, perhaps along the lines of the 14 May 1999 debacle at Downing Street.[22] After all, Clinton was not in the best of moods: in consequence of suspension, his last St Patrick's Day had not turned out to be the joyous celebration for which he had hoped.[23] Not going to Washington was not an option for Trimble. If he had absented himself, the UUP leader says, it would have been interpreted as evidence that he was scared to go.[24] But Trimble was not simply seeking to play the 'blame game' through an act of pre-emption; according to David Campbell, he was also trying to condition his 'own folk' to make another leap of faith, namely no prior decommissioning.[25] Trimble did not want people to say that he had concealed his position, and wanted the UUP to know that if the 'sequencing' was right, he would be tempted to go for a new deal.[26]

The response from the 'antis' was not long in coming: the sole question was who would be the 'stalking horse' to run against Trimble for the leadership at the March 2000 AGM of the UUC. In the end, the 'antis' settled upon a relatively emollient figure: Rev. Martin Smyth, MP for South Belfast, who had topped the poll in the ballot for honorary secretaries at the March 1999 AGM. Ross would have been too controversial, and had Donaldson run and lost, the 'noes' would have shot their best bolt. But the antis believed that any semi-decent showing by Smyth – dismissed by some, unfairly, as a 'stalking donkey' – would be a bonus for them. Daphne Trimble states that the UUP leader thought the margin would be similar to that at the November 1999 meeting at which it was decided to enter government with Sinn Fein after the Mitchell review (58% to 42%).[27] But most others in the Trimble camp were more optimistic and Denis Rogan calculated that the incumbent leader would win by a

70%–30% margin.[28] Matters were further complicated by the strength of feeling on the policing issue. David Burnside decided to resubmit a motion on the subject which he had withdrawn at his leader's request for the sake of party unity at the time of the UUC meeting in February 2000. Burnside believed that it was a terrible mistake to 'de-link' the issue of the RUC from the question of UUP participation in government and urged the party not to return to the executive until it had won concessions on policing.[29] Although Trimble readily acknowledged Burnside's sincerity, if the motion was passed at the UUC AGM it would represent an additional hurdle to re-entering government with Sinn Fein: like any leader, he never relished having his hands tied.[30] But even on the intrinsic merits of the RUC issue, Trimble was not sure if his old Vanguard colleague was right. According to David Campbell, Trimble thought that the Burnside motion was so maximalist in its demands that it wrecked the prospect of any agreed compromise with moderate nationalists, along the lines of Mgr Denis Faul's dual name proposal (NIPS/RUC), which might just come about in the Lords stages of the Patten legislation. Any nationalists willing to split the difference would have been frightened off by this motion, or so Trimble reasoned.[31]

Burnside, however, secured the support of John Taylor and a majority of Westminster MPs.[32] According to David Campbell, Trimble took the view that Taylor's support for the Burnside motion was his deputy's signal that the 'all-in' power-sharing experiment was on the rocks.[33] Worse was to come as Lord Molyneaux declared his support for Martin Smyth's challenge on the night of Thursday 23 March 2000, less than two days before the AGM, as did Jeffrey Donaldson.[34] So when the votes for the leadership contest were counted at the end of the morning session of the AGM on Saturday 25 March, Trimble beat the 'stalking donkey' by 457 votes to 348 – or 56.77% to 43.23%.[35] Considering the victory which Trimble had won by securing suspension, and the shortcomings of Smyth, it was a poor result. Denis Rogan, who was sitting beside Trimble on the platform when the vote was announced, recalls Trimble nodding to him and saying, 'We're in damage limitation mode now. I mightn't be here next year.' Pausing a moment, he added: 'As the IRA said about the Brighton bomb [of 1984]: "We only have to get lucky once."'[36] For him, there were no 'moral' defeats, such as Paisley inflicted upon O'Neill in Bannside in the 1969 General Election, when the incumbent Northern Ireland Prime Minister scraped by, but lost the political battle and thereupon resigned. Trimble would have to lose arithmetically before he did that. 'David always believed that one is enough,' states Daphne Trimble.[37] One close associate says that then, and only then, would he have contemplated setting up a breakaway Faulkner-style Unionist Party of Northern Ireland, on a minority of Unionist votes in the Assembly.[38] Trimble, though, always denied this and stated that if he lost in the UUC, that would be it. But he was also the most pragmatic and determined of politicians – and there appeared many things which he ruled out and subsequently embraced as a matter of last resort, when the alternative was his own obliteration and that of the institutions which he had laboured to create. The antis had more to rejoice about after lunch that Saturday, when Burnside's motion on the RUC was considered. After one of the rowdiest debates in years – which John Taylor, for one, believes was even more unpleasant than the UUC meetings which cumulatively led to the deposition of Faulkner – the Trimbleista amendment to the Burnside motion lost by 384 votes to 338.[39] But from Trimble's perspective, these reverses did have one great advantage: they proved beyond peradventure to Sinn Fein and to the Irish Government that his vulnerability was not feigned.

The combination of Trimble's Washington offer and his ensuing reverses at the UUC can also be said not to have hindered the subsequent intensification of contacts between the two Governments and the republicans. According to Jonathan Powell, it was clear by the first week in April 2000 that something was doable, though what exactly was unclear.[40] But there was only a narrow window of opportunity in which to achieve this. It would have to be after Easter, which fell on April 23: the Governments were now mindful of asking the Provisionals to do anything at that time of year, with all its significance in the republican calendar.[41] At the same time, it would also have to be before the marching season reached its height: Paddy Teahon recalls that Ahern would often say that 'when evenings get bright, you can't negotiate'.[42] And there was another factor: according to David Campbell, the Trimbleistas had intelligence which suggested that the Agreement-sceptical Union First group was going to make a major policy announcement to coincide with the second anniversary of the referendum on 22 May. Campbell states that the British also knew about this and that any continuing vacuum would only benefit Donaldson (though the latter emphatically denies any such initiative was ever planned).[43] The convergence between the protagonists took several forms. First, the Irish persuaded the British that the latter's goal of a declaration that the 'war is over' was unavailable for the moment. Second, the British persuaded the Irish they needed a much more public 'up front' IRA declaration than they received on 11 February if they were to take the risk of reciprocating on the question of policing demilitarisation, and other issues.[44] Thus, slowly, the concept had emerged of 'redefining' decommissioning. Jim Steinberg believed there was a useful precedent in the Kosovo Liberation Army's decision voluntarily to agree to have their arms sealed under international inspection, ensuring that they felt as if dignity was preserved.[45] But the redefinition of the arms issue also concerned its timing. Because the republican leadership had great difficulty in agreeing to a concrete timetable, Unionists might instead have to settle for an 'up-front' confidence-building measure (CBM) that would have certain features of an arms gesture but which was dressed up in as palatable a way as possible for the republican base.

A salient figure in brokering this redefinition was Powell. Partly, there were negative reasons for this: following suspension, says Jim Steinberg, Mandelson's relationship with nationalists was so damaged that he had ceased to be an *interlocuteur valable*. 'Stylistically, republicans felt comfortable with Blair,' recalls the former deputy US National Security Adviser. 'Mandelson is very smart but doesn't always bring people with him.'[46] There had already been hints of Powell's continuing role in Northern Ireland even before suspension: David Campbell recalls that at one meeting at the NIO's London offices at Millbank on 27 January 2000 to discuss Drumcree, Powell had openly contradicted Mandelson. As Campbell notes, it was startling to observe an unelected aide cut across this particular senior minister in front of outsiders. There was, Campbell felt, a keen rivalry between the two men. Republicans also detected what they saw as this rivalry and sought to exploit it ruthlessly in the coming months.[47] Contrary to what the Irish sometimes claimed, Mandelson would never be as marginalised in the coming months as Mowlam was during the nadir of her relationship with the Ulster Unionists, but he had undoubtedly lost some of his influence.[48] The result of all this was that Powell would make flying visits across the Irish Sea to negotiate with the Provisionals. When in Northern Ireland, he would be met by senior republicans at Aldergrove International Airport and from there would be taken to west Belfast safe-houses or hotels: initially, the RUC were not kept informed, but when they discovered this they insisted that they be kept in the loop lest the Prime Minister's chief of staff be embarrassed by being stopped at a road block or caught in some other routine operation. When the meetings were held in the Republic, Powell would be taken to the discreet setting of King's Hospital Old School in Kilmainham, Co. Dublin. Above all, it was a signal to republicans that Blair himself was becoming 're-engaged' after his initial period of post-Mowlam detachment. It was certainly to their advantage: one senior RUC officer of the period states that 'Jonathan was always more susceptible to the republicans' arguments than Peter.'[49]

Having played his part in 'breaking the log-jam' whilst in Washington, Trimble now became a largely passive player in the drama as attention focused upon the negotiation with Sinn Fein/IRA. Trimble states that whilst Blair had privately said to him in mid-April that a CBM might be the 'X factor' in the negotiations, there was no detail to the proposal and that he did not realise that there had been any serious progress until the last week of April.[50] The Ulster Unionist team as a whole received their first serious briefing on the emerging package at No. 10 on Tuesday 2 May – as part of a set of back-to-back meetings between the two governments and the local parties.[51] Trimble first had a five-minute meeting alone with Blair, reporting back to his colleagues in the dining room. He said that the Prime Minister was nervous about the process and that the British Government was contemplating asking a third party to act as a guarantor. The Provisionals, he claimed, wanted the ANC to do the verification of any forthcoming act, whereas Blair's inclination was for someone from a Nordic nation, since he knew that the Unionists would not accept the bona fides of one of the republican movement's foreign cognates. Blair then told the whole UUP delegation in his study that the IRA had not made a definite commitment to decommission all along and that the Government now wanted specific suggestions in the next few days. Those specifics, he said, were the need for unequivocal adherence to peaceful means; a verifiable process; and a re-engagement with de Chastelain. Trimble said that he read into what Blair said that the Prime Minister was not now looking at proper, permanent decommissioning – to which Blair replied that he was looking for the permanent removal of arms from the equation. He also indicated that the Government was considering a CBM.[52] Blair hoped for an IRA text by Wednesday night or at latest by Thursday morning. Blair asked the Ulster Unionists to return to No. 10 on the next day, Wednesday 3 May, this time for supper. At the supper, the Prime Minister started to indicate the contents of a potential 'sequence'. He revealed that the previously mooted CBM had become likelier – the implication being that this was because it was impossible to extract a timetable for concrete decommissioning.[53] But apart from that, there was little advance at this supper on the previous day's position and Blair's message was that it was very unlikely that matters would be advanced enough to make him risk coming to Northern Ireland for a summit meeting that would seal the accord.[54]

On Thursday 4 May, David Campbell was telephoned by John Sawers, who told him that the Prime Minister would be coming that day to Hillsborough.[55] According to Reg Empey, the UUP had a fairly good idea of what was coming, but important details were missing and there was still no IRA text nor a precise idea of when it would be delivered.[56] The two Governments then had a working dinner, which was only partly overshadowed by the leak of a document written by the British ambassador to Dublin, Ivor Roberts, concerning a discussion with senior Irish figures during Mandelson's visit to Dublin on 18 April. The diplomat stated that Cowen had no understanding of unionist concerns and that 'beyond the constitutional status acceptance that Northern Ireland remains part of the UK, there should be no further evidence of Britishness in the governance of Northern Ireland. It was an argument presented with all the subtlety and openmindedness that one would expect from a member of Sinn Fein. There was no disposition among members of his entourage or indeed by Martin Mansergh, who was also present, to water down this line.'[57] It certainly portended problems on the question of symbolism which almost undid the emerging deal – though, as things turned out, perhaps as much by accident as design. These matters were raised over a few glasses of whisky at Trimble's first meeting with Blair, Mandelson and Powell in the Lady Grey study at 10:30 p.m. that night. The Prime Minister told Trimble that the republicans were consulting widely that night and that they would know by mid-morning what the response was (though No. 10 believed that even Brian Keenan's commitment to the process was not to be underestimated: they saw him as a sophisticated hardliner, rather like McGuinness).[58] The Unionists asked for a text but the British claimed that they did not have one. Nonetheless, Blair indicated that he had obtained some movement from the Provisionals that would satisfy UUP requirements and sought to push the Unionists to accept the new 'sequencing'. Trimble tried to slow him down and sought to re-direct the discussion towards the flags issue. Blair pronounced himself to be sympathetic to Unionists on this subject: Unionists were seeking legislation to uphold the right of the devolved ministries (and of Stormont) to fly the Union Flag on designated days after Sinn Fein ministers had declined to do so during the brief life of the suspended Executive. Again, Blair sought to pull the discussion back to sequencing and, again, Trimble sought to focus on policing. No matter how good the sequencing was, the UUP leader said he needed a 'significant' concession relating to the name of the RUC (the urgency of which had been increased by the success of the Burnside motion on the RUC in March 2000). The Prime Minister fretted that the name of the new police force might turn out to be a 'deal-breaker' for republicans; it also emerged that the republicans had given guarantees to their own folk that they would not negotiate any compromises on Patten. Trimble disagreed with Blair and said they would moan and do little else. He understood that the republicans could not negotiate, so wanted the British to act of their own volition.[59] David Campbell pitched in and remarked that under Patten, the RUC had been subsumed rather than disbanded: therefore, its continued existence might find some legislative expression in the forthcoming Bill to give effect to the police reforms. The UUP, and particularly David Campbell, were already thinking along the lines of precedents in the British Army. Thus, the old Royal Irish Rangers were an amalgamation of previous units such as the 27th (Enniskillen), 83rd and 87th regiments.

Trimble and elements of the UUP leadership were then summoned from their temporary headquarters at the White Gables Hotel to see Blair at 10:30 a.m. on the next day, but they were kept waiting till 12:45 as meetings with Sinn Fein dragged on. In the room on this occasion were Blair, Mandelson, Powell, Bill Jeffrey and Ahern (again unaccompanied by his officials and as at No. 10 earlier in the week saying very little); on the UUP side were Trimble, Taylor, Maginnis, Empey, Michael McGimpsey, David Campbell, David Kerr and Philip Robinson. Looking at the two big leather chairs reminiscent of those in old Orange halls, John Taylor quipped, 'Come on, Bertie, you occupy the Deputy Master's chair!'[60] Once more, Blair stated that he hoped that an IRA statement would be available in an hour. He outlined the basic points of the deal. He mentioned that there would be a CBM of weapons dumps, to be inspected by the former ANC Secretary-General Cyril Ramaphosa.

Alongside him would be the former Finnish President Martti Ahtisaari: the latter was the idea of John Sawers, who had known him during the Namibian independence negotiations when he served in South Africa. Sawers and the rest of the British team were well aware that both sides of the Ulster divide needed a figure acceptable to each of them.

Between 3 and 3:30 p.m., Powell telephoned David Campbell and invited him and Trimble to come and see the IRA statement. The two insisted that the entire UUP team view it and they went to Mandelson's private drawing room on the first floor. Trimble gave the document a cursory glance and reacted: 'This isn't enough for us, you've misled us,' he told the Secretary of State. Mandelson was indignant though it was hard with him to know when he was really annoyed. 'David, I've worked my backside off for you. Would you rather have Mo Mowlam back doing all of this?[61] Taylor chimed in and said that the UUP needed time and calm; Trimble responded favourably and he proceeded to parse the text more closely. The UUP leader was able to refer back to his earlier notes and found that the latest proposals accorded with what Blair and Mandelson had previously told him. In consequence his demeanour changed utterly. There was no statement as such that the 'war is over', but Trimble consoled himself with the IRA's formulation that 'the full implementation, on a progressive and irreversible basis by the two Governments, especially the British Government of what they have agreed will provide a political context, in an enduring political process, with the potential to remove the causes of conflict, and in which Irish republicans and unionists can, as equals, pursue our respective political objectives peacefully'. As Trimble saw it, the acknowledgment of the unionists as 'equals' was ideologically significant: they were no longer *Untermenschen* – though to anti-Agreement unionists, this seemed a rather minimalistic aspiration on the UUP leader's part.[62] But upon closer examination, Trimble was attracted to other parts of the document as well. The UUP leader believed that whereas the IRA emissary's offer to de Chastelain on 11 February was conditioned both upon maintenance/restoration of the institutions and ending the 'causes of conflict', this offer of re-engagement with de Chastelain was predicated solely upon restoration of the institutions. Instead, the Provisionals had settled for something which merely had the *potential* to end the 'causes of conflict', thus reducing the ending of Partition to an aspiration.[63] Moreover, having broken off contact with the decommissioning body in February, they had now agreed to re-engage with de Chastelain following a unilateral suspension of the institutions that reiterated the sovereignty of Westminster. The Provisionals could not offer a timeframe for putting arms beyond use, so instead they offered – in the context of 'speedy and full implementation' of the Belfast Agreement – a CBM to confirm that their weapons remain secure. Such sites were to be inspected by third parties who were then to report to the de Chastelain body that they had done so. These dumps were to be regularly reinspected. Trimbleistas argued that whoever was doing the inspecting, and under whatever conditions, the CBM showed that the IRA's arsenal was no longer sacrosanct.[64] The conditional 'may' of February had now become 'will' (i.e. 'the IRA leadership will initiate a process that will completely and verifiably put IRA arms beyond use').[65] Mandelson also made much of the 'will' point in commending the deal to the Commons on Monday 8 May.[66] Moreover, it was made clear to Trimble in discussions with the British that the Irish and Sinn Fein had not succeeded in obtaining their goal of repeal of the suspension legislation: as one senior official observes, no Government ever likes to forswear any option in perpetuity.[67] That said, pan-nationalism secured a pledge that any future suspensions would be preceded by a fully consultative review; and, in practical terms, no British Secretary of State would ever again wish to risk the abuse meted out to Mandelson.[68] But overall, Trimble was pleased enough to be able to tell Paul Bew, 'I've got a document – it's much better than anything in the past.'[69] It was a further illustration of the UUP leader's mood swings.

But Trimble had to obtain some 'side orders' on both the RUC and on flags. Again, Trimble and Taylor went back to the Prime Minister and Secretary of State and said that these were a matter of survival. By the late afternoon of Friday 5 May, Campbell and others had worked up a paper giving flesh to their ideas on preserving the name of the RUC. The amalgamation of the old Northern Irish infantry regiments of the line to form the Royal Irish Rangers in 1968 had also caused much pain: after all, combined, they had suffered some 21,000 fatalities and around 70,000–80,000 other casualties in two world wars.[70] However, dignity had been preserved and old comrades could legitimately claim an institutional line of descent. Not all 'antis' were impressed. As one loyalist observed, there was no real comparison between these two events: the old regiments had not been abolished at the behest of the Germans, for the purpose of making Germans join those units! Nonetheless, Trimble needed this fig-leaf. According to Peter Mandelson, Blair believed that the issue of policing could not be renegotiated without the whole thing being unpicked and had said as much to republicans; but, equally, if the UUP could somehow persuade republicans to accept some formulation to ensure that the institutions were restarted, then he would have no objections. Mandelson duly drafted some words in his own hand on a yellow, lined piece of paper.[71] The 'Name option' for the Bill read, 'The name shall be the PSNI (incorporating the RUC)'; the 'Interpretation option' read, 'Police service means the PSNI (incorporating the RUC)'. And it added 'DT happy with either options [sic]'. He photocopied the document and gave it to Trimble and said that he would sort the matter out with Blair.[72] Indeed, Mandelson adds that at a subsequent meeting with republicans that afternoon, in the Lady Grey room, he tore off the piece of paper and told them 'this is harmless, see if it's something your people will go with. It's no skin off your nose, but it's absolutely essential. Otherwise, we can't get the UUC off the hook of the Burnside amendment.' According to Mandelson, he provided the same explanation to the Irish Government.[73] Certainly, Dublin did at various moments seem to be disposed to give Trimble something, though it was never clear exactly what.[74] Trimble and Taylor also met with Adams and McGuinness late that afternoon: they indicated to the UUP leader and his deputy that the IRA statement was the maximum which they could extract from the organisation, but stressed it represented a watershed. Then Adams volunteered a comment: 'We know you've got an issue on the RUC but there's nothing I can do to help you on that. I know that sometime between now and the [Ulster Unionist] Council meeting [to ratify UUP re-entry into government] the British will do something. I'll oppose it, of course.'[75] The UUP interpreted this as meaning that the Sinn Fein leadership were planning to offer rhetorical opposition to any Unionist gains on the name of the police force, but no more than that. Moreover, the way Adams phrased it suggested that he understood it was something that the British were doing off their own bat, but not as part of any overall renegotiation of Patten which the Sinn Fein president could not or would not do. Trimble told Blair and Mandelson about this conversation, but they appeared to be very cautious about this claim. It does, however, appear likely that the 'Shinners' knew that something was coming down the pike for the First Minister (suspended): when Adams and McGuinness met him again on Tuesday 9 May 2000, they said they noticed the tell-tale words in the two Governments' letter to the parties pledging only to implement rather than 'fully implement' Patten.[76]

The UUP leader also believed he had secured agreement for legislation on the flying of flags on appointed days and that this would be pushed through Parliament quickly, before any meeting of the UUC and before the Executive was restored. The Union Flag would be allowed to be flown over Government buildings and if the Assembly could not agree on the flying of flags, then the Secretary of State would be empowered to intervene.[77] Or, as Mandelson subsequently told the *Irish Times*, 'I am no more in favour of in-your-face flag-flying than I am in favour of its complete banishment.'[78] It was a victory which Trimble probably would not have won without Mandelson who was determined that Unionists had to feel a 'parity of esteem' if they were to move in a 'crab-like way' to inclusivity. It was not that Mandelson was pro-Unionist: he simply did not believe that there was any viable inclusive process – wherever that process was leading – in which the representatives of the Province's British majority lost ten-nil every time.[79] These were themes which he consistently and publicly articulated in a range of speeches and articles, notably his Institute of Directors speech at Stormont on 28 March 2000, in which he had spoken of the Belfast Agreement as upholding the legitimacy of Northern Ireland's position within the United Kingdom (of which Unionists had received several advance drafts); his British Irish Association keynote address in Oxford on 8 September 2000, when he warned that 'absolutist' demands by nationalists on the Patten legislation could destroy Trimble's leadership; and his *Times* article of 2 November 2000. But Mandelson had two other motivations in acting as he did. First, he spotted the arrogance of republicans and believed that if they over-reached themselves, the whole process could come crashing down (exemplified, subsequently, by the discovery of the alleged republican spy ring at Stormont). Therefore, he deemed them to be in need of 'tough love'.[80] Second, he always had an eye for mainland opinion. As Sir Ronnie Flanagan recalls, the then Secretary of State would say: 'My test is: what would my mother think if I was not allowing you to fly the Union Flag?'[81]

The Unionists left at 7:30 thinking they had secured these concessions, even if they had not been pinned down precisely.[82] When Trimble came home that night, he showed his family the still unpublished IRA statement. No one said anything, but when they reached the end of the text they all agreed, 'That's it. There's enough in that.'[83] The Unionists believed that Mandelson would tie up the loose ends with Blair who, in turn, would deal with Ahern. But on this occasion, the Prime Minister's negotiating style was even flakier than that of the UUP. The negotiations went on for several hours, but it is still unclear what precisely was or was not finally agreed there.[84] Reg Empey states that Blair only dealt with the matter in the broadest terms and that Adams was not 'squared' by the Prime Minister, though there was an understanding that something would be done. Blair also confirmed direct commitments to the republicans on the issue of OTRs – 'on the run' terrorists who were either escapees or else had never been brought to justice. These had been first offered at the end of the Mitchell review in November 1999. It would have been tantamount to an amnesty, and the Prime Minister did so outside of the declared Government negotiating position, and without the enthusiastic support of the Secretary of State.[85] Jim Steinberg states that Blair hoped that this 'amnesty' could be done through 'executive action'.[86] In fact, it would have necessitated primary legislation and a messy political battle in Parliament. Mandelson admitted to the Unionists at a subsequent meeting at Hillsborough on 30 August 2000 that Blair offered this concession in exchange for no apparent reciprocal move by the Provisionals.[87] Indeed, one civil servant states that the episode resembled Blair's intervention in the negotiations in December 1998 on the functions of cross-border bodies and the number of Northern Ireland government departments: the Prime Minister inserted himself into the talks, left the job unfinished lest the whole deal be unpicked. In consequence, 'the boulder rolled back down the slope again'.[88]

What is certain is that the Ulster Unionist leadership wanted nothing to leak: they believed, rightly or wrongly, that with a nudge and a wink the Sinn Fein president had afforded them the space they needed. If anything emerged before that, and especially before the IRA statement was issued on Saturday 6 May, it could be disastrous to the entire enterprise. As Trimble saw it, there were two dangers for Adams and McGuinness in this. If a deal on policing and flags was cooked up bilaterally between the British and the Unionists, then the republican grassroots – already paranoid about side-deals between the British and the Unionists such as Blair's letter on decommissioning of 10 April 1998 – might well then say to the Sinn Fein leadership and to the Irish Government, 'Why didn't you insert yourself into the negotiations between the Brits and the Unionists?' But at least then, Adams could claim that he had been a victim of

British perfidy and a surrender to a latter-day 'Orange card'. It was far worse if he had been a party to negotiation in defiance of the IRA position which forbade involvement in any talks implying a dilution of Patten. So delicate did the matter appear to the Unionist leadership that Empey even briefed the UUP Assembly group, who had been hanging round all day in Room 277 at Parliament Buildings at Stormont and told them that 'this is the last chance we have to do anything for the RUC, and if anybody says anything it will blow all out of the water'.[89] Taylor also did his round of briefings. He went out into the courtyard at Hillsborough and told some colleagues that the RUC was incorporated into the 'title deeds' of the new force and that the flags issue seemed to have been resolved satisfactorily.[90] On the next day, recalls Taylor, UTV had the exact wording of the policing concessions, revealing the incorporation of the title.[91] The trouble with these reports was that it made it appear as though the republican leadership had been engaged in a negotiation over the RUC – the very thing they had promised their 'board of directors' not to do. Empey was so angry – fearing that it would cause anger in nationalist Ireland and thus give the British Government an excuse not to honour their understanding – that he stormed out of a meeting of the Assembly group at Stormont that Saturday (6 May) and went into another room to 'cool down'. As he recalls, 'I lost it.'[92] That said, by Friday evening, so many people knew of at least part of the contents of the Hillsborough package that the leaks could have come from almost anyone.[93]

The leaks represented the start of a slide in Trimble's position. Indeed, even those elements which seemed to him so positive concerning IRA weapons – impressive enough to 'process junkies' – fell way short of the mark as far as many Unionists were concerned. Frank Millar summarised their case thus: 'There is nowhere yet any commitment to the actual destruction of weaponry; no promise to produce an inventory of all arms held; no indication of the percentage of dumps to be opened to inspection in relation to the total; no obvious sanction in the hands of the inspectors should they find weapons have been used; no suggestion as to how weapons in other dumps are deemed to be secure; and no cast-iron guarantee that they can never be used again.'[94] According to David Campbell, at a meeting of the Assembly group at 4 p.m. on Tuesday 9 May, many of the Ulster Unionist legislators stated that they and their constituents saw the CBM as a wholly inadequate substitute for actual decommissioning.[95] But it was policing which continued to give Trimble

the greatest difficulty.[96] Dublin, which had been inclined to give Trimble
something, suddenly started to backtrack in the face of this pressure and
pronounced that if there was to be a 'new beginning' for policing, then
the symbolism of the incoming force had to be free from associations
with the British or Irish states.[97] Indeed, following a meeting between
the SDLP and the British some weeks later, Sean Farren wrote in his
notebook that '[Mandelson] revealed that Irish Government had vetoed
the inclusion of "incorporation" [of the RUC into the police service] on
the face of the [policing] Bill and had appeared to have done so at Sinn
Fein's insistence; I am incensed at this given that we had spent considerable time with the Irish working on this idea at Hillsborough and had
understood that the UUP would have accepted it.' The problem for the
British and Irish Governments was that the SDLP could not afford to be
outflanked by the Provisionals who, in turn, could be outflanked by the
dissidents: according to Ed Moloney, pan-nationalism therefore needed
reforms so far-reaching as to be tantamount to disbandment.[98] Blair was
now caught and according to Trimble, he wobbled under the republican
threat that the CBM might be lost: the 'disappointed' UUP leader wondered why the Prime Minister was so susceptible to these pressures when
the IRA would have looked at fault if they had withdrawn their offer
after having granted it.[99] Blair then played the ultimate Prime Ministerial
card. According to the *Guardian* of 26 May, he called Clinton twice on
Wednesday 10 May asking him to lean on both the Irish Government
and Sinn Fein to make some compromise on the name to help Trimble;
but the American President refused, saying he had sympathy with the
Unionists on decommissioning but none on flags and policing (many in
the Administration saw the RUC as little more than equivalent to the
white police in the Deep South, whom they observed during their political
adolescence in the Civil Rights era). The story was completely denied by
No. 10, not least since it was one of the few known clashes between these
two ideological allies. But the *Guardian* was right on the essence of the
story, even though it appears that the actual conversation was rather
gentler than its report suggested. According to Dick Norland of the NSC
staff, Blair told Clinton that he had a problem and wondered whether
he had any ideas. Clinton replied that he did not, but that he would
come back to Blair after mulling it over and see what he could do.[100] Of
course, Clinton did not do so: it was as good as a rebuff, but it was
administered far more softly in the way of a master (southern) politician

towards an apparently close friend. Yet considering Blair's solidarity with Clinton over the Lewinsky affair of 1998 and the Kosovo War of 1999, this again was a poor result from the point of view of the British Government.

Trimble was made more nervous still by the Government's slowness in publishing the Bill and any possible amendments incorporating the RUC name, as well as the flags measure (which would be taken through by the 'fast track' method of an Order in Council).[101] The UUC meeting, scheduled for Saturday 20 May, was coming up very fast and he was not minded to start 'selling' any package unless he was confident that he was obtaining his own minimum guarantees. At this point, therefore, all he really had was Mandelson's statement to the Commons on the Hillsborough package on Monday 8 May, in which the Secretary of State reiterated his conviction that the CBM was merely the start of the process, not a substitute for it and certainly not its end. But, as has been seen, this currency had little purchasing power amongst unionists.[102] By the evening of Thursday 11 May, he was in the bleakest of moods. According to Michael McDowell's contemporaneous note of his telephone conversation with Trimble at 9:20 p.m. that night, the UUP leader believed that there had been massive pressure from the republicans. 'Downing Street has caved in,' Trimble lamented. 'It was fixed at the weekend. I am now left in a mess. The policing situation is nothing of substance, it's a minimalist gesture. That is all I have ... it's a fudge. The reality is it's not worth anything.' McDowell immediately alerted his old associate from Washington, Jonathan Powell, to the gravity of the crisis. 'I spoke to David Trimble at home an hour or two ago and I believe he is on the point of *resigning* [McDowell's emphasis]. He mentioned it as an option – and it is not an idle thought on his part. He is really thinking of doing so ... tonight I fear the worst. He believes he has been sold down the river by his own Government and he is most definitely seeing resignation as the only honourable way out. He is absolutely clear that he cannot sell the minimalist formula London is offering on the policing issue. It is, he says, a fudge which the UUC will not accept and he cannot in decency sell it to them. Well, he said he COULD do it and then *resign* [McDowell's emphasis]. David was thoroughly depressed and exhausted but his judgement is clear enough I think. I urged him to sleep on it and see if anything could be done tomorrow to save things. The deal will not work without him. And no future deal will be possible with another Unionist.' Shortly thereafter, Powell spoke to McDowell. 'He [Trimble] is very, very low,' the Prime Minister's chief of staff conceded.[103] Trimble also spoke with Blair from his home in Lisburn for six minutes at 10 p.m. that night and told the Prime Minister that it was 'all over' but that he would not abort the UUC meeting for 20 May: he would carry on regardless, and go down all guns blazing.[104] At a minimum, Trimble recalls he would have had to go to the UUC and say, 'sorry, folks'.[105] To David Campbell, this seemed like a death wish and he told Jonathan Powell that he would not allow Trimble to take it to the UUC simply to be beaten; the implication was that Campbell wanted postponement to buy more time. The two chiefs of staff spoke every couple of hours in those days, and on the morning of Friday 12 May Mandelson rang Campbell and told him that the UUP leader's conversation had a profound effect on the Prime Minister, who in consequence became rather emotional (Mandelson had been listening to the conversation, but was unable to speak). The effect was to strengthen Blair's determination to support Trimble and deliver the agreed formula-tion on the RUC name. If the UUC was still called for Saturday 20 May, the British would have an announcement ready by Friday 19 May.[106] All that Trimble will say of this conversation with Blair is that 'the penny dropped'.[107]

Trimble was nonetheless reluctant to postpone. He knew that No. 10's great worry was that if he postponed the UUC meeting, the Provisionals might use that as an excuse to withdraw their arms offer. And any delay would deny the Government the kudos of resuming devolution by the time of the two-year deadline for the implementation of the Belfast Agreement, on 22 May (the second anniversary of the referendum ratify-ing that accord).[108] Trimble did two stock-taking exercises, first with party officers on Friday 12 May and then with some party officers and Assemblymen on Monday 15 May at Stormont. The weekend reaction at the grassroots had not been good: there was still no evidence of 'saleable' product for next Saturday's UUC. The reaction was equally negative at a meeting of the Assembly group on Tuesday 16 May, despite Trimble's hardline noises on the previous day following his first meeting, in Belfast, with Ahtisaari and Ramaphosa.[109] David Campbell then telephoned Trimble and told him that the feeling after that morning's meeting of the Assembly group was that the UUP should run with the deal, but delay the UUC meeting by a week. Trimble became very cross with Campbell and asked him, 'If we delay, what are we delaying for? We've got the best we can on policing and flags.' 'Yes, but we've not yet heard much from many party figures about what's good about the package,' replied his chief of staff. 'If my job means anything to you, it's to give you honest advice. And if you go [to the UUC meeting] on Saturday, you'll lose.'[110] Barry White, his soon-to-depart Westminster assistant, says that he never saw Trimble so edgy as on that night of Tuesday 16 May. 'What are you going to do?' asked White. 'I want to go with it, but Belfast have lost their nerve,' replied the First Minister (suspended). 'Anyway, if it all goes wrong for you, we can have a joint leaving party,' suggested White. 'Sometimes, people can forget how tenacious I can be,' Trimble retorted.[111]

During the course of these internal UUP deliberations, Mandelson published the 64-page Police Bill on Tuesday 16 May: as expected, it deferred a final decision on the title of the new force, pending consultation between the Secretary of State and the soon-to-be-created Policing Board. Moreover, whereas Patten recommended that the Union Flag should no longer be flown from police buildings, the Bill did not close the matter and the Secretary of State would have the deciding role (Mandelson appears to have had in mind the possibility of flying the Union Flag over force headquarters during royal visits).[112] Thus, Mandelson was trying to help Trimble prior to the UUC meeting by creating as much ambiguity as possible to sway party doubters wavering over whether to back the package: he was holding out the prospect that some formulation could be found that would enable them to say that the terms of the Burnside motion had been satisfied. But there was, as yet, no firm assurance about incorporation of the RUC in the formal title of the successor organisation.[113] Mandelson was able to give Trimble more immediate assistance on the question of flags and stood up in the Commons at 10:26 p.m. on Tuesday 16 May to push through the draft Flags (Northern Ireland) Order 2000 – in terms that would have been far less likely in the Mowlam era.[114] But despite this relative success, the mood did not lighten in Belfast. Nor, for that matter, were many Unionists impressed with a letter from Mandelson to Trimble supplying him with reassurances on a variety of Unionist concerns. As well as reiterating that the RUC was not being disbanded and giving the new Policing Board the right to design a badge for the incoming force, Mandelson declared that punishment beatings were unacceptable; that the suspension legislation would not be revoked; that the North-South bodies would not survive a collapse of the Assembly; and that there would be action against electoral fraud.

But as with many British Government statements on the mainland concerning 'new' initiatives for this or that, it seemed to Unionists that the same old announcements were being recycled over and over again.[115]

On the evening of 17 May, Trimble again met with senior colleagues, this time at Reg Empey's home in east Belfast. Jim Wilson stated that until then he had been in favour of the original date of the UUC meeting. But now, he had come round to the view that another week was required. On Thursday 18 May, the Assembly group also met. David Campbell asked Taylor where he stood on the timing of the meeting. 'I'm very negative,' replied the MP for Strangford. 'The flags are sorted, but we need the RUC, too.'[116] Trimble still disliked the idea of postponement: he thought it a confession of failure and of weakness. But the evidence that he would be defeated – he now thought by a 70–30 margin – was so overwhelming that he relented and agreed to delay the UUC by one week to Saturday 27 May. Again, Taylor's assessment of the communal mood was very important to Trimble. However, the UUP leader consoled himself with the knowledge that things looked bad not because of the intrinsic demerits of the deal, but rather because 'we were not out there selling the thing'.[117] He telephoned both Blair and Ahern to let them know about postponement: according to one senior Irish source, the Prime Minister and Taoiseach understood entirely.[118]

All Trimble's efforts were now focused upon the internal dynamics of his party, and particularly towards handling John Taylor in the run-up to the UUC meeting. On Thursday 19 May, after delaying his departure to attend the meeting of the Assembly group, Taylor had gone abroad, to the Far East for the inauguration of the new Taiwanese President. Whilst in Taipei, he spoke to David Campbell and said that if the wording on the RUC was right, 'I'll be back for 10 a.m. on Saturday morning [for the UUC]. I've always turned up and backed you, haven't I?'[119] Certainly, Trimble was not especially worried, since he knew that Taylor was 'trying to help me by playing hard to get'; but the UUP leader nonetheless told David Campbell not to tell anyone, in order to maintain pressure on the British Government. Taylor duly did his bit making distinctly sceptical noises in the *Financial Times* on Tuesday 23 May (in fact, the NIO was not surprised by Taylor's stance, having seen him do this before).[120] Subsequently, Taylor went on to Japan and was telephoned by Mandelson. It was 8 a.m. in Tokyo and midnight in London. 'I've been sitting up to phone you,' said the Ulster Secretary. 'I hope it's not too early.' Mandelson confirmed that the name of the RUC would be incorporated into the title deeds of the new force. 'That is acceptable,' said Taylor, 'but I must have it in writing.'[121] Trimble then sent the form of wording to Taylor on Monday 22 May via Mandelson's fax. It read: 'The body of constables known as the RUC shall continue in being as the PSNI (incorporating the RUC) and shall be known for all purposes (including the purposes of any statutory provision) as the PSNI.' Trimble then added in his own hand 'John: I am going to suggest to Mandy [sic] that "shall" in line 3 should read "may".'

The stage was thus, quite literally, set for another grand performance: Josias Cunningham remembered that before the meeting began, he sat amongst papier mâché sarcophagi stored in tunnels ready for that night's performance of Aida at the Waterfront Hall. Cunningham reckoned the vote was too close to call: one third were 'pro', another third were 'anti' and rest were indeterminately in between.[122] Once more, the fate of the institutions rested in the hands of a group described by one irritated Cabinet minister as a group of 'old men, completely out of touch, holding up the whole process'.[123] The usual round of speeches was completed – as Adams had observed some time earlier, elements of the process really did resemble Groundhog Day in which each cycle was just like the last. As the voting began, Denis Rogan reckoned it would be about 60–40 in Trimble's favour and expected it would be a quick count; instead, he was faced with a recount. 'If I lose, I am resigning immediately,' Trimble told Rogan.[124] But when the result came out, Trimble had again won by 53.25% to 46.75%. Jeffrey Donaldson attributed the result to 'war-weariness', both internally in party terms and in society at large. 'Jeffrey, we agreed with every word you said, but . . .' was a familiar refrain in those days. Even his own constituency chairman, Donn McConnell, told the Lagan Valley MP that 'My grandchildren will never thank me for leaving this place in a mess.'[125] Trimble, though, left the scene of his latest triumph in the midst of much controversy. Anti-Agreement Unionists chanted, to the melody of 'What Shall We Do With the Drunken Sailor':

> 'What shall we do with the traitor Trimble/
> What shall we do with the traitor Trimble/
> What shall we do with the traitor Trimble/
> Early in the morning?
> Burn! Burn! Burn! the traitor . . .'

Of greater importance were Trimble's own remarks about the republican movement at the press conference immediately after the UUC. 'As far as democracy is concerned, these folk ain't house-trained yet,' he observed. 'It may take some time before they do become house-trained and I think we actually do need to see the Assembly running so that the checks and balances that are there eventually bring them to heel. We are dealing with a party that has not got accustomed to democratic procedures.'[126] It triggered much condemnation of the UUP leader in segments of nationalist Ireland for what they regarded as his patronising and disparaging characterisation of republicans – implicitly, they thought, as animals. In fact, it was not the first time that Trimble used the expression and he had employed it in his interview with Frank Millar in the *Irish Times* as recently as the day before.[127] But the twin sets of criticisms, from both anti-Agreement unionists and from nationalists, served as a reminder of how narrow a channel he had to navigate, and how miraculous it was that he had survived – despite his own lack of conventional political skills. Perhaps, indeed, he was perfectly suited for managing that peculiar body of men and women called the UUC. Paddy Teahon – who had just retired as Secretary-General of the Taoiseach's Department – reflected back on his years as a key southern negotiator and wondered aloud: 'Could even Ahern or Blair have pulled it off had they been in the UUP leader's shoes?'[128]

THIRTY-FOUR

In office but not in power

TRIMBLE'S prediction to Paul Bew – that 'it might take another crisis to get this thing right' – was soon vindicated.[1] Certainly, there were bonuses in the re-establishment of the suspended Executive. Just days after the Executive resumed its operations, it was announced that two major investment projects at Harland and Wolff and Bombardier Aerospace in east Belfast had gone ahead: Trimble attended the Bombardier announcement, and the message to voters was obvious.[2] There were also signs of cooperation between the two traditions in a number of areas: nationalists and unionists united to reject an extension to Northern Ireland of the mainland's more liberal 1967 Abortion Act.[3] More important, from the point of view of the Trimble project, was the apparent growth of 'structural unionism': of nationalists being sucked into operating British institutions. Thus, Sinn Fein and the UUP, represented by Pat Doherty and Sir Reg Empey, toured North America together for an investment tour.[4] Likewise, in the following year, Francie Molloy of Sinn Fein, chairman of the Assembly Finance Committee, was every bit as annoyed as Nigel Dodds of the DUP by John Prescott's talk of revising the Barnett formula whereby block grants are allocated to the component parts of the United Kingdom.[5] Thus, even the most hardline elements were seen to be playing the politics of the 'begging bowl' with the United Kingdom Treasury, in a fashion not dissimilar to the pre-1972 Stormont ministers. Indeed, the Education Minister, Martin McGuinness, embraced a controversial part of New Labour education policy when he announced he would support and expand the Private Finance Initiative as a means of raising capital for school building and maintenance – though he took care to make the announcement on 14 September at St Genevieve's RC Secondary School in the heart of Gerry Adams's 'fiefdom' in west Belfast.

Such apparent 'bedding down' of the Agreement prompted Blair to urge the Unionists at a private dinner with the UUP at No. 10 on 26 July 2000 to have a major public relations campaign in the run-up to and during the General Election (which was widely expected in the following year). In conjunction with Mandelson, he was very keen to assist. He was also keen to demonstrate that Northern Ireland was part of the new United Kingdom constitutional settlement and to that end was prepared to hold a Joint Ministerial Committee of the devolved countries of the United Kingdom in Belfast; he even talked of holding a British Cabinet meeting in one of the regions. Indeed, at a meeting of the JMC on health held in Glasgow on 16 June, Trimble disagreed on a matter of detail with the UK Health Secretary, Alan Milburn – and the Prime Minister made a point of backing up the First Minister of Northern Ireland. Trimble was so delighted by this that having been rather bored with the proceedings, he decided to stay for the whole day. Significantly, the Northern Ireland Health Minister, Bairbre De Brun, had already visited No. 10 with Trimble on 5 June to bid for more money.[6] Trimble could have repeatedly rammed home the point to his own supporters about De Brun attending the pan-British summit on health as exemplifying structural unionism; but, he chose not to do so. Indeed, according to Sean O'Callaghan, he pulled his punches at No. 10's behest, much as he did after suspension in not crowing about a dramatic reiteration of the sovereignty of Westminster.[7] Like the key figures in the British state, Trimble really believed he had 'won' the big constitutional argument. Having secured that, he felt that he ought not to rub it in and thus make life intolerably hard for the Sinn Fein politicos with their 'militaristic' comrades. He appeared to prefer for his own 'folk' to infer the structurally unionist meaning of events such as the JMC and quietly to derive satisfaction from them, much as he did. But even if he had sold structural unionism aggressively, it is by no means certain that ordinary unionists would have been much impressed. In so far as the Ulster-British population were aware of the concept of McGuinness and de Brun becoming 'structural unionists', they would have viewed it as a bogus concept. After all, it was a staple theme of much Protestant discourse throughout the Troubles that nationalists took British money whilst working to undermine the state. But Trimble did win one significant symbolic victory in this period in the shape of flags legislation: so much so that the sight of the Union flag fluttering atop Parliament Buildings, with the statue of Edward Carson visible in front, was subsequently displayed on the front of the UUP's 2001 election

The campaigner: Trimble presses the flesh on the Shankill Road during the 1998 referendum. The flamboyant Steven King, then John Taylor's aide-de-camp, is on the far right. King later became a star columnist on the *Belfast Telegraph*.

The saddest day: Trimble inspects the Omagh bomb damage with Willie Thompson, (second from the right) then Ulster Unionist MP for West Tyrone, 17 August 1998.

Eyeball to eyeball with the republicans: Trimble faces Gerry Kelly, Martin McGuinness and Gerry Adams, Hillsborough April 1999.

The changing of the guard:
Mo Mowlam hands over
the Ulster Secretaryship to
Peter Mandelson outside
No 10, October 1999.

From Red Hand to glad hand: Trimble receives an honorary Doctor of Law Degree
from the Jesuits of Boston College, Massachusetts

Reg Empey and Michael McGimpsey of the UUP, singing from the same hymn sheet as Martin McGuinness of Sinn Fein, at the launch of the Creativity Seed programme on 13 February 2002. This picture appeared on the front of the *News Letter* on the next day, prompting Nigel Dodds of the DUP to observe, 'that's one of the best pictures we've ever had'.

'We've educated Patten to the realities of policing!' The ever-positive Ken Maginnis, UUP security spokesman 1982–2001.

The don: Paul Bew, Professor of Politics at Queen's University Belfast. The prolific ex-Marxist became Trimble's foremost defender in academe.

A tower of strength: David Lavery, Trimble's Principal Private Secretary 1998–2001.

A gentleman and a
patriot: the late Sir Josias
Cunningham, President
of the UUP 1990–2000.

'The Undertaker':
David Campbell,
Trimble's Chief of Staff
from 1998. The UUP
leader came to rely
heavily on his judgement.

The internal Unionist divide: James Molyneaux with the two main rivals for the nomination for his old seat, David Burnside and Jim Wilson. Burnside was the victor.

Trimble shares a light moment with Rev Martin Smyth, MP for South Belfast and his rival for the UUP leadership in 1995 and 2000.

'You've betrayed Ulster, you wee bastard!' Willie Ross, sheep farmer, MP for Londonderry East 1974–2001 and Trimble's most forthright critic in the Parliamentary party, at home near Dungiven. When the author asked Ross if he actually said this to Trimble, the MP replied, 'I never said "wee", laddie!'

David Brewster, erstwhile Honorary Secretary of the Ulster Unionist Council, and one of Trimble's doughtiest opponents. Brewster would later leave for the DUP.

address. This, however, was undermined in the meantime by the continued refusal of McGuinness and de Brun to fly the flag until such time
as the matter was finally settled.[8] Eventually, it was agreed that the Union
flag would fly over seven government buildings and departmental headquarters on seventeen specified days, including the Queen's birthday.[9]

Such was the atmosphere in which the two independent international
inspectors, Ramaphosa and Ahtisaari, verified that the IRA had opened
two of its arms dumps as part of its 'up-front' contribution towards
resolving the arms issue.[10] But the lateness of the IRA offer on arms (and
the concessions which the Provisionals won in return for what unionists
regarded as a preposterously delayed and nugatory gesture) does much
to explain why it met with so indifferent a response in the majority
community. Nationalists believed that such churlishness was evidence
that *nothing* would satisfy unionists. The unionists had demanded that
the two Governments push the republican movement towards violating
the sacrosanctity of their arms dumps – a big shift in terms of IRA
theology. And having won that battle, the unionists had then moved on
to their next tranche of demands, this time on policing and other symbolic
issues. This analysis underlay Seamus Mallon's criticisms of the UUP
during the passage of the policing Bill which began its Second Reading
stage on 6 June 2000 – and, more particularly, his criticisms of what he
saw as Mandelson's propensity to indulge the UUP and its leader above
almost all other considerations. The SDLP and much of nationalist Ireland
had other problems with the Bill besides the high-profile symbolic matters
and as of 29 June had tabled 64 amendments: their demands included
radical surgery on the requirements for human-rights training in the new
force; the proposals for 50–50 Catholic-Protestant recruitment ratios; the
power of the Ombudsman to investigate alleged past abuses; the definition
in law of the powers of the Oversight Commissioner; the composition
and staffing of the new Policing Board; and the power of that board to
follow up reports from the Chief Constable by initiating inquiries.[11] As far
as Mallon was concerned, this highlighted that the Mandelson legislation
deviated from the Patten proposals in most of those instances. Similar
criticisms were also voiced by such academic commentators as Brendan
O'Leary of the LSE and Patten Commission members Gerard Lynch and
Clifford Shearing. O'Leary even warned that if the Bill was unamended,
there could be substantial defections from the Provisionals to the dissident
republicans. According to Chris Patten, Maurice Hayes and Peter Smith,

QC, also talked to him about their concerns. Patten, though, declines to state the content of his own subsequent intervention with the Government on the legislation.[12] Mallon was confident he would eventually obtain what he wanted. His confidence was derived, in part, from a 70-minute one-on-one meeting with Blair at Chequers on Sunday 28 May. Mallon made it quite clear that unless wide-ranging changes were made, the SDLP would not take its place on the new Policing Board: he recalls that the Prime Minister simply smiled.[13]

At Second Reading, Mandelson duly signalled that he would make a range of concessions when the Bill came to report stage.[14] Mandelson's original caution on Patten appears to have reflected his own period as a Lambeth councillor, when he witnessed the excesses of police liaison committees during the height of London Labour's 'loony left' phase in the 1970s and 1980s. One senior British official believes that 'in his early days as Secretary of State, Mandelson was genuinely motivated by considerations of good governance rather than "shall I back unionists or nationalists?". But, as time went on, Mandelson became increasingly convinced of the old adage that "humankind cannot bear too much reality", and especially the unionist portion of it. He knew that on both the flag and the name he would ultimately be arriving at a Patten-like destination, but he thought that it would be better to arrive slowly rather than overnight. His motivation was not the final outcome, but to make it less shocking.'[15] Another civil servant puts it even more starkly: 'The Brits stuck in changes [between Patten and the Bill] in order to take them out according to the needs of the moment.' The question, though, was how many of these changes would be removed and on what terms. Mandelson, though, never enjoyed the consistent support of No. 10 on this approach – especially when he tacked in a 'unionist' direction. This applies especially, Mandelson says, to the issue of the name of the force, but not exclusively so. Ironically, one of the few allies he had on matters of policing governance was the then Home Secretary, Jack Straw – which made it all the more disappointing to Mandelson when Straw played a 'tacitly instrumental' role in the Ulster Secretary's subsequent departure from office.[16] George Howarth, the Political Development Minister at the time, stated that 'in the course of 2000, Peter became increasingly tetchy about No. 10. It really started in the summer, when things went badly wrong with the policing Bill. He felt that Jonathan Powell was exerting too much influence and that deals were being struck with the Irish. There were times at Castle

Buildings when he would even say disobliging things about No. 10's handling of the legislation. And ultimately, Ronnie Flanagan was regarded as the arbiter of what was good policing practice and what wasn't.'[17] Indeed, the then GOC. Lt Gen, Sir Hew Pike, states that during that year, Mandelson's detractors in No. 10 concluded that the Secretary of State had 'gone native' and was listening too much to his security advisers: voluminous briefings would be sent to No. 10, and were apparently not read properly. According to Pike, the Irish Government, the SDLP and Sinn Fein were very persuasive and seemingly omnipresent in Downing Street at this time – and were far more powerful as an influence than the Unionists.[18] There was, of course, one other argument which advocates of a 'maximalist' or 'pro-nationalist' position on the issue of policing could deploy. What was the point of having inflicted all the 'pain' of symbolic change upon the RUC and unionist community for no compensating gain on the green side of the divide? This then became the rationale for further British moves in the direction of nationalist Ireland. But Trimble played little part in these debates – he was not present at Second Reading stage nor, unlike Mallon, did he sit on the Standing Committee – and acquiesced in some of these nationalist successes on matters of police governance as a matter of deliberate calculation. According to David Lavery, Trimble wanted to allow the SDLP to gain some ground vis-à-vis abstentionist Sinn Fein by letting them 'play the parliamentary card' and win victories for their community at Westminster.[19]

Curiously, this was one occasion when Trimble was determined to make a stand on symbolic issues. Ken Maginnis tabled his Committee stage amendments on the night of 12 June, the most important of which stated that the RUC would remain in the formal title of the new force, whilst acknowledging that it 'shall be styled for operational purposes the PSNI'.[20] But the Government hesitated on delivering this – partly because, as Joe Pilling told Paul Bew, it feared that if the UUP demands were granted there would be no CBM that autumn.[21] Trimble duly went to Blair and told the Prime Minister that the inevitable effect of not securing this was a successful challenge to himself in the UUC.[22] The Government consequently decided to accept the Maginnis amendment and made a further technical change of its own to embrace the RUC Reserve; there would also be a tight legal definition of the term 'operational purposes' that would effectively rule out any practical use of the term 'RUC'.[23] It duly received Conservative and Liberal Democrat backing. Although independent lawyers stated that the effect of the Maginnis amendment was to consign the name 'RUC' to the history books in any practical sense, and had only really made explicit in law Patten's own assertion that there was to be no disbandment of the force, Mallon was nonetheless deeply upset. He felt he had staked so much on the British Government's acceptance of the SDLP amendments – exemplified by his vote for the Bill at Second Reading – and duly denounced Mandelson for 'political chicanery' on the floor of the Commons.[24] In a subsequent address to the National Committee on Foreign Policy on 15 September, Mallon emphasised that the full implementation of Patten was more important that the survival of any one individual and that both himself and Trimble might go (i.e. depart office). He then was reported as saying that 'Peter, I hope, will.' Mallon denied it was a call for the Northern Ireland Secretary to depart, and stated that it was solely a reminder that everyone was dispensable. Then, when pushed as to why he hoped Mandelson would go, he added, intriguingly: 'Well, I think the reality is he will be going.'[25] Mallon said that he had good reason for saying this, though to this day he declines to name the source of his prescient remark. The sharp disagreements continued even when the First and Deputy First Ministers visited President Clinton in the Oval Office on 13 September. Subsequently, Clinton told Blair about how the First and Deputy First Ministers had conducted themselves in Washington: what struck him was how they had contradicted each other.[26]

The combination of policing reforms with continuing paramilitary activity ensured that by mid-summer, Unionism was again suffering a crisis of confidence. The headlines, both provincially and nationally, were dominated *inter alia* by a vicious internal loyalist feud that erupted between the UDA and UVF in the remaining Protestant portions of west Belfast, in which the key figure was the UDA godfather, Johnnie Adair.[27] Eventually, Mandelson employed his powers under the Sentences Act to recall the ever more outrageous Adair to prison; Trimble did not condemn the decision per se, and believed that the security forces should have been doing more to stop the disturbances, but thought that the apparent one-sidedness of the crack-down was destabilising in the absence of proper action against Real IRA and others.[28] Yet even if there were no apparent double standard, respectable 'middle Ulster' would have been profoundly disquieted by such violence – especially at a time of major upheaval in the police and demolition of watchtowers.[29] There was also plenty of dissident republican activity, such as a foiled 500lb 'spectacular', destined for an Army base in Londonderry on 12 August at the time of the city's Apprentice Boys' parade.[30] The Provisionals also continued their activities: on 13 June, Sir Ronnie Flanagan stated that there were 'intelligence indications' that they had shot dead a Belfast drugs dealer, Edmund McCoy, in Dunmurry (making it a total of sixteen to eighteen men shot for that reason by the IRA since the first ceasefire in 1994).[31] And then there was the refusal of the Irish Government to release the IRA killers of Garda Jerry McCabe: evidence, again, in the eyes of Unionists, of the greater value placed on the lives of southern policemen than of their northern counterparts.[32] This was quite apart from the relentless assaults by loyalists against Catholic homes, schools and churches. Above all, despite the CBM – which was deemed by Unionists to be a poor substitute for decommissioning – there was no sign that any actual destruction of arms would take place in the near future. Indeed, on 25 October, the IRA confirmed that whilst it had earlier resumed *contact* with the IICD, it had not recommenced *discussions* with de Chastelain because of British ill faith.

These were not the best conditions in which to fight a Westminster by-election in an overwhelmingly unionist seat with a large RUC vote. On 27 April, Clifford Forsythe, Ulster Unionist MP for South Antrim, had died suddenly; in the 1997 General Election, he had enjoyed a majority of 16,611 over the SDLP, and 57.49% of the total vote. In percentage terms, it was therefore the party's safest seat, so much so that the DUP had only stood once against Forsythe, at the time of the parliamentary division's creation in 1983. But now, the DUP would give the UUP no such free pass: the pre-Agreement world was another country, and all bets were off. The Paisleyites had already nominated Rev. Willie McCrea, MLA, of Magherafelt, Co. Londonderry, and the former MP for Mid-Ulster.[33] Many felt that he was not the strongest conceivable candidate. First, he was an outsider, not coming from any remotely contiguous area. Second, he was a sitting MLA and councillor in his native patch; he would thus have a dual mandate for two different constituencies, which could lead to potential conflicts of interest in terms of bidding for funding; and, third, he had publicly appeared on a platform with Billy Wright at a rally after Drumcree II in 1996. Perhaps this explains why Trimble thought that the UUP would be ultimately 'okay' in South Antrim.[34] Seven candidates put in for the Ulster Unionist nomination: Trimble's sometime Vanguard colleague David Burnside (who came from Ballymoney in North Antrim);

Jim Wilson, the then Ulster Unionist chief whip and another ex-Vanguardist (who came from Ballyclare in the constituency); David Campbell, from nearby Carrickfergus in East Antrim, who entered the race belatedly and reluctantly with Trimble's encouragement after the latter became worried about the consequences of a Burnside candidature; and four others.[35] In the final ballot at a meeting at the Dunadry Hotel near Templepatrick, Co. Antrim, on 19 June, Burnside beat Campbell by 90 votes to 70.[36] Once selected, Trimble weighed in behind the new candidate: it was still better to have a moderately hardline internal critic win the by-election in the person of Burnside than a very hardline outsider in the person of McCrea. But party unity suffered a serious blow on 9 August when Sir Josias Cunningham was killed in a car crash: the then party president was one of the few figures who commanded the respect of all factions and had a total grasp of the party's finances.[37] His death also diminished the chances of an amicable resolution of the UUP's links with the Orange Order.

Burnside rapidly found the going very hard indeed. The DUP deployed an army of well-disciplined activists, rather after the fashion of the Liberal Democrats' style of 'pavement politics' on the mainland. McCrea also enjoyed the support of such mainland friends of the Union as Andrew Hunter, who came to canvass (it was a sign of Trimble's remarkable magnanimity that when Hunter himself faced a very serious challenge from Labour in his Basingstoke constituency during the General Election of 2001 – in which the incumbent MP's opposition to the Belfast Agreement played a part – the UUP leader made a point of endorsing him).[38] By contrast, according to Burnside, less than half of the UUP Assembly party and only half of the Westminster MPs turned up.[39] Burnside sought – not inaccurately – to position himself as a one-time 'yes' voter disillusioned by Blair's pledges. He also made much of his genuine role in trying to save the RUC. But Blair Wallace, who went out canvassing on Burnside's behalf, soon discovered that in one home after another the reaction was: 'Oh? Is he Trimble's man? We'll not be voting for him.' As Wallace recalls, these were households in areas such as Ballyclare and Ballynure that had voted Ulster Unionist for generations.[40] It was an odd position for Burnside to find himself slated as 'Trimble's man' and pointed up the dilemmas for Agreement sceptic elements in the party: they were seen as neither one thing nor the other and Burnside in particular was accused of not 'selling' the deal hard enough. Whatever the truth of the matter, when the by-election was held on 21 September, McCrea emerged as the victor with 11,601 votes or 37.95% of the poll on a 43.02% turn-out; Burnside secured 10,779, or 35.26%, with the other candidates way behind. It appeared to represent one of the greatest earthquakes in unionism in years – certainly since Paisley and the Rev. William Beattie running as Protestant Unionists wrested the old Bannside and South Antrim seats from the UUP in the Stormont by-elections of April 1970.[41] Immediately afterwards, everybody had their explanations, and many were self-serving. Mandelson immediately blamed Burnside as a poor candidate: to have done otherwise would have implicitly conceded that policies, and specifically Government policies, had undermined pro-Agreement unionism.[42] Privately, Trimble also blamed Burnside's lack of political touch exemplified by his statement that he 'knew Bournemouth and Brighton better than Portrush' – in an attempt to show that he could communicate with the mainland (in fact, as was subsequently proven, Burnside was a perfectly viable candidate in conditions of a normal South Antrim turn-out). Trimble's public pronouncements were probably a more accurate analysis of what had happened: he ascribed the defeat to the Patten report.[43]

Once again, Trimble faced another 'greatest crisis' of his leadership. Indeed, he told Steven King on several occasions in this period in a quite cool, matter-of-fact way that it was a mistake to have gone back into the Executive with Sinn Fein in May 2000 and that he should have held out for more.[44] At times, he appeared almost resigned to his fate as the antis circled around him ominously. Thus, even the ever-loyal Ruth Dudley Edwards – whose catchphrase about Trimble was 'he's in a very difficult position, you know' – told Paul Bew that she thought the puff had gone out of the UUP leader.[45] In fact, Trimble's powers of recuperation were considerable and although he may not have had much of a grand strategy, he certainly had plenty of tactical ruses up his sleeve to see him through the coming weeks. He left all his principal interlocutors in no doubt as to the gravity of his predicament. When Sandy Berger, Clinton's National Security Adviser, telephoned him just before he appeared at a *Daily Telegraph* 'Question Time' panel in Bournemouth on 4 October, Trimble bluntly told him, 'you've got three weeks in which to save it' (that is, the Belfast Agreement).[46] He had already delivered much the same message to Blair at a breakfast in No. 10 on 2 October, at which the UUP leader told the Prime Minister that he would be damaged at his party's annual conference on Saturday 7 October.

But as occurred after the murder of Charles Bennett and the Florida arms importation in 1999, the 'antis' again did not move quickly enough to call a meeting of the UUC whilst the party was reeling from the blow of South Antrim (Donaldson says it was not logistically possible to have held a meeting that quickly).[47] They appear also to have hesitated on the manner of the challenge to Trimble: should it be specifically policy-related, thus tying the First Minister's hands, or a no confidence vote?[48] However, the behaviour of some of the pro-Agreement elements was even more vexing to the UUP leader. Ken Reid of UTV observed to a colleague that when he did a search of statements made by pro-Agreement colleagues during those weeks, he could barely find a pro-Trimble remark.[49] According to Frank Millar, there was a revival of the NIO-inspired talk of July 1999, when it was suggested that Trimble should follow the example of Mallon's resignation and that Empey might make a better leader of the UUP than Trimble.[50] Once again, the 'men in grey sashes' were said to be gearing up to tell Trimble to do the honourable thing – not on ideological grounds, but on personality grounds. He had become the issue, and was no longer the indispensable man. Yet for all the grumbling, this threat never materialised. Indeed, Trimble made it through the UUP annual conference on 7 October with one of his most forthright speeches to date in which he asked: 'The revolving door in Downing Street for any nationalist with a grievance gives the impression that some victims are more privileged than others. Is there really a moral vacuum at No. 10?'[51] No. 10 would not have liked it, but nor would they have been unduly alarmed: they recognised that such tactical, rhetorical escalations were the minimum necessary to tide Trimble through.

Some in Government believed that this crisis was about management of the UUC rather than a major issue of principle. Indeed, at a meeting on Monday 23 October, Blair alluded to a forthcoming *Belfast Telegraph* poll which showed that there was very substantial unionist support for Trimble remaining as leader and for staying inside the Northern Ireland Executive (Ed Curran, the editor, who is very protective of such data, states that he has no idea how findings of the survey leaked to Government, but is sure that it did not come from his journalists or from the pollsters. He is convinced that this was the only time such information ever seeped out).[52] Whatever the source of the leak, the numbers certainly underwrote Blair's conviction that Trimble's problems lay more within his party than the electorate as a whole.[53] Again, the UUP leader made it quite clear that he would do the minimum necessary to squeeze through the forthcoming UUC meeting – but no more than that, if he could possibly avoid it. The question, of course, was what was the minimum necessary? Trimble told Blair that he thought he could resist a leadership challenge more easily than a motion to tie his hands on policy. His problems were two-fold. First, some pro-Agreement colleagues were 'preparing the lifeboats'. Second, he had word that Donaldson was seeking to put together a composite motion for the sake of party unity which would be hard for him to resist. Donaldson's preference was for a shorter timetable for Unionist withdrawal from the Executive than Trimble thought desirable. Trimble had not yet decided what his own motion would be, but once he did he would be in touch with No. 10. Certainly, Trimble wanted to avoid naming specific dates and to stave that off would have liked de Chastelain to be more proactive and to issue regular reports. But, since it now seemed unlikely that there would even be a CBM that week – and, even if there was one, he noted, it would be so late and contrived as to be thoroughly counterproductive with the UUC – he would have to do something more.

Trimble's options were very limited. Indeed, even some of his best cards – the support of the British Prime Minister – were potentially counterproductive in this context. Thus, Blair offered to come to Belfast on Thursday 26 October for the next JMC, a forum which he knew the UUP leader greatly valued. Trimble accepted, but urged the Prime Minister publicly to demand decommissioning as the best way of reinforcing his (devalued) 1998 referendum pledges. And then there were some old tricks which he believed he could no longer play. Trimble knew by now that the British Government had come to believe that virtually all deadlines – *vide* the post-dated cheque – were counterproductive and only undermined Adams with his own 'militarists'. Indeed, the UUP leader himself had also come to accept elements of this analysis, especially after the suspension crisis. How, therefore, could he satisfy the UUC without at the same time upsetting Blair and incurring the rage of nationalist Ireland? Trimble had the device at the ready. Originally, Trimble had contemplated pulling out of the North-South Ministerial Council (NSMC), which was the all-Ireland portion of the new institutions most valued by nationalists and which they hoped over time would turn into a proto-government of a unified Republic. But after consulting colleagues, he concluded that withdrawal *tout court* would cause immense problems with the SDLP and the Irish Government. Instead, Trimble decided to focus on Sinn Fein and revealed to Blair that he was thinking of ceasing to nominate Sinn Fein ministers to the NSMC (the UUP leader believed that he had a legal right in his capacity as First Minister to determine whether such meetings can take place, under the terms of the Northern Ireland Act 1998). This gambit had the advantages of being unexpected and of not being time-sensitive – and thus a dreaded 'deadline'.[54]

In the meantime, Trimble continued to indulge talk of a 'unity motion'. He met twice with Donaldson in the week leading up to the UUC and authorised two 'swing' Assemblymen, Fred Cobain and Danny Kennedy, to try to cobble together a composite with Donaldson under the watchful eye of Empey. Whatever his private misgivings about its viability, Trimble at least had to be seen to be responding to the passion in a bruised party for a common approach. According to David Campbell, the Trimbleistas' (and, indeed, the British Government's) greatest fear in those days was that Donaldson would come up with something so reasonable-sounding that they could not refuse him, even though in practice it would tie the leadership's hands utterly: in other words, allowing the Executive to continue, but precipitating action if there was still no evidence of decommissioning by Christmas. Certainly, Fred Cobain derived the impression that something along these lines was going to be Donaldson's position and reported as much back to the Trimbleistas. But when Donaldson finally showed his hand in a mailing sent to delegates on the night of Wednesday 25 October, it emerged that his actual ideas were far more prescriptive. They would have entailed immediate withdrawal from the NSMC and effective withdrawal from the Executive by the end of November, with no resumption until there was substantial decommissioning and a reversal of the Patten reforms.[55] David Campbell et al. calculated that a quick closure of the Executive was something for which the critical centre ground of the UUC was not quite ready.[56] Despite Cobain's and Kennedy's attempts to achieve a compromise, Trimble responded on the next day with a withering attack on what he called 'Jeffrey's letter to Santa'.[57] Although there were further attempts at compromise on the day of the UUC meeting, this intervention may have damaged the prospects for a revival of the compromise proposal.[58]

Trimble was not safe yet, though. On the evening of Wednesday 25 October, the IRA issued a statement stating that it would allow the independent inspectors to verify that the organisation had undertaken another CBM and that they would contemplate re-engagement with de Chastelain – as promised on 6 May at Hillsborough – provided that it advanced the peace process.[59] The IRA had made the offer despite Trimble's personal plea to Martin McGuinness in the margins of a Northern Ireland Executive meeting on Thursday 19 October that such a step would be counterproductive; shortly after that plea, Ahern had telephoned Trimble to tell him that Adams was 'on the road' with republicans asking for the CBM. It confirmed to Trimble his own profound conviction from his security force sources that the republicans wanted Donaldson to win.[60] Worse still, Blair's visit to Belfast on Thursday 26 October – perhaps predictably – failed to give Trimble the necessary lift.[61] As Trimble saw it, Blair was 'unfocused' during the crucial press conference and did not make explicit that 'whatever happens, Northern Ireland will be governed as part of the United Kingdom'.[62] Perhaps the most significant part of the visit was the private session between the Government and the UUP teams in Castle Buildings at 5 p.m. Trimble gave Blair advanced notice that he would announce on Saturday the commencement of phased sanctions against Sinn Fein participation on the NSMC until such time as the IRA fully re-engaged with de Chastelain. 'Thanks for letting us know,' replied Blair. According to Trimble, Blair gave some indication of these plans to the Irish Government – and that they then urged Sinn Fein not to over-react.[63]

Trimble thus approached the twenty-fourth meeting of the UUC and party Executive to discuss the Belfast Agreement with quiet confidence. As the UUP leader unveiled his NSMC sanctions in response to the Donaldson motion, he noticed that the atmosphere in the Waterfront Hall was distinctly flat – as though the UUC did not think his measure amounted to very much.[64] When the votes were finally counted, Trimble had again won, this time by 445 to 374 votes, or 54% to 46%. This represented a mere percentage point improvement on the May 2000 UUC meeting but, as Trimble observed, 'never has one per cent had such an effect'.[65] Whilst Donaldson sought to put a brave face on it and claimed that Trimble had been forced on to his own ground, the reality was that the high-water mark of anti-Agreement Ulster Unionism was receding – at least for the time being.[66] The Trimbleistas calculated that they had bought themselves time within the party until the end of January 2001.[67] The public reaction of republicans was predictably robust. Adams denounced Trimble's 'arrogant' behaviour and stated that 'Sinn Fein does not hold executive position by dint of patronage from the UUP'.[68] The effects of what Tim Dalton of the Irish Department of Justice called the 'fatwa' were obvious: the creation of the NSMC had been sold to the republican grassroots by the Sinn Fein leadership as one of many positive aspects of the Belfast Agreement that made the traditional forms of 'armed struggle' unnecessary. Trimble had now thrown its workings into doubt by a mechanism which dissident republicans could characterise as a new version of the 'Unionist veto'.[69] But it was significant that neither the Irish Government nor the SDLP denounced the move in vociferous terms; and the much-feared republican political retaliation never materialised. Thus, Sinn Fein did not engage in any 'tit-for-tat' withdrawal from Assembly committees,[70] let alone leave the Assembly *tout court*, though they did launch a law-suit.[71] If Trimble's sanction was the mildest response available, so too was the republican leadership's *political* response. Instead, believed Trimble, the Provisionals' response to his NSMC sanctions was more sinister: they may have given the republican dissidents a bit of surreptitious help, as exemplified by the attempted murder of a Catholic RUC officer in Co. Fermanagh during this period.[72] Peter Mandelson states that in his view, whilst there was no operational coordination between the Provisionals and Real IRA, there was dialogue between the two which kept any splits very carefully managed.[73]

But the Irish Government's and SDLP's understanding of Trimble's predicament did not yet extend to an endorsement of the new policing arrangements – to the irritation of both himself and the British. This left Trimble dangerously exposed to another challenge in the UUC. So the First Minister sought to find a context in which he could break the cycle of 'battles royal' within his own party; or, at least, to provide him with sufficient cover to make it through to next year's expected General Election without having brought down the Executive. Trimble believed that the only viable 'context' for a resolution of the impasse would be a third, valedictory visit by Clinton before he formally left office on 20 January 2001. Nationalists would not respond to pressure from Unionists or the British Government, but they might just respond to the most hibernophile of American presidents as a kind of farewell gesture.[74] Of course, this was a high-risk strategy for him. Clinton was widely disliked by many Unionists for his perceived pro-nationalist tilt. If the UUP leader brought him in, thus associating himself again with the friend of their enemies, and still failed to obtain a result, it would further confirm the DUP's view that he was a 'patsy'.[75] Trimble, however, was prepared to take that risk. Not only did he think it would work, but he enjoyed such high-level political dealings. And he felt a degree of sympathy for Clinton as the man who brought him, no less than Gerry Adams, into the big league of international politics. 'I must be gracious to Clinton,' he told Ruth Dudley Edwards.[76]

Nothing, though, was finalised in light of the President's shifting schedule, which also included the possibility of an historic visit to North Korea. Doing something in Northern Ireland remained an option, as was evidenced by the recall of Jim Steinberg as an unofficial intermediary. Steinberg had formally left the NSC in August 2000 for a senior position at the Markle Foundation in New York and whilst visiting London in mid-November for his new employers breakfasted with Jonathan Powell at the Ritz. Powell described the sense of drift, which could become a 'waterfall' by the time of the next UUC meeting. This was expected in January 2001, and would result in further pressure on Trimble to 'up the ante' by then. Steinberg accepted the role – but says he told his former boss on the NSC, Sandy Berger, that whilst he did not believe that a Clinton visit would solve the problems, it could concentrate the minds of all of the parties and thus be the catalyst that led to a deal.[77] Therein, of course, lay the problem for Trimble: he had a very different conception of Clinton's place in history from that of the President himself.[78] Trimble believed their interests overlapped, namely in bringing about a grand act of decommissioning that set the seal on the 'constitutionalisation' of republicanism. But after the intense encounters of the Israeli-Palestinian summit at Camp David in July 2000 – which had then blown up in his face with the outbreak of the al-Aqsa intifada in September – Clinton seemed to seek the easy plaudits of the Irish crowds rather than to do the hard graft that was necessary to achieve a settlement. As Peter Mandelson recalls, 'Clinton's policy was to do everything to avoid closing down the channel of communications with republicans. He aimed to show, even in his last days in office, that they had a friend at court.'[79] In consequence, says Trimble, 'Clinton made no effort beforehand and did nothing.'[80] In fact, from a UUP perspective, it was worse than nothing. Trimble wrote to Clinton on 1 December and then gave an interview to Catherine Utley of the BBC World Service for the World Update programme. 'I am appealing to Bill Clinton to use his influence to persuade the IRA to fulfil the commitments it made in May.'[81] An angry Sandy

Berger telephoned Jonathan Powell on 3 December: Trimble's sin, in the eyes of the White House, was that he was 'putting it up' to Clinton and urging him to call in his 'debts' from the republican movement. As Berger saw it, Clinton was now being 'set up' for failure if there was no decommissioning.[82]

But it was not only substantive policy issues which divided the Ulster Unionists from the American Administration: it was the all-important questions of presidential symbolism and scheduling as well. As Trimble observed to the American Consul-General in Belfast, Ki Fort, 'You've never done a trip that's properly balanced.' He also said as much when Steinberg visited him at Stormont on 27 November 2000.[83] By this, he meant that Clinton had never yet visited a specifically 'unionist' town during his two previous visits. Trimble therefore requested that Clinton 'even up' the balance with a trip to Banbridge in his own constituency. After all, it had been bombed just prior to the Omagh blast in 1998. Mandelson, also, raised the issue of a Banbridge visit – but the White House schedulers said no.[84] According to Ki Fort, there were simply so may hours set aside for talks at Stormont that there was no time for a stop-over at other points en route.[85] Trimble was unpersuaded by this line of reasoning: Clinton had the time to visit Dundalk, Co. Louth, before flying north to Ulster – where the US President was expected to denounce the dissident republicans and proclaim that they and the related '32 County Sovereignty Committee' were now on the State Department's list of terrorist organisations.[86] But even this was by no means certain: Mandelson had been very annoyed with Dick Norland who he believed had dragged his feet on designation. The Americans retorted that this was no simple matter, requiring careful aforethought that would not expose them to legal challenge. The Clinton Administration also feared that such a step would give undue credibility to a marginal grouping in the United States. The matter of designation of the dissident groupings also became the subject of an exchange between Trimble and the Ulster Secretary at Northern Ireland Questions on 20 December 2000, when Mandelson came as close as was diplomatically possible to endorsing Trimble's attack on the 'dilatory' approach of the Americans.[87] Although privately Trimble never expressed his anger in quite the same way as Mandelson did to Norland, he viewed such reasoning as absurd: the Clinton Administration had over two years since Omagh to sort out its response to the dissidents. Trimble suspected that once again, the

Clintonistas had failed to move because Sinn Fein/IRA (and, more particularly, the Irish) had told them that precipitate counter-measures would trigger a wave of sympathy in the republicans' own base for the dissidents and thus weaken the Adams-McGuinness leadership.[88]

By the time that Clinton arrived in Dublin on 12 December, the three Governments were all playing down prospects of a breakthrough: the trip would, at most, be a catalyst for the 'choreography' of a 'mini-deal' that entailed the Unionists dropping NSMC sanctions in exchange for an IRA re-engagement with de Chastelain (plus further moves towards British 'demilitarisation' of south Armagh).[89] Certainly, the public aspects of the visit to the Republic were profoundly uncongenial to Unionists of all stripes. Clinton and his wife Hillary – just elected as junior US Senator from New York State – embraced Adams and McGuinness on stage at the Dublin headquarters of Guinness. According to Jim Steinberg, Gerry Adams sought out the opportunity of a public embrace by Clinton and the President responded in his characteristically bonhomous style.[90] To Unionists, nothing could have been more emblematic of the moral vacuum at the heart of the process than the respectability conferred by the leader of the Free World upon those whom they saw as the not-so-former men of violence who had not repented of their deeds.[91] Trimble believed this performance had far more to do with Clinton's 'demob-happiness' and the needs of his wife to keep the Irish American vote in New York contented, even though her next outing at the polls would be six years away.[92] As George Howarth recalls, 'The NIO were not as sensitive to the optics and the implications for Trimble as they might have been. Partly, it was because the southern leg of the trip was beyond their control and we were "blindsided", as it were. But there was also a sense that Her Majesty's Government couldn't deny him his lap of honour.'[93] Worse still from the UUP leader's viewpoint, the President delivered only the most indirect of rebukes to Real IRA.[94] 'In the event, what Clinton said in Dundalk was pathetic', states the UUP leader.[95]

Clinton flew that night to Belfast and at 9 a.m. on 13 December, he went to Stormont. But little came of those exchanges. The big set-piece event at the new Odyssey Centre, built on land near the Belfast shipyards, turned out to be rather more dramatic – albeit in a rather perverse way. Trimble employed the very language that Clinton had directed at the paramilitaries in 1995 ('you are the past; your day is over').[96] But from a UUP perspective, the President's subsequent address contained too much treacly Clintonic emoting about the future of the 'children of Northern Ireland', and too little in the way of concrete political help; even the talk of American security assistance to help the two Governments to deal with dissident violence seemed nugatory. Moreover, Clinton's reference to the need for exclusively peaceful means seemed less dramatic than in 1995. Many unionists would have bridled at what they saw as the 'moral equilateralism' of Clinton's meetings with victims of terror from each of the main communities.[97] Throughout this speech, Trimble kept looking at his watch; he then leant over to Blair and whispered some words in the Prime Minister's ear and walked off the platform. It appeared as though he had administered a massive snub to the President of the United States. Moreover, the White House had been deprived of an 'inclusive' photo opportunity on the platform. Some of those watching the scene, such as Ki Fort, thought he must be feeling unwell.[98] In fact, the truth was far more banal than any of those explanations. Trimble had to catch a plane to London so that he could then fly on to Sicily where the mafia-busting Mayor of Palermo, Leoluca Orlando, was hosting a conference on defeating the criminal-political nexus; Trimble was to be appointed as an Honorary Citizen of Palermo.[99] But because Clinton, as he so often did, was running close to two hours behind schedule – mostly dealing with political problems in America rather than the Northern Ireland peace process – Trimble now had to make a choice. He told Blair what was happening, who replied 'you must be joking'. Even though Blair offered a lift in the Prime Minister's aircraft, Trimble did not want to alter his plans because it would have gone to RAF Northolt rather than Heathrow and still not given him enough time to catch his next plane: according to Trimble there was only one connection available.[100] As one Northern Protestant associate of Trimble observes, far from having administered a grand political gesture or diplomatic *faux pas* – depending on your point of view – the UUP leader 'had simply fallen prey to what can only be described as "traditional Ulster Prod anal retentiveness". It's the old Ulster refrain, "Sure, I've made a booking, I'll not be changing it now, not even for the President of the US." Or, alternatively put, "I've cut the coupon." Of course, Trimble hadn't paid for the air ticket himself, but old habits die hard. At one level, it's appalling that the man who's carrying the flag for Northern Ireland, and the main ambassador of his own community, should do that. But at another level, the rigidity and unbiddability of these people is a great strength. And, at that moment, you got a truer flavour of the Ulster character than you would from a 1000 speeches.'[101] And, of course, it also was a further illustration of his frequent desire to escape from Northern Ireland, even with the President and Prime Minister present.

Trimble's rapid exit certainly illustrated the complexity of his character. On the one hand, here was the cosmopolitan who appeared to have transcended his provincial background; who loved mixing with the great and the good; who urged his 'own folk' to 'think politically' beyond the traditional confines of Unionist ideology; and to accept the internationalisation of the Ulster conflict. On the other hand, as was illustrated by this episode, he could sometimes behave as though he had never left Bangor. But when BBC Northern Ireland put a very negative interpretation upon his action – construing it as a deliberate snub to Clinton – Trimble was very upset and it appeared to make him much more cautious about political and cultural warfare for some time thereafter.[102] As his Northern Protestant, non-party, associate adds, this in itself was also reflective of another aspect of the middle-class Ulster mindset: the combination of truculent independence with a craving for respectability.[103] Of course, had Trimble been really cosmopolitan, he would have understood that the Clintonistas were now 'history' and that the incoming Administration might well have been amused if they had known that he had snubbed the outgoing President. For whilst Clinton was in Belfast, he received the news from his aide Bruce Lindsey, that Vice President Albert Gore, the Democratic nominee, had finally conceded to his US Republican rival, Governor George W. Bush of Texas, after weeks of legal wrangling; indeed, Clinton talked to Gore whilst in a holding room at the Odyssey Centre.[104] This conversation contributed to the late start in the programme and Trimble's subsequent 'walk off'. But there is no doubt that Gore's concession drove Clinton's Irish trip off the American front pages and, to a much lesser extent, in Northern Ireland as well.[105] This was fortunate for Trimble after the Clintons' embrace of the republicans: indeed, as one loyalist observed, even the supposed debacle of walking off the platform perversely worked to Trimble's advantage, since many unionists derived pleasure from the idea that the UUP leader had shown the American President exactly what they thought of 'Slick Willie'. And the Northern Protestant then mused: 'If cats have only nine lives, then David Trimble certainly ain't a cat. Or if he is, then he's a super-cat. And he's certainly the oddest cat I've ever met.'

THIRTY-FIVE

A narrow escape

FEVERISH efforts to put together a deal that would avert collapse of the Executive continued in the days immediately following Clinton's departure. Trimble firmly believed that the Provisionals would do nothing to disarm, and certainly not before the unofficial 'cut-off' at the end of January. As he saw it, they hoped that his 'boiler would burst' under internal party pressure and that he would then be forced by the UUC to withdraw from the Northern Ireland Executive (thus irritating the two governments and losing the 'blame game').[1] But the 'Groundhog Day' quality of the discussions on guns, government and policing was suddenly interrupted by a new set of claims concerning Peter Mandelson – this time relating to his alleged role in obtaining passports for the Hinduja brothers. Indeed, one senior UUP figure, arriving at No. 10 at 1 p.m. on Tuesday 23 January 2001 for a routine meeting, could not help noticing a very odd atmosphere and even a slight frisson of tension between Blair and Mandelson. Likewise, an Irish Government delegation also visited No. 10 at around this time, and noticed that everyone there seemed exercised by 'other matters' and would leave the room at regular intervals. By the next day, they all had their answer and it was clear that Mandelson was on the way out; Trimble was subsequently delighted to be able to offer a tribute to the outgoing Secretary of State on the floor of the Commons during his resignation statement, and whilst he was exiting the chamber met Blair behind the Speaker's chair.[2] A very upset Prime Minister then invited Trimble to come to his rooms. 'It's terrible, but he's finished now,' pronounced Blair.[3] When the news of the resignation came through, key Irish officials were meeting with Adams, McGuinness and Ted Howell in a west Belfast safe-house to try to secure a resolution of the stand-off. 'If Mandelson had been there, he would have been quite pleased with the reaction,' states one participant. 'Despite suspension and the policing Bill, there was no exultation over his departure, and they all knew that he was not all bad and had persuaded Trimble to make the jump, twice, in November 1999 and in May 2000.'[4]

Speculation immediately arose, including amongst some senior Ulster Unionists, as to whether Mandelson's departure would make it easier for the SDLP to sign up to the new policing structures.[5] Indeed, as one senior Irish official observes, if Mandelson had still been central to the peace process – a hugely important task of the modern British state – Blair would probably not have let him go. Whatever the truth of the matter, Trimble was undoubtedly the sorriest of the major Northern Ireland party leaders about Mandelson's departure. This was not because he imagined him to be a proto-Unionist. Indeed, quite apart from some memorable rows, he would have been well aware that Mandelson had wobbled over suspension in February 2000 and that it was No. 10 which had driven the process. Rather, Trimble's regrets stemmed from the loss of a man whom he regarded as a consummate professional. 'All facts, Ranke used to say, were equidistant from G-d,' noted Paul Bew in the April 2001 issue of *Parliamentary Brief*. 'For Mandelson, all Irish ideologies – unionist and nationalist – were equidistant from G-d, significant only in so far as they threatened to advance or inhibit the New Labour project . . . Particularly from February to May 2000, Mandelson tackled an unpromising situation with brilliant strategic realism. He had worked out Trimble's bottom line – that nationalist consent to the new devolved arrangements within the UK become visible – and made that part of the deal by his flag legislation.' Indeed, as he sat in his chair at the London headquarters of the NIO at 10 Millbank as he was preparing to leave office, Mandelson told his senior officials: 'Somebody has to look after the police.'[6] Likewise, at the launch of Trimble's collection of speeches and articles held at Politico's bookshop on 18 July 2001, Mandelson went up to his former Political Director at the NIO, Bill Jeffrey, and told him that he was keeping an eye on issues relating to the RUC.[7] Mandelson certainly stayed in touch with Trimble after his departure from office, and it was subsequently reported that they would have regular conversations – a kind of 'politicians anonymous' at which two embattled men could share their thoughts with one another.[8]

George Howarth states that Trimble was consulted on Mandelson's replacement: the final choice boiled down to Charles Clarke, then a Home Office Minister, or John Reid, the Scottish Secretary; Nick Brown, the then Agriculture Minister, and Adam Ingram were also briefly mooted. Trimble had no power of veto, but Blair was sensitive to the UUP leader's needs on this issue.[9] The UUP leader would have been happy with either of the main candidates, yet was contented enough when Reid was appointed: although Reid was a west of Scotland (Irish) Catholic and an ardent Celtic supporter, Trimble initially entertained hopes that the residual sectarian tensions of that region (not least of which was the 'Old Firm' rivalry of Glasgow's two main football teams) would give the new Ulster Secretary some feel for his own position.[10] Moreover, he would have been aware that as Armed Forces Minister from 1997–8, Reid had been sympathetic to the readmission of two Scots Guards to the Army following their conviction for shooting dead a Catholic in 1992. Their sentence of life imprisonment had, at the time, proved controversial on the mainland.[11] Better still, reasoned some of Trimble's advisers, Reid had been a Communist once: as the late Mick McGahey once said of Scottish Bolsheviks, they 'were caught between Holy Water and Boyne Water'.[12] If Reid was neutral, that would be enough for the UUP leader.

But just as the metropolitan Mandelson proved to be immeasurably better than the UUP could reasonably have expected, so Reid proved from their viewpoint to be immeasurably worse. Partly, this was connected with the circumstances of Reid's appointment and the lessons imbibed by 'the system' from the 'defenestration' of the outgoing Secretary of State (Mandelson's term). Reid first suspected he might be appointed after doing a round of television interviews in defence of Mandelson – 'not very successfully', he adds. 'So when I got a call from Tony Blair, it was pretty obvious that he didn't want a late-night briefing about Scotland.' The main focus of their discussion when they met was the relationship between the Prime Minister and the Northern Ireland Secretary – and that it was essential that they be at one and that no wedges be driven between them by either side of the divide in Northern Ireland.[13] The clear implication is that this is exactly what had happened – first under Mowlam, when the UUP had to appeal to No. 10 over her head, and then under Mandelson, when nationalists did so. Indeed, in December 2001, after a clash between Trimble and Reid, Jonathan Powell even telephoned David Campbell to tell him 'you shouldn't think that John Reid is another Mo Mowlam' – with, Campbell feels, the clear implication that if forced to chose between the UUP leader and Secretary of State, they would on this occasion opt for the latter.[14] But the NIO also felt that during Mandelson's tenure, they had not – in the words of one senior official – 'hit him hard enough with the idea of "Patten must be adhered to, right or wrong"', and had let him deviate from that template for understandable political and administrative reasons. Moreover, senior British officials also believed that the political class had drawn conclusions from the ferocious reaction to suspension and would think very carefully before 'dissing' nationalists again. Certainly, Reid was very careful not to offend nationalist sensibilities. Thus, in an interview with Frank Millar in the *Irish Times* on 14 May 2001, Reid declined to say whether he agreed with Blair's remarks in Belfast in 1997 that he valued the Union of Great Britain and Northern Ireland (an aside which brought no rebuke from the UUP leader). There were also personality clashes with Trimble. The UUP leader found that precisely because he was from the west of Scotland, Reid thought he knew all of the answers and above all, how to behave – and that by adopting a rough and ready manner (the 'we Celts understand each other' routine), he alienated rather than reconciled unionists. Thus, David McNarry of the UUP recalls that in July 2002 the Ulster Secretary walked into a meeting of the Loyalist Commission, comprised largely of senior paramilitaries. Reid took his jacket off and loosened his tie in an act of self-conscious informality and pronounced: 'I suppose you boys have never met a Taig before' (a pejorative term for a Catholic). As McNarry observes, if this was an attempt at humour, it failed miserably: many of those present knew loads of Catholics, including republicans, not least from prison and a host of other forums where paramilitaries were subsequently able to talk to each other. Many of them had found employment in mixed workplaces at various points in their lives. Everyone wanted to hear what he had to say as Secretary of State, not, McNarry felt, to witness him engage in an act of cultural empathy.[15] Likewise, Trimble recalls that Reid suggested that Douglas Alexander, a DTI minister, look into a matter of mutual concern. 'It'll be all right, he goes to Ibrox,' Reid reassured the UUP leader. Trimble did not much like football, but as he observed, it said something about Reid's perception of the First Minister – namely that to couch the matter in sectarian terms would somehow appeal to him. 'He didn't seem to realise that many decent, middle-class Protestant people in Ulster think that the "Old Firm" is awful, and that they think that Rangers fans are as bad as their opposite numbers,' says Trimble.[16] In the end, Trimble wondered: 'Why do Reid, Des Browne [MP for Kilmarnock and Loudoun and then Under Secretary at the NIO from 2001] and Ingram [MP for East Kilbride, then Security Minister and a Protestant] all share these aggressive characteristics? It's got something to do with the nature of the greater Glasgow Labour party and the arrogance bred by being effectively part of a one party state.'[17]

Most of the problems with Reid were not readily apparent at the time that the new Secretary of State assumed office. Some who subsequently observed the relationship between the UUP leader and the Secretary of State thought that the chemistry had far more to do with Trimble's personal moods (and Reid's prickliness) than any great issue of principle. Certainly, Trimble's moods were very variable in this period, and his conduct was often inexplicable in his own terms. His peculiar approach to public affairs and human relationships was most dramatically illustrated in his attitude towards the United States. The inauguration of George W. Bush as President should have represented a major opportunity. During the course of the previous year, he had made contact with leading Washington conservatives, and had attended several conferences of the American Enterprise Institute, perhaps the most influential think tank with the new Administration. Most of these conservatives were Atlanticists and Anglophiles who had utter contempt for the Clintonites' foreign policy; they thought it a disgrace that Clinton had granted a visa to Adams in 1994, a man they associated with the 1984 Brighton bomb blast that nearly killed their heroine, Margaret Thatcher. Thus, if not pro-Unionist, they were certainly anti-IRA and they believed that it was one of many terrorist groups across the world which the Clintonites had treated with kid gloves. At minimum, many Realpolitik conservatives, devoid of sentimentality, believed that Clinton personally had invested far too much time in a tiny jurisdiction, Northern Ireland, of little economic or geo-strategic concern to the United States. Better still, from Trimble's viewpoint, Congressman Peter King, one of the foremost friends of Sinn Fein on Capitol Hill, had shifted his support from Bush to the Texas Governor's main rival, Senator John McCain, in the bitter Republican primary campaign for the GOP nomination. This was after the devoutly Methodist Bush had visited Bob Jones University in South Carolina (where Ian Paisley obtained his doctorate) – an institution which many believed to be anti-Catholic.[18]

Yet despite all this – and the fact that the UUP leader was one of the few genuinely pro-American Nobel Peace Prize winners, even backing the Vietnam War – Trimble proved surprisingly reluctant to exploit these new circumstances.[19] Indeed, his behaviour was in some ways reminiscent of that of James Molyneaux in 1984–5 before the signing of the Anglo-Irish agreement: Molyneaux had an 'in' with Norman Tebbit and others in the Thatcher ministry, but was unable to make much of it. In the first instance, Trimble's problems were organisational: he kept in place Anne Smith, the part-time employee in the UUP's Washington office, who few could claim was a Washington heavyweight.[20] He was also slow off the mark in taking advantage of the new informal back-channels that were open to him. Thus, Steven King and others wrote a memorandum in late 2000, on Trimble's behalf, that advocated a shift in American policy and was meant to go to members of the incoming Administration. It drew attention to Sinn Fein/IRA's record of anti-Americanism and its support for many of the terrorist movements in the world that threatened US citizens; but although it contained no direct criticism of Blair or the British Government, Trimble was worried that it might be construed as such and requested that it not go in with his name attached.[21] Later, a further memorandum was sent directly, via a prominent Bush supporter, to the new US Secretary of State, Colin Powell. This document, much of it researched by C.D.C. Armstrong, drew attention to the neutral Irish Republic's historic lack of support for American foreign policy – a point which would have extra significance in the light of the fact that the Republic had recently been elected by the General Assembly for a two-year term as one of ten non-permanent members of the UN Security Council.[22] It arrived just in advance of Powell's first meeting with Brian Cowen, and also drew attention to a host of anti-American articles in *An Phoblacht*, one of which also accused Powell of helping to cover up the My Lai massacre (later, it emerged that some of the most anti-Bush articles were written in Irish).[23] The authors of the memorandum sent to Powell warned that the rise of Sinn Fein could make the southern state even less amenable to US interests.[24]

Trimble's eccentric behaviour reached its nadir during a visit to Washington from 15–18 February 2001. There, he attended one of the largest right-wing gatherings, the Conservative Political Action Committee conference in Arlington, Virginia. Thanks to the intercession of a prominent American activist, he sat on the platform with such luminaries as Vice President Cheney (with whom he was photographed) and the then chairman of the Senate Foreign Relations Committee, Jesse Helms of North Carolina. On the next night, the guest of honour was Karl Rove, the

President's main political strategist, who was widely credited with having crafted Bush's electoral game plan. Rove came over to the table where Trimble was sitting, but the UUP leader militantly – and inexplicably – refused to meet him; he had literally to be pushed into the presidential counsellor's arms and when they finally spoke he appeared to make little or no impression. That night, he also sat next to a prominent Washington conservative, Frank Gaffney, the president of the Centre for Security Policy, and expressed a very keen interest in meeting John Ashcroft, the incoming Attorney General – who would be a key figure in the event of any future prosecutions against Irish republicans. Gaffney knew Ashcroft and they had a very good mutual friend in the US Senate who could facilitate an introduction. Yet although Trimble had been briefed beforehand that one of Gaffney's main aims was to build an anti-missile shield for America and her allies, the UUP leader nonetheless made it clear that he thought that Russia had a good case against American withdrawal from the Anti-Balistic Missile Treaty that forbade widespread deployment of such systems. Indeed, it was an eccentric posture for him to adopt. Whether the Russians had a case on the 1972 ABM Treaty was not the point here: Trimble was carrying the flag for Ulster Unionism, and his views on the merits or demerits of arms control agreements were of no relevance to the task at hand. Indeed, despite Trimble's disquisition on the ABM Treaty, which he found distinctly underwhelming, Gaffney still sought via their mutual friend to arrange a meeting with Ashcroft. But, having emphasised to Gaffney the crucial importance of such an encounter, Trimble was somehow unable to make contact with the intermediary and the courtesy call fell through.[25] Partly, it may have had something to do with his embarrassment about 'cold-calling' people – the residue of his old shyness.[26] One of those who observed his performances during that visit wondered why anyone would have taken the trouble to help him at all (it certainly vindicated the observation of the writer F. Frankfort Moore in 1914 that 'whatever an Ulsterman may be, he is certainly never charming, and of that fact no one is more fully aware than the Ulsterman himself').[27] After all, there was a vocal pro-Sinn Fein constituency in Washington, albeit much smaller than many Britons realised, which made support for Trimble potentially risky. Yet here was a man who was neither personally engaging nor prepared to make an ideological appeal to secular conservatives, let alone to the Christian right. In fact, he was not even willing to make much of a moral appeal on behalf of a community tormented by terrorism and it was noticeable at an American Enterprise Institute event on the previous day that the former Reagan Administration official, Richard Perle, referred to Gerry Adams in more uncompromising terms than did Trimble.[28] Indeed, the only viable UUP message in the United States would have been to appeal to anglophile conservatives to put this anti-American national liberation movement beyond the pale. But Trimble did not want to do that: what he wanted was 'a wee bit more pressure' *within* the confines of the existing process – that is, to alter the terms of trade rather than to exclude Sinn Fein (indeed, Trimble's relatively mild approach was noted with some surprise by Sinn Fein's American counsellors, especially after September 11). But no one in America was going to go out on a limb, and potentially risk criticism from Irish-Americans, for the sake of so calibrated a policy. Trimble was the first Unionist politician of modern times fully to grasp the importance of the international dimensions of the Ulster crisis, but in practice was woefully slow when it came to implementing such a strategy. Thus, even after Gerry Adams had caused controversy in the United States by calling upon Fidel Castro in Havana in late 2001, Trimble was still reluctant to make common cause with Cuban-Americans in Miami – a fairly critical group in a key 'swing' state. But he was not alone in the laggardly quality of his responses: even well after September 11, officials at the British Embassy in Washington could not help noticing that the NIO behaved as if Clinton was still in power.[29]

Certainly, it is inconceivable to imagine that Adams or Hume – indeed, almost any normal political animal – would have made similar mistakes if placed in Trimble's shoes in the United States. It raises the obvious question – why? When asked about his performance with Rove, Trimble muttered something about not 'brown-nosing', even though he was supposed to be 'winning friends and influencing people'. As such, it was a very peculiar application of the traditional flinty, Ulster Protestant independent-mindedness. Moreover, as has been noted earlier, he had been reluctant during the Clinton years to link up with his obvious conservative Republican allies. Partly, it was because he was afraid of offending the then President (even though building up a bloc of support on Capitol Hill and inside the Beltway would have made Clinton *less*, not more likely to let him down). Then there was the self-consciously 'civilised' aspect of Trimble's new political persona: as he told me in October 2000, 'I can't be associated with yahoos', even though the 'yahoos' had enjoyed majorities in both houses of Congress in the world's only superpower since 1994. But there was another factor: because Trimble did not know America that well, he tended to give excessive credence to the message coming from State Department officials such as the US Consul-General in Belfast, Ki Fort. She told him that regardless of the outcome of the American presidential elections, she expected there would be no fundamental change of policy; Dick Norland, the NSC staffer, likewise told me 'basic continuity is the watchword'.[30] In declaratory terms, they were right: there was no change of policy per se. But informed observers knew that neither Bush, nor even Gore, would spend the same amounts of time on Northern Ireland that Clinton did: Senator Chris Dodd of Connecticut, for one, had said as much when he visited the Province in August 2000.[31] Thus, St Patrick's Day was still celebrated in the White House and Gerry Adams contrived a photo-opportunity with Bush on the steps of the Capitol building, but the event was self-evidently not what it had been for the past eight years.[32] The most important institutional manifestation of the down-grading was that Northern Ireland would now not be handled by the President and the most senior figures on the NSC, but rather by Richard Haass, head of policy planning in the State Department and ambasssador-at-large, who had served in the first Bush Administration.[33] Curiously, he was one of the few figures in the Washington foreign policy establishment with something of a track record on Northern Ireland: in his book *Unending Conflicts: The U.S. and Regional Disputes*, published in 1990, he had favourably remarked upon the RUC's growing acceptability amongst Catholics and had raised questions about the Anglo-Irish Agreement of 1985. In 1995, he also suggested that there was too much focus upon the nationalist community and the IRA, which he termed 'the squeakiest wheel'.[34] But despite these propitious circumstances, Trimble never really hit it off with Haass. Again, it may partly have been a matter of his moods, which could fluctuate dramatically, although Haass was not a particularly easy person to deal with, either.

More eccentric still was Trimble's approach to a four-part BBC drama series on the Easter Rising of 1916 and subsequent events, called *Rebel Heart*, written by the pro-republican author Ronan Bennett. Trimble's advisers drew his attention to the series, which they believed portrayed the British and the unionists in a most biased, negative light.[35] The UUP leader was militantly against doing anything about this, perhaps because of the pounding he had taken from BBC Northern Ireland after he walked off the platform at the Odyssey Centre during Clinton's visit. Eventually, after much persuasion, Trimble turned round and condemned the series, in a letter to the BBC's then Chairman Sir Christopher Bland (in which he called Bennett an 'active IRA apologist') and in an article for *The Daily Telegraph* on 15 January 2001.[36] But having entered the fray, he did so in the most inept manner possible. There was a perfectly respectable, liberal case for saying that *Rebel Heart* did very little to contribute to the 'decommissioning of mindsets', to use a favoured nationalist phrase of the mid-1990s. However, Trimble chose to take on the series on the weakest ground possible: he conducted a pedantic defence of District Inspector (or D.I.) Nixon, an RIC/RUC officer long suspected of a role in the murder of an innocent Belfast Catholic family, the McMahons, during the disturbances of 1922. But even if Nixon had not been responsible for that particular atrocity, on the basis of his public and highly sectarian pronouncements alone he was scarcely someone who merited much support from a New Unionist: he had been expelled from the RUC in 1924 for making a political speech at an Orange Lodge, thus falling foul of police disciplinary regulations, and later became an independent Unionist at Stormont.[37] It was not the first time that Trimble had put historical or legal detail ahead of what Blair always called 'the big picture'. Earlier, he had attacked the *Panorama* programme that named the four men suspected of involvement in the bombing of Omagh by Real IRA, on the grounds that it might prejudice a possible conviction.[38] As such, he had aligned himself with the Northern Ireland Human Rights Commission (whose bid to block the programme on those very grounds had just been quashed in the High Court) and Ahern (whose Government Trimble alleged was not doing enough against the dissidents) and against Mandelson (who stuck his neck out to support the film).[39] Trimble himself, of course, had done similar things in years gone by, naming leading figures in the IRA on the floor of the Commons. Bew, for one, conjectured that he was simply so fed up with the entire BBC that he would do nothing to help any enterprise connected with it.[40] It was not, in fact, the case – it was his old lawyer's instincts – but there is no doubt that Trimble believed BBC Northern Ireland to be profoundly hostile to him and he complained about its coverage when Greg Dyke, the then Director-General, came to Belfast in 2000 and in 2003 at the *House Magazine/BBC Parliamentary Awards*.[41] Certainly, he lacked what Louis Althusser might have called an 'ideological state apparatus' to pick up his message. Indeed many of his supporters believed that his three major speeches of late 2000 – to the British-Irish Association in September, to the UUC in October, and at the Odyssey in December – received relatively poor coverage (in contrast to claims that he had stormed off the platform when Clinton was speaking).[42]

Perhaps the most obvious reason why Trimble was not very good at such forms of longer-term political and cultural struggle was the punishing pace of managing the process and his party, day-in, day-out: the important frequently yielded pride of place to the urgent. Weeks were consumed by the arcana of a 'maxi', 'midi' and 'mini' deal to resolve the crisis of the institutions, leading up to the fourth Hillsborough summit of Blair's premiership on 8 March 2001. It all came to naught and the great issues were all 'parked' until after the General Election, still widely expected for 3 May.[43] The British and Irish Governments issued a statement to the effect that there would be no more demilitarisation until the Provisionals agreed specific schemes with the IICD and indicated that they expected an agreement; in exchange, demilitarisation would commence, plus concessions on the OTRs and the existing policing legislation. On that same day, the IRA indicated that its representative had been in touch with the IICD and on 14 March, in its third statement in a week, indicated that its representative had met with de Chastelain's body.[44] The outcome of Hillsborough was thus no disaster for the UUP, in the sense that they had not been pushed into abandoning their NSMC sanctions, but in the absence of decommissioning it was an insufficient basis on which credibly to fight the General Election. The point was further underlined when Paul Bew subsequently spoke to Bill Jeffrey. The NIO Political Director made clear that a further raft of concessions on policing, including probably on the badge of the new force, were on their way: one of the reasons for deferring final settlement of the issues raised at Hillsborough 2001 until after the General Election was simply to help Trimble. In other words, nationalists obtained substantial concessions; Unionist gains this time round would be solely procedural, relating to the timing.[45] The most significant 'procedural' item on the UUP's broader agenda was Trimble's goal of postponing the quadrennial local government elections, scheduled for 16 May 2001. The UUP feared that if there was a typically low unionist turn-out for these not-very-powerful bodies, then the result of the South Antrim by-election might be replicated Province-wide. The

DUP would mobilise their own highly motivated constituency, whereas the UUP might well not do so. Moreover, David Campbell feared that if the UUP leader went into any post-election UUC meeting with a raft of aggrieved, recently defeated councillors, the pro-Agreement forces would be greatly weakened.[46] But if Trimble could ensure that the local and Westminster elections were held on the same day, then the UUP turn-out would be increased because it was for a 'real' poll for a real Parliament and the chances of severe losses at municipal level would be much diminished. Indeed, in at least one case – that of William Ross in East Londonderry – Trimble believed that he had so alienated pro-Agreement unionists that the sitting Westminster MP would need the help of moderate UUP councillors such as David McClarty of Coleraine DC. Thus, pro-Agreement voters who would come out for McClarty in the locals might just hold their noses and vote for Ross in the general election.[47] Trimble originally asked for this step on 11 December 2000 in a meeting with Blair at No. 10 and claims that it had the support of Mandelson; but he believed it was held up by John Reid's Northern Ireland Office, who feared that it would be too much of a contrivance to save Trimble and that it lacked nationalist support.[48] In the end, the local poll was postponed to coincide with the general election, much to the annoyance of both the DUP and Sinn Fein: they were quite right to charge that it was a 'sop' to Trimble.[49] 'Sops', however, would be all he obtained from the British Government at this stage.

One senior NIO official observing Trimble in this period, not least at Hillsborough, was struck by how serene he was – despite obtaining so little from the two governments.[50] There were a number of reasons for this serenity. First, he had managed to make it well into the New Year without his 'boiler bursting'. Partly, this had been achieved through the mechanism of the internal consultation, which had allowed members to let off steam. Trimble had a further stroke of luck when the 24 March AGM of the UUC was postponed because of foot-and-mouth disease; this was subsequently rescheduled to 23 June, in other words well after the general election. This would make any leadership or policy challenge before the poll almost impossible. But the real reason for the serenity which the British official spotted in Trimble's behaviour at Hillsborough was because the UUP leader was by then fairly well resolved upon pulling another dramatic stroke. As he told Richard Haass on 9 May 2001, when they met at Winfield House in London, he felt that the IRA would need a 'real jolt' – that is, to help it on its way towards becoming a 'slightly constitutional party'. How, though, was he to achieve that? Trimble knew that there would be no second, open-ended suspension of the institutions after the fashion of February 2000, at least not without the support of the Irish (which would not, of course, be forthcoming).[51] The furious reaction of nationalist Ireland to the first suspensions had seen to that. And, as he noted, 'I didn't have Jo Cunningham to put the pressure on this time': someone who, as on that dramatic occasion, he trusted utterly.[52] He had, therefore, to do 'something else'. The nature of that 'something else' which Trimble needed to survive had first become apparent to his close associate, Eoghan Harris, some months earlier. During the course of a long interview in a hotel suite in Washington in February 2001, Harris suggested to Trimble that he was on course for a disaster in the forthcoming elections. Harris thought the UUP leader was too complacent about his constituency, that the British were doing nothing for him and that his own community would punish him for Blair's failures to adhere to the referendum pledges. Harris believed that in the past, the two Governments had been willing to facilitate Trimble's survival by giving him some sort of narrative to sell to his own community. But that, clearly, was no longer the case, since at Hillsborough, the Governments had given him nothing to sell. He would therefore have to think of the 'nuclear options' available to him – that is, various forms of post-dated resignation. The UUP leader contemplated the matter overnight. On the next day – at lunch with Ahmed Chalabi of the Iraqi National Congress, who entertained the guests with his account of the Drogheda talks of 1995 that attempted to compose differences between the country's Kurdish factions – Harris asked him: 'Are you going to do some sort of post-dated resignation?' 'The whole success of this depends on the secrecy of it,' Trimble replied with great velocity. 'I must now go completely underground on that.' It was hard to know the exact significance of such discussions with Trimble: often, he used them as a sounding-board for something he had in mind already.

Why did Trimble decide to take this step? Curiously, the state of opinion in the unionist population as a whole formed only a part of his calculations, despite the frequency with which many of his lieutenants referred to the threat of the DUP. Indeed, as has been noted, for some time he at least affected a rather optimistic view of his prospects: for instance, at Hillsborough on 8 March 2001, he told Blair that he would lose three seats (Martin Smyth in South Belfast, William Ross in East Londonderry and Willie Thompson in West Tyrone – of which only Ross's constituency would go to the DUP, and the other two to nationalists). But he was confident that the UUP would hold on to Fermanagh and South Tyrone, North Belfast and Strangford. In other words, Trimble obviously believed that an anti-Agreement posture was a loser for UUP candidates and a pro-Agreement stance was a winner. The Prime Minister expressed surprise at Trimble's projection: Government polling was much more pessimistic and in January 2001, Trimble says he was told by Ken Reid of UTV that the NIO reckoned that in a worst-case scenario the UUP could be reduced to a mere two seats after the election.[53] But Trimble had his own polling data from Pricewaterhouse Coopers to back up his instincts. The results were delivered on 3 April, on the basis of a sample of 1173 unionists across Northern Ireland (with special emphasis on Strangford, South Antrim and North Down). They indicated on the basis of first preferences that the pro-Agreement UUP voters remained the largest component of the pro-Union population at 38.4%, followed by the DUP at 24.6% and UUP anti-Agreement elements at 16.3%. UUP pro-Agreement voters pronounced themselves as likeliest to turn out on the day itself, at 62.9%. Health was deemed the most important issue by the total sample, at 38.9%, followed shortly thereafter by decommissioning, with education a close third; peace process-related issues, such as decommissioning and the threat of Real IRA mattered more to DUP and UUP anti-Agreement voters. David Campbell says that Trimble was most intrigued by results of the question, 'Should the next General Election be a referendum on the leadership of David Trimble as First Minister?' By 54.7% to 43.3%, those surveyed said 'no' (though 68.1% of Ulster Unionist anti-Agreement voters and 72.1% of DUP supporters backed the proposition that the election should be a referendum on Trimble's leadership). Indeed, on the basis of this data and of a subsequent telephone canvass of the Mourneview estate in Lurgan, Co. Armagh, Trimble was convinced that he would enjoy a 6000 majority in Upper Bann.[54] That said, Trimble was also well aware that as with so many previous samples over the years, the respondents to the Pricewaterhouse Coopers poll may well have been reluctant to admit their support for the DUP. According to David Campbell, the UUP leader therefore knew that he needed something more to squeeze by – and that to place his own personal position as First Minister on the line by some form of resignation might just do the trick.[55]

The polling evidence was therefore sufficiently contradictory not to be the sole, or even the main impetus behind Trimble's resignation strategy. There had to be an extra ingredient – principle. There was a strong case for suggesting that Trimble's Unionism was minimalistic, but it did have two irreducible cores. First, there was the consent principle. Second, that the IRA had to engage in some form of real disarmament if there was to be any stability of the institutions. At bottom, Trimble simply did not want to continue in office on the current debasing terms. Again, just as Harris focused his thoughts during his visit to the United States in February 2001, so he was much influenced by some correspondence which he received from a very different source. On 10 April 2001, a personal letter arrived in the First Minister's office from a Protestant minister known to be of impeccably moderate views. The minister had met with Martin McGuinness on a few occasions in recent months. He wrote: 'I regret to say that apart from conversation and consultation on educational matters, I did not get the slightest indication from the Education Minister that there was the remotest chance of decommissioning ... While one can, with dubious feelings, perhaps reluctantly accept the situation for a short time, to give every opportunity for Sinn Fein/IRA to deliver, I am now of the firm belief that if the present administration is to continue without imminent progress on decommissioning, that it will be an act of hypocrisy and against moral and upright standards ... I know many that only voted for the Belfast Agreement because the Prime Minister gave his additional handwritten pledges, which sadly now seem to be meaningless ... Speaking personally, I write to say that after much heart searching, that if you are unable to indicate to me that you will pull out of the Executive if there is still no verifiable progress on decommissioning by this summer, then come September I believe I will have no alternative but to refuse to attend any further meetings with the Minister of Education.' David Campbell showed the letter to Trimble and explained that the Protestant minister had been in favour of the Belfast Agreement. If this was the thinking in such circles, then it was a sure sign of trouble in middle Ulster; Campbell then sent it to Powell, asking him, in turn, to show it to Blair.[56] But Trimble was also undoubtedly influenced in the decision he intended to make by events much further away from home. From 2000–2001, he had tracked the progress of a man he had admired, Israel's premier Ehud Barak. Barak, Trimble believed, had made a very generous offer to Yasser Arafat at Camp David in July 2000 – only to be hit by a rising tide of ethno-religious rage from a still-unfulfilled Palestinian people who believed that their day had come.[57] Having taken the risk of making such an offer at the behest of Clinton, so exposing his own flank at home, Barak's position was then destroyed when he allowed his left wing to make yet more concessions to obtain a deal: he was duly defeated by Likud's Ariel Sharon.[58]

All that remained for Trimble was to decide the terms on which to deploy his resignation weapon. He waited until the announcement of the postponed general election, after which they would be in the middle of the marching season. And he had two basic options. The first was to resign *tout court*, which would administer a dramatic shock to the system but would make it extremely unlikely that he could ever reassemble the necessary coalition to be re-elected as First Minister. The second was to submit a post-dated letter to the Speaker, under the terms of the Northern Ireland Act 1998, which would only take irrevocable effect six weeks after its submission and thus would buy extra time to cobble something together. The first senior UUP colleagues whom Trimble took into his confidence were Empey and Taylor. Taylor was firmly of the view that Trimble should avail himself of the second option. Resignation *simpliciter*, the UUP deputy leader argued, would be demoralising to pro-Agreement unionists; by contrast, the latter would strike the right balance. Trimble agreed with Taylor and decided to hand a post-dated letter of resignation to Lord Alderdice, to be activated on 1 July, unless the IRA had begun to decommission its weapons. He would confine the resignation to himself: if he needed the rest of his team to resign, they could always follow suit.[59] On Thursday 3 May, he brought together some of his main aides – including David Campbell, David Kerr and Philip Robinson – in Jack Allen's room at Stormont to discuss the modalities. Kerr and Robinson were of the opinion that he ought to do a press conference in Glengall Street. Campbell disagreed: since he was resigning as First Minister, Trimble would have to do it in the Assembly chamber. Moreover, the DUP had tabled a vote of no confidence in Martin McGuinness for Tuesday 8 May and since the press would already be there, any major announcement by Trimble would inevitably knock it off the front pages. The date was also chosen because it was a year since the Provisionals promised to decommission. Later that day (3 May), Trimble summoned the full Assembly group to a meeting, but he was still not prepared to tell them of his plans; eventually, he was prevailed upon to take Jim

Wilson and a few others into his confidence. At 8:30 a.m. on Tuesday 8 May, Trimble convened a meeting in his office with Empey, McGimpsey, Jim Wilson and some senior aides, where he ran through his plans.[60] At 10 a.m., he met with Alderdice and asked if he could make a personal statement to the Assembly at 10:30 a.m., to which request the Speaker agreed. Then at 10:15 a.m., he made the most crucial call of all: to inform Blair himself. Before he did so, David Campbell had asked him: 'Have you thought about what you've to say if Blair asks you not to do it?' 'I'll say "Thanks, but no thanks, Tony."' But when his office tried to contact Blair, he discovered that the Prime Minister was unavailable: indeed, later that day Blair would go to Buckingham Palace to inform the Queen of the date of the postponed general election, to be held now on 7 June. Only Jonathan Powell was contactable. Did he still want to talk to him? A relieved Trimble seized on the opportunity and announced to Campbell: 'I think I'll just speak to Jonathan.' This was fortunate: he would have found it much harder to present such a *fait accompli* to Blair than to Blair's senior aide.[61] Indeed, Campbell subsequently told Paul Bew, 'as long as he lives, he'll never get into a room alone with Blair again' (in fact, this did not turn out to be the case, but it said something about Trimble's mood in that period).[62] When Trimble told Powell of his plans there was a sharp intake of breath – as though he was hearing them for the first time (though UUP representatives had hinted to the British Government that Trimble could not let matters drift beyond June, as did Trimble when he met privately with Ahern on 4 May. In both cases he had stopped well short of saying exactly what he would do). 'What will the letter say?' asked the Prime Minister's chief of staff. 'And on what grounds wouldn't it happen?' Trimble explained his case in a breathless, almost embarrassed way. 'Presumably you have to do this for electoral reasons?' Trimble made it clear that they were obviously not irrelevant, but that his principal reason was to force a resolution of the decommissioning issue. Powell asked if the letter had already been delivered, which Trimble confirmed.[63] 'I'm not going even to attempt to persuade you because I presume you'd not be open to persuasion.' 'That's why I'm telling you at the last minute,' replied Trimble, laughing nervously.[64] He then told the Assembly party, gathered in his office: 'Sorry, I don't have time to explain, but I think you'll like what I'm going to say.'[65] By now, Trimble was running a quarter of an hour behind schedule and thus was only able to give the Deputy First Minister, Seamus Mallon, 90 seconds' notice of his plans; he then virtually had to sprint to the Assembly chamber to make the statement.[66]

The reaction was swift and predictable, with Martin McGuinness denouncing Trimble's move as a 'wrecker's charter'.[67] Such condemnation suited Trimble fine. More gratifying still was the DUP's response. Trimble recalls Peter Robinson going 'white as a sheet' in the Assembly chamber as he, Trimble, appeared to be about to announce that he would resign altogether, along with his three UUP colleagues, thus making it impossible for the Paisleyites to remain in office. It was, he says, obvious that the DUP relaxed when it became clear that his sanction was of a more limited, calibrated variety; the deathly silence on the DUP benches then turned to cat-calls.[68] The DUP could still campaign on the theme of Trimble as the man who had brought unrepentant republicans into government, but the UUP leader derived pleasure from the belief that they might have to pulp thousands of leaflets denouncing the UUP leader for failing to collapse the Executive. In so doing, Trimble could argue that he had gone further than the DUP ever had: for all their anti-Agreement rhetoric, the DUP as a party had never yet actually resigned their ministerial positions altogether. The Paisleyites' response pointed up to Trimble the Janus-faced quality of the DUP's participation in the structures of the Belfast Agreement. He had taken the risk of creating the new structures, for better or for worse; they now wanted to 'collect the chips', blaming him for the unpalatable parts of the new dispensation but never themselves bringing the new structures down despite innumerable republican provocations.[69] Indeed, the DUP's slow immersion into the new structures had already been underlined when it was announced that the two DUP ministers, Gregory Campbell and Maurice Morrow, would meet bilaterally (rather than under the NSMC umbrella) with their southern counterparts.[70] During the General Election campaign, Gregory Campbell would also appear in a UTV debate with Pat Doherty of Sinn Fein – something which would have been unthinkable at the time of the 1998 referendum.[71] Indeed, Trimble believed that if the DUP was really trying to bring the new structures down, they would not have opposed one of his greatest foes inside the UUP – Willie Ross. Rather, as in February 1974, they would have sought to maximise anti-Agreement forces of whatever stripe.[72] But the most positive impact of Trimble's move was felt inside the UUP itself: even Ross welcomed his leader's action.[73] The UUP thus entered the General Election campaign perhaps more united than at any time since the 1997 Westminster poll.[74] Once again, Trimble had tacked, temporarily, in his internal opponents' direction – as during 'The Way Forward' debacle of July 1999 when he rejected the inter-governmental document. But contrary to what nationalists often alleged, he had not become the prisoner of the 'antis'; he was simply their guest for a brief period and would make his excuses as soon as was decently possible. Whatever else the resignation did, it improved Trimble's own morale and enabled him to say on the door-step, 'Look, I've done this – don't blame me for not holding the Provisionals to account for their failure on decommissioning, blame the two Governments.'[75]

Such public pronouncements on the verge of the election campaign were, however, only part of the story. Of equal importance were the UUP's discussions with the Alliance party to try to reach a mutual under-standing about standing down in certain seats in order to maximise the chances of pro-Agreement candidates. On the basis of the 1997 West-minster elections, there was a potential pool of 63,000 Alliance voters (largely in the east of the Province) who the Trimbleistas reckoned might be willing to vote for the UUP now that it had signed up to the long-term Alliance party goal of power-sharing with nationalists. Some Trimbleistas even thought that in the context of the Belfast Agreement, the Alliance had lost its *raison d'être* and ought even to think about winding itself up and joining the UUP – on which point they were wildly optimistic, since the overwhelming majority of Alliance activists wanted to retain their own party structures. David Campbell and Fred Cobain had begun preliminary discussions with David Ford, then the Alliance's chief whip in the Assembly, and the party's General Secretary, Stephen Farry, about possible arrangements in early 2001.[76] Subsequently, Trimble and the then Alliance leader, Sean Neeson, also discussed the issue, but no pact ever emerged as such. Instead, the Alliance say they voluntarily stood down in a number of seats. These included North Belfast – where the ageing UUP incumbent, Cecil Walker, was being challenged by the highly capable DUP Assemblyman and sometime minister, Nigel Dodds.[77] Walker would need every one of the Alliance's 2221 votes from 1997. In some ways, it was an easy decision for the Alliance to make: Walker was very pro-Agreement and in the highly polarised climate of North Belfast, the Alliance was not likely to do very well anyhow. Of equal importance in this context were the Alliance's calculations about the effect of their candidature on the contest between the SDLP and Sinn Fein: if they stood down, the chances of Alban Maginness outpolling the convicted IRA bomber Gerry Kelly would be considerably enhanced. Likewise, in West Tyrone, the Alliance voluntarily stood down so as to maximise the chances of the SDLP fending off a strong challenge from Sinn Fein.[78] But with other UUP candidates, such a choice would be much harder. Moreover, in at least one constituency, East Belfast, the Alliance party could make a real claim to have a clear run: in 1997, Peter Robinson of the DUP had topped the poll with 42.63%, followed by Reg Empey with 25.33% – a mere 600 votes ahead of Jim Hendron of the Alliance party with 23.8%. There was thus a theoretical pro-Agreement majority in East Belfast, if one or the other party would stand down. Trimble disagreed. If the UUP stood down for the Alliance party, the Alliance party would not win because Agreement-sceptic UUP supporters would not move across to the Alliance; but if the UUP had a free run, Alliance voters would be likelier to vote for the right UUP candidate to be rid of Peter Robinson. He wanted Empey – the party's best-known figure in the seat – to run again. Empey, though, was militantly against doing so: according to Trimble, he did not see why he should have to fight electoral battles all of the time.[79] The East Belfast Ulster Unionist Association then selected a comparative unknown as their candidate, but Empey was also against any UUP candidate standing down on the grounds that if the UUP gave the Alliance a free run, it would result in a reduction of the UUP in that constituency, thus worsening their position in the locals and in the Assembly elections of 2003.[80] This gave Trimble the worst of both worlds. He had an apparently weak UUP candidate who could not maximise the vote, but nor did he have the flexibility – had he so wanted – to stand down in East Belfast and thus trade it for an Alliance withdrawal in other UUP-held seats where the UUP would be hard-pressed to hold off DUP challengers. But if Trimble could not deliver to the Alliance, nor could they deliver for him. Thus, Trimble wanted David Ford to stand down in South Antrim. On the basis of the 21 September 2000 by-election, Ford's 2031 votes could be said to represent the difference between victory and defeat for the UUP's David Burnside, who had lost to Rev. Willie McCrea of the DUP by 822 votes (there had been no DUP candidate in 1997). Ford, though, was not willing to do so. For on 12 January 2001, Burnside beat three other candidates for the nomination. They included the very pro-Agreement Jim Wilson, who had been given special dispensation to stand exempting him from the party's 'no dual mandate' rule.[81] During the selection process, Burnside traded far more on his relationship with Molyneaux than with Trimble; Wilson subsequently conceded that a key factor in Burnside's success was the local association's belief that they had to show that unionists had a bottom line.[82] On the next day, at an American Enterprise Institute conference in London, Trimble expressed surprise at Burnside's victory: he declared that he would have to revise his view of his own sources.[83] However out of touch Trimble was about grassroots opinion, the selection of Burnside nonetheless had one obvious effect: it finished off any prospect that the Alliance party would stand down in South Antrim. He was seen as far too 'Orange' and hardline by many Alliance supporters in the constituency. Of course, this did not necessarily mean that in a tight contest ordinary Alliance voters would not go for Burnside in order to defeat an even greater affront to their sensibilities in the person of Willie McCrea. Nonetheless, Trimble believed that the presence of any Alliance candidate in this seat harmed the UUP's prospects. A similar process, Trimble contended, obtained in respect of the UUP's attempt to persuade Kieran McCarthy to stand down in Strangford. The 5467 votes obtained by McCarthy in 1997 would be the key to the UUP's attempt to hold off Iris Robinson of the DUP.[84] Once again, the internal UUP selection process made that task harder. In late 1999, shortly after the UUC meeting at which it was decided to enter government with Sinn Fein, Trimble informed David Campbell that Taylor had come to him and asked to be relieved of one of his tasks.[85] Despite winning reselection on 16 October 2000, Taylor announced on 29 January 2001 that he would stand down from his Westminster seat.[86] The victor in the selection contest was David McNarry, a prominent figure in the Loyal Orders. McCarthy, too, was unwilling to stand down. For McNarry, like Burnside, was regarded as insufficiently pro-Agreement by the Alliance.[87] In one instance – William Ross in East Londonderry – Trimble did not even try to persuade the Alliance party to stand down. As far as the UUP leader was concerned, Ross was simply too anti-Agreement to make such an entreaty to the pro-Agreement Alliance party ideologically viable. And in South Belfast, it was actually to Trimble's advantage that the Alliance did not stand down. Between 1992 and 1997, this heavily – though by no means exclusively – middle-class constituency with many mixed areas witnessed the largest percentage increase in the nationalist vote. Rev. Martin Smyth had held on with 14,201 votes (35.97%) against 9601 (24.32%) for Dr Alasdair McDonnell of the SDLP; the Alliance were in a strong fourth with 5112 votes or 12.95% (third position was held by

David Ervine of the PUP, the political wing of the UVF, then very much at the height of its voter-friendliness). It could be argued that there was at least a fair chance that if the Alliance party stood down, the bulk of its voters might plump for McDonnell, a noted moderate, in order to oust Smyth, who was a staunch opponent of the Belfast Agreement. Moreover, Alex Maskey of Sinn Fein – with his previous record of republican activity – was a weak candidate in this constituency. As Ed Moloney wryly observed, 'the pugnacious Alex Maskey from Andersonstown would possibly rank fairly high in the list of reasons new Catholic residents of South Belfast would give for having left West Belfast'.[88] But when nominations closed at 4 p.m. on Tuesday 22 May 2001, it emerged that there had been no discussions about any such pact and that the Alliance would run in the seat. The other way in which Smyth might have lost was through the South Belfast Ulster Unionist Association's selection procedures. Trimble duly gave Michael McGimpsey, an Assemblyman and councillor for the seat, dispensation from the 'no dual mandate' rule to oppose Smyth; but sentiment ran against this attempt at making an exception from the usual procedure. On 16 February, the incumbent duly won re-selection by 60–47.[89] Thus it was that Trimble, despite Smyth's anti-Agreement views, needed him to win if the UUP was to remain the largest pro-British party in the Province.

Yet Trimble's hopes were fulfilled in a number of seats. Most notably, on 21 May 2001, the Alliance withdrew its candidate in North Down, Dr Stephen Farry.[90] In 1997, Robert McCartney of the anti-Agreement UKUP had beaten Alan McFarland of the UUP by 12,817 (35.5%) to 11,368 (31.09%); Sir Oliver Napier of the Alliance came in third with 7554 (20.6%), having almost come second in the 1995 by-election. Obviously, if those Alliance voters went over in any numbers to the new and ardently pro-Agreement UUP candidate, Lady Hermon (Trimble's former colleague at Queen's and the wife of a much-respected one-time Chief Constable of the RUC), she would win and thus take the scalp of one of the UUP leader's most articulate critics. A less high-profile, but ultimately no less significant development was the decision of the Alliance party not to run in Trimble's own constituency of Upper Bann, where they had obtained 3017 votes in 1997 (or 6.31% of the poll). Likewise, in early April 2001 the Alliance party stood down in Fermanagh and South Tyrone. On 4 January 2001, Ken Maginnis announced that he would not be putting his name forward for re-election. The question of who would be the Ulster Unionist candidate was of more than usual significance. There was a slight nationalist majority in the seat as a whole, but the UUP candidate could normally expect to win because of the split in the Catholic vote; Trimble, for one, believed that Maginnis's moderate image meant that he never polarised the communities along the lines of Willie McCrea in Mid-Ulster, thus causing Catholics to bolt to Sinn Fein. Some thought that a few Catholics actually voted for Maginnis, or that others were sufficiently grateful for his constituency services to abstain. Maginnis believed that the party Executive's vice chairman, James Cooper, who came from a prominent family of Fermanagh Ulster Unionists, would be the ideal candidate to secure this legacy. Maginnis was greatly impressed by Cooper's virtues, one of which, as the ex-UDR major was fond of pointing out, was that 'he's a millionaire, you know'. Cooper was challenged for the nomination by the anti-Agreement Honorary Secretary of the UUP, Arlene Foster. It was widely assumed that if Foster was selected, there would be no other anti-Agreement candidate nominated to oppose her in the constituency; conversely, it was widely assumed that if Cooper won, assorted anti-Agreement unionists might encourage someone to run under another label. This would create a different set of circumstances in Fermanagh and South Tyrone, where there had not been a split pro-Union vote since 1979.[91] Trimble, however, believed that if Foster won, it would be so offensive to nationalists that the SDLP would stand down, thus leaving the way open for Sinn Fein to take the seat.[92] This was nonsense: Tommy Gallagher, the SDLP candidate, confirms that he would *not* have stood down in the event of Foster's selection. As he points out, when this last happened during the two by-elections held in the course of the 1981 Hunger Strikes, it had much more to do with the internal dynamics of the Catholic community than with the views of the then UUP candidates, Harry West and Ken Maginnis, respectively. Moreover, with the Assembly elections coming up in 2003, men such as Gallagher had every incentive to run to maintain their profile (quite apart from the obvious point that the SDLP believed themselves to be the only authentically pro-Agreement party in the race). Maginnis makes a subtler point. He claims that whilst Foster's candidature would not have caused Gallagher to stand down, her presence in the race would nonetheless so polarise Catholics as to prompt them to bolt to Sinn Fein. Gallagher, though, says that this is also wrong: Foster, unlike Willie McCrea when he was MP for Mid-Ulster, was not a particularly controversial figure amongst Catholics, despite her anti-Agreement views.[93] Nonetheless, the Trimble/Maginnis line of reasoning prevailed – just – and Cooper beat Foster by 178 to 169 (a third candidate won two votes).[94] Not merely was Trimble convinced that Cooper would hold the seat 'easily', but he conceived so high an opinion of him that whilst the latter was addressing the Ulster Unionist Executive on 10 February 2001, the UUP leader wrote a handwritten note to Denis Rogan: 'If James wins Fermanagh–South Tyrone and I happen to step in front of the proverbial bus, he would be the man.' But whilst Cooper was moderate enough to secure an Alliance party withdrawal, his problem was that any gains on the liberal end of the spectrum were more than cancelled out when Jim Dixon, a victim of the Enniskillen bomb and a former UKUP candidate, decided to run. Few thought Dixon could win, so the only issue was how many votes he would draw away from Cooper. Trimble, for one, believed that the DUP wanted Dixon to run as an independent in the hope that they would not then be blamed if the UUP lost and thus handed the constituency to a nationalist.[95]

The election campaign itself was punctuated by two memorable events: Paisley himself denounced 'line-dancing' as catering to the 'lust of the flesh . . .' much to the horror of some of the party's modernising contingent.[96] The DUP thus risked looking like a fundamentalist throw-back on an issue of minimal concern to the vast majority of unionist voters (and most of those who cared about line-dancing either were already in Paisley's camp or else were so religious as not to vote at all). More significantly, on 15 May, UTV *Insight* programme featured a *Question Time*-style interrogation of the four main candidates in North Belfast by a studio audience in the old Crumlin Road courthouse. It ranked as one of the poorest performances of all time for one of the candidates: the 76-year-old UUP incumbent, Cecil Walker, said that he could not hear the questions and appeared tongue-tied. When asked how he could purport to represent young people given the Young Unionists' and the Young Democrats' opposition to the Agreement (the youth wings of the UUP and DUP, respectively), Walker replied, 'I think that we do maintain a good decorum for young people in every way we can.' Later, he stated that he had a problem with his hearing aid.[97] The contrast with ultra-competent Nigel Dodds, the barrister with a double-first in law from Cambridge, was painfully obvious. Such was the scale of the disaster that some Trimbleistas, including John Taylor, David Kerr and Paul Bew, urged the UUP leader to persuade Walker to stand down. Their concerns did not solely relate to North Belfast, which Dodds was probably going to win anyway. Rather, an abysmal performance by Walker might incarnate a sense of decay Province-wide and thus reflect badly on UUP candidates elswhere (indeed, the programme was repeated on the next day, which according to David Kerr prompted complaining calls to Glengall Street).[98] 'Don't be so stupid,' Trimble exploded. 'We can still win this.'[99] Trimble had come to feel genuine affection for Walker on account of his loyalty in an unusually turbulent Westminster party. That said, Trimble had a very uneven grasp of the viability of his own preferred candidates in a number of constituencies – both in terms of their 'selectability' before Ulster Unionist Associations and the electorate at large. In some instances, most notably with Walker, some of his most ardent supporters thought he was simply 'in denial'. Likewise, he also believed that a visit by Blair could actually help him; some of his key aides, such as David Campbell and Barry White, were relieved when the proposed Prime Ministerial return to Coleraine – where Blair had made his referendum pledges in 1998 – did not come off.[100]

The question of the UUP leader's own role was, by comparison, a much more complex calculation. A glance at both the UUP and DUP campaign literature from 2001 shows that both sets of leaflets and adverts featured one individual above all others: David Trimble. Obviously, in the first case, Trimble was used positively, and in the second negatively. Thus, in the DUP adverts which appeared in the *Belfast Telegraph* on 5 June 2001, Paisley and his team were pictured once; but cartoons depicting a long-nosed Trimble as Pinocchio or as a secondhand car dealer appeared twice in each. In other words, Trimble appeared four times, Paisley on his own once and another time with the rest of the DUP candidates in a collective photograph. Likewise, the UUP's Province-wide literature was designed by Mark Fullbrook of PLS with a very heavy emphasis on Trimble – because of polling data which showed the First Minister to be more popular than the Belfast Agreement itself.[101] But whether Trimble was a net asset or a net liability to the UUP, notes Sydney Elliott, one thing is certain: it was the most personally polarised election ever held in Northern Ireland, even more so than the 1969 Stormont election which effectively finished off Terence O'Neill as Provincial premier.[102] The other notable feature of both the UUP's Province-wide literature and Trimble's own leaflets in Upper Bann was the degree to which they focus on the theme of 'Unionism delivering' on 'real issues' such as health and education, as much as on questions relating to the peace process. As Trimble's constituency agent, John Dobson, recalls: 'We really believed because we had delivered something to the voters – such as Craigavon Hospital being in our hands – that our core would come out and support us as they always had.'[103]

In fact, as Daphne Trimble recalls, 'it was the worst campaign ever, full of unpleasant incidents' – in which such 'real' issues played little part and the peace process was everything.[104] John Dobson now concedes that he should have seen it coming quicker. Before the election, he had urged that Trimble attend the British Pipe Band championship in Banbridge, where there would be thousands present. Trimble went into the tea tent. An ordinary-looking man came up to Trimble with his palm outstretched, as if to shake the First Minister's hand: instead, he grabbed Trimble's thumb, in an attempt to bend it backwards and to break it. The RUC rapidly intervened, but it represented a foretaste of what was to come. Normally, as Dobson notes, there was something of a 'cult of celebrity' as Trimble would do walkabouts in the three main towns of Upper Bann; but, by the end of the first week, the UUP were going into a very strong headwind and were 'getting it with both barrels' from their own folk with a far greater intensity than during the Assembly elections of 1998. Worse still, the abuse was emanating not just from well-known loyalist working-class estates such as Corcrain in Portadown or Mourneview in Lurgan, but also from all socio-economic strata and from all age groups – and whilst some of it was orchestrated, much of it was simply spontaneous. Often, shaven-headed 'wee nippers' would come up to Trimble and say 'hi, mister, my da [sic] says you're a traitor'.[105]

Northern Ireland results are counted on the day after the election itself. Trimble began Friday 8 June at Glengall Street with 'morning prayers'. According to his Westminster aide, Barry White, Trimble still thought that he had won between eight and nine seats – in other words, only one or two losses. This was well within the acceptable range, partly because turn-out was slightly up in key seats in the east of the Province (suggesting to the Trimbeistas that some pro-Agreement middle-class voters had bothered to vote UUP). But around lunchtime, somebody fed through the news that there were problems in Upper Bann, and the mood altered dramatically.[106] Between 2:30 and 3 p.m. worse news came through: Roy Beggs Sr, the eighteen-year incumbent MP for East Antrim, was now behind in his bid to hold the seat against a Paisleyite challenge. Nobody had thought he was in any difficulty at all, especially since the DUP candidate, East Belfast Assemblyman Sammy Wilson, was thought not to be the strongest opponent having come from outside of the constituency. Likewise, David Burnside was behind in his bid to regain the neighbouring South Antrim seat from McCrea. Similar rumours were reaching the UUP about Strangford. Assuming that Ross, Thompson and Walker had lost, this meant that if worst came to worst, the UUP would be down to just three or four seats: Donaldson in Lagan Valley, whose result was never in doubt; Sylvia Hermon in North Down, who was always in front; and either Martin Smyth in South Belfast or James Cooper in Fermanagh and South Tyrone. 'We're looking at meltdown,' Trimble said to David Kerr, quite clinically, but with a combination of sadness and exasperation.[107]

By mid-afternoon, John Dobson rang Trimble to say that it was still tight in Upper Bann and that the DUP candidate, David Simpson, was polling well everywhere. A large, hostile crowd, he said, was building up outside the Seapatrick Church of Ireland parish hall in Banbridge where the count was taking place; some, Dobson recognised as long-time DUP activists, but others he had never seen before and again came from all classes and age groups.[108] Trimble and his wife arrived at a side entrance with a few shouts of 'Judas' and 'you'll pay the price'; Barry White says that it was more comfortable to stand near Sinn Fein activists inside than alongside some of the DUP supporters.[109] Meanwhile, Simpson was walking about the hall, self-confidently. Eventually, a Sinn Fein activist who had looked at all of the boxes whispered to Dobson: 'You've got it, but not by much.'[110] The hall was sealed, the media were let in and the result was announced. Trimble had secured 17,095 votes, or 33.5% of the poll – down 10.1%. David Simpson was 2058 behind him with 15,037 or 29.46% – up 17.99%. Having obtained 59.0% in his first General Election in Upper Bann in 1992, it was a sign of what sacrifices Trimble was prepared to make in order to ensure that power-sharing worked: there can have been few other politicians who were willing to say goodbye to around two-fifths of their vote for sake of bringing their deadly foes into the fold! The extent of that risk would rapidly become apparent. John Dobson advised that Trimble leave as soon as possible as the hostile crowd had grown even further, but he declined to do so. 'No, there are people in the hall who have worked for me and I'm going to make the winner's speech,' he declared. In the meantime, though, some anti-Agreement voters had managed to make their way into the hall through a serving hatch and such was the din that Dobson who was standing four feet away from Trimble could not hear what he was saying.[111] When Trimble finished, he refused to go out of the side door and insisted on departing by the front entrance. 'I thought, "they're going to have a bit of fun" but that there was no serious risk,' recalls Trimble. 'I then paused, quite deliberately at the top of the steps, and I knew they would get angry and the images that were produced wouldn't reflect well on the DUP. I'm sorry to be so cynical about it.'[112] In fact, he did a double thumbs up.[113] As he made his way to the car, the crowd surged forward towards himself and Daphne Trimble. Both of them were spat at and kicked in the shins; one man tried to grab Trimble's head. By the time they reached the car, she was almost in tears.[114] When Trimble reached BBC Northern Ireland headquarters in Belfast, he was limping and there was mud on his jacket. The BBC staff tried to clear it off, but Trimble replied, 'No, let it stay.'[115]

By the time Trimble had returned to Belfast, the pall of gloom had begun to lift. Certainly, there were losses, but they were almost in the 'to be expected' category. Willie Thompson had been beaten in West Tyrone by Pat Doherty of Sinn Fein, leaving Brid Rodgers of the SDLP in a relatively poor third; the success of Sinn Fein in overhauling the SDLP as the largest nationalist party would have grave implications for the Trimble project in the months to come. Nigel Dodds obliterated Cecil Walker in North Belfast, who fell into fourth place with a mere 11.98% of the vote. Gregory Campbell, likewise, overhauled Willie Ross by a much smaller margin in East Londonderry – though both George Howarth and John Taylor saw this as a possible gain for Trimble since they regarded Ross as far more internally troublesome and even more opposed to the institutions than was Campbell.[116] Sylvia Hermon had handily defeated Robert McCartney in North Down. Curiously, McCartney put in his best performance ever, with 13,509 votes or 36.33% of the poll. It was thus almost as good as his by-election victory in 1995 on a 38.6% turn-out. The problem for him was that in the absence of candidates representing the 20.66% of voters who backed the Alliance in 1997, and the 3.39% of voters who had supported the Northern Ireland Women's Coalition, the bulk of their supporters appear to have transferred *en masse* to Hermon. According to the electoral analyst Nicholas Whyte, the Catholic portion of the electorate in North Down is 7–8%; since nationalist parties obtained 4.2% combined, it suggests that around 2000 Catholics voted

for Hermon. Burnside also regained South Antrim by 1011 votes from
McCrea, thus ending the DUP veteran's brief return to the Commons:
Burnside obtained 16,366 votes, or 37.05%, to McCrea's 15,355, or 34.77%;
the biggest loser was the Alliance party, which lost over half its vote in
absolute and percentage terms compared to the 1997 General Election.
Thus, despite David Ford's unwillingness to stand down, Alliance voters
clearly knew what to do and felt that Burnside was preferable to McCrea.
It was a remarkable achievement for a man who had been written off as
a 'loser' after the by-election and who some thought would never come
back after that; and although Burnside would subsequently become a
greater thorn in Trimble's side, at this moment the two men's fortunes
were inextricably linked. Likewise, Jeffrey Donaldson in Lagan Valley was
the only Ulster Unionist whose vote actually went up at the expense of
the DUP – with a 1.09% increase, to 56.52% (the DUP share was down
0.13% to 13.42%). If ever there was proof that Donaldson's position was
squarely in the middle of the Unionist consensus, this was it. Perhaps
even more surprising was the success of Rev. Martin Smyth. The odds
appeared to be against him: a divided association, a strong SDLP candidate – indeed, according to the electoral analyst Nicholas Whyte, perhaps
as many as 2000 Alliance voters, large numbers of them liberal Protestants,
defected to Alasdair McDonnell to try to defeat the anti-Agreement
incumbent. Yet Smyth still managed to increase his percentage share by
8.84% in South Belfast. Partly, this was because the PUP had a much
weaker candidate than in 1997, and lost three-quarters of its support. The
UUP had a close shave in East Antrim, where Roy Beggs won by 128
votes – 13,101 (36.39%) to the DUP's 12,973 (36.04%). The latter had thus
increased their share of the poll by 16.59%, partly because of local issues.
But there were two major disappointments. First, Iris Robinson defeated
David McNarry in Strangford by 1110 votes – 18,532 (42.84%) to 17,422
(40.28%). Again, as in South Antrim, the Alliance vote was down by
6.43%, but in this instance not by enough and if Kieran McCarthy's
remaining 2902 ballots cast had gone to the UUP they would have held
the seat. Of those who did shift from Alliance to the UUP, calculates
Nicholas Whyte, 600 or more would probably have been Catholics. Worse
still for Trimble was the result in Fermanagh and South Tyrone. Despite
his confidence that James Cooper would win, Sinn Fein's Michelle Gilder-
new squeaked ahead by 53 votes. The circumstances of that loss were
depressing for two reasons: first, there were allegations of republicans

keeping a polling station in Garrison, Co. Fermanagh, open for 45 minutes after voting officially ended, which resulted in an election petition to contest the validity of the ballot (though this challenge was later dismissed and the ballot was upheld).[117] Second, and perhaps more important was the independent anti-Agreement candidature of Jim Dixon, which syphoned off 6643 votes (13.17%). According to Daphne Trimble, Cooper's defeat upset her husband more than any other single result.[118]

The UUP thus held six seats to five for the DUP – compared to ten seats to two after the 1997 General Election. In percentage terms, the aggregate UUP Province-wide vote was 26.8%, compared to 22.5% for the DUP – 5.9% down and 8.9% up, respectively, on 1997. This was the worst result ever for the UUP at Westminster. By Tuesday 12 June, when the local election count was completed, it also emerged that the UUP was reduced from 185 seats in 1997 to 154 in 2001, but was still the largest party. Yet despite these losses, Trimble felt able to tell his wife, 'that's enough'. And he added, 'You know, I'm harder to get rid of than people think.'[119] He had not been 'Barakised', after the fashion of the former Israeli premier.[120] Partly, this was because of 'expectation management' – not that the overly-optimistic Trimble had engaged in much of that during the campaign. Rather, such 'expectation management' as went on was a matter of folk memory. For Trimble had not been destroyed, as was Faulkner in the February 1974 General Election. Indeed, considering that it could reasonably be argued that the 1998 Belfast Agreement was more disadvantageous to Unionists than the 1973 Sunningdale accords (*pace* Trimble's successes in revising the Irish Constitution and on North-South bodies) the UUP's limited success in 2001 was little short of miraculous. Indeed, if the DUP could not pull off a great victory under the 'cruel' first-past-the-post system – whereby relatively small shifts in the vote are often translated into large numbers of seats changing hands – it seemed hard at this point to envisage how they would inflict a knock-out blow in the rather gentler STV system that would be used in the forthcoming Assembly elections.[121]

The 2001 election results contained other, subtler dangers for the Trimble project. The first was the absence of much cross-community voting, even in areas where the winner could only come from one of two candidates from whichever was the majority community in that particular seat. This was despite an explicit appeal from the UUP leader to Catholic voters to save pro-Agreement candidates.[122] He appears to have over-estimated its potential. Partly, as Paul Bew observes, he did not fully grasp the extent of the decline of Catholic unionism (very much with a lower case 'u') in the face of the self-confidence arising from the success of the 'Celtic Tiger' in the south and repeated concessions to Sinn Fein. This decline was subsequently confirmed by the 2001 Northern Ireland Life and Times Survey.[123] Especially disappointing was the absence, except in tiny numbers, of Catholics crossing sectarian lines to vote for Trimble to avert a DUP victory. According to Nicholas Whyte, only in South Antrim did cross-community voting really make the difference between victory and defeat. Thus, the Alliance vote in the Westminster election was 1200 less than its total in the local elections held there on the same day. Likewise, the the SDLP vote was down 900. This suggests that at least 1000 Catholics voted for Burnside. There was a certain irony here. Burnside, who was not opposed to power-sharing in principle but had done relatively little to help bring it about, received a significant number of Catholic votes; whereas Trimble, who had done more than any Unionist before him to bring nationalists into the fold, received virtually none. It is perfectly possible that memories of Drumcree were too deeply seared into the nationalist consciousness to allow for such an act of generosity, or that the general nature of day-to-day sectarian conflict in that part of north Armagh made it an impossibility. Trimble appears to share this viewpoint. When asked why he received so few Catholic votes, Trimble replies bluntly, "This is Upper Bann we're talking about."[124] Certainly, this kind of bitterness would not have been nearly so widespread in South Antrim, making cross-community voting there an easier option. But it also suggested one other possibility: that voters are only really prepared to vote on a cross-community basis for a more moderate candidate from the opposing tradition where the choice is between that person and a high-profile figure who polarised people. Thus, some Shankill Protestants voted for Joe Hendron to defeat Gerry Adams in 1992, and some South Antrim Catholics voted for Burnside to throw out McCrea. But since David Simpson of the DUP was not quite so obviously controversial as those other two, Trimble could not benefit (this reasoning also suggests that Trimble might have been right in thinking that Catholics could have voted for him if Paisley, as was briefly rumoured, had come into Upper Bann and contested the seat).[125]

No less important to Trimble was the question of unionist turn-out, and especially middle-class unionist turn-out east of the Bann. After all, re-energising the Ulster Protestant bourgeoisie to participate in politics was one of the UUP leader's key goals. But, according to Sydney Elliott, whilst nationalist turn-out was at around 85% – huge in an epoch of declining participation across the United Kingdom – unionist turn-out hovered a little above the 60% mark.[126] Even when the subsequent discovery of voter over-registration in nationalist strongholds such as west Belfast is taken into account – which at a stroke removed almost 20% of 'electors' off the list in late 2002 – a very substantial differential remains.[127] The turn-out in Protestant areas was slightly up, but considering that there were a number of tightly fought contests between the various wings of unionism in such seats as East Antrim, North Down and Strangford, the increase was not impressive. Thus, in East Antrim, the turn-out rose from 58.26% in 1997 to 59.12% in 2001. In North Down, it rose from 58.03% in 1997 to 58.83% in 2001: this was still well short of the turn-out in Sir James Kilfedder's last two elections in 1987 and 1992, of 63% and 65.5% respectively and was the lowest of any Northern Ireland constituency (indeed, in the Harbour Ward of Bangor, where Trimble grew up, the local government election turn-out that day was a mere 54.69%).[128] In Strangford, turn-out rose from 59.47% in 1997 to 59.92% in 2001. Only in South Antrim, which had been the scene of McCrea's dramatic by-election victory, was there much change in the levels of participation – up from 57.91% to 62.5% (and, where unlike the other seats, there had been little history of the UUP being challenged at all; the increase can partly, perhaps, be put down to the novelty factor of a serious contest after the by-election in 2000).

Moreover, the evidence was very mixed on the question of who exactly was turning out to vote – and in whose interest. Thus, it was a cliché to say that Trimble's fortunes would depend upon ensuring that the 'nice', middle-class people who voted 'yes' in the 1998 referendum but failed to come out for the June 1998 Assembly elections now had to be mobilised to save the Agreement. Certainly, the Pricewaterhouse Coopers poll before the elections showed that middle-class pro-Agreement voters were intending to come out in greater numbers than anyone else. But according to Sydney Elliott, on the basis of the council elections, there was no massive difference in turn-out between middle- and working-class areas of East Antrim, South Antrim, Strangford and North Down.[129] Moreover, there was also some evidence to suggest that the DUP had overcome its 'respectability deficit' amongst those elements of the Protestant middle classes that still regarded themselves as 'Unionist' with an upper case 'U'. Thus, in the leafy University Electoral Area of Newtownabbey District Council – three of whose wards were in the Westminster seat of East Antrim and four of which were in South Antrim – Roger Hutchinson of the DUP secured the highest number of first preference votes at his first attempt for that authority. Although an 'outsider' from Larne at the other end of East Antrim, he nonetheless overhauled a long-time UUP councillor and MLA, Ken Robinson. Significantly, Hutchinson made inroads in the middle-class areas surrounding the Jordanstown campus, as well as recouping lost ground for the DUP in the more hardline sections of the area such as the estates of Monkstown.[130] Likewise, at an anecdotal level, David McNarry states that he encountered just as much hostility from some of the parents of children at the very middle-class grammar school of Regent House in Newtownards as he did on the nearby estates.[131] Another reason for the growth of DUP support amongst segments of the middle classes was the hostility of wide swathes of the RUC 'family' to Trimble, who they believed had let them down. Reports of such disaffection are legion: Daphne Trimble recalls that some of the frostiest receptions she received were from RUC officers and their wives in Banbridge: 'You sold us out and now we're going to teach you a lesson and vote DUP.'[132] Indeed, both David McNarry and Iris Robinson are agreed on one thing: that the RUC issue made the difference between victory and defeat for the DUP in Strangford.[133] The matter was sufficiently etched in Trimble's mind for the First Minister to raise it with Blair at their first post-election wrap-up in the Cabinet Room at No. 10 on 12 June 2001: both David Burnside and Sylvia Hermon gave examples, and the MP for North Down stated that voters had held up copies of *The Daily Telegraph* which depicted the bulk of the 301 RUC officers murdered in the course of their duties during the Troubles (it was significant that both of these successful UUP candidates had very strong profiles on the issue of policing, Burnside through his role in the Save the RUC campaign and Hermon also through her husband).[134] But although Trimble complained bitterly to Blair about the electoral effects of Army plaques being removed from RUC stations as part of the new police service's 'clean walls policy' – it was a tradition that every Army unit that had served in a joint base would leave a regimental crest – he did not grasp the significance of the issue until very late. Even after the election was well over, Trimble would still claim that policing only cost the

UUP a couple of thousand votes in the Province as a whole, though he conceded that in a close set of races it could make the difference.[135] Whilst there were probably only a few thousand RUC officers directly affected, they all had families and friends; and the issue was of profound importance to many thousands of unionists who had never donned a uniform.

Such comments raise an obvious question mark over Trimble's judgment as a politician. Certainly, he turned out to be highly optimistic about the overall outcome and he appears to have believed his own propaganda in respect of the viability of individual UUP candidates. Of these contests, it appears that his calculations were only really correct in respect of Sylvia Hermon. That said, on the big strategic issue of the campaign – his own post-dated resignation – Trimble had it more right than wrong. Yet for a brief moment, he appeared to entertain doubts about its efficacy as a strategy. On 22 May 2001, the *Belfast Telegraph* published a poll conducted by UMS which showed that nearly half of the Ulster Unionist supporters believed that Trimble had gone too far in his promise to resign by 1 July if there was no IRA decommissioning; more DUP supporters backed him than did those of his own party. 'The numbers are good,' Trimble told Bew in those days. 'But the only problem is on my decision to resign.'[136] In retrospect, the poll turned out to be off the mark, partly because the sample contained large numbers of disapproving nationalists as well as liberal Protestants.[137] It showed that the SDLP vote would outnumber Sinn Fein by 25%–16%. Likewise, it showed the UUP comfortably outnumbering the DUP by 25%–14%. Obviously, neither of these predictions was fulfilled and it appears that voters wanted to say the 'politically correct' thing rather than state their actual preferences. Indeed, with hindsight, Trimble regretted not going further and resigning *simpliciter* there and then in May. In part, he had not gone 'the whole hog' because he thought on the basis of the UUP's private Pricewaterhouse Coopers polling that he had enough in the 'kitty' and therefore did not need to bring down the institutions altogether.[138] The more slow-burn form of resignation contained two problems. First, it was probably too calibrated to be readily comprehensible. Second – partly deriving from the first point – many voters simply did not believe Trimble. Thus, Daphne Trimble recalls that even UUP supporters would say 'Youse [sic] are all the same – we don't believe you.'[139] David Burnside also found that if he could persuade voters that Trimble did mean it, he would have them 'in the bag' – but that it was often hard going. However, he confirms that without the post-dated letter, he could not have won back South Antrim for the UUP.[140] Jeffrey Donaldson also says that it helped him in Lagan Valley, as does Roy Beggs in East Antrim.[141] Trimble now believes that had he resigned *tout court*, he would have swung enough anti-Agreement voters in Fermanagh and South Tyrone, and in Strangford, to hold on to those seats.[142]

The one thing which the post-dated resignation undoubtedly did was to consolidate Trimble's leadership of the UUP. A core group of party grandees met in Denis Rogan's office in south Belfast on the Saturday after the election, including Trimble, Jack Allen, David Campbell, James Cooper, Ken Maginnis and Jim Nicholson. During this session, Trimble's mobile telephone rang. It was Blair on the line from Chequers, and Trimble asked for a meeting as soon as possible. 'Are we all agreed that David should continue?' asked Cooper. The universal feeling was that Trimble should stay on and fight any possible challenge to his position at the UUC AGM that had been postponed from March to 23 June. 'The party needs Trimble to remain and deliver before he can think of retiring,' declared Nicholson.[143] The much-touted visit from the 'men in grey sashes' did not materialise. Nonetheless, there still was much speculation about Trimble's longer-term future. Thus, Frank Millar and Gerry Moriarty reported in the *Irish Times* on 13 June 2001 that senior figures close to Trimble were saying that the UUP chief had 'almost certainly fought his last election' as UUP leader. As well as the obvious danger of a direct challenge by Donaldson or Smyth, there was also much speculation of a 'dream ticket' comprising both Donaldson and Empey. According to this scenario, Donaldson would lead the party and eventually join the Assembly after the next election in 2003 (or before, if a party worthy could be persuaded to stand down), with Empey as First Minister. Donaldson would then bide his time until such moment as Empey decided to pass on the baton. This putative coalition of interests would consist not just of 'antis' but would also comprise some 'pros' who were fed up with Trimble's moodiness and unpredictability; after all, the ex-Vanguardist had never, in many ways, really been one of the 'good ole' boys' (ironically, Empey was an ex-Vanguardist, too, but he was seen as somehow having a greater 'sense of party'). Moreover, Trimble's moodiness and unpredictability (and, Trimbleistas such as Bew argued, principles) also made the UUP leader rather too inclined to risk bringing down the institutions. Certain advocates of the 'dream ticket' believed that it was all very well for him to threaten to 'pull the plug' when he had his Nobel money and could now walk into just about any job he wanted – whereas some of them were dependent upon the Assembly for their status.[144] According to David Campbell, Empey denied having anything to do with such talk of 'dream tickets'. 'Does David think I'm conspiring against him?' asked the Enterprise and Investment Minister. 'I haven't stuck with him this far to let him down now.' He added he would only consider running for the leadership if Trimble stood down of his own accord.[145] This was in itself not entirely fanciful. According to Daphne Trimble, the UUP leader was at times tempted by the idea of not coming back. But, she says, this was as much a 'psychological device' to reassure himself that he was not serving a 'life sentence' as a serious option; in fact, 'he knew in his heart of hearts that he was lumbered with it'.[146] Nor did he discourage the idea that he might step down as First Minister – he was undoubtedly bored with the job – but carry on as party leader to forge a closer link between the UUP and the Conservatives. In this scenario, the IRA would fail to disarm by the time of his deadline in August and, as Ed Moloney conjectured, Trimble would then drape himself in the cloak of victimhood and play the role of the honourable man let down by a British Prime Minister who betrayed his referendum pledges. This would create the context in which he could cultivate that tighter connection with the Tories.[147] Indeed, on the day after the General Election – in which New Labour had been returned with a second successive landslide victory – Charles Moore, editor of *The Daily Telegraph*, even suggested that Trimble become a contender for the Tory leadership itself. Moore's reasoning was that the Tories were desperately short of heavyweight figures with positive name recognition (well-known figures such as Michael Howard and Michael Portillo had name recognition, but were unpopular because of their residual association with the Major ministry). Trimble, by contrast, was not associated with those failures, enjoyed the prestige of being a 'peacemaker' with a Nobel Prize and invariably received ecstatic receptions on the platform at the Conservative conference. Above all, the Tories often turned to improbable outsiders in moments of great trouble: Disraeli, who was racially Jewish, had returned the party to power in the 19th century and Thatcher, a woman, had done so in the 20th. Why not an Ulsterman in the 21st?[148] Daphne Trimble, who was in her car at the time that Moore was broadcasting, 'nearly drove off the road' when she heard his suggestion.[149] But

Moore was not alone in this: on 30 June 2001, the *Sun* made the same suggestion in its leader column, much to Trimble's delight.[150] Indeed, later that summer, Trimble endorsed the candidature of Iain Duncan Smith, subsequently the victor in the Conservative leadership race.[151] Jonathan Powell was concerned enough to ask some of the Ulster Unionists, half-jokingly, 'What's all this about David and the Tories?'[152] Whether or not the idea was viable in practice, it was certainly indicative of Trimble's prestige on the mainland: no Unionist leader had been spoken of in these terms since Carson. The subsequent award to Trimble of the 'Zurich/*Spectator* Parliamentarian of the Year' in November 2001 was a further indication of his high reputation.[153] In late 2001, Jack Straw, the new Foreign Secretary, invited him to talk to the Gibraltarians about the negotiations with Spain on the future status of the Rock ('Yes,' replied Trimble. 'But you might not like what I have to say on the importance of the consent principle').[154] And in the following year, he topped a poll of Westminster colleagues for election to the Executive of the all-party British-American Parliamentary Group. Everyone knew who Trimble was – even if this still-shy man knew relatively few of his fellow legislators.

Although such plaudits would have counted for little with the stalwarts of the UUC, Trimble did not in the end face a challenge for the leadership. 'It was Jeffrey's best chance – and I don't know why he didn't,' Trimble observed after the UUC meeting.[155] He later ascribed Donaldson's unwillingess to run to the Lagan Valley MP's desire to enter the Assembly.[156] Likewise, some of the more purist 'antis' were becoming disillusioned with Donaldson's reluctance to run; David Brewster was one of the few Ulster Unionists who insisted upon Trimble's resignation because of the electoral losses.[157] In fact, Donaldson calculated correctly on this occasion: precisely because of Trimble's post-dated resignation, which had shored up the centre ground, it was not the best time for him to make such a challenge. Moreover, some of the Young Unionists were drifting over to the DUP, thus diminishing Donaldson's natural constituency.[158] The attention then shifted to the officerial elections and, in particular, to the post of party president that had been left vacant since the death of Sir Josias Cunningham in the previous summer. The two candidates were Denis Rogan and Martin Smyth – pro- and anti-Agreement, respectively. Smyth won by 364 votes to 353, but Trimble could console himself with the fact that the balance on the officer team (including Smyth) was now 10–4 in his own favour. Moreover, the Ulster Unionist Executive, elected in the previous April, was solidly behind him.[159] Again, considering the internal and external odds against Trimble – the combination of the internal 'antis', the DUP and the unwillingness of the British Government to pay much of a price to help him, let alone the strength of pan-nationalism – the fact that he had survived was almost a miracle. It was often claimed that he had no strategy, save to survive week by week. If so, he was rather good at it, but would need much more luck in the coming months. And he, like everyone else, cannot have foreseen the dramatic form which that good fortune would take.

THIRTY-SIX

The luckiest politician

THE 1 July deadline set by Trimble for his resignation gave the British (and Irish) Governments two stark choices. Under section 16(8) of the Northern Ireland Act 1998, there was then a further period of six weeks during which time all the parties could try and resolve the dispute by 12 August. Obviously, if Trimble's resignation took effect on 30 June/ 1 July, and there was a satisfactory settlement of the outstanding issues during the cooling-off period, then Trimble (or his replacement) could risk standing for re-election in the Assembly. But once that period expired, the options narrowed. Trimble's favoured course of action was for the British to suspend – preferably, *before* 1 July. This held two attractions for him. First, it would put the Northern Ireland institutions into deep freeze, pending such time as the Provisionals moved under the pressure of the Governments, and would enable him to resume office without having to have another vote in the Assembly. Moreover, it would also be another dramatic reassertion of the sovereignty of Westminster, after the fashion of 11 February 2000, and which would have been done at his behest. Of course, it was these very features which made suspension so unpalatable to the republican movement (and to the Irish Government). In the event of no resolution by 12 August, they preferred that Reid avail himself of the other option under the Northern Ireland Act 1998: dissolution of the Assembly and fresh elections to that body. Considering that Sinn Fein had overhauled the SDLP in the latest Westminster elections in terms of numbers of MPs and the popular vote, to become the dominant force in northern nationalism, they would obviously stand to benefit from such a ballot. Therefore, reasoned Trimble, if the British Government wanted to persuade the republican movement to make a gesture, they would certainly not hold out to Sinn Fein the prospect of another poll. After all, why should Sinn Fein make any move to decommission – with all of the potential internal ructions which that might entail – when the effect of sitting on their hands would be to trigger an electoral process that would almost certainly leave Gerry Adams as Deputy First Minister? It was, Trimble believed, a 'no-brainer'.[1]

Unfortunately for Trimble, the British and Irish Governments did not see things that way. The Irish, particularly, believed that the costs of saving Trimble were too high. Thus, Frank Millar heard southern officials start to make asides about the UUP leader such as 'he's being very difficult, you know'.[2] Moreover, they were not even sure that suspension would actually succeed in liberating Trimble from his internal critics and blithely assumed that if either Donaldson or Robinson of the DUP took over the leadership of Unionism as a whole, they would eventually fit into the mould of past leaders who came to the job as hardliners and then had to make an accommodation.[3] Above all, they were determined that there be no suspension *before* Trimble resigned. The reaction of nationalist Ireland and its American allies to the Mandelson suspension of February 2000 also served to convince the British that some devices for propping up Trimble were simply too costly. Moreover, as far back as May, Jonathan Powell had warned the Ulster Unionists that they need not assume that suspension was there for the asking; Blair also repeatedly assured Ahern that 'we don't want to suspend', notably when they met in the Prime Minister's constituency in Sedgefield on 27 July. And whereas Mandelson between January and February 2000 made it absolutely clear that Trimble was the indispensable man, Reid offered no such reassurance between June and July 2001.

But there were other, more banal and short-term considerations that militated against suspension. When the UUP met with Blair at No. 10 on 12 June 2001 several of those present detected from his body language and his general demeanour a certain boredom, even irritation, at being unable to free himself from the perennial obligation of sustaining the Northern Ireland peace process. The Prime Minister had just finished his re-shuffle and had other issues such as the upcoming EU summit in Gothenburg to consider. 'He was present physically in the room,' recalls one of the participants, 'but in reality he appeared not there. There was little warmth and, for the first time, even a touch of arrogance about him. And, above all, he seemed not to be fully briefed.' Trimble then shocked Blair: he told the Prime Minister that there were now two and a half weeks left to solve the matter and that he wanted out of office since he was not relishing being First Minister. Blair immediately began to focus on the matter at hand and declared, 'The follow through from that is an [Assembly] election, isn't it?' It was obvious that he had been told to say this by Powell or Reid, possibly as an attempt to bluff Trimble into withdrawing his resignation. The UUP leader brassily stated that if elections were called, his party would have to campaign on the theme of Sinn Fein having dishonoured their pledges and that it would be very much harder, if not impossible, to elect a new Executive after fighting an election on that basis. The effect of Trimble's retort about fighting a campaign on such a platform was to leave Blair looking glum.[4] It may well have been the case that under the STV system, Trimble thought that the UUP would not lose much compared to the Westminster election. Rather, his worries about the proposed Assembly elections related to the SDLP. According to David Kerr's diary for 15 June 2001, Trimble told the Assembly group that day that 'we had a difficult [Westminster] election and the SDLP had a disastrous election' (Sinn Fein now outnumbered them 4–3 in the terms of Westminster seats won). If there were new Assembly elections, the UUP might well survive as a viable governing force to supply the First Minister (though many believed that the anti-Agreement forces would coalesce around the DUP and the two Unionist blocs would be of around equal size). But the SDLP would probably not survive in large enough form to provide a Deputy First Minister again; and since the unionist population would not tolerate a Sinn Fein 'co-premiership' when the republicans had not completed their journey to fully democratic politics, the Agreement would then collapse.

Before making the choice of elections or suspension, the Governments resolved to make one last attempt at saving the institutions. But the republican movement, pumped up by its recent electoral successes in Northern Ireland, was not going to move to save Trimble and believed that a serious negotiation would only begin once he was out of office.[5] Thus it was that the deadline expired on the night of 30 June/1 July. Ominously, the outgoing First Minister spent the weekend at the Somme commemoration in France.[6] He thus became the first provincial head of government to go there since Terence O'Neill visited during the 50th anniversary of the battle, in 1966, when the then Northern Ireland premier was caught unawares by both internal party ructions and the emergence of a paramilitary grouping styling itself as the 'UVF'.[7] This precedent seemed suitably bleak at the time. For the report of the IICD, published on 2 July, stated that there had been no decommissioning either by the IRA or, indeed, the UVF and UDA.[8] The reason for the Provisionals' reluctance was, as Trimble correctly predicted, that they would not start seriously to negotiate until after he had resigned. But where he was wrong was his belief that by resigning on the issue of decommissioning, he had 'put it up' to the republicans and the two Governments and that they would now have to convene another short, sharp round-table at which only the subject of arms would be addressed. Indeed, by the time the conference began on Monday 9 July 2001 at Weston Park in Shropshire – a 17th-century stately home that served as the model for P.G. Wodehouse's Blandings Castle – it was clear that there were no fewer than four issues in play. These included policing, demilitarisation, the stability of the institutions (that is, no more NSMC sanctions) as well as paramilitary weapons. It should certainly have been foreseen: at Prime Minister's Questions on 4 July, Blair told Hague at one of the latter's final appearances at the Dispatch Box before his resignation took effect that those were the four issues which needed to be resolved. Whilst he did not rule out use of any of the powers available to him (implying that suspension was still an option), arms was the last mentioned of the matters at hand.[9] It suggested, therefore, that there would be a tranche of concessions to the IRA in order to persuade them to move on weapons.[10] Trimble did, however, enjoy one crucial piece of political cover: Jeffrey Donaldson agreed to re-join his negotiating team for the first time since the failure of 'The Way Forward' proposals in June–July 1999. Donaldson says he did this in order to keep an eye on the UUP leadership, to ensure that it made no more concessions.[11]

As so often before, Sinn Fein skilfully hinted at all manner of flexibility on arms without irrevocably committing themselves to anything – if only they could see the 'colour of the British Government's money' on policing and demilitarisation. But their ability to read the British Government's intentions may have been based upon more than just sound intuition: in October 2002, it appeared that through a spy network in the NIO, republicans may have had access to the Blair ministry's negotiating position in the run-up to Weston Park.[12] Obviously, the UUP knew nothing of this at the time and proceeded merrily on their way. So after a first meeting with Blair on Tuesday 10 July, the UUP went to see Sinn Fein in their party room on the first floor. Those present included Adams, Gerry Kelly and McGuinness. According to the diary of David Kerr, it was a fairly routine exchange until Donaldson spoke up: 'This is not about the renegotiation of the Agreement,' declared the MP for Lagan Valley. 'It is about the implementation of the Agreement' (by this, he meant the IRA's failure to live up to their side of the bargain). The Agreement involved pain on both sides and he accepted there was hurt on the republican side. And, in a voice choking with emotion, he spoke of his cousin Constable Sam Donaldson of the RUC, who had been murdered in Crossmaglen, Co. Armagh. The Donaldson family never forgot the letters which they had received from ordinary Catholics in the 'Bandit Country' expressing sorrow and sympathy. More than anything else, Donaldson said, decommissioning would convey the message that the 'war is over' and the 'siege is lifted'. However much Sinn Fein alleged that he 'didn't want a Fenian about the place', the truth was that he was wedded to the principle of inclusivity. McGuinness then complained that the UUP leadership had not sufficiently praised their Sinn Fein counterparts and thus shown to both the unionist and nationalist communities that they were moving forward together. At this point, Adams declared that he was trying to bring an end to physical-force republicanism. 'The IRA is engaged with the IICD,' he explained. 'It might be slow, but it is happening. There is going to be a split in the republican community if Sinn Fein moves forward on [accepts] policing.' The two groups reconvened in the early afternoon and Adams said that he wanted to ask Trimble a 'very pertinent' question. 'If you stand for re-election, can you be re-elected?' 'I believe so,' replied the UUP leader. 'If I cannot then we will have to have a [fresh Assembly] election. We expect to make gains.' McGuinness stated baldly: 'So do we.' And, David Kerr added in his diary: 'He looks up our line to see our faces. Looks surprised at how relaxed we look.' Adams then came back at the UUP delegation: 'Why do you need us to do this if there is going to be an election anyway?' (which Unionists interpreted as meaning, 'Why should we take a risk with our base when you lot aren't in any real electoral danger?'). 'Because we need to solve the problem,' replied Trimble. 'We have to do it now anyway.' They then adjourned for 12 July celebrations in Ulster. But Trimble did not attend those: instead he went to a garden party later that day at Buckingham Palace. Shortly before Trimble left on 11 July, the Prime Minister told the UUP leader that he needed to secure the stability of the North-South institutions and produced a form of words. Trimble stated that he had no difficulty with this, so long as the bigger issues were resolved. On policing, Blair stated that it was unacceptable that unrepentant republicans should run the District Partnership Policing Boards in circumstances in which the movement as a whole contained a still active paramilitary wing. Nonetheless, he added that the Patten report had demanded four Belfast sub-groups, effectively meaning that the one in the west Belfast area could be dominated by republicans. It was a sure sign that Blair was thinking of giving Sinn Fein what they wanted in this area, if he had not already done so; Trimble said that he could not 'take in any more water on policing', but it was not a make-or-break issue for him now, and everyone knew it.

The prospect of such concessions greatly discomfited the UUP MPs. According to Frank Millar, on Wednesday 11 July at a meeting of the parliamentary party in London, five MPs plus Lord Laird concluded that the deal was shaping up to be a 'sell-out' and that the UUP should not return to Weston Park.[13] But a UUP delegation did return to Weston Park. At the final meeting with Blair on Saturday 14 July, the Prime Minister told them that Sinn Fein still had a 'long shopping list', adding 'I'm trying to whittle it down.' Once more, they returned to the subject of what would happen if there was no resolution of the impasse by the time of the 12 August, six-week deadline. Trimble was in favour of suspension and a review; but the Prime Minister said that if Reid did not suspend, there would have to be elections and everything that would flow from that. Trimble then suggested an alternative to open-ended suspension: what about a one-day suspension, to buy an additional six weeks? The UUP leader also said that if there was a suspension, then his party ought to benefit and he again raised the issue of whether himself and Mallon might continue as junior direct rule ministers superintending the Northern Ireland Civil Service (that is, devolved matters). It would certainly, he argued, represent a powerful signal to Sinn Fein. 'We can think about that,' replied Blair. 'And, as you say, there must be a penalty.' Subsequently, in the course of their last conversation in the garden, Blair reassured Trimble: 'We're fairly convinced that they're going to do something' (that is, the IRA would decommission). Trimble said they had received intelligence before suggesting that the Provisionals would 'do something', but they never had delivered. Was there any new intelligence to suggest a shift? Blair turned to Powell, as he so often did when intelligence was discussed. 'Are you optimistic this time?' the Prime Minister asked his chief of staff. 'Yes, I think they're going to do something.' They also reached two understandings at the end of Weston Park: first, that the two premiers would publicly state that a package was ready but they would only implement it if actual decommissioning occurred. In other words, the trigger for implementation would be a certification by de Chastelain that actual decommissioning had occurred. Second, that if no decommissioning occurred, the two Governments would publicly indict Sinn Fein. So on Saturday 14 July, the two Governments published their joint communiqué, in which arms was only one aspect of the negotiation and the last-mentioned item. Reid and Cowen would now go away and work on the detailed package.[14]

Many of these proposals in this package – including such incentives for republicans as the idea of an indemnity law to cover all crimes committed during the Troubles – soon seeped into the public domain.[15] No. 10 were told by the UUP that these leaks were making their lives very difficult, particularly if a package of proposed concessions to nationalists was published without a de Chastelain report first indicating an act of decommissioning. For once something was in the public domain, even if just billed as 'proposals', it could rarely, if ever, be clawed back. Indeed, Reid subsequently made clear that the proposals on policing were autonomous and would be offered almost irrespective of what republicans delivered on decommissioning.[16] But both Blair and Ahern kept reassuring Trimble that *something* would happen on that score. Any delays in publishing the package were to buy time in order to extract from the IRA a new statement.[17] Publication of the intergovernmental statement was thus postponed from Friday 27 July, when Blair and Ahern met in Sedgefield, Co. Durham, to Monday 30 July. That day, the UUP discovered from the NIO that it would probably only be published on Wednesday 1 August. It would be much the same as discussed, but with one caveat: decommissioning would not have to happen first for the concessions to be given to nationalists. Instead, the document merely referred to the *importance* of decommissioning. When Trimble met Reid at Hillsborough on Wednesday 1 August for a final 'pre-brief' on the intergovernmental package, before it was actually launched on Thursday 2 August, there was still no sign of any decommissioning, contrary to what Blair had told the UUP.[18] Nor, contrary to what Trimble had been told by Blair at the end of Weston Park, was there any indictment of Sinn Fein accompanying the package of concessions – effectively saying to republicans 'all this could have been yours, if only you had not been so intransigent'. The UUP leader asked the Northern Ireland Secretary: 'Why are you doing that? Once all this is published, it will simply be the starting point for another negotiation.' Reid said that if all this enabled the SDLP to sign up for the new PSNI, that would be a good result. 'You're taking leave of your senses,' replied Trimble. There was also a draft statement for the parties designed to ensure no further NSMC sanctions. 'I will not be making that statement,' Trimble added. When asked by the UUP what would happen if there was still no decommissioning after receiving all these 'goodies', Reid said that the two Governments would denounce Sinn Fein. But even this was not what it seemed, for Reid shortly thereafter added that Blair was still minded to call elections.

When the proposals were finally published, Trimble did not condemn them out of hand. There were some small gains: he obtained 'unionist' inquiries on allegations of Garda Siochana collusion with the IRA, and on the suspicious circumstances of the murder of Billy Wright, to match those of 'nationalist' victims. He also secured a review of the workings of the Parades Commission. But nobody could be under any illusion that in the round, the document represented bleak reading for unionists: only one out of 20 sub-headings in the ten-page Anglo-Irish text related to weapons.[19] It looked as though Trimble had been outmanoeuvred in the run-up to the 12 August deadline and that he had been left with two unacceptable choices: acceptance (meaning defeat) or rejection (meaning blame for failure).[20] Moreover, Adams had picked up the talk of Assembly elections. What better way of bringing them about, and averting suspension, than a display of republican good faith? Thus, on Thursday 9 August, an IRA statement appeared, stating that its representative had met with de Chastelain on eight occasions over the past five months and had agreed modalities for putting weapons beyond use. The IRA statement elicited much favourable comment in nationalist Ireland.[21] But the UUP leader still had a card to play: the status of his three remaining ministers. For if they pulled out, then the DUP would have to pull out as well. There would therefore be no Unionist ministers of any hue in the Executive, and without cross-community representation, the whole thing would have to fall, including the SDLP and Sinn Fein participants. Trimble made this strategy quite clear when he met with senior party colleagues at Glengall Street before he left for his holidays in Austria; Empey disagreed with this approach, stating 'I'm not up for it.' He said he wanted, instead, to try to persuade Reid to suspend.[22] Trimble agreed, but also left the appropriate dismissal letters with David McNarry, whom he had just appointed as his special adviser.[23] (One wag quipped that electoral defeat seemed to be a prerequisite for being rewarded by Trimble: David Campbell, David McNarry and Mark Neale, a Craigavon councillor who lost his seat in 2001, were all subsequently appointed as Stormont special advisers; and Cecil Walker was knighted for his services in 2002. Trimble says that the three men were appointed for their ability, and particularly for their feel for grassroots unionist opinion.)[24] The threat of resignation might just, Trimble concluded, force the British to suspend after the fashion of February 2000. And during discussions with the British, Trimble reminded them of one other relevant aspect of the 2000 suspension legislation: as well as open-ended suspensions, the Secretary of State could also suspend for a day, thus setting the six-week clock starting all over again. What the British appeared not to know – as Reid told a UUP delegation at Hillsborough Castle on 9 August – was what the Irish reaction to this 'technical' mini-suspension would be.

The Trimbleistas believed that the credibility of the UUP leader's resignation strategy was undermined by a senior colleague. Reg Empey had been designated by Trimble to exercise the functions of First Minister *ad interim*. He again made it clear at a meeting with senior colleagues at the White Gables Hotel in Hillsborough on 9 August, prior to a session with Reid, that he was very reluctant to follow Trimble's resignation. The reasons for this were as follows: Empey says he was concerned about the legality of it and claims that it looked tacky. Furthermore, he wondered what could be achieved by resigning in August, with so much of the British Government on holiday.[25] If Trimble felt sufficiently strongly, he would surely have resigned the ministers of his own accord. Empey argued that the UUP could not be seen to pull down the institutions by resigning at this stage (he had not, however, say David Campbell and David McNarry, made these arguments when Trimble himself resigned). As far as he was concerned, Trimble's resignation itself was the 'nuclear option' and thus placed quite sufficient pressure on the Government.[26] Why, he argued, should the UUP inflict this wound upon itself because republicans had defaulted? Empey preferred, rather, to withdraw from the Executive, after the fashion of the DUP's semi-detached status (in other words, the UUP ministers would remain in place). Empey believes he had the support of his colleagues Sam Foster, Michael McGimpsey and junior minister Dermott Nesbitt for this approach; Trimble, by contrast, claims that they backed him. Foster, McGimpsey and Nesbitt state that they would have been perfectly happy to resign had that been the collective view of the group – though they add that at this particular moment in time, they were in favour of 'keeping the powder dry for a bit longer' (that is, not resigning immediately) in order to obtain the result the UUP desired.[27] McNarry also reckons that initially, Empey was even reluctant to see the institutions suspended for a 24-hour period. According to McNarry's diary, Empey communicated some of this reluctance to Reid and senior British officials when they met shortly thereafter at Hillsborough Castle at 4:20 p.m. that day. The reason for his reluctance soon became clear to McNarry. Empey asked of Reid: 'If there was a suspension, what is the thinking on retaining the function of First Minister and Deputy First Minister? If it meant [Gerry] Loughran [head of the NICS] writing the [Executive] minutes, this would be legally okay. We don't have a party position, [!!] but if the proposition was put forward, would the Government give a response and what are the possibilities to suspend if the Unionists haven't withdrawn?' Reid replied: 'I can't suspend unilaterally, but I'm willing – if the UUP ministers stayed in position – to consider a 24-hour suspension in order to create six weeks where within that period, the Government would be prepared to look at the retention of the First and Deputy First Minister. I could give you an answer on this later this evening. I have John Hume waiting on me now.' According to David McNarry, Empey visibly relaxed when Reid suggested to him how the possible 'mini-suspension' might work. In this scenario, the acting First Minister would only be out of office for 24 hours. McNarry was nonetheless still profoundly worried about the signals which had been sent out by Empey. For McNarry believed that by giving an impression of differing approaches within the UUP, Empey had undermined the credibility of Trimble's resignation strategy and might have given the British an excuse not to suspend. He duly turned on his heels after the meeting had ended and returned, alone, to Reid. When McNarry returned to Reid's office, he found the Ulster Secretary with Bill Jeffrey, the Political Director of the NIO. 'Bill, I have a bit of a problem,' declared McNarry. 'What is it, David?' replied Reid, apparently surprised to see him. 'I need a few moments,' said McNarry, who explained that Trimble's own position was quite unambiguous and that he would have to contact the UUP leader immediately: whilst it would be internally messy for Trimble to submit the resignations of the ministers unilaterally, he would use his

power as nominating officer to do so if necessary. McNarry then telephoned Trimble and told him what had happened. 'Aha, this is what
happens when I'm not there,' commented the UUP leader. He was, says
McNarry, disappointed, but not surprised.[28] Later, an exasperated Trimble
opined to Steven King of some colleagues, including Empey, 'they're an
ungrateful bunch'; he could often say things in the heat of the moment,
which did not necessarily impede subsequent good relations with any of
the individuals in question.[29] McNarry next telephoned Campbell, who
was on holiday at Lake Garda in Italy. McNarry reiterated his view that
Empey was 'seriously off-side'. Trimble's chief of staff was sufficiently
concerned by this to call Empey that evening. Empey was hugely upset,
believing that he had not been adequately consulted beforehand on the
resignation gambit (though he had been well aware that this escalation
was very much the obvious next step for his leader and he certainly
knew that as nominating officer, Trimble, could pull the UUP ministers
unilaterally; Empey says that he recalls no such consultations or strategy,
and denies his aim was to undermine Trimble.)[30] And, in terms reminiscent of those he had employed towards the end of the negotiations
on the Belfast Agreement in April 1998, Empey argued that the UUP had
lost office in 1972 and had not regained it in 29 years. 'We'll never get
back,' he exclaimed.[31] 'Do you not see that potentially you're the main
beneficiary of all of this?' asked Campbell. Later in the conversation,
Campbell again sought to convince Empey in what he thought were the
acting First Minister's terms: 'David has made no secret that he doesn't
want to come back as First Minister. If we don't get decommissioning
sorted out, you'll never get the job anyway.'[32] On the next day, Campbell
spoke to Trimble and suggested the following deal. The UUP leader would
not resign his ministers, but in exchange, Reid would do a one-day
suspension, averting elections, thus keeping the SDLP alive.[33] Trimble
duly put this idea to Reid whilst on the road in Austria. The implied
threat of unilateral action by Trimble certainly helped to force Reid's
hand: despite declaring himself not to be a suspender, after all that had
befallen Mandelson, Reid froze the institutions for a day on 11 August,
much to the annoyance of republicans.[34]

Suspension inevitably upset the republicans. According to the
Guardian on 15 August 2001, Adams had been told privately by Blair that
the British would stand up to the Unionists and that the Mandelson
suspension of February 2000 would not be repeated.[35] No. 10 denies that

any such guarantee was made. But in spirit, the report was correct. The Mandelson suspension had been open-ended and was overtly opposed by the Irish Government. This suspension was just for one day and did not arouse anything like the same public opposition from the southern Government. And, of course, this suspension had taken place *after* Trimble had resigned: from a nationalist viewpoint, it would have been much worse if the UUP leader had 'put it up' to the two Governments without paying any price. Nonetheless, the one-day suspension represented a success for Trimble. The British and Irish Governments had sought to bluff him into withdrawing his resignation by threat of elections, much as they had tested his resolve in varying measures in the run-up to the Mandelson suspension in 2000. Once again, Trimble had bluffed them, calculating correctly that they would pull back from definitively undermining the centre ground. And as before, he had one secret weapon: the unwillingness of the DUP ministers to resign before him or his colleagues. 'If they had pulled the plug, I dread to think what would have happened,' recalls Trimble.[36]

The slow, grinding trench warfare of Ulster politics was then suddenly interrupted by dramatic news from several continents away. On 13 August, three Irishmen were paraded in handcuffs at police headquarters in Bogota, Colombia. The three were originally named as David Bracken, James Monaghan and Martin McCauley. The Colombians alleged that they had been travelling on false Irish or British passports and that they had been in the country's 'demilitarised' zone on behalf of the Provisional IRA, where they were engaged in training their fellow revolutionaries in the FARC (Colombia's largest insurrectionary force).[37] Monaghan was a well-known republican; McCauley had been convicted of weapons possession; 'Bracken' turned out to be Niall Connolly, a young middle-class Dubliner who was Sinn Fein's representative in Latin America, based in Cuba.[38] Initially, Adams denied that he had any association with the three men and denied that Sinn Fein even had a representative in Havana; but the Cuban authorities rapidly confirmed that Connolly did indeed hold this job and later, when it was safer to do so, Adams admitted as much as well.[39]

It was a public relations disaster for the republican movement, and nowhere more so than the United States. The US State Department described FARC as 'narco-terrorists' because of that organisation's involvement in the drugs trade and had poured several billion dollars over the years into the country as part of the economic, humanitarian and security assistance programme known as 'Plan Colombia'. Moreover, many American citizens were under threat there.[40] In fact, the three accused were found not guilty of 'training for illegal activities'.[41] They refused to appear in court, apparently in the belief that they would not get a fair trial. They were, however, all convicted of the charge of travelling on false passports. Before the conclusion of the trial, legislators such as William Delahunt, Democrat of Massachusetts, were demanding Congressional inquiries on the relationship between Sinn Fein and the FARC.[42]

Likewise, in the Republic of Ireland, both Fine Gael and Labour demanded that the republican movement come clean; John Hume also demanded that they clarify what had happened.[43] Curiously, the British Government's *public* response was far more subdued, which may have owed something to the internal politics of Whitehall. The security services had been on the trail of the three republicans for some time and had informed No. 10 of their movements. But at least one key British player in Colombia claims that during the Clinton years, he and his colleagues did not have the full confidence to inform their American counterparts. This was, he believed, because elements in the Democratic Administration might quietly inform Sinn Fein/IRA that they were being watched. Once Bush took over, the risks diminished dramatically, and they could work with an Administration where the normal imperatives of law enforcement and intelligence gathering had reasserted themselves. Blair had been briefed on events in Colombia at the time of Weston Park – but, as one security source notes, gave the republicans concessions on policing and demilitarisation anyhow.[44] When the three were arrested, however, there was a level of disbelief in the highest reaches of Government: Reid, for one, told Sir Ronnie Flanagan that he believed that the three men may have been in Colombia without the knowledge of Adams and McGuinness.[45] Furthermore, Jonathan Powell told Trimble on 29 August 2001 that he thought that Adams and McGuinness had lost an internal battle inside the movement.[46]

It was not just Blair's aides who were soft-pedalling the issue; it was the Prime Minister himself. Indeed, when Trimble met with Blair at No. 10 on 5 September, he thought the Prime Minister to be in a state of denial about what had happened.[47] All Blair could say was that the republican movement was 'in a muddle' and moved at the pace of the slowest vessel; he claimed that they knew that they had miscalculated in not decommissioning, and would act now. Blair told Trimble that he had to recognise that the UUP was 'in a very strong position' and implied that he should not do anything to heighten the crisis, such as resigning his party's remaining ministers. Trimble doubted that he could hold things for very much longer, but he did not want to push things very hard either at this point if he could possibly avoid it. Indeed, not only did he lack a first-rate operation in the United States to exploit the new circumstances to Unionism's advantage – for example, by making headway with Cuban-Americans in the wake of Adams' visit to Havana – but he did not really want to build one or to exploit the circumstances, either. 'If we were to come in and attack Adams vigorously – do we do him any damage or do we in fact rescue him?' asked Trimble. 'Others were doing it more effectively. It could look as though we were exploiting it, kicking the poor chap when he's down and encouraging a sectarian knee-jerk reaction on the other side.'[48] Certainly, if the roles had been reversed, it is impossible to imagine Sinn Fein forbearing to 'kick the poor chap when he's down'; rather, the Sinn Fein publicity machine would have been working overtime. Trimble's reluctance personally to land serious blows on Sinn Fein was a further illustration that he did not want republicans driven out of the process, if he could possibly avoid it.[49]

Whatever Trimble's calculations, the IRA responded swiftly following the arrest of the three Irishmen in Colombia. On 14 August, the IRA withdrew its offer of 9 August agreeing modalities for decommissioning. The new IRA statement referred to the UUP's 'rejection' of their 9 August offer (in fact, it was not rejected, though it was cool in the absence of actual decommissioning) and the alleged British failure to live up to their commitments. Others suggested that the IRA's withdrawal of its 9 August offer was caused by events in Colombia. Even then, however, seasoned observers could not help noticing that although the IRA withdrew a specific proposal, it did not withdraw the interlocutor himself, as it had after the Mandelson suspension of February 2000. This was taken as an indication that all the matters mentioned in the statement were up for negotiation.[50] And despite the moral and public relations disaster of loyalists' protests in north Belfast against what they saw as the ongoing retreat of Protestants in the Glenbryn area – when Catholic children were attacked on their way to the Holy Cross Primary School – the pressure increased relentlessly on republicans.[51] On 20 August 2001, the Roman

Catholic bishops endorsed the new policing arrangements. They were rapidly followed by the SDLP, which thus became the first of the main parties in Northern Ireland to sign up to the new policing arrangements and, more important, the first time that northern nationalists had done so. These moves also enjoyed the backing of the Irish Government. The SDLP did so after Reid had made clear that once the new Policing Board was in place the sweeping programme of symbolic change would be implemented very quickly; and Seamus Mallon pronounced the legislation to be 'de-Mandelised'.[52] Thus, by the end of September 2001, three out of the four major parties in Ulster had signed up, with varying measures of resistance, to the new policing arrangements. Only Sinn Fein remained outside the tent – and after their decision to join Stormont, few can have doubted where the leadership wanted to take them. The question now was at what price and over what timescale.

Trimble was again rescued by the completely unexpected. After the joint UUP-DUP delegation met with Reid to discuss policing issues at Hillsborough on 11 September – the first such cooperative action between the two parties since the DUP left the talks in protest at the admission of Sinn Fein to the all-party talks in September 1997 – the UUP leader returned to Stormont. When he arrived in the party rooms, he found David Kerr and his colleagues watching televised images of aircraft slamming into the twin towers of the World Trade Center. They were all as shell-shocked as anyone else. Once he had digested the full human dimensions of the tragedy, Trimble's thoughts inevitably turned to the implications for Northern Ireland. 'They can't go back to bombing London,' he concluded.[53] To Ulster Unionists, and indeed Unionists of any stripe, the lessons of 11 September were obvious. The difference between the Provisionals and al-Qaeda, Trimble told the UUP conference that year, was not one of morality, but simply one of scale. To him, the IRA was the prototype for terrorists globally, which showed how evil men could exploit discontented adolescents for their own ends and then glamorise their hideous misdeeds. After all, it was republicans who had perfected 'spectaculars': indeed, even the choice of high-rise, high-profile buildings as targets was eerily reminiscent of their practices. Trimble further observed that the noted republican Brendan (Bic) McFarlane had suggested that the IRA try to bring down Concorde with a SAM-7.[54] Maybe now, Unionists reasoned, the Americans would fully understand what they had been through over the last 30 years.[55]

Certainly, the international environment had suddenly become far more inhospitable to the Provisionals. Sinn Fein/IRA may have had nothing to do with al-Qaeda, but its sympathies lay squarely with a host of anti-American movements or states which would now be the targets of George W. Bush's broader war on terrorism. Its foreign cognates were the PLO, HB/ETA, the FARC, the Puerto Rican FALN and Macheteros and the Turkish DHKP-C.[56] During the course of the Troubles, the republican movement's state allies had included Cuba, Libya and Syria.[57] With Irish-Americans (not least some of the corporate chiefs who had bankrolled Sinn Fein) uniting behind the Commander-in-Chief along with all of their other compatriots, it was obvious that the republican movement was now facing international isolation. Adams well understood that if he was to avoid being swept away by this tide of moral and political indignation, he would have to move swiftly in some form.[58] The Sinn Fein president met with Blair on 17 September 2001 and told him that the republican movement would now do something on decommissioning and that he wanted to meet with Trimble to tell him what and when. At Trimble's meeting with Blair on 19 September 2001 the Prime Minister assured the UUP leader that the republicans would move in the next three weeks. 'Have they said it clearly?' asked Trimble. 'Yes, and they will tell you,' replied Blair. 'What happens if they don't?' inquired Empey. 'Oh, then we'll have to suspend and go into review,' said Blair. 'Well, what is the stick to be used if they don't?' Then came the shocking response from the Prime Minister: 'What stick can there be?' It was thus made clear to the UUP that even in these circumstances, the British were not prepared to consider the exclusion of Sinn Fein.

It was the first indication that the events of 11 September would not necessarily transform the landscape of Northern Ireland as completely as Trimble might have hoped. The problems for the UUP leader were two-fold. First, there was the tactical question of whether he could actually hold the UUP for another three weeks on the basis of a 'jam tomorrow' private assurance from Blair, let alone from Adams. Second, Blair's approach suggested that although he was aligning himself closely with Bush's war on terrorism, he nonetheless viewed Adams as a special case who still needed inducements to maintain his position against republican 'hardliners'.[59] Indeed, it soon became apparent that the British Government regarded 'global terrorism' launched against the United States for no discernible, rational objective as a quite different phenomenon from a much reduced campaign of armed struggle that had been launched for specific political objectives.[60] This approach found its most obvious expression in the Anti-Terrorism Crime and Security Bill, which created a distinction between international terrorists and domestic terrorists and which stated that 'international terrorism does not include terrorism concerned only with the affairs of a part of the United Kingdom'; as such it built on the precedents set by the 1998 post-Omagh legislation and the Terrorism Act 2000, which Trimble alleged drew distinctions between 'good' terrorists (who were 'on ceasefire' and engaged in political processes) and 'bad' terrorists (who were not).[61] Moreover, Blair believed that whereas al-Qaeda's campaign was based upon a desire to wreak destruction for no coherent political purpose, and was based upon a deeply flawed view of alleged injustice in the world, the grievances of Irish nationalists had some real validity (though, of course, the Prime Minister deplored the violent means used by republicans to undo those injustices). Thus, in Blair's Labour party conference speech, the Prime Minister stated that 'there will be no unification of Ireland except by consent. And there will be no return to the days of unionist or Protestant supremacy because those days have no place in the modern world. So the unionists must accept justice and equality for nationalists.'[62] The UUP leader was furious and told Daphne Trimble, 'Blair's lost the plot.'[63] When he visited No. 10 on the next day he was quick off the mark: 'I've never felt so insulted,' and quoted Blair's words back at him. 'I've never displayed any of that. We're not supremacists. We've always striven for justice and equality for all.' 'I'm sorry,' replied the Prime Minister. 'I apologise for that. I didn't intend to offend you.' But Trimble was not mollified and returned to the offensive. 'Well that's all very well, but I'm not a supremacist.' By now, Blair was shifting about uncomfortably. Here he was, fresh from his triumph at the party conference and his welcome from George W. Bush in the US Congress on 20 September, being berated by a provincial party leader. 'I'll find a way of making clear that I didn't mean you.' Powell then poured oil on troubled waters, declaring, 'Well, he did call for the IRA to give up their weapons.' As such, the speech supplied further evidence in support of the contention that the high-water marks of 'New Labour revisionism' took the longest time in reaching Northern Ireland policy. Like Gladstone, Blair was essentially in thrall to a nationalist interpretation of recent Irish history (subsequently, on the floor of the Commons, John Reid explicitly likened Blair's efforts to settle

Northern Ireland to those of the GOM – although more cynical observers believed that this lay more in the realm of flattery of the 'boss' than of serious historical analysis).[64]

Trimble swiftly grasped that such differentiation between 'good' and 'bad' terrorism – and the differing methods of dealing with them – was profoundly subversive of his position. It also explains why he spoke out so strongly about these distinctions in his article in *The Daily Telegraph* of 24 September and in his Conservative conference speech of 10 October.[65] But however disillusioned he became with Blair, Trimble could never quite break with the Prime Minister, either personally or politically (that summer, for instance, Blair had been talking to him about helping raise money for the centre parties in Northern Ireland in anticipation of the Assembly elections). Indeed, he strove as much as he possibly could to help Blair – and, by inference, Adams – on the timing of the wind-down of the institutions. Likewise, he stated in his *Daily Telegraph* article of 24 September that the Provisionals had committed 30 murders since the Belfast Agreement; but although this may 'have turned his stomach' (to adapt Major's phrase about discussions with the Provisionals in 1993), Trimble did not actually regard the republican movement as beyond the pale per se, so long as they began to decommission. Indeed, on 14 October, Trimble stated that '*the next time the IRA murders someone*, Dr Reid must take exactly the same action he took against the loyalist groups' (author's emphasis).[66] Ed Moloney was correct in stating that the British and Irish Governments were prepared to tolerate a degree of ambiguity for the longest time in the Adams-McGuinness position, to allow them gradually to wind down the IRA; there is also a case for suggesting that Trimble acquiesced in this game far more than is generally understood. His strong public pronouncements, such as in *The Daily Telegraph*, were partly about the process of managing the UUP. Indeed, on 19 September 2001, Trimble told Blair at No. 10 that 'my first duty is to preserve my leadership of the party. I will do what I have to do to preserve it and my colleagues.' It was also a way of signalling to Blair that he had other options open to him. However, he did not want to avail himself of those options (including bringing down the Executive altogether) if he could possibly avoid it. All he really wanted was 'a wee bit more pressure' on republicans. 'Have you got the Irish on board for Plan B?' Trimble asked Blair on 19 September. 'Well, I'm up for that, but I don't know if I can get the Irish to do that yet.' If Blair did try, he did not do so very hard – not least since Trimble appeared not to be pushing for it that hard, either.

Nonetheless, slowly but surely, the republican movement began to reposition itself. On 20 September it was announced in *An Phoblacht* that the IRA would now renew and intensify talks with the IICD. It was not enough even for the Irish Government, but it represented a start.[67] On 23 September, Reid signed a one-day suspension order for the second time; the Ulster Secretary had said in August that the first mini-suspension would be the last time such a device was used, but the events of 11 September made it possible for him to employ it again. The unionist community was inevitably sceptical of promises and procedural steps which simply restored the *status quo ante* of engagement with the IICD. Trimble knew that the longer it went on without actual decommissioning, the greater the pressure on him would be. Once again, the question was, whose boiler would burst first? Blair told Trimble on 19 September at No. 10 that 'they [Sinn Fein] need three weeks', implying that the UUP leader should take no precipitate steps to escalate such as resigning the ministers. The Prime Minister told Trimble that Adams wanted to meet with him, and Bill Jeffrey suggested that the Sinn Fein president be as open as possible. But when the two men met on 20 September 2001 at Parliament Buildings, Adams told the UUP leader nothing of substance. Essentially, the republican's message was that something might happen, and something might not. Trimble complained to Reid later that day that he had been led to believe that Adams would be forthright. The Secretary of State reassured the UUP leader that his own judgment was that the republicans would do something; likewise, when Trimble subsequently met with Ahern on 2 October, the Taoiseach told him that McGuinness needed another two weeks. Again, words were not enough for Trimble and he stated his intention to table an exclusion motion on Monday 24 September, to maintain the pressure. But he ensured that it would only be debated in the Northern Ireland Assembly two weeks hence, on 8 October, to buy the Governments and Sinn Fein a little more time. However, if the motion was carried (which seemed unlikely, since the SDLP was not ready to support it and thus to give it the necessary cross-community support) he would resign his ministers.[68] It seemed that he decided on this 'slow-burn' course of action following a call from Blair.[69]

The Ulster Unionist and DUP motions duly failed to obtain the required cross-community support and on 8 October the UUP withdrew their ministers from the Executive, as a preliminary to full resignation in the following week.[70] It was all increasingly moot, though. On 7 October, the UUP received an initial report from their own private sources, and on 9 October a fuller briefing – both of which suggested that under pressure from the Americans, the Provisionals had agreed to start decommissioning in the next two weeks. (The IRA had originally intended to delay decommissioning until just before the elections in the Irish Republic scheduled for 2002, but the current circumstances made that plan impossible.) If they did not do so, Sinn Fein/IRA would be treated in the same way as Real IRA and the 32 County Sovereignty Committee. On 16 October, Trimble met with David Montgomery and told him that he would be resigning his ministers. 'This will cause a terrible stink,' the former MGN chief observed. 'Gerry [Adams] will go ballistic.' 'I'm flying back in the morning and I don't think he will,' replied the UUP leader.[71] On 17 October, Trimble confirmed to Reid that he would have to resign his ministers on the next day. The Assembly was sitting in the next week, but then there would be a recess for Halloween and then the suspension would expire on 4 November. Trimble suggested another one-day suspension to restart the clock so that d'Hondt could be run and a new First and Deputy First Minister could be elected. Then Reid asked: 'To what extent will suspension affect them?' (that is, Sinn Fein). It was the first hint that the British were thinking of not employing that device – and it soon became apparent that whilst the Government had promised the Ulster Unionists that there would be no elections, it had also promised Sinn Fein no more painful suspensions.

As Trimble correctly predicted, the republicans decided to make their big move before their important fundraising event in New York on 1 November. Jonathan Powell duly telephoned David Campbell on Sunday 21 October and stated that he was confident of an act of decommissioning and that Adams would be meeting with Trimble; it was important that the UUP leader be positive. Campbell agreed, but expressed his worries that NIO officials were still talking about elections. Trimble put these in the form of a memorandum and on the next day, Powell informed Campbell that the Prime Minister had 'absolutely no tolerance of elections. They won't happen.'[72] On 22 October, in front of a west Belfast audience that included Brian Keenan and former hunger strikers, Adams announced that he had 'asked' the IRA to make a 'ground-breaking move on the arms issue'; at 8 p.m. that night, Trimble met with de Chastelain at the IICD headquarters at Rosepark House in east Belfast and after receiving the good news repaired to his offices. His colleagues, including Empey, then toasted him with Black Bush Irish whiskey.[73] On 23 October, in a carefully choreographed reply, the Provisionals stated that they had responded in the affirmative to Adams. According to de Chastelain, they had put a quantity of arms beyond use, including arms, ammunition and explosives. 'We were told this day would never happen and it has happened,' declared Trimble proudly.[74] On 24 October, he revoked the resignations of his three ministers.[75] Meanwhile, the British began to announce a programme of Army base closures in Co. Armagh and Co. Londonderry, along the lines of what had been discussed at Weston Park.[76]

At one level, the act of decommissioning represented a great triumph for Trimble. He had resigned in June/July, created a crisis, and with a massive amount of luck – including 11 September – had altered the terms of trade. As The Economist leader of 27 October noted, '[the IRA's] bad temper is an unintended tribute to Mr Trimble, and to his establishment friends. It is often said that Sinn Fein and the IRA never submit to pressure. This time, they have. By resigning over decommissioning, Mr Trimble forced Gerry Adams, Sinn Fein's leader to weigh what he stood to gain by keeping the new political institutions alive against what he stood to lose by allowing them to collapse.'[77] But the republican movement had also made bad errors, ignoring one of Blair's mottoes: 'The time when you're most successful is when you are most vulnerable.'[78] Back in July, the republicans were riding high: they had crushed the SDLP, had secured further concessions on policing and other issues at Weston Park and seemed to be on the verge of Assembly elections that would formally establish their hegemony inside the devolved institutions. If they had done the deal then, and decommissioned even in the most nugatory fashion, Trimble would have been in trouble. But, as so often, they had chiselled for more and were overtaken by events. These 'events' constituted a 'triple whammy': the first suspension on 10 August, the SDLP going on the new policing board without Sinn Fein and, of course, 11 September. Trimble could only really claim personal credit for the first of these, but Sinn Fein's pain was undoubtedly his gain and that would be enough for many of his supporters, at least for now. On the other hand, the UUP's position had not improved intrinsically in any *positive* sense. All that had happened was that republicans were being forced to do what they had promised anyway and the additional danger of Assembly elections – which the British Government had contemplated over the summer – seemed to have passed. Policing reform, overhaul of criminal justice, demilitarisation and a host of other changes were proceeding apace, as if 11 September had never happened. And even when Trimble attained a long-held objective, such as SDLP endorsement of the police, it was bought at a huge price. Trimble often said of the republicans that 'they know what they've got to do, so what is the point of Government paying them to do what they're going to have to do *anyway*?' But that was exactly what Government did – time and time again.

The consciousness of the price paid by the two Governments and by Trimble to secure these gains does much to explain why the UUP leader's achievement was not greeted with great rapture in much of his own community. And he still had one hurdle to jump: to secure re-election as First Minister in the Assembly before the final six-week deadline ran out on 4 November. He had toyed seriously with the idea of not returning as First Minister and wanted John Taylor – by now ennobled as Lord Kilclooney – to succeed him. After all, as has been noted, he was the only one of the four major party leaders to hold the additional burden of ministerial office. But Taylor was adamant that at 64 he was too old for the job.[79] After Empey's reaction to the prospect of resigning his post in August 2001, Trimble was less enthusiastic about him taking over than before. So once again, it came down to himself, alone. There was some polling evidence to suggest that he remained the most viable leader of the unionist community at large: when questioned in a Pricewaterhouse Coopers survey in September 2001 on the issue of 'in whose hands is the Union safest?' 48.0% answered Trimble, followed by Paisley on 32.2%. Amongst UUP supporters only, on the question of 'who do you think would be the best leader of the party?', Trimble topped the poll with 75.2%, followed by Donaldson with 16.3%, by Empey with 4.4%, with Burnside and Martin Smyth on 2% apiece. He was reinforced in his decision to resume the 'co-premiership' by another set of events over which he had no control whatsover. On 17 September John Hume announced he would step down as leader of the SDLP, which he had led since 1979. After some deliberation, only one candidate emerged as his successor: Mark Durkan, the current Northern Ireland Finance Minister and Hume's fellow Derryman (and the son of an RUC Inspector). Durkan was duly anointed in October. But what of Hume's deputy, Seamus

Mallon, who also served as Deputy First Minister? Trimble told me on 27 May 2001 that the UUP would not vote for Mallon again, alleging that 'he can't work with us'. Indeed, the UUP leader had earlier suggested that if Mallon again put himself forward for the post of Deputy First Minister, he would not put himself forward.[80] But in any event Mallon announced on 18 September that he, too, would step down – for his own reasons. Trimble was pleased: he felt that it should have been done long ago and on a personal basis looked forward to working with Durkan, whom he found much easier. 'David's much better tempered when he comes home now,' says Daphne Trimble.[81]

None of this greatly impressed Unionist critics of the Belfast Agreement and the DUP was soon predicting that it could succeed in blocking Trimble's re-election because he would be unable to secure a majority of his own community (that is, 30 of the 58 self-designated unionists in the Assembly).[82] Peter Weir, the rebel UUP Assemblyman for North Down, was an obvious defector, which would reduce Trimble's margins to 29–29 and thus deprive him of a majority. Another long-time sceptic, Pauline Armitage, who sat in the Assembly for East Londonderry, and had served as a Greenfinch in the UDR, was also listed as a potential 'anti'. She was profoundly upset by what had been done to the RUC.[83] Such sentiments would have been reinforced by her surreal encounter with de Chastelain in which the General could not state in which country the decommissioning act took place. Nor, for his part, did Trimble really want to do any deals with these 'antis', especially after the Ulster Unionist Executive on Saturday 27 October had endorsed his approach by 80%–20% and urged all those elected on the UUP ticket (whether in receipt of the party whip or not) to support Trimble's re-election as First Minister. In these circumstances, Trimble's aides started contemplating what means he could employ to secure re-election. Some options were definitely ruled out. At a dinner in the House of Lords on the occasion of Trimble's Castlereagh Lecture on Wednesday 31 October, the UUP leader turned to Philip Johnston of *The Daily Telegraph* and jested: 'In the old days [i.e. at Stormont from 1921–72] I could have tried to give them [the UUP 'antis'] a bridge or a factory for their constituencies.'[84] There was therefore only one avenue open to save the situation. The Alliance or one of the other smaller parties would have to redesignate themselves as a Unionist party, either temporarily or else in perpetuity, to give Trimble his margin. The Alliance was the most obvious choice.

But Trimble was very hostile to the redesignation option, which seemed to him like a contrivance. If he won by this 'tacky' means (his word to describe it) he feared he would lack legitimacy within his own community.[85]

Trimble then had to contend with another, procedural problem. The six-week suspension ran out on Saturday 3 November. Once again, this left the British Government with a choice of another one-day suspension (buying an additional six weeks) or elections. Both of these options appeared to have been ruled out by the British – and the Government was particularly reluctant to suspend *after* an act of IRA decommissioning.[86] The republicans had impressed upon them that every suspension, however short, was a humiliating reassertion of the sovereignty of Westminster and the British agreed with them in these circumstances. This meant that the only way to secure Trimble's re-election in the existing Assembly was by introducing emergency Westminster legislation – which, according to David Montgomery, the Government was prepared to introduce in the last analysis.[87] Trimble, though, wanted to avoid such delegitimising, retrospective legislation if at all possible. And since there was a danger of him losing the first vote owing to the opposition of Weir and Armitage, it was vital that there be enough time to hold a second vote through redesignation before suspension expired. But it turned out that there was only one day on which the vote could take place – on Friday 2 November.[88] By then, it seemed certain that Trimble would be down to just 28 votes out of 58 (the 28 included the two PUP Assemblymen plus the remaining 26 Ulster Unionists) and that none of the independent unionists would abstain. Reluctantly, and partly at the prompting of his wife Daphne, he decided that Friday morning to accept redesignation in the absence of any other options.[89] 'It was messy and horrible,' she recalls. 'But he had to do it. There was no alternative.'[90] First, Jane Morrice of the Women's Coalition had redesignated as a unionist. This took Trimble's total up to 29 – still one short. This meant that the Alliance's reaction would be crucial. David Ford, the party's new leader, was opposed to redesignation, not least because of feeling amongst his own grassroots. Curiously, although they had been alerted to this emerging crisis by the UUP, No. 10 had been very slow about asking the Alliance to help. When eventually Blair tried to ring Ford, the Alliance leader was already on his feet in the chamber. The UUP duly lost the first vote within the designated unionist community by 30–29 (although the overall result in the whole Assembly was 72–30 in favour of the re-election of Trimble).[91] Weir and Armitage had voted against Trimble's re-election. But there was now no time to hold another vote before the suspension ran out. Trimble left for a conference in Gleneagles, Scotland, on organised crime, not knowing exactly what would happen when the suspension expired at midnight on Saturday 3 November. Whilst there, Trimble sought out the British Attorney-General, Lord Goldsmith, for his opinion on the legalities of securing re-election under the Northern Ireland Act 1998. Were there any loopholes? It emerged that it would be lawful, or at least not explicitly *unlawful* to go ahead with another re-election of the First and Deputy First Ministers after the six-week suspension expired. Thus, whilst the Act said that re-election should occur within the six-week period, it did not say that it could *not* take place outside that time-frame. Trimble was nonetheless very tense and unhappy, fearing – on the basis of advice from David Lavery – that it would be *ultra vires* and thus expose the UUP to legal challenge. 'I don't know why I'm agreeing to this,' he snapped. 'It's very messy.' By dinner, the UUP leader had recovered his poise. 'We have to do what we have to do,' he told David Campbell. He was reinforced in this conviction by the 80% backing which he had obtained in the Ulster Unionist Executive and the support of 70% of the entire Assembly.[92] Why, Trimble reasoned to himself, should two recalcitrants flout the will of his party and the Province's main democratic institution? 'I'm not a Faulkner, lacking legitimacy,' he declared.[93]

A new vote was duly called for Tuesday 6 November. On the previous Friday evening, Ford had called a special meeting of the Alliance party executive at party headquarters in University Street, which agreed upon redesignation: his price was a review of the workings of the Assembly, which he duly obtained, and a revision of Standing Orders, permitting a swift 'tactical' redesignation of Alliance Assemblymen (as opposed to the original rules, which meant that a redesignated Assemblyman would have to remain in his/her new communal bloc until the end of the elected body's life).[94] On the day, three Alliance members classified themselves as Unionists, and Trimble accordingly obtained 31 'Unionist' votes to 29; the total in the Assembly was 70–29 in favour.[95] Armitage did not turn up, citing an overnight incident at her home in Portstewart, Co. London-derry.[96] She was suspended from the party and Weir was expelled.[97] Trimble and Durkan were thus elected as First and Deputy First Ministers.

Why, then, did Trimble embrace the option of redesignation, which only days earlier he had dismissed as 'tacky'? 'It's still tacky,' he explains. 'But sometimes you have to do tacky things. And who ever heard of anybody refusing votes? What should I do, stand in front of the voting lobby at Stormont and say "No, Jane [Morrice], I don't want your vote"?'[98] That said, Trimble's politically successful manoeuvre raised important questions of principle and law; the DUP shortly thereafter launched legal proceedings, stating that the delay in holding the vote until after the end of the suspension period was a violation of the Northern Ireland Act 1998.[99] The suit eventually went up to the House of Lords where the plaintiff, Peter Robinson, lost his case on 25 July 2002 by a 3–2 margin.[100] But the political ramifications were of greater significance still. As Frank Millar argued in a seminal article in the *Irish Times* on 5 November 2001, the crux of the Belfast Agreement was the concept of dual consent. John Hume had gifted the process with the idea that in a deeply divided society, majoritarianism was no longer enough. Consequently, he hit upon a political mechanism not dissimilar to the concept adopted in very different circumstances by the South Carolinian statesman, John C. Calhoun: the need for concurrent majorities in both distinctive sectors of the polity or, more crudely put, a mutual veto.[101] Since the unionist population was thought by many to be declining to the point that nationalists might soon overtake them, such protection might be supposed to be essential to Ulster-British interests. Its most obvious institutional expression in the context of the Belfast Agreement was the need to obtain simultaneous majorities in both the unionist and nationalist communities for the election of the First and Deputy First Ministers. It had been a key demand of Mallon in the closing hours of the April 1998 negotiations that this be included, but it also represented a further guarantee to unionists that there could be no repeat of the 1974 power-sharing Executive, when a minority of unionists sought to sustain that arrangement against a majority of the pro-Union population. Yet now, that key means of communal protection had been cast aside because of its inconvenience – simply to facilitate the momentary needs of David Trimble after he had lost the confidence of a majority of elected unionists in the Assembly.[102] Significantly, dilution of the rule about obtaining the support of majorities of elected members from both main communities had been proposed earlier in the year by Mitchel McLaughlin in the *Guardian*. He had suggested 're-evaluation of the basic architecture of the Good Friday Agreement' to ensure that anti-Agreement unionists could not block votes in the Assembly.[103] When asked about Millar's observations, Trimble answers: 'Is the existence of communal vetoes a good thing? Is it any more than a phase we have to go through – and we don't know how long that phase will be? All the safeguards were necessary in order to obtain nationalist agreement to an Assembly. Having safeguards and weighted majorities is fine, but not for ever and a day. I want to see more normal politics here.'[104] By this, Trimble means that now that the constitutional issue is settled in favour of the Union, mainland political parties ought to organise fully and properly in Northern Ireland. Once they do so, sufficient numbers of Protestants and Catholics will vote for British parties to make the communal vetoes unnecessary. John Taylor acknowledges the strength of Millar's points, but says 'those are matters for another day'.[105] Not for nothing did Millar in his Christmas-time 'London Letter' bestow upon the UUP leader the 'Escapologist of the Year' award 'for finally losing his mandate and becoming minority unionist leader at Stormont, tearing up the rules of the Belfast Agreement to get himself elected First Minister, and getting away with it'.[106] And it again raised the question: was Trimble the luckiest politician in these islands – or, like all successful politicians, did he make his own luck?

THIRTY-SEVEN

Another farewell to Stormont

'WE should aim for a really stable six months in the run-up to the [May 2003 Assembly] elections.' Such was Blair's unambiguous message for Trimble and Durkan when the new First and Deputy First Ministerial team visited No. 10 on 7 March 2002. The two men had gone to London to discuss a cross-departmental financial package that would help the two centre parties show to their respective communal electorates that they were 'delivering'. Its purpose was to demonstrate that the moderates, rather than the DUP or Sinn Fein, were the driving force behind the provision of tangible benefits to the man in the street.[1] Blair also indicated his willingness to back a fundraiser for a campaign on behalf of the two main centre parties: the event was subsequently held in the Clarence Room at Claridge's on 23 April 2002, and was attended by a number of businessmen, such as George Magan and Jonathan Rothermere.[2] The UUP leader obviously craved such stability too – and, in some ways, he was gratified in his wish. On 1 December 2001, he faced another motion in the UUC, this time put forward by David Burnside, which would have compelled UUP ministers to withdraw from the Executive if there was no further movement on decommissioning by early spring and if the word 'Royal' was not restored to the police name. Trimble argued that the best way to put pressure on the Provisionals was to wait until the remit of the de Chastelain body had expired in February, when it would be much harder for anyone to blame the UUP for precipitating another crisis.[3] When the votes were counted, Trimble had won by 409 votes to 320 – or 56% to 44%, compared to the 54% he had won in October 2000. There was better news still for Trimble in the coming months when UUP dissidents such as Peter Weir, and some Young Unionists, decided that the game was up and left for the DUP or dropped out of politics altogether.[4]

The wider picture seemed to be improving, too, from the UUP leader's viewpoint. Much to his delight, the Protestant residents of Glenbryn announced that they were suspending their protests outside the Holy Cross Primary School in north Belfast. Even on symbolic matters, where unionists had suffered great defeats, the picture seemed a little brighter. Following the DUP's decision to join the new Policing Board in September 2001, which afforded Trimble huge political coverage, the cross-community body was also able to choose a design which incorporated a much-reduced crown along with six other symbols clustered around a star (with the cross of St Patrick as the centrepiece).[5] And on 14 May 2002, the Queen visited Stormont as part of her Golden Jubilee celebrations and addressed Assemblymen in the Great Hall.[6] Trimble was pleased with her speech, which he thought to be 'an endorsement of all we had done', placing the new Assembly squarely in the context of the wider devolutionary project for the rest of the United Kingdom. He thought it hugely significant that the SDLP was there to welcome her: in 1953, during her post-Coronation tour, members of the old Nationalist party, the official Opposition at Stormont, had signed a petition in the *Derry Journal* against her visit. And although Sinn Fein was not present, the UUP leader noted approvingly that they did not vociferously protest against the tour, either.[7]

Blair was also keen to emphasise to the Ulster Unionists that the republicans were not having it all their own way: on 22 January 2002, at No. 10, he told them that he had met Adams and McGuinness the day before. The Prime Minister claimed that Trimble's good working relationship with Durkan was worrying them. But the Prime Minister sounded an ominous note, too. He worried that the Sinn Fein leaders were heading for difficulties in a few months' time and that there was a certain ambivalence about continuing the process of decommissioning. He had reiterated to Adams and McGuinness that the atmosphere was now totally different in the United States and that they had to think about ditching their 'ultra-leftists'. But in order to sustain Adams and McGuinness, and to make politics seem attractive to the republican movement, Blair had to maintain the pace of concessions. The most dramatic in terms of mainland opinion was the decision to grant the Sinn Fein Westminster MPs office facilities in the Commons – and an estimated £400,000 plus in taxpayers' money – despite their continuing abstentionism from the division lobbies and their refusal to swear the oath of allegiance to the

Sovereign like other MPs. Indeed, Robin Cook, then leader of the Commons, recalls in his diary for 17 December 2001 that 'much of the afternoon is spent wrestling with the challenge of producing a speech for tomorrow's debate that makes handing over a quarter of a million pounds of allowances over to the political allies of Britain's only home-grown terrorist organisation sound entirely reasonable. My rhetorical problem is that it was part of the price of persuading the IRA to commence decommissioning in October. However I am barred from letting that particular cat out of the bag . . .'[8] The *Daily Mail* front page of 22 January 2002 bore the headline 'SICKENING: Outrage as Adams & Co swagger in to Parliament and hoist the Irish flag'. It was accompanied by a 'Mac' cartoon of Adams and McGuinness drinking in plush offices as they looked out of the window, proudly boasting, 'What a view, eh Martin? From here you can see where Airey Neave was killed, the Old Bailey bomb site, the Hyde Park nailbomb site, the . . .'[9]

It was the kind of issue which obviously outraged opinion in Great Britain enough for so commercial an operation as the *Daily Mail* to 'splash' it. But as so often, Trimble's position was more complex than his own hostile rhetoric might have led the superficial observer to suppose. He had no *principled* objection to Sinn Fein MPs, whatever their past records, taking their seats: indeed, the historian in him would have relished what he saw as Adams' almost Redmondite belief in the centrality of Westminster in governing the destiny of these islands![10] Rather, he was against Sinn Fein obtaining such 'goodies' without further reciprocal moves towards constitutionalism – that is, not having to make the hard choices between violence and the full fruits of democratic politics. In a Commons debate on the subject on 18 December 2001, Trimble contrasted the British Government's approach with what he saw as the relative rigour and openness of the Irish Government in refusing dual membership in the Dail and Commons for Sinn Fein members elected for Northern Ireland constituencies. At this moment, the Ulster Secretary, John Reid, intervened. Obviously stung by the apparent suggestion by Trimble that the Government was 'pulling a fast one', Reid pulled out of his pocket a letter from Trimble to his predecessor, Peter Mandelson, making it clear that the UUP leader had been consulted along with everyone else in January 2000 on the issue of office facilities. The letter seemed to suggest that Trimble's one-time position against the measure was contingent upon Sinn Fein's living up to their obligations under the Mitchell review of

1999 (that is, a start to IRA decommissioning). Reid argued that whilst there was a possibility of discussion about the pace at which such progress was made, there was no question that the UUP leader had been kept in the dark.[11]

Trimble had been an assured parliamentary performer from his earliest days in the Commons, but as he later complained to David Campbell, 'I've never been as humiliated as that. I've never witnessed that type of behaviour in Parliament.'[12] He argued that Reid had not resumed Mandelson's January 2000 consultation about Sinn Fein offices with the UUP in the new and different circumstances of December 2001 and that he had been selectively quoted out of context. Whatever the rights and wrongs of Trimble's judgment, the fact remained that Reid's intervention was a gift to the DUP and Trimble's internal UUP opponents, who believed that there had always been a dissonance between his public hostility and his 'real' stance that was more calibrated. They believed that Trimble had effectively accepted that he could not stop such measures, but that he needed to go through the 'optics' of opposition on the floor of the House – and that Reid had blown this dissonance. Indeed, it could be argued that Reid had waived one of the unwritten conventions of the peace process: that whilst Secretaries of State can be punchbags for the various factions, they cannot attack those factions themselves in the same way. Or, as one official at No. 10 puts it, 'the role of the NIO is sometimes to be the "Aunt Sally" of the process, who takes the heat'. Even Mowlam had never directly tackled him in Parliament in so aggressive a fashion. After all, the UUP leader was the 'Fabergé egg' of the process – a delicate, but irreplaceable commodity to be handled with care. And it could be argued that Reid was understanding enough of Adams' and McGuinness's internal management problems never to have embarrassed them in such a manner.[13] According to NIO officials, it was a spontaneous, unplanned gesture: they had simply shoved the letter in Reid's folder for his information just before the debate.[14] On the next day, a UUP delegation met with Jonathan Powell, and the Prime Minister's chief of staff defended Reid and said that the Northern Ireland Secretary felt he was 'giving as good as he got'. David Campbell showed Powell the Hansard, which he felt supported his argument that Trimble had not attacked Reid personally on this occasion; nonetheless, Campbell believed that Reid was trying to 'get back' at Trimble for the personal attacks on him in front of the Prime Minister (where the Ulster Secretary was rarely able to answer back).[15] It may even have been the case that No. 10 gave the go-ahead for the move: at one point, as has been noted, Powell had telephoned Campbell to say that the UUP 'shouldn't think John Reid is another Mo Mowlam' (i.e. that Trimble could drive a wedge between him and No. 10).[16] Nonetheless, Powell asked Campbell to assist in the process of patching things up.[17] If nothing else a total breakdown would have scheduling implications for Blair's diary, forcing him to spend yet more time on Ulster and to handle routine matters that were usually the responsibility of a departmental chief. Reid and Trimble eventually met at the NIO offices in Millbank on 9 January where a modicum of civility was restored in the course of an hour-long tête-à-tête – but they would never be close.[18]

Meanwhile, despite Gerry Adams' talk at the World Economic Forum in New York of the need for unionist 'assent or consent' for a united Ireland, the Provisionals continued their activities unabated.[19] Sir Ronnie Flanagan revealed that he did not rule out Provisional IRA responsibility for the murder of a man in Castlewellan, Co. Down, on 21 February 2002.[20] Of far greater concern to Trimble were the stories appearing in the media – such as David McKittrick's article in The Independent of 11 February 2002 – which suggested, on the basis of conversations with unnamed demographers, that the Protestant majority had almost disappeared. Other reports, such as BBC Northern Ireland's Spotlight, stated that the ageing Protestant population accounted for two-thirds of the 15,000 deaths in the Province per annum. Likewise, the Irish Times obtained figures which showed that over half of the schoolchildren in Ulster were Catholic.[21] If such estimates were right, and Protestants felt themselves under siege, they could lash out (as at Glenbryn, but on a much larger scale). Trimble never believed that the upcoming ten-yearly census, to be published in late 2002, would reveal such near-parity and was delighted by the rebuttal of McKittrick in the Irish Times on 15 February 2002 penned by his former special adviser, Graham Gudgin.[22] But as David Campbell recalls, Trimble needed something more to becalm his own 'folk' in the face of what appeared to be statistical evidence of the further erosion of their position. That 'something more' turned out to be a Border Poll – or referendum on the constitutional status of the Province. Such a plebiscite had last been held on 8 March 1973 (when nationalists boycotted the ballot). As with the post-dated resignation cheque of November 1999, Trimble had initially not been keen on the idea when Paul Bew and others had urged that a Border Poll be held on the same day as the 2001 Westminster elections. Bew had several reasons for counselling this. First, there was the need to stabilise the pro-Union community – or, as Steven King noted, it 'would give Viagra to the consent principle'. It would also prove that there was still a substantial Catholic vote for the Union.[23] Second, if a Border Poll on Northern Ireland's future was held on the same day as the Westminster or Assembly elections, many of the pro-Agreement unionist middle classes who had come out for the May 1998 referendum on the Belfast Agreement but had stayed at home in the June 1998 Assembly elections would turn out and thus improve Trimble's electoral prospects. Third, any increased unionist turn-out would also increase the chances of an extra Executive seat for either unionist party in the Assembly elections – possibly tilting the balance from 5–5 to 6–4. This could turn out to be psychologically significant if, as Trimble feared, Sinn Fein became the majority party in the nationalist community. Thus, a Border Poll could, in certain circumstances, be the device which enabled unionists to continue with an inclusive Executive.[24] Not everyone was so convinced: Clifford Smyth, for one, has argued that the very suggestion of a Border Poll undermined a key tenet of Trimbleism, namely that the Belfast Agreement had secured the Union. If things were so safe, why call one at all?[25] Frank Millar also expressed doubts, but for different reasons. He argued that John Hume's central insight into the conflict was that majoritarianism was not right as a governing principle in a divided society: hence the dual consent principle under which the Assembly operated, whereby certain legislation could only pass if over 50% of designated unionists and nationalists supported it. If one needed the protection of the dual consent method for deciding so trivial a matter, say, as building a bridge over the Bann, why should a mere 50% plus one be enough to secure resolution of the ultimate constitutional issue?[26] It followed from that if dual consent applied, then the Union could endure in perpetuity – yet here was Trimble prepared to risk it for his short-term political needs. Others were not so sure about the political effect within the unionist community, and whether a Border Poll really would help the UUP if held on the same day as an Assembly election: whilst the first few percentage points of any increase in the unionist turn-out would probably aid the 'moderates', it was by no means axiomatic that a larger turn-out would do so. Far too little was known about the 40% or so of residents of 'unionist areas' who did not vote in the 2001 Westminster elections to make any certain predictions.

Trimble first put the idea forward at a private party meeting at Glengall Street in early February 2002: it aroused some enthusiasm, so much so that Trimble may even have seen it as serving the additional purpose of consolidating internal UUP unity. Indeed, Trimble's main worry was not that senior figures would oppose it but that Jeffrey Donaldson might run with it and make it his own before he was able to unveil the proposal at his next major address at the AGM of the UUC in March 2002 (for the longest time, Trimble sought to keep Donaldson as close as possible – on the basis of Lyndon Johnson's line about J. Edgar Hoover that it was 'probably better to have him inside the tent pissing out than outside the tent pissing in' – and later invited him onto the party's election strategy committee). Everything, therefore, was set fair for his speech on Saturday 9 March. But the unexpected then intervened. Steven King, who had drafted much of the speech, distributed the written version of the UUP leader's remarks to the gathered journalists. In it, Trimble blasted the Irish Republic as a 'pathetic, sectarian, mono-ethnic, mono-cultural State'. In fact, Trimble did not deliver the address as written – he had toned it down beforehand – but by then the text was effectively in the public domain. In consequence, the call for a Border Poll was lost in the massive controversy in nationalist Ireland over Trimble's attack on the south.[27] Thus, Sam Smyth observed in the *Sunday Tribune* of 17 March 2002 that '. . . the UUP leader could well be the political manifestation of boils on the back of an adolescent youth's neck'. John Reid also repudiated Trimble's remarks.[28] But they even incurred the displeasure of such long-time supporters of the UUP leader in the Republic such as Eoghan Harris. Quite apart from doubts about Trimble's tone – which validated the prejudices of the most tribal elements in the south about Unionists – Harris felt that Trimble was analytically wrong. The UUP leader's comments painted a ludicrously out of date portrait of the south which was utterly dismissive of the gains of progressive forces in the 26 counties over three or more decades. Moreover, the issue of southern sectarianism no longer really had much to do with the social power of the Roman Catholic Church, whose influence was waning by the year following a succession of scandals. Indeed, Trimble made these remarks in the very week that Ahern and the Roman Catholic Church had been on the losing side of a referendum which would have placed further restrictions on

abortion.[29] In Harris's opinion the problem was the residual tribal prejudice of some *post*-Catholics. He contended that, for them, Anglophobia
and anti-unionism were now the bases of their identity. He contrasted
them with such traditional Catholics as Mgr Denis Faul, whom he argued
were likeliest to do most for genuine reconciliation with their Protestant
neighbours.[30]

Trimble blamed Steven King for the crisis, by going 'over the top' in
his draft speech. In the normal course of events, Trimble would have
read the whole text well in advance.[31] But Friday 8 March was no normal
day. The sequence of events had begun on the day before that, when the
UUP leader stayed behind at No. 10 after he and Durkan had a meeting
with Blair. Trimble showed Blair the unfinished text, observing that there
was more to put in. The bit which remained to be added was a passage
on decommissioning. A second decommissioning act was thought to be
coming – following the first in November 2001 – but the British believed
that Adams had not yet told 'the movement'. 'The speech is good,' commented Blair, 'but we need to know what you're going to add.' Following
his conversations with Sinn Fein, the Prime Minister was obviously
worried that if Trimble issued a hard-edged demand on arms, it would
appear to the republican grassroots as if Adams and McGuinness had
jumped to the UUP's agenda when news of the second tranche of decommissioning emerged. At No. 10's behest, Trimble decided to give Adams
a sight of the relevant paragraph on Friday 8 March, and it was duly
delivered to Adams' office. Then a further unexpected event occurred.
He received word that Toby Harnden of *The Daily Telegraph* was working
on a report that some republicans had been arrested in Florida.[32] According to David Campbell, Trimble suspected Belfast Special Branch for
leaking it so as to inflict maximum damage on the eve of the UUC AGM,
though there was never any evidence to prove this was so and senior
officers denied it.[33] Valuable energy was therefore taken up with that
issue. Meanwhile, Adams had not come back with a response to the UUP
text. Only much later that day did Powell ring David Campbell to tell
him that Adams had contacted him – to say that he still did not know
what Trimble was going to say. Campbell duly faxed the text of the
relevant portion to Powell (but not the whole speech). Powell called
Campbell again and told him that the added section was problematic.
If Trimble delivered it as written, there would be no further acts of
decommissioning. 'I'm not going to phone Trimble,' said Campbell. 'He's

relaxing listening to music. I know what I'll get if I disturb him.' 'I'm just making you aware of what Gerry said,' replied Powell. Campbell knew full well that Trimble would not allow Adams to dictate what he said to the UUC. When Campbell saw Trimble the next day just before the meeting began, he relayed the events of the previous evening. 'I assume you're going to change your speech,' joked Campbell. Trimble laughed, but in the mêlée surrounding the passage on decommissioning and The Daily Telegraph story, he did not fully scrutinise those sections of the speech about the south which were destined to cause such uproar.[34] Although Trimble declined to bend to Adams' demand, the real revelation here is that relations between the two men were such that this sort of exchange of text could be contemplated in the first place.[35] The other intriguing aspect of the story is that Blair knew about the Border Poll proposal beforehand and did not then object loudly.[36] (The idea of a Border Poll proposal continued to float in the ether and eventually was placed again in the political deep freeze.)

The fuss over Trimble's UUC speech, which dogged him at the St Patrick's Day celebrations in America, was soon overshadowed by news that there had been a break-in at the Belfast regional headquarters of PSNI Special Branch based at Castlereagh on the night of 17 March 2002. It emerged that the intruders had obtained many of the code names of Special Branch sources in the area, though since these codes were mixed up with a lot of unimportant materials as well the burglars would not necessarily have discovered the identities. In consequence, large numbers of their police handlers, whose private numbers were also stolen, had to move their homes. The informer network appeared to be in grave danger – so much so that Reid called in Sir John Chilcot, previously Permanent Under Secretary at the NIO and now staff counsellor (or 'agony aunt') to the security and intelligence services to conduct two inquiries. One would focus on the immediate failings leading to the break-in and the other on the longer term implications for national security.[37] There was much speculation as to the identity of the burglars – Jonathan Powell, for one, wondered whether or not the break-in was the work of renegade members of the security forces – but it soon emerged that the principal suspects were known 'mainstream' republicans (as opposed to dissidents). This had been Trimble's contention all along, partly based on his conversations with Sean O'Callaghan. O'Callaghan said that the Provisionals spotted an opportunity and could not resist taking it (to which the UUP leader adverted in conversation with Blair). O'Callaghan's assessment was also vindicated by the findings of the Chilcot report, some of which were placed in the public domain on 16 July 2003.[38]

Thereafter, the tempo of bad news increased. Nor did events on the ground in Northern Ireland give much cause for optimism: the family of a Catholic taxi driver shot dead in Dungannon, Co. Tyrone, blamed the Provisionals; a bomb was planted under the car of a Catholic PSNI recruit by dissidents; and following raids on republican houses in the wake of the Castlereagh break-in, it was reported that the police had found intelligence documents on senior Conservatives. In the following year, Trimble was informed by the police that his personal details were found in IRA computer files and documents.[39] In consequence of all this, the second act of IRA decommissioning (announced in early April 2002) was greeted with little excitement. The climate was such that Trimble's internal party opponents felt able once again to contemplate taking their case to the UUC – despite their defeat of the previous December – and to demand withdrawal from the Northern Ireland Executive.[40] Again, Reid only worsened matters by stating that 'we assess that there is no imminent threat to the IRA ceasefire'.[41] Later, he would enrage Trimble at a meeting when he told the UUP in the Commons on 30 April that the proposed review of policing arrangements would go ahead – a concession granted to the republicans at the Weston Park talks of July 2001. 'You're a damn fool,' the UUP leader told Reid. Trimble did little better with Blair. When the First Minister met him at No. 10 on 24 April, Blair asked what the republicans were playing at. It was an odd question for a man to ask when he had all of the intelligence assets of the British state available to him. Like Reid, he believed that the Provisionals were not going back to violence, but that their recent actions could not be ignored. And he added: 'What do you want us to do?' Trimble said that the republicans had to be given the choice either of shutting down the IRA or else going into a review of the Belfast Agreement. He had little time left before the pot boiled over: the one obvious safety valve, in the shape of immediate NSMC sanctions was denied him since that entity could not meet till the end of May because of the forthcoming Irish General Election (Trimble had imposed NSMC sanctions in October 2000, after the South Antrim by-election, which was about the mildest course of action available to him). But, as he told me on 28 April 2002, he could not walk out then and there from the Northern Ireland Executive because public opinion was not prepared for such a course of action. And if he did pull the plug in those circumstances, without what the British would consider to be a 'smoking gun', then the Government would call Assembly elections for later in the year without any Border Poll. Worse still, from Trimble's viewpoint, was the brief meeting held in an office at Stormont on 26 April between himself and senior colleagues on the one side and Adams and McGuinness on the other. The Sinn Fein president denied the Colombia, Castlereagh and ongoing east Belfast street agitation allegations. 'No one believes you,' said Trimble, 'and our ability to sustain things is brought into question.'[42] The impression was reinforced when Adams later stated that he had never been a member of the IRA.[43]

The Irish General Election turned out to be less bad than Trimble might have feared: if Sinn Fein had become the third or fourth largest party, they might have exercised a destabilising influence on Northern Ireland policy, notwithstanding Ahern's pledge that he would not enter a coalition Government with republicans as the junior partner.[44] In the event, they quintupled their representation to five out of 166 TDs, including Martin Ferris, who obtained the highest number of first preferences in Kerry North despite a past conviction for gun-running. This was, however, still well behind the two main parties, plus Labour, the Progressive Democrats and the Greens.[45] In other words, Sinn Fein had obtained a middle-of-the-range result of the kind that senior British and Irish officials had wanted: good enough not to undermine the Adams-McGuinness project, but not so good as to destabilise Unionism. As Trimble told Jonathan Powell on 20 May at No. 10, even a middling result by Sinn Fein alarmed ordinary Ulster Unionists and the success of republicans such as Ferris would reinforce the impression that republicans did not have to make hard choices. Trimble was, however, more worried about the street disorders in east Belfast, between residents of the Catholic enclave of Short Strand and Protestants in nearby Cluan Place. Trimble believed that the disturbances were part of a republican strategy to ratchet up the tension and to destabilise the UVF leadership. At this stage, with Adair poised to seize control of the UDA, the UVF was the last remaining substantial element within the loyalist family that was wholly committed to the ceasefire.[46] Indeed, Trimble had specifically told Ahern when they met at Government Buildings on 29 April that he believed the republicans' strategy of tension had the further aim of forcing the two PUP-UVF

Assemblymen – notably David Ervine, who sat for East Belfast – to pull out of Stormont.[47] If so, Trimble would lack the necessary 30 votes in the Assembly, or over half of designated unionists, to sustain himself. In the ensuing polarisation of opinion on both sides, the centre parties would lose out and the DUP and Sinn Fein would acquire hegemony in their respective communities: the Executive would then never be re-formed and Sinn Fein would then seek to cut a new deal over the union-ists' heads with the two Governments.[48] At one point, Trimble even asked No. 10, 'Are Adams and McGuinness in control any longer?'[49] The UUP would need a dramatic confidence-building measure before the summer was out to sustain participation in the process – namely, legislation to exclude Sinn Fein in the event of breaches of the ceasefire. This had, of course, been suggested in the Blair side-letter to Trimble in the final hours of the negotiations on the Belfast Agreement on 10 April 1998. As things stood at present, the only power which the British Government currently had under Section 30 of the Northern Ireland Act 1998 was to refer a motion to the Northern Ireland Assembly for exclusion of a defaulting party from the Executive, which would take effect if majorities in both communities voted for it. Since nobody thought the SDLP had the stomach for doing this to Sinn Fein, the motion would duly fail and the Executive would collapse: an extension of Fergus Finlay's dictum about a process without Sinn Fein not being worth a 'penny candle'. Whilst such a referral would effectively mean that the UUP had won the 'blame game', at least as far as the British Government was concerned, the UUP still did not see why it should repeatedly be punished for republican misbehaviour by successive suspensions. Therefore, Trimble wanted the British Government to assume the responsibility for exclusion. After all, they had once acted unilaterally, and against the wishes of nationalist Ireland, in suspending in February 2000 and could do so again.[50]

From mid-2002 onwards, Blair appears increasingly to have grasped the gravity of the crisis and the failure of Sinn Fein to cross the Rubicon. He thought they were further away than ever from full-scale armed struggle, but wished to retain a residual capacity for violence. Thus, Blair informed Trimble at No. 10 on 5 June 2002 that 'if the IRA are not prepared to make the definite leap to democracy, but have merely changed their tactics, then it's important that you realise that I will not tolerate it for ever'. Likewise, at Jersey airport on Friday 14 June 2002, the Prime Minister asked: 'Are the Provisionals in transition or are they messing us about? Plainly, things aren't right.' Blair was doing no more than to state the obvious: on the previous night (Thursday 13 June) east Belfast witnessed some of the worst street disorders in the Province since the ceasefires began. Trimble feared that such disorder might play into the hands of Donaldson, who was bringing forward a motion for UUP withdrawal from the institutions at the meeting of the Ulster Unionist Executive on Saturday 15 June (though privately he was rather more confident). Trimble also told Blair in the car on the way from the airport to the conference that if nothing had been done by the time of the summer recess of Parliament, the UUP would have to withdraw from the provincial Executive. Indeed, Trimble added that a September crisis would skewer the upcoming round of selection meetings for UUP nominations for the Assembly in the direction of the 'antis'. But persuading the Prime Minister to take concrete action proved rather harder than to persuade him that there was a problem in the first place. 'I need to think carefully about this,' Blair observed to the UUP in Jersey. 'I have to think whether I go for the nuclear option [that is, expulsion].' Essentially, Blair seemed to take an Augustinian line on exclusion – 'Give me chastity and continency – but not yet!' Indeed, when Trimble showed Blair the headline in the *Belfast Telegraph* at the Hillsborough summit of 4 July 2002, of 'PMs unwilling to sanction SF', Blair replied, 'I'm not unwilling to sanction them, but I'm not going to say that today.' But he did authorise his senior officials to start to develop a paper recommitting all the parties to the Mitchell principles of non-violence of January 1996. It was not much, since as Reid told Trimble on 3 July at No. 10, Sinn Fein would happily sign up whilst the IRA would assert that the Mitchell principles were nothing to do with them. Nonetheless, the UUP believed it was highly significant that the British Government was at least talking for the first time about exclusion, even if they had no game plan to bring it about. Trimble won the vote in the Ulster Unionist Executive handily, as he privately knew he would: he believed that the meeting exposed Donaldson's flawed strategy, which would have resulted in fresh elections in September 2002 (and which the critical centre ground of the UUP would not willingly endorse in those adverse circumstances).[51] 'My one problem was that Jeffrey put it to the vote – thus creating the impression that I was stronger than I actually was,' recalls Trimble.[52] In consequence, the British were even less disposed to give him something than if he had been clinging on by the barest of margins.

The British began to work on eliciting another IRA statement – which Trimble feared would be the occasion for another raft of concessions to republicans at the all-party round-table to be held on 4 July 2002 at Hillsborough. Blair claimed that no such concessions would be forthcoming. At the conclusion of their meeting on 3 July 2002 at No. 10, Trimble raised the issue of a mechanism for verifying violations of the ceasefire and for triggering exclusion. Trimble suggested the idea of an independent international observer or ceasefire monitor. The two Governments, the Chief Constable and General de Chastelain all lacked credibility in the eyes of ordinary unionists: as Trimble later told Reid, the average voter did not believe that the Government would act against republicans. Something new was now needed. The auditor had originally been the idea of Trimble's informal adviser in Washington, Michael McDowell, in consultation with his friends in the Alliance party. McDowell relentlessly bombarded Jonathan Powell with faxes on the subject, almost after the fashion of Sinn Fein's perpetual campaigning. On 21 July, McDowell made his most detailed summary of the case for a monitor: '. . . if the Wednesday [24 July pre-recess] Commons statements consist only of an announcement of the *possibility* of John Reid sending a motion to the Northern Ireland Assembly to debate exclusion of Sinn Fein (or the Prod paras) then we are sunk and the deal is dead . . . the NIO instinct is to minimalise . . . Only establishing an Auditor/Overseer who is truly independent and robust and who will not be pushed around by anybody in his determinations will save the pass. Reid's role under the advice of the Chief Const is not being undermined under this mechanism. I for one (and I am hardly a mainstream UUP voter) would not put faith in John Reid ultimately doing this or the Prime Minister countenancing it. I have spoken to DT today, and to David Campbell, and reluctantly agree that they have little choice other than pulling out of the Executive if we only have the John Reid route . . . An International Auditor/Overseer, given even a modest amount of the treasure trove of intelligence out there, would note breaches in the Mitchell principles, including continuing purchases and importations of weapons by the IRA, and would have no difficulty in furnishing evidence to the SoS. It would be a huge form of pressure on SF and the Prod paras and would rebuild the credibility of the GFA, the PM and DT. The SoS would not have to act right away but it would restore some confidence in the process. Any intelligence would be given on the same basis that we brief allies like the US, i.e. broad terms, not specifics, e.g. "intell indicates that senior members of PIRA were involved in Castlereagh" without going into names or sources so that no one in the field is compromised or endangered; it would then be up to the SoS to take this additional and independent advice and use it in determining breaches of the ceasefire . . . Finally, there will never be a better time to pressure the Shinners. What are they going to do anyway? Where are they going to go? Does anybody seriously believe they would "retaliate" by going back to bombing in England? They would be finished in the US, especially under this Administration.'

Yet Powell, to whom Blair often deferred on intelligence matters relating to Northern Ireland, was concerned about the provision of classified materials to any outsider, however distinguished. The list of names mentioned as possible auditors over the coming months was diverse: Trimble suggested Blair's old friend, the former Israeli premier Ehud Barak: but whilst Jonathan Powell expressed interest, John Reid later told the UUP that no Israeli was, in the current circumstances, a runner from the Government's point of view.[53] Trimble also suggested Judge Baltazar Garzon, the highly acclaimed Spanish judge who had been responsible both for returning Pinochet to Chile and for hammering ETA.[54] But the independent-mindedness which attracted the UUP leader made him a more problematic choice for Blair, quite apart from the supposed effect of such an appointment upon Anglo-Spanish relations. 'The Spanish guy is a non-starter,' Blair told Trimble on 12 September 2002. 'On a personal level, I had a lot to do with him over Pinochet and the man's a complete nightmare.' When Trimble mentioned Garzon's work in the Basque country, Blair replied: 'He's an excellent bloke, but we don't know what he's going to do or say next.' Trimble was told that Richard Haass had vociferously objected to Garzon because of the Spaniard's pursuit of Henry Kissinger for the former US Secretary of State's alleged role in the 1973 coup in Chile.[55] As Trimble had correctly told McDowell when they spoke on the telephone on 21 July, 'the outsider would see that much is [being] hidden'.[56] In consequence, Trimble alighted upon the idea first advocated by David Burnside of a team of Privy Counsellors who had been cleared to examine classified data – and forwarded the South Antrim MP's letter to Jonathan Powell. Such an approach would have the additional advantage of being more acceptable to the UUP Assembly group and grassroots, who were likelier to trust an all-British team than even the most robust foreigner. Indeed, as the prospect of another IRA statement receded, the chances of some kind of audit mechanism being introduced increased – or so the UUP were led to believe.

But as Frank Millar had predicted in the *Irish Times* of 6 July 2002, the idea both of an independent monitor and legal sanctions was not gaining much traction in official circles on either side of the Irish Sea. When the UUP met with Reid at Castle Buildings on 22 July – a mere two days before he and the Prime Minister were scheduled to make statements to the Commons that were meant to steady unionist opinion – the Secretary of State was blunt. 'I don't believe that there is a problem with my judgment.' It was possible that he was worried that his powers might be usurped by the audit mechanism. Trimble explained that he was not trying to take powers away from Reid; rather, he was trying to assist the Northern Ireland Secretary by giving him added international political cover for any action he might have to take. Again, Reid averred that 'I don't believe there's any credibility problem with me – and I would bet that I would win any popularity poll with any Northern Ireland politician'. 'You're dealing with a misconception,' replied Trimble. 'The perception amongst the average unionists is that unless the Provisionals kill a policeman or a soldier, they're safe.' Reid's apparent departmental *amour propre* was indeed a major problem for Trimble and, as the UUP leader argued, was out of date in the new Northern Ireland. For example, the Patten legislation had created a police oversight commissioner (Tom Constantine, a former head of the US Drugs Enforcement Agency).

Why did the idea of the monitor gain so little ground? Partly, as has been noted, because of concerns about disseminating intelligence and partly because of what Trimble saw as Reid's reluctance. But there were other, longer-term, factors at play. The Irish Government – so often more solicitous of the republicans' internal needs than those of Trimble – weighed in against the monitor as, obviously, did Sinn Fein.[57] Elements in the NIO were also not sure why the Government should take the risk with nationalist Ireland when such a measure might not extricate Trimble from the weak position in which he then found himself. At the same time, Blair himself was rather sanguine, if not naive, about the UUP leader's prospects. When they met on 12 September at No. 10, the Prime Minister stated that he believed that a lot of unionists would fear the prospect of Paisley as the main representative of their community! Yes, there was the precedent of the British acting unilaterally to suspend the Executive in February 2000 – but the recollection of that trauma was seared on the Government's memory. And then there was what one writer has called 'the international ideology of Northern Ireland': the Ulster peace process was increasingly held up by Blair as a model of conflict resolution.[58] Why, wondered Mary Holland in her *Irish Times* column of 4 July, would he endanger that model for the sake of Trimble? Such was the slippage that the UUP was almost blind-sided when the time came for Blair and Reid to deliver their respective remarks in the Commons on 24 July. On 23 July, David Campbell telephoned Bill Jeffrey, the Political Director of the NIO, to say that the manner in which Reid presented the statement to Parliament was critical – and, no less important, how he answered supplementary questions. He knew by then that the UUP would probably not obtain the exclusion legislation it craved, but it might just obtain a monitor with real teeth that would clearly point the finger at malefactors. And if not that, some robust language about paramilitarism from both the Prime Minister and Secretary of State might just help Trimble through a very difficult summer. But when Campbell came to London the next morning, he could neither find Jeffrey nor make contact on the telephone – despite ringing every ten minutes. Changes were constantly being made to the text, he was told. Consequently, the UUP only obtained a copy of the statement when Barry White, Trimble's Westminster assistant, collected it from the Government whips' office about three-quarters of an hour before it was due to be delivered at 3:30 p.m. Trimble read it and noticed there was a reference of sorts to a kind of auditor to 'shine a light' on paramilitary activity, after the fashion of the advisory role of Professor Ron Goldstock on the issue of organised crime in Northern Ireland. The Ulster Secretary undertook to consult widely about such an appointment and to report back after the summer. Reid also raised the prospect – under the existing Northern Ireland Act 1998 – of the referral of an exclusion motion to the Assembly in the event of further acts of violence (the tests for which, Reid claimed, would become increasingly rigorous). Thus, the basic message on ceasefire violations was 'the future starts tomorrow': the Provisionals had been given another 'last warning'. When Campbell asked Trimble what he thought of it, the UUP leader replied, 'It all depends on how he answers the questions.' But Trimble did not condemn the statement out of hand, even though it fell far short of what he had originally believed was the minimum necessary to sustain his position.[59]

Trimble might have read the written text accurately, but he misread the mood-music of the Reid statement as it was delivered in the House. Stung by a ferocious attack by the Conservative spokesman on Northern Ireland, Quentin Davies, Reid responded combatively to interventions – in particular, slapping down Kate Hoey with noticeable brusqueness when she requested the creation of an independent mechanism.[60] As Trimble recalls, the body language of Reid was 'I'm in charge and I'm not going to do anything.'[61] But as he came out of the chamber, Trimble was worried that he had been too positive about the statement.[62] David Campbell says that when Trimble heard about the fall-out at home – the six o'clock news broadcasts gave the impression that Reid had humiliated the unionists by giving vastly less than had been expected – Trimble realised that he had to obtain something more. Moreover, Quentin Davies had left Trimble exposed by taking so hard a line.[63] Or, as Barry White puts it, 'I thought that it was all over. How many times can you say enough is enough without losing all credibility?'[64] The law-abiding population certainly needed reassurance: two nights before, a 19-year-old Catholic, Gerard Lawlor, was murdered by the UFF in Belfast.[65] David Campbell duly rang Jonathan Powell. Blair's answer to Sylvia Hermon's question at PMQs had been well received, argued Campbell, but for the unionists Reid had undermined any good that might have come out of the afternoon. Powell responded by blaming the Tories for anything which happened, but Campbell cut him short. 'That's beside the point,' replied Trimble's chief of staff. 'We hear that Tony Blair is going to be doing a "state of the nation" press conference tomorrow. Can he do anything to retrieve the situation?' Powell responded in the affirmative. 'Can you give us language?' the Prime Minister's chief of staff asked. It was, as far as Campbell was concerned, the first sign of British Government recognition that the day had not been a great success. And it left Campbell with the feeling that for all the UUP's regular contact with No. 10, Trimble had to resign (or threaten to resign) before they could obtain what they needed.[66] Michael McDowell also faxed Powell that night. 'Words, words, words ... not enough by half. Note the comfortable, arrogant body language of the Shinners this afternoon after the statement ... I spoke to DT an hour ago ... Frustrated, pissed off as blazes as well, but not ready, G-d bless him, to throw in the towel – yet. Note that last word. He says Tony and you now know the Commons show didn't work and that you are prepared to do operation rescue.'[67] Blair was as good as his word, and pledged to move against Sinn Fein if the ceasefire was breached. And, he added, there could be 'no twin track of politics and violence'. He would be looking carefully at some mechanism to give extra credibility. The difference in tone was clear – even if, as David Campbell told Jonathan Powell, the comments were still not enough to avert a summer of violence.[68] But there would be no UUC this side of summer. This was not because Blair's remarks had bought Trimble time, but because of the social calendar of Northern Ireland. The combination of the marching season and the holidays effectively precluded the calling of a Special General Meeting. Had the 'antis' sought to do so, Trimble argued, it would have been greatly resented at this time of year.[69]

Considering that Trimble had marched his troops to the top of the hill and back again for no apparent purpose, in the shape of the monitor, he left for his holidays in remarkably cheerful mood. So much seemed to be conspiring against him. Many – though not all – of his difficulties were beyond his control. For the fifth successive year, the Drumcree march was stopped: Trimble condemned those who rioted as doing nothing for the brethren of Portadown District.[70] That much, though, was predictable. Of greater concern to him, considering his support for President Bush's foreign policy, was his worsening relationship with Richard Haass. Trimble had initially been encouraged by Haass's writings on Ulster and his lack of 'beery' ethnic sentimentalism. Haass had even consulted with Trimble before delivering his address to the National Committee on Foreign Policy in New York on 7 January 2002 on the theme of 'Protestant alienation', in contrast to Reid who had not conferred with him personally before his speech at Liverpool University.[71] But the relationship deteriorated thereafter, despite Haass's profession of admiration of Trimble. There were a number of reasons for this. Haass disliked what he saw as Trimble's inept and intemperate attack on the Irish Republic at his UUC AGM in March 2002, and similar remarks which the UUP leader made in a meeting with the editorial board of the *Chicago Sun-Times* on 15 November 2002 (which Trimble thought was off-the-record).[72] He also resented the UUP leader's attempt to compare Adams to bin Laden, as was made clear by the American at their breakfast meeting at the Culloden

Hotel, Cultra, on 13 September 2002.[73] For his part, Trimble disliked what he saw as Haass's 'moral equilateralism' between anti-American paramilitaries such as Sinn Fein/IRA on the one side and pro-American democrats such as the UUP on the other; every time the US envoy gave Irish republicans a 'kicking', he would then apparently compensate for it by attacking the UUP. Thus, stern warnings about the consequences of further alleged republican activity would be followed by attacks on the UUP for not having 'sold' the Belfast Agreement hard enough – as though, in Trimble's view, even if true, those two 'wrongs' were in any way 'crimes' of equal seriousness. 'The criticism of us is manufactured,' opines Trimble.[74]

Trimble believed that there was a highly personal aspect to this shift in Haass's thinking – namely, the American's close relationship with Reid (at one point, Haass organised a bluegrass band to perform at a buffet in honour of the Northern Ireland Secretary at his home in Chevy Chase).[75] Indeed, some of the favourite themes of British officials seemed to arise frequently in Haass's discourse. When Trimble met with Haass on 11 September 2002, he told the American envoy that only a winding-down of the IRA would avert breakdown in the process. Haass replied: 'How do you avoid a mass exodus to Real IRA?'[76] Whatever the ideological or personal origins of Trimble's estrangement from Haass, the policy effects for the UUP were very clear. Shortly after David Campbell met with Haass and his assistant on Northern Ireland matters, Meghan O'Sullivan, at the State Department on 26 July, Trimble's chief of staff spoke to Michael McDowell. According to McDowell's note of the conversation, 'Haass was clearly not convinced about the independent mechanism. I said we were not trying to usurp John Reid in any way. I said if he was not happy with our model would he come back with his own?' Campbell was escorted out by Meghan O'Sullivan. 'It came across how much he talks to Reid rather than to Jonathan Powell,' observed Campbell to McDowell. And, O'Sullivan added: 'One worry we have is that does [the independent auditor] not lead to exclusion?' 'Well, if they're genuine then it won't be a problem. But if they're not genuine, then we all have a problem,' replied Campbell.[77]

The Trimbleistas felt they had further reason to take umbrage with the American approach in this period. Rumours had been circulating in Belfast for some time that the Americans were facilitating a dialogue between the DUP and Sinn Fein: according to Jack Holland in the *Irish*

Echo of 23 October 2002, the US Consulate in Belfast confirmed that middle-ranking representatives of the two parties were in the US during the year and could easily have met under those conditions. Later Martin McGuinness claimed the two parties had tentative contact via an intermediary – a claim denied by the DUP as a 'smear'.[78] But the 'Molotov-Ribbentrop Pact by the Lagan', as Paul Bew termed it, was not just a twinkle in the eye of American diplomats. For during the course of 2002, elements of both the Irish Government and the NIO – and at least one No. 10 official – looked seriously at the DUP. According to this analysis, patience with Trimble was at an end. 'We've done so much for him but he's lost control to Donaldson,' observed one civil servant at No. 10. 'What's the point in doing things to help Trimble if he's not going to be the main man after the Assembly elections?' Elements in the Governments of both states found the task of propping up both moderate unionism and moderate nationalism exhausting, politically costly and debilitating. The issue had first been raised in a different form by Frank Millar at the time of the suspension crisis of February 2000, when he wondered whether they would let Trimble hang out to dry; the article had occasioned an angry call from Mandelson, who denied it fervently.[79] But if the name of the game was bringing in the extremes – and it was always inherent in the process that a slightly constitutionalised Sinn Fein might replace an ageing SDLP – why not extend that to the Unionist side, too? Trimble could often be awkward and unpredictable, and above all could not deliver permanent stability without being accused of betrayal by the DUP. The kind of repeated challenges which Trimble faced within the UUP forced the British to rescue him through devices such as successive suspensions, at what they saw as a considerable cost to their relations with nationalist Ireland (and to the internal balance of forces within the republican movement, which was perturbed by Trimble's endless playing of the 'Orange card' that reiterated British sovereignty).[80]

Some British panjandrums were particularly excited by what might happen if Paisley were to retire, or worse. As one senior NIO official said of the DUP leader, 'Where there's death, there's hope.'[81] Their attention focused particularly on Paisley's deputy, Peter Robinson, and his fellow minister, Nigel Dodds. Although Robinson's rhetoric was more hardline – and, unlike such UUP moderates as Empey and Michael McGimpsey, he had the craft not to be photographed on the front page of the *News*

Letter grinning away with the likes of Martin McGuinness – British man-darins hoped that if he took over, he might not be susceptible to endless challenges to his authority within the DUP. Indeed, he might just make a deal stick.[82] Moreover, if anti-Agreement elements within the UUP succeeded in toppling Trimble, then the Belfast Agreement would be finished. The DUP could not then step into the breach. But, the officials reasoned, the DUP might just be able to step into the breach *after* defeating the UUP in any Assembly election and after a renegotiation of the Agreement. Why not, therefore, implicitly dangle before the DUP the prospect of becoming the majority party within unionism, in exchange for a more full-blooded *structural* (as opposed to ideological) acceptance of much of the new current institutional set-up? The two most hardline advocates of each side's interests would become the hegemonic forces inside their respective communities, but critically then would be ever more bound *within* the new system. Senior figures in the NIO believed that in assessing Trimble's prospects as coldly as they did, they were ultimately to do their political masters a favour; they thought that No. 10, whatever its momentary frustrations with the UUP leader, ultimately had an excessively personalised, even romantic view of Trimble. Indeed, one senior ex-mandarin who remained involved in the affairs of Northern Ireland described this as tantamount to the policy of Western leaders holding on to a discredited Gorbachev long after the initiative had passed to others. For those self-proclaimed cynics, the issue was preserving the process, not Trimble. They simply saw him as a means, not an end in himself, however important he may have been at one point.

Some Irish diplomats also came to believe that the more 'pragmatic' elements in the DUP represented a better bet than Trimble.[83] Although the Taoiseach denied to Trimble when they met at the Irish Embassy in London on 23 January 2003 that there was such a policy – 'we've only ever sought to do business with you, they're our opposition as well' – a senior DFA official subsequently admitted to the UUP in front of Brian Cowen at Iveagh House on 25 February 2003 that the Irish Government did have contact 'with some of their more progressive middle-rankers'. Trimble understood the reasoning behind such thinking. He believed that Robinson and others were sending out emollient signals so as to persuade the British not to make concessions to save him. According to the UUP leader's analysis, Robinson was effectively saying to the British, 'Why use up valuable capital on rescuing a doomed Trimble? Why not wait till I'm there and you can then give me things that enable me to present myself as having renegotiated the Agreement?' And Trimble also wondered whether the British and Irish were not toying with the 'Robinson option' so as to pressure the UUP to adjust its bottom line.[84]

There was certainly a rash of speculation about Robinson as the 'coming man': a host of flattering profiles appeared in such unlikely publications as *The Economist*, the *Irish Times* and the *Sunday Business Post*, which made much of his abilities as a minister.[85] Indeed, he later told the *Irish Times* that the DUP's secret alternative to the Belfast Agreement 'will recognise the size of the Sinn Fein vote'.[86] Such signals were not, however, confined to Robinson. The DUP Assemblyman for Foyle, William Hay, said that the DUP may be prepared to work with Sinn Fein; it was hedged with the caveat about Sinn Fein becoming a normal political party, but the novelty lay in the fact that a senior DUP figure was prepared to contemplate such action. As was pointed out, DUP and Sinn Fein councillors were already actively cooperating on a number of local authorities.[87] Senior DUP figures such as Robinson and Gregory Campbell would also appear on television programmes with Sinn Fein politicians.[88] And at the Sinn Fein *Ard Fheis* in March 2003, Martin McGuinness predicted that the DUP would eventually deal with Sinn Fein.[89] So prevalent were the rumours of DUP figures dancing a *quadrille* with sections of nationalist Ireland that Ian Paisley declared at his party's annual conference in Belfast on 23 November 2002 that any member of his party caught making contact with Sinn Fein would be expelled.[90] Trimble certainly took the rumours of Anglo-Irish interest in Robinson seriously enough to mock the idea in his own party conference speech on 19 October 2002.[91] But there was no evidence that Blair himself ever subscribed to the 'Robinson boomlet': for so long as this Prime Minister was in office, politics would be conducted on a highly personal basis. Looking back at it, one official observes that the flirtation of some in Government with the idea of the DUP deputy leader as the 'man with whom we can do business' had far more to do with the ebbs and flows of irritation with Trimble than any genuine admiration for Robinson. 'Our line was, "he [Trimble] may be a prat, but he's the only prat we've got".'[92]

Trimble's difficulties were not all external. Once again, there was talk of visits to Trimble from the 'men in grey sashes' and his replacement by a 'dream ticket' of Empey and Donaldson to unify the party. According to this analysis, much of the unpopularity of the Belfast Agreement could be put down to dislike of Trimble himself. If only he would fall on his sword quietly, Paisley and Robinson would be propitiated and unionists could work more closely together – or, if not, at least the UUP would be in a better position to contest the Assembly elections.[93] Indeed, when members of the Assembly group protested vociferously about Trimble's decision to apply for a researcher's pass for Sean O'Callaghan at the Commons – a decision made in retaliation for the Government granting Sinn Fein parliamentary office facilities – the UUP leader commented, 'For some, it's just a cover for disillusionment with me.'[94] Certainly, Trimble's thinning margins did not hinder him in his pursuit of other objectives, notably closer links with the Conservative party. These had assumed an extra urgency after it emerged that some SDLP figures were talking to Fianna Fail about a formal link.[95] If nationalist parties could make north-south linkages, asked Trimble, why could the UUP not enhance east-west connections? Whilst a full re-affiliation of UUP Associations was too complex to effect quickly, Trimble reckoned that a parliamentary alliance – entailing the receipt of the Tory whip at Westminster – might be possible. There was talk, once again, of Trimble joining the shadow Cabinet or even becoming the Conservative leader.[96] But this more limited link-up proved equally difficult to arrange. At an officers' meeting on 14 June 2002, Trimble raised the subject, but several colleagues, notably Empey, were against it. Donaldson, who had backed the move in principle, was reported to be against such a step before the Assembly elections of 2003 and until the internal problems of the UUP were resolved.[97] Indeed, there was as much discussion at that meeting about the source of the leak for Frank Millar's article concerning these divisions, in the *Irish Times* of 13 June 2002, as there was about the intrinsic merits of the proposal.[98] Partly, Trimble had himself to blame. He had done little of the preparatory groundwork with his own party to explain why this was a good thing, in the way that a Blair or an Ahern might have done with their supporters. Certainly, there was little in the way of a public campaign to 'educate' the party along the lines of: 'Sinn Fein are now a 32-county, cross-border party. We need to do the same and reinforce links across the Irish Sea.' Trimble was brilliant at 'solo runs', but the kind of sustained teamwork and organisational skill required to effect knotty internal reforms were not his *forte*. Nor were they Duncan Smith's *forte*, either: despite a visit to the UUP conference in Londonderry in October 2002, Duncan Smith did not give the issue a high priority and his Northern Ireland spokesman, Quentin Davies, was considered to be no great fan either of Trimble or a closer relationship with the UUP.[99] And, as Trimble notes, there were also doubts amongst some Tories about whether he would survive: they were, he says, effectively asking themselves, 'Why should we move in Trimble's direction when he may be yesterday's man?'[100] Of more immediate concern, though, was the round of UUP selection meetings for the forthcoming Assembly elections. Four pro-Agreement Assemblymen – Joan Carson, Sam Foster (both from Fermanagh-South Tyrone), Duncan Shipley-Dalton (South Antrim) and Sir John Gorman (North Down) – announced their retirements. And three pro-Trimble Assemblymen, Ian Adamson (East Belfast), Ivan Davis (Lagan Valley) and James Leslie (North Antrim) were not reselected by their Associations.[101] Adamson and Leslie were replaced by candidates who were equally pro-Agreement.[102] In three cases, well-known opponents of Trimble with a serious chance of winning went on to the ticket: David Burnside (South Antrim), Jeffrey Donaldson (Lagan Valley) and Arlene Foster (Fermanagh-South Tyrone).[103] The 'no dual mandate' rule was not invoked on this occasion. There was, says Trimble, a widespread opinion in hindsight that had Donaldson been allowed to enter the Assembly in 1998, the UUP would have been spared much bother in the intervening years.[104] Thus, it was possible to argue that both quantitatively and qualitatively, Trimble would face a more hostile Assembly group after the next election – to the point that some thought that if he put himself forward, he might not win re-election as First Minister.[105]

Yet when Trimble returned from his holidays in late August, he gave the impression that there was no basic crisis of the institutions. Indeed, his message was 'devolution is here to stay' – prompting Frank Millar to wonder why he had demanded so much of the Government before the recess.[106] It was not obvious in terms of immediate events, either, why the UUP leader sounded so confident. On 1 August, a civilian died after an explosion at a TA base in Londonderry.[107] On 28 August, Trimble went to look at first-hand at the intimidation suffered by residents of Cluan Place in Belfast, which was under siege from nearby republicans: a shower of missiles was hurled, some of which nearly hit the UUP leader.[108] According to the Assistant Chief Constable for Belfast, Alan McQuillan, the IRA and the UVF were orchestrating the street violence in the city.[109] It made another UUC meeting inevitable, which was duly called for 21 September. But when some of his advisers asked for his guidance on the drafting of a letter to be sent to the UUC delegates in the week running up to the meeting, they were shocked at how weak the message was: again, as upon his return from the summer holidays, it was 'steady as she goes', and emphasised that provided republicans were moving towards democratic means, they should be in government. As such, it represented further evidence of his strong idealistic commitment to inclusive government as means of civilising republicans (though not on any terms).[110] But as he put out feelers amongst the delegates, his mood changed. One Trimble stalwart, Ivan Davis, reported a noticeable number of unhappy delegates, including some amongst pro-Agreement types.[111] It was obvious that many activists, and especially Assembly candidates, were deeply concerned about their survival prospects for the forthcoming elections. Indeed, when Henry Patterson interviewed a leading pro-Agreement activist in the East Belfast Ulster Unionist Association on Friday 20 September for his research project on the UUP and devolution, he found that the man was full of admiration for what he saw as Trimble's success in persuading republicans 'to administer British rule' in Northern Ireland. Nevertheless, the activist was intensely concerned about the prospect of his party remaining in government with Sinn Fein – especially when republicans had not made their transition to fully democratic politics this side of an election.[112] Trimble was also impressed by his meeting with de Chastelain at the IICD's headquarters at Rosepark House in east Belfast: the General could not put his hand on his heart and say that there was any decommissioning process going on.[113]

Trimble realised he would have to try to seek a common motion with his adversaries. But when he met for two hours with Donaldson and Burnside at Hillsborough on Friday 20 September, no compromise was reached.[114] Donaldson crafted a motion designed to appeal to the middle ground: rather than pushing for an immediate withdrawal of UUP ministers from the Executive, he instead advocated immediate withdrawal from the NSMC, with the date for a full pull-out from the Executive left vague. This formula had certainly succeeded in winning over some previously pro-Agreement elements, notably Bertie Kerr of Fermanagh, who had been appointed by Trimble as chairman of the advisory panel of the cross-border Food Safety Promotion Board: on the next day, Kerr would be one of the main supporters of the Donaldson motion. On the basis of his delegate soundings, and what he knew of Donaldson's motion, Trimble saw his chance. He believed that Donaldson's paragraph on withdrawal from the Northern Ireland Executive was very weak. He duly settled upon a short, sharp timeframe and if there was no movement by republicans by then, he would resign. He initially wanted to set the March 2003 AGM of the UUC as the deadline, but Empey thought that was too tight. He did not want a crisis on the eve of the Assembly elections, and instead argued for January.[115] Trimble duly decided upon a pull-out from the Executive by 18 January if the IRA had not demonstrated by then that a 'real and genuine transition (to non-violence and democracy) is proceeding to a conclusion'.[116] He kept the final motion to a tiny group – Campbell, Cooper, Empey and Michael McGimpsey – so as to achieve maximum surprise on Donaldson.[117]

Over 700 delegates attended, with eleven speakers on either side. By then, things were so finely balanced that neither side could be sure of winning. 'He was going to win or I was going to win by a 51%–49% margin,' observed Donaldson. 'And that sort of policy mandate is no use to anyone.'[118] In any case, there was also a considerable pre-election impetus for party unity from much of the centre ground. Empey asked for an adjournment and, once again, the two factions met to consider a composite motion, this time in one of the hallways of the hotel. The unity motion was duly put, without a vote: Trimble made sure to announce it himself, even though much of the wording was that of his adversary. He wanted it to be made quite clear, both inside and outside the party, that he had placed himself at the forefront of this movement. So as the cycle of challenges to Trimble repeated itself, Gerry Adams again denounced the UUP leader for embracing a 'wreckers' charter'. Likewise, Martin McGuinness claimed that he had become the prisoner of the rejectionists. The SDLP, Alliance and Women's Coalition all criticised him.[119] Richard Haass, speaking in Washington, said he was 'concerned' that the UUP threat to withdraw from the Executive by 18 January could undermine the Agreement – though he did finally endorse the concept of the ceasefire monitor.[120] The Irish Government also privately expressed its disappointment to the UUP. John Reid, speaking to *Guardian Unlimited Politics* on 3 October, also claimed that the process was in 'grave difficulties because of the deadline imposed by the Ulster Unionists. If it were to fall, and if G-d forbid, we were to go back to conflict, all that would happen is that a lot more people would die.' But, crucially, No. 10 did not engage in the 'politics of condemnation' upon Trimble in quite the same way. The reason for the relatively gentle British response soon became apparent.

On Friday 4 October, the PSNI raided the Sinn Fein offices at Stormont in the full glare of TV cameras which happened to be there. The investigation into the Castlereagh break-in had led them to investigate other alleged republican operations, giving them reason to believe that the republicans had spies inside the Northern Ireland Office.[121] It was alleged that a large store of sensitive confidential information was found in a house in Belfast.[122] It also appeared as if the republicans may have had advance sight of the Government's bottom line in the negotiations at the time of the Weston Park talks of July 2001.[123] According to one report, Blair's codename on some of the IRA documents seized in the raid was 'the naive idiot'.[124] The entire episode was redolent of Ned Broy, Michael Collins' top agent in Dublin Castle from 1920–21.[125] One of those arrested was Denis Donaldson, Sinn Fein's chief administrator at Stormont, who was charged with possessing documents useful to terrorists in carrying out acts of violence. Under the Terrorism Act 2002, Donaldson pleaded not guilty and the other defendant had not entered a plea at the time of writing.[126] As the UUP leader observed of the initial revelations, 'I think that's bigger than Watergate.' The remark was, as Trimble himself would say, 'a wee bit over the top' – but there was no doubting that the Northern Ireland institutions were facing their biggest crisis yet.[127] Some senior Provisionals were so angry about the Stormont raid that they advocated a 'military response'; only the intervention of some veteran 'hardline' republicans prevented it from occurring. Eventually, the republicans settled for an IRA statement which suspended further contact between the Provisionals and the de Chastelain body.[128]

Trimble was travelling by car in his constituency when he learned about the raid from his special adviser, David McNarry. 'I was in a great mood by lunch-time,' recalls the UUP leader. 'I realised we were going into a crisis smelling of roses.'[129] Trimble was also much amused by a quip that did the rounds those days in party circles: 'Finally, a Donaldson brought down the Assembly!' But in his more reflective moments, Trimble felt that it vindicated the threat which he made at the UUC of 21 September to leave the institutions by January 2003. 'Imagine if he had gone to the UUC on a "trust me" ticket, scraped through by one or two percentage points, and then this had happened,' says David Campbell. 'Basically, he would have had to resign.'[130] Some sixth sense had led Trimble to take the protective action he did in outflanking Jeffrey Donaldson 'on the right', though he denies he was quietly tipped off either by Blair or a British official, or any security sources. Perhaps he was simply lucky, but Trimble certainly made his own luck when it came to his personal political survival. Indeed, according to David Campbell, his customary British Government channels of communication went unusually quiet both before and after the UUC meeting. 'There was almost a lack of interest,' recalls Trimble's chief of staff.[131] The absence of a warning from the British does, however, raise the question of why they were willing to let him go 'naked into the conference chamber', to use Aneurin Bevan's famous phrase.[132] The First Minister of Northern Ireland was allowed to remain totally ignorant of an alleged illegal operation which directly affected him – in contrast to Richard Haass, who according to both Trimble and one American Administration source was informed (the NIO says it would have been wholly inappropriate to inform one of the Northern Ireland party leaders in the course of a police investigation).[133] Reid had certainly known about aspects of the alleged spy ring before he made his 24 July statement – and claimed that his remarks that day were intended as a warning that terrorism was incompatible with involvement in the democratic process (it is noteworthy that whilst the statement dealt with a range of paramilitary activity, it omitted specific mention of intelligence gathering).[134] If, in retrospect, it was a warning, it seemed to the UUP to be so banal and vague as to be worthless. When Trimble asked Reid at No. 10 on 8 October 2002, 'Why did you not let me know about this before 24 July?', Reid apparently stated that he did not know of the full seriousness of the investigation of the spy ring until three weeks before the raid. But other elements of the system were profoundly concerned by the effect on Trimble. According to Billy Lowry, then head of Belfast Special Branch, a senior MI5 officer indicated to him that to conduct the raid before the 21 September UUC would make things very difficult for the then First Minister. The MI5 officer believed that if the raid took place beforehand, Trimble would lose the vote and the institutions would be permanently scuppered. Lowry declined to make operational considerations dependent upon the needs of the politicians; he adds that it was difficult to know whether the MI5 officer was actually worried about Trimble's fate, or whether he was simply trying to persuade Lowry not to take a course of action that would be politically inconvenient under whatever circumstances, by couching it in terms which he imagined might appeal to the policeman.[135]

But when the UUP delegation met with the Prime Minister at No. 10 on 8 October 2002, Blair asserted that the Provisionals were further from violence than before: they had to give their militants something to do. They were managing a process of change, and were still letting the IRA do a certain amount. 'No,' retorted Trimble. 'They've initiated an intelligence operation to gain advantage over you and us. It's now impossible for me to have any further trust in them.' Blair, as so often before, emphasised that he thought that Adams and McGuinness 'want this to work'. 'Be careful about putting your faith in them,' replied Trimble. 'They are not moral or honest people. They will cheerfully tell you one thing and do another. I do believe that they have a strategy but don't confuse it with our strategy or your strategy.' 'How, then, do we put it up to them to disband the IRA?' asked the Prime Minister. 'The IRA threat of violence holds no fear for me. I have told them that. I think they are prepared to accept a partitioned Ireland.' Trimble said that 'putting it up to them' meant the threat of them losing their political strategy – that is, ultimately, exclusion. He was not alone in this wish: as he noted in the Commons, both the Alliance party and the Liberal Democrats favoured such an option.[136] In concrete terms, said the UUP leader, there would be a plenary of the Assembly on the 14 or 15 October: he recommended that the Government send an exclusion motion to the Northern Ireland Assembly – even if the SDLP were to oppose it, and thus prevent it from coming about – simply as a sign of who was to blame for the crisis of the institutions. As for elections, to hold them now would simply reward Sinn Fein for what they had done. And he added: 'Just for the avoidance of doubt, I will say that you asked for two weeks. I will give you one week [to take action]. We will not wait beyond Tuesday [15 October].' (that is, before resigning the UUP ministers.) 'Can you not work with Sinn Fein again?' asked Blair. 'They need to do something dramatic,' replied Trimble. Further decommissioning would now not be enough.[137] Most of his party seemed to agree with his stance: according to a *Sunday Times* poll of 100 delegates at the UUP annual conference on 19 October 2002, 80% of them wanted him to be the leader at the forthcoming Assembly elections.[138] And a BBC Northern Ireland poll for the *Hearts and Minds* programme released on 17 October 2002 indicated that if a referendum were held again on the Belfast Agreement, the 'no' vote would rise to 44%. Perhaps even more significantly, 58% of unionists did not wish to share power with either the SDLP or Sinn Fein. In other words, they effectively preferred direct rule. If accurate, it suggested that ordinary unionists were much less hooked on devolution, at this price, than many of their political representatives. Trimble always disliked this line of reasoning. Rather, he believed it was a statement along the lines of 'we hate the current crowd up there', not 'we hate Stormont per se'.[139] Whichever reading of the polls is right, one thing is certain: unlike 1972, there were no mass demonstrations or strikes against the suspension of 'our wee Stormont'.[140]

There was only one other way to keep the institutions going: to secure the support of the SDLP for exclusion. Trimble certainly believed, on the basis of 'intelligence' from within the SDLP, that a serious debate was going on within Mark Durkan's party about whether Ulster's constitutional nationalists should vote for exclusion. But if there was such a debate going on – and sources within the SDLP say that Trimble's perception of serious internal discussion about this option was much exaggerated – the constitutional nationalists would have received little support from elsewhere in nationalist Ireland had they opted for such a course.[141] For the Government of the Republic was deeply unhappy about the turn of events. First, there was the manner of the Stormont raid, which Ahern's former special adviser, Martin Mansergh, claimed was the sort of thing 'you might associate more with Turkey and President Mugabe'.[142] Second, as Ahern told Trimble at Government Buildings in Dublin on 11 October, he hated the idea of exclusion as a way of managing the crisis. Though he did not say so explicitly, ruling this option out effectively made another suspension inevitable – and, in the circumstances of this crisis, suspension looked like the least bad of the alternatives. When Michael McGimpsey asked why the UUP should be punished for Sinn Fein's transgressions, he was met with stony Irish faces. The Ulster Unionists suggested that if there were republican 'moles' at Stormont, there could also be similar such infiltrators in the Irish state. 'Actually, it's very pertinent,' replied Ahern. Despite Ahern's hostility, Blair did raise the subject of exclusion with the SDLP. But according to British officials, the Prime Minister concluded that the SDLP simply were not serious about exclusion and therefore saw no reason to go through a 'charade' of remitting an exclusion motion to the Assembly that would not pass with cross-community consent just to point the finger at Sinn Fein. In any case, No. 10 believed that Sinn Fein had in effect already been identified as the malefactor.[143]

Trimble soon moved to revive another idea which he had first put forward at the time of the Mandelson suspension of February 2000: that both himself and Mark Durkan should keep alive the 'spirit of devolution' by serving as junior ministers in the Labour Government handling the work of the Northern Ireland Department pending the return of the Executive. Blair looked favourably upon this suggestion but, again, Durkan resisted the concept of a 'shadow role', according to Frank Millar. DFA officials in Dublin also feared that this proposal would undermine 'inclusivity' by a backdoor route.[144] Indeed, even now, the NIO was still not sure about suspension: Paul Bew recalls attending a supper at Hillsborough in honour of the Belgian ambassador, hosted by the Permanent Under Secretary, Sir Joe Pilling, at which not a single voice was raised in favour of suspension save his own.[145] But despite such reluctance, the Government did respond to Trimble's one-week deadline and on 14 October, Reid suspended the institutions.[146] Significantly, Bush issued a statement in support of the suspension. This was in marked contrast to Clinton's behaviour in February 2000, though according to the *Irish Echo*, Haass declined to lay the blame for breakdown explicitly at the door of Sinn Fein.[147] On his last day in office, Trimble met with Miss Northern Ireland – a constituent, Miss Gail Williamson, from Lurgan. One of the rules of the contest was that all entrants must have the support of their own Government. Trimble was immensely courteous to her, rushing ahead to open doors in a way that he would for few others – prompting one of his police protection unit to comment, 'G-d, he is human after all.'[148] He had survived perhaps the most difficult year of his leadership – but at the cost of his First Minister's salary. He would henceforth only receive his Westminster salary, plus a third of his reduced Assemblyman's salary (£56,358 plus £6,887). This meant a loss of over £40,000.

But where now? Blair claimed to the UUP that he would not engage in another agonising negotiation in exchange for a major move from paramilitarism – in other words, there would be no additional raft of concessions on policing and demilitarisation to persuade the republicans to move. It was, he concluded, no longer right to ask unionists to keep waiting for republicans to complete their transition at the slow pace at which it had occurred hitherto. His way of 'putting it up to republicans' came in the form of a speech delivered at the Belfast Harbour Commissioner's office on 17 October. It was a highly personalised address:

the Prime Minister drafted it in his own hand on the way back from his summit with President Putin of Russia. At one level, it made for uncomfortable reading for unionists. First, there was the implied 'moral equilateralism' between all sides. Thus, the pain of the innocent victim of terrorism was placed on a par with the anguish of republicans who were prepared to die for a united Ireland now entering Stormont. Second, there was the politically correct presentation of the recent past: 'For our part, the purpose of the British security response, often harsh . . .' And as one unionist observed, the words 'remove the threat of violence and the peace process is on an unstoppable path' would have represented to republicans a clear signal that the status quo was not a final settlement, merely a staging post to something better. But Blair had another message, too: that republicans could no longer derive negotiating leverage through retention of their arsenal and a capacity for violence, as Blair effectively admitted they had done. '[Such a capacity] no longer acts to remove Unionist intransigence, but to sustain it,' commented the Prime Minister. 'It no longer pushes the British Government forward, but delays us. It doesn't any longer justify David Trimble's engagement; it thwarts it. I used to say we had to be sure all sides wanted the Agreement to work. I am sure everyone does. Unionism, certainly as represented by David Trimble, does. I believe that. They know the past has to be laid to rest. In any event, even if some don't, the British Government will simply not countenance any path other than implementing the Agreement. I also believe that Gerry Adams and Martin McGuinness want the Agreement to work . . . But the crunch is the crunch. There is no parallel track left. The fork in the road has finally come. Whatever guarantees we need to give that we will implement the Agreement, we will. Whatever commitment to the end we all want to see, of a normalised Northern Ireland, I will make. But we cannot carry on with the IRA, half in, half out of this process. Not just because it isn't right any more. It won't work any more.' In other words, Blair believed that residual paramilitarism had to be abandoned because its main effect was to strengthen Trimble's Unionist opponents.[149] Blair subsequently also ruled out Joint Authority in the event of a republican failure to move: he was seeking to convey the message that IRA intransigence would not be rewarded on this occasion.[150] From a UUP perspective, it was probably the most reassuring speech that Blair had delivered since his first address in Belfast as Prime Minister on

16 May 1997. Yes, they had lost Stormont – but at least they were not seen by the Government and mainland opinion as the malefactors in its demise.

THIRTY-EIGHT

A pyrrhic victory

BLAIR'S 'Harbour Commissioner' speech undoubtedly set the tone for much of the discourse on Northern Ireland in the coming months. Trimble liked it – but wondered whether the Prime Minister would stick to his public pledge about no more 'inch by inch' negotiations. Indeed, when asked about the speech at a meeting of the UUP Assembly group on 28 October 2002, his verdict was 'carrots, more carrots'.[1] The observation seemed to be confirmed by the Government's decision to persist with the introduction of another policing Bill to reform the constabulary in Northern Ireland, which proposed, *inter alia*, giving more powers to the Province-wide Policing Board and to the Ombudsman; and, subject to acts of completion, to allow ex-prisoners to sit on new district policing committees after a quarantine period.[2] But although Trimble lamented such carrots, he did not threaten to leave the process over them so long as other things were set right: indeed, Frank Millar commented in the *Irish Times* of 27 November 2002 that 'shortly before the most recent meeting of the UUC, senior party sources were privately dismissive of the threatened resignations [of certain unionist members of the Policing Board in protest against further reforms], suggesting that the imminent British concessions would prove but a fig-leaf to cover Sinn Fein's embarrassment at finally signing up to the Policing Board'.

There were reservations inside Government, too, over aspects of Blair's Belfast speech – though for rather different reasons. At least one senior NIO official thought that whilst it was prudent of the Prime Minister not to technically use the 'd' word – for disbandment – he had nonetheless 'set the bar so high' that the Provisionals could not jump it. But, the official believed, that was what Blair in effect was asking for. At that stage, there was still a hope that whilst a shadow organisation called 'PIRA' might exist, it might metamorphose into something akin to a kind of republican version of the Royal British Legion. Indeed, Trimble himself soon came round to this way of thinking and in his address to the UUC AGM of 1 March 2003, and acknowledged that the 'd' word might be too 'neuralgic' for republicans.[3] 'If I push on the "d" word,' Trimble told me, 'everyone will say that what I really want is surrender.' And, he believed, 'disbandment' would be a hard thing to prove.[4] One issue which Blair did not address in his speech was the crucial question of whether the Assembly elections would still be held in May 2003 – in which everyone expected Sinn Fein to overhaul the SDLP, if not the DUP to overhaul the UUP. Trimble believed that a British Government threat to cancel them would be the greatest available spur to republican action. If republicans had not moved by May 2003, there would be no point in holding elections when an Executive could not be re-formed in those conditions (even if the UUP were still the main party on the unionist side of the divide, which Trimble firmly believed it would be). And, of course, success at the polls in those circumstances might make republicans even more intransigent.[5]

The British responded with a policy of 'creative ambiguity'. As they saw it, there were two extreme courses of action. One was 'unless you, the IRA do "X", there will be no election'. At the other extreme was the proposition, 'these elections will go ahead willy-nilly, whatever happens'. Such attitudes were reflected in John Reid's statement to the Commons of 15 October announcing suspension which was hedged about with qualifications on the subject.[6] The British knew they might at some point have to take such action, but with the Taoiseach already militantly opposed in public to any rescheduling of the poll, they did not wish to commit themselves so soon one way or another.[7] Indeed, as Blair told the UUP delegation at No. 10 on 3 December 2002, when they asked about postponing the elections, 'We need to be careful – I want to use that tactically at my discretion.' Adams, for one, picked up on this ambiguity: when he met Trimble at Stormont on 4 November, he told the UUP leader that he did not regard a May 2003 Assembly election as a certainty (he added that republicans were not planning to join the Policing Board this side of the poll).[8]

But in the early days after suspension, it seemed to many in the UUP as if the familiar pattern would repeat itself and that new negotiations would resume leading to restoration of the institutions. They had two reasons for thinking as much: first, Gerry Adams' apparently emollient speech in Monaghan on 26 October, which impressed some in London as well as in Dublin.[9] Moreover, another unexpected development prompted one veteran Trimble-watcher to wonder whether the UUP leader might be more willing to move again. For on 23 October, the Education Secretary Estelle Morris resigned, stating that she was not as good at dealing with the modern media as she should have been.[10] In the ensuing reshuffle, John Reid left Northern Ireland to become chairman of the Labour party – to be replaced by the Welsh Secretary, Paul Murphy. Trimble was astonished by Reid's departure, and then pleased. The two men had clashed bitterly again at No. 10, in front of the Prime Minister, on 8 October – when John Taylor had to intervene to soothe tempers. Certainly, there were sound reasons of internal Cabinet and Labour management to move Reid, but one Whitehall source believes that a factor in John Reid's departure was his behaviour on 24 July in the Commons and also in subsequent private exchanges. Other Government sources deny this was so, but observe that all Secretaries of State for Northern Ireland have limited shelf-life – and, since he had outlived his usefulness, Reid's departure came at a happy juncture. Indeed, one official looking back on Reid's period in office was hard-pushed to say what, exactly, he had achieved. In terms of the peace process, Brooke had helped create the 'three-stranded' structures in 1991–2; Mayhew had set up the talks, with an American chairman, in 1996; Mowlam could be said to have brought the Provisionals in from the cold as never before in 1997–8; and Mandelson could be credited with persuading Trimble to make the leap into government with republicans twice over, and kept the UUP on board for a very radical set of the policing reforms in 1999–2000. Reid, by contrast, left little in the way of an obvious legacy – though this may have more to do with the phase of the process which he superintended.

Paul Murphy was about as different from Reid as it was possible to be. Although both were Catholics of Irish origin, Reid was more of a west of Scotland 'cultural Catholic' (without being religious), whereas Murphy was no 'cultural Catholic' but was religious. And, obviously, he was as emollient as Reid was blunt. As Trimble observes, 'He's the first person as Secretary of State who's managed to avoid offending either side.'[11] Barry White, Trimble's Westminster assistant, who has watched his boss return from innumerable meetings at No. 10 or the NIO over the years, notes: 'Murphy has been great for him. Mandelson treated Trimble seriously; Reid treated him like a child.' But they had one other thing in common: a love of classical music. 'I'm going to see the Secretary of State for supper tonight,' Trimble told White. 'I know I'm not going to get any work done.' Trimble had been out shopping and every pocket was bulging with opera CDs. 'Paul has this one I didn't have, but I have this one he doesn't have,' cooed Trimble.[12] On one occasion, Trimble went down to Hillsborough for a meeting with Adams, at the Sinn Fein president's request. The UUP leader arrived early and they soon began listening to the new recording of George Dyson's *Quo Vadis*, by the BBC National Chorus of Wales and the BBC National Orchestra of Wales: Murphy had his copy ahead of Trimble. As they sat there, taking it in, Adams came into the room and looked at the CD. 'I've never heard of that label before,' said Adams, who promptly wrote it down.[13] It all contributed to an unusual level of trust between Trimble and another politician – especially for Trimble and a Northern Ireland Secretary. For example, on 24 July 2002, Trimble received a fax of the Government statement just minutes before Reid was due to deliver it; under Murphy, he would enjoy what he saw as much greater levels of genuine consultation.[14] Just as Mandelson was able to persuade Trimble to make what an official calls 'imaginative leaps' because the UUP leader trusted him more than Mowlam, so it was assumed that Murphy might be able to do the same this time round.

Indeed, some Trimbleistas believed that the unionist communal mood was, overall, better at the end of 2002 than it had been for some time – even if the effects did not last for very long. Not only did it appear that republicans had been 'caught with their hands in the cookie jar', but the result of the ten-yearly census, published in December 2002, was better from a Protestant/unionist viewpoint than many of them had feared. The adjusted figures showed that there was a 53%–44% Protestant majority (this, of course, omitted the still-significant numbers of pro-Union Catholics). Whilst it was the best result for nationalists since the foundation of the state of Northern Ireland, it was still well short of the 46% anticipated by some, and certainly it suggested – contrary to the hopes of some republicans – that the superior Catholic birth rate would not end Partition any time soon.[15] One senior British mandarin was delighted with the outcome: 'We gulled them [the republicans] into believing that they were going to be the majority by 2020.' By this, he meant that he believed they had been sucked into constitutional politics on the basis of delusions about an imminent demographic triumph – and now could not return to armed struggle to make good the short-fall.[16] But if republicans had been gulled on the basis of a false prospectus, there was little evidence in the coming months that Adams and McGuinness were on the receiving end of recriminations from their grassroots – along the lines of 'you sold us a pup'. For his part, Trimble was not in the least bit surprised by the census result. And he welcomed the stabilising effect on the psychology of the unionist community.[17]

Trimble thus entered 2003 with two great advantages. He had again won the 'blame game' and Sinn Fein/IRA were under pressure. Trimble's requirements were clear: a statement from the IRA that 'the war is over', an end to all paramilitary activity and moves that amounted to disbandment. And the Prime Minister was prepared to give plenty of time to the Northern Ireland peace process, even on the verge of a war with Saddam Hussein, to bring such an outcome about. Such was the optimism that a further increment of Prime Ministerial will might do the trick that one No. 10 official thought at the start of the year that the title of the book written about the period would be 'Peace and War', imagining that the business would be done by early spring. The Irish – and especially the DFA – maintained with even greater fervour that Adams and McGuinness were up for 'it', though 'it' was never very clearly defined. The Dublin Government thought that a clear statement from the IRA that 'the war is over' was do-able, but was doubtful about the 'deliverability' of effective disbandment. The best that they appeared to think was available was more decommissioning, though as Cowen told the UUP at Iveagh House on 25 February 2003, '[the republicans] can't deliver a Steven Spielberg' (that is, a highly public act of disarmament). At other stages, the Irish Government also toyed with the idea of the IRA 'standing to' – a concept modelled on de Valera's order to the IRA of 1923. At Trimble's behest, David Campbell asked Paul Bew to supply a memorandum on the analogy. He believed that the precedent was not helpful to the UUP in the current circumstances. Even five years after the order, de Valera was still referring to the Free State as an illegal entity – because it had been set up under a British threat of war – and continued to behave in a destabilising way. Indeed, violence dragged on for years thereafter, most notably in the form of the assassination of Kevin O'Higgins in 1927. Yet despite this, Trimble, too, felt he had reasons for optimism. He derived hope from the absence of 'diatribes' in his own dealings with Adams and McGuinness at Parliament Buildings on 13 January 2003 (a read-out confirmed by the British from their meeting with Adams on 14 January, when they were impressed by the fact that Adams had admitted for the first time that actions by republicans had undermined unionist confidence). Certainly, Adams and McGuinness were not ruling things out and had by now been told that if they wanted their May 2003 elections, they would have to sort everything out by February.

Trimble believed that if he was to persuade the UUP to return to the Executive, he also needed an independent mechanism to verify any movement on their part and a 'sanctions regime' to punish any future republican breaches of faith. After October 2002, he returned to the concept in the 10 April 1998 side-letter from Blair on possible exclusion legislation. As part of that 'sanctions regime', the UUP leader secured acceptance from the British Government for his idea that the independent ceasefire monitor needed 'teeth' – that is, access to classified data. This was, of course, a concept which the British had resisted in the previous summer. On 28/29 January 2003, at the Irish state guest house at Farmleigh in Dublin – previously the home of the Earl of Iveagh – a British delegation led by Jonathan Powell and Jonathan Phillips of the NIO persuaded the Irish that such a safeguard was a prerequisite for any progress. Of course, the devil was always in the details of such arrangements, and on both of those the British and Trimble proved flexible. So as to make it 'sellable', the British agreed to have representatives of all of the main players in the process on the monitoring panel. It would thus include nominees of the Irish Government and the US Administration as well as the British Government. There would also be someone from Northern Ireland. Trimble agreed to build in a system of 'Yellow Cards' or warnings prior to the 'Red Card' being administered, thus diluting 'automaticity': even now, he wanted to preserve inclusivity if he could, but via the means of a footballing metaphor that the man in the street could understand.[18] The 'Yellow Cards', as Trimble saw it, might include withdrawal of parties' allowances at Stormont. To that end, he also joined the Government in referring to 'safeguards' rather than 'sanctions', a word which upset republican sensibilities. Again, Trimble, like the British Government, and unlike so many unionists, was prepared to give Sinn Fein a 'soft landing' if the substance was right. And, as the Irish Government saw it, the monitoring body had one other advantage for Trimble. Up till now, any republican recidivism created a crisis for him and his leadership. With a monitoring body in place, he could say to his own supporters, 'Look, a credible international monitor is in place. Let's wait for them to decide before rushing to conclusions.'[19]

But there was another aspect of the 'sanctions regime' which was not immediately apparent. It applied not just to Sinn Fein, but to any party which was in some way deemed to be in default of its obligations under the Belfast Agreement. Thus, as *quid pro quo* for monitoring the paramilitary-linked parties, the body would also monitor whether the British Government was living up to its obligations on demilitarisation. The British did not like such 'moral equivalence', yet in the end accepted the Irish argument that the monitoring committee could not otherwise be sold to republicans. At the behest of the Dublin Government, this sanctions regime was then further widened. Not only would it include all 'military' matters, but it would also comprise political infractions of the Belfast Agreement. Accordingly, the DUP could be fined or punished in some other way for failing to attend Executive meetings – their so-called 'Hokey-Cokey' strategy of one foot in, and one foot out, which opponents alleged was designed to appear as if they were not sitting in Government with Sinn Fein. Indeed, David Campbell states that the UUP leader had it in mind that the sanctions regime could be used against the DUP as early as the autumn of 2002.[20] But once the idea was extended beyond purely paramilitary offences, it was impossible to limit its application to the DUP. Indeed, in an attempt to sell the sanctions regime to the British and more especially the Irish during several sessions at Hillsborough on 3 March 2003, Empey suggested that it could apply to any party – including the UUP – which was undermining, say, North-South institutions. This, of course, was what nationalists alleged Trimble had done by imposing his NSMC sanctions in October 2000.[21] 'When Reg is volunteering for punishment, he's speaking for himself,' quipped an irritated Trimble. According to Trimble, it subsequently became apparent that Empey had talked himself into a very substantial concession which would give Donaldson and the rejectionists the best card they had in the coming months.[22] Empey says he does not recall any of his colleagues disagreeing with his comments: 99% of the necessity for this body was because of republicans and any extension to unionists was purely theoretical.[23]

But Empey was doing no more than point out the obvious. And however uncongenial its timing, it did not cause Trimble to walk away from the sanctions regime. Indeed, to the surprise of the Irish Government, Trimble appeared to be prepared to live with this application of the sanctions regime to fully constitutional as well as paramilitary-linked parties.[24] They were surprised because the sanctions regime, in their eyes, represented a major leap forward in terms of the theology of the process. It entailed a further dilution of British sovereignty by admitting foreigners as part of a panel of independent monitors. John Taylor, for one, criticised the proposed sanctions regime for giving Dublin a role in 'Strand I' – the internal governance of Northern Ireland – from which it had been excluded during the 1996–8 talks.[25] In and of itself, though, foreign involvement in decisions regarding Northern Ireland was scarcely novel: by now, the list was very long and included the Anglo-Irish Agreement of 1985, George Mitchell's report on arms of January 1996, Mitchell's chairmanship of the talks from 1996–8, the Mitchell review of 1999, the international component of the Patten Commission, and Tom Constantine's role as police oversight commissioner. What was novel about this new 'sanctions regime' was that it posited the idea that a set of purely political actions taken by a purely democratic political party with no paramilitary wing could trigger punishment – no less than the violent actions of the armed wing of a paramilitary-linked party. Thus, the legitimate doubts and activities of a Nigel Dodds or a Jeffrey Donaldson, who had never been involved in terrorism, were effectively deemed as threatening to political stability as the paramilitarism of the Provisionals or the UVF. If ever there was an illustration of the 'moral equilateralism' in the process, Trimble's critics argued, this was surely it. And, they believed, here was Trimble acquiescing in such a regime for his own political convenience. The UUP leader says he did not particularly want this regime, but settled for it because he saw it had a silver lining. He believed he could not keep the SDLP on board for such a sanctions regime if only republican wrongdoing was punished. Moreover, if Sinn Fein were excluded, the SDLP could not serve alone in an Executive with two unionist parties. Trimble therefore had to make the conditions as unwelcome as possible for the DUP if he was to keep the SDLP in – a further illustration that he preferred power-sharing to pan-unionism.[26]

Even a diluted sanctions regime came at a price, though. Before Christmas 2002, the republicans submitted a 57-page document to the British Government on such 'reserved' matters as OTRs (on the run prisoners who either had or had not been convicted), the home service battalions of the Royal Irish Regiment and policing.[27] As Ahern told the UUP when the two heads of Government visited Hillsborough on 12 February, 'it [the sanctions regime] has to be verifiable and punishable – but we have to face the fact that we can't do this without giving them something'. Thus, the Prime Minister was, indeed, engaged in just the kind of 'inch by inch' negotiation which he had appeared to repudiate in his October 2002 Belfast speech. Many British officials (and a few Trimbleistas) believed that it would contain little which was new beyond the raft of concessions already offered at Weston Park in July 2001, and that it seemed unlikely that it would be implemented in full without IRA movement on 'disbandment'.[28] That, of course, would be scant consolation to many unionists, and partly explains why Trimble temporarily walked out of the talks on 19 December 2002: he had to show that he was not a 'soft touch'. But he also regarded the inter-party discussions as foolish in and of themselves. These talks would inevitably become the means by which Blair's 'no inch by inch' pledge would be unpicked.[29] Indeed, he could turn up the rhetoric, and in the past had expressed 'revulsion' at the idea of an amnesty for OTRs which, he alleged, would have a 'devastating impact on public confidence in the Agreement'.[30] Likewise, he told a meeting of the Liaison Group between Westminster MPs and Stormont Assemblymen at Cunningham House (the UUP's new headquarters) on 7 March that as far as the OTRs were concerned, 'we haven't signed up to anything'.[31] Yet whilst Trimble opposed concessions to republicans on 'reserved' issues, he was never prepared to stymie them in the only way possible – by threatening to leave the talks permanently. His critics believed that hostile language or even a vote against in the division lobbies of the Commons were meaningless gestures against a Government with a massive majority.[32] Trimble replied to these criticisms in the *Irish Times* on 31 March 2002, accusing those who counselled such an approach of wanting him to resign every other day on any issue they could think of – their 'concealed and primary objective' being 'to remove the present First Minister and to bring down the Assembly'. The UUP leader's highly calibrated position was also based upon a calculation that these unpleasant things would probably happen anyhow, so he might as well 'make the best of a bad job' (author's term). Thus, on 22 February 2002, he told the Prime Minister that he was against the concept of allowing OTRs back and he would vigorously oppose it – but that if this were to happen, then the Government needed to bring in legislation to ensure that there was a greater discretionary element in it than had operated in the Sentences Act of 1998 on the main batch of prisoner releases. Then, the Government had effectively signed away its rights and forfeited almost all its leverage over Sinn Fein by not making those releases conditional upon progress on decommissioning (although Trimble himself had been angered during the debates on that Bill about some of the amendments to tighten up the linkage between prisoner releases and disarmament).[33] Trimble now wanted the Secretary of State to have the say on each and every OTR – and for them to go through a process of being charged, tried and sentenced so that justice was seen to be done (even though the individual in question would not actually serve a single day in prison). He also hoped that the OTRs scheme could be used as a model for the treatment of members of the security forces accused of crimes. It was classic Trimble. He did not believe that there was any great moral issue at stake here so long as the legal niceties were in order and so long as the carrots and sticks were being properly administered. Of course, it raised another issue: was his decision to advertise early the fact that he had no principled objection to the return of the OTRs the best negotiating strategy? Whilst he was trying to make the best of things that he knew were very likely to happen, would he have been better off delaying such a concession until much later? In other words, should he have privately and publicly made the maximum of this further emotional trauma for the unionist community – as Sinn Fein might have done in his position – and then cashed it in at the last minute for something else, forcing the two Governments to give him 'collateral'?[34]

But that was not Trimble's style, and when he received a fleeting early glimpse of what eventually became the Joint Declaration in mid-February, he did not 'go ballistic' and remained focused on the absolute necessity of the 'sanctions regime' at both the Hillsborough summits of 13 February and 3/4 March 2003.[35] For all his insistence that there was only one issue on the agenda – as at Weston Park in July 2001 – the negotiations were now very wide-ranging indeed. By this point, both Blair and Ahern had come to the conclusion that devolution could only be restored by a full, permanent cessation of violence, by a verifiable end to all activity – including punishment beatings – and by re-engagement with the de Chastelain body (broken in the previous year). But the package also included items that could only alarm unionists: extensive demilitarisation and reduction of the Army to pre-Troubles levels; a British commitment to rapid devolution of criminal justice and policing to the Northern Ireland Executive; Sinn Fein joining the Policing Board; the return of

OTRs; and the scrapping of the 2000 suspension legislation.[36] When the UUP arrived for their first meeting with Blair and Ahern at 12:30 p.m. on 3 March 2003 at Hillsborough, the Prime Minister exuded a brisk confidence. 'They're prepared to do it,' he declared. 'You need to go through it with them to find out what it means.' The British assumption was that the republicans were serious. Indeed, according to the Irish, senior Sinn Fein figures had begun to tour the IRA's Active Service Units towards the end of February and in early March – but that they needed another month to put their house in order. Trimble responded that this also applied to the UUP, since any deal would have to make it through the UUC (where Trimble was engaged in his own 'act of completion', partly including an attempt to reform the Orange link). But there was still too little flesh on what exactly the Provisionals were going to do, and when, partly because they needed to call an Army Convention. Such timing was no good for Trimble: if the elections were to be held on 1 May, that would mean dissolution by 28 March, and he would thus be entering the campaign without anything concrete from republicans and if the IRA statement or actions turned out to be insufficient he would look like a soft touch. Alternatively, the actions of republicans could end up dominating the first week of the campaign, to the detriment of the Unionist party which had sought to do business with them. Until he saw the IRA statement and an act of decommissioning, he would not call a special meeting of the UUC. Blair responded that if the UUP leader wanted postponement, that would be very hard indeed without an agreement with other parties. The next morning the UUP and Sinn Fein – represented by Trimble and Empey and Adams and McGuinness – met as Blair had suggested in Paul Murphy's study on the first floor. When they emerged, the body language and 'mood-music' of the participants greatly encouraged British officials. Indeed, the senior SDLP negotiator, Sean Farren, observed in his notebook that '[Trimble is] not interested in the SDLP. [He] flicked through a book . . . and played with a thing in his hand. He looked out of the window.' According to Trimble, there was one immediate effect of his encounter with Adams: a shared understanding between the parties that everyone needed more time. Sinn Fein needed an extra month, which meant that elections would have to be postponed. As far as Trimble was concerned, 'Sinn Fein effectively asked for the first postponement.'[37] Trimble may be exaggerating here, but the British believed that Sinn Fein certainly acquiesced in this delay.[38] Meanwhile, other UUP figures were brought in and working parties were set up to deal with detailed aspects of policy, such as on normalisation and sanctions. The UUP wanted the sanctions regime, with its independent monitoring commission, to be enshrined in Westminster legislation: once the commission reported, the British Government would be required to act as the final arbiter. Sinn Fein vigorously stated their discomfort with the package. But, if it was going to happen, they were determined that it have no legislative background at Westminster. Instead, they wanted its recommendations to go to the Northern Ireland Assembly rather than to the British Government (where, they hoped, any proposed punishments might die a death through insufficient cross-community support).[39]

It was during these discussions that events took a bizarre turn. As so often during this period, Blair was obliged to interrupt Northern Ireland business to deal with the Iraq crisis.[40] Indeed, by staying at Hillsborough for another day to complete the negotiation, he was already missing his audience with the Queen and was obliged to reschedule his meeting with Igor Ivanov, the Russian Foreign Minister. Activity was frantic in the run-up to the anticipated vote in the UN Security Council on the second resolution concerning military action – a decision which would be crucial for Blair's credibility both at home and abroad. The Prime Minister was on the telephone lobbying the Prime Minister of Sweden, Göran Persson, in an attempt to secure an EU consensus on the issue. Tom Kelly, the No. 10 spokesman, suddenly came into the room and went up to Jonathan Powell, who was listening in on his mobile telephone after being 'patched in' by the Downing Street switchboard. 'You'll never guess what I've just heard,' Kelly told Powell. 'Trimble's about to leave.'[41] Powell duly sought to tell Blair what Trimble was planning to do and tried to coax his boss off the telephone. 'Shut up, I've got to speak to this person,' replied Blair – who then started to explain to his Swedish counterpart the reason for the interruption.[42] When eventually he did end the conversation, the Prime Minister asked, 'Has David gone?' He was astonished to be told that Trimble was leaving for parliamentary business in London. Trimble's account is slightly different. He says he went in and told Blair that he would be departing for London. The UUP had completed its last meeting with Sinn Fein, in which the republicans had raised no further issues that the two parties would need to talk about. Why stay, Trimble reasoned, when there was already an understanding that the Assembly elections would have to be temporarily postponed? But Blair revealed to the UUP leader that Sinn Fein were now kicking up a fuss about the proposed sanctions and that he was, accordingly, seeking to amend them. Trimble, though, would not budge and he says he told Empey and Michael McGimpsey to stand firm on the sanctions issue in his absence (Empey, for one, was stunned by his departure).[43]

It was, nonetheless, an odd decision for Trimble to take – rather like his decision to walk off the platform at the Odyssey Centre during Clinton's speech in December 2000, to attend a conference in Palermo. And, as in December 2000, he had a booking which he would not change. Presumably, he could have changed it, but by now he was fed up with just the sort of 'word by word' or even 'inch by inch' negotiation which he was so desperate to avoid. He believed his walk-out worked, because by the time he disembarked from the aircraft in London, the draft was more satisfactory to him. The latest draft said that the Government would act in a manner consistent with the recommendations of the monitoring body, whereas immediately before that it had solely pledged the Government to consider taking action if the Assembly did not resolve the matter.[44] Retrospectively, some British officials saw Trimble's move as a good, if rather unorthodox form of party management: by giving his colleagues 'ownership' of the proposals, he had effectively bound them to his strategy (that is, the very opposite of what he had done on 14 May 1999 at No. 10, when he negotiated alone and found himself way in advance of their position on setting up the Executive). As the British saw it, nobody in the UUP who was there that day could credibly distance themselves from Trimble by saying that the leader had acquiesced in the proposals all by himself. But Trimble was not the only leader to engage in such brinkmanship: more conventionally, perhaps, Sinn Fein made a point of revving up their cars twice as the Prime Minister fought to obtain agreement on the monitoring body. The discussion ended after 30 hours at 11:30 p.m. on 4 March and the Prime Minister and Taoiseach held their press conference at 11:45; Blair then ate supper with the Irish team, left at 1:30 a.m. and returned to No. 10 at 3:00 a.m. for a rescheduled breakfast with the Russian Foreign Minister later that day.[45] The big matters were not resolved between the parties, however. Accordingly, the two thorniest for Sinn Fein and the UUP – sanctions and the OTRs, respectively – would now be dealt with by inter-governmental fiat.[46] The British and Irish would duly come to their best judgments on those, and they would be separated from the rest of the Joint Declaration, to be published in the following month, when the two heads of Government would return with a final blueprint.[47] The 'equality of pain' for both Sinn Fein and the UUP on sanctions and the OTRs provided a context in which both parties would need more time to consult. But the headlines were dominated by the announcement that the two Governments had agreed on a post-ponement of the Assembly elections from 1 May to 29 May. And if the poll was postponed once – proving that the original election date enshrined in the Northern Ireland Act 1998 was no longer sacrosanct – then it could presumably be postponed again.[48] Certainly, the British did not want to postpone again on an indefinite basis unless they absolutely had to – and especially if the Irish were reluctant to do so. Indeed, as one senior Irish figure observed at the time, 'we support elections as a discipline'.[49] By this, they meant that the threat of holding a poll which it might lose would force the UUP into what the southerners regarded as a more flexible posture, which they believed would be to the UUP's benefit: cobble together another deal which would enable the UUP to fight the Assembly elections inside the Northern Ireland Executive as the party which brought unionists both devolution and decommissioning, rather than trying to outbid the DUP at a game they could not win. It was an extension of the old line that the UUP should try to 'sell' the Agreement harder and that any attempt by Trimble to show that he had a bottom line could only strengthen his rejectionists. In an ideal world, Trimble would have liked to have fought the election from within the Executive and he toyed with the idea on several occasions after October 2002. But circumstances would not permit. And the UUP again feared that republi-cans would do just enough to convince the two Governments to give them their election, but not enough to satisfy a sceptical unionist electorate.

That said, Trimble told Haass when they met in Washington in the following week during the St Patrick's Day celebrations that all the indi-cations were that the Provisionals were definitely going to do something. He met with Ahern at the Mayflower Hotel and at the urging of Michael McDowell in Washington – who had received representations from Irish officials – toned down his use of the word 'sanctions' in his remarks to the National Press Club. Instead, he used the expression 'full compliance' and 'safeguards'. The visit was overshadowed by the Iraq crisis, and for the first time it looked as though Blair's own position was imperilled. Indeed, when one senior British official was asked what the departure of Blair might mean for Northern Ireland, he replied, 'the end of personalised politics'.[50]

That, of course, would be bad for Trimble (it was, recalls the UUP leader, indicative of how embattled No. 10 felt at this time that when Trimble queried the wisdom of some proposal, Blair quipped darkly, 'Oh, you're not against me as well?').[51] Whilst he was there, he volunteered his services to Jonathan Powell to make whatever representations he could with senior Americans about the coming conflict in Iraq. It was a useful card which few northern nationalists could play, since most of them were opposed to the war: McGuinness, for one, demanded that US military stop-overs at Shannon be halted.[52] Indeed, when a trio of anti-war Nobel Laureates from the Freie Universität Berlin sent out a petition for signature, Trimble rebutted them with his own letter of support in favour of Anglo-American action.[53] But in the short run, at least, such assistance seemed to profit him little. In late March, Trimble wrote to Blair to express his worry about reports which he was receiving that the Government was conceding on almost all fronts. It had been something of a pattern in the process that such concessions were offered when republicans 'flashed a bit of thigh' in the two Governments' direction – in this instance, Adams' hint that Sinn Fein could join the Policing Board.[54] The Governments publicly denied that there was such a negotiation going on about policing and Paul Murphy indicated that there would be no further policing legislation.[55] On 31 March at No. 10, Trimble observed that his understanding arising out of the 3/4 March Hillsborough summit was that the first move was an IRA statement, to be followed by the Joint Declaration with all its proposed 'goodies' for nationalists. Now, there were suggestions it was going to be the other way round. If published in that order, he argued, it would enable republicans effectively to say, 'fine, but give us some more'. Blair sought to reassure unionists that he would not return to Belfast unless there was something concrete on the table from Adams. Trimble duly went back to Adams and the two men met in the UUP leader's old office at Stormont on Wednesday 2 April: the Sinn Fein president said he would have great difficulty delivering if the institutions were not up and running first. Sinn Fein also needed to know if any republican proposal would be rejected or not. Trimble, obviously, said no to this 'sequencing'. But he agreed to meet the republicans again on Saturday 5 April at Stormont – when Adams would give the UUP leader the crucial detail of the language and actions which republicans were planning to use to restart the institutions.

The plan was, however, interrupted by dramatic news from America.

On 27 March, Tony Blair was sitting with his aides on the aircraft after his visit to Camp David and was musing about where the next Anglo-American summit on the war and the reconstruction of Iraq might take place. Bush was obviously greatly indebted to the Prime Minister for his support in that conflict and would travel to see his British friend and ally. 'What about Hillsborough?' Blair asked his team. Blair made the suggestion both because of the value which a Presidential visit would add to his efforts in Northern Ireland itself and because of its utility as a model for 'conflict resolution' elsewhere, notably in the Middle East.[56] Jonathan Powell duly took senior Irish officials into his confidence on 1 April: if Ahern came up for the summit, would Hillsborough suit them as a venue? Despite considerable opposition to the Iraq war in the Republic, the Irish agreed to the proposal. The location remained secret until some of the President's security detail were spotted on Friday 4 April at the Laganside Hilton, three days before Bush's arrival on Monday 7 April.[57] The British were surprised, and pleased, that Bush agreed to stay at Hillsborough: Clinton had opted for the more 'neutral' venue of the Europa or the Laganside Hilton. It was not, however, the largest of residences, and it would be difficult to squeeze in both the Presidential and Prime Ministerial entourages, including Colin Powell and Condoleezza Rice. 'I just about managed to stay in my bedroom,' quips Paul Murphy, the Northern Ireland Secretary.[58] Bush peppered Blair with questions about what the Northern Ireland model meant, such as what a prolonged commitment to managing such a process entailed – though when the President declared that he was prepared to invest the same amount of energy to the Middle East as the Prime Minister did to Ulster, there were giggles from some of the more experienced Whitehall hands.[59] The bulk of the time was taken up with Iraq and the Middle East. But in the afternoon of Tuesday 8 April, Bush did go round the Throne Room meeting all of the parties: the President thanked Trimble for his support on the war.[60] According to Peter Stothard's eyewitness account, *30 Days: A Month at the Heart of Blair's War*, the President had earlier looked at a chessboard on which the pieces were carved representations of all of the players in the Troubles. 'Tony Blair moves in quickly to explain that the black Republicans [pawns], whom Americans have traditionally financed, are against the war in Iraq, while the white Unionists, whom the Americans like to see as colonial oppressors, are in favour of it,' recalls Stothard. 'The President nods.'[61] Relatively little of substance was achieved on Northern Ireland *per se*. But after the Presidential helicopter had lifted off from the grounds of Hillsborough, Blair and Ahern sat and talked on the bench outside the main drawing room. They were gripped by two conflicting emotions. On the one hand, the visit had gone well and Bush had given Blair the assurances he needed on the Middle East peace process and the role of the UN in the future of Iraq. But on Northern Ireland, the outlook was bleaker. The Irish had seen language from the Provisionals which was way short of the mark. A judgment would have to be made if this was for real, or whether this posture was simply a 'try-on' to secure further concessions. Blair was not going to take 'no' for an answer, but it represented the first darkening of the intergovernmental mood.[62] Indeed, Trimble's own meeting with Adams on Saturday 5 April was a damp squib: the Sinn Fein president was going to hold something back for the Presidential visit, rather than expend his capital early for the UUP leader. Trimble later speculated Sinn Fein 'played things so very fine [in the run-up to the revised poll date of 29 May] because they had lost four to five critical days in the run-up to and during the Bush visit'. What might have happened, he wondered, if they had the extra time?[63]

The two heads of Government had planned to return to Northern Ireland on Thursday 10 April, barely 48 hours after Bush's departure, to issue an intergovernmental blueprint of steps to restart the Executive. But because the IRA's proposed 'acts of completion' were still so vague, they decided not to publish the list of concessions to nationalists on policing and normalisation. Had they done so, says Trimble, it would have been all over for him, because it would have proven that republicans had been rewarded in exchange for nothing.[64] If the Provisionals were going to be vague in these circumstances, Blair and Ahern were not going to be specific, either, and the publication of the document – scheduled for the fifth anniversary of the signing of the Belfast Agreement – was aborted. The Irish were also determined not to commit Ahern's prestige to so uncertain an endeavour. But the two Governments also believed that momentum had to be maintained and it was decided that an Irish delegation led by Ahern would go to London. The British and Irish teams duly met in the packed 'den', where they went over a revised draft of the IRA statement: they insisted upon an 'eleventh-hour rewrite' that gave greater 'clarity' and 'certainty'.[65] Blair told Adams on the telephone at midday that the problem with the IRA statement was that it did not state that the 'war is over' in terms that others might understand; it did not clearly say that paramilitarism was incompatible with the Belfast Agreement; and it did not commit with sufficient clarity on decommissioning. Adams appeared to accept that the republican movement was not there yet, but pointed out that only an IRA Army Convention could pronounce that 'the war is over' (where he might have great difficulties in pushing such a statement through, or so the British and Irish believed). Ahern allegedly also described the draft IRA statement to one associate as 'a joke' and David Campbell received a call from a senior DFA official on the morning of Thursday confirming that the statement fell far short of the mark. Campbell believed that if this diplomat thought it was woefully inadequate, then there must be massive problems![66] Shortly after he spoke to Adams, Blair left the room to test the revised intergovernmental draft of the IRA statement on Trimble; he also made sure that Empey was briefed later as well. The UUP leader responded that the proposals were in the right area (subsequently, Adams would call Blair to complain that Trimble was briefing journalists to say that 'the war is over' – and he wished the UUP leader would keep out of it). Enough progress was made to enable Ahern to drop off some of his key officials in Belfast that night before heading on to Dublin, where they would put the new proposals to the republicans. Whereas the previous draft said that 'the IRA leadership is determined to ensure our activities, disciplines and strategies will be consistent with the further development of this process', the new statement read that 'the IRA is determined to ensure our activities, disciplines and strategies will be consistent [only] with the Good Friday Agreement'. From a UUP perspective, this would have the advantage of implying that the Belfast Agreement was the end-point of the struggle, rather than just another phase in the relentless republican march to a united Ireland. So total was the confidence between the British and Irish delegations that when Blair left the meeting at 6 p.m. to put his young son Leo to bed, the Irish were left alone for a period in the Prime Minister's study.

The Irish met that night with a surly Adams and McGuinness at the British-Irish Secretariat at Windsor House. They went over the text from 9 p.m. till 11 p.m. Ahern again met with Adams and McGuinness at St Luke's in Drumcondra (his constituency office) on the morning of Saturday 12 April. The republicans demanded a statement from both Governments reaffirming their commitment to the Northern Ireland institutions, which they duly issued. The Irish informed Jonathan Powell at midday that Adams and McGuinness were going back to the IRA and would deliver a response on the following day: if all went well, the two heads of Government might be able to return to Hillsborough on Monday 14 April and revive their cancelled summit. So promising did things appear that despite the impediments of bad flu and a dying mother, Powell flew to Dublin on Sunday 13 April to meet with Irish colleagues. After being collected at the airport by Brendan Scannell, head of the Anglo-Irish Division of the DFA, Powell went to St Luke's. There, Powell, the Taoiseach, two southern Cabinet ministers and a number of senior Irish officials waited with increasing impatience for six hours for Adams and McGuinness to turn up: great secrecy attended their efforts to persuade other republicans to make some kind of move. Eventually, at around 6:15 p.m., the Irish were able to speak to Adams, who said that he was coming from Drogheda and would be there in around an hour. But despite some incremental improvements in the text, the republicans' draft was still short of what was required. When he arrived at about 7:15 p.m., Adams was quite explicit about the limits of what the IRA could say 'up front' to break the impasse. But the IRA statement of that day still did not bring paramilitarism to an end. Rather, it pledged that 'we are resolved to see the complete and final closure of this conflict. The IRA leadership is determined to ensure that our activities, disciplines and strategies *will be* [author's emphasis] consistent with this. Furthermore, the full and irreversible implementation of the agreement *and other commitments will provide* a context in which the IRA can proceed to definitively set aside arms to further our political objectives. When there is such a context this decision can be taken only by a general army convention representing all volunteers.'[67]

For the two Governments, let alone the UUP, this was all rather 'futuristic' and conditional upon further concessions. This statement was not, however, released until 6 May. Instead, republicans issued a holding statement on the night of Sunday 13 April, pledging themselves to make another pronouncement on their future intentions and guaranteeing a third decommissioning act under the aegis of the de Chastelain body.[68] By this point, such a concession seemed virtually worthless in the eyes of unionist opinion. Indeed, the UUP would have taken the statement as simply an effort to do the minimum to appear reasonable, and put the onus back on themselves and the British to make the next move. Or else, they would have taken it as a ruse to divide the Irish Government (which was often inclined to ask less of the Provisionals) from its British counterpart. In this, they did not really succeed, save in one sense: the Irish, at the behest of the republicans, wanted the elections to go ahead even if the IRA did not deliver enough. Once again, as during the suspension crisis of February 2000, the Irish preferred to let Trimble 'face the music' than to cause a major rupture in their relationship with Sinn Fein. Indeed, when Trimble explained to Ahern on 21 April why Assembly elections would be a disaster, the Irish delegation did not respond. The only question, as in February 2000, was whether the Blair–Trimble relationship remained solid enough to trump that. Even there, things did not look entirely rosy: when the UUP leader explained to Blair the case for postponing the poll when they met at No. 10 on 17 April, the Prime Minister put his head in his hands and confessed that such a course of action was very difficult.

Still, the two Governments would not give up. Just after the Drumcondra meeting, Blair told Trimble over the telephone that he had resolved to ask three questions of his republican interlocutors, and Powell did the same with David Campbell.[69] But these were not placed immediately in the public domain: instead, there was a gap of time during which period the British Government waited for a republican response. If Adams was going to address these issues, they wondered, why make life more complicated for him? David Campbell thought that the questions were good – but was disturbed that it seemed as though the questions would be asked only of Adams and not of the IRA. The UUP had seen enough in the past of 'leadership positions' or 'clarifications' from the Sinn Fein president which may or may not have been the settled position of the entire 'movement'.[70] They had reason to be worried, since Adams was said to be under great pressure internally and not feeling well; there were also rumours that he had been rebuffed by senior Provisionals at a more informal republican gathering in the margins of the Sinn Fein Ard Fheis in Dublin.[71] Certainly, Adams made the necessary gestures to the republican base, addressing an Easter commemoration in north Belfast at which wreaths were laid by such IRA legends as Sean Kelly, the man convicted of planting the Shankill bomb of 1993 that killed nine Protestants.[72]

Despite talk of Adams' difficulties, Blair pushed ahead with his three questions and finally put them in the public domain at a press conference at No. 10 on Wednesday 23 April. Would the IRA end all activities inconsistent with the Belfast Agreement, including targeting, procurement, punishment beatings, etc? When they say that they are committed to putting weapons beyond use through the de Chastelain body, does that mean all arms so the process is complete? And when they say that they support the Belfast Agreement and want it to work, if the two Governments and the other parties fulfil their obligations under the 1998 accord and Joint Declaration (the document listing the further concessions which Blair would make but which was held back on 10 April for want of republican reciprocity), does that mean the complete and final closure of the conflict? The three questions arose out of paragraph 13 of the then unpublished Joint Declaration, which itself arose out of the requests made by Blair in his October 2002 Belfast speech: 'We need to see an immediate, full and permanent cessation of all paramilitary activity, including military attacks [sic], training, targeting, intelligence gathering, acquisition or development of arms or weapons, other preparations for terrorist campaigns, punishment beatings and attacks and involvement in riots.' The IRA was enraged that in asking these questions, Blair had appeared to breach what they considered to be the protocol by quoting from aspects of their unpublished 13 April statement, and later roundly criticised the Prime Minister for doing so.[73] In the meantime, Adams came back with his reply in a speech at Stormont on the afternoon of Sunday 27 April. The prelude to it was, in some ways, even more interesting than the actual event itself. The two men met that morning at Hillsborough Castle, under the watchful eye of Paul Murphy. Just as Trimble had faxed a text of his March 2002 UUC address to Adams, so Adams now showed his proposed remarks to Trimble. The UUP leader said it was not enough. Trimble suggested that they should now, perhaps, have a break until the autumn and try for a deal and elections in the autumn: it was the first time that Adams had consulted Trimble in this way.[74] But the Sinn Fein president's response really only dealt with question two – on decommissioning – which was of least value now to a fed-up UUP and unionist community (especially since no cameras would be present for the third decommissioning act – that is, 'no Spielbergs'). Trimble also viewed question three as a 'dud', since it effectively gave the republicans a say in determining whether the Governments and the parties had fulfilled their obligations under the Agreement. Thus, from a UUP perspective, Adams had only satisfactorily answered one question out of two, and the less important one at that.[75] It was therefore a source of great vexation to him when the No. 10 spokesman pronounced that day that Adams had answered two out of three questions satisfactorily. Whilst question one had not been answered fully – 'We need assurances that activity *will* not happen, not *should* not happen,' pronounced the British – the other two responses constituted progress in the Government's eyes. The Government also noted that Adams said that he was representing the views of the IRA leadership. It did not want to give Sinn Fein the excuse not to address the crucial third question, by failing to acknowledge any progress. If it had been totally dismissive, it feared that Sinn Fein could then turn to their constituency and spin a narrative of having 'gone the extra mile' – but that their generosity had been spurned by a British Government that still caved in before the 'Orange card'. As the British saw it, 'telling the truth' in fact made things harder for Sinn Fein on the one question that really mattered. Trimble, though, thought he was being 'shafted' because of No. 10's insatiable need for positive 'spin', and feared that nationalist Ireland would turn round and say, 'Look, they've done two out of three, please cut the Provies a bit of slack.' The UUP leader was particularly worried that the Irish would say that whilst not perfect, the republicans had certainly moved enough to earn them their much-craved Assembly elections. And he feared that in this mood, the British might be susceptible to such arguments – especially in the light of earlier polling done for No. 10 by Millward Brown which was very optimistic about the UUP's prospects.[76] So was the Trimble–Blair axis finally going to break down, as so many observers expected?

Trimble duly telephoned Jonathan Powell on the morning of Monday 28 April. It was one of the sharpest exchanges ever between the two men: such conversations were hard for the British, since at other times they would be bearing the burden of arguing Trimble's case with the Irish and the republicans. By early afternoon, Blair spoke with the UUP leader and sought to mollify him. Trimble also sought, and obtained, a guarantee that he would be informed in future about pronouncements such as the response to the Sinn Fein president's speech. The UUP leader publicly said that on the basis of Adams' answers, he still could not nominate or vote for a First or Deputy First Minister after any new Assembly elections.[77] The British maintained that they did not consider this to be his last word on the subject, and that the Prime Minister could still secure a deal on IRA 'acts of completion' by maintaining the pressure on question one (though they publicly kept their options open, and at a press conference on Monday 28 April, Blair sidestepped a question about the date of elections, merely saying that they should take place in a 'positive' atmosphere).[78] Adams accordingly sought to make one last heave on Tuesday 29 April. According to Gerry Moriarty's account in the *Irish Times* of 3 May 2003, they alighted upon the following formulation: that Adams should confirm on the basis of his contacts with the IRA leadership that they agreed with his clarifications on their future intentions as outlined in his Stormont address of Sunday 27 April. It was also suggested that Adams should confirm that on the basis of his contacts with the IRA leadership, the kind of activity raised by Blair in question one cannot and will not be authorised by the IRA. Significantly, the Governments believed that this formula was acceptable to Trimble (the UUP leader says that was not so – and draws attention to his news conference at UUP headquarters on Monday 28 April, in which he noted that 'if the two Governments have had an IRA statement for over two weeks and still can't get any changes to it, and have to go to a third party for clarification, the statement must be deficient'). But, in any case, the IRA would not allow Adams' Stormont clarifications to appear as an addendum to the text of its 13 April statement.[79] Instead, as the Sinn Fein president told an Irish official, 'I can't put it in the language that you want, but I can tell you that my belief is that the intent [behind the IRA pronunciamento] is as the Governments want it.' This, obviously, was not enough for the UUP, nor was it enough for the Irish Government.[80]

Why could republicans not give enough this time round? Some reports suggested that Adams and McGuinness were 'rolled over' at an IRA meeting of about 40 to 50 republican activists, held in the margins of the Sinn Fein *Ard Fheis* between 28 and 30 March. As has been noted, the Irish believed that Adams and McGuinness could not risk taking any 'act of completion' to a full IRA Army Convention for fear of losing. The British were never quite so convinced about this narrative of vulnerability – which sat oddly with the DFA's relentless optimism about the republican movement's willingness to do the deal – but noticed that Adams and McGuinness never really squared away their 'middle management'. One senior British official wondered whether they never really intended to 'get into the ball park' and simply hoped that everyone else would settle for less. At some level, they did not seem to take the Prime Minister's October 2002 speech seriously. Their greatest single problem appears to have been signing up to policing – a difficulty about which they were quite explicit to journalists such as Frank Millar from the latter part of 2002. For they were asking for further radical changes which the British were not prepared to grant at this stage and in these circumstances. As Sinn Fein saw it, the PSNI would have to show more 'representativeness' – that is, recruit more known republicans – before the 'peelers' would become acceptable in areas such as Ballymurphy and the Bogside.[81] Sinn Fein also claimed to be very nervous about the supposed impact upon their electoral fortunes in an 'act of completion': they were privately not so much worried about the SDLP, as about the core republican vote staying at home.[82]

Such 'realities' were on everyone's mind when Trimble arrived at No. 10 at 2:30 p.m. on Wednesday 30 April. Blair made it clear that Adams had not yet given enough, but he still wanted to know what, now, would satisfy the UUP leader. Trimble replied that the moment had come to close down the negotiation. Mechanically, time had just run out: if there were to be Assembly elections on 29 May, nomination papers had to be in by the end of the week, a UUC had to be called and there was a risk that the campaign would be dominated by the issues in the Joint Declaration. If Blair drew a line in the sand now, argued Trimble, he would have a different context in which to extract further statements from republicans. 'Even if you got everything you wanted from republicans, are the atmospherics so bad as to [make any concessions] of no value to you?' Trimble agreed: it was now quite clear that Blair was inclining heavily towards postponement of the poll. As one observer notes, under these circumstances Trimble would have been entering Assembly elections without decommissioning or devolution – having campaigned in the 2001 Westminster poll as the party that had brought about both these things. By postponing the elections, Blair was implictly admitting failure and was also protecting Trimble from the consequences of that failure. 'The meeting with Trimble convinced Tony that moderate Unionism was not in a shape to fight the election,' recalls one official.[83] The Prime Minister also indicated that he was 'astonished' by Paisley's attack in this period on Brian Cowen's physical features.[84] Whether or not the DUP leader contributed materially to Blair's decision to pull the elections, it certainly served as a reminder to him of what the alternative was to Trimble. Later that afternoon, a host of top officials – including Powell, Jonathan Phillips, Matthew Rycroft and Tom Kelly – met with Blair and Paul Murphy in 'the den', or Prime Ministerial study next to the Cabinet Room. The mood was as dark as the afternoon. Trimble's stance had made an impression. The question now was how to handle the Irish – or, as Paul Murphy told the UUP on 15 April 2003, how to 'let them down gently'.[85] Would it cause a rift? And how would both Irish-Americans and the US Administration respond? The NIO believed that the state of Anglo-American relations ought not to be judged solely by the sense of transatlantic solidarity that obtained in connection with the war on terrorism or even the excellent personal relations between President and Prime Minister. In any case, the NIO thought that 'the Americans had an emotional attachment to this thing called democracy' and would not, therefore, understand why a poll was being postponed. It was an ongoing NIO concern, though very much exaggerated, and especially so in the days after the Anglo-American victory in Iraq.[86]

The NIO's worst fears turned out to be misplaced. Blair spoke to Ahern after this meeting, and again after he took the final decision to postpone on Thursday 1 May. The first call to the Taoiseach was to give the Irish an indication of where his mind was going: effectively, Blair was saying, 'We feel we have no option but to postpone, so if you're going to come up with something to avert this outcome you had better move quickly.' The second call was quite definitive and its message was, 'We know you're not going to like this, but we're going to postpone.'[87] The Irish were still very much opposed to postponement, but according to one British official the message from Dublin, as he understood it, was, 'We will disagree with you publicly and privately, but we see why you did what you did.' In consequence, says the official, the Irish objections were of a totally different order of magnitude from that of the suspension crisis of February 2000. Thus, in February 2000, Paddy Teahon was handed the telephone by the Taoiseach and told Blair in very uncompromising terms exactly what he thought about Peter Mandelson. The difference between the two crises owed something to the fact that Murphy was a far less controversial and flamboyant personality than Mandelson. In 2000, much of nationalist Ireland believed that the Northern Ireland Executive would be gone for ever, whereas in 2003 the Irish at least had the hope that it would be restarted soon. Moreover, even the Irish found the republican statement to be inadequate. As Dublin sources subsequently noted, the IRA failure to declare in time that Adams' clarifications to the 'P. O'Neill' statement were authoritative effectively meant that the Assembly elections could not go ahead as planned (though republican sources did say on the night of 6 May, some five days after postponement, that Adams did accurately reflect the Provisionals' position).[88]

Blair then telephoned Trimble just after lunch, at 2:15 p.m. on Thursday 1 May, to inform him of the decision. 'After all, at the end of the day, this is the right thing to do,' the UUP leader told him at the conclusion of the conversation. 'Yes, it is the right thing,' replied the Prime Minister. 'I wouldn't do it otherwise.'[89] Blair proceeded to tell a press conference at 2:40 p.m. in the Pillared Room in No. 10 that the Provisionals' statement and Adams' subsequent clarification did not amount to an 'act of completion'. He wished to leave no one in any doubt that 'had we got clear answers to those questions [to republicans] a few weeks ago, David Trimble would have cut the deal and we would have been in a very different position' – a clear rejoinder to those in nationalist Ireland who believed that the UUP leader was not serious. And he went on: 'We are now five years on from the Agreement. Five years ago it was in my view acceptable for us to say to David Trimble, "Look, that IRA is going through a process of transition, you should be prepared to be in government even though that process has to work its way through" . . . I think it is not unreasonable for him [Trimble] to say after five years that the process of transition has to end, and actually, from the two Governments' point of view, it is as important to us as it is to him.' In these circumstances, no Northern Ireland Executive could be formed and elections would 'frustrate the very purpose of the Good Friday Agreement'.[90] According to No. 10, the reference to Trimble was included precisely because the Blairites anticipated that it would be the instinctive response of nationalist Ireland to blame the UUP leader.

Ahern duly expressed his public opposition to the postponement and later strongly criticised Trimble for his part in the failure to restore the institutions.[91] In so doing, he appeared to be in line with southern public opinion. According to an *Irish Times*/TNS MRBI poll published on 19 May, a plurality of voters believed that the IRA had not made clear its intentions to abandon paramilitarism – but only 15% of them believed that republicans were responsible for the breakdown, in contrast to the 35% who blamed the UUP. Adams declared that the postponement was evidence that the 'Unionist veto' was still very much in operation and that northern nationalists were still being denied even 'very modest entitlements'. But beyond nationalist Ireland, Blair's decision caused little controversy. Despite Conservative objections to the postponement – for reasons which baffled some observers – there was no great rumpus about it in the Commons.[92] Even the *Guardian*, which in the past had been understanding of the internal difficulties of Adams and McGuinness, effectively blamed the republicans for the breakdown in its leader of 2 May 2003. Bush also expressed his support for the postponement. The contrast with Clinton, who did not publicly back up Blair in February 2000, could not have been greater. Once the decision to postpone was taken by a firm British Government, the Americans fell into line, whatever their own feelings in favour of elections. Thus, when Trimble's friend Michael McDowell met an unshaven Richard Haass the next weekend at the check-out at a supermarket near their homes in Chevy Chase, Maryland, and pronounced the postponement to be the 'right decision', the US envoy could only say 'maybe' – and later called for elections to be held as soon as possible.[93]

It was nonetheless a remarkable political achievement for Trimble. Once again, in order to sustain the UUP leader, Blair had defied the Government of the Irish Republic, Sinn Fein, the SDLP, the DUP, the Tories and substantial portions of the UUP.[94] For all the frustrations with Trimble – exemplified by his walk-out at Hillsborough in March 2003 – life without him was a leap in the dark. Or, as one senior British official put it, 'the alternative was the election of the extremes, and we were looking at five to ten years of ice age'. That was why Blair was so unrepentant in the face of nationalist accusations that it was all about 'saving Private Trimble'.[95] 'You're expecting me to bring Trimble along,' one Irish official recalls Blair telling the republicans. 'That's a huge task. Even if I believe in your intentions, I just can't bring him across the floor.'[96] But although the British stood by Trimble, they were unrepentant about their strategy in the negotiations between October 2002 and May 2003. Trimble wanted them to be much more rigorous in the application of carrots and sticks. He believed that if they had explicitly threatened postponement much sooner and had pulled other levers – such as asking the Americans to ban Sinn Fein fundraising in the United States, or at least threatening to do so – the republicans would have moved in time. If the British had acted promptly, asserted the UUP leader, they would consequently never have needed to postpone. But the British believed that the kind of things which Trimble wanted them to do would only have been on the cards in the event of another South Quay bomb (a reference to the attack of 9 February 1996, which ended the first IRA ceasefire).

Had the British accepted the advice of the Irish on either the occasion of the suspension of February 2000 or the postponement of May 2003, the effect would have been to destroy Trimble. As has been noted, the southerners wanted Trimble to survive, but were not prepared to pay much of a price to help him do so. Partly, as some figures on the British side believed, it was a case of 'clientism': years after the Belfast Agreement was signed, the Irish still believed that they had to look after northern nationalists. But it was also the case that the Irish really believed that postponement of the Assembly elections would not help Trimble. They thought that delay would not help him and that he could not outbid Paisley at the hardline game and that he needed to 'sell' the Agreement more. Trimble was philosophical about the Irish stance. He had taken the advice of the British and remained in touch with Ahern throughout the crisis: he, too, was grateful to the Taoiseach for not making things even worse. Rather, in the Commons debate of 12 May 2003 on the legislation postponing the elections the UUP leader reserved his scorn for the DFA alone.[97] As so often before, Trimble was exculpating the sovereign, instead blaming the wicked advisers.

One other familiar pattern also reasserted itself: the ambiguous response of the unionist community to what Trimble had done. Some Trimbleistas feared that the UUP leader's success in the realm of high politics, in persuading Blair to stand up to pan-nationalism, would not be understood by the public at large. By contrast, unionist 'defeats', as exemplified by substantial elements of the Joint Declaration and the statement on OTRs, were all too comprehensible. But such fears appear to have been misplaced. A survey of 900 people carried out by Millward Brown Ulster for the *News Letter* and published on 19 May showed that 61% of unionists believed that Blair was justified in postponing the elections (the poll also revealed that a surprisingly high 31% of nationalists supported the Prime Minister's decision – as was also evidenced by the failure of Sinn Fein to bring nationalists out on to the streets to protest against what republicans saw as a denial of democracy).[98] More gratifyingly still from Trimble's viewpoint, he remained the most popular of unionist leaders, despite the growth in support for the DUP. The figures suggest thus that most unionists did grasp that the Provisionals had, on this occasion, come off worst. But many of Trimble's foes *within* the UUP were not so indulgent. As David Brewster observes, 'Some of us wanted an election more than anything else – and we didn't get it.'[99] They had been deprived of the ballot which they thought would finally rid them of him and enable them to move the party in a more pan-unionist direction. Many more were further angered by the publication of the Joint Declaration on 1 May and the subsequent announcement that parts of it would be implemented in advance of any IRA 'act of completion'.[100] There was, in fact, debate within the British Government about whether to issue it. Some officials were worried that if it was issued and any one side rejected it, the whole thing would be unpicked and would have to be renegotiated. But in the end, it was decided to go ahead with publication. It was reasoned that much of it had already leaked anyhow; that publication would help to calm some of the wilder rumours about its contents; and that it would help keep the pressure on Sinn Fein by showing to the world that republicans had spurned another set of concessions made in good faith. However, it also showed that there had been another 'inch by inch' negotiation of the kind which Blair had pledged not to indulge in and against which Trimble had counselled.[101] Privately, many Trimbleistas believed that there was little that was new in the Joint Declaration over and above what was in the Weston Park package of July 2001 – which, as they pointed out, contained no sanctions regime whatsoever to deal with republican misbehaviour. Therein, of course, lay the essence of their differences with the 'antis'. Many of the Trimbleistas had a very high 'pain threshold'. They disliked much of what was in the Joint Declaration, but they could, at a pinch, live with most aspects of it for the sake of a bigger prize: the prospect of political stability through the 'defanging' of the republican movement. With the exception of the OTRs there was little there beyond 'verbiage'. Anyhow, Trimble did not think there was that much that he as UUP leader could do about many of its provisions. Why throw good money after bad? In consequence, as one British official observes, 'David was not a big player in the Joint Declaration and was most sensitive to matters of how it was presented rather than the substance.'[102] But the 'antis' did not take so philosophical a view of such concessions to nationalists: indeed, David Burnside contended that in this period, the Alliance party seemed at times to be more critical of the concessions to republicans in the Joint Declaration than was Trimble.[103] And the 'antis' also knew that because of the broadness of the proposed sanctions regime they could be as much the targets as their republican foes. Even if the Joint Declaration contained little that was new – as both Trimble and the British contended – everyone had their line in the sand. Claire Short had hers, after the war on Iraq, when she pronounced enough was enough and resigned from the Government. Now, it was Jeffrey Donaldson's turn.[104] The way was thus open for a dramatic 'parting of the ways' between pro- and anti-Agreement Ulster Unionism.

THIRTY-NINE

Paisley triumphant

TRIMBLE was soon thrown on the defensive in the UUP's renewed civil war – but in a quite unexpected way. In late May, a briefing from the GOC Northern Ireland, Lt Gen. Philip Trousdell, was leaked to the press. The reports suggested that the nearly 4000-strong home service battalions of the Royal Irish Regiment (previously the Ulster Defence Regiment) should prepare for major reductions in the event of an 'act of completion'.[1] Under the normalisation programme outlined in one of the annexes to the Joint Declaration, the total number of servicemen would be reduced from the current 14,800 to 5000 troops by 2007, assuming republicans did what they were supposed to do. When the UUP leader discussed the matter of the RIR with British officials at the Hillsborough summit in March 2003, he understood that the permanent garrison of 5000 would be in addition to the home service RIR units. Coming on the heels of the Patten reforms to the RUC, the reports, if true, would have represented another great blow to the Province's pro-British population – depriving them of yet another legitimate outlet through which to express their patriotism.[2]

Whatever the Army's actual intentions, the political effects were obvious. The leaks gave a considerable boost to Donaldson's campaign to reject the Joint Declaration *tout court* at the next meeting of the UUC on 16 June, thus tying Trimble's hands completely. The UUP leader rapidly swung into action. After a testy encounter with Gen. Trousdell at Thiepval Barracks on 28 May, Trimble took his case to Jonathan Powell at Downing Street on 4 June: according to Trimble, No. 10 knew nothing of the leaked plans. The UUP leader also met with Geoff Hoon in the Ministry of Defence on 10 June and was critical of what he saw as the GOC's lack of political sensitivity to his own predicament; he was reassured and gratified when the Chief of the General Staff, Gen. Sir Michael Jackson, joined the meeting and recalled from his own service as a Colonel in Northern Ireland that some UDR part-timers were amongst the best soldiers he had ever met. 'I am one of the RIR's greatest fans,' declared 'Jacko'. Trimble thus obtained a reprieve of sorts for the home service battalions: Hoon's statement (which the UUP leader helped to amend) affirmed that no definite plans had been made regarding the long-term composition of the Army's garrison in Ulster. Trimble believed that the assurances were as good as could ever be obtained from the MoD on the future of any regiment.[3]

But Trimble's foes remained unimpressed – and the internal strife was redoubled. The UUP leader faced a motion of no confidence in his association in Upper Bann from 'antis', whilst Donaldson was faced with the prospect of a challenge by Trimble loyalists in Lagan Valley. Donaldson raised the temperature when he suggested that he might leave the party if he again lost in the UUC, describing the forthcoming meeting as a 'defining moment'.[4] Donaldson further suggested that a pan-unionist coalition be formed with the DUP as a precursor to a renegotiation of the Belfast Agreement. The present UUP leadership, he told Frank Millar in the *Irish Times* on 13 June 2003, cannot represent majority unionist opinion in any talks on the future of Northern Ireland. It was one of the first signs of how personalised the debate was to become: hitherto, at least, both men had been outwardly respectful towards each other and were even surprisingly quite generous towards each other in private (much to the irritation of some pro-Agreement elements, who had wanted the UUP leader to be much less forgiving). Indeed, as late as the end of 2002, Trimble spoke to me of the possibility of Donaldson eventually succeeding him – and did not seem horrified by the prospect.

All was now changed utterly. Trimble disliked bits of the Joint Declaration, yet he feared that wholesale rejection of the document would be a tactical mistake that would make the UUP appear unreasonable. He had set up party working groups to come up with responses to the Joint Declaration, but in his eyes Donaldson had jumped the gun by calling for another UUC. 'I couldn't be seen to be doing what Jeffrey dictated,' recalls Trimble. 'At the end of the day, it all came down to the question: are you with Trimble or Donaldson? All of these UUC meetings were, in one way or another, concealed leadership challenges.'[5] Moreover, a group of militantly pro-Agreement elements were starting to make their presence felt in the party. Men such as Bob Little, a prospective UUP

Assembly candidate for Strangford, were demanding that Trimble be more aggressive towards internal dissent. As David Campbell recalls, 'I had been defending DT against accusations that he had not been doing enough to deal with Jeffrey. For five years, these pro-Agreement people had been coming and organising for the leader at UUCs and were fed up with being on the defensive. And if the price of cleaning up the party and reconstructing it as a force of the centre ground were electoral setbacks in the near term, that was a risk that some of them were prepared to take.'[6] So despite the discovery of a 1200 lb bomb in Londonderry on the day before the UUC meeting, which Donaldson cited as evidence of the enduring paramilitary threat, Trimble won again by 440 votes to 369 (54%–46%). Significantly, one of the first callers after Trimble won was none other than Gerry Adams. If a split was avoided in the UUP, believed Trimble, it would make it likelier that the republicans would 'divvy up' on winding down paramilitarism. By this, he meant that the republicans would be much likelier to respond positively if they knew that Trimble had broken the cycle of challenges to his leadership and could deliver stable government.[7]

Donaldson was in doubt as to what the result meant. 'This leaves people like myself, and those who supported me, in a position where we have to decide if this party now represents what we believe in,' lamented the Lagan Valley MP. 'Does it represent the principles of unionism?'[8] But after considering his options, Donaldson decided not to leave the UUP altogether. Instead, along with his parliamentary colleagues David Burnside and Martin Smyth, he just resigned the UUP *whip* at Westminster on 23 June – leaving them with the option of carrying on the struggle inside the party. In consequence, with half its MPs gone, the UUP was no longer the fourth largest party at Westminster, but now was smaller than the DUP, the Scottish and Welsh Nationalists (indeed, the UUP was now the smallest party in the Commons, along with the SDLP).[9] The only leadership loyalists left were Trimble himself, Roy Beggs Sr and Lady Hermon. Trimble was especially angry with Smyth, who as party president oversaw the UUC meeting, and with Donaldson, a party vice president: the constitution of the UUP stated that officers must implement decisions of the UUC. Trimble also threw into doubt whether he would sign Burnside's and Donaldson's nomination papers for any forthcoming Assembly elections. 'Their press conference was like the launch of a manifesto in an election campaign,' recalls Trimble. 'It couldn't be ignored.'[10] Trimble called upon the UUP chairman, James Cooper, to convene a meeting of the party officers to deal with the whipless three. On 26 June, the 14-strong officer team voted by 5–2 to have the case of the whipless three referred to a disciplinary body chaired by a prominent Fermanagh Unionist, Raymond Ferguson. On the next day, the disciplinary committee informed the rebels that they were suspended, pending a hearing on 17 July. Donaldson denounced Ferguson as unsuitable, since the latter had spoken strongly against his position at the UUC, whilst Arlene Foster announced that she was resigning as a party officer.[11] But it was not just the 'antis' who were concerned: some of those who were normally Trimble stalwarts in the centre ground of the party believed that with such narrow margins in the UUC, the leader was in no position to engage in high-handed actions against the rebellious faction. Indeed, Frank Millar was told by these erstwhile supporters that they would vote against action when the matter was scheduled for a final decision at the Ulster Unionist Executive in September.[12] Others were surprisingly equivocal. Thus, James Nicholson, MEP, a party vice president, told the *Irish Times* when asked whether he would support Trimble that 'as far as I am concerned at this stage I am making no comment. Things are at such a fluid state in the party after what has happened it would do well for many people in the party to step back and reflect on what the situation is.' And when asked if Trimble should consider his position as leader, Nicholson remarked: 'It is too early to look at that. He has just come through and did win another situation in the UUC. We have to wait and see what plays out.'[13]

The whipless three soon hit back, and on 3 July began legal proceedings to overturn their suspension. On 7 July, Mr Justice Girvan ruled that the moves against the trio were unlawful. The disciplinary committee had not been properly constituted and Trimble himself was rebuked for voting since he was not technically an officer of the party.[14] It was a grave blow: as Trimble later observed, 'The UUP shambles hurt us – we had tried to do something and we had failed.'[15] The internal crisis also put on hold any serious negotiation with Sinn Fein to re-establish the institutions until at least September, though Trimble continued to meet with Adams throughout this period. On 8 July, Trimble survived a motion of no confidence in Upper Bann, but with 69 out of 184 voting against him (or 37.5% of the total).[16] Even George Savage, a long-time supporter of Trimble and his Assembly colleague, declined to say in a media interview before the meeting if he was supporting the leader.[17] On 11 July, the UUP officers met for two and a half hours and this time, by a 6–3 margin, opted to reconvene a new disciplinary panel; significantly, Empey abstained.[18] Though he disagreed with what Donaldson was doing, Empey felt that it was a huge strategic error to let the crisis drift to the point where the Lagan Valley MP might leave the party and was soon conducting a 'peace process' with another party officer, Jim Rodgers, designed to heal the internal divide between the factions. The peace process was launched without Trimble's approval; according to Empey, Trimble did not try to stop him from launching this initiative, but concedes that the UUP leader became increasingly sceptical of the exercise.[19] Trimble now believes that one of the key planks of any such reconciliation could only be his own head, though Rodgers denies absolutely that this was the purpose or the effect of the exercise.[20] The 'peace process' was eventually suspended after Donaldson supporters put in a requisition for another UUC meeting to overturn the disciplinary proceedings. The meeting was scheduled for 6 September; it would be the 13th such gathering since the Belfast Agreement of 1998.[21]

Trimble had been keen for the Commons legislation on his cherished International Monitoring Commission (IMC), to adjudicate on paramilitarism, to be published before 6 September: he had been working with the British Government to ensure that there were safeguards against the Irish Republic's nominee to the body enjoying a say on the internal governance of Northern Ireland. Maintaining this 'line in the sand' over Strand I was critical to John Taylor, who pronounced that the draft Bill as originally constituted failed to do so.[22] Trimble believed that he had managed to tidy up the legislation and was pleased with the nominees to the body – who included John Grieve, a former commander of the Metropolitan Police's anti-terrorist squad. Grieve had played a key part in catching the Docklands bombers and was a great admirer of the RUC and its last Chief Constable, Sir Ronnie Flanagan. The Government regarded the IMC as central to Trimble's willingness to re-engage with Sinn Fein; but given the atmosphere which then obtained within the UUP, it was of little immediate use to the embattled Ulster Unionist leader.[23] In the event, the IMC turned out to be an electoral irrelevance for Trimble – neither an asset nor a liability.

By the eve of the UUC, Trimble's thoughts were a long way from the minutiae of legislative draftsmanship. That night, on 5 September, UTV reported that under the cover of the internal 'peace process', Empey and

Donaldson had agreed that the current leadership had to be replaced.[24] Empey says that he and Donaldson never agreed anything, let alone the question of leadership posts.[25] Many Trimbleistas were shocked. 'Things can never be the same between Empey and us again,' recalls David Campbell. 'We were really good friends. He always spoke for the leader and that disappeared overnight. He can no longer be trusted.' The two men subsequently also exchanged a heartfelt correspondence.[26] Empey responds: 'It's sad that people have got themselves into a laager mentality about an individual person. It's nothing to do with policy, it's about management of the party.' But Empey told another associate, 'Nobody has shovelled more shit for Trimble than me – and on £240 a month!'[27] Nor did John Taylor ride to the rescue on this occasion, believing that disciplinary action would only create greater division.[28] But when the votes were counted, these 'big beasts' seemed to count for little: Trimble's majority had gone up to 443–359, or 55.2% to 44.8%. Significantly, Donaldson was heckled for the first time.[29] 'At the September 2003 UUC, the hostility to Jeffrey outstripped the hostility to DT – and that's saying something!' recalls David Brewster. 'If you lose again and again you wonder: can I go on?'[30] Empey did not speak that day: he says he decided to take a vow of silence, like his fellow mediator in the internal 'peace process', Jim Rodgers.[31]

The better-than-expected result proved to the British and Irish states – and to Gerry Adams – that Trimble was still an *interlocuteur valable*. As Powell had observed to him when they met at No. 10 on 1 July, 'If things go the right way, you could actually clean up the party and make real progress.' In fact, a kind of stalemate obtained between the factions: as Trimble observes, Donaldson could not beat him in the UUC, but nor, under these circumstances, could he expel Donaldson once and for all.[32] However, far from encouraging him to put party first and to bind the wounds within his own community – along the lines suggested by Frank Millar in the *Irish Times* on 8 September – the stalemate actually encouraged him to take a new risk. Rather than sticking rigidly to the position of no Assembly elections without a republican 'act of completion', Trimble decided instead to enter another negotiation with the republicans. He would place his chips on a final, grand attempt to negotiate all-round 'acts of completion'. 'What's the point of securing another postponement of the election if the result is another six months of these people taking pops at me?' asked Trimble. 'I'd got no credit for the efforts I'd made in exposing republicans.'[33] Whilst some colleagues thought that the UUP would be better off fighting an election with no deal, Trimble disagreed – especially after the internal feuds of the summer.[34] Indeed, having obtained a republican 'act of completion', Trimble's intention was to write a UUP manifesto for the Assembly elections that was so explicit about re-establishing the Executive as to force Donaldson et al. either to buckle down or else to rebel again (under which circumstances Trimble would have used his legal powers as nominating officer under the Northern Ireland Act 1998 to deny the 'antis' the party label).[35] Thus, in one bound he would be free of his detractors.

Trimble had other reasons for considering renewed talk of Assembly elections even before the republicans had moved. First, he received word from a highly reliable journalistic source who was telling him that the Government was planning to resile from its own position of 1 May delaying the poll and to grant an election – the very same source who had correctly predicted the earlier postponement. 'If I'd sat back and done nothing and said, "I'm sticking to my demands for completion", there's a serious danger that I would have been seen as being in default and then I was fighting on a terrain that was indistinguishable from the DUP,' recalls Trimble. 'And, I had to ask myself: were things going to get any better for me if I stood still? If I continued to delay the elections, it would appear as if the Ulster Unionists were afraid of seeking the opinion of the voters. It already looked to loads of nationalists as if the whole thing was a "save Dave" campaign. And without elections, the Government would find it increasingly hard to maintain the existing institutions, which were being kept on ice, albeit on reduced salaries. It was becoming ever more difficult to sustain things and the Assembly was starting to resemble the Long Parliament [which sat in the era of the English Civil War and Commonwealth, from 1640–60].[36] Second, Trimble was profoundly affected by the quiet on the key sectarian interfaces that summer – which made the 2003 marching season the most peaceful in years. He partly credited this outcome to the impending arrival of the IMC, but he also knew that it owed much to the entirely separate meetings which were held between a UUP delegation (including himself, Fred Cobain and Reg Empey) and Sinn Fein at a Redemptorist retreat called St Clement's on the Antrim Road (other individuals were also present). As Trimble saw it, Adams had gone out of his way to help ensure that republicans complied with the proscription of the kind of activity described in paragraph

13 of the Joint Declaration. If republicans could show that they were willing to make a real difference on the ground, reasoned Trimble, they were clearly in the market for some deal. Indeed, he told Jonathan Powell at No. 10 on 21 May that he had said as much to Adams. So impressed was he that towards the end of the summer, when it was clear that all had gone well, he shook the Sinn Fein President's hand for the first time.[37]

The quiet on the interfaces had an even greater effect upon the two Governments. 'The summer could have been very nasty,' notes one No. 10 official. 'But the positive outcome certainly weighed heavily with Blair and with Jonathan Powell'[38] (later, Trimble would lament that Government gave the republicans their much-sought-after election for so little in the way of 'acts of completion'; however, as has been noted, he himself was part of the process whereby the republicans were able to set up the issue of interfaces as a key criterion for their good faith). Ministers also noted that with the exception of some intra-communal 'civil adminis-tration' – as exemplified by the Provisionals' suspected role in the murder of the dissident south Armagh republican Gareth O'Connor – the level of paramilitary activity was as low as it had been in years.[39] Nor was the Government unduly distressed by allegations by the Chief Constable of the PSNI, Hugh Orde, that elements of the Provisional IRA had been engaged in intimidation of nationalist members of the District Policing Partnership Board in Cookstown, Co. Tyrone (allegations denied by Martin McGuinness).[40] After all, the NIO argued, Orde was the first Chief Constable since the Troubles began not to have to bury one of his officers who had been murdered. And one minister posed a philosophical ques-tion: if Italian democracy could survive the presence in government of the mafia in the person of Giulio Andreotti, why could Northern Ireland not survive the presence in the Executive of the political wing of the IRA?[41]

But there was still the problem of squaring such approaches with Blair's public pronouncements on ending paramilitarism, as embodied in paragraph 13 of the intergovernmental Joint Declaration of 1 May. 'No. 10 came to conclude that if we were looking for a black-and-white statement from republicans that "the war is over" we weren't going to get it,' recalls one official. 'We had made our point through postponement and it was now a law of diminishing returns. We were trying to strike a balance between literal-minded Prods and republicans who can't say explicitly that they are surrendering. The question then was: how do we try and re-create the same reality [that is, Blair's October 2002 speech and paragraph 13] in less direct language that republicans can live with. Adams and McGuinness couldn't sell paragraph 13 to their grassroots. Were they ready to say what had to be said in as plain a language as we would wish? No. Were they ready to try? Yes. And they did.' Irish officials also came to the conclusion that if Adams and McGuinness were asked to fulfil the very words of paragraph 13, then they would have to take the matter to an IRA Army Convention, where the Sinn Fein leadership was likely to lose. Senior civil servants in both states, and their political masters, came to believe that if there was no political movement in the autumn, and the Assembly elections were postponed again, it would 'semi-automatically' bring about the demise of the Belfast Agreement. And the slide from the clarity of Blair's position of October 2002 and May 2003 was further helped by what one senior civil servant described as 'the Prime Minister's utter lack of embarrassment over inconsistency'. The Harbour Commissioner's address thus became an ideal, an aspiration, the manner and timing of which could be refined according to the needs of the moment. And the particular need of the moment was the republican movement's unequivocal message to both Governments that they would only begin to 'show the colour of their money' once they had a guarantee that Assembly elections would be held.

Other, still more prosaic calculations impelled the Government towards the granting of an election. The emollient Ulster Secretary, Paul Murphy, was terrified of having to stand up in the Commons and defy the opinion of all the Northern Ireland parties (barring the UUP leadership) and the Tories and Liberal Democrats to renew the postponement for a further six months under the 'sunset clause' of the relevant legislation. Most unexpected was the behaviour of the Conservative Party: far from supporting Trimble and Blair over the 1 May postponement, its eccentric and prolix Northern Ireland spokesman, Quentin Davies, attacked the decision as an 'abomination' and a denial of democracy.[42] Thus, instead of providing Trimble with supporting fire, as it had done for much of the time in the previous Parliament, the Tories were now effectively siding against him and with the DUP and Sinn Fein. And the then Tory leader, Iain Duncan Smith, declined to rein Davies in: although Davies was from the Europhile wing of the party, he was one of the most ardent supporters of his increasingly embattled chief.[43] The lack of Tory backing for postponement mattered to a Government that tried to maintain bi-partisan support for key decisions, and thus removed a further potential restraint for resuming the push towards elections. And, as before, the US Administration in the person of Richard Haass was at best sceptical on the postponement of the elections. Thus, Trimble and the British Government were without two potential allies whose support they might reasonably have expected. In Haass's case, it was because he was convinced that the logic of the process was leading to DUP–Sinn Fein hegemony: why delay the inevitable, especially when Haass believed that both of sets of hardliners were now prepared to operate the new institutions? British officials were anxious not to offend Haass, though they subsequently acknowledged that they had over-estimated Haass's importance in the scheme of things: he had not come out on top in key Washington policy debates and duly departed for the presidency of the Council on Foreign Relations in 2003. A telephone call from Blair's foreign policy adviser, Sir David Manning, to Condoleezza Rice would certainly have been enough to stop Haass pushing the idea of an election, but no such call was ever made. No 10 obviously preferred to expend valuable credit with the US Administration on obtaining support for such cherished initiatives as the Middle East Road Map than on shoring up the UUP leader. And Paul Bew recalls that such was the fastidious disdain of key British diplomats in Washington for prominent Administration neo-conservatives that UK diplomats never rallied those figures who might have been most inclined to restrain Haass.[44] So supporting Trimble came at a considerable price and in any case, ministers believed, they had already given him quite enough help – not just by postponing the election but also by putting anti-electoral fraud measures and the IMC on to the statute book. As one minister recalled, 'Postponing elections was rather like the left's argument against One Member One Vote [OMOV] in the 1980s. Every time they argued against it, their reasoning looked thinner.' In fact, the keenest demands for Assembly elections came largely from the Northern Ireland political classes whom the Government were so anxious to sustain by paying part of their salaries. By contrast, polling evidence showed that a substantial majority of Protestants supported postponement in May 2003 and opposed the calling of the poll in November.[45]

But even if the worst came to the worst and the DUP triumphed, asked many in the NIO at both the political and official level, was it such a catastrophe? As they saw it, there were further signs of change in the DUP, exemplified by Gregory Campbell's speech at the West Belfast Festival.

Of course, he was there to 'confront' the nationalist audience, just as Trimbleistas had done some years before when they started appearing on television programmes to debate with republicans: but, as has been noted, the really crucial point to the Government was that such encounters were taking place at all. Aspects of the DUP's programme were perfectly tolerable and worthy as far as the British state was concerned, exemplified by Sammy Wilson's call for reducing the bloated size of the Office of First and Deputy First Ministers.[46] And the Government would have known that at the fringes of the DUP there were one or two well-connected figures who believed – as one told me – that 'Trimble sold the pass and administered the death blow to the Union. All that remains is for us to go in and to negotiate a Protestant homeland within a united Ireland on as advantageous a basis as possible.'[47] All in all, many in the Government concluded that the DUP was a very different organisation from the party which had helped bring down the Sunningdale accord in the UWC strike of 1974. After all, even Paisley had been down to Government Buildings in Dublin, albeit in his capacity as head of the Free Presbyterian Church rather than as DUP leader. As one wag on the Shankill put it, it was 'easier to get shit off a woollen blanket than the DUP out of Stormont'.[48]

Blair himself carried no such torch for the DUP. He did not want an election for its own sake – 'to process' or a review of the Belfast Agreement – but rather one that was part of an overall understanding between the UUP and Sinn Fein that would lead to the re-creation of the Executive. To that end, both Governments refined their negotiating strategy. They concluded from the failed talks of March/April/May that they had 'micro-managed' things excessively. Much better, it was decided, to let Trimble and Adams sort things out between them and then to give them such support as they needed. Inevitably, though, the two Governments were an integral part of the process from the outset, and they defined its parameters. Thus, Blair met with Adams on 3 September at No. 10, during the course of which the Sinn Fein president again told the Prime Minister that he required 'certainty' on an election date for his own people before he could move; Blair was not yet willing to name a date, but for the first time affirmed that he had made his mind up in principle that there should be an election in the context of an overall deal with the UUP. He was '95% certain' that it would be this year, probably with November as the preferred date. But as Adams told him, 'We can't go back to our people with 95%.'[49] Adams' pressure worked, for by the time that Jonathan Powell and senior Irish officials met with a Sinn Fein delegation on 11 September at Windsor House in Belfast, the two Governments were willing to give the republicans greater 'clarity'. Sinn Fein received a statement in writing from the British side committing London to an election before the end of the year, with 4 December as the last practical date. Significantly, the British made a further commitment that once the election date was announced, it would not be postponed again. But Adams was not yet fully appeased: unless there was an absolute commitment to an election, he could not go back to the republican movement and ask them to release a new draft statement to No. 10. Adams also gave Trimble much the same message: he had been rebuked by the IRA and needed further guarantees.[50] On 13 September, Ahern visited Blair at Chequers after watching his beloved Manchester United defeat Charlton Athletic two-nil away at The Valley: for the first time, Blair gave the Irish a written commitment to hold an election and, in turn, he received the first form of words from republicans. But the latter was a disappointment and represented no improvement on the formula of that April. Trimble, though, was not to be deterred: he told the Taoiseach when they met at Government Buildings in Dublin on 15 September that it was in the IRA's interest to do a proper 'act of completion' so that the Ulster Unionists could go into the election with a positive manifesto. And the two men further agreed that 25 November was the last viable date for elections that year.[51] Ahern was particularly keen to refute suggestions that he wanted the election postponed to coincide with the European poll in June 2004: there had been some talk that Fianna Fail wanted to stretch Sinn Fein by holding elections on both sides of the border on the same day.

Certainly, the UUP–Sinn Fein dialogue that autumn appeared to be of unparalleled intensity – although, as Gerry Adams recalls, the discussions earlier in the summer concerning the interfaces were probably of even greater significance in the apparent building of trust between the two sides.[52] The discussions were wide-ranging: Adams wanted the devolution of policing and criminal justice within six months of an election, whereas Trimble wanted Sinn Fein first to endorse the PSNI by coming on the Policing Board and only then to devolve security powers. Anyhow, said the UUP leader, nothing could be contemplated without clear 'acts of completion'. To advance the process, they agreed on the creation of joint

UUP–Sinn Fein working parties on these matters. Above all, the UUP leader made clear from early on that the *visibility* of decommissioning would be critical to his ability to sell the deal to his own people: indeed, according to Trimble, Adams appeared to understand this point when they met at Stormont on 18 September. Trimble had long since abandoned disbandment of the IRA as an immediate demand and even accepted that there could be 'no Spielbergs', as republicans put it (that is, filmed decommissioning), but he thought his bottom line was clear.[53] Blair also made his demands clear: in a telephone conversation with Adams on 23 September, he emphasised that the Sinn Fein leader's words had to be endorsed by the IRA and they had to find a form of words that would effectively mean the same thing as paragraph 13 of the Joint Declaration. But critically, he added: 'Of course, you can stick to your position that you don't endorse the Joint Declaration in full – for instance that you don't accept the Monitoring Commission – but you must refer to activities that will stop. You can list them or refer to them, but it can't mean a narrower list.' Adams said that he would discuss this with Trimble – and if the UUP leader could agree to it, that was fine as far as the British were concerned.

But the task of dragging the necessary words out of Sinn Fein was arduous – even for the two Governments. After receiving multiple drafts and forms of language from such leading republicans as Leo Green and Ted Howell, the British and Irish reconvened with a Sinn Fein delegation on 1 October in the Cabinet Room at No. 10. There were some positive developments, such as the IRA's commitment to endorse Adams' words in his capacity as Sinn Fein president. But on paragraph 13, the outcome was still way short of the mark: the IRA leadership was only prepared to state that it would accept that it should not authorise any activity that was inconsistent with a successful outcome of the peace process. At one point, Powell had a shouting match with Adams, declaring that the republicans' wording was not up to the mark on an end of paramilitarism; matters became so heated that it became necessary to take a break. Later that day, a UUP delegation also met with Powell and NIO officials. The Prime Minister's chief of staff told Trimble that Adams would give him more words concerning an end to paramilitarism when they met at Hillsborough on the following weekend. 'We think they're on the cusp of getting that,' Powell reassured the UUP leader. Trimble said that he would rewrite the Adams statement and give Powell a copy. And he added that he, too, believed that Adams intended to have his words endorsed by the IRA as part of a sequence of events, including the announcement of an election. IRA action on arms would be very substantial, Trimble predicted, with de Chastelain being able to say what he wanted about the next decommissioning act. But once again, Trimble said that he needed transparency, adding: 'Seeing is believing.' If the transparent act could not be in pictures, then at least it would have to be verified by independent assessors such as church leaders (both of these ideas would, however, be vetoed by the Provisionals).[54]

The tempo increased further in the coming days. On 4 October, Ahern and Blair met in the margins of the EU summit in Rome after the 'family photo' of the heads of Government. The Irish sensed that the British were becoming very impatient with Sinn Fein and the two men duly resolved to send a joint Anglo-Irish letter to the republicans, signed by both of them, setting out their requirement for an end to paramilitarism. In addition to a public statement, the IRA would also be expected to perform certain private actions, such as instructions to the 'volunteers' – instructions that were never sent. Trimble and Michael McGimpsey (who was rapidly emerging as one of the UUP leader's favourite colleagues as Reg Empey appeared to fade out of the picture) met with Adams and McGuinness on the weekend of 4/5 October at Hillsborough and again at Stormont on 7 October. On Friday 10 October, Powell rang David Campbell to say that decommissioning had been 'all set up'. The arms issue was becoming even more important as time went on, since Trimble now feared that the republicans would use language that was incomprehensible to the ordinary unionists. If saying 'the war is over' proved theologically impossible, then the UUP leader would need some 'collateral'. But how much would he receive of that?

Trimble resumed the search for answers on the weekend of 11/12 October at Hillsborough. The two Governments were sufficiently impressed by the progress made to turn a heads-of-Government meeting into a round-table of all of the key parties at No. 10 on Monday 13 October (the exclusion of the SDLP greatly annoyed its leader Mark Durkan, and appeared to set the seal on the party's irrelevance).[55] Indeed, on Sunday 12 October, Adams had assured the Irish Government that all was going well on the issue of decommissioning. But in the first meeting at 10:30 a.m., the UUP leader expressed unhappiness with the draft text which, he asserted, lacked clarity. Moreover, Trimble said that whilst Sinn

Fein were telling the UUP that there would be greater transparency in the expected third decommissioning act, journalists were now informing the UUP that republicans were telling their own supporters at the grassroots that there would be no such visibility. 'What could you live with?' asked Ahern. 'De Chastelain needs to be as open as possible,' replied Trimble. 'Yes,' chimed in Blair. 'De Chastelain has to say what he has seen.' And Trimble replied: 'De Chastelain needs to be really tough with them. We need visibility and a clear timetable to completion.' 'That's fair,' concluded Ahern. At 12:30 p.m., the UUP obtained sight of the revised Adams statement and its endorsement by the IRA: in Trimble's view, the IRA pronouncement was sufficient. Bilaterals between the Governments and Sinn Fein were followed by bilaterals between the UUP and Sinn Fein; the former were placed in the Terracotta Room on the first floor overlooking Horse Guards, whilst the latter were placed in the first-floor study (with the White Room as 'no man's land'). At one point, the double doors opened and the Sinn Fein delegation burst into the UUP room. 'There was Gerry Adams doing his cheeky chappy routine, ostensibly friendly. I didn't really want to talk to him about politics at this moment. So I was delighted to give the republicans an impromptu guided tour of the pictures – and took particular delight in pointing out the site of the portrait of a girl on a tricycle by Sir John Lavery. And of course the sub-text of my remarks was, "Here's a good Belfast Catholic who ended up a happy member of the British establishment."'[56] Alex Maskey, who had recently concluded his term as the first Sinn Fein Lord Mayor of Belfast, soon joined them. 'David left his colleagues and started explaining about the paintings – the Lavery, and some Lord I had never heard of before,' recalls the veteran republican. 'And I thought to myself: "This is surreal. Here we are in the middle of a really high stakes negotiation and here we are getting a guided tour of No. 10 from David Trimble!" It was quite unexpected because David can be very formalised at times, perhaps stuffy, and you can see him at a meeting and then he can pass you in the corridor and say nothing. It's as though he's insecure, though he's not. But he also can go off at tangents, particularly when he's feeling comfortable, and he certainly felt comfortable in London that day – perhaps more so than in Belfast. And that day in London, we could all do with a bit of light relief.'[57] At the final meeting, Blair told the UUP that he believed that the republicans really wanted a deal. If so, a sequence of events would start on Monday 20 October. The sequence would comprise, in no particular order, the announcement of the election; a decommissioning act; an Adams statement endorsed by the IRA; a pronouncement by Trimble reaffirming his commitment to stable Northern Ireland institutions; and remarks by the two heads of Government. 'We need, though, to tie up the language,' concluded the Prime Minister. 'And de Chastelain's report will have to be credible.' 'Yes,' replied Trimble. 'And we need both him and you to prescribe a timetable for completion.'

Trimble was sufficiently reassured by what he heard at the Downing Street summit to inform the UUP Assembly group at Stormont on the next day that Sinn Fein were keen to do the deal and that for the first time he saw it as 'game on'. There would, he said, be a statement on the IRA's future as well as decommissioning now and a timetable for further acts. Or, as Trimble told Frank Millar on Thursday 16 October, 'You will see a quantum leap beyond [the IRA statement of] April.' And, after a pause, he added, 'Yes, it is enough, though I will need some commentary as well' (that is, a credible gloss from all the parties concerned).[58] On Tuesday 14 October, de Chastelain returned to Belfast and at 4:30 p.m. met at his headquarters at Rosepark House with an Ulster Unionist delegation composed of Alan McFarland, Michael McGimpsey and David McNarry.[59] The UUP team made it clear that the timetable for completion was crucial. Moreover, the deal could only work if it 'sold itself': in other words, that the act of decommissioning would have to be utterly transparent to the unionist population. 'If there's no visibility here, you might as well tell the Provisionals not to do it,' concluded Michael McGimpsey. De Chastelain, the UUP believed, had taken on board their concerns.[60] British officials say that they also emphasised to de Chastelain the need for transparency in this period – particularly since they were aware that since 2001 the General had a private confidentiality agreement with the Provisionals concerning how much he could say (when a revised decommissioning scheme gave him extra latitude).[61] Still, no serious alarm bells rang and the British and Irish aver that as long as the UUP and Sinn Fein appeared to be making progress on other fronts, they had no reason to interfere. The two Governments were especially impressed with the emerging understanding on the Q&A session for the day the sequence would be run. The UUP had been particularly concerned about how the deal would be presented, especially since they knew that Adams' text was going to fall short of their original aspirations: they feared that some Provisionals might be inclined to minimise the significance of the Sinn

Fein statement in an attempt to reassure their grassroots, and thus make it harder to sell to the unionists.

A working group was duly set up comprising Alan McFarland, Michael McGimpsey and Mark Neale on the UUP side, and with Leo Green, Aidan McAteer and Richard McAuley on the Sinn Fein side. Meeting Green was always difficult for Mark Neale: Green had been convicted of the murder of a family friend, RUC Inspector Harry Cobb (some time earlier, Neale was walking with his 8-year-old daughter in a Craigavon supermarket and ran into Green. 'Who was that man?' asked the child. 'That man murdered a friend of your daddy,' replied Neale. The girl simply could not comprehend why Green was not still in prison).[62] But the two men now had business to do. The UUP were particularly interested in answers to potential questions to Adams following his statement, such as 'Does it mean that the war is over?' and 'Does it mean that paramilitarism is over?' It was a good way to test Sinn Fein's bona fides, since if they equivocated or said no in those sessions, there was no point in proceeding with the sequence. The groups met at Stormont on Friday 17 October and Monday 20 October, and at Hillsborough on Sunday 19 October. The UUP were satisfied with some of the republicans' answers. Thus, on the issue of a total end to punishment beatings and exilings, the planned answer for Adams was, 'I do not want to see anything which in any way undermines the peace process. Today's initiative shows that the IRA supports the peace process and they want full and immediate implementation of the Good Friday Agreement in all its aspects and they are determined that their strategies and actions are consistent with this objective.' On whether the statement fulfilled the two heads of Governments' demands on paragraph 13 of the Joint Declaration, the Sinn Fein president would reply: 'You need to put that question to the British Prime Minister . . . actions on the ground speak louder than words.' On the question of whether the IRA's weapons would now be put beyond use, the UUP accepted that 'the issue of weapons is for the IICD [the de Chastelain body] and the armed groups. Sinn Fein wants to see all the guns taken out of Irish society.' At one point, the republicans sought to have a reference to 'unionist guns' included; the UUP said no, and substituted 'loyalist guns' instead.[63] Negotiations also continued on a statement that Trimble would have to issue to show to republicans that he had 'crossed the Rubicon' and was genuinely committed to inclusive government, to 'equality' and a range of other measures. Sinn Fein sought, *inter alia*, an Irish language commission; a commitment to erode differentials between Catholic and Protestant unemployment in a measurable way; a subcommittee of the Northern Ireland Executive to monitor the sensitive use of symbols; and the establishment of a North-South inter-parliamentary forum. Trimble was prepared to give them much of it (barring the Irish language commission) because he thought it largely 'guff' and verbiage. In other words, it was a price well worth paying to secure the big prize – an end to republican paramilitarism.

But by Friday 17 October – the eve of the UUP's annual conference in Armagh City – Trimble found himself profoundly depressed. As he looked at the papers strewn over the hotel bed, he realised he did not have enough. In particular, Blair's draft statement was woefully lacking in substance, notably on holding republicans to a timetable to wind down the IRA. And it was also increasingly clear to him that for all his words on Monday 13 October at No. 10, Blair had not done enough to urge upon de Chastelain the kind of transparency that the UUP leader needed. Indeed, he told Paul Bew on the morning ot Saturday 18 October that 'the nature of the IRA's endorsement of peaceful means is unclear, as I feared'.[64] On the next day, from the hotel car park, he telephoned Adams to say that the republicans were still not in the right terrain – though his conference speech was emollient enough.[65] By the time the two delegations met again at Hillsborough on Sunday 19 October, Trimble felt that he had to take decisive action. This is how an internal UUP paper summarised the position at midday:

1. Settle IRA statement with Adams and McGuinness.
2. Settle Ulster Unionist and Sinn Fein statement with Sinn Fein.
3. Dissatisfied with draft government statements – too bland, needs more substance (needs to include paragraph 13 and decommissioning of all weapons . . .).
4. Need to see and have assurances regarding the content of the Secretary of State's statement to the Commons and the Q&A. The issues covered there are:
   – paragraph 13 reiterated
   – timetable for decommissioning
   – monitoring – robust, immediate continuing look at all criminality by paramilitaries
   – De Chastelain – transparency, verification, timetables, openness

At lunchtime, the UUP faxed a memorandum to de Chastelain, starting with the sentence: 'Transparency is absolutely vital so that unionist support can be carried; a picture is worth a thousand words. If the IICD's statement was along the same lines as previous acts of putting weapons "beyond use", then the UUP would not be able to proceed even if other elements (IRA, government statements) were satisfactory. Unionists require the maximum possible transparency. The IICD's statement should include an inventory, both from past and present acts, as well as qualitative assessment of their ordnance; its age, condition and effectiveness . . . It must also dispel the suspicion that materials decommissioned were old, rusty or unusable. Moreover, the statement should include confirmation of the timing of the most recent act of decommissioning . . .' De Chastelain received this memo on the Sunday; the UUP received no reply, but de Chastelain says that it was his understanding that no reply was needed.[66] Trimble realised he would also have to mobilise Blair. He wrote a memorandum to Jonathan Powell in which he told the No. 10 chief of staff that he expected to see elements of paragraph 13 reiterated in the Government statement, with particular emphasis given to the words calling for an immediate, full and permanent cessation of all paramilitary activity. He duly attached the memo to de Chastelain, and reaffirmed the UUP's need for a timescale for all acts of completion, including decommissioning. He drew attention to paragraph 14 of the Joint Declaration on decommissioning, stating that the IICD had been too reluctant to impose a timetable on disarmament: he wanted completion sooner than the earliest timescale for devolution of policing and justice. Trimble also sought further guarantees that if the IRA did carry out further activities forbidden under paragraph 13, then Sinn Fein ministers would be excluded from office; that the IMC investigate Castlereagh; and assurances that the standards for entry into the PSNI would not be reduced to admit ex-prisoners into the force and that criminal records of convicted terrorists not be expunged. The memorandum was faxed to Powell at 4 p.m., but Trimble could not raise him: Blair had his heart flutter that day and had gone to hospital and he understood that the Downing Street aide had gone with him (in fact, contrary to what the UUP leader believed, Powell had not gone to the hospital but was working from home, not least contacting de Chastelain).[67] As Trimble saw it, critical hours in the attempt to set things right were thus lost. But he also spent much of the afternoon taking Reg Empey through the text of the Adams statement: his former ministerial colleague was back on board for the first time since the current round of UUP–Sinn Fein talks began.[68]

Shortly before Trimble commenced the concluding sessions with Sinn Fein, the UUP leader reviewed his progress that day: the British statement was inadequate; Blair was unavailable; and he had endured a fraught party conference, with Donaldson criticising him in the margins. Trimble duly told Adams – who had left with McGuinness in the late morning for a meeting with the IRA in the 'field' to arrange the decommissioning act and had only just returned to Hillsborough – that he needed more time to sort things out with the British. It would probably require a 24-hour delay in running the sequence that was originally due to run from the time de Chastelain disappeared to begin his inspections on the night of Sunday 19 October through Monday 20 October. Adams was shocked. 'I played for time,' states Trimble. 'It caused huge problems for the republicans, who were already proceeding with the decommissioning act. I told Adams, "I'm not ready to roll on Monday."' The two men then spoke from Hillsborough in a four-way conference call with Powell and Michael Collins, second secretary-general of the Taoiseach's Department and a former ambassador to the Czech Republic. Adams agreed to go ahead – provided that the UUP stuck to the sequence. As Trimble understood it, the plan was that the decommissioning would still take place on Monday 20 October, but would now be announced along with the rest of the sequence on Tuesday 21 October.[69] In any case, the republicans were also having their own technical problems with the decommissioning act, so a day's delay suited them, too. And it suited the British as well: one senior UUP figure claims to have been told authoritatively that Blair was advised not to fly on Monday 20 October, but rather to wait until Tuesday 21 October (though Government officials vehemently deny that the Prime Minister's health had anything to do with the temporary postponement).

Trimble met again with the Ulster Unionist Assembly group on the morning of Monday 20 October: he predicted 'helicopters on the lawn' from the two heads of Government on the next day, but was not notably pessimistic in this forum. In fact, the most memorable bit of the session came when Dr Ian Adamson, the outgoing Assemblyman for East Belfast, drew beautiful diagrams of the human heart to illustrate Blair's aortal fibrillations.[70] Later that day, Trimble received a reply to his *aide-mémoire* to Powell from Paul Murphy: it gave assurances of sorts to all of his queries (on Castlereagh and Stormontgate, for instance, the Ulster Secretary's letter stated that these were matters for the police and the courts and that 'in similar cases *in future* [author's emphasis] it would depend, in the first instance, on any recommendations from the IMC'. But the Murphy letter omitted the issue of decommissioning. It was, Trimble recalls, extremely difficult to obtain a response from No. 10 on decommissioning that day, but he did receive some text of what Blair might say. As so often before, that would only be finalised on the flight over to Belfast.[71] By now, Ahern was also worried about again investing his prestige in an abortive venture. After telephoning Blair that morning to wish him well, the Taoiseach proposed that the two men make a joint call to de Chastelain at around 6:30 p.m. Tim Dalton, Secretary-General of the Irish Department of Justice, called de Chastelain in mid-morning to inquire whether he could be descriptive on the contents of the decommissioning act. 'I have no indications that I can,' replied de Chastelain. 'I will be going away shortly and I will be off-line.' By 5 p.m., Ahern had repaired with key officials to his constituency office at St Luke's in Drumcondra. The Irish aides liaised constantly with Jonathan Powell and the No. 10 switchboard until 11:30 p.m., but to no avail: de Chastelain had turned off his mobile by Monday night at the insistence of the IRA, who did not want him to be traceable as he inspected the destruction of the arms dumps.[72] What appears to have happened was that once Trimble delayed the sequence, to the irritation of the republicans, the IRA decided to delay the decommissioning act until such time as they were certain the election would be announced. To quicken that process, the British were willing at one point to announce the holding of the election at 10 p.m. on Monday 20 October. But Trimble soon learned of this plan and contacted Powell. Powell said that the announcement was for the next day's newspapers; the UUP leader replied this was not realistic, since the announcement would run immediately on the Northern Ireland bulletins. Moreover, if there was a substantial gap between the declaration of the election and the decommissioning, it would appear to unionists as if the IRA had called the tune rather than as part of a pre-arranged choreography of equals carried out on a very tight timeframe. Powell accepted the point, and this part of the revised sequence ran according to schedule.[73]

Thus it was that Trimble embarked upon what he had earlier described to Sean O'Callaghan as 'the biggest gamble I've ever taken'.[74] Although he had far less certainty than he would have wished, and by the morning of Tuesday 21 October believed that No. 10 had done too little work to retrieve the situation because of Blair's health scare, he still felt that he could not 'pull the plug' at this stage. 'There's a world of difference between unease and knowing it will be wrong,' says Trimble.[75] Shortly before 7 a.m. on Tuesday 21 October, Jonathan Powell spoke to Michael Collins of the Taoiseach's Department. Even now, neither Government could reach de Chastelain. Should they go ahead with the announcement of the election, scheduled for 7 a.m.? They took the view that the election was now an irreversible part of the 'choreography'; Powell would also have been well aware that at Windsor House in Belfast on 11 September his side had given the republicans guarantees about holding the elections whatever happened once they were announced. It was accordingly announced that the poll would be held on Wednesday 26 November, despite the fact that no one knew for sure what the IRA had done. There was thus a slight feel of A.J.P. Taylor's 'war by timetable' to the day's events: nobody felt they could stop it because the wheels of the 'peace train' were already in motion.[76] Shortly before an Irish Cabinet meeting began, Blair spoke to Ahern. The Taoiseach was of the mind not to go to Hillsborough till they had spoken to de Chastelain; at a minimum, de Chastelain would have to come to Hillsborough on this occasion to talk to the heads of Government afterwards (something he had not done when the two previous decommissioning acts had occurred). But Blair was of the view that with everything set up, the two heads of Government now had to fly to Belfast. If they did not go, nothing would happen; if they did go, there was at least a chance of a deal. Senior British officials felt they could not abort the summit now, even though the two Governments had done just that on 10 April 2003 when the Provisionals failed to give enough: they believed that this was a trick that could be pulled only once, without doing irreparable damage to the process. Ahern, though, was still nervous. 'I'm not going up to this,' the Taoiseach told his aides later that morning. Even when he arrived at the Ceremonial Suite at Dublin airport, he delayed the departure for as long as possible and argued with them about the wisdom of the event. As one senior Irish official recalls, 'He was way ahead of the rest of us.'

Shortly before take-off in the early afternoon, whilst the Irish Government jet's engines were revving up, Tim Dalton made a last effort to reach de Chastelain and successfully made the connection; at around the same time, Jonathan Powell also heard from de Chastelain as he was arriving in Belfast.[77] 'Will you be able to be more descriptive?' asked Dalton. 'No,' replied de Chastelain. After a turbulent 20-minute flight, during the course of which the Irish plane was hit by lightning ('We feared it was the first real act of decommissioning that day,' recalls one Irish official), the southern delegation arrived in Northern Ireland. They sped to Hillsborough, where the two Prime Ministers discussed the Adams statement of that morning – and the effects on Trimble's position. Shortly thereafter, de Chastelain and his colleague on the IICD, the former American diplomat Andrew Sens, joined them in the Lady Grey room. De Chastelain was evidently exhausted after a lengthy stretch in the field. 'He looked like he had been dragged through a hedge backwards,' says one senior British official. According to some reports, de Chastelain also had no change of clothes whilst being ferried about by circuitous routes to remote arms dumps somewhere in the Republic.[78] Blair peppered de Chastelain with questions and took out his 'legal pad' to try to write out formulations about what the two inspectors could say at the press conference that was still within the remit of their confidentiality agreement with the Provisionals. How de Chastelain presented his work was now crucial to the success of the venture and its acceptability to unionists and laymen generally. 'Could you say that these weapons could cause a lot of mayhem and destruction in the hands of terrorists?' asked Dalton. 'Yes, they could,' replied de Chastelain. But as one British figure recalls, de Chastelain was a military man of a particular generation with a code of honour about his undertaking. Accordingly, he would not breach any understandings with the republicans concerning the publication of details of quantities of weapons decommissioned – although senior British sources claim that if he had said to the media what he had said to them in private, the deal might have been 'sellable'. Before de Chastelain went out to deliver his remarks to the assembled press, Powell called David Campbell to tell him that the General would be sticking to his confidentiality agreement with the IRA.[79]

Whilst this drama was unfolding at Hillsborough, Trimble had been at Stormont. According to the diary of Mark Neale, at 10:55 a.m. he told Assembly colleagues, 'We have the potential of a successful Assembly election', though he did warn them how much hung on the de Chastelain report.[80] Michael McGimpsey was also concerned and recalls asking himself, 'Why would Blair fly to Belfast to let himself be humiliated?'[81] Quite why Trimble should have been comparatively optimistic at this point is unclear: perhaps he was simply seeking to keep up the morale of his colleagues. Adams' speech represented an advance on the state of affairs in April 2003. On this occasion, the words of the Sinn Fein president loomed far larger than those of the IRA statement endorsing him, thus implying that the Provisionals were becoming the junior partner in the republican movement. Adams' reference to 'the Good Friday Agreement, with its vision of a fair and just society operating exclusively demo-cratically and peacefully, was democratically endorsed by the vast majority of the people of *both states* [author's emphasis] on the island of Ireland' represented an acknowledgment of the reality of Partition. It represented an acknowledgment that Ireland was as much a geographic as a political entity. It also accepted the Belfast Agreement, in relatively unfanciful terms, as the theological end point of value – in contrast to the IRA statement after the 1998 accord, which saw the deal as falling short of presenting a solid basis for a lasting settlement. Later, in a commemor-ation speech at Milltown cemetery in Belfast, Adams would also refer to the IRA in the past tense.[82]

But all of this was much too obscure for the residents of the loyalist estates – and many others besides. Adams had succeeded in deleting any reference to any specific paramilitary activities as outlined in the Joint Declaration, such as targeting, training and punishment beatings.[83] Or, as one British official observed, 'They spoke in Irish, not English.' It was a million miles removed, also, from the words of Blair's press conference in the Pillared Room at No. 10 on 23 April: 'In the end, I don't care what language they use provided the language is clear, and it has got to be clear in the way that any ordinary member of the public in the republican community, the nationalist community, the unionist community, and members of no particular grouping can understand. And that's the heart of it.' Indeed, when Frank Millar asked a senior British official what had happened to these minimum standards, it was patiently explained to him that he had to cross-reference Adams' words to paragraph 7 of the Joint Declaration, which held that it was 'essential that each party has complete confidence in the commitment of the representatives of the others to the full operation and implementation of the agreement in all its aspects and accords respect to each other's democratic mandate'. Adams had fulfilled the requirements of paragraph 13 by declaring that 'actions and lack of actions on the ground speak louder than words and I believe that everyone – including the two Governments and the unionists – can now move forward with confidence'.[84] Even then, the 'good bits' of the Adams statement that Trimble had been negotiating with the Sinn Fein leader were larded about throughout the text – thus diluting its effect. It was further devalued by what the UUP leader thought was 'patronising rubbish' about the sufferings of the Protestant working classes.[85] Moreover, in line with Blair's generous offer in his telephone conversation with Adams of 23 September, Adams had rejected the IMC as standing outside of the terms of the Belfast Agreement: it thus gave him a potential opt-out clause on his own obligations.

The rejection of the IMC was not in the draft text of Adams' remarks which Trimble had seen on the morning of Saturday 18 October and he found out about its inclusion only hours before Adams' speech was actually delivered.[86] But by this stage, sitting in the boardroom of UUP headquarters at Cunningham House, Trimble was much more disturbed by broadcasts from BBC Northern Ireland's Security Correspondent, Brian Rowan. It was clear to him that senior Provisionals were neither minimising nor boosting the Adams statement: they were simply saying nothing beyond the IRA statement. As Trimble saw it, if the Provisionals were operating within the spirit of the understanding which he thought had been achieved, then they would have been heralding something 'significant' here. To him, the Provisionals' omission implied that they were going little beyond their 13 April statement.[87] Trimble also thought it noteworthy and indicative of the nervousness on the republican side, that Adams had not stuck around to answer questions, but had left the podium at the Balmoral Hotel in Dunmurry straight after his statement.[88] According to Richard McAuley of Sinn Fein, there never was a plan for Adams to give a press conference after his statement and that any 'glosses' from republicans would, therefore, have to come after the sequence had run its full course.[89] But the *coup de grâce* was yet to come. Trimble and his colleagues watched de Chastelain's statement with a mixture of amazement and horror. It turned out to be the very opposite of Downing Street or Millbank-style 'spin'. 'It is a short report and if you're taking notes you won't have to write very long,' the tired General told the assembled press corps. The IRA had opted for confidentiality, so he would do the best he could under the terms of reference. The amount of arms put beyond use was larger than previous events. The decommissioning act had included light, medium and heavy ordnance, such as automatic weapons, ammunition and explosives. But he refused to say how many weapons were destroyed, nor what proportion of the IRA's total arsenal (later, de Chastelain would tell the Toronto *Globe and Mail* on 23 October that even the IRA quartermaster might not know precisely the full inventory of weapons). From Trimble's viewpoint it was all far too vague and the terminology employed by the General was incomprehensible to the non-military layman. 'Spell out what you mean!' UUP Assemblymen shouted at the television screen.[90] Indeed, one of the General's assertions that was comprehensible – that the decommissioning act did not include tanks – was invested with a touch of farce. And when asked about completion of decommissioning, de Chastelain inadvertently gave an answer that Trimble thought was dangerously close to the traditional republican formulation: 'I would like to have seen the whole issue of decommissioning handled much faster by both the loyalist and republican groups,' responded the General. 'I can't say when it is going to finish, but I believe it will proceed more swiftly as the politicians get to grips with the problems.'[91] The Governments – and Trimble – thought that Andrew Sens's parting shot at the end of the press conference was much closer to what was needed in the circumstances. 'What we saw [decommissioned] this morning could have caused death and destruction on a huge scale if it had been used.' Had this been said at the beginning, and had the rest followed in the same spirit, Trimble believed that everything might have been very different.[92] But by then it was too late. The impression of lack of clarity, and of the Provisionals setting the pace of the process, was indelibly etched on the minds of the UUP. 'It was like a Greek tragedy unfolding before your very eyes,' recalls one senior British official. 'You have two possible outcomes. You know that you can get to a happy ending, but thanks to one wrong step there are now bodies on stage. And the one wrong step was de Chastelain's confidentiality agreement with the Provisionals.'[93]

'We're in deep trouble and the only thing that can save this is if the IRA authorises de Chastelain to give a full report on decommissioning,' Trimble told his colleagues.[94] 'Reg – you phone McGuinness immediately and tell him he's destroyed it. I'm going to phone Adams. David [Campbell], you phone Powell.'[95] Adams informed Trimble that he had not been at the de Chastelain press conference but that he had been told it had gone badly. Nonetheless, Adams was not going to move. 'Oh, that can't be done,' he told Trimble repeatedly. The UUP leader said he would have to call Blair.[96] But even there, it was an uphill struggle. When David Campbell had telephoned Powell at 4:40 p.m., the Prime Minister's chief of staff was still chancing his arm. 'We're waiting for your statement,' the No. 10 aide said tersely. 'Jonathan, the party will not be buying this,' said Campbell. Powell rang off but two minutes later had come back on the line. 'Look, I'll let you speak to DT,' said Campbell.' 'There's a queue of people here who would like to decommission some spare bullets into John de Chastelain – and I'm at the head of it,' quipped Trimble. Powell soon put Blair on the line to the UUP leader.[97] Blair was to the point. 'You've got to do it,' he said. 'We've come this far. I know it isn't perfect.' Trimble stood firm. The UUP leader told Blair that if he could not obtain a full inventory of weapons decommissioned from de Chastelain, then at least there should be a list of headings with categories. Blair asked for some more time to consider what to do next. He spoke twice to Adams ('Is there any way we can open up on this?' the Prime Minister asked) and again to Trimble. 'Okay, you're not going to make your original statement [committing himself to 'equality' and 'inclusivity']. Can you not just make it and link it [to improved republican performance on weapons]?'[98] By now, time was running out and Blair was desperate: such feelings were always worse when politicians were expecting a good day. He knew that Trimble would have to deliver his press conference in time for the six o'clock news bulletins, or else many of his 'own folk' would think the UUP leader was running with this flawed sequence. Trimble effectively gave the Prime Minister a rehearsal of what he would say to the media. 'He didn't try and talk me out of it,' recalls Trimble.[99] But British and Irish officials were concerned that Trimble might say something that would make it very hard to retrieve things later. 'We were hoping he would say nothing,' says one No. 10 panjandrum.

Trimble duly gave his press conference at Cunningham House. As he had indicated to Blair, he would let the notices go out for another meeting of the UUC to consider the package – giving republicans 'who foolishly imposed obligations of confidentiality on the IICD the opportunity to repair the damage that has been done to the process this afternoon'. With that, he formally put the sequence on hold *ad interim*. Adams and McGuinness headed for Hillsborough, where they slipped in through the back entrance at about 6 p.m.: had they gone in through the front, it would have prompted questions that they were going to go back to the IRA and thus raise expectations again. The Sinn Fein president was in a high state of agitation: the Irish had not seen him in such a condition since the Hillsborough summit of Easter 1999. One British official thought that the republicans had fallen prey to what Peter Mandelson described as their greatest diplomatic vice – over-negotiating for that last 10% bit of advantage and thus over-estimating what their opposition could live with. The two republicans could do nothing that night, but agreed to resume the search for a way out in the coming days. De Chastelain was summoned back to Hillsborough as well, but he too felt he could not move things forward substantially without the agreement of the IRA. 'I can't make any of this public,' he repeated. The only person who was determined not to go to Hillsborough that day was Trimble: as he observes, it would have played badly with ordinary unionists who would have said, 'Oh dear, he's been called in to have his arm twisted again.'[100] The effects of this decision and of his press conference were positive, Trimble says. As a result of his action, the dominant image of the day was not that he had run with an inadequate deal, but that he had said 'this isn't good enough, I'm stopping this' – not unhelpful in the run-up to an Assembly election campaign. And he felt a degree of gratitude to both the IRA and de Chastelain for making his task so easy on the day (by unreasonableness in the first case, and lack of media savvy in the second).[101] But Trimble's sense of relief over this narrow escape was not felt by the British and Irish teams: the 'wash-up' dinner afterwards was one of the most depressing that any of the participants could recall and in the words of a senior Irish mandarin 'felt more like the last supper'.

Ahern and Blair, duly chastened, returned to their respective capitals to deliver statements to the national legislatures. The Taoiseach's comments were perhaps the most remarkable: he revealed to the Dail on Wednesday 22 October that he had only spoken to de Chastelain some 20 hours after he had intended and that he had entertained the profoundest misgivings about going up to Hillsborough. There were some issues which 'we have no control over', since the 'one person with whom we were not dealing was the IRA representative in the area of decommissioning'. Ahern gave the impression that he and Blair were in possession of important additional information about the decommissioning act that had not been released – but that he and the Prime Minister had decided against publishing it lest it end the process. He did not exclude the possibility of saying more if that could be agreed (a Sinn Fein delegation subsequently lambasted senior Irish officials for these remarks when they met outside

Dublin on Tuesday 28 October. They thought he was taking the UUP's side and minimising the extent of the generous offer they had made).[102] And Blair told the Commons on the same day that although he was not at liberty to say more without de Chastelain's permission, 'We are working hard to try to find a way in which we can do so, because I believe, on the basis of what we know, that people would be satisfied if they knew the full details.'[103] But what was in the public domain was obviously not enough to resume the sequence. Indeed, one senior British official derived a degree of wry amusement from the 'innocent truthfulness' of Blair's remarks. 'If there's one group for whom the "trust me, I'm a pretty straight kind of a guy" routine had little appeal, it's Ulster Protestants,' noted the mandarin.[104] Their scepticism would have been confirmed when a DUP delegation led by Paisley met with de Chastelain and the General told 'the Doc' that he had given the two Governments no information beyond what he had said in public. Subsequently, though, a spokesman for de Chastelain refused to confirm or deny the two leaders' statements.[105]

Contact between the UUP and Sinn Fein resumed on Wednesday 22 October, as Trimble sought to establish a timescale for the completion of IRA disarmament in addition to the necessary transparency on the decommissioning act. If he did not obtain what he needed, he would fight the Assembly elections without any commitment to reforming the Northern Ireland Executive and the poll would effectively become an election to 'process' (that is a review/renegotiation).[106] In an attempt to persuade the Provisionals and de Chastelain to refine their confidentiality agreement, Trimble also sought legal advice on the General's statutory obligations. On the basis of the counsel he received, Trimble contended that the confidentiality agreement was a private understanding between de Chastelain and the IRA and not a legal obligation under the Decommissioning Act 1997 and subsequent provisions. Confidentiality, believed the UUP leader, existed for the purposes of reassuring those who were doing the decommissioning that they would not be prosecuted and was not an automatic statutory ban on the release of information if the relevant paramilitary group did not want it. Trimble was particularly struck by paragraph 26 of the Decommissioning Scheme of June 1998, which stated that disclosure of information received by the Commission may occur for the following reasons: first, where disclosure is necessary for reasons of public safety; second, to confirm the legitimate participation in the decommissioning process by those eligible to do so; and third, to fulfil the Commission's duty to report to the two Governments. Trimble further noted that the two Governments, to whom the IICD reported, were not bound by the confidentiality agreements.[107] But neither Government made much use of any of these arguments. Above all, they feared that if the IICD was forced to disclose an inventory without the IRA agreeing to it, then de Chastelain would have to resign – a point which was confirmed by a spokesman for the General.[108]

The parties agreed to meet for a final fling at Hillsborough on the weekend of 25/26 October. Blair spoke again to Adams on the Saturday morning. 'The IRA can't do any more,' said the Sinn Fein president. 'The real problem is Trimble's handling of the situation within Unionism.' 'No, it's not,' snapped the Prime Minister. 'The real problem is the IRA's inability to move on definitively.' Significantly, the IRA issued an apology on the previous day to families of those it had murdered and whose bodies were buried secretly: it was a characteristic of the process that the Provisionals would sometimes make that sort of gesture when under pressure.[109] The two sides worked away on the Saturday on a new formulation. Michael Collins came up from Dublin and Powell flew in from London to chair the meetings on the Sunday. Powell arrived full of optimism, with his shirtsleeves rolled up, and pronounced his now-familiar watchwords: 'Let's see if we can find a way through all this.' Indeed, one senior British official asserts that had all of that been on offer on Tuesday 21 October, the sequence might well have worked. In fact, though it represented an improvement, the republicans were still too vague about timetables for 'acts of completion'. 'Could we just take some time out here and look at the big picture?' asked David Campbell of his colleagues assembled in the Lady Grey room. 'We're on the verge of an imperfect deal and we need to think what the reaction of the electorate is going to be to this. To my mind, we need to hold tight and fight the poll on the basis of what we require as opposed to what's being offered.' Campbell reckoned that on the basis of what the UUP team was discussing with Sinn Fein that weekend, Trimble would lose in the UUC – and most of his party comrades concurred.[110] Indeed, when Blair telephoned Trimble on Monday 27 October, the Prime Minister did not really disagree with the latter's assertion that the deal was unrescuable for now. In retrospect, perhaps the most significant aspect of the weekend was that the two sides came to a tacit understanding about the Assembly elections. 'Even when I stopped the sequence, I took care not to piss on the project,' recalls the UUP leader. 'In my remarks on 21 October, I took care to acknowledge the good things that Adams had said. And they did not engage in "yah-boo-sucks" either. And when we met the following weekend, there was an absence of recrimination.' Something might be salvageable after the poll, so why burn bridges irrevocably by slugging it out in the campaign?[111] Indeed, Gerry Adams recalls that 'the [2003 Assembly] election was David's best yet. He did more to sell the Agreement than ever before – and if he'd done more of that earlier he would have motivated a critical section of [pro-Agreement unionist] voters and done better.'[112]

As Frank Millar subsequently observed, the abortive sequence of 21 October 'was probably one of the greatest failures of Anglo-Irish diplomacy in recent years'.[113] Trimble's unionist opponents, such as Donaldson and Paisley, took it as further evidence of what they believed was his lack of negotiating skill.[114] 'It would have been better if there was no sequence than an aborted sequence,' notes Gerry Adams. 'The time for David to have said no was the day before, not after it had begun.'[115] But who was to blame? As the record shows, Trimble had flagged up the issue of transparency of the decommissioning act early on in the process. The British and the Irish Governments (and the republican movement, for that matter) were in no doubt as to what he needed. Yet although they all repeatedly raised the issue in general terms with Sinn Fein, none of them (including the UUP leader) appears to have nailed down Adams on what exactly the IRA would let de Chastelain say on this occasion under their confidentiality agreement. In Trimble's case, this omission appears to have been a matter of deliberate calculation. 'I didn't ask Adams what he could ask the IRA because I didn't think I would get a useful answer,' says the UUP leader. 'If I accepted, it would seem that I was settling for ambiguity – that is, for less. And if I broke off on discussions because of uncertainty, I would be blamed by London. So rather than ask him and then be left having to rely on his word or to take an awkward decision, I took out a different insurance policy. I made him aware of the need for transparency, so then when they don't live up to their moral obligations, I have freedom of manoeuvre to pull the plug. It was similar to the basic operating method I've had since the Mitchell review of 1999' (when he obtained a general understanding with republicans that if he formed an inclusive Executive for the first time, they would follow with decommissioning). And Trimble maintained his freedom of manoeuvre in one other way: from early on in the process, he made sure that the UUP's own statement would not be released until *after* the decommissioning act was announced. It would have been disastrous for him if he had released his pre-planned statement of undertakings and then to have been 'stiffed' by the Provisionals.[116]

If Trimble's negotiation failed in technical terms, as his unionist opponents have alleged, then it was a failure which was shared by the two Governments. After all, the two states enjoyed vastly greater resources than did he – an out-of-office politician leading a bitterly divided party. Where he is more open to criticism is for what one loyalist calls 'ideological low-balling': being too easily contented with crumbs off the table of the Governments and the republicans.[117] He also frequently over-estimated his own position, partly because he believed that the republicans had lost by accepting a Partitionist settlement. Moreover, he feared that he could not be totally heedless of Adams' internal management problems in winding down armed struggle. Thus, in the year between the suspension of Stormont in October 2002 and the abortive sequence of October 2003, he concluded that there could be no immediate disbandment of the IRA, partly because of problems to do with its verification; he accepted that the transformation of the IRA into a Royal British Legion-style Old Comrades Association, or 'Irish Republican Brotherhood', was not available for the moment; he accepted that there could be no stark IRA statement that 'the war is over' for the time being; he accepted for now that the republicans could not list by name the paramilitary activities that would have to stop, as outlined in paragraph 13 of the Joint Declaration; he accepted that they would have to speak in 'their own language'; he accepted that the republican movement could not on this occasion decommission on film ('no Spielbergs', as Martin McGuinness put it); and he accepted that the decommissioning act would not be witnessed by independent clergymen. Overall, he did a poor job of holding the British Government to the letter and spirit of Blair's 'Harbour Commissioner' address of October 2002 and of holding the Irish Government to the Joint Declaration of 1 May. Trimble too rarely sought to condition the ideological *Zeitgeist*.

British and Irish mandarins contend that if Trimble was prepared to live with the terms of sequence, how could they then ask for more than the UUP leader? But key figures in the two states were also well aware of Trimble's tendency to 'low-ball' – born partly of the Unionists' post-1985 poverty of political aspiration, partly of his own over-confidence about how much political capital he had in the kitty, and partly because of his fear of losing the 'blame game' with London (which partly explains his reluctance to say 'game off' well before 21 October). Yet despite being aware of Trimble's 'low-balling' tendencies, the Governments did nothing to compensate for that in their own behaviour. As Paul Bew has observed, 'The two governments ruthlessly exploited David Trimble's fidelity to the Agreement but failed in their basic responsibility when he took such a huge risk on behalf of their common project.'[118] Especially after laying it on the line to the republicans in the Joint Declaration of 1 May, it was primarily the job of the two states to uphold democratic standards. Yet no sooner had they issued it than they were already pulling the rug from under Trimble's feet with talk of elections, especially on the Irish side. Indeed, for all Ahern's much-advertised doubts about running the sequence on 20/21 October, the fact remains that he played a critical role in persuading the British to give away the one great card they possessed – the threat not to hold an election.[119] The republican movement refused to move until they had a guarantee of a poll, and the two Governments gave that pledge for very little in return. Quite simply, Adams and McGuinness out-stared the leaders of two western democracies. And they were able to do so because the two states would do nothing to jeopardise their standing inside the republican movement – even though, as Ed Moloney and others have contended, the IRA cannot return to armed struggle in the post-September 11 world. When given a choice of cutting Trimble adrift or cutting the Sinn Fein leadership adrift, the two states still opted for the former. It was the easier option, partly because Trimble made it so.

Compared to the dramatic gap between what the Governments were asking of the Provisionals in April/May 2003 and what was on offer on 21 October, the issue of de Chastelain's presentational shortcomings appears insignificant. Even if de Chastelain had delivered a press conference of Kennedy-esque standards, the sequence would probably not have been sellable to unionists. But assuming that the Governments were right and de Chastelain's report was critical, their conduct was still hard to fathom. Even now, many officials are astonishingly vague on what exactly they knew about the confidentiality arrangements between de Chastelain and the Provisionals. If the transparency of decommissioning was so important, why did the Governments let the whole weight of the sequence fall on that segment of it over which they had least control – and which was in the gift of a secretive militaristic elite, namely the IRA's Army Council? Why did they rely so heavily upon the media skills of an exhausted, ageing general at a press conference? And why did they let so much of the weight of selling the deal fall upon Trimble, who was much more electorally vulnerable to the DUP than Sinn Fein was to the SDLP? Would Sinn Fein seriously have been punished by ordinary Catholics at the polls for a genuinely transparent act of decommissioning?

After such high drama, the Assembly election campaign was relatively anti-climatic – perhaps because the results were so predictable. In line with the shared understanding between the UUP and Sinn Fein on that last weekend at Hillsborough on 25/26 October, Trimble and Adams did not recriminate with one another on the stump. Indeed, the Ulster Unionist manifesto and 'mini-manifesto' were remarkably soft-edged. When Sean O'Callaghan suggested to Trimble that his election slogan should be, 'The Man Who Spiked the IRA's Guns', the UUP leader laughed. 'That sounds a bit triumphalist,' Trimble observed. Instead, he opted for the slogan 'The Future not the Past'. As O'Callaghan observes, it was further evidence of Trimble's belief that the IRA's war was over: he wanted to proceed with 'normal politics' now that the 'national question' had been settled (exemplified by the manifesto's heavy emphasis on the achievements of devolution).[120] And as in 2001, Trimble was the central figure of the campaign: Nigel Dodds offered a compliment of sorts when he commented that 'Mr Trimble has very little support out on the ground and within his own party. He surrounds himself with nodding dogs which he can't even allow on TV. In every TV programme that I've seen it is Mr Trimble, Mr Trimble, Mr Trimble. Nobody else can be trusted to deliver the message and half his party and candidates won't even be seen anywhere near him.'[121] Tensions between the two parties came to a head eight days before the poll, when the DUP unveiled a mobile billboard outside Cunningham House. Trimble emerged from party headquarters to confront Paisley and his deputy, Peter Robinson, and again challenged 'the Doc' to a debate; Robinson described the UUP leader as 'yesterday's man'. The 'fuss on the bus', as it came to be known, was probably not the greatest exchange ever heard, but from Trimble's viewpoint it served one useful purpose: to knock the statement issued by the three rebel Ulster Unionist MPs off the front pages.[122] Donaldson et al. had pledged, amongst other things, to prevent the appointment of a Sinn Fein representative such as Gerry Kelly as Policing and Justice Minister in the event of a devolution of security powers in the lifetime of the next Assembly.[123] Later, whilst Trimble was broadcasting on Radio Ulster's *Talkback* phone-in programme, Donaldson rang in to contradict the UUP leader's assertion that the party was united behind the manifesto.[124] It was closest thing that the electorate had to a real debate between pro- and anti-Agreement unionist factions during the campaign – but the obvious disunity probably cost the UUP votes when the poll was held on Wednesday 26 November 2003.[125]

When the votes were counted, the DUP had won 30 seats to the UUP's 27; Sinn Fein had overhauled the SDLP by 24–18. Ian Paisley had won his first Stormont election (the DUP had of course come top in terms of the popular vote once before, in the local government elections of 1981, though the UUP narrowly retained their edge in seats; and Paisley had always won the largest number of first preferences in European elections, but never in the big tests for the Provincial Parliament or Westminster). The DUP had picked up seven of the eight seats won by the smaller anti-Agreement parties in the 1998 Assembly elections (UKUP, United Unionists) and Peter Weir held on to his seat in North Down following his defection to the Paisleyites. They secured the highest number of first preferences of any party, rising from 18.22% in 1998 to 25.71% in 2003. However, considering the very adverse circumstances, Trimble had also done remarkably well to lose only one seat out of the UUP's 1998 total of 28. Indeed, the UUP's overall percentage of first preferences had actually gone up from 21.24% in 1998 to 22.67% this time. It was a source of particular satisfaction to him that he secured the highest number of first preferences in Upper Bann (9158) and was easily elected on the first count, though that represented a reduction of about 25% on his 1998 total of 12,338.[126] And both he and Daphne Trimble were pleasantly surprised that there was none of the abuse that had been levelled at them upon their departure from the count in the 2001 Westminster poll.[127]

Overall, the UUP did best in a geographical and sociological corridor in the greater Belfast area – stretching from South Belfast, through East Belfast and into North Down. Whilst the 1998 Assembly elections were the obvious benchmark for assessing performance, it is also worth looking at the 1996 Forum elections (the first held in the current eighteen constituencies). For in 1998, the turn-out (though lower than in the previous month's referendum) was still exceptionally high by Northern Ireland standards. This was especially so in seats held by Unionists at Westminster. Thus, in South Belfast, the UUP share of first preferences went from 23% in 1996, to 23% in 1998, to 27% in 2003 – compared to 15%, 13% and 21% for the DUP over the same period. The Alliance share dropped from 12%, to 10% and then to 6%. In East Belfast, the UUP share rose from 22% in 1996, to 24% in 1998, to 33% in 2003; the DUP share rose from 29% to 31% to 39%; the Alliance share dropped from 19%, to 18% and then to 9% (if Alliance votes were added to UUP votes, it again showed that there was a possibility of a serious pro-Agreement challenge to Robinson at Westminster, if the two parties could ever agree a joint candidate). In North Down, the UUP went from 26% in 1996 to 33% in 1998 and to 32% in 2003; the DUP went from 18% to 7% and then up to 23%; the Alliance went from 17% to 14% and down to 9% over the same period. Thus, Trimble's performance echoed that of Terence O'Neill in the last of the old Stormont elections in 1969: there were suggestions of a real appeal amongst segments of the middle classes in parts of the greater Belfast area. The figures appeared to suggest that in those constituencies, if nowhere else, a pro-Agreement UUP could probably replenish a good portion of its lost support from the Alliance party.

The DUP and anti-Agreement UUP candidates did best in what might be termed the 'new Protestant heartlands' – areas where there was a lot of new housing and the combined pan-unionist party totals tended to go up between the Westminster and local elections of 1997 and 2001. In such areas, the loss of traditional UUP voters to the DUP massively outweighed gains amongst middle-class Alliance voters. Thus, the DUP forged ahead in East Antrim, going from 29% in 1996, to 22% in 1998 (partly because of a successful UKUP candidature), to 34% in 2003; the UUP went from 30%, to 29.6% and down to 28.7%. Likewise, in South Antrim, the DUP went from 24% in 1996, to 20% in 1998 (again, because of a successful UKUP candidature), to 31% in 2003; the UUP went from 30.1% in 1996, to 29.9% in 1998 and to 29.8% in 2003. The most dramatic DUP gains were in Strangford, where the Paisleyites went from 29% in 1996, to 28% in 1998, to 48% in 2003; the UUP dropped from 31.3%, to 29.2% and then to 28.9%. Likewise, the DUP made very solid gains in East Londonderry, where they rose from 24% in 1996, to 24% in 1998 and up to 32% in 2003; the UUP dropped over the same period from 31% to 25% and then down to 23%. But perhaps the most intriguing result was in Lagan Valley: Donaldson secured the largest number of first preferences of any candidate in the election, in vote or percentage terms – 14,104 or 34.2%. The UUP's percentage total went from 37.7% in 1996, to 31% in 1998 (partly, perhaps, because Donaldson was not allowed to run) to 46.2% in 2003. The DUP total went from 22.1%, to 18% and back to 20.5%. It was probably the only seat where the vote of the small anti-Agreement parties went not to the DUP but to the UUP, and confirmed Donaldson's particular appeal to traditional unionists of all hues, especially DUP supporters. Significantly, in none of the seats held by unionists at Westminster – whether favourable or unfavourable to the Trimble project – was there much evidence of higher turn-out. Indeed, the ten lowest turn-outs were in constituencies held by Unionist MPs: North Down, East Antrim and Strangford were still down there at 54%, 56% and 57.1% respectively, whereas the lowest turn-out in a nationalist-held seat at Westminster was in Foyle, where 63.5% voted. Neither the DUP nor the UUP had yet solved the problem of low unionist participation in the political process, even though the differentials with nationalists were partially eroded in this election because of lower turn-out in areas with heavy Catholic majorities such as West Belfast (this may in part be attributable to the measures against electoral fraud brought in during 2002). Nor, observes the Queen's University political scientist Dr Sydney Elliott, was there much evidence of cross-community voting five and a half years after the signing of the Belfast Agreement, at least if terminal transfers are anything to go by. In so far as there was any cross-community voting, it came mostly in the form of UUP to SDLP, and to a lesser degree vice versa. There was certainly precious little sign of nationalist voters heeding Sinn Fein's call to vote for pro-Agreement unionist candidates.[128]

The Paisleyites' progress was thus very solid – but not sensational. The NIO claimed to be surprised by the results in the days that followed, but they should not have been. Sydney Elliott had predicted a year earlier on the basis of analysis of the 2001 local elections – when the UUP had a lead of 1.5% – that the DUP would do little more than to pick up the small anti-Agreement parties (Elliott forecast the result would be 29 DUP to 28 UUP). As such, these figures confirmed the trend that had been observable subsequent to the Assembly elections of 1998 – that Trimble was the minority shareholder in unionism as whole, albeit by a narrow margin.[129] It proved there was still a substantial unionist constituency for a compromise with nationalism – and that its leadership could have squeaked by again if the British and Irish Governments had done more to help it. Indeed, the RTE exit poll conducted by Millward Brown Ulster on the day of the vote shows that as many as 29% of DUP voters only decided upon their choice *after* the Assembly elections were called – which in a narrow race may well have made the difference.[130] Yet as so often before, Trimble defied the laws of political gravity, partly because he was lucky in his opponents. According to David Campbell, Trimble was concerned that after these electoral reverses Donaldson would call another UUC meeting.[131] But instead, Donaldson hesitated. The reason for his apparent prevarication soon became obvious. On 18 December, he finally left for the DUP along with the other newly elected MLAs, Arlene Foster of Fermanagh-South Tyrone and Norah Beare from Lagan Valley, thus turning the balance in the Assembly to 33–24 in favour of the DUP. The combined total of the anti-Agreement and pro-Agreement factions amongst designated unionists was now 34–25.[132] It also made the DUP the largest unionist party in the Commons, by a 6–5 margin.[133] William Ross, for one, was furious with Donaldson. 'Like Bill Craig [Trimble's mentor, who left the UUP to found Vanguard in protest at Brian Faulkner's policies], he's leaving just at the moment that he was on the verge of victory,' commented the former MP for East Londonderry.[134] With his most formidable opponent gone, Trimble might just be able to rebuild the party along the lines he wanted. For a man who professed such indifference to political life, he was remarkably difficult to dislodge – and to discourage. Indeed, some observers, such as Frank Millar, reckoned that Trimble's insouciance about the election results and the subsequent defections of Donaldson et al. verged on complacency.[135] A little humility might have been in order, even though the UUP leader was no Faulkner.

So much for Trimble's own fortunes. But what did the DUP's victory mean for the unionist population? Mitchel McLaughlin insisted that Paisley's triumph required that the British and Irish Governments spell out 'the options to the rejectionists' – that is, sign up for the Belfast Agreement or else face another intergovernmental imposition along the lines of 1985. And, critically, he added: 'No longer can Mr Blair use David Trimble's precarious hold on the leadership of majority unionism to justify prevarication. He must act decisively now to disavow rejectionists of the notion that they can renegotiate the agreement.'[136] It was another tribute, of sorts, to the frustrations which republicans felt when dealing with Trimble's prolonged rearguard action. Everything, though, would now depend on the British reaction, and the Government seemed in the weeks immediately thereafter to have little idea what to do next. They were regretful, but not particularly remorseful about their own role in bringing about the result. One minister observed that now Blair faced a serious leader of the Opposition in the person of Michael Howard (who had replaced Iain Duncan Smith in October 2003), he would have less time for Ulster. 'At least he can say " 'eaven knows, I've tried".' For the first time, Blair had behaved in a fashion quite heedless of Trimble's core political interests. The UUP leader's personal reputation was still unscathed on the British mainland – but as for the Trimble-Blair project, it was hard to imagine that Humpty-Dumpty could be put together again any time soon.[137]

FORTY

Conclusion

WHO and what is David Trimble? Like William Safire's description of Richard Nixon, Trimble is as complex as a 'layer cake' – strip away one level and you find another which completely alters your view of the man.[1] Consider the apparent contradictions: the anti-populist who was propelled to the UUP leadership by a street protest; the intellectual leading one of the least intellectual political movements in these islands; the cool, logical land law lecturer who can go red in the face with anger and emotion and whose behaviour could be very moody; the 'knowledge snob' who remembers much but who bears remarkably few grudges; the middle-class professional who laboured so hard to lure his peer group back into Unionist politics but who resented them for opting out for so long from public life; the hyperactive academic whose political posture could often be very passive; the highly articulate parliamentarian who left relatively few memorable phrases or sound-bites behind him; the leader who wanted to communicate the Unionist case to the mainland and the outside world but created no serious organisation to disseminate that message; the often indiscreet gossip who plays his cards very close to his chest; the chameleon who has often gone with the most powerful forces around him throughout his career, but who in Herb Wallace's words also 'derives a perverse satisfaction from adopting unpopular causes'; the ambitious man who for much of his career took risks which no 'careerist' would dream of taking; the flatterable provincial who militantly declines to 'brown-nose' powerful, natural allies; the UUP leader who wants his people to 'think politically' but who after a dozen or more years in the Commons knows relatively few MPs; the terrifyingly direct Ulsterman who likes 'others to do my dirty work for me'; the cosmopolitan who enjoyed relatively little foreign travel till comparatively late in life; the quintessential Ulsterman who cannot wait to escape the Province; the lover of Westminster who was willing to pay a very high price for return of provincial self-government at Stormont; the master of detail who let the details slip from his grasp on two crucial issues, namely the negotiations on the Strand I aspects of the internal governance of Northern Ireland and on the creation and deliberations of the Patten Commission; and the moderate Tory who talks of a closer relationship with the Conservatives, occasionally voting Liberal Democrat in local elections, but whose closest mainland collaboration is with Tony Blair and who wanted to serve *ad interim* as a junior direct-rule minister in his Government.

And then, of course, there was the biggest 'contradiction' of all: the loyalist hardliner who became a pillar of inclusive government. During the course of my researches, I often asked his one-time close associate, John Hunter, who broke with him over the Belfast Agreement, 'Did Trimble change? Or did he knowingly take you for a ride? Or did you deceive yourself – much as the Tory right deceived itself about John Major as an appropriate successor to Thatcher? Or a bit of all three?' John Hunter is absolutely certain that the man for whom he worked has changed beyond recognition. '"A pluralist Parliament for a pluralist people"? [A reference to Trimble's speech on 1 July 1998 at the opening of the Assembly.] That certainly isn't the Trimble I knew.'[2] At times, Trimble appears to have endorsed this interpretation: 'I've changed, you know,' he told Herb Wallace after signing the Belfast Agreement.[3] Such sentiments as a 'pluralist Parliament for a pluralist people' certainly formed little part of the *public* Trimble before he became leader. But there was greater consistency in his approach than the remark to Herb Wallace suggests. First, there is no evidence of anti-Catholic bigotry during his period at Queen's University, even at the height of his activism in Vanguard and the UWC strike of 1974. He was never anything other than entirely professional in his conduct; indeed, considering the world of hardline loyalism in which he mixed, and the near-civil war conditions which obtained in Northern Ireland in the early to mid-1970s, this lack of bigotry is remarkable. If he was cold, he was impartially cold towards all or, as Gerry Adams put it to John Reid and his officials in the summer of 2002, 'Well, of course, the thing about David Trimble is he treats everyone like shite.'[4] He still lives in a mixed part of Lisburn and is most comfortable relaxing in London with lapsed southern Catholics such as Ruth Dudley Edwards and Sean O'Callaghan. Second, he always held quirky views – and a great multiplicity of them. During the 1970s and

1980s, Trimble occupied a great many positions on the unionist/loyalist spectrum: he was at various times a devolutionist, an integrationist, an advocate of Dominion status and also appeared to flirt with Ulster independence. No doubt, he would argue that all of these stances were means to ends, rather than ends in themselves: tactics rather than principles to secure the future of the Ulster-British nation. Partly, this variety of stances owed something to intellectual gamesmanship, for he loved tossing an idea up in the air, playing about with it and then discarding it almost as quickly as he embraced it. As A.J.P. Taylor once said of himself when accused of having no firm opinions on anything, he had 'strong views, weakly held'.[5] Indeed, when William Ross sharply attacked Trimble to his face at a meeting of the parliamentary party in early 1998, accusing the UUP leader of having 'no principles', the latter replied, 'No, but I do have opinions.'[6]

What, then, were those opinions? Trimble appears to have abandoned the starkest forms of Unionist majoritarianism at a quite early stage in his career – although he did not always make a song and dance about it and at times objected vociferously to specific power-sharing schemes. The absence of principled opposition to power-sharing was partly a pragmatic calculation, based upon what he reckoned the British state – the key player in the Ulster crisis – would allow. If Northern Ireland was to regain a measure of self-government after the prorogation of Stormont in 1972, Unionists would have to share power with Catholics and suck them in to operating British institutions. The question, especially after 1985, was what price nationalist Ireland would ask for acceptance of Northern Ireland as the relevant unit of government. But such considerations and debates were staples of internal Unionist discourse in this period: none of them per se were unique to Trimble. What made Trimble different in his willingness to take the risk to do the deal with Irish nationalism were two things. First, he was a genuine *political eccentric*. His priorities were almost *sui generis* amongst Unionists. Thus, from his Vanguard days he was a long-time enthusiast for a British-Irish Council (sometimes called the Council of the Isles) as an east-west counterbalance to the North-South bodies on the island of Ireland. The BIC mattered much more to him, at least during the negotiations leading up to the Belfast Agreement, than the fate of the RUC, even though he did not obtain a single vote out of the former issue and lost plenty in consequence of his (perceived) failure on the latter. Indeed, many years previously he expressed unusual

views about the RUC, too, describing in unconcerned fashion the Craig–
Collins pacts of 1922 which had proposed arrangements for the separate
policing of Catholic areas by Catholics and Protestant areas by Protestants.[7] Ultimately, he acquiesced in a set of policing structures which
brought Northern Ireland closer to that vision of cantonised law enforcement than at any time since the existence of the state was secured
(although he denied that his views on Craig–Collins played any part in
his approach to the RUC).

So much for Trimble's long-held views. If not 'liberal', they were certainly 'accommodationist' in the sense of being willing to make an
arrangement of sorts with Irish nationalism. Indeed, one of the curiosities
of Trimble's political behaviour was the way in which he combined lack
of personal bigotry against Catholics with a recognition of the durability
of sectarian sentiment in the public space. It was this long-time 'realism'
about inter-communal strife, especially on his own side, which made him
so suitable a candidate to do a deal with Irish nationalism. Simply by
recognising the existence of these communal sentiments, and at least
appearing to his 'own folk' to share them, and by giving them intellectual
expression, he gained the credibility to rise to the leadership of the UUP
and to hold on to just enough of the grassroots to push through a
settlement. There was a measure of opportunism in all this. But it was
also a genuine assessment of what he saw as the durability of communal
strife in the public space. This cold calculation – combined with lack of
sentiment and emotion about certain outworkings of the end of the
terrorist campaign such as prisoner releases – made him promising raw
material to become a leading player in the 'top-down' consociational settlement of the kind which emerged in Northern Ireland. His behaviour in
office thus conformed, in some important respects, to the classical pattern
of the mutual accommodation of sectarian elites in divided societies that
was described in the writings of the political scientist Arend Lijphart.[8]

Lijphart would also have recognised his remark to Sean Farren in the
margins at one of the Duisburg seminars in the late 1980s. The senior
SDLP politician and fellow academic asked him point blank, 'What do
you want for your people?' 'To be left alone,' replied Trimble, in almost
Garboesque fashion.[9] Again, this response at least appears to conform to
another of Lijphart's defining characteristics of consociational settlements:
a substantial degree of segmental autonomy.[10] For example, so strong was
Trimble's recognition of such communal 'realities' that he was reluctant

to embrace with much ardour the concept of integrated education – even though there was a civic unionist case of a kind for suggesting that the Catholic school system would find such an agenda more challenging than 'Protestant' state schools. Thus, a campaign for integrated education would have enabled Trimble to look 'liberal' (allowing him to present himself, say, in America as the foe of 'segregated schooling') *and* to annoy wide swathes of northern nationalism. But he never did so and Martin McGuinness was able to associate himself with that campaign far more than the UUP leader (Trimble says that he was sceptical because he was never quite sure what culture pupils were being integrated into).[11] Perhaps, indeed, the old nationalist allegation about Unionists was right in respect of Trimble, but in a quite different sense from which they meant it: that he 'did not want a Fenian about the place'. The allegation is used by nationalists to claim that bigoted Unionists do not want to share power with them and wish to maintain a supremacist regime. As has been seen, this claim in its traditional sense was nonsense. Trimble took enormous risks to share power with both constitutional and unconstitutional nationalists, admitting the latter into the heart of government long before they even began to contemplate disbandment of their paramilitary structures. Indeed, following the suspension of the Northern Ireland Executive in October 2002 after allegations concerning a republican spy ring at Stormont, he effectively admitted to John Humphrys on *On the Record* of 1 December 2002 that Sinn Fein had wiped his eye three times in a row (and, arguably, on a fourth occasion, if the negotiations which he conducted in the run-up to the abortive sequence of 21 October 2003 are included as well).[12] He wanted them in government, but not at any price, and certainly not at a price that would entirely destroy his own position. He also, as has been noted, was more than happy physically to live alongside Catholics, to teach them, to work with them professionally and to socialise with a few of them in so far as he socialised with anyone. Trimble's remark to Sean Farren about being 'left alone' is of lasting significance not because of any bigotry, or 'not wanting a Fenian about the place', but because he did not want to have to endure endless 'in your face' triumphalism from unrepentant, militant republicans. He was perfectly happy that they should be up at Stormont on an equal basis, but it was a hard-nosed business arrangement, not a marriage or a group therapy session. Or, as he observed in response to a liberal Protestant critic, Norman Porter, the Agreement was not 'a foundational event allowing the radical reconstruction of a new politics in Northern Ireland'; instead, it was 'an honourable historic compromise between unionism and nationalism which involves acceptance of the consent principle . . .'[13] Nor, obviously, did he conceive of himself as an actor in a political morality play, whose pre-ordained role is to bring down the curtain on a rotten discriminatory system (after the fashion of the popular Irish nationalist analogy with F.W. de Klerk).[14] Essentially, his message was: 'You've got much of what you want. Now please let me go about my daily routine undisturbed.' As such, his attitude was squarely in line with the proverbial 'Prod in the garden centre'.[15] They were moving in ever greater numbers into Protestant redoubts in the eastern part of the Province, as was also suggested by studies concerning the rise in residential segregation.[16] Likewise, polling evidence for Cooperation Ireland showed that Protestants were as uninterested as ever in learning more about the affairs of the Irish Republic.[17]

The other aspect of Trimble's persona which pre-dated his leadership bid was much more humdrum: ambition. Like many politicians, Trimble's career represented a mixture of idealism and self-aggrandisement. Many of his one-time Unionist admirers would say that the second of those elements rose very much into the ascendant after he won the UUP leadership in 1995. Certainly, before 1995, or even 1990 (when he was elected to the Commons), Trimble behaved in a highly *uncareeristic* fashion for a Queen's academic or indeed any middle-class Ulster Protestant professional of the period. Even if his role in hardline protests in 1974 and after 1985 was part of a master strategy to acquire long-term credibility to do a deal with nationalism much later on, as some loyalists have subsequently alleged to me, it was certainly costly for him at the time in academic terms. Truly, he cannot be accused of 'opting out', after the fashion of so many of the Protestant middle classes – a stratum of society with whom his relationship remained highly ambiguous, even after he did the deal. Indeed, there was a streak of genuine public-spiritedness in his political makeup, as well as opportunism. But what is possible is that because Trimble often lived in a world of his own – and certainly possessed less 'craft' than he later acquired – he misunderstood the effect which his early actions would have and was therefore surprised by the price which he paid for his convictions. He may also have misunderstood these movements and did not realise that they would be poor vehicles for his ambitions. It is also possible that he fully understood that they were poor vehicles for his ambitions; but they were the only ones available and if politics offered few big prizes, he might as well stick to his ideological guns. If this analysis is correct, then he only compromised when the prizes were big enough. Or, deep down, did he conclude after the failure of the protests against the Anglo-Irish Agreement of 1985 that such forms of hardline activity were doomed, that Unionism would have to come to terms with nationalism, and that he might as well make the best of it in personal and political terms? Thus, before 1995, Trimble had relatively few outlets for his ambitions: his constituency then was Vanguard or Ulster Clubs branch suppers. After 1995, his constituency, in the broadest sense, also comprised the British Prime Minister and the American President. Thus, despite his self-conscious penchant for unfashionable causes, which he sometimes adopted to show how clever he was, he tended to respond to the most powerful forces around him at any given time. That trait mixed interestingly with the above-mentioned element of intellectual gamesmanship. He could always rationalise things to himself, and to others, with considerable fluency. Moreover, as Jeffrey Donaldson insightfully notes, people too often listened to the high volume at which Trimble often delivered his remarks, rather than their actual content. Thus, Trimble vaulted to national and international prominence because of his role in opposing the detail of the Frameworks Documents in 1995 and in successive sieges of Drumcree in 1995 and 1996 (the latter largely because he was constituency MP for the area). But Paisley, for one, had correctly discerned that despite such tactical rhetorical and symbolic escalations, Trimble was never a purist opponent of the peace process. Thus, he had accepted the Downing Street Declaration of 1993. Many of his key ideas had been worked out before he obtained the leadership, although he would evolve further under the pressure of events. Indeed, within days of becoming head of the UUP, he engaged in correspondence with Ruth Dudley Edwards which suggested to her at least that he was planning some 'surprises'. Dudley Edwards had written to Trimble just after his election as leader, outraged by some of the unpleasant press coverage which he had received. In particular, she was thinking of David McKittrick's article in *The Independent* on 11 September 1995, in which the prominent journalist pronounced that '25 years in politics have left no real indication that he has a vision beyond Unionism and Orangeism'. 'I don't recognise you in what I've been reading,' ventured Dudley Edwards. Trimble replied: 'All will soon become clear.'[18] He thus had a

'He's in a very difficult position, you know'. Ruth Dudley Edwards, historian and journalist, argued Trimble's case the length and breadth of these islands.

A party loyalist: David McNarry, Trimble's special adviser from 2001 who was elected Stormont assemblyman for Strangford in 2003.

The boy from the Co. Cork: Eoghan Harris, ex-Marxist and Republican who wrote Trimble's Nobel Prize speech in Oslo.

Some candid advice: Michael McDowell, Alliance party supporter and Trimble's informal counsellor in Washington, lays it on the line.

The informer: Sean O'Callaghan, the former head of IRA Southern Command and one-time Garda agent, advised Trimble on republican personalities and strategy following his release from gaol in 1996.

But would he approve? Sir James Craig, the first Prime Minister of Northern Ireland, looks down on the then First Minister of the new Northern Ireland. Trimble chose Sir John Lavery's portrait of Craig – a personal hero – for his office in Stormont Castle. Both men courted controversy amongst their own supporters by negotiating with republicans.

The sash my father never wore: Seamus Mallon and David Trimble, Deputy First Minister and First Minister of Northern Ireland, don the Tibetan kata in the presence of the Dalai Lama and Peter Mandelson, then Ulster Secretary.

A welcome break from Belfast: Trimble meets the former ANC Secretary-General, Cyril Ramaphosa, who inspected the IRA's weapons dumps, in South Africa, September 2002.

Trimble treats with the Tories at the annual dinner of Wycombe Conservative Association in 2000, flanked by Sir Ray Whitney (left), MP from 1978–2001 and his successor, Paul Goodman. Despite talk of a parliamentary alliance, the UUP leader was not able formally to link up with the Conservatives.

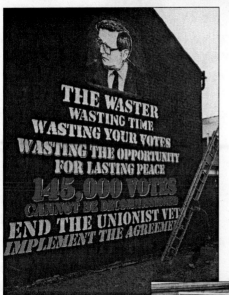

A back-handed compliment to Trimble: a republican wall mural in west Belfast.

The political is personal: the DUP targets Trimble at Stormont during the 2001 General Election.

'A prophet without honour' in his own constituency: Trimble runs the gauntlet of anti-agreement unionists in Banbridge, Co. Down, after narrowly winning re-election for Upper Bann in the 2001 Westminster Election.

'Structural unionism' in action: Tony Blair and Gordon Brown announce an investment package in the shadow of the Harland and Wolff shipyard in Belfast. Mark Durkan, SDLP leader and Deputy First Minister 2001–2002, is second from the left.

'The fuss on the bus': Trimble confronts the DUP after the Paisleyites had parked their campaign vehicle outside UUP headquarters at Cunningham House, east Belfast, during the November 2003 Assembly Election.

'Do I need to take you by the neck to say that I am not talking to Sinn Fein, my party is not talking to Sinn Fein, and anybody who talks to Sinn Fein will be out of my party?' Ian Paisley leaves Ivan Little of UTV in no doubt as to his intentions in Ballymoney, Co. Antrim, after the DUP emerged victorious in the November 2003 Assembly Election.

broad sense of what he wanted to do quite early, but no detailed game plan – and for all his love of gossip, kept it close to his chest.

Certainly, the British Government knew that Trimble was more flexible than the conventional wisdom allowed. Moreover, they would soon have discovered that he was susceptible to flattery. Once he reached a position of responsibility, he could not have enough of the attention. It started early in his leadership: shortly before Christmas 1995, he asked Major's Private Secretary for Foreign Affairs, Rod Lyne, to give him and his family a tour of No. 10. Likewise, he later asked Larry Butler of the NSC to show his children round the White House. Nor, as John Taylor observes, did he make much of a secret that he loved visits to Buckingham Palace.[19] These were sure signs that he was determined to enjoy the baubles and perks of office for as long as he could. 'I would never have done that,' says one Trimbleista of the request of Lyne. 'When the only card you've got to play is that you're a wild man from Portadown who is capable of doing anything, why throw it away by showing that you're impressed?'[20] As Sean O'Callaghan observes, 'David Trimble was exposed to new influences relatively late in life and he enjoyed them. By contrast, his own folk are narrow and bite your arse the whole time. Who would you have gone with in his position?'[21] These 'new influences' included a greater range of things – from near-daily top-level governmental dealings to offers of membership of the Athenaeum to invitations to such events as the 40th birthday party of the historian Andrew Roberts at the Royal Hospital (for which he made a particular point of clearing his diary).[22] He was bored by provincial politics – which partly explains his multiple away-days – and according to Ruth Dudley Edwards would have liked to have been part of a British Cabinet.[23]

If any one individual helped to encourage Trimble along the path he took, it was Blair. Blair was undoubtedly the most important influence upon the UUP leader's career, with the possible exception of his early mentor, William Craig, and he succeeded with the UUP leader where Major had failed. There were obvious superficial similarities: both were lawyers and modernisers who took over their own parties at relatively young ages. Trimble certainly admired what Blair had done to New Labour. In fact, their life experiences and political outlooks and styles were worlds apart. Blair's upbringing was, quite simply, far more privileged: public school, Oxford, the move to the London Bar, and then always in the fast track politically before becoming Labour leader aged

41. Trimble was a *petit bourgeois* grammar-school boy, a late-comer to a provincial university, who then suffered multiple disappointments as an academic and politician and who only entered the Commons at the age of 45 (thereafter, however, his rise was even more meteoric). Although Trimble had a better and more original intellect than the Prime Minister, he was relatively lacking in the kind of 'emotional intelligence' which Blair possessed in ample quantities. This obviously mattered a great deal in modern politics everywhere – and especially in Northern Ireland. And though Trimble took great risks to do the deal as a kind of hard-nosed communal accommodation, his conception of 'modernisation' of the UUP and the methodologies to achieve that goal was far removed from Blair's *modus operandi*. Moreover, their views of the Ulster crisis were also light years apart. Like Gladstone, Blair appeared to be in thrall to a basically Irish nationalist interpretation of Irish history, but for rather different reasons than the GOM.[24]

Yet despite such differences, Trimble stuck to Blair. Why? Initially, he may not have realised how incompatible their respective views of Northern Ireland actually were, and when things went wrong tended to blame Mo Mowlam or the NIO. Indeed, at least for the first two years of the New Labour Government, Trimble was in thrall to an imagined Blair who existed largely in his own mind. But even when he woke up to this, he would not break with Blair. Obviously, this was partly a function of the fact that he had to 'stay in' with a very powerful Prime Minister with a massive majority. Thus, the exigencies of the 'blame game' – and being blamed by Blair was about the worst fate which could befall him – impelled him much further down roads along which he had taken some tentative steps. He would occasionally tease New Labour that he had other options, such as appearing on the platform at Conservative conferences, writing an article with Iain Duncan Smith, and suggesting a closer relationship with the Tories.[25] But Blair, as a powerful incumbent Prime Minister, always had something more to offer, even if he did not deliver in the manner or timeframe that Trimble wanted. The most obviously deliverable of the 'goodies' was constant personal attention and virtually unlimited access to No. 10. Amazingly, the intoxicating effects of this potion never quite wore off, no matter how much of it was consumed: even as late as 2 September 2002, Trimble was delighted when Blair delayed his departure from South Africa to talk to him at the Earth summit in Johannesburg. At one level, Trimble was well aware of the dangers of being sucked in by the Blair machine and would sometimes recount the story told by T.E. Utley, the pre-eminent High Tory critic of the Heath Government's Ulster policy. 'I remember long afterwards a characteristically friendly comment from William Whitelaw about my past disagreements with him,' wrote Utley in his last column before he died. '"Utley," he said, "you always told me that I was driving Faulkner too far. My G-d you were right! But what a damned fool he was to allow himself to be driven!"'[26] Inevitably, though, Trimble was driven, if not quite as far or at as fast a pace as Blair wanted. And it was an association which Trimble knew was costly at home in Northern Ireland. At the State Banquet for President Bush on 19 November 2003, the Prime Minister teased the UUP leader about his reluctance to support the Government on the issue of foundation hospitals, on which Blair was facing a tight Commons division. 'People already think I'm too close to you,' replied Trimble.[27]

How detached is Trimble from the Unionist community?[28] Contrary to what some anti-Agreement loyalists have asserted to me, he has never become a 'guilty Prod' – a breed he loathed.[29] And he never succumbed to any belief in the inevitability of, and still less the desirability of Irish unity as expressed by the likes of a Gordon Wilson.[30] No one who exploded with a powerful Labour Prime Minister over his characterisation of Northern Ireland society could be deemed a 'guilty Prod'. Indeed, he could still stand out against the crowd – quite literally. During the first period of suspension from February to May 2000, George Howarth recalls attending a concert at the Waterfront Hall, which culminated in a resounding chorus of 'Fields of Athenry', a popular and inspiring love song set in the Famine. Howarth looked down from the box and saw the entire audience on their feet, singing their hearts out – except David Trimble, who remained firmly and sternly rooted to his seat.[31] Trimble believed that the tune has been appropriated by some aggressively nationalistic elements for their own ends – namely, the perpetuation of an anti-British narrative. Certainly, to be seen to be singing along would have been a political mistake on Trimble's part, but he was also genuinely unenthused by what he saw as the song's message. The question here is not whether Trimble's assessment of 'Fields of Athenry' was right or wrong. Rather, it is to show that the man who founded the Ulster Society in the 1980s, for the preservation of Ulster-British culture, had not really changed his views per se by 2000 (whether on cultural warfare or on the necessity of an accommodation of sorts with nationalism). What had changed was his willingness, or rather lack of willingness, to wage such cultural warfare in the public domain on a sustained, coherent basis – despite such occasional sallies as his speech in October 2002 at the launch of Henry Patterson's book, *Ireland Since 1939*, and his voluble opposition to the renaming of Londonderry by the nationalist majority on the city council in early 2003.[32]

This new-found unwillingness was not what his advisers such as Graham Gudgin and Sean O'Callaghan prescribed. O'Callaghan, in particular, urged Trimble publicly to prepare his people to engage in new forms of cultural and political struggle, now that the terrorist campaign against them was over. Trimble listened carefully to their advice, but rarely implemented it. Partly, this was because of how he conceived of his own role as First Minister and even as UUP leader post-Agreement. Far from using it as a 'bully pulpit' relentlessly to promote his vision of Britishness, he preferred a 'softly, softly' approach. Thus, on 13 January 2001, whilst at an American Enterprise Institute conference in London, Trimble told Paul Bew that he could not push the Belfast Agreement in a 'Unionist way' lest such apparent triumphalism give the republican movement an excuse not to decommission.[33] He also believed that if he took the lead on certain issues, it would 'discredit' those causes in the eyes of nationalists: for instance, at a conference in Sicily in December 2000 to celebrate the signing of the UN Convention against Transnational Crime, he explained his reluctance to take up the 'culture of lawfulness' agenda in those terms.[34] Thus, far from liberating Trimble to push Unionist causes, the Belfast Agreement actually constrained him much of the time. Most notably, after the first suspension in February 2000, No. 10 urged Trimble not to celebrate too loudly about this unilateral reassertion of the sovereignty of Westminster lest it make it impossible to re-assemble the Northern Ireland Executive – and the UUP leader acquiesced. Indeed, as Henry Patterson observed in his study of the UUP Assembly group, 'in his desire to disprove the republican charge that they "don't want a Fenian about the place", Mr Trimble and his main lieutenants have tended to avoid saying anything that might be regarded as too abrasive to their new colleagues in government'.[35] Although he did not think that Northern Ireland was a 'failed political entity' per se, he nonetheless also believed that the only viable future which the existing Province had in the current circumstances was by governing in conjunction with republicans.[36] Moreover, he also felt increasingly constricted about the allies he could seek abroad. It was a subset of his concern with the 'blame game'. Thus, he believed that he could not associate with 'yahoos' in America; by this, he did not mean far-right militias or the KKK, but perfectly respectable Republican US Congressmen who would likely have loathed the Provisionals because they were aligned with anti-American terrorists all over the world. Even after September 11, he simply wanted the Americans to apply 'a wee bit more pressure' on Irish republicans – that is, a shift in the terms of trade *within* the existing process, rather vigorously pushing their exclusion (indeed, some of Sinn Fein's American counsellors were surprised at how little trouble he actually caused them considering the changed ideological climate).[37] Some American conservatives might well have been prepared to risk relations with the most purist elements of the rump Irish lobby, for the sake of a morally clear stance on the Provisionals. No one, though, was going to stick their necks out for so exquisitely calibrated a policy when even the Provisionals' main victims – namely, the Unionists – were not seeking to place them beyond the pale.

Trimble also did not take O'Callaghan's advice about the need for Unionists to engage in new forms of political and cultural struggle for a far simpler, personal reason: he was exhausted. The years of struggle and protest meetings, from the 1970s onwards, and above all after 1985, had exacted their toll. He had been there, and done that, and in middle age could not maintain the struggle at the same tempo. Viewing him over the years, Viscount Cranborne even wondered whether Trimble, like Margaret Thatcher, had not expended his reserves of courage: Cranborne believed that political courage was a finite, not a replenishable resource.[38] It was not that he had abandoned the Ulster Society's agenda. Rather, he simply could not carry it forward any more on a sustained, day-to-day basis. Partly, this was because he used up his energies in combating relentless internal challenges to his authority, in which he inevitably invested much emotional and political capital. Thus, in October 2002, Trimble appeared to be at least as excited by the success of his chief whip, Jim Wilson, in coming ahead of David Burnside in the ballot of the South Antrim Ulster Unionist Association for selection as Assembly candidates as he was by the uncovering of the alleged republican spy ring at Stormont. And stylistically, he increasingly doubted the value of what he called 'American-style campaigning' at Westminster (after all, he adds, few others do this in the Commons). Thus, Trimble never formally followed up, either in writing or in person, with the 27 Labour and Liberal Democrat MPs who voted against the Government's decision in December 2001 to grant Commons office facilities to Sinn Fein.[39] Indeed, of that score of MPs, Trimble knew only three of them – Gwyneth Dunwoody, Frank Field and Kate Hoey – whose views were already well known. He would not even have recognised many of the others, though everyone knew who he was. But whatever the cause of his shortcomings in conducting ideological and cultural struggles, there can be no doubt that his *modus operandi* was the polar opposite of Irish republicans. Thus, Trimble took the view that he had limited political resources and would therefore concentrate his efforts in those areas which mattered most to him (and where he did quite well). For the rest, he appeared to show a certain unwillingness to 'throw good money after bad'. Sinn Fein, by contrast, campaigned on almost *everything*. Thus, when they launched their 'No Return To Stormont' campaign of 1997–8, Adams and McGuinness must have known that the end result of any settlement would be some kind of Northern Ireland Assembly; but although they were bound to lose, the fuss which they made helped to convince the two Governments that the republican movement had made a massive sacrifice which required 'collateral' in other areas.

The end result in policy terms was not so much 'New Unionism' as 'Minimalistic Unionism' or, at times, something which can only be described as 'Trimbleism'. Its lodestar was the consent principle, and the outworkings thereof. Along with the British state, he believed that the IRA campaign to bring about a united Ireland had failed and that Adams and McGuinness knew it. They had structurally, if not ideologically, accepted the consent principle by entering Stormont. Thus, he told me with great pleasure that he once observed Gerry Kelly proprietorially taking some schoolchildren round Stormont: 'he was not there to tell them how evil this place was'.[40] He believed that they were so comfortable there that to withdraw access to those institutions had 'become a pressure point on them'.[41] Acceptance of that consent principle, whether structurally or ideologically, required that the republican movement also – eventually – abandon the means of coercion. And, if republicans no longer had the option of bombing London, they would lose their 'supplementary mandate' of violence, resulting in the creation of a political level playing field. This helps to explain why Trimble was prepared to devote so much time to securing decommissioning. Essentially, he accepted Quentin

Thomas's colourful analogy: that republicans were the lobsters who had to be enticed into the lobster pots. But in order to entrap such creatures, you need bait – and the only problem was that the bait in this case came off the hide of the unionist community, and sometimes from very sensitive spots in the unionist body politic. Partly, as has been noted, Trimble was prepared to live with such concessions because he genuinely believed that unionism had won – in the sense that the Union endured and because republicans were operating British institutions. It was a variant of Eoghan Harris's line to the UUP conference in Enniskillen in 1999: 'Look, Sinn Fein fought for 30 years. It's like a kid wanting a bike for Christmas. The bike they wanted was a united Ireland. They didn't get the bike. Please give them a few stickers.'[42] Likewise, he believed that the Irish Republic was re-entering the British family of nations, partly through the mechanisms of the British-Irish Council and through greater economic integration such as the gradual creation of a single energy market for both countries.[43] Indeed, he often couched his arguments for the Agreement not in traditional Unionist terms, but in terms of how much it would upset purist republicans. Thus, UUP literature in the 1998 referendum and the 2001 Westminster elections quoted liberally from former IRA prisoners such as Brendan ('Darkie') Hughes and Anthony McIntyre. But for many of Trimble's one-time natural supporters, the vexation of such foes was not enough. Since when, they asked, did men like Hughes and McIntyre set the gold standards of unionism?

Thanks both to its actual provisions, and to the skill of Sinn Fein in using Stormont as that 'bully pulpit', the Belfast Agreement did not look like a unionist victory at all to much of the majority population. Thus, the Union may have endured, but it would be a very different kind of Northern Ireland from that which obtained even under direct rule from 1972. Ultimately, it was a Union for which Trimble was prepared to settle. Like Faulkner, he believed that these were the only terms on which the Union could last. 'It is simply not possible to run Northern Ireland on the basis that excludes the 40% plus who regard themselves as nationalists,' he told the UUP conference on 17 November 2001. 'Like it or not, by fair means and foul, Sinn Fein does have 20% of the vote.'[44] Northern Ireland could only continue as an entity whole and undivided – as opposed to a re-partition or cantonisation – on this inclusive basis.[45] Indeed, according to *Ha'aretz* of 15 November 2002 he opined that after almost 30 years of violent conflict, most Protestants have recognised that the status quo was unacceptable and that they, too, wanted change. What was curious about Trimble was the apparent ease with which he adjusted to the changes. Thus, he was quite unsentimental about prisoner releases per se. Rather, his anger was mostly directed at the NIO for not foreseeing the optical problems for him during the 1998 referendum arising out of the republican triumphalism upon the freeing of the Balcombe Street gang. Likewise, at a breakfast meeting on the first floor at No. 10 on 2 October 2000, his worries were about public perceptions of how the issue of republican prisoners who were 'On the Run' (OTRs) was handled: his message was not that a scheme for resolving the OTRs issue was wrong in principle, simply that he wanted 'no more nasty surprises' of which he was not informed.[46]

Vexing as these were, they hardly went to the core of the problems that were upsetting much of his community. As Robin Wilson has noted, many unionists – and this extends way beyond the core support of the DUP – have a semi-religious world view. For them, freeing murderers, both loyalist and republican, was unconscionable.[47] Much the same went for the presence of Sinn Fein ministers in government, and the reforms of the RUC. Sometimes, he would even brush aside some of the anger over such measures – outworkings of the end of the Provisionals' campaign of armed struggle – as mere 'emotion'. At a minimum, he thought that those who focused on these matters were allowing their hearts to rule over their heads.[48] We often heatedly debated his acquiescence in such aspects of the Belfast Agreement: more than once, he described objections to some of its controversial provisions as the reaction of 'someone who is looking for an excuse to oppose change' or even as evidence of incipient 'Paisleyism'. Likewise, he sometimes claimed that the doubts of *The Daily Telegraph* about the accord could be ascribed to its supposedly partisan 'Tory' hostility to a Labour Government and all its works. It is hard to know if he seriously believed this – after all, some of the most articulate critics of the accord such as Dennis Kennedy and Conor Cruise O'Brien could hardly be said to base their objections upon 'Paisleyism' – or whether these were just the easiest arguments that came to hand for a hard-pressed politician. Likewise, he was also scornful of Jeffrey Donald-son's electoral successes, even when the Lagan Valley MP had scored the highest number of first preferences of any candidate in the 2003 Assembly elections. 'He's just getting the support of Paisleyites,' Trimble remarked.[49] His dismissive approach towards aspects of the unionist communal mood, because certain institutional arrangements had been settled to his satisfaction, was one of his greatest weaknesses as UUP leader. In one leap, without any disarmament or wholesale apology for their past violence, Trimble had taken republicans into the heart of government. Maybe, thought Unionists, they were destined to suffer defeats. But as Mohamed Heikal observed of the long-time Arab policy of boycotting the Jewish state, '[we] could not in the short term defeat Israel in a major battle, but it could make the moral force of the Arab position felt by refusing to acknowledge, recognise or negotiate with Israel . . . the strategy of ostracisation had entered the psyche of the humiliated masses, becoming a solace for their shock and impotence'.[50] If ostracism was the solace of the unionist masses, then Trimble assuredly threw away that card – not that he regarded it as of great value.

The British drew the appropriate conclusions and pressed ahead with their policies. By virtue of his reluctant acquiescence in those policies, Trimble also became part of the 'moral vacuum' which he discerned in Blair's handling of the process. Thus, despite the involvement of mainstream republicans in 30 murders since the Belfast Agreement was struck, and their refusal to condemn the attempted murder by dissidents of a Catholic PSNI recruit, he did not collapse the institutions in protest – even though support for the forces of law and order might have been supposed to be a prerequisite for initial entry into government, let alone two and a half years after it.[51] Like the British state, Trimble believed that it would be a stabler Northern Ireland with republicans inside the tent and towards achieving that end was prepared to give Adams and McGuinness time to sort themselves out. His problem was that whereas the British Government could afford to do that, much of his sceptical constituency was not so understanding. This forced him to jink to the right, and then to the left in a kind of 'Ali shuffle', but much of it was pure survivalism on a day-to-day basis. Thus, he ended up embracing two concepts which he had initially rejected as 'tacky', or worse: the post-dated resignation letter to Josias Cunningham of November 1999 and the temporary redesignation of the Alliance party as Unionists in the Assembly to secure his own re-election as First Minister in November 2001. Like Malcolm X, his operating slogan could be said to be 'by any means necessary'.[52] And by virtue of representing one of the most polarised constituencies in Northern Ireland, Trimble was forced constantly to attend to the needs of the Orange Order on the issue of Drumcree. So despite his admonition that unionists 'think politically', and communicate a viable modern case to the mainland and the wider world, Trimble ended up spending rather more time in 1998–9 on parades (which are incomprehensible and/or unacceptable to many outside of Northern Ireland) than on the RUC or even prisoner releases (where unionists would have enjoyed a measure of sympathy on the mainland). Even his genuine desire to reform the UUP's link with the Orange Order was often deferred because the important so often yielded pride of place to the urgent.[53] Trimble's unique circumstances thus meant that he was rarely able to enunciate a civic unionist identity on a coherent or consistent basis. But even if Trimble had done so, would nationalist Ireland have responded generously?[54] If the bitter, churlish response of many nationalist commentators concerning his remarkable Nobel Prize speech in Oslo in December 1998 and thereafter is anything to go by, he was probably best off doing what he had to do at his own pace.

'Doing what he had to do' meant, in this case, managing the unionist community and, specifically, the UUP. But was Trimble any good at it? Was he, to put it quite bluntly, a quality politician? Gerry Adams told the British that he was baffled and mystified that anyone as charmless and inept as Trimble could pull off any sort of political trick.[55] Jim Steinberg believed that Trimble was not a politician in any conventional sense at all, and certainly not compared to the far more 'smooth' Gerry Adams.[56] Likewise, Jonathan Powell told one associate that the UUP leader's negotiating style was bizarre: he would either ask for favours that were so inconsequential as to be worthless or else demand what by that point was impossible (such as 'save the RUC').[57] Peter Mandelson also recalls of Trimble's negotiating style that 'David was mostly rational; but he could, at times, be either casual to the point of jocularity and abandon or else be red in the face.'[58] Yet at another level, Trimble was sufficient unto the task at hand. Paddy Teahon, who observed him during many sessions from 1995–2000, eventually concluded that in the narrowest sense, Trimble was in fact very good and that his bizarre skills were perfectly matched to the bizarre, sometimes gothic ways of an ageing and decrepit UUP.[59] After all, Trimble survived repeated challenges, internally and externally, despite forging an accord that administered the *coup de grâce* to the old Ulster. Even Adams came to the conclusion that for all his awkwardness, Trimble was not entirely deficient in political tradecraft: 'At times, after difficult meetings with him, yes, I felt like blowing my gasket. You think, "I wouldn't do it this way or that way if I were in his shoes." But at some point you just take a vow of silence. Some of it's just him and is nothing to do with the nature of Unionism – such as when you see him exiting the stage with Clinton [at the Odyssey in December 2000] or leaving Hillsborough in the middle of a negotiation [in March 2003]. But whether he's done what he's done for purely tactical reasons, in order to maintain unionism's influence with London, or genuinely because he wants to develop a pluralist unionism, Trimble has the really difficult task, of making some sort of relationship with your neighbours. To do that, you have to do the hardest thing of all – to negotiate with your own side. In his own way, David did it. The easy job is Paisley's job.'[60]

Trimble certainly proved the validity of the old Ulster expression – that 'the creaking door hangs long'. Of course, he had enjoyed the support of the British and Irish states, and the US Administration, but those were frequently dubious assets for the task at hand. What Trimble had was a certain academic plausibility, notwithstanding the anti-intellectualism of much of the party. Few activists would have understood the arcana of the three-stranded process, yet Trimble somehow conveyed to enough of them the sense that he would not be outwitted by the 'wily', 'fork-tongued' nationalists. Even so redoubtable an opponent of Trimble as Ernie Baird acknowledged this quality: 'What keeps him there is that he appears to know what's going on in the outside world. And a lot of our folk will say, "Oh, Mr Trimble is very clever, he's a lecturer, you know." There's still a certain respect for people of learning, and especially so the further west you go.'[61] And because so many aspects of the emerging dispensation would have been very hard to swallow, he treated them gently, through the softer medium of seminars, rather than lectures. If Trimble had 'educated' his constituency or 'sold' the Belfast Agreement as nationalists and their allies often urged him to do – that is, rammed the necessity of concessions down their throats – he would have been doomed.[62] Because he did it gently, effecting it in ambiguous increments, and because of where he seemed to have come from in ideological terms, they accepted it more readily. As Chris McGimpsey, a Maginnis supporter in the 1995 leadership election observes, 'Ken would have been slaughtered for even attempting a quarter of what Trimble's done!'[63] Where he was a poor politician was at the level of personal relations, unlike James Molyneaux or even Ian Paisley. Indeed, Trimble's achievement in rising to, and staying at the top for so long, is all the more remarkable when one considers his personality. He was no hail-fellow-well-met backslapper with the party faithful or constituents – after the boisterous fashion of Paisley – nor did he display the natural, low-key courtesy of Molyneaux.[64] He was simply not that interested in other people and their problems, although he was not altogether unobservant about human foibles and could, on occasion, display flashes of insight. Partly, this owed much to his shyness, and partly also to a genuine sense of mission about what was and was not important. The sense of mission meant that he had far less time for personal, non-political friends. I would sometimes tell him that I had interviewed some old school friend or former colleague. His eyes would light up and his crooked teeth would flash in an engaging grin; he would invariably ask me to pass on warm regards to the individual in question. But so far as I am aware, he never sought to contact the old friend and in most cases had not been in touch for years, even before his life became dramatically busier as UUP leader. His emotional and personal needs appear to have been quite satisfied by his family life – and by his music.

Because of his shyness and powerful sense of mission and what was and was not important, he developed only a few meaningful relationships with figures in the highest reaches of the Governments with which he had to deal: Blair (and his *alter egos* John Holmes and Jonathan Powell), Ahern and Clinton. As one senior British official observes, 'Adams knows that the important thing is to have contact at the top, namely at No. 10, but also to cover all other angles. Trimble, by contrast, thinks that if you have a relationship with No. 10, that's it.' The UUP leader never forged a similar relationship with his SDLP 'co-president' at Stormont, Seamus Mallon. Maybe so: but there is no doubt that Trimble genuinely found Mallon very difficult (and vice versa). Their failed relationship remains one of the 'might-have-beens' of the process, and there was little of the mutual regard which characterised the relationship between Sir James Craig and Joe Devlin, the leader of northern nationalism, in the 1920s. But then neither man had to work with each other in the same cheek-by-jowl fashion as Trimble and Mallon.[65] In this sense, the relationship between Faulkner, on the one side, and Paddy Devlin on the other – who worked with each other during the 1974 Sunningdale experiment – is perhaps a more relevant comparison. Again, a great mutual regard grew up as they worked cheek-by-jowl with each other in embattled circumstances.[66]

Nor did Trimble have many political intimates within his own community. He admired John Taylor and took him very seriously as a bellwether of unionist opinion. Likewise, he would regularly sound out party officers such as Jack Allen, James Cooper, Reg Empey and Denis Rogan and amongst civil servants he particularly admired David Lavery and Maura Quinn. He trusted and respected the abilities of younger political appointees around him, such as his chief of staff, David Campbell, and his Westminster aide, Barry White: affording an insight to those junior to himself was a way of repaying his own debt to William Craig, who had encouraged young talent in his time. However, he most enjoyed unwinding with knowledgeable and entertaining associates from outside the party, such as Ruth Dudley Edwards. But he had no one intimate or counsellor, after the fashion of Paisley and Desmond Boal. One of his deepest traits was his desire to be the smartest kid on the block and he therefore liked to work things out for himself. Trimble's lack of sustained interest in other people also contributed to the debacle which befell the RUC. Thus, his failure to find out anything about Peter Smith's views on policing when he approved the former UUC Honorary Secretary's appointment to the Patten Commission turned out to be disastrous for him. This lack of *sustained* interest in people and what motivated them probably made his task harder than it otherwise might have been. Indeed, Lord Fraser of Kilmorack's observation about the very different personality and style of R.A. Butler can also be applied to Trimble: '. . . like many very clever people, Rab was rather naïf about the simpler aspects of life'.[67] On the other hand, a more gregarious person would probably have been too sensitive to keep at it for so long in adversity and especially in the face of such disapproval from their own community and party. Thus, these faults did not prevent him from carrying on his project much further than many friends and foes thought possible: his tenacity was one of his most under-rated qualities.

Where Trimble can seriously be faulted is in his judgment of mainland politics. This prevented him from doing the deal under more advantageous circumstances, in 1995–7, when both the Tories and the Fine Gael-led 'Rainbow Coalition' were in power, than after 1997, when New Labour and the Fianna Fail-led coalition were in power. His unwillingness to strike the bargain was governed by considerations of principle and of circumstances. He believed that any deal with nationalist Ireland would only stick if it was sponsored by the 'Greener' parties in both Britain and the Republic. Certainly, any treaty sponsored by the likes of John Bruton, especially in respect of the revision of Articles 2 and 3, would have encountered greater difficulty in the Republic. But Trimble's assessment was certainly not true of any treaty sponsored by Major – if only because Blair, in opposition, was prepared to back up the Tories against the wishes of nationalist Ireland (exemplified by his backing for Major's response to the Mitchell report in January 1996). His unwillingness to do the deal under the Conservatives also owed something to residual mistrust of what they had done during their long period in office, exemplified most recently by the Frameworks Documents of 1995. But in the light of the subsequent Belfast Agreement, it may be asked whether that paper was really so bad from a unionist viewpoint. Indeed, following conversations with senior officials such as Quentin Thomas in late 1997, Paul Bew wondered whether the Trimble of 1995 (and, indeed, the whole UUP) had allowed themselves to be 'spooked' by some of the more removable provisions of the Frameworks. Thomas told Bew that the most contro-versial Strand II proposals on cross-border bodies – which were meant to be invested with 'dynamic', 'executive' and 'harmonising' powers – were going to be severely diluted in negotiations with the Irish, if only because the UK Treasury saw grave cost implications for the Exchequer in the maximalist conceptions for all-Ireland institutions. Likewise, Con-servative euro-sceptics were bound to have minimised the nationalist-friendly EU dimensions of the Frameworks. In other words, Bew believed that Trimble was so fixated upon the *remediable* deficiencies of the Frame-works that he rejected them and subsequently was forced to pay an enormous price in other areas to rid the Unionists of a (mostly) phantom threat. The most costly of these were the arrangements in the 1998 Belfast Agreement on prisoners and the RUC. Trimble contends that 'the Tories would have been tougher on the RUC' than New Labour, but there is not a whit of evidence to support this assertion. New Labour's differences with the Conservatives' Northern Ireland policy lay not in the realm of the consent principle, the constitutional issues or the institutional arrangements, where there was broad agreement between the two major parties. Rather, they lay in the domain of 'reserved' issues such as parades, policing and prisoners. John Major's testimony suggests that even if he had wanted to be very radical in those areas when in office – and he avers that this was not so – the balance of forces within the Tory party would have prevented him from implementing such policies.

But the UUP did not only pay in 'reserved' matters for its obsession with the 'paper tiger' of the Strand II provisions of the Frameworks. It also paid in the Strand I provisions of the internal governance of the Province. Thus, the Frameworks Documents of 1995 envisaged an Assembly without a full Executive. In other words, the emotional pain for unionists would have been little greater than accepting a republican vice chairman of Fermanagh District Council. Moreover, under the Frameworks proposals of 1995 there was complete gridlock: departments could barely sneeze without obtaining cross-community consent in the relevant committee and full Assembly. By contrast, under the Belfast Agreement, republicans sat in a full Executive with law-making powers, and the individual ministers were afforded considerable latitude in their bailiwicks. Trimble gave generously in Strand I because, once again, he over-estimated his own position. He believed in his own mind that he had won a great victory on minimising the cross-border provisions of the Belfast Agreement – and, at a political level, he was right since the DUP was never able to gain much traction on this subject in the way they did under Faulkner. Therefore, he felt he had to give the SDLP something to fend off the attacks of Sinn Fein for entering office alongside the UUP. Indeed, Trimble's other great strategic miscalculation, along with his pathological mistrust of the Tories, was his belief that the SDLP was savable. This was perhaps understandable in the context of 1998; but he continued to cling to this delusion after Sinn Fein had overhauled the SDLP in the Westminster elections of 2001 and to pay a high price for it. He ideally wanted Sinn Fein inside the tent, but preferably as the minority party in nationalism.

So much for Trimble's qualities as a politician. But what of his inheritance? He became leader well after the debacles of the prorogation of Stormont in 1972 and the Anglo-Irish Agreement of 1985. Moreover, he inherited a party which during the long years of devolution, from 1921 to 1972, had become parochial and inward-looking when cut off from the day-to-day currents of mainland politics. Party and state became fused during the 50-plus years of UUP rule and there was no need to think politically because Unionist majorities were guaranteed; the NICS did all of the thinking, so when the UUP lost power, it was partially lobotomised. Although concerns about deficiencies in what used to be called 'publicity' were expressed in party circles both before and after 1972, these were never remedied in a serious way – and certainly not by the UUP MPs at Westminster, despite the accession of so distinguished an orator as Enoch Powell to their ranks.[68] Indeed, as Peter Catterall and Sean McDougall have observed, a quarter-century of IRA terrorism had been far more successful in integrating the politics of Northern Ireland and Great Britain than the constitutionalism of Unionist MPs at Westminster. Whatever conclusions could be derived from this analysis about the efficacy of the strategies of nationalists and republicans respectively, Catterall and McDougall are undoubtedly accurate in their assessment of the *inefficacy* of Unionists.[69] Other peoples (or culturally distinctive groups from particular sub-national regions) that had suffered major defeats had learned to send their best politicians to the centre and cultivated high levels of parliamentary skills: the example of the American Deep South, which dispatched Congressmen or Senators to Washington at a young age to accumulate seniority in the federal capital in order to roll back the effects of Reconstruction, comes particularly to mind.[70] But 30 years of defeats did not administer a cathartic shock to the Unionist body politic to shake them out of their complacency.

The bulk of the middle classes opted out after the UUP's loss of patronage powers in 1972. What remained was the Third Eleven, if that. Thus, Ken Maginnis states that 'the Robert Babingtons and the Dick Fergusons left [Stormont MP for North Down and subsequently a County Court judge; Stormont MP for South Tyrone 1969–72 and subsequently an eminent silk in London] leaving a primary school teacher like myself to do the business. I did the utmost that I could. Those who never got stuck in can't really criticise.'[71] In other words, those who might have communicated best with mainland audiences, such as the old aristocracy and the *bourgeoisie*, did not do so, leaving the field to Paisley and UUP mediocrities. Indeed, Paisley's platform style – which to many on the mainland became synonymous with the cause of Ulster – made politics even less respectable and desirable to much of the Province's middle classes. What remained was a disproportionately *petit bourgeois* cadre (many of the most public-spirited of the *petit bourgeoisie* joined the RUC and the UDR and would have nothing to do with politics). Indeed, as has been noted, of the sitting UUP MPs at the time of the 1995 leadership election, only Martin Smyth, Taylor and Trimble had attended university. The non-graduates had many qualities, such as staying power, but many of them were beset by a certain lack of intellectual self-confidence and a conviction that those wily nationalists would somehow outwit them in any negotiations. As such, their attitude was reminiscent of Will Rogers' famous quip encapsulating US isolationist attitudes, 'America never lost a war and never won a conference.'[72]

So much for Trimble's inheritance. But what were his real achievements? He undoubtedly got the best of the North-South arrangements, at least to the extent that they never became an issue for him within the unionist family as the Council of Ireland did for Faulkner at the time of Sunningdale. The revision of Articles 2 and 3, so elusive under the Tories, was secured on his watch with the help of the British Government. Despite Adams' bluster, the reciprocal scrapping of Section 75 of the Government of Ireland Act 1920 was nothing like of equivalent value – as was proven by the subsequent suspensions of the institutions by successive Northern Ireland Secretaries. The consent principle had been reiterated under a New Labour Government. As Paul Bew has noted, this had been a constant of British state thinking since the time of Gladstone. But it has waxed and waned since and in its modern form, it had been successfully renegotiated by officials such as Chilcot and Thomas during the course of discussions with nationalist Ireland on the Downing Street Declaration of 1993.[73] Likewise, Blair accepted consent in Opposition for his own reasons. Nonetheless, although such developments predated Trimble's leadership, it was not a negligible achievement – especially considering the degree to which Blair was in thrall to a republican interpretation of Irish history. By staying close to the Prime Minister, inside the Blairite tent, he had avoided losing the 'blame game', at least on the British mainland, by the time of the fourth suspension of the institutions in October 2002 and the second postponement of the Assembly elections scheduled for May 2003. So complete was his success in Great Britain that Paul Murphy, the Northern Ireland Secretary, even employed Trimble's arguments in the Commons on 12 May 2003 in justifying the relevant legislation giving effect to that decision.[74] Whatever Blair thought that Unionists had been responsible for in the past, he could not pin much on them in the present (even though he did not 'punish' Sinn Fein for any defaults and by extension did not confer any benefits upon the UUP). In part, Trimble's success in not losing the 'blame game' owed much to mainland perceptions of his reasonable demeanour. A typical reaction to the UUP leader can be found in the diary of Victor Stock, then Rector of St Mary-Le-Bow, on 4 June 1996: 'David Trimble came for his Dialogue, not as an important politician in an armoured vehicle or chauffeur-driven car, but on the Underground. He is clever, funny, foxy, easily roused and astute. He talked to me about how he had been a Christian Fundamentalist, but had begun to move on and open up. He's very worried for his four-year-old-child and doesn't want to be in politics for ever . . . I think he has enough bravery and intelligence to be of real assistance to the cause of peace. In public, in the pulpit, he was an excellent ambassador for Unionism. In England we never hear the Unionist case put in a compelling way.'[75] Few, if any, unionists elicited such positive responses during the Troubles – although he never fully exploited this prestige. But there was one other, negative reason which potentially justified Trimble's course of action. If unionism was in cultural, demographic and political decline – a presumption which Trimble utterly rejected – then he did well to sign the deal before the slide became yet more precipitate.[76] Thus, there was at least a chance that the Belfast Agreement, with its multiple safeguards and checks and balances, could end up being a kind of last refuge for the Ulster-British population. In that sense, the Belfast Agreement might eventually resemble the Lebanese National Pact of 1943 – which was regarded as a great defeat for the Christian Maronites when it was signed, but which in the changed circumstances of the late 1950s was worth defending to the death.[77] If this turned out to be so, it would be a tremendous retrospective vindication for Trimble.

So much for the credit side. On the debit side, he had not resolved the issue of Ulster's anomalous status within the United Kingdom nor, indeed, in Europe and the wider world. Thus, following the second postponement of the May 2003 Stormont elections, Paul Murphy was able to tell the Commons that 'the nature of the Assembly that was suspended and eventually dissolved is different from that of any other Assembly in the United Kingdom . . . If the Assembly had not had those special rules and had become an ordinary Assembly like any other in the United Kingdom, the Belfast Agreement would not have worked.'[78] Indeed, as Donald Horowitz has noted, Northern Ireland is unique amongst consociational settlements in requiring a grand coalition of all of the major parties.[79] After 11 September, the differential treatment of Ulster continued: everywhere, there was a new-found vigour in the war against terrorism, except in Northern Ireland, where in the eyes of many unionists policy continued to be made to keep potential insurgents quiet (a policy alternatively described by both the Prime Minister and Paul Murphy as 'five years of "creative ambiguity"').[80] And despite Victor Stock's favourable observations concerning Trimble's advocacy skills, there was no adequate mechanism for disseminating the unionist message. Such activity as took place was terribly *ad hoc*. Occasionally, as in his UUC speech of March 2002, Trimble would make rude remarks about the Irish Republic, but even he rarely put forward a positive case for the Union from first principles – asserting that Ulster was geologically, ethnically and religiously apart from the rest of the island with linkages to England and Scotland as least as strong as elsewhere in Ireland.[81] Certainly, the intellectual hegemony of unionism within the Conservative party increased after it went into Opposition in 1997, and the support for the unionist case in substantial sections of mainland print journalism was arguably at least as great as at any time since Partition; but these were mostly the consequences of autonomous forces which long pre-dated Trimble's accession to the leadership, such as the influence of Enoch Powell's thought on sovereignty and the nation state, or the rise to journalistic prominence of several disciples of T.E. Utley. But because of his own personal shyness, Trimble was too rarely in touch with these forces, and thus Unionism punched beneath its weight. And whilst his own appearances and reasonable demeanour formed a most pleasant contrast with Paisley in terms of the sensibilities of television audiences on the mainland, he frequently failed to land effective blows for his cause. Too often, he was caught up in the 'wonkery' of the process; the audience might have thought he was decent, but they would have lost him in the detail. In that sense, although he intellectually recognised its importance, he never really internalised Eoghan Harris's advice to the UUP in his contribution to the Ulster Young Unionist Council's pamphlet *Selling Unionism: Home and Away*, published in 1995. Harris believed that Unionists were hopeless with the media because they wanted to win their case as if in a court of law, not tell a story after the fashion of southern Catholics as if in a theatre (amongst Unionists, perhaps only Ken Maginnis was able to do that reasonably competently for a southern audience). Indeed, it was striking how little credit Trimble received from southern opinion, even after signing the deal. Thus, when Blair postponed the May 2003 Assembly elections because the IRA had not definitively abandoned paramilitary activity, an *Irish Times*/TNS poll showed that Irishmen were twice as inclined to blame Trimble for the crisis as they were Sinn Fein (even though 45% of respondents simultaneously also said that the IRA had not made clear its intentions to end violence).[82]

Further afield, Unionism had failed successfully to align itself with potential sympathisers, such as southern evangelicals in America – despite the
enduring, post-September 11, anti-Americanism of Sinn Fein that annoyed
even Niall O'Dowd during the war on Iraq.[83] Nor, despite Trimble's
own grasp of such Unionist-friendly precedents such as the South Tyrol
question, did the UUP find a vocabulary or readily graspable set of
analogies to dramatise their case. Thus, there was nothing to compare
with Irish nationalist successes in comparing their cause with the American civil rights movement – or tarring their opponents with the brush
of the French Algerian *pieds noirs* or Afrikaners.[84]

At home, as has been noted, Trimble inherited an antiquated party
structure. In purely technical terms – printed literature, the website, agent
training – the UUP improved considerably during his leadership. Where
Trimble failed was to use the UUP machine in the same way that the
republican leadership uses the Sinn Fein machine, namely to maintain
communal morale. Such sentiments were exemplified by the remark made
by an elderly resident of the Glenbryn estate in north Belfast: 'I wish to
G-d Gerry Kelly was a Prod.'[85] In such an environment in which nationalists increasingly enjoyed cultural hegemony, it was scarcely surprising
that middle-class Protestants – the breed with which Trimble had so
ambiguous a relationship – did not want to opt back into politics. Even
within Unionist politics, the atmosphere was so poisonous and divisive
that only those with the strongest stomachs would dare enter the arena.
And, of course, Northern Irish society, after the ceasefires, was not noticeably peaceful. According to police sources, at least 79 people were murdered by paramilitaries between 1999 and 2002. Nor would public
confidence have been greatly increased by the reports of the Policing
Board, the Police Oversight Commissioner or the Northern Ireland Affairs
Select Committee of the Commons. The collective impression – at least
from the media accounts of their work – was of endemic criminality
combined with an over-stretched police force.[86] Indeed, a private survey
carried out for Belfast City Council revealed that the respondents saw
the paramilitaries as more influential than the politicians.[87] If a key aspect
of the Trimble project was to re-energise and re-involve them in public
life, thus ensuring that Unionism did not punch beneath its weight and
generated a political class capable of communicating with the wider
world, then he cannot be said to have succeeded particularly well. Despite
some UUP gains in the 2003 Assembly elections in parts of the greater

Belfast area (and the growth of membership in some UUP branches such as Castlereagh in the East Belfast Westminster constituency) the re-engagement of the provincial *bourgeoisie* with unionist politics remained patchy.[88] And if middle-class re-engagement is judged by the levels of turn-out in elections, then Trimble made little or no difference save possibly in the referendum – though the DUP did not resolve the conundrum of differential nationalist-unionist turn-out either.

The broader demographic trend was also mixed. Certainly, there was some evidence of Protestants deciding to remain in Northern Ireland to attend universities at home rather than in Britain itself. Thus, before the Belfast Agreement around half of those from the non-Catholic sector who went on to higher education attended Northern Ireland institutions. By 2000/2001, this had increased to 61% (the percentage of Catholics who went on to higher education choosing to stay in the Province also rose by similar numbers during this period, from 71% to 82%).[89] That said, this 'trend' may have been as much the consequence of the imposition of university tuition fees imposed by central government in 1998–9 (which gave a financial incentive not to leave Ulster) as it was the consequence of the return of local self-government.[90] But for all that, the ten-yearly census published at the end of 2002 further suggested that the Protestant 'brain drain' still remained very substantial: it revealed that there had been a net out-migration of Protestants of around 1600 per annum, many of whom, it could be surmised, were bright children from state grammar schools who were attending mainland universities and not returning to Ulster (by contrast, there was an average net in-migration of Catholics of around 700 per annum over the same period, adding half a per cent to the Catholic population).[91] Again, this suggested that Northern Ireland was becoming a 'colder house' for Protestants, to use Trimble's phrase in the 1998 Nobel speech – and a warmer, more welcoming one for Catholics.[92] Whilst the overall 2001 census was better for unionists than many of them had feared, the results nonetheless still implied profound *qualitative* as opposed to *quantitative* problems for the future make-up of the pro-British community.

Indeed, wide swathes of the unionist middle classes remained ambiguous about Trimble. Brian Lennon SJ wrote in his insightful *Irish News* column of 14 September 1995 that his liberal Protestant friends were a little annoyed by Trimble's victory in the recent leadership election but that they could scarcely complain since they had opted out whilst the new UUP chief had put up with the drudgery over the years. In fact, little changed in terms of the attitudes of some liberal Protestants in the intervening nine years. For them, Trimble remained too 'Orange', and still the supposedly gloating victor of Drumcree. Norman Porter spoke for a segment of liberal Protestant opinion when he asserted in *The Elusive Quest: Reconciliation in Northern Ireland* that the UUP leader remained far too wedded to a notion of the Agreement as underwriting British sovereignty and insufficiently appreciative of the leap made so far by republicans by participating in Northern Ireland's institutions by his 'continued use of confrontational language in his current demand for disbandment by the IRA'. Rather, Porter asserted, there was 'a space for a serious unionist-republican dialogue over arms and related issues that never occurred because of unionism's confrontational tactics' (in fact, as has been seen, there was a remarkable private dialogue between Trimble and his republican counterparts).[93] But for others, including some who also regarded themselves as liberals, Trimble went way too far in treating with republicanism and did far too little to save the RUC – a blow which some regarded as even greater than the Anglo-Irish Agreement. Indeed, if there were routes open to Unionism other than the peace process – and in 1995, the protest against the abolition of the playing of the National Anthem at the Queen's University graduation ceremony, the by-election victory of Robert McCartney, and the surprisingly strong middle-class support for the Drumcree demonstrations suggested that elements of the Protestant *bourgeoisie* were willing to back more radical options – then Trimble played a major part in closing down those alternatives. Thus, for a variety of reasons, there was little affection for Trimble, save in a small coterie of non-party admirers, though there was much grudging respect. As Paul Bew noted, the adage that 'no man is a hero to his valet' is never truer than in the world of Northern Ireland's Unionist politics.[94]

How much power did Trimble regain, both for himself and the Unionist people? The Strand I settlement suggests not very much, in so far as Unionists had to share power not merely with nationalists but republicans as well, who in the political circumstances that then obtained were well-nigh un-ejectable. Moreover, despite the apparent requirement for dual consent of both communities on key issues, the settlement was organised in such a way as to give individual ministers considerable autonomy in their own fiefdoms, at least rhetorically. As Alex Kane observed, in some ways the democratic deficit was as wide after the Agreement, with devol-

ution, as it had been under direct-rule ministers.[95] Thus, Sinn Fein ministers could use their portfolios as a kind of platform for conditioning the
public space, exemplified by McGuinness's decision to scrap the 11-plus
examination. No doubt this experience does much to explain why Protestants, in a poll published in the *Belfast Telegraph* on 20 February 2003,
gave the barest of majorities to the proposition that devolved rule was
best for Northern Ireland: for many of them, local self-government was
not worth having on such terms and they believed that the grammars
were for the time being safer under the cautious team of junior direct-rule
ministers that took over after suspension.[96] Many people also believed
that the devolved institutions were massively overblown and costly for
an area whose population was smaller than that of West Yorkshire. Such
sentiments were reinforced when it was learned that Assemblymen were
still being paid a large chunk of their salaries, even though the institutions
were suspended.[97] But the latitude afforded departmental ministers did
not appear, however, to concern Trimble unduly. Indeed, for much of
the time, he appears not to have been interested in driving through any
very ambitious policy agenda, despite his reputation as a 'policy wonk'.
And although he played a key part in the return of provincial self-
government, he leaves little in the way of a personally distinctive administrative legacy. Thus, unlike Sir James Craig, he cannot be said to have
created a provincial bureaucracy largely from scratch; he merely inherited
pre-existing NICS structures from the direct-rule ministers. Nor could
he boast anything like Brookeborough's achievement in the 1940s of
securing from Whitehall parity between Northern Irish and mainland
levels of welfare provision.[98] But whatever his skills as an administrator,
there can be no doubt that Trimble considerably over-rated the popularity
of devolution amongst unionists, which partly explains why he was willing
to take a risk on another negotiation with the republican movement in
the autumn of 2003.

Trimble's real function was never as a state-builder. Rather, it was to
negotiate the high politics of the new dispensation. But here, too, his
power was limited and he was often 'out of the loop'. For although he
was the Province's foremost elected official, he was kept totally in the
dark about the IRA spy ring at Stormont that led to the suspension of
the institutions in October 2002, and potentially at the cost of his own
job. There was a widespread suspicion in Unionist circles, Paul Bew's
phrase, that Unionists may have won the moral high ground, but republi-

cans had the inside track. Given the choice of losing Trimble or the republicans, many anti-Agreement Unionists argued, the British Government would always opt to lose the UUP leader, if only because of the fear of bombs in London. In other words, the Blair ministry would always give priority to the 'peace process', which was between the state and the paramilitaries, over the 'political process', which was inclusive of all parties. Certainly, in his speech at the Belfast Harbour Commissioner's offices on 17 October 2002, Blair came perilously close to admitting that the Provisionals' residual capacity for threatening violence had won them considerable concessions.[99]

Yet despite that, and despite the considerable irritation which some officials at No. 10 and in the NIO felt about Trimble's unpredictability and stubbornness, Blair seemed for the longest time unwilling to risk the political destruction of the UUP leader – as exemplified by his decision to postpone the Assembly elections of May 2003 over the objections of Sinn Fein, the SDLP, the Irish Government, the DUP, the Conservative party and wide swathes of the UUP. Whatever the attractions of Peter Robinson or Nigel Dodds in the minds of some British panjandrums, losing Trimble still represented a leap in the dark. This was referred to derisively by some nationalist commentators as 'saving Private Trimble'.[100] Such criticisms were a back-handed tribute to the potency of the 'Trimble card' *vis-à-vis* the Prime Minister. Some nationalists regarded this as little more than an updated version of the 'Orange card', rejigged for the Blair era. As Gerry Adams observes: 'If you look back at the books, on Chichester-Clark or on Faulkner, as I've been doing recently, you see that the big worry of the British has been to stay on good terms with whoever is the leader of Unionism. You see it all the time in those memoirs, "Faulkner's going down the tubes or whatever". Trimble has done it, just like the rest of them. And fair play to him.'[101] But it was a very personalised kind of 'Orange card' and without Trimble's relationship to Blair, it is highly unlikely that it could ever have been played as successfully by any other leader of Unionism in these times. For the most part, these were procedural victories, such as postponing the 2001 local elections so that they would coincide with the Westminster poll, and four suspensions. They were designed to keep Trimble and the pro-Agreement UUP political class in play, rather than as concrete Unionist victories in terms of the actual governance of the Province. Yet at the time, they were victories nonetheless. And, on each occasion, the legislative mechanics required to push through these procedural, political successes reaffirmed British sovereignty in a manner that was painful to republicans. In that sense, Trimble's interpretation of the Belfast Agreement was triumphantly vindi- cated. Blair only ceased to protect Trimble in September/October 2003 by finally calling the twice-postponed Assembly elections – but it could be argued that Trimble played a part in that Prime Ministerial miscalcu- lation by wanting to hold the poll for his own reasons.

Trimble's successes thus lay largely in the realm of high *politics*, rather than in the realm of *policy* – whether towards the PSNI, criminal justice or other aspects of public administration. In all these areas, policy remained very 'Green'. And on the few occasions that Trimble did succeed in translating his personal relationship into a policy shift, such as the reprieve which he won for the home service battalions of the Royal Irish Regiment in May–June 2003, it was clearly done by the Government to try to help him through a difficult period within the party rather than because anyone in London thought that the RIR units were especially worth saving. As one loyalist observes, that made the reprieve even more insulting to many unionists: Trimble's political hide counted for more than the sacrifices made by the 206 RIR/UDR soldiers who lost their lives.[102] It was an extension of the point made earlier about Trimble's appeal in America. His message there was a highly personalised manifesto rather than a Unionist appeal per se. Essentially, it ran as follows. 'I'm David Trimble, I'm a decent civilised guy, and unless you help me those nasty mean Paisleyites will take over.' Thus, the Unionist cause had been whittled down to one rather slender thread – Trimble and Trimble's needs. It worked in its own terms, just, for a very long time. But it provided little intellectual or ideological basis for Unionism in the longer run, post-Trimble (or post-Blair, for that matter).

Even this limited strategy required a lot of hard pounding on Trimble's part. He had to force the pace himself, most notably in his threat to walk out over the draft Mitchell document at the start of Holy Week 1998 and in the run-up to the first suspension in February 2000. At other times, Trimble was the passive beneficiary of sheer luck: September 11; the PSNI raid on the Sinn Fein offices at Stormont in October 2002 which led to the fourth suspension of the institutions later that month; and, from a unionist perspective, the better-than-expected ten-yearly census result in December 2002 (indeed, he only contributed to the last-mentioned of these by virtue of producing four intelligent, Protestant, children). But whether accomplished by accident or design, Trimble lasted for the longest time. Judged by the Paisleyite standard – namely, that the process was about the transfer of Ulster into a united Ireland – Trimble did rather well to interpolate himself into Anglo-Irish deliberations. And, of course, the UUP was frequently at the centre of international media attention whenever its Executive or full Council met in order to decide whether to proceed with the next phase of the Belfast Agreement. Trimble's opponents thus underestimated one other key advantage which he as leader enjoyed: that at critical moments in the 'inclusive' process, the British state would, for whatever reason, give him just enough to ensure that he had a semi-plausible narrative to sell to his own people.

But judged by his own standards – namely, that this was a genuinely inclusive process across the board – Trimble did rather less well. The most notable instance of this was his failure to make any real impact upon the deliberations of the Patten Commission. He almost ceased to object to the routinisation of southern interference in the most sensitive areas of day-to-day governance of the Province. Thus he did not dissent loudly when the Taoiseach appeared to prefer the version of events offered by the republican movement to that of the Acting Chief Constable of the PSNI following the break-in at the Belfast Special Branch headquarters at Castlereagh on 17 March 2002.[103] With the exception of the question of the RIR home service battalions in 2003, he was a relatively passive player in the debate on demilitarisation, where his concerns often revolved around the timing of base closures and the need to avoid discomfiting surprises in the unionist community rather than the principle thereof. Partly, he was a secondary player in these discussions because he may have calculated that he could not greatly affect the outcome himself and if the British Government wanted to take risks with national security by pulling down watchtowers, let it be on their head. Why, then, throw good money after bad, as it were, by expending his limited chips pointlessly? At other times, he simply sold himself short. Thus, at the conclusion of the Mitchell review in November 1999, when Trimble took the leap of entering the Executive with Sinn Fein before they began disarming, he secured little or nothing in return at that moment of his maximum leverage. There was a certain lack of ruthlessness in his political conduct – or, more precisely, towards the 'big boys' in the political game. Thus, he was at times very understanding of the multiple considerations with which Blair, and even Clinton, had to juggle. As one No. 10 official observes, 'David Trimble, unlike Sinn Fein, is not a chiseller.' Partly, as one aide observes, this was a product of his dislike of asking for favours. How much this profited him, or his community, is open to question.

Ultimately, Trimble will be assessed on whether he strengthened the Union. Like Faulkner before him, Trimble concluded that the terms on offer from the two Governments were the only basis for sustaining the existing constitutional framework. Arthur Aughey has suggested that the UUP leader's predicament resembled that of the Sicilian Prince Don Fabrizio in Lampedusa's historical novel *The Leopard*. Faced with the Risorgimento, his nephew Tancredi suggests that 'unless we ourselves take a hand now, they'll foist a republic on us. If you want things to stay the same things will have to change.'[104] Thus, in order to maintain what really mattered – the Union – Trimble was prepared to tolerate very wide-ranging changes to the way Northern Ireland was governed. And it was a Northern Ireland which was subject to constant rolling change. This was effected through the work of the Equality and Human Rights Commissions, not to mention a further review of policing legislation and the ongoing work of the Police Ombudsman.[105] In short, as Blair observed in October 2002, in a speech largely directed at Adams and the Provisionals, there was an ongoing 'process'. This meant only one thing to his target audience. That the Belfast Agreement, far from representing an end point – a settlement, in other words – contained a transformative *dynamic* for what the Prime Minister believed had been a discriminatory society. If this interpretation is correct, then there is little stability in the process, for Trimble or any Unionist who might seek to do a deal with Irish nationalism. Thus, Trimble had airbrushed the 'd' word (standing for 'dynamic') – which had so offended him in the Frameworks Documents – out of the Strand II segments of the Belfast Agreement only to see it re-emerge in other provisions of the accord.

Ironically, both Trimble and Adams believed in the necessity of stability in order to attain their respective ends. But the definitions of 'stability' differed in each case. Trimble, obviously, wanted real stability so as to secure the Union, to bring the middle classes back into politics – and maybe even to bring about the political integration of Northern Ireland into the rest of the United Kingdom via the mechanism of Labour organising in the Province and a closer relationship between the UUP and the Tories. In Adams' case, stability meant principally an IRA ceasefire. Essentially, this would create a set of conditions that would answer John

Hume's question of some years previously: 'How do we end the British presence in Ireland in a manner that leaves behind a stable and peaceful Ireland?'[106] It was the kind of question which was also asked, in a different form, by republicans such as Jim Gibney.[107] The implication was that too precipitate a British withdrawal would so alarm unionists as to trigger a dramatic response that could set back the process. Far better slowly to acclimatise unionists to the inevitable 'Greening' of Northern Ireland, with the help of a British state that was prepared to reward an end to full-scale armed struggle with a very wide-ranging set of reforms. Some anti-Agreement Unionists were so impressed by these arguments that they came to believe that the Ulster-British cause was akin to the fate of a boiling frog. Throw a frog into boiling water and it will immediately jump out; throw a frog into cold water and slowly turn up the temperature, and the creature will not know that it is being boiled alive.[108] If this was the inevitable destination of the process, then even Trimble's victories could be said to have played their part in acclimatising unionists to the new dispensation – by slowing the pace at which the temperature was turned up. According to this analysis, all that Trimble was doing by demanding decommissioning Sinn Fein/IRA and 'holding their feet to the fire' was assisting Adams in what he wanted to do anyhow – constitutionalising republicanism and receiving a massive political pay-off in exchange.

All this was a matter of intense, unprovable debate. But even by the principal scientific measurement of political success in democratic societies – election results – Trimble's legacy was ambiguous. In the 1999 and 2004 European Parliament elections, the UUP plummeted to its lowest percentage shares of the vote since the foundation of Northern Ireland; in the 2001 Westminster poll it secured its lowest number of Commons seats ever; and in the 2003 Assembly election, it fell into third place in terms of first preferences cast (26% for the DUP, 24% for Sinn Fein and 23% for the UUP, though the mathematics of the STV voting system meant that the UUP was in second place in terms of seats).[109] So as the UUP approaches its 100th birthday in 2005, it appears that the party had finally lost its leading position in the politics of the unionist community and is now only ahead of the DUP in the relatively unimportant domain of local government.[110] Since Trimble obviously believes that a strong UUP is essential to the continuation of the Union of Great Britain and Northern Ireland, this precipitate decline represents a fairly damning indictment of his leadership. But there is much more to it than that. The point was made most succinctly by Henry Patterson, who wondered whether Trimble's legacy to Unionism would not be rather like that of John Hume to constitutional nationalism: yes, the UUP and SDLP were severely damaged, perhaps beyond repair, but their opponents within their own communities were forced to accept the revised rules of the political game as defined by those two individuals. In other words, parties were effectively sacrificed for principles.[111] Trimble may have dished the UUP in the course of taking the risk of pushing through the Belfast Agreement, but the DUP tacitly accepted surprising amounts of the new order. Thus, DUP criticisms of North-South bodies focused on their alleged cost and bloated size as much as upon the ideological threat which they posed to the Union; Paisleyites now appeared in TV studios with republicans; and Peter Robinson even cited Trimble's refusal to engage in bilaterals with Sinn Fein during the 1997–8 talks as a possible model for how the DUP might take the process forward.[112] Other DUP figures privately conceded that they could not undo much of what they saw as Trimble's rotten handiwork, now that the wicked deed of the Belfast Agreement was done. Instead, the task of ridding Ulster of Trimble resembled that of the scapegoat ritual in the ancient world. Thus, Joe Klein, surveying the impeachment of Bill Clinton, quoted the Stanford scholar Rene Girard: 'In Greek mythology, the scapegoat is never wrongfully accused. But he is always magical. He has the capacity to relieve the burden of guilt from a society . . . in this way tension is relieved and change takes place.' But though the DUP and many in the UUP desperately wanted Trimble as the sacrifice, so that change could take place, Trimble – like Clinton – somehow managed to slip his captors time and again.[113] Indeed, by Patterson's standard, Trimble could be said to have done better than John Hume. Certainly, the UUP was in better shape than the SDLP following the 2003 Assembly elections. And it could be argued that he had played a greater part in securing DUP acquiescence in the new structures than Hume did *vis-à-vis* republicans. If Ed Moloney is right about Gerry Adams' 'revisionism', then the Sinn Fein president's evolution owed more to his own autonomous thought processes and ambitions (as well as his long-time dialogue with the British) than it did to Hume's persuasive skills. Of course, the more pragmatic elements in the DUP played their part in bringing the Paisleyites on board, but Trimble seized the initiative against them for much of this period in a way that Hume never did to republicans. Indeed, it could be argued that the very fact that the UUP survived at all during this period, considering the scale of the communal reversals, in itself was a real achievement: as with so much that Trimble did, it is hard to know whether to describe the glass as half empty or half full. Indeed, the party political effects of his legacy are particularly unclear. As of the time of writing this book, there is growing talk in Ulster circles of the UUP and DUP coming together in the post-Trimble and the post-Paisley era to form a pan-unionist bloc to counter the dominance of Sinn Fein on the nationalist side. Such a project would be impossible as long as the two 'big beasts' of Unionist politics are around. But on what terms it might eventually come about, no one can be sure. And to do what exactly?[114]

What can, however, be said beyond peradventure is that Trimble transformed himself and his image during his years as leader. Indeed, his achievement in becoming the youngest-ever leader of the UUP is all the more remarkable when one compares his background to those of his predecessors (the word 'predecessor' is used here in the broadest sense, to include leaders of the Unionists at Westminster before Partition). Trimble was perhaps the least 'privileged' of the group; his great obvious advantage, intellect, was for much of the time an object of suspicion in one of the least intellectual political movements in these islands. Thus, Unionism was led by representatives of the land-owning classes such as Edward Saunderson (1886–1906), Viscount Brookeborough (1943–63), Terence O'Neill (1963–9), and James Chichester-Clark (1969–71); by representatives of the substantial business or farming classes, such as Sir James Craig (1921–40), John Miller Andrews (1940–3) Brian Faulkner (1971–4) and Harry West (1974–9). James Molyneaux (1979–95) came from a not-dissimilar lower-middle-class background to Trimble, but had the substantial advantages of a 'good war' record and much greater long-term 'Orange cred' as Imperial Grand Master of the Orange Order and Sovereign Commonwealth Grand Master of the Royal Black Institution; such 'Orange cred' as Trimble acquired was largely belated and short-lived, deriving from two successive stand-offs at Drumcree. Two 'outsiders' had also led Unionism before Partition: the half-English Walter Long (1906–10), and a Dubliner, Sir Edward Carson (1910–21). But both men already had distinguished careers in politics (and, in Carson's case, at the Bar) before they assumed the mantle of leadership. By virtue of his upbringing in England following the death in combat of his father in the First World War, Terence O'Neill was psychologically something of an outsider in Ulster; but he enjoyed material and class advantages that Trimble never possessed, as well as a war record in the Irish Guards.[115]

Considering that in 1990, Trimble was a struggling, marginalised, land law lecturer and aspirant politician – who had failed to obtain either a professorial chair or a UUP parliamentary nomination – his subsequent successes were very remarkable. For the first time, in his capacity as First Minister, he enjoyed an excellent salary; well over £250,000 in Nobel Prize money. He kept this bounty, despite early indications that it would be used for the establishment of a Trimble foundation. Then there was the prestige of the Nobel Prize itself, and scores of other tokens of recognition such as the Zurich/*Spectator* Parliamentarian of the Year award; the Legion of Honour; frequent visits to the White House and the President during the Clinton years, commensurate with if not well in excess of that normally accorded to the head of Government in a small-to-medium-sized sovereign country; a visit to the Renaissance Weekend in Charleston, South Carolina; an appearance in the New Labour manifesto of 2001; and unlimited access to No. 10 and to Dublin. In the process, he became the most respected and prestigious figure thrown up by the Unionist movement – at least on the British mainland and abroad – since the foundation of Northern Ireland. Anthony McIntyre has observed that the process has been bad for *republicanism*, but extremely good for *individual republicans*. Likewise, the process may have been bad for Unionism, at least as traditionally defined, but it was very good for certain individual Unionists – and for no one more than David Trimble. He thus achieved an extraordinary personal liberation. Whether he had liberated his own people is far more open to question: perhaps, like Chou En Lai's response when asked about the effects of the French Revolution, it is simply too early to tell.[116]

NOTES

AUTHOR'S NOTE

1. See Henry McDonald, *Trimble* (London, 2000).
2. For a full list, see the catalogue of the Northern Ireland Political Collection at the Linen Hall Library; see the website at www.linenhall.com
3. Austen Morgan claims that 'Belfast Agreement' is the correct legal term. See Austen Morgan, *The Belfast Agreement: A Practical Legal Analysis* (London, 2000), pp. 5–6, 9–10.
4. See Frank Ormsby (ed.), *The Collected Poems of John Hewitt* (Belfast, 1992), p. 141.

CHAPTER ONE: *Floreat Bangoria*

1. See Liam Kennedy's essay on the Protestants of Longford and Westmeath, 'The Long Retreat' in *Colonialism, Religion and Nationalism in Ireland* (Belfast, 1996), pp. 1–34. For another perspective, see Marie Coleman, *Co. Longford and the Irish Revolution* (Dublin, 2003), pp. 96–116, 135.
2. George F. Black, *The Surnames of Scotland* (New York, 1962), pp. 779 and 782–783.
3. On the increasing pressures on lower-middle-class and middle-class Protestants in Co. Longford, see Kerby A. Miller, 'The Lost World of Andrew Johnston' in J.S. Donnelly Jr and Kerby A. Miller, *Popular Culture in Ireland 1650–1850* (Dublin, 1998).
4. See J.J. Lee, 'Patterns of Rural Unrest in Nineteenth-Century Ireland: A Preliminary Survey' in L.M. Cullen and F. Furet (eds), *Ireland and France 17th–20th Centuries: Towards a Comparative Study of Rural History* (Paris, 1980), pp. 223–237. See David Fitzpatrick, 'The Geography of Irish Nationalism 1910–21', *Past and Present*, 78, 1978, p. 144.
5. Rev. Janet Catterall interview 30/01/03.
6. See Kennedy, *Colonialism, Religion and Nationalism in Ireland*, pp. xii–xiii. For another perspective, see Peter Hart, 'The Protestant Experience of Revolution in Southern Ireland' in Hart, *The IRA at War 1916–1923* (Oxford, 2003), pp. 223–241.
7. DT interview 29/11/98. Information about George Trimble comes from

RIC and RUC records. I am grateful to Constable David Lockhart of the RUC Historical Society for his help.

8. DT interview 29/11/98.

9. DT interview 04/03/02.

10. Maureen Irwin interview 01/12/98.

11. Maureen Irwin interview 01/12/98.

12. DT interview 29/11/98.

13. See Adam Loughridge, *The Covenanters in Ireland* (Belfast, 1984), pp. 120–123. I am grateful to Rev. Professor Robert McCollum for his advice on this matter.

14. DT interview 29/11/98. See also W.H. Jack's obituary notice in the *Belfast Telegraph* 23/01/37.

15. John Hume interview 21/12/98.

16. DT interview 29/11/98. Trimble is not far wrong: according to the investigation by Templegrove Action Research to be found on the CAIN website, the total Protestant population of the cityside declined from 8459 in 1971 to 1407 in 1991, an 83.4% drop. See CAIN website http://cain.ulst.ac.uk/issues/segregat/temple/areaplan.htm and *Belfast Telegraph* 18/01/02.

17. DT interview 29/11/98. See Trimble's foreword to C. Davis Milligan, *The Walls of Derry: Their Building, Defending and Preserving* (Lurgan, 1996).

18. John Hume interview 21/12/98. For Hume's family background, see Paul Routledge, *John Hume: A Biography* (London, 1997), p. 20.

19. DT interview 20/02/02.

20. DT interview 20/02/02.

21. Iain Trimble interview 27/02/02.

22. DT interview 20/02/02.

23. Iain Trimble interview 27/02/02.

24. DT interview 20/02/02.

25. Daphne Trimble interview 20/06/00.

26. DT interview 20/02/02.

27. David Montgomery interview 03/12/98. See also Henry Patterson's letter in the *Guardian* 23/01/04

28. Christopher Ricks (ed.), *The Poems of Tennyson* (London, 1969), p. 1126.

29. For one description of a traditional Ulster Presbyterian upbringing of a slightly earlier era, see W.R. Rodgers' account of his childhood in Michael Longley (ed.), *Poems: W.R. Rodgers* (Oldcastle, Co. Meath, 1993), p.11.

30. Iain Trimble interview 01/03/02.

31. DT interview 24/02/02.

32. DT interview 22/02/02.

33. Iain Trimble interview 01/03/02.

34. DT interview 29/11/98.

35. Iain Trimble interview 21/11/98; Rosemary Trimble interview 23/11/98.

36. Daphne Trimble interview 25/01/99.

37. I am grateful to Maurice McCord, then head of history at Bangor Grammar, and Errol Steele, then head of languages, for their reminiscences of the young Trimble on 24/11/98.

38. Jim Driscoll interview 25/11/98.

39. See James Hamilton, *Bangor Abbey through Fourteen Centuries* (Belfast, 1958) p. 18.

40. Jim Driscoll interview 25/11/98.

41. *The Gryphon* 1971.

42. David Montgomery interview 03/12/98.

43. Terry Higgins interview 23/12/98.

44. DT interview 29/11/98.

45. DT interview 20/02/02.

46. Iain Trimble interview 21/11/98.

47. Martin Mawhinney interview 30/11/98.

48. Leslie Cree interview 13/12/98.

49. DT interviews 20/12/98 and 22/12/98.

50. Leslie Cree interview 13/12/98.

51. David Montgomery interview 23/12/98.

52. DT interview 27/09/98.

53. Leslie Cree interview 13/12/98.

54. I am grateful to Ian Wilson of the North Down Heritage Centre for these insights.

55. DT interview 20/02/02.

56. See *The Dictionary of National Biography Missing Persons*, ed. C.S. Nicholls (Oxford, 1993), pp. 18–19.

57. DT interview 20/02/02.

58. DT interviews 27/09/98 and 29/11/98.

CHAPTER TWO: *A don is born*

1. Information on Trimble's Land Registry days comes from interviews with his colleagues: Herb Wallace 25/11/98 and 02/12/98; Sam Beattie 24/11/98; John Orr, QC 25/11/98; Derek Reade; and DT interviews 27/09/98 and 29/11/98.

2. See T.W. Moody and J.C. Beckett, *Queen's, Belfast 1845–1949: The History of a University* (2 volumes, London, 1959), especially Volume I, pp. 1–39. See also Sean Farren's entry on Irish universities in Robert Welch (ed.), *The Oxford Companion to Irish Literature*(Oxford, 1996), pp. 581–583.

3. DT interview 27/09/98.

4. Herb Wallace interview 25/11/98.

5. DT interviews 29/11/98 and 20/12/98.
6. On Calvert, see Brian Faulkner, *Memoirs of a Statesman* (London, 1978), pp. 228, 232.
7. See Edward Heath, *The Course of My Life: My Autobiography* (London, 1998), pp. 22–23.
8. Herb Wallace interview 25/11/98.
9. Private information.
10. DT interviews 29/11/98 and 10/01/98.
11. DT interview 23/02/03.
12. DT interview 20/02/02.
13. DT interview 27/02/02 and Iain Trimble interview 27/02/02.
14. *Belfast Telegraph* 14/11/73.
15. DT interview 27/02/02.
16. DT interview 02/11/03.
17. DT interview 29/11/98.
18. Claire Palley interviews 27/11/98 and 04/12/98.
19. Alex Attwood interview 07/12/98.
20. Alban Maginness interview 30/11/98.
21. Judith Eve interview 30/11/98.
22. Claire Palley interviews 27/11/98 and 04/12/98.
23. DT interview 17/06/02.
24. Alban Maginness interview 30/11/98.
25. Claire Palley interview 16/05/02. Other female colleagues, such as Valerie Mitchell and Sylvia Hermon, have also confirmed this point to me.
26. Kevin Boyle interview 23/12/98.
27. Trimble also wrote a series of articles for the *Northern Ireland Legal Quarterly* (hereinafter referred to as *NILQ*). He also delivered lectures and contributed to other publications. The following is a representative list:

   - 'Review of C.D. Drake, "Law of Partnership"', *NILQ*, 23, 1972, pp. 537–538.
   - 'The Procedure Governing Compulsory Acquisition of Land in Northern Ireland', *NILQ*, 24, 1973, pp. 466–490, 576–577.
   - 'Living in a No Scheme World', *NILQ*, 27, 1976, pp. 357–370.
   - 'Consolidation, Housing and the Government of Ireland Act 1920: Form Preferred to Substance', *NILQ*, 33, 1982, pp. 396–398.
   - 'Planning Blight', *NILQ*, 33, 1982, pp. 60–69.
   - 'Repairing Obligations in Regulated Tenancies', *NILQ*, 35, 1984, pp. 104–106.
   - 'The Taxes on Development: A Lecture Delivered to the Belfast Solicitors' Association' (Belfast, 1975).

- 'Compensation for Compulsory Purchase: Some Recent Developments: A Lecture' (Belfast, 1976).
- Northern Ireland section in J. Alder, *Effective Enforcement of Planning Control* (Oxford, 1989), pp. 136–144.

28. Sylvia Hermon interview 02/12/98.
29. Tom Hadden interview 01/12/98.
30. David Moore interview 07/12/98.

CHAPTER THREE: *In the Vanguard*

1. The figure of 318 goes back to 1966. See David McKittrick, Seamus Kelters, Brian Feeney and Chris Thornton, *Lost Lives: The Stories of the Men, Women and Children who Died as a Result of the Northern Ireland Troubles* (Edinburgh, 1999). This book is hereafter referred to as *Lost Lives*.
2. *Parliament Buildings Stormont* (Belfast, 1999), p. 19.
3. See Nicholas Mansergh, *The Unresolved Question: The Anglo-Irish Settlement and its Undoing, 1912–72* (London, 1991), pp. 137–140.
4. For the full speech see Northern Ireland Commons Debates 18/12/33 to 14/11/34, col. 1091.
5. DT interview 24/02/03. Quoted in the Vanguard pamphlet *Community of the British Isles* (Belfast, 1973), p. 9. See also Brian Follis, *A State Under Siege: The Establishment of Northern Ireland 1920–1925* (Oxford, 1995).
6. DT interview 20/12/98.
7. For the disdain of senior Army officers towards Stormont, see Peter Jenkins, *Guardian* 17/01/72 and 18/01/72.
8. DT interview 20/02/02.
9. See Basil McIvor, *Hope Deferred: Experiences of an Irish Unionist* (Belfast, 1998).
10. John Harbinson, *The Ulster Unionist Party 1882–1973: Its Development and Organisation* (Belfast, 1973), pp. 90–91.
11. DT interviews 29/11/98 and 20/12/98. See also Harbinson, *The Ulster Unionist Party*, p. 92.
12. See also Harbinson, *The Ulster Unionist Party*, pp. 46–7.
13. DT interview 23/02/03.
14. St John Ervine, *Craigavon: Ulsterman* (London, 1949). But see also Thomas Wilson (ed.), *Ulster under Home Rule: A Study of the Political and Economic Problems of Northern Ireland* (Oxford, 1955); Hugh Shearman, *Northern Ireland: Its History, Resources, and People* (1948); Cyril Falls, *Northern Ireland as an Outpost of Defence* (London, 1952).

15. See Clifford Smyth, *Ian Paisley: Voice of Protestant Ulster* (Edinburgh, 1987), pp. 129–130.

16. DT interviews 29/11/98 and 20/12/98.

17. DT interviews 29/11/98 and 20/12/98.

18. *Sunday News* 18/06/72.

19. *News Letter* 21/10/72 and the *Guardian* 20/10/72. For earlier comments, see *Irish News* 17/05/72.

20. DT interview 20/12/98.

21. David Burnside interview 07/01/99.

22. See *News Letter* 13/02/73.

23. See Boal's article in the *Sunday News* 06/01/74.

24. *News Letter* 20/03/72.

25. See Henry McDonald, *Trimble* (London, 2001), pp. 39–41; DT telephone interview 20/05/02; *Irish News* 28/02/00.

26. *Sunday Press* 20/02/72.

27. DT interviews 20/12/98 and 22/12/98.

28. DT interviews 20/12/98 and 22/12/98.

29. Estimates vary, but the 40,000 figure comes from Sydney Elliott and W.D. Flackes, *Northern Ireland: A Political Directory 1968–99* (Belfast, 1999), p. 474.

30. DT interview 22/12/98.

31. See *Northern Ireland Constitutional Proposals* Cmnd 5259 (London, 1973) and Patrick Buckland, *The Factory of Grievances: Devolved Government in Northern Ireland* (Dublin, 1979), pp. 221–240.

32. See Enid Lakeman, *How Democracies Vote* (4th edition, London, 1974).

33. DT interview 29/11/98.

34. Trimble urged the anti-Agreement Young Unionists at their conference in October 1998 to read Popper.

35. Stewart O'Fee interview 10/01/99. I am also grateful to James O'Fee for reminiscences of his father, July 2001.

36. See Faulkner, *Memoirs of a Statesman*, p. 62.

37. DT interview 20/12/98.

38. See *Lost Lives*, pp. 328–329.

39. See Elliott and Flackes, *Northern Ireland*, pp. 533–538.

40. DT interview 10/01/99.

41. DT interview 10/01/99.

42. Isobel McCulloch interview 08/03/02.

43. William Craig interview 24/12/98.

44. Andy Tyrie interview 07/01/99.

45. DT interview 20/02/02.

46. DT interview 03/11/03.

CHAPTER FOUR: *Ulster will fight*

1. *County Down Spectator* 09/11/73.

2. For the abortive Council of Ireland of the 1920s, see Dennis Kennedy, *The Widening Gulf: Northern Attitudes to the Independent Irish State 1919–49* (Belfast, 1988) pp. 60–63, and Kennedy's essay 'Politics of North–South Relations in Post-Partition Ireland' in Patrick J. Roche and Brian Barton (eds), *The Northern Ireland Question: Nationalism, Unionism and Partition* (Aldershot, 1999), pp. 71–95.

3. See Paul Bew and Henry Patterson, *The British State and the Ulster Crisis* (London, 1985), pp. 61–68.

4. The phrase has also been credited to Mark Durkan. See *Sunday Times* (Irish edition) 23/09/01.

5. See McIvor, *Hope Deferred* pp. 103–104.

6. *The Observer* 12/04/98.

7. See Faulkner, *Memoirs of a Statesman*, p. 25. See also David Bleakley, *Faulkner: Conflict and Consent in Irish Politics* (London, 1974), p. 28.

8. David Bleakley interview 08/01/99.

9. DT interview 22/12/98.

10. Molyneaux interview 13/01/99.

11. DT interview 22/12/98.

12. See Paul Bew and Gordon Gillespie, *Chronology of the Troubles* (London, 1998), p. 77 (hereafter referred to as *Chronology*).

13. *Chronology*, pp. 77–82.

14. *Chronology*.

15. See Paul Bew, Peter Gibbon and Henry Patterson, *Northern Ireland 1921–1996: Political Forces and Social Classes* (London, 1996), pp. 164–175.

16. Sean O'Callaghan, *The Informer* (London, 1998), pp. 65–66.

17. See J.A. McKibbin, 'Ulster Vanguard: A Sociological Profile', unpublished MSc thesis for Queen's University, Belfast, 1990.

18. DT interview 10/01/99.

19. DT interviews 20/02/02 and 29/05/03.

20. DT interview 10/01/99.

21. See *Lost Lives*, pp. 631–632.

22. DT interview 20/02/02.

23. Private information.

24. Herb Wallace interview 25/11/98.

25. DT interview 10/01/99.

26. Later, Trimble also provided advice on 'constitutional' matters to the Ulster Loyalist Central Coordinating Committee for the pamphlet *Your Future? Ulster Can Survive Unfettered* – a pro-independence document.

See also *Hibernia* 07/06/74, which incorrectly stated that Trimble was a member of the UWC.

27. *Chronology*, pp. 87–88.
28. See McIvor, *Hope Deferred*, p. 119.
29. Andy Tyrie interview 07/01/99. See also the profile of Ernest Baird in *Fortnight*, 09/08/74.
30. DT interview 23/02/03.

CHAPTER FIVE: *The changing of the Vanguard*

1. Cmnd 5675. Quoted in Elliott and Flackes, *Northern Ireland*, p. 101.
2. DT interview 05/01/99.
3. David Burnside interview 07/01/99.
4. Sir Reg Empey interview 06/01/99.
5. DT interview 05/01/99.
6. Elliott and Flackes, *Northern Ireland*, p. 542.
7. DT interview 05/01/99. See *Northern Ireland Convention Report of Debates* 11/06/75, pp. 171–173. Trimble was answering questions in the absence of the chairman of the Rules Committee, Ian Paisley.
8. Maurice Hayes interview 06/01/99.
9. Sir Frank Cooper interview 12/01/99.
10. See *Northern Ireland Convention Report of Debates*, 01/10/75, cols. 645–646; 30/11/75 col. 811; 03/03/76 col. 1065.
11. Anthony Alcock interview 03/04/99; DT interview 05/01/99.
12. DT interview 23/02/03.
13. See *Northern Ireland Convention Report of Debates*, 22/05/75, pp. 40–42.
14. DT interview 05/01/99. See also Devlin's memoir, *Straight Left: An Autobiography* (Belfast, 1993), p. 261, and the *Irish Times* 24/01/76.
15. DT interview 05/01/99.
16. *Belfast Telegraph* 04/03/76.
17. DT interview 10/01/99.
18. Press release from Vanguard 25/10/76.
19. DT interview 05/01/99.
20. Ibid. See also Clifford Smyth, *Ian Paisley*, p. 38.
21. William Craig interview 24/12/98; DT interview 05/01/99.
22. Isobel McCulloch interview 08/03/02.
23. Quoted in unpublished Vanguard paper 'The Case For Voluntary Coalition'.
24. William Beattie interview 16/02/02.
25. William Beattie interview 16/02/02.
26. Hugh Logue interview 04/01/99.

27. DT interview 05/01/99.
28. Private Vanguard paper.
29. Vanguard press release of DT speech at Saintfield, 25/02/76.
30. Sir Reg Empey interview 06/01/99.
31. *Lost Lives*, pp. 571–572.
32. See Clifford Smyth, *Ian Paisley*, p. 102.
33. See Clifford Smyth, *Ian Paisley*, pp. 100–105.
34. Maurice Hayes interview 06/01/99.
35. DT interview 10/01/99.
36. DT interview 10/01/99.
37. DT interviews 05/01/99 and 10/01/99.
38. *Belfast Telegraph* 30/09/75 and 23/10/99. Also DT interview 03/11/03.
39. DT interview 10/01/99.
40. DT interview 10/01/99.
41. DT interview 17/02/04. See also *Irish Times* 01/02/04.
42. *Northern Ireland Convention Proceedings*, 03/03/76 col. 1064.
43. DT interview 23/02/03.
44. *Northern Ireland Convention Proceedings*, 03/03/76 col. 1069.
45. John Kennedy interview 20/01/00.
46. DT interviews 22/12/98 and 10/01/99.
47. Ian Paisley interview 24/01/00.
48. See Micheal O Cuinneagain, *On the Arm of Time* (Donegal, 1992), pp. 39–40 and 44–47.
49. DT interviews 22/12/98 and 10/01/99.
50. Daphne Trimble interview 25/01/99.
51. Daphne Trimble interview 30/11/98.
52. Aiken had been responsible for the massacre of Protestants at Altnaveigh, Co. Armagh, in 1922. See Toby Harnden, *Bandit Country: The IRA & South Armagh* (London, 1999), pp. 93–106.
53. Ibid. See also *Sunday Tribune* 01/10/95.
54. Ibid.
55. Herb Wallace interview 02/12/98.
56. Sam Beattie interview 24/11/98.
57. DT interview 20/02/02.
58. DT interview 24/02/02.

CHAPTER SIX: *Death At Queen's*

1. Private information.
2. DT interview 26/03/02; *News Letter* 03/05/77.
3. *News Letter* 23/10/78.

4. James Molyneaux interview 13/01/99. See also Ann Purdy, *Molyneaux: The Long View* (Antrim, 1989).

5. DT interview 24/01/99.

6. *News Letter* 11/04/79 and *County Down Spectator* 13/04/79.

7. Tom Hadden interview 10/05/02. Trimble's last column was on 7 July 1986, after which he was dropped.

8. *Fortnight* 13 May 1977; April 1985; and 23 September 1985. James Molyneaux interview 02/04/03.

9. *Fortnight* 23 September 1985.

10. *Fortnight* March, April 1981.

11. See *Fortnight* November 1983 and 18 January 1984.

12. Cmnd 7763 (London, 1979).

13. See *Fortnight* December 1979/January 1980 and July/August 1980.

14. See Elliott and Flackes, *Northern Ireland*, pp. 548–551. See also Purdy, *Molyneaux*, pp. 123–124.

15. See *Fortnight* May 1981.

16. DT interview 24/01/99. See *Fortnight* July/August 1981.

17. See Edgar Graham, *Ireland and Extradition* (Belfast, 1982).

18. See also Frank Millar's remarks in the *Belfast Telegraph* 07/12/83.

19. Ian Clark interview 24/03/02.

20. *Ulster Star* 29/05/81.

21. Marianne Elliott, *The Catholics of Ulster* (London, 2000), pp. 376–377.

22. James Cooper interview 28/01/99.

23. See Whyte, p. 149.

24. David Blatherwick interview 25/02/99.

25. DT interview 24/01/99.

26. See Commons Hansard, Vol. 26, 21 June–2 July 1982, cols. 769–771 and 788–790, and Simon Heffer, *Like the Roman* (London, 1998), pp. 864–866.

27. DT interview 24/01/99.

28. David Blatherwick interview 25/02/99.

29. DT interview 24/01/99.

30. *News Letter* 03/03/82. On Lord McDermott, see *Dictionary of National Biography 1971–81* (Oxford, 1986).

31. Brian Garrett interview 25/11/98.

32. Sylvia Hermon interview 02/12/98.

33. DT interviews 20/02/02 and 26/03/02. Peter Froggatt telephone interview 20/05/02.

34. See *Lost Lives*, pp. 830–831.

35. See *Northern Ireland Assembly Official Report of Debates* Volume 7 (Part 2), 01/11/83–07/12/83, cols. 930–945.

36. DT interview 26/03/02.

37. *Combat*, Vol. 4, Issue 64, 1983. See also *Belfast Telegraph* report of 08/12/83 on the UDA statement after the killing and *Irish News* 08/12/83.

38. Sylvia Hermon interview 02/12/98.

39. Dermott Nesbitt interview 02/12/98.

40. Sandra Maxwell interview 01/12/98.

41. Sylvia Hermon interview 02/12/98.

42. See *Irish Times* 09/12/83.

43. *Lost Lives*, p. 967.

44. Sir Colin Campbell interview 12/03/02.

45. DT interview 23/02/03.

46. Sir Colin Campbell interview 12/03/02.

47. DT interview 23/02/03.

48. Sir Colin Campbell interview 12/03/02. In fact, another colleague, Valerie Mitchell, had offered a personal tribute on the night before.

49. See also *Belfast Telegraph* 15/12/83 and 16/12/83.

50. Sir Colin Campbell interview 12/03/02.

51. DT interview 24/01/99.

52. I am grateful to Anne Graham, sister of the deceased, for providing me with these details, which are taken from Rev. McAloney's funeral address. See also memorial address by D.S. Greer in *Northern Ireland Legal Quarterly*, Vol. 34, No. 4, Winter 1983, pp. 267–268.

53. According to Anne Graham, the only jarring note from the point of view of her family was sounded years later, in Ann Purdy's biography of Molyneaux. He claimed that he had to terminate the proceedings in the church hall afterwards, where some local ladies had laid on tea and sandwiches. Molyneaux believed that the event was becoming 'like a parish social', with a great din. The then UUP leader clearly thought that he was sparing a broken family further hurt and upset; in fact, says Anne Graham, the event did not upset them and they were enormously gratified by the turn-out. She was far more irritated by Molyneaux's subsequent claims than by any noise at the post-funeral reception. Anne Graham interview 11/05/02. See Purdy, *Molyneaux*, p. 39.

54. Private information.

55. DT interview 23/02/03.

56. Dermott Nesbitt interview 02/12/98.

57. DT interview 23/02/03.

CHAPTER SEVEN: *He doth protest too much*

1. Ian Clark interview 19/01/99 and DT interview 20/02/02.

2. I am grateful to Anne Smyth, chairman of the Ulster-Scots Language

Society, for helping me to find the spelling. See *Concise Ulster Dictionary* (Oxford, 1996).

3. John Taylor interview 08/01/99.

4. See Trimble's essay in M. Crozier (ed.), *Cultural Traditions in Northern Ireland*, Proceedings of the Cultural Traditions Group Conference, 3–4 March 1989 (Belfast, 1989), pp. 45–50.

5. DT interview 23/02/03.

6. Ronnie Hanna, *Land of the Free: Ulster and the American Revolution* (Lurgan, 1992).

7. See *Belfast Telegraph* 18/01/02.

8. See *New Ulster* No. 5, Winter 1987–8 and No. 17, Summer 1992.

9. Cmnd 9690 (London, 1985).

10. See DT's article in Charles Townshend (ed.), *Consensus in Ireland: Approaches and Recessions* (Oxford, 1998), pp. 73–94.

11. *Northern Ireland Assembly Committee on the Government of Northern Ireland, First Report, Proceedings and Appendices* (Belfast, 1986), pp. 72–73.

12. *News Letter* 20/11/84.

13. DT interview 14/02/99.

14. Frank Millar interview 18/01/99. See also Henry McDonald's account of how Trimble and William Craig sought to warn Molyneaux and Paisley in June 1985 – after Craig had, allegedly, been tipped off by some Conservatives of what the Government was planning. McDonald, *Trimble*, pp. 91–91.

15. See Margaret Thatcher, *The Downing Street Years* (London, 1993), pp. 413–415.

16. See Garrett Fitzgerald, *All in a Life: An Autobiography* (Dublin, 1991), p. 532.

17. See Sean O'Callaghan, *The Informer* (London, 1999), pp. 197–212. Garrett Fitzgerald has confirmed the value of O'Callaghan's work in this period in his *Irish Times* column of 04/01/97. See also Percy Cradock, *In Pursuit of British Interests: Reflections on Foreign Policy under Margaret Thatcher and John Major* (London, 1997), p. 205.

18. John A. Farrell, *Tip O'Neill and the American Century* (Boston, 2001), pp. 623–4.

19. DT interview 14/02/99.

20. Daphne Trimble interview 25/01/99.

21. DT interview 14/02/99. See also his Calvin Macnee article in *Fortnight* 2–15 December 1985.

22. See *Chronology*, p. 194.

23. *Northern Ireland Assembly Debates 16/11/85*, Vol. 18, pp. 127–128.

24. DT interview 14/02/99.

25. Lord Armstrong interview 22/02/01.

26. The UDA was not proscribed as a terrorist organisation until 1992.

27. John Oliver interview 25/01/99.

28. Nelson McCausland interview 19/03/02.

29. DT interview 14/02/99.

30. DT interview 14/02/99.

31. See also *Ulster Star* 04/04/86.

32. DT interview 14/02/99.

33. Private information.

34. Lord Armstrong interview 22/02/01.

35. Private information.

36. *Observer* 27/04/86 and Paul Bew and Henry Patterson, 'The New Stalemate: Unionism and the Anglo-Irish Agreement' in Paul Teague (ed.), *Beyond the Rhetoric: Politics, the Economy and Social Policy in Northern Ireland* (London, 1987), p. 46.

37. Frank Millar interview 19/01/99.

38. *Irish Times* 22/05/98.

39. DT interview 03/11/03.

40. Smyth, *Ian Paisley*, pp. 129–130.

41. Alex Attwood interview 07/12/98.

42. Sir Colin Campbell interview 12/03/02.

43. Quoted in Patrick Cosgrave, *R.A. Butler: An English Life* (London, 1981), p. 21.

44. Judith Eve interview 30/11/98; Herb Wallace interview 02/12/98.

45. Sylvia Hermon interview 02/12/98; *News Letter* 18/06/86. See also *Ulster Star* 20/06/86.

46. Brian Childs interview 26/11/98.

47. DT interview 14/12/98.

48. See Justine McCarthy, *Mary McAleese: The Outsider* (Dublin, 1999), pp. 36–44.

49. Ibid.

50. DT interview 14/02/99.

CHAPTER EIGHT: *Mr Trimble goes to London*

1. Jack Allen interview 22/01/99.

2. Jim Wilson interview 19/02/99. Also DT interview 03/11/03.

3. Jack Allen interview 22/01/99.

4. *News Letter* 12/04/90.

5. *Irish Times* 13/06/98 and *Belfast Telegraph* 31/12/98.

6. Jack Allen interview 13/03/02. See also the collection of McCusker's

speeches, with foreword by his widow, entitled *Harold McCusker: 'The Apprentice Politician'.*

7. Daphne Trimble interview 25/01/99.

8. The account of the selection is taken partly from the private diary of Robert Creane and Robert Creane interview 16/02/99; DT interview 14/02/99.

9. Victor Gordon interview 28/01/99.

10. *Craigavon Echo* 07/03/90; *Portadown Times* 16/03/90.

11. *Portadown Times* 23/03/90.

12. Jack Allen interview 13/03/02.

13. Gary Kennedy interview 16/02/99.

14. Gary Kennedy interview 16/02/99.

15. Gary Kennedy interview 16/02/99; *Belfast Telegraph* 20/04/99; George Savage interview 08/03/02.

16. See Alvin Jackson, *Colonel Edward Saunderson: Land and Loyalty in Victorian Ireland* (Oxford, 1995).

17. See also R.D. Jones, J.S. Kane, R. Wallace, D. Sloan, B. Courtney, *The Orange Citadel: A History of Orangeism in the Portadown District* (Armagh, 1996), p. 103.

18. Drew Nelson interview 28/01/99.

19. DT interview 14/02/99.

20. See also *Craigavon Echo* 16/05/90.

21. *Portadown Times* 25/05/90.

22. *Irish Times* 22/05/90. See also Ed Gorman, *The Times* 19/05/90.

23. Private information.

24. John Kennedy interview 05/03/02.

25. DT interview 23/02/03.

26. Trimble learned about the the significance of the Ulster custom from the B&ICO pamphlet *The Economics of Partition* (Belfast, 1972). Others are not so sure, claiming that similar forms of tenant right obtained in the south, which enjoyed less dramatic levels of industrial development. See Barbara Lewis Solow, *The Land Question and the Irish Economy, 1870–1903* (Cambridge, Mass., 1971), pp. 30–32.

27. Commons Hansard, Vol. 173, 21 May–8 June 1990, cols. 355–359.

28. *The Daily Telegraph* 15/05/97.

29. DT interview 04/08/99.

30. See also Trimble's solicitude for Blair in the debate on asylum, Commons Hansard, Vol. 213, 2–13 November 1992, cols. 68–70.

31. Frank Millar interview 18/01/99.

32. See Commons Hansard, Vol. 193, 17–28 June 1991, cols. 658–662 and Vol. 219, 15–26 February 1993, cols. 533–543. Trimble further addressed the

subject of the Northern Ireland Select Committee in an article in the *Guardian*, 09/03/94. See also Trimble's remarks on other aspects of Ulster's anomalous treatment within the United Kingdom in the debate on the renewal of the Prevention of Terrorism Act, Commons Hansard, Vol. 220, 1–12 March 1993, cols. 986–988 and during the Criminal Justice and Public Order Bill, Commons Hansard, Vol. 235, 11–21 January 1994, col. 30.

33. See Trimble's comments in Commons Hansard, Vol. 181, 19–30 Nov. 1990, col. 299; on the Oder-Neisse line, Vol. 175, 25 June–6 July 1990, cols. 1202–1203; Vol. 193, 17–28 June 1991, cols. 554–555; Vol. 183, 17 December 1990–18 January 1991, col. 856. Trimble also returned to a favourite theme, the South Tyrol question. See Commons Hansard, Vol. 175, 25 June–6 July 1990, col. 1203 and Vol. 200, 2–13 December 1991, col. 575. See also *News Letter* 19/03/90.

34. *Portadown Times* 24/09/93; 08/10/95; 15/10/95.

35. Sir Bob Cooper interview 27/01/99. See also *Irish News* 29/04/94. See also Trimble's remarks in the discussion on the Fair Employment (Amendment) (Northern Ireland) Order 1991, Commons Hansard, Vol. 195, 15–25 July 1991, cols. 186–190.

36. See *Chronology*, pp. 255, 257 and 275.

37. *Orange Standard* March 1992 and *Lost Lives*, pp. 960–961.

38. Commons Hansard, Vol. 183, 17 December 1990–18 January 1991, cols. 67–69 and 113–128; Vol. 238, 21 February–4 March 1994, cols. 66–74.

39. Commons Hansard, Vol. 187, 4–15 March 1991, cols. 54–59.

40. See Ed Moloney, *A Secret History of the IRA* (London, 2002), pp. 246–260.

41. For the conventional account of what happened, see E. Mallie and D. McKittrick, *The Fight For Peace: The Secret Story behind the Irish Peace Process* (London, 1996), pp. 102–105. See also Anthony Seldon, *Major: A Political Life* (London, 1997), pp. 263–268.

42. See David Bloomfield, *Political Dialogue in Northern Ireland: The Brooke Initiative* (London, 1998), pp. 51–53 and Thomas Hennessey, *The Northern Ireland Peace Process: Ending the Troubles* (Dublin, 2000), p. 69.

43. Patrick Mayhew interview 20/01/99.

44. *News Letter* 10/01/90.

45. See Trimble's earlier letter in *The Times* on the Brooke initiative, 27/01/92.

46. See Bew, Gibbon and Patterson, *Northern Ireland 1921–1996*, p. 220.

47. Ken Maginnis interview 18/02/99.

48. See also DT speech to Friends of the Union, 09/10/91.

49. Ken Maginnis interview 18/02/99.

CHAPTER NINE: *Framework or straitjacket?*

1. Dr Alvin Jackson of Queen's University has stated in his book, *Home Rule: An Irish History 1800–2000* (London, 2003), p. 310 that 'Trimble has contributed two short skilful and polemical volumes on the 1916 rising and the foundation of the Northern Irish state'. Paul Bew also acknowledges Trimble's scholarship in *Ideology and the Irish Question,* (Oxford, 1994) pp. 105, 154.
2. See Foster, op cit p. 420.
3. See, for instance, Powell's review of Foster's *Modern Ireland* in *The Spectator* 26/11/88.
4. See J.G. Simms, *Jacobite Ireland 1685–91* (London, 1969), p. 101 and Patrick Macrory, *The Siege of Derry* (London, 1980), pp. 192–193.
5. Michael Ancram interview 11/03/99; Michael Mates interview 22/03/99.
6. Patrick Mayhew interview 18/03/99.
7. Andy Wood interview 06/06/99.
8. Michael Ancram interview 11/03/99.
9. Michael Ancram interview 11/03/99.
10. DT interview 21/02/99.
11. Commons Hansard, Vol. 234, 6–17 December 1993, cols. 1087–1088.
12. DT interview 21/02/99.
13. For McCusker's speech, see Commons Hansard, Vol. 87, 18–29 November 1985, col. 912.
14. *Banbridge Chronicle* 17/02/94.
15. See Commons Hansard, Vol. 241, 12–22 April 1994, cols. 141–151.
16. See also Commons Hansard, Vol. 240, 21–31 March 1994, cols. 627–628.
17. DT interview 21/02/99.
18. See *Irish Times* 23/02/95 and *News Letter* 23/02/95.
19. *Irish News* 28/06/02.
20. *Impartial Reporter and Farmers' Journal* 06/10/94.
21. See *Sunday Business Post* 23/10/94 and 30/10/94.
22. DT interview 21/02/99.
23. See, for instance, Max Hastings, *Editor* (London, 2002), p. 258.
24. DT interview 21/02/99.
25. John Major interview 09/02/00.
26. Pauline Neville-Jones interview 13/01/01.
27. DT interview 03/11/03 and Reg Empey interview 22/11/03.
28. James Molyneaux interview 13/01/99.
29. David Burnside interview 07/01/99.
30. *The Times* 01/02/95.
31. DT interview 14/02/99.

32. See Trimble in *Ulster Review*, Summer 1995.

33. See Commons Hansard, Vol. 252, 10–20 January 1995, cols. 814–822 and Frank Millar, *Irish Times* 19/01/95.

34. Quoted in Paul Bew and Gordon Gillespie, *The Northern Ireland Peace Process 1993–96: A Chronology* (London, 1996), pp. 89–90.

35. Cmnd 2964 (London, 1995).

36. James Molyneaux interview 24/03/02; private information.

37. Michael Ancram interview 11/03/99.

38. Sir Quentin Thomas interviews 18/02/02 and 29/03/02.

39. Peter Bell interview 02/04/02.

40. John Bruton notebook 17/01/00.

41. *News Letter* 21/12/94 and 22/12/94.

42. *News Letter* 16/06/95. See also Feargal Cochrane, 'The 1995 North Down By-Election' in *Irish Political Studies*, 11, 1996, pp. 168–173.

43. DT interview 21/02/99.

CHAPTER TEN: *The Siege of Drumcree (I)*

1. Quoted in Kenneth McConkey, *Sir John Lavery* (Edinburgh, 1993), p. 162. See also F. Frankfort Moore, *The Truth About Ulster* (London, 1914), p. 45.

2. John Hermon, *Holding the Line* (Dublin, 1997), p. 173.

3. DT interview 23/03/02.

4. See Chris Ryder and Vincent Kearney, *Drumcree* (London, 2001), p. 95. Trimble first raised the matter in the Commons, in a written question, as far back as November 1990. See Commons Hansard, Vol. 181, 19–30 November 1990, col. 223.

5. John Hunter interview 23/02/99.

6. See Ryder and Kearney, *Drumcree*, p. 133.

7. See Ryder and Kearney, *Drumcree*, pp. 103–127 and Gordon Lucy, *Stand-Off!: Drumcree 1995 and 1996* (Lurgan, 1996). Lucy was a witness to some of these events, but his account is also derived from a lengthy interview in the summer of 1995 at Glengall Street with Trimble and others.

8. Lucy, *Stand-Off!*, p. 8.

9. Lucy, *Stand-Off!*, p. 58. See also Gracey's obituary in *The Daily Telegrph* 02/02/04.

10. Blair Wallace interview 20/03/02; *Chronology*, p. 308. *Belfast Telegraph* 31/01/00.

11. Blair Wallace interview 20/03/02.

12. John Pickering interview 16/02/99.

13. DT interview 23/11/03.

14. Jim Blair interview 20/02/99.

15. Harold Gracey interview 16/02/99.

16. Martin Smyth interview 11/04/02.

17. See Ryder and Kearney, *Drumcree*, p. 113.

18. Jim Blair interview 04/04/02.

19. *Belfast Telegraph* 10/07/95.

20. Lucy, *Stand-Off!*, p. 12.

21. Jim Blair interview 20/02/99; John Pickering interview 16/02/99.

22. Terry Houston interview 18/02/99.

23. Jim Blair interview 04/04/02.

24. Terry Houston interview 18/05/02.

25. Harold Gracey interview 16/02/99.

26. Ryder and Kearney, *Drumcree* pp. 114–115.

27. Terry Houston interview 18/05/02.

28. Brendan McAllister interview 19/03/02.

29. Ryder and Kearney, *Drumcree* pp. 116–117.

30. Ryder and Kearney, *Drumcree* pp. 123–125.

31. Jim Blair interview 20/02/99 and Sir Ronnie Flanagan interview 01/07/02.

32. Jim Blair interview 20/02/99.

33. Jim Blair interview 20/02/99.

34. DT interview 21/02/99.

35. Ian Paisley interview 24/01/00.

36. DT interview 21/02/99.

37. See the tribute to the RUC's 'commendable professionalism' in the second editorial in the *Belfast Telegraph* 11/07/95.

38. Patrick Mayhew interview 10/03/99.

39. Fergus Finlay interview 06/04/99.

40. *Irish Times* 15/07/95.

41. *Irish Times* 17/07/95.

42. See N. Kochan, *Ann Widdecombe: Right from the Beginning* (London, 2000), p. 222.

43. See *The Times* 12/07/95.

44. Jim Blair interview 20/02/99.

45. DT interview 21/02/99.

46. Gordon Lucy interview 26/01/99.

47. John Taylor interview 08/01/99.

48. Ruth Dudley Edwards interview 08/03/02; Gordon Lucy interview 26/01/99; DT interview 25/05/03. On Dolly's Brae, see Jonathan Bardon, *A History of Ulster*, (Belfast, 1992) pp. 302–304; and Elliott, *The Catholics of Ulster*, pp. 349–351. The Dolly's Brae analogy was not the happiest of comparisons: the inquiry set up by the Liberal Government of the day

estimated that at least 30 Catholics were killed. By comparison, therefore, Drumcree was a relatively mild affair!

49. See also Trimble's article in *The Independent* 12/07/95.
50. Private information.
51. Joel Patton interview 12/03/02.
52. DT interview 23/11/03.
53. John Major interview 09/02/00.
54. Sir Robin Butler interview 01/03/01.
55. Paul Bew interview 23/02/03.
56. Peter Bell interview 21/12/03.
57. See *Irish Times* 13/07/96.

CHAPTER ELEVEN: *Now I am the Ruler of the UUP!*

1. John Major interview 09/02/00.
2. John Hunter interview 24/01/99.
3. Daphne Trimble interview 12/04/99.
4. DT interview 21/02/99.
5. Jack Allen interview 13/03/02.
6. Sir John Wheeler interview 05/03/02.
7. DT interview 11/04/99.
8. *The Times* 29/08/95.
9. Gordon Lucy interview 20/02/99.
10. Steven King interview 15/05/99.
11. Gordon Lucy interview 16/12/03.
12. David Brewster interview 03/04/99.
13. Daphne Trimble interview 12/04/99.
14. See R.F. Foster, 'To the Northern Counties Station: Lord Randolph Churchill and the Prelude to the Orange Card' in F.S.L. Lyons R.A.J. and Hawkins (eds.), *Ireland under the Union: Varieties of Tension* (Oxford, 1980), pp. 237–287.
15. Denis Rogan interview 05/03/02.
16. Steven King interview 16/02/99.
17. John Taylor interview 07/02/03.
18. Gordon Lucy interview 16/12/03.
19. DT interview 21/02/99.
20. Mark Neale interview 28/02/02.
21. Jim Wilson interview 19/02/99.
22. DT interview 14/02/99; Daphne Trimble interview 12/04/99.
23. See Faulkner, *Memoirs of a Statesman* p. 13.
24. Caroline Nimmons interview 07/06/99.

25. See *Portadown Times* 15/09/95; Jim Wilson interview 09/03/02.
26. Ruth Dudley Edwards interview 09/03/02. See also Arthur Aughey, 'Ulster Unionist Party Leadership Election', *Irish Political Studies*, 11, 1996.
27. *Irish Times* 09/09/95.
28. *The Daily Telegraph* 11/09/95.
29. *The Independent* 12/09/95; Andrew Marr interview 03/01/02.
30. Matthew d'Ancona interview 16/05/03.

CHAPTER TWELVE: *The Establishment takes stock*

1. Frank Millar interview 18/01/99.
2. Marigold Johnson interview 10/04/02.
3. See also *The Times* 03/10/95.
4. Elements of Trimble's personality are to be found in the composite character of Strachan, the fictitious UUP leader described by Douglas Hurd in his novel *The Shape of Ice* (London, 1998), p. 194. 'Strachan had been in professional Ulster politics all his life since leaving Queen's University with a law degree,' wrote the former Northern Ireland Secretary. 'He knew, in amazing detail, from the Unionist angle the facts of every conference, every statute, every initiative, every agreement or disagreement which Northern Ireland had encountered since partition in 1922. Indeed his knowledge stretched back through the centuries, regiment after regiment of marching Protestant facts.'
5. Woodrow Wyatt (S. Curtis, ed.), *The Journals of Woodrow Wyatt*, Vol. 3, (London, 2000), p. 553.
6. George Bridges interview 07/03/02. See Major's memoirs, pp. 479–480; Seldon, *Major*, pp. 620–621.
7. Patrick Mayhew interview 20/01/99.
8. Patrick Mayhew interview 20/01/99 and DT interview 14/01/04.
9. Peter Bell interview 15/02/99.
10. DT interviews 11/04/99 and 20/02/02.
11. Daphne Trimble interview 14/06/99.
12. Sir John Kerr interview 15/05/99.
13. Andrew Hunter interview 24/03/99.
14. DT interview 03/11/03.
15. Chris McGimpsey interview 23/11/98.
16. The poll appeared in *The Sunday Times* (Ireland Edition) 22/10/95. See also Steven King, 'The Third Man', *Ulster Review*, 20, Summer 1996.
17. DT interview 11/04/99.
18. Proinsias De Rossa interview 07/04/99.
19. Fergus Finlay interview 06/04/99.

20. See the *Irish Times* 02/10/95.
21. *News Letter* 12/10/93 and 13/10/93.
22. DT interview 03/11/03 and Ken Maginnis interview 18/02/99.
23. DT interview 11/04/99.
24. William Ross interview 08/03/02.
25. Steven King interview 11/03/02.
26. DT interview 03/11/03.
27. Reg Empey interview 06/01/99.
28. DT interview 11/04/99.
29. Sir John Chilcot interview 31/07/02.
30. *Belfast Telegraph* 09/09/95.
31. *Irish Times* 11/09/95.
32. DT interview 11/04/99.
33. DT interview 11/04/99.
34. DT interview 11/04/99; Andrew Hunter interview 24/03/99.
35. Commons Hansard, Vol. 126, 25 January–5 February 1988, cols. 21–35.
36. Patrick Mayhew interview 10/03/99.
37. Andrew Hunter interview 24/03/99. See also Mo Mowlam, *Momentum* (London, 2002), pp. 25–26. Mayhew declines to comment on any aspect of Mowlam's memoirs. Patrick Mayhew interview 04/07/02.
38. Daphne Trimble interview 14/06/99.
39. Andrew Hunter interview 24/03/99.
40. Patrick Mayhew interview 10/03/99.
41. Andrew Hunter interview 24/03/99.
42. Sir John Wheeler interview 12/03/99.
43. Michael Ancram interview 11/03/99.
44. DT interview 03/11/03.
45. Viscount Cranborne interview 14/01/99. Thomas was surprised that Cranborne was able to reach this judgment, since the erstwhile NIO Political Director has no recollection of meeting him.
46. See John Campbell, *F.E. Smith* (London, 1984), pp. 548–585.
47. Private information.
48. Viscount Cranborne interview 14/01/99.
49. Patrick Mayhew interview 10/03/99.
50. DT interview 11/04/99. Cranborne acknowledges that because he was not always in the loop, he could not necessarily tell Trimble the whole story.

CHAPTER THIRTEEN: *Something funny happened on the way to the Forum election*

1. Gordon Lucy interview 26/01/99; John Hunter interview 23/02/99; DT interview 25/05/03.
2. See UUP Press Release 22/09/95. See also Trimble in the *Irish Times* 02/10/95 and the *Sunday Tribune* 24/12/95.
3. DT interview 11/04/99.
4. William Ross interview 08/03/02.
5. *Irish News* 25/09/95.
6. *News Letter* 26/01/96.
7. Fergus Finlay interview 06/04/99.
8. Sean O hUiginn interview 23/04/99. See also Oliver MacDonagh, *The Emancipist: Daniel O'Connell 1830–1847* (London, 1989), pp. 268–272.
9. DT interview 11/04/99.
10. DT interview 11/04/99.
11. *Irish Times* 23/10/95.
12. See Terence O'Neill, *The Autobiography of Terence O'Neill*, p. 74.
13. See Dean Godson in *The Daily Telegraph* 29/05/96.
14. *Irish Times* 03/10/95.
15. John Bruton interview 06/04/99.
16. *The Times* 03/10/95.
17. *Irish Times* 05/10/95.
18. See *Lost Lives*, pp. 426–428.
19. John Bruton interview 06/04/99.
20. See Stephen Collins, *Spring and the Labour Story* (Dublin, 1993), pp. 24–25.
21. Spring also welcomed Trimble's election as UUP leader in this address. See *Irish Times* 28/09/95.
22. See, for example, Garrett Fitzgerald, *All in a Life: An Autobiography* (London, 1991), p. 225 and *Reflections on the Irish State* (Dublin, 2003), p. 98.
23. DT interview 11/04/99. Trimble later changed his view of the DFA, as exemplified by his remarks in the Commons on 12/05/03, following the second postponement of the May 2003 Assembly Elections. See Commons Hansard, Vol. 405, 12–22 May 2003, cols. 101–104.
24. *Irish Times* 05/02/96; Nora Owen interview 08/04/99.
25. Fergus Finlay interview 06/04/99. See also *Irish Times* 23/10/95.
26. Maginnis says that he wanted to be the one to cause the row, in order 'to prevent Trimble from letting himself down' and to allow him to develop as a more accommodating sort of UUP leader. Maginnis felt Trimble's

greatest weakness in his early days as leader was his inability to 'plan his rows' but instead he would explode spontaneously. Ken Maginnis interview 16/11/03.

27. Ken Maginnis interview 16/11/03.
28. Fergus Finlay interview 06/04/99.
29. DT interview 29/02/04.
30. See *News Letter* 15/09/95; DT interview 03/11/03.

CHAPTER FOURTEEN: *Go West, young man!*

1. Conor Cruise O'Brien interview 08/04/99.
2. Fergus Finlay interview 06/04/99.
3. Jim Wilson interview 17/11/03.
4. Jack Allen interview 21/12/03
5. John Hunter interview 23/02/99.
6. Denis Rogan interview 22/02/99.
7. James Cooper interview 28/01/99.
8. Jim Nicholson interview 19/02/99.
9. Jeffrey Donaldson interview 17/02/99.
10. Jack Allen interview 22/02/99.
11. DT interview 21/02/99.
12. Jack Allen interview 22/02/99.
13. Denis Rogan interview 22/02/99.
14. *News Letter* 23/10/95.
15. *News Letter* 23/10/95.
16. *Orange Standard* October 1995.
17. *News Letter* 23/10/95.
18. DT interview 21/02/99.
19. See James Cooper's remarks, *Irish Times* 19/11/01.
20. *Irish Times* 15/09/95.
21. DT interviews 21/02/99 and 03/11/03.
22. David Brewster interview 03/04/99.
23. David Brewster interview 03/04/99.
24. *News Letter* 19/09/95.
25. See also *Irish Times* 11/09/95.
26. Robert McCartney interview 28/04/99.
27. Nancy Soderberg interview 26/04/99.
28. Anthony Lake, *Nightmares* (New York, 2000), pp. 122–123.
29. Nancy Soderberg interview 26/04/99.
30. See *Belfast Telegraph* 18/03/64 and *Belfast Telegraph* editorial 19/06/65 and a complaining private letter from O'Neill to Jack Sayers, then editor of the

Belfast Telegraph, dated 24/06/65. I am grateful to Dennis Kennedy for supplying me with this correspondence. See also Ken Bloomfield, *Stormont in Crisis: A Memoir* (Belfast, 1994), pp. 42–63.

31. Lady Faulkner interview 19/05/03. See also *News Letter* 03/07/72.
32. See *News Letter* 08/12/81; *Belfast Telegraph* 12/01/82, 12/03/84, 15/05/84 and 29/05/84. See also *Irish Times* 20/01/82.
33. Anne Smith interview 19/03/02. See also Anthony Lake, *Nightmares* (New York, 2000), pp. 122–123.
34. See Earl J. Hess, *Pickett's Charge – The Last Attack at Gettysburg* (London, 2001), pp. 64–65 and 256–257.
35. Nancy Soderberg interview 26/04/99.
36. David Burnside interview 07/01/99.
37. DT interview 20/03/02.
38. Sir John Kerr interview 05/05/99.
39. Sir John Wheeler interview 12/03/99.
40. Private information.
41. DT interview 11/04/99.
42. DT interview 11/04/99.
43. *News Letter* 01/11/95.
44. *News Letter* 02/11/95.
45. Anthony Lake interview 18/03/02.
46. Anne Smith interview 19/03/02.
47. Anne Smith interview 19/03/02.
48. DT interview 05/10/00.

CHAPTER FIFTEEN: *'Binning Mitchell'*

1. Seldon, *Major*, pp. 580–582.
2. Patrick Mayhew interview 20/01/99.
3. Andrew Hunter interview 24/03/99.
4. See *Irish Times* 30/11/95 and George Mitchell, *Making Peace* (London, 1999), pp. 25–27.
5. *The Times* 06/09/95 and 07/09/95. See also Paul Bew and Gordon Gillespie, *The Northern Ireland Peace Process 1993–1996: A Chronology* (London, 1996), pp. 118–119, 128, 134.
6. Jeffrey Donaldson interview 20/06/02.
7. Anthony Lake interview 18/03/02.
8. *Irish Times* 21/10/96.
9. *News Letter* 01/12/95. See *The Times* 14/03/96.
10. DT interview 11/04/99.
11. Jeffrey Donaldson interview 17/02/99.

12. George Mitchell interview 22/04/99.
13. Mitchell, *Making Peace*, p. 37.
14. *News Letter* 26/06/98.
15. Commons Hansard, Vol. 270, 22 January–2 February 1995–6, cols. 354–370.
16. Fergus Finlay interview 06/04/99.
17. Commons Hansard, Vol. 270, 22 January–2 February 1995–6, cols. 359–360.

CHAPTER SIXTEEN: *'Putting manners on the Brits'*

1. Quentin Thomas interview 29/03/02. See also Kevin Rafter, *Martin Mansergh: A Biography* (Dublin, 2002), p. 239.
2. Seldon, *Major*, pp. 624–625.
3. Anthony Lake interview 18/03/02.
4. John Wheeler interview 12/03/99.
5. Viscount Cranborne interview 07/03/02.
6. Paul Bew interview 13/05/02. See also Conor Cruise O'Brien, *Memoir: My Life and Themes* (London, 1998), pp. 439–447.
7. John Steele interview 05/04/99.
8. Viscount Cranborne interview 14/01/99.
9. Patrick Mayhew interview 20/01/99.
10. Fergus Finlay interview 07/04/99.
11. Toby Harnden interview 03/03/03. See also Conor O'Clery, *Irish Times* 14/06/96 and Trimble's review of Ed Moloney's *A Secret History of the IRA*, *The Spectator* 14/21 December 2002.
12. *Irish News* 01/03/96.
13. See Thomas Hennessey, *The Northern Ireland Peace Process: Ending the Troubles?* (Dublin, 2000), p. 101.
14. John Bruton interview 06/04/99.
15. DT interview 11/04/99.
16. Private information.
17. DT interview 11/04/99.
18. Cmd 3232 15/03/96.
19. *Mail on Sunday* 21/01/96.
20. See Commons Hansard, Vol. 214, 1992–3, cols. 861–862.
21. See *Mail on Sunday, Night and Day Magazine*, 21/01/96.
22. Peter Robinson interview 30/03/03.
23. Quentin Thomas interview 19/02/02.
24. DT interview 11/04/99.
25. DT interview 11/04/99.

26. Brian Mawhinney interview 28/03/02.

27. Private information.

28. See Commons Hansard, Vol. 272, 19 February–1 March 1996, cols. 689–694.

29. Patrick Mayhew interview 20/01/99.

30. Paddy Ashdown, *The Ashdown Diaries, Volume One 1988–97* (London, 2000), p. 406.

31. Woodrow Wyatt (S. Curtis, ed.), *The Journals of Woodrow Wyatt*, Vol. 3 (London, 2000), p. 689.

32. DT telephone interview 14/06/01.

33. Ashdown, *The Ashdown Diaries*, p. 355.

34. John Bruton interview 06/04/99. See F.S.L. Lyons, *Charles Stewart Parnell* (London, 1977), pp. 283–288, 309.

35. DT interview 17/06/02.

36. Anthony Lake interview 18/03/02.

37. *Irish News* 15/05/96.

38. *News Letter* 26/05/96; 27/05/96; 28/05/96.

39. Elaine McClure interview 27/01/99.

40. *Irish Times* 21/10/96.

41. On the issue of Catholic candidates before 1972, see Harbinson, *The Ulster Unionist Party*, pp. 43–44. See also Gorman's autobiography, *The Times of My Life: An Autobiography* (Barnsley, 2002).

42. *The Unionist*, Autumn 1997.

43. I am grateful to Hazel Legge at UUP headquarters for looking up these statistics for me.

44. Quoted in Paul Bew and Gordon Gillespie, *Northern Ireland: A Chronology of the Troubles 1968–99* (Dublin, 1999), p. 328.

45. John Bruton interview 22/11/03.

46. Fergus Finlay interview 07/04/99.

47. John Oliver interview 25/01/99.

48. *Sunday Independent* 16/06/96.

49. See Elliott and Flackes, *Northern Ireland*, pp. 579–589.

50. Michael Ancram interview 11/03/99.

CHAPTER SEVENTEEN: *The Yanks are coming*

1. Viscount Cranborne interview 14/01/99.

2. John Major interview 09/02/00.

3. DT interview 06/04/03.

4. DT interview 17/04/99.

5. John Hunter interview 23/02/99.

6. Andrew Hunter interview 24/03/99.
7. *News Letter* 04/06/96.
8. DT interview 17/04/99.
9. *Irish News* 08/06/96 and 14/06/96.
10. Mitchell, *Making Peace*, p. 46.
11. DT interview 17/04/99.
12. Robert McCartney interview 28/04/99.
13. DT interview 17/04/99.
14. Robert McCartney interview 28/04/99.
15. *Irish News* 11/06/96.
16. See Mitchell, *Making Peace*, pp. 49–53; George Mitchell interview 22/04/99.
17. Nora Owen interview 08/04/99.
18. George Mitchell, *Making Peace* pp. 47–48. See Commons Hansard, Vol. 226, 7–18 June, col. 566; Vol. 251, 5–20 December 1994, col. 922; Vol. 260, 15–31 May 1995, cols. 1042–1044. See also Brendan Simms, *Unfinest Hour: Britain and the Destruction of Bosnia* (London, 2002), pp. 287–288.
19. Private information.
20. Nora Owen interview 08/04/99.
21. Nigel Dodds interview 12/04/99.
22. DT interview 11/04/99.
23. Robert McCartney interview 28/04/99.
24. Nora Owen interview 08/04/99.
25. Patrick Mayhew interview 20/01/99.
26. Private information.
27. *News Letter* 13/06/96.
28. Mitchell, *Making Peace*, pp. 76–83.
29. Peter Bell interview 09/06/99.
30. Sean Farren interview 16/06/99.
31. Nigel Dodds interview 12/04/99.

CHAPTER EIGHTEEN: *The Siege of Drumcree (II)*

1. William Ross interview 08/03/02. On Drumcree II see Ryder and Kearney, *Drumcree*, pp. 128–175.
2. *Irish Times* 08/06/96; *The Sunday Telegraph* 16/06/96.
3. Harold Gracey interview 16/02/99.
4. DT interview 17/04/99.
5. Denis Watson interview 18/02/99; DT interview 06/04/03.
6. Gordon Lucy interview 20/02/99.
7. DT interview 17/04/99; *The Scotsman* 10/07/96.

8. *Irish Times* 07/09/96.
9. Lucy, *Stand-Off!*, p. 133.
10. Lucy, *Stand-Off!*, p. 75; *Irish News* 08/07/96.
11. *Irish News* 16/07/96.
12. Private information.
13. Sir John Wheeler interview 12/03/99.
14. DT interview 17/04/99.
15. Lucy, *Stand-Off!*, pp. 77–78; *Irish Times* 09/07/96.
16. *Irish Times* 09/07/96.
17. See *Irish Times* 10/07/96.
18. *Irish News* 09/07/96.
19. *Irish Times* 09/07/96.
20. David Kerr interview 10/09/00.
21. David Campbell interview 16/01/02.
22. John Hunter interview 09/02/02.
23. David Campbell interview 16/01/02.
24. Harold Gracey interview 16/02/99.
25. DT interview 17/04/99.
26. James Molyneaux interview 13/01/99.
27. *Irish News* 11/07/96.
28. DT interview 17/04/99.
29. Robert McCartney interview 28/04/99.
30. Robert McCartney interview 28/04/99.
31. DT interview 17/04/99.
32. *Irish Times* 11/07/99; *News Letter* 11/07/96.
33. DT interview 17/04/99; Jeffrey Donaldson interview 17/02/99.
34. Jeffrey Donaldson interview 17/02/99; DT interview 17/04/99; John Major interview 09/02/00.
35. John Pickering private diary 16/02/99.
36. Denis Watson interview 18/02/99.
37. Harold Gracey interview 16/02/99.
38. Stephanie Roderick interview 07/06/99.
39. See, for instance, *The Sunday Times* 09/08/92.
40. Commons Hansard, Vol. 216, 14 December 1992–15 January 1993, col. 574.
41. See *Lost Lives*, pp. 611–614.
42. See Chris Anderson, *The Billy Boy: The Life and Death of Billy Wright* (Edinburgh, 2002); Jim Cusack and Henry McDonald, *The UVF* (Dublin, 1997), p. 230; *Fortnight*, October 1996.
43. DT interview 17/04/99; David Kerr interview 10/09/00.
44. *News Letter* 17/07/96.
45. Interview with senior RUC officer.

46. Jim Blair interview 02/07/02.
47. DT interview 17/04/99.
48. Daphne Trimble interview 12/04/99.
49. Patrick Mayhew interview 23/05/03.
50. Rupert Smith interview 12/04/02.
51. Patrick Mayhew interviews 20/01/99 and 03/04/02.
52. Viscount Cranborne interview 18/03/99.
53. Nora Owen interview 08/04/99.
54. Fergus Finlay interview 07/04/99.
55. Lucy, *Stand-Off!* pp. 87–89.
56. Peter Bell interview 09/04/99.
57. *Irish News* 13/07/96.
58. Commons Hansard, Vol. 281, 8–19 July 1996, col. 786.
59. Report of the Independent Review of Parades and Marches, January 1997.
60. For Steel's remarks, see Commons Hansard, Vol. 281, 8–19 July 1996, col. 790.
61. *News Letter* 15/10/96.
62. *Irish Times* 17/07/96 and 18/07/96.
63. *Irish Times* 07/09/96.
64. *Irish Times* 07/09/96; *News Letter* 29/07/96.
65. Maurice Hayes interview 06/01/99.
66. DT interview 17/04/99.
67. *Belfast Telegraph* 05/09/96.
68. *Belfast Telegraph* 31/08/96 and 02/09/96.
69. *Irish Times* 06/09/96.
70. George Mitchell, *Making Peace*, p. 73; Bew and Gillespie, p. 338.
71. *Chronology*, p. 338.
72. Gary McMichael interview 14/06/99.
73. Gary McMichael interview 14/06/99.

CHAPTER NINETEEN: *Fag end Toryism*

1. See Moloney, *A Secret History of the IRA*, p. 454.
2. *Lost Lives*, pp. 1400–1401.
3. See Seldon, *Major* pp. 620–621, 631 and 661–662; Major, pp. 479–480.
4. *Belfast Telegraph* 09/10/96 and DT interview 03/11/03.
5. DT interview 17/04/99.
6. Sir John Wheeler interview 12/03/99.
7. Sir John Wheeler interview 12/03/99.
8. Viscount Cranborne interview 14/01/99.
9. Commons Hansard, Vol. 286, 25 November–6 December 1996, cols. 460–461.

10. *The Scotsman* 28/02/97; *News Letter* 28/02/97.

11. DT interview 06/04/03.

12. See *The Daily Telegraph* 24/12/96.

13. Nigel Dodds interview 25/03/02.

14. DT interview 13/06/99.

15. See *News Letter* 12/04/97; *Belfast Telegraph* 11/04/97; *News Letter* 08/10/99 and 01/03/01; *Belfast Telegraph* 24/01/01.

16. *Irish Times* 29/04/97.

17. Elliott and Flackes, *Northern Ireland*, p. 590.

18. DT interview 13/06/99.

CHAPTER TWENTY: *The unlikeliest Blair babe*

1. DT interview 13/06/99.

2. Tony Blair interview 07/02/00.

3. DT interview 13/06/99.

4. I am again grateful to George MacDonald McAllister for drawing my attention to these references.

5. Private information. See also Geoffrey Levy in the *Daily Mail* 06/12/98, Jackie Ashley, *Guardian* 22/07/02.

6. See Andy McSmith, *Faces of Labour: The Inside Story* (London, 1997), p. 228.

7. John Lloyd interview 22/06/99.

8. I am grateful to Gary Kent and Bert Ward for digging up this reference.

9. *News Letter* 31/03/92.

10. Commons Hansard, Vol. 239, 7–18 March 1994, col. 338. See Mo Mowlam, *Momentum* (London, 2002), p. 26.

11. Commons Hansard, Vol. 234, 6–17 December 1993, cols. 1073–1074.

12. See Trimble's remarks on McNamara, Commons Hansard, Vol. 235, 11–21 January 1994, col. 1217.

13. Julia Langdon, *Mo Mowlam* (London, 2000), p. 269.

14. Mowlam, *Momentum*, p. 71; private information; David Brewster interview 27/06/02.

15. *Belfast Telegraph* 02/09/96.

16. DT interview 17/04/99.

17. Mo Mowlam, *Momentum*, pp. 150, 267, 347–348.

18. See Liam Clarke and Kathryn Johnston, *Martin McGuinness: From Guns to Government* (Edinburgh, 2003), pp. 310–311. See also Gerry Adams, *Hope and History: Making Peace in Ireland* (Co. Kerry, 2003), p. 352.

19. Daphne Trimble interview 14/06/99.

20. See Mo Mowlam, *Momentum*, p. 3.

21. Daphne Trimble interview 14/06/99.

22. Peter Bell interviews 16/01/00 and 25/03/02.

23. Daphne Trimble interview 14/06/99; DT interview 06/04/03.

24. Tony Worthington interview 21/05/03.

25. Mo Mowlam interview 06/07/99. See also *Irish News* 04/05/02 and Mowlam, *Momentum*, p. 116.

26. Frank Millar interview 08/06/02.

27. Tony Worthington interview 28/07/99.

28. Frank Millar interview 08/06/02.

29. *New Left Review*, November–December 1996, pp. 153–159.

30. See Ed Moloney in *The Sunday Tribune* 05/05/02. See also Mo Mowlam, *Momentum*, p. 18.

31. Tony Worthington interview 28/07/99.

32. *News Letter* 15/09/95. See *Sunday Times* and *Independent on Sunday* 17/09/95.

33. See Bew and Gillespie, *The Northern Ireland Peace Process 1993–1996: A Chronology*, p. 119.

34. Private information.

35. John Taylor interview 18/03/02. Michael Farrell, *Northern Ireland: The Orange State* (London, 1980).

36. *Irish News* 16/06/99.

37. See Ed Moloney in *The Sunday Tribune* 05/05/02.

38. See Paul Bew in *The Daily Telegraph* 02/01/01.

39. I am grateful to Arthur Aughey for pointing this out on the FCO's web-site.

40. Langdon, *Mo Mowlam*, p. 4.

41. See *Belfast Telegraph* 08/12/95.

42. Commons Hansard, Vol. 272, 19 February–1 March 1996, col. 95.

43. Commons Hansard, Vol. 281, 8–19 July 1996, cols. 786–787; *News Letter* 07/02/97; *Financial Times* 16/07/96; *The Guardian* 16/07/96. See also Trimble's comments in 1997, Commons Hansard, Vol. 296, 16–27 June 1997, cols. 1039–1045.

44. See DT interview, *New Statesman* 25/04/97.

45. Mo Mowlam interview 06/07/99.

46. Fergus Finlay interview 06/04/99. See also Paddy Ashdown, *The Ashdown Diaries, Volume One 1988–97*, p. 355.

47. David Montgomery interview 21/07/99.

48. Gary Kent interview 19/07/99.

49. David Montgomery interview 21/07/99.

50. Calum Macdonald interview 03/07/02.

51. Gary Kent interview 19/07/99.

52. DT interview 26/03/02.
53. David Montgomery interview 21/07/99.
54. DT interview 13/06/99.
55. Private information; David Montgomery interview 21/07/99.
56. DT interview 17/04/99.
57. *News Letter* 12/12/96; *Irish Times* 12/12/96 and 13/07/96.
58. *Belfast Telegraph* 14/12/96.
59. Alastair Campbell interview 06/03/00.
60. Private information.
61. DT interview 17/04/99.
62. DT interview 13/06/99.
63. Bernard Donoughue, *Prime Minister: The Conduct of Policy Under Harold Wilson and James Callaghan* (London: Jonathan Cape, 1987), p. 129.
64. Bernard Donoughue interview 22/03/02.
65. Bernard Donoughue interview 22/03/02.
66. Private information.
67. David Montgomery interview 21/07/99.
68. Daphne Trimble interview 20/06/00.
69. Reg Empey interview 08/01/00.
70. Bernard Donoughue interview 22/03/02. Peter Hennessey thinks that this figure is probably right; the only precedent for such an investment of Prime Ministerial time was during the Heath years. See Peter Hennessey, *The Prime Minister: The Office and its Holders since 1945* (London, 2000), pp. 346–347.
71. Tony Blair interview 07/02/00.
72. See Robert Kee, *Ireland: A History* (London, 1980).
73. Jonathan Powell interview 18/02/00. See also Powell's interview in *The Telegraph Magazine*, 05/05/01.
74. DT interview 13/06/99.
75. DT interview 13/06/99.
76. DT interview 13/06/99.
77. David Montgomery interview 21/07/99.
78. Kate Hoey interview 22/03/02.
79. Norman Godman interview 29/01/04.
80. George Robertson interview 19/07/99.
81. The speech is reprinted in Paul Bew, Henry Patterson and Paul Teague, *Northern Ireland between War And Peace: The Political Future of Northern Ireland* (London, 1997), pp. 217–224.
82. Andy Wood interview 06/06/99.
83. DT interview 13/06/99.
84. John Lloyd interview 22/06/99.

CHAPTER TWENTY-ONE: *The pains of peace*

1. *News Letter* 24/05/97 and 03/06/97.
2. *Irish Times* 07/06/97.
3. Stephanie Roderick interview 14/06/99.
4. *The Daily Telegraph* 17/06/97.
5. *Daily Telegraph* 17/06/97; *News Letter* 17/06/97.
6. *Irish News* 19/06/97.
7. John Steele interview 05/04/99.
8. On Begley, see Mallie and McKittrick, *The Fight for Peace*, pp. 201–202.
9. *Belfast Telegraph* 17/06/97; *Irish Times* 19/06/97.
10. *Belfast Telegraph* 24/06/97.
11. *News Letter* 24/06/97.
12. For Drumcree III and the events leading up to it, see Ryder and Kearney, *Drumcree*, pp. 170–226 and Mowlam, *Momentum*, pp. 87–109.
13. *Irish News* 08/07/97.
14. DT interview 13/06/99.
15. *Belfast Telegraph* 07/07/97.
16. DT interview 13/06/99.
17. *Irish Times* 12/07/97.
18. Private information.
19. Private information; *Daily Telegraph* 30/06/97; *Sunday Tribune* 05/05/02.
20. Commons Hansard, Vol. 297, 30 June–11 July 1997, cols. 63–65. Also DT interview 03/11/03.
21. DT interview 13/06/99. On Jackson's record, see *Irish Post* 06/11/93 and *An Phoblacht/Republican News* 04/11/93.
22. *Daily Telegraph* 18/07/97.
23. *Belfast Telegraph* 18/07/97.
24. *Daily Telegraph* 21/07/97.
25. Les Rodgers interview 30/03/03.
26. Sean O'Callaghan interview 12/11/99.
27. *Irish Times* 19/07/99.
28. DT interview 13/06/99.
29. DT interview 13/06/99.
30. Jeffrey Donaldson interview 15/06/99.
31. John Taylor interview 18/03/02.
32. DT interview 13/06/99.
33. Frank Millar interview 07/11/99.
34. *Belfast Telegraph* 04/09/97.
35. *Irish Times* 23/07/97.
36. Sean O'Callaghan interview 01/07/02.

37. William Hague interview 15/06/00; Andrew Mackay interview 13/04/00.
38. See *The Independent* 26/07/99.
39. *Belfast Telegraph* 18/09/97.
40. *News Letter* 28/08/97.
41. Denis Rogan interview 03/08/99.
42. Dr Seamus Hegarty interview 22/03/02; DT interview 06/04/03.
43. *Irish Times* 02/09/97; DT interview 13/06/99.
44. *News Letter* 01/09/07; *The Daily Telegraph* 30/09/97 and 23/09/97.
45. Private information.
46. DT interview 04/08/99.
47. Sean O'Callaghan interview 08/01/02.
48. DT interview 20/02/02.
49. Peter Weir interview 18/04/02; *Belfast Telegraph* 30/09/97.
50. Paul Bew interview 20/06/02.
51. Quentin Thomas interview 16/05/02.
52. Peter Bell interview 02/04/02.
53. Jeffrey Donaldson interview 15/06/99.
54. Robert McCartney interview 28/04/99.
55. DT interview 13/06/99.
56. DT interview 12/02/04.
57. DT interview 13/06/99.
58. Jeffrey Donaldson interview 15/06/99.
59. Mo Mowlam interviews 06/07/99 and 17/06/02.
60. Jeffrey Donaldson interview 15/06/99.
61. *News Letter* 18/09/99. See also Mowlam, *Momentum*, pp. 167–168.

CHAPTER TWENTY-TWO: *When Irish eyes are smiling*

1. DT interview 13/06/99. See also *Parliamentary Brief* January 1998.
2. DT interview 07/11/99.
3. *An Phoblacht/Republican News* 11/09/97.
4. *Daily Telegraph* 13/09/97; *News Letter* 15/09/97.
5. *The Times* 17/09/97.
6. Antony Alcock diary 16/09/97.
7. *Daily Telegraph* 17/09/97.
8. DT interview 06/04/03.
9. Peter Weir interview 05/04/99.
10. Private information.
11. Daphne Trimble interview 14/06/99.
12. DT interview 03/08/99.

13. Clifford Smyth interview 07/04/03.
14. Sean Farren interview 03/04/99.
15. *Guardian Saturday Magazine* 25/11/00.
16. DT interview 27/05/03.
17. Austen Morgan, unpublished autobiography.
18. Austen Morgan interview 21/06/99.
19. Thomas Hennessey interview 27/05/03. See C.D.C. Armstrong's book review in *The Daily Telegraph* 06/01/01.
20. John Hunter interview 23/02/99.
21. Reg Empey interview 06/01/99.
22. Peter Weir interview 05/04/99.
23. DT interview 17/06/02.
24. DT interview 03/08/99.
25. Peter King interview 25/10/00.
26. Larry Butler interview 23/04/99.
27. *News Letter* 08/10/97.
28. Stephen Collins (ed.), *The Sunday Tribune Guide to Politics* (Dublin, 1997), p. 237.
29. DT interview 06/04/03.
30. David Andrews interview 31/01/01.
31. See Ken Whelan and Eugene Masterson, *Bertie Ahern: Taoiseach and Peacemaker* (Dublin, 1998), pp. 9–10.
32. Ahern had first visited UUP HQ at Glengall Street in January 1995, and had met with senior Ulster Unionists. See Whelan and Masterson, *Bertie Ahern*, p. 150.
33. Bertie Ahern interview 12/05/99. Ahern's British-Irish Association address is reprinted in Paul Bew, Henry Patterson and Paul Teague, *Northern Ireland: Between War and Peace* (London, 1997), pp. 225–231.
34. Bertie Ahern interview 12/05/99.
35. *Irish Times* 22/11/97.
36. *Irish Times* 09/12/97; Private information; Sean Farren interview 16/06/99.
37. Ken Maginnis interview 09/06/99.
38. Bertie Ahern interview 12/05/99.
39. *Irish Times* 22/11/97.
40. See also the account of Jack Lynch's views on re-unification in an article by Eamonn McCann in the *Sunday Tribune* 25/05/03.
41. Paddy Teahon interview 18/03/02.
42. Bertie Ahern interview 12/05/99.
43. Austen Morgan interview 21/06/99.
44. *Irish Times* 22/11/97.
45. David Trimble interview 13/06/99.

CHAPTER TWENTY-THREE: *Murder in the Maze (or the way out of it)*

1. Commons Hansard, Vol. 302, 1–12 December 1997, cols. 1215–1216.
2. *Irish News* 17/11/97.
3. DT interview 04/08/99.
4. *News Letter* 17/10/97.
5. DT interview 04/08/99.
6. *The Daily Telegraph* 18/12/99.
7. *News Letter* 01/12/97.
8. *Irish Times* 27/10/97.
9. *Irish News* 03/12/97.
10. DT interview 04/08/99; *Belfast Telegraph* 12/11/97. See also Ed Moloney in the *Sunday Tribune* 00/00/00.
11. Ruth Dudley Edwards interview 10/03/02.
12. DT interview 03/08/99.
13. Sean O'Callaghan interview 12/12/99. See also Ed Moloney, 'O'Callaghan Joins the Aristocracy', *Sunday Tribune* 30/11/97.
14. See *Fortnight* No. 385 May 2000; DT interview 06/04/03.
15. *Sunday Independent* 12/03/00. See Mansergh's review of Henry McDonald's *Trimble*, the *Irish Times* 26/02/00.
16. Ruth Dudley Edwards interview 05/04/02; DT interview 03/08/99.
17. DT interview 03/08/99; Paul Bew interview 25/12/99.
18. Sir John Holmes interview 22/07/99.
19. Ruth Dudley Edwards interview 10/03/02. See John Lloyd, 'Good Traitors' *Prospect*, January 2000.
20. DT interview 03/08/99.
21. *Daily Telegraph* 06/12/97.
22. Jeffrey Donaldson interview 15/06/99.
23. Dail Debates, Vol. 483, 19 November–2 December 1997, cols. 1246–1252 and *Financial Times* 05/12/97.
24. *Sunday Tribune* 18/01/98.
25. Bertie Ahern interview 12/05/99.
26. See *Lost Lives*, pp. 1416–1420 and the Narey report, 'Report of an Inquiry into the Escape of a Prisoner from HMP Maze on 10 December 1997 and the Shooting of a Prisoner on 27 December 1997', House of Commons Paper HC 1997–98 658 (London, 1998) and 'HMP The Maze (Northern Ireland): Report of a Full Inspection 23 March–3 April 1998' (London, 1998); *Belfast Telegraph* 29/12/97 and 30/12/97.
27. See *Lost Lives*, pp. 1420–1422; *Belfast Telegraph* 02/01/98.
28. *Irish News* 06/01/98.
29. Gary McMichael interview 14/06/99; DT interview 03/08/99.

30. *Irish Times* 13/10/96.
31. Jeffrey Donaldson interview 15/06/99.
32. John White interview 25/03/02.
33. DT interviews 03/08/99 and 04/08/99.
34. Private information; Mowlam, *Momentum*, pp. 182–184.
35. Private information.
36. David Adams interview 14/06/99; John White interview 25/03/02.
37. DT interview 03/08/99.
38. Paddy Teahon interview 10/06/99.
39. George Mitchell interview 22/04/99.
40. *Sunday Tribune* 18/01/98.
41. DT interview 20/02/02.
42. DT interview 03/08/99.
43. UUP submission to the Inter-Party Talks 17/02/98.
44. *News Letter* 24/01/98.
45. Peter Weir interview 05/04/99; DT interview 03/08/99.
46. Antony Alcock diary 27/01/98; *Irish Times* 04/02/98.
47. *The Daily Telegraph* 11/02/98.
48. See *News Letter* 12/02/98, 13/02/98, 16/02/98; *Irish Times* 14/02/98; *News Letter* 14/02/98 and 16/02/98.
49. *Irish Times* 26/02/98.
50. *News Letter* 17/02/98 and 19/02/98.
51. *Lost Lives*, pp. 1428–1430.
52. Seamus Mallon interview 14/01/00.
53. *The Daily Telegraph* 05/03/98.
54. *Daily Telegraph* 26/03/98.
55. Private information.
56. *Irish Times* 20/03/98.
57. *Irish Times* 21/03/98.
58. Private information.
59. Jeffrey Donaldson interview 15/06/99.
60. *Irish Times* 23/03/98.

CHAPTER TWENTY-FOUR: *Long Good Friday*

1. DT interview 03/08/99.
2. *The Sunday Times* 05/04/98.
3. *The Daily Telegraph* 03/04/98.
4. George Mitchell, *Making Peace* (New York, 1999), p. 159.
5. John de Chastelain interview 24/01/00.
6. John de Chastelain interview 24/01/00.

7. Paul Bew interview 08/01/00.
8. DT interview 04/08/99.
9. *The Daily Telegraph* 13/04/98.
10. *The Daily Telegraph* 06/04/98.
11. Daphne Trimble interview 14/06/99.
12. DT interview 04/08/99.
13. Reg Empey interview 08/03/02.
14. Paddy Teahon interview 09/06/99.
15. John Taylor interview 22/06/02.
16. *The Independent* 08/04/98. See Hennessey, *The Northern Ireland Peace Process* p. 164.
17. *Daily Telegraph* 08/04/98.
18. Paddy Teahon interview 09/06/99.
19. DT interview 04/08/99.
20. DT interview 04/08/99.
21. DT interview 11/11/00 and 16/02/04.
22. John de Chastelain interview 20/01/00.
23. Mitchell, *Making Peace*, p. 169.
24. See *RTE Guide*, 8/5/98.
25. Mitchell, *Making Peace*, p. 171; Bertie Ahern interview 12/05/99.
26. Bertie Ahern interview 12/05/99.
27. Paddy Teahon interview 09/06/99.
28. *RTE Guide* 08/05/98.
29. Private information.
30. Tony Blair interview 07/02/00.
31. DT interview 04/08/99.
32. Paul Bew interview 08/01/00.
33. Mitchell, *Making Peace* p. 175.
34. Thomas Hennessey interview 15/03/02; Tony Blair interview 07/02/00.
35. DT interview 04/08/99.
36. George Mitchell interview 22/04/99.
37. Jeffrey Donaldson interview 30/07/99.
38. DT interview 04/08/99.
39. DT interview 03/08/99.
40. David Andrews interview 01/02/01.
41. Tony Blair interview 07/02/00.
42. Quentin Thomas interview 06/03/03.
43. Peter Bell interview 07/04/03.
44. Paddy Teahon interview 09/06/99.
45. John Holmes interview 12/03/02.

46. See Anthony McIntyre, 'Modern Irish Republicanism: The Product of British State Strategies' in *Irish Political Studies*, 10, 1995, p. 104.
47. DT interview 03/01/00.
48. John Taylor interview 18/03/02.
49. Bertie Ahern interview 12/05/99.
50. Seamus Mallon interview 14/01/00.
51. Hennessey, *The Northern Ireland Peace Process* pp. 125–126.
52. Mark Durkan interview 11/05/02.
53. Thomas Hennessey interview 15/03/02.
54. See also Rick Wilford, 'A Healthy Democracy?' *Parliamentary Brief*, June 2002.
55. Sir Reg Empey interview 12/05/02.
56. DT interview 20/02/02.
57. DT interview 04/08/99.
58. Sydney Elliott interview 30/04/03.
59. Private information.
60. DT interview 04/08/99.
61. Sean O'Callaghan interview 28/03/02.
62. *Irish Times* 17/05/01.
63. See also Faulkner, *Memoirs of a Statesman*, p. 229; private information.
64. See Frank Millar in the *Irish Times* 01/03/01.
65. Peter Weir interview 05/04/99.
66. *Irish Times* 18/05/98.
67. Henry Patterson, 'Words for Peace', *Times Change*, Summer/Autumn 1997.
68. See Brigid Hadfield in *Public Law*, Winter 1998.
69. Willie Ross interviews 08/03/02 and 05/01/04; private information.
70. DT interviews 05/01/99 and 04/08/99.
71. *Irish News* 10/04/98.
72. Jeffrey Donaldson interview 11/03/02.
73. *Belfast Telegraph* 10/04/98.
74. Ken Maginnis interview 19/01/00.
75. Paul Bew interview 08/01/00.
76. *Belfast Telegraph* 17/04/98.
77. Paul Bew interview 08/01/00.
78. DT interview 03/12/00.
79. Denis Rogan interview 11/03/02.
80. David Kerr interview 13/09/00.
81. Paddy Teahon interview 10/06/99.
82. DT interview 04/08/99.
83. Denis Rogan interview 29/05/03.
84. Private information.

85. Private information.
86. John Steele interview 05/04/99.
87. Private information.
88. DT interview 04/08/99.
89. Ken Maginnis interview 11/03/02.
90. DT interview 04/08/99.
91. Jeffrey Donaldson interview 30/07/99.
92. Thomas Hennessey interview 28/01/00.
93. Anthony Alcock interview 03/04/99.
94. Jonathan Powell interview 18/02/00.
95. DT interview 04/08/99.
96. Jonathan Powell interview 18/02/00.
97. Austen Morgan interview 21/06/99.
98. See *Endgame in Ireland*, p. 248.
99. DT interview 04/08/99. See also Trimble's comments to Frank Millar, *Irish Times* 17/04/00.
100. Austen Morgan interview 21/06/99.
101. DT interview 04/08/99.
102. David Montgomery interview 22/03/02.
103. Private information.
104. DT 04/08/99.
105. Denis Rogan interview 11/03/02.
106. Jeffrey Donaldson interview 30/07/99.
107. Sean O'Callaghan interview 25/03/02.
108. See *Lost Lives*, pp. 56–57 and 1011–1012.
109. Jeffrey Donaldson interview 14/04/02.
110. Arlene Foster interview 08/03/02.
111. David Brewster interview 14/04/02.
112. Daphne Trimble interview 14/06/99.
113. DT interview 04/08/99.
114. Mitchell, *Making Peace*, pp. 4–5.
115. Thomas Hennessey interview 03/07/02.
116. DT interview 04/08/99.
117. Barry White interview 13/03/02.
118. Reg Empey interview 16/03/02.
119. John Taylor interview 18/03/02.
120. DT interview 04/08/99; *Irish Times* 11/04/99.
121. Daphne Trimble interview 14/06/99.
122. Jonathan Powell interview 18/02/00.
123. *Irish News* 13/04/98.
124. Ruth Dudley Edwards interview 02/07/02.

125. Private information.
126. DT interview 28/01/03.
127. Daphne Trimble interview 14/06/99.
128. Private information.
129. *Sunday Telegraph* 30/01/00.
130. See, for instance, Sean Mac Arthaigh in the *Sunday Business Post* 20/04/03; DT interview 11/05/03; Jonathan Powell interview 23/05/03.
131. See also *Irish Times* 19/11/01.
132. See Anthony McIntyre, 'Modern Irish Republicanism: The Product of British State Strategies', p. 104.
133. See *Irish Times* 11/03/02.
134. *The Orange Standard* October 1994.
135. See www.ark.ac.uk/nilt/
136. The figures are cited by Trimble in an interview with British Airways' *Voyager* magazine, June 1998.
137. For claims about the 'chill factor' see Drew Nelson in the *Irish Times* 04/07/95; a *Belfast Telegraph* survey 12/12/97 and letters in the *Belfast Telegraph* on 26/06/98 and 19/04/01.
138. DT interview 24/03/02. See also Graham Gudgin in the *Belfast Telegraph* 20/12/02.
139. Chris McGimpsey interview 08/04/02.
140. Jeffrey Donaldson interview 25/03/02.
141. Reg Empey interview 09/03/02.
142. Reg Empey interview 09/03/02.

CHAPTER TWENTY-FIVE: *'Let the people sing'*

1. DT interview 04/08/99.
2. Denis Rogan interview 11/03/02; *News Letter* 13/04/98.
3. *Irish News* 17/04/98.
4. *Irish Times* 17/04/98.
5. *Belfast Telegraph* 17/04/98.
6. *Irish Times* 20/04/98.
7. DT interview 04/08/99.
8. DT interview 04/08/99.
9. Private information.
10. Ken Maginnis interview 11/03/02.
11. Thomas Hennessey interview 14/04/99; Jack Allen interview 22/02/99.
12. DT interview 04/08/99.
13. *The Daily Telegraph* 20/04/98.
14. *The Daily Telegraph* 09/05/98.

15. *News Letter* 20/05/98.
16. Jeffrey Donaldson interview 30/07/99.
17. Arlene Foster interview 09/06/99.
18. *The Daily Telegraph* 13/05/98.
19. *News Letter* 18/05/98, 19/05/98.
20. DT interview 04/08/99.
21. DT interview 03/08/99.
22. Private information.
23. See *Lost Lives*, pp. 567–568; 588; 599.
24. *The Daily Telegraph* 06/05/98.
25. DT interview 06/04/03.
26. DT interview 04/08/99; *Irish Times* 20/05/98.
27. See Ulster Marketing Surveys, *Northern Ireland Agreement: Referendum Exit Poll 22 May 1998* (Belfast, 1998), p. 9. UMS survey stated that support for the Agreement amongst unionists was 51%. The 55% figure comes from a Cooper and Lybrand exit survey, also on 22 May 1998. I am grateful to Dr Sydney Elliott for supplying me with these statistics.
28. *Belfast Telegraph* 14/05/98; *The Daily Telegraph* 21/05/98.
29. *The Daily Telegraph* 15/05/98.
30. *The Daily Telegraph* 20/05/98.
31. Viscount Cranborne interview 04/02/00.
32. *Irish Times* 19/05/98.
33. DT interview 04/08/99.
34. Sean Farren interview 16/01/00.
35. Bono interview 07/06/00.
36. DT interview 26/03/02.
37. *Irish Times* 21/05/98; DT interview 04/08/99.
38. Kate Hoey interview 24/06/99.
39. Kate Hoey interview 24/06/99.
40. *Irish Times* 21/05/98.
41. Alastair Campbell interview 06/03/00.
42. *The Daily Telegraph* 22/05/98.
43. Sydney Elliott interview 16/06/99.
44. Bew and Gillespie, p. 365.
45. *Irish News* 27/04/98.
46. Private information.
47. Herb Wallace interview 02/12/98.
48. DT interview 04/08/99. The concept of 'no dual mandate' had been operated informally by the party since the days of Sir James Craig, until the UUC adopted new rules on 18 March 1989. This custom was not always observed and Westminster MPs such as Molyneaux served in the

Prior Assembly. I am grateful to Jack Allen, Honorary Treasurer of the UUC, for this information.

49. Denis Rogan interview 30/04/03.

50. Jeffrey Donaldson interview 30/07/99.

51. Mark Fullbrook interview 23/06/99.

52. Private information.

53. *Belfast Telegraph* 11/11/96.

54. Jane Wells interview 08/03/02.

55. DT interview 04/08/99; *News Letter* 04/06/98.

56. *Irish Times* 10/06/98.

57. *Irish Times* 06/06/98.

58. Jeffrey Donaldson interview 30/07/99; DT interview 04/08/99.

59. Commons Hansard, Vol. 314, 15–25 June 1998, cols. 456–458.

60. *The Daily Telegraph* 06/06/98.

61. See *Irish Times* 01/05/02.

62. *News Letter* 12/06/98; *Irish Times* 12/06/98.

63. *Irish Times* 19/06/98.

64. *Irish Times* 18/06/98, 19/06/98.

65. John Dobson interview 28/01/99.

66. Daphne Trimble interview 14/06/98.

67. Elliott and Flackes, *Northern Ireland*, pp. 596–602.

68. *Irish Times* 27/06/98.

69. Victor Gordon interview 28/01/99.

70. Stephanie Roderick interview 30/04/03; *The Daily Telegraph* 27/06/98.

71. *The Daily Telegraph* 27/06/98; *Irish Times* 29/07/98.

72. *Irish Times* 12/10/02.

73. Sam Lutton interview 25/01/99.

74. Sydney Elliott interview 16/06/99.

75. Elliott and Flackes, *Northern Ireland*, pp. 596–602.

76. *Irish Times* 22/06/99.

77. Frank Millar interview 28/04/02.

78. DT interview 26/03/02.

79. DT interview 02/04/99.

80. *Irish Times* 14/11/98.

81. Sean Farren interview 16/06/99.

82. *Belfast Telegraph* 07/10/98.

83. See Ervine *Craigavon*, pp. 420–423 and 525–526; *Financial Times* 02/07/99 and 27/05/99.

84. See http://www.ni-assembly.gov.uk/commission/minutes/010403

85. See D.S. Johnson, 'The Northern Ireland Economy, 1914–39' in Liam

Kennedy and Philip Ollerenshaw (eds.), *An Economic History of Ulster 1820–1939* (Manchester, 1985), pp. 184–223.

86. DT interview 28/05/03.

87. Assembly Hansard, Vol. 1 (1 July 1998 to 1 February 1999) pp. 16–17; *Irish Times* 02/07/98.

88. For the real quote, see NI Commons Hansard, Vol. 16, 18 December–14 November 1934, col. 1095.

89. Denis Rogan interview 11/03/02.

90. *Belfast Telegraph* 31/07/98.

91. See Ryder and Kearney, *Drumcree*, pp. 226–314.

92. *News Letter* 30/06/98; DT interviews 04/08/99 and 15/01/00.

93. *News Letter* 01/07/98.

94. DT interview 15/01/00.

95. Private information.

96. *The Daily Telegraph* 01/07/98; private information.

97. See *The Daily Telegraph* 06/07/98 and 07/07/98.

98. DT interview 15/01/00.

99. John Steele interview 18/01/00.

100. Bew and Gillespie, p. 371.

101. Ruth Dudley Edwards, *The Faithful Tribe* (London, 1999), p. 414.

102. DT interview 06/04/03; *Observer* 12/07/98; *News Letter* 13/07/98.

103. *Irish Times* 13/07/98.

104. DT interview 15/01/00.

105. DT interview 18/02/04.

CHAPTER TWENTY-SIX: *A Nobel calling*

1. *News Letter* 03/08/98.

2. David Campbell interview 22/05/03.

3. See *Lost Lives*, pp. 1437–1460; private information.

4. Daphne Trimble interview 14/06/99.

5. DT interview 15/01/00.

6. DT interview 15/01/00; Denis Rogan interview 11/03/02; *Irish Times* 17/12/98.

7. See *News Letter* 13/06/68.

8. See *The Times* 09/03/18; *Irish News* 22/01/34, 07/05/46; and *Irish Press* 11/02/70. See also Enda Staunton, *The Nationalists of Northern Ireland 1918–1973* (Dublin, 2001), pp. 83–86. I am grateful to C.D.C. Armstrong for making these points to me.

9. Seamus Hegarty interview 24/03/02; *Irish Times* 20/08/98.

10. DT interview 15/01/00.

11. Whelan and Masterson, *Bertie Ahern*, p. 210.

12. *Irish Times* 20/08/98.

13. Commons Hansard, Vol. 317, 27 July–27 October 1998, cols. 700–702. Trimble's speech is to be found in cols. 787–795.

14. *Irish Times* 28/09/98, 01/10/98.

15. DT interview 15/01/00; *Irish Times* 05/09/98. The discussions with Blair on the Prime Ministerial jet are also recounted in *To Raise Up a New Northern Ireland: Articles and Speeches 1998–2000 by David Trimble* (Belfast, 2001), pp. 165–166.

16. Blair Hall interview 27/05/03.

17. DT interview 15/01/00.

18. *Belfast Telegraph* 02/09/98.

19. *Irish Times* 17/08/98.

20. *The Daily Telegraph* 07/09/98.

21. DT interview 03/11/03; private information.

22. DT interview 15/01/00.

23. Reg Empey interview 08/01/00; *Irish Times* 03/09/98.

24. Denis Rogan interview 11/03/02.

25. *Belfast Telegraph* 02/09/98.

26. *News Letter* 07/09/98 and 11/09/98.

27. *The Independent* 27/03/02.

28. DT interview 15/01/00.

29. See Winston Churchill, *The World Crisis: The Aftermath* (London, 1929), p. 317.

30. Steven King interview 16/01/00.

31. See John Campbell, pp. 560–561.

32. Ken Reid interview 20/06/99.

33. Private information.

34. DT interview 1999. Verified as accurate 13/04/03. For more on Trimble's view of republicanism, see his review of Ed Moloney's *A Secret History of the IRA*, *The Spectator* 14/21 December 2002.

35. DT interview 04/12/99. See David Sharrock and Mark Devenport, *Man of War, Man of Peace? The Unauthorised Biography of Gerry Adams* (London, 1997), pp. 20, 32, 94 and 246.

36. Sean O'Callaghan interview 12/11/99.

37. Maura Quinn interview 22/03/02.

38. DT interview 22/01/00.

39. *Belfast Telegraph* 16/10/98 and 08/12/98.

40. Daphne Trimble interview 16/12/98; *Irish Times* 07/12/98.

41. *Irish Times* 09/12/98.

42. *Irish Times* 09/12/98.

43. *News Letter* 04/12/98.

44. DT interview 22/1/00.

45. *Irish Times* 16/12/98.

46. See also Tom McGurk, *Sunday Business Post* 29/12/98.

47. *Irish Times* 21/12/98.

48. Jim Nicholson interview 22/03/02.

49. *Irish Times* 12/12/98.

50. *Belfast Telegraph* 25/09/98.

51. *Irish Times* 20/10/98.

52. See also *The Sunday Times* 21/10/98.

53. *Sunday Tribune* 22/11/98.

54. DT interview 22/01/00.

55. *Irish Times* 21/11/98.

56. DT interview 22/01/99. See also *To Raise up a New Northern Ireland*, pp. 81–91.

57. *Irish Times* 24/11/98 and 25/11/98.

58. DT interview 22/01/00.

59. DT interview 22/01/00.

60. Private information.

61. *Financial Times* 08/11/01.

62. DT interview 22/01/00.

63. Seamus Mallon interview 14/01/00.

64. Seamus Mallon interview 14/01/00.

65. *Irish News* 23/12/98.

66. *Irish Times* 19/12/98.

67. DT interview 22/01/00.

68. *Irish Times* 19/12/98.

69. See Paul Bew in the *Irish Times* 10/12/98.

70. See Conor Cruise O'Brien, *Memoir*, pp. 439–442.

71. I am grateful to Jonathan Isaby, then of the BBC, for confirming this point. Adams led in the first half of 1998, but Trimble pulled ahead in the second half of 1998.

72. DT interview 22/01/00; Ken Maginnis interview 19/01/00.

73. John de Chastelain interview 24/01/00.

74. *Irish Times* 14/12/98.

CHAPTER TWENTY-SEVEN: *The blame game speeds up*

1. *Irish News* 01/02/99.

2. *Irish Times* 15/03/99.

3. *Irish News* 02/02/99. See also *Irish News* 20/01/99.

4. See also Eamon Collins (and Mick McGovern), *Killing Rage* (London, 1998).

5. *Irish Times* 04/03/99.

6. *Irish Times* 25/01/99; Denis Rogan interview 23/01/00.

7. See also Ed Moloney, *Sunday Tribune* 10/01/99.

8. *Irish Times* 09/03/99.

9. DT interview 25/05/03; *Belfast Telegraph* 09/03/99.

10. Peter Bell interview 25/03/02.

11. DT interview 22/01/00.

12. See the *Irish News*' editorial on Trimble's reaction to the killing, 18/03/99.

13. DT interview 22/01/00; *Irish Times* 19/03/99.

14. *News Letter* 22/03/99.

15. *News Letter* 22/03/99.

16. Ken Maginnis interview 19/01/00.

17. Denis Rogan interview 11/03/02.

18. Denis Rogan interview 24/01/00.

19. Steven King interview 16/01/00. See also Steven King profile in *Magill*, June 2000.

20. DT interview 30/01/00.

21. John Taylor interview 22/06/02; *News Letter* 29/03/99.

22. David Campbell interview 14/03/02.

23. DT interview 30/01/00; John Taylor interview 20/01/00.

24. *Lost Lives*, p. 789.

25. Billy Armstrong interview 27/03/02.

26. Private information.

27. Graham Gudgin interview 19/01/00.

28. Sean Farren interview 16/01/00.

29. Ken Maginnis interview 19/01/00.

30. Steven King interview 16/01/00.

31. Private information.

32. DT interview 30/01/00.

33. Seamus Mallon interview 14/01/00; Sean Farren interview 16/01/00.

34. See *An Phoblacht* 01/04/99.

35. DT interview 27/02/00.

36. *Sunday Tribune* 11/04/99.

37. Private information.

38. DT interview 22/01/00.

39. *Belfast Telegraph* 16/04/99.

40. *The Guardian* 14/04/99.

41. DT interview 30/01/00.

42. See also Adams in the *Belfast Telegraph* 11/05/99.

43. DT interview 30/01/00.

44. Reg Empey interview 08/01/00.

45. DT interview 30/01/00.
46. David Kerr interview 10/09/00
47. *Irish Times* 22/05/99.
48. Private information.
49. David Campbell interview 10/11/03; David Kerr interview 16/12/03.
50. Private information.
51. Jim Wilson interview 05/04/00.
52. DT telephone interview 22/06/02.
53. DT interview 24/12/03.
54. Private information.
55. David Andrews interview 31/01/01.
56. Tony Blair interview 07/02/00.
57. DT interview 30/01/00.
58. Alastair Campbell interview 06/03/00. See also *Irish Times* 19/05/99.
59. DT interview 30/01/00.
60. Denis Rogan interview 23/01/00.
61. DT interview 05/04/00.
62. Seamus Mallon interview 14/01/00.
63. Private information.
64. DT interview 22/01/00.
65. David Kerr 10/09/00.
66. Reg Empey interview 08/01/00.
67. DT interview 30/01/00.
68. *Irish Times* 17/05/99.
69. Daphne Trimble interview 14/06/99.
70. DT interview 30/01/00.
71. Reg Empey interview 08/01/00.
72. Paul Bew interview 09/04/00; *Irish Times* 22/05/99.
73. Ken Reid interview 15/06/99.
74. Graham Gudgin interview 01/05/03.
75. Paul Bew interview 09/04/00.
76. Reg Empey interviews 08/01/00 and 24/03/02.
77. *Belfast Telegraph* 31/05/99.
78. Quoted in *Belfast Telegraph* 21/05/99.
79. Paul Bew interview 08/04/00.
80. Paul Bew interview 02/04/00.
81. Reg Empey interview 15/01/00; private information; *Irish Times* 04/06/99.
82. *Irish Times* 31/05/99.
83. Daphne Trimble interview 14/06/99.
84. Steven King interview 16/01/00.
85. Reg Empey interview 15/01/00.

86. DT interview 30/01/00; Reg Empey interview 15/01/00.
87. DT interview 30/01/00.
88. Steven King interview 16/01/00.
89. John Taylor interview 09/12/03.
90. Ken Maginnis interview 19/01/00.
91. *Daily Telegraph* 19/06/99.
92. DT interview 30/01/00.
93. Sean Farren interview 16/01/00.
94. *Daily Telegraph* 15/06/99.
95. DT interview 30/01/00.
96. Reg Empey interview 15/01/00.

CHAPTER TWENTY-EIGHT: *No way forward*

1. Kate Hoey interview 24/06/99.
2. DT interview 27/02/00.
3. Ken Reid interview 15/06/99.
4. *News Letter* 16/06/99.
5. *Irish Times* 13/07/99.
6. *Irish Times* 01/07/99; DT interview 27/02/00.
7. *Irish Times* 28/06/99.
8. *Sunday Independent* 27/06/99.
9. Sean O'Callaghan interview 18/03/02.
10. *Belfast Telegraph* 17/06/99.
11. *News Letter* 23/06/99.
12. *Irish Times* 01/07/99.
13. *News Letter* 23/06/99.
14. David Montgomery interviews 22/03/02 and 19/12/03.
15. Paul Murphy interview 12/01/00.
16. Kate Hoey interview 23/06/99.
17. DT interview 30/01/00.
18. *Irish Times* 21/06/99.
19. Denis Rogan interview 23/01/00.
20. Jeffrey Donaldson interview 11/01/00.
21. DT interview 30/01/00.
22. *Irish Times* 23/06/99.
23. Commons Hansard, Vol. 333, 14–25 June 1999, cols. 1161–1162.
24. *Irish Times* 30/06/99.
25. *News Letter* 23/06/99.
26. *Irish Times* 21/06/99.
27. *News Letter* 28/06/99.

28. DT interview 22/01/00.
29. *Belfast Telegraph* 26/02/99; DT interview 30/01/00.
30. David Campbell interview 14/03/02.
31. *Irish News* 04/01/99; private information.
32. *Belfast Telegraph* 29/06/99.
33. David Campbell interview 14/03/02.
34. *Irish Times* 03/07/99; *The Guardian* 05/07/99.
35. DT interview 30/01/00.
36. David Campbell interview 22/05/99.
37. *Guardian* 05/07/99.
38. *Irish News* 28/06/99; *The Sunday Telegraph* 04/07/99.
39. John de Chastelain interview 24/01/00.
40. *The Sunday Telegraph* 04/07/99; Ken Reid interview 15/06/99.
41. Private information.
42. Private information.
43. Private information.
44. Peter Bell interview 16/01/00.
45. *The Sunday Telegraph* 04/07/99.
46. Peter Bell interview 16/01/00.
47. Tony Blair interview 08/02/00.
48. DT interview 27/02/00.
49. *Irish Times* 01/07/99.
50. *Irish Times* 07/07/99.
51. See Tim Pat Coogan, *De Valera: Long Fellow, Long Shadow* (London, 1993), pp. 354–355.
52. DT interview 30/01/00.
53. Ken Maginnis interview 19/01/00.
54. Reg Empey interview 15/01/00.
55. Private information.
56. DT interview 27/02/00.
57. Ken Maginnis interview 19/01/00.
58. DT interview 27/02/00.
59. Ken Maginnis interview 19/01/00.
60. *Mail on Sunday* 04/07/99.
61. *The Daily Telegraph* 05/07/99.
62. DT interview 30/01/00.
63. Ken Reid interview 01/05/03.
64. Alastair Campbell interview 06/03/00.
65. DT interview 27/02/00.
66. Steven King interview 16/01/00.
67. DT interview 30/01/00.

68. David Lavery interview 19/01/00. See also *Lost Lives*, p. 803.
69. Steven King interview 16/01/00.
70. *The Observer* 04/07/99.
71. Private information.
72. *Irish Times* 05/07/99.
73. Private information.
74. DT interviews 30/01/00 and 27/02/00.
75. DT interview 30/01/00.
76. *Irish Times* 02/07/99.
77. *Irish Times* 02/07/99.
78. Private information.
79. *Irish Times* 03/07/99.
80. *Irish Times* 03/07/99.
81. DT interview 27/02/00.
82. *Irish Times* 15/07/99.
83. *Irish Times* 03/07/99.
84. Robert McCartney interview 13/03/02.
85. Private information.
86. Commons Hansard, Vol. 334, 28 June–8 July 1999, cols. 639–653.
87. Commons Hansard, Vol. 334, 28 June–8 July 1999, cols. 639–643; *Irish Times* 05/07/99.
88. *Irish Times* 19/07/99.
89. *Irish Times* 14/07/99.
90. Jeffrey Donaldson interview 11/01/00.
91. *Irish Times* 10/07/99.
92. *News Letter* 13/07/99.
93. *Guardian* 13/07/99.
94. Commons Hansard, Vol. 335, 12–23 July 1999, cols. 274–276.
95. *Irish Times* 13/07/99.
96. Commons Hansard, Vol. 334, 28 June to 8 July 1999, cols. 639–641.
97. Commons Hansard, Vol. 281, 8–19 July 1996, cols. 786–787.
98. Paul Bew interview 01/06/00.
99. Commons Hansard, Vol. 335, 12–23 July 1999, cols. 187–283.
100. DT interview 27/02/00.
101. *The Sunday Telegraph* 18/07/99.
102. Commons Hansard, Vol. 335, 12–23 July 1999, cols. 195–198.
103. *News Letter* 15/07/99.
104. *The Daily Telegraph* 15/07/99.
105. *Irish Times* 13/07/99.
106. *Irish Times* 15/07/99.
107. DT interview 27/02/00.

108. David Montgomery interview 17/07/99.
109. DT interview 13/04/03.
110. Jonathan Powell interview 16/03/02. See also Clarke and Johnston op cit, pp. 307–309.
111. DT interview 27/02/00; Jeffrey Donaldson interview 03/06/00; *Irish Times* 16/07/99.
112. Commons Hansard, Vol. 335, 12–23 July 1999, cols. 210–214.
113. DT interview 27/02/00; Seamus Mallon interview 14/01/00.
114. Private information. Confirmed by Seamus Mallon.
115. Seamus Mallon interview 14/01/00.
116. Assembly Hansard Vol. 2, 15/07/99, p. 324.
117. Barry White interview 14/05/03.
118. DT interview 27/02/00.
119. Private information; *Irish Times* 16/07/99.
120. Private information; *Irish Times* 16/07/99.
121. *Irish Times* 16/07/99 and 19/07/99.
122. Paul Bew interview 01/06/00.
123. See, for instance, Deaglan de Breadun, *Irish Times* 16/07/99.
124. Clarke and Johnston, op cit, p. 308.
125. DT interview 13/06/99.
126. DT interview 27/02/00.
127. *Irish Times* 13/07/99.
128. DT interview 27/02/00; private information.
129. *Irish Times* 13/07/99.
130. *Daily Mail* 16/07/99.
131. *Irish Times* 16/07/99.
132. *Daily Mail* 16/07/99.
133. *Irish Times* 15/07/99; *The Economist* 17/07/99.
134. Commons Hansard, Vol. 335, 12–23 July 1999, col. 572.
135. See also Frank Millar, *Irish Times* 17/05/01.
136. Commons Hansard, Vol. 335, July 12–23 1999, col. 571.
137. Commons Hansard, Vol. 335, 12–23 July 1999, cols. 237–238.
138. *The Independent* 16/07/99.
139. Private information.
140. See Geoffrey Goodman, *The Awkward Warrior: Frank Cousins, His Life and Times* (London, 1979).

CHAPTER TWENTY-NINE: *RUC RIP*

1. George Mitchell interview 22/03/02.
2. DT interview 13/05/02.

3. DT interview 27/02/00.
4. See the *Daily Telegraph* 18/07/01. See also *News Letter* 17/07/01 and 23/07/01; the *Daily Telegraph* 18/07/01.
5. *Irish Times* 28–30/07/99.
6. *News Letter* 31/07/99.
7. Reg Empey interview 08/01/00.
8. DT interview 09/01/00; *Belfast Telegraph* 11/09/99.
9. DT interview 09/01/00.
10. DT interview 11/11/00.
11. *Irish Times* 30/07/99, 27/08/99.
12. *Irish News* 27/08/99.
13. DT interview 13/04/03; *News Letter* 03/09/99.
14. Private information.
15. *Irish News* 24/08/99.
16. *News Letter* 13/09/99.
17. *Belfast Telegraph* 25/08/99. For Trimble's reaction to the leaks, see his article in *The Times* 27/08/99.
18. DT interview 09/01/00.
19. *A New Beginning: Policing in Northern Ireland: The Report of the Independent Commission on Policing for Northern Ireland* (London, 1999).
20. See also Maurice Hayes' letter in *The Times* 06/09/02.
21. *Irish Times* 15/02/01.
22. Commons Hansard, Vol. 337, 1–11 November 1999, cols. 34–35.
23. Sean O'Callaghan interview 22/03/02.
24. *News Letter* 10/09/99.
25. *Irish Times* 17/04/00.
26. *Irish Times* 10/09/99.
27. Private information.
28. Henry Patterson interview 23/03/02.
29. *Irish Times* 13/05/00.
30. Private information.
31. Private information.
32. Andrew Mackay interview 13/04/00.
33. Viscount Cranborne interview 14/03/02.
34. See, for example, Ewan Macaskill in *The Guardian* 12/03/98; Frank Millar in the *Irish Times* 18/03/98; Trimble's comments in *Ha'aretz* 15/11/02; DT interview 23/05/03.
35. Ken Maginnis interview 17/11/03.
36. Maginnis says that Rodgers also knew by this point that the name would change; Rodgers confirms this but says that he did not think that the

name change and other symbolic alternations would be quite so sweeping. Leslie Rodgers interview 30/03/03.

37. DT interview 23/05/03.
38. Colin Cramphorn interview 03/07/03.
39. Private information.
40. Chris Patten interview 21/03/02; Peter Mandelson interview 21/05/03.
41. Chris Patten interview 21/03/02.
42. Andrew Mackay interview 13/04/00.
43. See *The Daily Telegraph* 06/10/99.
44. Patrick Mayhew interview 07/03/02.
45. *The Guardian* 29/04/98; *Irish Times* 29/04/98 and 24/01/97.
46. Ken Maginnis interview 19/01/00.
47. John Steele interview 18/02/04; Ken Maginnis interview 18/02/04.
48. Ken Maginnis interview 10/06/00.
49. Peter Smith interview 20/06/00.
50. See Peter Smith's pamphlet *Why Unionists Say No* in Linen Hall Political Collection.
51. John Steele interview 18/01/00.
52. Ken Maginnis interview 16/03/02.
53. Sir John Wheeler interview 18/03/02.
54. Peter Smith interview 20/06/00.
55. See *Sunday Tribune* 05/05/02.
56. Peter Smith interview 20/06/00.
57. Private information; Peter Smith interview 20/06/00.
58. David Campbell interview 06/06/03.
59. *A Police Ombudsman for Northern Ireland?* (Belfast, 1997).
60. See, for instance, Patten's review of Hayes' memoir *Sweet Killough: Let Go Your Anchor* in *The Financial Times Weekend*, 16–17/07/94.
61. Maurice Hayes interview 29/04/03.
62. Mike Brogden and Clifford Shearing, *Policing for a New South Africa* (London, 1993), p. 156. See also Adrian Guelke, 'Policing and the South African Miracle', *Social and Legal Studies*, 4, 1995, pp. 413–419. Ken Maginnis interview 19/01/00.
63. Ken Maginnis interview 19/01/00 and Chris Patten interview 21/03/02.
64. Chris Patten interview 21/03/02.
65. See Mansergh's remarks in the *Irish Times* 23/11/98.
66. Chris Patten interview 21/03/02; see Chris Ryder, *The RUC 1922–2000: A Force under Fire* (London, 2000), pp. 347–349.
67. Private information.
68. Chris Patten interview 21/03/02.
69. *Belfast Telegraph* 08/06/00; *Irish Times* 09/06/00.

70. See also Liam Clarke, *Sunday Times* (Irish edition) 18/06/00.

71. Peter Smith interview 17/11/03.

72. I am grateful to Professor Trevor Hartley of the LSE and Professor Erika Szyszczak of Leicester University for their advice concerning EU law. See also Austen Morgan in *The Observer* 23/07/00.

73. Ken Maginnis interview 10/06/00.

74. Chris Patten interview 21/03/02.

75. DT interview 09/01/00.

76. DT interview 09/01/00. See also *The Daily Telegraph* 09/06/00.

77. Chris Patten letter to the author 24/07/02.

78. Chris Patten interview 21/03/02.

79. *Irish Times* 06/09/99.

80. *Northern Ireland Forum Debates* 17/04/98, No. 70. p. 5.

81. *The Daily Telegraph* 23/03/00.

82. Sean O'Callaghan interview 28/07/02.

83. See Commons Hansard, Vol. 337, 1–11 November 1999, col. 34. See also Ryder, *The RUC 1922–2000: A Force Under Fire*, p. 99.

84. See *Belfast Telegraph* 05/04/00.

85. See also Commons Hansard, Vol. 253, 23 January–3 February 1995, cols. 1006–1008, for Trimble's remarks on Lee Clegg. See Commons Hansard, Vol. 259, 1–11 May 1995, for Trimble's remarks on the RUC. See Commons Hansard, Vol. 261, 6–15 June 1995, cols. 119–123, for Trimble's views on disabled police officers. See also Trimble's letter in *The Times*, 27/02/90. Additionally, Trimble spoke in the Second Reading of the Army Bill that wound up the Ulster Defence Regiment. See Commons Hansard, Vol. 203, 3–14 February 1992, cols. 1172–1178.

86. Herb Wallace interview 22/06/02.

87. Sir Ronnie Flanagan interview 30/03/03.

88. David Campbell interview 22/05/03.

89. Ken Maginnis interview 19/01/00.

90. Sir Ronnie Flanagan interview 01/07/02.

91. Sir Ronnie Flanagan interview 01/07/02.

92. Sir Ronnie Flanagan interview 20/06/02.

93. *Irish Times* 07/09/00.

94. Private information.

95. Herb Wallace interview 10/03/02.

96. David Lavery interview 18/02/04 and DT interview 23/11/03.

97. Sean O'Callaghan interview 29/04/03.

98. DT interview 09/01/00.

99. For Mgr Faul's suggestion, see *News Letter* 10/09/99.

100. DT interview 23/05/03.

101. Commons Hansard, Vol. 347, 27 March–7 April, cols. 1210–1216.
102. Peter Mandelson interview 06/05/01.
103. Private information.
104. Denis Rogan interview 23/01/00.
105. Contemporaneous note by author following conversation with one of those present. DT does not disagree with this account.
106. See *Daily Mail* 09/09/99; 10/09/99; 11/09/99; 24/11/99; 18/12/99; 13/01/00; 20/01/00; 28/03/00.
107. See Commons Hansard, Vol. 342, 10–20 January 2000, cols. 843–844; DT interview 22/01/00.
108. John Major interview 09/02/00.
109. Private information.

CHAPTER THIRTY: *By George*

1. *News Letter* 23/09/99.
2. *News Letter* 13/09/99.
3. DT interview 30/01/00.
4. Nigel Dodds interview 29/04/03.
5. John Taylor interview 20/01/00.
6. DT interview 09/01/00.
7. Jim Wilson interview 18/01/00.
8. *The Observer* 26/09/99.
9. DT interview 09/01/00.
10. *Irish Times* 11/10/99.
11. Jim Wilson interview 18/01/00.
12. Ruth Dudley Edwards interview 02/07/02.
13. *Irish Times* 11/10/99.
14. Reg Empey interview 08/01/00.
15. Trimble's recollection of Stewart is only slightly inaccurate. See Stewart's *The Ulster Crisis*, pp. 248–249; DT interview 09/01/00.
16. *Irish Times* 05/10/99.
17. DT interview 09/01/00.
18. David Montgomery interview 22/03/02.
19. See Clarke and Johnston, *Martin McGuinness*, pp. 310–311.
20. DT interviews 09/01/00 and 27/02/00.
21. See Donald Macintyre, *Mandelson and the Making of New Labour* (London, 2000), p. 519.
22. DT interview 09/01/00; Peter Mandelson interview 13/01/00.
23. *New Statesman* 18/10/99. See also Brian Barton, 'The Impact of World War II on Northern Ireland and on Belfast–London Relations' in Peter

Catterall and Sean McDougall (eds.), *The Northern Ireland Question in British Politics* (Basingstoke, 1996), pp. 61–67.

24. *Sunday Independent* 17/10/99.
25. DT interview 09/01/00.
26. See Macintyre, *Mandelson*, p. 521.
27. DT interview 09/01/00.
28. Hew Pike interview 30/04/03.
29. Peter Mandelson interview 18/02/02.
30. Reg Empey interview 08/01/00.
31. Philip Lader interview 13/01/00.
32. DT interview 09/01/00; Reg Empey interviews 08/01/00 and 15/01/00.
33. See *Endgame*, p. 263; *Irish Times* 19/11/99.
34. DT interview 09/01/00.
35. Private information.
36. DT interview 09/01/00.
37. Sean O'Callaghan interview 12/11/99.
38. DT interview 13/11/99.
39. See Geoff Martin in the *News Letter* 26/02/00.
40. *Irish Times* 28/10/99.
41. *Irish Times* 29/10/99.
42. Reg Empey interview 15/01/00.
43. DT interview 15/01/00.
44. Private information.
45. DT interview 13/04/03.
46. DT interview 09/01/00.
47. DT interview 13/11/99.
48. See *News Letter* 08/11/99; *Irish Times* 02/08/00; *Belfast Telegraph* 05/01/01; *Sunday Tribune* 14/07/02.
49. Rev. Robert Coulter interview 15/03/02.
50. DT interview 24/03/02.
51. Rev. Robert Coulter interview 15/03/02; DT interview 24/03/02; Reg Empey interview 15/01/00.
52. DT interview 09/01/00.
53. Jim Steinberg interview 25/10/00.
54. Reg Empey interview 18/06/00.
55. DT interview 23/11/03.
56. Paul Bew interview 20/06/02.
57. *The Daily Telegraph* 18/11/99.
58. Daphne Trimble interview 10/03/02.
59. DT interview 09/01/00.
60. *Irish Times* 08/11/99 and 11/11/99.

61. David Campbell interview 30/05/01.
62. Private information.
63. Michael McGimpsey interview 15/03/02.
64. Private information.
65. Macintyre, *Mandelson*, pp. 529–530.
66. DT interviews 12/01/02; 22/06/02; 23/06/02.
67. DT interview 22/06/02.
68. Peter Mandelson interview 13/01/00.
69. Reg Empey interview 15/01/00.
70. Peter Mandelson interview 13/01/00.
71. Reg Empey interview 13/01/00.
72. Peter Mandelson interview 13/01/00.
73. DT interview 09/01/00.
74. *Irish Times* 12/11/99.
75. *Irish Times* 13/11/99.
76. Private information.
77. Jim Wilson interview 18/01/00.
78. DT telephone interview 12/01/02.
79. Reg Empey interview 15/01/00.
80. Private information.
81. Peter Mandelson interview 13/01/00.
82. Peter Mandelson interview 13/01/00.
83. Private information.
84. DT interview 15/01/00.
85. DT interview 09/01/00.
86. DT telephone interview 12/01/02.
87. DT interview 15/01/00.
88. Private information.
89. DT interviews 09/01/00 and 15/01/00; *Irish Times* 12/11/99.
90. *Irish Times* 13/11/99.
91. DT interview 13/11/99.
92. DT interview 15/01/00.
93. Clifford Smyth interview 14/03/02.
94. See *Irish Times* 29/08/98.
95. *Irish Times* 18/11/99.
96. Commons Hansard, Vol. 339, 17–26 November 1999, cols. 345–359.
97. *Irish Times* 26/11/99.
98. Steven King interview 16/01/00.
99. Paul Bew interview 20/06/02.
100. DT interviews 15/01/00 and 22/01/00.
101. *Irish Times* 25/11/99.

102. DT interview 15/01/00.
103. *Sunday Independent* 14/11/99.
104. Steven King interview 26/11/99.
105. *Irish Times* news service 15/11/99.
106. DT interview 15/01/00.
107. *Belfast Telegraph* 23/11/99.
108. *Belfast Telegraph* 24/11/99.
109. Peter Mandelson interview 04/02/04.
110. DT interview 09/01/00.
111. DT interview 15/01/00.
112. Paul Bew interview 20/06/02.
113. *Irish News* 22/11/99.
114. Congressman Peter King interview 25/10/00.
115. *Irish Times* 23/11/99.
116. *Irish Times* 26/11/99.
117. *Irish Times* 25/11/99.
118. *News Letter* 23/11/99.
119. DT interviews 20/02/02 and 24/02/02.
120. *Irish Times* 16/11/99.
121. *Irish Times* 23/11/99.
122. Denis Rogan interview 23/01/00.
123. DT interview 15/01/00.
124. David Campbell interview 17/11/03.
125. Ruth Dudley Edwards interview 16/03/02.
126. Steven King interview 16/01/00.
127. Denis Rogan interview 23/01/00.
128. DT interview 15/01/00.
129. *Irish Times* 17/11/99.
130. John Taylor interview 20/01/00.
131. Sir Nicholas Browne interview 04/07/02.
132. John Taylor interview 20/01/00.
133. DT interview 20/02/02.
134. John Taylor interview 20/01/00.
135. Steven King interview 11/12/99.
136. John Taylor interview 20/01/00.
137. Jeffrey Donaldson interview 19/11/03.
138. DT interview 09/01/00.
139. Jeffrey Donaldson interview 11/01/00.
140. *The Daily Telegraph* 26/11/99.
141. Commons Hansard, Vol. 87, 18–26, November 1985, col. 912.
142. DT interview 09/01/00.

143. *Irish Times* 27/11/99.
144. Josias Cunningham interview 18/01/00.
145. DT interview 15/01/00.
146. DT interview 09/01/00.
147. Private information.
148. DT interviews 09/01/00 and 15/01/00; Josias Cunningham interview 18/01/00.
149. *Irish Times* 29/11/99.
150. Barry White interview 07/03/02.
151. Jeffrey Donaldson interview 11/01/00.
152. DT interview 15/01/00.
153. Barry White interview 07/03/02.
154. *Irish Times* 29/11/99.
155. DT interview 09/01/00.
156. Dick Norland interview 20/10/00.
157. Anne Smith interview 22/10/00.
158. Jim Steinberg interview 30/04/03.

CHAPTER THIRTY-ONE: *'And the lion shall lie down with the lamb'*

1. *Irish Times* 04/12/99.
2. DT interview 11/06/00.
3. *Irish Times* 16/12/99. I am grateful to Dr Graham Gudgin for his help on these figures.
4. DT interview 13/04/03.
5. See Bew, Gibbon and Patterson, *Northern Ireland 1921–1996: Political Forces and Social Classes*, pp. 55–109.
6. *Irish Times* 04/12/99, 29/12/99, 01/12/99.
7. DT interview 25/05/03; *Irish Times* 30/11/99.
8. Private information.
9. Steven King interview 16/01/00. See also Paul Bew in the *Irish Times* 15/01/02.
10. DT interview 20/02/02.
11. DT interview 11/06/00.
12. Reg Empey interview 18/01/00.
13. *Irish Times* 03/12/99.
14. Steven King interview 11/12/99.
15. See *The Times* 11/01/01; *Irish News* 11/01/01; *Irish Times* 25/10/01.
16. Private information.
17. *Irish Times* 14/12/99.
18. *Irish Times* 14/12/99.

19. Private information.
20. DT interview 11/06/00.
21. See also Tom Nairn, *After Britain: New Labour and the Return of Scotland* (London, 2000), p. 4.
22. *Irish Times* 18/12/99.
23. *Irish Times* 06/01/00.
24. *Irish Times* 17/12/99 and 18/12/99.
25. *Irish Times* 18/12/99.
26. DT interview 11/06/00.
27. See *Memorandum of Understanding and Supplementary Agreements*, Cmd 4444, Part I paras. 22–25 and Part II Section A (London, 1999). See also Trimble's article in the *News Letter* 16/09/00.
28. *Irish Times* 23/12/99.
29. Ken Maginnis interview 19/01/00.
30. DT interview 11/06/00.
31. Graham Gudgin interview 10/02/02.
32. See Patrick Buckland, *James Craig* (Dublin, 1980), p. 118.
33. *News Letter* 09/12/99.
34. DT interview 11/06/00.
35. DT interviews 09/01/00 and 11/06/00.
36. *Irish Times* 27/12/99.
37. See also Faulkner, *Memoirs of a Statesman*, p. 278.
38. Steven King interview 16/01/00.
39. Daphne Trimble interview 20/06/00.
40. Private information.
41. Daphne Trimble interview 20/06/00. On Lavery's portrait of Sir James Craig, see St John Ervine, *Craigavon*, p. 477.
42. *Irish News* 15/03/99; Graham Gudgin interview 10/02/02.
43. *The Daily Telegraph* 24/05/00.
44. Steven King interview 11/12/99; Reg Empey interview 30/04/03.
45. Graham Gudgin interview 10/02/02. For Gudgin's writings, see 'Discrimination in Housing and Employment under the Stormont Administration' in P.J. Roche and Brian Barton (eds.), *The Northern Ireland Question* (Aldershot, 1999), pp. 97–121.
46. Graham Gudgin interview 10/02/02. See also Trimble in *Parliamentary Brief*, December 2001.
47. Michael Farrell interview 31/01/01. See also Henry Patterson, 'The Ulster Unionist Party since the Belfast Agreement', paper for workshop session on the State of the Key Parties, ESRC conference on Devolution in Northern Ireland, Belfast 04/03/03, and Patterson's unpublished paper, 'The Limits of "New Unionism": The Ulster Unionist Assembly Party',

delivered to the Irish Political Studies Association conference, Galway, November 2001.

48. DT interview 16/02/02.
49. See *Northern Ireland Assembly Official Report*, Vol. 4 No. 4 pp. 132–133. For Trimble's speech see pp. 127–128.
50. *Irish Times* 12/02/00.
51. DT interviews 29/01/04 and 11/06/00.
52. See Northern Ireland Assembly Official Report, 31/01/00, p. 303 and *Belfast Telegraph* 20/01/00, 21/01/00.
53. David Lavery interview 30/01/01.
54. See Rick Wilford, 'A Healthy Democracy?', *Parliamentary Brief*, June 2002.
55. Paul Bew interview 10/06/02.
56. Reg Empey interview 18/06/00.
57. Reg Empey interview 18/06/00.
58. See Rick Wilford, 'A Healthy Democracy?'.

CHAPTER THIRTY-TWO: *Mandelson keeps his word*

1. Barry White interview 18/07/00.
2. Daphne Trimble interview 20/06/00.
3. Denis Rogan interview 10/07/00.
4. DT interview 11/06/00. See also the *Irish Times*/MRBI poll 22/01/00.
5. Private information.
6. *Irish Times* 27/01/00.
7. Peter Mandelson interview 06/05/00.
8. Peter Mandelson interview 06/05/00.
9. Private information; Irish Times 06/01/00.
10. *Irish News* 24/01/00.
11. *Daily Mail* 24/01/00.
12. Peter Mandelson interview 06/05/00.
13. Private information.
14. Paul Bew interview 06/11/03.
15. Jonathan Powell interview 18/02/00.
16. *Sunday Times* 30/01/00.
17. Eoghan Harris interview 31/01/00.
18. See Northern Ireland Assembly Hansard, Vol. 4, 6 December 1999– 8 February 2000, pp. 189–190; *Irish Times* 01/12/99, 19/01/00 and 25/01/00.
19. Paul Bew interview 18/01/02.
20. Commons Hansard, Vol. 342, 10–22 January 2000, cols. 845–864.
21. Peter Mandelson interview 06/05/00.

22. See Dail Debates, Vol. 511, 17–30 November 1999, cols. 451–465.
23. Paul Bew interview 15/11/03.
24. DT interview 18/06/00.
25. *Irish Times* 27/01/00.
26. See also *Belfast Telegraph* 27/01/00.
27. See Ed Moloney in the *Sunday Tribune* 07/05/00.
28. DT interviews 11/06/00 and 16/11/03.
29. *Irish Times* 31/01/00.
30. Private information.
31. Private information.
32. DT interview 11/06/00.
33. Peter Mandelson interview 21/11/03.
34. DT interview 18/06/00.
35. Josias Cunningham interview 20/06/00.
36. See Maurice Hayes in the *Irish Independent* 18/08/00.
37. See Steven King's obituary in *The Independent* 12/08/00.
38. David Campbell interview 17/03/02.
39. Paul Bew interview 20/06/02.
40. *News Letter* 31/01/00.
41. *Irish Times* 31/01/00.
42. *Irish News* 29/01/00.
43. *Irish Times* 02/02/00.
44. John de Chastelain interview 19/06/00.
45. John de Chastelain interview 19/06/00.
46. *Irish Times* 02/02/00 and 03/02/00.
47. Dail Debates, Vol. 513, 26 January–8 February 2000, col. 697.
48. *Irish Times* 02/02/00.
49. *Irish Times* 03/02/00.
50. Steven King interview 01/02/00.
51. *Irish Times* 05/02/00.
52. Barry White interview 06/02/00.
53. Ruth Dudley Edwards interview 29/04/03.
54. Commons Hansard, Vol. 343, 24 January–4 February 2000, cols. 1316–1324.
55. *Irish Times* 04/02/00.
56. *Irish Times* 12/02/00; 09/02/00; 05/02/00.
57. *Irish Times* 09/02/00.
58. DT interview 18/06/00; private information.
59. *Irish Times* 09/02/00.
60. DT interview 18/06/00.
61. Commons Hansard, Vol. 344, 7–22 February 2000, col. 133.

62. See, for example, *Los Angeles Times* 02/02/00; *Washington Post* 03/02/00.

63. Commons Hansard, Vol. 344, 7–22 February 2000, cols. 206–207.

64. Commons Hansard, Vol. 344, 7–22 February 2000, cols. 206–207.

65. Commons Hansard, Vol. 344, 7–22 February 2000, col. 155.

66. DT interview 18/06/00.

67. Private information.

68. DT interview 09/02/00.

69. DT interview 11/06/00.

70. *Irish Times* 11/02/00; Dail Debates, Vol. 514, 9–22 February 2000, cols. 325–326; *Belfast Telegraph* 10/02/00.

71. DT interview 18/06/00.

72. DT interview 18/06/00; *Irish Times* 05/02/00.

73. Barry White interview 18/07/00.

74. Reg Empey interview 18/06/00.

75. Private information.

76. Mitchel McLaughlin interview 20/06/00.

77. Peter Mandelson interview 06/05/00.

78. *Sunday Tribune* 20/02/00.

79. DT interview 11/06/00.

80. Paddy Teahon interview 12/03/02.

81. Reg Empey interview 18/06/00.

82. Josias Cunningham interview 20/02/00.

83. *Irish Times* 14/02/00.

84. Private information.

85. *Irish Times* 14/02/00.

86. Peter Mandelson interview 06/05/00.

87. Daphne Trimble interview 20/06/00.

88. DT interview 13/04/03.

89. Private information.

90. On Assad, see, for instance, *Financial Times* 31/03/00; *The Independent* 02/04/00. On Arafat, see the *New York Times* 20/07/00; *The Independent*, 26/07/00; *Financial Times* 05/10/00. Private information.

91. Private information.

92. Jonathan Powell interview 18/02/00.

93. *Irish Times* 25/02/00; DT interview 18/06/00.

94. DT interview 18/06/00.

95. *Irish News* 14/02/00.

96. DT interview 18/06/00.

97. John de Chastelain interview 21/03/02.

98. John de Chastelain interview 19/06/00.

99. Mitchel McLaughlin interview 20/06/00.

100. *Irish Times* 03/02/00.
101. Peter Mandelson interview 06/05/00.
102. Private information.
103. Mitchel McLaughlin interview 20/06/00.
104. Private information.
105. DT interview 18/02/00.
106. Stephen Collins interview 14/03/02.
107. *The Daily Telegraph* 11/03/00; private information.
108. *The Daily Telegraph* 14/03/00.
109. *Irish Times* 17/02/00.
110. *Irish Times* 15/02/00.
111. Peter Bell interview 30/04/03.
112. DT interview 18/06/00.
113. Private information.
114. Private information.
115. Reg Empey interview 08/07/00.
116. *Irish Times* 13/04/00.
117. David Campbell interview 20/06/00.
118. DT interview 09/07/00.
119. Private information.
120. DT interview 13/04/03.
121. DT interview 18/06/00.
122. Jim Steinberg interview 25/10/00.
123. Macintyre *Mandelson*, p. 557.
124. Jim Steinberg interview 30/04/03.
125. Peter Mandelson interview 29/01/04.
126. *Irish Times* 17/02/00; *International Herald Tribune* 30/07/00.
127. DT interview 18/06/00.
128. David Campbell interview 25/07/00.
129. *Irish Times* 12/02/00.
130. DT interview 18/06/00.
131. Paul Bew interview 11/06/00.
132. Peter Mandelson interview 06/05/00.
133. *News Letter* 01/03/00.
134. *Newsweek* 06/03/00; *Belfast Telegraph* 03/03/00.

CHAPTER THIRTY-THREE: *The Stormont soufflé rises again*

1. Peter Mandelson interview 21/11/03. See also Macintyre, *Mandelson*, pp. 560 and 568.
2. Cyril Ramaphosa interview 16/05/02.

3. *Irish Times* 18/03/00.
4. *Irish Times* 23/03/00.
5. See, for example, *Irish Times* 18/03/00.
6. Quoted in Macintyre, *Mandelson*, p. 569.
7. Macintyre, *Mandelson*, pp. 564–565. See also Mandelson's speech at the CBI dinner in Belfast, *Irish Times* 07/04/00.
8. See also *Irish Times* 22/03/00.
9. David Campbell interview 20/06/00.
10. DT interview 18/06/00.
11. Reg Empey interview 18/06/00.
12. David Lavery interview 19/06/00.
13. *Irish Times* 18/03/00.
14. Daphne Trimble interview 20/06/00; DT interview 18/06/00.
15. Jim Steinberg interview 25/10/00.
16. DT interview 11/06/00; *Irish Times* 18/03/00.
17. Interview with senior NIO official; *Irish Times* 18/03/00.
18. Michael McDowell interview 29/04/03.
19. DT interview 18/06/00.
20. Daphne Trimble interview 20/06/00.
21. Frank Millar interview 22/03/00.
22. DT interview 18/06/00; David Campbell interview 20/06/00.
23. See also Mallie and McKittrick, *Endgame*, p. 274.
24. DT interview 18/06/00.
25. David Campbell interview 20/06/00.
26. DT interview 18/06/00.
27. Daphne Trimble interview 20/06/00.
28. Denis Rogan interview 10/07/00.
29. Private correspondence from David Burnside to Sir Josias Cunningham 27/01/00 and 08/03/00.
30. DT interview 18/06/00.
31. David Campbell interview 20/06/00. See also *Irish Times* 23/03/00.
32. *Irish Times* 16/03/00.
33. David Campbell interview 20/06/00.
34. *Irish Times* 24/03/00.
35. *Irish Times* 27/03/00.
36. Denis Rogan interview 10/07/00.
37. Daphne Trimble interview 20/06/00.
38. Private information.
39. John Taylor interview 04/07/00.
40. Jonathan Powell interview 23/05/03.
41. Private information.

42. Paddy Teahon interview 22/06/00.
43. David Campbell interview 20/06/00.
44. *Irish Times* 08/04/00. See also Macintyre, *Mandelson* pp. 570–576.
45. See Mallie and McKittrick, *Endgame*, p. 276.
46. Jim Steinberg interview 25/10/00.
47. David Campbell interview 20/06/00.
48. Private information.
49. Private information.
50. DT interview 09/07/00.
51. *Irish Times* 02/05/00.
52. Private information.
53. DT interview 09/07/00.
54. David Campbell interview 20/06/00.
55. David Campbell interview 10/07/00.
56. Reg Empey interview 08/07/00.
57. Quoted in *Irish Times* 05/05/00.
58. Private information.
59. DT interview 09/07/00.
60. DT interview 09/07/00.
61. Peter Mandelson interview 21/11/03.
62. DT interview 09/07/00.
63. DT interview 18/06/00.
64. See also Trimble in the *Irish Times* 26/05/00.
65. DT interview 18/06/00.
66. Commons Hansard, Vol. 349, 2–12 May 2000, col. 502.
67. Private information.
68. See Trimble in the *Irish Times* 26/05/00.
69. Paul Bew interview 11/06/00.
70. David Campbell interview 20/06/00. I am grateful to J.A. Creaney, QC, for checking these figures with Royal Irish Regiment sources.
71. Peter Mandelson interview 20/03/01.
72. Private information.
73. Peter Mandelson interview 20/03/01.
74. *Irish Times* 11/05/00.
75. DT interview 09/07/00.
76. Dt interview 09/07/00; *News Letter* 08/05/00.
77. *Irish Times* 17/05/00.
78. *Irish Times* 07/06/00.
79. Peter Mandelson interview 06/05/00.
80. Private information.
81. Sir Ronnie Flanagan interview 20/06/02.

82. See Frank Millar in the *Irish Times* 12/05/00.
83. Daphne Trimble interview 20/06/00.
84. *Irish Times* 08/05/00.
85. Peter Mandelson interview 20/03/01.
86. Jim Steinberg interview 12/02/01.
87. Private information.
88. Private information.
89. Reg Empey interview 08/07/00.
90. John Taylor interview 04/07/00.
91. Ibid.
92. Reg Empey interview 08/07/00.
93. David Campbell interview 20/06/00.
94. *Irish Times* 08/05/00. See also Dennis Kennedy, *Irish Times* 10/05/00.
95. David Campbell interview 20/06/00.
96. *Irish Times* 10/05/00. See also *Irish Times* 23/05/00.
97. *Irish Times* 11/05/00.
98. *Sunday Tribune* 20/08/00.
99. DT interview 09/07/00.
100. Dick Norland interview 20/10/00.
101. DT interview 09/07/00. See John Taylor's remarks, *Irish Times* 09/05/00.
102. Commons Hansard, Vol. 349, 2–12 May 2000, cols. 501–503.
103. Note of Michael McDowell conversation with Jonathan Powell 11/05/00.
104. David Campbell interview 20/06/00.
105. DT interview 09/07/00.
106. David Campbell interview 20/06/00.
107. DT interview 09/07/00.
108. David Campbell interview 20/06/00.
109. David Campbell interview 20/06/00; *Irish Times* 16/05/00.
110. David Campbell interview 20/06/00.
111. Barry White interview 07/02/02. White later returned to Trimble's employ after a short stint in the private sector: the UUP leader had the highest regard for his abilities.
112. See Frank Millar in the *Irish Times* 13/06/00; Gerry Moriarty's interview 07/06/00.
113. *Irish Times* 17/05/00. See Mandelson in the *Irish Times* 16/05/00.
114. Commons Hansard, Vol. 350, 15–25 May 2000, cols. 263–269.
115. Commons Hansard, Vol. 350, 15–25 May 2000, cols. 319–321.
116. David Campbell interview 20/06/00.
117. DT interview 09/07/00. See also *Irish Times* 19/05/00.
118. Private information; David Campbell interview 10/07/00.
119. David Campbell interview 10/07/00.

120. David Campbell interview 10/07/00; DT interview 13/04/03.
121. John Taylor interview 04/07/00.
122. Josias Cunningham interview 20/06/00.
123. *Irish Times* 20/05/00.
124. Denis Rogan interview 10/07/00.
125. Donn McConnell interview 16/12/03.
126. *Irish Times* 30/05/00.
127. *Irish Times* 26/05/00; see also *News Letter* 31/05/00.
128. Paddy Teahon interview 22/06/00.

CHAPTER THIRTY-FOUR: *In office but not in power*

1. Paul Bew interview 11/06/00.
2. *The Financial Times* 01/06/00; *Irish Times* 01/06/00.
3. See Northern Ireland Assembly Hansard, Vol. 5, 5 June–4 July 2000, p. 236; *Irish Times* 21/06/00.
4. *The Financial Times* 17/08/00.
5. *Guardian* 24/04/01.
6. Private information. See also *The Financial Times* 06/06/00; Mary Holland, *Irish Times* 05/10/00. See also William Graham, *Irish News* 20/12/00.
7. Sean O'Callaghan interview 02/09/02.
8. *Irish Times* 09/09/00.
9. *Irish Times* 25/10/00.
10. *Irish Times* 27/06/00.
11. *Irish Times* 06/06/00 and 07/06/00.
12. See O'Leary in *Guardian* 15/06/00 and 28/07/00; *Irish Times* 13/07/00; *Guardian* 14/11/00. Chris Patten interview 22/03/02 and letter to the author 24/07/02.
13. Seamus Mallon interview 14/05/03.
14. Commons Hansard, Vol. 351, 5–15 June 2000, cols. 177–184.
15. Private information.
16. Peter Mandelson interview 20/03/01.
17. George Howarth interview 06/02/02.
18. Hew Pike interview 05/03/01.
19. David Lavery interview 30/01/01.
20. This was listed on the Amendment paper as of 13 June 2000 as New Clause 8.
21. Paul Bew interview 29/04/03.
22. DT interview 27/01/01.
23. See Frank Millar in the *Irish Times* 11/07/00.

24. Commons Hansard, Vol. 353, 3–13 July 2000, col. 824.

25. *Irish Times* 18/11/00.

26. Private information.

27. *Sunday Tribune* 09/07/00.

28. *Irish Times* 23/08/00 and 31/08/00.

29. *Irish Independent* 23/07/00 and *Irish Times* 01/08/00, 01/07/00.

30. See *The Sunday Times* 13/08/00.

31. See Jim Cusack in the *Irish Times* 14/06/00.

32. *Sunday Independent* 06/08/00.

33. *News Letter* 28/04/00.

34. DT interview 27/01/01.

35. DT interview 27/01/01.

36. Sir Josias Cunningham interview 20/06/00; *Irish Times* 21/07/00.

37. DT interview 27/01/01; *Irish Times* 10/08/00.

38. See UUP press release 05/06/01.

39. See David Burnside's letter to the South Antrim Ulster Unionist Association 03/10/00.

40. Blair Wallace interview 27/09/00.

41. Elliott and Flackes *Northern Ireland*, p. 529.

42. *Irish Times* 23/09/00.

43. See also Paul Bew, *Irish Times* 07/10/00.

44. Paul Bew interview 22/09/00.

45. Paul Bew interview 18/10/00.

46. DT interview 04/10/00.

47. Jeffrey Donaldson interview 06/09/02.

48. *Irish Times* 25/09/00 and 02/10/00.

49. Ken Reid interview 21/01/03.

50. Frank Millar interview 18/10/00.

51. *Irish Times* 09/10/00.

52. Ed Curran interview 23/01/03.

53. *Belfast Telegraph* 27/10/00.

54. DT interview 03/02/01.

55. *Irish Times* 27/10/00.

56. David Campbell interview 05/02/01. See also Frank Millar in the *Irish Times* 26/10/00.

57. See Frank Millar in the *Irish Times* 27/10/00.

58. See Frank Millar in the *Irish Times* 30/10/00.

59. *Irish Times* 26/10/00.

60. DT interview 11/11/01.

61. *Irish Times* 27/10/00.

62. DT interview 03/02/02.

63. DT interview 03/02/02.
64. DT interviews 30/10/00, 03/02/01.
65. DT interview 03/02/01.
66. *Irish Times* 30/10/00.
67. David Campbell interview 05/02/01.
68. *Guardian* 30/10/00; *Irish News* 31/10/00.
69. See also *Irish Times* 30/10/00; *Irish News* 04/11/00.
70. *Irish Times* 16/11/00.
71. *Irish News* 05/12/00.
72. DT interview 06/12/00; *The Daily Telegraph* 08/01/01.
73. Peter Mandelson interview 20/03/01.
74. DT interview 11/11/00.
75. Paul Bew interview 08/01/01.
76. Contemporaneous note of conversation with Ruth Dudley Edwards. Confirmed 30/01/03.
77. Jim Steinberg interview 12/02/01.
78. See also David Halberstam, *War in a Time of Peace: Bush, Clinton, and the Generals* (New York, 2001), p. 482.
79. Peter Mandelson interview 20/03/01.
80. DT interview 28/04/01.
81. *Irish News* 04/12/00; DT interview 03/02/02.
82. Private information; DT interview 06/12/00.
83. DT interview 03/02/02.
84. Peter Mandelson interview 20/03/01.
85. Ki Fort interview 02/02/01.
86. See also Jim Cusack, *Irish Times* 12/12/00.
87. Commons Hansard, Vol. 360, 18 December 2000–11 January 2001, cols. 347–348.
88. DT interview 17/11/03.
89. *Irish Times* 12/12/00 and 13/12/00.
90. Jim Steinberg interview 12/02/01.
91. See Boris Johnson, *Daily Telegraph* 14/12/00.
92. DT interview 03/02/02.
93. George Howarth interview 06/02/02.
94. See Ed Moloney in *The Sunday Tribune* 17/12/00.
95. DT interview 03/02/01.
96. *Irish Times* 14/12/00.
97. See the full text of Clinton's address in the *Irish News* 14/12/00.
98. Ki Fort interview 02/02/01.
99. See Chris McGimpsey, *Belfast Telegraph* 15/12/00.
100. Private information; DT interview 03/02/02.

101. Private information.
102. Paul Bew interview 20/12/00.
103. Private information.
104. Jim Steinberg interview 12/02/01.
105. *Irish Times* 14/12/00.

CHAPTER THIRTY-FIVE: *A narrow escape*

1. DT interview 03/02/02.
2. Commons Hansard, Vol. 361, 15–26 January 2001, col. 908.
3. DT interview 27/01/01.
4. Private information.
5. See Ed Moloney in *Sunday Tribune* 18/01/01.
6. Private information.
7. See Mandelson's subsequent interventions in Commons Hansard, Vol. 370, 13–28 June 2001, cols. 74–79; Vol. 372 (part 1), 16 July–8 October 2001, col. 276; and in the Police (NI) Bill (Lords) on 10 February 2003, Commons Hansard, Vol. 399, February 2003, cols. 680–687.
8. See *The Observer* 12/08/01.
9. George Howarth interview 06/02/02.
10. See Trimble's interview in *The Observer* 13/05/01.
11. *Daily Mail* 14/05/98.
12. I am grateful to Mark Dingwall for this reference which appeared in a BBC documentary on the life of the NUM Vice President.
13. John Reid interview 06/03/02.
14. David Campbell interview 22/01/02.
15. David McNarry interview 21/01/03.
16. DT interview 16/02/02.
17. DT interview 16/02/02.
18. See *Daily News* (NY) 21/02/00; *The Times* 18/02/00.
19. See also Trimble's concluding remarks in his interview in the *Sunday Business Post* 18/05/03.
20. David Campbell interview 21/01/03.
21. Steven King interview 22/12/00.
22. See also Patrick Smyth in the *Irish Times* 14/08/02.
23. *An Phoblacht* 14/09/95 and *Sunday Independent* 31/03/02.
24. See also *Sunday Independent* 03/11/02.
25. Frank Gaffney interview 19/01/03.
26. DT interview 26/01/03.
27. See F. Frankfort Moore, *The Truth About Ulster* (London, 1914), p. 102.

28. See Jack Holland, *Irish Echo* 28 February–6 March 2001.

29. See Ray O'Hanlon in the *Irish Echo* 5–12 December 2001. At some point after September 11, Trimble 'upped the ante', as was exemplified by his article on the opinion pages of the *Washington Post* of 30 November 2002. Such comments annoyed elements of the Irish lobby. See, for instance, Trina Vargo in the *Irish Times* 13/01/03.

30. Ki Fort interview. Fort also rang Steven King to deliver much the same message. Paul Bew interview 21/12/00.

31. *Irish Times* 22/08/00.

32. *The Daily Telegraph* 16/03/01.

33. *The Daily Telegraph* 12/03/01.

34. See *Boston Globe* website 17/03/95 and the *Irish Voice* 14/03/01.

35. See Philip Johnston, *The Daily Telegraph*, 01/12/00.

36. See also Malachi O'Doherty in the *Belfast Telegraph* 14/11/00.

37. See Harbinson, *The Ulster Unionist Party* p. 94. See also Moloney and Pollak, pp. 29–32.

38. DT interview 27/01/01.

39. *Irish Times* 10/10/00.

40. Paul Bew interview 29/04/03.

41. DT interview 13/07/03.

42. See Louis Althusser, 'Ideology and Ideological State Apparatuses' in *Lenin and Philosophy and Other Essays* (London, 1971), pp. 121–173; DT interview 13/04/03. See also Eoghan Harris in *The Daily Telegraph* 23/07/03.

43. *Irish Times* 09/03/01.

44. See Ed Moloney in the *Sunday Tribune* 11/04/01; *Irish Times* 15/03/01.

45. Paul Bew interview 07/05/01.

46. David Campbell interview 21/05/01.

47. David Campbell interview 21/05/01.

48. Paul Bew interview 11/05/02.

49. *Irish Times* 03/04/01 and 21/05/01.

50. Paul Bew interview 10/05/01.

51. DT interview 07/08/01.

52. DT interview 16/02/02.

53. DT interviews 11/03/01 and 27/01/01; Paul Bew interview 07/05/01. See also Ed Moloney in the *Sunday Tribune* 04/03/01.

54. DT interview 28/04/01.

55. David Campbell interview 21/05/01.

56. David Campbell interviews 21/05/01 and 21/01/03.

57. DT interview 28/04/01.

58. See Steven King in the *Belfast Telegraph* 13/02/01.

59. See Frank Millar in the *Irish Times* 10/05/01.

60. See Vincent Kearney in *The Sunday Times* (Irish edition) 13/05/01; David Campbell interview 21/01/03.
61. David Campbell interview 21/05/01.
62. Paul Bew interview 18/07/01.
63. Private information.
64. DT interview 09/05/01.
65. David Campbell interview 21/01/03.
66. Barry White interview 07/02/02; Assembly Hansard 08/05/01 p. 1.
67. *Belfast Telegraph* 08/05/01.
68. DT interview 09/05/02; Paul Bew interview 16/02/02.
69. DT interview 28/04/01; *Sunday Times* 13/05/01. See also Robinson's remarks in the *Belfast Telegraph* 08/05/01.
70. *Irish News* 29/01/01.
71. *Irish Times* 04/06/01. See also Ed Moloney in the *Sunday Tribune* 04/06/01.
72. DT interview 28/04/01.
73. UTV website 11/05/01.
74. See also Frank Millar, *Irish Times* 09/05/01.
75. DT interview 20/02/02.
76. Fred Cobain interview 30/01/01.
77. DT interview 28/04/01. See also Frank Millar in the *Irish Times* 17/04/01.
78. Stephen Farry interview 21/01/03.
79. DT interview 28/04/01.
80. Barry White interview 07/02/02.
81. *Irish Times* 12/01/01.
82. Paul Bew interview 18/01/01.
83. Paul Bew interview 14/01/01; DT interview 30/01/01.
84. See Ed Moloney in the *Sunday Tribune* 07/02/01.
85. David Campbell interview 21/01/03; DT interview 03/02/01.
86. *Irish News* 30/01/01.
87. DT interview 16/02/02.
88. See the *Sunday Tribune* 20/05/01.
89. *Irish Times* 17/02/01. See Ed Moloney in the *Sunday Tribune* 18/02/01.
90. *Irish Times* 22/05/01.
91. *Irish News* 05/01/01.
92. DT interview 27/01/01.
93. Tommy Gallagher interview 23/01/03.
94. *Irish News* 30/01/01.
95. DT interview 17/11/03.
96. *Guardian* 18/05/01.
97. *Irish Times* 17/05/01 and UTV internet site 16/05/01.

98. John Taylor interview 06/02/02; David Kerr interview 14/02/02.

99. David Kerr interview 14/02/02.

100. Barry White interview 07/02/02.

101. Mark Fullbrook interview 03/06/01.

102. Sydney Elliott interview 12/02/02.

103. John Dobson interview 13/02/02.

104. Daphne Trimble interview 10/02/02.

105. *The Times* 29/03/01; John Dobson interview 13/02/02.

106. Barry White interview 07/02/02.

107. David Kerr interview 14/02/02.

108. John Dobson interview 13/02/02.

109. Barry White interview 07/02/02.

110. John Dobson interview 13/02/02.

111. John Dobson interview 13/02/02.

112. DT interview 16/02/02.

113. Barry White interview 07/02/02.

114. Daphne Trimble interview 10/02/02.

115. Barry White interview 07/02/02.

116. George Howarth interview 06/02/02; John Taylor interview 06/02/02.

117. *Sunday Life* 17/06/01 and *Irish Times* 20/10/01.

118. Daphne Trimble interview 10/02/02.

119. Daphne Trimble interview 10/02/02.

120. See Paul Bew in *The Sunday Times* 10/06/02.

121. Sydney Elliott interview 22/01/03. See also Sydney Elliott, 'The Governance of Northern Ireland', *Economic Outlook & Business Review*, Vol. 16.3, August–September 2001, pp. 64–70.

122. *The Observer* 13/05/01.

123. Paul Bew interview 29/04/03; www.ark.ac.uk/nilt/

124. DT interview 16/02/02.

125. *Irish Times* 09/04/01 and 26/05/01; *Irish News* 02/06/01.

126. Sydney Elliott interview 12/02/02.

127. See *Irish Times* 02/12/02.

128. I am grateful to Councillor Roberta Dunlop for these statistics.

129. Sydney Elliott interview 22/01/03.

130. Ken Robinson interview 16/03/02.

131. David McNarry interview 10/02/02.

132. Daphne Trimble interview 10/02/02.

133. David McNarry interview 10/02/02; Iris Robinson interview 03/03/02.

134. *The Daily Telegraph* 22/04/98.

135. DT interview 16/02/02.

136. Paul Bew interview 29/04/03.

137. See Ed Moloney, *Sunday Tribune* 30/05/01.
138. DT interview 16/02/02.
139. Daphne Trimble interview 10/02/02.
140. David Burnside interview 22/01/03.
141. Jeffrey Donaldson interview 22/01/03; Roy Beggs interview 26/01/03.
142. DT interviews 16/02/02 and 20/02/02; Paul Bew interview 18/02/02.
143. David Campbell interview 18/06/01.
144. See also Frank Millar in the *Irish Times* 19/06/01 and Ed Moloney in the *Sunday Tribune* 24/06/01.
145. David Campbell interview 18/06/01.
146. Daphne Trimble interview 10/02/02.
147. See Ed Moloney in the *Sunday Tribune* 19/06/01.
148. Charles Moore interview 24/01/03. See Ed Moloney in the *Sunday Tribune* 24/06/01.
149. *The Daily Telegraph* 23/06/01.
150. Barry White interview 07/02/02.
151. *The Daily Telegraph* 15/08/01.
152. David Campbell interview 21/01/03.
153. *Irish Times* 11/09/01.
154. DT interview 11/05/03. At the time, the British Government was moving towards a form of Joint Sovereignty with Spain. Gibraltarians and Unionists found it ominous that ministers such as Peter Hain were citing the Northern Ireland precedent. See Commons Hansard, Vol. 376, 3–13 December 2001, Written Answers, col. 825W; Commons Hansard, Vol. 379, 28 January–8 February 2002, Westminster Hall Debates, cols. 136WH, col. 141WH, 143WH; and Commons Hansard, Vol. 387, 17–27 June 2002, Westminster Hall Debates, col. 40WH.
155. DT interview 24/06/01.
156. DT interview 16/02/02.
157. *The Observer* 24/06/01; *Belfast Telegraph* 14/06/01; David Brewster interview 21/01/03.
158. DT interview 24/06/01.
159. DT interview 24/06/01; *Irish Times* 25/06/01.

CHAPTER THIRTY-SIX: *The luckiest politician*

1. See the *Irish Times* 19/06/01 and Ed Moloney, *Sunday Tribune* 08/07/01.
2. Frank Millar interview 20/01/03.
3. See also Frank Millar in the *Irish Times* 28/06/01.
4. Private information.
5. See Frank Millar, *Irish Times* 30/06/01.

6. *The Sunday Times* 01/07/01.
7. See Terence O'Neill, *The Autobiography of Terence O'Neill* (London, 1972), pp. 80–81.
8. *Irish Times* 03/07/01.
9. Commons Hansard, Vol. 371, 2–13 July 2001, cols. 253–254.
10. *Irish Times* 07/07/01.
11. Jeffrey Donaldson interview 19/01/03.
12. *The Daily Telegraph* 08/10/02.
13. Frank Millar interview 11/07/01. Trimble says he was not present at this meeting.
14. *Irish Times* 16/07/01.
15. *The Sunday Times* 22/07/01.
16. See Frank Millar, *Irish Times* 30/07/01.
17. *Irish Times* 03/08/01.
18. Private information.
19. See the text reprinted in the *Irish Times* 02/08/01; Gerry Moriarty in the *Irish Times* 04/08/01.
20. See also *Irish Times* 08/08/01.
21. *Guardian* 15/08/01.
22. DT interview 29/01/03.
23. David McNarry interview 26/01/03.
24. *News Letter* 15/06/02.
25. Reg Empey interview 22/11/03.
26. David McNarry interview 21/01/03; David Campbell interview 26/01/03. See also *Irish Times* 27/06/01, 29/06/01 and 02/07/01.
27. Reg Empey interview 02/02/03; DT interview 13/04/03; Sam Foster interview 29/04/03; Michael McGimpsey interview 01/05/03; Dermott Nesbitt interview 14/05/03.
28. David McNarry interview 21/01/03.
29. Steven King interview 10/02/02.
30. Reg Empey interview 22/11/03.
31. David Campbell interview 16/01/02; DT interview 16/02/02.
32. David Campbell interview 10/07/02.
33. David Campbell interview 21/01/03.
34. See also Ed Moloney in the *Sunday Tribune* 07/10/01.
35. See also *Irish Times* 10/08/01.
36. DT interview 16/02/02.
37. *Irish Times* 14/08/01.
38. *News Letter* 18/10/02.
39. *News Letter* 16/08/01; *Irish Times* 29/08/01; and Ed Moloney in the *Sunday Tribune* 16/09/01; *Irish Times* 22/04/02. See also the article by

Andres Pastrana, then President of Colombia, *Washington Post* 10/04/02.

40. See also *Guardian* website 12/08/02.

41. *Guardian* 27/04/04.

42. *Belfast Telegraph* 30/08/01.

43. *Irish Times* 17/08/01. See also John Bruton in the *Washington Post* 30/08/01. See also *Sunday Business Post* 02/09/01.

44. Private information.

45. Sir Ronnie Flanagan interview 20/06/02.

46. See also Ed Moloney in the *Sunday Tribune* 19/08/01.

47. DT interview 05/09/01.

48. DT interview 26/01/03.

49. See also Trimble's remarks in the *Irish Times* 01/09/01.

50. See Jim Cusack in the *Irish Times* 15/08/01.

51. *Guardian* 06/09/01. Blair told Trimble on 5 September at No. 10 that the Glenbryn protests were 'manna from heaven' for the Provisionals following Colombia. Subsequently, Trimble, with David McNarry, played a part in an interim resolution of the Glenbryn dispute. McNarry had also helped to create the 'Loyalist Commission' to address social and political concerns of working-class Protestants. David McNarry interview 29/01/03. See *News Letter* 22/10/01.

52. See Jim Cusack in the *Irish Times* 21/08/01.

53. DT interview 16/02/02.

54. See *Irish Times* 19/11/01 and David Beresford, *Ten Men Dead: The Story of the 1981 Irish Hunger Strike* (London, 1994), p. 216.

55. See also Trimble's remarks in Commons Hansard, Vol. 372, 14 September 2001, cols. 611–612.

56. See Trimble's comments in Commons Hansard, Vol. 372, cols. 683–4; *Irish Times* 17/09/01; *Daily Telegraph* 28/09/01, 20/09/01; *An Phoblacht* 27/09/01.

57. See Sean O'Callaghan, *The Informer* (London, 1998), p. 103; Tim Pat Coogan, *The IRA* (London, 1997), pp. 460, 539, 543; and Moloney.

58. See also Ed Moloney in the *Sunday Tribune* 23/09/01.

59. See Trimble's article in *The Daily Telegraph* 24/09/01.

60. The point was also made by Peter Mandelson in a Channel 4 programme on 30/12/01. See *Irish Times* 29/12/01.

61. See Trimble and Iain Duncan Smith in *The Daily Telegraph* 21/11/01 and Duncan Smith's remarks in Commons Hansard, Vol. 372, 16 July–19 October 2001, cols. 675–684.

62. *Irish Times* 03/10/01.

63. Daphne Trimble interview 10/02/02.

64. Commons Hansard, Vol. 389, part 1, 15–24 July 2002, col. 996.

65. *The Independent* 11/10/01.

66. *Irish Times* 15/10/01.

67. *Irish Times* 21/09/01.

68. See also *Irish Times* 24/09/01 and 03/10/01.

69. Frank Millar interview 26/09/01.

70. See Northern Ireland Assembly Hansard, Vol. 12, 10 September–6 November 2001, cols. 287–293.

71. David Montgomery interview 12/11/01.

72. David Campbell interview 16/01/02.

73. David Campbell interview 21/01/03.

74. *Irish Times* 23/10/01 and *New York Times* 24/10/01.

75. *Irish Times* 25/10/01.

76. *Irish Times* 25/10/01.

77. See also the leader, 'Trimble's Triumph', in *The Washington Times* 26/10/01.

78. DT interview 16/02/02.

79. John Taylor interview 29/04/03.

80. DT interview 27/05/01 and confirmed by DT 13/04/03.

81. Daphne Trimble interview 10/02/02.

82. *Irish Times* 28/10/01.

83. *The Sunday Telegraph* 04/11/01; *Irish Times* 05/11/01.

84. Philip Johnston interview 01/11/01.

85. Graham Gudgin interview 10/02/02.

86. DT interview 16/02/02.

87. David Montgomery interview 23/01/03.

88. David Campbell interview 22/01/02.

89. David Campbell interview 03/11/01.

90. Daphne Trimble interview 10/02/02.

91. Northern Ireland Assembly Hansard, Vol. 12, 10 September–6 November 2001, cols. 454–455.

92. See also *The Daily Telegraph* 03/11/01.

93. David Campbell interview 22/01/02.

94. *The Guardian* 06/11/01; *Irish News* 06/11/01.

95. See Northern Ireland Assembly Hansard, Vol. 12, 10 September–6 November 2001, cols. 527–529.

96. *News Letter* 07/11/01.

97. *Irish Times* 10/11/01; *Belfast Telegraph* 30/04/02.

98. DT interview 16/02/02.

99. *Irish Times* 09/11/01.

100. http://www.lawreports.co.uk and *Belfast Telegraph* 26/07/02. See also the

essay by Trimble's former colleague, Professor Brigid Hadfield, 'Does the Devolved Northern Ireland Need an Independent Judicial Arbiter?' in N. Bamforth and P. Leyland (eds.), *The Multilayered Constitution* (Oxford, 2003).

101. See Arend Lijphart, *Democracy in Plural Societies: A Comparative Exploration* (London, 1977), p. 37.

102. See also Brian Feeney in the *Irish News* 07/11/01.

103. *Guardian* 12/04/01.

104. DT interview 16/02/02.

105. John Taylor interview 06/02/02.

106. *Irish Times* 20/12/01.

CHAPTER THIRTY-SEVEN: *Another farewell to Stormont*

1. See Paul Bew's interview with Trimble in *Parliamentary Brief*, June 2002.

2. See *The Independent* 30/04/02; private information; David Montgomery interview 15/06/03.

3. See Ed Moloney in the *Sunday Tribune* 23/11/01.

4. See Henry McDonald in *The Observer* 02/12/01; *Belfast Telegraph* 17/05/02.

5. Private information; *News Letter* 13/12/01.

6. See *Irish News* 15/05/02; *Belfast Telegraph* 15/05/02.

7. A point which Trimble also made at a critical meeting of his constituency party in Upper Bann on 8 July 2003, when he successfully fought off a no confidence motion. Private information and DT interview 11/05/03. See also Official Report of Debates, Parliament of Northern Ireland, Vol. 37, 24 February–29 September 1953, col. 1306.

8. See Robin Cook, *The Point of Departure* (London, 2003), pp. 69–71. See also *The Independent* 22/01/02.

9. See also Frank Millar in the *Irish Times* 22/01/02.

10. See Paul Bew, *Ideology and the Irish Question* (Oxford, 1994).

11. Commons Hansard, Vol. 377, 17 December 2001–11 January 2002, cols. 203–204.

12. David Campbell interview 21/01/02.

13. See also Ruth Dudley Edwards in the *Sunday Independent* 30/12/01.

14. DT interview 11/05/03; private information.

15. David Campbell interview 21/01/02.

16. David Campbell interview 21/01/02.

17. David Campbell interview 21/01/02.

18. See also Frank Millar in the *Irish Times* 22/11/01 and Reid's interview with David Sharrock, *The Daily Telegraph* 30/11/01.

19. *Irish Times* 04/02/02 and 07/02/02. See also the decision of Alex Maskey

– the first Sinn Fein Lord Mayor of Belfast – to lay a wreath at the Somme in honour of the war dead. See *Irish Times* 16/09/02 and *Belfast Telegraph* 04/09/02.

20. See *Sunday Mirror* 24/02/02.

21. Irish Times 14/02/02.

22. See also *Financial Times* 11/02/02.

23. *Irish Times* 21/09/02.

24. *Belfast Telegraph* 06/09/02. In fact, the results of the 2003 Assembly election would have brought about a 6–4 unionist–nationalist balance in the Executive if one were ever formed, and without recourse to a Border Poll. Intriguingly, the SDLP also advocated a Border Poll during the 2003 elections.

25. Clifford Smyth interview 15/03/02.

26. See *Irish Times* 27/07/02. See also Martin Mansergh's reply in the *Sunday Business Post* 10/11/02.

27. David Campbell interview 14/03/02.

28. *Irish Independent* 15/03/02.

29. *The Daily Telegraph* 08/03/02.

30. See also *Irish Times* 13/03/02. See also Ruth Dudley Edwards in the *Irish Times* 14/03/02.

31. DT interviews 18/03/02 and 11/05/03.

32. See *The Daily Telegraph* 09/03/02.

33. Paul Bew interview 11/05/03.

34. David Campbell interview 20/03/02.

35. See Trimble's comments in Commons Hansard, Vol. 388, 1–12 July 2002, col. 270WH.

36. See also the *Guardian* 11/03/02 and *Belfast Telegraph* 15/03/02. The Irish Government had its own reasons for opposing this move: one senior official asked me shortly after the UUP leader put forward the idea in the public domain, 'Please G-d, tell me Trimble won't lose the Border Poll.' See *Irish Times* 12/03/02.

37. Private information; Commons Hansard, Vol. 384, 22 April–2 May 2002, col. 931.

38. See Commons Hansard, Vol. 409, 14 July–1 Sept 2003, cols. 40WS–1WS; *The Observer* 31/03/02.

39. See *Irish Times* 19/04/02 and 20/04/02; *The Times* 08/06/02; *Guardian* 27/06/02. See also *The Daily Telegraph* 04/07/02 and 07/03/02; *Belfast Telegraph* 28/02/03.

40. *The Observer* 21/04/02.

41. *Irish Times* 23/04/02.

42. Private information.

43. *Scotland on Sunday* 21/07/02.
44. See *The Daily Telegraph* 29/04/02.
45. See Stephen Collins, *The Sunday Tribune Guide to Irish Politics 2002* (Dublin, 2002).
46. DT interview 24/06/03.
47. According to the *Belfast Telegraph*'s report of Housing Executive statistics, nearly 1000 people were forced from their homes in the seven months up till December 2002. See *Belfast Telegraph* 14/12/02.
48. DT interview 11/05/03 and private information.
49. Private information.
50. *Irish Times* 20/06/02.
51. *Irish Times* 17/06/02.
52. DT interview 24/06/03.
53. David Campbell interview 29/06/03.
54. See *The Times* 18/01/99.
55. *Guardian* 17/04/02; DT interview 12/09/02; private information.
56. I am grateful to Michael McDowell for supplying me with a contemporaneous note of this conversation.
57. See BBC News website 19/07/02 and 9/09/02.
58. See Charles Moore in the *Wall Street Journal* 08/03/02.
59. David Campbell interview 29/06/03.
60. Commons Hansard, Vol. 389, 15–24 July 2002, cols. 998–999.
61. DT interview 11/05/03; Barry White interview 15/05/03. See also *The Times* 30/07/02.
62. Barry White interview 15/05/03. See also Frank Millar in the *Irish Times* 25/07/02.
63. David Campbell interview 29/06/03.
64. Barry White interview 15/05/03.
65. *The Daily Telegraph* 23/07/02.
66. David Campbell interview 15/08/02. See also *Guardian* 22/07/02.
67. See also Trimble's article in *The Daily Telegraph* 25/07/02.
68. BBC News website 25/07/02; DT interview 24/06/03.
69. DT interview 11/05/03.
70. *The Daily Telegraph* 09/07/02.
71. DT interview 16/02/02. For the Haass speech, see http://www.state.gov/s/p/rem/7300.htm
72. See also *Chicago Sun-Times* 17/11/02; *Belfast Telegraph* 26/11/02 and Ruth Dudley Edwards in the *Belfast Telegraph* 22/11/02.
73. Jim Deasy, a Fine Gael TD, also spotted the disjuncture between the US approach to international terrorism and its attitude to the IRA. See *Irish Times* 04/11/02.

74. DT interview 11/05/03. See the criticisms of Trimble by William J. Flynn, of the US National Committee on Foreign Policy, BBC News website 28/02/03.

75. *Irish Echo* 10–16 July 2002.

76. David Campbell interview 29/06/03. See also Haass's comment in the *Irish Times* 25/04/03.

77. David Campbell interview 15/08/02.

78. See also *Belfast Telegraph* 05/02/03.

79. Frank Millar interview 20/01/03.

80. Private information.

81. Private information. See, too, Frank Millar in the *Irish Times* 02/12/03.

82. See *News Letter* 14/02/02 and *Irish News* 30/07/03.

83. See Frank Millar in the *Irish Times* 15/10/02.

84. DT interview 24/06/03.

85. *The Times* 28/12/02; *The Economist* 19/10/02; *Sunday Business Post* 17/11/02; and *Irish Times* 13/02/02. See also *Irish Times* 18/01/03 and Robinson's article in the *Belfast Telegraph* 30/08/02.

86. *Irish Times* 04/12/02.

87. *Sunday Business Post* 12/10/03.

88. See *Irish Echo* 23–29 October 2002.

89. *Irish Times* 29/03/03.

90. See UTV website 23/11/02.

91. An edited version of this was reprinted in the *Irish Times* 21/10/02. See also Paul Bew in *The Daily Telegraph* 22/04/03.

92. Private information.

93. See Frank Millar in the *Irish Times* 10/08/02 and 07/09/02.

94. David Campbell interview 30/01/02.

95. See BBC News website 29/06/02.

96. See *Irish Times* 09/12/02 and *The Daily Telegraph* 09/12/02.

97. See Jeffrey Donaldson's letter in *The Daily Telegraph* 18/06/01.

98. DT interview 24/06/03.

99. *Irish Times* 19/12/02.

100. DT interview 11/05/03. Indeed, the only major organisational change of the period was the move in May 2002 from the party's historic headquarters at Glengall Street in the city centre to a new building – Cunningham House, named for the late Sir Josias Cunningham – in the heart of east Belfast. It was far more convenient for Stormont and City airport and, to Trimble's surprise, caused relatively little controversy. Trimble also pursued the issue of Labour membership in Northern Ireland. See Commons Hansard, Vol. 399, 3–13 February 2002, cols. 269–270.

101. See *Belfast Telegraph* 26/09/02.

102. DT interview 24/06/03.

103. See *Sunday Business Post* 22/09/02 and *News Letter* 26/09/02, 07/10/02.

104. DT interview 24/06/03.

105. Trimble himself was comfortably reselected in Upper Bann on 30 October 2002 at the Craigavon Civic Centre. However, Trimbleistas believed that some anti-Agreement members voted for the other pro-Agreement incumbent Assemblyman George Savage, in order to deny the UUP leader the satisfaction of topping the poll. Trimble was thus the runner-up.

106. UTV website 27/08/02; Frank Millar interview 08/09/02.

107. *Belfast Telegraph* 02/08/02.

108. *The Daily Telegraph* 29/08/02.

109. *Irish Times* 30/08/02.

110. Private information; DT interview 11/05/03. See also Henry Patterson in *The Sunday Times* (Ireland) 22/09/02.

111. David Campbell interview 29/06/03.

112. *The Sunday Times* (Ireland) 22/09/02.

113. DT interview 11/05/03; David Campbell interview 28/09/02.

114. *Irish Times* 21/09/02.

115. David Campbell interview 29/06/03.

116. *Irish Times* 23/09/02.

117. DT interview 17/11/03.

118. Jeffrey Donaldson interview 21/09/02.

119. *Irish Times* 24/09/02.

120. BBC News website 26/09/02 and *Irish Echo* 16–22 October 2002. Haass backed the idea of a ceasefire monitor after Reid announced that a monitor would be nominated. See *Irish Times* 13/09/02.

121. *Irish Times* 05/10/02.

122. See *The Daily Telegraph* 08/10/02; *The Observer* 13/10/02.

123. See *The Daily Telegraph* 07/10/02.

124. *The Sunday Telegraph* 06/10/02.

125. *The Daily Telegraph* 05/10/02. See Michael Hopkinson, *The Irish War of Independence* (Dublin, 2002), p. 69.

126. *Irish Times* 07/10/02 and *Belfast Telegraph* 08/11/02 and 09/11/02.

127. *Irish Times* 05/10/02.

128. See *Irish Times* 31/10/02.

129. DT interview 11/05/03.

130. David Campbell interview 03/07/03. Trimble's decision was also vindicated by the attack by a group of hammer-wielding Provisionals on a Catholic bus driver in Londonderry. *The Daily Telegraph* 01/10/02; *Irish Times* 03/10/02.

131. David Campbell interview 03/07/03.

132. Quoted in John Campbell, *Nye Bevan and the Mirage of British Socialism* (London, 1987), p. 337.

133. DT interview 11/05/02. Private information.

134. *Irish Times* 05/10/02.

135. Billy Lowry interview 29/06/03. See *The Daily Telegraph* 13/01/03.

136. Commons Hansard, Vol. 390, 24 September–17 October 2002, cols. 199–200. See also David Ford's article in the *Belfast Telegraph* 24/10/02.

137. See also *The Daily Telegraph* 09/10/02 and *Irish Times* 09/10/02.

138. See *The Sunday Times* 20/10/02.

139. DT interview 13/05/03. See BBC Northern Ireland website 17/10/02. See also the QUB/Rowntree polls in the *Belfast Telegraph* 19/02/03 and 20/02/03.

140. See also *News Letter* 19/02/03 and Graham Gudgin in the *Belfast Telegraph* 11/11/02.

141. Trimble later attacked the SDLP for refusing to 'cut the umbilical cord that appears to link them with Sinn Fein' in a speech to the Institute of Irish Studies at Liverpool University on 05/11/02.

142. *Irish Times* 08/10/02.

143. *News Letter* 02/11/02.

144. See *Irish Times* 14/10/02.

145. Paul Bew interview 07/07/03.

146. *Irish Times* 12/10/02.

147. *Irish Echo* 16–22 October 2002.

148. Mark Neale interview 13/05/03.

149. See edited version in the *Irish Times* 18/10/02.

150. See Frank Millar's interview with Blair in the *Irish Times* 08/11/02. See also Paul Murphy's remarks in Dublin, as reported in the *Irish Times* 06/02/02.

CHAPTER THIRTY-EIGHT: *A pyrrhic victory*

1. DT interview 11/05/03; Mark Neale interview 13/05/03.

2. *Irish Times* 26/10/02; *Guardian* 26/11/02.

3. *Irish Times* 03/03/03.

4. DT interview 13/05/03. See also Frank Millar in the *Irish Times* 02/12/02.

5. See also Paul Bew's remarks to the Meath Peace Group, *Irish Times* 02/10/02 and David McNarry's remarks as reported in the *Irish Times* 28/01/02.

6. Commons Hansard, Vol. 390, 24 September–17 October 2002, cols. 191–194.

7. *Irish Times* 11/10/02.

8. On the Assembly elections, see Frank Millar in the *Irish Times* 10/01/03; 13/01/03; 01/02/03. On Sinn Fein's approach to policing, see also Frank Millar in the *Irish Times* 27/11/02 and 03/04/03.

9. *The Times* 28/10/02.

10. *The Guardian* 24/10/02.

11. DT interview 11/05/03.

12. Barry White interview 15/05/03.

13. DT interview 11/05/03.

14. DT interview 11/05/03.

15. *The Guardian* 20/12/02. See also Graham Gudgin in the *Belfast Telegraph* 20/12/02. For nationalist perspectives on the census, see Brian Feeney in the *Irish News* 01/01/03; Garrett Fitzgerald in the *Irish Times* 21/12/02; and Denis Bradley in the *Irish Times* 04/07/03.

16. Private information.

17. DT interview 11/05/03.

18. Trimble also struck a populistic note in the debate on the draft Northern Ireland Arms Decommissioning Act 1997 (Amnesty Period) Order 2003 on 11/02/03. Why, he asked, should Iraq's disarmament be pursued through a sanctions regime, but not that of the IRA on the island of Ireland? Commons Hansard, Vol. 399, 3–13 February 2003, cols. 817–820.

19. Private information.

20. David Campbell interview 15/07/03.

21. David Campbell interview 18/07/03.

22. DT interviews 11/05/03 and 16/07/03.

23. Reg Empey interview 20/07/03.

24. Private information.

25. See *Irish Times* 05/03/03; 15/03/03; John Taylor press release 11/06/03. See also Garrett Fitzgerald in the *Irish Times* 08/03/03.

26. DT interview 11/05/03. See also Trimble's remarks at the National Press Club as reported in the *Irish Times* 15/03/03.

27. BBC News website 29/01/03.

28. See Frank Millar in the *Irish Times*. See also Seamus Mallon in Commons Hansard, Vol. 402, 24 March–4 April 2003, cols. 339–342 and Trimble's remarks, Commons Hansard, Vol. 403, 7–14 April 2003, col. 640.

29. DT interview 13/05/03; *Irish Times* 20/12/02.

30. BBC News website 20/03/02 and *Irish Times* 23/01/02.

31. Mark Neale interview 13/05/03.

32. See, for example, Trimble's contribution to the Police (Northern Ireland) Bill [Lords], Commons Hansard, Vol. 402, 24 March–4 April 2003, cols. 346–349 and at Second Reading, Commons Hansard, Vol. 399, 3–13 February 2003, col. 662.

33. Commons Hansard, Vol. 313, 1–11 June 1998, cols. 1096–1101.
34. For a victim's reaction to the OTRs proposal, see Christopher Walker in *The Times* 05/03/03.
35. *News Letter* 24/02/03 and 22/03/03; *Belfast Telegraph* 25/02/03.
36. *Irish Times* 03/03/03. See Trimble's comments on the need to be cautious about the swift devolution of criminal justice and policing in Strabane on 13 December 2002, quoted in *Irish Times* 14/12/02. See also Martin McGuinness's comments on the possibility of Sinn Fein holding the Justice portfolio, as reported in the *Irish Times* 26/03/03.
37. DT interview 13/05/03.
38. DT interview 14/07/03.
39. DT interview 16/07/03.
40. On the interaction between the Iraq crisis and Northern Ireland in these weeks, see Peter Stothard, *30 Days: A Month at the Heart of Blair's War* (London, 2003), pp. 140–143 and 190–191.
41. Tom Kelly interview 04/06/03.
42. Jonathan Powell interview 30/05/03.
43. DT interview 06/07/03; Reg Empey interview 20/07/03.
44. DT interview 13/05/03; David Campbell interview 03/07/03.
45. Paul Murphy interview 04/06/03.
46. *Irish Times* 06/03/03.
47. *Irish Times* 05/03/03 and 06/03/03.
48. See Commons Hansard, Vol. 401, 10–21 March 2003, cols. 629–702 and *The Daily Telegraph* 05/03/02.
49. Private information.
50. Private information.
51. DT interview 11/05/03.
52. *Irish Times* 30/01/03.
53. See UUP press release 18/02/03.
54. *Belfast Telegraph* 29/03/03.
55. *Irish Times* 28/03/03; Commons Hansard, Vol. 402, 24 March–4 April 2003, col. 316.
56. Private information.
57. *Irish Times* 05/04/03.
58. Paul Murphy interview 04/06/03. For the Blair-Bush summit at Hillsborough, see Stothard, *30 Days*, pp. 213–228.
59. See also *Belfast Telegraph* 10/04/03 and *Washington Post* 09/04/03.
60. DT interview 11/05/03. See also Adams' remarks on UTV website 06/04/03.
61. See Stothard, *30 Days*, pp. 216–217.
62. Private information.
63. DT interview 04/07/03.

64. DT interview 13/05/03.
65. See Mark Brennock in the *Irish Times* 11/04/03 and 01/05/03.
66. David Campbell interview 03/07/03.
67. Reprinted in the *Irish Times* 07/05/03.
68. *Irish Times* 14/04/03.
69. DT interview 13/05/03.
70. David Campbell interview 03/07/03.
71. Private information.
72. *Irish Times* 23/04/03.
73. Reprinted in *Irish Times* 07/05/03.
74. DT interview 23/11/03.
75. DT interview 27/04/03. For the full text of Adams' remarks, see *Irish Times* 28/04/03.
76. David Campbell 03/07/03. See Gerry Moriarty, *Irish Times* 28/04/03. See also *Guardian* 28/04/03 and Gerry Moriarty and Mark Brennock in the *Irish Times* 29/04/03.
77. *Guardian* 29/04/03.
78. See Frank Millar in the *Irish Times* 29/04/03.
79. See Gerry Moriarty in the *Irish Times* 03/05/03.
80. See also Steven King in the *Belfast Telegraph* 30/04/03 and *Irish Times* 10/05/03.
81. See Frank Millar in the *Irish Times* 27/11/02.
82. See also Suzanne Breen in the *Irish Times* 01/05/03.
83. Private information.
84. See Fionnuala O'Connor, *Irish Times* 02/05/03.
85. Private information.
86. Private information.
87. Private information.
88. See Dan Keenan and Mark Brennock in the *Irish Times*. See also *Irish Times* 10/05/03.
89. DT interview 13/05/03.
90. See Frank Millar in the *Irish Times* 02/05/03.
91. BBC News website 09/05/03.
92. See Commons Hansard, Vol. 404, 28 April–8 May 2003, cols. 459–468.
93. Michael McDowell interview 29/06/03; BBC website 19/05/03.
94. See Commons Hansard 01/05/03 and Vol. 405, 12–22 May 2003, cols. 78–124. See also Dan Keenan in the *Irish Times* 30/05/03 and BBC News website 21/05/03.
95. See, for instance, Maurice Hayes in the *Irish Independent* 02/05/03 and Paul Donovan in the *Guardian* 11/05/03.
96. Private information.

97. Commons Hansard, Vol. 405, 12–22 May 2003, col. 101.
98. See Brian Feeney in the *Irish News* 14/08/03.
99. David Brewster interview 08/06/03.
100. *Irish Times* 06/05/03 and 07/05/03. The full text is reprinted in the *Irish Times* 02/05/03.
101. See, for instance, *Guardian* 22/04/03.
102. See also Jeffrey Donaldson's question to Paul Murphy on the matter, Commons Hansard, Vol. 405, 12–22 May 2003, cols. 71–72.
103. David Burnside interview 23/01/04. See also *Belfast Telegraph* 16/06/03.
104. The comparison with Clare Short was first suggested by Frank Millar in an interview with Donaldson in the *Irish Times* on 13/07/03.

CHAPTER THIRTY-NINE: *Paisley triumphant*

1. *The Daily Telegraph* 04/06/03.
2. See *Daily Telegraph* 29/05/03. DT interview 27/05/03. The RIR was never actually referred to in the Joint Declaration.
3. BBC News 10/06/03.
4. *Irish Times* 16/06/03/
5. DT interview 11/01/04. For a nationalist perspective on Trimble's motives, see Brian Feeney in the *Irish News* 09/06/03.
6. David Campbell interview 17/11/02.
7. DT interview 24/06/03.
8. *Irish Times* 17/06/03.
9. *Irish Times* 23/06/03 and 24/06/03.
10. DT interview 18/12/03.
11. *Irish Times* 27/06/03.
12. *Irish Times* 26/06/03.
13. *Irish Times* 25/06/03.
14. *Irish Times* 08/07/03.
15. DT interview 18/12/03.
16. *Irish Times* 09/07/03.
17. BBC News 08/07/03 and *Irish Times* 10/07/03.
18. See *Irish Times* 11/07/03 and 12/07/03; *News Letter* 24/07/03.
19. Reg Empey interview 23/01/04.
20. Jim Rodgers interview 25/01/04.
21. *Irish Times* 20/08/03 and 27/08/03.
22. *Irish Times* 12/06/03 and the letter of John Taylor (Lord Kilclooney) in *The Times* 18/07/03.
23. *Irish Times* 02/07/03. See also Commons Hansard, Vol. 410, 8–18 September 2003, cols. 900–1011.

24. See also *Irish Times* 06/09/03.
25. Reg Empey interview 23/01/04.
26. David Campbell interview 17/12/03.
27. Private information.
28. BBC News 05/09/03.
29. DT interview 11/01/04.
30. David Brewster interview 03/01/04.
31. Reg Empey interviews 23/01/04 and 25/01/04; Jim Rodgers interview 25/01/04; BBC News 07/09/03.
32. DT interview 28/10/03. See also Adams' interview in the *Sunday Business Post* 28/09/03.
33. DT interviews 18/12/03 and 11/01/04.
34. See Frank Millar in the *Irish Times* 13/09/03.
35. DT interview 30/11/03.
36. DT interviews 18/12/03 and 21/12/03.
37. DT interviews 18/12/03, 11/01/04, 18/01/04 and 25/01/04; *Belfast Telegraph* 30/09/03; see also Anne Cadwallader in the *Christian Science Monitor* 29/08/03.
38. Private information.
39. See *Irish Echo* 10–16 September 2003 and *Irish News* 14/01/04.
40. *Irish Times* 16/09/03. See also the comments of PSNI Deputy Chief Constable Paul Leighton on RTE Interactive News 01/10/03.
41. See Dean Godson in *The Spectator* 06/12/03.
42. See Frank Millar in the *Irish Times* 10/05/03 and Commons Hansard, Vol. 404, 28 April–May 8 2003, cols. 460–462.
43. Dean Godson in *The Spectator* 06/12/03.
44. Paul Bew interview 31/12/03.
45. See Millward Brown Ulster survey for RTE exit poll on 26/11/03. I am grateful to Richard Moore for supplying me with this data.
46. See *Belfast Telegraph* 26/09/03 and 12/11/03.
47. See Dean Godson in *The Spectator* 06/12/03.
48. See also Fionnuala O'Connor in the *Irish Times* 30/01/04 and Frank Millar in the *Irish Times* 07/02/04.
49. Private information. See also *Irish Times* 10/09/03.
50. DT interview 25/01/04.
51. See also Frank Millar in the *Irish Times* 27/09/03.
52. Gerry Adams interview 07/01/04.
53. See also Trimble's speech to the UUP annual conference, as reported in the *Irish Times* 20/10/03.
54. DT interviews 22/01/04 and 24/01/04; David Campbell interview 22/01/04.
55. See *Irish Times* 15/10/03.

56. DT interview 11/01/04.
57. Alex Maskey interview 30/01/04.
58. Frank Millar interview 23/01/04.
59. See also *Irish Times* 15/10/03.
60. Alan McFarland interview 01/01/04.
61. DT interview 11/01/04.
62. Mark Neale interview 07/01/04. *Lost Lives*, p. 730.
63. Mark Neale interview 07/10/03.
64. Paul Bew interview 31/12/03.
65. DT interview 18/12/03.
66. John de Chastelain interview 02/01/04.
67. Jonathan Powell interview 20/01/04.
68. DT interview 18/01/04.
69. DT interview 20/01/04.
70. Mark Neale interview 07/01/04.
71. DT interview 11/01/04.
72. John de Chastelain interview 02/01/04.
73. DT interview 20/01/04.
74. Sean O'Callaghan interview 24/01/04.
75. DT interview 18/12/03.
76. See A.J.P. Taylor, *War by Timetable: How the First World War Began* (London, 1969).
77. Jonathan Powell interview 20/01/04.
78. See Liam Clarke and Stephen O'Brien in *The Sunday Times* (Ireland) 26/10/03.
79. DT interview 11/01/04.
80. Mark Neale interview 07/01/04 and DT interview 11/01/04.
81. Michael McGimpsey interview 31/12/03.
82. *Belfast Telegraph* 08/12/03.
83. See *Irish Times* 21/10/03.
84. See Frank Millar in the *Irish Times* 17/12/03.
85. DT interviews 18/12/03, 21/12/03.
86. DT interview 18/12/03.
87. DT interview 25/01/04.
88. DT interview 11/01/04.
89. Richard McAuley interview 26/01/04.
90. Mark Neale interview 07/01/04.
91. DT interview 18/12/03.
92. DT interview 11/01/04.
93. See also the leader in *The Times* of 22/10/03.
94. DT interview 18/12/03.
95. David Campbell interview 17/12/03.

96. DT interviews 18/12/03 and 11/01/04.
97. David Campbell interview 17/12/03.
98. Private information.
99. DT interviews 18/12/03 and 11/01/04.
100. DT interview 11/01/04.
101. DT interview 18/12/03.
102. See http://www.irlgov/debates-03/22Oct/Sect1.htm Vol. 573, No.1.
103. Commons Hansard, Vol. 411, 14–23 October 2003, cols. 633–634.
104. For the differing Protestant and Catholic attitudes to Blair, see the RTE exit poll on 26/11/03 conducted by Millward Brown Ulster.
105. See Commons Hansard, Vol. 412, 27 October–6 November 2003, cols. 21–30 and *Irish Times* 25/10/03.
106. See *Irish Times* 23/10/03/ and 24/10/03.
107. See Thomas Harding in *The Daily Telegraph* 30/10/03.
108. See Frank Millar in the *Irish Times* 24/10/03 and *Ottawa Citizen* 25/10/03.
109. *Irish Times* 25/10/03 and *Guardian* 25/10/03.
110. David Campbell interview 17/12/03.
111. DT interview 11/01/04.
112. Gerry Adams interview 07/01/04.
113. Frank Millar interview 28/10/03.
114. See Gerry Moriarty in the *Irish Times* 23/10/03.
115. Gerry Adams interview 07/01/04. See also Adams' remarks as reported in the *Irish Times* 27/10/03.
116. DT interview 18/01/04.
117. See Frank Millar in the *Irish Times* 23/10/03.
118. The *Sunday Times* (Ireland) 26/10/03.
119. See also Frank Millar in the *Irish Times* 17/12/03.
120. Sean O'Callaghan interview 24/01/04; Paul Bew interview 25/01/04.
121. *Irish News* 15/11/03.
122. DT interview 11/01/04.
123. See BBC News and UTV website 18/11/03.
124. See Liam Clarke in *The Sunday Times* (Ireland) 23/11/03.
125. See *Belfast Telegraph* 22/11/03.
126. David Campbell interview 17/12/03.
127. Daphne Trimble interview 11/01/04.
128. Sydney Elliott interview 31/12/03.
129. Sydney Elliott interview 31/12/03. See also Sydney Elliott, 'The Northern Ireland Assembly Election of 26 November 2003: Looking Back or Looking Forward?' in *Economic Outlook and Business*, Vol. 18.4, November/December 2003.
130. Shortly after the poll was called, Paul Murphy commended the

International Monitoring Commission to Trimble. It would, he said, make a significant difference. Possibly so in the longer run; but it proved electorally worthless in the short term. It reminded the UUP leader that the Government's idea of doing him favours was very different from his own! DT interviews 18/12/03 and 21/12/03.

131. David Campbell interview 17/12/03.

132. *Irish Times* 19/12/03.

133. See Frank Millar in the *Irish Times* 03/12/03.

134. William Ross interview 06/01/04. See also David Burnside's remarks as reported by the BBC Northern Irleland website 20/12/03.

135. See Frank Millar in the *Irish Times* 29/11/03 and 02/12/03, *Belfast Telegraph* 19/12/03 and 04/02/04.

136. See Frank Millar in the *Irish Times* 12/12/03.

137. See also James Downey in the *Irish Independent* 29/11/03.

CHAPTER FORTY: *Conclusion*

1. William Safire, *Before the Fall: An Inside View of the pre-Watergate White House* (New York, 1975), p. 97.

2. John Hunter interview 22/01/03.

3. Herb Wallace interview 13/12/99.

4. Private information.

5. See Alan Watkins, *Brief Lives* (London, 1982), p. 178.

6. Barry White interview 07/02/02.

7. See Paul Bew, 'The Political History of Northern Ireland Since Partition: The Prospects for North-South Cooperation' in A.F. Heath, R. Breen and C.T. Whelan (eds.), *Ireland North and South Perspectives from Social Science* (Oxford, 1999), pp. 401–418.

8. Lijphart, *Democracy in Plural Societies: A Comparative Exploration*, pp. 25 and 40.

9. Sean Farren interview 19/01/03.

10. Lijphart, *Democracy in Plural Societies: A Comparative Exploration*, p. 51.

11. DT interview 28/01/03.

12. See BBC transcript of 01/12/02.

13. See Trimble's article in *The Times Literary Supplement* 18/04/03 and Norman Porter, *The Elusive Quest: Reconciliation in Northern Ireland* (Belfast, 2003).

14. DT interview 22/01/00. See also Martin Mansergh in the *Sunday Business Post* 20/07/03.

15. The phrase is often credited to Professor Henry Patterson, but was in fact first invented by Dr Greta Jones.

16. See, for example, *The Times* 04/01/02. Professor Fred Boal of Queen's University is dubious about these figures, but residential segregation has certainly not diminished in consequence of the peace process. However, other statistics pointed in a different direction: according to the Institute of Conflict Research, mixed marriages now amounted to one in ten of new unions. See *The Observer* 25/11/01.

17. *Irish Examiner* 13/08/01.

18. Ruth Dudley Edwards interview 30/01/03.

19. John Taylor interview 23/01/03.

20. Private information.

21. Sean O'Callaghan interview 26/02/00.

22. Barry White interview 30/04/03.

23. Ruth Dudley Edwards interview 18/12/99.

24. See, for instance, J.R. Vincent, 'Gladstone and Ireland', Raleigh Lecture, 1977 (London, 1977).

25. *The Daily Telegraph* 21/11/01; *Guardian* 11/10/01; *Irish Times* 11/10/01.

26. See Charles Moore and Simon Heffer (eds.), *A Tory Seer: The Selected Journalism of T.E. Utley* (London, 1989), p. 256.

27. DT interview 11/01/04.

28. On the perils of detachment for communal leaders, see Lijphart, *Democracy in Plural Societies: A Comparative Exploration*, pp. 169–170.

29. See, for example, Trimble's interview in the *Sunday Business Post* 18/05/03 and his critical remarks about the human rights industry at a conference in Madrid as reported in the *Guardian* 29/01/04.

30. See Arthur Aughey's essay in *Selling Unionism: Home and Away* (Belfast, 1995), pp. 7–8.

31. George Howarth interview 06/02/02.

32. *Irish News* 01/02/03.

33. Paul Bew interview 13/01/01.

34. Roy Godson interview 21/12/00.

35. See Henry Patterson, 'The Limits of "New Unionism": The UUP'. Paper for the Political Studies Association Annual Conference, Galway, 2–4 November 2001.

36. See Trimble's remarks in *Ha'aretz* 15/11/02.

37. See also Trimble's remarks in the *Cape Times* of South Africa 06/09/02.

38. Viscount Cranborne interview 22/01/03.

39. Commons Hansard, Vol. 377, 17 December 2001–11 January 2002, cols. 258–262.

40. DT interview 09/01/00.

41. See Trimble in *Ha'aretz* 15/11/02.

42. *Irish Times* 11/10/99.

43. *Parliamentary Brief* December 2001.

44. Quoted in *The Observer* 18/11/01.

45. See, for example, Trimble's interview in the *Sunday Business Post* 18/05/03.

46. See *Belfast Telegraph* 30/09/00.

47. Robin Wilson interview 26/01/03.

48. DT interview 29/05/03.

49. DT interview 18/12/03.

50. Mohamed Heikal, *Secret Channels: The Inside Story of Arab-Israeli Peace Negotiations* (London, 1996), pp. 3–4.

51. See Trimble in *The Daily Telegraph* 24/09/01. See also *Irish News* 16/01/02.

52. See Walter Dean Myers, *Malcolm X: By Any Means Necessary* (1993).

53. See *News Letter* 15/02/03.

54. See Malachi O'Doherty in the *Belfast Telegraph* 10/06/03.

55. Private information.

56. Jim Steinberg interview 22/01/03.

57. Private information.

58. Peter Mandelson interview 20/03/01.

59. Paddy Teahon interview 27/01/03.

60. Gerry Adams interview 07/01/04.

61. Ernie Baird interview 07/01/99.

62. See Congressman Peter King's remarks in the *Irish Echo*, 18–24 April 2001, and Pat Doherty quoted in the *Belfast Telegraph* 20/02/03.

63. Chris McGimpsey interview 25/01/03.

64. For Paisley's style with constituents, see Clifford Smyth, *Ian Paisley* p. 146.

65. See St John Ervine, *Craigavon*, pp. 369–370 and 528–529.

66. Paddy Devlin, *Straight Left: An Autobiography*, p. 250 and Faulkner, *Memoirs of a Statesman* p. 240.

67. Howard, *RAB: The Life of R.A. Butler* (London, 1987), pp. 369–370.

68. See Harbinson, *The Ulster Unionist Party*, pp. 45–47 and Sean McDougall in Peter Catterall and Sean McDougall (eds.), *The Northern Ireland Question in British Politics* (London, 1996), pp. 29–46.

69. See Catterall and McDougall, *The Northern Ireland Question*, pp. 2 and 130. See also Philip Norton, 'Conservative Politics and the Abolition of Stormont' in Catterall and McDougall, *The Northern Ireland Question*, p. 130.

70. See Robert Caro, *The Years of Lyndon Johnson*, Volume 3, *Master of the Senate* (London, 2002), pp. 78–105.

71. Ken Maginnis interview 26/01/03.

72. Quoted in Henry Kissinger, *The White House Years* (London, 1979), p. 59.

73. See Paul Bew 'Where is Burke's Vision of the Union?', *The Times Literary Supplement* 16/03/01 and Owen Bowcott in the *Guardian* 01/01/02.

74. See Paul Murphy's remarks in the Commons on 12 May 2003 in the Northern Ireland Assembly (Elections and Periods of Suspension) Bill in Commons Hansard, Vol. 405, 12–23 May 2003, cols. 64–77. See also Liam Clarke in *The Sunday Times* (Ireland) 20/05/01.

75. See Victor Stock, *Taking Stock: Confessions of a City Priest* (London, 2001), p. 266.

76. For a Trimbleista perspective on the demographics, see Graham Gudgin in the *Irish Times* 21/02/02.

77. See Donald Horowitz, *Ethnic Groups in Conflict* (London, 1985), p. 588.

78. See Commons Hansard, Vol. 405, 12–23 May 2003, col. 67.

79. See Donald Horowitz, 'The Northern Ireland Agreement: Clear, Consociational and Risky' in McGarry, pp. 104–105.

80. See Commons Hansard, Vol. 405, 12–23 May 2003, cols. 64–67.

81. See, for instance, M.W. Heslinga, *The Irish Border as a Cultural Divide* (Aseen, 1962).

82. See *Irish Times* 19/05/03 and Fergus Finlay's comment in 'Coffee Circle Papers: Papers and Responses from the Series of Political Forums Organised during 1998 by Democratic Left'.

83. See *Irish Voice* 03/04/03.

84. For a recent example of Sinn Fein's ability to engender international solidarity, see the report in the *Belfast Telegraph* on 16/10/03 on Adams' meeting with the East Timorese President, Dr Kay Rala Xanana Gusmao.

85. Quoted in Mary Holland, *Irish Times* 08/11/01. See also the work of Dr Joanne Hughes and Dr Caitlin Donnelly of the University of Ulster, which comprised part of the Northern Ireland Life and Times Survey. *Belfast Telegraph* 18/06/01.

86. See Barry McCaffrey and Sharon O'Neill in the *Irish News* 16/01/02 and the first annual report of the Policing Board, http://www.nipolicingboard.org.uk; the fifth report of the Police Oversight Commissioner, Tom Constantine, http://www.oversightcommissioner.org/reports; and the Northern Ireland Affairs Select Committee, Fourth Report 2001–2002, *The Financing of Terrorism in Northern Ireland*, HC 978-I (London, 2002).

87. *Irish Times* 11/01/02.

88. The UUP managed to increase its complement of councillors in Castlereagh District Council from two to five in the 2001 local elections, thanks in part to an energetic ex-UDR 2nd Lieutenant called Michael Copeland.

89. Figures supplied by Northern Ireland Department of Education.

90. *Financial Times* 13/01/00.

91. I am grateful to Dr Graham Gudgin for his help in interpreting these statistics.

92. See also Graham Gudgin in the *Belfast Telegraph* 20/12/02.

93. See Norman Porter, *The Elusive Quest: Reconciliation in Northern Ireland* (Belfast, 2003), pp. 216–232, and Trimble's review of Porter in *The Times Literary Supplement* 18/04/03.

94. *Irish Times* 06/06/01.

95. *News Letter* 09/12/00.

96. *Belfast Telegraph* 03/10/03.

97. See Eric Waugh in the *Belfast Telegraph* 15/10/03; Brian Feeney in the *Irish News* 14/08/03; and Noel McAdam in the *Belfast Telegraph* 13/08/03 and 15/08/03.

98. See Bew, Gibbon and Patterson, *Northern Ireland 1921–96: Political Forces and Social Classes*, pp. 99–107.

99. Paul Murphy introducing the Northern Assembly (Elections and Periods of Suspension) Bill in the Commons on 12 May 2003 also spoke of five years of 'creative ambiguity' in respect of commitment to fully democratic methods. Commons Hansard. Vol. 405, 12–23 May 2003, col. 64.

100. See also Kevin McNamara's comments in Commons Hansard, Vol. 405, 12–23 May 2003, cols. 87–90.

101. Gerry Adams interview 07/01/04.

102. See *Lost Lives*, p. 1478.

103. See *The Daily Telegraph* 22/04/02 and *Irish News* 22/04/02.

104. See Arthur Aughey, 'Learning from "The Leopard"' in Rick Wilford (ed.), *Aspects of the Belfast Agreement* (Oxford, 2001), p. 189.

105. *Parliamentary Brief* December 2001.

106. See Paul Routledge, *John Hume* (London, 1998), p. 224.

107. See also Jim Gibney's comments in Routledge, *John Hume*, p. 242.

108. In fact, the 'boiling frog' metaphor had first been employed by a republican critic of Adams, Anthony McIntyre, to describe what he believed the Sinn Fein leadership had done to the traditional ideology of the movement. Experts on frogs are not wholly convinced about the analogy!

109. At the time, the 1998 Assembly elections – in which the UUP secured 21.3% of first preferences – was its worst performance ever. See Paul Mitchell, 'Transcending an Ethnic Party System?' in Wilford, *Aspects of the Belfast Agreement* p. 35.

110. See Henry Patterson, 'The UUP since the Belfast Agreement', paper delivered to ESRC conference on 'Devolution in Northern Ireland'.

111. *The Sunday Times* (Ireland) 22/09/02.

112. See Frank Millar's interview with Robinson in the *Irish Times* 04/12/02;

Adams' remarks in Frank Millar's article in the *Irish Times* 29/11/03; Frank Millar in the *Irish Times* 07/02/04.

113. See Joe Klein, *The Natural: The Misunderstood Presidency of Bill Clinton* (London, 2002), p. 184.

114. See David McNarry's remarks as reported by Liam Clarke in *The Sunday Times* (Ireland) 25/01/04. For a DUP perspective on the UUP's 'Lost Generation' see Peter Weir's remarks as reported in the *Belfast Telegraph* 24/01/04.

115. See Terence O'Neill, *The Autobiography of Terence O'Neill* (London, 1972).

116. Quoted in Simon Schama, *Citizens: A Chronicle of the French Revolution* (London, 1989), p. xiii.

ILLUSTRATIONS

Section 2

Page 1: (top) Trimble and John Major at Conservative Party conference 1998.
© Stefan Rousseau/PA Photos.
(bottom) Dick Spring and Sir Patrick Mayhew. © John Coghill.

Page 2: (top) John Bruton with Trimble. © Pacemaker Press.
(bottom) Trimble presents the Clintons with bath-robes. © Anne Smith.

Page 3: Billy Wright © Kevin Boyes

Page 4: (top) David, Daphne and Sarah Trimble © Harriet Logan/Network
Photographers.
(bottom) Tony Blair and David Montgomery. Reproduced courtesy of
Scottish Daily Record.

Page 5: (top) Tony Blair, John Holmes and John Sawers. © The Times.
(bottom) Jonathan Powell © Jeremy Young/Rex Features

Page 6: (top) Bertie Ahern and Martin Mansergh © Photocall
(bottom) Trimble talks to Tony Blair at Hillsborough on 7 April 1998
© John Giles/PA Photos

Page 7: (top) Unionist opposition to Trimble. © Mirror Syndication International.
(bottom) The campaign for a 'yes' vote in the 1998 referendum.
© Belfast Telegraph Newspapers Ltd.

Page 8: (top) Trimble receives a makeover. © Harriet Logan/Network
Photographers.
(bottom) Trimble, Blair and Hume during the 1998 referendum.
© Belfast Telegraph Newspapers Ltd.

Section 3

Page 1: Trimble on the Shankill Road during the 1998 referendum. © Mirror
Syndication International.

Page 2: (top) Trimble with Willie Thompson at Omagh, 17 August 1998.
© Dan Chung/Popperfoto/Reuters.
(bottom) Hillsborough Castle in April 1999. © Peter Morrison/AP

Page 3: (top) Mo Mowlam and Peter Mandelson outside No. 10, October 1999.
© Matthew Fearn/PA Photos
(bottom) Trimble is congratulated by Boston College President, Leahy.
© Brian Synder/Reuters.

Page 4: (top) Launch of the Creativity Seed programme in February 2002.
© Pacemaker Press.
(bottom) Ken Maginnis © Paul Faith/PA Photos.

Page 5: (top) Paul Bew. Reproduced courtesy of Paul Bew.
(bottom) David Lavery. © Colm Campbell/Northern Ireland Court
Service.

Page 6: (top) Sir Josias Cunningham. © Jim Moreland/J. M. Photography.
(bottom) David Campbell. © Belfast Telegraph Newspapers Ltd

Page 7: (top) James Molyneaux with David Burnside and Jim Wilson.
Reproduced courtesy of David Burnside.
(bottom) Rev Martin Smith and David Trimble. © Pacemaker
Press.

Page 8: (top) William Ross. © Paul Faith/Pacemaker Press.
(bottom) David Brewster (c)Margaret McLaughlin

Section 4

Page 1: (top) Ruth Dudley Edwards © Bobbie Hanvey.
(bottom) David McNarry © Belfast Telegraph Newspapers Ltd.

Page 2: (top) Eoghan Harris. (c)Mike Bunn.
(bottom) Trimble with Michael McDowell © Michael McDowell.

Page 3: Sean O'Callaghan. © Maxwell Photography.
(bottom) Trimble in front of Sir James Craig portrait. © Bobbie
Hanvey.

Page 4: (top) Trimble, Seamus Mallon and Peter Mandelson in the presence of
the Dalai Lama. © Pacemaker Press.
(bottom) Trimble meets Cyril Ramaphosa. © Belfast Telegraph
Newspapers Ltd.

Page 5: (top) Trimble at the Wycombe Conservative Association annual dinner.
© Bucks Free Press Group.
(middle) Republican wall mural. © Peter Morrison/AP
(bottom) DUP election poster 2001. © Alan Lewis/Photopress Belfast.

Page 6: (top) Trimble meets anti-agreement protest in Banbridge, 2001. © Paul
Faith/PA Photos.
(bottom) Blair and Brown announce an investment package in Belfast.
© Paul Faith/PA Photos.

Page 7: Trimble confronts the DUP during the Assembly Election, November 2003. © Belfast Telegraph Newspapers Ltd.
(bottom) Iain Paisley meets Ivan Little. © PA Photos.

Page 8: Portrait of David Trimble. © John Harrison Photography.

GLOSSARY

ABM Treaty	The Anti-Ballistic Missile Treaty signed by the USA and USSR on 26 May 1972.
AEI	American Enterprise Institute (for Public Policy Research) A leading conservative think-tank based in Washington DC, founded in 1943.
AFL-CIO	American Federation of Labor-Congress of Industrial Organizations. The US trade union movement.
AIA	Anglo–Irish Agreement This agreement signed by Margaret Thatcher and Garret FitzGerald on 15 November 1985, which gave the Republic a say in the affairs of Northern Ireland for the first time through the Anglo–Irish Intergovernmental Conference.
al-Qaeda	Fundamentalist Islamic terrorist group, headed by Osama bin Laden, which was responsible for the attacks on the US on 11 September 2001.
An Phoblacht/Republic News	The weekly newspaper of the republican movement.
ANC	African National Congress South African political party representing the black majority, formerly headed by Nelson Mandela.
APNI	Alliance Party of Northern Ireland Founded in 1970 out of the New Ulster Movement, the Alliance absorbed supporters from the NILP as well as disillusioned

unionists. Attracting support from both Catholics and Protestants, it is a non-sectarian party whose voters are mainly middle-class. It had representation on the short-lived Sunningdale Executive, although in recent years its support has slumped. Its sister party in Great Britain is the Liberal Democrats.

Apprentice Boys of Derry An organization, structured in a similar way to the Orange Order, which commemorates the Williamite resistance of the Siege of Derry.

Ard Fheis The Gaelic Word for the annual conferences held by Sinn Fein and several of the poliktical parties in the Republic of Ireland.

Articles 2 and 3 The two articles of the 1937 Constitution of the old Irish Free State which laid territorial claim to Northern Ireland. The Republic of Ireland withdrew the claim under the terms of the 1998 Belfast Agreement.

Atkins Talks The short-lived Constitutional Conference set up in early 1980 by then Secretary of State for Northern Ireland, Humphrey Atkins, which discussed possibilities for devolution. The SDLP, DUP and Alliance participated in the talks, which the UUP boycotted.

B Specials *See* Ulster Special Constabulary

Balcombe Street Gang An IRA unit. Its members – jailed for a campaign of mainland terror – were amongst the prisoners released for the day of the special Sinn Fein and Fheis on 10 May 1998.

Bar Library The base of practising barristers in Northern Ireland.

Belfast Agreement The accord forged by the British and Irish Governments along with the UUP, SDLP, SF, APNI and several smaller parties – but not the DUP or UKUP – at 5.36pm on Good Friday, 10 April 1998. It set up a new Northern Ireland Assembly, a power-sharing

Executive, the NSMC, various cross-border implementation bodies, the BIC and the BIIGC. It also provided for the release of paramilitary prisoners, reform of the RUC, a review of the criminal justice system, gradual normalisation of security arrangements in Northern Ireland, and the setting up of the NIHRC. It also committed the Irish Government to revoking Articles 2 and 3 of its Constitution. Also referred to as the Good Friday Agreement.

Belfast Harbour Commissioner's Office Address

Speech by Tony Blair in Belfast on 17 October 2002 in which he told republicans that 'the fork in the road has finally come'.

BIA

British-Irish Association
An organisation, founded in 1972, which annually brings together politicians, journalists, academics and others from London, Belfast and Dublin to discuss the political situation in Northern Ireland.

BIC

British–Irish Council
Sometimes referred to as the Council of the Isles, the body set up under Strand III of the Belfast Agreement, bringing together representatives of the British and Irish Governments, the various devolved administrations within the UK, the Channel Islands and the Isle of Man.

BIIGC

British–Irish Intergovernmental Conference
Set up under the Belfast Agreement, the reformed successor to the Anglo–Irish Intergovernmental Conference.

Bipartisanship

The word used for the cooperative attitude sometimes displayed by Labour and the Conservatives, as Government and Opposition (or vice versa), as regards Northern Ireland policy.

Blair's Handwritten Pledges

A reference to the five pledges publicly signed

by Tony Blair after a speech at the University of Ulster at Coleraine on 20 May 1998, during the referendum campaign on the Belfast Agreement. They included promises on excluding those using or threatening violence from government and keeping prisoners detained unless violence is given up for good.

Border Campaign
: The campaign of the IRA between 1956 and 1962.

Bow Group
: Founded in 1951, a think-tank and political research group associated with the Conservative Party.

Brooke–Mayhew Talks
: The talks initiative begun under the auspices of the Secretary of State for Northern Ireland, Peter Brooke, in April 1991, continuing until November 1992, by which time Patrick Mayhew had taken over from Brooke. The UUP, DUP, SDLP and APNI all participated, and it is here that the three-stranded approach of the Belfast Agreement was born.

B&ICO
: British and Irish Communist Organisation. A pressure group formed in 1969, which regularly published pamphlets.

CBM
: Confidence Building Measure

CDU/CSU
: Christlich Demokratische Union/Christlich Soziale Union
The Christian Democratic Parties which are the main centre-right political force in Germany.

Chequers
: The British Prime Minister's country residence in Buckinghamshire.

Commander-in-Chief
: A title sometimes used to denote the American President of the day.

Constitutional Convention
: The 78-member body elected on 1 May 1975 to consider how to govern Northern Ireland. With a majority of its members coming from

parties in the UUUC umbrella (including David Trimble in Belfast South), it was wound up in March 1976 without any proposals acceptable to Westminster having been agreed.

CIRA	Continuity IRA dissident republican terrorist group, which splintered from the Provisional IRA.
Craig–Collins Pact	The agreements of 1922 between the first Northern Ireland Prime Minister, Sir James Craig, and Michael Collins, the IRA leader and head of the new provisional Irish Government. They attempted to bring about an accommodation around the principles of recognition of Northern Ireland within the UK and cooperation between North and South.
Cross-Border Implementation Bodies	The bodies set up under the Belfast Agreement to coordinate the execution of policy in certain areas of mutual interest to Northern Ireland and the Republic of Ireland.
CWU	Communication Workers' Union. The main trade union for those working in the communications industry which was formed in January 1995 when two longstanding unions, the Union of Communication Workers and National Communications Union, merged.
Dail Eireann	The lower House of the Irish Parliament, whose members are TDs.
de Chastelain Commission	*See* IICD Defend the RUCA campaign set up to oppose parts of police reform as proposed by the Patten Report – particularly the abolition of the RUC's name.
Democratic Left	A small party in the Irish Republic and Northern Ireland, which resulted from a split in the Workers' Party in 1992.

Devolution Group

A group within the UUP formed by Trimble and others in the early 1980s to counterbalance the integrationist elements within the party.

DFA

Department of Foreign Affairs
The Department within the Irish Government, based at Iveagh House in central Dublin, which deals with matters pertaining to Northern Ireland.

d'Hondt

The formula by which the number of Ministers that each party receives on the Executive is calculated, making it broadly proportional to the number of MLAs they have. It was created in 1878 by the Belgian mathematician and lawyer, Victor d'Hondt.

Down Orange Welfare

A 1970s Co. Down-based loyalist paramilitary group led by Colonel Brush, which was especially active during the loyalist strike of 1974.

Downtown Radio

A popular Northern Irish commercial radio station.

DPPB

District Police Partnership Board
The Patten legislation to reform policing in Northern Ireland stated that each district council area would have a DPPB, i.e. a committee with an elected membership to hold the local police to account.

Drumcree

Drumcree parish church, near Portadown, has in recent years been the scene of the most contentious Orange Order parade of the marching season. After 1997, the march has not been allowed to pass along the mainly nationalist Garvaghy Road.

DSD

Downing Street Declaration
The Joint Declaration signed by John Major and Albert Reynolds for the British and Irish Governments at Downing Street on

15 December 1993, which set out broad principles for bringing peace to the province by reconciling the two political traditions.

DUP

Democratic Unionist Party
The more hardline of the two main unionist parties in Northern Ireland, it was formed out of the Protestant Unionist Party of the late 1960s, which opposed the direction being taken by the Ulster Unionist Party. It was founded in 1971 by Ian Paisley, who has been leader ever since. The DUP was part of the UUUC which opposed Sunningdale, and in more recent years has been a leading opponent of the Belfast Agreement. It registered particular electoral gains at both the 2001 general election and the 2003 Assembly election, where the DUP became the largest party. Also referred to as Paisleyites, or the Ulster Democratic Unionist Party.

Easter Rising/Rebellion

On Easter Monday in Dublin in 1916, militant republicans occupied many buildings in the city, declaring the establishment of an Irish Republic. There was much street fighting and about 450 people died. Six days later, on 29 April, the leaders surrendered to the British, and fifteen of their number were executed.

EDM

Early Day Motion
A motion signed by MPs which never gets debated, but nonetheless signals strength of feeling on a particular issue.

EPP

European People's Party
A centre-right/Christian Democratic grouping within the European Parliament.

Failsafe Legislation

A bill rushed through its initial stages in Parliament in July 1999 (although then dropped after UUUP opposition) to allow for suspension of devolution if the IICD ruled that decommissioning was not taking place.

FARC	Fuerzas Armadas Revolucionarias de Colombia A Colombian terrorist group, the paramilitary wing of the Colombian Communist Party.
FDP	Freie Demokratische Partei The centrist German Liberal Party, which spent some of the post-war years in government, forming coalitions with left- and right-wing parties.
FEA	Fair Employment Agency The FEA was set up in 1976 to try to solve the problem of direct discrimination in the workplace on religious or political grounds. Under the Fair Employment Act 1989 it became the Fair Employment Commission.
FF	Fianna Fail One of the two main political parties in the Republic of Ireland, founded by those opposed to the Anglo–Irish Treaty of 1921.
FG	Fine Gael One of the two main political parties in the Republic of Ireland, formed out of Cumann na nGaedhal, which supported the Anglo–Irish Treaty of 1921.
Fortnight	A monthly current affairs magazine in Northern Ireland.
Forum for Peace and Reconciliation	A forum organised by then Taoiseach Albert Reynolds in Dublin in 1994, which brought together the various nationalist parties.
Framework Document	Released by the British and Irish Governments on 22 February 1995, it set out a vision of how Northern Ireland could be governed in the future, including provision for an all-Ireland authority with executive powers.
Free Presbyterian Church	Founded by Ian Paisley in 1951, in a split from the mainstream Presbyterian Church.

GAA	Gaelic Athletic Association The body which oversees a variety of sports which are popular in the Irish Republic and predominantly amongst Catholics in Northern Ireland, particularly Gaelic football and hurling.
Garda Siochana	The police force of the Republic of Ireland. An individual officer is called a garda (pl. gardai).
Gardiner Committee	A committee, headed by Lord Gardiner, which looked into terrorism in Northern Ireland, reporting its conclusions in January 1975. Amongst these were that detention without trial was necessary in the short term, that prisoners should lose their special category status, and that for the time being, terrorist offences should be subject to non-jury trials.
Garvaghy Road Residents' Coalition	An organisation representing views of Catholic residents on the Garvaghy Road as regards the Drumcree Orange Parade. Its principal spokesman is Breandan Mac Cionnaith.
GFA	Good Friday Agreement. See Belfast Agreement
GOC	General Officer Commanding
GOP	Grand Old Party A nickname for the Republican Party in the US.
Greenfinches	A term used for the female members of the UDR.
HB/ETA	Herri Batasuna/Euskadi Ta Askatasuna The Basque separatist movement, of which HB is the political wing and ETA the paramilitary wing.
Hillsborough Castle	In Hillsborough, Co. Down, formerly the official residence of the Governor-General for Northern Ireland; since 1972, the official residence of the Secretary of State for

Northern Ireland and a regular location for talks. It is also the Queen's official residence in Northern Ireland and a location for royal garden parties.

Hillsborough Declaration
Made by Tony Blair and Bertie Ahern on 1 April 1999, it aimed to set out a sequence of events that would lead to the transfer of powers from Westminster to Stormont.

HMG
Her Majesty's Government
An abbreviation denoting the British Government.

Home Rule
The term given to the proposal in the late 19th and early 20th century to give self-government to the island of Ireland. Two Home Rules Bills failed to be passed by the British Parliament at Westminster – in 1886 and 1893 – and the enactment of a third was interrupted by the outbreak of World War I interrupted its enactment.

Housing Executive
The organisation in Northern Ireland responsible for public housing, established in 1971.

Hume–Adams Talks
The dialogue in the late 1980s and early 1990s between then SDLP leader John Hume and SF President, Gerry Adams, believed by many to have brought the republicans into the peace process.

Hunger Strikes
In 1980 and 1981, republican prisoners inside the Maze Prison conducted several hunger strikes in protest, amongst other issues, at the Government's refusal to grant them special status or the right to wear their own clothes. Ten prisoners (7 IRA, 3 INLA) died as a result of their fasting, including Bobby Sands, leader of the IRA prisoners, who won the Fermanagh-South Tyrone by-election on 9 April 1981.

IICD	Independent International Commission on Decommissioning The body established under the chairmanship of retired Canadian General John de Chastelain in August 1997 to oversee decommissioning of illegal weapons by paramilitaries.
IMC	International Monitoring Commission The body promised in the Joint Declaration of 1 May 2003 and legislated for in September 2003 to monitor paramilitary ceasefires and progress on security normalisation by the British Government.
Independent Commission on Policing	The body set up under the terns of the Belfast Agreement to look at reforming the RUC, chaired by former Conservative Party Chairman and former Governor of Hong Kong, Chris Patten. Its report, published on 9 September 1999, contained 175 recommendations for change, not least the abolition of the RUC's name and symbols.
INLA	Irish National Liberation Army A republican terrorist group dating back to 1975.
IRA	Irish Republican Army The organisation contemporarily known as the IRA is more properly called the Provisional IRA, dating back to a split in the republican movement in late 1969/early 1970 (*See also* Official IRA). IRA policy is decided by a seven-member Army Council, and its political wing is Sinn Fein. It is the largest of the republican terrorist organisations. All statements are signed by the fictitious P. O'Neill. Also known as Provisionals, 'Provos' or 'Provies'.
Irish Association	In full, the Irish Association for Cultural, Economic and Social Relations. Founded in 1938, it brings together people from different

viewpoints across Ireland to hear addresses from politicians, clergymen and academics. It aims to remove passion and prejudice from Irish politics and replace it with reconciliation and understanding between the two traditions.

Irish Free State
: The precursor to the Republic of Ireland; it was known as such from 1921 until the foundation of the Republic in April 1949, when all remaining constitutional ties with Britain and the Commonwealth were cut.

Irish News
: The main nationalist-inclined newspaper in Northern Ireland.

JMC
: Joint Ministerial Committee
A committee comprising representatives of the British Government, the Northern Ireland Executive, the Scottish Executive and Welsh Executive, primarily to consider non-devolved matters which impinge upon devolved responsibilities.

Joint Declaration
: Although there have been many Joint Declarations by the British and Irish Governments regarding the peace process, the one known by this simple title dates from 1 May 2003. It covered many areas in which progress needed to be made, although probably most significant was paragraph 13, which set out precise demands for a cessation of paramilitary activity.

Long Kesh
: *See* Maze Prison

Loyal Orders
: The collective name for a number of Protestant organisations, such as the Orange Order and the Royal Black Preceptory, so called due to their loyalty to the Crown.

Loyalist Commission
: A body created in October 2001, bringing together Church, community and political figures from across the loyalist community. It was established to attempt to ensure that all

factions within the community worked towards conflict resolution via peaceful means.

LVF

Loyalist Volunteer Force
A loyalist paramilitary group, which was formed by dissident members of the UVF in 1996. Once led by Billy Wright, its support is concentrated around the Portadown area in Co. Armagh.

Macpherson Report

The report of an inquiry chaired by Sir William Macpherson, published in February 1999, into events surrounding the murder of Stephen Lawrence. It concluded that the Metropolitan Police was 'institutionally racist'.

Maryfield

The Belfast base of the secretariat to the Anglo–Irish Intergovernmental Conference, which existed under the AIA, until superseded under the terms of the Belfast Agreement.

Maze Prison

The prison near Lisburn which housed most convicted terrorists during the course of 'The Troubles'. As a result of their shape, its cell blocks were known as H-Blocks. Many republicans referred to it as Long Kesh, the name of a camp in which some of their number were interned at that site in the early 1970s.

Millbank

This sometimes refers to the Labour Party, which had offices and its election 'war-room' in Millbank Tower in the late 1990s and early 2000s. It is also the road in Westminster where the NIO has its London office.

Mitchell Principles

The six principles of non-violence laid down by George Mitchell in a report on 26 January 1996, which prepared the ground for those associated with paramilitaries participating in the peace process.

Mitchell Review

A review of the implementation of the Belfast Agreement conducted by George Mitchell from September to November 1999, which

	precipitated the setting up of the Executive and the transfer of power from Westminster to Northern Ireland in December 1999.
MLA	Member of the Legislative Assembly The suffix which appears after the names of those elected to the Assembly set up under the Belfast Agreement.
National Assembly for Wales (or Welsh Assembly)	The devolved Assembly in Wales, first elected in 1999.
Nationalism	In a Northern Ireland context, the political philosophy of those who want to see a united Ireland, although through exclusively peaceful means. In Northern Ireland, the main nationalist party was the SDLP.
New Dialogue	A non-partisan organisation for those interested in Northern Ireland politics, with a particular interest in promoting an integrated education system in the province.
New Ireland Forum	The brainchild of John Hume, this was the body which in 1983 brought together the four main nationalist parties on the island of Ireland – FF, FG, SDLP and the Irish Labour Party.
New Ulster Movement	Founded in 1969, and calling for non-sectarian politics, many of its members then went on to form the APNI the following year.
News Letter (or *Belfast News Letter*)	The main unionist-inclined newspaper in Northern Ireland.
NICRA	Northern Ireland Civil Rights Association The organisation formed in 1967, calling for equal rights for Catholics in Northern Ireland.
NICS	Northern Ireland Civil Service
NIHRC	Northern Ireland Human Rights Commission The body set up under the Belfast Agreement to protect the human rights of all in Northern Ireland.

NILP

Northern Ireland Labour Party
A socialist party which was founded in the
province in 1924 and existed in its own right
until 1987.

NIO

Northern Ireland Office
The British Government Department that was
founded in 1972 after the collapse of
Stormont, and is responsible for administering
direct rule of the province from London. It is
headed by a Secretary of State, who sits in the
Cabinet and is assisted by several junior
ministers. Fourteen people have served as
Secretary of State since 1972: Willie Whitelaw,
Francis Pym, Merlyn Rees, Roy Mason,
Humphrey Atkins, Jim Prior, Douglas Hurd,
Tom King, Peter Brooke, Patrick Mayhew, Mo
Mowlam, Peter Mandelson, John Reid and
Paul Murphy.

NIPS

Northern Ireland Police Service
The name suggested by the Patten Report for
Northern Ireland's reformed police force, but
rejected by the British Government in favour
of the PSNI.

NIUP

Northern Ireland Unionist Party
A fringe hardline unionist party, set up by
four MLAs defecting from the UKUP in
January 1999. It failed to win any Assembly
seats in 2003.

NIWC

Northern Ireland Women's Coalition
A small non-sectarian party founded in 1996. It
had two MLAs in the 1998–2003 Assembly, both
of whom lost their seats at the 2003 election.

North Committee

The committee under the chairmanship of
Peter North, then ViceChancellor of Oxford
University, set up by then Secretary of State
for Northern Ireland, Patrick Mayhew, in
1996, to look at the issue of parades in
Northern Ireland.

Northern Ireland Assembly	Three bodies have been so called: the first, elected on 28 June 1973, fell in 1974 as part of the collapse of the Sunningdale Executive. The second, elected on 20 October 1982, existed until 1986 and scrutinised the work of the NIO, although had no power of its own and was boycotted by the SDLP and SF. The third Northern Ireland Assembly was set up under the Belfast Agreement and was first elected on 25 June 1998, with all parties represented there taking part in its proceedings. A second election was held on 26 November 2003.
Northern Ireland Executive	The Ministers, drawn from the Assembly through the d'Hondt formula, running the departments under the devolved administration in Northern Ireland as set up under the Belfast Agreement. It is headed by a First Minister and Deputy First Minister.
Northern Ireland Forum (for Political Dialogue)	The body of representatives, elected on 30 May 1996, to consider issues relevant to promoting dialogue and understanding within Northern Ireland.
NSC	National Security Council. The American body, set up under the National Security Council Act 1947, to coordinate US foreign policy and defence policy, and reconcile diplomatic and military commitments and requirements.
NSMC	North-South Ministerial Council The body set up under Strand II of the Belfast Agreement, bringing together ministers from the Northern Ireland Executive and the Irish Government to discuss cross-border matters of mutual interest.
Official IRA	After the split in the republican movement in late 1969/early 1970, the wing of the IRA that gradually wound down its campaign of armed struggle. It has effectively been on ceasefire since 1972. Also known as Officials, 'Stickies' or 'Sticks'.

Oireachtas	The Gaelic word for the Irish Parliament.
Orange Order	One of the loyal orders, it is the largest Protestant organisation in Northern Ireland and dates back to 1795, taking its name from William of Orange, who defeated the Catholic James II in 1690.
Orange Volunteers	A loyalist paramilitary group.
Order in Council	Passing an Order in (Privy) Council is the means by which the British Government can pass legislation without full discussion of the measure in Parliament being required.
OTR	On-the-Runs A term for those who committed or were suspected of committing terrorist offences before the signing of the Belfast Agreement who have either escaped from prison or were never imprisoned, for whom an amnesty was proposed in an annex to the Joint Declaration of 2003.
OUP	Official Unionist Party. *See* UUP
(Police) Oversight Commissioner	A post established as a result of proposals in the Patten Report, to oversee the implementation of the changes to the police force in Northern Ireland.
Parades Commission	An independent, quasi-judicial body legislated for in 1997, which has the power to place restrictions on parades in Northern Ireland.
Patten Commission/Report	*See* Independent Commission on Policing
People's Democracy	A radical left-wing group which campaigned for civil rights in Northern Ireland.
PIRA	Provisional Irish Republican Army. *See* IRA
PLO	Palestine Liberation Organisation
PLP	Parliamentary Labour Party
PPS	Parliamentary Private Secretary An MP serving as an unpaid aide to a British Government Minister.

Progressive Democrats	One of the smaller parties in the Republic of Ireland, formed by a faction splitting from FF in 1985, calling for, amongst other things, the withdrawal of the territorial claim on Northern Ireland.
Protestant Telegraph	A newspaper set up by Ian Paisley in the spring of 1966.
PSNI	Police Service of Northern Ireland The police force which replaced the RUC in the wake of the legislation which followed the Patten Report. It came into being at midnight on 4 November 2001 and its new uniform was introduced on 5 April 2002.
PTA	Prevention of Terrorism Act 1974 A piece of legislation conferring emergency powers on the police where terrorism was suspected, following IRA bombing campaigns on the mainland in 1974. It was renewed annually until being superseded by the Terrorism Act in 2000.
PUP	Progressive Unionist Party A small loyalist party founded in the late 1970s, based around Belfast's Shankill Road. It is the political wing of the UVF and its main spokesman is David Ervine. It had two seats in the 1998–2003 Assembly, but only retained one of them (Ervine's) in 2003. Its support is concentrated in loyalist, working-class areas of Belfast.
RBP	Royal Black Preceptory or Royal Black Institution Another of the loyal orders, it is more correctly called the Imperial Grand Black Chapter of the British Commonwealth. It was originally formed in 1797.
Real IRA	A dissident republican terrorist group which broke away from the IRA in November 1997.

Red Hand Defenders	A dissident loyalist terrorist group formed in 1998, which claimed responsibility for the murder of lawyer Rosemary Nelson in 1999.
Referendum Party	The political party founded by Sir James Goldsmith, which fought the 1997 British general election on a platform of demanding a referendum on Britain's relationship with the European Union.
Republicanism	In a Northern Ireland context, the political philosophy of those who want to see a united Irish Republic.
RIC	Royal Irish Constabulary The all-Ireland police force which was disbanded with effect from 31 May 1922.
RIR	Royal Irish Regiment Formed in July 1992 by merging the regular Army's Royal Irish Rangers with the home service battalions of the Ulster Defence Regiment.
RTE	Radio Telefis Eireann The Irish state broadcaster.
RUC	Royal Ulster Constabulary Northern Ireland's police force from 1 June 1922 until 4 November 2001, when it was replaced by the PSNI in the wake of legislation following the Patten Report.
SAM-7	A Soviet Surface-to-Air Missile.
'The Sash'	One of the most popular Orange songs.
Saville Inquiry	An Inquiry, chaired by Lord Saville of Newdigate, set up by the British Government in 1998 to investigate 'Bloody Sunday', when thirteen civilians were shot dead by members of the Parachute Regiment.
Scott Report	The report published in February 1996 by Lord Justice Scott into the 'Arms-to-Iraq' affair.

Scottish Parliament	The devolved Parliament in Scotland, first elected in 1999, which has some primary legislative powers.
SDLP	Social Democratic and Labour Party The main nationalist party in Northern Ireland, founded in 1970 by people who had been involved in the Nationalist Party, the National Democratic Party, the Republican Labour Party and the Northern Ireland Labour Party. It takes a left-of-centre view and has close links with the Labour Party in Great Britain. At the 1998 Assembly Election, it won the largest number of first preference votes of any party, although by the 2001 general election, they had been eclipsed by SF amongst the nationalist/republican community – which was repeated at the 2003 Assembly election.
Seanad Eireann	The Senate, the upper house of the Irish Parliament.
Sentences Act 1998	More properly, the Northern Ireland (Sentences) Act 1998, which enacted the sections of the Belfast Agreement relating to prisoner releases.
Sentence Review Commission	The body, set up under the above Act in 1998, charged with overseeing and regulating the early release of terrorist prisoners convicted during the Troubles.
SF	Sinn Fein The main republican party in Northern Ireland, which also organises in the Republic of Ireland. It can trace its roots to a party of the same name formed in 1905, although its modern-day incarnation dates back to 1970, when a split occurred over whether to recognise the Belfast and Dublin Parliaments: those refusing to do so formed Provisional Sinn Fein, now known merely as Sinn Fein, whilst those remaining went on to form the Workers' Party. Over the

years, it began standing in elections, but its MPs do not take their seats at Westminster, although its TDs do sit in the Dail. It won enough seats at the 1998 Assembly election to have two ministers on the Executive, and in 2001 won four seats to the SDLP's three at the Westminster election, similarly eclipsing them in the 2003 Assembly election. It is the political wing of the IRA and in Gaelic, Sinn Fein translates as 'Ourselves Alone'. Colloquially, its members are sometimes referred to as 'Shinners'.

Siege of Derry	On 18 December 1688, thirteen apprentice boys shut the gates to Derry, as a way of resisting Jacobite forces set on taking the city. The siege proper – which lasted 105 days – began in April when the Catholic James II arrived at the walled city, but was refused entry. Possibly two-thirds of Derry's inhabitants died before the siege finally ended on 12 August 1689, when a fleet of British ships sailed up Lough Foyle into the city.
SIPTU	Services, Industrial, Professional and Technical Union Ireland's largest trade union.
Socialist International	An international organisation bringing together socialist and left-wing political parties, including the British Labour Party and the SDLP.
SPD	Sozialdemokratische Partei Deutschlands Germany's main left-of-centre, Social Democratic party.
Spirit of Drumcree	A hardline faction within the Orange Order.
Stormont	The name used to refer to the devolved Northern Ireland Parliament which existed from 1921 until 1972, comprising a 52-member House of Commons and a 26-member Senate. It was so called as it had sat since 1932 at Parliament Buildings on the Stormont estate in east Belfast, a building faced with Portland stone, set on a

plinth of Mourne granite. It has been used for various of the failed devolved assemblies and has been the base of the Northern Ireland Assembly since 1998. There are also other official buildings on the estate at Stormont Castle, Stormont House and Castle Buildings.

Strands I, II and III

A concept dating back to the Brooke–Mayhew talks, and borne out in the Belfast Agreement, the three strands are: I – internal governance of Northern Ireland; II – the north–south dimension, i.e. relations between Northern Ireland and the Republic; and III – the east–west dimension, i.e. relations between the various constituent parts of the UK and the Republic.

Stranmillis Address

Tony Blair's speech at Stranmillis University College, South Belfast, on 15 June 1999, in which he said to Trimble's unionist critics: 'He has taken the hard road and he has more integrity doing so than those who undermine him'.

STV

Single Transferable Vote
The system of proportional representation used for elections in Northern Ireland to local councils, the Assembly and the European Parliament.

Sunningdale Agreement

The Agreement reached after a conference at Sunningdale Civil Service College in Berkshire in December 1973, leading to an attempt at power-sharing government in Northern Ireland in 1974. It included many Ulster Unionists (under Brian Faulkner), the SDLP and Alliance; it was known as the Sunningdale Executive, but collapsed after the UWC strike of May 1974.

Supergrass System

A system used in the 1980s by the RUC and British Government in which terrorist informers – some of whom were given immunity from prosecution – provided information in order to convict other terrorists.

Tanaiste	The Gaelic word for the Irish Deputy Prime Minister.
Taoiseach	The Gaelic word for the Irish Prime Minister.
TD	Teachta Dala The suffix which appears after the names of members of the lower house of the Irish Parliament, the Dail.
Thatcher–Haughey Talks	A landmark meeting held between a British delegation, led by Margaret Thatcher, and Charles Haughey, the Irish Taoiseach, in Dublin in December 1980, at which a review was promised of 'the totality of relations between the two countries'.
Tribune Group	A left wing pressure group within the British Labour Party.
'The Twelfth'	12 July is the day when the Orange Order celebrate the victory on that day in 1690 of William of Orange over James II at the Battle of the Boyne. It is a Bank Holiday in Northern Ireland and there are many parades. The evening before, 'Eleventh Night', many bonfires are lit by Protestants across Northern Ireland.
UDA	Ulster Defence Association A loyalist paramilitary group, which dates back to 1971 but was not proscribed until 1992.
UDP	Ulster Democratic Party Formed in 1989 out of the Ulster Loyalist Democratic Party, it was the political wing of the UDA. It was represented in the Northern Ireland Forum from 1996–8, but failed to win any seats in the Assembly election in 1998 and was wound up in November 2001. Many involved went on to form the Ulster Political Research Group in 2002.
UDR	Ulster Defence Regiment A locally-raised militia under regular Army control, founded in 1970 effectively as a

replacement for the B Specials, with the aim of attracting wider cross-community support. Eventually merged into the RIR in 1992.

UFF
Ulster Freedom Fighters
A component part of, and a name often used by, the UDA.

UIO
Unionist Information Office
The London-based organisation aimed at promoting Ulster Unionism on the British mainland, which was established with David Burnside as director in July 1996.

UKUP
United Kingdom Unionist Party
A small hardline unionist party which opposed the Belfast Agreement. It was formed in 1996 by former UUP member Robert McCartney, who won the North Down by-election in 1995 – a seat he held until 2001 as the party's only MP. UKUP won five seats at the 1998 Assembly election, although it suffered four defections (See NIUP). McCartney was the UKUP's only MLA at the 2003 Assembly election.

Ulster Clubs
Formed in 1985 to oppose the rerouting of loyalist parades, before going on to fervently oppose the AIA.

Ulster Covenant
More correctly, Ulster's Solemn League and Covenant. It was signed on 28 September 1912 by 450,000 people in Ulster opposed to the idea of Home Rule for Ireland.

Ulster Independence Committee
Formed by a Presbyterian Minister, Hugh Ross, in 1988, with the aim of ending sectarian politics in Northern Ireland by unifying its residents under an Ulster identity.

Ulster Society
More correctly, the Ulster Society for the Promotion of Ulster-British Heritage and Culture, it was formed by David Trimble and others in 1985.

Ulster Special Constabulary	An all-Protestant force formed in 1920 to supplement the full-time security forces, of which by far the largest contingent were the B Specials, numbering over 10,000 part-timers. It was disbanded in 1970.
Union First Group	A faction in the UUP critical of David Trimble in the wake of signing the Belfast Agreement.
Unionism	The political philosophy of those in Northern Ireland who believe that it should remain united with Great Britain but do not employ violent means to that end. Its main proponents are the UUP and DUP.
Unionist Labour Group	A faction within the UUP, formed in 1995, which is supportive of the Labour Movement.
Unionist Party of Northern Ireland	A breakaway party formed by those who continued to support Brian Faulkner and the Sunningdale Agreement after the UUP had rejected it. However, it failed to win any seats in the October 1974 general election, and only won five of the 78 seats on the Constitutional Convention. After limited electoral success, it was wound up in 1981.
United Ulster Unionist Movement	A breakaway faction from the VUPP during the Constitutional Convention which was opposed to the idea of a voluntary coalition. It subsequently became the United Ulster Unionist Party and although fighting a few elections in the late 1970s and early 1980s, it had been wound up by 1983.
UTV	Ulster Television The regional commercial television station in Northern Ireland, which is part of the ITV network.
UUC	Ulster Unionist Council The 860-strong governing council of the UUP, whose current membership includes 600–700 delegates from UUP constituency associations;

34 delegates from the Young Unionists; 122 delegates from the Orange Order; 12 delegates from the Association of Loyal Orange Women; 5 delegates from the Queen's University Belfast Ulster Unionist Association; 26 delegates from the Ulster Unionist Councillors Association. All UUP MPs, MLAs, peers and MEPs are ex-officio members. Its annual meeting elects the 13 party officers, plus the leader. A petition signed by 60 members of the UUC is enough to demand a meeting of the body.

UUP

Ulster Unionist Party
The less hardline of the two main unionist parties in Northern Ireland, it was effectively founded as the Unionist Party in 1905 on the formation of the UUC. During the existence of Stormont, from 1921 to 1972, it had a majority of the seats, hence forming the Government of Northern Ireland. It suffered from a significant internal split in 1973–74 over the participation of then leader (and the last Prime Minister of Northern Ireland) Brian Faulkner in the Sunningdale Executive. Similar – though not so fatal – splits have also befallen David Trimble, the party leader since 1995, over the party's support for the Belfast Agreement in 1998. At the 2003 Assembly election, the DUP eclipsed it as the largest unionist party in terms of seats at Stormont. The party was also sometimes referred to as the Official Unionist Party (OUP).

UUP Executive Committee

This comprises the party leader as elected by the UUC; the party officers; the chief whip of the parliamentary party; the chief whip of the UUP in the Assembly; any UUP MEPs; the leader and one other member of the parliamentary party; the leader and three other members of the UUP in the Assembly; 1 UUP peer; 60–72 delegates from the UUP constituency associations; 8 delegates from the Ulster Women's Unionist Council; 4 delegates from the Young Unionists;

12 delegates from the Orange Institution Central Committee; 2 delegates from the Association of Loyal Orange Women; 1 delegate from the Queen's University Belfast Ulster Unionist Association; and 3 delegates from the Ulster Unionist Councillors Association. Amongst its functions are to act on behalf of the UUC between UUC meetings; to consider all aspects of party policy and discuss the formulation of policy with the party leader; and to approve major property, financial and publicity decisions.

UUP Officers	The thirteen party officers are elected by the annual general meeting of the UUC and are responsible for implementing decisions of the Executive Committee, regularly consulting with the party leader, as well as taking responsibility for all property and financial matters on behalf of the UUC. They act on behalf of the Executive Committee between meetings. They comprise: the President, four Vice-Presidents, Four Honorary Secretaries, the Honorary Treasurer, the Chairman and Vice-Chairman of the Executive Committee and the Assistant Treasurer.
UUUC	United Ulster Unionist Council The coalition of elements of the UUP along with the DUP and VUPP which opposed the Sunningdale Agreement. The UUUC won 11 of Northern Ireland's 12 seats at the February 1974 general election and 10 of the 12 seats at the October 1974 general election. It also won a majority of seats on the Constitutional Convention, before effectively collapsing in 1977.
UVF	Ulster Volunteer Force A loyalist paramilitary organisation, whose modern-day incarnation dates back to the late 1960s. Its political wing is the PUP.
UWC	Ulster Workers Council The body that ran the May 1974 loyalist strike.

(Ulster Vanguard)   A unionist pressure group launched in early
1972, with William Craig as leader, which was
unhappy at the prospect of direct rule from
Westminster. It became a fully-fledged party,
the VUPP, in March 1973.

Vanguard Service Corps   An organisation which used to provide escorts
for the Ulster Vanguard leadership.

VUPP   Vanguard Unionist Progressive Party
A political party formed out of Ulster
Vanguard which existed from 1973 until 1978
and was led by William Craig. It was part of
the UUUC and David Trimble represented
Belfast South for the VUPP in the 1975–6
Constitutional Convention.

Way Forward Document   In the wake of the failure of the Hillsborough
Declaration, this document was published by
the British and Irish Governments on 2 July
1999 as a further attempt at trying to prompt
the setting up of the Executive and the
devolution of power to Northern Ireland.

Weston Park Talks   The talks held at Weston Park in Shropshire
in July 2001, which attempted to solve the
impasse in the wake of David Trimble's
resignation as First Minister.

White Paper   A document produced by the British
Government in advance of solid legislative
proposals being finalised.

Windsor House   The central Belfast base of the British–Irish
secretariat, set up under the Belfast
Agreement, most of whose staff had
previously worked at Maryfield.

Winfield House   The official residence of the US Ambassador
to London in Regent's Park.

Young Citizen Volunteers   The youth wing of the UVF.

Young Democrats   The youth wing of the DUP.

Young Unionists   The youth wing of the UUP.

INDEX

Printed by RR Donnelley at Glasgow, UK